Portable Literature

READING ▪ REACTING ▪ WRITING

Ninth Edition
2016 MLA Update Edition

Laurie G. Kirszner
University of the Sciences, Emeritus

Stephen R. Mandell
Drexel University

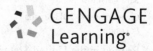

Australia • Brazil • Mexico • Singapore • United Kingdom • United States

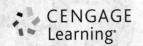
CENGAGE
Learning®

**Portable Literature:
Reading, Reacting,
Writing, Ninth Edition
2016 MLA Update Edition**
Laurie G. Kirszner,
Stephen R. Mandell

Product Director: Monica Eckman

Product Team Manager: Nicole Morinon

Product Manager: Kate Derrick

Senior Content Developer: Leslie Taggart

Content Developer: Karen Mauk

Associate Content Developer: Erin Bosco

Product Assistant: Claire Branman

Media Developer: Janine Tangney

Marketing Manager: Erin Parkins

Senior Content Project Manager: Michael Lepera

Senior Art Director: Marissa Falco

Manufacturing Planner: Betsy Donaghey

IP Analyst: Ann Hoffman

IP Project Manager: Farah Fard

Production Service/ Compositor: Cenveo® Publisher Services

Text Designer: Cenveo® Publisher Services

Cover Designer: Sarah Bishins

Cover Image: © 2013 Aryana B. Londir

For product information and technology assistance, contact us at
Cengage Learning Customer & Sales Support, 1-800-354-9706

For permission to use material from this text or product, submit all requests online at **www.cengage.com/permissions.**
Further permissions questions can be emailed to
permissionrequest@cengage.com.

Library of Congress Control Number: On file

ISBN: 978-1-337-28101-0

Cengage Learning
20 Channel Center Street
Boston, MA 02210
USA

Cengage Learning is a leading provider of customized learning solutions with employees residing in nearly 40 different countries and sales in more than 125 countries around the world. Find your local representative at: **www.cengage.com.**

Cengage Learning products are represented in Canada by Nelson Education, Ltd.

To learn more about Cengage Learning Solutions, visit **www.cengage.com.**

Purchase any of our products at your local college store or at our preferred online store **www.cengagebrain.com.**

Printed in the United States of America
Print Number: 05   Print Year: 2019

BRIEF CONTENTS

PART 4   DRAMA   801

CONTENTS

Julia Alvarez

2   Writing Literary Arguments 31

Alice Walker

3 Documenting Sources and Avoiding Plagiarism 49

To cite information from an online database, supply the publication information (including page numbers, if available) followed by the italicized name of the database and the DOI or URL. Include the date of access if the source is subject to change.

Luckenbill, Trent. "Environmental Litigation: Down the Endless Corridor." *Environment.* 17 July 2001, pp. 34-42. *ABI/INFORM GLOBAL.*

31. A scholarly journal article from an online database
Schaefer, Richard J. "Editing Strategies in Television News Documentaries." *Journal of Communication,* vol. 47, no. 4, 1997, pp. 69-89. *InfoTrac OneFile Plus.*

32. A monthly magazine article from an online database
Livemore, Beth. "Meteorites on Ice." *Astronomy,* July 1993, pp. 54-58. *Expanded Academic ASAP Plus.*

33. A newspaper article from an online database
Meyer, Greg. "Answering Questions about the West Nile Virus." *Dayton Daily News,* 11 July 2002, pp. Z3-7. *LexisNexis.*

34. A reference book article from an online database
Laird, Judith. "Geoffrey Chaucer." *Cyclopedia of World Authors,* 1997. *MagillOnLiterature.* Accessed 2 Oct. 2015.

35. A dictionary definition from an online database
"Migraine." *Mosby's Medical, Nursing and Allied Health Dictionary,* 1998 ed. *Health Reference Center.*

Sample MLA works-cited entries

Kate Chopin

Zadie Smith

Sherman Alexie

10 Point of View 226

Edwidge Danticat

11 Style, Tone, and Language 281

James Joyce

Illustration of Trojan horse
from Virgil's *Aeneid*

Janice Mirikitani

17   Word Choice, Word Order   534

E. E. Cummings

18   Imagery   560

Jane Flanders

19 Figures of Speech 575

Marge Piercy

20 Sound　　　　　　　　　　　　　　　　　　　609

Emily Dickinson

21 Form 632

Elizabeth Bishop

22 Symbol, Allegory, Allusion, Myth 671

W. H. Auden

23   Discovering Themes in Poetry   702

Dylan Thomas

24 Poetry for Further Reading 732

Linda Pastan

The Bedroom (1888) by
Vincent Van Gogh

Anton Chekhov

Harold Pinter

Warren Leight

William Shakespeare

Sophocles

30 Theme   1229

August Wilson

Appendix   Using Literary Criticism in Your Writing   1332

PREFACE

In Alice Walker's short story "Everyday Use" (p. 344), two sisters—one rural and traditional, one urban and modern—compete for possession of two quilts that have been in their family for years. At the end of the story, the narrator's description of the quilts suggests their significance—as a link between the old and the new, between what was and what is:

> One was in the Lone Star pattern. The other was Walk Around the Mountain. In both of them were scraps of dresses that Grandma Dee had worn fifty and more years ago. Bits and pieces of Grandpa Jarrell's Paisley shirts. And one teeny faded blue piece, about the size of a penny matchbox, that was from Great Grandpa Eza's uniform that he wore in the Civil War. (350)

In a sense, *Portable Literature: Reading, Reacting, Writing* is a kind of literary quilt, one that places nontraditional works alongside classics, integrates the familiar with the unfamiliar, and invites students to see well-known works in new contexts. To convey this message, each edition of the book integrates imagery from a handmade quilt. The quilt designed for this new edition uses contemporary as well as traditional quilting techniques to reflect our own increased focus on contemporary and emerging writers as well as on writers from diverse cultures and backgrounds.

The ninth edition of *Portable Literature: Reading, Reacting, Writing*, like the previous editions, is designed to demystify the study of literature and to prepare students to explore the literary works collected here. Our goal in this edition remains what it has been from the start: to expand students' personal literary boundaries. To this end, we have fine-tuned the reading selections and expanded the pedagogical features that support the study of literature, acting in response to thoughtful comments from our reviewers and from our students. Having class-tested this book in our own literature classrooms, we have learned what kinds of selections and features best help our students to read, think about, understand, and write about literature in ways that make it meaningful to their lives in the twenty-first century.

To help instructors engage their students with literature and guide them in becoming better thinkers and writers, we have added new readings and enhanced key elements that have made *Portable Literature: Reading, Reacting, Writing* a classroom success.

Unparalleled Writing Coverage

The first college literature anthology to address writing as a major component of the introductory literature course, *Portable Literature: Reading, Reacting, Writing* begins with a comprehensive writing guide. **Part 1, "A Guide to Writing about Literature,"** consists of three chapters that help students see writing about literature as a process of discovering, testing, and arguing about ideas. In addition, comprehensive writing coverage is integrated throughout the book in the following features:

- **A general introduction to the writing process** Chapter 1, "Reading and Writing about Literature," explains and illustrates the process of planning, drafting, and revising essays about literary works, concluding with an exercise asking students to evaluate and compare two student essays that examine the same three short stories.

- **A chapter on literary argument** Chapter 2, "Writing Literary Arguments," helps students to think critically about their writing and build convincing and insightful arguments about literary works. Chapter 2 takes students through the process of writing a literary argument and concludes with two annotated student essays.

- **Extensive research and documentation coverage** Chapter 3, "Documenting Sources and Avoiding Plagiarism," includes strategies for avoiding plagiarism. Chapter 3 also includes the updated documentation guidelines put forth in the eighth edition of the *MLA Handbook* (2016). The style has been simplified to emphasize a common approach to a wide variety of source types, and the updated chapter introduces the new approach while continuing to offer numerous citation examples for students.

- **Five complete model student essays** Because our own experience in the classroom has shown us that students often learn most easily from models, the text includes five model student essays written in response to the kinds of topics that are frequently assigned in Introduction to Literature classes.

- **Checklists** Most chapter introductions end with a checklist designed to help students measure their understanding of concepts introduced in the chapter. These checklists can also guide students as they generate, explore, focus, and organize ideas for writing about works of literature.

- **Writing suggestions** Imaginative suggestions for essay topics are included at the end of each chapter to spark students' interest and inspire engaged writing.

 ## Fresh, Balanced Selections

The short stories, poems, and plays collected in this book represent a balance of old and new as well as a wide variety of nations and cultures and a full range of writing styles.

- **Extensive selection of fiction** The fiction section includes not only perennial classics ("The Lottery," "A Rose for Emily," "The Cask of Amontillado") and stories we introduced to readers in the first edition, such as David Michael Kaplan's "Doe Season" and Charles Baxter's "Gryphon," but also a number of works never previously collected in a college literature anthology, such as Amanda Brown's "Love and Other Catastrophes: A Mix Tape." The 11 new stories that appear in this edition include several popular contemporary works, such as Lorrie Moore's "Referential" and Ed Park's "Slide to Unlock." In addition, Chapter 6, "Fiction Sampler: Graphic Fiction," engages students with visual examples from the literary canon.

- **Blend of contemporary and classic poetry** The poetry section balances works by classic poets (such as Robert Frost, Emily Dickinson, and Langston Hughes) with works by more contemporary poets (such as Linda Pastan and Francisco X. Alarcón) and also introduces students to exciting twenty-first-century works by poets such as Richard Blanco and Claire Lee. Now offering an even broader range of diverse works, the poetry section has been expanded with 46 new works by poets such as Agha Shahid Ali, Wendell Berry, Gwendolyn Brooks, Lewis Carroll, Sandra M. Castillo, Hart Crane, Rita Dove, Rhina Espaillat, David Hernandez, Nancy Mercado, Deborah Paredez, Sylvia Plath, Lola Ridge, Jacob Saenz, Carl Sandburg, Virgil Suárez, May Swenson, Jean Toomer, and Pamela Spiro Wagner. In addition, unique visual glossary items appear throughout the poetry section, clarifying and illuminating unfamiliar terms and concepts within poems.

- **Varied selection of plays** The drama section juxtaposes classic selections—William Shakespeare's *Hamlet,* August Wilson's *Fences,* Milcha Sanchez-Scott's *The Cuban Swimmer*—with contemporary plays, such as Earl T. Roske's *Zombie Love* and David Ives's *The Blizzard.* Five plays are new to the ninth edition, including Kimberly Pau's *Magic 8 Ball* and Michael Salomon's *The Date.*

- **Innovative "sampler" chapters** Chapter 5, "Fiction Sampler: The Short-Short Story"; Chapter 6, "Fiction Sampler: Graphic Fiction"; the full-color "Poetry Sampler: Poetry and Art"; and Chapter 26, "Drama Sampler: Ten-Minute Plays," showcase representative selections from four popular literary subgenres, introducing students to the variety and diversity of literature with brief, accessible works.

 ## Thorough Background Information

As we have learned in our classrooms over the years, part of helping students to demystify literature is helping them to understand the context in which the stories, poems, and plays were written. To achieve this goal, we continue to include contextual and background materials throughout the book in various forms:

- **Cultural context notes** A cultural context section follows each author headnote in the fiction and drama sections, providing vital background about the social and historical climate in which the work was written.

- **Accessible discussion of literary history** "Origins of Modern Fiction" in Chapter 4, "Understanding Fiction"; "Origins of Modern Poetry" in Chapter 15, "Understanding Poetry"; and "Origins of Modern Drama" in Chapter 25, "Understanding Drama," are fully illustrated with visuals that trace each genre's development and bring the history of literature to life.

 ## Other Pedagogical Features

A number of other pedagogical features appear throughout the text to prompt students to think critically about reading and to stimulate class discussions and energetic, thoughtful writing:

- **Reading and Reacting questions** Reading and Reacting questions, including journal prompts, follow many selections throughout the text. These questions ask students to interpret and evaluate what they have read—sometimes encouraging them to make connections between the literary work being studied and other works in the text.

- **Critical Perspectives** Critical Perspective questions (included in most sets of Reading and Reacting questions) ask students to respond to analytical, interpretive, or evaluative comments that writers and critics have made about the work. This feature encourages students to apply their own critical thinking skills to literary criticism as well as to the work of literature itself.

- **Literary criticism appendix** The appendix, "Using Literary Criticism in Your Writing," explains and illustrates the key schools of literary criticism and shows how each can be applied to a typical student writing assignment inspired by a literary work.

- **Related Works** A Related Works section following the Reading and Reacting questions lists works linked (by theme, author, or genre) to the particular work under study. This feature encourages students to see connections between works by different writers, between works in different genres, or between two themes—connections they can explore in class discussion and in writing.

 ## A Full Package of Supplementary Materials

To support students and instructors who use the ninth edition of *Portable Literature: Reading, Reacting, Writing*, these ancillary materials are available from Cengage Learning:

- **Instructor's Resource Manual** A comprehensive instructor's manual provides all the materials necessary to support a variety of teaching styles. This resource includes discussion and activities for every short story, poem, and play in the anthology; a thematic table of contents; semester and quarter sample syllabi; and articles on the evolution of the literary canon and reader-response theory. In addition, many selections include a section called "Do Your Students Know?"—brief, entertaining notes that provide interesting, sometimes offbeat contextual information.

- **MindTap™ Literature** MindTap is a personalized teaching and learning experience with relevant assignments that guide students to analyze, apply, and improve thinking, allowing instructors to measure skills and outcomes with ease. By seamlessly integrating course material with videos, activities, apps, and much more, MindTap creates a unique learning path that fosters increased comprehension and efficiency.

 Acknowledgments

From start to finish, this book has been a true collaboration, not only with each other, but also with our students and colleagues. We have worked hard on this book, and many people have worked hard along with us.

We would like to begin by thanking our incredibly creative and talented Content Developer, Karen Mauk, who has always been there for us (and who we hope always will be there). She is one of a kind, and we are simply in awe of her abilities.

At Cengage, we thank Nicole Morinon, Product Team Manager; Kate Derrick, Product Manager; Leslie Taggart, Senior Content Developer; Erin Bosco, Associate Content Developer; Claire Branman, Product Assistant; Janine Tangney, Media Developer; and Michael Lepera, Content Project Manager. We also thank the team at Cenveo® Publisher Services, especially Karen Oemler, our talented Project Manager and Copyeditor.

We also very much appreciate the help we got on this project from William Coyle on the poetry selections and apparatus as well as the Instructor's Resource Manual, and from Karen Mauk on updating the headnotes, footnotes, Cultural Contexts, and Critical Perspective questions.

We would like to thank the following reviewers of the ninth edition: Emory Abbott, Georgia Perimeter College; Lisa Angius, Farmingdale State College; Carolyn Ayers, Saint Mary's University of Minnesota; Alyce Baker, Lock Haven University of Pennsylvania; Annalisa Buerke, University of Northwestern—St. Paul; Robert Canipe, Catawba Valley Community College; Jill Channing, Mitchell Community College; Sheila Chase, Arkansas State University—Beebe; Sheryl Chisamore, SUNY—Ulster; Susan Chism, Greenville College; Ellen Feig, Bergen Community College; Joanne Gabel, Reading Area Community College; Barbara Goldstein, Hillsborough Community College; Joseph Granitto, Farmingdale State College; Michael Hedges, Horry-Georgetown Technical College; Margaret Hosty, Tarrant

County College; Robert Hurd, Anne Arundel Community College; Kristin Jacobson, Richard Stockton College of New Jersey; Alyssa Johnson, Horry-Georgetown Technical College; Lisa Jones, Hillsborough Community College—Dale Mabry and Pasco-Hernando State College—West; Carol Kushner, Dutchess Community College; Pete Landino, Terra State Community College; Elizabeth Langemak, La Salle University; Richard Larschan, University of Massachusetts—Dartmouth; Dawn Lattin, Idaho State University; Andrea Laurencell Sheridan, SUNY—Orange; Kristin Le Veness, Nassau Community College; Angie Macri, Pulaski Technical College; Boyd Minner, Navarro College; Lisa Moslow, Erie Community College—North; Karen O'Donnell, Finger Lakes Community College; Paula Rash, Caldwell Community College and Technical Institute; Joan Reeves, Northeast Alabama Community College; Shewanda Riley, Tarrant County College; Nancy Risch, Caldwell Community College and Technical Institute; Gregory Sargent, Quinsigamond Community College; James Scruton, Bethel University; Roy Seeger, University of South Carolina—Aiken; Amy Smith, Hilbert College; Susan St. Peters, Riverside City College; Karl Terryberry, Daemen College; Stephanie Tingley, Youngstown State University; Andrew Tomko, Bergen Community College; Heather Weiss, Technical College of the Lowcountry; Stephen Whited, Piedmont College; Winona Winkler Wendth, Quinsigamond Community College; and Kristy Wooten, Catawba Valley Community College.

We would also like to thank our families for being there when we needed them. And finally, we each thank the person on the other side of the ampersand for making our collaboration work one more time.

1 | A GUIDE TO WRITING ABOUT LITERATURE

CHAPTER 1

READING AND WRITING ABOUT LITERATURE

 Reading Literature

Much of the time, reading is a passive process; readers expect the text to give them everything they need, and they do not expect to contribute much to the reading process. In contrast, **active reading** means participating in the reading process: thinking about what you read, asking questions, challenging ideas, and forming judgments. Active reading is excellent preparation for the discussion and writing you will do in college literature classes. And, because it helps you understand and appreciate the works you read, active reading will continue to be of value to you long after your formal classroom study of literature has ended.

Previewing

You begin active reading by **previewing** a work to get a general idea of what to look for later on, when you read it more carefully.

Start previewing by observing the work's most obvious visual characteristics. How long is a short story? How many acts and scenes does a play have? Is a poem divided into stanzas? The answers to these and similar questions will help you begin to notice more subtle aspects of the work's form. For example, previewing may reveal that a contemporary short story is presented entirely in a question-and-answer format, that it is organized as diary entries, or that it is divided into sections by headings. Previewing may identify poems that seem to lack formal structure, such as E. E. Cummings's unconventional "l(a" (p. 496); poems written in traditional forms (such as **sonnets**) or in experimental forms, such as Richard Blanco's **prose poem** "Mexican Almuerzo in New England" (p. 666); or **concrete poems**, such as George Herbert's 1663 poem "Easter Wings." Your awareness of these and other distinctive features at this point may help you gain insight into a work later on.

Perhaps the most distinctive visual element of a work is its title. Not only can the title give you a general idea of what the work is about, as straightforward titles like "Miss Brill" and "The Cask of Amontillado" do, but it can also call attention to a word or phrase that emphasizes an important idea. For example, the title of Amy Tan's short story "Two Kinds" (p. 471) refers to two kinds of daughters—Chinese and American—identifying the two perspectives that create the story's conflict. A title can also be an allusion to another work. Thus, *The Sound and the Fury*, the title of a novel by William Faulkner, alludes to a speech from Shakespeare's *Macbeth* that reinforces a major theme of the novel. Finally, a title can introduce a symbol that will gain meaning in the course of a work—as the quilt does in Alice Walker's "Everyday Use" (p. 344).

Other visual elements—such as paragraphing, capitalization, italics, and punctuation—can also provide clues about how to read a work. In William Faulkner's short story "Barn Burning" (p. 256), for instance, previewing would help you to notice passages in italic type, indicating the protagonist's thoughts, which occasionally interrupt the narrator's story.

Finally, previewing can enable you to identify some of the more obvious structural features of a work—how long a story is, how many acts a play has, or the shape of a poem, for example. Such features may or may not be important; at this stage, your goal is to observe, not to analyze or evaluate.

Previewing is a useful strategy not because it provides answers but because it suggests questions to ask later, as you read more closely. For instance, *why* does Faulkner use italics in "Barn Burning," and *why* does Herbert shape his poem like a pair of wings? Elements such as those described above will gain significance as you read more carefully.

Highlighting

When you read a work closely, you will notice additional, more subtle, elements that you may want to examine further. At this point, you should begin **highlighting**—physically marking the text to identify key words or details and to note relationships among ideas.

For example, you might notice that particular words or phrases are repeated, as in Tim O'Brien's short story "The Things They Carried" (p. 310), in which the word *carried* appears again and again. Because this word appears so frequently, and because it appears at key points in the story, it helps to reinforce a key theme: that soldiers carry heavy burdens and responsibilities in wartime. Repeated words and phrases are particularly important in poetry. In Dylan Thomas's "Do not go gentle into that good night" (p. 710), for example, the repetition of two of the poem's nineteen lines four times each enhances the poem's rhythmic, almost monotonous, cadence. As you read, highlight your text to identify such repeated words and phrases. Later, you can consider *why* these elements are repeated.

During the highlighting stage, you might also pay particular attention to **patterns of imagery** that can help you to interpret the work. When highlighting Robert Frost's "Stopping by Woods on a Snowy Evening" (p. 765), for instance, you might identify the related images of silence, cold, and darkness. Later on, you can consider their significance.

✔ **CHECKLIST   Using Highlighting Symbols**

When you highlight a text, try these strategies:

- Underline important ideas.
- Box or circle words, phrases, or images that you want to think more about.
- Put question marks beside confusing passages, unfamiliar references, or words that need to be defined.
- Circle related words, ideas, or images and draw lines or arrows to connect them.
- Number incidents that occur in sequence.
- Mark a key portion of the text with a vertical line in the margin.
- Star particularly important ideas.

The following poem by Julia Alvarez has been highlighted by a student preparing to write about it. Notice how the student uses highlighting symbols to identify key ideas and patterns that she plans to examine later.

JULIA ALVAREZ (1950–   )

Dusting (1984)

Each morning I wrote my name
On the dusty cabinet, then crossed
The dining table in script, scrawled
In capitals on the backs of chairs,
Practicing signatures like scales ?

5

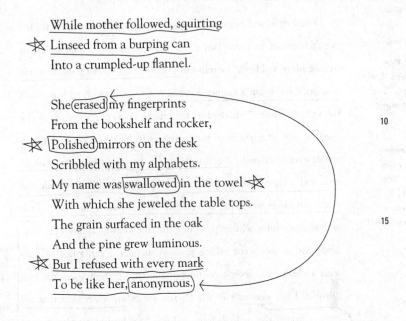

While mother followed, squirting
Linseed from a burping can
Into a crumpled-up flannel.

She erased my fingerprints
From the bookshelf and rocker,   10
Polished mirrors on the desk
Scribbled with my alphabets.
My name was swallowed in the towel
With which she jeweled the table tops.
The grain surfaced in the oak   15
And the pine grew luminous.
But I refused with every mark
To be like her, anonymous.

The student boxes and stars words that she thinks are important ("polished" and "swallows"). In addition, she boxes a simile ("like scales") that she wants to think more about. She also circles two words ("erased" and "anonymous") that she believes express an important theme and draws an arrow to connect them. Finally, she underlines what she tentatively thinks are the poem's key ideas. When she rereads her poem, her highlighting will make it easier for her to react to and interpret the poem's ideas.

Annotating

As you highlight a text, you also **annotate** it, recording your reactions in the form of marginal notes. In these notes, you may define new words, identify **allusions** and patterns of language or imagery, summarize key events, list a work's possible themes, suggest a character's motivation, examine the possible significance of a particular symbol, or record questions that occur to you as you read. Ideally, your annotations will help you find ideas to write about.

The following paragraph from John Updike's 1961 short story "A&P" (p. 160) was highlighted and annotated by a student in an Introduction to Literature course who was responding to the question, "Why does Sammy really quit his job?"

Lengel sighs and begins to look very patient and old and gray. He's been a friend of my parents for years. "Sammy, you don't want to do this to your Mom and Dad," he tells me. It's true, I don't. But it seems to me that once you begin a gesture it's fatal not to go through with it. I fold the apron, "Sammy" stitched in red on the pocket, and put it on the counter, and drop the bow tie on top of it. The bow tie is theirs, if you've ever wondered. "You'll feel this for the rest of your life," Lengel * says, and I know that's true, too, but remembering how he made the pretty girl blush makes me so scrunchy inside I punch the No Sale tab and the machine whirs "pee-pul" and the drawer splats out. One advantage to this scene taking place in summer, I can follow this up with a clean exit, there's no fumbling around getting your coat and galoshes, I just saunter into the electric eye in my white shirt that my mother ironed the night before, and the door heaves itself open, and outside the sunshine is skating around on the asphalt.

Margin annotations (handwritten):
- Action isn't the Result of thought.
- Sammy Reacts to the girl's embaRRassment.
- Need for a clean exit Romantic idea.
- →Romantic cowboy, but his mother iRons his shiRt (iRony).

Because the instructor had discussed the story in class and given students a specific assignment, these annotations are quite focused. In addition to high-lighting important information, the student notes her reactions to the story and tries to interpret the main character's actions.

Sometimes, however, you annotate a work before you have decided on a topic. In fact, the process of reading and responding to the text can help you find a topic to write about. If you don't yet have a topic, your annotations are likely to be somewhat unfocused, so you will probably need to make additional annotations when your essay's direction is clearer.

 ## Writing about Literature

Writing about literature—or about anything else—is an idiosyncratic pro-cess during which many activities occur at once: as you write, you think of ideas; as you think of ideas, you clarify the focus of your essay; and as you clarify your focus, you reshape your paragraphs and sentences and refine your word choice. Even though this process may sound disorganized, it has three distinct stages: *planning, drafting,* and *revising and editing.*

Planning an Essay

Considering Your Audience

Sometimes you write primarily for yourself—for example, when you write a journal entry. At other times, you write for others. As you write an essay, consider the special requirements of your **audience**. Is your audience your classmates or your instructor? Can you assume your readers are familiar with your essay's topic and with any technical terms you will use, or should you include brief plot summaries or definitions of key terms? If your audience is your instructor, remember that he or she is a representative of a larger academic audience that expects accurate information, logical arguments, and a certain degree of stylistic fluency—as well as standard English and correct grammar, mechanics, and spelling. In addition, your instructor expects you to support your statements with specific information, to express yourself clearly and unambiguously, and to document your sources. In short, your instructor wants to see how clearly you think and whether you are able to arrange your ideas into a well-organized, coherent essay.

In addition to being a member of a general academic audience, your instructor is also a member of a particular community of scholars—in this case, those who study literature. By writing about literature, you engage in a dialogue with this community. For this reason, you need to follow certain specific **conventions**—procedures that by habitual use have become accepted practice. Many of the conventions that apply specifically to writing about literature—matters of style, format, and the like—are discussed in this book. (The checklist on pages 20–21 addresses some of these conventions.)

Understanding Your Purpose

Sometimes you write with a single **purpose** in mind. At other times, you may have more than one purpose. In general terms, you may write for any of the following three reasons:

1. *Writing to respond*   When you write to **respond**, your goal is to discover and express your reactions to a work. To record your responses, you engage in relatively informal activities, such as brainstorming and journal writing (see pp. 9–11). As you write, you explore your own ideas, forming and re-forming your impressions of the work.

2. *Writing to interpret*   When you write to **interpret**, your aim is to explain a work's possible meanings. As you interpret a work of literature, you may summarize, give examples, or compare and contrast the work with other works or with your own experiences. Then, you may go on to analyze the work: as you discuss each of its elements, you put complex statements into your own words, define difficult concepts, and place ideas in context.

3. *Writing to evaluate*   When you write to evaluate, your purpose is to assess a work's literary merits. You may consider not only its aesthetic appeal but also its ability to retain that appeal over time and across national or cultural boundaries. As you write, you use your own critical sense and the opinions of experts to help you make judgments about the work.

█ NOTE   When you write a **literary argument**, your purpose is to **persuade**. See Chapter 2.

Choosing a Topic

When you write an essay about literature, you develop and support an idea about one or more literary works. Before you begin writing, you should make certain that you understand your assignment. Do you know how much time you have to complete your essay? Are you expected to rely on your own ideas, or are you able to consult outside sources? Is your essay to focus on a specific work or on a particular element of literature? Do you have to write on an assigned topic, or are you free to choose a topic? About how long should your essay be? Do you understand exactly what the assignment is asking you to do? Do you know what format to use?

Sometimes your assignment limits your options by telling you what you should discuss:

- Analyze Thomas Hardy's use of irony in his poem "The Man He Killed."
- Discuss Hawthorne's use of allegory in his short story "Young Goodman Brown."
- Explain Nora's actions at the end of Ibsen's *A Doll House*.

At other times, your instructor may give you few guidelines other than an essay's required length and format. In such situations, when you must choose a topic on your own, you can often find a topic by brainstorming or by writing journal entries. As you engage in these activities, keep in mind that you have many options to choose from:

- You can **explicate** a poem or a passage of a play or short story, doing a close reading and analyzing the text.
- You can **compare two works** of literature. (The Related Works lists that follow many of the selections in this book suggest possible connections.)
- You can **compare two characters** or discuss some trait those characters share.
- You can **trace a common theme**—jealousy, revenge, power, coming of age—in two or more works.
- You can **discuss a common subject**—war, love, nature—in two or more works.

- You can **analyze a single literary element** in one or more works—for instance, plot, point of view, or character development.
- You can **focus on a single aspect** of a literary element, such as the use of flashbacks, the effect of a shifting narrative perspective, or the role of a minor character.
- You can **apply a critical theory** to a work of literature—for instance, a feminist perspective to Tillie Olsen's "I Stand Here Ironing" (p. 217).
- You can **consider a work's cultural context**, examining connections between an issue treated in a work of literature—for instance, racism in Richard Wright's "Big Black Good Man" (p. 236) or postpartum psychosis in Charlotte Perkins Gilman's "The Yellow Wallpaper" (p. 434)—and that same issue as it is treated in professional journals or in the popular press.
- You can **examine some aspect of history or biography** and consider its relationship to a literary work—for instance, the influence of World War I on Wilfred Owen's poems.
- You can **explore a problem within a work and propose a possible solution**—for example, consider Montresor's possible motives for killing Fortunato in Edgar Allan Poe's "The Cask of Amontillado" (p. 249) and suggest the most likely one.
- You can **compare fiction and film**, exploring similarities and differences between a literary work and a film version of the work—for example, the different endings in Joyce Carol Oates's short story "Where Are You Going, Where Have You Been?" (p. 453) and *Smooth Talk*, the film version of the story.

Finding Something to Say

Once you have a topic, you have to find something to say about it. The ideas you came up with as you highlighted and annotated can help you formulate a statement that will be the central idea of your essay and will help you find material that can support that statement.

You can use a variety of strategies to find supporting material:

- You can **freewrite**—that is, write on a topic for a given period of time without pausing to consider style, structure, or content.
- You can discuss ideas with others—friends, classmates, instructors, parents, and so on.
- You can do research, either in print sources or online.

Two additional strategies—*brainstorming* and *keeping a journal*—are especially helpful at this stage of the writing process.

Brainstorming When you **brainstorm**, you record ideas—single words, phrases, or sentences (in the form of statements or questions)—as they occur to you, moving as quickly as possible. Your starting point may be a general assignment, a particular work (or works) of literature, or a specific topic. You can brainstorm at any stage of the writing process—alone or with other students—and you can repeat this activity as often as you like.

A student preparing to write an essay on the relationships between children and parents in four poems brainstormed about each poem. The following excerpt from her notes shows her preliminary reactions to one of the four poems, Adrienne Rich's "A Woman Mourned by Daughters."

> Memory: then and now
>
>   Then: leaf, straw, dead insect (= light);
>
>   ignored
>
>   Now: swollen, puffed up, weight (= heavy);
>
>   focus of attention controls their
>
>   movements.
>
> * Kitchen = a "universe"
>
>   Teaspoons, goblets, etc. = concrete
>
>   representations of mother; also =
>
>   obligations, responsibilities (like
>
>   plants and father)
>
>   (weigh on them, keep them under her spell)
>
>   Milestones of past: weddings, being fed as
>
>   children, "You breathe upon us now"
>
>   PARADOX? (Dead, she breathes, has weight,
>
>   fills house and sky. Alive, she was a dead
>
>   insect, no one paid attention to her.)

Keeping a Journal   You can record ideas in a journal (a notebook, a small notepad, or a computer file)—and, later, you can use these ideas in your essay. In a **journal**, you expand your marginal annotations, recording your responses to works you have read, noting questions, exploring emerging ideas, experimenting with possible essay topics, trying to paraphrase or summarize difficult concepts, or speculating about a work's ambiguities. A journal is the place to take chances, to try out ideas that may initially seem frivolous or irrelevant; here you can write until connections become clear or ideas crystallize.

As he prepared to write an essay analyzing the role of Jim—the "gentle-man caller" who is invited to meet Laura—the shy, lonely sister of the pro-tagonist in Tennessee Williams's 1945 play *The Glass Menagerie*, a student explored ideas in the following journal entry.

When he tells Laura that being disappointed is not the same as being discouraged, and that he's disappointed but not discouraged, Jim reveals his role as a symbol of the power of newness and change—a "bulldozer" that will clear out whatever is in its path, even delicate people like Laura. But the fact that he is disappointed shows Jim's human side. He has run into problems since high school, and these problems have blocked his progress toward a successful future. Working at the warehouse, Jim needs Tom's friendship to remind him of what he used to be (and what he still can be?), and this shows his inse-curity. He isn't as sure of himself as he seems to be.

Seeing Connections

As you review your notes, you try to discover patterns—to see repeated images, similar characters, recurring words and phrases, and interrelated themes or ideas. Identifying these patterns can help you to decide which points to make in your essay and what information you will use to support these points.

A student preparing an essay about D. H. Lawrence's short story "The Rocking-Horse Winner" (p. 409) made the following list of related ideas.

Secrets
  Mother can't feel love
  Paul gambles
  Paul gives mother money
  Family lives beyond means
  Paul gets information from horse
Religion
  Gambling becomes like a religion
  They all worship money
  Specific references: "serious as a church"; "It's as if he had it from heaven";
  "secret, religious voice"
Luck
  Father is unlucky
  Mother is desperate for luck
  Paul is lucky (ironic)

Deciding on a Thesis

When you are ready, you will express the main idea of your emerging essay in a **thesis statement**—an idea, usually expressed in a single sentence, that the rest of your essay will support. This idea should emerge logically out of your highlighting, annotating, brainstorming notes, journal entries, and lists of related ideas. Eventually, you will write a **thesis-and-support essay**: stating your thesis in your introduction, supporting the thesis in the body paragraphs of your essay, and reinforcing the thesis in your conclusion.

An effective thesis statement tells readers what your essay will discuss and how you will approach your material. For this reason, it should be precisely worded, making its point clear to your readers, and it should contain no vague words or imprecise phrases that will make it difficult for readers to follow your discussion.

In addition to being specific, your thesis statement should give your readers an accurate sense of the scope and direction of your essay. It should not make promises that you do not intend to fulfill or include extraneous details that might confuse your readers. If, for example, you are going to write an essay about the dominant image in a poem, your thesis should not imply that you will focus on the poem's setting or tone.

Remember that as you organize your ideas and as you write, you will probably modify and sharpen your thesis. Sometimes you will even begin planning your essay with one thesis in mind and end up with an entirely different one. If this happens, be sure to revise your body paragraphs so that they support your new thesis. If you find that your ideas about your topic are changing, don't be concerned; this is how the writing process works. (See p. 32 for more on stating a thesis.)

Preparing an Outline

Once you have decided on a thesis and have some idea how you will support it, you can begin to plan your essay's structure. At this stage of the writing process, an **outline** can help you to clarify your ideas and show how these ideas relate to one another.

A **scratch outline** is perhaps the most useful kind of outline for a short essay. An informal list of the main points you will discuss in your essay, a scratch outline is more focused than a simple list of related ideas because it presents ideas in the order in which they will be introduced. As its name implies, however, a scratch outline lacks the detail and the degree of organization of a more formal outline. The main purpose of a scratch outline is to give you a sense of the shape and order of your essay and thus enable you to begin writing.

A student writing a short essay on Edwin Arlington Robinson's use of irony in his poem "Miniver Cheevy" (1910) used the following scratch outline as a guide.

Speaker's Attitude
   Ironic
   Cynical
   Critical

Diction
  Formal
  Detached
Allusions
  Thebes
  Camelot
  Priam
  Medici
Repeated Words
  "Miniver"
  "thought"
Regular Rhyme Scheme

Drafting an Essay

A first draft is a preliminary version of your essay, something to react to and revise. Even before you actually begin drafting your essay, however, you should review the material you have collected. To make sure you are ready to begin drafting, take the following three steps:

1. ***Make sure you have collected enough information to support your thesis.*** The points you make are only as convincing as the evidence you present to support them. As you read and take notes, you collect supporting examples from the work or works about which you are writing. How many of these examples you need to use in your draft depends on the scope of your thesis. In general, the broader your thesis, the more material you need to support it. For example, if you were supporting the rather narrow thesis that the speech of a certain character in one scene of a play reveals important information about his motivation, only a few examples would be needed. However, if you wanted to support the broader thesis that Nora and Torvald Helmer in Henrik Ibsen's *A Doll House* (p. 881) are trapped in their roles, you would need to present a wide range of examples.

2. ***See if the work includes any details that contradict your thesis.*** Before you begin writing, test the validity of your thesis by looking for details that contradict it. For example, if you plan to support the thesis that in *A Doll House*, Ibsen makes a strong case for the rights of women, you should look for counterexamples. Can you find subtle hints in the play that suggest women should remain locked in their traditional roles and continue to defer to their fathers and husbands? If so, you will want to modify your thesis accordingly.

3. ***Consider whether you need to use outside sources to help you support your thesis.*** You could, for example, strengthen the thesis that *A Doll House* challenged contemporary attitudes about marriage by including

the information that when the play first opened, Ibsen was convinced by an apprehensive theater manager to write an alternative ending. In this new ending, Ibsen had Nora decide, after she stopped briefly to look in at her sleeping children, that she could not leave her family. Sometimes information from a source can even lead you to change your thesis. For example, after reading A Doll House, you might have decided that Ibsen's purpose was to make a strong case for the rights of women. In class, however, you might learn that Ibsen repeatedly said that his play was about the rights of all human beings, not just of women. This information could lead you to a thesis that suggests Torvald is just as trapped in his role as Nora is in hers. Naturally, Ibsen's interpretation of his own work does not invalidate your first judgment, but it does suggest another conclusion that is worth investigating.

After carefully evaluating the completeness, relevance, and validity of your supporting material, you can begin drafting your essay, using your scratch outline as a guide. In this first draft, your focus should be on the body of your essay; this is not the time to worry about constructing the "perfect" introduction and conclusion. (In fact, many writers, knowing that their ideas will change as they write, postpone writing these paragraphs until a later draft, preferring instead to begin simply by stating their thesis.) As you write, remember that your first draft will probably not be as clear as you would like it to be; still, it will enable you to see your ideas begin to take shape.

Revising and Editing an Essay

Revision

When you **revise**, you literally "re-see" your draft; sometimes you then go on to reorder and rewrite substantial portions of your essay. Before you are satisfied with your essay, you will probably write several drafts—each more closely focused and more coherent than the previous one.

Strategies for Revision

Two strategies can help you to revise your drafts: *peer review* and *a dialogue with your instructor*:

1. **Peer review** is a process in which students assess each other's work-in-progress. This activity may be carried out in informal sessions during which one student comments on another's draft, or it may be a formal process in which students respond to specific questions on a form supplied by the instructor or participate in a discussion online. In either case, one student's reactions can help another student revise.

2. **A dialogue with your instructor**—in a face-to-face conference or by email—can give you a sense of how to proceed with your revision. Establishing such an oral or written dialogue can help you learn how to respond critically to your own writing, and your reactions to your instructor's comments on any draft can help you to clarify your essay's goals and write drafts that are increasingly consistent with these goals. (If your instructor is not available, try to schedule a conference with a writing center tutor.)

As you move through successive drafts, the task of revising your essay will be easier if you follow a systematic process. As you read and react to your essay, begin by assessing the effectiveness of the larger elements—for example, your thesis statement and your key supporting ideas—and then move on to examine increasingly smaller elements.

Thesis Statement First, reconsider your **thesis statement**. Is it carefully and precisely worded? Does it provide a realistic idea of what your essay will cover? Does it make a point that is worth supporting?

Vague: Many important reasons exist to explain why Margot Macomber's shooting of her husband was probably intentional.

Revised: Although Hemingway's text states that Margot Macomber "shot at the buffalo," a careful analysis of her relationship with her husband suggests that in fact she intended to kill him.

Vague: Dickens's characters are a lot like those of Addison and Steele.

Revised: With their familiar physical and moral traits, Charles Dickens's minor characters are similar to the "characters" created by the eighteenth-century essayists Joseph Addison and Richard Steele for the newspaper the *Spectator*.

Supporting Ideas Next, assess the appropriateness of your **supporting ideas,** considering whether you present enough support for your thesis and whether all the details you include are relevant to that thesis. Make sure you have supported your key points with specific, concrete examples from the work or works you are discussing, briefly summarizing key events, quoting dialogue or description, and describing characters or settings. Make certain, however, that your own ideas are central to the essay and that you have not substituted plot summary for analysis and interpretation. Your goal is to draw a conclusion about one or more works and to support that conclusion with pertinent details. If an event in a story you are analyzing supports a point you wish to make, include a *brief* summary; then, explain its relevance to the point you are making.

In the following excerpt from an essay on a short story by James Joyce, the first sentence briefly summarizes a key event, and the second sentence explains its significance.

> At the end of James Joyce's "Counterparts," when Farrington returns home after a day of frustration and abuse at work, his reaction is to strike out at his son Tom. This act shows that although he and his son are similarly victimized, Farrington is also the counterpart of his tyrannical boss.

Topic Sentences   Now, turn your attention to the **topic sentences** that present the main ideas of your body paragraphs. Make sure that each topic sentence is clearly worded and that it signals the direction of your discussion.

Be especially careful to avoid abstractions and vague generalities in topic sentences. Also avoid words and phrases such as *involves, deals with, concerns, revolves around,* and *pertains to,* which are likely to make your topic sentences wordy and imprecise.

Vague: One similarity involves the dominance of the men by women. (What is the similarity?)

Revised: In both stories, a man is dominated by a woman.

Vague: There is one reason for the fact that Jay Gatsby remains a mystery. (What is the reason?)

Revised: Because *The Great Gatsby* is narrated by the outsider Nick Carraway, Jay Gatsby himself remains a mystery.

When revising topic sentences that are intended to move readers from one point (or one section of your essay) to another, be sure the relationship between the ideas they link is clear. A topic sentence should include transitions that look back at the previous paragraphs as well as ahead to the paragraph it introduces.

Unclear: Now, the poem's imagery will be discussed.

Revised: <u>Another reason</u> for the poem's effectiveness is its unusual imagery.

Unclear: The sheriff's wife is another interesting character.

Revised: <u>Like her friend Mrs. Hale</u>, the sheriff's wife also has mixed feelings about what Mrs. Wright has done.

Introduction and Conclusion   When you are satisfied with the body of your essay, you can turn your attention to your essay's *introduction* and *conclusion*.

The **introduction** of an essay about literature should identify the works to be discussed and their authors and indicate the emphasis of the discussion to follow. Depending on your purpose and on your essay's topic, you may want to provide some historical background or biographical information or briefly discuss the work in relation to similar works. Like all introductions, the one you write for an essay about literature should create interest in your topic and should include a clear thesis statement.

The following introduction, though acceptable for a first draft, is in need of revision.

> **Draft:**   Revenge, which is defined as "the chance to retaliate, get satisfaction, take vengeance, or inflict damage or injury in return for an injury, insult, etc.," is a major theme in many of the stories we have read. The stories that will be discussed here deal with a variety of ways to seek revenge. In my essay, I will consider some of these differences.

Although the student clearly identifies her essay's topic, she does not identify the works she will discuss or the particular point she will make about revenge. Her tired opening strategy, a dictionary definition, is not likely to create interest in her topic, and her announcement of her intention in the last sentence is awkward and unnecessary. The following revised introduction is much more effective.

> **Revised:**   In Edgar Allan Poe's "The Cask of Amontillado," Montresor vows revenge on Fortunato for an unspecified "insult"; in Ring Lardner's "Haircut," Paul, a young mentally challenged man, gets even with a cruel practical joker who has taunted him for years. Both of these stories present characters who seek revenge, and both stories end in murder. However, the murderers' motivations are presented very differently. In "Haircut," the narrator is unaware of the significance of many events, and his ignorance helps to create sympathy for the murderer; in "The Cask of Amontillado," where the narrator is actually the murderer, Montresor's inability to offer a convincing motive turns the reader against him.

In your **conclusion**, you reinforce your thesis and perhaps sum up your essay's main points; then, you make a graceful exit.

The conclusion that follows is acceptable for a first draft, but it needs further development.

> **Draft:**   Although the characters of Montresor and Paul were created by different authors at different times, they do have similar motives and goals. However, they are portrayed very differently.

The following revised conclusion reinforces the essay's main point, effectively incorporating a brief quotation from "The Cask of Amontillado":

Revised: What is significant is not whether each murderer's act is justified, but rather how each murderer, and each victim, is portrayed by the narrator. Montresor—driven by a thirst to avenge a "thousand injuries" as well as a final insult—is shown to be sadistic and unrepentant; in "Haircut," it is Jim, the victim, whose sadism and lack of remorse are revealed to the reader.

Sentences and Words Now, focus on the individual sentences and words of your essay. Begin by evaluating your **transitions**, the words and phrases that link sentences and paragraphs. Be sure that every necessary transitional element has been supplied and that each word or phrase you have selected accurately conveys the exact relationship (sequence, contradiction, and so on) between ideas.

When you are satisfied with the clarity and appropriateness of your essay's transitions, consider sentence variety and word choice:

- Be sure you have varied your sentence structure. You will bore your readers if all your sentences begin with the subject ("He…He…"; "The story…The story…").
- Make sure that all the words you have selected communicate your ideas accurately and that you have not used vague, inexact diction. For example, saying that a character is *bad* is not as helpful as describing him or her as *ruthless, conniving,* or *malicious.*
- Eliminate subjective expressions, such as *I think, in my opinion, I believe, it seems to me,* and *I feel.* These phrases weaken your essay by suggesting that its ideas are "only" your opinions and have no objective validity.

Documentation Make certain that all references to sources are integrated smoothly into your sentences and that all information that is not your own is documented appropriately. For specific information on using and documenting sources, see Chapter 3.

✔ **CHECKLIST** **Using Sources**

When you incorporate source material into your essays, follow these guidelines:

☐ Acknowledge all material from sources, including the literary work or works under discussion, using the documentation style of the Modern Language Association (MLA).

- Combine paraphrases, summaries, and quotations with your own interpretations, weaving quotations smoothly into your essay. Introduce the words or ideas of others with a phrase that identifies their source ("According to Richard Wright's biographer, . . . "), and end with appropriate parenthetical documentation.

- Use quotations *only* when something vital would be lost if you did not reproduce the author's exact words.

- Integrate short quotations (four lines or fewer of prose or three lines or fewer of poetry) smoothly into your essay. Use a slash (/) with one space on either side to separate lines of poetry. Be sure to enclose quotations in quotation marks.

- Set off quotations of more than four lines of prose or more than three lines of poetry by indenting one-half inch from the left-hand margin. Double-space, and do not use quotation marks. If you are quoting just one paragraph, do not indent the first line.

- Use ellipses—three spaced periods—to indicate that you have omitted material within a quotation (but never use ellipses at the beginning of a quoted passage).

- Use brackets to indicate that you have added words to a quotation: As Earl notes, "[Willie] is a modern-day Everyman" (201). Use brackets to alter a quotation so that it fits grammatically into your sentence: Wilson says that Miller "offer[s] audiences a dark view of the present" (74).

- Place commas and periods *inside* quotation marks: According to Robert Coles, the child could "make others smile."

- Place punctuation marks other than commas and periods *outside* quotation marks: What does Frost mean when he says, "a poem must ride on its own melting"? However, if the punctuation mark is part of the quoted material, place it *inside* the quotation marks: In "Mending Wall," Frost asks, "Why do they make good neighbors?"

- When citing part of a short story or novel, supply the page number (143). For a poem, supply line numbers (3–5), including the word *line* or *lines* in just the first reference. For a play, supply act, scene, and line numbers in arabic numerals (2.2.17-22).

- Include a works-cited list.

Editing and Proofreading

Once you have finished revising, you **edit**—that is, you make certain that your essay's grammar, punctuation, spelling, and mechanics are correct. Always run a spell check, but remember that you still have to **proofread**—look carefully for errors that the spell checker will not identify. These include homophones (*brake* incorrectly used instead of *break*), typos that create correctly spelled words (*work* instead of *word*), and words (such as a technical or foreign term or a writer's name) that may not be in your computer's dictionary. If you use a grammar checker, remember that although grammar programs may identify potential problems—long sentences, for example—they may not be able to determine whether a particular long sentence is grammatically correct (let alone stylistically pleasing). Always keep a style handbook nearby so that you can double-check any problems a spell checker or grammar checker highlights in your writing.

As you edit, pay particular attention to the special conventions of literary essays, some of which are addressed in the checklist below. When your editing is complete, give your essay a descriptive title. Before you print your final copy, be sure that its format conforms to your instructor's requirements.

✔ **CHECKLIST**   Conventions of Writing about Literature

When you write about works of literature, follow these guidelines:

- Use present-tense verbs when discussing works of literature: "The character of Mrs. Mallard's husband is not developed...."

- Use past-tense verbs only when discussing historical events ("Owen's poem conveys the destructiveness of World War I, which at the time the poem was written was considered to be..."); when presenting historical or biographical data ("Her first novel, which was published in 1811 when Austen was thirty-six,..."); or when identifying events that occurred prior to the time of the story's main action ("Miss Emily is a recluse; since her father's death she has lived alone except for a servant").

- Avoid unnecessary plot summary. Your goal is to draw a conclusion about one or more works and to support that conclusion with pertinent details. If a plot detail supports a point you wish to make, a *brief* summary is acceptable. But remember, plot summary is no substitute for analysis.

- Use literary terms accurately. For example, be careful not to confuse *narrator* or *speaker* with *author;* feelings or opinions expressed by a narrator or character do not necessarily represent those of the author.

You should not say, "In the poem's last stanza, *Frost* expresses his indecision" when you mean that the poem's *speaker* is indecisive.

- Italicize titles of novels and plays; place titles of short stories and poems within quotation marks.

- Refer to authors of literary works by their full names (*Edgar Allan Poe*) in your first reference to them and by their last names (*Poe*) in subsequent references. Never refer to authors by their first names, and never use titles that indicate marital status (*Flannery O'Connor* or *O'Connor*, never *Flannery* or *Miss O'Connor*).

- Be careful not to make sweeping or unrealistic claims. Remember that the support you present cannot "prove" that what you are saying is true, so choose verbs like *demonstrate, show, suggest*, and *indicate* rather than *prove*.

Three Model Student Essays

The three papers in this section were written by students in an Introduction to Literature course. The first, by John Frei, analyzes the short story "The Secret Lion" (p. 466); the second, by Catherine Whittaker, compares the poems "Those Winter Sundays" (p. 705) and "Digging" (p. 706); the third, by Kimberly Allison, discusses the play *Trifles* (p. 867). As they planned, drafted, and revised these essays, the students followed the writing process described in this chapter.

Frei 1

John Frei

Professor Nyysola

English 102

14 January 2015

"The Secret Lion": Everything Changes

The first paragraph of Alberto Alvaro Ríos's "The Secret Lion" presents a twelve-year-old's view of growing up: everything changes. When the magician pulls a tablecloth out from under a pile of dishes, the child is amazed at the "staying-the-same part" (467); adults focus on the tablecloth. As adults, we have the benefit of experience; we know the trick will work as long as the technique is correct.

Opening paragraph identifies work and author. Parenthetical documentation identifies source of quotation.

Frei 2

We gain confidence, but we lose our innocence, and we lose our sense of wonder. The price we pay for knowledge is a permanent sense of loss, and this trade-off is central to "The Secret Lion," a story whose key symbols reinforce its central theme: that change is inevitable and that change is always accompanied by loss.

Thesis statement

    The golf course is one symbol that helps to convey this theme. When the boys first see the golf course, it is "heaven" (470). Lush and green and carefully tended, it is very different from the dry, brown Arizona landscape and the polluted arroyo. In fact, to the boys it is another world, as exotic as Oz and ultimately as unreal. Before long, the Emerald City becomes black and white again. They learn that there is no such thing as a "Coke-holder," that their "acting 'rich'" is just an act, and that their heaven is only a golf course (471). As the narrator acknowledges, "Something got taken away from us that moment. Heaven" (471).

Topic sentence identifies one key symbol.

    The arroyo, a dry gulch that can fill up with water, is another symbol that reflects the idea of the inevitability of change and of the loss that accompanies change. It is a special, Edenlike place for the boys—a place where they can rebel by shouting forbidden words and by swimming in forbidden waters. Although it represents a retreat from the disillusionment of the golf course, and it is clearly second choice, it is still their "personal Mississippi" (467), full of possibilities. Eventually, though, the arroyo too disappoints the boys, and they stop going there. As the narrator says, "Nature seemed to keep pushing us around one way or another, teaching us the same thing every place we ended up" (468). The lesson they keep learning is that nothing is permanent.

Topic sentence identifies another key symbol.

    The grinding ball, round and perfect, suggests permanence and stability. But when the boys find it, they realize at once that they cannot keep it forever, just as they cannot remain balanced forever between childhood and adulthood. Like a child's life, the ball is perfect but temporary. Burying it is their desperate attempt to stop time, to preserve perfection in an imperfect world, innocence in an adult world. But the boys are already twelve years old, and they have learned nature's lesson well enough to know that this action will not work.

Topic sentence identifies another key symbol.

Even if they had been able to find the ball, the perfection and the innocence it suggests to them would still be unattainable. Perhaps that is why they do not try very hard to find it.

Like the story's other symbols, the secret lion itself suggests the most profound kind of change: the movement from innocence to experience, from childhood to adulthood, from expectation to disappointment to resignation. The narrator explains that when he was twelve, "something happened that we didn't have a name for, but it was there nonetheless like a lion, and roaring, roaring that way the biggest things do. Everything changed" (466). School was different, girls were different, language was different. Despite its loud roar, the lion remained paradoxically "secret," unnoticed until it passed. Like adolescence, the secret lion is a roaring disturbance that unsettles everything for a brief time and then passes, leaving everything changed.

> Topic sentence identifies final (and most important) symbol.

In an attempt to make things stay the same, to make time stand still, the boys bury the grinding ball "because it was perfect.... It was the lion" (471). The grinding ball is "like that place, that whole arroyo" (468): secret and perfect. The ball and the arroyo and the lion are all perfect, but all, ironically, are temporary. The first paragraph of "The Secret Lion" tells us, "Everything changed" (466); by the last paragraph, we learn what this change means: "Things get taken away" (471). In other words, change implies loss. Heaven turns out to be just a golf course; the round, perfect object is only "a cannonball thing used in mining" (467); the arroyo is just a polluted stream; and childhood is just a phase. "Things get taken away," and this knowledge that things do not last is the lion, secret yet roaring.

> Conclusion

Work Cited

Ríos, Alberto Alvaro. "The Secret Lion." *Portable Literature: Reading, Reacting, Writing*, edited by Laurie G. Kirszner and Stephen R. Mandell, 9th ed., Wadsworth, 2016, pp. 466-71.

Whittaker 1

Catherine Whittaker

Professor Jackson

English 102

5 January 2015

Digging for Memories

Robert Hayden's "Those Winter Sundays" and Seamus Heaney's **[Introduction]**
"Digging" are two poems that are tributes to the speakers' fathers.
Although the depiction of the families and the tones of the two **[Thesis statement]**
poems are different, the common thread of love between fathers
and children extends through the two poems, and each speaker is
inspired by his father's example.

Many other poets have written about children and their fathers. Some
of these poems express regret and gratitude. For example, Judith Ortiz Cofer
in "My Father in the Navy: A Childhood Memory" writes a touching **[References to poems include complete authors' names and titles.]**
tribute to her father, whose homecomings were so eagerly awaited.
In other poems, such as Theodore Roethke's "My Papa's Waltz,"
fathers are depicted as imperfect, vulnerable people who try to
cope with life as well as possible.

As these and other poems reveal, reflections on childhood can bring
complex memories to light, as they do for Hayden's and Heaney's speakers.
Now adults, they reminisce about their childhoods with a mature sense of
enlightenment not found in children. Both speakers describe their **[First point of similarity: both poems focus on memory.]**
fathers' hard work and dedication to their families. For example,
Hayden's speaker remembers that even after working hard all week,
his father would get up early on Sunday to warm the house in
preparation for his sleeping children. The speaker vividly portrays
his father's hands, describing "cracked hands that ached / from **[First reference to lines of poetry includes *line* or *lines*. Subsequent references include just line numbers.]**
labor in the weekday weather" (lines 3-4). And yet, these same
hands not only built the fires that drove out the cold but also polished his children's good shoes. In a similar way, Heaney's speaker
reminisces about his father's and grandfather's digging of soil and
sod, pointing out their skill and their dedication to their tasks.

Whittaker 2

The fathers in these poems appear to be hard workers, laborers who struggled to support their families. Not only were they dedicated to their work, but they also loved their children. Looking back, Hayden's speaker realizes that, although his childhood may not have been perfect and his family life was not entirely without problems, his father loved him. Heaney's description of the potato picking allows us to imagine a loving family led by a father and grandfather who worked together and included the children in both work and celebration. Heaney's speaker grows into a man who has nothing but respect for his father and grandfather, wishing to be like them and to somehow fill their shoes.

> Second point of similarity: both fathers are hard workers.

Although some similarities exist between the fathers (and the sons) in the poems, the family life the two poems depict is very different. Perhaps it is the tone of each poem that best reveals the family atmosphere. The tone of "Digging" is wholesome, earthy, natural, and happy, emphasizing the healthy and caring nature of the speaker's childhood. Heaney's speaker seems to have no bad memories of his father or family. In contrast, the tone of Hayden's poem is very much like the coldness of the Sunday mornings. Even though the father warmed the house, the "chronic angers of that house" (9) did not leave with the cold. The speaker, as a child, seems to have resented his father, blaming him for the family's problems. The warm relationship readers see between the father and the son in Heaney's poem is absent in Hayden's.

> Focus shifts to contrast between the two poems.

In spite of these differences, readers cannot go away from either poem without the impression that both speakers learned important lessons from their fathers. Both fathers had a great amount of inner strength and were dedicated to their families. As the years have passed, Hayden's speaker has come to realize the depth of his father's devotion to his family. He uses the image of the "blueblack cold" (2) that was splintered and broken by the fires lovingly prepared by his father to suggest the father's efforts to keep his family free from harm. The cold suggests the tensions of the

> Focus returns to parallels between the two poems. Third point of similarity: both speakers learn from fathers (discussed in two paragraphs).

3

family, but the father is determined to force these tensions out of the house through his "austere and lonely offices" (14).

In Heaney's poem, the father—and the grandfather—also had a profound impact on the young speaker. As the memories come pouring back, the speaker's admiration for the men who came before him forces him to reflect on his own life and work. He realizes that he will never have the ability (or the desire) to do the physical labor of his relatives: "I've no spade to follow men like them" (28). However, just as the spade was the tool of his father and grandfather, the pen will be the tool with which the speaker will work. The shovel suggests the hard work, effort, and determination of the men who came before him, and the pen is the literary equivalent of the shovel. Heaney's speaker has been inspired by his father and grandfather, and he hopes to accomplish with a pen in the world of literature what they accomplished with a shovel on the land.

"Digging" and "Those Winter Sundays" are poems written from the perspective of adult sons who admire and appreciate their fathers. Childhood memories not only evoke vivid images of the past but also lead the speakers to insight and enlightenment. Long after childhood, the fathers' influence over their sons is evident; only now, however, do the speakers appreciate its true importance.

Conclusion reinforces thesis.

Whittaker 4

Works Cited

Hayden, Robert. "Those Winter Sundays." Kirszner and Mandell, pp. 705-06.

Heaney, Seamus. "Digging." Kirszner and Mandell, pp. 706-07.

Kirszner, Laurie G., and Stephen R. Mandell, editors. *Portable Literature: Reading, Reacting, Writing*. 9th ed., Wadsworth, 2016.

Allison 1

Kimberly Allison

Professor Johnson

English 1013

3 January 2015

Desperate Measures: Acts of Defiance in Trifles

Susan Glaspell wrote her best-known play, *Trifles*, in 1916, at a time when married women were beginning to challenge their socially defined roles, realizing that their identities as wives kept them in a subordinate position in society. Because women were demanding more autonomy, traditional institutions such as marriage, which confined women to the home and made them mere extensions of their husbands, were beginning to be reexamined.

> Opening sentence identifies author and work.

> Introduction places play in historical context.

Evidently touched by these concerns, Glaspell chose as her play's protagonist a married woman, Minnie Wright, who challenged society's expectations in a very extreme way: by murdering her husband. Minnie's defiant act has occurred before the action begins; during the play, two women, Mrs. Peters and Mrs. Hale, who accompany their husbands on an investigation of the murder scene, piece together the details of the situation surrounding the murder. As the events unfold, however, it becomes clear that the focus of *Trifles* is not on who killed John Wright but on the themes of the subordinate role of women, the confinement of the wife in the home, and the experiences all women share. With these themes, Glaspell shows her audience the desperate measures women had to take to achieve autonomy.

> Thesis statement

The subordinate role of women, particularly Minnie's role in her marriage, becomes evident in the first few minutes of the play, when Mr. Hale observes that the victim, John Wright, had little concern for his wife's opinions: "I didn't know as what his wife wanted made much difference to John—" (869). Here Mr. Hale suggests that Mrs. Wright was powerless against the wishes of her husband. Indeed, as these characters imply, Mrs. Wright's every act and thought was

> Topic sentence identifies first point essay will discuss: women's subordinate role.

Allison 2

controlled by her husband, who tried to break her spirit by forcing her
to stay alone in the house, performing repetitive domestic chores.
Mrs. Wright's only source of power in the household was her kitchen work,
a situation that Mrs. Peters and Mrs. Hale understand because their own
behavior is also determined by their husbands. Therefore, when Sheriff
Peters makes fun of Minnie's concern about her preserves, saying, "Well,
can you beat the women! Held for murder and worryin' about her preserves"
(871), he is, in a sense, criticizing all three of the women for worrying
about domestic matters rather than about the murder that has been committed. Indeed, the sheriff's comment suggests that he assumes women's
lives are trivial, an attitude that influences the thoughts and speech of all
three men.

    Mrs. Peters and Mrs. Hale are similar to Minnie Wright in
another way as well: throughout the play, they are confined to the
kitchen of the Wrights' house. As a result, the kitchen becomes the
focal point of the play—and, ironically, the women find that the
kitchen holds the clues to Mrs. Wright's loneliness and to the details
of the murder. Mrs. Peters and Mrs. Hale remain confined to the
kitchen while their husbands enter and exit the house at will. This
situation mirrors Minnie Wright's daily life, as she remained in the
home while her husband went to work and into town. As they move about
the kitchen, the two women discuss Minnie Wright's isolation: "Not having
children makes less work—but it makes a quiet house, and Wright out to
work all day, and no company when he did come in" (876). Beginning to
identify with Mrs. Wright's loneliness, Mrs. Peters and Mrs. Hale recognize
that, busy in their own homes, they have participated in isolating and
confining Minnie Wright. Mrs. Hale declares, "Oh, I *wish* I'd come over here
once in a while! That was a crime! That was a crime! Who's going to punish
that?...I might have known she needed help!" (879).

    Soon the two women discover that Mrs. Wright's only connection to
the outside world was her bird, the symbol of her confinement; she herself

> Topic sentence introduces second point essay will discuss: women's confinement in the home.

Allison 3

was a caged bird who was kept from singing and communicating with others because of her husband. And piecing together the evidence—the disorderly kitchen, the misstitched quilt pieces, and the dead canary—the women come to believe that John Wright broke the bird's neck, just as he had broken his wife's spirit. At this point, Mrs. Peters and Mrs. Hale understand the connection between the dead canary and Minnie Wright's motivation. The stage directions describe the moment when the women become aware of the truth behind the murder: "*Their eyes meet,*" and the women share "*A look of growing comprehension, of horror*" (877).

> Transitional paragraph discusses women's observations and conclusions.

Through their observations and discussions in Mrs. Wright's kitchen, Mrs. Hale and Mrs. Peters come to understand the commonality of women's experiences. Mrs. Hale speaks for both of them when she says, "I know how things can be—for women....We all go through the same thing—it's all just a different kind of the same thing" (879). And once the two women realize the experiences they share, they begin to recognize that they must join together in order to challenge their male-oriented society; although their experiences may seem trivial to the men, the "trifles" of their lives are significant to them. They realize that Minnie's independence and identity were crushed by her husband and that their own husbands also believe that women's lives are trivial and unimportant. This realization leads them to commit an act as defiant as the one that got Minnie into trouble: they conceal their discovery from their husbands and from the law.

> Topic sentence introduces third point essay will discuss: experiences women share.

Significantly, Mrs. Peters does acknowledge that "the law is the law" (874), yet she still seems to believe that because Mr. Wright treated his wife badly, she is justified in killing him. They also realize, however, that for men the law is black and white and that an all-male jury will not take into account the extenuating circumstances that prompted Minnie Wright to kill her husband. And even if Mrs. Wright were allowed to communicate to the all-male court the psychological abuse she has suffered, the law would

Allison 4

undoubtedly view her experience as trivial because a woman who complained about how her husband treated her would be seen as ungrateful.

Nevertheless, because Mrs. Hale and Mrs. Peters empathize with Mrs. Wright's situation, they suppress the evidence they find, enduring their husbands' condescension rather than standing up to them. And through this desperate action, the women break through the boundaries of their social role, just as Minnie Wright has done. Although Mrs. Wright is imprisoned for her crime, she has freed herself; and although Mrs. Peters and Mrs. Hale conceal their knowledge, fearing the men will laugh at them, these women are really challenging society and, in this way, freeing themselves as well.

In *Trifles*, Susan Glaspell addresses many of the problems shared by early-twentieth-century women, including their subordinate status and their confinement in the home. In order to emphasize the pervasiveness of these problems and the desperate measures women had to take to break out of restrictive social roles, Glaspell does more than focus on the plight of a woman who has ended her isolation and loneliness by committing a heinous crime against society. By presenting characters who demonstrate the vast differences between male and female experience, she illustrates how men define the roles of women and how women must challenge these roles in search of their own significance in society and their eventual independence.

Conclusion places play in historical context.

Allison 5

Work Cited

Glaspell, Susan. *Trifles. Portable Literature: Reading, Reacting, Writing*, edited by Laurie G. Kirszner and Stephen R. Mandell, 9th ed., Wadsworth, 2016, pp. 867-80.

CHAPTER 2

WRITING LITERARY ARGUMENTS

Many of the essays you write about literature are **expository**—that is, you write to give information to readers. For example, you might discuss the rhyme or meter of a poem or examine the interaction of two characters in a play. Other essays you write, however, may be **literary arguments**—that is, you take a position on a debatable topic and attempt to change readers' minds about it. For example, you might argue that the boy's quest in James Joyce's short story "Araby" (p. 288) has symbolic meaning or that Sammy, the main character in John Updike's short story "A&P" (p. 160), is sexist.

When you write a literary argument, you follow the same process you do when you write any essay about a literary topic. However, because the purpose of an argument is to convince readers, you need to use some additional strategies to present your ideas.

 Planning a Literary Argument

Choosing a Topic

Your first step in writing a literary argument will be to decide on a topic to write about. Ideally, your topic should be one that you really want to explore further. It stands to reason that the more your topic interests you, the more willing you will be to do some serious research and some hard thinking.

Your topic should also be narrow enough for you to develop within your page limit. After all, in an argumentative essay, you will have to present your own ideas and supply convincing support while possibly also addressing opposing arguments. If your topic is too broad, you will not be able to discuss it in enough detail.

Finally, your topic should be interesting to your readers. Keep in mind that some topics—such as the significance of the wall in Robert Frost's poem "Mending Wall" (p. 764)—have been written about so often that you will probably not be able to say anything new or interesting about them. Instead of relying on an overused topic, choose one that allows you to write something original.

Developing an Argumentative Thesis

After you have chosen a topic, your next step is to develop an **argumentative thesis**—one that takes a strong stand on an issue. Because an argumentative essay attempts to change the way readers think, it should focus on a thesis about which reasonable people disagree. In other words, it must be **debatable**; that is, it must have at least two sides. A factual statement—one about which reasonable people do not disagree—is therefore not appropriate as a thesis for an argumentative essay.

Factual Statement: Linda Loman is Willie's long-suffering wife in Arthur Miller's play *Death of a Salesman*.

Debatable Thesis: More than a stereotype of the long-suffering wife, Linda Loman in Arthur Miller's play *Death of a Salesman* is a complex character.

One way to make sure that your thesis actually does take a stand is to try to formulate an **antithesis**—a statement that takes an arguable position opposite from yours. If you can construct an antithesis, you can be certain that your thesis statement is debatable. If you cannot, your thesis statement needs further revision.

Thesis Statement: The last line of Richard Wright's short story "Big Black Good Man" indicates that Jim was fully aware all along of Olaf's deep-seated racial prejudice.

Antithesis: The last line of Richard Wright's short story "Big Black Good Man" indicates that Jim remained unaware of Olaf's feelings toward him.

█ NOTE   Your thesis statement is an assertion that your entire essay supports. Keep in mind, however, that you can never prove an argumentative thesis conclusively—if you could, there would be no argument. The best you can do is provide enough evidence to establish a high probability that your thesis is reasonable.

✔ CHECKLIST   Developing an Argumentative Thesis

To make sure you have an effective argumentative thesis, consider these questions:

▢ Does your thesis statement make clear to readers what position you are taking?

▢ Can you formulate an antithesis?

▢ Can you support your thesis with evidence from the text and from research?

Defining Your Terms

You should always define the key terms you use in your argument. For example, if you are using the term *narrator* in an essay, make sure that readers know whether you are referring to a first-person or a third-person narrator. In addition, you may need to clarify the difference between an **unreliable narrator**—someone who misrepresents or misinterprets events—and a **reliable narrator**—someone who accurately describes events. Without a clear definition of the terms you are using, readers may have a difficult time understanding the point you are making.

Defining Your Terms

Be especially careful to use precise terms in your thesis statement. Avoid vague and judgmental words, such as *wrong, bad, good, right,* and *immoral.*

Vague: The poem "Birmingham Sunday (September 15, 1963)" by Langston Hughes shows how bad racism can be.

Clearer: The poem "Birmingham Sunday (September 15, 1963)" by Langston Hughes makes a moving statement about how pervasive and dehumanizing racism can be.

Considering Your Audience

As you plan your essay, keep your audience in mind. For example, if you are writing about a work that has been discussed in class, you can assume that your readers are familiar with it; include plot summary only when it is needed to explain a point you are making. Keep in mind that you will be addressing an academic audience—your instructor and possibly some students. For this reason, you should be sure to follow the conventions of writing about literature as well as the conventions of standard written English. (For information on the conventions of writing about literature, see the checklist in Chapter 1, pp. 20–21.)

When you write an argumentative essay, you should assume that you are addressing a **skeptical audience**—one that is not easily convinced. Remember, your thesis is debatable, so not everyone will agree with you—and even if your readers are sympathetic to your position, you cannot assume that they will accept your ideas without question.

The strategies you use to convince your readers will vary according to your relationship with them. Somewhat skeptical readers may need to see only that your argument is logical and that your evidence is solid. More skeptical readers, however, may need to see that you understand their reservations and that you concede some of their points. Of course, you may never be able to convince hostile readers that your conclusions are legitimate. The best you can hope for is that these readers will acknowledge the strengths of your argument even if they do not accept your conclusion.

Refuting Opposing Arguments

As you develop your literary argument, you may often need to **refute**—that is, to disprove or raise doubts about—opposing arguments by demonstrating that they are false, misguided, exaggerated, or illogical. By summarizing and refuting opposing views, you make opposing arguments seem less credible to readers; thus, you strengthen your case. When an opposing argument is so strong that it cannot be easily dismissed, however, you should acknowledge the strength of the argument and then point out its limitations.

Notice in the following paragraph how a student refutes the argument that Homer Barron, a character in William Faulkner's short story "A Rose for Emily," is gay.

Summary of opposing argument	A number of critics have suggested that Homer Barron, Miss Emily's suitor, is gay. Actually, there is some evidence in the story to support this interpretation. For example, the narrator points out that Homer "liked men" and that he
Acknowledgment of argument's strengths	was not "a marrying man" (Faulkner 224). In addition, the narrator describes Homer as wearing yellow gloves when he took Emily for drives. According to the critic William Greenslade, in the 1890s yellow was associated with homosexuality (24). This evidence does not in itself establish that Homer is gay, however.
Refutation	During the nineteenth century, many men preferred the company of other men (as many do today). This, in itself, did not mean they were gay. Neither does the fact that Homer wore yellow gloves. According to the narrator, Homer was a man who liked to dress well. It is certainly possible that he wore these gloves to impress Miss Emily, a woman he was trying to attract.

 ## Using Evidence Effectively

Supporting Your Literary Argument

Many literary arguments are built on **assertions**—statements made about a debatable topic—backed by **evidence**—supporting examples in the form of references to the text, quotations, and the opinions of literary critics. For example, if you stated that Torvald Helmer, Nora's husband in Henrik Ibsen's play *A Doll House*, is as much a victim of society as his wife is, you could support this assertion with relevant quotations and examples from the play. You could also paraphrase, summarize, or quote the ideas of literary critics who also hold this opinion. Remember, only assertions that are **self-evident** ("All plays include characters and dialogue.") or **factual** ("*A Doll House* was published in 1879.") need no supporting evidence. All other kinds of assertions require support.

Establishing Credibility

Some people bring **credibility** with them whenever they write. When a well-known literary critic evaluates the contributions of a particular writer, you can assume that he or she speaks with authority. (Although you might question the critic's opinions, you do not question his or her expertise.) But most people do not have this kind of credibility. When you write a literary argument, you must constantly work to establish credibility. You do this by *demonstrating knowledge, maintaining a reasonable tone,* and *presenting yourself as someone worth listening to.*

Demonstrating Knowledge One way to establish credibility is by presenting your own carefully considered ideas about a subject. A clear argument and compelling support can demonstrate to readers that you know what you are talking about.

You can also show readers that you have thoroughly researched your subject. By referring to important research sources and by providing accurate documentation for your information, you present evidence that you have done the necessary background reading. Including a range of sources—not just one or two—suggests that you are well acquainted with your subject. Remember, however, that questionable sources, inaccurate (or missing) documentation, and factual errors can undermine your credibility. For some readers, an undocumented quotation or even an incorrect date can call an entire argument into question.

Maintaining a Reasonable Tone Your **tone**—your attitude toward your readers or subject—is almost as important as the information you convey. Talk *to* your readers, not *at* them. If you lecture your readers or appear to talk down to them, you will alienate them. Generally speaking, readers are more likely to respond to a writer who seems fair and respectful than one who seems strident or condescending.

As you write your essay, use moderate language, and qualify your statements so that they seem reasonable. Avoid words and phrases such as *all, never, always, definitely,* and *in every case,* which can make your points seem simplistic, exaggerated, or unrealistic. Also, avoid absolute statements. For example, the statement, In "Doe Season," the ocean definitely symbolizes Andy's attachment to her mother, leaves no room for other possible interpretations. A more measured and accurate statement might be, In "Doe Season," the use of the ocean as a symbol suggests Andy's identification with her mother and her realization that she is becoming a woman.

Presenting Yourself as Someone Worth Listening To   When you write a literary argument, you should present yourself as someone your readers will want to listen to. Make your argument confidently, and don't apologize for your views. For example, do not use phrases such as "In my opinion," "It seems to me," and "Although I am not an expert," which undercut your credibility. Be consistent, and be careful not to contradict yourself. Finally, avoid the use of *I* (unless you are asked to give your opinion or to write a response), and avoid slang and colloquialisms.

Being Fair

Because argument promotes one position over all others, it is seldom objective. However, college writing requires that you stay within the bounds of fairness and that you avoid **bias**—opinions based on preconceived ideas rather than on evidence. To make sure that the support for your argument is not misleading or distorted, follow these guidelines:

- *Avoid misrepresenting evidence.* You **misrepresent evidence** when you exaggerate the extent to which critical opinion supports your thesis. For example, don't try to make a weak case stronger than it actually is by saying that "many critics" think that something is so when only one or two do.
- *Avoid quoting out of context.* You **quote out of context** when you take a passage out of its original setting in order to distort its intended meaning. For example, you are quoting out of context if you say, Emily Dickinson's poems are so idiosyncratic that they do not appeal to readers when your source says, "Emily Dickinson's poems are so idiosyncratic that they do not appeal to readers *who are accustomed to safe, conventional subjects.*" By eliminating a key portion of the sentence, you unfairly alter the meaning of the original.
- *Avoid slanting.* When you select only information that supports your case and ignore information that does not, you are guilty of **slanting**. You can eliminate this problem by including a full range of examples, not just examples that support your thesis. Be sure to consult books and articles that represent a cross-section of critical opinion about your subject.
- *Avoid using unfair appeals.* Traditionally, writers of arguments use three types of appeals to influence readers: **logical appeals**, which address a reader's sense of reason; **emotional appeals**, which play on a reader's emotions; and **ethical appeals**, which emphasize the credibility of

the writer. Problems arise, however, when these appeals are used unfairly. For example, writers can use **logical fallacies**—flawed arguments—to fool readers into thinking a conclusion is logical when it is not. Writers can also use inappropriate emotional appeals—appeals to prejudice, for example—to influence readers. And finally, writers can undercut their credibility if they use questionable support—books and articles written by people who have little or no expertise on the topic. This is especially true when information is obtained from the Internet, where the credentials of the writer may be difficult or impossible to assess. If you want your readers to accept your position, you should be careful to avoid logical fallacies and unfair appeals.

Using Visuals as Evidence

Visuals—pictures, drawings, diagrams, and the like—can add a persuasive element to your essay. Because visual images have an immediate impact, they can sometimes make a strong literary argument even stronger. In a sense, visuals are another type of evidence that can support your thesis. For example, suppose you are writing an essay about the play *Trifles* in which you argue that Mrs. Wright's quilt is an important symbol in the play. In fact, your research leads you to conclude that the process of creating the quilt by piecing together its log cabin pattern parallels the process by which the two female characters in the play determine why Mrs. Wright murdered her husband. The addition of a photograph of a quilt with a log cabin pattern could not only eliminate several paragraphs of description but also help support your conclusion.

Of course, not all visuals will be appropriate or effective for a literary argument. Before using a visual, make certain it actually supports the point you want to make. If it does not, it will distract readers and undercut your argument. To ensure that readers understand the purpose of the visual, introduce it with a sentence that establishes its context; then, discuss its significance, paying particular attention to how it helps you make your point. Finally, be sure to include full documentation for any visual that is not your original creation. (See pp. 40, 41, and 46 for examples of visuals used as evidence in student essays.)

 ## Organizing a Literary Argument

In its simplest form, a literary argument—like any argumentative essay—consists of a thesis statement and supporting evidence. Literary arguments, however, frequently use additional strategies to win audience approval and to overcome potential opposition.

Elements of a Literary Argument

- **Introduction:** The introduction should orient readers to the subject of your essay, presenting the issue you will discuss and explaining its significance.
- **Thesis statement:** In most literary arguments, you will present your thesis statement in your introduction. However, if you think your readers may not be familiar with the issue you are discussing (or if it is very controversial), you may want to postpone stating your thesis until later in the essay.
- **Background:** In this section, you can survey critical opinion about your topic, perhaps pointing out the shortcomings of these opinions. You can also define key terms, review basic facts, or briefly summarize the plot of the work or works you will discuss.
- **Arguments in support of your thesis:** Here you present your arguments and the evidence to support them. It makes sense to move from the least controversial to the most controversial point or from the most familiar to the least familiar idea. In other words, you should begin with arguments that your readers are most likely to accept and then deal with those that require more discussion and more evidence.
- **Refutation of opposing arguments:** In a literary argument, you should summarize and refute the most obvious arguments against your thesis. If you do not address these opposing arguments, doubts about your position will remain in your readers' minds. If the opposing arguments are relatively weak, refute them after you have presented your own arguments. However, if the opposing arguments are strong, you may want to concede their strengths and discuss their limitations *before* you present your own arguments.
- **Conclusion:** Your conclusion will often restate your thesis as well as the major arguments you have made in support of it. Your conclusion can also summarize key points, remind readers of the weaknesses of opposing arguments, or underscore the logic of your position. Many writers like to end their essays with a strong last line—for example, a quotation or a memorable statement that they hope will stay with readers after they finish the essay.

Writing a Literary Argument

The following student essay and the one that begins on page 44 present literary arguments.

The first essay focuses on Dee, a character in Alice Walker's short story "Everyday Use." The student author supports her thesis with ideas she developed as she read the story and watched a DVD that dramatized it. She also includes information she found when she did research. (Note that her essay includes two visuals from a DVD version of the story.)

Chase 1

Margaret Chase

Professor Sierra

English 1001

6 January 2015

The Politics of "Everyday Use"

Alice Walker's "Everyday Use" focuses on a mother,   Introduction

Mrs. Johnson, and her two daughters, Maggie and Dee, and how they

view their heritage. The story's climax comes when Mrs. Johnson rejects

Dee's request to take a hand-stitched quilt with her so that she can hang

it on her wall. Knowing that Maggie will put the quilt to "everyday use,"

Dee is horrified, and she tells her mother and Maggie that they do not

understand their heritage. Although many literary critics see Dee's   Thesis

desire for the quilt as materialistic and shallow, a closer examination   statement

of this story, written in 1973, suggests a more positive interpretation

of Dee's character.

On the surface, "Everyday Use" is about two sisters, Dee   Background

and Maggie, and Mrs. Johnson, their mother. Mrs. Johnson tells the

reader that "Dee, . . . would always look anyone in the eye. Hesitation was no

part of her nature" (346). Unlike her sister Dee, Maggie is shy and intro-

verted. She is described as looking like a lame animal that has been run over

by a car. According to the narrator, "She has been like this, chin on chest,

eyes on ground, feet in shuffle" (346) ever since she was burned in a fire.

Unlike Dee, Mrs. Johnson never got an education. After second

grade, she explains, the school closed down. She says, "Don't ask me

why: in 1927 colored asked fewer questions than they do now" (347).

Mrs. Johnson admits that she accepts the status quo even though she knows

Chase 2

that it is unjust. This admission further establishes the difference between Mrs. Johnson and Dee: Mrs. Johnson has accepted her circumstances, while Dee has worked to change hers. Their differences are illustrated in a film version of the story by their contrasting styles of dress. As shown in fig. 1, Dee and her boyfriend Hakim-a-barber dress in clothes that celebrate their African heritage; Mrs. Johnson and Maggie dress in plain, conservative clothing.

© Denna Bendall/Worn Path Productions

Fig. 1. Dee and Hakim-a-barber arrive at the family home; *The Wadsworth Original Film Series in Literature: "Everyday Use,"* directed by Bruce R. Schwartz, Wadsworth, 2005.

When Dee arrives home with her new boyfriend, other differences soon become obvious. As she eyes her mother's belongings and asks Mrs. Johnson if she can take the top of the butter churn home with her, it is clear that she is materialistic. However, her years away from home have also politicized her. Dee now wants to be called "Wangero" because she believes (although mistakenly) that her given name comes from whites who owned her ancestors. In addition, she talks about how a new day is dawning for African Americans.

> Background continued

The meaning and political importance of Dee's decision to adopt an African name and wear African clothing cannot be fully appreciated without a knowledge of the social and political context in which Walker wrote this story. Walker's own comments about this

> First argument in support of thesis

Chase 3

time period explain Dee's behavior and add meaning to it. In her interview with White, Walker explains that the late 1960s was a time of cultural and intellectual awakening for African Americans. Many turned ideologically and culturally to Africa, adopting the dress, hairstyles, and even the names of their African ancestors. Walker admits that as a young woman she too became interested in discovering her African heritage. (In fact, she herself was given the name *Wangero* during a visit to Kenya in the late 1960s.) Walker tells White that she considered keeping this new name but eventually realized that to do so would be to "dismiss" her family and her American heritage. When she researched her American family, she found that her great-great-grandmother had walked from Virginia to Georgia carrying two children. "If that's not a Walker," she says, "I don't know what is." Thus, Walker realized that, over time, African Americans had actually transformed the names they had originally taken from their enslavers. To respect the ancestors she knew, Walker says, she decided it was important to keep her given name.

Along with adopting symbols of their African heritage, many African Americans also elevated these symbols, such as the quilt shown in fig. 2, to the status of art. According to Salaam,

> Second argument in support of thesis

© Suzanne English/Worn Path Productions

Fig. 2. Traditional hand-stitched quilt; Evelyn C. White, "Alice Walker: Stitches in Time," interview, *The Wadsworth Original Film Series in Literature: "Everyday Use,"* directed by Bruce R. Schwartz, Wadsworth, 2005.

Chase 4

one way of doing this was to put these objects in museums; another was to hang them on the walls of their homes. Such acts were aimed at convincing whites that African Americans had an old and rich culture and that, consequently, they deserved respect. These gestures were also meant to improve self-esteem and pride within black communities (Salaam 42-43).

Admittedly, as some critics have pointed out, Dee is more materialistic than political. For example, although Mrs. Johnson makes several statements throughout the story that suggest her admiration of Dee's defiant character, she also identifies incidents that highlight Dee's materialism and selfishness. When their first house burned down, Dee watched it burn while she stood under a tree with "a look of concentration" (346) rather than grief. Mrs. Johnson knows that Dee hated their small, dingy house, and she knows too that Dee was glad to see it destroyed. Furthermore, Walker acknowledges in an interview with her biographer, Evelyn C. White, that as she was writing the story, she imagined that Dee might even have set the fire that destroyed the house and scarred her sister. Even now, Dee is ashamed of the tin-roofed house her family lives in, and she has said that she would never bring her friends there. Mrs. Johnson has always known that Dee wanted "nice things" (346); even at sixteen, "she had a style of her own, and knew what style was" (346). However, although Dee is materialistic and self-serving, she is also proud and strong willed. Knowing that she will encounter opposition wherever she goes, she works to establish power. Thus, her desire for the quilt can be seen as an attempt to establish herself and her African-American culture in a society dominated by whites.

> Summary and refutation of opposing argument

Even though Mrs. Johnson knows Dee wants the quilt, she gives it to Maggie. According to literary critics Houston Baker and

> Analysis of Mrs. Johnson's final act

Chase 5

Charlotte Pierce-Baker, when Mrs. Johnson decides to give the quilt to Maggie, she is challenging Dee's understanding of her heritage. Unlike Dee, Mrs. Johnson recognizes that quilts signify "sacred generations of women who have made their own special kind of beauty separate from the traditional artistic world" (qtd. in Piedmont-Marton 45). According to Baker and Pierce-Baker, Mrs. Johnson realizes that her daughter Maggie, whom she has long dismissed because of her quiet nature and shyness, understands the true meaning of the quilt in a way that Dee never will (Piedmont-Marton 45).

Unlike Dee, Maggie has paid close attention to the traditions and skills of her mother and grandmother: she has actually learned to quilt. More important, by staying with her mother instead of going to school, she has gotten to know her family. She underscores this fact when she tells her mother that Dee can have the quilt because she does not need it to remember her grandmother. Even though Maggie's and Mrs. Johnson's understanding of heritage may be more emotionally profound than Dee's, it is important not to dismiss Dee's interest in elevating the quilt to the level of art. The political stakes of defining an object as art in the late 1960s and early 1970s were high, and the fight for equality went beyond basic civil rights.

Although there is much in the story that indicates Dee's materialism, her desire to hang the quilt should not be dismissed as selfish. Like Mrs. Johnson and Maggie, Dee is a complicated character. In 1973, when "Everyday Use" was written, displaying the quilt would have been not only a personal act, but also a political act—an act with important implications. The final message of "Everyday Use" may just be that an accurate understanding of the quilt (and, by extension, of African-American culture) requires both views—Maggie's and Mrs. Johnson's "everyday use" and Dee's elevation of the quilt to art.

Conclusion (restating thesis)

Chase 6

Works Cited

Piedmont-Marton, Elisabeth. "An Overview of 'Everyday Use.'" *Short Stories for Students*, vol. 2, 1997, pp. 42-45. *Literature Resource Center*, www. go.galegroup.com/ps/i.do?id=Gale%7CH1420002698&V=2.

Salaam, Kalamu Ya. "A Primer of the Black Arts Movement: Excerpts from *The Magic of Juju: An Appreciation of the Black Arts Movement.*" *Black Renaissance/Renaissance Noire*, 2002, pp. 40-59.

Walker, Alice. "Alice Walker: Stitches in Time." Interview by Evelyn C. White. *The Wadsworth Original Film Series in Literature: "Everyday Use,"* directed by Bruce R. Schwartz, Wadsworth, 2005.

---. "Everyday Use." *Portable Literature: Reading, Reacting, Writing*, edited by Laurie G. Kirszner and Stephen R. Mandell, 9th ed., Wadsworth, 2016, pp. 345-52.

The following literary argument addresses the question of why video games should be considered literature. The student who wrote this essay supports her argument with her own experience with video games as well as with information that she found online and in her college library. (Note that her essay includes a visual from the video game *World of Warcraft* to illustrate one of her points.)

Linde 1

Danielle Linde

Professor Smith

English 1001

15 January 2015

The Literary Merit of Video Games

In recent years, some critics have begun to view video games   Introduction

not just as entertainment but also as a form of literature. While

some claim that video games will bring about the death of traditional

literature, others argue that they will bring new life to literature. More than

one literary critic has observed that many of the games that are available

today have much in common with traditional forms of literature. In
fact, some video games create fictionalized worlds that share many
of the characteristics of traditional literature. For this reason, video
games should be given the respect they deserve and be considered a
legitimate form of imaginative literature.

> Thesis statement

The basic function of video games is to tell a story. Critic
Marie-Laure Ryan argues that "a text of fiction invites its readers to
imagine a world" and that a video game presents the same
experience to players. Like a traditional author of a literary work, a
video game creator invents a world that can be inhabited by the
imagination as players interact with the game. Ryan observes that players
can "transport themselves in imagination from the world they regard as
actual toward an alternative possible world—a virtual reality—which they
regard as actual for the duration of their involvement in the text, game, or
spectacle." Similarly, Geoffrey Rockwell refers to video games as a "form of
fiction consumed through the computer" (345). Like fiction, these video
games contain their own casts of characters, including heroes and villains
the player can interact with or even become. In many ways, this experience
is the same one a reader has when he or she chooses to identify with or
disapprove of the characters in a novel.

> First argument in support of thesis

Like all forms of literature, video games create a world. Just
like those of novels, the worlds of video games can mirror current
events, as is the case with *Medal of Honor*, which takes place on
the battlefields of Afghanistan, or they can be highly imaginative,
such as the fantasy world of *World of Warcraft*. Just as many novels do,
video games often contain allusions to mythology and history as well as
to literary works—such as Dante's *Inferno* and Poe's "The Gold Bug." Critic
Tanya Krzywinska points out that some parts of the narrative of *World of
Warcraft* are based on classical myth, while others are based on the typical
stories told in fantasy novels, and still others are based on events drawn
from popular culture (124). She also notes that the narratives of games
such as *World of Warcraft* which tend to have a hero who is in conflict

> Second argument in support of thesis

Linde 3

with an evil villain and often feature magic, are similar to classical myths
(126). Mythical creatures, such as the dragons (see fig. 1) that are
common in video games, are also common in fantasy literature and
fairy tales.

Fig. 1. Screen shot from *World of Warcraft: Cataclysm;* Blizzard Entertainment,
2015.

Like novels, the plots of video games follow certain conventional patterns or plots. According to Krzywinska, "the primary and
highly recognizable mythic pattern that informs and structures the
game [*World of Warcraft*] is the epic hero quest, wherein various forces
work to help and hinder the hero–player en route to achieving particular goals"
(126). It is clear that in terms of both of setting and narrative, video games
can bear striking similarities to conventional literary works.

> Third argument in support of thesis

Despite these similarities, however, some critics claim that video
games are fundamentally different from literature, and for this reason
should not be considered art, let alone literature. Roger Ebert, the
celebrated film critic, says, "In principle, video games cannot be art."
He expands his statement by focusing on the features that define art,

> Summary and refutation of opposing argument

Linde 4

calling it "the fruition of a long gestation." He concludes that video games have their origins in such artistic reflection but from commercial interests. Furthermore, Ebert argues that the fact that video games are an emerging form of media does not mean that they should not be judged by the same standards as other arts. His main point, however, is that video games are fundamentally different from art forms such as literature and film. "One obvious difference between art and games," he says, "is that you can win a game. It has rules, points, objectives, and an outcome". Although Ebert's analysis is fundamentally correct, he seems to ignore the many similarities that exist between literature and video games. Because video games have highly developed settings, characters, and plots, it does not seem unreasonable to see some video games as forms of literary expression.

The main difference between video games and traditional litera-   Summary
ture is the fact that games involve multimedia interaction. After all,   and
refutation
novels do not come with controllers, nor do they allow readers to   of opposing
argument
choose what a character does next. Novelist Don Zancanella points
out that "console game narratives are more of a mosaic than a linear
recounting of time-ordered events" (99). Whereas a reader of a literary work
is told a story, a video game player takes a direct role in determining the outcome of the story, making choices that can result in either a favorable or an
unfavorable outcome. This more interactive model does not mean that video
games are not literature. However, it does mean that they should be analyzed
differently from traditional literature. Geoffrey Rockwell observes that because
of their popularity and similarity to literature, video games require further
attention and study. He concludes by saying that we need a "critical framework" for discussing video games (350). This new framework should take into
consideration the specific types of interaction that make video games unique.
For instance, in video games, characters can interact with a variety of other
characters, creating an experience in which "consideration of multiple points
of view is central to interpretation" (Zancanella 99). Clearly, as the study of
video games as literature becomes more academically accepted, scholars will
have to develop new, more suitable ways of evaluating this genre.

Linde 5

Despite some arguments to the contrary, video games have much   Conclusion
in common with works of literature. Video games, like literature,   (restating
serve the basic function of transporting readers to other worlds by   thesis)
creating characters, plots, and settings. Video games also draw from and
contribute to the larger literary canon, frequently integrating references
and allusions to literary works into their stories. As video games continue
to increase in popularity and the variety of subjects covered by the games
continues to grow, the value of studying the genre as a form of literature
will become more obvious both to players and to critics. In analyzing and
evaluating video games, however, scholars will have to take into account
the interactivity and the less linear plots that characterize these games.
The result will be not just new forms of criticism, but also new forms of
games that will expand the definition of literature.

Linde 6

Works Cited

Ebert, Roger. "Video Games Can Never Be Art." *Roger Ebert's Journal*, 16 Apr. 2010,
    www.rogerebert.com/rogers-journal/video-games-can-never-be-art.

Krzywinska, Tanya. "World Creation and Lore: *World of Warcraft* as Rich Text."
    Digital Culture, Play, and Identity: A Critical Anthology of World of
    Warcraft *Research*, edited by Hilde Walker Corneliussen and Jill
    Rettberg, MIT P, 2008, pp. 123-42.

Rockwell, Geoffrey. "Gore Galore: Literary Theory and Computer Games."
    Computers and the Humanities, vol. 36, no. 3, 2002, pp. 345-58.

Ryan, Marie-Laure. "Fictional Worlds in the Digital Age." *A Companion to
    Digital Literary Studies*, edited by Susan Schreibman and
    Ray Siemens, Blackwell, 2008. *Wiley Online Library*,
    doi:10.1002/9781405177504.ch13.

Zancanella, Don, et al. "Computer Games as Literature." *English in the Digital
    Age: Information and Communications Technology (ICT) and the Teaching
    of English*, edited by Andrew Goodwyn, Continuum, 2000, pp. 87-102.

CHAPTER 3

DOCUMENTING SOURCES AND AVOIDING PLAGIARISM

Documentation is the formal acknowledgment of the sources in an essay. This chapter explains and illustrates the documentation style recommended by the Modern Language Association (MLA), the style used by students of literature.

What to Document

In general, you must document the following types of information from a source (print or electronic):

- **All word-for-word quotations from a source.** Whenever you use a writer's exact words, you must document them. Even if you quote only a word or two within a paraphrase or summary, you must document the quoted words separately, after the final quotation marks.
- **All ideas from a source that you put into your own words.** Be sure to document all paraphrases or summaries of a source's ideas, including the author's judgments, conclusions, and debatable assertions.
- **All visuals—tables, charts, and photographs—from a source.** Because visuals are almost always someone's original creation, they must be documented.

NOTE Certain items do not require documentation: **common knowledge** (information most readers probably know), facts available from a variety of reference sources, familiar sayings and well-known quotations, and your own ideas and conclusions.

Avoiding Plagiarism

Plagiarism is the presentation of another person's words or ideas as if they were your own. Most plagiarism is **unintentional plagiarism**—for example, pasting a passage from a downloaded document directly into your essay and forgetting to include quotation marks and documentation. However, there is a difference between an honest mistake and **intentional plagiarism**—for example, copying sentences from a journal article or submitting as your own an essay that someone else has written. The penalties for unintentional plagiarism may sometimes be severe, but intentional plagiarism is intellectual theft and is almost always dealt with harshly.

The guidelines that follow can help you avoid the most common mistakes that lead to unintentional plagiarism.

Document All Material That Requires Documentation

Original: In Oates's stories there are no safe relationships, but the most perilous of all possibilities is sex. Sex is always destructive. (Tierce, Mike, and John Michael Crafton. "Connie's Tambourine Man: A New Reading of Arnold Friend.")

Plagiarism: In many of Oates's stories, relationships—especially sexual relationships—are dangerous.

In the example above, the writer uses an idea from a source but does not include documentation. As a result, she gives readers the mistaken impression that the source's idea is actually her own.

Correct: Tierce and Crafton point out that in many of Oates's stories, relationships—especially sexual relationships—are dangerous (220).

Enclose Borrowed Words in Quotation Marks

Original: "The Yellow Wallpaper," which Gilman herself called "a description of a case of nervous breakdown," recalls in the first person the experiences of a woman who is evidently suffering from postpartum psychosis. (Gilbert, Sandra M., and Susan Gubar. *The Madwoman in the Attic: The Woman Writer and the Nineteenth-Century Literary Imagination.*)

Plagiarism: As Gilbert and Gubar point out, the narrator in "The Yellow Wallpaper" is evidently suffering from postpartum psychosis (212).

Even though the writer documents the passage, he uses the source's exact words without putting them in quotation marks.

Correct: As Gilbert and Gubar point out, the narrator in "The Yellow Wallpaper" is "evidently suffering from postpartum psychosis" (212).

Do Not Imitate a Source's Syntax and Phrasing

Original: Tennessee Williams's *The Glass Menagerie*, though it has achieved a firmly established position in the canon of American plays, is often distorted, if not misunderstood, by readers, directors, and audiences. (King, Thomas. "Irony and Distance in *The Glass Menagerie*.")

Plagiarism: Although *The Glass Menagerie* has a well-established place in the American theater, it is frequently misinterpreted by those who read it, direct it, and see it (King 125).

Although the student does not use the exact words of his source, he closely follows the sentence structure of the original and simply substitutes synonyms for the writer's key words. Remember, acceptable paraphrases and summaries do more than change words; they use original phrasing and syntax to convey the source's meaning.

Correct: According to Thomas King, although *The Glass Menagerie* has become an American classic, it is still not fully appreciated (125).

Differentiate Your Words from Those of Your Source

Original: At some colleges and universities, traditional survey courses of world and English literature...have been scrapped or diluted....What replaces them is sometimes a mere option of electives, sometimes "multicultural" courses introducing material from Third World cultures and thinning out an already thin sampling of Western writings, and sometimes courses geared especially to issues of class, race, and gender. (Howe, Irving. "The Value of the Canon.")

Plagiarism: At many universities, the Western literature survey courses have been edged out by courses that emphasize minority concerns. These courses are "thinning out an already thin sampling of Western writings" in favor of "courses geared especially to issues of class, race, and gender" (Howe 40).

Because the student writer does not differentiate his ideas from those of his source, it appears that only the two quotations in the last sentence are borrowed when, in fact, the first sentence also borrows ideas from the original. The student should have identified the boundaries of the borrowed material by introducing it with an identifying phrase and ending with documentation. (Note that a quotation always requires its own documentation.)

Correct: According to Irving Howe, at many universities the Western literature survey courses have been edged out by courses that emphasize minority concerns (41). These courses, says Howe, are "thinning out an already thin sampling of Western writings" in favor of "courses geared especially to issues of class, race, and gender" (40).

NOTE It is easy to become overwhelmed by any research project. For example, you can run out of time, lose track of your sources, or confuse your own ideas with those of your sources.

✔ CHECKLIST   Avoiding Unintentional Plagiarism

Any of these problems can result in unintentional plagiarism—to avoid this problem, keep the following suggestions in mind:

▪ *Formulate a research plan.* List the steps you intend follow and estimate how much time they will take.

▪ *Set Up a Schedule.* Set up a realistic schedule that allows you enough time to complete your assignment. Include extra time just in case any unexpected problems occur.

▪ *Ask for help.* If you run into trouble, don't panic; ask your instructor or a college reference librarian for help.

▪ *Don't paste downloaded text directly into your essay.* Summarize or paraphrase downloaded material that you intend to use. Boldface or highlight quotation marks to remind you that you are using the exact words of your sources.

▪ *Keep track of your sources.* Create one set of files for downloaded material and another set of files for your notes. Make sure you label and date these files so that you'll know what they contain and when they were created.

▪ *Record full documentation information for every source.* Make sure you have all the source information you will need to create your works-cited list.

▪ *Document your sources.* As you write your first draft, document each piece of information that comes from a source. Don't make the mistake of thinking you will be able to find this information later on. If you don't keep track of your sources as you draft, you may forget which words and ideas are your own and which require documentation.

▪ *Keep a list of the sources you are using.* Keep an up-to-date list of all the sources you are using. This list will enable you to create a works-cited list when you have finished writing your essay.

Documenting Sources

MLA documentation has two main parts: parenthetical references in the body of the essay (in-text citations) and a works-cited list.* In addition, there may be content notes.

Parenthetical References in the Text

MLA documentation style uses parenthetical references within the text to refer to an alphabetical works-cited list at the end of the essay. A parenthetical reference should contain just enough information to guide readers to the appropriate entry in your works-cited list.

A typical parenthetical reference consists of the author's last name and a page number.

> Gwendolyn Brooks uses the sonnet form to create poems that have a wide social and aesthetic range (Williams 972).

✔ CHECKLIST Guidelines for Punctuating Parenthetical References

To punctuate parenthetical references correctly, follow these guidelines:

Paraphrases and Summaries

■ Place the parenthetical reference *after* the last word of the sentence and *before* the final punctuation.

> In her poems, Brooks combines the pessimism of modernist poetry with the optimism of the Harlem Renaissance (Smith 978).

Direct Quotations Run in with the Text

■ Place the parenthetical reference *after* the quotation marks and *before* the final punctuation.

> According to Gary Smith, Brooks's *A Street in Bronzeville* "conveys the primacy of suffering in the lives of poor Black women" (980).

> According to Gary Smith, the poems in *A Street in Bronzeville* "served notice that Brooks had learned her craft..." (978).

> Along with Thompson, we must ask, "Why did it take so long for critics to acknowledge that Gwendolyn Brooks is an important voice in twentieth-century American poetry" (123)?

---

*For more information, see the *MLA Handbook*, 8th ed. (MLA, 2016). You can also consult the MLA website at style.mla.org.

Quotations Set Off from the Text

- Omit the quotation marks, and place the parenthetical reference one space *after* the final punctuation.

For Gary Smith, the identity of Brooks's African American women is inextricably linked with their sense of race and poverty:

> For Brooks, unlike the Renaissance poets, the victimization of poor Black women becomes not simply a minor chord but a predominant theme of *A Street in Bronzeville*. Few, if any, of her female characters are able to free themselves from a web of poverty that threatens to strangle their lives. (980)

If you mention the author's name or the title of the work in your essay, only a page reference is needed.

According to Gladys Margaret Williams in "Gwendolyn Brooks's Way with the Sonnet," Brooks combines a sensitivity to poetic forms with a depth of emotion appropriate for her subject matter (972-73).

If you use more than one source by the same author, include a shortened title in the parenthetical reference.

Brooks knows not only Shakespeare, Spenser, and Milton, but also the full range of African American poetry (Williams, "Brooks's Way" 972).

SAMPLE PARENTHETICAL REFERENCES

An entire work

When citing an entire work, state the name of the author in your essay instead of in a parenthetical reference.

August Wilson's play *Fences* treats many themes frequently expressed in modern drama.

A work by two authors

Myths cut across boundaries and cultural spheres and reappear in strikingly similar forms from country to country (Feldman and Richardson 124).

A work by three or more authors

State the last name of the first author, and use the abbreviation et al. (Latin for "and others") for the rest.

Hawthorne's short stories frequently use a combination of allegorical and symbolic methods (Guerin et al. 91).

A work in an anthology

In his essay "Flat and Round Characters," E. M. Forster distinguishes between one-dimensional characters and those that are well developed (Stevick 223-31).

Note that the parenthetical reference cites the anthology (edited by Stevick) that contains Forster's essay; full information about the anthology appears in the works-cited list.

A work with volume and page numbers

Critics consider *The Zoo Story* to be one of Albee's best plays (Eagleton 2: 17).

An indirect source

Use the abbreviation qtd. in ("quoted in") to indicate that the quoted material was not taken directly from the original source.

Wagner observed that myth and history stood before him "with opposing claims" (qtd. in Winkler 10).

A play with numbered lines

The parenthetical reference should contain the act, scene, and line numbers (in arabic numerals), separated by periods. When included in parenthetical references, titles of the books of the Bible and well-known literary works are often abbreviated—Gen. for Genesis and *Ham.* for *Hamlet*, for example.

"Give thy thoughts no tongue," says Polonius, "Nor any unproportioned thought his act" (*Ham.* 1.3.64-65).

A poem

Use a slash (/) to separate lines of poetry run in with the text. (The slash is preceded and followed by one space.) Use a double slash (//) to separate stanzas. The parenthetical reference should cite the lines quoted. Include the word line or lines in the first reference but just the numbers in subsequent references.

"I muse my life-long hate, and without flinch / I bear it nobly as I live my part," says the speaker in Claude McKay's bitterly ironic poem "The White City" (lines 3-4).

An electronic source

If you are citing a source from the Internet or from an online database, use page numbers if they are available. If the source uses paragraph, section, or screen numbers, use the abbreviation par. or sec. or the full word screen.

The earliest type of movie censoring came in the form of licensing fees, and in Deer River, Minnesota, "a licensing fee of $200 was deemed not excessive for a town of 1000" (Ernst, par. 20).

If an Internet source has no page, paragraph, section, or screen markers, cite the entire work.

In her article "Limited Horizons," Lynne Cheney says that schools do best when students read literature not for practical information but for its insights into the human condition.

Because of its parody of communism, the film *Antz* is actually an adult film masquerading as a child's tale (Clemin).

The Works-Cited List

Parenthetical references refer to a **works-cited list** that includes all the sources you refer to in your essay:

- Begin the works-cited list on a new page, continuing the page numbers of the essay. For example, if the text of the essay ends on page 6, the works-cited list will begin on page 7.
- Center the title Works Cited one inch from the top of the page.
- Arrange entries alphabetically, according to the last name of each author. Use the first word of the title if the author is unknown (articles—*a, an,* and *the*—at the beginning of a title are not considered first words).
- Double-space the entire works-cited list between and within entries.
- Begin typing each entry at the left margin, and indent subsequent lines one-half inch.
- A typical works-cited entry has three core elements—author, title, and publishing information—separated by periods. If there is another source that "contains" the original published source (for example, a database or website containing a journal article), that information is also followed by a period. The *MLA Handbook* shows a single space after all end punctuation.

Below is a directory listing the sample MLA works-cited list entries that begin on page 58.

DIRECTORY OF MLA WORKS-CITED LIST ENTRIES

Print Sources: Entries for Articles

1. An article in a scholarly journal
2. An article in a magazine
3. An article in a daily newspaper
4. An article in a reference book

Print Sources: Entries for Books

5. A book by a single author
6. A book by two authors
7. A book by three or more authors
8. Two or more works by the same author
9. An edited book
10. A book with a volume number
11. A short story, poem, or play in a collection of the author's work
12. A short story in an anthology
13. A poem in an anthology
14. A play in an anthology
15. An essay in an anthology
16. More than one item from the same anthology
17. A translation

Entries for Other Sources

18. An interview
19. A lecture or an address

Electronic Sources: Entries from Internet Sites

20. A scholarly project or information database on the Internet
21. A document within a scholarly project or information database on the Internet
22. A personal site on the Internet
23. A book on the Internet
24. An article in a scholarly journal on the Internet
25. An article in an encyclopedia on the Internet
26. An article in a newspaper on the Internet
27. An article in a magazine on the Internet
28. A painting or photograph on the Internet
29. An email
30. A blog or online forum

Electronic Sources: Entries from Online Databases

31. A scholarly journal article from an online database
32. A monthly magazine article from an online database
33. A newspaper article from an online database
34. A reference book article from an online database
35. A dictionary definition from an online database

Entries for Other Electronic Sources

36. A nonperiodical publication on DVD-ROM or CD-ROM
37. A periodical publication on DVD-ROM or CD-ROM
38. A film, videocassette, DVD, or CD-ROM

MLA • Print Sources: Entries for Articles

Article citations include the author's name; the title of the article (in quotation marks); the name of the periodical (italicized); the volume and issue numbers (if applicable; see below); the month, if applicable (abbreviated, except for May, June, and July); the year; and the pages on which the full article appears (with the abbreviations *p.* or *pp.*).

1. An article in a scholarly journal
Grossman, Robert. "The Grotesque in Faulkner's 'A Rose for Emily.'" *Mosaic*, vol. 20, no. 3, 1987, pp. 40-55.

In the citation above, *no. 3* signifies issue 3. Note that some scholarly journals do not have volume numbers.

2. An article in a magazine
Milosz, Czeslaw. "A Lecture." *The New Yorker*, 22 June 1992, p. 32.

An article with no listed author is entered by title in the works-cited list.

"Solzhenitsyn: An Artist Becomes an Exile." *Time*, 25 Feb. 1974, pp. 34+.

Note that *34+* indicates that the article appears on pages that are not consecutive; in this case, the article begins on page 34 and continues on page 37.

3. An article in a daily newspaper
Oates, Joyce Carol. "When Characters from the Page Are Made Flesh on the Screen." *The New York Times*, late ed., 23 Mar. 1986, pp. C1+.

Note that *C1+* indicates that the article begins on page 1 of Section C and continues on a subsequent page.

4. An article in a reference book

"Dance Theatre of Harlem." *The New Encyclopaedia Britannica: Micropaedia*, Encyclopaedia Britannica, 2008.

Grimstead, David. "Fuller, Margaret Sarah." *Encyclopedia of American Biography*, edited by John A. Garraty, HarperCollins, 1996.

MLA • Print Sources: Entries for Books

Book citations include the author's name; book title and subtitle (italicized); and publication information (place, only if relevant; publisher; and date). Capitalize all major words in the title except articles, prepositions, and the *to* of an infinitive (unless it is the first or last word of the title or subtitle). Write publishers' names in full, with the following exceptions: Omit business words like *Company (Co.)*, *Corporation (Corp.)*, *Incorporated (Inc.)*, and *Limited (Ltd.)*. In the names of academic presses, replace *University Press* with *UP* (or, if the words are separated by other words or appear alone, replace them with *U* and *P*: *U of Chicago P*, *MIT P*.

5. A book by a single author

Kingston, Maxine Hong. *The Woman Warrior: Memoirs of a Girlhood among Ghosts*. Alfred A. Knopf, 1976.

6. A book by two authors

Feldman, Burton, and Robert D. Richardson. *The Rise of Modern Mythology*. Indiana UP, 1972.

Note that only the *first* author's name is in reverse order.

7. A book by three or more authors

Guerin, Wilfred, et al., editors. *A Handbook of Critical Approaches to Literature*. 5th ed., HarperCollins, 2004.

8. Two or more works by the same author

List two or more works by the same author in alphabetical order by *title*. Include the author's full name in the first entry; use three unspaced hyphens followed by a period to take the place of the author's name in second and subsequent entries.

Novoa, Juan-Bruce. *Chicano Authors: Inquiry by Interview.* U of Texas P, 1980.

---. "Themes in Rudolfo Anaya's Work." Literature Colloquium, New Mexico State U, Las Cruces, 11 Apr. 2002. Address.

9. An edited book

Oosthuizen, Ann, editor. *Sometimes When It Rains: Writings by South African Women.* Pandora, 1987.

10. A book with a volume number

When all the volumes of a multivolume work have the same title, list the number of the volume you used.

Eagleton, T. Allston. *A History of the New York Stage.* Vol. 2, Prentice Hall, 1987.

When each volume of a multivolume work has a separate title, list the title of the volume you used.

Durant, Will, and Ariel Durant. *The Age of Napoleon: A History of European Civilization from 1789 to 1815.* Simon & Schuster, 1975.

(*The Age of Napoleon* is volume 2 of *The Story of Civilization.* You need not provide documentation for the entire multivolume work unless this information is relevant to your essay.)

11. A short story, poem, or play in a collection of the author's work

Gordimer, Nadine. "Once upon a Time." *"Jump" and Other Stories,* Farrar, Straus and Giroux, 1991, pp. 23-30.

12. A short story in an anthology

Salinas, Marta. "The Scholarship Jacket." *Nosotros: Latina Literature Today,* edited by Maria del Carmen Boza et al., Bilingual, 1986, pp. 68-70.

13. A poem in an anthology

Simmerman, Jim. "Child's Grave, Hale County, Alabama." *The Pushcart Prize, X: Best of the Small Presses,* edited by Bill Henderson, Penguin, 1986, pp. 198-99.

14. A play in an anthology

Hughes, Langston. *Mother and Child. Black Drama Anthology,* edited by Woodie King and Ron Miller, New American Library, 1986, pp. 399-406.

15. An essay in an anthology

Forster, E. M. "Flat and Round Characters." *The Theory of the Novel,* edited by Philip Stevick, Free Press, 1980, pp. 223-31.

16. More than one item from the same anthology

If you are using more than one selection from an anthology, cite the anthology in a separate entry. Then, list each individual selection separately, including the author and title of the selection, the anthology editor's last name, and the inclusive page numbers.

> Baxter, Charles. "Gryphon." Kirszner and Mandell, pp. 173-86.
>
> Kirszner, Laurie G., and Stephen R. Mandell, editors. *Portable Literature: Reading, Reacting, Writing*. 9th ed., Cengage Learning, 2016.
>
> Rich, Adrienne. "Living in Sin." Kirszner and Mandell, pp. 538-39.

17. A translation

> Carpentier, Alejo. *Reasons of State*. Translated by Francis Partridge, W. W. Norton, 1976.

Entries for Other Sources

18. An interview

> Brooks, Gwendolyn. "An Interview with Gwendolyn Brooks." *Triquarterly*, no. 60, 1984, pp. 405-10.

19. A lecture or an address

> Novoa, Juan-Bruce. "Themes in Rudolfo Anaya's Work." Literature Colloquium, New Mexico State U, Las Cruces, 11 Apr. 2002. Address.

MLA • Electronic Sources: Entries from Internet Sites

MLA style recognizes that full publication information is not always available for electronic sources. Include in your citation whatever information you can reasonably obtain: the author or editor of the source (if available); the title of site (italicized); the version number of the source (if applicable); the name of the publisher (if available); and the date of electronic publication. MLA recommends including digital object identifiers (DOIs) or URLs, preferably permalinks (stable Internet addresses), in the works-cited list. The date of access may be included if there is a possibility that the source may change or be removed from the site, or if the source provides no date specifying when it was published.

20. A scholarly project or information database on the Internet

> Nelson, Cary, editor. *Modern American Poetry*. Dept. of English, U of Illinois, Urbana-Champaign, 1999-2014, www.english.illinois.edu/maps/index.htm.

21. A document within a scholarly project or information database on the Internet

"D-Day: June 6th, 1944." *History.com*. History Channel, 1999, www.history.com/ topics/world-war-ii/d-day.

22. A personal site on the Internet

Yerkes, James. *The Centaurian: John Updike Home Page*. Prexar, 15 June 2009, userpages.prexar.com/joyerkes. Accessed 19 June 2015.

23. A book on the Internet

Douglass, Frederick. *My Bondage and My Freedom*. Boston, 1855. *Google Book Search*, books.google.com/books?id=AbUgrcBdsncC&dq=editions: ISBN1593083572.

24. An article in a scholarly journal on the Internet

DeKoven, Marianne. "Utopias Limited: Post-Sixties and Postmodern American Fiction." *Modern Fiction Studies*, vol. 41, no. 1, 1995, pp. 75-97. *Project Muse*, doi:10.1353/mfs.1995.0002.

25. An article in an encyclopedia on the Internet

"Hawthorne, Nathaniel." *Encyclopaedia Britannica Online*, 2010, www.britannica.com/ biography/Nathaniel-Hawthorne.

26. An article in a newspaper on the Internet

Cave, Damien. "Election Day May Look Familiar." *The New York Times*, 28 Apr. 2008, www.nytimes.com/2008/04/28/us/politics/ 28voting.html?_r=0.

27. An article in a magazine on the Internet

Anolik, Lili. "How Joan Didion the Writer Became Joan Didion the Legend." *Vanity Fair*, Feb. 2016, www.vanityfair.com/culture/2016/02/ joan-didion-writer-los-angeles.

28. A painting or photograph on the Internet

Lange, Dorothea. *Looking at Pictures*. 1936, Museum of Modern Art, New York. *MoMA*, www.moma.org/collection/artists/3373/.

29. An email

Mauk, Karen. "Re: Manuscript." Received by Stephanie Carpenter, 3 Mar. 2016.

30. A blog or online forum

Berg, Kirsten. "Bright Angel." *PowellsBooks.Blog*, 17 June 2009, www.powellsbook. blog.com. Accessed 18 June 2014.

MLA • Electronic Sources:
Entries from Online Databases

To cite information from an online database, supply the publication information (including page numbers, if available) followed by the italicized name of the database and the DOI or URL. Include the date of access if the source is subject to change.

> Witze, Alexandra. "Climate Change: Losing Greenland." *Nature*, 17 Apr. 2008, pp. 798-802. *ProQuest*, doi:10.1038/452798a.

31. A scholarly journal article from an online database

> Schaefer, Richard J. "Editing Strategies in Television News Documentaries." *Journal of Communication*, vol. 47, no. 4, 1997, pp. 69-89. *InfoTrac OneFile Plus*, doi:10.1111/j.1460-2466.1997.tb02726.x.

32. A monthly magazine article from an online database

> Livermore, Beth. "Meteorites on Ice." *Astronomy*, July 1993, pp. 54-58. *Expanded Academic ASAP Plus*, ezproxy.cul.columbia.edu/login?url=http://search. proquest.com.ezproxy.cul.columbia.edu/docview/215935960?accountid=10226.

33. A newspaper article from an online database

> Meyer, Greg. "Answering Questions about the West Nile Virus." *Dayton Daily News*, 11 July 2002, pp. Z3-7. *LexisNexis*, ezproxy.cul.columbia.edu/login?url=http://search. proquest.com.ezproxy.cul.columbia.edu/docview/254487263?accountid=10226.

34. A reference book article from an online database

> "Food Chain/Web." *Environmental Encyclopedia*, 2011. *Biography in Context*, ic.galegroup. com/ic/bic1/ReferenceDetailsPage/ReferenceDetailsWindow?failOverType=&query=& prodId=BIC1&windowstate=normal&contentModules=&display-query=&mode= view&displayGroupName=Reference&limiter=&currPage=&disableHighlighting= false&displayGroups=&sortBy=&search_within_results=&p=BIC1&action=e&catId=& activityType=&scanId=&documentId=GALE%7CCV2644150565&source=Bookmark&u= columbiau&jsid=79e21d41751c4f6bc5a337d3e22d61fa.

35. A dictionary definition from an online database

> "Migraine." *Columbia Electronic Encyclopedia*, 6th ed. *Literary Reference Center*, web.a.ebscohost.com/ehost/detail/detail?vid=8&sid=a0d05779-c5ea-4daf-b800-1e0f8e09ecde%40sessionmgr4001&hid=4104&bdata=JnNpdGU9ZWhvc3 QtbGl2ZQ%3d%3d#db=lfh&AN=39021787.

MLA • Electronic Sources:
Entries for Other Electronic Sources

36. A nonperiodical publication on DVD-ROM or CD-ROM

> "Windhover." *Concise Oxford English Dictionary*, 11th ed., CD-ROM ed., Oxford UP, 2009.

37. A periodical publication on DVD-ROM or CD-ROM

Zurbach, Kate. "The Linguistic Roots of Three Terms." *Linguistic Quarterly*, vol. 30,
1994, pp. 12-47. *InfoTrac: Magazine Index Plus.*

38. A film, videocassette, DVD, or CD-ROM

The Heinle Original Film Series in Literature: Eudora Welty's "A Worn Path." Directed by
Bruce R. Schwartz, DVD ed., Wadsworth, 2003.

NOTE Using information from Internet sources (especially blogs and
online forums) can be risky. Contributors are not necessarily experts.
Unless you can verify that the information you are obtaining from these
sources is reliable, do not use it. You can check the reliability of an Internet
source by asking your instructor or librarian for guidance.

Content Notes

Use **content notes**, indicated by a superscript (a raised number) in the text,
to cite several sources at once or to provide commentary or explanations that
do not fit smoothly into your essay. The full text of these notes appears on the
first numbered page following the last page of the essay. (If your essay has no
content notes, the works-cited page follows the last page of the essay.) Like
works-cited entries, content notes are double-spaced within and between
entries. However, the first line of each explanatory note is indented one-half
inch, and subsequent lines are flush with the left-hand margin.

To Cite Several Sources

In the essay

Surprising as it may seem, there have been many attempts to define literature.[1]

In the note

1. For an overview of critical opinion, see Arnold 72; Eagleton 1-2; Howe 43-44; and
Abrams 232-34.

To Provide Explanations

In the essay

In recent years, gothic novels have achieved great popularity.[3]

In the note

3. Gothic novels, works written in imitation of medieval romances, originally relied
on supernatural occurrences. They flourished in the late eighteenth and early nineteenth
centuries.

2| FICTION

CHAPTER 4

UNDERSTANDING FICTION

A **narrative** tells a story by presenting events in some logical or orderly way. A work of **fiction** is a narrative that originates in the imagination of the author rather than in history or fact. Of course, some fiction—historical or autobiographical fiction, for example—focuses on real people and is grounded in actual events, but the way the characters interact, what they say, and how the plot unfolds are largely the author's invention.

Even before they know how to read, most people learn how narratives are structured. As children learn how to tell a story, they start to experiment with its form, learning the value of exaggerating, adding or deleting details, rearranging events, and bending facts. In other words, they learn how to *fictionalize* a narrative to achieve a desired effect. This kind of informal personal narrative is similar in many respects to more structured literary narratives.

 Origins of Modern Fiction

People have always had stories to tell, and as we evolved, so did our means of self-expression. Our early ancestors depicted the stories of their daily lives and beliefs in primitive drawings that used pictures as symbols. As language evolved, so too did our means of communicating—and our need to preserve what we understood to be our past.

Stories and songs emerged as an oral means of communicating and preserving the past: tales of heroic battles or struggles, myths, or religious beliefs. In a society that was not literate, and in a time before mass communication, the oral tradition enabled people to pass down these stories, usually in the form of long rhyming poems. These poems used various literary devices—including **rhyme** and **alliteration** as well as **anaphora** (the repetition of key words or phrases)—to make them easier to remember. Thus, the earliest works of fiction were in fact poetry.

Eventually written down, these extended narratives developed into **epics**—long narrative poems about heroic figures whose actions determine the fate of a nation or of an entire race. Homer's *Iliad* and *Odyssey*, the ancient Babylonian *Epic of Gilgamesh*, the Hindu *Bhagavad Gita*, and the Anglo-Saxon *Beowulf* are examples of epics. Many of the tales of the Old Testament also came out of this tradition. The setting of an epic is vast—sometimes worldwide or cosmic, including heaven and hell—and the action commonly involves a battle or a perilous journey. Quite often, divine beings participate in the action and influence the outcome of events, as they do in the Trojan War in the *Iliad* and in the founding of Rome in Virgil's *Aeneid*.

During the Middle Ages, these early epics were supplanted by the **romance**. Written initially in verse and later in prose, the romance replaced the gods, goddesses, and central heroic characters of the epic with knights, kings, and damsels in distress. Events were controlled by enchantments rather than by the will of divine beings. The anonymously written *Sir Gawain and the Green Knight* and

Engraving of Ulysses slaying Penelope's suitors, from Homer's *Odyssey*
Source: ©Bettmann/Corbis

Thomas Malory's *Le Morte d'Arthur* are romances based on the legend of King Arthur and the Knights of the Round Table.

Engraving of the Trojan horse from Homer's *Odyssey*
Source: ©Bettmann/Corbis

The Lady Guinevere

Portrait of Queen Guinevere, King Arthur's wife and Sir Lancelot's mistress
Source: ©Bettmann/Corbis

Other significant texts of the Middle Ages include Geoffrey Chaucer's *The Canterbury Tales* and Giovanni Boccaccio's *The Decameron*, both written in the fourteenth century. These two works are made up of poems and stories, respectively, integrated into a larger narrative framework. They share similarities with modern collections of linked short stories—stories set in the same town or featuring the same characters, such as Sherwood Anderson's 1919 *Winesburg, Ohio* and Amy Tan's 1989 *The Joy Luck Club*.

The History of the Novel

The evolution of the **novel** has been a gradual but steady process. Early forms of literature share many of the characteristics of the novel (although not necessarily sharing its recognizable form). Epics and romances, for instance, often had unified plots, developed characters, and complex themes, and in this way, they were precursors of what today we call the novel.

The First Printing Press.

Nineteenth-century woodcut depicting Johannes Gutenberg's printing press
Source: North Wind Picture Archives/Alamy

Perhaps the most notable event in the development of the novel, and of literature as a whole, was the invention of the printing press by Johannes Gutenberg in 1440. Before this milestone, printing was a costly and impractical process that was largely reserved for medical books and sacred texts. However, this invention made the production and distribution of longer works a practical possibility and forever expanded the scope of what we consider literature to be—and how we access it. In fact, the printing press was one of the factors that made the Renaissance possible. During this period, philosophy, science, literature, and the arts flowered. The **pastoral romance**, a prose tale set in an idealized rural world, and the **character**, a brief satirical sketch illustrating a type of personality, both became popular in Renaissance England. The **picaresque novel**, an episodic, often satirical work about a rogue or rascal (such as Miguel de Cervantes's *Don Quixote*), emerged in seventeenth-century Spain. Other notable Renaissance-era texts included Sir Philip Sidney's *Arcadia*, Edmund Spenser's *The Faerie Queen*, and John Bunyan's *The Pilgrim's Progress*. Each of these texts included features now associated with the novel—longer narratives, extended plots, the development of characters over time, and a hero/protagonist—and the form continued to evolve.

The English writer Daniel Defoe is commonly given credit for writing the first novel. His *Robinson Crusoe* (1719) is an episodic narrative similar to a picaresque but unified by a single setting as well as by a central character. Another early novel, Jonathan Swift's *Gulliver's Travels* (1726), is a satirical commentary on the undesirable outcomes of science. During this time, the **epistolary novel** also flourished. This kind of novel told a story in letters or included letters as a means of disseminating information. Samuel Richardson's *Clarissa* (1748) is an example from the eighteenth century; a contemporary example is Alice Walker's *The Color Purple* (1982).

By the nineteenth century, the novel had reached a high point in its development, and its influence and importance were widespread. During the Victorian era in England (1837–1901), many novels reflected the era's preoccupation with propriety and manners. The most notable examples of

An 1863 engraving by Gustave Doré depicting a scene from Miguel de Cervantes's *Don Quixote*
Source: ©Timewatch Images/Alamy

Nineteenth-century woodcut by J. Mahoney depicting a scene from Charles
Dickens's *Oliver Twist*
Source: ©Bettmann/Corbis

these **novels of manners** were Jane Austen's *Sense and Sensibility* (1811)
and *Pride and Prejudice* (1813). Beyond the world of the aristocracy, members
of the middle class clamored for novels that mirrored their own experiences, and writers such as George Eliot, Charles Dickens, William Thac-
keray, and Charlotte and Emily Brontë appealed to this desire by creating
large fictional worlds populated by many different characters who reflected
the complexity—and at times the melodrama—of Victorian society.

Scene from the 1931 film *Frankenstein*
Source: Bettmann/Corbis

Other writers addressed the dire consequences of science and ambition, as
Mary Wollstonecraft Shelley did in
her Gothic tale *Frankenstein* (1817).

In the United States, the early nineteenth century was marked by novels
that reflected the concerns of a growing
country with burgeoning interests. James
Fenimore Cooper (*Last of the Mohicans*)
and Nathaniel Hawthorne (*The Scarlet
Letter*) wrote historical fiction, while
Herman Melville (*Moby-Dick*) examined good and evil, madness and sanity.
Realism, which strove to portray
everyday events and people in a realistic fashion, began in France with Hon-
oré de Balzac and Gustav Flaubert and

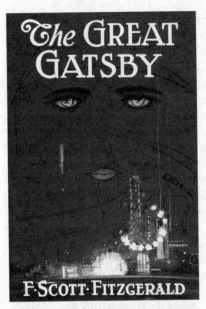

Source: Courtesy, Charles Scribner's Sons, an imprint of Simon & Schuster

Cover images of *The Great Gatsby, The Sun Also Rises,* **and** *The Sound and the Fury*
Source: Courtesy, Charles Scribner's Sons, an imprint of Simon & Schuster

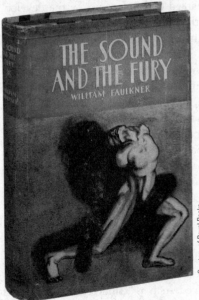

Courtesy of Royal Books

spread to the United States, influencing writers such as Henry James, Stephen Crane, and Mark Twain. Other nineteenth-century writers addressed social and even feminist themes in their work. In the United States, writers who addressed such concerns included Harriet Beecher Stowe (*Uncle Tom's Cabin*) and Kate Chopin (*The Awakening*). Meanwhile, in Russia, novelists such as Fyodor Dostoyevsky (*Crime and Punishment*) and Leo Tolstoy (*War and Peace*) examined the everyday lives, as well as the larger political struggles and triumphs, of their people.

The early twentieth century marked the beginning of a literary movement known as **modernism,** in which writers reacted to the increasing complexity of a changing world and mourned the passing of old ways under the pressures of modernity.

World War I, urbanization, and the rise of industrialism all contributed to a sense that new ideas needed to be expressed in new ways, and writers such as James Joyce (*Ulysses*), Virginia Woolf (*To the Lighthouse*), and D. H. Lawrence (*Sons and Lovers*) experimented with both form and content.

In the United States, the Roaring Twenties and the Great Depression inspired numerous novelists who set out to write the "Great American Novel" and capture the culture and concerns of the times, often in very gritty and realistic ways. These authors included F. Scott Fitzgerald (*The Great Gatsby*), Ernest Hemingway (*The Sun Also Rises*), William Faulkner (*The Sound and the Fury*), and John Steinbeck (*The Grapes of Wrath*). A little later, novelists such as Richard Wright (*Native Son*) and Ralph Ellison (*Invisible Man*) made important literary contributions by addressing the sociopolitical climate for African Americans in a segregated society.

In the aftermath of modernism, a movement called **postmodernism** emerged. Postmodern artists reacted against the limitations placed on them by modernist ideas as well as the carnage of World War II. Often, the search for meaning in a postmodern text became an end in itself, and in this way, a work's meaning became relative and subjective. Postmodern novelists, such as Donald Barthelme, Margaret Atwood, Thomas Pynchon, Salman Rushdie, and Kurt Vonnegut, confronted the fragmentation of society and rejected the idea of a unified plot or the possibility of a reliable narrator.

Contemporary fiction has been marked and influenced by the developments of the latter part of the twentieth century, including globalization, the rise of technology, and the advent of the Internet and the Age of Communication. As our ability to interact and communicate with other societies has increased exponentially, so too has our access to the literature of other cultures. Contemporary fiction is a world that mirrors the diversity of its participants in terms of form, content, theme, style, and language. There are many writers worthy of mention, as each culture makes its own invaluable contributions. Some particularly noteworthy contemporary writers include the Nobel Prize–winning novelists Orhan Pamuk, José Saramago, Doris Lessing, Gabriel García Márquez, Nadine Gordimer, Saul Bellow, Toni Morrison, and V. S. Naipul. As we continue into the twenty-first century, the only thing that remains certain about the future of the novel, and of fiction in general, is its past.

The History of the Short Story

Early precursors of the short story include **anecdotes**, **parables**, **fables**, **folk tales**, and **fairy tales**. What all of these forms have in common is brevity and a moral. The ones that have survived, such as "Cinderella" and Aesop's *Fables*, are contemporary versions of old, even ancient, tales that can be traced back centuries through many different cultures.

Folktales and fairy tales share many characteristics. First, they feature simple characters who illustrate a quality or trait that can be summed up in a few words. Much of the appeal of "Cinderella," for example, depends on the contrast between the selfish, sadistic stepsisters and the poor, gentle, victimized Cinderella. In addition, the folktale or fairy tale has an obvious theme or **moral**—good triumphing over evil, for instance. The stories move directly to their conclusions, never interrupted by ingenious or unexpected plot twists. (Love is temporarily thwarted, but the prince eventually finds Cinderella and marries her.) Finally, these tales are anchored not in specific times or places but in "once upon a time" settings, green worlds of prehistory filled with royalty, talking animals, and magic.

Undated woodcut of Cinderella
Source: ©Bettmann/Corbis

The thematically linked stories in Giovanni Boccaccio's *The Decameron* and Geoffrey Chaucer's *The Canterbury Tales*, both written in the fourteenth century, were precursors of the modern short story. *Grimm's Fairy Tales* (1824–1826), an early collection of short narratives and folk stories, also helped to pave the way for the development of the genre, but it was not until the nineteenth century that the contemporary version of the short story emerged.

During the last quarter of the nineteenth century, a proliferation of literary and popular magazines and journals created a demand for short fiction (between 3,000 and 15,000 words) that could be published in their entirety rather than in serial installments, as most novels at the time were. Nathaniel Hawthorne's *Twice Told Tales* (1842) and Edgar Allan Poe's *Tales of the Grotesque and Arabesque* (1836) were early collections of short stories. Americans in particular hungrily consumed the written word, and short stories soared in popularity. In fact, because the short story was embraced so readily and developed so quickly in the United States, it is commonly (although not quite accurately) thought of as an American literary form.

Defining the Short Story

Like the novel, the short story evolved from various forms of narrative and has its roots in an oral tradition. However, whereas the novel is an extended piece of narrative fiction, the **short story** is distinguished by its relative brevity, which creates a specific set of expectations and possibilities as well as certain limitations. Unlike the novelist, the short story writer cannot devote a great deal of space to developing a highly complex plot or a large number of characters. As a result, the short story often begins close to or at the height of action and develops a limited number of characters. Usually focusing on a single incident, the writer develops one or more characters by showing their reactions to events. This attention to character development, as well as its detailed description of setting, is what distinguishes the short story from earlier short narrative forms.

In many contemporary short stories, a character experiences an **epiphany**, a moment of illumination in which something hidden or not understood becomes immediately clear. In other short stories, the thematic significance, or meaning, is communicated through the way in which the characters develop, or react. Regardless of the specifics of its format or its theme, a short story offers readers an open window to a world that they can enter—if only briefly.

The short story that follows, Ernest Hemingway's "Hills Like White Elephants" (1927), illustrates many of the characteristics of the **modern short story**. Although it is so brief that it might be more accurately called a **short-short story**, it uses its limited space to establish a distinct setting and develop two characters. From the story's first paragraph, readers know where the story takes place and whom it is about: "The American and the girl with him sat at a table in the shade, outside the building. It was very hot and the express from Barcelona would come in forty minutes." As time elapses and the man and woman wait for the train to Madrid, their strained dialogue reveals the tension between them and hints at the serious conflict they must resolve.

ERNEST HEMINGWAY (1898–1961) grew up in Oak Park, Illinois, and after high school graduation began his writing career as a reporter on the *Kansas City Star*. While working as a volunteer ambulance driver in World War I, eighteen-year-old Hemingway was wounded. As Hemingway himself told the story, he was hit by machine-gun fire while carrying an Italian soldier to safety. (Hemingway biographer Michael Reynolds, however, reports that Hemingway was wounded when a mortar shell fell and killed the man next to him.)

Success for Hemingway came early, with publication of the short story collection *In Our Time* (1925) and his first and most acclaimed novel, *The Sun Also Rises* (1926), a portrait of a postwar "lost generation" of Americans adrift in Europe. This novel established Hemingway as a writer who was able to create fiction out of his own life experiences. *For Whom the Bell Tolls* (1940) emerged out of his experiences as a journalist in Spain during the Spanish Civil War. Later in life, he made his home in Key West, Florida, and then in Cuba, where he wrote *The Old Man and the Sea* (1952). In 1954 he won the Nobel Prize in Literature. In 1961, plagued by poor health and mental illness—and perhaps also by the difficulty of living up to his own image—Hemingway took his own life.

Cultural Context At the time this story was written, Ernest Hemingway was part of a group of American expatriates living in Paris. Disillusioned by World War I and seeking a more bohemian lifestyle, free from the concerns of American materialism, this group of artists, intellectuals, poets, and writers were known as the "Lost Generation." Some of the group's most famous members included F. Scott Fitzgerald, Gertrude Stein, and John Dos Passos. The literary legacy they left behind is arguably one of the greatest of the twentieth century.

Hills Like White Elephants (1927)

The hills across the valley of the Ebro[1] were long and white. On this side there was no shade and no trees and the station was between two lines of rails in the sun. Close against the side of the station there was the warm shadow of the building and a curtain, made of strings of bamboo beads, hung across the open door into the bar, to keep out flies. The American and the girl with him sat at a table in the shade, outside the building. It was very hot and the express from Barcelona would come in forty minutes. It stopped at this junction for two minutes and went on to Madrid.

"What should we drink?" the girl asked. She had taken off her hat and put it on the table.

"It's pretty hot," the man said.

"Let's drink beer."

"Dos cervezas," the man said into the curtain.   5

"Big ones?" a woman asked from the doorway.

"Yes. Two big ones."

The woman brought two glasses of beer and two felt pads. She put the felt pads and the beer glasses on the table and looked at the man and the girl. The girl was looking off at the line of hills. They were white in the sun and the country was brown and dry.

"They look like white elephants," she said.

"I've never seen one," the man drank his beer.   10

"No, you wouldn't have."

"I might have," the man said. "Just because you say I wouldn't have doesn't prove anything."

The girl looked at the bead curtain. "They've painted something on it," she said. "What does it say?"

"Anis del Toro.[2] It's a drink."

"Could we try it?"   15

---

[1] *Ebro:* A river in northern Spain.

[2] *Anis del Toro:* Spanish for *bull's anisette,* a dark alcoholic drink made from anise, an herb that tastes like licorice.

The man called "Listen" through the curtain. The woman came out from the bar.

"Four reales."[3]

"We want two Anis del Toro."

"With water?"

20 "Do you want it with water?"

"I don't know," the girl said. "Is it good with water?"

"It's all right."

"You want them with water?" asked the woman.

"Yes, with water."

25 "It tastes like licorice," the girl said and put the glass down.

"That's the way with everything."

"Yes," said the girl. "Everything tastes of licorice. Especially all the things you've waited so long for, like absinthe."[4]

"Oh, cut it out."

"You started it," the girl said. "I was being amused. I was having a fine time."

30 "Well, let's try and have a fine time."

"All right. I was trying. I said the mountains looked like white elephants. Wasn't that bright?"

"That was bright."

"I wanted to try this new drink. That's all we do, isn't it—look at things and try new drinks?"

"I guess so."

35 The girl looked across at the hills.

"They're lovely hills," she said. "They don't really look like white elephants. I just meant the coloring of their skin through the trees."

"Should we have another drink?"

"All right."

The warm wind blew the bead curtain against the table.

40 "The beer's nice and cool," the man said.

"It's lovely," the girl said.

"It's really an awfully simple operation, Jig," the man said. "It's not really an operation at all."

The girl looked at the ground the table legs rested on.

"I know you wouldn't mind it, Jig. It's really not anything. It's just to let the air in."

45 The girl did not say anything.

---

[3]*reales:* Spanish coins.

[4]*absinthe:* A green alcoholic drink made from wormwood, anise, and other herbs.

"I'll go with you and I'll stay with you all the time. They just let the air in and then it's all perfectly natural."

"Then what will we do afterward?"

"We'll be fine afterward. Just like we were before."

"What makes you think so?"

"That's the only thing that bothers us. It's the only thing that's made 50 us unhappy."

The girl looked at the bead curtain, put her hand out and took hold of two of the strings of beads.

"And you think then we'll be all right and be happy."

"I know we will. You don't have to be afraid. I've known lots of people that have done it."

"So have I," said the girl. "And afterward they were all so happy."

"Well," the man said, "if you don't want to you don't have to. I wouldn't 55 have you do it if you didn't want to. But I know it's perfectly simple."

"And you really want to?"

"I think it's the best thing to do. But I don't want you to do it if you don't really want to."

"And if I do it you'll be happy and things will be like they were and you'll love me?"

"I love you now. You know I love you."

"I know. But if I do it, then it will be nice again if I say things are like 60 white elephants, and you'll like it?"

"I'll love it. I love it now but I just can't think about it. You know how I get when I worry."

"If I do it you won't ever worry?"

"I won't worry about that because it's perfectly simple."

"Then I'll do it. Because I don't care about me."

"What do you mean?" 65

"I don't care about me."

"Well, I care about you."

"Oh, yes. But I don't care about me. And I'll do it and then everything will be fine."

"I don't want you to do it if you feel that way."

The girl stood up and walked to the end of the station. Across, on the 70 other side, were fields of grain and trees along the banks of the Ebro. Far away beyond the river, were mountains. The shadow of a cloud moved across the field of grain and she saw the river through the trees.

"And we could have all this," she said. "And we could have everything and every day we make it more impossible."

"What did you say?"

"I said we could have everything."

"We can have everything."

75 "No, we can't."

"We can have the whole world."

"No, we can't."

"We can go everywhere."

"No, we can't. It isn't ours any more."

80 "It's ours."

"No, it isn't. And once they take it away, you never get it back."

"But they haven't taken it away."

"We'll wait and see."

"Come on back in the shade," he said. "You mustn't feel that way."

85 "I don't feel any way," the girl said. "I just know things."

"I don't want you to do anything that you don't want to do—."

"Nor that isn't good for me," she said. "I know. Could we have another beer?"

"All right. But you've got to realize—"

"I realize," the girl said. "Can't we maybe stop talking?"

90 They sat down at the table and the girl looked across at the hills on the dry side of the valley and the man looked at her and at the table.

"You've got to realize," he said, "that I don't want you to do it if you don't want to. I'm perfectly willing to go through with it if it means anything to you."

"Doesn't it mean anything to you? We could get along."

"Of course it does. But I don't want anybody but you. I don't want anyone else. And I know it's perfectly simple."

"Yes, you know it's perfectly simple."

95 "It's all right for you to say that, but I do know it."

"Would you do something for me now?"

"I'd do anything for you."

"Would you please please please please please please please stop talking?"

He did not say anything but looked at the bags against the wall of the station. There were labels on them from all the hotels where they had spent nights.

100 "But I don't want you to," he said, "I don't care anything about it."

"I'll scream," the girl said.

The woman came out through the curtains with two glasses of beer and put them down on the damp felt pads. "The train comes in five minutes," she said.

"What did she say?" asked the girl.

"That the train is coming in five minutes."

105 The girl smiled brightly at the woman, to thank her.

"I'd better take the bags over to the other side of the station," the man said. She smiled at him.

"All right. Then come back and we'll finish the beer."

He picked up the two heavy bags and carried them around the station to the other tracks. He looked up the tracks but could not see the train. Coming back, he walked through the barroom, where people waiting for the train were drinking. He drank an Anis at the bar and looked at the people. They were all waiting reasonably for the train. He went out through the bead curtain. She was sitting at the table and smiled at him.

"Do you feel better?" he asked.

"I feel fine," she said. "There's nothing wrong with me. I feel fine."   110

*   *   *

Like many short stories, "Hills Like White Elephants" has a single setting, contains a straightforward plot, involves few characters, starts at the height of the action, and reaches its climax quickly. Even so, this story is anything but simple. From the beginning, readers can sense the tension that exists between the two characters, "the girl" and "the American." For almost half the story, they talk about anything except what concerns them most—the question of whether the girl should have an unspecified "simple operation"—presumably an abortion. When they finally confront the issue, the man trivializes the situation by saying that the procedure is "natural" and "not really an operation at all." Eventually, the girl pleads, "Would you please please please please please please please stop talking?" She is clearly hurt by the American's condescending tone and is frightened by her circumstances. Although at the end of the story she assures him that she is "fine," they both sense that no matter what she decides to do, their relationship will never be the same. In this brief, seemingly uncomplicated story, Hemingway manages to convey, almost entirely through dialogue, the inability of the two main characters to communicate, as well as the moral bankruptcy of their world.

The Boundaries of Fiction

As noted above, a **short story** is a work of fiction that is marked by its brevity, its relatively limited number of characters, its short time frame, and its ability to achieve thematic significance in a relatively short space. A **novella** (such as Franz Kafka's "The Metamorphosis" and Herman Melville's "Bartleby, the Scrivener") is an extended short story that shares some characteristics (for example, concentrated action) with a short story while retaining some qualities of a novel, including greater character development. At the other end of the spectrum are **short-short stories**, which are under 1,500 words (about five pages) in length. (Examples of those very brief stories are included in Chapter 5.) **Prose poems**, such as Richard Blanco's "Mexican Almuerzo in New England" (p. 666), are hybrid versions of literature that have characteristics of both prose (being written in paragraphs) and poetry (being written in verse form, often using imagery, meter, and rhyme to convey lyrical beauty). In addition, **graphic stories**—sometimes complete in themselves, sometimes part of longer works of **graphic fiction**—have proliferated in recent years. (Examples of such works are included in Chapter 6.)

Finally, the Internet—along with computers, smartphones, and tablets—offers numerous possibilities for arranging and disseminating texts. Currently, writers are experimenting with fictional forms that are every bit as revolutionary as those modernist works created by James Joyce, John Dos Passos, Virginia Woolf, and Gertrude Stein nearly a century ago. For example, "Black Box" (an excerpt appears below), a science fiction short story written by Pulitzer Prize–winning author Jennifer Egan, was originally presented as tweets over a ten–night period.

> Some powerful men actually call their beauties "Beauty."
>
> Contrary to reputation, there is a deep camaraderie among beauties.
>
> If your Designated Mate is widely feared, the beauties at the house party where you've gone undercover to meet him will be especially kind.
>
> Kindness feels good, even when it's based on a false notion of your identity and purpose.

Egan has also written a story in the form of a PowerPoint presentation. The writer Alex Epstein has created a story made up of Facebook photos, and other writers are experimenting with blog-post fiction as well as with stories on websites devoted to specific kinds of fiction—for example, flash fiction or graphic short stories. Perhaps the most experimental fictional form is **hypertext fiction**—stories, such as Catlin Fisher's "These Waves of Girls" and Paul La Farge's "Luminous Airplanes"—that contains text and links to pictures, film clips, and other texts. Readers create "paths" through hypertext stories by following links in any order they choose. In this way, a single work of hypertext fiction can contain many possible plots, and readers can move through them at will.

There are, it seems, as many different ways to tell a story as there are stories to be told. A short story may be comic or tragic; its subject may be growing up, marriage, crime and punishment, war, sexual awakening, death, or any number of other human concerns. The setting can be an imaginary world, the old West, rural America, the jungles of Uruguay, nineteenth-century Russia, pre-communist China, or modern Egypt. The story may have a conventional form, with a definite beginning, middle, and end, or it may be structured as a letter, as a diary entry, or even as a collection of random notes. The story may use just words, or it may juxtapose conventional text with symbols, pictures, or empty space. The narrator of a story may be trustworthy or unreliable, involved in the action or a disinterested observer, sympathetic or deserving of scorn, extremely ignorant or highly insightful, limited in vision or able to see inside the minds of all the characters. As the selections in this anthology show, the possibilities of the short story are almost endless.

CHAPTER 5

FICTION SAMPLER:
THE SHORT-SHORT STORY

Julia Alvarez
AP Images/Ramon Espinosa

Stephen Graham Jones
Gary Isaacs

Jamaica Kincaid
Taro Yamasaki//Time Life Pictures/
Getty Images

Ed Park
Sylvia Plachy

This chapter focuses on the **short-short story**, a short story that is fewer than 1,500 words in length. Short-shorts are often divided into subcategories according to their overall length. For example, **micro fiction**, at approximately 250 words or fewer, is one of the shortest kinds of short-short fiction, followed by **flash fiction** (fewer than approximately 1,000 words) and then by **sudden fiction** (fewer than approximately 1,500 words). Short-shorts are sometimes also categorized according to how long they take to read or how long they take to write. Regardless of their individual characteristics, all short-short stories compress ideas into a small package and, to varying degrees, test the limits of the short story genre. Some short-shorts are quite conventional (that is, they include recognizable characters and have an identifiable beginning, middle, and end); others are experimental, perhaps lacking a definite setting or a clear plot. As defined by Robert Shapard (who, along with James Thomas, edited the short-short story collections *Sudden Fiction* and *New Sudden Fiction*), short-short stories are "Highly compressed, highly charged, insidious, protean, sudden, alarming, tantalizing"; they can "confer form on small corners of chaos, can do in a page what a novel does in two hundred." One of the most extreme examples is Ernest Hemingway's famous six-word story: "For sale: baby shoes, never worn."

The stories in this sampler represent a wide range of short-short fiction. Of the ten stories collected here, Julia Alvarez's "Snow" and Bret Anthony Johnston's "Encounters with Unexpected Animals" perhaps most closely resemble traditional short stories in that they develop familiar characters in recognizable settings. Similarly, Sandra Cisneros's "Pilón" explores a theme that is familiar in literary works: the narrator's attempt to recapture long-ago memories.

Other stories in this sampler are somewhat more experimental. Although their plots may unfold in conventional ways, their treatment of time is sometimes surprising. For example, in "Discovering America," Stephen Graham Jones summarizes the events of several years of the narrator's life in three pages; George Saunders's two-paragraph "Sticks" covers several decades; and Ed Park's "Slide to Unlock" unfolds in just a few minutes. Dave Eggers's "Accident" and Lydia Davis's "Television" are perhaps even more unpredictable: although they resemble conventional short stories in some respects, both maintain an unusual narrative distance through their unexpected use of point of view.

Finally, Jamaica Kincaid's "Girl," a **stream-of-consciousness monologue**, is unique in its style and form (the entire story is a single sentence), as is Amanda Brown's "Love and Other Catastrophes: A Mix Tape," consisting entirely of a list of song titles.

Despite their brevity, the stories in this chapter have much in common with the stories that appear elsewhere in this book. Each, in its own distinctive way, "tells a story."

JULIA ALVAREZ (1950–   ) was born in New York City. Soon after her birth, Alvarez's family relocated to the Dominican Republic, where they lived for ten years until they emigrated back to New York. Alvarez describes herself as "a Dominican, hyphen, American....As a fiction writer, I find that the most exciting things happen in the realm of that hyphen—the place where two worlds collide or blend together." Alvarez's works explore the experiences and emotions of immigrants, particularly female Hispanic immigrants, as they struggle to redefine themselves in the context of a new culture. She has published many highly regarded works of fiction and poetry,

Source: © AP Photo/Ramon Espinosa

including *Homecoming* (1984 and 1996), *How the García Girls Lost Their Accents* (1991), *In the Time of Butterflies* (1995), and *¡Yo!* (1997). She is also the author of the children's book *How Tía Lola Saved the Summer* (2011), and the memoir *A Wedding in Haiti* (2012). Alvarez is currently a writer-in-residence at Middlebury College in Vermont.

Snow (1984)

Our first year in New York we rented a small apartment with a Catholic school nearby, taught by the Sisters of Charity, hefty women in long black gowns and bonnets that made them look peculiar, like dolls in mourning. I liked them a lot, especially my grandmotherly fourth grade teacher, Sister Zoe. I had a lovely name, she said, and she had me teach the whole class how to pronounce it. *Yo-lan-da.* As the only immigrant in my class, I was put in a special seat in the first row by the window, apart from the other children so that Sister Zoe could tutor me without disturbing them. Slowly, she enunciated the new words I was to repeat: *laundromat, cornflakes, subway, snow.*

Soon I picked up enough English to understand holocaust was in the air. Sister Zoe explained to a wide-eyed classroom what was happening in Cuba. Russian missiles were being assembled, trained supposedly on New York City. President Kennedy, looking worried too, was on the television at home, explaining we might have to go to war against the Communists. At school, we had air-raid drills: an ominous bell would go off and we'd file into the hall, fall to the floor, cover our heads with our coats, and imagine our hair falling out, the bones in our arms going soft. At home, Mami and my sisters and I said a rosary for world peace. I heard new vocabulary: *nuclear bomb, radioactive fallout, bomb shelter.* Sister Zoe explained how it would happen. She drew a picture of a mushroom on the blackboard and dotted a flurry of chalkmarks for the dusty fallout that would kill us all.

The months grew cold, November, December. It was dark when I got up in the morning, frosty when I followed my breath to school. One morning as I sat at my desk daydreaming out the window, I saw dots in the air like the ones Sister Zoe had drawn—random at first, then lots and lots. I shrieked, "Bomb Bomb!" Sister Zoe jerked around, her full black skirt ballooning as she hurried to my side. A few girls began to cry.

But then Sister Zoe's shocked look faded. "Why, Yolanda dear, that's snow!" She laughed. "Snow."

"Snow," I repeated. I looked out the window warily. All my life I had 5 heard about the white crystals that fell out of American skies in the winter. From my desk I watched the fine powder dust the sidewalk and parked cars below. Each flake was different, Sister Zoe said, like a person, irreplaceable and beautiful.

*   *   *

AMANDA BROWN (1981–   ), a graduate of Emerson College, co-owns the independent record label Not Not Fun. "Love and Other Catastrophes" was first published in 2002 in *Story Quarterly* and was reprinted in *The Best American Nonrequired Reading 2003*.

Love and Other Catastrophes:
A Mix Tape (2002)

"All By Myself" (Eric Carmen). "Looking for Love" (Lou Reed). "I Wanna Dance With Somebody" (Whitney Houston). "Let's Dance" (David Bowie). "Let's Kiss" (Beat Happening). "Let's Talk About Sex" (Salt N' Pepa). "Like A Virgin" (Madonna). "We've Only Just Begun" (The Carpenters). "I Wanna Be Your Boyfriend" (The Ramones). "I'll Tumble 4 Ya" (Culture Club). "Head Over Heels" (The Go-Go's). "Nothing Compares To You" (Sinéad O'Connor). "My Girl" (The Temptations). "Could This Be Love?" (Bob Marley). "Love and Marriage" (Frank Sinatra). "White Wedding" (Billy Idol). "Stuck in the Middle with You" (Steelers Wheel). "Tempted" (The Squeeze). "There Goes My Baby" (The Drifters). "What's Going On?" (Marvin Gaye). "Where Did You Sleep Last Night?" (Leadbelly). "Whose Bed Have Your Boots Been Under?" (Shania Twain). "Jealous Guy" (John Lennon). "Your Cheatin' Heart" (Tammy Wynette). "Shot Through the Heart" (Bon Jovi). "Don't Go Breaking My Heart" (Elton John and Kiki Dee). "My Achy Breaky Heart" (Billy Ray Cyrus). "Heartbreak Hotel" (Elvis Presley). "Stop, In the Name of Love" (The Supremes). "Try a Little Tenderness" (Otis Redding). "Try (Just a Little Bit Harder)" (Janis Joplin). "All Apologies" (Nirvana). "Hanging on the Telephone" (Blondie). "I Just Called to Say I Love You" (Stevie Wonder). "Love Will Keep Us Together" (Captain and Tennille). "Let's Stay Together" (Al Green). "It Ain't Over 'Till It's Over" (Lenny Kravitz). "What's Love Got To Do With It?" (Tina Turner). "You Don't Bring Me Flowers Anymore" (Barbara Streisand and Neil Diamond). "I Wish You Wouldn't Say That" (Talking Heads). "You're So Vain" (Carly Simon). "Love Is a Battlefield" (Pat Benatar). "Heaven Knows I'm Miserable Now" (The Smiths). "(Can't Get No) Satisfaction" (Rolling Stones). "Must Have Been Love (But It's Over Now)" (Roxette). "Breaking Up Is Hard to Do" (Neil Sedaka). "I Will Survive" (Gloria Gaynor). "Hit the Road, Jack" (Mary McCaslin and Jim Ringer). "These Boots Were Made for Walking" (Nancy Sinatra). "All Out of Love" (Air Supply). "All By Myself" (Eric Carmen).

*   *   *

SANDRA CISNEROS (1954–   ) was born and raised in Chicago. Her fiction, poems, and essays explore Mexican–American heritage and identity. She is the author of *The House on Mango Street* (1983), *My Wicked Wicked Ways* (1987), *Woman Hollering Creek and Other Stories* (1991), *Loose Woman: Poems* (1994), and *Caramelo, or, Puro Cuento: A Novel* (2002). Cisneros is the recipient of numerous awards and fellowships, including a MacArthur Foundation Fellowship and two national Endowment of the Arts Fellowships for fiction and poetry.

Alicia Wagner Calzada/ZUMA Press/Newscom

Pilón (2002)

Like the Mexican grocer who gives you a pilón, something extra tossed into your bag as a thank-you for your patronage just as you are leaving. I give you here another story in thanks for having listened to my cuentó[1] . . .

On Cinco de Mayo Street, in front of Café la Blanca, an organ grinder playing "Farolito." Out of a happy grief, people give coins for shaking awake the memory of a father, a beloved, a child whom God ran away with.

And it was as if that music stirred up things in a piece of my heart from a time I couldn't remember. From before. Not exactly a time, a feeling. The way sometimes one remembers a memory with the images blurred and rounded, but has forgotten the one thing that would draw it all into focus. In this case, I'd forgotten a mood. Not a mood—a state of being, to be more precise.

How before my body wasn't my body. I didn't have a body. I was a being as close to a spirit as a spirit. I was a ball of light floating across the planet. I mean the me I was before puberty, that red Rio Bravo[2] you have to carry yourself over.

I don't know how it is with boys. I've never been a boy. But girls somewhere between the ages of, say, eight and puberty, girls forget they have bodies. It's the time she has trouble keeping herself clean, socks always drooping, knees pocked and bloody, hair crooked as a broom. She doesn't look in mirrors. She isn't aware of being watched. Not aware of her body causing men to look at her yet. There isn't the sense of the female body's volatility, its rude weight, the nuisance of dragging it about. There isn't the world to bully you with it, bludgeon you, condemn you to a life sentence of fear. It's the time when you look at a young girl and notice she is

---

[1] *cuento:* Spanish for *story.*
[2] *Rio Bravo:* The Rio Grande river.

at her ugliest, but at the same time, at her happiest. She is a being as close to a spirit as a spirit.

5   Then that red Rubicon. The never going back there. To that country, I mean.

And I remember along with that feeling fluttering through the notes of "Farolito," so many things, so many, all at once, each distinct and separate, and all running together. The taste of a *caramelo* called Glorias on my tongue. At la Caleta beach, a girl with skin like *cajeta*, like goat-milk candy. The *caramelo* color of your skin after rising out of the Acapulco foam, salt water running down your hair and stinging the eyes, the raw ocean smell, and the ocean running out of your mouth and nose. My mother watering her dahlias with a hose and running a stream of water over her feet as well, Indian feet, thick and square, *como de barro*, like the red clay of Mexican pottery.

And I don't know how it is with anyone else, but for me these things, that song, that time, that place, are all bound together in a country I am homesick for, that doesn't exist anymore. That never existed. A country I invented. Like all emigrants caught between here and there.

*   *   *

Geraint Lewis/Alamy

LYDIA DAVIS (1947–   ) has published one novel and seven story collections, including, most recently, *Can't and Won't* (2014). She is the recipient of the 2013 Man Booker International Prize as well as other awards and honors. The author of numerous short-short stories, Davis has also translated works by Maurice Blanchot, Michel Leiris, and Marcel Proust.

Television (1989)

1.

We have all these favorite shows coming on every evening. They say it will be exciting and it always is.

They give us hints of what is to come and then it comes and it is exciting. If dead people walked outside our windows we would be no more excited. We want to be part of it all.

5   We want to be the people they talk to when they tell what is to come later in the evening and later in the week.

We listen to the ads until we are exhausted, punished with lists: they want us to buy so much, and we try, but we don't have a lot of money. Yet we can't help admiring the science of it all.

How can we ever be as sure as these people are sure? These women are women in control, as the women in my family are not.

Yet we believe in this world.

We believe these people are speaking to us.

Mother, for example, is in love with an anchorman. And my husband 10 sits with his eyes on a certain young reporter and waits for the camera to draw back and reveal her breasts.

After the news we pick out a quiz show to watch and then a story of detective investigation.

The hours pass. Our hearts go on beating, now slow, now faster.

There is one quiz show which is particularly good. Each week the same man is there in the audience with his mouth tightly closed and tears in his eyes. His son is coming back on stage to answer more questions. The boy stands there blinking at the television camera. They will not let him go on answering questions if he wins the final sum of a hundred and twenty-eight thousand dollars. We don't care much about the boy and we don't like the mother, who smiles and shows her bad teeth, but we are moved by the father: his heavy lips, his wet eyes.

And so we turn off the telephone during this program and do not answer the knock at the door that rarely comes. We watch closely, and my husband now presses his lips together and then smiles so broadly that his eyes disappear, and as for me, I sit back like the mother with a sharp gaze, my mouth full of gold.

2.

It's not that I really think this show about Hawaiian policemen is very 15 good, it's just that it seems more real than my own life.

Different routes through the evening: Channels 2, 2, 4, 7, 9, or channels 13, 13, 13, 2, 2, 4, etc. Sometimes it's the police dramas I want to see, other times the public television documentaries, such as one called *Swamp Critters*.

It's partly my isolation at night, the darkness outside, the silence outside, the increasing lateness of the hour, that makes the story on television seem so interesting. But the plot, too, has something to do with it: tonight a son comes back after many years and marries his father's wife. (She is not his mother.)

We pay a good deal of attention because these shows seem to be the work of so many smart and fashionable people.

I think it is a television sound beyond the wall, but it's the honking of wild geese flying south in the first dark of the evening.

You watch a young woman named Susan Smith with pearls around 20 her neck sing the Canadian National Anthem before a hockey game. You listen to the end of the song, then you change the channel.

Or you watch Pete Seeger's legs bounce up and down in time to his *Reuben E. Lee* song, then change the channel.

It is not what you want to be doing. It is that you are passing the time.

You are waiting until it is a certain hour and you are in a certain condition so that you can go to sleep.

There is some real satisfaction in getting this information about the next day's weather—how fast the wind might blow and from what direction, when the rain might come, when the skies might clear—and the exact science of it is indicated by the words "40 percent" in "40 percent chance."

25   It all begins with the blue dot in the center of the dark screen, and this is when you can sense that these pictures will be coming to you from a long way off.

3.

Often, at the end of the day, when I am tired, my life seems to turn into a movie. I mean my real day moves into my real evening, but also moves away from me enough to be strange and a movie. It has by then become so complicated, so hard to understand, that I want to watch a different movie. I want to watch a movie made for TV, which will be simple and easy to understand, even if it involves disaster or disability or disease. It will skip over so much, it will skip over all the complications, knowing we will understand, so that major events will happen abruptly: a man may change his mind though it was firmly made up, and he may also fall in love suddenly. It will skip all the complications because there is not enough time to prepare for major events in the space of only one hour and twenty minutes, which also has to include commercial breaks, and we want major events.

One movie was about a woman professor with Alzheimer's disease; one was about an Olympic skier who lost a leg but learned to ski again. Tonight it was about a deaf man who fell in love with his speech therapist, as I knew he would because she was pretty, though not a good actress, and he was handsome, though deaf. He was deaf at the beginning of the movie and deaf again at the end, while in the middle he heard and learned to speak with a definite regional accent. In the space of one hour and twenty minutes, this man not only heard and fell deaf again but created a successful business through his own talent, was robbed of it through a company man's treachery, fell in love, kept his woman as far as the end of the movie, and lost his virginity, which seemed to be hard to lose if one was deaf and easier once one could hear.

All this was compressed into the very end of a day in my life that as the evening advanced had already moved away from me...

*   *   *

DAVE EGGERS (1970–   ) grew up near Chicago. In addition to many short stories, he has also published the memoir *A Heartbreaking Work of Staggering Genius* (2000), a finalist for the Pulitzer Prize, as well as several novels, including, most recently, *Your Fathers, Where Are They? And the Prophets, Do They Live Forever?* (2014). As the founder of McSweeney's (a literary group that publishes the journal *McSweeney's*, the magazine *The Believer*, and the DVD magazine *Wholphin*) and as editor of *The Best American Nonrequired Reading 2002, 2003,* and *2004,* Eggers has helped to popularize experimental, irreverent literature in print and electronic formats.

Accident (2005)

You all get out of your cars. You are alone in yours, and there are three teenagers in theirs, an older Camaro in new condition. The accident was your fault, and you walk over to tell them this. Walking over to their car, which you have ruined, it occurs to you that if the three teenagers are angry teenagers, this encounter could be very unpleasant. You pulled into an intersection, obstructing them, and their car hit yours. They have every right to be upset, or livid, or even violence-contemplating. As you approach, you see that their driver's side door won't open. The driver pushes against it, and you are reminded of scenes where drivers are stuck in submerged cars. Soon they all exit through the passenger side door and walk around the Camaro, inspecting the damage. None of them is hurt, but the car is wrecked. "Just bought this today," the driver says. He is 18, blond, average in all ways. "Today?" you ask. You are a bad person, you think. You also think: what a dorky car for a teenager to buy in 2005. "Yeah, today," he says, then sighs. You tell him that you are sorry. That you are so, so sorry. That it was your fault and that you will cover all costs. You exchange insurance information, and you find yourself, minute by minute, ever more thankful that none of these teenagers has punched you, or even made a remark about your being drunk, which you are not, or being stupid, which you are, often. You become more friendly with all of them, and you realize that you are much more connected to them, particularly to the driver, than possible in perhaps any other way. You have done him and his friends harm, in a way, and you jeopardized their health, and now you are so close you feel like you share a heart. He knows your name and you know his, and you almost killed him and, because you got so close to doing so but didn't, you want to fall on him, weeping, because you are so lonely, so lonely always, and all contact is contact, and all contact makes us so grateful we want to cry and dance and cry and cry. In a moment of clarity, you finally understand why boxers, who want so badly to hurt each other, can rest their heads on the shoulders of their opponents, can lean against one another like tired lovers, so thankful for a moment of peace.

*   *   *

BRET ANTHONY JOHNSTON (1971–   ) is the director of creative writing at Harvard University. He is the author of the story collection *Corpus Christi* (2004), the documentary *Waiting for Lightning* (2012), and the novel *Remember Me Like This* (2014). Johnston has received several honors and prizes, including the Pushcart Prize, a National Endowment for the Arts Literature Fellowship, and the National Book Foundation 5 Under 35 award.

Brian Birzer/Getty Images

Encounters with Unexpected Animals (2012)

Lambright had surprised everyone by offering to drive his son's girlfriend home. The girl was three months shy of seventeen, two years older than Robbie. She'd been held back in school. Her driver's license was currently suspended. She had a reputation, a body, and a bar code tattooed on the back of her neck. Lambright sometimes glimpsed it when her green hair was ponytailed. She'd come over for supper this evening, and though she volunteered to help Robbie and his mother with the dishes, Lambright had said he'd best deliver her home, it being a school night. He knew this pleased his wife and Robbie, the notion of him giving the girl another chance.

Driving, Lambright thought the moon looked like a fingerprint of chalk. They headed south on Airline Road. A couple of miles and he'd turn right on Saratoga, then left onto Everhart, and eventually they'd enter Kings Crossing, the subdivision with pools and sprinkler systems. At supper, Robbie and the girl had told, in tandem, a story about playing hide-and-seek on the abandoned country club golf course. Hide-and-seek, Lambright thought, is that what y'all call it now? Then they started talking about wildlife. The girl had once seen a blue-and-gold macaw riding on the headrest of a man's passenger seat, and another time, in a pasture in the Rio Grande Valley, she'd spotted zebras grazing among cattle. Robbie's mother recalled finding goats in the tops of peach trees in her youth. Robbie told the story of visiting the strange neighborhood in San Antonio where the muster of peacocks lived, and it led the girl to confess her desire to get a fan of peacock feathers tattooed on her lower back. She wanted a tattoo of a busted magnifying glass hovering over the words FIX ME.

Lambright couldn't figure what she saw in his son. Until the girl started visiting, Robbie had superhero posters on his walls and a fleet of model airplanes suspended from the ceiling with fishing wire. Lambright had actually long been skeptical of the boy's room, worrying it looked too childish, worrying it confirmed what might be called "softness" of character. But now the walls were stripped and all that remained of the fighter fleet was the fishing-wire stubble on the ceiling.

Two weeks ago, one of his wife's necklaces disappeared. Last week, a bottle of her nerve pills. Then, over the weekend, he'd caught Robbie and the girl with a flask of whiskey in the backyard. She'd come to supper tonight to make amends.

Traffic was light. When he stopped at the intersection of Airline and   5
Saratoga, the only headlights he saw were far off, like buoys in the bay. The turn signal dinged. He debated, then clicked it off. He accelerated straight across Saratoga.

"We were supposed to turn—"

"Scenic route," he said. "We'll visit a little."

But they didn't. There was only the low hum of the tires on the road, the noise of the truck pushing against the wind. Lambright hadn't contributed anything to the animal discussion earlier, but now he considered mentioning what he'd read a while back, how bald-eagle nests are often girded with cat collars, strung with the little bells and tags of lost pets. He stayed quiet, though. They were out near the horse stables now. The air smelled of alfalfa and manure. The streetlights had fallen away.

The girl said, "I didn't know you could get to Kings Crossing like this."

They crossed the narrow bridge over Oso Creek, then came into a   10
clearing, a swath of clay and patchy brush, gnarled mesquite trees.

He pulled onto the road's shoulder. Caliche pinged against the truck's chassis. He doused his headlights, and the scrub around them silvered, turned to moonscape. They were outside the city limits, miles from where the girl lived. He killed the engine.

"I know you have doubts about me. I know I'm not—"

"Cut him loose," Lambright said.

"Do what?"

"Give it a week, then tell him you've got someone else."   15

Her eyes scanned the night through the windshield. Maybe she was getting her bearings, calculating how far out they were. Cows lowed somewhere in the darkness. She said, "I love Rob—"

"You're a pretty girl. You've been to the rodeo a few times. You'll do all right. But not with him."

The chalky moon was in and out of clouds. A wind buffeted the truck and kicked up the odor of the brackish creek. The girl was picking at her cuticles, which made her look docile.

"Is there anything I can say here? Is there something you're wanting to hear?"

"You can say you'll quit him," Lambright said. "I'd like to have your   20
word on that subject."

"And if I don't, you'll leave me on the side of the road?"

"We're just talking. We're sorting out a problem."

"Or you'll beat me up and throw me in the creek?"

"You're too much for him. He's overmatched."

25   "And so if I don't dump him, you'll, what, rape me? Murder me? Bury me in the dunes?"

"Lisa," he said, his tone pleasingly superior. He liked how much he sounded like a father.

Another wind blew, stiff and parched, rustling the trees. To Lambright, they appeared to shiver, like they'd gotten cold. A low cloud unspooled on the horizon. The cows were quiet.

"I see how you look at me, you know," she said, shifting toward him. She unbuckled her seat belt, the noise startlingly loud in the truck. Lambright's eyes went to the rearview mirror: no one around. She scooted an inch closer. Two inches. Three. He smelled lavender, her hair or cool skin. She said, "Everyone sees it. Nobody'll be surprised you drove me out here."

"I'm telling you to stay away from my son."

30   "In the middle of the night, in the middle of nowhere."

"There's no mystery here," Lambright said.

"Silly," she said.

"Do what?"

"I said you're silly. There's mystery all around us. Goats in trees. Macaws in cars."

35   Enough, Lambright thought. He cranked the ignition, switched on his headlights.

"A man who drives his son's underage girl into remote areas, that's awfully mysterious."

"Just turn him loose," he said.

"A girl who flees the truck and comes home dirty and crying. What will she tell her parents? Her boyfriend? The man's depressed wife?"

"Just leave him be," he said. "That's the takeaway tonight."

40   "Will the police be called? Will they match the clay on her shoes to his tires?"

"Lisa—"

"Or will she keep it to herself? Will it be something she and the man always remember when they see each other? When she marries his son, when she bears his grandbabies? These are bona fide mysteries, Mr. Lambright."

"Lisa," he said. "Lisa, let's be clear."

But she was already out of the truck, sprinting toward the creek. She flashed through the brush and descended the bank, and Lambright was shocked by the languid swiftness with which she crossed the earth. Blood was surging in his veins, like he'd swerved to miss something in the road and his truck had just skidded to a stop and he didn't yet know if he was hurt, if the world was changed. The passenger door was open, the interior light burning, pooling. The girl jumped across the creek and bolted alongside it. She cut to and fro. He wanted to see her as an animal he'd managed to avoid, a rare and dangerous creature he'd describe for Robbie when he got home, but really her movement reminded him of a trickle of water tracking through pebbles. It stirred in him a floating sensation, the curious and scattered feeling of being born on waves or air or wings. He was disoriented, short of breath. He knew he was at the beginning of something, though just then he couldn't say exactly what.

*   *   *

Gary Isaacs

STEPHEN GRAHAM JONES (1972–   ) is a Blackfoot Native American who grew up in Texas. Currently a professor of English at the University of Colorado at Boulder, Jones has published five story collections and fifteen novels. His novel *The Last Final Girl* was recognized as the 2012 Novel of the Year by the online publication *This Is Horror*. The recipient of a National Endowment for the Arts Literature Fellowship, Jones also won the 2001 Independent Publishers Award for Multicultural Fiction.

Discovering America (2001)

Because I'm Indian in Tallahassee Florida the girl behind the counter feels compelled to pull the leather strap ($1.19 per foot) around her neck, show me her medicine pouch, how authentic it is. "Yeah," I say, "hmm," and don't tell her about the one-act play I'm writing, about this Indian in the gift shop at the bottom of Carlsbad Caverns. His name isn't Curio but that's what the lady calls him when she sighs into line with her Germanic accent and her Karl May[1] childhood. "You should do a rain dance or something," she tells him, she's never seen heat like this, like New Mexico. In the play she's sweating, he's sweating, and there's uncounted tons of rock above them, all this pressure.

In Tallahassee it rained all the time.

I stayed there for eleven months, nineteen days, and six hours.

Because I'm Indian at a party in Little Rock Arkansas, a group of students approaches me out of a back room of the house, ceremony still thick on their breath. In a shy voice their leader asks me what kind of animal my spirit helper is, and when I can't quite get enough tact into my mouth

---

[1] *Karl May*: German author (1842–1912).

to answer, they make a show of respect, say they understand if I can't tell them, really. They tell me theirs, though: a grasshopper, a dragonfly, three wolves, and somewhere in there I become that tall, silent Indian in Thomas Pynchon's "Mortality and Mercy in Vienna," right before he goes cannibalistic in the middle of an otherwise happening party. The working title of the play I'm still writing is *The Time That Indian Started Killing Everybody*, and standing there with my beer I don't revise it.

5   In Little Rock there were all kinds of bugs I hadn't seen before.

I stayed there for five months, four days, and twenty-two hours.

Because I'm Indian in Odessa Texas the guy who picks me up off the side of the road asks me what kind. He's an oilfield worker. His dashboard is black with it. When I say *Blackfeet* he finishes for me with *Montana*, says yeah, he drilled up there for a while. Cold as hell. "Yeah," I say, thinking this is going to be an all right ride. He drives and tells me how when he was up there he used to ride a helicopter to the rig every morning, it was *that* cold. In trade I tell him how the National Guard had to airlift hay and supplies a couple of winters back. He nods as if this is all coming back to him, and then, with both arms draped over the wheel real casual, asks me if they still run over Indians up there? I turn to him and he explains the sport, even hangs a tire into the ditch to show me how it's done.

In Odessa the butane pumps go all night, and it's hard to sleep.

I stayed there for three months, fourteen days, and fourteen hours.

Because I'm Indian the guys at the warehouse in Clovis New Mexico add a single feather to the happy face that's been carved into the back of my locker ever since I got there. It's not like looking in a mirror. Every time it's not like looking in a mirror. My second week there we're sweeping rat droppings into huge piles, and when I lean over one to see what Butch is pointing at he slams his broom down, drives it all into my face. That weekend I start coughing it all up, become sure it's the hantavirus that's been killing Indians all over. My whole check goes into the pay phone, calling everyone, talking to them one last time, reading them my play, the part where Curio kills one of the gift-shop people the old way, which means he hits him across the face with a log of Copenhagen, then follows him down to finish it, out of mercy.

10   In Clovis they don't turn their trucks off so you can talk on the phone, so you have to scream.

I stayed there for four weeks, one day, and two and a half hours.

Because I'm Indian in Carlsbad New Mexico the crew I'm working with calls me Chief, motions me over every time there's another animal track in the dirt. "I don't know," I tell them about the tracks, even though I do, and for a couple of hours we work in silence, up one row, down another. Once I find strange and cartoonish tracks in my row—traced with the sharp corner of a hoe—but I pretend to miss them, pretend no one's watching me miss them. All this pretending. Towards the end of the day I pass one of the crew and, without looking up, he asks if I've scalped anybody today, Chief?

I unplant a weed from his row, look up for the briefest moment, long enough to say it: "Nobody you know." He doesn't laugh, and neither do I, and then later that night in a gas station I finish the play I started writing in Florida. It starts when the clerk wipes the sweat from his forehead, says how damn hot it is. And dry. I neither nod nor don't nod, just wait for him to say it.

In Carlsbad New Mexico the law is sluggish, slow to respond.

I stay there for sixteen hours, nine minutes, and fifty-two seconds, and when the rain comes it's not because I danced it up, but because I brought it with me.

*   *   *

JAMAICA KINCAID (1949–   ) was born Elaine Potter Richardson on the island of Antigua, where she received a British education and was often at the top of her class. In early childhood, she was very close to her mother, but when her mother gave birth to three sons in quick succession, it altered their relationship forever. According to Kincaid, she was treated badly and neglected, and she left Antigua in 1965 to work as an au pair in Westchester county, near New York City. She went on to study photography at the New School for Social Research and attended Franconia College in New Hampshire for a year. In 1973, after having begun her writing career, she changed her name to Jamaica Kincaid because her family disapproved of her writing. She soon began writing a regular column for the *New Yorker*. Her best-known works include the novel *Annie John* (1986) and the nonfiction book *A Small Place* (1988), which criticizes British Colonialism in Antigua. Her most recent books include *Talk Stories* (2001), *Among Flowers: A Walk in the Himalaya* (2005), *My Favorite Tool* (2005), and *See Now Then* (2013).

Source: Taro Yamasaki//Time Life Pictures/Getty Images

Girl (1984)

Wash the white clothes on Monday and put them on the stone heap; wash the color clothes on Tuesday and put them on the clothesline to dry; don't walk barehead in the hot sun; cook pumpkin fritters in very hot sweet oil; soak your little clothes right after you take them off; when buying cotton to make yourself a nice blouse, be sure that it doesn't have gum on it, because that way it won't hold up well after a wash; soak salt fish overnight before you cook it; is it true that you sing benna[1] in Sunday

---

[1] *benna:* Calypso music.

School?; always eat your food in such a way that it won't turn someone else's stomach; on Sundays try to walk like a lady and not like the slut you are so bent on becoming; don't sing benna in Sunday School; you mustn't speak to wharf-rat boys, not even to give directions; don't eat fruits on the street—flies will follow you; *but I don't sing benna on Sundays at all and never in Sunday school;* this is how to sew on a button; this is how to make a buttonhole for the button you have just sewed on; this is how to hem a dress when you see the hem coming down and so to prevent yourself from looking like the slut I know you are so bent on becoming; this is how you iron your father's khaki shirt so that it doesn't have a crease; this is how you iron your father's khaki pants so that they don't have a crease; this is how you grow okra—far from the house, because okra tree harbors red ants; when you are growing dasheen, make sure it gets plenty of water or else it makes your throat itch when you are eating it; this is how you sweep a corner; this is how you sweep a whole house; this is how you sweep a yard; this is how you smile to someone you don't like too much; this is how you smile to someone you don't like at all; this is how you smile to someone you like completely; this is how you set a table for tea; this is how you set a table for dinner; this is how you set a table for dinner with an important guest; this is how you set a table for lunch; this is how you set a table for breakfast; this is how to behave in the presence of men who don't know you very well, and this way they won't recognize immediately the slut I have warned you against becoming; be sure to wash every day, even if it is with your own spit; don't squat down to play marbles—you are not a boy, you know; don't pick people's flowers—you might catch something; don't throw stones at blackbirds, because it might not be a blackbird at all; this is how to make a bread pudding; this is how to make doukona;[2] this is how to make pepper pot; this is how to make a good medicine for a cold; this is how to make a good medicine to throw away a child before it even becomes a child; this is how to catch a fish; this is how to throw back a fish you don't like, and that way something bad won't fall on you; this is how to bully a man; this is how a man bullies you; this is how to love a man, and if this doesn't work there are other ways, and if they don't work don't feel too bad about giving up; this is how to spit up in the air if you feel like it, and this is how to move quick so that it doesn't fall on you; this is how to make ends meet; always squeeze bread to make sure it's fresh; *but what if the baker won't let me feel the bread?;* you mean to say that after all you are really going to be the kind of woman who the baker won't let near the bread?

*   *   *

---

[2]*doukona:* Spicy plantain pudding.

Sylvia Plachy

ED PARK (1970–   ) teaches in the graduate writing program at Columbia University. An avid blogger and tweeter, Park has published numerous stories and short works of creative nonfiction. Recognized as one of *Time*'s top ten fiction books of the year and one of *The Atlantic*'s top ten pop culture moments of the decade, his 2008 novel *Personal Days* was a finalist for the PEN Hemingway Award, the Asian American Literary Award, and the John Sargent Sr. First Novel Prize.

Slide to Unlock (2013)

You cycle through your passwords. They tell the secret story. What's most important to you, the things you think can't be deciphered. Words and numbers stored in the lining of your heart.

Your daughter's name.

Your daughter's name backward.

Your daughter's name backward plus the year of her birth.

Your daughter's name backward plus the last two digits of the year of   5
her birth.

Your daughter's name backward plus the current year.

They keep changing. They blur in the brain. Every day you punch in three or four of these memory strings to access the home laptop, the work laptop. The e-mail, the Facebook, the voice mail. Frequent-flyer account. Every week, you're asked to change at least one, to increase the security. You feel virtuous when the security meter changes from red to green.

Your home town backward.

Your home town plus the year you were born.

Your home town backward plus the year you were born.   10

Olaf Fub 1970.

There are hints when you forget. Mother's maiden name. First car, favorite color, elementary school.

First girl you kissed—that should be one.

First boy.

Can the hints just be the passwords?   15

Stop stalling.

First sex. You remember the day, month, year. The full year or just the last two digits?

First concert you attended.

Name of hospital where you were born.

You wonder who writes these prompts. Someone has to write them.   20

Tip: Never use the same password for more than one account.

Last four digits of first phone number.
Last four digits of first work number.
Your daughter's best friend's name backward.
25   Your boss's first name.
Your first boss's last name plus the year you were born.

If you could type out all your passwords, their entire silent history, they
would fill a book you could read in a minute.
Last four digits of your cell backward.
Favorite sports team.
30   Favorite sports team backward.
Serbas.
Pet's name.
You knew a guy who had a dog named Serbas. You knew two guys
with dogs named Serbas. They didn't like each other. The guys, that is.
The dogs, who knows. You're pretty sure one was female, the other male.
Pet's name backward plus current year.
35   Favorite sibling—sibling who never let you down—plus last two digits
of current year.
Mix of capitals and lowercase.
Six to eight characters long.
Ten to fourteen.
Stop stalling.
40   Mix of numerals and letters.
At least one symbol: #, %,*,!.!
Father's home town.
Mother's maiden name backward.
The girl at work you can't stop thinking about.
45   The girl at work plus current year.
The girl at work backward.
The girl at work backward and lowercase plus last two digits of current
year.

Passwords mean nothing to the machine. The machine lets you in to do
what you need to do. It doesn't judge. It doesn't care.
Your password appears as a row of dots.
50   Favorite film. But that keeps changing.
"Vertigo." "Groundhog Day."
Favorite actor.
Actress who first made you hard, backward, plus current year.
Best friend from high school.
Best friend from college.
55   *Stop stalling.*
Year you last saw your daughter.
Year you last saw your daughter plus her name.

There's a file on your work computer called PASSWORDS. But what if you forget the password to get into your work computer?

Her favorite toy.

What she named her bike.   60

First girl you dated in college backward and lowercase.

"The Shop Around the Corner." "Buffalo '66."

Date of first death in the family.

Grandfather's name backward plus birth year.

Year you finally started getting your shit together.   65

"Citizen Kane." "Ace Ventura: Pet Detective."

Year of First Communion plus name of priest.

Stop stalling.

Favorite author backward and lowercase with middle letter capped for no reason save randomness.

Street address of the house you grew up in.   70

Sibling you don't talk to.

Spouse of sibling you don't talk to, whom you text when you're drunk.

Stop stalling.

Your last name backward plus the day, month, and year you find yourself at an A.T.M. at the ass end of Hertel Avenue with the tip of a gun pressed between your shoulder blades, the gun in the hand of the guy who followed you from down the street, affecting a limp, a big guy in a black windbreaker and a Bills Starter cap, who stepped behind you, quiet as a shadow, the big guy with dead eyes behind five-dollar sunglasses who already has your phone and wallet and the bottle of wine you thought it would be a good idea to run out and get, at ten in the evening, she said she'd stay inside and you said you would hurry, and it was a good night for a walk, so, while you're at it, taking in the cool night air, why not get some cash for the week to come?

The big guy with the very hard gun who is saying *Password* and *Right* 75 *now* and *Stop stalling.*

*   *   *

GEORGE SAUNDERS (1958–   ) teaches in the MFA program at Syracuse University and was named one of *Time's* 100 most influential people in the world. He has published several story and essay collections, including *Tenth of December* (2013), in which the following story appeared. Saunders is the recipient of a Guggenheim Fellowship, a MacArthur Fellowship, and an Academy Award from the American Academy of Arts and Letters.

Eamonn McCabe/Getty Images

Sticks (1995)

Every year Thanksgiving night we flocked out behind Dad as he dragged the Santa suit to the road and draped it over a kind of crucifix he'd built out of metal pole in the yard. Super Bowl week the pole was dressed in a jersey and Rod's helmet and Rod had to clear it with Dad if he wanted to take the helmet off. On Fourth of July the pole was Uncle Sam, on Veterans Day a soldier, on Halloween a ghost. The pole was Dad's one concession to glee. We were allowed a single Crayola from the box at a time. One Christmas Eve he shrieked at Kimmie for wasting an apple slice. He hovered over us as we poured ketchup, saying, Good enough good enough good enough. Birthday parties consisted of cupcakes, no ice cream. The first time I brought a date over she said, What's with your dad and that pole? and I sat there blinking.

We left home, married, had children of our own, found the seeds of meanness blooming also within us. Dad began dressing the pole with more complexity and less discernible logic. He draped some kind of fur over it on Groundhog Day and lugged out a floodlight to ensure a shadow. When an earthquake struck Chile he laid the pole on its side and spray-painted a rift in the earth. Mom died and he dressed the pole as Death and hung from the crossbar photos of Mom as a baby. We'd stop by and find odd talismans from his youth arranged around the base: army medals, theater tickets, old sweatshirts, tubes of Mom's makeup. One autumn he painted the pole bright yellow. He covered it with cotton swabs that winter for warmth and provided offspring by hammering in six crossed sticks around the yard. He ran lengths of string between the pole and the sticks, and taped to the string letters of apology, admissions of error, pleas for understanding, all written in a frantic hand on index cards. He painted a sign saying LOVE and hung it from the pole and another that said FORGIVE? and then he died in the hall with the radio on and we sold the house to a young couple who yanked out the pole and left it by the road on garbage day.

*   *   *

Reading and Reacting

1. Which of the stories in this chapter do you see as the most conventional? Which seems the *least* conventional? Why?
2. Does every story seem complete? What, if anything, seems to be missing from each story that might be present in a longer story?
3. If you were going to add material to "Snow" or "Sticks," what would you add? Why?

4. Some stories in this chapter—for example, "Encounters with Unexpected Animals"—include dialogue; others include none (or very little). How would these stories—for example, "Pilón"—be different if dialogue (or more dialogue) were added? What kind of dialogue would be useful?

5. **CRITICAL PERSPECTIVE** Writing for *Studies in Short Fiction*, William C. Hamlin describes the essential characteristics of the short-short story.

> Perhaps in no kind of fiction other than the short-short can Poe's "rules" for the "tale" be so fully adapted and realized. He wrote about organic unity and singleness of effect and the totality of that effect. In the short-short there is simply no room for sub-plotting, for Jamesian penetration, for slowly developing tensions, for any kind of byplay. The writer is trying to go from A to B in the shortest time consistent with purpose and reason. If he or she is successful, then the reader is richer by a minor masterpiece.

Do you think all the stories in this sampler meet Hamlin's criteria for success? Why or why not?

WRITING SUGGESTIONS: The Short-Short Story

1. Write a **response** expressing your reactions to the ending of "Slide to Unlock."
2. Write an **explication** of any short-short story in this chapter—or of a short-short story located elsewhere in this book—for example, Kate Chopin's "The Story of an Hour" (p. 127).
3. Write a character analysis of the narrator in "Accident" or "Television."
4. Write a **comparison-contrast essay** comparing "Love and Other Catastrophes: A Mix Tape" with one of the love poems in Chapter 23.
5. Write a **comparison-contrast essay** comparing "Encounters with Unexpected Animals" to Joyce Carol Oates's "Where Are You Going, Where Have You Been?" (p. 453).
6. Write an essay about the **cultural context** of "Pilón," "Girl," or "Discovering America."
7. Write a "mix tape" story about an experience in your own life.

CHAPTER 6

FICTION SAMPLER:
GRAPHIC FICTION

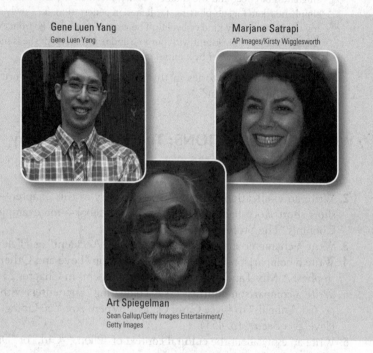

Gene Luen Yang
Gene Luen Yang

Marjane Satrapi
AP Images/Kirsty Wigglesworth

Art Spiegelman
Sean Gallup/Getty Images Entertainment/
Getty Images

The term *graphic fiction* can be applied to a wide range of visual material, including individual and collected comics and cartoons. As graphic novelist Ivan Brunetti explains, when creating graphic fiction, "The cartoonist uses his own particular set of marks (or 'visual handwriting') to establish a consistent visual vocabulary in which to communicate experience, memory, and imagination—in short, the stuff of narratives."

Like the **short-short stories** (see p. 81), works of graphic fiction pack ideas into small spaces (in this case, the "cells" or "panels" on a page).

While many graphic works are fictional narratives, others—such as graphic essays, biographies, autobiographies, historical accounts, and journalistic pieces—actually qualify as nonfiction. Works of graphic fiction appear in printed books, magazines, newspapers, and pamphlets, and many are published online as **Web comics**. Two of today's most popular kinds of graphic fiction are **manga** (Japanese comics translated into English) and **superhero comic books**. In the genre's volatile history, graphic novels have taken various forms, appealing to popular and literary audiences alike. In fact, the genre is constantly being redefined. As graphic novelist Eddie Campbell argues, the graphic novel genre "signifies a movement rather than a form" as it strives "to take the form of the comic book, which has become an embarrassment, and raise it to a more ambitious and meaningful level."

Graphic fiction had its origins in comic strips. In the late nineteenth and early twentieth centuries, American newspapers started to feature comic strips that ranged in variety from popular, slapstick, and sci-fi (*The Yellow Kid*, 1895; *Happy Hooligan*, 1900; *Thimble Theatre* [later renamed *Popeye*], 1929; *Flash Gordon*, 1934) to literary and artistic (*Little Nemo*, 1905; *Krazy Kat*, 1913). Comic books, or collections of previously published comic strips, appeared in the mid 1930s, and shortly thereafter the superhero comic emerged and exploded. Comic book characters like Superman, Batman, Wonder Woman, and Captain Marvel began to dominate the genre in the 1940s, and contemporary superhero comics such as *Spider-Man* (1962) and *X-Men* (1963) have achieved international fame both in traditional print formats and in major motion pictures.

In response to the superhero subgenre, **underground** or **alternative comics** appeared in the 1960s, challenging the status quo and depicting taboo topics such as drugs and sex. These unconventional comics, created by artists such as Robert Crumb (1943–) and S. Clay Wilson (1941–), have experienced ups and downs throughout their sales history, unlike their consistently best-selling superhero counterparts. Alternative comics helped usher in the more acclaimed literary graphic novels of the 1980s and 1990s, including Art Spiegelman's Pulitzer Prize–winning *Maus* (1986) and Daniel Clowes's *Ghost World* (1993).

Will Eisner's *A Contract with God* (1978) is generally acknowledged to be the first graphic novel. Actually a collection of four short stories, the book displayed the label "graphic novel" on its cover, establishing this new genre as a literary form fundamentally different from mainstream comics. The graphic novel continues to evolve today in its attempt to contribute in fresh, new ways to the changing literary canon.

This chapter includes four works of graphic fiction, narratives that use words as well as images to tell their stories and weave together fiction, his-

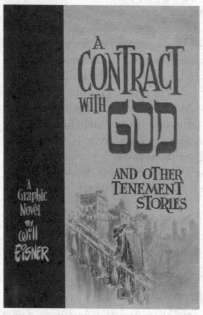

Cover image of the first graphic novel, Eisner's *A Contract with God* (1978)

Source: © Baronet Books 1978

tory, and memoir. Max Brooks's *The Harlem Hellfighters* recounts the struggles and triumphs of an African American army regiment in World War I; like the book as a whole, the two excerpts reprinted here juxtapose the men's courage in combat with the discrimination they faced at home. The excerpt from Marjane Satrapi's *Persepolis* presents an episode from Satrapi's life as a rebellious child in Iran during the Islamic Revolution; in an excerpt from his Pulitzer Prize–winning book *Maus: A Survivor's Tale*, Art Spiegelman reimagines an episode from the life of his father, a Polish Jew who survived the Holocaust. Finally, the brief excerpt from Gene Luen Yang's *American Born Chinese* explores the familiar American theme of reinvention through a young boy's struggles with his identity.

MAX BROOKS (1972–   ) is the author of the 2006 novel *World War Z*, which was adapted into a film starring Brad Pitt. He has also published *The Zombie Survival Guide: Complete Protection from the Living Dead* (2003), *The Zombie Survival Guide: Recorded Attacks* (2009), and, most recently, *The Harlem Hellfighters* (2014), from which the following excerpts were taken.

Cultural Context The 369th infantry regiment (nicknamed the Harlem Hellfighters by German soldiers) was an African American unit of the U.S. Army that fought in World Wars I and II. When the unit returned home from Europe in 1919 after a long and heroic tour of duty, they faced the same racial discrimination and violence that other African American citizens experienced at that time.

from The Harlem Hellfighters (2014)

Another excerpt from The Harlem Hellfighters begins on the following page.

IT'D BE A NICE STORY IF I COULD SAY THAT OUR PARADE OR EVEN OUR VICTORIES CHANGED THE WORLD OVERNIGHT, BUT TRUTH'S GOT AN UGLY WAY OF KILLIN' NICE STORIES. THE TRUTH IS THAT WE CAME HOME TO IGNORANCE, BITTERNESS, AND SOMETHIN' CALLED "THE RED SUMMER OF 1919," SOME OF THE WORST RACIAL VIOLENCE AMERICA'S EVER SEEN. THE TRUTH IS THAT OUR FIGHT, AND THE FIGHT OF THOSE WHO LOOKED UP TO US AS HEROES, DIDN'T END WITH THE "THE WAR TO END ALL WARS."

WAS IT ALL
FOR NOTHING?

ONLY IF WE'RE
FORGOTTEN

MARJANE SATRAPI (1969–   ), raised in Tehran, Iran, has published numerous graphic fiction books in both English and French, including the award-winning graphic memoir *Persepolis* (2003) and its sequel, *Persepolis 2* (2004). The *Persepolis* works, from which the following excerpt is taken, depict Satrapi's experiences growing up in Tehran during the Islamic Revolution and Iran's war with Iraq. Satrapi cowrote and codirected the animated feature film *Persepolis* (2007), which tied for a Special Jury Prize at the 2007 Cannes Film Festival and was nominated for an Academy Award for best animated feature film. Like *Persepolis*, Satrapi's graphic novel *Embroideries* (2005) also portrays the female experience in modern-day Iran.

Cultural Context Persepolis was an ancient Persian city located in modern-day Iran. King of Persia from 522–486 B.C., Darius I named Persepolis the capital of Persia. The city is known for its monumental architecture, including several royal palaces and an audience hall, the ruins of which can still be seen today. Named after the ancient city, Satrapi's graphic novel, from which the following excerpt is taken, alludes to Iran's epic past and makes an ironic statement about the cultural climate of today.

from Persepolis (2003)

Source: ©2003 Marjane Satrapi. Used courtesy of Pantheon Books at Random House.

This graphic story starts on the next page ➡

Source: ©2003 Marjane Satrapi. Used courtesy of Pantheon Books at Random House.

Sean Gallup/Getty Images Entertainment/Getty Images

ART SPIEGELMAN (1948–   ) was born in Stockholm, Sweden, and raised in Queens, New York. He is arguably one of the most influential comic artists of the underground movement, which began in the 1960s. In collaboration with his wife, Spiegelman founded the comics magazine *RAW* in 1980, and his comics have been featured in such publications as the *New Yorker*, the *New York Times*, and the *Village Voice*. The following graphic story comes from his two-part masterpiece, the Pulitzer Prize–winning *Maus* (1986) and *Maus II* (1991), which are based on his parents' struggle for survival during the Holocaust. Collections of Spiegelman's work include *In the Shadow of No Towers* (2004), one of the *New York Times* Book Review's 100 Notable Books of 2004.

Cultural Context This graphic story depicts the heartrending process in which Jews were separated from their families and forced into concentration and death camps during the Nazi regime. Between 1933 and 1945, an estimated fifteen thousand camps throughout Nazi-occupied countries killed approximately 3.5 million people. The camps were originally established to incarcerate political adversaries, such as Communists and Social Democrats, but soon began imprisoning Jews, Jehovah's Witnesses, Gypsies, homosexuals, the mentally ill, and anyone who opposed the Nazi regime. Chelmno, the first of six death camps established in Poland, opened in 1941. At these camps, the Nazis carried out the systematic murder of millions of Jews and other innocent people.

from Maus (1973)

Art Spiegelman, from MAUS I. Copyright © 1973, 1980, 1982, 1983, 1984, 1985, 1986 by Art Spiegelman. Used by permission of Pantheon Books, a division of Random House, Inc.

AFTER WHAT HAPPENED TO THE GRANDPARENTS, IT WAS A FEW MONTHS QUIET.
THEN IT CAME POSTERS EVERYWHERE AND SPEECHES FROM THE GEMEINDE[1]...

Art Spiegelman, from MAUS I. Copyright © 1973, 1980, 1982, 1983, 1984, 1985, 1986 by Art Spiegelman. Used by permission of Pantheon Books, a division of Random House, Inc.

[1]*Gemeinde:* Local government in Germany.

MY FATHER—HE HAD 62 YEARS—CAME BY STREETCAR TO ME FROM DABROWA, THE VILLAGE NEXT DOOR FROM SOSNOWIEC.

HERE'S A COOKIE, RICHIEU. AUNT FELA BAKED IT FOR YOU.

SAY THANK YOU TO GRANDPA.

AFTER MY MOTHER DIED WITH CANCER, HE LIVED THERE IN THE HOUSE OF MY SISTER FELA, AND HER FOUR SMALL CHILDREN.

I NEED YOUR ADVICE, VLADEK. SHOULD I GO TO THE STADIUM ON WEDNESDAY, OR HIDE AT HOME?

I DON'T KNOW. I'M NOT EVEN SURE WHAT WE'RE GOING TO DO. ...ANJA'S MOTHER SAYS SHE ISN'T GO-ING. SHE'S SICK AND AFRAID.

AT LEAST ANJA'S FATHER, LOLEK AND I ALL WORK AT THE GERMAN WOODSHOP. WE'RE A LITTLE SAFER. BUT YOU DON'T WORK. YOU HAVE NO PAPERS. YOU DON'T HAVE ANYTHING!

WELL, OUR COUSIN MORDECAI SAYS HE'LL BE AT ONE OF THE INSPECTION TABLES. I COULD BRING MY PAPERS TO HIM...

WHAT DOES FELA SAY?

SHE'S NOT SURE...BUT IF FELA DECIDES TO GO, OF COURSE I'LL GO WITH HER.

CAN I HAVE ANOTHER COOKIE?

RICHIEU!

REALLY, I DIDN'T KNOW HOW TO ADVISE HIM.

BUT FINALLY HE DID GO. PEOPLE WERE AFRAID TO NOT SHOW UP.

SO IT CAME TO THE STADIUM ALMOST ALL THE JEWS OF SOSNOWIEC, AND FROM THE OTHER VILLAGES NEAR, MAYBE 25 OR 30,000 PEOPLE.

EVERYONE CAME VERY NICE DRESSED. THEY TRIED SO THAT THEY WOULD LOOK YOUNG AND ABLE TO WORK, IN ORDER TO GET A GOOD STAMP ON THEIR PASSPORT.

WHEN WE WERE EVERYBODY INSIDE, GESTAPO WITH MACHINE GUNS SURROUNDED THE STADIUM.

THEN WAS A SELECTION, WITH PEOPLE SENT EITHER TO THE LEFT, EITHER TO THE RIGHT.

LINE UP BY FAMILY AT THE TABLES TO REGISTER! QUICKLY!

OLD PEOPLE, FAMILIES WITH LOTS OF KIDS, AND PEOPLE WITHOUT WORK CARDS ARE ALL GOING TO THE LEFT!

WE UNDERSTOOD THIS MUST BE VERY BAD.

ME AND ANJA CAME TO THE TABLE WHERE MY COUSIN WAS SITTING...

AH, YOU WORK AT THE CARPENTRY SHOP. GO TO THE RIGHT.

SO WE GOT STAMPED OUR PASSPORTS AND CAME QUICK TO THE GOOD SIDE OF THE STADIUM. THOSE THEY SENT LEFT, THEY DIDN'T GET ANY STAMP.

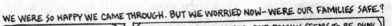

WE WERE SO HAPPY WE CAME THROUGH. BUT WE WORRIED NOW—WERE OUR FAMILIES SAFE?

LOOK! THERE'S POPPA, WITH LOLEK AND LONIA!

WE SAW WOLFE AND TOSHA. OUR FAMILY SEEMS TO BE OKAY.

DID YOU SEE MY FATHER?

I COULDN'T SEE ANYWHERE MY FATHER.

BUT LATER SOMEONE WHO SAW HIM TOLD ME... HE CAME THROUGH THIS SAME COUSIN OVER TO THE GOOD SIDE.

HER, THEY SENT TO THE LEFT. FOUR CHILDREN WAS TOO MANY.

SPIEGELMAN... TO THE RIGHT.

THEN CAME FELA TO REGISTER...

FELA!

MY DAUGHTER! HOW CAN SHE MANAGE ALONE—WITH FOUR CHILDREN TO TAKE CARE OF?

AND, WHAT DO YOU THINK? HE *SNEAKED* ON TO THE BAD SIDE!

AND THOSE ON THE BAD SIDE NEVER CAME ANYMORE HOME.

THOSE WITH A STAMP *WERE* LET TO GO HOME. BUT THERE WERE VERY FEW JEWS NOW LEFT IN SOSNOWIEC...

WELL.... IT'S ENOUGH FOR TODAY. YES, ARTIE?...

ONE FROM THREE THEY KEPT AT THE STADIUM.... MAYBE 10,000 PEOPLE—AND WITH THEM, MY FATHER.

Gene Luen Yang

GENE LUEN YANG (1973–   ) teaches for Hamline University's MFA program in writing for children and young adults. He has published several graphic novels, including *American Born Chinese* (2006), from which the following excerpt was taken. *American Born Chinese* was the first graphic novel to win the American Library Association's Printz Award and to be nominated for a National Book Award. Yang has also been honored with two Eisner Awards.

Cultural Context This excerpt from *American Born Chinese* refers to the Transformers toys, which were originally developed by a Japanese company and purchased in 1984 by the American company Hasbro. Transformers are robot action figures with movable parts that can be shaped into animals as well as land and space vehicles. The toys have been popular among generations of children around the world and were spun off into a comic book series as well as TV shows and feature films. The young boy in this excerpt quotes two Transformers taglines, "Robot in Disguise" and "More than Meets the Eye." Here, the boy plays with the robot/truck as he plays with transforming his identity.

from American Born Chinese (2006)

Reading and Reacting

1. What specific visual elements establish the setting of the excerpt from *Persepolis* as harsh and restrictive for Marji? How do these visual elements help to move readers from one panel of the story to the next?

2. Write a plot summary of the excerpt from *Maus* or one of the excerpts from *The Harlem Hellfighters*. Include as much specific detail as you can.

3. Create a graphic fiction sequel (or prequel) to the excerpt from *American Born Chinese*.

4. In *Maus*, the Jews are portrayed as mice, and the Nazis are depicted as cats. Why do you think Spiegelman chose to portray his characters as animals—and, specifically, as *these* animals? What does he gain (or lose) by doing so?

5. **CRITICAL PERSPECTIVE:** Writing for *Wilson Quarterly*, Ken Chen describes the relationship of graphic fiction to the broader literary canon in this way: "Because comics traditionally have been a pulp medium, they've been able to portray the world with a liberating strangeness, unconstrained by taste or codified literary standards." In what sense do the graphic stories in this sampler "portray the world with a liberating strangeness"? Do these stories break any literary rules?

WRITING SUGGESTIONS: Graphic Fiction

1. Write a **response** expressing your reactions to the excerpt from *Maus*.

2. Write an **explication** of one of the graphic fiction selections in this chapter.

3. Write a **comparison-contrast essay** comparing the excerpts from *The Harlem Hellfighters* to "The Things They Carried" (p. 310)—or to one of the war poems in Chapter 23.

4. Write a **character analysis** of Marji in the excerpt from *Persepolis*.

5. Write an essay about the **cultural context** of the excerpt from *Maus* or the excerpt from *American Born Chinese*.

PLOT

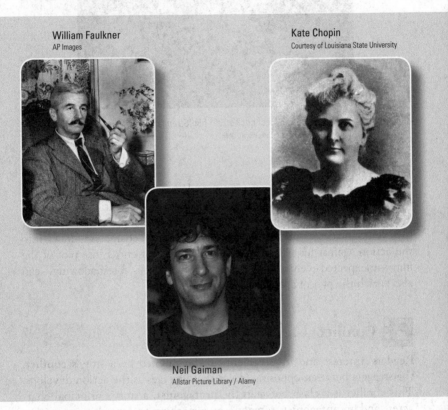

William Faulkner
AP Images

Kate Chopin
Courtesy of Louisiana State University

Neil Gaiman
Allstar Picture Library / Alamy

Alfred Hitchcock's 1951 film *Strangers on a Train*, based on a suspense novel by Patricia Highsmith, offers an intriguing premise: two men, strangers, each can murder someone the other wishes dead; because they have no apparent connection to their victims, both can escape suspicion. Many people would describe this ingenious scheme as the film's "plot," but in fact it is simply the gimmick around which the complex plot revolves. Certainly a clever twist can be an important ingredient of a story's plot, but **plot** is more than "what happens": it is how what happens is revealed, the way in which a story's events are arranged.

Scene from Alfred Hitchcock's 1951 film *Strangers on a Train*
Warner Bros/The Kobal Collection/Picture Desk

Plot is shaped by causal connections—historical, social, and personal—by the interaction between characters, and by the juxtaposition of events. In *Strangers on a Train*, the plot that unfolds is complex: one character directs the events and determines their order while the other character is drawn into the action against his will. The same elements that enrich the plot of the film—unexpected events, conflict, suspense, flashbacks, foreshadowing—can also enrich the plot of a work of short fiction.

Conflict

Readers' interest and involvement are heightened by a story's **conflict**, the struggle between opposing forces that emerges as the action develops. This conflict is a clash between the **protagonist**, a story's principal character, and an **antagonist**, someone or something presented in opposition to the protagonist. Sometimes the antagonist is a villain; more often, it is a character who represents a conflicting point of view or advocates a course of action different from the one the protagonist follows. Sometimes the antagonist is not a character at all but a situation (for instance, war or poverty) or an event (for example, a natural disaster, such as a flood or a storm) that challenges the protagonist. In some stories, the protagonist may struggle against a supernatural force, or the conflict may occur within a character's mind. It may, for example, be a struggle between two moral choices, such as whether to stay at home and care for an aging parent or to leave and make a new life.

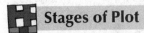

Stages of Plot

A work's plot explores one or more conflicts, moving from *exposition* through a series of *complications* to a *climax* and, finally, to a *resolution*.

During a story's **exposition**, the writer presents the basic information readers need to understand the events that follow. Typically, the exposition sets the story in motion: it establishes the scene, introduces the major characters, and perhaps suggests the major events or conflicts to come.

Sometimes a single sentence can present a story's exposition clearly and economically, giving readers information vital to their understanding of the plot that will unfold. For example, the opening sentence of Amy Tan's "Two Kinds" (p. 471)—"My mother believed you could be anything you wanted to be in America"—reveals an important trait of a central character. Similarly, the opening sentence of Shirley Jackson's "The Lottery" (p. 335)—"The morning of June 27th was clear and sunny, with the fresh warmth of a full-summer day; the flowers were blossoming profusely and the grass was richly green"—introduces the picture-perfect setting that is essential to the story's irony. At other times, as in John Updike's "A&P" (p. 160), a more fully developed exposition section establishes the story's setting, introduces the main characters, and suggests possible conflicts. Finally, in some experimental stories, a distinct exposition component may be absent, as it is in Amanda Brown's "Love and Other Catastrophes: A Mix Tape" (p. 84).

As the plot progresses, the story's conflict unfolds through a series of complications that eventually lead readers to the story's climax. As it develops, the story may include several crises. A **crisis** is a peak in the story's action, a moment of considerable tension or importance. The **climax** is the point of greatest tension or importance, the scene that presents a story's decisive action or event.

The final stage of plot, the **resolution** or **denouement** (French for "untying of the knot"), draws the action to a close and accounts for all remaining loose ends. Sometimes this resolution is achieved with the help of a *deus ex machina* (Latin for "god from a machine"), an intervention of some force or agent previously extraneous to the story—for example, the sudden arrival of a long-lost relative or a fortuitous inheritance, the discovery of a character's true identity, or a surprise last-minute rescue. Usually, however, the resolution is more plausible: all the events lead logically and convincingly (though not necessarily predictably) to the resolution. Sometimes the ending of a story is indefinite—that is, readers are not quite sure what the protagonist will do or what will happen next. This kind of resolution, although it may leave some readers feeling cheated, has its advantages: it mirrors the complexity of life, where closure rarely occurs, and it can keep readers involved in the story as they try to understand the significance of its ending or to decide how conflicts should have been resolved.

Order and Sequence

A writer may introduce a story's events in strict chronological order, presenting each event in the sequence in which it actually takes place. More often, however, especially in relatively modern fiction, writers do not introduce events chronologically. Instead, they present incidents out of expected order, or in no apparent order. For example, a writer may choose to begin *in medias res* (Latin for "in the midst of things"), starting with a key event and later going back in time to explain events that preceded it, as Tillie Olsen does in "I Stand Here Ironing" (p. 217). Or, a writer can decide to begin a work of fiction at the end and then move back to reconstruct events that led up to the final outcome, as William Faulkner does in "A Rose for Emily" (p. 143). Many sequences are possible as the writer manipulates events to create interest, suspense, confusion, shock, or some other effect.

Writers who wish to depart from strict chronological order can use *flashbacks* and *foreshadowing*. A **flashback** moves out of sequence to examine an event or situation that occurred before the time in which the story's action takes place. A character can remember an earlier event, or a story's narrator can re-create an earlier situation. For example, in Alberto Alvaro Ríos's "The Secret Lion" (p. 466), the adult narrator looks back at events that occurred when he was twelve years old and then moves further back in time to consider related events that occurred when he was five. In Edgar Allan Poe's "The Cask of Amontillado" (p. 249), the entire story is told as a flashback. Flashbacks are valuable because they can substitute for or supplement formal exposition by presenting background readers need to understand a story's events. One disadvantage of flashbacks is that if they interrupt the natural flow of events, they may be intrusive or distracting. Such distractions, however, can be an advantage if the writer wishes to reveal events gradually and subtly or to obscure causal links.

Foreshadowing is the introduction early in a story of comments, situations, events, characters, or objects that hint at things to come. Typically, a seemingly simple element—a chance remark, a natural occurrence, a trivial event—is eventually revealed to have great significance. For example, a dark cloud passing across the sky during a wedding can foreshadow future problems for the marriage. Foreshadowing allows a writer to hint provocatively at what is to come so that readers only gradually become aware of a particular detail's role in a story. Thus, foreshadowing helps readers sense what will occur and grow increasingly involved as they see the likelihood (or even the inevitability) of a particular outcome.

In addition to using conventional techniques like flashbacks and fore-shadowing, writers may experiment with sequence by substantially tampering with—or even dispensing with—chronological order. (An example is the scrambled chronology of "A Rose for Emily.") In such instances, the experimental form enhances interest and encourages readers to become involved with the story as they work to untangle or reorder the events and determine their logical and causal connections.

In recent years, the Internet has given a new fluidity to the nature of plot, with readers actually able to participate in creating a story's plot. For more on such innovations, see page 80.

✔ CHECKLIST   Writing about Plot

- What happens in the story?

- Where does the story's formal exposition section end? What do readers learn about characters in this section? What do readers learn about setting? What possible conflicts are suggested here?

- What is the story's central conflict? What other conflicts are presented? Who is the protagonist? Who (or what) serves as the antagonist?

- Identify the story's crisis or crises.

- Identify the story's climax.

- How is the story's central conflict resolved? Is this resolution plausible? satisfying?

- Which part of the story constitutes the resolution? Do any problems remain unresolved? Does any uncertainty remain? If so, does this uncertainty strengthen or weaken the story? Would another ending be more effective?

- How are the story's events arranged? Are they presented in chronological order? What events are presented out of logical sequence? Does the story use foreshadowing? flashbacks? Are the causal connections between events clear? logical? If not, can you explain why?

Source: Courtesy of Louisiana State University

KATE CHOPIN (1851–1904) was born Katherine O'Flaherty, the daughter of a wealthy Irish-born merchant and his aristocratic Creole wife. She was married at nineteen to Oscar Chopin, a Louisiana cotton broker, who took her to live first in New Orleans and later on a plantation in central Louisiana. Chopin's representations of the Cane River region and its people in two volumes of short stories—*Bayou Folk* (1894) and *A Night in Arcadie* (1897)—are the foundation of her reputation as a local colorist, a writer dedicated to creating an accurate picture of a particular region and its people.

Her honest, sexually frank stories (many of them out of print for more than half a century) were rediscovered in the 1960s and 1970s, influencing a new generation of writers. Though she was a popular contributor of stories and sketches to the magazines of her day, Chopin scandalized many critics with her outspoken novel *The Awakening* (1899), in which a woman seeks sexual and emotional fulfillment with a man who is not her husband. The book was removed from the shelves of the public library in St. Louis, where Chopin was born.

"The Story of an Hour" depicts a brief event in a woman's life, but in this single hour, Chopin reveals both a lifetime's emotional torment and the momentary joy of freedom.

Cultural Context   During her marriage, Chopin lived in Louisiana, the only civil-law state in the United States. Whereas the legal systems of all other states are based on common law, the laws of Louisiana have their roots in the Napoleonic Code, the civil code enacted in France in 1804 to regulate issues of property, marriage, and divorce. This patriarchal code favored the husband in all domestic affairs and left women without many legal or fiscal rights. In "The Story of an Hour," the concept of freedom is closely tied to the prospect of escaping these restrictions.

The Story of an Hour (1894)

Knowing that Mrs. Mallard was afflicted with a heart trouble, great care was taken to break to her as gently as possible the news of her husband's death.

It was her sister Josephine who told her, in broken sentences, veiled hints that revealed in half concealing. Her husband's friend Richards was there, too, near her. It was he who had been in the newspaper office when intelligence of the railroad disaster was received, with Brently Mallard's name leading the list of "killed." He had only taken the time to assure himself of its truth by a second telegram, and had hastened to forestall any less careful, less tender friend in bearing the sad message.

She did not hear the story as many women have heard the same, with a paralyzed inability to accept its significance. She wept at once, with sudden, wild abandonment, in her sister's arms. When the storm of grief had spent itself she went away to her room alone. She would have no one follow her.

There stood, facing the open window, a comfortable, roomy armchair. Into this she sank, pressed down by a physical exhaustion that haunted her body and seemed to reach into her soul.

5   She could see in the open square before her house the tops of trees that were all aquiver with the new spring life. The delicious breath of rain was in the air. In the street below a peddler was crying his wares. The notes of a distant song which some one was singing reached her faintly, and countless sparrows were twittering in the eaves.

There were patches of blue sky showing here and there through the clouds that had met and piled one above the other in the west facing her window.

She sat with her head thrown back upon the cushion of the chair, quite motionless, except when a sob came up into her throat and shook her, as a child who has cried itself to sleep continues to sob in its dreams.

She was young, with a fair, calm face, whose lines bespoke repression and even a certain strength. But now there was a dull stare in her eyes, whose gaze was fixed away off yonder on one of those patches of blue sky. It was not a glance of reflection, but rather indicated a suspension of intelligent thought.

There was something coming to her and she was waiting for it, fearfully. What was it? She did not know; it was too subtle and elusive to name. But she felt it, creeping out of the sky, reaching toward her through the sounds, the scents, the color that filled the air.

Now her bosom rose and fell tumultuously. She was beginning to rec- 10 ognize this thing that was approaching to possess her, and she was striving to beat it back with her will—as powerless as her two white slender hands would have been.

When she abandoned herself a little whispered word escaped her slightly parted lips. She said it over and over under her breath: "Free, free, free!" The vacant stare and the look of terror that had followed it went from her eyes. They stayed keen and bright. Her pulses beat fast, and the coursing blood warmed and relaxed every inch of her body.

She did not stop to ask if it were not a monstrous joy that held her. A clear and exalted perception enabled her to dismiss the suggestion as trivial.

She knew that she would weep again when she saw the kind, tender hands folded in death; the face that had never looked save with love upon her, fixed and gray and dead. But she saw beyond that bitter moment a long procession of years to come that would belong to her absolutely. And she opened and spread her arms out to them in welcome.

There would be no one to live for during those coming years; she would live for herself. There would be no powerful will bending her in that blind persistence with which men and women believe they have a right to impose a private will upon a fellow creature. A kind intention or a cruel intention made the act seem no less a crime as she looked upon it in that brief moment of illumination.

And yet she had loved him—sometimes. Often she had not. What did 15 it matter! What could love, the unsolved mystery, count for in the face of this possession of self-assertion which she suddenly recognized as the strongest impulse of her being.

"Free! Body and soul free!" she kept whispering.

Josephine was kneeling before the closed door with her lips to the key-hole, imploring for admission. "Louise, open the door! I beg; open the door—you will make yourself ill. What are you doing, Louise? For heaven's sake open the door."

"Go away. I am not making myself ill." No; she was drinking in a very elixir of life through that open window.

Her fancy was running riot along those days ahead of her. Spring days, and summer days, and all sorts of days that would be her own. She breathed a quick prayer that life might be long. It was only yesterday she had thought with a shudder that life might be long.

20   She arose at length and opened the door to her sister's importunities. There was a feverish triumph in her eyes, and she carried herself unwittingly like a goddess of Victory. She clasped her sister's waist, and together they descended the stairs. Richards stood waiting for them at the bottom.

Some one was opening the front door with a latchkey. It was Brently Mallard who entered, a little travel-stained, composedly carrying his grip-sack and umbrella. He had been far from the scene of the accident, and did not even know there had been one. He stood amazed at Josephine's piercing cry; at Richards' quick motion to screen him from the view of his wife.

But Richards was too late.

When the doctors came they said she had died of heart disease—of joy that kills.

Reading and Reacting

1. The story's basic exposition is presented in its first two paragraphs. What additional information about character or setting would you like to know? Why do you suppose Chopin does not supply this information?

2. "The Story of an Hour" is a very economical story, with little action or dialogue. Do you see this economy as a strength or a weakness? Explain.

3. When "The Story of an Hour" was first published in *Vogue* magazine in 1894, the magazine's editors titled it "The Dream of an Hour." A film version, echoing the last words of the story, is called *The Joy That Kills*. Which of the three titles do you believe most accurately represents what happens in the story? Why?

4. Do you think Brently Mallard physically abused his wife? Did he love her? Did she love him? Exactly why was she so relieved to be rid of him? Can you answer any of these questions with certainty?

5. What is the nature of the conflict in this story? Who, or what, do you see as Mrs. Mallard's antagonist?

6. What emotions does Mrs. Mallard experience during the hour she spends alone in her room? What events do you imagine take place during this same period outside her room? outside her house?

7. Do you find the story's ending satisfying? believable? contrived?

8. Was the story's ending unexpected, or were you prepared for it? What elements in the story foreshadow this ending?

9. JOURNAL ENTRY Rewrite the story's ending, substituting a few paragraphs of your own for the last three paragraphs.

10. CRITICAL PERSPECTIVE Kate Chopin is widely viewed today as an early feminist writer whose work often addressed the social injustices and inequalities that women faced during the second half of the nineteenth century. According to literary critic Elaine Showalter, "The Story of an Hour" was written during a period in which women writers were able to "reject the accommodating postures of femininity and to use literature to dramatize the ordeals of wronged womanhood."

Do you think this story rejects the "postures of femininity"? What "ordeals of wronged womanhood" are being dramatized here?

Related Works: "The Storm" (p. 199), "The Yellow Wallpaper" (p. 434), "If I should learn, in some quite casual way" (p. 592), *Trifles* (p. 867), *A Doll House* (p. 881)

NEIL GAIMAN (1960–   ) grew up in England and currently lives in Minnesota. The author of numerous critically acclaimed stories, novels, and graphic fiction for children and adults, Gaiman is also a screenwriter, film director, and essayist. Largely dealing with fantasy and science fiction subjects, his work has been translated into numerous languages. Gaiman is also the author of the award-winning comics series *Sandman*. In discussing his novel *Anansi Boys* (2005), Gaiman provides a description that applies to much of his work: "It's a scary, funny sort of a story, which isn't exactly a thriller, and isn't really horror, and doesn't quite qualify as a ghost story (although it has at least one ghost in it), or a romantic comedy (although there are several romances in there, and it's certainly a comedy, except for the scary bits)."

Cultural Context The concept of "aliens living among us" is a popular subject in the science fiction genre. Classic science fiction films that explore this theme include *The Day the Earth Stood Still* (originally released in 1951 and remade in 2008), *The Thing* (originally released in 1951 and remade in 1982 and 2011), *Invasion of the Body Snatchers* (1956), and *The Blob* (1958). More recent "aliens among us" films include *E.T.: The Extra-Terrestrial* (1982) and the *Men in Black* movies (1997, 2002, and 2012). While the classics tend to depict aliens as evil and scary, some of the newer films show the "human" side of our alien counterparts. In "How to Talk to Girls at Parties," Gaiman builds on this science fiction tradition by depicting young, enticing girls as aliens who forever change the male protagonists' attitudes toward lust and temptation.

How to Talk to Girls at Parties (2007)

"Come on," said Vic. "It'll be great."

"No, it won't," I said, although I'd lost this fight hours ago, and I knew it.

"It'll be brilliant," said Vic, for the hundredth time. "Girls! Girls! Girls!" He grinned with white teeth.

We both attended an all-boys' school in South London. While it would be a lie to say that we had no experience with girls—Vic seemed to have had many girlfriends, while I had kissed three of my sister's friends— it would, I think, be perfectly true to say that we both chiefly spoke to, interacted with, and only truly understood, other boys. Well, I did, anyway. It's hard to speak for someone else, and I've not seen Vic for thirty years. I'm not sure that I would know what to say to him now if I did.

5   We were walking the back streets that used to twine in a grimy maze behind East Croydon station—a friend had told Vic about a party, and Vic was determined to go whether I liked it or not, and I didn't. But my parents were away that week at a conference, and I was Vic's guest at his house, so I was trailing along beside him.

"It'll be the same as it always is," I said. "After an hour you'll be off somewhere snogging the prettiest girl at the party, and I'll be in the kitchen listening to somebody's mum going on about politics or poetry or something."

"You just have to *talk* to them," he said. "I think it's probably that road at the end here." He gestured cheerfully, swinging the bag with the bottle in it.

"Don't you know?"

"Alison gave me directions and I wrote them on a bit of paper, but I left it on the hall table. S'okay. I can find it."

10   "How?" Hope welled slowly up inside me.

"We walk down the road," he said, as if speaking to an idiot child. "And we look for the party. Easy."

I looked, but saw no party: just narrow houses with rusting cars or bikes in their concreted front gardens; and the dusty glass fronts of newsagents, which smelled of alien spices and sold everything from birthday cards and second-hand comics to the kind of magazines that were so pornographic that they were sold already sealed in plastic bags. I had been there when Vic had slipped one of those magazines beneath his sweater, but the owner caught him on the pavement outside and made him give it back.

We reached the end of the road and turned into a narrow street of terraced houses. Everything looked very still and empty in the Summer's evening. "It's all right for you," I said. "They fancy you. You don't actually *have* to talk to them." It was true: one urchin grin from Vic and he could have his pick of the room.

"Nah. S'not like that. You've just got to talk."

The times I had kissed my sister's friends I had not spoken to them. They had been around while my sister was off doing something elsewhere, and they had drifted into my orbit, and so I had kissed them. I do not remember any talking. I did not know what to say to girls, and I told him so.

"They're just girls," said Vic. "They don't come from another planet."

As we followed the curve of the road around, my hopes that the party would prove unfindable began to fade: a low pulsing noise, music muffled by walls and doors, could be heard from a house up ahead. It was eight in the evening, not that early if you aren't yet sixteen, and we weren't. Not quite.

I had parents who liked to know where I was, but I don't think Vic's parents cared that much. He was the youngest of five boys. That in itself seemed magical to me: I merely had two sisters, both younger than I was, and I felt both unique and lonely. I had wanted a brother as far back as I could remember. When I turned thirteen, I stopped wishing on falling stars or first stars, but back when I did, a brother was what I had wished for.

We went up the garden path, crazy paving leading us past a hedge and a solitary rose bush to a pebble-dashed facade. We rang the doorbell, and the door was opened by a girl. I could not have told you how old she was, which was one of the things about girls I had begun to hate: when you start out as kids you're just boys and girls, going through time at the same speed, and you're all five, or seven, or eleven, together. And then one day there's a lurch and the girls just sort of sprint off into the future ahead of you, and they know all about everything, and they have periods and breasts and makeup and God-only-knew-what-else—for I certainly didn't. The diagrams in biology textbooks were no substitute for being, in a very real sense, young adults. And the girls of our age were.

Vic and I weren't young adults, and I was beginning to suspect that even when I started needing to shave every day, instead of once every couple of weeks, I would still be way behind.

The girl said, "Hello?"

Vic said, "We're friends of Alison's." We had met Alison, all freckles and orange hair and a wicked smile, in Hamburg, on a German Exchange. The exchange organizers had sent some girls with us, from a local girls' school, to balance the sexes. The girls, our age, more or less, were raucous and funny, and had more or less adult boyfriends with cars and jobs and motorbikes and—in the case of one girl with crooked teeth and a raccoon coat, who spoke to me about it sadly at the end of a party in Hamburg, in, of course, the kitchen—a wife and kids.

"She isn't here," said the girl at the door. "No Alison,"

"Not to worry," said Vic, with an easy grin. "I'm Vic. This is Enn." A beat, and then the girl smiled back at him. Vic had a bottle of white wine in a plastic bag, removed from his parents' kitchen cabinet. "Where should I put this, then?"

25   She stood out of the way, letting us enter. "There's a kitchen in the back," she said. "Put it on the table there, with the other bottles." She had golden, wavy hair, and she was very beautiful. The hall was dim in the twilight, but I could see that she was beautiful.

"What's your name, then?" said Vic.

She told him it was Stella, and he grinned his crooked white grin and told her that that had to be the prettiest name he had ever heard. Smooth bastard. And what was worse was that he said it like he meant it.

Vic headed back to drop off the wine in the kitchen, and I looked into the front room, where the music was coming from. There were people dancing in there. Stella walked in, and she started to dance, swaying to the music all alone, and I watched her.

This was during the early days of punk. On our own record players we would play the Adverts and the Jam, the Stranglers and the Clash and the Sex Pistols. At other people's parties you'd hear ELO or 10cc or even Roxy Music. Maybe some Bowie, if you were lucky. During the German Exchange, the only LP that we had all been able to agree on was Neil Young's *Harvest*, and his song "Heart of Gold" had threaded through the trip like a refrain; *I crossed the ocean for a heart of gold.* . . .

30   The music playing in that front room wasn't anything I recognized. It sounded a bit like a German electronic pop group called Kraftwerk, and a bit like an LP I'd been given for my last birthday, of strange sounds made by the BBC Radiophonic Workshop. The music had a beat, though, and the half-dozen girls in that room were moving gently to it, although I only looked at Stella. She shone.

Vic pushed past me, into the room. He was holding a can of lager. "There's booze back in the kitchen," he told me. He wandered over to Stella and he began to talk to her. I couldn't hear what they were saying over the music, but I knew that there was no room for me in that conversation.

I didn't like beer, not back then. I went off to see if there was something I wanted to drink. On the kitchen table stood a large bottle of Coca-Cola, and I poured myself a plastic tumblerful, and I didn't dare say anything to the pair of girls who were talking in the underlit kitchen. They were animated and utterly lovely. Each of them had very black skin and glossy hair and movie star clothes, and their accents were foreign, and each of them was out of my league.

I wandered, Coke in hand.

The house was deeper than it looked, larger and more complex than the two-up two-down model I had imagined. The rooms were underlit—I doubt there was a bulb of more than forty watts in the building—and each room I went into was inhabited: in my memory, inhabited only by girls. I did not go upstairs.

A girl was the only occupant of the conservatory. Her hair was so fair 35 it was white, and long, and straight, and she sat at the glass-topped table, her hands clasped together, staring at the garden outside, and the gathering dusk. She seemed wistful.

"Do you mind if I sit here?" I asked, gesturing with my cup. She shook her head, and then followed it up with a shrug, to indicate that it was all the same to her. I sat down.

Vic walked past the conservatory door. He was talking to Stella, but he looked in at me, sitting at the table, wrapped in shyness and awkwardness, and he opened and closed his hand in a parody of a speaking mouth. *Talk.* Right.

"Are you from around here?" I asked the girl.

She shook her head. She wore a low-cut silvery top, and I tried not to stare at the swell of her breasts.

I said, "What's your name? I'm Enn."   40

"Wain's Wain," she said, or something that sounded like it. "I'm a second."

"That's uh. That's a different name."

She fixed me with huge liquid eyes. "It indicates that my progenitor was also Wain, and that I am obliged to report back to her. I may not breed."

"Ah. Well. Bit early for that anyway, isn't it?"

She unclasped her hands, raised them above the table, spread her fin- 45 gers. "You see?" The little finger on her left hand was crooked, and it bifurcated at the top, splitting into two smaller fingertips. A minor deformity. "When I was finished a decision was needed. Would I be retained, or eliminated? I was fortunate that the decision was with me. Now, I travel, while my more perfect sisters remain at home in stasis. They were firsts. I am a second.

"Soon I must return to Wain, and tell her all I have seen. All my impressions of this place of yours."

"I don't actually live in Croydon," I said. "I don't come from here." I wondered if she was American. I had no idea what she was talking about.

"As you say," she agreed, "neither of us comes from here." She folded her six-fingered left hand beneath her right, as if tucking it out of sight. "I had expected it to be bigger, and cleaner, and more colorful. But still, it is a jewel."

She yawned, covered her mouth with her right hand, only for a moment, before it was back on the table again. "I grow weary of the journeying, and I wish sometimes that it would end. On a street in Rio, at Carnival, I saw them on a bridge, golden and tall and insect-eyed and winged, and elated I almost ran to greet them, before I saw that they were only

people in costumes. I said to Hola Colt, 'Why do they try so hard to look
like us?' and Hola Colt replied, 'Because they hate themselves, all shades
of pink and brown, and so small.' It is what I experience, even me, and I
am not grown. It is like a world of children, or of elves." Then she smiled
and said, "It was a good thing they could not any of them see Hola Colt."

50   "Um," I said, "do you want to dance?"
        She shook her head immediately. "It is not permitted," she said. "I can
do nothing that might cause damage to property. I am Wain's."
        "Would you like something to drink, then?"
        "Water," she said.
        I went back to the kitchen and poured myself another Coke, and filled
a cup with water from the tap. From the kitchen back to the hall, and from
there into the conservatory, but now it was quite empty.

55   I wondered if the girl had gone to the toilet, and if she might change
her mind about dancing later. I walked back to the front room and stared
in. The room was filling up. There were more girls dancing, and several
lads I didn't know, who looked older than me and Vic. The lads and the
girls all kept their distance, but Vic was holding Stella's hand as they
danced, and when the song ended he put an arm around her, casually,
almost proprietorially, to make sure that nobody else cut in.
        I wondered if the girl I had been talking to in the conservatory was
now upstairs, as she did not appear to be on the ground floor.
        I walked into the living room, which was across the hall from the room
where the people were dancing, and I sat down on the sofa. There was a
girl sitting there already. She had dark hair, cut short and spiky, and a
nervous manner.
        Talk, I thought. "Um, this mug of water's going spare," I told her, "if
you want it?"
        She nodded, and reached out her hand and took the mug, extremely
carefully, as if she were unused to taking things, as if she could trust neither her vision nor her hands.

60   "I love being a tourist," she said, and smiled hesitantly. She had a gap
between her two front teeth, and she sipped the tap water as if she were
an adult sipping a fine wine. "The last tour, we went to sun, and we swam
in sunfire pools with the whales. We heard their histories and we shivered
in the chill of the outer places, then we swam deepward where the heat
churned and comforted us.
        "I wanted to go back. This time, I wanted it. There was so much I had
not seen. Instead we came to world. Do you like it?"
        "Like what?"
        She gestured vaguely to the room—the sofa, the armchairs, the cur-
tains, the unused gas fire.
        "It's all right, I suppose."

"I told them I did not wish to visit world," she said, "My parent-teacher 65 was unimpressed. 'You will have much to learn,' it told me. I said 'I could learn more in sun, again. Or in the deeps. Jessa spun webs between galaxies. I want to do that.'

"But there was no reasoning with it, and I came to world. Parent-teacher engulfed me, and I was here, embodied in a decaying lump of meat hanging on a frame of calcium. As I incarnated I felt things deep inside me, fluttering and pumping and squishing. It was my first experience with pushing air through the mouth, vibrating the vocal cords on the way, and I used it to tell parent-teacher that I wished that I would die, which it acknowledged was the inevitable exit strategy from world."

There were black worry beads wrapped around her wrist, and she fiddled with them as she spoke. "But knowledge is there, in the meat," she said, "and I am resolved to learn from it."

We were sitting close at the center of the sofa now. I decided I should put an arm around her, but casually. I would extend my arm along the back of the sofa and eventually sort of creep it down, almost imperceptibly, until it was touching her. She said, "The thing with the liquid in the eyes, when the world blurs. Nobody told me, and I still do not understand. I have touched the folds of the Whisper and pulsed and flown with the tachyon[1] swans, and I still do not understand."

She wasn't the prettiest girl there, but she seemed nice enough, and she was a girl, anyway. I let my arm slide down a little, tentatively, so that it made contact with her back, and she did not tell me to take it away.

Vic called to me then, from the doorway. He was standing with his 70 arm around Stella, protectively, waving at me. I tried to let him know, by shaking my head, that I was onto something, but he called my name, and, reluctantly, I got up from the sofa, and walked over to the door. "What?"

"Er. Look. The party," said Vic, apologetically. "It's not the one I thought it was. I've been talking to Stella and I figured it out. Well, she sort of explained it to me. We're at a different party."

"Christ. Are we in trouble? Do we have to go?"

Stella shook her head. He leaned down and kissed her, gently, on the lips. "You're just happy to have me here, aren't you darlin'?"

"You know I am," she told him.

He looked from her back to me, and he smiled his white smile: roguish, 75 loveable, a little bit Artful Dodger, a little bit wide-boy Prince Charming. "Don't worry. They're all tourists here anyway. It's a foreign exchange thing, innit? Like when we all went to Germany."

"It is?"

---

[1]tachyon: A hypothetical particle moving faster than light.

"Enn. You got to *talk* to them. And that means you got to listen to them too. You understand?"

"I *did*. I already talked to a couple of them."

"You getting anywhere?"

80   "I was till you called me over."

"Sorry about that. Look, I just wanted to fill you in. Right?"

And he patted my arm and he walked away with Stella. Then, together, the two of them went up the stairs.

Understand me, all the girls at that party, in the twilight, were lovely; they all had perfect faces, but, more important than that, they had whatever strangeness of proportion, of oddness or humanity it is that makes a beauty something more than a shop-window dummy. Stella was the most lovely of any of them, but she, of course, was Vic's, and they were going upstairs together, and that was just how things would always be.

There were several people now sitting on the sofa, talking to the gap-toothed girl. Someone told a joke, and they all laughed. I would have had to push my way in there to sit next to her again, and it didn't look like she was expecting me back, or cared that I had gone, so I wandered out into the hall. I glanced in at the dancers and found myself wondering where the music was coming from. I couldn't see a record player or speakers.

85   From the hall I walked back to the kitchen.

Kitchens are good at parties. You never need an excuse to be there, and, on the good side, at this party I couldn't see any signs of someone's mum. I inspected the various bottles and cans on the kitchen table, then I poured a half an inch of Pernod into the bottom of my plastic cup, which I filled to the top with Coke. I dropped in a couple of ice cubes, and took a sip, relishing the sweet-shop tang of the drink.

"What's that you're drinking?" A girl's voice.

"It's Pernod," I told her. "It tastes like aniseed balls, only it's alcoholic." I didn't say that I only tried it because I'd heard someone in the crowd ask for a Pernod on a live Velvet Underground LP.

"Can I have one?" I poured another Pernod, topped it off with Coke, passed it to her. Her hair was a coppery auburn, and it tumbled around her head in ringlets. It's not a hair style you see much now, but you saw it a lot back then.

90   "What's your name?" I asked.

"Triolet," she said.

"Pretty name," I told her, although I wasn't sure that it was. She was pretty, though.

"It's a verse form," she said, proudly. "Like me."

"You're a poem?"

95   She smiled and looked down and away, perhaps bashfully. Her profile was almost flat—a perfect Grecian nose that came down from her

forehead in a straight line. We did *Antigone* in the school theater the previous year. I was the messenger who brings Creon the news of Antigone's death. We wore half-masks that made us look like that. I thought of that play, looking at her face, in the kitchen, and I thought of Barry Smith's drawings of women in the *Conan* comics: five years later I would have thought of the Pre-Raphaelites, of Jane Morris and Lizzie Siddall. But I was only fifteen, then.

"You're a poem?" I repeated.

She chewed her lower lip. "If you want. I am a poem, or I am a pattern, or a race of people whose world was swallowed by the sea."

"Isn't it hard to be three things at the same time?"

"What's your name?"

"Enn." 100

"So you are Enn," she said. "And you are a male. And you are a biped. Is it hard to be three things at the same time?"

"But they aren't different things. I mean, they aren't contradictory." It was a word I had read many times but never said aloud before that night, and I put the stresses in the wrong places. *Contradictory.*

She wore a thin dress, made of a white, silky fabric. Her eyes were a pale green, a color that would now make me think of colored contact lenses; but this was thirty years ago; things were different then. I remember wondering about Vic and Stella, upstairs. By now, I was sure that they were in one of the bedrooms, and I envied Vic so much it hurt.

Still, I was talking to this girl, even if we were talking nonsense, even if her name wasn't really Triolet (my generation had not been given hippie names: all the Rainbows and the Sunshines and the Moons, they were only six, seven, eight years old back then). She said, "We knew that it would soon be over, and so we put it all into a poem, to tell the universe who we were, and why we were here, and what we said and did and thought and dreamed and yearned for. We wrapped our dreams in words and patterned the words so that they would live forever, unforgettable. Then we sent the poem as a pattern of flux, to wait in the heart of a star, beaming out its message in pulses and bursts and fuzzes across the electromagnetic spectrum, until the time when, on worlds a thousand sun systems distant, the pattern would be decoded and read, and it would become a poem once again."

"And then what happened?" 105

She looked at me with her green eyes, and it was as if she stared out at me from her own Antigone half-mask; but as if her pale green eyes were just a different, deeper, part of the mask. "You cannot hear a poem without it changing you," she told me. "They heard it, and it colonized them. It inherited them and it inhabited them, its rhythms becoming part of the way that they thought; its images permanently transmuting their metaphors; its verses, its outlook, its aspirations becoming their lives. Within a generation their children would be born already knowing the poem, and, sooner rather than later, as these things go, there were no more children born. There was no need for them, not any longer. There was only a poem, which took flesh and walked and spread itself across the vastness of the known."

I edged closer to her, so I could feel my leg pressing against hers. She seemed to welcome it: she put her hand on my arm, affectionately, and I felt a smile spreading across my face.

"There are places that we are welcomed," said Triolet, "and places where we are regarded as a noxious weed, or as a disease, something immediately to be quarantined and eliminated. But where does contagion end and art begin?"

"I don't know," I said, still smiling. I could hear the unfamiliar music as it pulsed and scattered and boomed in the front room.

110   She leaned into me then and—I suppose it was a kiss.... I suppose. She pressed her lips to my lips, anyway, and then, satisfied, she pulled back, as if she had now marked me as her own.

"Would you like to hear it?" she asked, and I nodded, unsure what she was offering me, but certain that I needed anything she was willing to give me.

She began to whisper something in my ear. It's the strangest thing about poetry—you can tell it's poetry, even if you don't speak the language. You can hear Homer's Greek without understanding a word, and you still know it's poetry. I've heard Polish poetry, and Iniut poetry, and I knew what it was without knowing. Her whisper was like that. I didn't know the language, but her words washed through me, perfect, and in my mind's eye I saw towers of glass and diamond; and people with eyes of the palest green; and, unstoppable, beneath every syllable, I could feel the relentless advance of the ocean.

Perhaps I kissed her properly. I don't remember. I know I wanted to.

And then Vic was shaking me violently. "Come on!" he was shouting. "Quickly. Come on!"

115   In my head I began to come back from a thousand miles away.

"Idiot. Come on. Just get a move on," he said, and he swore at me. There was fury in his voice.

For the first time that evening I recognized one of the songs being played in the front room. A sad saxophone wail followed by a cascade of liquid chords, a man's voice singing cut-up lyrics about the sons of the silent age. I wanted to stay and hear the song.

She said, "I am not finished. There is yet more of me."

"Sorry love," said Vic, but he wasn't smiling any longer. "There'll be another time," and he grabbed me by the elbow and he twisted and pulled, forcing me from the room. I did not resist. I knew from experience that Vic could beat the stuffing out me if he got it into his head to do so. He wouldn't do it unless he was upset or angry, but he was angry now.

Out into the front hall. As Vic pulled open the door, I looked back 120
one last time, over my shoulder, hoping to see Triolet in the doorway to
the kitchen, but she was not there. I saw Stella, though, at the top of the
stairs. She was staring down at Vic, and I saw her face.

This all happened thirty years ago. I have forgotten much, and I will
forget more, and in the end I will forget everything; yet, if I have any
certainty of life beyond death, it is all wrapped up not in psalms or hymns,
but in this one thing alone: I cannot believe that I will ever forget that
moment, or forget the expression on Stella's face as she watched Vic hurrying away from her. Even in death I shall remember that.

Her clothes were in disarray, and there was makeup smudged across
her face, and her eyes—

You wouldn't want to make a universe angry. I bet an angry universe
would look at you with eyes like that.

We ran then, me and Vic, away from the party and the tourists and the
twilight, ran as if a lightning storm was on our heels, a mad helterskelter
dash down the confusion of streets, threading through the maze, and we
did not look back, and we did not stop until we could not breathe; and
then we stopped and panted, unable to run any longer. We were in pain. I
held onto a wall, and Vic threw up, hard and long, in the gutter.

He wiped his mouth.   125

"She wasn't a—" He stopped.

He shook his head.

Then he said, "You know...I think there's a thing. When you've gone
as far as you dare. And if you go any further, you wouldn't be *you* anymore?
You'd be the person who'd done *that*? The places you just can't go...I
think that happened to me tonight."

I thought I knew what he was saying, "Screw her, you mean?" I said.

He rammed a knuckle hard against my temple, and twisted it vio- 130
lently. I wondered if I was going to have to fight him—and lose—but after
a moment he lowered his hand and moved away from me, making a low,
gulping noise.

I looked at him curiously, and I realized that he was crying: his face
was scarlet; snot and tears ran down his cheeks. Vic was sobbing in the
street, as unselfconsciously and heartbreakingly as a little boy.

He walked away from me then, shoulders heaving, and he hurried
down the road so he was in front of me and I could no longer see his face.
I wondered what had occurred in that upstairs room to make him behave
like that, to scare him so, and I could not even begin to guess.

The streetlights came on, one by one. Vic stumbled on ahead, while I
trudged down the street behind him in the dusk, my feet treading out the
measure of a poem that, try as I might, I could not properly remember and
would never be able to repeat.

Reading and Reacting

1. Consider the story's exposition. Where does it take place? What do we know about Enn? about Vic?

2. What is Enn's impression of Vic at the beginning of the story? Has it changed by the end? Explain.

3. In paragraph 7, Vic tells Enn that he needs to *talk* to girls if he is going to make any headway with them. Does Enn follow Vic's advice? Does the story actually explain or illustrate "how to talk to girls at parties"?

4. In paragraph 16, Vic says, "They're just girls, ... They don't come from another planet." How does this statement foreshadow the events to come? What other instances of foreshadowing can you identify?

5. What is your initial reaction to Wain? to the dark-haired girl? to Triolet? How do your own reactions differ from Enn's? How do you explain why you respond differently?

6. Reread paragraph 119. Do you think the narrator is exaggerating when he says he will remember forever the expression on Stella's face?

7. In what respects is this a realistic story? In what respects is it *not* realistic? Is it an initiation story? Is it a horror story?

8. What, if anything, does this story say about the differences between male and female college students? about college parties? Is the story about college students' social interactions, or is it about something else entirely?

9. **JOURNAL ENTRY** What do you think Vic sees at the end of the story that upsets him so much?

10. **CRITICAL PERSPECTIVE** Literary critic David Rudd describes Gaiman's children's novel *Coraline* (2003) as "a rich and powerful work that explores areas seen by many as inappropriate for children, although other critics, such as Bruno Bettelheim in *The Uses of Enchantment* (1976), argue that children not only *want* to but *need* to explore matters that affect their lives, albeit in their own time and fashion (issues to do with death, sex, ontology, evil, desire, violence, and so on)."

    In what ways are Enn and Vic expressing their "need to explore matters that affect their lives" in "How to Talk to Girls at Parties"? How does this need help to drive the story's plot?

Related Works: "Gryphon" (p. 172), "Young Goodman Brown" (p. 367), "Greasy Lake" (p. 425), "The Secret Lion" (p. 466), "You Fit into Me" (p. 598), "La Belle Dame Sans Merci: A Ballad" (p. 771), *Zombie Love* (p. 884)

AP Images

WILLIAM FAULKNER (1897–1962), winner of the 1949 Nobel Prize in Literature and the 1955 and 1963 Pulitzer Prizes for fiction, was a Southern writer whose work transcends the regional label. His nineteen novels, notably *The Sound and the Fury* (1929), *As I Lay Dying* (1930), *Light in August* (1932), *Absalom, Absalom!* (1936), and *The Reivers* (1962), explore a wide range of human experience—from high comedy to tragedy—as seen in the life of one community, the fictional Yoknapatawpha County (modeled on the area around Faulkner's own hometown of Oxford, Mississippi). Faulkner's Yoknapatawpha stories—a fascinating blend of complex Latinate prose and primitive Southern dialect—paint an extraordinary portrait of a community bound together by ties of blood, by a shared belief in moral "verities," and by an old grief (the Civil War). Faulkner's grandfather raised "Billy" on Civil War tales and local legends, including many about the "Old Colonel," the writer's great-grandfather, who was a colorful Confederate officer. Although Faulkner's stories elegize the agrarian virtues of the Old South, they look unflinchingly at that world's tragic flaw: the "peculiar institution" of slavery.

Local legends and gossip frequently served as the spark for Faulkner's stories. As John B. Cullen, writing in *Old Times in Faulkner Country*, notes, "A Rose for Emily," Faulkner's first nationally published short story, was based on the tale of Oxford's aristocratic "Miss Mary" Neilson, who married Captain Jack Hume, the charming Yankee foreman of a street-paving crew, over her family's shocked protests. According to Cullen, one of Faulkner's neighbors said he created his story "out of fears and rumors"—the dire predictions of what *might* happen if Mary Neilson married her Yankee.

Cultural Context For many years, the pre–Civil War South was idealized as a land of prosperous plantations, large white houses, cultured and gracious people, and a stable economy based on farming. Central to the myth of the Old South was an adherence to the code of chivalry and a belief in the natural superiority of the white aristocracy, led by men who made their fortunes by owning and running plantations that depended on slave labor. Once the South lost the Civil War, the idealized image of the Old South fell by the wayside, making room for the New South, which, like the North, was industrialized. In this story, Faulkner contrasts notions of the Old South and its decaying values with the newer ideas and innovations of the post-Reconstruction South.

A Rose for Emily (1930)

I

When Miss Emily Grierson died, our whole town went to her funeral: the men through a sort of respectful affection for a fallen monument, the women mostly out of curiosity to see the inside of her house, which no one save an old manservant—a combined gardener and cook—had seen in at least ten years.

It was a big, squarish frame house that had once been white, decorated with cupolas[1] and spires[2] and scrolled balconies in the heavily lightsome style of the seventies, set on what had once been our most select street. But garages and cotton gins had encroached and obliterated even the august names of that neighborhood; only Miss Emily's house was left, lifting its stubborn and coquettish decay above the cotton wagons and the gasoline pumps—an eyesore among eyesores. And now Miss Emily had gone to join the representatives of those august names where they lay in the cedar-bemused cemetery among the ranked and anonymous graves of Union and Confederate soldiers who fell at the battle of Jefferson.

Alive, Miss Emily had been a tradition, a duty, and a care; a sort of hereditary obligation upon the town, dating from that day in 1894 when Colonel Sartoris, the mayor—he who fathered the edict that no Negro woman should appear on the streets without an apron—remitted her taxes, the dispensation dating from the death of her father on into perpetuity. Not that Miss Emily would have accepted charity. Colonel Sartoris invented an involved tale to the effect that Miss Emily's father had loaned money to the town, which the town, as a matter of business, preferred this way of repaying. Only a man of Colonel Sartoris' generation and thought could have invented it, and only a woman could have believed it.

When the next generation, with its more modern ideas, became mayors and aldermen, this arrangement created some little dissatisfaction. On the first of the year they mailed her a tax notice. February came, and there was no reply. They wrote her a formal letter, asking her to call at the sheriff's office at her convenience. A week later the mayor wrote her himself, offering to call or to send his car for her, and received in reply a note on paper of an archaic shape, in a thin, flowing calligraphy in faded ink, to the effect that she no longer went out at all. The tax notice was also enclosed, without comment.

5   They called a special meeting of the Board of Aldermen. A deputation waited upon her, knocked at the door through which no visitor had passed since she ceased giving china-painting lessons eight or ten years earlier. They were admitted by the old Negro into a dim hall from which a stairway mounted into still more shadow. It smelled of dust and disuse—a close, dank smell. The Negro led them into the parlor. It was furnished in heavy, leather-covered furniture. When the Negro opened the blinds of one window, they could see that the leather was cracked; and when they sat down, a faint dust rose sluggishly about their thighs, spinning

---

[1] *cupolas:* Rounded structures on roofs.
[2] *spires:* Tapered structures on roofs.

with slow motes in the single sun-ray. On a tarnished gilt easel before the fireplace stood a crayon portrait of Miss Emily's father.

They rose when she entered—a small, fat woman in black, with a thin gold chain descending to her waist and vanishing into her belt, leaning on an ebony cane with a tarnished gold head. Her skeleton was small and spare; perhaps that was why what would have been merely plumpness in another was obesity in her. She looked bloated, like a body long submerged in motionless water, and of that pallid hue. Her eyes, lost in the fatty ridges of her face, looked like two small pieces of coal pressed into a lump of dough as they moved from one face to another while the visitors stated their errand.

She did not ask them to sit. She just stood in the door and listened quietly until the spokesman came to a stumbling halt. Then they could hear the invisible watch ticking at the end of the gold chain.

Her voice was dry and cold. "I have no taxes in Jefferson. Colonel Sartoris explained it to me. Perhaps one of you can gain access to the city records and satisfy yourselves."

"But we have. We are the city authorities, Miss Emily. Didn't you get a notice from the sheriff, signed by him?"

"I received a paper, yes," Miss Emily said. "Perhaps he considers him- 10 self the sheriff...I have no taxes in Jefferson."

"But there is nothing on the books to show that, you see. We must go by the—"

"See Colonel Sartoris. I have no taxes in Jefferson."

"But, Miss Emily—"

"See Colonel Sartoris." (Colonel Sartoris had been dead almost ten years.) "I have no taxes in Jefferson. Tobe!" The Negro appeared. "Show these gentlemen out."

II

So she vanquished them, horse and foot, just as she had vanquished their 15 fathers thirty years before about the smell. That was two years after her father's death and a short time after her sweetheart—the one we believed would marry her—had deserted her. After her father's death she went out very little; after her sweetheart went away, people hardly saw her at all. A few of the ladies had the temerity to call, but were not received, and the only sign of life about the place was the Negro man—a young man then—going in and out with a market basket.

"Just as if a man—any man—could keep a kitchen properly," the ladies said; so they were not surprised when the smell developed. It was another link between the gross, teeming world and the high and mighty Griersons.

A neighbor, a woman, complained to the mayor, Judge Stevens, eighty years old.

"But what will you have me do about it, madam?" he said.

"Why, send her word to stop it," the woman said. "Isn't there a law?"

20 "I'm sure that won't be necessary," Judge Stevens said. "It's probably just a snake or a rat that nigger of hers killed in the yard. I'll speak to him about it."

The next day he received two more complaints, one from a man who came in diffident deprecation. "We really must do something about it, Judge. I'd be the last one in the world to bother Miss Emily, but we've got to do something." That night the Board of Aldermen met—three gray-beards and one younger man, a member of the rising generation.

"It's simple enough," he said. "Send her word to have her place cleaned up. Give her a certain time to do it in, and if she don't . . ."

"Dammit, sir," Judge Stevens said, "will you accuse a lady to her face of smelling bad?"

So the next night, after midnight, four men crossed Miss Emily's lawn and slunk about the house like burglars, sniffing along the base of the brickwork and at the cellar openings while one of them performed a regular sowing motion with his hand out of a sack slung from his shoulder. They broke open the cellar door and sprinkled lime there, and in all the outbuildings. As they recrossed the lawn, a window that had been dark was lighted and Miss Emily sat in it, the light behind her, and her upright torso motionless as that of an idol. They crept quietly across the lawn and into the shadow of the locusts that lined the street. After a week or two the smell went away.

25 That was when people had begun to feel really sorry for her. People in our town, remembering how old lady Wyatt, her great-aunt, had gone completely crazy at last, believed that the Griersons held themselves a little too high for what they really were. None of the young men were quite good enough for Miss Emily and such. We had long thought of them as a tableau, Miss Emily a slender figure in white in the background, her father a spraddled silhouette in the foreground, his back to her and clutching a horsewhip, the two of them framed by the back-flung front door. So when she got to be thirty and was still single, we were not pleased exactly, but vindicated; even with insanity in the family she wouldn't have turned down all of her chances if they had really materialized.

When her father died, it got about that the house was all that was left to her; and in a way, people were glad. At last they could pity Miss Emily. Being left alone, and a pauper, she had become humanized. Now she too would know the old thrill and the old despair of a penny more or less.

The day after his death all the ladies prepared to call at the house and offer condolence and aid, as is our custom. Miss Emily met them at the door, dressed as usual and with no trace of grief on her face. She told them that her father was not dead. She did that for three days, with the ministers calling on her, and the doctors, trying to persuade her to let them dispose of the body. Just as they were about to resort to law and force, she broke down, and they buried her father quickly.

We did not say she was crazy then. We believed she had to do that. We remembered all the young men her father had driven away, and we knew that with nothing left, she would have to cling to that which had robbed her, as people will.

III

She was sick for a long time. When we saw her again, her hair was cut short, making her look like a girl, with a vague resemblance to those angels in colored church windows—sort of tragic and serene.

The town had just let the contracts for paving the sidewalks, and in   30
the summer after her father's death they began the work. The construction company came with niggers and mules and machinery, and a foreman named Homer Barron, a Yankee—a big, dark, ready man, with a big voice and eyes lighter than his face. The little boys would follow in groups to hear him cuss the niggers, and the niggers singing in time to the rise and fall of picks. Pretty soon he knew everybody in town. Whenever you heard a lot of laughing anywhere about the square, Homer Barron would be in the center of the group. Presently we began to see him and Miss Emily on Sunday afternoons driving in the yellow-wheeled buggy and the matched team of bays from the livery stable.

At first we were glad that Miss Emily would have an interest, because the ladies all said, "Of course a Grierson would not think seriously of a Northerner, a day laborer." But there were still others, older people, who said that even grief could not cause a real lady to forget *noblesse oblige*[3]— without calling it *noblesse oblige*. They just said, "Poor Emily. Her kinsfolk should come to her." She had some kin in Alabama; but years ago her father had fallen out with them over the estate of old lady Wyatt, the crazy woman, and there was no communication between the two families. They had not even been represented at the funeral.

And as soon as the old people said, "Poor Emily," the whispering began. "Do you suppose it's really so?" they said to one another. "Of course it is. What else could..." This behind their hands; rustling of craned silk and satin behind jalousies closed upon the sun of Sunday afternoon as the thin, swift clop-clop-clop of the matched team passed: "Poor Emily."

She carried her head high enough—even when we believed that she was fallen. It was as if she demanded more than ever the recognition of her dignity as the last Grierson; as if it had wanted that touch of earthiness

---

[3]*noblesse oblige:* The obligation of those of high birth or rank to behave honorably.

to reaffirm her imperviousness. Like when she bought the rat poison, the arsenic. That was over a year after they had begun to say "Poor Emily," and while the two female cousins were visiting her.

"I want some poison," she said to the druggist. She was over thirty then, still a slight woman, though thinner than usual, with cold, haughty black eyes in a face the flesh of which was strained across the temples and about the eye-sockets as you imagine a lighthouse-keeper's face ought to look. "I want some poison," she said.

35   "Yes, Miss Emily. What kind? For rats and such? I'd recom—"

"I want the best you have. I don't care what kind."

The druggist named several. "They'll kill anything up to an elephant. But what you want is—"

"Arsenic," Miss Emily said. "Is that a good one?"

"Is . . . arsenic? Yes, ma'am. But what you want—"

40   "I want arsenic."

The druggist looked down at her. She looked back at him, erect, her face like a strained flag. "Why, of course," the druggist said. "If that's what you want. But the law requires you to tell what you are going to use it for."

Miss Emily just stared at him, her head tilted back in order to look him eye for eye, until he looked away and went and got the arsenic and wrapped it up. The Negro delivery boy brought her the package; the druggist didn't come back. When she opened the package at home there was written on the box, under the skull and bones: "For rats."

IV

So the next day we all said, "She will kill herself"; and we said it would be the best thing. When she had first begun to be seen with Homer Barron, we had said, "She will marry him." Then we said, "She will persuade him yet," because Homer himself had remarked—he liked men, and it was known that he drank with the younger men in the Elks' Club—that he was not a marrying man. Later we said, "Poor Emily" behind the jalousies[4] as they passed on Sunday afternoon in the glittering buggy, Miss Emily with her head high and Homer Barron with his hat cocked and a cigar in his teeth, reins and whip in a yellow glove.

Then some of the ladies began to say that it was a disgrace to the town and a bad example to the young people. The men did not want to interfere, but at last the ladies forced the Baptist minister—Miss Emily's people were Episcopal—to call upon her. He would never divulge what happened during that interview, but he refused to go back again. The next Sunday they again drove about the streets, and the following day the minister's wife wrote to Miss Emily's relations in Alabama.

---

[4]*jalousies:* Blinds or shutters with adjustable horizontal slats.

So she had blood-kin under her roof again and we sat back to watch 45 developments. At first nothing happened. Then we were sure that they were to be married. We learned that Miss Emily had been to the jeweler's and ordered a man's toilet set in silver, with the letters H. B. on each piece. Two days later we learned that she had bought a complete outfit of men's clothing, including a nightshirt, and we said, "They are married." We were really glad. We were glad because the two female cousins were even more Grierson than Miss Emily had ever been.

So we were not surprised when Homer Barron—the streets had been finished some time since—was gone. We were a little disappointed that there was not a public blowing-off, but we believed that he had gone on to prepare for Miss Emily's coming, or to give her a chance to get rid of the cousins. (By that time it was a cabal, and we were all Miss Emily's allies to help circumvent the cousins.) Sure enough, after another week they departed. And, as we had expected all along, within three days Homer Barron was back in town. A neighbor saw the Negro man admit him at the kitchen door at dusk one evening.

And that was the last we saw of Homer Barron. And of Miss Emily for some time. The Negro man went in and out with the market basket, but the front door remained closed. Now and then we would see her at a window for a moment, as the men did that night when they sprinkled the lime, but for almost six months she did not appear on the streets. Then we knew that this was to be expected too; as if that quality of her father which had thwarted her woman's life so many times had been too virulent and too furious to die.

When we next saw Miss Emily, she had grown fat and her hair was turning gray. During the next few years it grew grayer and grayer until it attained an even pepper-and-salt iron-gray, when it ceased turning. Up to the day of her death at seventy-four it was still that vigorous iron-gray, like the hair of an active man.

From that time on her front door remained closed, save for a period of six or seven years, when she was about forty, during which she gave lessons in china-painting. She fitted up a studio in one of the downstairs rooms, where the daughters and granddaughters of Colonel Sartoris' contemporaries were sent to her with the same regularity and in the same spirit that they were sent to church on Sundays with a twenty-five-cent piece for the collection plate. Meanwhile her taxes had been remitted.

Then the newer generation became the backbone and the spirit of the 50 town, and the painting pupils grew up and fell away and did not send their children to her with boxes of color and tedious brushes and pictures cut from the ladies' magazines. The front door closed upon the last one and remained closed for good. When the town got free postal delivery, Miss Emily alone refused to let them fasten the metal numbers above her door and attach a mailbox to it. She would not listen to them.

Daily, monthly, yearly we watched the Negro grow grayer and more stooped, going in and out with the market basket. Each December we sent her a tax notice, which would be returned by the post office a week later, unclaimed. Now and then we would see her in one of the downstairs windows—she had evidently shut up the top floor of the house—like the carven torso of an idol in a niche, looking or not looking at us, we could never tell which. Thus she passed from generation to generation—dear, inescapable, impervious, tranquil, and perverse.

And so she died. Fell ill in the house filled with dust and shadows, with only a doddering Negro man to wait on her. We did not even know she was sick; we had long since given up trying to get any information from the Negro. He talked to no one, probably not even to her, for his voice had grown harsh and rusty, as if from disuse.

She died in one of the downstairs rooms, in a heavy walnut bed with a curtain, her gray head propped on a pillow yellow and moldy with age and lack of sunlight.

V

The Negro met the first of the ladies at the front door and let them in, with their hushed, sibilant voices and their quick, curious glances, and then he disappeared. He walked right through the house and out the back and was not seen again.

55   The two female cousins came at once. They held the funeral on the second day, with the town coming to look at Miss Emily beneath a mass of bought flowers, with the crayon face of her father musing profoundly above the bier and the ladies sibilant and macabre; and the very old men—some in their brushed Confederate uniforms—on the porch and the lawn, talking of Miss Emily as if she had been a contemporary of theirs, believing that they had danced with her and courted her perhaps, confusing time with its mathematical progression, as the old do, to whom all the past is not a diminishing road but, instead, a huge meadow which no winter ever quite touches, divided from them now by the narrow bottle-neck of the most recent decade of years.

Already we knew that there was one room in that region above stairs which no one had seen in forty years, and which would have to be forced. They waited until Miss Emily was decently in the ground before they opened it.

The violence of breaking down the door seemed to fill this room with pervading dust. A thin, acrid pall as of the tomb seemed to lie everywhere upon this room decked and furnished as for a bridal: upon the valance curtains of faded rose color, upon the rose-shaded lights, upon the dressing table, upon the delicate array of crystal and the man's toilet things backed with tarnished silver, silver so tarnished that the monogram was obscured.

Among them lay collar and tie, as if they had just been removed, which, lifted, left upon the surface a pale crescent in the dust. Upon a chair hung the suit, carefully folded; beneath it the two mute shoes and the discarded socks.

The man himself lay in the bed.

For a long while we just stood there, looking down at the profound and fleshless grin. The body had apparently once lain in the attitude of an embrace, but now the long sleep that outlasts love, that conquers even the grimace of love, had cuckolded him. What was left of him, rotted beneath what was left of the nightshirt, had become inextricable from the bed in which he lay; and upon him and upon the pillow beside him lay that even coating of the patient and biding dust.

Then we noticed that in the second pillow was the indentation of a 60 head. One of us lifted something from it, and leaning forward, that faint and invisible dust dry and acrid in the nostrils, we saw a long strand of iron-gray hair.

Reading and Reacting

1. Arrange these events in the sequence in which they actually occur: Homer's arrival in town, the aldermen's visit, Emily's purchase of poison, Colonel Sartoris's decision to remit Emily's taxes, the development of the odor around Emily's house, Emily's father's death, the arrival of Emily's relatives, Homer's disappearance. Then, list the events in the sequence in which they are introduced in the story. Why do you suppose Faulkner presents these events out of their actual chronological order?

2. Despite the story's confusing sequence, many events are foreshadowed. Give some examples of this technique. How does foreshadowing enrich the story?

3. Where does the exposition end and the movement toward the story's climax begin? Where does the resolution stage begin?

4. Emily is clearly the story's protagonist. In the sense that he opposes her wishes, Homer is the antagonist. What other characters—or what larger forces—are in conflict with Emily?

5. Explain how each of these phrases moves the story's plot along: "So she vanquished them, horse and foot…" (par. 15); "After a week or two the smell went away" (par. 24); "And that was the last we saw of Homer Barron" (par. 47); "And so she died" (par. 52); "The man himself lay in the bed" (par. 58).

6. The narrator of the story is an observer, not a participant. Who might this narrator be? Do you think the narrator is male or female? How do you suppose the narrator might know so much about Emily? Why do you think the narrator uses *we* instead of *I*?

7. The original version of "A Rose for Emily" included a two-page death-bed scene revealing that Tobe, Emily's servant, has shared her terrible secret all these years and that Emily has left her house to him. Why do you think Faulkner deleted this scene? Do you think he made the right decision?

8. Some critics have suggested that Miss Emily Grierson is a kind of symbol of the Old South, with its outdated ideas of chivalry, formal manners, and tradition. In what sense is she also a victim of those values?

9. **JOURNAL ENTRY** When asked at a seminar at the University of Virginia about the meaning of the title "A Rose for Emily," Faulkner replied, "Oh, it's simply the poor woman had no life at all. Her father had kept her more or less locked up and then she had a lover who was about to quit her, she had to murder him. It was just 'A Rose for Emily'—that's all." In another interview, asked the same question, he replied, "I pitied her and this was a salute, just as if you were to make a gesture, a salute, to anyone; to a woman you would hand a rose, as you would lift a cup of *sake* to a man." What do you make of Faulkner's responses? What else might the title suggest?

10. **CRITICAL PERSPECTIVE** In his essay "William Faulkner: An American Dickens," literary critic Leslie A. Fiedler characterizes Faulkner as "primarily . . . a sentimental writer; not a writer with the occasional vice of sentimentality, but one whose basic mode of experience is sentimental." Fiedler continues, "In a writer whose very method is self-indulgence, that sentimentality becomes sometimes downright embarrassing." Fiedler also notes Faulkner's "excesses of maudlin feelings and absurd indulgences in overripe rhetoric."

    Do you think these criticisms apply to "A Rose for Emily"? If so, does the "vice of sentimentality" diminish the story, or do you agree with Fiedler—who calls Faulkner a "supereminently good 'bad' writer"—that the author is able to transcend these excesses?

Related Works: "Miss Brill" (p. 166), "Barn Burning" (p. 256), "Porphyria's Lover" (p. 520), "Richard Cory" (p. 783), *Trifles* (p. 867)

WRITING SUGGESTIONS: Plot

1. Write a sequel to "The Story of an Hour," telling the story in the voice of Brently Mallard. Use flashbacks to provide information about his view of the Mallards' marriage.

2. Find a newspaper or magazine article that presents a story that you find disturbing. Then, write a fictionalized version of the article in which you retell the story's events in a detached tone, without adding analysis or

commentary. Expand the original article by creating additional characters and settings.

3. "The Story of an Hour" includes a *deus ex machina*, an outside force or agent that suddenly appears to change the course of events. Consider the possible effects of a *deus ex machina* on the other stories in this chapter. What might this outside force be in each story? How might it change the story's action? How plausible would such a dramatic turn of events be in each case?

4. Both "The Story of an Hour" and "How to Talk to Girls at Parties" create a dreamlike, disorienting atmosphere that has an unsettling effect on the protagonists. However, "The Story of an Hour" is essentially a realistic story while "How to Talk to Girls at Parties" is something quite different. Compare and contrast these two stories, focusing on how the stories' events affect the two protagonists and their perceptions of reality.

5. Read the following article from the January 30, 1987, *Philadelphia Inquirer*. After listing some similarities and differences between the events in the article's story and those in "A Rose for Emily," write an essay in which you discuss how the presentation of events differs. Can you draw any conclusions about the differences between journalistic and fictional treatments of similar incidents?

DICK POTHIER AND THOMAS J. GIBBONS JR.

A Woman's Wintry Death Leads to a Long-Dead Friend

For more than two years, Frances Dawson Hamilton lived with the body of her long-time companion, draping his skeletonized remains with palm fronds and rosary beads.

Yesterday, the 70-year-old woman was found frozen to death in the home in the 4500 block of Higbee Street where she had lived all her life—the last year without heat or hot water. Her body was found by police accompanying a city social worker who came bearing an order to have her taken to a hospital.

Police investigators said the body of Bernard J. Kelly, 84, was found in an upstairs bedroom of the two-story brick home in the Wissinoming section, on the twin bed where he apparently died at least two years ago.

Two beds had been pushed together, and Hamilton apparently had been sleeping beside Kelly's remains since he died of unknown causes, police said.

Kelly's remains were clothed in long johns and socks, investigators said. The body was draped with rosary beads and palm fronds, and on the bed near his body were two boxes of Valentine's Day candy.

"It was basically a funeral—we've seen it before in such cases," said one investigator who was at the scene but declined to be identified.

Neighbors and investigators said Hamilton and Kelly had lived together in the house for at least 15 years. Several neighbors said Hamilton came from an affluent family, was educated in Europe, and lived on a trust fund until a year or so ago.

Last winter, said John Wasniewski, Hamilton's next-door neighbor, the basement of the home was flooded and the heater destroyed. "There was no heat in that house last winter or this winter," he said.

An autopsy will be performed on Hamilton today, but she apparently froze to death sometime since Monday, when a friend spoke to her on the telephone, investigators said.

Over the last two years, neighbors said, Hamilton had become increasingly reclusive and irrational. Just last week, a city social worker summoned by a friend arranged for a Philadelphia Gas Works team to visit the home and try to repair the furnace—but she refused to let them in.

The friend was James Phillips, 44, of Horsham, a salesman for Apex Electric in Souderton.

In October 1985, he said, Hamilton visited the Frankford Avenue electrical shop where he was then working, told him that she had an electrical problem in her house and had no lights, and asked whether he could help.

Phillips said he visited the house, fixed the problem and gave her some light bulbs.

"She was really paranoid," Phillips said. "She believed that all her problems were from people doing things to her. For some reason or other, she took to me."

Phillips said that he began visiting her, taking her shopping and doing some shopping for her. But, he said, he never saw the body on the second floor.

Hamilton told him there was a man up there. "I thought it was a story she was telling to protect herself," Phillips said.

He provided her with electric heaters and also contacted a caseworker with the city's Department of Human Services whom Phillips identified as Albert Zbik.

Between the two of them, he said, "we got her through last winter." Phillips said Zbik helped her obtain food stamps and Social Security assistance.

When the snowstorm hit last week, Phillips became concerned because he knew Hamilton would have trouble getting food. On Saturday, he took her a plate of hot food and bought more food from a local store.

On Monday, she telephoned him. "I didn't like the way she sounded," he said. He called Zbik and told him he felt it was time that they forced her to go to a hospital.

Phillips said Zbik went to her home yesterday, carrying a form authorizing an involuntary admission to a hospital for observation or required medical treatment.

Phillips told police that he was never allowed above the first floor and was often told by Hamilton that "Bernie is not feeling well today."

Neighbors and police investigators said Kelly was last seen alive about two years ago, and appeared to be quite ill at the time.

"As recently as last month, I asked Frances how Bernard was and whether she should get a doctor, and she said it wasn't necessary. She said 'He's sick, but I'm taking care of him—I'm feeding him with an eyedropper,'" Wasniewski said.

"I told her in December that if he was that sick, she should call a doctor, but she'd say she was taking care of him very well," Wasniewski said.

CHAPTER 8

CHARACTER

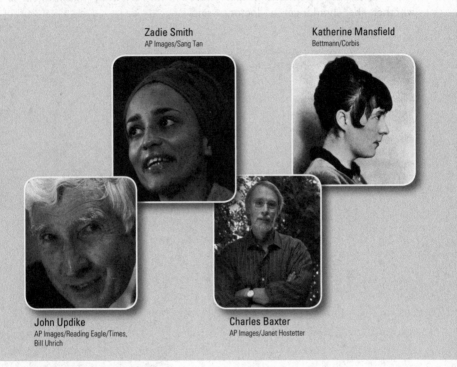

Zadie Smith
AP Images/Sang Tan

Katherine Mansfield
Bettmann/Corbis

John Updike
AP Images/Reading Eagle/Times,
Bill Uhrich

Charles Baxter
AP Images/Janet Hostetter

A **character** is a fictional representation of a person—usually (but not necessarily) a psychologically realistic depiction. Writers may develop characters through their actions, through their reactions to situations or to other characters, through their physical appearance, through their speech and gestures and expressions, and even through their names.

Generally speaking, characters' personality traits, as well as their appearances and their feelings and beliefs, are communicated to readers in two ways. First, readers can be *told* about characters. Third-person narrators can provide information about what characters are doing, saying, and thinking; what experiences they have had; what they look like; how they are dressed;

and so on. Sometimes these narrators also offer analysis of and judgments about a character's behavior or motivation. Similarly, first-person narrators can tell us about themselves or about other characters. Thus, Sammy in John Updike's "A&P" (p. 160) tells readers what he thinks about his job and about the girls who come into the supermarket where he works. He also tells us what various characters look like and describes their actions, attitudes, speech, and gestures. (For more information about first-person narrators, see Chapter 10, "Point of View.")

Alternatively, aspects of a character's personality and beliefs may be revealed through his or her actions, dialogue, or thoughts. For instance, Sammy's vivid fantasies and his disapproval of his customers' lives suggest to readers that he is something of a nonconformist; however, Sammy himself does not actually tell us this.

 ## Round and Flat Characters

In his influential 1927 work *Aspects of the Novel*, English novelist E. M. Forster classifies characters as either **round** (well developed, closely involved in and responsive to the action) or **flat** (barely developed or stereotypical). To a great extent, these categories are still useful today. In an effective story, the major characters are usually complex and fully developed; if they are not, readers will not care what happens to them. Sometimes readers are encouraged to become involved with the characters, even to identify with them, and this empathy is possible only when we know something about the characters—their strengths and weaknesses, their likes and dislikes. In some cases, of course, a story can be effective even when its central characters are not well developed. Sometimes, in fact, a story's effectiveness is enhanced by an *absence* of character development, as in Shirley Jackson's "The Lottery" (p. 335).

Readers often expect characters to behave as "real people" in their situation might behave. Real people are not perfect, and realistic characters cannot be perfect either. The flaws that are revealed as round characters are developed—greed, gullibility, naïveté, shyness, a quick temper, or a lack of insight or judgment or tolerance or even intelligence—make them believable. In modern fiction, the protagonist is seldom if ever the noble "hero"; more often, he or she is at least partly a victim, someone to whom unpleasant things happen and someone who is sometimes ill-equipped to cope with events.

Unlike major characters, minor characters are frequently not well developed. Often they are flat, perhaps acting as *foils* for the protagonist. A **foil** is a supporting character whose role in the story is to highlight a major character by presenting a contrast with him or her. For instance, in "A&P," Stokesie, another young checkout clerk, is a foil for Sammy. Because he is a little older than Sammy and seems to have none of Sammy's imagination, restlessness, or nonconformity, Stokesie suggests what Sammy might become if he were to continue to work at the A&P. Some flat characters are **stock characters**, easily identifiable types who behave so predictably that readers can readily recognize them. The kindly old priest, the tough young bully, the ruthless business executive, and the reckless adventurer are all stock characters. Some flat characters can even be **caricatures**, characterized by a single dominant trait, such as miserliness, or even by one physical trait, such as nearsightedness.

 ## Dynamic and Static Characters

Characters may also be classified as either *dynamic or static*. A **dynamic character** grows and changes in the course of a story, developing as he or she reacts to events and to other characters. In "A&P," for instance, Sammy's decision to speak out in defense of the girls—as well as the events that lead him to do so—changes him. His view of the world has changed at the end of the story, and as a result his position in the world may change too. A **static character** may face the same challenges a dynamic character might face but will remain essentially unchanged: a static character who was selfish and arrogant will remain selfish and arrogant, regardless of the nature of the story's conflict. In the fairy tale "Cinderella," for example, the title character is as sweet and good-natured at the end of the story—despite her mistreatment by her family—as she is at the beginning. Her situation may have changed, but her character has not.

Whereas round characters tend to be dynamic, flat characters tend to be static. But even a very complex, well-developed major character may be static; sometimes, in fact, the point of a story may hinge on a character's inability to change. A familiar example is the title character in William Faulkner's "A Rose for Emily" (p. 143), who lives a wasted, empty life, at least in part because she is unwilling or unable to accept that the world around her and the people in it have changed.

A story's minor characters are often static; their growth is not usually relevant to the story's development. Moreover, we usually do not learn enough about a minor character's traits, thoughts, actions, or motivation to determine whether the character changes significantly.

 ## Motivation

Because round characters are complex, they are not always easy to understand. They may act unpredictably, just as real people do. They wrestle with decisions, resist or succumb to temptation, make mistakes, ask questions, search for answers, hope and dream, rejoice and despair. What is important is not whether we approve of a character's actions but whether those actions are *plausible*—whether the actions make sense in light of what we know about the character. We need to understand a character's **motivation**—the reasons behind his or her behavior—or we will not believe or accept that behavior. In "A&P" for instance, given Sammy's age, his dissatisfaction with his job, and his desire to impress the young woman he calls Queenie, the decision he makes at the end of the story is perfectly plausible. Without having established his motivation, Updike could not have expected readers to accept Sammy's actions.

Of course, even when readers get to know a character, they still are not able to predict how a complex, round character will behave in a given situation; only a flat character is predictable. The tension that develops as readers wait to see how a character will act or react, and thus how a story's conflict will be resolved, is what holds readers' interest and keeps them involved as a story's action unfolds.

✔ **CHECKLIST   Writing about Character**

☐ Who is the story's main character? Who are the other major characters?

☐ Who are the minor characters? What roles do they play in the story? How would the story be different without them?

☐ What do the major characters look like? Is their physical appearance important?

☐ What are the major characters' most notable personality traits?

☐ What are the major characters' likes and dislikes? their strengths and weaknesses?

☐ What are the main character's most strongly held feelings and beliefs?

☐ What are we told about the major characters' backgrounds and prior experiences? What can we infer?

☐ Are the characters round or flat?

☐ Are the characters dynamic or static?

☐ Does the story include any stock characters? Does any character serve as a foil?

☐ Do the characters act in a way that is consistent with how readers expect them to act?

☐ With which characters are readers likely to be most sympathetic? least sympathetic?

JOHN UPDIKE (1932–2009) was a prolific writer of novels, short stories, essays, poems, plays, and children's tales. Updike's earliest ambition was to be a cartoonist for the *New Yorker*. He attended Harvard hoping to draw cartoons for the *Harvard Lampoon*, studied drawing and fine art at Oxford, and in 1955 went to work for the *New Yorker*—not as a cartoonist but as a "Talk of the Town" reporter. Updike left the *New Yorker* after three years to write full time but continued to contribute stories, reviews, and essays to the magazine for over forty years. Among his novels are *Rabbit, Run* (1960), *The Centaur* (1963), *Rabbit Redux* (1971), *Rabbit Is Rich* (1981), *The Witches of Eastwick* (1985), and *Rabbit at Rest* (1990). His last novels are *Seek My Face* (2002), *Villages* (2004), *Of the Farm* (2004), *Terrorist* (2006), and *The Widows of Eastwick* (2008). In 1998, Updike received the National Book Foundation Medal for Distinguished Contribution to American Letters.

In early stories such as "A&P" (1961), Updike draws on memories of his childhood and teenage years for the sort of "small" scenes and stories for which he quickly became famous. "There is a great deal to be said about almost anything," Updike comments in an interview in *Contemporary Authors*. "All people can be equally interesting. . . . Now either nobody is a hero or everybody is. I vote for everybody. My subject is the American Protestant small-town middle class. I like middles. It is in middles that extremes clash."

Cultural Context   The 1950s were a decade of prosperity for the United States. Soldiers returned from World War II, women who had worked in defense plants returned to their homes, and the population soared as a result of a "baby boom." Part of this prosperity manifested itself materially: Americans tried to "keep up with the Joneses" in terms of their possessions, and manufacturers raced to produce the latest consumer goods. Conformity became the norm, with the advent of mass-produced suburban tract houses and a conservative code of dress and behavior that dictated what was appropriate. This atmosphere is the context for the manager's disapproval in "A&P"—and Sammy's reaction foreshadows the mood of the rebellious generation to come.

A&P (1961)

In walks these three girls in nothing but bathing suits. I'm in the third checkout slot, with my back to the door, so I don't see them until they're over by the bread. The one that caught my eye first was the one in the plaid green two-piece. She was a chunky kid, with a good tan and a sweet broad softlooking can with those two crescents of white just under it, where the sun never seems to hit, at the top of the backs of her legs. I stood there with my hand on a box of Hi Ho crackers trying to remember if I rang it up or not. I ring it up again and the customer starts giving me hell. She's one of these cash-register-watchers, a witch about fifty with rouge on her cheekbones and no eyebrows, and I know it made her day to trip me up. She'd been watching cash registers for fifty years and probably never seen a mistake before.

By the time I got her feathers smoothed and her goodies into a bag—she gives me a little snort in passing, if she'd been born at the right time they would have burned her over in Salem—by the time I get her on her way the girls had circled around the bread and were coming back, without a push-cart, back my way along the counters, in the aisle between the check-outs and the Special bins. They didn't even have shoes on. There was this chunky one, with the two-piece—it was bright green and the seams on the bra were still sharp and her belly was still pretty pale so I guessed she just got it (the suit)—there was this one, with one of those chubby berry-faces, the lips all bunched together under her nose, this one, and a tall one, with black hair that hadn't quite frizzed right, and one of these sunburns right across under the eyes, and a chin that was too long—you know, the kind of girl other girls think is very "striking" and "attractive" but never quite makes it, as they very well know, which is why they like her so much—and then the third one, that wasn't quite so tall. She was the queen. She kind of led them, the other two peeking around and making their shoulders round. She didn't look around, not this queen, she just walked straight on slowly, on these long white prima-donna legs. She came down a little hard on her heels, as if she didn't walk in her bare feet that much, putting down her heels and then letting the weight move along to her toes as if she was testing the floor with every step, putting a little deliberate extra action into it. You never know for sure how girls' minds work (do you really think it's a mind in there or just a little buzz like a bee in a glass jar?) but you got the idea she had talked the other two into coming in here with her, and now she was showing them how to do it, walk slow and hold yourself straight.

She had on a kind of dirty-pink—beige maybe, I don't know—bathing suit with a little nubble all over it and, what got me, the straps were down. They were off her shoulders looped loose around the cool tops of her arms, and I guess as a result the suit had slipped a little on her, so all around the top of the cloth there was this shining rim. If it hadn't been there you wouldn't have known there could have been anything whiter than those shoulders. With the straps pushed off, there was nothing between the top of the suit and the top of her head except just *her*, this clean bare plane of the top of her chest down from the shoulder bones like a dented sheet of metal tilted in the light. I mean, it was more than pretty.

She had sort of oaky hair that the sun and salt had bleached, done up in a bun that was unravelling, and a kind of prim face. Walking into the A&P with your straps down, I suppose it's the only kind of face you *can* have. She held her head so high her neck, coming up out of those white shoulders, looked kind of stretched, but I didn't mind. The longer her neck was, the more of her there was.

5   She must have felt in the corner of her eye me and over my shoulder Stokesie in the second slot watching, but she didn't tip. Not this queen. She kept her eyes moving across the racks, and stopped, and turned so slow it made my stomach rub the inside of my apron, and buzzed to the other two, who kind of huddled against her for relief, and they all three of them went up the cat-and-dog-food-breakfast-cereal-macaroni-rice-raisins-seasonings-spreads-spaghetti-soft-drinks-crackers-and-cookies aisle. From the third slot I look straight up this aisle to the meat counter, and I watched them all the way. The fat one with the tan sort of fumbled with the cookies, but on second thought she put the packages back. The sheep pushing their carts down the aisle—the girls were walking against the usual traffic (not that we have one-way signs or anything)—were pretty hilarious. You could see them, when Queenie's white shoulders dawned on them, kind of jerk, or hop, or hiccup, but their eyes snapped back to their own baskets and on they pushed. I bet you could set off dynamite in an A&P and the people would by and large keep reaching and checking oatmeal off their lists and muttering "Let me see, there was a third thing, began with A, asparagus, no, ah, yes, applesauce!" or whatever it is they do mutter. But there was no doubt, this jiggled them. A few houseslaves in pin curlers even looked around after pushing their carts past to make sure what they had seen was correct.

You know, it's one thing to have a girl in a bathing suit down on the beach, where what with the glare nobody can look at each other much anyway, and another thing in the cool of the A&P, under the fluorescent lights, against all those stacked packages, with her feet paddling along naked over our checkerboard green-and-cream rubber-tile floor.

"Oh Daddy," Stokesie said beside me. "I feel so faint."

"Darling," I said. "Hold me tight." Stokesie's married, with two babies chalked up on his fuselage already, but as far as I can tell that's the only difference. He's twenty-two, and I was nineteen this April.

"Is it done?" he asks, the responsible married man finding his voice. I forgot to say he thinks he's going to be manager some sunny day, maybe in 1990 when it's called the Great Alexandrov and Petrooshki Tea Company or something.

10   What he meant was, our town is five miles from a beach, with a big summer colony out on the Point, but we're right in the middle of town, and the women generally put on a shirt or shorts or something before they get out of the car into the street. And anyway these are usually women with six children and varicose veins mapping their legs and nobody, including them, could care less. As I say, we're right in the middle of town, and if you stand at our front doors you can see two banks and the Congregational church and the newspaper store and three real-estate offices and about twenty-seven old freeloaders tearing up Central Street because the sewer

broke again. It's not as if we're on the Cape; we're north of Boston and there's people in this town haven't seen the ocean for twenty years.

The girls had reached the meat counter and were asking McMahon something. He pointed, they pointed, and they shuffled out of sight behind a pyramid of Diet Delight peaches. All that was left for us to see was old McMahon patting his mouth and looking after them sizing up their joints. Poor kids, I began to feel sorry for them, they couldn't help it.

Now here comes the sad part of the story, at least my family says it's sad but I don't think it's sad myself. The store's pretty empty, it being Thursday afternoon, so there was nothing much to do except lean on the register and wait for the girls to show up again. The whole store was like a pinball machine and I didn't know which tunnel they'd come out of. After a while they come around out of the far aisle, around the light bulbs, records at discount of the Caribbean Six or Tony Martin Sings or some such gunk you wonder they waste the wax on, sixpacks of candy bars, and plastic toys done up in cellophane that fall apart when a kid looks at them anyway. Around they come, Queenie still leading the way, and holding a little gray jar in her hand. Slots Three through Seven are unmanned and I could see her wondering between Stokes and me, but Stokesie with his usual luck draws an old party in baggy gray pants who stumbles up with four giant cans of pineapple juice (what do these bums *do* with all that pineapple juice? I've often asked myself) so the girls come to me. Queenie puts down the jar and I take it into my fingers icy cold. Kingfish Fancy Herring Snacks in Pure Sour Cream: 49. Now her hands are empty, not a ring or a bracelet, bare as God made them, and I wonder where the money's coming from. Still with that prim look she lifts a folded dollar bill out of the hollow at the center of her nubbled pink top. The jar went heavy in my hand. Really, I thought that was so cute.

Then everybody's luck begins to run out. Lengel comes in from haggling with a truck full of cabbages on the lot and is about to scuttle into that door marked MANAGER behind which he hides all day when the girls touch his eye. Lengel's pretty dreary, teaches Sunday school and the rest, but he doesn't miss that much. He comes over and says, "Girls, this isn't the beach."

Queenie blushes, though maybe it's just a brush of sunburn I was noticing for the first time, now that she was so close. "My mother asked me to pick up a jar of herring snacks." Her voice kind of startled me, the way voices do when you see the people first, coming out so flat and dumb yet kind of tony, too, the way it ticked over "pick up" and "snacks." All of a sudden I slid right down her voice into her living room. Her father and the other men were standing around in ice-cream coats and bow ties and the women were in sandals picking up herring snacks on toothpicks off a big plate and they were all holding drinks the color of water with olives and sprigs of mint in them.

When my parents have somebody over they get lemonade and if it's a real racy affair Schlitz in tall glasses with "They'll Do It Every Time" cartoons stencilled on.

15   "That's all right," Lengel said. "But this isn't the beach." His repeating this struck me as funny, as if it had just occurred to him, and he had been thinking all these years the A&P was a great big dune and he was the head lifeguard. He didn't like my smiling—as I say he doesn't miss much—but he concentrates on giving the girls that sad Sunday-school-superintendent stare.

Queenie's blush is no sunburn now, and the plump one in plaid, that I liked better from the back—a really sweet can—pipes up, "We weren't doing any shopping. We just came in for the one thing."

"That makes no difference," Lengel tells her, and I could see from the way his eyes went that he hadn't noticed she was wearing a two-piece before. "We want you decently dressed when you come in here."

"We *are* decent," Queenie says suddenly, her lower lip pushing, getting sore now that she remembers her place, a place from which the crowd that runs the A&P must look pretty crummy. Fancy Herring Snacks flashed in her very blue eyes.

"Girls, I don't want to argue with you. After this come in here with your shoulders covered. It's our policy." He turns his back. That's policy for you. Policy is what the kingpins want. What the others want is juvenile delinquency.

20   All this while, the customers had been showing up with their carts but, you know, sheep, seeing a scene, they had all bunched up on Stokesie, who shook open a paper bag as gently as peeling a peach, not wanting to miss a word. I could feel in the silence everybody getting nervous, most of all Lengel, who asks me, "Sammy, have you rung up this purchase?"

I thought and said "No" but it wasn't about that I was thinking. I go through the punches, 4, 9, GROC, TOT—it's more complicated than you think, and after you do it often enough, it begins to make a little song, that you hear words to, in my case "Hello (*bing*) there, you (*gung*) hap-py pee-pul (*splat*)!"—the *splat* being the drawer flying out. I uncrease the bill, tenderly as you may imagine, it just having come from between the two smoothest scoops of vanilla I had ever known were there, and pass a half and a penny into her narrow pink palm, and nestle the herrings in a bag and twist its neck and hand it over, all the time thinking.

The girls, and who'd blame them, are in a hurry to get out, so I say "I quit" to Lengel quick enough for them to hear, hoping they'll stop and watch me, their unsuspected hero. They keep right on going, into the electric eye; the door flies open and they flicker across the lot to their car, Queenie and Plaid and Big Tall Goony-Goony (not that as raw material she was so bad), leaving me with Lengel and a kink in his eyebrow.

"Did you say something, Sammy?"

"I said I quit."

"I thought you did."   25

"You didn't have to embarrass them."

"It was they who were embarrassing us."

I started to say something that came out "Fiddle-de-doo." It's a saying of my grandmother's, and I know she would have been pleased.

"I don't think you know what you're saying," Lengel said.

"I know you don't," I said. "But I do." I pull the bow at the back of my   30
apron and start shrugging it off my shoulders. A couple customers that had been heading for my slot begin to knock against each other, like scared pigs in a chute.

Lengel sighs and begins to look very patient and old and gray. He's been a friend of my parents for years. "Sammy, you don't want to do this to your Mom and Dad," he tells me. It's true, I don't. But it seems to me that once you begin a gesture it's fatal not to go through with it. I fold the apron, "Sammy" stitched in red on the pocket, and put it on the counter, and drop the bow tie on top of it. The bow tie is theirs, if you've ever wondered. "You'll feel this for the rest of your life," Lengel says, and I know that's true, too, but remembering how he made that pretty girl blush makes me so scrunchy inside I punch the No Sale tab and the machine whirs "pee-pul" and the drawer splats out. One advantage to this scene taking place in summer, I can follow this up with a clean exit, there's no fumbling around getting your coat and galoshes, I just saunter into the electric eye in my white shirt that my mother ironed the night before, and the door heaves itself open, and outside the sunshine is skating around the asphalt.

I look around for my girls, but they're gone, of course. There wasn't anybody but some young married screaming with her children about some candy they didn't get by the door of a powder-blue Falcon station wagon. Looking back in the big windows, over the bags of peat moss and aluminum lawn furniture stacked on the pavement, I could see Lengel in my place in the slot, checking the sheep through. His face was dark gray and his back stiff, as if he'd just had an injection of iron, and my stomach kind of fell as I felt how hard the world was going to be to me hereafter.

Reading and Reacting

1. Summarize the information Sammy gives readers about his tastes and background. Why is this exposition vital to the story's development?

2. List some of the most obvious physical characteristics of the A&P's customers. How do these characteristics make them foils for Queenie and her friends?

3. What is it about Queenie and her friends that appeals to Sammy?

4. Is Queenie a stock character? Explain.

5. What rules and conventions are customers expected to follow in a supermarket? How does the behavior of Queenie and her friends violate these rules?

6. Is the supermarket setting vital to the story? Could the story have been set in a car wash? in a fast-food restaurant? in a business office?

7. How accurate are Sammy's judgments about the other characters? How might the characters be portrayed if the story were told by Lengel?

8. Given what you learn about Sammy during the course of the story, what do you see as his *primary* motivation for quitting his job? What other factors motivate him?

9. JOURNAL ENTRY Where do you think Sammy will find himself in ten years? Why?

10. CRITICAL PERSPECTIVE In her 1976 book *The Necessary Blackness*, critic Mary Allen observes, "Updike's most tender reverence is reserved for women's bodies. The elegant style with which he describes female anatomy often becomes overwrought, as his descriptions do generally. But it always conveys wonder."

In what passages in "A&P" does Updike (through Sammy) convey this sense of wonder? Do you think today's audience, reading the story more than fifty years after Updike wrote it, and more than thirty years after Allen's essay was published, would still see such passages as conveying "tender reverence"? Or do you think readers might now see Sammy (and, indeed, Updike) as sexist? How do you react to these passages?

Related Works: "How to Talk to Girls at Parties" (p. 131), "New York Day Women" (p. 273), "Araby" (p. 288), "A Supermarket in California" (p. 605), "The Road Not Taken" (p. 624), "Short-Order Cook" (p. 751)

KATHERINE MANSFIELD (1888–1923), one of the pioneers of the modern short story, was born in New Zealand and educated in England. Very much a "modern young woman," she began living on her own in London at the age of nineteen, soon publishing stories and book reviews in many of the most influential literary magazines of the day.

A short story writer of great versatility, Mansfield produced sparkling social comedies as well as more intellectually and technically complex works intended for "perceptive readers." According to one critic, her best works "[w]ith delicate plainness . . . present elusive moments of decision, defeat, and small triumph." Her last two story collections—*Bliss and Other Stories* (1920) and *The Garden Party and Other Stories*

(1922)—were met with immediate critical acclaim, but Mansfield's career was cut short in 1923 when she died of complications from tuberculosis at the age of thirty-five.

One notable theme in Mansfield's work is the *dame seule*, the "woman alone," which provides the basis for the poignant "Miss Brill."

Cultural Context During the nineteenth century, the task of spinning wool was typically given to unmarried women as a way for them to earn their keep in the home. Thus, the term *spinster* came into existence. Over time, the word acquired a negative stereotype, conjuring up the image of a lonely, childless, frumpy middle-aged woman who longs to be like other "normal" women—wives and mothers. Today, the word *spinster* is rarely used, reflecting the changed perception of unmarried women and the wider lifestyle choices open to them.

Miss Brill (1922)

Although it was so brilliantly fine—the blue sky powdered with gold and great spots of light like white wine splashed over the Jardins Publiques[1]— Miss Brill was glad that she had decided on her fur. The air was motionless, but when you opened your mouth there was just a faint chill, like a chill from a glass of iced water before you sip, and now and again a leaf came drifting—from nowhere, from the sky. Miss Brill put up her hand and touched her fur. Dear little thing! It was nice to feel it again. She had taken it out of its box that afternoon, shaken out the moth-powder, given it a good brush, and rubbed the life back into the dim little eyes. "What has been happening to me?" said the sad little eyes. Oh, how sweet it was to see them snap at her again from the red eiderdown! . . . But the nose, which was of some black composition, wasn't at all firm. It must have had a knock, somehow. Never mind—a little dab of black sealing-wax when the time came—when it was absolutely necessary. . . . Little rogue! Yes, she really felt like that about it. Little rogue biting its tail just by her left ear. She could have taken it off and laid it on her lap and stroked it. She felt a tingling in her hands and arms, but that came from walking, she supposed. And when she breathed, something light and sad—no, not sad, exactly—something gentle seemed to move in her bosom.

There were a number of people out this afternoon, far more than last Sunday. And the band sounded louder and gayer. That was because the Season had begun. For although the band played all year round on Sundays, out of season it was never the same. It was like some one playing with only the family to listen; it didn't care how it played if there weren't any strangers present. Wasn't the conductor wearing a new coat, too? She

---

[1] *Jardins Publiques:* "Public Gardens" (French).

was sure it was new. He scraped with his foot and flapped his arms like a rooster about to crow, and the bandsmen sitting in the green rotunda blew out their cheeks and glared at the music. Now there came a little "flutey" bit—very pretty!—a little chain of bright drops. She was sure it would be repeated. It was; she lifted her head and smiled.

Only two people shared her "special" seat: a fine old man in a velvet coat, his hands clasped over a huge carved walking-stick, and a big old woman, sitting upright, with a roll of knitting on her embroidered apron. They did not speak. This was disappointing, for Miss Brill always looked forward to the conversation. She had become really quite expert, she thought, at listening as though she didn't listen, at sitting in other people's lives just for a minute while they talked round her.

She glanced, sideways, at the old couple. Perhaps they would go soon. Last Sunday, too, hadn't been as interesting as usual. An Englishman and his wife, he wearing a dreadful Panama hat and she button boots. And she'd gone on the whole time about how she ought to wear spectacles; she knew she needed them; but that it was no good getting any; they'd be sure to break and they'd never keep on. And he'd been so patient. He'd suggested everything—gold rims, the kind that curved round your ears, little pads inside the bridge. No, nothing would please her. "They'll always be sliding down my nose!" Miss Brill wanted to shake her.

5   The old people sat on the bench, still as statues. Never mind, there was always the crowd to watch. To and fro, in front of the flower-beds and the band rotunda, the couples and groups paraded, stopped to talk, to greet, to buy a handful of flowers from the old beggar who had his tray fixed to the railings. Little children ran among them, swooping and laughing; little boys with big white silk bows under their chins, little girls, little French dolls, dressed up in velvet and lace. And sometimes a tiny staggerer came suddenly rocking into the open from under the trees, stopped, stared, as suddenly sat down "flop," until its small high-stepping mother, like a young hen, rushed scolding to its rescue. Other people sat on the benches and green chairs, but they were nearly always the same, Sunday after Sunday, and—Miss Brill had often noticed—there was something funny about nearly all of them. They were odd, silent, nearly all old, and from the way they stared they looked as though they'd just come from dark little rooms or even—even cupboards!

Behind the rotunda the slender trees with yellow leaves down drooping, and through them just a line of sea, and beyond the blue sky with gold-veined clouds.

Tum-tum-tum tiddle-um! tiddle-um! tum tiddley-um tum ta! blew the band.

Two young girls in red came by and two young soldiers in blue met them, and they laughed and paired and went off arm-in-arm. Two peasant women with funny straw hats passed, gravely, leading beautiful smoke-colored donkeys. A cold, pale nun hurried by. A beautiful woman came along and dropped her bunch of violets, and a little boy ran after to hand them to her, and she took them and threw them away as if they'd been poisoned. Dear me! Miss Brill didn't know whether to admire that or not! And now an ermine toque[2] and a gentleman in grey met just in front of her. He was tall, stiff, dignified, and she was wearing the ermine toque she'd bought when her hair was yellow. Now everything, her hair, her face, even her eyes, was the same color as the shabby ermine, and her hand, in its cleaned glove, lifted to dab her lips, was a tiny yellowish paw. Oh, she was so pleased to see him—delighted! She rather thought they were going to meet that afternoon. She described where she'd been—everywhere, here, there, along by the sea. The day was so charming—didn't he agree? And wouldn't he, perhaps? . . . But he shook his head, lighted a cigarette, slowly breathed a great deep puff into her face, and, even while she was still talking and laughing, flicked the match away and walked on. The ermine toque was alone; she smiled more brightly than ever. But even the band seemed to know what she was feeling and played more softly, played tenderly, and the drum beat, "The Brute! The Brute!" over and over. What would she do? What was going to happen now? But as Miss Brill wondered, the ermine toque turned, raised her hand as though she'd seen some one else, much nicer, just over there, and pattered away. And the band changed again and played more quickly, more gaily than ever, and the old couple on Miss Brill's seat got up and marched away, and such a funny old man with long whiskers hobbled along in time to the music and was nearly knocked over by four girls walking abreast.

Oh, how fascinating it was! How she enjoyed it! How she loved sitting here, watching it all! It was like a play. It was exactly like a play. Who could believe the sky at the back wasn't painted? But it wasn't till a little brown dog trotted on solemn and then slowly trotted off, like a little "theatre" dog, a little dog that had been drugged, that Miss Brill discovered what it was that made it so exciting. They were all on the stage. They weren't only the audience, not only looking on; they were acting. Even she had a part and came every Sunday. No doubt somebody would have noticed if she hadn't been there; she was part of the performance after all. How strange she'd never thought of it like that before! And yet it explained why she made such a point of starting from home at just the same time each week—so as not to be late for the performance—and it also explained why she had quite a queer, shy feeling at telling her English pupils how she spent her Sunday afternoons. No wonder! Miss Brill nearly

---

[2] *ermine toque:* Small, close-fitting woman's hat made from the fur of an ermine, a type of weasel.

laughed out loud. She was on the stage. She thought of the old invalid gentleman to whom she read the newspaper four afternoons a week while he slept in the garden. She had got quite used to the frail head on the cotton pillow, the hollowed eyes, the open mouth and the high pinched nose. If he'd been dead she mightn't have noticed for weeks; she wouldn't have minded. But suddenly he knew he was having the paper read to him by an actress! "An actress!" The old head lifted; two points of light quivered in the old eyes. "An actress—are ye?" And Miss Brill smoothed the newspaper as though it were the manuscript of her part and said gently: "Yes, I have been an actress for a long time."

10   The band had been having a rest. Now they started again. And what they played was warm, sunny, yet there was just a faint chill—a something, what was it?—not sadness—no, not sadness—a something that made you want to sing. The tune lifted, lifted, the light shone; and it seemed to Miss Brill that in another moment all of them, all the whole company, would begin singing. The young ones, the laughing ones who were moving together, they would begin, and the men's voices, very resolute and brave, would join them. And then she too, she too, and the others on the benches—they would come in with a kind of accompaniment—something low, that scarcely rose or fell, something so beautiful—moving.... And Miss Brill's eyes filled with tears and she looked smiling at all the other members of the company. Yes, we understand, we understand, she thought—though what they understood she didn't know.

Just at that moment a boy and a girl came and sat down where the old couple had been. They were beautifully dressed; they were in love. The hero and heroine, of course, just arrived from his father's yacht. And still soundlessly singing, still with that trembling smile, Miss Brill prepared to listen.

"No, not now," said the girl. "Not here, I can't."

"But why? Because of that stupid old thing at the end there?" asked the boy. "Why does she come here at all—who wants her? Why doesn't she keep her silly old mug at home?"

"It's her fu-fur which is so funny," giggled the girl. "It's exactly like a fried whiting."[3]

15   "Ah, be off with you!" said the boy in an angry whisper. Then: "Tell me, my petite chérie—"[4]

"No, not here," said the girl. "Not yet."

On her way home she usually bought a slice of honeycake at the baker's. It was her Sunday treat. Sometimes there was an almond in her slice,

---

[3]*whiting:* Food fish related to the cod.

[4]*petite chérie:* "Little darling" (French).

sometimes not. It made a great difference. If there was an almond it was like carrying home a tiny present—a surprise—something that might very well not have been there. She hurried on the almond Sundays and struck the match for the kettle in quite a dashing way.

But to-day she passed the baker's by, climbed the stairs, went into the little dark room—her room like a cupboard—and sat down on the red eiderdown. She sat there for a long time. The box that the fur came out of was on the bed. She unclasped the necklet quickly; quickly, without looking, laid it inside. But when she put the lid on she thought she heard something crying.

Reading and Reacting

1. What specific details can you infer about Miss Brill's character (and, perhaps, about her life) from this statement: "She had become really quite expert, she thought, at listening as though she didn't listen, at sitting in other people's lives just for a minute while they talked round her" (par. 3)?

2. How do Miss Brill's observations of the people around her give us insight into her own character? Why do you suppose she doesn't interact with any of the people she observes?

3. In paragraph 9, Miss Brill realizes that the scene she observes is "exactly like a play" and that "Even she had a part and came every Sunday." What part does Miss Brill play? Is she a stock character in this play, or is she a three-dimensional character? Does she play a lead role or a supporting role?

4. What do you think Miss Brill means when she says, "I have been an actress for a long time" (par. 9)? What does this comment reveal about how she sees herself? Is her view of herself similar to or different from the view the other characters have of her?

5. What role does Miss Brill's fur piece play in the story? In what sense, if any, does it function as a character?

6. What happens in paragraphs 11–16 to break Miss Brill's mood? Why is the scene she observes so upsetting to her?

7. At the end of the story, has Miss Brill changed as a result of what she has overheard, or is she the same person she was at the beginning? Do you think she will return to the park the following Sunday?

8. The story's last paragraph describes Miss Brill's room as being "like a cupboard." Where else has this image appeared in the story? What does its reappearance in the conclusion tell us?

9. **JOURNAL ENTRY** Write a character sketch of Miss Brill, inventing a plausible family and personal history that might help to explain the character you see in the story.

10. CRITICAL PERSPECTIVE Critic Gillian Boddy, in *Katherine Mansfield: The Woman, The Writer*, offers the following analysis of Mansfield's fiction:

> The story evolves through the characters' minds. The external narrator is almost eliminated. As so often in her work, the reader is dropped into the story and simply confronted by a particular situation. There is no preliminary establishing and identification of time and place. The reader is immediately involved; it is assumed that he or she has any necessary prerequisite knowledge and is, in a sense, part of the story too.

Do you see this absence of conventional exposition as a problem in "Miss Brill"? Do you think the story would be more effective if Mansfield had supplied more preliminary information about setting and character? Or do you believe that what Boddy calls Mansfield's "concentration on a moment or episode" is a satisfactory substitute for the missing exposition, effectively shifting interest from "*what* happens" to "*why* it happens"?

Related Works: "Rooming houses are old women" (p. 579), "Aunt Jennifer's Tigers" (p. 617), *Trifles* (p. 867)

Source: © AP Photo/Janet Hostetter

CHARLES BAXTER (1947–   ) was born in Minneapolis and educated at Macalester College and at the State University of New York, Buffalo. Currently teaching in the creative writing program at the University of Minnesota, Baxter is the author of six critically praised collections of short stories: *Harmony of the World* (1984), *Through the Safety Net* (1985), *A Relative Stranger: Stories* (1990), *Believers: A Novella and Stories* (1997), *Gryphon: New and Selected Stories* (2011), and *There's Something I Want You to Do* (2014). He is also the author of five novels, *First Light* (1987), *Shadow Play* (1993), *The Feast of Love* (2002), *Saul and Patsy* (2003), and *The Soul Thief* (2008), and one book of poetry, *Imaginary Paintings and Other Poems* (1989). Baxter has also written *Burning Down the House* (1997), a collection of essays on fiction.

Baxter's critics often mention the compassion he shows in writing about his fictional characters: a couple who lose their child, a hospital worker who wants to be famous, a tired businessman who really wants to paint. In many of his short stories in *Through the Safety Net* (in which "Gryphon" appeared), unexpected events jar Baxter's characters out of their routines, forcing them to consider different choices, to call on inner strength, or to swim against the tide of "middle America's" conventions.

Cultural Context One of the key elements of this story is a character's use of a deck of tarot cards to predict the future. Originating more than 500 years ago in northern Italy in a game called "Triumphs," the Tarot was quickly adopted as a tool for divining the future. With deep roots in the symbolism of medieval and Renaissance Europe, the Tarot is today the singular most popular tool for spiritual introspection and prophesy. While the death card in particular is often feared, many interpreters argue that it hardly ever points to literal death but rather symbolizes the ending of something significant and the beginning of something new. In "Gryphon," the accuracy of the Tarot's prediction is less important than the young students' reactions to it.

Gryphon (1985)

On Wednesday afternoon, between the geography lesson on ancient Egypt's hand-operated irrigation system and an art project that involved drawing a model city next to a mountain, our fourth-grade teacher, Mr. Hibler, developed a cough. This cough began with a series of muffled throat clearings and progressed to propulsive noises contained within Mr. Hibler's closed mouth. "Listen to him," Carol Peterson whispered to me. "He's gonna blow up." Mr. Hibler's laughter—dazed and infrequent—sounded a bit like his cough, but as we worked on our model cities we would look up, thinking he was enjoying a joke, and see Mr. Hibler's face turning red, his cheeks puffed out. This was not laughter. Twice he bent over, and his loose tie, like a plumb line, hung down straight from his neck as he exploded himself into a Kleenex. He would excuse himself, then go on coughing. "I'll bet you a dime," Carol Peterson whispered, "we get a substitute tomorrow."

Carol sat at the desk in front of mine and was a bad person—when she thought no one was looking she would blow her nose on notebook paper, then crumble it up and throw it into the wastebasket—but at times of crisis she spoke the truth. I knew I'd lose the dime.

"No deal," I said.

When Mr. Hibler stood us up in formation at the door just prior to the final bell, he was almost incapable of speech. "I'm sorry, boys and girls," he said. "I seem to be coming down with something."

"I hope you feel better tomorrow, Mr. Hibler," Bobby Kryzanowicz, the   5 faultless brown-noser said, and I heard Carol Peterson's evil giggle. Then Mr. Hibler opened the door and we walked out to the buses, a clique of us starting noisily to hawk and cough as soon as we thought we were a few feet beyond Mr. Hibler's earshot.

Five Oaks being a rural community, and in Michigan, the supply of substitute teachers was limited to the town's unemployed community college graduates, a pool of about four mothers. These ladies fluttered, provided easeful class days, and nervously covered material we had mastered weeks earlier. Therefore it was a surprise when a woman we had never seen came into the class the next day, carrying a purple purse, a checkerboard lunchbox, and a few books. She put the books on one side of Mr. Hibler's desk and the lunchbox on the other, next to the Voice of Music phonograph. Three of us in the back of the room were playing with Heever, the chameleon that lived in the terrarium and on one of the plastic drapes, when she walked in.

She clapped her hands at us. "Little boys," she said, "why are you bent over together like that?" She didn't wait for us to answer. "Are you tormenting an animal? Put it back. Please sit down at your desks. I want no cabals this time of the day." We just stared at her. "Boys," she repeated, "I asked you to sit down."

I put the chameleon in his terrarium and felt my way to my desk, never taking my eyes off the woman. With white and green chalk, she had started to draw a tree on the left side of the blackboard. She didn't look usual. Furthermore, her tree was outsized, disproportionate, for some reason.

"This room needs a tree," she said, with one line drawing the suggestion of a leaf. "A large, leafy, shady, deciduous . . . oak."

10   Her fine, light hair had been done up in what I would learn years later was called a chignon, and she wore gold-rimmed glasses whose lenses seemed to have the faintest blue tint. Harold Knardahl, who sat across from me, whispered "Mars," and I nodded slowly, savoring the imminent weirdness of the day. The substitute drew another branch with an extravagant arm gesture, then turned around and said, "Good morning. I don't believe I said good morning to all of you yet."

Facing us, she was no special age—an adult is an adult—but her face had two prominent lines, descending vertically from the sides of her mouth to her chin. I knew where I had seen those lines before: *Pinocchio*. They were marionette lines. "You may stare at me," she said to us, as a few more kids from the last bus came into the room, their eyes fixed on her, "for a few more seconds, until the bell rings. Then I will permit no more staring. Looking I will permit. Staring, no. It is impolite to stare, and a sign of bad breeding. You cannot make a social effort while staring."

Harold Knardahl did not glance at me, or nudge, but I heard him whisper "Mars" again, trying to get more mileage out of his single joke with the kids who had just come in.

When everyone was seated, the substitute teacher finished her tree, put down her chalk fastidiously on the phonograph, brushed her hands, and faced us. "Good morning," she said. "I am Miss Ferenczi, your teacher for the day. I am fairly new to your community, and I don't believe any of you know me. I will therefore start by telling you a story about myself."

While we settled back, she launched into her tale. She said her grandfather had been a Hungarian prince; her mother had been born in some place called Flanders, had been a pianist, and had played concerts for people Miss Ferenczi referred to as "crowned heads." She gave us a knowing look. "Grieg," she said, "the Norwegian master, wrote a concerto for piano that was," she paused, "my mother's triumph at her debut concert in London." Her eyes searched the ceiling. Our eyes followed. Nothing up there but ceiling tile. "For reasons that I shall not go into, my family's fortunes took us to Detroit, then north to dreadful Saginaw, and now here I am in Five Oaks, as your substitute teacher, for today, Thursday, October the eleventh. I believe it will be a good day: All the forecasts coincide. We shall start with your reading lesson. Take out your reading book. I believe it is called *Broad Horizons*, or something along those lines."

Jeannie Vermeesch raised her hand. Miss Ferenczi nodded at her.   15 "Mr. Hibler always starts the day with the Pledge of Allegiance," Jeannie whined.

"Oh, does he? In that case," Miss Ferenczi said, "you must know it *very* well by now, and we certainly need not spend our time on it. No, no allegiance pledging on the premises today, by my reckoning. Not with so much sunlight coming into the room. A pledge does not suit my mood." She glanced at her watch. "Time *is* flying. Take out *Broad Horizons*."

She disappointed us by giving us an ordinary lesson, complete with vocabulary word drills, comprehension questions, and recitation. She didn't seem to care for the material, however. She sighed every few minutes and rubbed her glasses with a frilly perfumed handkerchief that she withdrew, magician style, from her left sleeve.

After reading we moved on to arithmetic. It was my favorite time of the morning, when the lazy autumn sunlight dazzled its way through ribbons of clouds past the windows on the east side of the classroom, and crept across the linoleum floor. On the playground the first group of children, the kindergartners, were running on the quack grass just beyond the monkey bars. We were doing multiplication tables. Miss Ferenczi had made John Wazny stand up at his desk in the front row. He was supposed to go through the tables of six. From where I was sitting, I could smell the Vitalis soaked into John's plastered hair. He was doing fine until he came to six times eleven and six times twelve. "Six times eleven," he said, "is sixty-eight. Six times twelve is . . ." He put his fingers to his head, quickly and secretly sniffed his fingertips, and said, "seventy-two." Then he sat down.

"Fine," Miss Ferenczi said. "Well now. That was very good."

"Miss Ferenczi!" One of the Eddy twins was waving her hand desper-   20 ately in the air. "Miss Ferenczi! Miss Ferenczi!"

"Yes?"

"John said that six times eleven is sixty-eight and you said he was right!"

"*Did* I?" She gazed at the class with a jolly look breaking across her marionette's face. "Did I say that? Well, what *is* six times eleven?"

"It's sixty-six!"

She nodded. "Yes. So it is. But, and I know some people will not   25 entirely agree with me, at some times it is sixty-eight."

"When? When is it sixty-eight?"

We were all waiting.

"In higher mathematics, which you children do not yet understand, six times eleven can be considered to be sixty-eight." She laughed through her nose. "In higher mathematics numbers are . . . more fluid. The only thing a number does is contain a certain amount of something. Think of water. A cup is not the only way to measure a certain amount of water, is it?" We were staring, shaking our heads. "You could use saucepans or thimbles. In either case, the water *would be the same*. Perhaps," she started again, "it would be better for you to think that six times eleven is sixty-eight only when I am in the room."

"Why is it sixty-eight," Mark Poole asked, "when you're in the room?"

30 "Because it's more interesting that way," she said, smiling very rapidly behind her blue-tinted glasses. "Besides, I'm your substitute teacher, am I not?" We all nodded. "Well, then, think of six times eleven equals sixty-eight as a substitute fact."

"A substitute fact?"

"Yes." Then she looked at us carefully. "Do you think," she asked, "that anyone is going to be hurt by a substitute fact?"

We looked back at her.

"Will the plants on the windowsill be hurt?" We glanced at them. There were sensitive plants thriving in a green plastic tray, and several wilted ferns in small clay pots. "Your dogs and cats, or your moms and dads?" She waited. "So," she concluded, "what's the problem?"

35 "But it's wrong," Janice Weber said, "isn't it?"

"What's your name, young lady?"

"Janice Weber."

"And you think it's wrong, Janice?"

"I was just asking."

40 "Well, all right. You were just asking. I think we've spent enough time on this matter by now, don't you, class? You are free to think what you like. When your teacher, Mr. Hibler, returns, six times eleven will be sixty-six again, you can rest assured. And it will be that for the rest of your lives in Five Oaks. Too bad, eh?" She raised her eyebrows and glinted herself at us. "But for now, it wasn't. So much for that. Let us go to your assigned problems for today, as painstakingly outlined, I see, in Mr. Hibler's lesson plan. Take out a sheet of paper and write your names in the upper left-hand corner."

For the next half hour we did the rest of our arithmetic problems. We handed them in and went on to spelling, my worst subject. Spelling always came before lunch. We were taking spelling dictation and looking at the clock. "Thorough," Miss Ferenczi said. "Boundary." She walked in the aisles between the desks, holding the spelling book open and looking down at our papers. "Balcony." I clutched my pencil. Somehow, the way she said those words, they seemed foreign, Hungarian, mis-voweled and mis-consonanted. I stared down at what I had spelled. *Balconie.* I turned my pencil upside down and erased my mistake. *Balconey.* That looked better, but still incorrect. I cursed the world of spelling and tried erasing it again and saw the paper beginning to wear away. *Balkony*. Suddenly I felt a hand on my shoulder.

"I don't like that word either," Miss Ferenczi whispered, bent over, her mouth near my ear. "It's ugly. My feeling is, if you don't like a word, you don't have to use it." She straightened up, leaving behind a slight odor of Clorets.

At lunchtime we went out to get our trays of sloppy joes, peaches in heavy syrup, coconut cookies, and milk, and brought them back to the classroom, where Miss Ferenczi was sitting at the desk, eating a brown sticky thing she had unwrapped from tightly rubber-banded wax paper. "Miss Ferenczi," I said, raising my hand. "You don't have to eat with us. You can eat with the other teachers. There's a teachers' lounge," I ended up, "next to the principal's office."

"No, thank you," she said. "I prefer it here."

"We've got a room monitor," I said. "Mrs. Eddy." I pointed to where 45 Mrs. Eddy, Joyce and Judy's mother, sat silently at the back of the room, doing her knitting.

"That's fine," Miss Ferenczi said. "But I shall continue to eat here, with you children. I prefer it," she repeated.

"How come?" Wayne Razmer asked without raising his hand.

"I talked with the other teachers before class this morning," Miss Ferenczi said, biting into her brown food. "There was a great rattling of the words for the fewness of ideas. I didn't care for their brand of hilarity. I don't like ditto machine jokes."

"Oh," Wayne said.

"What's that you're eating?" Maxine Sylvester asked, twitching her 50 nose. "Is it food?"

"It most certainly *is* food. It's a stuffed fig. I had to drive almost down to Detroit to get it. I also bought some smoked sturgeon. And this," she said, lifting some green leaves out of her lunchbox, "is raw spinach, cleaned this morning before I came out here to the Garfield-Murry school."

"Why're you eating raw spinach?" Maxine asked.

"It's good for you," Miss Ferenczi said. "More stimulating than soda pop or smelling salts." I bit into my sloppy joe and stared blankly out the window. An almost invisible moon was faintly silvered in the daytime autumn sky. "As far as food is concerned," Miss Ferenczi was saying, "you have to shuffle the pack. Mix it up. Too many people eat . . . well, never mind."

"Miss Ferenczi," Carol Peterson said, "what are we going to do this afternoon?"

"Well," she said, looking down at Mr. Hibler's lesson plan, "I see that 55 your teacher, Mr. Hibler, has you scheduled for a unit on the Egyptians."

Carol groaned. "Yessss," Miss Ferenczi continued, "that is what we will do: the Egyptians. A remarkable people. Almost as remarkable as the Americans. But not quite." She lowered her head, did her quick smile, and went back to eating her spinach.

After noon recess we came back into the classroom and saw that Miss Ferenczi had drawn a pyramid on the blackboard, close to her oak tree. Some of us who had been playing baseball were messing around in the back of the room, dropping the bats and the gloves into the playground box, and I think that Ray Schontzeler had just slugged me when I heard Miss Ferenczi's high-pitched voice quavering with emotion. "Boys," she said, "come to order right this minute and take your seats. I do not wish to waste a minute of class time. Take out your geography books." We trudged to our desks and, still sweating, pulled out *Distant Lands and Their People.* "Turn to page forty-two." She waited for thirty seconds, then looked over at Kelly Munger. "Young man," she said, "why are you still fossicking in your desk?"

Kelly looked as if his foot had been stepped on. "Why am I what?"

"Why are you . . . burrowing in your desk like that?"

"I'm lookin' for the book, Miss Ferenczi."

60   Bobby Kryzanowicz, the faultless brown-noser who sat in the first row by choice, softly said, "His name is Kelly Munger. He can't ever find his stuff. He always does that."

"I don't care what his name is, especially after lunch," Miss Ferenczi said. "*Where is your book?*"

"I just found it." Kelly was peering into his desk and with both hands pulled at the book, shoveling along in front of it several pencils and crayons, which fell into his lap and then to the floor.

"I hate a mess," Miss Ferenczi said. "I hate a mess in a desk or a mind. It's . . . unsanitary. You wouldn't want your house at home to look like your desk at school, now, would you?" She didn't wait for an answer. "I should think not. A house at home should be as neat as human hands can make it. What were we talking about? Egypt. Page forty-two. I note from Mr. Hibler's lesson plan that you have been discussing the modes of Egyptian irrigation. Interesting, in my view, but not so interesting as what we are about to cover. The pyramids and Egyptian slave labor. A plus on one side, a minus on the other." We had our books open to page forty-two, where there was a picture of a pyramid, but Miss Ferenczi wasn't looking at the book. Instead, she was staring at some object just outside the window.

"Pyramids," Miss Ferenczi said, still looking past the window. "I want you to think about the pyramids. And what was inside. The bodies of the pharaohs, of course, and their attendant treasures. Scrolls. Perhaps," Miss Ferenczi said, with something gleeful but unsmiling in her face, "these scrolls were novels for the pharaohs, helping them to pass the time in their long voyage through the centuries. But then, I am joking." I was looking at the lines on Miss Ferenczi's face. "Pyramids," Miss Ferenczi went on, "were the repositories of special cosmic powers. The nature of a pyramid is to guide cosmic energy forces into a concentrated point. The Egyptians knew that; we have generally forgotten it. Did you know," she asked, walking to the side of the room so that she was standing by the coat closet, "that George Washington had Egyptian blood, from his grand-mother? Certain features of the Constitution of the United States are notable for their Egyptian ideas."

Without glancing down at the book, she began to talk about the movement of souls in Egyptian religion. She said that when people die, their souls return to Earth in the form of carpenter ants or walnut trees, depending on how they behaved—"well or ill"—in life. She said that the Egyptians believed that people act the way they do because of magnetism produced by tidal forces in the solar system, forces produced by the sun and by its "planetary ally," Jupiter. Jupiter, she said, was a planet, as we had been told, but had "certain properties of stars." She was speaking very fast. She said that the Egyptians were great explorers and conquerors. She said that the greatest of all the conquerors, Genghis Khan, had had forty horses and forty young women killed on the site of his grave. We listened. No one tried to stop her. "I myself have been in Egypt," she said, "and have witnessed much dust and many brutalities." She said that an old man in Egypt who worked for a circus had personally shown her an animal in a cage, a monster, half bird and half lion. She said that this monster was called a gryphon and that she had heard about them but never seen them until she traveled to the outskirts of Cairo. She said that Egyptian astronomers had discovered the planet Saturn, but had not seen its rings. She said that the Egyptians were the first to discover that dogs, when they are ill, will not drink from rivers, but wait for rain, and hold their jaws open to catch it.

*   *   *

"She lies."

We were on the school bus home. I was sitting next to Carl Whiteside, who had bad breath and a huge collection of marbles. We were arguing. Carl thought she was lying. I said she wasn't, probably.

"I didn't believe that stuff about the bird," Carl said, "and what she told us about the pyramids? I didn't believe that either. She didn't know what she was talking about."

"Oh yeah?" I had liked her. She was strange. I thought I could nail him. "If she was lying," I said, "what'd she say that was a lie?"

70   "Six times eleven isn't sixty-eight. It isn't ever. It's sixty-six, I know for a fact."

"She said so. She admitted it. What else did she lie about?"

"I don't know," he said. "Stuff."

"What stuff?"

"Well." He swung his legs back and forth. "You ever see an animal that was half lion and half bird?" He crossed his arms. "It sounded real fakey to me."

75   "It could happen," I said. I had to improvise, to outrage him. "I read in this newspaper my mom bought in the IGA about this scientist, this mad scientist in the Swiss Alps, and he's been putting genes and chromosomes and stuff together in test tubes, and he combined a human being and a hamster." I waited, for effect. "It's called a humster."

"You never." Carl was staring at me, his mouth open, his terrible bad breath making its way toward me. "What newspaper was it?"

"The *National Enquirer*," I said, "that they sell next to the cash registers." When I saw his look of recognition, I knew I had bested him. "And this mad scientist," I said, "his name was, um, Dr. Frankenbush." I realized belatedly that this name was a mistake and waited for Carl to notice its resemblance to the name of the other famous mad master of permutations, but he only sat there.

"A man and a hamster?" He was staring at me, squinting, his mouth opening in distaste. "Jeez. What'd it look like?"

When the bus reached my stop, I took off down our dirt road and ran up through the back yard, kicking the tire swing for good luck. I dropped my books on the back steps so I could hug and kiss our dog, Mr. Selby. Then I hurried inside. I could smell Brussels sprouts cooking, my unfavorite vegetable. My mother was washing other vegetables in the kitchen sink, and my baby brother was hollering in his yellow playpen on the kitchen floor.

80   "Hi, Mom," I said, hopping around the playpen to kiss her, "Guess what?"

"I have no idea."

"We had this substitute today, Miss Ferenczi, and I'd never seen her before, and she had all these stories and ideas and stuff."

"Well. That's good." My mother looked out the window behind the sink, her eyes on the pine woods west of our house. Her face and hairstyle always reminded other people of Betty Crocker, whose picture was framed inside a gigantic spoon on the side of the Bisquick box; to me, though, my mother's face just looked white. "Listen, Tommy," she said, "go upstairs and pick your clothes off the bathroom floor, then go outside to the shed and put the shovel and ax away that your father left outside this morning."

"She said that six times eleven was sometimes sixty-eight!" I said.
"And she said she once saw a monster that was half lion and half bird." I
waited. "In Egypt, she said."

"Did you hear me?" my mother asked, raising her arm to wipe her fore- 85
head with the back of her hand. "You have chores to do."

"I know," I said. "I was just telling you about the substitute."

"It's very interesting," my mother said, quickly glancing down at me,
"and we can talk about it later when your father gets home. But right now
you have some work to do."

"Okay, Mom." I took a cookie out of the jar on the counter and was
about to go outside when I had a thought. I ran into the living room,
pulled out a dictionary next to the TV stand, and opened it to the G's.
Gryphon: "variant of griffin." *Griffin:* "a fabulous beast with the head and
wings of an eagle and the body of a lion." Fabulous was right. I shouted
with triumph and ran outside to put my father's tools back in their place.

Miss Ferenczi was back the next day, slightly altered. She had pulled her
hair down and twisted it into pigtails, with red rubber bands holding them
tight one inch from the ends. She was wearing a green blouse and pink
scarf, making her difficult to look at for a full class day. This time there
was no pretense of doing a reading lesson or moving on to arithmetic. As
soon as the bell rang, she simply began to talk.

She talked for forty minutes straight. There seemed to be less connec- 90
tion between her ideas, but the ideas themselves were, as the dictionary
would say, fabulous. She said she had heard of a huge jewel, in what she
called the Antipodes, that was so brilliant that when the light shone into it
at a certain angle it would blind whoever was looking at its center. She said
that the biggest diamond in the world was cursed and had killed everyone
who owned it, and that by a trick of fate it was called the Hope diamond.
Diamonds are magic, she said, and this is why women wear them on their
fingers, as a sign of the magic of womanhood. Men have strength, Miss
Ferenczi said, but no true magic. That is why men fall in love with women
but women do not fall in love with men; they just love being loved. George
Washington had died because of a mistake he made about a diamond.
Washington was not the first *true* President, but she did not say who was.
In some places in the world, she said, men and women still live in the trees
and eat monkeys for breakfast. Their doctors are magicians. At the bottom
of the sea are creatures thin as pancakes which have never been studied
by scientists because when you take them up to the air, the fish explode.

There was not a sound in the classroom, except for Miss Ferenczi's voice,
and Donna DeShano's coughing. No one even went to the bathroom.

Beethoven, she said, had not been deaf; it was a trick to make himself
famous, and it worked. As she talked, Miss Ferenczi's pigtails swung back

and forth. There are trees in the world, she said, that eat meat: their leaves are sticky and close up on bugs like hands. She lifted her hands and brought them together, palm to palm. Venus, which most people think is the next closest planet to the sun, is not always closer, and, besides, it is the planet of greatest mystery because of its thick cloud cover. "I know what lies underneath those clouds," Miss Ferenczi said, and waited. After the silence, she said, "Angels. Angels live under those clouds." She said that angels were not invisible to everyone and were in fact smarter than most people. They did not dress in robes as was often claimed but instead wore formal evening clothes, as if they were about to attend a concert. Often angels *do* attend concerts and sit in the aisles where, she said, most people pay no attention to them. She said the most terrible angel had the shape of the Sphinx. "There is no running away from that one," she said. She said that unquenchable fires burn just under the surface of the earth in Ohio, and that the baby Mozart fainted dead away in his cradle when he first heard the sound of a trumpet. She said that someone named Narzim al Harrardim was the greatest writer who ever lived. She said that planets control behavior, and anyone conceived during a solar eclipse would be born with webbed feet.

"I know you children like to hear these things," she said, "these secrets, and that is why I am telling you all this." We nodded. It was better than doing comprehension questions for the readings in *Broad Horizons*.

"I will tell you one more story," she said, "and then we will have to do arithmetic." She leaned over, and her voice grew soft. "There is no death," she said. "You must never be afraid. Never. That which is, cannot die. It will change into different earthly and unearthly elements, but I know this as sure as I stand here in front of you, and I swear it: you must not be afraid. I have seen this truth with these eyes. I know it because in a dream God kissed me. Here." And she pointed with her right index finger to the side of her head, below the mouth, where the vertical lines were carved into her skin.

95   Absent-mindedly we all did our arithmetic problems. At recess the class was out on the playground, but no one was playing. We were all standing in small groups, talking about Miss Ferenczi. We didn't know if she was crazy, or what. I looked out beyond the playground, at the rusted cars piled in a small heap behind a clump of sumac, and I wanted to see shapes there, approaching me.

On the way home, Carl sat next to me again. He didn't say much, and I didn't either. At last he turned to me. "You know what she said about the leaves that close up on bugs?"

"Huh?"

"The leaves," Carl insisted. "The meat-eating plants. I know it's true. I saw it on television. The leaves have this icky glue that the plants have got smeared all over them and the insects can't get off, 'cause they're stuck. I saw it." He seemed demoralized. "She's tellin' the truth."

"Yeah."

"You think she's seen all those angels?"   100

I shrugged.

"I don't think she has," Carl informed me. "I think she made that part up."

"There's a tree," I suddenly said. I was looking out the window at the farms along County Road H. I knew every barn, every broken windmill, every fence, every anhydrous ammonia tank, by heart. "There's a tree that's . . . that I've seen . . ."

"Don't you try to do it," Carl said. "You'll just sound like a jerk."

I kissed my mother. She was standing in front of the stove. "How was your   105
day?" she asked.

"Fine."

"Did you have Miss Ferenczi again?"

"Yeah."

"Well?"

"She was fine. Mom," I asked, "can I go to my room?"   110

"No," she said, "not until you've gone out to the vegetable garden and picked me a few tomatoes." She glanced at the sky. "I think it's going to rain. Skedaddle and do it now. Then you come back inside and watch your brother for a few minutes while I go upstairs. I need to clean up before dinner." She looked down at me. "You're looking a little pale, Tommy." She touched the back of her hand to my forehead and I felt her diamond ring against my skin. "Do you feel all right?"

"I'm fine," I said, and went out to pick the tomatoes.

Coughing mutedly, Mr. Hibler was back the next day, slipping lozenges into his mouth when his back was turned at forty-five minute intervals and asking us how much of the prepared lesson plan Miss Ferenczi had followed. Edith Atwater took the responsibility for the class of explaining to Mr. Hibler that the substitute hadn't always done exactly what he would have done, but we had worked hard even though she talked a lot. About what? he asked. All kinds of things, Edith said. I sort of forgot. To our relief, Mr. Hibler seemed not at all interested in what Miss Ferenczi had said to fill the day. He probably thought it was woman's talk; unserious and not suited for school. It was enough that he had a pile of arithmetic problems from us to correct.

For the next month, the sumac turned a distracting red in the field, and the sun traveled toward the southern sky, so that its rays reached Mr. Hibler's Halloween display on the bulletin board in the back of the room, fading the scarecrow with a pumpkin head from orange to tan. Every three days I measured how much farther the sun had moved toward the southern horizon by making small marks with my black Crayola on the north wall, ant-sized marks only I knew were there, inching west.

115 And then in early December, four days after the first permanent snowfall, she appeared again in our classroom. The minute she came in the door, I felt my heart begin to pound. Once again, she was different: this time, her hair hung straight down and seemed hardly to have been combed. She hadn't brought her lunchbox with her, but she was carrying what seemed to be a small box. She greeted all of us and talked about the weather. Donna DeShano had to remind her to take her overcoat off.

When the bell to start the day finally rang, Miss Ferenczi looked out at all of us and said, "Children, I have enjoyed your company in the past, and today I am going to reward you." She held up the small box. "Do you know what this is?" She waited. "Of course you don't. It is a tarot pack."

Edith Atwater raised her hand. "What's a tarot pack, Miss Ferenczi?"

"It is used to tell fortunes," she said. "And that is what I shall do this morning. I shall tell your fortunes, as I have been taught to do."

"What's fortune?" Bobby Kryzanowicz asked.

120 "The future, young man. I shall tell you what your future will be. I can't do your whole future, of course. I shall have to limit myself to the five-card system, the wands, cups, swords, pentacles, and the higher arcanes. Now who wants to be first?"

There was a long silence. Then Carol Peterson raised her hand.

"All right," Miss Ferenczi said. She divided the pack into five smaller packs and walked back to Carol's desk, in front of mine. "Pick one card from each of these packs," she said. I saw that Carol had a four of cups, a six of swords, but I couldn't see the other cards. Miss Ferenczi studied the cards on Carol's desk for a minute. "Not bad," she said. "I do not see much higher education. Probably an early marriage. Many children. There's something bleak and dreary here, but I can't tell what. Perhaps just the tasks of a housewife life. I think you'll do very well, for the most part." She smiled at Carol, a smile with a certain lack of interest. "Who wants to be next?"

Carl Whiteside raised his hand slowly.

"Yes," Miss Ferenczi said, "let's do a boy." She walked over to where Carl sat. After he picked his five cards, she gazed at them for a long time. "Travel," she said. "Much distant travel. You might go into the Army. Not too much romantic interest here. A late marriage, if at all. Squabbles. But the Sun is in your major arcana, here, yes, that's a very good card." She giggled. "Maybe a good life."

Next I raised my hand, and she told me my future. She did the same 125
with Bobby Kryzanowicz, Kelly Munger, Edith Atwater, and Kim Foor.
Then she came to Wayne Razmer. He picked his five cards, and I could
see that the Death card was one of them.

"What's your name?" Miss Ferenczi asked.

"Wayne."

"Well, Wayne," she said, "you will undergo a *great* metamorphosis, the
greatest, before you become an adult. Your earthly element will leap away,
into thin air, you sweet boy. This card, this nine of swords here, tells of
suffering and desolation. And this ten of wands, well, that's certainly a
heavy load."

"What about this one?" Wayne pointed to the Death card.

"That one? That one means you will die soon, my dear." She gath- 130
ered up the cards. We were all looking at Wayne. "But do not fear," she
said. "It's not really death, so much as change." She put the cards on Mr.
Hibler's desk. "And now, let's do some arithmetic."

At lunchtime Wayne went to Mr. Faegre, the principal, and told him
what Miss Ferenczi had done. During the noon recess, we saw Miss
Ferenczi drive out of the parking lot in her green Rambler. I stood under
the slide, listening to the other kids coasting down and landing in the
little depressive bowl at the bottom. I was kicking stones and tugging at
my hair right up to the moment when I saw Wayne come out to the playground. He smiled, the dead fool, and with the fingers of his right hand
he was showing everyone how he had told on Miss Ferenczi.

I made my way toward Wayne, pushing myself past two girls from
another class. He was watching me with his little pinhead eyes.

"You told," I shouted at him. "She was just kidding."

"She shouldn't have," he shouted back. "We were supposed to be
doing arithmetic."

"She just scared you," I said. "You're a chicken. You're a chicken, 135
Wayne. You are. Scared of a little card," I singsonged.

Wayne fell at me, his two fists hammering down on my nose. I gave
him a good one in the stomach and then I tried for his head. Aiming my
fist, I saw that he was crying. I slugged him.

"She was right," I yelled. "She was always right! She told the truth!"
Other kids were whooping. "You were just scared, that's all!"

And then large hands pulled at us, and it was my turn to speak to
Mr. Faegre.

In the afternoon Miss Ferenczi was gone, and my nose was stuffed with
cotton clotted with blood, and my lip had swelled, and our class had been
combined with Mrs. Mantei's sixth-grade class for a crowded afternoon

science unit on insect life in ditches and swamps. I knew where Mrs. Mantei lived: she had a new house trailer just down the road from us, at the Clearwater Park. She was no mystery. Somehow she and Mr. Bodine, the other fourth-grade teacher, had managed to fit forty-five desks into the room. Kelly Munger asked if Miss Ferenczi had been arrested, and Mrs. Mantei said no, of course not. All that afternoon, until the buses came to pick us up, we learned about field crickets and two-striped grasshoppers, water bugs, cicadas, mosquitoes, flies, and moths. We learned about insects' hard outer shell, the exoskeleton, and the usual parts of the mouth, including the labrum, mandible, maxilla, and glossa. We learned about compound eyes and the four-stage metamorphosis from egg to larva to pupa to adult. We learned something, but not much, about mating. Mrs. Mantei drew, very skillfully, the internal anatomy of the grasshopper on the blackboard. We learned about the dance of the honeybee, directing other bees in the hive to pollen. We found out about which insects were pests to man, and which were not. On lined white pieces of paper we made lists of insects we might actually see, then a list of insects too small to be clearly visible, such as fleas; Mrs. Mantei said that our assignment would be to memorize these lists for the next day, when Mr. Hibler would certainly return and test us on our knowledge.

Reading and Reacting

1. In classical mythology, a gryphon (also spelled *griffin*) is a monster that has the head and wings of an eagle and the body of a lion. Why is this story called "Gryphon"?
2. Describe Miss Ferenczi's physical appearance. Why is her appearance important to the story? How does it change as the story progresses?
3. How is Miss Ferenczi different from other teachers? from other substitute teachers? from other people in general? How is her differentness communicated to her pupils? to the story's readers?
4. What is the significance of the narrator's comment, in paragraph 11, that the lines on Miss Ferenczi's face remind him of Pinocchio?
5. Is Miss Ferenczi a round or a flat character? Explain.
6. In what sense is the narrator's mother a foil for Miss Ferenczi?
7. Why does the narrator defend Miss Ferenczi, first in his argument with Carl Whiteside and later on the playground? What does his attitude toward Miss Ferenczi reveal about his own character?
8. Are all of Miss Ferenczi's "substitute facts" lies, or is there some truth in what she says? Is she correct when she says that substitute facts cannot hurt anyone? Could it be argued that much of what is taught in schools today could be viewed as "substitute facts"?

9. JOURNAL ENTRY Is Miss Ferenczi a good teacher? Why or why not?

10. CRITICAL PERSPECTIVE Writing in the *New York Times Book Review*, critic William Ferguson characterizes *A Relative Stranger*, a more recent collection of Baxter's short stories than the one in which "Gryphon" appeared, as follows:

> The thirteen stories in *A Relative Stranger*, in all quietly accomplished, suggest a mysterious yet fundamental marriage of despair and joy. Though in one way or another each story ends in disillusionment, the road that leads to that dismal state is so richly peopled, so finely drawn, that the effect is oddly reassuring.

Do you think this characterization of Baxter's work in *A Relative Stranger* applies to "Gryphon" as well? For example, do you see a "marriage of despair and joy"? Do you find the story reassuring in any way, or does it convey only a sense of disillusionment?

Related Works: "A&P" (p. 160), "A Worn Path" (p. 386), "The Secret Lion" (p. 466), "When I Heard the Learn'd Astronomer" (p. 536), "On First Looking into Chapman's Homer" (p. 640), "Isla" (p. 679)

Source: ©AP Photo/Sang Tan

ZADIE SMITH (1975–   ), born in London as Sadie Smith, changed her name at a young age "because," she said in an interview, "it seemed right, exotic, different." The author of four novels, she has published short stories in such publications as the *New Yorker, McSweeney's, and Granta.* Her highly praised first novel, *White Teeth* (2000), winner of numerous awards, was later followed by *On Beauty* (2005), winner of the 2006 Orange Prize for Fiction. In 2009, she published a collection of essays, *Changing My Mind.* Smith wrote "The Girl with Bangs" in response to the song "Bangs" by They Might Be Giants.

Cultural Context As a cultural trend, bangs have come and gone and come again with American women throughout the latter part of the twentieth century and into the twenty-first century. The hairstyle has evolved from the long "mall bangs" of the 1960s, which start at the crown of the head, to a range of subtler styles used to frame the face. Today, popular styles of bangs among twenty- and thirty-something women include side-swept bangs, angled bangs, short choppy bangs, classic blunt bangs, straight bangs, super-short bangs, curly bangs, and eyebrow-skimming bangs. Celebrities helping to repopularize the look include Jessica Simpson, Lara Flynn Boyle, Kim Cattrall, Ashlee Simpson, Jennifer Lopez, Paris Hilton, and Nicole Richie.

The Girl with Bangs (2001)

I fell in love with a girl once. Some time ago, now. She had bangs. I was twenty years old at the time and prey to the usual rag-bag of foolish ideas. I believed, for example, that one might meet some sweet kid and like them a lot—maybe even marry them—while all the time allowing that kid to sleep with other kids, and that this could be done with no fuss at all, just a chuck under the chin, and no tears. I believed the majority of people to be bores, however you cut them; that the mark of their dullness was easy to spot (clothes, hair) and impossible to avoid, running right through them like a watermark. I had made mental notes, too, on other empty notions—the death of certain things (socialism, certain types of music, old people), the future of others (film, footwear, poetry)—but no one need be bored with those now. The only significant bit of nonsense I carried around in those days, the only one that came from the gut, if you like, was this feeling that a girl with soft black bangs falling into eyes the color of a Perrier bottle must be good news. Look at her palming the bangs away from her face, pressing them back along her hairline, only to have them fall forward again! I found this combination to be good, *intrinsically* good in both form and content, the same way you think of cherries (life is a bowl of; she was a real sweet) until the very center of one becomes lodged in your windpipe. I believed Charlotte Greaves and her bangs to be good news. But Charlotte was emphatically bad news, requiring only eight months to take me entirely apart; the kind of clinically efficient dismembering you see when a bright child gets his hand on some toy he assembled in the first place. I'd never dated a girl before, and she was bad news the way boys can never be, because with boys it's always possible to draw up a list of pros and cons, and see the matter rationally, from either side. But you could make a list of cons on Charlotte stretching to Azerbaijan,[1] and "her bangs" sitting solitary in the pros column would out-weigh all objections. Boys are just boys after all, but sometimes girls *really seem to be* the turn of a pale wrist, or the sudden jut of a hip, or a clutch of very dark hair falling across a freckled forehead. I'm not saying that's what they really are. I'm just saying sometimes it seems that way, and that those details (a thigh mole, a full face flush, a scar the precise shape and size of a cashew nut) are so many hooks waiting to land you. In this case, it was those bangs, plush and dramatic, curtains opening on to a face one would queue up to see. All women have a backstage, of course, of course. Labyrinthine, many-roomed, no doubt, no doubt. But you come to see the show, that's all I'm saying.

---

[1]*Azerbaijan:* Country on the coast of the Caspian Sea, bordered by Russia, Armenia, and Iran.

I first set eyes on Charlotte when she was seeing a Belgian who lived across the hall from me in college. I'd see her first thing, shuffling around the communal bathroom looking a mess—undone, always, in every sense—with her T-shirt tucked in her knickers, a fag[2] hanging out of her mouth, some kind of toothpaste or maybe mouthwash residue by her lips and those bangs in her eyes. It was hard to understand why this Belgian, Maurice, had chosen to date her. He had this great accent, Maurice, *elaborately* French, like you couldn't *be* more French, and a jaw line that seemed in fashion at the time, and you could tick all the boxes vis-à-vis personal charms; Maurice was an impressive kind of a guy. Charlotte was the kind of woman who has only two bras, both of them gray. But after a while, if you paid attention, you came to realize that she had a look about her like she just got out of a bed, no matter what time of day you collided with her (she had a stalk of a walk, never looked where she was going, so you had no choice) and this tendency, if put under the heading "QUALITIES THAT GIRLS SOMETIMES HAVE," was a kind of poor relation of "BEDROOM EYES" or "LOOKS LIKE SHE'S THINKING ABOUT SEX ALL THE TIME"—and it worked. She seemed always to be stumbling away from someone else, toward you. A limping figure smiling widely, arms outstretched, dressed in rags, a smouldering city as backdrop. I had watched too many films, possibly. But still: a bundle of precious things thrown at you from a third-floor European window, wrapped loosely in a blanket, chosen frantically and at random by the well-meaning owner slung haphazardly from a burning building; launched at you; it could hurt, this bundle, but look! You have caught it! A little chipped, but otherwise fine. Look what you have saved! (You understand me, I know. This is how it feels. What is the purpose of metaphor, anyway, if not to describe women?)

Now, it came to pass that this Maurice was offered a well-paid TV job in Thailand as a newscaster, and he agonized, and weighed Charlotte in one hand and the money in the other and found he could not leave without the promise that she would wait for him. This promise she gave him, but he was still gone, and gone is gone, and that's where I came in. Not immediately—I am no thief—but by degrees, studying near her in the library, watching her hair make reading difficult. Sitting next to her at lunch watching the bangs go hither, and, I suppose, thither, as people swished by with their food trays. Befriending her friends and then her; making as many nice noises about Maurice as I could. I became a boy for the duration. I stood under the window with my open arms. I did all the old boy tricks. These tricks are not as difficult as some boys will have you believe, but they are indeed slow, and work only by a very gradual process

---

[2] *fag:* Cigarette.

of accumulation. You have sad moments when you wonder if there will ever be an end to it. But then, usually without warning, the hard work pays off. With Charlotte it went like this: she came by for a herbal tea one day, and I rolled a joint and then another and soon enough she was lying across my lap, spineless as a mollusk, and I had my fingers in those bangs—teasing them, as the hairdressers say—and we had begun.

Most of the time we spent together was in her room. At the beginning of an affair you've no need to be outside. And it was like a filthy cocoon, her room, ankle deep in rubbish; it was the kind of room that took you in and held you close. With no clocks and my watch lost and buried, we passed time by the degeneration of things, the rotting of fruit, the accumulation of bacteria, the rising-tideline of cigarettes in the vase we used to put them out. It was a quarter past this apple. The third Saturday in the month of that stain. These things were unpleasant and tiresome. And she was no intellectual; any book I gave her she treated like a kid treats a Christmas present—fascination for a day and then the quick pall of boredom; by the end of the week it was flung across the room and submerged; weeks later when we made love I'd find the spine of the novel sticking into the small of my back, paper cuts on my toes. There was no bed to speak of. There was just a bit of the floor that was marginally clearer than the rest of it. (But wait! Here she comes, falling in an impossible arc, and here I am by careful design in just the right spot, under the window, and here she is, landing and nothing is broken, and I cannot believe my luck. You understand me. Every time I looked at the bangs, the bad stuff went away.)

5   Again: I know it doesn't sound great, but let's not forget the bangs. Let us not forget that after a stand-up row, a real screaming match, she could look at me from underneath the distinct hairs, separated by sweat, and I had no more resistance. *Yes, you can leave the overturned plant pot where it is. Yes, Rousseau is an idiot if you say so.* So this is what it's like being a boy. The cobbled street, the hopeful arms hugging air. There is nothing you won't do.

Charlotte's exams were coming up. I begged her to look through her reading list once more, and plan some strategic line of attack, but she wanted to do it her way. Her way meant reading the same two books— Rousseau's *Social Contract* and Plato's *Republic* (her paper was to be on people, and the way they organize their lives, or the way they did, or the way they should, I don't remember; it had a technical title, I don't remember that either)—again and again, in the study room that sat in a quiet corner of the college. The study room was meant to be for everyone but since Charlotte had moved in, all others had gradually moved out. I recall one German graduate who stood his ground for a month or so, who cleared his throat regularly and pointedly picked up things that she had dropped—but she got to him, finally. Charlotte's papers all over the floor, Charlotte's old lunches on every table, Charlottes clothes and my clothes (now indistinguishable) thrown over every chair. People would come up to me in the bar and say, "Look, Charlotte did X. Could you please, for the love of God, stop Charlotte doing X, *please?*" and I would try, but Charlotte's bangs kept Charlotte in the world of Charlotte and she barely heard me. And now, please, before we go any further: tell me. Tell me if you've ever stood under a window and caught an unworthy bundle of chintz.[3] Gold plating that came off with one rub; faked signatures, worthless trinkets. Have you? Maybe the bait was different—not bangs, but deep pockets either side of the smile or unusually vivid eye pigmentation. Or some other bodily attribute (hair, skin, curves) that recalled in you some natural phenomenon (wheat, sea, cream). Some difference. So: have you? Have you ever been out with a girl like this?

Some time after Charlotte's exams, after the 2.2 that had been stalking her for so long finally pounced, there was a knock on the door. My door—I recall now that we were in my room that morning. I hauled on a dressing-gown and went to answer it. It was Maurice, tanned and dressed like one of the Beatles when they went to see the Maharashi,[4] a white suit with a Nehru collar, his own bangs and tousled hair, slightly long at the back. He looked terrific. He said, "Someone in ze bar says you might have an idea where Charlotte is. I need to see 'er—it is very urgent. Have you seen 'er?" I had seen her. She was in my bed, about five feet from where Maurice stood, but obscured by a partition wall. "No..." I said. "No, not this morning. She'll probably be in the hall for breakfast though, she usually is. So, Maurice! When did you get back?" He said, "All zat must come later. I 'ave to find Charlotte. I sink I am going to marry 'er." And I thought, *Christ, which bad movie am I in?*

I got Charlotte up, shook her, poured her into some clothes, and told her to run around the back of the college and get to the dining hall before Maurice. I saw her in my head, the moment the door closed—no great feat of imagination, I had seen her run before, like a naturally uncoordinated animal (a panda?) that somebody has just shot—I saw her dashing incompetently past the ancient walls, catching herself on ivy, tripping up steps, and finally falling through the swing doors, looking wildly round the dining hall like those movie time-travellers who know not in which period they have just landed. But still she managed it, apparently she got there in time, though as the whole world now knows, Maurice took one look at her strands matted against her forehead, running in line with the ridgeways of sleep left by the pillows, and said, "You're sleeping with her?"

---

[3] *chintz:* A usually brightly printed and glazed cotton fabric.

[4] *Maharashi:* Maharishi Mahesh Yogi (1911?–2008), Hindu religious leader revered by the British rock group the Beatles.

(Or maybe, "You're sleeping with *her?*"—I don't know; this is all reported speech) and Charlotte, who, like a lot of low-maintenance women, cannot tell a lie, said "Er... yes. Yes" and then made that signal of feminine relief; bottom lip out, air blown upward; bangs all of a flutter.

Later that afternoon, Maurice came back round to my room, looking all the more noble, and seemingly determined to have a calm man-to-man "you see, I have returned to marry her/I will not stand in your way" type of a chat, which was very reasonable and English of him. I let him have it alone. I nodded when it seemed appropriate; sometimes I lifted my hands in protest but soon let them fall again. You can't fight it when you've been replaced: a simple side-step and here is some old/new Belgian guy standing in the cobbled street with his face upturned, and his arms wide open, judging the angles. I thought of this girl he wanted back, who had taken me apart piece by piece, causing me nothing but trouble, with her bangs and her antisocial behaviour. I was all (un)done, I realized. I sort of marvelled at the devotion he felt for her. From a thousand miles away, with a smoldering city as a backdrop, I watched him beg me to leave them both alone; tears in his eyes, the works. I agreed it was the best thing, all round. I had the impression that here was a girl who would be thrown from person to person over years, and each would think they had saved her by some miracle when in actual fact she was in no danger at all. Never even for a second.

10   He said, "Let us go, zen, and tell 'er the decision we have come to," and I said yes, let's, but when we got to Charlotte's room, someone else was putting his fingers through her curls. Charlotte was always one of those people for whom sex is available at all times—it just happens to her, quickly, and with a minimum of conversation. This guy was some other guy that she'd been sleeping with on the days when she wasn't with me. It had been going on for four months. This all came out later, naturally.

Would you believe he married her anyway? And not only that, he married her after she'd shaved her head that afternoon just to spite us. All of us—even the other guy no one had seen before. Maurice took a bald English woman with a strange lopsided walk and a temper like a gorgon back to Thailand and married her despite friends' complaints and the voluble protest of Aneepa Kapoor, who was the woman he read the news with. The anchorwoman, who had that Hitchcock style: hair tied back tight in a bun, a spiky nose and a vicious red mouth. The kind of woman who doesn't need catching. "Maurice," she said, "you *owe* me. You can't just throw four months away like it wasn't worth a bloody thing!" He emailed me about it. He admitted that he'd been stringing Aneepa along for a while, and she'd been expecting something at the end of it. For in the real world, or so it seems to me, it is almost always women and not men who are waiting under windows, and they are almost always disappointed. In this matter, Charlotte was unusual.

Reading and Reacting

1. At what point did you realize that the narrator was female? Do you think her feelings and behavior would have been any different if she were male?
2. What exactly is it about Charlotte that fascinates the narrator? Do you share this fascination?
3. What do we learn in paragraph 1 about the narrator's tastes, feelings, and beliefs? Is this information enough to explain her obsession with Charlotte?
4. Why do you think the narrator focuses on Charlotte's bangs? What other physical traits does Charlotte have?
5. In paragraph 2, the narrator characterizes Charlotte as "the kind of woman who has only two bras, both of them gray." What does this tell readers about Charlotte? What does the description of Charlotte's room in paragraph 4 reveal about her?
6. What role does Maurice play in the story? What do we know about him? Is he a flat or a round character? Is he essential to the story?
7. At the end of paragraph 4, the narrator tells us, "Every time I looked at the bangs, the bad stuff went away." What do you think this "bad stuff" is?
8. In the story's last lines, the narrator explains that "in the real world, or so it seems to me, it is almost always women and not men who are waiting under windows, and they are almost always disappointed. In this matter, Charlotte was unusual." What does the narrator mean? How do these words help to explain her infatuation with Charlotte?

9. **JOURNAL ENTRY** Write a farewell email to the narrator from Charlotte. Try to explain her feelings for the narrator as well as her motivation for shaving her head and for deciding to marry Maurice.

10. **CRITICAL PERSPECTIVE** Writing about Zadie Smith's novel *On Beauty*, Max Watman makes the following comments:

> Smith's characters are expertly portrayed....She can blow them up in all their chalky whites and lively pinks. She is one of the best character writers working. . . . *On Beauty* is one of the few contemporary novels that feels as if it is stuffed with fully formed people rather than tics and mannerisms.

Do you think Charlotte in "The Girl with Bangs" is depicted as a "fully formed" person, or do you think she is really just "tics and mannerisms"?

Related Works: "Love and Other Catastrophes: A Mix Tape" (p. 84), "Araby" (p. 288), "My mistress' eyes are nothing like the sun" (p. 572), "Love is not all" (p. 642), "General Review of the Sex Situation" (p. 721), "She Walks in Beauty" (p. 747), *Beauty* (p. 831), *The Date* (p. 1160)

WRITING SUGGESTIONS: Character

1. In both "A&P" and "Gryphon," the main characters (Sammy and Tommy, respectively) struggle against rules, authority figures, and inflexible social systems. Compare and contrast the struggles in which these two characters are engaged.

2. Write an essay in which you contrast the character of Miss Brill (p. 166) with Emily Grierson in "A Rose for Emily" (p. 143) or with Phoenix Jackson in "A Worn Path" (p. 386). Consider how each character interacts with those around her as well as how each seems to see her role or mission in the world.

3. Sammy, Miss Brill, and Miss Ferenczi all use their active imaginations to create scenarios that help get them through the day. None of them is able to sustain the illusion, however. As a result, all three find out how harsh reality can be. How are these scenarios alike, and how are they different? What steps could these three characters take to fit more comfortably into the worlds they inhabit? *Should* they take such steps? Are they able to do so?

4. Write an analysis of a minor character in one of this chapter's stories—for example, Stokesie in "A&P" or Maurice in "The Girl with Bangs."

5. In "A&P," "Gryphon," and "The Girl with Bangs," each narrator is fascinated by another character—Queenie, Miss Ferenczi, and Charlotte, respectively. What exactly is each narrator attracted to? How do you account for these almost obsessive attachments?

CHAPTER 9

SETTING

Sherman Alexie
J. Vespa/WireImage/Getty Images

Tillie Olsen
Chris Felver/Archive Photos/Getty Images

The **setting** of a work of fiction establishes its historical, geographical, and physical context. *Where* a work is set—on a tropical island, in a dungeon, at a crowded party, in the woods—influences our reactions to the story's events and characters. *When* a work takes place—during the French Revolution, during the Vietnam War, today, or in the future—is equally important. Setting, however, is more than just the approximate time and place in which a work is set; setting also encompasses a wide variety of other elements.

Clearly, setting is more important in some works than in others. In some stories, no particular time or place is specified or even suggested, perhaps because the writer does not consider a specific setting to be important or because the writer wishes the story's events to seem timeless and universal. In other stories, a writer may provide only minimal information about setting, telling readers little more than where and when the action takes place. In many cases, however, a particular setting is vital to the story, perhaps influencing characters' feelings or behavior, as it does in the stories in this chapter.

Sometimes a story's central conflict is between the protagonist and the setting—for example, *Alice in Wonderland*, a northerner in the South, an unsophisticated American tourist in an old European city, a sane person in a psychiatric hospital, a moral person in a corrupt environment, an immigrant in a new world, or a city dweller in the country. Such a conflict may drive the story's plot and also help to define the characters. A conflict between *events* and setting—for example, the arrival of a mysterious stranger in a typical suburban neighborhood, the intrusion of modern social ideas into an old-fashioned world, or the intrusion of a brutal murder into a peaceful village—can also enrich a story.

 ## Historical Setting

A particular historical period, and the events and customs associated with it, can be important to your understanding of a story; therefore, some knowledge of the period in which a story is set may be useful (or even essential) for readers. The historical setting establishes a story's social, cultural, economic, and political environment. Knowing, for instance, that Charlotte Perkins Gilman's "The Yellow Wallpaper" (p. 434) was written in the late nineteenth century, when doctors treated women as delicate and dependent creatures, helps to explain the narrator's emotional state. Likewise, it may be important to know that a story is set during a particularly volatile (or static) political era, during a time of permissive (or repressive) attitudes toward sex, during a war, or during a period of economic prosperity or recession. Any one of these factors may help to explain why events occur as well as why characters act (and react) as they do. Historical events or cultural norms may, for instance, limit or expand a character's options, and our knowledge of history may reveal to us a character's incompatibility with his or her milieu. For example, in F. Scott Fitzgerald's "Bernice Bobs Her Hair" (1920) set in the 1920s in a midwestern town, a young girl is goaded into cutting her long hair. To understand the significance of Bernice's act—and to understand the reactions of others to that act—readers must know that during that era only racy "society vampires," not nice girls from good families, bobbed their hair.

Knowing the approximate year or historical period during which a story takes place can help readers to better understand characters and events. This knowledge can explain forces that act on characters and account for their behavior, clarify circumstances that influence the story's action, and justify a writer's use of plot devices that might otherwise seem improbable. Thus, stories set before the development of modern transportation and communication networks may hinge on plot devices readers would not accept in a modern story. For example, in "Paul's Case," a 1904 story by Willa Cather, a young man who steals a large sum of money in Pittsburgh is able to spend several days enjoying his newfound wealth before the news of the theft reaches New York, where he has fled. In other stories, we see characters threatened by diseases that have now been eradicated (or subjected to outdated medical or psychiatric treatment) or constrained by social conventions very different from those that operate in our own society.

Geographical Setting

In addition to knowing *when* a work takes place, readers need to know *where* it takes place. Knowing whether a story is set in the United States, in Europe, or in a developing nation can help to explain anything from why language and customs are unfamiliar to us to why characters act in ways we find surprising or hold beliefs that are alien to us. Even in stories set in the United States, regional differences may account for differences in plot development and characters' motivation. For example, knowing that William Faulkner's "A Rose for Emily" (p. 143) is set in the post–Civil War American South helps to explain why the townspeople are so chivalrously protective of Miss Emily. Similarly, the fact that Bret Harte's classic story "The Outcasts of Poker Flat" (1869) is set in a California mining camp accounts for its varied cast of characters—including a gambler, a prostitute, and a traveling salesman.

The size of the town or city in which a story takes place may also be important. In a small town, for example, a character's problems are more likely to be subject to intense scrutiny by other characters, as they are in stories of small-town life such as "A Rose for Emily." In a large city, characters may be more likely to be isolated and anonymous, like Mrs. Miller in Truman Capote's gothic short story "Miriam" (1945), who is so lonely that she creates an imaginary companion. Characters may also be alienated by their big-city surroundings, as Gregor Samsa is in Franz Kafka's classic 1915 novella "The Metamorphosis," about a man who turns into a bug.

Of course, a story may not have a recognizable geographical setting: its location may not be specified, or it may be set in a fantasy world. Choosing unusual settings may free writers from the constraints placed on them by familiar environments, thus allowing them to experiment with situations and characters, unaffected by readers' expectations or associations with familiar settings.

Physical Setting

Physical setting can influence a story's mood as well as its development. For example, *time of day* can be important. The gruesome murder described in Edgar Allan Poe's "The Cask of Amontillado" (p. 249) takes place in an appropriate setting: not just underground but in the darkness of night. Conversely, the horrifying events of Shirley Jackson's "The Lottery" (p. 335) take place in broad daylight, contrasting dramatically with the darkness of the society that permits—and even participates in—a shocking ritual. Many stories, of course, move through several time periods as the action unfolds, and changes in time may also be important. For instance, the approach of evening (or of dawn) can signal the end of a crisis in the plot.

Whether a story is set primarily *indoors* or *out-of-doors* may also be significant: characters may be physically constrained by a closed-in setting or liberated by an expansive landscape. Some interior settings may be psychologically limiting. For instance, the narrator in "The Yellow Wallpaper" feels suffocated by her room, whose ugly wallpaper comes to haunt her. In many of Poe's stories, the central character is trapped, physically or psychologically, in a confined, suffocating space. In other stories, an interior setting may have a symbolic function. For example, in "A Rose for Emily," the house is for Miss Emily a symbol of the South's past glory as well as a refuge, a fortress, and a hiding place. Similarly, a building or house may represent society, with its rules, norms, and limitations, as in John Updike's "A&P" (p. 160), where the supermarket establishes social as well as physical limits.

Conversely, an outdoor setting can free a character from social norms of behavior, as it does for Ernest Hemingway's Nick Adams, a war veteran who, in "Big Two-Hearted River" (1925), finds order, comfort, and peace only when he is away from civilization. An outdoor setting can also expose characters to physical dangers, such as untamed wilderness, uncharted seas, and frighteningly empty open spaces, as is the case in Stephen Crane's "The Open Boat" (1897).

Weather can be another important aspect of setting. A storm can threaten a character's life or just make the character—and readers—*think* danger is present, distracting us from other, more subtle threats. Extreme weather conditions can make characters act irrationally or uncharacteristically, as in Kate Chopin's "The Storm" (p. 199), where a storm provides the story's complication and sets in motion the characters' actions. In numerous stories set in hostile landscapes, where extremes of heat and cold influence the action, weather may serve as a test for characters, as it does in Jack London's "To Build a Fire" (1908), in which the main character struggles unsuccessfully against the brutally cold, hostile environment of the Yukon.

The various physical attributes of setting combine to create a story's **atmosphere** or **mood**. In "The Cask of Amontillado," for example, several factors work together to create the story's eerie, intense atmosphere: it is nighttime; it is the hectic carnival season; and the catacombs are dark, damp, and filled with the bones of the narrator's ancestors. Sometimes the mood or atmosphere that is created helps to convey a story's central theme—as the ironic contrast between the pleasant atmosphere and the shocking events that unfold communicates the theme of "The Lottery." A story's atmosphere may also be linked to a character's mental state, perhaps reflecting his or her mood. For example, darkness and isolation can reflect a character's depression, whereas an idyllic, peaceful atmosphere can express a character's joy. And, of course, a story's atmosphere can also *influence* the characters' state of mind, causing them to react one way in a crowded, hectic city but to react very differently in a peaceful rural atmosphere.

✔ **CHECKLIST   Writing about Setting**

- Is the setting specified or unspecified? Is it fully described or only suggested?

- Is the setting just background, or is it a key force in the story?

- Are any characters in conflict with their environment?

- How does the setting influence the story's plot? Does it cause characters to act?

- In what time period does the story take place? How can you tell? What social, political, or economic situations or events of the historical period might influence the story?

- In what geographical location is the story set? Is this location important to the story?

- At what time of day is the story set? Is time important to the development of the story?

- Is the story set primarily indoors or out-of-doors? What role does this aspect of the setting play in the story?

- What role do weather conditions play in the story?

- What kind of atmosphere or mood does the physical setting create?

- How does the story's atmosphere influence the characters? Does it affect (or reflect) their emotional state? Does it help to explain their motivation?

- Does the atmosphere change as the story progresses? Is this change significant?

KATE CHOPIN (1851–1904) (picture and biography on p. 127) wrote in a style that was realistic yet infused with a dense, sensual texture that was perhaps, in part, her artistic response to her memories of the exotic Louisiana bayou country. Like her contemporary Gustave Flaubert (Chopin's short novel *The Awakening* has often been called a "Creole *Bovary*"), Chopin used the physical world—as in the charged atmosphere of "The Storm"—to symbolize the inner truths of her characters' minds and hearts. Unlike Flaubert, however, she depicted sex not as a frantic and destructive force but as a joyous, elemental part of life. Apparently Kate Chopin knew how daring "The Storm" was: she never submitted it for publication.

Cultural Context In the following story, which presumably takes place in Louisiana, the character Calixta expresses fear that the powerful storm will break the levees, the raised embankments kept in place to prevent the river from overflowing. In August 2005, more than one hundred years after this story was written, the levees in New Orleans gave way to the sheer force of Hurricane Katrina, which flooded the city, destroyed the area's economic and cultural foundation, and displaced hundreds of thousands of residents.

The Storm (c. 1899)

I

The leaves were so still that even Bibi thought it was going to rain. Bobinôt, who was accustomed to converse on terms of perfect equality with his little son, called the child's attention to certain sombre clouds that were rolling with sinister intention from the west, accompanied by a sullen, threatening roar. They were at Friedheimer's store and decided to remain there till the storm had passed. They sat within the door on two empty kegs. Bibi was four years old and looked very wise.

"Mama'll be 'fraid, yes," he suggested with blinking eyes.

"She'll shut the house. Maybe she got Sylvie helpin' her this evenin'," Bobinôt responded reassuringly.

"No; she ent got Sylvie. Sylvie was helpin' her yistiday," piped Bibi.

5   Bobinôt arose and going across to the counter purchased a can of shrimps, of which Calixta was very fond. Then he returned to his perch on the keg and sat stolidly holding the can of shrimps while the storm burst. It shook the wooden store and seemed to be ripping great furrows in the distant field. Bibi laid his little hand on his father's knee and was not afraid.

II

Calixta, at home, felt no uneasiness for their safety. She sat at a side window sewing furiously on a sewing machine. She was greatly occupied and did not notice the approaching storm. But she felt very warm and often stopped to mop her face on which the perspiration gathered in beads. She unfastened her white sacque at the throat. It began to grow dark, and suddenly realizing the situation she got up hurriedly and went about closing windows and doors.

Out on the small front gallery she had hung Bobinôt's Sunday clothes to air and she hastened out to gather them before the rain fell. As she stepped outside, Alcée Laballière rode in at the gate. She had not seen him very often since her marriage, and never alone. She stood there with Bobinôt's coat in her hands, and the big rain drops began to fall. Alcée rode his horse under the shelter of a side projection where the chickens had huddled and there were plows and a harrow piled up in the corner.

"May I come and wait on your gallery till the storm is over, Calixta?"
he asked.

"Come 'long in, M'sieur Alcée."

His voice and her own startled her as if from a trance, and she seized 10
Bobinôt's vest. Alcée, mounting to the porch, grabbed the trousers and
snatched Bibi's braided jacket that was about to be carried away by a sudden gust of wind. He expressed an intention to remain outside, but it was
soon apparent that he might as well have been out in the open: the water
beat in upon the boards in driving sheets, and he went inside, closing the
door after him. It was even necessary to put something beneath the door
to keep the water out.

"My! what a rain! It's good two years sence it rain' like that," exclaimed
Calixta as she rolled up a piece of bagging and Alcée helped her to thrust
it beneath the crack.

She was a little fuller of figure than five years before when she married;
but she had lost nothing of her vivacity. Her blue eyes still retained their
melting quality; and her yellow hair, dishevelled by the wind and rain,
kinked more stubbornly than ever about her ears and temples.

The rain beat upon the low, shingled roof with a force and clatter that
threatened to break an entrance and deluge them there. They were in the
dining room—the sitting room—the general utility room. Adjoining was
her bed room, with Bibi's couch along side her own. The door stood open,
and the room with its white, monumental bed, its closed shutters, looked
dim and mysterious.

Alcée flung himself into a rocker and Calixta nervously began to
gather up from the floor the lengths of a cotton sheet which she had been
sewing.

"If this keeps up, *Dieu sait*[1] if the levees[2] goin' to stan' it!" she exclaimed. 15

"What have you got to do with the levees?"

"I got enough to do! An' there's Bobinôt with Bibi out in that storm—
if he only didn't left Friedheimer's!"

"Let us hope, Calixta, that Bobinôt's got sense enough to come in out
of a cyclone."

She went and stood at the window with a greatly disturbed look on
her face. She wiped the frame that was clouded with moisture. It was
stiflingly hot. Alcée got up and joined her at the window, looking over
her shoulder. The rain was coming down in sheets obscuring the view of
far-off cabins and enveloping the distant wood in a gray mist. The playing
of the lightning was incessant. A bolt struck a tall chinaberry tree at the

---

[1] *Dieu sait:* "God knows" (French).

[2] *levees:* Raised embankments designed to keep a river from overflowing.

edge of the field. It filled all visible space with a blinding glare and the crash seemed to invade the very boards they stood upon.

20   Calixta put her hands to her eyes, and with a cry, staggered backward. Alcée's arm encircled her, and for an instant he drew her close and spasmodically to him.

"*Bonté!*"[3] she cried, releasing herself from his encircling arm and retreating from the window, "the house'll go next! If I only knew w'ere Bibi was!" She would not compose herself; she would not be seated. Alcée clasped her shoulders and looked into her face. The contact of her warm, palpitating body when he had unthinkingly drawn her into his arms, had aroused all the old-time infatuation and desire for her flesh.

"Calixta," he said, "don't be frightened. Nothing can happen. The house is too low to be struck, with so many tall trees standing about. There! aren't you going to be quiet? say, aren't you?" He pushed her hair back from her face that was warm and steaming. Her lips were as red and moist as pomegranate seed. Her white neck and a glimpse of her full, firm bosom disturbed him powerfully. As she glanced up at him the fear in her liquid blue eyes had given place to a drowsy gleam that unconsciously betrayed a sensuous desire. He looked down into her eyes and there was nothing for him to do but to gather her lips in a kiss. It reminded him of Assumption.

"Do you remember—in Assumption, Calixta?" he asked in a low voice broken by passion. Oh! she remembered; for in Assumption he had kissed her and kissed and kissed her; until his senses would well nigh fail, and to save her he would resort to a desperate flight. If she was not an immaculate dove in those days, she was still inviolate; a passionate creature whose very defenselessness had made her defense, against which his honor forbade him to prevail. Now—well, now—her lips seemed in a manner free to be tasted, as well as her round, white throat and her whiter breasts.

They did not heed the crashing torrents, and the roar of the elements made her laugh as she lay in his arms. She was a revelation in that dim, mysterious chamber; as white as the couch she lay upon. Her firm, elastic flesh that was knowing for the first time its birthright, was like a creamy lily that the sun invites to contribute its breath and perfume to the undying life of the world.

25   The generous abundance of her passion, without guile or trickery, was like a white flame which penetrated and found response in depths of his own sensuous nature that had never yet been reached.

---

[3]Bonté: "Goodness!" (French).

When he touched her breasts they gave themselves up in quivering ecstasy, inviting his lips. Her mouth was a fountain of delight. And when he possessed her, they seemed to swoon together at the very borderland of life's mystery.

He stayed cushioned upon her, breathless, dazed, enervated, with his heart beating like a hammer upon her. With one hand she clasped his head, her lips lightly touching his forehead. The other hand stroked with a soothing rhythm his muscular shoulders.

The growl of the thunder was distant and passing away. The rain beat softly upon the shingles, inviting them to drowsiness and sleep. But they dared not yield.

The rain was over; and the sun was turning the glistening green world into a palace of gems. Calixta, on the gallery, watched Alcée ride away. He turned and smiled at her with a beaming face; and she lifted her pretty chin in the air and laughed aloud.

III

Bobinôt and Bibi, trudging home, stopped without at the cistern to make **30** themselves presentable.

"My! Bibi, w'at will yo' mama say! You ought to be ashame'. You oughtn' put on those good pants. Look at 'em! An' that mud on yo' collar! How you got that mud on yo' collar, Bibi? I never saw such a boy!" Bibi was the picture of pathetic resignation. Bobinôt was the embodiment of serious solicitude as he strove to remove from his own person and his son's the signs of their tramp over heavy roads and through wet fields. He scraped the mud off Bibi's bare legs and feet with a stick and carefully removed all traces from his heavy brogans. Then, prepared for the worst—the meeting with an over-scrupulous housewife, they entered cautiously at the back door.

Calixta was preparing supper. She had set the table and was dripping coffee at the hearth. She sprang up as they came in.

"Oh, Bobinôt! You back! My! but I was uneasy. W'ere you been during the rain? An' Bibi? he ain't wet? he ain't hurt?" She had clasped Bibi and was kissing him effusively. Bobinôt's explanations and apologies which he had been composing all along the way, died on his lips as Calixta felt him to see if he were dry, and seemed to express nothing but satisfaction at their safe return.

"I brought you some shrimps, Calixta," offered Bobinôt, hauling the can from his ample side pocket and laying it on the table.

"Shrimps! Oh, Bobinôt! you too good fo' anything!" and she gave him **35** a smacking kiss on the cheek that resounded. "*J'vous réponds,*[4] we'll have a feas' tonight! umph-umph!"

---

[4] *J'vous réponds:* "I tell you" (French).

Bobinôt and Bibi began to relax and enjoy themselves, and when the three seated themselves at table they laughed much and so loud that anyone might have heard them as far away as Laballière's.

IV

Alcée Laballière wrote to his wife, Clarisse, that night. It was a loving letter, full of tender solicitude. He told her not to hurry back, but if she and the babies liked it at Biloxi, to stay a month longer. He was getting on nicely; and though he missed them, he was willing to bear the separation a while longer—realizing that their health and pleasure were the first things to be considered.

V

As for Clarisse, she was charmed upon receiving her husband's letter. She and the babies were doing well. The society was agreeable; many of her old friends and acquaintances were at the bay. And the first free breath since her marriage seemed to restore the pleasant liberty of her maiden days. Devoted as she was to her husband, their intimate conjugal life was something which she was more than willing to forego for a while.

So the storm passed and everyone was happy.

Reading and Reacting

1. Trace the progress of the storm through the five parts of the story. Then trace the stages of the story's plot. How does the progress of the storm parallel the developing plot?

2. How does the weather help to create the story's atmosphere? How would you characterize this atmosphere?

3. In Part I, the "sombre clouds . . . rolling with sinister intention" introduce the storm. In what sense does this description introduce the story's action as well?

4. In what respects does the storm *cause* the events of the story? List specific events that occur because of the storm. Is the presence of the storm essential to the story?

5. In what sense does the storm act as a character in the story?

6. The weather is the most obvious element of the story's setting. What other aspects of setting are important to the story?

7. After Part II, the storm is not mentioned again until the last line of the story. What signs of the storm remain in Parts III, IV, and V?

8. Besides referring to the weather, what else might the title suggest?

9. **JOURNAL ENTRY** The storm sets in motion the chain of events that leads to the characters' adultery. Do you think the storm excuses the characters in any way from responsibility for their actions?

10. CRITICAL PERSPECTIVE Kate Chopin is widely considered to be a regional, or "local color" writer. This term refers to writing in which descriptions of a particular geographic region are prominent. Local color writers strive to incorporate accurate speech patterns and dialects—as well as descriptions of local scenery, dress, and social customs—into their writing. Writing for the *Southern Literary Journal* and quoting Chopin critic Helen Taylor, Sylvia Bailey Shurbutt notes, "Of the regional stories, Taylor writes, ['Chopin's] ironic and resonant use of historical, topographical, and mythical Louisiana materials...functions to interrogate both the Southern ideology of womanhood and contradictory constructions of Southern femininity in the 1890's.'"

In what respects is "The Storm" an example of local color writing? How does it challenge "the southern ideology of womanhood"?

Related Works: "Hills Like White Elephants" (p. 74), "Love is not all" (p. 642), "What lips my lips have kissed" (p. 720), "General Review of the Sex Situation" (p. 721)

SHERMAN ALEXIE (1966–   ), a Spokane/Coeur d'Alene Indian, grew up on the Spokane Indian Reservation in Wellpinit, Washington, about fifty miles northwest of Spokane, where approximately 2,400 Spokane Tribal members live. Alexie has published short stories, novels, and poetry. He was named one of *Granta's* Best of Young American Novelists, and his first novel, *Reservation Blues* (1995), won the Before Columbus Foundation's American Book Award and the Murray Morgan Prize. His second novel, *Indian Killer* (1996), was named one of *People's* Best of Pages and was a *New York Times* Notable Book. "This Is What It Means to Say Phoenix, Arizona" (from his 1993 short story collection *The Lone Ranger and Tonto Fistfight in Heaven*) eventually became the movie *Smoke Signals*, which was released in 1998. His most recent books are the young adult novel *The Absolutely True Diary of a Part-Time Indian* (2007), for which he won the National Book Award for Young People's Literature; the novel *Flight* (2007); the story collection *Blasphemy* (2012); and the poetry collections *Face* (2009) and *What I've Stolen, What I've Earned* (2013).

Commenting on Native American culture, Alexie has said, "One of the biggest misconceptions about Indians is that we're stoic, but humor is an essential part of our culture." "This Is What It Means to Say Phoenix, Arizona" demonstrates this unique use of humor to transcend the harsh realities of life on the reservation and of the struggle to adapt to contemporary American life.

Cultural Context The United States policy of creating Native American reservations can be traced back to the administration of President Ulysses S. Grant, who determined that establishing such reservations was the best way to handle the "Indian problem" between white settlers and the Native Americans they encountered. (Even supporters of Native Americans believed that they were incapable of assimilating into the wider American society and that only on reservations would they be able to survive as a people.) Today, about forty percent of America's 4.9 million Native Americans continue to live on reservations, where unemployment rates soar and more than twenty-eight percent of families live below the federal poverty line. At the same time, reservations are the one place where members of a tribe can live together and retain their culture, language, and heritage. The characters in "This Is What It Means to Say Phoenix, Arizona" experience both the positive and negative aspects of reservation life.

This Is What It Means to Say
Phoenix, Arizona (1993)

Just after Victor lost his job at the Bureau of Indian Affairs,[1] he also found out that his father had died of a heart attack in Phoenix, Arizona. Victor hadn't seen his father in a few years, had only talked to him on the telephone once or twice, but there still was a genetic pain, which was as real and immediate as a broken bone. Victor didn't have any money. Who does have money on a reservation, except the cigarette and fireworks salespeople? His father had a savings account waiting to be claimed, but Victor needed to find a way to get from Spokane to Phoenix. Victor's mother was just as poor as he was, and the rest of his family didn't have any use at all for him. So Victor called the tribal council.

"Listen," Victor said. "My father just died. I need some money to get to Phoenix to make arrangements."

"Now Victor," the council said, "you know we're having a difficult time financially."

"But I thought the council had special funds set aside for stuff like this."

5   "Now, Victor, we do have some money available for the proper return of tribal members' bodies. But I don't think we have enough to bring your father all the way back from Phoenix."

"Well," Victor said. "It ain't going to cost all that much. He had to be cremated. Things were kind of ugly. He died of a heart attack in his trailer and nobody found him for a week. It was really hot, too. You get the picture."

"Now, Victor, we're sorry for your loss and the circumstances. But we can really only afford to give you one hundred dollars."

"That's not even enough for a plane ticket."

"Well, you might consider driving down to Phoenix."

---

[1] *Bureau of Indian Affairs:* The division of the U.S. Department of the Interior that manages Native American matters; the bureau is operated by government officials, not tribal leaders.

"I don't have a car. Besides, I was going to drive my father's pickup 10 back up here."

"Now, Victor," the council said, "we're sure there is somebody who could drive you to Phoenix. Or could anybody lend you the rest of the money?"

"You know there ain't nobody around with that kind of money."

"Well, we're sorry, Victor, but that's the best we can do."

Victor accepted the tribal council's offer. What else could he do? So he signed the proper papers, picked up his check, and walked over to the Trading Post to cash it.

While Victor stood in line, he watched Thomas Builds-the-Fire stand- 15 ing near the magazine rack talking to himself. Like he always did. Thomas was a storyteller whom nobody wanted to listen to. That's like being a dentist in a town where everybody has false teeth.

Victor and Thomas Builds-the-Fire were the same age, had grown up and played in the dirt together. Ever since Victor could remember, it was Thomas who had always had something to say.

Once, when they were seven years old, when Victor's father still lived with the family, Thomas closed his eyes and told Victor this story: "Your father's heart is weak. He is afraid of his own family. He is afraid of you. Late at night, he sits in the dark. Watches the television until there's nothing but that white noise. Sometimes he feels like he wants to buy a motorcycle and ride away. He wants to run and hide. He doesn't want to be found."

Thomas Builds-the-Fire had known that Victor's father was going to leave, known it before anyone. Now Victor stood in the Trading Post with a one-hundred-dollar check in his hand, wondering if Thomas knew that Victor's father was dead, if he knew what was going to happen next.

Just then, Thomas looked at Victor, smiled, and walked over to him.

"Victor, I'm sorry about your father," Thomas said.   20

"How did you know about it?" Victor asked.

"I heard it on the wind. I heard it from the birds. I felt it in the sun-light. Also, your mother was just in here crying."

"Oh," Victor said and looked around the Trading Post. All the other Indians stared, surprised that Victor was even talking to Thomas. Nobody talked to Thomas anymore because he told the same damn stories over and over again. Victor was embarrassed, but he thought that Thomas might be able to help him. Victor felt a sudden need for tradition.

"I can lend you the money you need," Thomas said suddenly. "But you have to take me with you."

"I can't take your money," Victor said. "I mean, I haven't hardly talked 25 to you in years. We're not really friends anymore."

"I didn't say we were friends. I said you had to take me with you."

"Let me think about it."

Victor went home with his one hundred dollars and sat at the kitchen table. He held his head in his hands and thought about Thomas Builds-the-Fire, remembered little details, tears and scars, the bicycle they shared for a summer, so many stories.

*   *   *

Thomas Builds-the-Fire sat on the bicycle, waiting in Victor's yard. He was ten years old and skinny. His hair was dirty because it was the Fourth of July.

30   "Victor," Thomas yelled. "Hurry up. We're going to miss the fireworks."

After a few minutes, Victor ran out of his family's house, vaulted over the porch railing, and landed gracefully on the sidewalk.

Thomas gave him the bike and they headed for the fireworks. It was nearly dark and the fireworks were about to start.

"You know," Thomas said, "it's strange how us Indians celebrate the Fourth of July. It ain't like it was our independence everybody was fighting for."

"You think about things too much," Victor said. "It's just supposed to be fun. Maybe Junior will be there."

35   "Which Junior? Everybody on this reservation is named Junior."

The fireworks were small, hardly more than a few bottle rockets and a fountain. But it was enough for two Indian boys. Years later, they would need much more.

Afterward, sitting in the dark, fighting off mosquitoes, Victor turned to Thomas Builds-the-Fire.

"Hey," Victor said. "Tell me a story."

Thomas closed his eyes and told this story: "There were these two Indian boys who wanted to be warriors. But it was too late to be warriors in the old way. All the horses were gone. So the two Indian boys stole a car and drove to the city. They parked the stolen car in the front of the police station and then hitchhiked back home to the reservation. When they got back, all their friends cheered and their parents' eyes shone with pride. 'You were very brave,' everybody said to the two Indian boys. 'Very brave.'"

40   "Ya-hey," Victor said. "That's a good one. I wish I could be a warrior."

"Me too," Thomas said.

Victor sat at his kitchen table. He counted his one hundred dollars again and again. He knew he needed more to make it to Phoenix and back. He knew he needed Thomas Builds-the-Fire. So he put his money in his wallet and opened the front door to find Thomas on the porch.

"Ya-hey, Victor," Thomas said. "I knew you'd call me."

Thomas walked into the living room and sat down in Victor's favorite chair.

"I've got some money saved up," Thomas said. "It's enough to get us 45 down there, but you have to get us back."

"I've got this hundred dollars," Victor said. "And my dad had a savings account I'm going to claim."

"How much in your dad's account?"

"Enough. A few hundred."

"Sounds good. When we leaving?"

When they were fifteen and had long since stopped being friends, Victor 50 and Thomas got into a fistfight. That is, Victor was really drunk and beat Thomas up for no reason at all. All the other Indian boys stood around and watched it happen. Junior was there and so were Lester, Seymour, and a lot of others.

The beating might have gone on until Thomas was dead if Norma Many Horses hadn't come along and stopped it.

"Hey, you boys," Norma yelled and jumped out of her car. "Leave him alone."

If it had been someone else, even another man, the Indian boys would've just ignored the warnings. But Norma was a warrior. She was powerful. She could have picked up any two of the boys and smashed their skulls together. But worse than that, she would have dragged them all over to some tepee and made them listen to some elder tell a dusty old story.

The Indian boys scattered, and Norma walked over to Thomas and picked him up.

"Hey, little man, are you O.K.?" she asked. 55

Thomas gave her a thumbs-up.

"Why they always picking on you?"

Thomas shook his head, closed his eyes, but no stories came to him, no words or music. He just wanted to go home, to lie in his bed and let his dreams tell the stories for him.

Thomas Builds-the-Fire and Victor sat next to each other in the airplane, coach section. A tiny white woman had the window seat. She was busy twisting her body into pretzels. She was flexible.

"I have to ask," Thomas said, and Victor closed his eyes in embarr- 60 assment.

"Don't," Victor said.

"Excuse me, miss," Thomas asked. "Are you a gymnast or something?"

"There's no something about it," she said. "I was first alternate on the 1980 Olympic team."

"Really?" Thomas asked.

65   "Really."

"I mean, you used to be a world-class athlete?" Thomas asked.

"My husband thinks I still am."

Thomas Builds-the-Fire smiled. She was a mental gymnast too. She pulled her leg straight up against her body so that she could've kissed her kneecap.

"I wish I could do that," Thomas said.

70   Victor was ready to jump out of the plane. Thomas, that crazy Indian storyteller with ratty old braids and broken teeth, was flirting with a beautiful Olympic gymnast. Nobody back home on the reservation would ever believe it.

"Well," the gymnast said. "It's easy. Try it."

Thomas grabbed at his leg and tried to pull it up into the same position as the gymnast's. He couldn't even come close, which made Victor and the gymnast laugh.

"Hey," she asked. "You two are Indian, right?"

"Full-blood," Victor said.

75   "Not me," Thomas said. "I'm half magician on my mother's side and half clown on my father's."

They all laughed.

"What are your names?" she asked.

"Victor and Thomas."

"Mine is Cathy. Pleased to meet you all."

80   The three of them talked for the duration of the flight. Cathy the gymnast complained about the government, how they screwed the 1980 Olympic team by boycotting the games.

"Sounds like you all got a lot in common with Indians," Thomas said. Nobody laughed.

After the plane landed in Phoenix and they had all found their way to the terminal, Cathy the gymnast smiled and waved goodbye.

"She was really nice," Thomas said.

85   "Yeah, but everybody talks to everybody on airplanes," Victor said.

"You always used to tell me I think too much," Thomas said. "Now it sounds like you do."

"Maybe I caught it from you."

"Yeah."

Thomas and Victor rode in a taxi to the trailer where Victor's father had died.

90   "Listen," Victor said as they stopped in front of the trailer. "I never told you I was sorry for beating you up that time."

"Oh, it was nothing. We were just kids and you were drunk."

"Yeah, but I'm still sorry."

"That's all right."

Victor paid for the taxi, and the two of them stood in the hot Phoenix summer. They could smell the trailer.

"This ain't going to be nice," Victor said. "You don't have to go in."   95
"You're going to need help."

Victor walked to the front door and opened it. The stink rolled out and made them both gag. Victor's father had lain in that trailer for a week in hundred-degree temperatures before anyone had found him. And the only reason anyone found him was the smell. They needed dental records to identify him. That's exactly what the coroner said. They needed dental records.

"Oh, man," Victor said. "I don't know if I can do this."
"Well, then don't."
"But there might be something valuable in there."   100
"I thought his money was in the bank."
"It is: I was talking about pictures and letters and stuff like that."
"Oh," Thomas said as he held his breath and followed Victor into the trailer.

When Victor was twelve, he stepped into an underground wasps' nest. His foot was caught in the hole and no matter how hard he struggled, Victor couldn't pull free. He might have died there, stung a thousand times, if Thomas Builds-the-Fire had not come by.

"Run," Thomas yelled and pulled Victor's foot from the hole. They ran   105
then, hard as they ever had, faster than Billy Mills, faster than Jim Thorpe, faster than the wasps could fly.

Victor and Thomas ran until they couldn't breathe, ran until it was cold and dark outside, ran until they were lost and it took hours to find their way home. All the way back, Victor counted his stings.

"Seven," Victor said. "My lucky number."

*   *   *

Victor didn't find much to keep in the trailer. Only a photo album and a stereo. Everything else had that smell stuck in it or was useless anyway. "I guess this is all," Victor said. "It ain't much."

"Better than nothing," Thomas said.
"Yeah, and I do have the pickup."   110
"Yeah," Thomas said. "It's in good shape."
"Dad was good about that stuff."
"Yeah, I remember your dad."
"Really?" Victor asked. "What do you remember?"

Thomas Builds-the-Fire closed his eyes and told this story: "I remem-   115
ber when I had this dream that told me to go to Spokane, to stand by the falls in the middle of the city and wait for a sign. I knew I had

to go there but I didn't have a car. Didn't have a license. I was only thirteen. So I walked all the way, took me all day, and I finally made it to the falls. I stood there for an hour waiting. Then your dad came walking up. 'What the hell are you doing here?' he asked me. I said, 'Waiting for a vision.' Then your father said, 'All you're going to get here is mugged.' So he drove me over to Denny's, bought me dinner, and then drove me home to the reservation. For a long time, I was mad because I thought my dreams had lied to me. But they hadn't. Your dad was my vision. *Take care of each other* is what my dreams were saying. *Take care of each other*."

Victor was quiet for a long time. He searched his mind for memories of his father, found the good ones, found a few bad ones, added it all up, and smiled.

"My father never told me about finding you in Spokane," Victor said.

"He said he wouldn't tell anybody. Didn't want me to get in trouble. But he said I had to watch out for you as part of the deal."

"Really?"

120   "Really. Your father said you would need the help. He was right."

"That's why you came down here with me, isn't it?" Victor asked.

"I came because of your father."

Victor and Thomas climbed into the pickup, drove over to the bank, and claimed the three hundred dollars in the savings account.

Thomas Builds-the-Fire could fly.

125   Once, he jumped off the roof of the tribal school and flapped his arms like a crazy eagle. And he flew. For a second he hovered, suspended above all the other Indian boys, who were too smart or too scared to jump too.

"He's flying," Junior yelled, and Seymour was busy looking for the trick wires or mirrors. But it was real. As real as the dirt when Thomas lost altitude and crashed to the ground.

He broke his arm in two places.

"He broke his wing, he broke his wing, he broke his wing," all the Indian boys chanted as they ran off, flapping their wings, wishing they could fly too. They hated Thomas for his courage, his brief moment as a bird. Everybody has dreams about flying. Thomas flew.

One of his dreams came true for just a second, just enough to make it real.

*   *   *

130 Victor's father, his ashes, fit in one wooden box with enough left over to fill a cardboard box.

"He always was a big man," Thomas said.

Victor carried part of his father out to the pickup, and Thomas carried the rest. They set him down carefully behind the seats, put a cowboy hat on the wooden box and a Dodgers cap on the cardboard box. That was the way it was supposed to be.

"Ready to head back home?" Victor asked.

"It's going to be a long drive."

"Yeah, take a couple days, maybe."   135

"We can take turns," Thomas said.

"O.K.," Victor said, but they didn't take turns. Victor drove for sixteen hours straight north, made it halfway up Nevada toward home before he finally pulled over.

"Hey, Thomas," Victor said. "You got to drive for a while."

"O.K."

Thomas Builds-the-Fire slid behind the wheel and started off down the   140 road. All through Nevada, Thomas and Victor had been amazed at the lack of animal life, at the absence of water, of movement.

"Where is everything?" Victor had asked more than once.

Now, when Thomas was finally driving, they saw the first animal, maybe the only animal in Nevada. It was a long-eared jackrabbit.

"Look," Victor yelled. "It's alive."

Thomas and Victor were busy congratulating themselves on their discovery when the jackrabbit darted out into the road and under the wheels of the pickup.

"Stop the goddamn car," Victor yelled, and Thomas did stop and   145 backed the pickup to the dead jackrabbit.

"Oh, man, he's dead," Victor said as he looked at the squashed animal. "Really dead."

"The only thing alive in this whole state and we just killed it."

"I don't know," Thomas said. "I think it was suicide."

Victor looked around the desert, sniffed the air, felt the emptiness and   150 loneliness, and nodded his head.

"Yeah," Victor said. "It had to be suicide."

"I can't believe this," Thomas said. "You drive for a thousand miles and there ain't even any bugs smashed on the windshield. I drive for ten seconds and kill the only living thing in Nevada."

"Yeah," Victor said. "Maybe I should drive."

"Maybe you should."

Thomas Builds-the-Fire walked through the corridors of the tribal school   155 by himself. Nobody wanted to be anywhere near him because of all those stories. Story after story.

Thomas closed his eyes and this story came to him: "We are all given one thing by which our lives are measured, one determination. Mine are the stories that can change or not change the world. It doesn't matter which, as long as I continue to tell the stories. My father, he died on Okinawa[2] in World War II, died fighting for this country, which had tried to kill him for years. My mother, she died giving birth to me, died while I was still inside her. She pushed me out into the world with her last breath. I have no brothers or sisters. I have only my stories, which came to me before I even had the words to speak. I learned a thousand stories before I took my first thousand steps. They are all I have. It's all I can do."

Thomas Builds-the-Fire told his stories to all those who would stop and listen. He kept telling them long after people had stopped listening.

Victor and Thomas made it back to the reservation just as the sun was rising. It was the beginning of a new day on earth, but the same old shit on the reservation.

"Good morning," Thomas said.

160   "Good morning."

The tribe was waking up, ready for work, eating breakfast, reading the newspaper, just like everybody else does. Willene LeBret was out in her garden, wearing a bathrobe. She waved when Thomas and Victor drove by.

"Crazy Indians made it," she said to herself and went back to her roses.

Victor stopped the pickup in front of Thomas Builds-the-Fire's HUD[3] house. They both yawned, stretched a little, shook dust from their bodies.

"I'm tired," Victor said.

165   "Of everything," Thomas added.

They both searched for words to end the journey. Victor needed to thank Thomas for his help and for the money, and to make the promise to pay it all back.

"Don't worry about the money," Thomas said. "It don't make any difference anyhow."

"Probably not, enit?"

"Nope."

170   Victor knew that Thomas would remain the crazy storyteller who talked to dogs and cars, who listened to the wind and pine trees. Victor knew that he couldn't really be friends with Thomas, even after all that had happened. It was cruel but it was real. As real as the ash, as Victor's father, sitting behind the seats.

---

[2]*Okinawa:* Largest island of the Ryukyus, a chain of Japanese islands in the western Pacific Ocean.

[3]*HUD:* The U.S. Department of Housing and Urban Development.

"I know how it is," Thomas said. "I know you ain't going to treat me any better than you did before. I know your friends would give you too much shit about it."

Victor was ashamed of himself. Whatever happened to the tribal ties, the sense of community? The only real thing he shared with anybody was a bottle and broken dreams. He owed Thomas something, anything.

"Listen," Victor said and handed Thomas the cardboard box that contained half of his father. "I want you to have this."

Thomas took the ashes and smiled, closed his eyes, and told this story: "I'm going to travel to Spokane Falls one last time and toss these ashes into the water. And your father will rise like a salmon, leap over the bridge, over me, and find his way home. It will be beautiful. His teeth will shine like silver, like a rainbow. He will rise, Victor, he will rise."

Victor smiled.   175

"I was planning on doing the same thing with my half," Victor said. "But I didn't imagine my father looking anything like a salmon. I thought it'd be like cleaning the attic or something. Like letting things go after they've stopped having any use."

"Nothing stops, cousin," Thomas said. "Nothing stops."

Thomas Builds-the-Fire got out of the pickup and walked up his driveway. Victor started the pickup and began the drive home.

"Wait," Thomas yelled suddenly from his porch. "I just got to ask one favor."

Victor stopped the pickup, leaned out the window, and shouted 180 back.

"What do you want?" he asked.

"Just one time when I'm telling a story somewhere, why don't you stop and listen?" Thomas asked.

"Just once?"

"Just once."

Victor waved his arms to let Thomas know that the deal was good. It 185 was a fair trade. That's all Thomas had ever wanted from his whole life. So Victor drove his father's pickup toward home while Thomas went into his house, closed the door behind him, and heard a new story come to him in the silence afterward.

Reading and Reacting

1. In paragraph 1, readers are told that Victor lives on a reservation. What details elsewhere in the story establish this setting? What associations does this setting have for you? Do you think the story could take place anywhere else?

2. In addition to various locations on the reservation, the story's settings include an airplane, a trailer in Phoenix, and a road through Nevada. What does each of these settings contribute to the story's plot?

3. Is the scene on the plane necessary? intrusive? distracting? far-fetched?

4. How would you characterize the story's mood or atmosphere? How do Thomas's stories help to create this mood? How do they help to establish his character? Do you think the story should have included more of Thomas's stories?

5. Why do you suppose Victor and Thomas cannot be friends when they get back to the reservation? Why are they able to be friends when they are traveling to Phoenix?

6. Do the flashbacks to the two men's childhood add something vital to the story? What purpose do these flashbacks serve?

7. In Native American culture, the storyteller holds an important position, telling tales that transmit and preserve the tribe's basic beliefs. Do you think Thomas's stories serve such a function? Or, do you think that he is, as Victor characterizes him, simply "the crazy storyteller who talked to dogs and cars, who listened to the wind and pine trees" (par. 170)?

8. What do you think the story's title means?

9. **JOURNAL ENTRY** At the end of the story, when Thomas returns home, he hears "a new story come to him in the silence" after he closes the door. What kind of story do you think comes to him at this point?

10. **CRITICAL PERSPECTIVE** In the introduction to a collection of Native American literature, Clifford E. Trafzer, the collection's editor, discusses the unique characteristics of Native American writers:

> Due to their grounding in the oral tradition of their people, Native American writers do not follow the literary canon of the dominant society in their approach to short stories. Rather than focusing on one theme or character in a brief time frame, or using one geographical area, they often use multiple themes and characters with few boundaries of time or place. Their stories do not always follow a linear and clear path, and frequently the past and present, real and mythic, and conscious and unconscious are not distinguishable. Multidimensional characters are common, and involved stories usually lack absolute conclusions. Native American writers may also play tricks with language, deliberately misusing grammar, syntax, and spelling—sometimes in defiance of the dominant culture—in order to make English reflect the language of their peoples.

Do you think "This Is What It Means to Say Phoenix, Arizona" displays the characteristics Trafzer associates with Native American writers?

Related Works: "Discovering America" (p. 93), "Evolution" (p. 523), "Defending Walt Whitman" (p. 732), "Indian Boarding School: The Runaways" (p. 763)

TILLIE OLSEN (1912 or 1913–2007) is known for her works of fiction about working-class Americans. Her short stories and one novel are inhabited by those she called the "despised people"—coal miners, farm laborers, packinghouse butchers, and housewives. Olsen was born in Nebraska into a working-class family. According to an account in her nonfiction work *Silences* (1978), she was inspired at age fifteen to write about working-class people when she read Rebecca Harding Davis's *Life in the Iron Mills*, a tale of the effects of industrialization on workers, in an 1861 issue of *Atlantic Monthly* bought for ten cents in a junk shop.

Shortly after she left high school, Olsen was jailed for helping to organize packinghouse workers. Motivated by her experiences, she began to write a novel, *Yonnondio*. Under her maiden name, Tillie Lerner, she published two poems, a short story, and part of her novel during the 1930s. After her marriage, she did not publish again for twenty-two years, spending her time raising four children and working at a variety of jobs. The collection of short stories *Tell Me a Riddle* (1961), which includes "I Stand Here Ironing" (originally titled "Help Her to Believe"), was published when she was fifty. Her only other work of fiction is *Yonnondio* (1974), which she pieced together from drafts she wrote in the 1930s and edited for publication in 1974.

In 1984, she edited *Mother to Daughter, Daughter to Mother: Mothers on Mothering*, a collection of poems, letters, short fiction, and diary excerpts written by famous and not-so-famous women, and in 1987, she collaborated with photographer Estelle Jussim on *Mothers & Daughters: An Exploration in Photographs*.

Cultural Context During the Great Depression of the 1930s, jobs were scarce throughout the United States, and many people who managed to keep their jobs were forced to take pay cuts. At the height of the Depression in 1933, almost twenty-five percent of the total workforce—more than eleven million people—were unemployed. The displacement of the American worker and the destruction of farming communities caused families such as the one in this story to split up or to migrate from their homes in search of work. In 1935, the Social Security Act established public assistance, unemployment insurance, and social security, which offered economic relief to American workers and their families.

I Stand Here Ironing (1961)

I stand here ironing, and what you asked me moves tormented back and forth with the iron.

"I wish you would manage the time to come and talk with me about your daughter. I'm sure you can help me understand her. She's a youngster who needs help and whom I'm deeply interested in helping."

"Who needs help." . . . Even if I came, what good would it do? You think because I am her mother I have a key, or that in some way you could use me as a key? She has lived for nineteen years. There is all that life that has happened outside of me, beyond me.

And when is there time to remember, to sift, to weigh, to estimate, to total? I will start and there will be an interruption and I will have to gather it all together again. Or I will become engulfed with all I did or did not do, with what should have been and what cannot be helped.

5   She was a beautiful baby. The first and only one of our five that was beautiful at birth. You do not guess how new and uneasy her tenancy in her now-loveliness. You did not know her all those years she was thought homely, or see her poring over her baby pictures, making me tell her over and over how beautiful she had been—and would be, I would tell her— and was now, to the seeing eye. But the seeing eyes were few or nonexistent. Including mine.

I nursed her. They feel that's important nowadays. I nursed all the children, but with her, with all the fierce rigidity of first motherhood, I did like the books then said. Though her cries battered me to trembling and my breasts ached with swollenness, I waited till the clock decreed.

Why do I put that first? I do not even know if it matters, or if it explains anything.

She was a beautiful baby. She blew shining bubbles of sound. She loved motion, loved light, loved color and music and textures. She would lie on the floor in her blue overalls patting the surface so hard in ecstasy her hands and feet would blur. She was a miracle to me, but when she was eight months old I had to leave her daytimes with the woman downstairs to whom she was no miracle at all, for I worked or looked for work and for Emily's father, who "could no longer endure" (he wrote in his good-bye note) "sharing want with us."

I was nineteen. It was the pre-relief, pre-WPA[1] world of the depression. I would start running as soon as I got off the streetcar, running up the stairs, the place smelling sour, and awake or asleep to startle awake, when she saw me she would break into a clogged weeping that could not be comforted, a weeping I can hear yet.

10   After a while I found a job hashing at night so I could be with her days, and it was better. But it came to where I had to bring her to his family and leave her.

It took a long time to raise the money for her fare back. Then she got chicken pox and I had to wait longer. When she finally came, I hardly knew her, walking quick and nervous like her father, looking like her father, thin, and dressed in a shoddy red that yellowed her skin and glared at the pockmarks. All the baby loveliness gone.

---

[1] *WPA:* The Works Progress Administration, created in 1935 as part of President Franklin D. Roosevelt's New Deal program. The purpose of the WPA (renamed the Works Projects Administration in 1939) was to provide jobs for the unemployed during the Great Depression.

She was two. Old enough for nursery school they said, and I did not know then what I know now—the fatigue of the long day, and the lacerations of group life in the kinds of nurseries that are only parking places for children.

Except that it would have made no difference if I had known. It was the only place there was. It was the only way we could be together, the only way I could hold a job.

And even without knowing, I knew. I knew the teacher that was evil because all these years it has curdled into my memory, the little boy hunched in the corner, her rasp, "why aren't you outside, because Alvin hits you? that's no reason, go out, scaredy." I knew Emily hated it even if she did not clutch and implore "don't go Mommy" like the other children, mornings.

She always had a reason why we should stay home. Momma, you look 15 sick. Momma, I feel sick. Momma, the teachers aren't there today, they're sick. Momma, we can't go, there was a fire there last night. Momma, it's a holiday today, no school, they told me.

But never a direct protest, never rebellion. I think of our others in their three-, four-year-oldness—the explosions, the tempers, the denunciations, the demands—and I feel suddenly ill. I put the iron down. What in me demanded that goodness in her? And what was the cost, the cost to her of such goodness?

The old man living in the back once said in his gentle way: "You should smile at Emily more when you look at her." What *was* in my face when I looked at her? I loved her. There were all the acts of love.

It was only with the others I remembered what he said, and it was the face of joy, and not of care or tightness or worry I turned to them—too late for Emily. She does not smile easily, let alone almost always as her brothers and sisters do. Her face is closed and sombre, but when she wants, how fluid. You must have seen it in her pantomimes, you spoke of her rare gift for comedy on the stage that rouses laughter out of the audience so dear they applaud and applaud and do not want to let her go.

Where does it come from, that comedy? There was none of it in her when she came back to me that second time, after I had had to send her away again. She had a new daddy now to learn to love, and I think perhaps it was a better time.

Except when we left her alone nights, telling ourselves she was old 20 enough.

"Can't you go some other time, Mommy, like tomorrow?" she would ask. "Will it be just a little while you'll be gone? Do you promise?"

The time we came back, the front door open, the clock on the floor in the hall. She rigid awake. "It wasn't just a little while. I didn't cry. Three times I called you, just three times, and then I ran downstairs to open the door so you could come faster. The clock talked loud. I threw it away, it scared me what it talked."

She said the clock talked loud again that night I went to the hospital to have Susan. She was delirious with the fever that comes before red measles, but she was fully conscious all the week I was gone and the week after we were home when she could not come near the new baby or me. She did not get well. She stayed skeleton thin, not wanting to eat, and night after night she had nightmares. She would call for me, and I would rouse from exhaustion to sleepily call back: "You're all right, darling, go to sleep, it's just a dream," and if she still called, in a sterner voice, "now go to sleep, Emily, there's nothing to hurt you." Twice, only twice, when I had to get up for Susan anyhow, I went in to sit with her.

25   Now when it is too late (as if she would let me hold and comfort her like I do the others) I get up and go to her at once at her moan or restless stirring. "Are you awake, Emily? Can I get you something?" And the answer is always the same: "No, I'm all right, go back to sleep, Mother."

They persuaded me at the clinic to send her away to a convalescent home in the country where "she can have the kind of food and care you can't manage for her, and you'll be free to concentrate on the new baby." They still send children to that place. I see pictures on the society page of sleek young women planning affairs to raise money for it, or dancing at the affairs, or decorating Easter eggs or filling Christmas stockings for the children.

They never have a picture of the children so I do not know if the girls still wear those gigantic red bows and the ravaged looks on the every other Sunday when parents can come to visit "unless otherwise notified"—as we were notified the first six weeks.

Oh it is a handsome place, green lawns and tall trees and fluted flower beds. High up on the balconies of each cottage the children stand, the girls in their red bows and white dresses, the boys in white suits and giant red ties. The parents stand below shrieking up to be heard and the children shriek down to be heard, and between them the invisible wall: "Not to Be Contaminated by Parental Germs or Physical Affection."

There was a tiny girl who always stood hand in hand with Emily. Her parents never came. One visit she was gone. "They moved her to Rose Cottage," Emily shouted in explanation. "They don't like you to love anybody here."

30   She wrote once a week, the labored writing of a seven-year-old. "I am fine. How is the baby. If I write my leter nicly I will have a star. Love." There never was a star. We wrote every other day, letters she could never hold or keep but only hear read—once. "We simply do not have room for children to keep any personal possessions," they patiently explained when we pieced one Sunday's shrieking together to plead how much it would

mean to Emily, who loved so to keep things, to be allowed to keep her letters and cards.

Each visit she looked frailer. "She isn't eating," they told us.

(They had runny eggs for breakfast or mush with lumps, Emily said later, I'd hold it in my mouth and not swallow. Nothing ever tasted good, just when they had chicken.)

It took us eight months to get her released home, and only the fact that she gained back so little of her seven lost pounds convinced the social worker.

I used to try to hold and love her after she came back, but her body would stay stiff, and after a while she'd push away. She ate little. Food sickened her, and I think much of life too. Oh she had physical lightness and brightness, twinkling by on skates, bouncing like a ball up and down up and down over the jump rope, skimming over the hill; but these were momentary.

She fretted about her appearance, thin and dark and foreign-looking 35 at a time when every little girl was supposed to look or thought she should look a chubby blonde replica of Shirley Temple. The doorbell sometimes rang for her, but no one seemed to come and play in the house or be a best friend. Maybe because we moved so much.

There was a boy she loved painfully through two school semesters. Months later she told me how she had taken pennies from my purse to buy him candy. "Licorice was his favorite and I brought him some every day, but he still liked Jennifer better'n me. Why, Mommy?" The kind of question for which there is no answer.

School was a worry to her. She was not glib or quick in a world where glibness and quickness were easily confused with ability to learn. To her overworked and exasperated teachers she was an overconscientious "slow learner" who kept trying to catch up and was absent entirely too often.

I let her be absent, though sometimes the illness was imaginary. How different from my now-strictness about attendance with the others. I wasn't working. We had a new baby, I was home anyhow. Sometimes, after Susan grew old enough, I would keep her home from school, too, to have them all together.

Mostly Emily had asthma, and her breathing, harsh and labored, would fill the house with a curiously tranquil sound. I would bring the two old dresser mirrors and her boxes of collections to her bed. She would select beads and single earrings, bottle tops and shells, dried flowers and pebbles, old postcards and scraps, all sorts of oddments; then she and Susan would play Kingdom, setting up landscapes and furniture, peopling them with action.

Those were the only times of peaceful companionship between her 40 and Susan. I have edged away from it, that poisonous feeling between them, that terrible balancing of hurts and needs I had to do between the two, and did so badly, those earlier years.

Oh there are conflicts between the others too, each one human, needing, demanding, hurting, taking—but only between Emily and Susan, no, Emily toward Susan that corroding resentment. It seems so obvious on the surface, yet it is not obvious. Susan, the second child, Susan, golden- and curly-haired and chubby, quick and articulate and assured, everything in appearance and manner Emily was not; Susan, not able to resist Emily's precious things, losing or sometimes clumsily breaking them; Susan telling jokes and riddles to company for applause while Emily sat silent (to say to me later: that was *my* riddle, Mother, I told it to Susan); Susan, who for all the five years' difference in age was just a year behind Emily in developing physically.

I am glad for that slow physical development that widened the difference between her and her contemporaries, though she suffered over it. She was too vulnerable for that terrible world of youthful competition, of preening and parading, of constant measuring of yourself against every other, of envy, "If I had that copper hair," "If I had that skin. . . ." She tormented herself enough about not looking like the others, there was enough of the unsureness, the having to be conscious of words before you speak, the constant caring—what are they thinking of me? without having it all magnified by the merciless physical drives.

Ronnie is calling. He is wet and I change him. It is rare there is such a cry now. That time of motherhood is almost behind me when the ear is not one's own but must always be racked and listening for the child cry, the child call. We sit for a while and I hold him, looking out over the city spread in charcoal with its soft aisles of light. "*Shoogily*," he breathes and curls closer. I carry him back to bed, asleep. *Shoogily*. A funny word, a family word, inherited from Emily, invented by her to say: *comfort*.

In this and other ways she leaves her seal, I say aloud. And startle at my saying it. What do I mean? What did I start to gather together, to try and make coherent? I was at the terrible, growing years. War years. I do not remember them well. I was working, there were four smaller ones now, there was not time for her. She had to help be a mother, and housekeeper, and shopper. She had to set her seal. Mornings of crisis and near hysteria trying to get lunches packed, hair combed, coats and shoes found, everyone to school or Child Care on time, the baby ready for transportation. And always the paper scribbled on by a smaller one, the book looked at by Susan then mislaid, the homework not done. Running out to that huge school where she was one, she was lost, she was a drop; suffering over the unpreparedness, stammering and unsure in her classes.

45   There was so little time left at night after the kids were bedded down. She would struggle over books, always eating (it was in those years she

developed her enormous appetite that is legendary in our family) and I would be ironing, or preparing food for the next day, or writing V-mail[2] to Bill, or tending the baby. Sometimes, to make me laugh, or out of her despair, she would imitate happenings or types at school.

I think I said once: "Why don't you do something like this in the school amateur show?" One morning she phoned me at work, hardly understandable through the weeping: "Mother, I did it. I won, I won; they gave me first prize; they clapped and clapped and wouldn't let me go."

Now suddenly she was Somebody, and as imprisoned in her difference as she had been in anonymity.

She began to be asked to perform at other high schools, even in colleges, then at city and statewide affairs. The first one we went to, I only recognized her that first moment when thin, shy, she almost drowned herself into the curtains. Then: Was this Emily? The control, the command, the convulsing and deadly clowning, the spell, then the roaring, stamping audience, unwilling to let this rare and precious laughter out of their lives.

Afterwards: You ought to do something about her with a gift like that—but without money or knowing how, what does one do? We have left it all to her, and the gift has as often eddied inside, clogged and clotted, as been used and growing.

She is coming. She runs up the stairs two at a time with her light grace-   50
ful step, and I know she is happy tonight. Whatever it was that occasioned your call did not happen today.

"Aren't you ever going to finish the ironing, Mother? Whistler painted his mother in a rocker. I'd have to paint mine standing over an ironing board." This is one of her communicative nights and she tells me everything and nothing as she fixes herself a plate of food out of the icebox.

She is so lovely. Why did you want me to come in at all? Why were you concerned? She will find her way.

She starts up the stairs to bed. "Don't get me up with the rest in the morning." "But I thought you were having midterms." "Oh, those," she comes back in, kisses me, and says quite lightly, "in a couple of years when we'll all be atom-dead they won't matter a bit."

She has said it before. She *believes* it. But because I have been dredging the past, and all that compounds a human being is so heavy and meaningful in me, I cannot endure it tonight.

I will never total it all. I will never come in to say: She was a child   55
seldom smiled at. Her father left me before she was a year old. I had to work her first six years when there was work, or I sent her home and to

---

[2] *V-mail:* Mail sent to or from members of the armed forces during World War II. Letters were reduced onto microfilm and enlarged and printed out at their destination.

his relatives. There were years she had care she hated. She was dark and thin and foreign-looking in a world where the prestige went to blondeness and curly hair and dimples, she was slow where glibness was prized. She was a child of anxious, not proud, love. We were poor and could not afford for her the soil of easy growth. I was a young mother, I was a distracted mother. There were other children pushing up, demanding. Her younger sister seemed all that she was not. There were years she did not want me to touch her. She kept too much in herself, her life was such she had to keep too much in herself. My wisdom came too late. She has much to her and probably little will come of it. She is a child of her age, of depression, of war, of fear.

Let her be. So all that is in her will not bloom—but in how many does it? There is still enough left to live by. Only help her to know—help make it so there is cause for her to know—that she is more than this dress on the ironing board, helpless before the iron.

Reading and Reacting

1. "I Stand Here Ironing" focuses on incidents that took place in the "pre-relief, pre-WPA world" of the Depression (par. 9). In light of social, political, and economic changes that have occurred since the 1930s, do you think the events the story presents could occur today? Explain.

2. In what sense is the image of a mother at an ironing board appropriate for this story?

3. The narrator is overwhelmed by guilt. What does she believe she has done wrong? What, if anything, do *you* think she has done wrong? Do you think she has been a good mother? Why or why not?

4. Who, or what, do you blame for the narrator's problems? For example, do you blame Emily's father? the Depression? the social institutions and "experts" to which the narrator turns?

5. Do you see the narrator as a victim limited by the times in which she lives? Do you agree with the narrator that Emily is "a child of her age, of depression, of war, of fear" (par. 55)? Or do you believe both women have some control over their own destinies, regardless of the story's historical setting?

6. What do you think the narrator wants for her daughter? Do you think her goals for Emily are realistic? Why or why not?

7. Paragraph 28 describes the physical setting of the convalescent home to which Emily was sent. What does this description add to the story?

8. To whom do you think the mother is speaking in this story?

9. **Journal Entry** Put yourself in Emily's position. What do you think she would like to tell her mother?

10. CRITICAL PERSPECTIVE Writing in *The Red Wheelbarrow*, psychologist Robert Coles discusses the complex family relationships depicted in "I Stand Here Ironing" and reaches an optimistic conclusion:

> But the child did not grow to be a mere victim of the kind so many of us these days are rather eager to recognize—a hopeless tangle of psychopathology. The growing child, even in her troubled moments, revealed herself to be persistent, demanding, and observant. In the complaints we make, in the "symptoms" we develop, we reveal our strengths as well as our weaknesses. The hurt child could summon her intelligence, exercise her will, smile and make others smile.

Do you agree with Coles's psychological evaluation of Emily? Do you find the story's ending as essentially uplifting as he seems to? Why or why not?

Related Works: "Everyday Use" (p. 344), "Two Kinds" (p. 471), "Those Winter Sundays" (p. 705), "Dusting" (p. 706), *Post-its* (p. 955)

WRITING SUGGESTIONS: Setting

1. In "The Storm" and "I Stand Here Ironing," social constraints determined by the story's historical setting limit a woman's options. Explore the options each woman might reasonably exercise in order to break free of the limits that social institutions impose on her.

2. Write an essay in which you consider how "This Is What It Means to Say Phoenix, Arizona" would be different if its geographical and physical setting were changed to a setting of your choice. In your essay, examine the changes (in plot development as well as in the characters' conflicts, reactions, and motivation) that might occur as a result of the change in setting.

3. Select a story from another chapter, and write an essay in which you consider how setting affects its plot—for example, how it creates conflict or crisis, how it forces characters to act, or how it determines how the plot is resolved.

4. "The Storm" uses rich descriptive language to create a mood that dominates the story. This is also true of James Joyce's "Araby" (p. 288). Analyze this use of language in one of these stories. Or, explicate a short passage from each story, and then compare the two passages, analyzing the two writers' use of language to create a mood.

CHAPTER 10

POINT OF VIEW

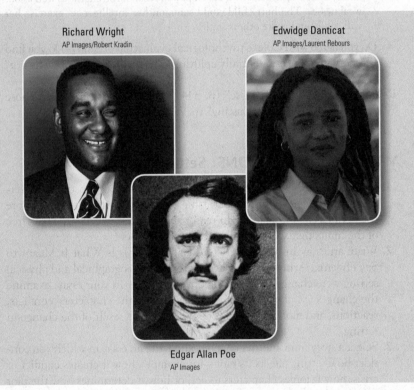

Richard Wright
AP Images/Robert Kradin

Edwidge Danticat
AP Images/Laurent Rebours

Edgar Allan Poe
AP Images

One of the first choices writers make is who tells the story. This choice determines the story's **point of view**—the vantage point from which events are presented. The implications of this choice are far-reaching.

Consider the following scenario. Five people witness a crime and are questioned by the police. Their stories agree on certain points: a crime was committed, a body was found, and the crime occurred at noon. But in other ways their stories are different. The man who fled the scene was either tall or of average height; his hair was either dark or light; he either was carrying an object or was empty-handed. The events that led up to the crime and even the description of the crime itself are markedly different, depending on who tells the story. Thus, the **narrator**—the person telling the story—determines what details are included in the story and how they are arranged—in short, the plot. In addition, the perspective of the narrator affects the story's style, language, and themes.

The narrator of a work of fiction is not the same as the writer—even when a writer uses the first-person *I*. Writers create narrators to tell their stories. Often the personalities and opinions of narrators are far different from those of the author. The term **persona**—which literally means "mask"—is used for such narrators. By assuming this mask, a writer expands the creative possibilities of a work.

When deciding on a point of view for a work of fiction, a writer can choose to tell the story either in the **first person** or in the **third person**.

 ## First-Person Narrators

Sometimes the narrator is a character who uses the **first person** (*I* or sometimes *we*) to tell the story. Often this narrator is a **major character**—Sammy in John Updike's "A&P" (p. 160) and the boy in James Joyce's "Araby" (p. 288), for example—who tells his or her own story and is the focus of that story. Sometimes, however, a first-person narrator tells a story that is primarily about someone else. Such a narrator may be a **minor character** who plays a relatively small part in the story or simply an **observer** who reports events experienced or related by others. The narrator of William Faulkner's "A Rose for Emily" (p. 143), for example, is an unidentified witness to the story's events. By using *we* instead of *I*, this narrator speaks on behalf of all the town's residents, expressing their shared views of their neighbor, Emily Grierson, as the following excerpt illustrates:

> We did not say she was crazy then. We believed she had to do that. We remembered all the young men her father had driven away, and we knew that with nothing left, she would have to cling to that which had robbed her, as people will.

Writers gain a number of advantages when they use first-person narrators. First, they are able to present incidents convincingly. Readers are more willing to accept a statement like "My sister changed a lot after that day" than they are the impersonal observations of a third-person narrator. The first-person narrator also simplifies a writer's task of selecting details. Only the events and details that the narrator could actually have observed or experienced can be introduced into the story.

Another major advantage of first-person narrators is that their restricted view can create **irony**—a discrepancy between what is said and what readers believe to be true. Irony may be *dramatic, situational,* or *verbal.* **Dramatic irony** occurs when a narrator (or a character) perceives less than readers do; **situational irony** occurs when what happens is at odds with what readers are led to expect; **verbal irony** occurs when the narrator says one thing but actually means another.

"Gryphon," by Charles Baxter (p. 172), illustrates all three kinds of irony. Baxter creates **dramatic irony** when he has his main character see less than readers do. For example, at the end of the story, the young boy does not yet realize what readers already know—that he has learned more from Miss Ferenczi's way of teaching than from Mr. Hibler's. The setting of the story—a conventional school—creates **situational irony** because it contrasts with the unexpected events that unfold there. In addition, many of the narrator's comments create **verbal irony** because they convey the opposite of their literal meaning. At the end of the story, for example, after the substitute, Miss Ferenczi, has been fired, the narrator relates another teacher's comment that life will now return to "normal" and that their regular teacher will soon return to test them on their "knowledge." This comment is ironic in light of all Miss Ferenczi has done to redefine the narrator's ideas about "normal" education and about "knowledge."

Unreliable Narrators

Sometimes first-person narrators are self-serving, mistaken, confused, unstable, or even insane. These **unreliable narrators**, whether intentionally or unintentionally, misrepresent events and misdirect readers. In Edgar Allan Poe's "The Cask of Amontillado" (p. 249), for example, the narrator, Montresor, tells his story to justify a crime he committed fifty years before. Montresor's version of what happened is not accurate, and perceptive readers know it: his obvious self-deception, his sadistic manipulation of Fortunato, his detached description of the cold-blooded murder, and his lack of remorse lead readers to question his sanity and, therefore, to distrust his version of events. This distrust creates an ironic distance between readers and narrator.

The narrator of Charlotte Perkins Gilman's "The Yellow Wallpaper" (p. 434) is also an unreliable narrator. Suffering from "nervous depression," she unintentionally distorts the facts when she says that the shapes in her bedroom wallpaper are changing and moving. Moreover, she does not realize what is wrong with her or why, or how her husband's "good intentions" are hurting her. Readers, however, see the disparity between the narrator's interpretation of events and their own, and this irony enriches their understanding of the story.

Some narrators are unreliable because they are naive. Because they are immature, sheltered, or innocent of evil, these narrators are not aware of the significance of the events they are relating. Having the benefit of experience, readers interpret events differently from the way these narrators do.

When we read a passage by a child narrator—such as the following one from J. D. Salinger's classic 1951 novel *The Catcher in the Rye*—we are aware of the narrator's innocence, and we know his interpretation of events is flawed:

> Anyway, I keep picturing all these little kids playing some game in this big field of rye and all. Thousands of little kids, and nobody's around— nobody big, I mean—except me. And I'm standing on the edge of some crazy cliff. What I have to do, I have to catch everybody if they start to go over the cliff—I mean if they're running and they don't look where they're going I have to come out from somewhere and catch them. I'd just be the catcher in the rye....

The irony in the preceding passage comes from our knowledge that the naive narrator, Holden Caulfield, cannot stop children from growing up. Ultimately, they all fall off the "crazy cliff" and mature into adults. Although Holden is not aware of the futility of trying to protect children from the dangers of adulthood, readers know that his efforts are doomed from the start.

A naive narrator's background can also limit his or her ability to understand a situation. The narrator in Sherwood Anderson's 1922 short story "I'm a Fool," for example, lies to impress a rich girl he meets at a racetrack. At the end of the story, the boy regrets the fact that he lied, believing that if he had told the truth, he could have seen the girl again. The reader knows, however, that the narrator (a laborer at the racetrack) is deceiving himself because the social gap that separates him and the girl could never be bridged.

Keep in mind that all first-person narrators are, in a sense, unreliable because they present a situation as only one person sees it. When you read, you should look for discrepancies between a narrator's view of events and your own. Discovering that a story has an unreliable narrator enables you not only to question the accuracy of the narrative but also to recognize the irony in the narrator's version of events. In this way, you gain insight into the story and learn something about the writer's purpose.

 ## Third-Person Narrators

Sometimes a writer uses the **third person** (*he, she, they*) to tell the story from the point of view of a narrator who is not a character. Third-person narrators fall into three categories: **omniscient**, **limited omniscient**, and **objective**.

Omniscient Narrators

Some third-person narrators are **omniscient** (all-knowing) narrators, moving at will from one character's mind to another's. One advantage of omniscient narrators is that they have none of the naïveté, dishonesty, gullibility, or mental instability that can characterize first-person narrators. In addition, because omniscient narrators are not characters in the story, their perception is not limited to what any one character can observe or comprehend. As a result, they can present a more inclusive view of events and characters than first-person narrators can.

Omniscient narrators can also convey their attitude toward their subject matter. For example, the omniscient narrator in the South African writer Nadine Gordimer's 1989 short story "Once upon a Time" uses sentence structure, word choice, repetition, and sarcasm to express disdain for the scene being described:

> In a house, in a suburb, in a city, there were a man and his wife who loved each other very much and were living happily ever after. They had a little boy, and they loved him very much. They had a cat and a dog that the little boy loved very much. They had a car and a caravan trailer for holidays, and a swimming-pool which was fenced so that the little boy and his playmates would not fall in and drown. They had a housemaid who was absolutely trustworthy and an itinerant gardener who was highly recommended by the neighbours. For when they began to live happily ever after they were warned, by that wise old witch, the husband's mother, not to take on anyone off the street.

Occasionally, omniscient narrators move not only in and out of the minds of the characters but also in and out of a **persona** (representing the voice of the author) who speaks directly to readers. This narrative technique was popular with writers during the eighteenth century, when the novel was a new literary form. It permitted writers to present themselves as masters of artifice, able to know and control all aspects of experience. Few contemporary writers would give themselves the license that Henry Fielding does in the following passage from *Tom Jones* (1749):

> And true it was that [Mr. Alworthy] did many of these things; but had he done nothing more I should have left him to have recorded his own merit on some fair freestone over the door of that hospital. Matters of a much more extraordinary kind are to be the subject of this history, or I should grossly misspend my time in writing so voluminous a work; and you my sagacious friend, might with equal profit and pleasure travel through some pages which certain droll authors have been facetiously pleased to call *The History of England*.

A contemporary example of this type of omniscient point of view occurs in Ursula K. LeGuin's "The Ones Who Walk Away from Omelas." This story presents a description of a city that in the narrator's words is "like a city in a fairy tale." As the story proceeds, however, the description of Omelas changes, and the narrator's tone changes as well: "Do you believe? Do you accept the festival, the city, the joy? No? Then let me describe one more thing." By undercutting her own narrative, the narrator underscores the ironic theme of the story, which suggests that it is impossible for human beings to ever achieve an ideal society.

Limited Omniscient Narrators

Third-person narrators can have **limited omniscience**, focusing on only what a single character experiences. In other words, nothing is revealed that the character does not see, hear, feel, or think.

Limited omniscient narrators, like all third-person narrators, have certain advantages over first-person narrators. When a writer uses a first-person narrator, the narrator's personality and speech color the story, creating a personal or even an idiosyncratic narrative. Also, the first-person narrator's character flaws or lack of knowledge may limit his or her awareness of the significance of events. Limited omniscient narrators are more flexible: they take readers into a particular character's mind just as a first-person narrator does, but without the first-person narrator's subjectivity, self-deception, or naïveté. In the following example from Anne Tyler's "Teenage Wasteland" (1984), the limited omniscient narrator presents the story from the point of view of a single character, Daisy:

> Daisy and Matt sat silent, shocked. Matt rubbed his forehead with his fingertips. Imagine, Daisy thought, how they must look to Mr. Lanham: an overweight housewife in a cotton dress and a too-tall, too-thin insurance agent in a baggy, frayed suit. Failures, both of them—the kind of people who are always hurrying to catch up, missing the point of things that everyone else grasps at once. She wished she'd worn nylons instead of knee socks.

Here the point of view gives readers the impression that they are standing off to the side watching Daisy and her husband Matt. However, at the same time that we have the advantage of this objective view, we are also able to see into the mind of one character.

Objective Narrators

Third-person **objective narrators**, who tell a story from an objective (or dramatic) point of view, remain entirely outside the characters' minds. With objective narrators, events unfold the way they would in a play or a movie: narrators tell the story by presenting dialogue and recounting events; they do not reveal the characters' (or their own) thoughts or attitudes. Thus, they allow readers to interpret the actions of the characters without any interference. Ernest Hemingway uses the objective point of view in his short story "A Clean, Well-Lighted Place" (1933):

> The waiter took the brandy bottle and another saucer from the counter inside the café and marched out to the old man's table. He put down the saucer and poured the glass full of brandy.
> "You should have killed yourself last week," he said to the deaf man. The old man motioned with his finger. "A little more," he said. The waiter poured on into the glass so that the brandy slopped over and ran

down the stem into the top saucer of the pile. "Thank you," the old man said. The waiter took the bottle back inside the café. He sat down at the table with his colleague again.

The story's narrator is distant, seemingly emotionless, and this perspective is consistent with the author's purpose: for Hemingway, the attitude of the narrator reflects the stunned, almost anesthetized condition of people in the post–World War I world.

 ## Selecting an Appropriate Point of View

The main criterion writers use when they decide on a point of view from which to tell a story is how the point of view they select will affect their narrative. The passages that follow illustrate the options available to writers.

Limited Omniscient Point of View

In the following passage from the short story "Doe Season" (p. 395), David Michael Kaplan uses a third-person limited omniscient narrator to tell the story of Andy, a nine-year-old girl who is going hunting with her father for the first time:

> They were always the same woods, she thought sleepily as they drove through the early morning darkness—deep and immense, covered with yesterday's snowfall, which had frozen overnight. They were the same woods that lay behind her house, *and they stretch all the way to here,* she thought, *for miles and miles, longer than I could walk in a day, or a week even, but they are still the same woods.* The thought made her feel good: it was like thinking of God; it was like thinking of the space between here and the moon; it was like thinking of all the foreign countries from her geography book where even now, Andy knew, people were going to bed, while they—she and her father and Charlie Spoon and Mac, Charlie's eleven-year-old son—were driving deeper into the Pennsylvania country-side, to go hunting.
>
> They had risen long before dawn. Her mother, yawning and not try-ing to hide her sleepiness, cooked them eggs and French toast. Her father smoked a cigarette and flicked ashes into his saucer while Andy listened, wondering *Why doesn't he come?* and *Won't he ever come?* until at last a car pulled into the graveled drive and honked. "That will be Charlie Spoon," her father said; he always said "Charlie Spoon," even though his real name was Spreun, because Charlie was, in a sense, shaped like a spoon, with a large head and a narrow waist and chest.

Here the limited omniscient point of view has the advantage of allowing the narrator to focus on the thoughts, fears, and reactions of the child while at the same time giving readers information about Andy that she herself is too immature or unsophisticated to know. Rather than simply presenting the thoughts of the child (represented in the story by italics), the third-person narrator makes connections between ideas and displays a level of language and a degree of insight that readers would not accept from Andy as a first-person narrator. In addition, the limited omniscient perspective enables the narrator to maintain some distance.

First-Person Point of View (Child)

Consider how different the passage would be if it were narrated by nine-year-old Andy:

> "I like the woods," I thought. "They're big and scary. I wonder if they're the same woods that are behind my house. They go on for miles. They're bigger than I could walk in a day, or a week even." It was neat to think that while we were driving into the woods people were going to bed in other countries.
>
> When I woke up this morning, I couldn't wait to go hunting. My mother was cooking breakfast, but all I could think of was, "When will he come?" and "Won't he ever come?" Finally, I heard a car honk. "That will be Charlie Spoon," my father said. I think he called him "Charlie Spoon" because he thought Charlie was shaped like a big spoon.

As a first-person narrator, nine-year-old Andy must have the voice of a child; moreover, she is restricted to only those observations that a nine-year-old could reasonably make. Because of these limitations, the passage lacks the level of vocabulary, syntax, and insight necessary to develop the central character and the themes of the story. This point of view could succeed only if Andy's words established an ironic contrast between her naive sensibility and the reality of the situation.

First-Person Point of View (Adult)

The writer could have avoided these problems and still gained the advantages of using a first-person narrator by having Andy tell her story as an adult looking back on a childhood experience. (This technique is used by James Joyce in "Araby" [p. 288], Charles Baxter in "Gryphon" [p. 172], and Alberto Alvaro Ríos in "The Secret Lion" [p. 466].)

> "They are always the same woods," I thought sleepily as we drove through the early morning darkness—deep and immense, covered with yesterday's snowfall, which had frozen overnight. "They're the same woods that lie behind my house, and they stretch all the way to here," I thought. I knew that they stretched for miles and miles, longer than I could walk in a day, or even in a week but that they were still the same woods. Knowing this made me feel good: I thought it was like thinking of God; it was like thinking of the space between that place and the moon; it was like thinking of all the foreign countries from my geography book where even then, I knew, people were going to bed, while we—my father and I and Charlie

Spoon and Mac, Charlie's eleven-year-old son—were driving deeper into
the Pennsylvania countryside, to go hunting.
We had risen before dawn. My mother, who was yawning and not
trying to hide her sleepiness, cooked us eggs and French toast. My father
smoked a cigarette and flicked ashes into his saucer while I listened,
wondering, "Why doesn't he come?" and "Won't he ever come?" until
at last a car pulled into our driveway and honked. "That will be Charlie
Spoon," my father said. He always said "Charlie Spoon," even though
his real name was Spreun, because Charlie was, in a sense, shaped like a
spoon, with a large head and a narrow waist and chest.

Although this passage presents the child's point of view, it does not use a
child's voice; the language and scope of the passage are too sophisticated for
a child. By using a mature style, the adult narrator considers ideas that a child
could not possibly understand, such as the symbolic significance of the woods.
In so doing, however, he sacrifices the objectivity and detachment that characterize the third-person limited omniscient narrator of the original story.

Omniscient Point of View

The writer could also have used an omniscient narrator to tell his story. In
this case, the narrator would be free to reveal and comment not only on
Andy's thoughts but also on those of her father, and possibly even on the
thoughts of her mother and Charlie Spoon.

In the following passage, the omniscient narrator interprets the behavior
of the characters and tells what each one is thinking.

They were always the same woods, she thought sleepily as they drove
through the early morning darkness—deep and immense, covered with
yesterday's snowfall, which had frozen overnight. They were the same
woods that lay behind her house, and they stretch all the way to here, she
thought, for miles and miles, longer than I could walk in a day, or a week
even, but they are still the same woods.
They had risen before dawn. The mother, yawning and not trying to hide
her sleepiness, cooked them eggs and French toast. She looked at her husband
and her daughter and wondered if she was doing the right thing by allowing
them to go hunting together. "After all," she thought, "he's not the most
careful person. Will he watch her? Make sure that no harm comes to her?"
The father smoked a cigarette and flicked ashes into his saucer. He was
listening to the sounds of the early morning. "I know everything will be all
right," he thought. "It's about time Andy went hunting. When I was her
age...." Andy listened, wondering Why doesn't he come? and Won't he ever
come? until at last a car pulled into the graveled drive and honked. Suddenly
the father cocked his head and said, "That will be Charlie Spoon."
Andy thought it was funny that her father called Charlie "Spoon"
even though his real name was Spreun, because Charlie was, in a sense,
shaped like a spoon, with a large head and a narrow waist and chest.

Certainly this point of view has its advantages; for example, the wide scope of this perspective provides a great deal of information about the characters. However, the use of an omniscient point of view deprives the story of its focus on Andy.

Objective Point of View

Finally, the writer could have used an objective narrator. This point of view would eliminate all interpretation by the narrator and force readers to make judgments solely on the basis of what the characters say and do.

> Andy sat sleepily staring into her cereal. She played with the dry flakes of bran as they floated in the surface of the milk.
>
> Andy's mother, yawning, cooked them eggs and French toast. She looked at her husband and her daughter, paused for a second, and then went about what she was doing.
>
> Andy's father smoked a cigarette and flicked ashes into his saucer. He looked out the window and said, "I wonder where Charlie Spoon is?"
>
> Andy squirmed restlessly and repeatedly looked up at the clock that hung above the stove.

The disadvantage of this point of view is that it creates a great deal of distance between the characters and the readers. Instead of gaining the intimate knowledge of Andy that the limited omniscient point of view provides—knowledge even greater than she herself has—readers must infer what she thinks and feels without any help from the narrator.

✔ **CHECKLIST**   **Selecting an Appropriate Point of View: Review**

First-Person Narrators (use *I* or *WE*)

▶ *Major character telling his or her own story* "Every morning I lay on the floor in the front parlour watching her door." (James Joyce, "Araby")

▶ *Minor character as witness* "And so she died....We did not even know she was sick; we had long since given up trying to get information...." (William Faulkner, "A Rose for Emily")

Third-Person Narrators (use *HE, SHE,* and *THEY*)

▶ *Omniscient—able to move at will from character to character and comment about them* "In a house, in a suburb, in a city, there were a man and his wife who loved each other very much...." (Nadine Gordimer, "Once upon a Time")

continued on next page

▶ *Limited omniscient—restricts focus to a single character* "The wagon went on. He did not know where they were going." (William Faulkner, "Barn Burning")

▶ *Objective (dramatic)—simply reports the dialogue and the actions of characters* "'You'll be drunk,' the waiter said. The old man looked at him. The waiter went away." (Ernest Hemingway, "A Clean, Well-Lighted Place")

✔ CHECKLIST Writing about Point of View

▢ What is the dominant point of view from which the story is told?

▢ Is the narrator a character in the story? If so, is he or she a participant in the story's events or just a witness?

▢ Does the story's point of view create irony?

▢ If the story has a first-person narrator, is the narrator reliable or unreliable?

▢ If the story has a third-person narrator, is he or she omniscient? Does he or she have limited omniscience? Is the narrator objective?

▢ What are the advantages of the story's point of view? What are the disadvantages?

▢ Does the point of view remain consistent throughout the story, or does it shift?

▢ How might a different point of view change the story?

Source: © AP Photo/Robert Kradin

RICHARD WRIGHT (1908–1960) was born near Natchez, Mississippi, the son of sharecroppers. He had little formal schooling but as a young man was a voracious reader, especially of naturalistic fiction. Relocating to Chicago in the late 1920s, Wright worked as a postal clerk until 1935, when he joined the Federal Writers' Project. Deeply troubled by the economic and social oppression of African Americans, Wright joined the Communist Party in 1932, and his early poems and stories reflect a distinctly Marxist perspective. In 1944, he broke with the party because of its stifling effect on his creativity.

Wright began to reach a mainstream audience when a group of four long stories on the theme of racial oppression and violence was judged best manuscript in a contest sponsored by

Story magazine; these stories were published as *Uncle Tom's Children* in 1938. Two years later, Wright published his most famous work, *Native Son*, an angry and brutal novel exploring the moral devastation wrought by a racist society. The autobiographical *Black Boy* was published in 1945. Wright eventually left the United States for Paris in protest against the treatment of African Americans in his native country. His later work was concerned with national independence movements in Africa and elsewhere in the third world.

The following story, published in the posthumous collection *Eight Men* (1961), is uncharacteristic of Wright's work in a number of ways—not least of which is that it is told through the eyes of a white protagonist.

Cultural Context   In 1957, the year "Big Black Good Man" was written, President Dwight D. Eisenhower sent paratroopers to Little Rock, Arkansas, to forestall violence over desegregation of the public schools. The crisis began on September 2, when Governor Orval Faubus ordered the Arkansas National Guard to blockade Central High School in Little Rock to prevent the entrance of nine black students. On September 20, NAACP lawyers Thurgood Marshall and Wiley Brandon obtained an injunction from the federal district court that ordered the troops removed. On September 25, the students entered the school, escorted by members of the 101st Airborne Division of the United States Army.

Big Black Good Man   (1957)

Through the open window Olaf Jenson could smell the sea and hear the occasional foghorn of a freighter; outside, rain pelted down through an August night, drumming softly upon the pavements of Copenhagen,[1] inducing drowsiness, bringing dreamy memory, relaxing the tired muscles of his work-wracked body. He sat slumped in a swivel chair with his legs outstretched and his feet propped atop an edge of his desk. An inch of white ash tipped the end of his brown cigar and now and then he inserted the end of the stogie[2] into his mouth and drew gently upon it, letting wisps of blue smoke eddy from the corners of his wide, thin lips. The watery gray irises behind the thick lenses of his eyeglasses gave him a look of abstraction, of absentmindedness, of an almost genial idiocy. He sighed, reached for his half-empty bottle of beer, and drained it into his glass and downed it with a long slow gulp, then licked his lips. Replacing the cigar, he slapped his right palm against his thigh and said half aloud:

"Well, I'll be sixty tomorrow. I'm not rich, but I'm not poor either... Really, I can't complain. Got good health. Traveled all over the world and had my share of girls when I was young...And my Karen's a good wife. I own my home. Got no debts. And I love digging in my garden in the spring...Grew the biggest carrots of anybody last year. Ain't saved much

---

[1] *Copenhagen:* The capital of Denmark.

[2] *stogie:* A cheap cigar.

money, but what the hell…Money ain't everything. Got a good job. Night portering ain't too bad." He shook his head and yawned. "Karen and I could of had some children, though. Would of been good company…'Specially for Karen. And I could of taught 'em languages…English, French, German, Danish, Dutch, Swedish, Norwegian, and Spanish…" He took the cigar out of his mouth and eyed the white ash critically. "Hell of a lot of good language learning did me…Never got anything out of it. But those ten years in New York were fun…Maybe I could of got rich if I'd stayed in America…Maybe. But I'm satisfied. You can't have everything."

Behind him the office door opened and a young man, a medical student occupying room number nine, entered.

"Good evening," the student said.

5   "Good evening," Olaf said, turning.

The student went to the keyboard and took hold of the round, brown knob that anchored his key.

"Rain, rain, rain," the student said.

"That's Denmark for you," Olaf smiled at him.

"This dampness keeps me clogged up like a drainpipe," the student complained.

10   "That's Denmark for you," Olaf repeated with a smile.

"Good night," the student said.

"Good night, son," Olaf sighed, watching the door close.

Well, my tenants are my children, Olaf told himself. Almost all of his children were in their rooms now…Only seventy-two and forty-four were missing…Seventy-two might've gone to Sweden…And forty-four was maybe staying at his girl's place tonight, like he sometimes did…He studied the pear-shaped blobs of hard rubber, reddish brown like ripe fruit, that hung from the keyboard, then glanced at his watch. Only room thirty, eighty-one, and one hundred and one were empty…And it was almost midnight. In a few moments he could take a nap. Nobody hardly ever came looking for accommodations after midnight, unless a stray freighter came in, bringing thirsty, women-hungry sailors. Olaf chuckled softly. Why in hell was I ever a sailor? The whole time I was at sea I was thinking and dreaming about women. Then why didn't I stay on land where women could be had? Hunh? Sailors are crazy…

But he liked sailors. They reminded him of his youth, and there was something so direct, simple, and childlike about them. They always said straight out what they wanted, and what they wanted was almost always women and whisky…"Well, there's no harm in that…Nothing could be more natural," Olaf sighed, looking thirstily at his empty beer bottle. No; he'd not drink any more tonight; he'd had enough; he'd go to sleep…

15   He was bending forward and loosening his shoelaces when he heard the office door crack open. He lifted his eyes, then sucked in his breath.

He did not straighten; he just stared up and around at the huge black thing that filled the doorway. His reflexes refused to function; it was not fear; it was just simple astonishment. He was staring at the biggest, strangest, and blackest man he'd ever seen in all his life.

"Good evening," the black giant said in a voice that filled the small office. "Say, you got a room?"

Olaf sat up slowly, not to answer but to look at this brooding black vision; it towered darkly some six and a half feet into the air, almost touching the ceiling, and its skin was so black that it had a bluish tint. And the sheer bulk of the man!... His chest bulged like a barrel; his rocklike and humped shoulders hinted of mountain ridges; the stomach ballooned like a threatening stone; and the legs were like telephone poles... The big black cloud of a man now lumbered into the office, bending to get its buffalolike head under the door frame, then advanced slowly upon Olaf, like a stormy sky descending.

"You got a room?" the big black man asked again in a resounding voice.

Olaf now noticed that the ebony giant was well dressed, carried a wonderful new suitcase, and wore black shoes that gleamed despite the raindrops that peppered their toes.

"You're American?" Olaf asked him.   20

"Yeah, man; sure," the black giant answered.

"Sailor?"

"Yeah. American Continental Lines."

Olaf had not answered the black man's question. It was not that the hotel did not admit men of color; Olaf took in all comers—blacks, yellows, whites, and browns...To Olaf, men were men, and, in his day, he'd worked and eaten and slept and fought with all kinds of men. But this particular black man...Well, he didn't seem human. Too big, too black, too loud, too direct, and probably too violent to boot...Olaf's five feet seven inches scarcely reached the black giant's shoulder and his frail body weighed less, perhaps, than one of the man's gigantic legs...There was something about the man's intense blackness and ungainly bigness that frightened and insulted Olaf; he felt as though this man had come here expressly to remind him how puny, how tiny, and how weak and how white he was. Olaf knew, while registering his reactions, that he was being irrational and foolish; yet, for the first time in his life, he was emotionally determined to refuse a man a room solely on the basis of the man's size and color...Olaf's lips parted as he groped for the right words in which to couch his refusal, but the black giant bent forward and boomed:

"I asked you if you got a room. I got to put up somewhere tonight, man."   25

"Yes, we got a room," Olaf murmured.

And at once he was ashamed and confused. Sheer fear had made him yield. And he seethed against himself for his involuntary weakness. Well, he'd look over his book and pretend that he'd made a mistake; he'd tell this hunk of blackness that there was really no free room in the hotel, and that he was so sorry... Then, just as he took out the hotel register to make believe that he was poring over it, a thick roll of American bank notes, crisp and green, was thrust under his nose.

"Keep this for me, will you?" the black giant commanded. "Cause I'm gonna get drunk tonight and I don't wanna lose it."

Olaf stared at the roll; it was huge, in denominations of fifties and hundreds. Olaf's eyes widened.

30   "How much is there?" he asked.

"Two thousand six hundred," the giant said. "Just put it into an envelope and write 'Jim' on it and lock it in your safe, hunh?"

The black mass of man had spoken in a manner that indicated that it was taking it for granted that Olaf would obey. Olaf was licked. Resentment clogged the pores of his wrinkled white skin. His hands trembled as he picked up the money. No; he couldn't refuse this man... The impulse to deny him was strong, but each time he was about to act upon it something thwarted him, made him shy off. He clutched about desperately for an idea. Oh yes, he could say that if he planned to stay for only one night, then he could not have the room, for it was against the policy of the hotel to rent rooms for only one night...

"How long are you staying? Just tonight?" Olaf asked.

"Naw. I'll be here for five or six days, I reckon," the giant answered off handedly.

35   "You take room number thirty," Olaf heard himself saying. "It's forty kroner a day."

"That's all right with me," the giant said.

With slow, stiff movements, Olaf put the money in the safe and then turned and stared helplessly up into the living, breathing blackness looming above him. Suddenly he became conscious of the outstretched palm of the black giant; he was silently demanding the key to the room. His eyes downcast, Olaf surrendered the key, marveling at the black man's tremendous hands... He could kill me with one blow, Olaf told himself in fear.

Feeling himself beaten, Olaf reached for the suitcase, but the black hand of the giant whisked it out of his grasp.

"That's too heavy for you, big boy; I'll take it," the giant said.

40   Olaf let him. He thinks I'm nothing... He led the way down the corridor, sensing the giant's lumbering presence behind him. Olaf opened the door of number thirty and stood politely to one side, allowing the black giant to enter. At once the room seemed like a doll's house, so dwarfed and filled and tiny it was with a great living blackness... Flinging his suitcase upon a chair, the giant turned. The two men looked directly at each other now. Olaf saw that the giant's eyes were tiny and red, buried,

it seemed, in muscle and fat. Black cheeks spread, flat and broad, topping the wide and flaring nostrils. The mouth was the biggest that Olaf had ever seen on a human face; the lips were thick, pursed, parted, showing snow-white teeth. The black neck was like a bull's... The giant advanced upon Olaf and stood over him.

"I want a bottle of whiskey and a woman," he said. "Can you fix me up?"

"Yes," Olaf whispered, wild with anger and insult.

But what was he angry about? He'd had requests like this every night from all sorts of men and he was used to fulfilling them; he was a night porter in a cheap, water-front Copenhagen hotel that catered to sailors and students. Yes, men needed women, but this man, Olaf felt, ought to have a special sort of woman. He felt a deep and strange reluctance to phone any of the women whom he habitually sent to men. Yet he had promised. Could he lie and say that none was available? No. That sounded too fishy. The black giant sat upon the bed, staring straight before him. Olaf moved about quickly, pulling down the window shades, taking the pink coverlet off the bed, nudging the giant with his elbow to make him move as he did so... That's the way to treat 'im... Show 'im I ain't scared of 'im... But he was still seeking for an excuse to refuse. And he could think of nothing. He felt hypnotized, mentally immobilized. He stood hesitantly at the door.

"You send the whiskey and the woman quick, pal?" the black giant asked, rousing himself from a brooding stare.

"Yes," Olaf grunted, shutting the door.   45

Goddamn, Olaf sighed. He sat in his office at his desk before the phone. Why did *he* have to come here?... I'm not prejudiced... No, not at all... But... He couldn't think any more. God oughtn't make men as big and black as that... But what the hell was he worrying about? He'd sent women of all races to men of all colors... So why not a woman to the black giant? Oh, only if the man were small, brown, and intelligent-looking... Olaf felt trapped.

With a reflex movement of his hand, he picked up the phone and dialed Lena. She was big and strong and always cut him in for fifteen per cent instead of the usual ten per cent. Lena had four small children to feed and clothe. Lena was willing; she was, she said, coming over right now. She didn't give a good goddamn about how big and black the man was...

"Why you ask me that?" Lena wanted to know over the phone. "You never asked that before..."

"But this one is *big*," Olaf found himself saying.

"He's just a man," Lena told him, her voice singing stridently, laugh-   50
ingly over the wire. "You just leave that to me. You don't have to do anything. *I'll* handle 'im."

Lena had a key to the hotel door downstairs, but tonight Olaf stayed awake. He wanted to see her. Why? He didn't know. He stretched out on the sofa in his office, but sleep was far from him. When Lena arrived, he told her again how big and black the man was.

"You told me that over the phone," Lena reminded him.

Olaf said nothing. Lena flounced off on her errand of mercy. Olaf shut the office door, then opened it and left it ajar. But why? He didn't know. He lay upon the sofa and stared at the ceiling. He glanced at his watch; it was almost two o'clock...She's staying in there a long time...Ah, God, but he could do with a drink...Why was he so damned worked up and nervous about a nigger and a white whore?...He'd never been so upset in all his life. Before he knew it, he had drifted off to sleep. Then he heard the office door swinging creakingly open on its rusty hinges. Lena stood in it, grim and businesslike, her face scrubbed free of powder and rouge. Olaf scrambled to his feet, adjusting his eyeglasses, blinking.

"How was it?" he asked her in a confidential whisper.

55   Lena's eyes blazed.

"What the hell's that to you?" she snapped. "There's your cut," she said, flinging him his money, tossing it upon the covers of the sofa. "You're sure nosy tonight. You wanna take over my work?"

Olaf's pasty cheeks burned red.

"You go to hell," he said, slamming the door.

"I'll meet you there!" Lena's shouting voice reached him dimly.

60   He was being a fool; there was no doubt about it. But, try as he might, he could not shake off a primitive hate for that black mountain of energy, of muscle, of bone; he envied the easy manner in which it moved with such a creeping and powerful motion; he winced at the booming and commanding voice that came to him when the tiny little eyes were not even looking at him; he shivered at the sight of those vast and clawlike hands that seemed always to hint of death...

Olaf kept his counsel. He never spoke to Karen about the sordid doings at the hotel. Such things were not for women like Karen. He knew instinctively that Karen would have been amazed had he told her that he was worried sick about a nigger and a blonde whore...No; he couldn't talk to anybody about it, not even the hard-bitten[3] old bitch who owned the hotel. She was concerned only about money; she didn't give a damn about how big and how black a client was as long as he paid his room rent.

Next evening, when Olaf arrived for duty, there was no sight or sound of the black giant. A little later after one o'clock in the morning he

---

[3] *hard-bitten:* Stubborn, tough.

appeared, left his key, and went out wordlessly. A few moments past two the giant returned, took his key from the board, and paused.

"I want that Lena again tonight. And another bottle of whiskey," he said boomingly.

"I'll call her and see if she's in," Olaf said.

"Do that," the black giant said and was gone. 65

He thinks he's God, Olaf fumed. He picked up the phone and ordered Lena and a bottle of whiskey, and there was a taste of ashes in his mouth. On the third night came the same request: Lena and whiskey. When the black giant appeared on the fifth night, Olaf was about to make a sarcastic remark to the effect that maybe he ought to marry Lena, but he checked it in time... After all, he could kill me with one hand, he told himself.

Olaf was nervous and angry with himself for being nervous. Other black sailors came and asked for girls and Olaf sent them, but with none of the fear and loathing that he sent Lena and a bottle of whiskey to the giant... All right, the black giant's stay was almost up. He'd said that he was staying for five or six nights; tomorrow night was the sixth night and that ought to be the end of this nameless terror.

On the sixth night Olaf sat in his swivel chair with his bottle of beer and waited, his teeth on edge, his fingers drumming the desk. But what the hell am I fretting for?... The hell with 'im... Olaf sat and dozed. Occasionally he'd awaken and listen to the foghorns of freighters sounding as ships came and went in the misty Copenhagen harbor. He was half asleep when he felt a rough hand on his shoulder. He blinked his eyes open. The giant, black and vast and powerful, all but blotted out his vision.

"What I owe you, man?" the giant demanded. "And I want my money."

"Sure," Olaf said, relieved, but filled as always with fear of this living 70 wall of black flesh.

With fumbling hands, he made out the bill and received payment, then gave the giant his roll of money, laying it on the desk so as not to let his hands touch the flesh of the black mountain. Well, his ordeal was over. It was past two o'clock in the morning. Olaf even managed a wry smile and muttered a guttural "Thanks" for the generous tip that the giant tossed him.

Then a strange tension entered the office. The office door was shut and Olaf was alone with the black mass of power, yearning for it to leave. But the black mass of power stood still, immobile, looking down at Olaf. And Olaf could not, for the life of him, guess at what was transpiring in that mysterious black mind. The two of them simply stared at each other for a full two minutes, the giant's tiny little beady eyes blinking slowly as they seemed to measure and search Olaf's face. Olaf's vision dimmed for a second as terror seized him and he could feel a flush of heat overspread his body. Then Olaf sucked in his breath as the devil of blackness commanded:

"Stand up!"

Olaf was paralyzed. Sweat broke on his face. His worst premonitions about this black beast were coming true. This evil blackness was about to attack him, maybe kill him...Slowly Olaf shook his head, his terror permitting him to breathe:

75   "What're you talking about?"

"Stand up, I say!" the black giant bellowed.

As though hypnotized, Olaf tried to rise; then he felt the black paw of the beast helping him roughly to his feet.

They stood an inch apart. Olaf's pasty-white features were glued to the giant's swollen black face. The ebony ensemble of eyes and nose and mouth and cheeks looked down at Olaf, silently; then, with a slow and deliberate movement of his gorillalike arms, he lifted his mammoth hands to Olaf's throat. Olaf had long known and felt that this dreadful moment was coming; he felt trapped in a nightmare. He could not move. He wanted to scream, but could find no words. His lips refused to open; his tongue felt icy and inert. Then he knew that his end had come when the giant's black fingers slowly, softly encircled his throat while a horrible grin of delight broke out on the sooty face...Olaf lost control of the reflexes of his body and he felt a hot stickiness flooding his underwear... He stared without breathing, gazing into the grinning blackness of the face that was bent over him, feeling the black fingers caressing his throat and waiting to feel the sharp, stinging ache and pain of the bones in his neck being snapped, crushed...He knew all along that I hated 'im...Yes, and now he's going to kill me for it, Olaf told himself with despair.

The black fingers still circled Olaf's neck, not closing, but gently massaging it, as it were, moving to and fro, while the obscene face grinned into his. Olaf could feel the giant's warm breath blowing on his eyelashes and he felt like a chicken about to have its neck wrung and its body tossed to flip and flap dyingly in the dust of the barnyard...Then suddenly the black giant withdrew his fingers from Olaf's neck and stepped back a pace, still grinning. Olaf sighed, trembling, his body seeming to shrink; he waited. Shame sheeted him for the hot wetness that was in his trousers. Oh, God, he's teasing me...He's showing me how easily he can kill me...He swallowed, waiting, his eyes stones of gray.

80   The giant's barrel-like chest gave forth a low, rumbling chuckle of delight.

"You laugh?" Olaf asked whimperingly.

"Sure I laugh," the giant shouted.

"Please don't hurt me," Olaf managed to say.

"I wouldn't hurt you, boy," the giant said in a tone of mockery. "So long."

85   And he was gone. Olaf fell limply into the swivel chair and fought off losing consciousness. Then he wept. He was showing me how easily

he could kill me... He made me shake with terror and then laughed and left... Slowly, Olaf recovered, stood, then gave vent to a string of curses: "Goddamn 'im! My gun's right there in the desk drawer; I should of shot 'im. Jesus, I hope the ship he's on sinks... I hope he drowns and the sharks eat 'im..."

Later, he thought of going to the police, but sheer shame kept him back; and, anyway, the giant was probably on board his ship by now. And he had to get home and clean himself. Oh, Lord, what could he tell Karen? Yes, he would say that his stomach had been upset... He'd change clothes and return to work. He phoned the hotel owner that he was ill and wanted an hour off; the old bitch said that she was coming right over and that poor Olaf could have the evening off.

Olaf went home and lied to Karen. Then he lay awake the rest of the night dreaming of revenge. He saw that freighter on which the giant was sailing; he saw it springing a dangerous leak and saw a torrent of sea water flooding, gushing into all the compartments of the ship until it found the bunk in which the black giant slept. Ah, yes, the foamy, surging waters would surprise that sleeping black bastard of a giant and he would drown, gasping and choking like a trapped rat, his tiny eyes bulging until they glittered red, the bitter water of the sea pounding his lungs until they ached and finally burst... The ship would sink slowly to the bottom of the cold, black, silent depths of the sea and a shark, a *white* one, would glide aimlessly about the shut portholes until it found an open one and it would slither inside and nose about until it found that swollen, rotting, stinking carcass of the black beast and it would then begin to nibble at the decomposing mass of tarlike flesh, eating the bones clean... Olaf always pictured the giant's bones as being jet black and shining.

Once or twice, during these fantasies of cannibalistic revenge, Olaf felt a little guilty about all the many innocent people, women and children, all white and blonde, who would have to go down into watery graves in order that that white shark could devour the evil giant's black flesh... But, despite feelings of remorse, the fantasy lived persistently on, and when Olaf found himself alone, it would crowd and cloud his mind to the exclusion of all else, affording him the only revenge he knew. To make me suffer just for the pleasure of it, he fumed. Just to show me how strong he was... Olaf learned how to hate, and got pleasure out of it.

Summer fled on wings of rain. Autumn flooded Denmark with color. 90 Winter made rain and snow fall on Copenhagen. Finally spring came, bringing violets and roses. Olaf kept to his job. For many months he feared the return of the black giant. But when a year had passed and the giant had not put in an appearance, Olaf allowed his revenge fantasy to peter out, indulging in it only when recalling the shame that the black monster had made him feel.

Then one rainy August night, a year later, Olaf sat drowsing at his desk, his bottle of beer before him, tilting back in his swivel chair, his feet resting atop a corner of his desk, his mind mulling over the more pleasant aspects of his life. The office door cracked open. Olaf glanced boredly up and around. His heart jumped and skipped a beat. The black nightmare of terror and shame that he had hoped that he had lost forever was again upon him...Resplendently dressed, suitcase in hand, the black looming mountain filled the doorway. Olaf's thin lips parted and a silent moan, half a curse, escaped them.

"Hi," the black giant boomed from the doorway.

Olaf could not reply. But a sudden resolve swept him: this time he would even the score. If this black beast came within so much as three feet of him, he would snatch his gun out of the drawer and shoot him dead, so help him God...

"No rooms tonight," Olaf heard himself announcing in a determined voice.

95   The black giant grinned; it was the same infernal grimace of delight and triumph that he had had when his damnable black fingers had been around his throat...

"Don't want no room tonight," the giant announced.

"Then what are you doing here?" Olaf asked in a loud but tremulous voice.

The giant swept toward Olaf and stood over him; and Olaf could not move, despite his oath to kill him...

"What do you want then?" Olaf demanded once more, ashamed that he could not lift his voice above a whisper.

100   The giant still grinned, then tossed what seemed the same suitcase upon Olaf's sofa and bent over it; he zippered it open with a sweep of his clawlike hand and rummaged in it, drawing forth a flat, gleaming white object done up in glowing cellophane. Olaf watched with lowered lids, wondering what trick was now being played on him. Then, before he could defend himself, the giant had whirled and again long, black, snakelike fingers were encircling Olaf's throat...Olaf stiffened, his right hand clawing blindly for the drawer where the gun was kept. But the giant was quick.

"Wait," he bellowed, pushing Olaf back from the desk.

The giant turned quickly to the sofa and, still holding his fingers in a wide circle that seemed a noose for Olaf's neck, he inserted the rounded fingers into the top of the flat, gleaming object. Olaf had the drawer open and his sweaty fingers were now touching the gun, but something made him freeze. The flat, gleaming object was a shirt and the black giant's circled fingers were fitting themselves into its neck...

"A perfect fit!" the giant shouted.

Olaf stared, trying to understand. His fingers loosened about the gun.
A mixture of a laugh and a curse struggled in him. He watched the giant
plunge his hands into the suitcase and pull out other flat, gleaming shirts.

"One, two, three, four, five, six," the black giant intoned, his voice 105
crisp and businesslike. "Six nylon shirts. And they're all yours. One shirt
for each time Lena came...See, Daddy-O?"

The black, cupped hands, filled with billowing nylon whiteness, were
extended under Olaf's nose. Olaf eased his damp fingers from his gun and
pushed the drawer closed, staring at the shirts and then at the black giant's
grinning face.

"Don't you like 'em?" the giant asked.

Olaf began to laugh hysterically, then suddenly he was crying, his eyes
so flooded with tears that the pile of dazzling nylon looked like snow in
the dead of winter. Was this true? Could he believe it? Maybe this too was
a trick? But, no. There were six shirts, all nylon, and the black giant had
had Lena six nights.

"What's the matter with you, Daddy-O?" the giant asked. "You blowing your top? Laughing and crying..."

Olaf swallowed, dabbed his withered fists at his dimmed eyes; then he 110
realized that he had his glasses on. He took them off and dried his eyes
and sat up. He sighed, the tension and shame and fear and haunting dread
of his fantasy went from him, and he leaned limply back in his chair...

"Try one on," the giant ordered.

Olaf fumbled with the buttons of his shirt, let down his suspenders,
and pulled the shirt off. He donned a gleaming nylon one and the giant
began buttoning it for him.

"Perfect, Daddy-O," the giant said.

His spectacled face framed in sparkling nylon, Olaf sat with trembling
lips. So he'd not been trying to kill me after all.

"You want Lena, don't you?" he asked the giant in a soft whisper. "But 115
I don't know where she is. She never came back here after you left—"

"I know where Lena is," the giant told him. "We been writing to each
other. I'm going to her house. And, Daddy-O, I'm late." The giant zippered the suitcase shut and stood a moment gazing down at Olaf, his tiny
little red eyes blinking slowly. Then Olaf realized that there was a compassion in that stare that he had never seen before.

"And I thought you wanted to kill me," Olaf told him. "I was scared
of you..."

"Me? Kill you?" the giant blinked. "When?"

"That night when you put your fingers around my throat—"

"What?" the giant asked, then roared with laughter. "Daddy-O, you're 120
a funny little man. I wouldn't hurt you. I like you. You a *good* man. You
helped me."

Olaf smiled, clutching the pile of nylon shirts in his arms.

"You're a good man too," Olaf murmured. Then loudly, "You're a big black good man."

"Daddy-O, you're crazy," the giant said.

He swept his suitcase from the sofa, spun on his heel, and was at the door in one stride.

125   "Thanks!" Olaf cried after him.

The black giant paused, turned his vast black head, and flashed a grin.

"Daddy-O, drop dead," he said and was gone.

Reading and Reacting

1. Why do you suppose Wright presents events through Olaf's eyes? How would the story be different if Jim told it?

2. This story was published in 1957. What attitudes about race does Wright expect his American readers to have? Do these attitudes predispose readers to identify with Jim or with Olaf? Explain.

3. Why does Olaf dislike Jim? What does the narrator mean in paragraph 24 when he says that Jim's "intense blackness and ungainly bigness... frightened and insulted Olaf"?

4. In what ways do Jim's words and actions contribute to Olaf's fears? Do you think Olaf's reactions are reasonable, or do you believe he is overreacting?

5. The sailor's name is hardly mentioned in the story. Why? List some words used to describe Jim. Why are these words used? How do they affect your reaction to him?

6. Do you think the story's title is ironic? In what other respects is the story ironic?

7. Why do you think Wright set the story in Copenhagen? Could it have been set in the United States in 1957?

8. What do you think Jim thinks of Olaf? Do you suppose he realizes the effect he has on him? How do you explain Jim's last comment?

9. **JOURNAL ENTRY** What point do you think the story makes about racial prejudice? Do you think Wright seems optimistic or pessimistic about race relations in the United States?

10. **CRITICAL PERSPECTIVE** In his 1982 article "The Short Stories: *Uncle Tom's Children, Eight Men*," Edward Margolies notes that "Big Black Good Man" was somewhat of a departure for Wright:

> "Big Black Good Man," which first appeared in *Esquire* in 1957, is the last short story Wright published in his lifetime. Possibly it is the last he ever wrote. In any event it represents a more traditional approach to storytelling

in that Wright here avoids confining himself exclusively to dialogue. On the other hand, "Big Black Good Man" deviates from the usual Wright short story. For one thing, the narrative, by Wright's standards at least, is practically pointless. Scarcely anything "happens." There is no violence, practically no external narrative action, and no change of milieu.

Do you agree that the story is "practically pointless"? If not, what point do you think the story makes?

Related Works: "The Cask of Amontillado" (p. 249), "The *Chicago Defender* Sends a Man to Little Rock" (p. 742), *Fences* (p. 1270)

Source: AP Images

EDGAR ALLAN POE (1809–1849) profoundly influenced many writers all over the world. His tales of psychological terror and the macabre, his hauntingly musical lyric poems, and his writings on the craft of poetry and short story writing affected the development of symbolic fiction, the modern detective story, and the gothic horror tale. In most of Poe's horror tales (as in "The Cask of Amontillado"), readers vicariously "live" the story through the first-person narrator who tells the tale.

Poe was born in 1809, the son of a talented English-born actress who, deserted by her actor husband, died of tuberculosis before her son's third birthday. Although Poe was raised in material comfort by foster parents in Richmond, Virginia, his life was increasingly uncertain: his foster mother loved him, but her husband became antagonistic. He kept the young Poe so short of money at the University of Virginia (and later at West Point) that Poe resorted to gambling to raise money for food and clothing. Finally, disgraced and debt-ridden, he left school.

Poe found work as a magazine editor, gaining recognition as a literary critic. In 1836, he married his frail thirteen-year-old cousin, Virginia Clemm. Poe produced many of his most famous stories and poems over the next few years, working feverishly to support his tubercular wife, but although his stories were widely admired, he never achieved financial success. His wife died in 1847. Less than two years after her death, Poe was found barely conscious on a Baltimore street; three days later, he was dead at age forty. To this day, the cause of Poe's death remains a mystery.

Cultural Context Throughout antiquity, catacombs, such as those in Poe's story, were used to bury the dead. Catacombs are underground cemeteries composed of passages with recesses for tombs. The early Christian catacombs of Rome, consisting of approximately forty known chambers located in a rough circle about three miles from the center of the city, are the most extensive of all known catacombs. (Besides being used for burial, these catacombs were also used by early Christians as a refuge from persecution.) Funeral feasts were often celebrated in family vaults on the day of burial and on anniversary dates of the deaths of loved ones.

The Cask of Amontillado (1846)

The thousand injuries of Fortunato I had borne as I best could, but when he ventured upon insult I vowed revenge. You, who so well know the nature of my soul, will not suppose, however, that I gave utterance to a threat. *At length* I would be avenged; this was a point definitely settled— but the very definitiveness with which it was resolved precluded the idea of risk. I must not only punish but punish with impunity. A wrong is unre- dressed when retribution overtakes its redresser. It is equally unredressed when the avenger fails to make himself felt as such to him who has done the wrong.

It must be understood that neither by word nor deed had I given Fortunato cause to doubt my good will. I continued, as was my wont, to smile in his face, and he did not perceive that my smile *now* was at the thought of his immolation.

He had a weak point—this Fortunato—although in other regards he was a man to be respected and even feared. He prided himself on his con- noisseurship in wine. Few Italians have the true virtuoso spirit. For the most part their enthusiasm is adopted to suit the time and opportunity, to practise imposture upon the British and Austrian *millionaires*. In painting and gemmary, Fortunato, like his countrymen, was a quack, but in the matter of old wines he was sincere. In this respect I did not differ from him materially;—I was skillful in the Italian vintages myself, and bought largely whenever I could.

It was about dusk, one evening during the supreme madness of the car- nival season, that I encountered my friend. He accosted me with excessive warmth, for he had been drinking much. The man wore motley.[1] He had on a tight-fitting parti-striped dress, and his head was surmounted by the conical cap and bells. I was so pleased to see him that I thought I should never have done wringing his hand.

5   I said to him—"My dear Fortunato, you are luckily met. How remark- ably well you are looking to-day. But I have received a pipe[2] of what passes for Amontillado,[3] and I have my doubts."

"How?" said he. "Amontillado? A pipe? Impossible! And in the middle of the carnival!"

"I have my doubts," I replied; "and I was silly enough to pay the full Amontillado price without consulting you in the matter. You were not to be found, and I was fearful of losing a bargain."

---

[1] *motley:* The many-colored attire of a court jester.

[2] *pipe:* In the United States and England, a cask containing a volume equal to 126 gallons.

[3] *Amontillado:* A pale, dry sherry; literally, a wine "from Montilla" (Spain).

"Amontillado!"

"I have my doubts."

"Amontillado!" 10

"And I must satisfy them."

"Amontillado!"

"As you are engaged, I am on my way to Luchresi. If any one has a critical turn it is he. He will tell me—"

"Luchresi cannot tell Amontillado from Sherry."

"And yet some fools will have it that his taste is a match for your own." 15

"Come, let us go."

"Whither?"

"To your vaults."

"My friend, no; I will not impose upon your good nature. I perceive you have an engagement. Luchresi—"

"I have no engagement;—come." 20

"My friend, no. It is not the engagement, but the severe cold with which I perceive you are afflicted. The vaults are insufferably damp. They are encrusted with nitre."[4]

"Let us go, nevertheless. The cold is merely nothing. Amontillado! You have been imposed upon. And as for Luchresi, he cannot distinguish Sherry from Amontillado."

Thus speaking, Fortunato possessed himself of my arm; and putting on a mask of black silk and drawing a *roquelaire*[5] closely about my person, I suffered him to hurry me to my palazzo.

There were no attendants at home; they had absconded to make merry in honor of the time. I had told them that I should not return until the morning, and had given them explicit orders not to stir from the house. These orders were sufficient, I well knew, to insure their immediate disappearance, one and all, as soon as my back was turned.

I took from their sconces two flambeaux, and giving one to Fortunato, 25 bowed him through several suites of rooms to the archway that led into the vaults. I passed down a long and winding staircase, requesting him to be cautious as he followed. We came at length to the foot of the descent, and stood together upon the damp ground of the catacombs of the Montresors.

The gait of my friend was unsteady, and the bells upon his cap jingled as he strode.

"The pipe," he said.

"It is farther on," said I; "but observe the white web-work which gleams from these cavern walls."

---

[4]*nitre:* Mineral deposits.
[5]roquelaire: A short cloak.

He turned towards me, and looked into my eyes with two filmy orbs that distilled the rheum of intoxication.

30   "Nitre?" he asked at length.

"Nitre," I replied. "How long have you had that cough?"

"Ugh! ugh! ugh!—ugh! ugh! ugh!—ugh! ugh! ugh!—ugh! ugh! ugh!— ugh! ugh! ugh!"

My poor friend found it impossible to reply for many minutes.

"It is nothing," he said at last.

35   "Come," I said, with decision, "we will go back; your health is precious. You are rich, respected, admired, beloved; you are happy, as once I was. You are a man to be missed. For me it is no matter. We will go back; you will be ill, and I cannot be responsible. Besides, there is Luchresi—"

"Enough," he said; "the cough is a mere nothing; it will not kill me. I shall not die of a cough."

"True—true," I replied; "and, indeed, I had no intention of alarming you unnecessarily—but you should use all proper caution. A draught of this Médoc[6] will defend us from the damps."

Here I knocked off the neck of a bottle which I drew from a long row of its fellows that lay upon the mould.

"Drink," I said, presenting him the wine.

40   He raised it to his lips with a leer. He paused and nodded to me familiarly, while his bells jingled.

"I drink," he said, "to the buried that repose around us."

"And I to your long life."

He again took my arm, and we proceeded.

"These vaults," he said, "are extensive."

45   "The Montresors," I replied, "were a great and numerous family."

"I forget your arms."

"A huge human foot d'or, in a field azure; the foot crushes a serpent rampant whose fangs are imbedded in the heel."

"And the motto?"

"*Nemo me impune lacessit.*"[7]

50   "Good!" he said.

The wine sparkled in his eyes and the bells jingled. My own fancy grew warm with the Médoc. We had passed through long walls of piled skeletons, with casks and puncheons[8] intermingling, into the inmost recesses of the catacombs. I paused again, and this time I made bold to seize Fortunato by an arm above the elbow.

---

[6]*Médoc:* A red wine from the Médoc district, near Bordeaux, France.

[7]*"Nemo me impune lacessit":* "No one insults me with impunity" (Latin); this is the legend on the royal coat of arms of Scotland.

[8]*puncheons:* Barrels.

"The nitre!" I said; "see, it increases. It hangs like moss upon the vaults. We are below the river's bed. The drops of moisture trickle among the bones. Come, we will go back ere it is too late. Your cough—"

"It is nothing," he said; "let us go on. But first, another draught of the Médoc."

I broke and reached him a flagon of De Grâve.[9] He emptied it at a breath. His eyes flashed with a fierce light. He laughed and threw the bottle upwards with a gesticulation I did not understand.

I looked at him in surprise. He repeated the movement—a grotesque 55 one.

"You do not comprehend?" he said.

"Not I," I replied.

"Then you are not of the brotherhood."

"How?"

"You are not of the masons."[10] 60

"Yes, yes," I said; "yes, yes."

"You? Impossible! A mason?"

"A mason," I replied.

"A sign," he said, "a sign."

"It is this," I answered, producing from beneath the folds of my 65 *roquelaire* a trowel.

"You jest," he exclaimed, recoiling a few paces. "But let us proceed to the Amontillado."

"Be it so," I said, replacing the tool beneath the cloak and again offering him my arm. He leaned upon it heavily. We continued our route in search of the Amontillado. We passed through a range of low arches, descended, passed on, and descending again, arrived at a deep crypt, in which the foulness of the air caused our flambeaux rather to glow than flame.

At the most remote end of the crypt there appeared another less spacious. Its walls had been lined with human remains, piled to the vault overhead, in the fashion of the great catacombs of Paris. Three sides of this interior crypt were still ornamented in this manner. From the fourth side the bones had been thrown down, and lay promiscuously upon the earth, forming at one point a mound of some size. Within the wall thus exposed by the displacing of the bones, we perceived a still interior crypt or recess, in depth about four feet, in width three, in height six or seven. It seemed to have been constructed for no especial use within itself, but formed merely the interval between two of the colossal supports of the roof of the catacombs, and was backed by one of their circumscribing walls of solid granite.

---

[9]*De Grâve:* Correctly, "Graves," a light wine from the Bordeaux area.

[10]*masons:* Freemasons (members of a secret fraternity). The trowel is a symbol of their alleged origin as a guild of stonemasons.

It was in vain that Fortunato, uplifting his dull torch, endeavored to pry into the depth of the recess. Its termination the feeble light did not enable us to see.

70 "Proceed," I said; "herein is the Amontillado. As for Luchresi—"

"He is an ignoramus," interrupted my friend, as he stepped unsteadily forward, while I followed immediately at his heels. In an instant he had reached the extremity of the niche, and finding his progress arrested by the rock, stood stupidly bewildered. A moment more and I had fettered him to the granite. In its surface were two iron staples, distant from each other about two feet, horizontally. From one of these depended a short chain, from the other a padlock. Throwing the links about his waist, it was but the work of a few seconds to secure it. He was too much astounded to resist. Withdrawing the key I stepped back from the recess.

"Pass your hand," I said, "over the wall; you cannot help feeling the nitre. Indeed, it is *very* damp. Once more let me *implore* you to return. No? Then I must positively leave you. But I must first render you all the little attentions in my power."

"The Amontillado!" ejaculated my friend, not yet recovered from his astonishment.

"True," I replied; "the Amontillado."

75 As I said these words I busied myself among the pile of bones of which I have before spoken. Throwing them aside, I soon uncovered a quantity of building stone and mortar. With these materials and with the aid of my trowel, I began vigorously to wall up the entrance of the niche.

I had scarcely laid the first tier of the masonry when I discovered that the intoxication of Fortunato had in a great measure worn off. The earliest indication I had of this was a low moaning cry from the depth of the recess. It was *not* the cry of a drunken man. There was a long and obstinate silence. I laid the second tier, and the third, and the fourth; and then I heard the furious vibrations of the chain. The noise lasted for several minutes, during which, that I might hearken to it with the more satisfaction, I ceased my labors and sat down upon the bones. When at last the clanking subsided, I resumed the trowel, and finished without interruption the fifth, the sixth, and the seventh tier. The wall was now nearly upon a level with my breast. I again paused, and holding the flambeaux over the mason-work, threw a few feeble rays upon the figure within.

A succession of loud and shrill screams, bursting suddenly from the throat of the chained form, seemed to thrust me violently back. For a brief moment I hesitated, I trembled. Unsheathing my rapier, I began to grope with it about the recess; but the thought of an instant reassured me. I placed my hand upon the solid fabric of the catacombs, and felt satisfied. I reapproached the wall; I replied to the yells of him who clamoured. I re-echoed, I aided, I surpassed them in volume and in strength. I did this, and the clamourer grew still.

It was now midnight, and my task was drawing to a close. I had completed the eighth, the ninth and the tenth tier. I had finished a portion of the last and the eleventh; there remained but a single stone to be fitted and plastered in. I struggled with its weight; I placed it partially in its destined position. But now there came from out the niche a low laugh that erected the hairs upon my head. It was succeeded by a sad voice, which I had difficulty in recognizing as that of the noble Fortunato. The voice said—

"Ha! ha! ha!—he! he! he!—a very good joke, indeed—an excellent jest. We will have many a rich laugh about it at the palazzo—he! he! he!—over our wine—he! he! he!"

"The Amontillado!" I said. 80

"He! he! he!—he! he! he!—yes, the Amontillado. But is it not getting late? Will not they be awaiting us at the palazzo, the Lady Fortunato and the rest? Let us be gone."

"Yes," I said, "let us be gone."

"For the love of God, Montresor!"

"Yes," I said, "for the love of God."

But to these words I hearkened in vain for a reply. I grew impatient. I 85 called aloud—

"Fortunato!"

No answer. I called again—

"Fortunato!"

No answer still. I thrust a torch through the remaining aperture and let it fall within. There came forth in return only a jingling of the bells. My heart grew sick on account of the dampness of the catacombs. I hastened to make an end of my labour. I forced the last stone into its position; I plastered it up. Against the new masonry I re-erected the old rampart of bones. For the half of a century no mortal has disturbed them. *In pace requiescat!*[11]

Reading and Reacting

1. Montresor cites a "thousand injuries" and an "insult" as his motives for murdering Fortunato. Given what you learn about the two men during the course of the story, what do you suppose the "injuries" and "insult" might be?

2. Do you find Montresor to be a reliable narrator? If not, what makes you question his version of events?

3. What is Montresor's concept of personal honor? Is it consistent or inconsistent with the values of contemporary American society? How relevant are the story's ideas about revenge and guilt to present-day society? Explain.

---

[11]In pace requiescat: "May he rest in peace" (Latin).

4. Does Fortunato ever understand why Montresor hates him? What is Fortunato's attitude toward Montresor?

5. What is the significance of Montresor's family coat of arms and motto? What is the significance of Fortunato's costume?

6. In what ways does Montresor manipulate Fortunato? What weaknesses does Montresor exploit?

7. Why does Montresor wait fifty years to tell his story? How might the story be different if he had told it the morning after the murder?

8. Why does Montresor wait for a reply before he puts the last stone in position? What do you think he wants Fortunato to say?

9. **JOURNAL ENTRY** Do you think the use of a first-person point of view makes you more sympathetic toward Montresor than you would be if his story were told by a third-person narrator? Why or why not?

10. **CRITICAL PERSPECTIVE** In his discussion of this story in *Edgar Allan Poe: A Study of the Short Fiction*, Charles E. May says, "We can legitimately hypothesize that the listener is a priest and that Montresor is an old man who is dying and making final confession...."

Do you agree or disagree with May's hypothesis? Do you think that Montresor has atoned for his sin? Who else could be listening to Montresor's story?

Related Works: "A Rose for Emily" (p. 143), "Porphyria's Lover" (p. 520), "The Wolf's Postscript to 'Little Red Riding Hood'" (p. 527)

WILLIAM FAULKNER (1897–1962) (picture and biography on p. 143) "Barn Burning" (1939) marks the first appearance of the Snopes clan in Faulkner's fiction. These ruthless, conniving, and unappealing poor white tenant farmers and traders run roughshod over the aristocratic families of Yoknapatawpha County in three Faulkner novels: *The Hamlet* (1940), *The Town* (1957), and *The Mansion* (1959). According to Ben Wasson in *Count No Count*, Faulkner once told a friend that "somebody said I was a genius writer. The only thing I'd claim genius for is thinking up that name *Snopes*." In Southern literary circles, at least, the name "Snopes" still serves as a shorthand term for the graceless and greedy (but frequently successful) opportunists of the "New South."

Cultural Context Tenant farming is a system of agriculture in which workers (tenants) live on a landowner's property while providing labor. One form of tenant farming, which developed in the post–Civil War South, was known as sharecropping. Although white men, such as Ab Snopes, worked as sharecroppers, the majority of these workers were freed slaves. Sharecropping required a landowner to furnish land and housing, while a tenant supplied labor. In theory, sharecropping was supposed to benefit both the owners of the land and the people who farmed it.

In practice, however, a sharecropper was lucky to end the year without owing money for seeds, tools, and so on to the landowner. As a result, a sharecropper would often find himself (and his family) tied to the land in a never-ending cycle of debt.

Barn Burning (1939)

The store in which the Justice of the Peace's court was sitting smelled of cheese. The boy, crouched on his nail keg at the back of the crowded room, knew he smelled cheese, and more: from where he sat he could see the ranked shelves close-packed with the solid, squat, dynamic shapes of tin cans whose labels his stomach read, not from the lettering which meant nothing to his mind but from the scarlet devils and the silver curve of fish—this, the cheese which he knew he smelled and the hermetic[1] meat which his intestines believed he smelled coming in intermittent gusts momentary and brief between the other constant one, the smell and sense just a little of fear because mostly of despair and grief, the old fierce pull of blood. He could not see the table where the Justice sat and before which his father and his father's enemy (*our enemy* he thought in that despair; *ourn! mine and hisn both! He's my father!*) stood, but he could hear them, the two of them that is, because his father had said no word yet:

"But what proof have you, Mr. Harris?"

"I told you. The hog got into my corn. I caught it up and sent it back to him. He had no fence that would hold it. I told him so, warned him. The next time I put the hog in my pen. When he came to get it I gave him enough wire to patch up his pen. The next time I put the hog up and kept it. I rode down to his house and saw the wire I gave him still rolled on to the spool in his yard. I told him he could have the hog when he paid me a dollar pound fee. That evening a nigger came with the dollar and got the hog. He was a strange nigger. He said, 'He say to tell you wood and hay kin burn.' I said, 'What?' 'That whut he say to tell you,' the nigger said. 'Wood and hay kin burn.' That night my barn burned. I got the stock out but I lost the barn."

"Where is the nigger? Have you got him?"

"He was a strange nigger, I tell you. I don't know what became of 5 him."

"But that's not proof. Don't you see that's not proof?"

"Get that boy up here. He knows." For a moment the boy thought too that the man meant his older brother until Harris said, "Not him.

---

[1] *hermetic:* Canned.

The little one. The boy," and, crouching, small for his age, small and wiry like his father, in patched and faded jeans even too small for him, with straight, uncombed, brown hair and eyes gray and wild as storm scud, he saw the men between himself and the table part and become a lane of grim faces, at the end of which he saw the Justice, a shabby, collarless, graying man in spectacles, beckoning him. He felt no floor under his bare feet; he seemed to walk beneath the palpable weight of the grim turning faces. His father, stiff in his black Sunday coat donned not for the trial but for the moving, did not even look at him. *He aims for me to lie,* he thought, again with that frantic grief and despair. *And I will have to do hit.*

"What's your name, boy?" the Justice said.

"Colonel Sartoris Snopes," the boy whispered.

10   "Hey?" the Justice said. "Talk louder. Colonel Sartoris? I reckon any-body named for Colonel Sartoris in this country can't help but tell the truth, can they?" The boy said nothing. *Enemy! Enemy!* he thought; for a moment he could not even see, could not see that the Justice's face was kindly nor discern that his voice was troubled when he spoke to the man named Harris: "Do you want me to question this boy?" But he could hear, and during those subsequent long seconds while there was absolutely no sound in the crowded little room save that of quiet and intent breathing it was as if he had swung outward at the end of a grape vine, over a ravine, and at the top of the swing had been caught in a prolonged instant of mesmerized gravity, weightless in time.

"No!" Harris said violently, explosively. "Damnation! Send him out of here!" Now time, the fluid world, rushed beneath him again, the voices coming to him again through the smell of cheese and sealed meat, the fear and despair and the old grief of blood:

"This case is closed. I can't find against you, Snopes, but I can give you advice. Leave this country and don't come back to it."

His father spoke for the first time, his voice cold and harsh, level, with-out emphasis: "I aim to. I don't figure to stay in a country among people who..." he said something unprintable and vile, addressed to no one.

"That'll do," the Justice said. "Take your wagon and get out of this country before dark. Case dismissed."

15   His father turned, and he followed the stiff black coat, the wiry figure walking a little stiffly from where a Confederate provost's man's[2] musket ball had taken him in the heel on a stolen horse thirty years ago, followed the two backs now, since his older brother had appeared from somewhere in the crowd, no taller than the father but thicker, chewing tobacco steadily, between the two lines of grim-faced men and out of the store and

---

[2]*provost's man's:* Military policeman's.

across the worn gallery and down the sagging steps and among the dogs and half-grown boys in the mild May dust, where as he passed a voice hissed:

"Barn burner!"

Again he could not see, whirling; there was a face in a red haze, moon-like, bigger than the full moon, the owner of it half again his size, he leaping in the red haze toward the face, feeling no blow, feeling no shock when his head struck the earth, scrabbling up and leaping again, feeling no blow this time either and tasting no blood, scrabbling up to see the other boy in full flight and himself already leaping into pursuit as his father's hand jerked him back, the harsh, cold voice speaking above him: "Go get in the wagon."

It stood in a grove of locusts and mulberries across the road. His two hulking sisters in their Sunday dresses and his mother and her sister in calico and sunbonnets were already in it, sitting on and among the sorry residue of the dozen and more movings which even the boy could remember—the battered stove, the broken beds and chairs, the clock inlaid with mother-of-pearl, which would not run, stopped at some fourteen minutes past two o'clock of a dead and forgotten day and time, which had been his mother's dowry. She was crying, though when she saw him she drew her sleeve across her face and began to descend from the wagon. "Get back," the father said.

"He's hurt. I got to get some water and wash his..."

"Get back in the wagon," his father said. He got in too, over the tail-gate. His father mounted to the seat where the older brother already sat and struck the gaunt mules two savage blows with the peeled willow, but without heat. It was not even sadistic; it was exactly that same quality which in later years would cause his descendants to overrun the engine before putting a motor car into motion, striking and reining back in the same movement. The wagon went on, the store with its quiet crowd of grimly watching men dropped behind; a curve in the road hid it. *Forever* he thought. *Maybe he's done satisfied now, now that he has...* stopping himself, not to say it aloud even to himself. His mother's hand touched his shoulder.

"Does hit hurt?" she said.

"Naw," he said. "Hit don't hurt. Lemme be."

"Can't you wipe some of the blood off before hit dries?"

"I'll wash to-night," he said. "Lemme be, I tell you."

The wagon went on. He did not know where they were going. None 25 of them ever did or ever asked, because it was always somewhere, always a house of sorts waiting for them a day or two days or even three days away. Likely his father had already arranged to make a crop on another farm before he... Again he had to stop himself. He (the father) always did. There was something about his wolf-like independence and even courage when the advantage was at least neutral which impressed strangers, as if they got from his latent ravening ferocity not so much a sense of dependability as a feeling that his ferocious conviction in the rightness of his own actions would be of advantage to all whose interest lay with his.

That night they camped, in a grove of oaks and beeches where a spring ran. The nights were still cool and they had a fire against it, of a rail lifted from a nearby fence and cut into lengths—a small fire, neat, niggard almost, a shrewd fire; such fires were his father's habit and custom always, even in freezing weather. Older, the boy might have remarked this and wondered why not a big one; why should not a man who had not only seen the waste and extravagance of war, but who had in his blood an inherent voracious prodigality with material not his own, have burned everything in sight? Then he might have gone a step farther and thought that that was the reason: that niggard blaze was the living fruit of nights passed during those four years in the woods hiding from all men, blue or gray, with his strings of horses (captured horses, he called them). And older still, he might have divined the true reason: that the element of fire spoke to some deep mainspring of his father's being, as the element of steel or of powder spoke to other men, as the one weapon for the preservation of integrity, else breath were not worth the breathing, and hence to be regarded with respect and used with discretion.

But he did not think this now and he had seen those same niggard blazes all his life. He merely ate his supper beside it and was already half asleep over his iron plate when his father called him, and once more he followed the stiff back, the stiff and ruthless limp, up the slope and on to the starlit road where, turning, he could see his father against the stars but without face or depth—a shape black, flat, and bloodless as though cut from tin in the iron folds of the frockcoat which had not been made for him, the voice harsh like tin and without heat like tin:

"You were fixing to tell them. You would have told him." He didn't answer. His father struck him with the flat of his hand on the side of the head, hard but without heat, exactly as he had struck the two mules at the store, exactly as he would strike either of them with any stick in order to kill a horse fly, his voice still without fear or anger: "You're getting to be a man. You got to learn. You got to learn to stick to your own blood or you ain't going to have any blood to stick to you. Do you think either of them, any man there this morning, would? Don't you know all they wanted was a chance to get at me because they knew I had them beat? Eh?" Later, twenty years later, he was to tell himself, "If I had said they wanted only truth, justice, he would have hit me again." But now he said nothing. He was not crying. He just stood there. "Answer me," his father said.

"Yes," he whispered. His father turned.

30   "Get on to bed. We'll be there tomorrow."

Tomorrow they were there. In the early afternoon the wagon stopped before a paintless two-room house identical almost with the dozen others it had stopped before even in the boy's ten years, and again, as on the other dozen occasions, his mother and aunt got down and began to unload the wagon, although his two sisters and his father and brother had not moved.

"Likely hit ain't fitten for hawgs," one of the sisters said.

"Nevertheless, fit it will and you'll hog it and like it," his father said. "Get out of them chairs and help your Ma unload."

The two sisters got down, big, bovine, in a flutter of cheap ribbons; one of them drew from the jumbled wagon bed a battered lantern, the other a worn broom. His father handed the reins to the older son and began to climb stiffly over the wheel. "When they get unloaded, take the team to the barn and feed them." Then he said, and at first the boy thought he was still speaking to his brother: "Come with me."

"Me?" he said.

"Yes," his father said. "You."

"Abner," his mother said. His father paused and looked back—the harsh level stare beneath the shaggy, graying, irascible brows.

"I reckon I'll have a word with the man that aims to begin tomorrow owning me body and soul for the next eight months."

They went back up the road. A week ago—or before last night, that is—he would have asked where they were going, but not now. His father had struck him before last night but never before had he paused afterward to explain why; it was as if the blow and the following calm, outrageous voice still rang, repercussed, divulging nothing to him save the terrible handicap of being young, the light weight of his few years, just heavy enough to prevent his soaring free of the world as it seemed to be ordered but not heavy enough to keep him footed solid in it, to resist it and try to change the course of its events.

Presently he could see the grove of oaks and cedars and the other flowering trees and shrubs, where the house would be, though not the house yet. They walked beside a fence massed with honeysuckle and Cherokee roses and came to a gate swinging open between two brick pillars, and now, beyond a sweep of drive, he saw the house for the first time and at that instant he forgot his father and the terror and despair both, and even when he remembered his father again (who had not stopped) the terror and despair did not return. Because, for all the twelve movings, they had sojourned until now in a poor country, a land of small farms and fields and houses, and he had never seen a house like this before. *Hit's big as a courthouse* he thought quietly, with a surge of peace and joy whose reason he could not have thought into words, being too young for that: *They are safe from him. People whose lives are a part of this peace and dignity are beyond his touch, he no more to them than a buzzing wasp: capable of stinging*

35

40

for a little moment but that's all; the spell of this peace and dignity rendering
even the barns and stable and cribs which belong to it impervious to the puny
flames he might contrive...this, the peace and joy, ebbing for an instant as
he looked again at the stiff black back, the stiff and implacable limp of
the figure which was not dwarfed by the house, for the reason that it had
never looked big anywhere and which now, against the serene columned
backdrop, had more than ever that impervious quality of something cut
ruthlessly from tin, depthless, as though, sidewise to the sun, it would cast
no shadow. Watching him, the boy remarked the absolutely undeviating
course which his father held and saw the stiff foot come squarely down in
a pile of fresh droppings where a horse had stood in the drive and which
his father could have avoided by a simple change of stride. But it ebbed
only for a moment, though he could not have thought this into words
either, walking on in the spell of the house, which he could even want
but without envy, without sorrow, certainly never with that ravening and
jealous rage which unknown to him walked in the ironlike black coat
before him: *Maybe he will feel it too. Maybe it will even change him now*
from what maybe he couldn't help but be.

They crossed the portico. Now he could hear his father's stiff foot
as it came down on the boards with clocklike finality, a sound out of all
proportion to the displacement of the body it bore and which was not
dwarfed either by the white door before it, as though it had attained to a
sort of vicious and ravening minimum not to be dwarfed by anything—
the flat, wide, black hat, the formal coat of broadcloth which had once
been black but which had now that friction-glazed greenish cast of the
bodies of old house flies, the lifted sleeve which was too large, the lifted
hand like a curled claw. The door opened so promptly that the boy knew
the Negro must have been watching them all the time, an old man with
neat grizzled hair, in a linen jacket, who stood barring the door with his
body, saying, "Wipe yo foots, white man, fo you come in here. Major ain't
home nohow."

"Get out of my way, nigger," his father said, without heat too, flinging
the door back and the Negro also and entering, his hat still on his head.
And now the boy saw the prints of the stiff foot on the doorjamb and saw
them appear on the pale rug behind the machinelike deliberation of the
foot which seemed to bear (or transmit) twice the weight which the body
compassed. The Negro was shouting "Miss Lula! Miss Lula!" somewhere
behind them, then the boy, deluged as though by a warm wave by a suave
turn of carpeted stair and a pendant glitter of chandeliers and a mute
gleam of gold frames, heard the swift feet and saw her too, a lady—perhaps
he had never seen her like before either—in a gray, smooth gown with
lace at the throat and an apron tied at the waist and the sleeves turned
back, wiping cake or biscuit dough from her hands with a towel as she

came up the hall, looking not at his father at all but at the tracks on the blond rug with an expression of incredulous amazement.

"I tried," the Negro cried, "I tole him to..."

"Will you please go away?" she said in a shaking voice. "Major de Spain is not at home. Will you please go away?"

His father had not spoken again. He did not speak again. He did not 45 even look at her. He just stood stiff in the center of the rug, in his hat, the shaggy iron-gray brows twitching slightly above the pebble-colored eyes as he appeared to examine the house with brief deliberation. Then with the same deliberation he turned; the boy watched him pivot on the good leg and saw the stiff foot drag round the arc of the turning, leaving a final long and fading smear. His father never looked at it, he never once looked down at the rug. The Negro held the door. It closed behind them, upon the hysteric and indistinguishable woman-wail. His father stopped at the top of the steps and scraped his boot clean on the edge of it. At the gate he stopped again. He stood for a moment, planted stiffly on the stiff foot, looking back at the house. "Pretty and white, ain't it?" he said. "That's sweat. Nigger sweat. Maybe it ain't white enough yet to suit him. Maybe he wants to mix some white sweat with it."

Two hours later the boy was chopping wood behind the house within which his mother and aunt and the two sisters (the mother and aunt, not the two girls, he knew that; even at this distance and muffled by walls the flat loud voices of the two girls emanated an incorrigible idle inertia) were setting up the stove to prepare a meal, when he heard the hooves and saw the linen-clad man on a fine sorrel mare, whom he recognized even before he saw the rolled rug in front of the Negro youth following on a fat bay carriage horse—a suffused, angry face vanishing, still at full gallop, beyond the corner of the house where his father and brother were sitting in the two tilted chairs; and a moment later, almost before he could have put the axe down, he heard the hooves again and watched the sorrel mare go back out of the yard, already galloping again. Then his father began to shout one of the sisters' names, who presently emerged backward from the kitchen door dragging the rolled rug along the ground by one end while the other sister walked behind it.

"If you ain't going to tote, go on and set up the wash pot," the first said.

"You, Sarty!" the second shouted. "Set up the wash pot!" His father appeared at the door, framed against that shabbiness, as he had been against that other bland perfection, impervious to either, the mother's anxious face at his shoulder.

"Go on," the father said. "Pick it up." The two sisters stooped, broad, lethargic; stooping, they presented an incredible expanse of pale cloth and a flutter of tawdry ribbons.

50 "If I thought enough of a rug to have to git hit all the way from France I wouldn't keep hit where folks coming in would have to tromp on hit," the first said. They raised the rug.

"Abner," the mother said. "Let me do it."

"You go back and git dinner," his father said. "I'll tend to this."

From the woodpile through the rest of the afternoon the boy watched them, the rug spread flat in the dust beside the bubbling wash-pot, the two sisters stooping over it with that profound and lethargic reluctance, while the father stood over them in turn, implacable and grim, driving them though never raising his voice again. He could smell the harsh homemade lye[3] they were using; he saw his mother come to the door once and look toward them with an expression not anxious now but very like despair; he saw his father turn, and he fell to with the axe and saw from the corner of his eye his father raise from the ground a flattish fragment of field stone and examine it and return to the pot, and this time his mother actually spoke: "Abner. Abner. Please don't. Please, Abner."

Then he was done too. It was dusk; the whippoorwills had already begun. He could smell coffee from the room where they would presently eat the cold food remaining from the mid-afternoon meal, though when he entered the house he realized they were having coffee again probably because there was a fire on the hearth, before which the rug now lay spread over the backs of the two chairs. The tracks of his father's foot were gone. Where they had been were now long, water-cloudy scoriations resembling the sporadic course of a Lilliputian mowing machine.

55 It still hung there while they ate the cold food and then went to bed, scattered without order or claim up and down the two rooms, his mother in one bed, where his father would later lie, the older brother in the other, himself, the aunt, and the two sisters on pallets on the floor. But his father was not in bed yet. The last thing the boy remembered was the depthless, harsh silhouette of the hat and coat bending over the rug and it seemed to him that he had not even closed his eyes when the silhouette was standing over him, the fire almost dead behind it, the stiff foot prodding him awake. "Catch up the mule," his father said.

When he returned with the mule his father was standing in the black door, the rolled rug over his shoulder. "Ain't you going to ride?" he said.

"No. Give me your foot."

He bent his knee into his father's hand, the wiry, surprising power flowed smoothly, rising, he rising with it, on to the mule's bare back (they had owned a saddle once; the boy could remember it though not when or where) and with the same effortlessness his father swung the rug up in

---

[3] *lye:* A soap made from wood ashes and water, unsuitable for washing fine fabrics.

front of him. Now in the starlight they retraced the afternoon's path, up the dusty road rife with honeysuckle, through the gate and up the black tunnel to the drive to the lightless house, where he sat on the mule and felt the rough warp of the rug drag across his thighs and vanish.

"Don't you want me to help?" he whispered. His father did not answer and now he heard again that stiff foot striking the hollow portico with that wooden and clocklike deliberation, that outrageous overstatement of the weight it carried. The rug, hunched, not flung (the boy could tell that even in the darkness) from his father's shoulder struck the angle of wall and floor with a sound unbelievably loud, thunderous, then the foot again, unhurried and enormous; a light came on in the house and the boy sat, tense, breathing steadily and quietly and just a little fast, though the foot itself did not increase its beat at all, descending the steps now; now the boy could see him.

"Don't you want to ride now?" he whispered. "We kin both ride now," 60 the light within the house altering now, flaring up and sinking. *He's coming down the stairs now,* he thought. He had already ridden the mule up beside the horse block; presently his father was up behind him and he doubled the reins over and slashed the mule across the neck, but before the animal could begin to trot the hard, thin arm came round him, the hard, knotted hand jerking the mule back to a walk.

In the first red rays of the sun they were in the lot, putting plow gear on the mules. This time the sorrel mare was in the lot before he heard it at all, the rider collarless and even bareheaded, trembling, speaking in a shaking voice as the woman in the house had done, his father merely looking up once before stooping again to the hame[4] he was buckling, so that the man on the mare spoke to his stooping back:

"You must realize you have ruined that rug. Wasn't there anybody here, any of your women..." he ceased, shaking, the boy watching him, the older brother leaning now in the stable door, chewing, blinking slowly and steadily at nothing apparently. "It cost a hundred dollars. But you never had a hundred dollars. You never will. So I'm going to charge you twenty bushels of corn against your crop. I'll add it in your contract and when you come to the commissary you can sign it. That won't keep Mrs. de Spain quiet but maybe it will teach you to wipe your feet off before you enter her house again."

Then he was gone. The boy looked at his father, who still had not spoken or even looked up again, who was now adjusting the loggerhead in the hame.

"Pap," he said. His father looked at him—the inscrutable face, the shaggy brows beneath which the gray eyes glinted coldly. Suddenly the

---

[4]*hame:* Harness.

boy went toward him, fast, stopping as suddenly. "You done the best you could!" he cried. "If he wanted hit done different why didn't he wait and tell you how? He won't git no twenty bushels! He won't git none! We'll gether hit and hide hit! I kin watch…"

65   "Did you put the cutter back in that straight stock like I told you?"

"No, sir," he said.

"Then go do it."

That was Wednesday. During the rest of that week he worked steadily, at what was within his scope and some which was beyond it, with an industry that did not need to be driven nor even commanded twice; he had this from his mother, with the difference that some at least of what he did he liked to do, such as splitting wood with the half-size axe which his mother and aunt had earned, or saved money somehow, to present him with at Christmas. In company with the two older women (and on one afternoon, even one of the sisters), he built pens for the shoat and the cow which were a part of his father's contract with the landlord, and one after-noon, his father being absent, gone somewhere on one of the mules, he went to the field.

They were running a middle buster now, his brother holding the plow straight while he handled the reins, and walking beside the straining mule, the rich black soil shearing cool and damp against his bare ankles, he thought *Maybe this is the end of it. Maybe even that twenty bushels that seems hard to have to pay for just a rug will be a cheap price for him to stop forever and always from being what he used to be;* thinking, dreaming now, so that his brother had to speak sharply to him to mind the mule: *Maybe he even won't collect the twenty bushels. Maybe it will all add up and balance and vanish—corn, rug, fire; the terror and grief, the being pulled two ways like between two teams of horses—gone, done with for ever and ever.*

70   Then it was Saturday; he looked up from beneath the mule he was harnessing and saw his father in the black coat and hat. "Not that," his father said. "The wagon gear." And then, two hours later, sitting in the wagon bed behind his father and brother on the seat, the wagon accomplished a final curve, and he saw the weathered paintless store with its tattered tobacco- and patent-medicine posters and the tethered wagons and saddle animals below the gallery. He mounted the gnawed steps behind his father and brother, and there again was the lane of quiet, watching faces for the three of them to walk through. He saw the man in spectacles sitting at the plank table and he did not need to be told this was a Justice of the Peace; he sent one glare of fierce, exultant, partisan defiance at the man in collar and cravat now, whom he had seen but twice before in his life, and that on a galloping horse, who now wore on his face an expression not of rage but of amazed unbelief which the boy could not have known was at the incredible circumstance of being sued

by one of his own tenants, and came and stood against his father and cried at the Justice: "He ain't done it! He ain't burnt..."

"Go back to the wagon," his father said.

"Burnt?" the Justice said. "Do I understand this rug was burned too?"

"Does anybody here claim it was?" his father said. "Go back to the wagon." But he did not, he merely retreated to the rear of the room, crowded as that other had been, but not to sit down this time, instead, to stand pressing among the motionless bodies, listening to the voices:

"And you claim twenty bushels of corn is too high for the damage you did to the rug?"

"He brought the rug to me and said he wanted the tracks washed out 75 of it. I washed the tracks out and took the rug back to him."

"But you didn't carry the rug back to him in the same condition it was in before you made the tracks on it."

His father did not answer, and now for perhaps half a minute there was no sound at all save that of breathing, the faint, steady suspiration of complete and intent listening.

"You decline to answer that, Mr. Snopes?" Again his father did not answer. "I'm going to find against you, Mr. Snopes. I'm going to find that you were responsible for the injury to Major de Spain's rug and hold you liable for it. But twenty bushels of corn seems a little high for a man in your circumstances to have to pay. Major de Spain claims it cost a hundred dollars. October corn will be worth about fifty cents. I figure that if Major de Spain can stand a ninety-five dollar loss on something he paid cash for, you can stand a five-dollar loss you haven't earned yet. I hold you in damages to Major de Spain to the amount of ten bushels of corn over and above your contract with him, to be paid to him out of your crop at gathering time. Court adjourned."

It had taken no time hardly, the morning was but half begun. He thought they would return home and perhaps back to the field, since they were late, far behind all other farmers. But instead his father passed on behind the wagon, merely indicating with his hand for the older brother to follow with it, and crossed the road toward the blacksmith shop opposite, pressing on after his father, overtaking him, speaking, whispering up at the harsh, calm face beneath the weathered hat: "He won't git no ten bushels neither. He won't git one. We'll..." until his father glanced for an instant down at him, the face absolutely calm, the grizzled eyebrows tangled above the cold eyes, the voice almost pleasant, almost gentle:

"You think so? Well, we'll wait till October anyway." 80

The matter of the wagon—the setting of a spoke or two and the tightening of the tires—did not take long either, the business of the tires accomplished by driving the wagon into the spring branch behind the shop and letting it stand there, the mules nuzzling into the water from time to time, and the boy on the seat with the idle reins, looking up the slope and through the sooty tunnel of the shed where the slow hammer rang and where his father sat on an upended cypress bolt, easily, either talking or listening, still sitting there when the boy brought the dripping wagon up out of the branch and halted it before the door.

"Take them on to the shade and hitch," his father said. He did so and returned. His father and the smith and a third man squatting on his heels inside the door were talking, about crops and animals; the boy, squatting too in the ammoniac dust and hoof-parings and scales of rust, heard his father tell a long and unhurried story out of the time before the birth of the older brother even when he had been a professional horsetrader. And then his father came up beside him where he stood before a tattered last year's circus poster on the other side of the store, gazing rapt and quiet at the scarlet horses, the incredible poisings and convolutions of tulle and tights and the painted leers of comedians, and said, "It's time to eat."

But not at home. Squatting beside his brother against the front wall, he watched his father emerge from the store and produce from a paper sack a segment of cheese and divide it carefully and deliberately into three with his pocket knife and produce crackers from the same sack. They all three squatted on the gallery and ate, slowly, without talking; then in the store again, they drank from a tin dipper tepid water smelling of the cedar bucket and of living beech trees. And still they did not go home. It was a horse lot this time, a tall rail fence upon and along which men stood and sat and out of which one by one horses were led, to be walked and trotted and then cantered back and forth along the road while the slow swapping and buying went on and the sun began to slant westward, they—the three of them—watching and listening, the older brother with his muddy eyes and his steady, inevitable tobacco, the father commenting now and then on certain of the animals, to no one in particular.

It was after sundown when they reached home. They ate supper by lamplight, then, sitting on the doorstep, the boy watched the night fully accomplish, listening to the whippoorwills and the frogs, when he heard his mother's voice: "Abner! No! No! Oh, God. Oh, God. Abner!" and he rose, whirled, and saw the altered light through the door where a candle stub now burned in a bottle neck on the table and his father, still in the hat and coat, at once formal and burlesque as though dressed carefully for some shabby and ceremonial violence, emptying the reservoir of the lamp back into the five-gallon kerosene can from which it had been filled, while the mother tugged at his arm until he shifted the lamp to the other hand and flung her back, not savagely or viciously, just hard, into the wall, her hands flung out against the wall for balance, her mouth open and in her face the same quality of hopeless despair as had been in her voice. Then his father saw him standing in the door.

"Go to the barn and get that can of oil we were oiling the wagon with," 85 he said. The boy did not move. Then he could speak.

"What..." he cried. "What are you..."

"Go get that oil," his father said. "Go."

Then he was moving, running, outside the house, toward the stable: this the old habit, the old blood which he had not been permitted to choose for himself, which had been bequeathed him willy nilly and which had run for so long (and who knew where, battening on what of outrage and savagery and lust) before it came to him. *I could keep on,* he thought. *I could run on and on and never look back, never need to see his face again. Only I can't. I can't,* the rusted can in his hand now, the liquid sploshing in it as he ran back to the house and into it, into the sound of his mother's weeping in the next room, and handed the can to his father.

"Ain't you going to even send a nigger?" he cried. "At least you sent a nigger before!"

This time his father didn't strike him. The hand came even faster than 90 the blow had, the same hand which had set the can on the table with almost excruciating care flashing from the can toward him too quick for him to follow it, gripping him by the back of his shirt and on to tiptoe before he had seen it quit the can, the face stooping at him in breathless and frozen ferocity, the cold, dead voice speaking over him to the older brother who leaned against the table, chewing with that steady, curious, sidewise motion of cows:

"Empty the can into the big one and go on. I'll catch up with you."

"Better tie him to the bedpost," the brother said.

"Do like I told you," the father said. Then the boy was moving, his bunched shirt and the hard, bony hand between his shoulderblades, his toes just touching the floor, across the room and into the other one, past the sisters sitting with spread heavy thighs in the two chairs over the cold hearth, and to where his mother and aunt sat side by side on the bed, the aunt's arms about his mother's shoulders.

"Hold him," the father said. The aunt made a startled movement. "Not you," the father said. "Lennie. Take hold of him. I want to see you do it." His mother took him by the wrist. "You'll hold him better than that. If he gets loose don't you know what he is going to do? He will go up yonder." He jerked his head toward the road. "Maybe I'd better tie him."

"I'll hold him," his mother whispered. 95

"See you do then." Then his father was gone, the stiff foot heavy and measured upon the boards, ceasing at last.

Then he began to struggle. His mother caught him in both arms, he jerking and wrenching at them. He would be stronger in the end, he knew that. But he had no time to wait for it. "Lemme go!" he cried. "I don't want to have to hit you!"

"Let him go!" the aunt said. "If he don't go, before God, I am going up there myself!"

"Don't you see I can't?" his mother cried. "Sarty! Sarty! No! No! Help me, Lizzie!"

100 Then he was free. His aunt grasped at him but it was too late. He whirled, running, his mother stumbled forward on to her knees behind him, crying to the nearest sister: "Catch him, Net! Catch him!" But that was too late too, the sister (the sisters were twins, born at the same time, yet either of them now gave the impression of being, encompassing as much living meat and volume and weight as any other two of the family) not yet having begun to rise from the chair, her head, face, alone merely turned, presenting to him in the flying instant an astonishing expanse of young female features untroubled by any surprise even, wearing only an expression of bovine interest. Then he was out of the room, out of the house, in the mild dust of the starlit road and the heavy rifeness of honeysuckle, the pale ribbon unspooling with terrific slowness under his running feet, reaching the gate at last and turning in, running, his heart and lungs drumming, on up the drive toward the lighted house, the lighted door. He did not knock, he burst in, sobbing for breath, incapable for the moment of speech; he saw the astonished face of the Negro in the linen jacket without knowing when the Negro had appeared.

"De Spain!" he cried, panted. "Where's..." then he saw the white man too emerging from a white door down the hall. "Barn!" he cried. "Barn!"

"What?" the white man said. "Barn?"

"Yes!" the boy cried. "Barn!"

"Catch him!" the white man shouted.

105 But it was too late this time too. The Negro grasped his shirt, but the entire sleeve, rotten with washing, carried away, and he was out that door too and in the drive again, and had actually never ceased to run even while he was screaming into the white man's face.

Behind him the white man was shouting, "My horse! Fetch my horse!" and he thought for an instant of cutting across the park and climbing the fence into the road, but he did not know the park nor how high the vine-massed fence might be and he dared not risk it. So he ran on down the drive, blood and breath roaring; presently he was in the road again though he could not see it. He could not hear either: the galloping mare was almost upon him before he heard her, and even then he held his course, as if the very urgency of his wild grief and need must in a moment more find him wings, waiting until the ultimate instant to hurl himself aside and into the weed-choked roadside ditch as the horse thundered past and on, for an instant in furious silhouette against the stars, the tranquil early summer night sky which, even before the shape of the horse and rider vanished, stained abruptly and violently upward: a long, swirling roar incredible and soundless, blotting the stars, and he springing up and into the road again, running again, knowing it was too late yet still running even after he heard the shot and, an instant later, two shots, pausing now without knowing he had ceased to run, crying "Pap! Pap!", running again before he knew he had begun to run, stumbling, tripping over something and scrabbling up again without ceasing to run, looking backward over his shoulder at the glare as he got up, running on among the invisible trees, panting, sobbing, "Father! Father!"

At midnight he was sitting on the crest of a hill. He did not know it was midnight and he did not know how far he had come. But there was no glare behind him now and he sat now, his back toward what he had called home for four days anyhow, his face toward the dark woods which he would enter when breath was strong again, small, shaking steadily in the chill darkness, hugging himself into the remainder of his thin, rotten shirt, the grief and despair now no longer terror and fear but just grief and despair. *Father. My father*, he thought. "He was brave!" he cried suddenly, aloud but not loud, no more than a whisper: "He was! He was in the war! He was in Colonel Sartoris' cav'ry!" not knowing that his father had gone to that war a private in the fine old European sense, wearing no uniform, admitting the authority of and giving fidelity to no man or army or flag, going to war as Malbrouck[5] himself did: for booty—it meant nothing and less than nothing to him if it were enemy booty or his own.

The slow constellations wheeled on. It would be dawn and then sunup after a while and he would be hungry. But that would be tomorrow and now he was only cold, and walking would cure that. His breathing was easier now and he decided to get up and go on, and then he found that he had been asleep because he knew it was almost dawn, the night almost over. He could tell that from the whippoorwills. They were everywhere now among the dark trees below him, constant and inflectioned and ceaseless, so that, as the instant for giving over to the day birds drew nearer and nearer, there was no interval at all between them. He got up. He was a little stiff, but walking would cure that too as it would the cold, and soon there would be the sun. He went on down the hill, toward the dark woods within which the liquid silver voices of the birds called unceasing—the rapid and urgent beating of the urgent and quiring heart of the late spring night. He did not look back.

---

[5]*Malbrouck:* A character in a popular eighteenth-century nursery rhyme about a famous warrior.

Reading and Reacting

1. Is the third-person narrator of "Barn Burning" omniscient, or is his omniscience limited? Explain.

2. What is the point of view of the italicized passages? What do readers learn from them? Do they create irony? How would the story have been different without these passages?

3. "Barn Burning" includes a great deal of dialogue. How would you characterize the level of diction of this dialogue? What information about various characters does it provide?

4. What conflicts are presented in "Barn Burning"? Are any of these conflicts avoidable? Which, if any, are resolved in the story? Explain.

5. Why does Ab Snopes burn barns? Do you think his actions are justified? Explain your reasoning.

6. What role does the Civil War play in "Barn Burning"? What does Ab Snopes's behavior during the war tell readers about his character?

7. In the First and Second books of Samuel in the Old Testament, Abner was a relative of King Saul and commander in chief of his armies. Abner supported King Saul against David and was killed as a result of his own jealousy and rage. What, if any, significance is there in the fact that Faulkner names Ab Snopes—loyal to no man, fighter "for booty, and father of the Snopes clan"—after this mighty biblical leader?

8. Why does Sarty Snopes insist that his father was brave? How does your knowledge of events unknown to the boy create **irony**?

9. **JOURNAL ENTRY** How would the story be different if it were told from Ab's point of view? From Sarty's? From the point of view of Ab's wife? From the point of view of a member of a community in which the Snopeses have lived?

10. **CRITICAL PERSPECTIVE** Critic Edmond L. Volpe argues in his article "'Barn Burning': A Definition of Evil" that "Barn Burning" is not really about the class conflict between the sharecropping Snopeses and landowners like the de Spains but rather about Sarty:

> The story is centered upon Sarty's emotional dilemma. His conflict would not have been altered in any way if the person whose barn Ab burns had been a simple poor farmer, rather than an aristocratic plantation owner. . . . Sarty's struggle is against the repressive and divisive force his father represents. The boy's anxiety is created by his awakening sense of his own individuality. Torn between strong emotional attachment to the parent and his growing need to assert his own identity, Sarty's crisis is psychological and his battle is being waged far below the level of his intellectual and moral awareness.

Do you believe "Barn Burning" is, as Volpe suggests, essentially a coming-of-age story, or do you believe it is about something else—class conflict, for example?

Related Works: "A Worn Path" (p. 386), "Baca Grande" (p. 545), "Daddy" (p. 589), "Digging" (p. 706), *Fences* (p. 1270)

EDWIDGE DANTICAT (1969–   ) was born in Port-au-Prince, Haiti, and immigrated as a child with her parents to New York. Her work focuses largely on Haitian culture and the immigrant experience. In an interview, Danticat explained her motivation for writing the story collection *Krik? Krak!* (1995), a finalist for the National Book Award: "I wanted to raise the voice of a lot of the people that I knew growing up, and this was, for the most part…poor people who had extraordinary dreams but also very amazing obstacles." Winner of the 1995 Pushcart Short Story Prize and other fiction awards, Danticat has written the novels *The Dew Breaker* (2004) and *Claire of the Sea Light* (2013); the memoir *Brother, I'm Dying* (2007); the nonfiction collection *Create Dangerously: The Immigrant Artist at Work* (2010); and three young adult novels.

Source: AP Images/Laurent Rebours

Cultural Context   Haiti is a country that has been marked by authoritarian dictators, political unrest, crushing poverty, turbulent weather conditions, and a devastating earthquake in 2010 that killed over 230,000 people and injured another 300,000. These situations have led many Haitian immigrants to seek refuge in the United States. According to the 2009 American Community Survey, about 535,000 Haitians live in the United States, primarily in Florida and New York. In recent years, Haitian asylum seekers have encountered increased difficulty upon entering the United States, due in large part to the government's efforts to monitor immigration more closely after the 9/11 terrorist attacks.

New York Day Women (1991)

Today, walking down the street, I see my mother. She is strolling with a happy gait, her body thrust toward the DON'T WALK sign and the yellow taxicabs that make forty-five-degree turns on the corner of Madison and Fifty-seventh Street.

I have never seen her in this kind of neighborhood, peering into Chanel and Tiffany's and gawking at the jewels glowing in the Bulgari windows. My mother never shops outside of Brooklyn. She has never seen the advertising office where I work. She is afraid to take the subway, where you may meet those young black militant street preachers who curse black women for straightening their hair.

Yet, here she is, my mother, who I left at home that morning in her bathrobe, with pieces of newspapers twisted like rollers in her hair. My mother, who accuses me of random offenses as I dash out of the house.

* * *

Would you get up and give an old lady like me your subway seat? In this state of mind, I bet you don't even give up your seat to a pregnant lady.

* * *

5   My mother, who is often right about that. Sometimes I get up and give my seat. Other times, I don't. It all depends on how pregnant the woman is and whether or not she is with her boyfriend or husband and whether or not *he* is sitting down.

As my mother stands in front of Carnegie Hall, one taxi driver yells to another, "What do you think this is, a dance floor?"

My mother waits patiently for this dispute to be settled before crossing the street.

* * *

In Haiti when you get hit by a car, the owner of the car gets out and kicks you for getting blood on his bumper.

* * *

My mother who laughs when she says this and shows a large gap in her mouth where she lost three more molars to the dentist last week. My mother, who at fifty-nine, says dentures are okay.

* * *

10   **You can take them out when they bother you. I'll like them. I'll like them fine.**

* * *

Will it feel empty when Papa kisses you?

* * *

Oh no, he doesn't kiss me that way anymore.

*   *   *

My mother, who watches the lottery drawing every night on channel 11 without ever having played the numbers.

*   *   *

A third of that money is all I would need. We would pay the mortgage, and your father could stop driving that taxicab all over Brooklyn.

*   *   *

I follow my mother, mesmerized by the many possibilities of her jour-   15
ney. Even in a flowered dress, she is lost in a sea of pinstripes and gray suits, high heels and elegant short skirts, Reebok sneakers, dashing from building to building.

My mother, who won't go out to dinner with anyone.

*   *   *

If they want to eat with me, let them come to my house, even if I boil water and give it to them.

*   *   *

My mother, who talks to herself when she peels the skin off poultry.

*   *   *

Fat, you know, and cholesterol. Fat and cholesterol killed your aunt Hermine.

*   *   *

My mother, who makes jam with dried grapefruit peel and then puts in   20
cinnamon bark that I always think is cockroaches in the jam. My mother, whom I have always bought household appliances for, on her birthday. A nice rice cooker, a blender.

I trail the red orchids in her dress and the heavy faux leather bag on her shoulders. Realizing the ferocious pace of my pursuit, I stop against a wall to rest. My mother keeps on walking as though she owns the sidewalk under her feet.

As she heads toward the Plaza Hotel, a bicycle messenger swings so close to her that I want to dash forward and rescue her, but she stands dead in her tracks and lets him ride around her and then goes on.

My mother stops at a corner hot-dog stand and asks for something. The vendor hands her a can of soda that she slips into her bag. She stops by another vendor selling sundresses for seven dollars each. I can tell that she is looking at an African print dress, contemplating my size. I think to myself, Please Ma, don't buy it. It would be just another thing that I would bury in the garage or give to Goodwill.

*   *   *

Why should we give to Goodwill when there are so many people back home who need clothes? We save our clothes for the relatives in Haiti.

*   *   *

25   Twenty years we have been saving all kinds of things for the relatives in Haiti. I need the place in the garage for an exercise bike.

*   *   *

You are pretty enough to be a stewardess. Only dogs like bones.

*   *   *

This mother of mine, she stops at another hot-dog vendor's and buys a frankfurter that she eats on the street. I never knew that she ate frankfurters. With her blood pressure, she shouldn't eat anything with sodium. She has to be careful with her heart, this day woman.

*   *   *

I cannot just swallow salt. Salt is heavier than a hundred bags of shame.

*   *   *

She is slowing her pace, and now I am too close. If she turns around, she might see me. I let her walk into the park before I start to follow again.

My mother walks toward the sandbox in the middle of the park. There 30
a woman is waiting with a child. The woman is wearing a leotard with
biker's shorts and has small weights in her hands. The woman kisses the
child good-bye and surrenders him to my mother; then she bolts off, running on the cemented stretches in the park.

The child given to my mother has frizzy blond hair. His hand slips
into hers easily, like he's known her for a long time. When he raises his
face to look at my mother, it is as though he is looking at the sky.

My mother gives this child the soda that she bought from the vendor on the street corner. The child's face lights up as she puts a straw
in the can for him. This seems to be a conspiracy just between the two
of them.

My mother and the child sit and watch the other children play in
the sandbox. The child pulls out a comic book from a knapsack with Big
Bird on the back. My mother peers into his comic book. My mother, who
taught herself to read as a little girl in Haiti from the books that her brothers brought home from school.

My mother, who has now lost six of her seven sisters in Ville Rose[1] and
has never had the strength to return for their funerals.

*   *   *

Many graves to kiss when I go back. Many graves to kiss.   35

*   *   *

She throws away the empty soda can when the child is done with it. I
wait and watch from a corner until the woman in the leotard and biker's
shorts returns, sweaty and breathless, an hour later. My mother gives the
woman back her child and strolls farther into the park.

I turn around and start to walk out of the park before my mother can
see me. My lunch hour is long since gone. I have to hurry back to work. I
walk through a cluster of joggers, then race to a *Sweden Tours* bus. I stand
behind the bus and take a peek at my mother in the park. She is standing
in a circle, chatting with a group of women who are taking other people's
children on an afternoon outing. They look like a Third World Parent-
Teacher Association meeting.

I quickly jump into a cab heading back to the office. Would Ma have
said hello had she been the one to see me first?

---

[1] *Ville Rose:* Fictional Haitian town.

As the cab races away from the park, it occurs to me that perhaps one day I would chase an old woman down a street by mistake and that old woman would be somebody else's mother, who I would have mistaken for mine.

*   *   *

40   **Day women come out when nobody expects them.**

*   *   *

Tonight on the subway, I will get up and give my seat to a pregnant woman or a lady about Ma's age.

My mother, who stuffs thimbles in her mouth and then blows up her cheeks like Dizzy Gillespie[2] while sewing yet another Raggedy Ann doll that she names Suzette after me.

*   *   *

I will have all these little Suzettes in case you never have any babies, which looks more and more like it is going to happen.

*   *   *

My mother who had me when she was thirty-three—*l'âge du Christ*—at the age that Christ died on the cross.

*   *   *

45   **That's a blessing, believe you me, even if American doctors say by that time you can make retarded babies.**

*   *   *

My mother, who sews lace collars on my company softball T-shirts when she does my laundry.

*   *   *

Why can't you look like a lady playing softball?

*   *   *

---

[2] *Dizzy Gillespie:* American jazz trumpeter (1917–1993).

My mother, who never went to any of my Parent-Teacher Association meetings when I was in school.

*   *   *

You're so good anyway. What are they going to tell me? I don't want to make you ashamed of this day woman. Shame is heavier than a hundred bags of salt.

Reading and Reacting

1. Who is the narrator of the story? How does the narrative point of view shape the story?
2. How is the narrator different from her mother? What details in the story lead you to your conclusion?
3. The story consists of alternating passages—one in standard type and then one in boldface type. How does the point of view of the story shift between these two kinds of passages?
4. The story begins when the narrator says, "Today, walking down the street, I see my mother." What motivates the narrator to follow her mother?
5. The narrator tells her story in the present tense. What would she have gained or lost by telling it in the past tense?
6. Why does the narrator hide from her mother? Why doesn't she greet her?
7. How would you characterize the relationship between the narrator and her mother?
8. In paragraph 28, the narrator's mother says, "Salt is heavier than a hundred bags of shame." However, the story ends with her saying, "Shame is heavier than a hundred bags of salt" (par. 49). What does she mean? What is the significance of this shift?
9. **JOURNAL ENTRY** Write a paragraph in which you define "day woman." Include some examples from the story to help you develop your definition.
10. **CRITICAL PERSPECTIVE** In a 2000 interview with the literary journal *Brick*, Edwidge Danticat explains how, as a Haitian immigrant living in the United States, she has a dualistic relationship with Haiti:

   > I have come to terms with the fact that my relationship with Haiti is different than someone who lives there...I love being there, there's a kind of peace about it that I can't explain. But I realize that I'm not living, I'm staying for a certain period of time, at the end of which I travel back. And so, it's a relationship of insider/outsider.

   How does "New York Day Women" convey the narrator's "insider/outsider" relationship with her mother and with Haiti?

Related Works: "Girl" (p. 95), "I Stand Here Ironing" (p. 217), "Two Kinds" (p. 471), "'Mexican' Is Not a Noun" (p. 542), "Those Winter Sundays" (p. 705), *The Cuban Swimmer* (p. 1166)

WRITING SUGGESTIONS: Point of View

1. How would Poe's "The Cask of Amontillado" be different if it were told by a minor character who observed the events? Rewrite the story from this point of view—or tell the story that precedes the story, explaining the "thousand injuries" and the "insult."

2. Assume that you are Jim, the sailor in "Big Black Good Man," and that you are keeping a journal of your travels. Write the journal entries for the time you spent in Copenhagen. Include your impressions of Olaf, Lena, the hotel, and anything else that caught your attention. Make sure you present your version of the key events described in the story—especially Olaf's reaction to you.

3. Both "The Cask of Amontillado" and "Barn Burning" deal with crimes that essentially go unpunished and with the emotions that accompany these crimes. In what sense does each story's use of point of view shape its treatment of the crime in question? For instance, how does point of view determine how much readers know about the motives for the crime, the crime's basic circumstances, and the extent to which the crime is justified?

4. Write a story in which you retell "New York Day Women" from the mother's point of view. Be true to the original story. Be sure to reveal what she is thinking at various points in the story.

CHAPTER 11

STYLE, TONE, AND LANGUAGE

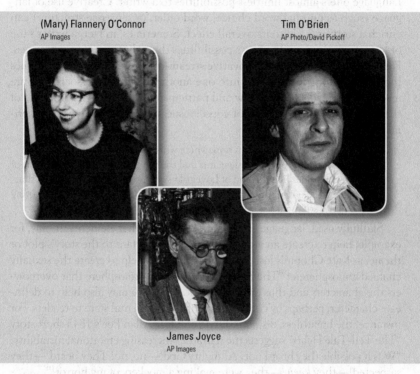

(Mary) Flannery O'Connor
AP Images

Tim O'Brien
AP Photo/David Pickoff

James Joyce
AP Images

Style and Tone

One of the qualities that gives a work of literature its individuality is its **style**, the way in which a writer uses language, selecting and arranging words to say what he or she wants to say. Style encompasses elements such as word choice; syntax; sentence length and structure; and the presence, frequency, and prominence of imagery and figures of speech.

Closely related to style is **tone**, the attitude of the narrator or author of a work toward the subject matter, characters, or audience. Word choice and sentence structure help to create a work's tone, which may be intimate or distant, bitter or affectionate, straightforward or cautious, supportive or critical, respectful or condescending. (Tone may also be **ironic**; see Chapter 10, "Point of View," for a discussion of irony.)

The Uses of Language

Language offers almost limitless possibilities to a writer. Creative use of language (such as unusual word choice, word order, or sentence structure) can enrich a story and add to its overall effect. Sometimes, in fact, a writer's use of language can expand a story's possibilities through its very inventiveness. For example, James Joyce's innovative **stream-of-consciousness** style mimics thought, allowing ideas to run into one another as random associations are made so that readers may follow and participate in the thought processes of the narrator. Here is a stream-of-consciousness passage from Joyce's experimental 1922 novel *Ulysses*:

> frseeeeeeeefronnnng train somewhere whistling the strength those engines have in them like big giants and the water rolling all over and out of them all sides like the end of Loves old sweet sonnnng the poor men that have to be out all the night from their wives and families in those roasting engines stifling it was today. . . .

Skillfully used, language can enhance a story's other elements. It may, for example, help to create an atmosphere that is important to the story's plot or theme, as Kate Chopin's lush, rhythmic sentences help to create the sexually charged atmosphere of "The Storm" (p. 199)—an atmosphere that overpowers the characters and thus drives the plot. Language may also help to delineate character, perhaps by conveying a character's mental state to readers. For instance, the breathless, disjointed style of Edgar Allan Poe's 1843 short story "The Tell-Tale Heart" suggests the narrator's increasing emotional instability: "Was it possible they heard not? Almighty God!—no, no! They heard!—they suspected!—they *knew!*—they were making a mockery of my horror!"

In his 1925 short story "Big Two-Hearted River," Ernest Hemingway uses short, unconnected sentences to create a flat, emotionless prose style that reveals his character's alienation and fragility as he struggles to maintain control: "Now things were done. There had been this to do. Now it was done. It had been a hard trip. He was very tired. That was done. He had made his camp. He was settled. Nothing could touch him."

Language that places emphasis on the sounds and rhythm of words and sentences can also enrich a work of fiction. Consider the use of such language in the following sentence from James Joyce's "Araby" (p. 288):

> The light from the lamp opposite our door caught the white curve of her neck, lit up her hair that rested there and, falling, lit up the hand upon the railing.

Here the narrator is describing his first conversation with a girl who fascinates him, and the lyrical, almost musical language reflects his enchantment. Note in particular the **alliteration** (*l*ight/*l*amp; *c*aught/*c*urve; *h*air/*h*and), the repetition (lit up/lit up), and the rhyme (lit up her *hair*/that rested *there*) and **near rhyme** (falling/railing); these poetic devices weave the words of the sentence into a smooth, rhythmic whole.

Another example of this emphasis on sound may be found in the measured **parallelism** of this sentence from Nathaniel Hawthorne's 1843 story "The Birthmark":

> He had left his laboratory to the care of an assistant, cleared his fine countenance from the furnace smoke, washed the stain of acids from his fingers, and persuaded a beautiful woman to become his wife.

The style of this sentence, conveying methodical precision and order, reflects the compulsive personality of the character being described.

The following passage from Alberto Alvaro Ríos's story "The Secret Lion" (p. 466) illustrates the power of language to enrich a story:

> We had read the books, after all; we knew about bridges and castles and wildtreacherousraging alligatormouth rivers. We wanted them. So we were going to go out and get them. We went back that morning into that kitchen and we said, "We're going out there, we're going into the hills, we're going away for three days, don't worry." She said, "All right."
>
> "You know," I said to Sergio, "if we're going to go away for three days, well, we ought to at least pack a lunch."
>
> But we were two young boys with no patience for what we thought at the time was mom-stuff: making sa-and-wiches. My mother didn't offer. So we got out little kid knapsacks that my mother had sewn for us, and into them we put the jar of mustard. A loaf of bread. Knivesforksplates, bottles of Coke, a can opener. This was lunch for the two of us. And we were weighed down, humped over to be strong enough to carry this stuff. But we started walking anyway, into the hills. We were going to eat berries and stuff otherwise. "Goodbye." My mom said that.

Through language, the adult narrator of the preceding paragraphs recaptures the bravado of the boys in search of "wildtreacherousraging alligatormouth rivers" even as he suggests to readers that the boys are not going far. The story's use of language is original and inventive: words are blended together ("getridofit," "knivesforksplates"), linked to form new words ("mom-stuff"), and drawn out to mimic speech ("sa-and-wiches"). These experiments with language show the narrator's willingness to move back into a child's frame of reference while maintaining the advantage of distance. The adult narrator uses sentence fragments ("A loaf of bread."), colloquialisms ("kid," "mom," "stuff"), and contractions. He also includes conversational elements such as *you know* and *well* in the story's dialogue, accurately recreating the childhood scene even as he sees its folly and remains aware of the disillusionment that awaits him. Thus, the unique style permits the narrator to bring readers with him into the child's world while he maintains his adult stance: "But we were two young boys with no patience for what we thought at the time was mom-stuff. . . ."

Although many stylistic options are available to writers, a story's language must be consistent with the writer's purpose and with the effect he or she hopes to create. Just as writers may experiment with point of view or manipulate events to create a complex plot, so they can adjust language to suit a particular narrator or character or to convey a particular theme. In addition to the creative uses of language described above, writers also frequently experiment with *formal and informal diction, imagery,* and *figures of speech.*

 ## Formal and Informal Diction

The level of diction—how formal or informal a story's language is—can reveal a good deal about a story's narrator and characters.

Formal diction is characterized by elaborate, complex sentences; a learned vocabulary; and a serious, objective, detached tone. It does not generally include contractions, shortened word forms (like *phone*), regional expressions, or slang, and it may substitute *one* or *we* for *I*. At its most extreme, formal language is stiff and stilted, far removed from everyday speech.

When formal diction is used by a narrator or by a character, it may indicate erudition, a high educational level, a superior social or professional position, or emotional detachment. When one character's language is significantly more formal than others', he or she may seem old-fashioned or stuffy; when language is inappropriately elevated or complex, it may reveal the character to be pompous or ridiculous; when a narrator's language is noticeably more formal than that of the story's characters, the narrator may seem superior or even condescending. Thus, the choice of a particular level (or levels) of diction in a story can convey information about characters and about the narrator's attitude toward them.

The following passage from Hawthorne's "The Birthmark" illustrates formal style:

> In the latter part of the last century there lived a man of science, an eminent proficient in every branch of natural philosophy, who not long before our story opens had made experience of a spiritual affinity more attractive than any chemical one. He had left his laboratory to the care of an assistant, cleared his fine countenance from the furnace smoke, washed the stain of acids from his fingers, and persuaded a beautiful woman to become his wife. In those days when the comparatively recent discovery of electricity and other kindred mysteries of Nature seemed to open paths into the region of miracle, it was not unusual for the love of science to rival the love of woman in its depth and absorbing energy. The higher

intellect, the imagination, the spirit, and even the heart might all find
their congenial ailment in pursuits which, as some of their ardent votaries
believed, would ascend from one step of powerful intelligence to another,
until the philosopher should lay his hand on the secret of creative force
and perhaps make new worlds for himself.

The long and complex sentences, learned vocabulary ("countenance," "ailment," "votaries"), and absence of colloquialisms suit Hawthorne's purpose
well, recreating the formal language of the earlier era in which his story is
set. The narrator is aloof and controlled, and his diction makes this clear
to readers.

Informal diction, consistent with everyday speech, is characterized by
slang, contractions, colloquial expressions like *you know* and *I mean*, shortened word forms, incomplete sentences, and a casual, conversational tone.
A first-person narrator may use an informal style, or characters may speak
informally; in either case, informal style tends to narrow the distance
between readers and text.

One kind of informal language is illustrated in Joyce Carol Oates's
"Where Are You Going, Where Have You Been?" (p. 453) by the casual,
slangy style of the dialogue between the teenager Connie and her older
stalker, Arnold Friend:

> "I ain't late, am I?" he said.
> "Who the hell do you think you are?" Connie said.
> "Toldja I'd be out, didn't I?"
> "I don't even know who you are."

Here, the level of the characters' diction is a key element of the story:
because Arnold seems to speak Connie's language, she lets down her guard
and becomes vulnerable to his advances.

Another kind of informal language is seen in the regionalisms and dialect used in Flannery O'Connor's "A Good Man Is Hard to Find" (p. 295),
where speech patterns and individual words ("aloose"; "you all"; "britches")
help to identify the region in which the characters live and their social class.

Informal diction may also include language readers find offensive. In such
cases, a character's use of obscenities may suggest anything from crudeness
to adolescent bravado, and the use of racial or ethnic slurs indicates that a
character is insensitive or bigoted.

The following passage from John Updike's "A&P" (p. 160) illustrates
informal style:

> She had sort of oaky hair that the sun and salt had bleached, done up in a
> bun that was unravelling, and a kind of prim face. Walking into the A&P
> with your straps down, I suppose it's the only kind of face you *can* have.
> She held her head so high her neck, coming out of those white shoulders,
> looked kind of stretched, but I didn't mind. The longer her neck was, the
> more of her there was.

Here, the first-person narrator, a nineteen-year-old supermarket checkout clerk, uses a conversational style, including colloquialisms ("sort of," "I suppose," "kind of"), contractions ("it's," "didn't"), and the imprecise, informal *you* ("Walking into the A&P with *your* straps down...."). The narrator uses neither elaborate syntax nor a learned vocabulary.

 ## Imagery

Imagery—words and phrases that describe what is seen, heard, smelled, tasted, or touched—can have a significant impact in a story. A writer may use a pattern of repeated imagery to convey a particular impression about a character or situation or to communicate or reinforce a story's theme. For example, a character's newly discovered sense of freedom or sexuality can be conveyed through repeated use of words and phrases suggesting blooming or ripening, as in the two stories in this text by Kate Chopin.

In T. Coraghessan Boyle's "Greasy Lake" (p. 425), the narrator's vivid description of Greasy Lake uses rich visual imagery to evoke a scene:

> Through the center of town, up the strip, past the housing developments and shopping malls, street lights giving way to the thin streaming illumination of the headlights, trees crowding the asphalt in a black unbroken wall: that was the way out to Greasy Lake. The Indians had called it Wakan, a reference to the clarity of its waters. Now it was fetid and murky, the mud banks glittering with broken glass and strewn with beer cans and the charred remains of bonfires. There was a single ravaged island a hundred yards from shore, so stripped of vegetation it looked as if the air force had strafed it. We went up to the lake because everyone went there, because we wanted to snuff the rich scent of possibility on the breeze, watch a girl take off her clothes and plunge into the festering murk, drink beer, smoke pot, howl at the stars, savor the incongruous full-throated roar of rock and roll against the primeval susurrus of frogs and crickets. This was nature.

By characterizing a bucolic natural setting with surprising words like "fetid," "murky," and "greasy" and unpleasant images such as the "glittering of broken glass," the "ravaged island," and the "charred remains of bonfires," Boyle creates a picture that is completely at odds with the traditional view of nature. The incongruous images are nevertheless perfectly consistent with the sordid events that take place at Greasy Lake.

 ## Figures of Speech

Figures of speech—such as *similes*, *metaphors*, and *personification*—can enrich a story, subtly revealing information about characters and themes.

By using **metaphors** and **similes**—figures of speech that compare two dissimilar items—writers can indicate a particular attitude toward characters and events. Thus, Flannery O'Connor's many grotesque similes in "A Good Man Is Hard to Find" help to dehumanize her characters; the children's mother, for instance, has a face "as broad and innocent as a cabbage." In Tillie Olsen's "I Stand Here Ironing" (p. 217), an extended metaphor in which a mother compares her daughter to a dress waiting to be ironed expresses the mother's attitude toward her child, effectively suggesting the daughter's vulnerability. Similes and metaphors are used throughout in Kate Chopin's "The Storm" (p. 199). In a scene of sexual awakening, Calixta's skin is "like a creamy lily," her passion is "like a white flame," and her mouth is "a fountain of delight"; these figures of speech add a lushness and sensuality to the story.

Personification—a figure of speech, closely related to metaphor, that endows inanimate objects or abstract ideas with life or with human characteristics—is used in "Araby" (p. 288), where houses, "conscious of decent lives within them, gazed at one another with brown imperturbable faces." This use of figurative language expands readers' vision of the story's setting and gives a dreamlike quality to the passage. (Other figures of speech, such as **hyperbole** and **understatement**, can also enrich works of fiction. See Chapter 19, "Figures of Speech," for further information.)

Allusions—references to familiar historical, cultural, literary, or biblical texts, figures, or events—may also expand readers' understanding and appreciation of a work. An allusion widens a work's context by bringing it into the context of a related subject or idea. For instance, in Charles Baxter's short story "Gryphon" (p. 172), the narrator's allusions to *Pinocchio* and Betty Crocker enable readers who recognize the references to gain a deeper understanding of what certain characters are really like. (For information on the use of allusion in poetry, see Chapter 22.)

█ NOTE   In analyzing the use of language in a work of fiction, you may occasionally encounter unfamiliar allusions (or foreign words and phrases or regional expressions), particularly in works treating cultures and historical periods other than your own. Frequently, such language will be clarified by the context or by explanatory notes in your text. If it is not, always look up the meaning.

✔ **CHECKLIST   Writing about Style, Tone, and Language**

■ Does the writer make any unusual creative use of word choice, word order, or sentence structure?

■ Is the story's tone intimate? distant? ironic? How does the tone advance the writer's purpose?

continued on next page

- Does the style emphasize the sound and rhythm of language? For example, does the writer use alliteration and assonance? repetition and parallelism? What do such techniques add to the story?

- Is the level of diction generally formal, informal, or somewhere in between?

- Is there a difference between the diction used by the narrator and the diction used in the characters' speech? If so, what is the effect of this difference?

- Do any of the story's characters use regionalisms, colloquial language, or nonstandard speech? If so, what effect does this language have?

- What do different characters' levels of diction reveal about them?

- What kind of imagery predominates? Where, and why, is imagery used?

- Does the story develop a pattern of imagery? How does this pattern of imagery help to convey the story's themes?

- Does the story use simile and metaphor? personification? What is the effect of these figures of speech?

- Do figures of speech reinforce the story's themes? reveal information about characters?

- Does the story make any historical, literary, or biblical allusions? What do these allusions contribute to the story?

- Are any unfamiliar, obscure, or foreign words, phrases, or images used in the story? What do these words or expressions contribute to the story?

Source: © AP Images

JAMES JOYCE (1882–1941) was born in Dublin but lived his entire adult life in self-imposed exile from his native Ireland. Though his parents sent him to schools that trained young men for the priesthood, Joyce saw himself as a religious and artistic rebel and fled to Paris soon after graduation in 1902. Recalled briefly to Dublin by his mother's fatal illness, Joyce returned to the Continent in 1904, taking with him an uneducated Irish country girl named Nora Barnacle, who became his wife in 1931. In dreary quarters in Trieste, Zurich, and Paris, Joyce struggled to support a growing family, sometimes teaching classes in Berlitz language schools.

Though Joyce never again lived in Ireland, he continued to write about Dublin. Publication of *Dubliners* (1914), a collection of short stories that included "Araby," was delayed for seven years because the Irish publisher feared libel suits from local citizens who were thinly disguised as characters in the stories. Joyce's autobiographical *Portrait of the Artist as a Young Man* (1916) tells of a young writer's rejection of family, church, and country. *Ulysses* (1922), the comic tale of eighteen hours in the life of a wandering Dublin advertising salesman, was banned when the United States Post Office brought charges of obscenity against the book, and it remained banned in the United States and England for more than a decade. With *Ulysses*, Joyce began a revolutionary journey away from traditional techniques of plot and characterization to the interior monologues and stream-of-consciousness style that mark his last great novel, *Finnegans Wake* (1939).

Cultural Context   In the early twentieth century, as world travel and the shipment of goods around the globe expanded at a dizzying pace, the West experienced a fascination with the "Orient." To peddle their wares, immigrants from the East established bazaars reminiscent of the ones in their homelands, displaying a dazzling array of spices, foods, and material goods. This exotic appeal to the senses, representing the allure of the distant and unknown, became a highlight of many towns and cities. In this story, the bazaar represents the allure of the strange and exotic for the young narrator.

Araby (1914)

North Richmond Street, being blind,[1] was a quiet street except at the hour when the Christian Brothers' School set the boys free. An uninhabited house of two storeys stood at the blind end, detached from its neighbours in a square ground. The other houses of the street, conscious of decent lives within them, gazed at one another with brown imperturbable faces.

The former tenant of our house, a priest, had died in the back drawing-room. Air, musty from having been long enclosed, hung in all the rooms, and the waste room behind the kitchen was littered with old useless papers. Among these I found a few paper-covered books, the pages of which were curled and damp: *The Abbot*, by Walter Scott, *The Devout Communicant* and *The Memoirs of Vidocq.*[2] I liked the last best because its leaves were yellow. The wild garden behind the house contained a central apple-tree and a few straggling bushes under one of which I found the late tenant's rusty bicycle-pump. He had been a very charitable priest; in his will he had left all his money to institutions and the furniture of his house to his sister.

---

[1] *blind:* Dead-end.

[2] The Abbot . . . Vidocq: Sir Walter Scott (1771–1832)—an English Romantic novelist; *The Devout Communicant*—a variant title for *Pious Meditations*, written by an eighteenth-century English Franciscan friar, Pacifus Baker; *The Memoirs of Vidocq*—an autobiography of François-Jules Vidocq (1775–1857), a French criminal turned police agent.

When the short days of winter came dusk fell before we had well eaten our dinners. When we met in the street the houses had grown sombre. The space of sky above us was the colour of ever-changing violet and towards it the lamps of the street lifted their feeble lanterns. The cold air stung us and we played till our bodies glowed. Our shouts echoed in the silent street. The career of our play brought us through the dark muddy lanes behind the houses where we ran the gauntlet of the rough tribes from the cottages, to the back doors of the dark dripping gardens where odours arose from the ashpits, to the dark odorous stables where a coach-man smoothed and combed the horse or shook music from the buckled harness. When we returned to the street light from the kitchen windows had filled the areas. If my uncle was seen turning the corner we hid in the shadow until we had seen him safely housed. Or if Mangan's sister came out on the doorstep to call her brother in to his tea we watched her from our shadow peer up and down the street. We waited to see whether she would remain or go in and, if she remained, we left our shadow and walked up to Mangan's steps resignedly. She was waiting for us, her figure defined by the light from the half-opened door. Her brother always teased her before he obeyed and I stood by the railings looking at her. Her dress swung as she moved her body and the soft rope of her hair tossed from side to side.

Every morning I lay on the floor in the front parlour watching her door. The blind was pulled down to within an inch of the sash so that I could not be seen. When she came out on the doorstep my heart leaped. I ran to the hall, seized my books and followed her. I kept her brown figure always in my eye and, when we came near the point at which our ways diverged, I quickened my pace and passed her. This happened morning after morning. I had never spoken to her, except for a few casual words, and yet her name was like a summons to all my foolish blood.

5   Her image accompanied me even in places the most hostile to romance. On Saturday evenings when my aunt went marketing I had to go to carry some of the parcels. We walked through the flaring streets, jostled by drunken men and bargaining women, amid the curses of labourers, the shrill litanies of shop-boys who stood on guard by the barrels of pigs' cheeks, the nasal chanting of street-singers, who sang a *come-all-you* about O'Donovan Rossa,[3] or a ballad about the troubles in our native land. These noises converged in a single sensation of life for me: I imagined that I bore my chalice safely through a throng of foes. Her name sprang to my lips at moments in strange prayers and praises which I myself did not understand. My eyes were often full of tears (I could not

[3] *O'Donovan Rossa:* Any popular song beginning "Come all you gallant Irishmen . . ."; O'Donovan Rossa was an Irish nationalist who was banished in 1870 for advocating violent rebellion against the British.

tell why) and at times a flood from my heart seemed to pour itself out into my bosom. I thought little of the future. I did not know whether I would ever speak to her or not or, if I spoke to her, how I could tell her of my confused adoration. But my body was like a harp and her words and gestures were like fingers running upon the wires.

One evening I went into the back drawing-room in which the priest had died. It was a dark rainy evening and there was no sound in the house. Through one of the broken panes I heard the rain impinge upon the earth, the fine incessant needles of water playing in the sodden beds. Some distant lamp or lighted window gleamed below me. I was thankful that I could see so little. All my senses seemed to desire to veil themselves and, feeling that I was about to slip from them, I pressed the palms of my hands together until they trembled, murmuring: "O love! O love!" many times.

At last she spoke to me. When she addressed the first words to me I was so confused that I did not know what to answer. She asked me was I going to *Araby*. I forgot whether I answered yes or no. It would be a splendid bazaar, she said she would love to go.

"And why can't you?" I asked.

While she spoke she turned a silver bracelet round and round her wrist. She could not go, she said, because there would be a retreat that week in her convent.[4] Her brother and two other boys were fighting for their caps and I was alone at the railings. She held one of the spikes, bowing her head towards me. The light from the lamp opposite our door caught the white curve of her neck, lit up her hair that rested there and, falling, lit up the hand upon the railing. It fell over one side of her dress and caught the white border of a petticoat, just visible as she stood at ease.

"It's well for you," she said.

10

"If I go," I said, "I will bring you something."

What innumerable follies laid waste my waking and sleeping thoughts after that evening! I wished to annihilate the tedious intervening days. I chafed against the work of school. At night in my bedroom and by day in the classroom her image came between me and the page I strove to read. The syllables of the word *Araby* were called to me through the silence in which my soul luxuriated and cast an Eastern enchantment over me. I asked for leave to go to the bazaar on Saturday night. My aunt was surprised and hoped it was not some Freemason[5] affair. I answered few questions in class. I watched my master's face pass from amiability to sternness; he hoped I was not beginning to idle. I could not call my

---

[4]*convent:* Her convent school.

[5]*Freemason:* At the time the story takes place, many Catholics in Ireland thought the Masonic Order was a threat to the church.

wandering thoughts together. I had hardly any patience with the serious work of life which, now that it stood between me and my desire, seemed to me child's play, ugly monotonous child's play.

On Saturday morning I reminded my uncle that I wished to go to the bazaar in the evening. He was fussing at the hallstand, looking for the hatbrush, and answered me curtly:

"Yes, boy, I know."

15   As he was in the hall I could not go into the front parlour and lie at the window. I left the house in bad humour and walked slowly towards the school. The air was pitilessly raw and already my heart misgave me. When I came home to dinner my uncle had not yet been home. Still it was early. I sat staring at the clock for some time and, when its ticking began to irritate me, I left the room. I mounted the staircase and gained the upper part of the house. The high cold empty gloomy rooms liberated me and I went from room to room singing. From the front window I saw my companions playing below in the street. Their cries reached me weakened and indistinct and, leaning my forehead against the cool glass, I looked over at the dark house where she lived. I may have stood there for an hour, seeing nothing but the brown-clad figure cast by my imagination, touched discreetly by the lamplight at the curved neck, at the hand upon the railings and at the border below the dress.

When I came downstairs again I found Mrs. Mercer sitting at the fire. She was an old garrulous woman, a pawnbroker's widow, who collected used stamps for some pious purpose. I had to endure the gossip of the tea-table. The meal was prolonged beyond an hour and still my uncle did not come. Mrs. Mercer stood up to go: she was sorry she couldn't wait any longer, but it was after eight o'clock and she did not like to be out late, as the night air was bad for her. When she had gone I began to walk up and down the room, clenching my fists. My aunt said:

"I'm afraid you may put off your bazaar for this night of Our Lord."

At nine o'clock I heard my uncle's latchkey in the halldoor. I heard him talking to himself and heard the hallstand rocking when it had received the weight of his overcoat. I could interpret these signs. When he was midway through his dinner I asked him to give me the money to go to the bazaar. He had forgotten.

20   "The people are in bed and after their first sleep now," he said.

I did not smile. My aunt said to him energetically:

"Can't you give him the money and let him go? You've kept him late enough as it is."

My uncle said he was very sorry he had forgotten. He said he believed in the old saying: "All work and no play makes Jack a dull boy." He asked me where I was going and, when I had told him a second time he asked me did I know *The Arab's Farewell to his Steed*.[6] When I left the kitchen he was about to recite the opening lines of the piece to my aunt.

I held a florin tightly in my hand as I strode down Buckingham Street towards the station. The sight of the streets thronged with buyers and glaring with gas recalled to me the purpose of my journey. I took my seat in a third-class carriage of a deserted train. After an intolerable delay the train moved out of the station slowly. It crept onward among ruinous houses and over the twinkling river. At Westland Row Station a crowd of people pressed to the carriage doors; but the porters moved them back, saying that it was a special train for the bazaar. I remained alone in the bare carriage. In a few minutes the train drew up beside an improvised wooden platform. I passed out on to the road and saw by the lighted dial of a clock that it was ten minutes to ten. In front of me was a large building which displayed the magical name.

I could not find any sixpenny entrance and, fearing that the bazaar 25 would be closed, I passed in quickly through a turnstile, handing a shilling to a weary-looking man. I found myself in a big hall girdled at half its height by a gallery. Nearly all the stalls were closed and the greater part of the hall was in darkness. I recognised a silence like that which pervades a church after a service. I walked into the centre of the bazaar timidly. A few people were gathered about the stalls which were still open. Before a curtain, over which the words *Café Chantant*[7] were written in coloured lamps, two men were counting money on a salver. I listened to the fall of the coins.

Remembering with difficulty why I had come I went over to one of the stalls and examined porcelain vases and flowered tea-sets. At the door of the stall a young lady was talking and laughing with two young gentlemen. I remarked their English accents and listened vaguely to their conversation.

"O, I never said such a thing!"

"O, but you did!"

"O, but I didn't!"

"Didn't she say that?"

"Yes. I heard her." 30

"O, there's a . . . fib!"

Observing me the young lady came over and asked me did I wish to buy anything. The tone of her voice was not encouraging; she seemed to have spoken to me out of a sense of duty. I looked humbly at the great jars

---

[6]The Arab's Farewell to his Steed: A sentimental poem by Caroline Norton (1808–1877) that tells the story of a nomad's heartbreak after selling his much-loved horse.

[7]Café Chantant: A Paris café featuring musical entertainment.

that stood like eastern guards at either side of the dark entrance to the stall and murmured:

"No, thank you."

35   The young lady changed the position of one of the vases and went back to the two young men. They began to talk of the same subject. Once or twice the young lady glanced at me over her shoulder.

I lingered before her stall, though I knew my stay was useless, to make my interest in her wares seem the more real. Then I turned away slowly and walked down the middle of the bazaar. I allowed the two pennies to fall against the sixpence in my pocket. I heard a voice call from one end of the gallery that the light was out. The upper part of the hall was now completely dark.

Gazing up into the darkness I saw myself as a creature driven and derided by vanity; and my eyes burned with anguish and anger.

Reading and Reacting

1. How would you characterize the story's level of diction? Is this level appropriate for a story about a young boy's experiences? Explain.

2. Identify several figures of speech in the story. Where is Joyce most likely to use this kind of language? Why?

3. What words and phrases express the boy's extreme idealism and romantic view of the world? How does such language help to communicate the story's major theme?

4. In paragraph 4, the narrator says, "her name was like a summons to all my foolish blood." In the story's last sentence, he sees himself as "a creature driven and derided by vanity." What other expressions does the narrator use to describe his feelings? How would you characterize these feelings?

5. How does the narrator's choice of words illustrate the contrast between his day-to-day life and the exotic promise of the bazaar?

6. What does each of the italicized words suggest: "We walked through the *flaring* streets" (par. 5); "I heard the rain *impinge* upon the earth" (par. 6); "I *chafed* against the work of school" (par. 12); "I found myself in a big hall *girdled* at half its height by a gallery" (par. 25)? What other examples of unexpected word choice can you identify in the story?

7. What is it about the events in this story that causes the narrator to remember them years later?

8. Identify words and phrases in the story that are associated with religion. What purpose do these references to religion serve? Do you think this pattern of words and phrases is intentional?

9. **JOURNAL ENTRY** Rewrite a brief passage from this story in the voice of the young boy. Use informal style, simple figures of speech, and vocabulary appropriate for a child.

10. Critical Perspective In *Notes on the American Short Story Today*, Richard Kostelanetz discusses the **epiphany**, one of Joyce's most significant contributions to literature:

> In Joyce's pervasively influential theory of the short story we remember, the fiction turned upon an epiphany, a moment of revelation in which, in [critic] Harry Levin's words, "amid the most encumbered circumstances it suddenly happens that the veil is lifted, the . . . mystery laid bare, and the ultimate secret of things made manifest." The epiphany, then, became a technique for jelling the narrative and locking the story's import into place. . . . What made this method revolutionary was the shifting of the focal point of the story from its end . . . to a spot within the body of the text, usually near (but not at) the end.

Where in "Araby" does the story's epiphany occur? Does it do all that Kostelanetz believes an epiphany should do? Do you think that—at least in the case of "Araby"—the epiphany may not be as significant a force as Kostelanetz suggests?

Related Works: "Snow" (p. 82), "A&P" (p. 160), "Gryphon" (p. 172), "The Girl with Bangs" (p. 187), "Doe Season" (p. 395), "The Secret Lion" (p. 466), "Shall I compare thee to a summer's day?" (p. 575), "How Do I Love Thee?" (p. 719), *Beauty* (p. 831)

Source: © AP Images

(MARY) FLANNERY O'CONNOR (1925–1964) was born to a prosperous Catholic family in Savannah, Georgia, and spent most of her adult life on a farm near the town of Milledgeville. She left the South to study writing at the University of Iowa, moving to New York to work on her first novel, *Wise Blood* (1952). On a train going south for Christmas, O'Connor became seriously ill; she was diagnosed as having lupus, the immune system disease that had killed her father and would cause O'Connor's death when she was only thirty-nine years old.

While her mother ran the farm, O'Connor spent mornings writing and afternoons wandering the fields with cane or crutches. Her short story collection *A Good Man Is Hard to Find* (1955) and an excellent French translation of *Wise Blood* established her international reputation, which was solidified with the publication of a second novel, *The Violent Bear It Away* (1960), and a posthumously published book of short stories, *Everything That Rises Must Converge* (1965).

O'Connor, said a friend, believed that an artist "should face all the truth down to the worst of it." Yet however dark, her stories are infused with grim humor and a fierce belief in the possibility of spiritual redemption, even for her most tortured characters. A line from her short story "A Good Man Is Hard to Find" says much about what O'Connor perceived about both natural things and her characters: "The trees were full of silver-white sunlight and the meanest of them sparkled." In O'Connor's work, the "meanest" things and people can sparkle, touched by a kind of holy madness and beauty.

Cultural Context   Some readers consider O'Connor a Christian writer, and indeed the Christian concepts of free will, original sin, and the need for spiritual redemption appear throughout her work. According to Christian theology, humanity was created with free will—the freedom to choose to obey or to disobey God, the freedom to follow right or wrong. Human beings fell from their original state of innocence, however, and this fall allowed sin and corruption to enter the world. Thus, a "good man"—one who is perfectly upright—is not simply "hard to find" but *impossible* to find: *all* have sinned and fall short of the glory of God, says the Bible (Romans 3.23). Because of that first disobedience (original sin), humanity stands in need of redemption—a reuniting with God—which, according to Christian theology, comes through Jesus Christ.

A Good Man Is Hard to Find (1955)

The grandmother didn't want to go to Florida. She wanted to visit some of her connections in east Tennessee and she was seizing at every chance to change Bailey's mind. Bailey was the son she lived with, her only boy. He was sitting on the edge of his chair at the table, bent over the orange sports section of the *Journal*. "Now look here, Bailey," she said, "see here, read this," and she stood with one hand on her thin hip and the other rattling the newspaper at his bald head. "Here this fellow that calls himself The Misfit is aloose from the Federal Pen and headed toward Florida and you read here what it says he did to these people. Just you read it. I wouldn't take my children in any direction with a criminal like that aloose in it. I couldn't answer to my conscience if I did."

Bailey didn't look up from his reading so she wheeled around then and faced the children's mother, a young woman in slacks, whose face was as broad and innocent as a cabbage and was tied around with a green headkerchief that had two points on the top like a rabbit's ears. She was sitting on the sofa, feeding the baby his apricots out of a ja r. "The children have been to Florida before," the old lady said. "You all ought to take them somewhere else for a change so they would see different parts of the world and be broad. They never have been to east Tennessee."

The children's mother didn't seem to hear her but the eight-year-old boy, John Wesley, a stocky child with glasses, said, "If you don't want to go to Florida, why dontcha stay at home?" He and the little girl, June Star, were reading the funny papers on the floor.

"She wouldn't stay at home to be queen for a day," June Star said without raising her yellow head.

5   "Yes and what would you do if this fellow, the Misfit, caught you?" the grandmother asked.

"I'd smack his face," John Wesley said.

"She wouldn't stay at home for a million bucks," June Star said. "Afraid she'd miss something. She has to go everywhere we go."

"All right, Miss," the grandmother said. "Just remember that the next time you want me to curl your hair."

June Star said her hair was naturally curly.

The next morning the grandmother was the first one in the car, ready 10 to go. She had her big black valise that looked like the head of a hippopotamus in one corner, and underneath it she was hiding a basket with Pitty Sing, the cat, in it. She didn't intend for the cat to be left alone in the house for three days because he would miss her too much and she was afraid he might brush against one of the gas burners and accidentally asphyxiate himself. Her son, Bailey, didn't like to arrive at a motel with a cat.

She sat in the middle of the back seat with John Wesley and June Star on either side of her. Bailey and the children's mother and the baby sat in front and they left Atlanta at eight forty-five with the mileage on the car at 55890. The grandmother wrote this down because she thought it would be interesting to say how many miles they had been when they got back. It took them twenty minutes to reach the outskirts of the city.

The old lady settled herself comfortably, removing her white cotton gloves and putting them up with her purse on the shelf in front of the back window. The children's mother still had on slacks and still had her head tied up in a green kerchief, but the grandmother had on a navy blue straw sailor hat with a bunch of white violets on the brim and a navy blue dress with a small white dot in the print. Her collars and cuffs were white organdy trimmed with lace and at her neckline she had pinned a purple spray of cloth violets containing a sachet. In case of an accident, anyone seeing her dead on the highway would know at once that she was a lady.

She said she thought it was going to be a good day for driving, neither too hot nor too cold, and she cautioned Bailey that the speed limit was fifty-five miles an hour and that the patrolmen hid themselves behind billboards and small clumps of trees and sped out after you before you had a chance to slow down. She pointed out interesting details of the scenery: Stone Mountain; the blue granite that in some places came up to both sides of the highway; the brilliant red clay banks slightly streaked with purple; and the various crops that made rows of green lace-work on the ground. The trees were full of silver-white sunlight and the meanest of them sparkled. The children were reading comic magazines and their mother had gone back to sleep.

"Let's go through Georgia fast so we won't have to look at it much," John Wesley said.

15   "If I were a little boy," said the grandmother, "I wouldn't talk about
my native state that way. Tennessee has the mountains and Georgia has
the hills."

"Tennessee is just a hillbilly dumping ground," John Wesley said, "and
Georgia is a lousy state too."

"You said it," June Star said.

"In my time," said the grandmother, folding her thin veined fingers,
"children were more respectful of their native states and their parents and
everything else. People did right then. Oh look at the cute little pickaninny!" she said and pointed to a Negro child standing in the door of a
shack. "Wouldn't that make a picture, now?" she asked and they all turned
and looked at the little Negro out of the back window. He waved.

"He didn't have any britches on," June Star said.

20   "He probably didn't have any," the grandmother explained. "Little
niggers in the country don't have things like we do. If I could paint, I'd
paint that picture," she said.

The children exchanged comic books.

The grandmother offered to hold the baby and the children's mother
passed him over the front seat to her. She set him on her knee and
bounced him and told him about the things they were passing. She rolled
her eyes and screwed up her mouth and stuck her leathery thin face into
his smooth bland one. Occasionally he gave her a faraway smile. They
passed a large cotton field with five or six graves fenced in the middle
of it, like a small island. "Look at the graveyard!" the grandmother said,
pointing it out. "That was the old family burying ground. That belonged
to the plantation."

"Where's the plantation?" John Wesley asked.

"Gone with the Wind,"[1] said the grandmother. "Ha. Ha."

25   When the children finished all the comic books they had brought,
they opened the lunch and ate it. The grandmother ate a peanut butter
sandwich and an olive and would not let the children throw the box and
the paper napkins out the window. When there was nothing else to do
they played a game by choosing a cloud and making the other two guess
what shape it suggested. John Wesley took one the shape of a cow and
June Star guessed a cow and John Wesley said, no, an automobile, and
June Star said he didn't play fair, and they began to slap each other over
the grandmother.

The grandmother said she would tell them a story if they would
keep quiet. When she told a story, she rolled her eyes and waved her head
and was very dramatic. She said once when she was a maiden lady she

---

[1] *Gone with the Wind: Gone with the Wind* is a 1936 novel by Margaret Mitchell about the Civil War.

had been courted by a Mr. Edgar Atkins Teagarden from Jasper, Georgia. She said he was a very good-looking man and a gentleman and that he brought her a watermelon every Saturday afternoon with his initials cut in it, E. A. T. Well, one Saturday, she said, Mr. Teagarden brought the watermelon and there was nobody at home and he left it on the front porch and returned in his buggy to Jasper, but she never got the watermelon, she said, because a nigger boy ate it when he saw the initials, E. A. T.! This story tickled John Wesley's funny bone and he giggled and giggled but June Star didn't think it was any good. She said she wouldn't marry a man that just brought her a watermelon on Saturday. The grandmother said she would have done well to marry Mr. Teagarden because he was a gentleman and had bought Coca-Cola stock when it first came out and that he died only a few years ago, a very wealthy man.

They stopped at The Tower for barbecued sandwiches. The Tower was a part stucco and part wood filling station and dance hall set in a clearing outside of Timothy. A fat man named Red Sammy Butts ran it and there were signs stuck here and there on the building and for miles up and down the highway saying, TRY RED SAMMY'S FAMOUS BARBECUE. NONE LIKE FAMOUS RED SAMMY'S! RED SAM! THE FAT BOY WITH THE HAPPY LAUGH. A VETERAN! RED SAMMY'S YOUR MAN!

Red Sammy was lying on the bare ground outside The Tower with his head under a truck while a gray monkey about a foot high, chained to a small chinaberry tree, chattered nearby. The monkey sprang back into the tree and got on the highest limb as soon as he saw the children jump out of the car and run toward him.

Inside, The Tower was a long dark room with a counter at one end and tables at the other and dancing space in the middle. They all sat down at a board table next to the nickelodeon and Red Sam's wife, a tall burnt-brown woman with hair and eyes lighter than her skin, came and took their order. The children's mother put a dime in the machine and played "The Tennessee Waltz," and the grandmother said that tune always made her want to dance. She asked Bailey if he would like to dance but he only glared at her. He didn't have a naturally sweet disposition like she did and trips made him nervous. The grandmother's brown eyes were very bright. She swayed her head from side to side and pretended she was dancing in her chair. June Star said play something she could tap to so the children's mother put in another dime and played a fast number and June Star stepped out onto the dance floor and did her tap routine.

"Ain't she cute?" Red Sam's wife said, leaning over the counter. 30 "Would you like to come be my little girl?"

"No I certainly wouldn't," June Star said. "I wouldn't live in a broken-down place like this for a million bucks!" and she ran back to the table.

"Ain't she cute?" the woman repeated, stretching her mouth politely.

"Aren't you ashamed?" hissed the grandmother.

Red Sam came in and told his wife to quit lounging on the counter and hurry up with these people's order. His khaki trousers reached just to his hip bones and his stomach hung over them like a sack of meal swaying under his shirt. He came over and sat down at a table nearby and let out a combination sigh and yodel. "You can't win," he said. "You can't win," and he wiped his sweating red face off with a gray handkerchief. "These days you don't know who to trust," he said. "Ain't that the truth?"

35   "People are certainly not nice like they used to be," said the grandmother.

"Two fellers come in here last week," Red Sammy said, "driving a Chrysler. It was a old beat-up car but it was a good one and these boys looked all right to me. Said they worked at the mill and you know I let them fellers charge the gas they bought? Now why did I do that?"

"Because you're a good man!" the grandmother said at once.

"Yes'm, I suppose so," Red Sam said as if he were struck with this answer.

His wife brought the orders, carrying the five plates all at once without a tray, two in each hand and one balanced on her arm. "It isn't a soul in this green world of God's that you can trust," she said. "And I don't count nobody out of that, not nobody," she repeated, looking at Red Sammy.

40   "Did you read about that criminal, The Misfit, that's escaped?" asked the grandmother.

"I wouldn't be a bit surprised if he didn't attack this place right here," said the woman. "If he hears about it being here, I wouldn't be none surprised to see him. If he hears it's two cent in the cash register, I wouldn't be at all surprised if he..."

"That'll do," Red Sam said. "Go bring these people their Co'-Colas," and the woman went off to get the rest of the order.

"A good man is hard to find," Red Sammy said. "Everything is getting terrible. I remember the day you could go off and leave your screen door unlatched. Not no more."

He and the grandmother discussed better times. The old lady said that in her opinion Europe was entirely to blame for the way things were now. She said the way Europe acted you would think we were made of money and Red Sam said it was no use talking about it, she was exactly right. The children ran outside into the white sunlight and looked at the monkey in the lacy chinaberry tree. He was busy catching fleas on himself and biting each one carefully between his teeth as if it were a delicacy.

45   They drove off again into the hot afternoon. The grandmother took cat naps and woke up every few minutes with her own snoring. Outside of Toombsboro she woke up and recalled an old plantation that she had

visited in this neighborhood once when she was a young lady. She said the house had six white columns across the front and that there was an avenue of oaks leading up to it and two little wooden trellis arbors on either side in front where you sat down with your suitor after a stroll in the garden. She recalled exactly which road to turn off to get to it. She knew that Bailey would not be willing to lose any time looking at an old house, but the more she talked about it, the more she wanted to see it once again and find out if the little twin arbors were still standing. "There was a secret panel in this house," she said craftily, not telling the truth but wishing that she were, "and the story went that all the family silver was hidden in it when Sherman came through but it was never found . . ."

"Hey!" John Wesley said. "Let's go see it! We'll find it! We'll poke all the woodwork and find it! Who lives there? Where do you turn off at? Hey Pop, can't we turn off there?"

"We never have seen a house with a secret panel!" June Star shrieked. "Let's go to the house with the secret panel! Hey Pop, can't we go see the house with the secret panel!"

"It's not far from here, I know," the grandmother said. "It wouldn't take over twenty minutes."

Bailey was looking straight ahead. His jaw was as rigid as a horseshoe. "No," he said.

The children began to yell and scream that they wanted to see the   50
house with the secret panel. John Wesley kicked the back of the front seat and June Star hung over her mother's shoulder and whined desperately into her ear that they never had any fun even on their vacation, that they could never do what THEY wanted to do. The baby began to scream and John Wesley kicked the back of the seat so hard that his father could feel the blows in his kidney.

"All right!" he shouted and drew the car to a stop at the side of the road. "Will you all shut up? Will you all just shut up for one second? If you don't shut up, we won't go anywhere."

"It would be very educational for them," the grandmother murmured.

"All right," Bailey said, "but get this: this is the only time we're going to stop for anything like this. This is the one and only time."

"The dirt road that you have to turn down is about a mile back," the grandmother directed. "I marked it when we passed."

"A dirt road," Bailey groaned.   55

After they had turned around and were headed toward the dirt road, the grandmother recalled other points about the house, the beautiful glass over the front doorway and the candle-lamp in the hall. John Wesley said that the secret panel was probably in the fireplace.

"You can't go inside this house," Bailey said. "You don't know who lives there."

"While you all talk to the people in front, I'll run around behind and get in a window," John Wesley suggested.

"We'll all stay in the car," his mother said.

60   They turned onto the dirt road and the car raced roughly along in a swirl of pink dust. The grandmother recalled the times when there were no paved roads and thirty miles was a day's journey. The dirt road was hilly and there were sudden washes in it and sharp curves on dangerous embankments. All at once they would be on a hill, looking down over the blue tops of trees for miles around, then the next minute, they would be in a red depression with the dust-coated trees looking down on them.

"This place had better turn up in a minute," Bailey said, "or I'm going to turn around."

The road looked as if no one had traveled on it in months.

"It's not much farther," the grandmother said and just as she said it, a horrible thought came to her. The thought was so embarrassing that she turned red in the face and her eyes dilated and her feet jumped up, upsetting her valise in the corner. The instant the valise moved, the newspaper top she had over the basket under it rose with a snarl and Pitty Sing, the cat, sprang onto Bailey's shoulder.

The children were thrown to the floor and their mother, clutching the baby, was thrown out the door onto the ground; the old lady was thrown into the front seat. The car turned over once and landed right-side-up in a gulch off the side of the road. Bailey remained in the driver's seat with the cat—gray-striped with a broad white face and an orange nose—clinging to his neck like a caterpillar.

65   As soon as the children saw they could move their arms and legs, they scrambled out of the car, shouting, "We've had an ACCIDENT!" The grandmother was curled up under the dashboard, hoping she was injured so that Bailey's wrath would not come down on her all at once. The horrible thought she had had before the accident was that the house she had remembered so vividly was not in Georgia but in Tennessee.

Bailey removed the cat from his neck with both hands and flung it out the window against the side of a pine tree. Then he got out of the car and started looking for the children's mother. She was sitting against the side of the red gutted ditch, holding the screaming baby, but she only had a cut down her face and a broken shoulder. "We've had an ACCIDENT!" the children screamed in a frenzy of delight.

"But nobody's killed," June Star said with disappointment as the grandmother limped out of the car, her hat still pinned to her head but the broken front brim standing up at a jaunty angle and the violet spray hanging off the side. They all sat down in the ditch, except the children, to recover from the shock. They were all shaking.

"Maybe a car will come along," said the children's mother hoarsely.

"I believe I have injured an organ," said the grandmother, pressing her side, but no one answered her. Bailey's teeth were clattering. He had on a yellow sport shirt with bright blue parrots designed in it and his face was as yellow as the shirt. The grandmother decided that she would not mention that the house was in Tennessee.

The road was about ten feet above and they could see only the tops 70 of the trees on the other side of it. Behind the ditch they were sitting in there were more woods, tall and dark and deep. In a few minutes they saw a car some distance away on top of a hill, coming slowly as if the occupants were watching them. The grandmother stood up and waved both arms dramatically to attract their attention. The car continued to come on slowly, disappeared around a bend and appeared again, moving even slower, on top of the hill they had gone over. It was a big black battered hearse-like automobile. There were three men in it.

It came to a stop just over them and for some minutes, the driver looked down with a steady expressionless gaze to where they were sitting, and didn't speak. Then he turned his head and muttered something to the other two and they got out. One was a fat boy in black trousers and a red sweat shirt with a silver stallion embossed on the front of it. He moved around on the right side of them and stood staring, his mouth partly open in a kind of loose grin. The other had on khaki pants and a blue striped coat and a gray hat pulled down very low, hiding most of his face. He came around slowly on the left side. Neither spoke.

The driver got out of the car and stood by the side of it, looking down at them. He was an older man than the other two. His hair was just beginning to gray and he wore silver-rimmed spectacles that gave him a scholarly look. He had a long creased face and didn't have on any shirt or undershirt. He had on blue jeans that were too tight for him and was holding a black hat and a gun. The two boys also had guns.

"We've had an ACCIDENT!" the children screamed.

The grandmother had the peculiar feeling that the bespectacled man was someone she knew. His face was as familiar to her as if she had known him all her life but she could not recall who he was. He moved away from the car and began to come down the embankment, placing his feet carefully so that he wouldn't slip. He had on tan and white shoes and no socks, and his ankles were red and thin. "Good afternoon," he said. "I see you all had you a little spill."

"We turned over twice!" said the grandmother. 75

"Oncet," he corrected. "We seen it happen. Try their car and see will it run, Hiram," he said quietly to the boy with the gray hat.

"What you got that gun for?" John Wesley asked. "Watcha gonna do with that gun?"

"Lady," the man said to the children's mother, "would you mind calling them children to sit down by you? Children make me nervous. I want all you all to sit down right together there where you're at."

"What are you telling US what to do for?" June Star asked.

80 Behind them the line of woods gaped like a dark open mouth. "Come here," said their mother.

"Look here now," Bailey began suddenly, "we're in a predicament! We're in . . . ."

The grandmother shrieked. She scrambled to her feet and stood staring. "You're The Misfit!" she said. "I recognized you at once!"

"Yes'm," the man said, smiling slightly as if he were pleased in spite of himself to be known, "but it would have been better for all of you, lady, if you hadn't of reckernized me."

Bailey turned his head sharply and said something to his mother that shocked even the children. The old lady began to cry and The Misfit reddened.

85 "Lady," he said, "don't you get upset. Sometimes a man says things he don't mean. I don't reckon he meant to talk to you thataway."

"You wouldn't shoot a lady, would you?" the grandmother said and removed a clean handkerchief from her cuff and began to slap at her eyes with it.

The Misfit pointed the toe of his shoe into the ground and made a little hole and then covered it up again. "I would hate to have to," he said.

"Listen," the grandmother almost screamed, "I know you're a good man. You don't look a bit like you have common blood. I know you must come from nice people!"

"Yes mam," he said, "finest people in the world." When he smiled he showed a row of strong white teeth. "God never made a finer woman than my mother and my daddy's heart was pure gold," he said. The boy with the red sweat shirt had come around behind them and was standing with his gun at his hip. The Misfit squatted down on the ground. "Watch them children, Bobby Lee," he said. "You know they make me nervous." He looked at the six of them huddled together in front of him and he seemed to be embarrassed as if he couldn't think of anything to say. "Ain't a cloud in the sky," he remarked, looking up at it. "Don't see no sun but don't see no cloud neither."

90 "Yes, it's a beautiful day," said the grandmother. "Listen," she said, "you shouldn't call yourself The Misfit because I know you're a good man at heart. I can just look at you and tell."

"Hush!" Bailey yelled. "Hush! Everybody shut up and let me handle this!" He was squatting in the position of a runner about to sprint forward but he didn't move.

"I pre-chate that, lady," The Misfit said and drew a little circle in the ground with the butt of his gun.

"It'll take a half a hour to fix this here car," Hiram called, looking over the raised hood of it.

"Well, first you and Bobby Lee get him and that little boy to step over yonder with you," The Misfit said, pointing to Bailey and John Wesley. "The boys want to ast you something," he said to Bailey. "Would you mind stepping back in them woods there with them?"

"Listen," Bailey began, "we're in a terrible predicament! Nobody real- 95 izes what this is," and his voice cracked. His eyes were as blue and intense as the parrots in his shirt and he remained perfectly still.

The grandmother reached up to adjust her hat brim as if she were going to the woods with him but it came off in her hand. She stood staring at it and after a second she let it fall on the ground. Hiram pulled Bailey up by the arm as if he were assisting an old man. John Wesley caught hold of his father's hand and Bobby Lee followed. They went off toward the woods and just as they reached the dark edge, Bailey turned and supporting himself against a gray naked pine trunk, he shouted, "I'll be back in a minute, Mamma, wait on me!"

"Come back this instant!" his mother shrilled but they all disappeared into the woods.

"Bailey Boy!" the grandmother called in a tragic voice but she found she was looking at The Misfit squatting on the ground in front of her. "I just know you're a good man," she said desperately. "You're not a bit common!"

"Nome, I ain't a good man," The Misfit said after a second as if he had considered her statement carefully, "but I ain't the worst in the world neither. My daddy said I was a different breed of dog from my brothers and sisters. 'You know,' Daddy said, 'it's some that can live their whole life out without asking about it and it's others has to know why it is, and this boy is one of the latters. He's going to be into everything!'" He put on his black hat and looked up suddenly and then away deep into the woods as if he were embarrassed again. "I'm sorry I don't have on a shirt before you ladies," he said, hunching his shoulders slightly. "We buried our clothes that we had on when we escaped and we're just making do until we can get better. We borrowed these from some folks we met," he explained.

"That's perfectly all right," the grandmother said. "Maybe Bailey has 100 an extra shirt in his suitcase."

"I'll look and see terrectly," The Misfit said.

"Where are they taking him?" the children's mother screamed.

"Daddy was a card himself," The Misfit said. "You couldn't put anything over on him. He never got in trouble with the Authorities though. Just had the knack of handling them."

"You could be honest too if you'd only try," said the grandmother. "Think how wonderful it would be to settle down and live a comfortable life and not have to think about somebody chasing you all the time."

105   The Misfit kept scratching in the ground with the butt of his gun as if he were thinking about it. "Yes'm, somebody is always after you," he murmured.

The grandmother noticed how thin his shoulder blades were just behind his hat because she was standing up looking down on him. "Do you ever pray?" she asked.

He shook his head. All she saw was the black hat wiggle between his shoulder blades. "Nome," he said.

There was a pistol shot from the woods, followed closely by another. Then silence. The old lady's head jerked around. She could hear the wind move through the tree tops like a long satisfied insuck of breath. "Bailey Boy!" she called.

"I was a gospel singer for a while," The Misfit said. "I been most everything. Been in the arm service, both land and sea, at home and abroad, been twict married, been an undertaker, been with the railroads, plowed Mother Earth, been in a tornado, seen a man burnt alive oncet," and he looked up at the children's mother and the little girl who were sitting close together, their faces white and their eyes glassy; "I even seen a woman flogged," he said.

110   "Pray, pray," the grandmother began, "pray, pray..."

"I never was a bad boy that I remember of," The Misfit said in an almost dreamy voice, "but somewheres along the line I done something wrong and got sent to the penitentiary. I was buried alive," and he looked up and held her attention to him by a steady stare.

"That's when you should have started to pray," she said. "What did you do to get sent to the penitentiary that first time?"

"Turn to the right, it was a wall," The Misfit said, looking up again at the cloudless sky. "Turn to the left, it was a wall. Look up it was a ceiling, look down it was a floor. I forget what I done, lady. I set there and set there, trying to remember what it was I done and I ain't recalled it to this day. Oncet in a while, I would think it was coming to me, but it never come."

"Maybe they put you in by mistake," the old lady said vaguely.

115   "Nome," he said. "It wasn't no mistake. They had the papers on me."

"You must have stolen something," she said.

The Misfit sneered slightly. "Nobody had nothing I wanted," he said. "It was a head-doctor at the penitentiary said what I had done was kill my daddy but I known that for a lie. My daddy died in nineteen ought nineteen of the epidemic flu and I never had a thing to do with it. He was buried in the Mount Hopewell Baptist churchyard and you can go there and see for yourself."

"If you would pray," the old lady said, "Jesus would help you."

"That's right," The Misfit said.

"Well then, why don't you pray?" she asked trembling with delight 120 suddenly.

"I don't want no hep," he said. "I'm doing all right by myself."

Bobby Lee and Hiram came ambling back from the woods. Bobby Lee was dragging a yellow shirt with bright blue parrots in it.

"Thow me that shirt, Bobby Lee," The Misfit said. The shirt came flying at him and landed on his shoulder and he put it on. The grandmother couldn't name what the shirt reminded her of. "No, lady," The Misfit said while he was buttoning it up, "I found out the crime don't matter. You can do one thing or you can do another, kill a man or take a tire off his car, because sooner or later you're going to forget what it was you done and just be punished for it."

The children's mother had begun to make heaving noises as if she couldn't get her breath. "Lady," he asked, "would you and that little girl like to step off yonder with Bobby Lee and Hiram and join your husband?"

"Yes, thank you," the mother said faintly. Her left arm dangled help- 125 lessly and she was holding the baby, who had gone to sleep, in the other. "Hep that lady up, Hiram," The Misfit said as she struggled to climb out of the ditch, "and Bobby Lee, you hold onto that little girl's hand."

"I don't want to hold hands with him," June Star said. "He reminds me of a pig."

The fat boy blushed and laughed and caught her by the arm and pulled her off into the woods after Hiram and her mother.

Alone with The Misfit, the grandmother found that she had lost her voice. There was not a cloud in the sky nor any sun. There was nothing around her but woods. She wanted to tell him that he must pray. She opened and closed her mouth several times before anything came out. Finally she found herself saying, "Jesus, Jesus," meaning, Jesus will help you, but the way she was saying it, it sounded as if she might be cursing.

"Yes'm," The Misfit said as if he agreed. "Jesus thown everything off balance. It was the same case with Him as with me except He hadn't committed any crime and they could prove I had committed one because they had the papers on me. Of course," he said, "they never shown me my papers. That's why I sign myself now. I said long ago, you get you a signature and sign everything you do and keep a copy of it. Then you'll know what you done and you can hold up the crime to the punishment and see do they match and in the end you'll have something to prove you ain't been treated right. I call myself The Misfit," he said, "because I can't make what all I done wrong fit what all I gone through in punishment."

There was a piercing scream from the woods, followed closely by a 130 pistol report. "Does it seem right to you, lady, that one is punished a heap and another ain't punished at all?"

"Jesus!" the old lady cried. "You've got good blood! I know you wouldn't shoot a lady! I know you come from nice people! Pray! Jesus, you ought not to shoot a lady. I'll give you all the money I've got!"

"Lady," The Misfit said, looking beyond her far into the woods, "there never was a body that give the undertaker a tip."

There were two more pistol reports and the grandmother raised her head like a parched old turkey hen crying for water and called, "Bailey Boy, Bailey Boy!" as if her heart would break.

"Jesus was the only One that ever raised the dead," The Misfit continued, "and He shouldn't have done it. He thown everything off balance. If He did what He said, then it's nothing for you to do but thow away everything and follow Him, and if He didn't, then it's nothing for you to do but enjoy the few minutes you got left the best way you can—by killing somebody or burning down his house or doing some other meanness to him. No pleasure but meanness," he said and his voice became almost a snarl.

135   "Maybe He didn't raise the dead," the old lady mumbled, not knowing what she was saying and feeling so dizzy that she sank down in the ditch with her legs twisted under her.

"I wasn't there so I can't say He didn't," The Misfit said. "I wisht I had of been there," he said, hitting the ground with his fist. "It ain't right I wasn't there because if I had of been there I would of known. Listen, lady," he said in a high voice, "if I had of been there I would of known and I wouldn't be like I am now." His voice seemed about to crack and the grandmother's head cleared for an instant. She saw the man's face twisted close to her own as if he were going to cry and she murmured, "Why you're one of my babies. You're one of my own children!" She reached out and touched him on the shoulder. The Misfit sprang back as if a snake had bitten him and shot her three times through the chest. Then he put his gun down on the ground and took off his glasses and began to clean them.

Hiram and Bobby Lee returned from the woods and stood over the ditch, looking down at the grandmother who half sat and half lay in a puddle of blood with her legs crossed under her like a child's and her face smiling up at the cloudless sky.

Without his glasses, The Misfit's eyes were red-rimmed and pale and defenseless-looking. "Take her off and thow her where you thown the others," he said, picking up the cat that was rubbing itself against his leg.

"She was a talker, wasn't she?" Bobby Lee said, sliding down the ditch with a yodel.

140   "She would of been a good woman," The Misfit said, "if it had been somebody there to shoot her every minute of her life."

"Some fun!" Bobby Lee said.

"Shut up, Bobby Lee," The Misfit said. "It's no real pleasure in life."

Reading and Reacting

1. How are the style and tone of the narrator's voice different from those of the characters? What, if anything, is the significance of this difference?

2. The figures of speech used in this story sometimes create unflattering, even grotesque, pictures of the characters. Find several examples of such negative figures of speech. Why do you think O'Connor uses them?

3. What does the grandmother's use of the words *pickaninny* and *nigger* reveal about her? How are readers expected to reconcile this language with her very proper appearance and her preoccupation with manners? How does her use of these words affect your reaction to her?

4. Explain the **irony** in this statement: "In case of an accident, anyone seeing her dead on the highway would know at once that she was a lady" (par. 12).

5. How does The Misfit's dialect characterize him?

6. What does the **allusion** to *Gone with the Wind* (par. 24) contribute to the story?

7. How do the style and tone of the two-paragraph description of the three men in the car (pars. 71–72) help to prepare readers for the events that follow?

8. When The Misfit tells the grandmother about his life, his language takes on a measured, rhythmic quality: "Been in the arm service, both land and sea, at home and abroad, been twict married, been an undertaker, been with the railroads, plowed Mother Earth, been in a tornado, seen a man burnt alive oncet . . ." (par. 109). Find other examples of rhythmic repetition and parallelism in this character's speech. How does this style help to develop The Misfit's character?

9. **JOURNAL ENTRY** Why do you think the grandmother tells The Misfit that she recognizes him? Why does she fail to realize the danger of her remark?

10. **CRITICAL PERSPECTIVE** In his 2002 essay "Light and Shadow: Religious Grace in Two Stories by Flannery O'Connor," David Allen Cook writes:

> The literary works of Flannery O'Connor often contend that religious belief can only be consummated by direct confrontation with evil, and for those uncommitted and unprepared, tragedy seems inevitable. For O'Connor's religious "pretenders," a moment of religious grace—a revelation of Truth— often does come, but at a devastating price. In…"A Good Man Is Hard to Find," we are presented with main characters that experience a deep epiphany after being spiritually challenged by the darker side of human nature.

In this story, who are the religious "pretenders," and who has true faith? What is the price of achieving a moment of religious grace? What role does violence play in this equation?

Related Works: "Accident" (p. 89), "Slide to Unlock" (p. 97), "The Lottery" (p. 335), "Where Are You Going, Where Have You Been?" (p. 453), "Bullet in the Brain" (p. 480), "Hitler's First Photograph" (p. 530)

Source: © AP Photo/David Pickoff

TIM O'BRIEN (1946–   ) is sometimes described as a writer whose books are on the short list of essential fiction about the Vietnam War. After graduating *summa cum laude* from Macalester College in 1968, O'Brien was immediately drafted into the United States Army and sent to Vietnam, where he served with the 198th Infantry Brigade. He was promoted to sergeant and awarded a Purple Heart after receiving a shrapnel wound in a battle near My Lai. In 1970, after his discharge from the army, he attended Harvard graduate school to study government. He worked as a reporter for the *Washington Post* before pursuing a full-time career as a writer.

O'Brien's plots focus on danger, violence, courage, endurance, despair, and other topics often associated with war fiction, but he treats these topics with an emphasis on the contemporary dilemmas faced by those who may be unwilling participants in an unpopular war. O'Brien calls *If I Die in a Combat Zone, Box Me Up and Ship Me Home* (1979) a memoir because it relates his war experiences as a naive young college graduate who suddenly finds himself facing bullets and land mines rather than sitting behind a desk. *Northern Lights* (1975) concentrates on the wilderness survival experiences of two brothers, one of whom has just returned from the Vietnam War. A fantastic daydream of an American soldier, *Going after Cacciato* (1978), won a National Book Award. *The Things They Carried* (1990) is a quasi-fictional collection of interrelated stories that deal with a single platoon. *The Vietnam in Me* (1994) emphasizes the destructive effects of war on a soldier, even after he has returned home, and *In the Lake of the Woods* (1994) tells a dramatic story of a couple missing in Minnesota. O'Brien's most recent books are *Tomcat in Love* (1998) and *July, July* (2002).

Cultural Context United States involvement in the Vietnam War lasted from the early 1960s until the mid 1970s. By the war's end, more than 47,000 Americans had been killed in action, nearly 11,000 had died of other causes, and more than 303,000 had been wounded. Estimates of South Vietnamese army casualties range from 185,000 to 225,000 killed and 500,000 to 570,000 wounded. The North Vietnamese and the Viet Cong, the guerrilla force that fought against South Vietnam and the United States, lost about 900,000 troops. In addition, more than 1 million North and South Vietnamese civilians were killed during the war. In 1975, North Vietnam's communist forces defeated the South, and in 1976, North and South Vietnam reunified to form the Socialist Republic of Vietnam. By 2000, Vietnam had established diplomatic relations with most other nations around the world.

The Things They Carried (1986)

First Lieutenant Jimmy Cross carried letters from a girl named Martha, a junior at Mount Sebastian College in New Jersey. They were not love letters, but Lieutenant Cross was hoping, so he kept them folded in plastic at the bottom of his rucksack. In the late afternoon, after a day's march, he would dig his foxhole, wash his hands under a canteen, unwrap the letters, hold them with the tips of his fingers, and spend the last hour of light pretending. He would imagine romantic camping trips into the White Mountains in New Hampshire. He would sometimes taste the envelope flaps, knowing her tongue had been there. More than anything, he wanted Martha to love him as he loved her, but the letters were mostly chatty, elusive on the matter of love. She was a virgin, he was almost sure. She was an English major at Mount Sebastian, and she wrote beautifully about her professors and roommates and midterm exams, about her respect for Chaucer and her great affection for Virginia Woolf. She often quoted lines of poetry; she never mentioned the war, except to say, Jimmy, take care of yourself. The letters weighed ten ounces. They were signed "Love, Martha," but Lieutenant Cross understood that "Love" was only a way of signing and did not mean what he sometimes pretended it meant. At dusk, he would carefully return the letters to his rucksack. Slowly, a bit distracted, he would get up and move among his men, checking the perimeter, then at full dark he would return to his hole and watch the night and wonder if Martha was a virgin.

The things they carried were largely determined by necessity. Among the necessities or near necessities were P-38 can openers, pocket knives, heat tabs, wrist watches, dog tags, mosquito repellent, chewing gum, candy, cigarettes, salt tablets, packets of Kool-Aid, lighters, matches, sewing kits, Military Payment Certificates, C rations, and two or three canteens of water. Together, these items weighed between fifteen and twenty pounds, depending upon a man's habits or rate of metabolism. Henry Dobbins, who was a big man, carried extra rations; he was especially fond of canned peaches in heavy syrup over pound cake. Dave Jensen, who practiced field hygiene, carried a toothbrush, dental floss, and several hotel-size bars of soap he'd stolen on R&R in Sydney, Australia. Ted Lavender, who was scared, carried tranquilizers until he was shot in the head outside the village of Than Khe in mid-April. By necessity, and because it was SOP,[1] they all carried steel helmets that weighed five pounds including the liner and camouflage cover. They carried the standard fatigue jackets and trousers. Very few carried underwear. On their feet they carried

---

[1] *SOP:* Standard operating procedure.

jungle boots—2.1 pounds—and Dave Jensen carried three pairs of socks and a can of Dr. Scholl's foot powder as a precaution against trench foot. Until he was shot, Ted Lavender carried six or seven ounces of premium dope, which for him was a necessity. Mitchell Sanders, the RTO,[2] carried condoms. Norman Bowker carried a diary. Rat Kiley carried comic books. Kiowa, a devout Baptist, carried an illustrated New Testament that had been presented to him by his father, who taught Sunday school in Oklahoma City, Oklahoma. As a hedge against bad times, however, Kiowa also carried his grandmother's distrust of the white man, his grandfather's old hunting hatchet. Necessity dictated. Because the land was mined and booby-trapped, it was SOP for each man to carry a steel-centered, nylon-covered flak jacket, which weighed 6.7 pounds, but which on hot days seemed much heavier. Because you could die so quickly, each man carried at least one large compress bandage, usually in the helmet band for easy access. Because the nights were cold, and because the monsoons were wet, each carried a green plastic poncho that could be used as a raincoat or ground sheet or makeshift tent. With its quilted liner, the poncho weighed almost two pounds, but it was worth every ounce. In April, for instance, when Ted Lavender was shot, they used his poncho to wrap him up, then to carry him across the paddy, then to lift him into the chopper that took him away.

They were called legs or grunts.

To carry something was to "hump" it, as when Lieutenant Jimmy Cross humped his love for Martha up the hills and through the swamps. In its intransitive form, "to hump" meant "to walk," or "to march," but it implied burdens far beyond the intransitive.

5   Almost everyone humped photographs. In his wallet, Lieutenant Cross carried two photographs of Martha. The first was a Kodachrome snapshot signed "Love," though he knew better. She stood against a brick wall. Her eyes were gray and neutral, her lips slightly open as she stared straight-on at the camera. At night, sometimes, Lieutenant Cross wondered who had taken the picture, because he knew she had boyfriends, because he loved her so much, and because he could see the shadow of the picture taker spreading out against the brick wall. The second photograph had been clipped from the 1968 Mount Sebastian yearbook. It was an action shot—women's volleyball—and Martha was bent horizontal to the floor, reaching, the palms of her hands in sharp focus, the tongue taut, the expression frank and competitive. There was no visible sweat. She wore white gym shorts. Her legs, he thought, were almost certainly the

---

[2] *RTO:* Radio telephone operator.

legs of a virgin, dry and without hair, the left knee cocked and carrying her entire weight, which was just over one hundred pounds. Lieutenant Cross remembered touching that left knee. A dark theater, he remembered, and the movie was *Bonnie and Clyde*, and Martha wore a tweed skirt, and during the final scene, when he touched her knee, she turned and looked at him in a sad, sober way that made him pull his hand back, but he would always remember the feel of the tweed skirt and the knee beneath it and the sound of the gunfire that killed Bonnie and Clyde, how embarrassing it was, how slow and oppressive. He remembered kissing her good night at the dorm door. Right then, he thought, he should've done something brave. He should've carried her up the stairs to her room and tied her to the bed and touched that left knee all night long. He should've risked it. Whenever he looked at the photographs, he thought of new things he should've done.

What they carried was partly a function of rank, partly of field specialty.

As a first lieutenant and platoon leader, Jimmy Cross carried a compass, maps, code books, binoculars, and a .45-caliber pistol that weighed 2.9 pounds fully loaded. He carried a strobe light and the responsibility for the lives of his men.

As an RTO, Mitchell Sanders carried the PRC-25 radio, a killer, twenty-six pounds with its battery.

As a medic, Rat Kiley carried a canvas satchel filled with morphine and plasma and malaria tablets and surgical tape and comic books and all the things a medic must carry, including M&M's for especially bad wounds, for a total weight of nearly twenty pounds.

As a big man, therefore a machine gunner, Henry Dobbins carried 10 the M-60, which weighed twenty-three pounds unloaded, but which was almost always loaded. In addition, Dobbins carried between ten and fifteen pounds of ammunition draped in belts across his chest and shoulders.

As PFCs or Spec 4s, most of them were common grunts and carried the standard M-16 gas-operated assault rifle. The weapon weighed 7.5 pounds unloaded, 8.2 pounds with its full twenty-round magazine. Depending on numerous factors, such as topography and psychology, the riflemen carried anywhere from twelve to twenty magazines, usually in cloth bandoliers, adding on another 8.4 pounds at minimum, fourteen pounds at maximum. When it was available, they also carried M-16 maintenance gear—rods and steel brushes and swabs and tubes of LSA oil—all of which weighed about a pound. Among the grunts, some carried the M-79 grenade launcher, 5.9 pounds unloaded, a reasonably light weapon except for the ammunition, which was heavy. A single round weighed ten ounces. The typical load was twenty-five rounds. But Ted Lavender, who was scared, carried thirty-four rounds when he was shot and killed outside Than Khe, and he went down under an exceptional burden, more than twenty pounds of ammunition, plus the flak jacket and helmet and rations and water and toilet paper and tranquilizers and all the rest, plus the unweighed fear. He was dead weight. There was no twitching or flopping. Kiowa, who saw it happen, said it was like watching a rock fall, or a big sandbag or something—just boom, then down—not like the movies where the dead guy rolls around and does fancy spins and goes ass over teakettle—not like that, Kiowa said, the poor bastard just flat-fuck fell. Boom. Down. Nothing else. It was a bright morning in mid-April. Lieutenant Cross felt the pain. He blamed himself. They stripped off Lavender's canteens and ammo, all the heavy things, and Rat Kiley said the obvious, the guy's dead, and Mitchell Sanders used his radio to report one U.S. KIA and to request a chopper. Then they wrapped Lavender in his poncho. They carried him out to a dry paddy, established security, and sat smoking the dead man's dope until the chopper came. Lieutenant Cross kept to himself. He pictured Martha's smooth young face, thinking he loved her more than anything, more than his men, and now Ted Lavender was dead because he loved her so much and could not stop thinking about her. When the dust-off arrived, they carried Lavender aboard. Afterward they burned Than Khe. They marched until dusk, then dug their holes, and that night Kiowa kept explaining how you had to be there, how fast it was, how the poor guy just dropped like so much concrete. Boom-down, he said. Like cement.

*   *   *

In addition to the three standard weapons—the M-60, M-16, and M-79—they carried whatever presented itself, or whatever seemed appropriate as a means of killing or staying alive. They carried catch-as-catch-can. At various times, in various situations, they carried M-14s and CAR-15s and Swedish Ks and grease guns and captured AK-47s and Chi-Coms and RPGs and Simonov carbines and black-market Uzis and .38-caliber Smith & Wesson handguns and 66 mm LAWs and shotguns and silencers and blackjacks and bayonets and C-4 plastic explosives. Lee Strunk carried a slingshot; a weapon of last resort, he called it. Mitchell Sanders carried brass knuckles. Kiowa carried his grandfather's feathered hatchet. Every third or fourth man carried a Claymore antipersonnel mine—3.5 pounds with its firing device. They all carried fragmentation grenades—fourteen ounces each. They all carried at least one M-18 colored smoke grenade—twenty-four ounces. Some carried CS or tear-gas grenades. Some carried white-phosphorus grenades. They carried all they could bear, and then some, including a silent awe for the terrible power of the things they carried.

In the first week of April, before Lavender died, Lieutenant Jimmy Cross received a good-luck charm from Martha. It was a simple pebble, an ounce at most. Smooth to the touch, it was a milky-white color with flecks of orange and violet, oval-shaped, like a miniature egg. In the accompanying letter, Martha wrote that she had found the pebble on the Jersey shoreline, precisely where the land touched water at high tide, where things came together but also separated. It was this separate-but-together quality, she wrote, that had inspired her to pick up the pebble and to carry it in her breast pocket for several days, where it seemed weightless, and then to send it through the mail, by air, as a token of her truest feelings for him. Lieutenant Cross found this romantic. But he wondered what her truest feelings were, exactly, and what she meant by separate-but-together. He wondered how the tides and waves had come into play on that afternoon along the Jersey shoreline when Martha saw the pebble and bent down to rescue it from geology. He imagined bare feet. Martha was a poet, with the poet's sensibilities, and her feet would be brown and bare, the toenails unpainted, the eyes chilly and somber like the ocean in March, and though it was painful, he wondered who had been with her that afternoon. He imagined a pair of shadows moving along the strip of sand where things came together but also separated. It was phantom jealousy, he knew, but he couldn't help himself. He loved her so much. On the march, through the hot days of early April, he carried the pebble in his mouth, turning it with his tongue, tasting sea salts and moisture. His mind wandered. He had difficulty keeping his attention on the war. On occasion he would yell at his men to spread out the column, to keep their eyes open, but then he would slip away into daydreams, just pretending, walking barefoot along the Jersey shore, with Martha, carrying nothing. He would feel himself rising. Sun and waves and gentle winds, all love and lightness.

What they carried varied by mission.

When a mission took them to the mountains, they carried mosquito 15 netting, machetes, canvas tarps, and extra bug juice.

If a mission seemed especially hazardous, or if it involved a place they knew to be bad, they carried everything they could. In certain heavily mined AOs,[3] where the land was dense with Toe Poppers and Bouncing Betties, they took turns humping a twenty-eight-pound mine detector. With its headphones and big sensing plate, the equipment was a stress on the lower back and shoulders, awkward to handle, often useless because of the shrapnel in the earth, but they carried it anyway, partly for safety, partly for the illusion of safety.

[3]*AOs:* Areas of operation.

On ambush, or other night missions, they carried peculiar little odds and ends. Kiowa always took along his New Testament and a pair of moccasins for silence. Dave Jensen carried night-sight vitamins high in carotin. Lee Strunk carried his slingshot; ammo, he claimed, would never be a problem. Rat Kiley carried brandy and M&M's. Until he was shot, Ted Lavender carried the starlight scope, which weighed 6.3 pounds with its aluminum carrying case. Henry Dobbins carried his girlfriend's panty-hose wrapped around his neck as a comforter. They all carried ghosts. When dark came, they would move out single file across the meadows and paddies to their ambush coordinates, where they would quietly set up the Claymores and lie down and spend the night waiting.

Other missions were more complicated and required special equipment. In mid-April, it was their mission to search out and destroy the elaborate tunnel complexes in the Than Khe area south of Chu Lai. To blow the tunnels, they carried one-pound blocks of pentrite high explosives, four blocks to a man, sixty-eight pounds in all. They carried wiring, detonators, and battery-powered clackers. Dave Jensen carried earplugs. Most often, before blowing the tunnels, they were ordered by higher command to search them, which was considered bad news, but by and large they just shrugged and carried out orders. Because he was a big man, Henry Dobbins was excused from tunnel duty. The others would draw numbers. Before Lavender died there were seventeen men in the platoon, and whoever drew the number seventeen would strip off his gear and crawl in head first with a flashlight and Lieutenant Cross's .45-caliber pistol. The rest of them would fan out as security. They would sit down or kneel, not facing the hole, listening to the ground beneath them, imagining cobwebs and ghosts, whatever was down there—the tunnel walls squeezing in—how the flashlight seemed impossibly heavy in the hand and how it was tunnel vision in the very strictest sense, compression in all ways, even time, and how you had to wiggle in—ass and elbows—a swallowed-up feeling—and how you found yourself worrying about odd things—will your flashlight go dead? Do rats carry rabies? If you screamed, how far would the sound carry? Would your buddies hear it? Would they have the courage to drag you out? In some respects, though not many, the waiting was worse than the tunnel itself. Imagination was a killer.

On April 16, when Lee Strunk drew the number seventeen, he laughed and muttered something and went down quickly. The morning was hot and very still. Not good, Kiowa said. He looked at the tunnel opening, then out across a dry paddy toward the village of Than Khe. Nothing moved. No clouds or birds or people. As they waited, the men smoked and drank Kool-Aid, not talking much, feeling sympathy for Lee Strunk but also feeling the luck of the draw. You win some, you lose some, said Mitchell Sanders, and sometimes you settle for a rain check. It was a tired line and no one laughed.

Henry Dobbins ate a tropical chocolate bar. Ted Lavender popped a 20 tranquilizer and went off to pee.

After five minutes, Lieutenant Jimmy Cross moved to the tunnel, leaned down, and examined the darkness. Trouble, he thought—a cave-in maybe. And then suddenly, without willing it, he was thinking about Martha. The stresses and fractures, the quick collapse, the two of them buried alive under all that weight. Dense, crushing love. Kneeling, watching the hole, he tried to concentrate on Lee Strunk and the war, all the dangers, but his love was too much for him, he felt paralyzed, he wanted to sleep inside her lungs and breathe her blood and be smothered. He wanted her to be a virgin and not a virgin, all at once. He wanted to know her. Intimate secrets—why poetry? Why so sad? Why that grayness in her eyes? Why so alone? Not lonely, just alone—riding her bike across campus or sitting off by herself in the cafeteria. Even dancing, she danced alone—and it was the aloneness that filled him with love. He remembered telling her that one evening. How she nodded and looked away. And how, later, when he kissed her, she received the kiss without returning it, her eyes wide open, not afraid, not a virgin's eyes, just flat and uninvolved.

Lieutenant Cross gazed at the tunnel. But he was not there. He was buried with Martha under the white sand at the Jersey shore. They were pressed together, and the pebble in his mouth was her tongue. He was smiling. Vaguely, he was aware of how quiet the day was, the sullen paddies, yet he could not bring himself to worry about matters of security. He was beyond that. He was just a kid at war, in love. He was twenty-two years old. He couldn't help it.

A few moments later Lee Strunk crawled out of the tunnel. He came up grinning, filthy but alive. Lieutenant Cross nodded and closed his eyes while the others clapped Strunk on the back and made jokes about rising from the dead.

Worms, Rat Kiley said. Right out of the grave. Fuckin' zombie.

The men laughed. They all felt great relief. 25

Spook City, said Mitchell Sanders.

Lee Strunk made a funny ghost sound, a kind of moaning, yet very happy, and right then, when Strunk made that high happy moaning sound, when he went *Ahhooooo*, right then Ted Lavender was shot in the head on his way back from peeing. He lay with his mouth open. The teeth were broken. There was a swollen black bruise under his left eye. The cheekbone was gone. Oh shit, Rat Kiley said, the guy's dead. The guy's dead, he kept saying, which seemed profound—the guy's dead. I mean really.

The things they carried were determined to some extent by superstition. Lieutenant Cross carried his good-luck pebble. Dave Jensen carried a rabbit's foot. Norman Bowker, otherwise a very gentle person, carried a thumb that had been presented to him as a gift by Mitchell Sanders. The thumb was dark brown, rubbery to the touch, and weighed four ounces at most. It had been cut from a VC corpse, a boy of fifteen or sixteen. They'd found him at the bottom of an irrigation ditch, badly burned, flies in his mouth and eyes. The boy wore black shorts and sandals. At the time of his death he had been carrying a pouch of rice, a rifle, and three magazines of ammunition.

You want my opinion, Mitchell Sanders said, there's a definite moral here.

30   He put his hand on the dead boy's wrist. He was quiet for a time, as if counting a pulse, then he patted the stomach, almost affectionately, and used Kiowa's hunting hatchet to remove the thumb.

Henry Dobbins asked what the moral was.

Moral?

You know. *Moral.*

Sanders wrapped the thumb in toilet paper and handed it across to Norman Bowker. There was no blood. Smiling, he kicked the boy's head, watched the flies scatter, and said, It's like with that old TV show—Paladin. Have gun, will travel.

35   Henry Dobbins thought about it.

Yeah, well, he finally said. I don't see no moral.

There it *is*, man.

Fuck off.

They carried USO stationery and pencils and pens. They carried Sterno, safety pins, trip flares, signal flares, spools of wire, razor blades, chewing tobacco, liberated joss sticks and statuettes of the smiling Buddha, candles, grease pencils, *The Stars and Stripes*, fingernail clippers, Psy Ops leaflets, bush hats, bolos, and much more. Twice a week, when the resupply choppers came in, they carried hot chow in green Mermite cans and large canvas bags filled with iced beer and soda pop. They carried plastic water containers, each with a two-gallon capacity. Mitchell Sanders carried a set of starched tiger fatigues for special occasions. Henry Dobbins carried Black Flag insecticide. Dave Jensen carried empty sandbags that could be filled at night for added protection. Lee Strunk carried tanning lotion. Some things they carried in common. Taking turns, they carried the big PRC-77 scrambler radio, which weighed thirty pounds with its battery. They shared the weight of memory. They took up what others could no longer bear. Often, they carried each other, the wounded or weak. They carried infections. They carried chess sets, basketballs, Vietnamese-English dictionaries, insignia of rank, Bronze Stars and Purple Hearts, plastic cards imprinted with the Code of Conduct. They carried diseases, among them malaria and dysentery. They carried lice and ring-worm and leeches and paddy algae and various rots and molds. They car-ried the land itself—Vietnam, the place, the soil—a powdery orange-red dust that covered their boots and fatigues and faces. They carried the sky. The whole atmosphere, they carried it, the humidity, the monsoons, the stink of fungus and decay, all of it, they carried gravity. They moved like mules. By daylight they took sniper fire, at night they were mortared, but it was not battle, it was just the endless march, village to village, without purpose, nothing won or lost. They marched for the sake of the march. They plodded along slowly, dumbly, leaning forward against the heat, unthinking, all blood and bone, simple grunts, soldiering with their legs, toiling up the hills and down into the paddies and across the rivers and up again and down, just humping, one step and then the next and then another, but no volition, no will, because it was automatic, it was anat-omy, and the war was entirely a matter of posture and carriage, the hump was everything, a kind of inertia, a kind of emptiness, a dullness of desire and intellect and conscience and hope and human sensibility. Their prin-ciples were in their feet. Their calculations were biological. They had no sense of strategy or mission. They searched the villages without knowing what to look for, not caring, kicking over jars of rice, frisking children and old men, blowing tunnels, sometimes setting fires and sometimes not, then forming up and moving on to the next village, then other villages, where it would always be the same. They carried their own lives. The pres-sures were enormous. In the heat of early afternoon, they would remove their helmets and flak jackets, walking bare, which was dangerous but which helped ease the strain. They would often discard things along the route of march. Purely for comfort, they would throw away rations, blow their Claymores and grenades, no matter, because by nightfall the resup-ply choppers would arrive with more of the same, then a day or two later still more, fresh watermelons and crates of ammunition and sunglasses and woolen sweaters—the resources were stunning—sparklers for the Fourth of July, colored eggs for Easter. It was the great American war chest—the fruits of science, the smokestacks, the canneries, the arsenals at Hartford, the Minnesota forests, the machine shops, the vast fields of corn and wheat—they carried like freight trains; they carried it on their backs and shoulders—and for all the ambiguities of Vietnam, all the mysteries and unknowns, there was at least the single abiding certainty that they would never be at a loss for things to carry.

*   *   *

After the chopper took Lavender away, Lieutenant Jimmy Cross led his 40 men into the village of Than Khe. They burned everything. They shot chickens and dogs, they trashed the village well, they called in artillery and watched the wreckage, then they marched for several hours through the hot afternoon, and then at dusk, while Kiowa explained how Lavender died, Lieutenant Cross found himself trembling.

He tried not to cry. With his entrenching tool, which weighed five pounds, he began digging a hole in the earth.

He felt shame. He hated himself. He had loved Martha more than his men, and as a consequence Lavender was now dead, and this was something he would have to carry like a stone in his stomach for the rest of the war.

All he could do was dig. He used his entrenching tool like an ax, slashing, feeling both love and hate, and then later, when it was full dark, he sat at the bottom of his foxhole and wept. It went on for a long while. In part, he was grieving for Ted Lavender, but mostly it was for Martha, and for himself, because she belonged to another world, which was not quite real, and because she was a junior at Mount Sebastian College in New Jersey, a poet and a virgin and uninvolved, and because he realized she did not love him and never would.

Like cement, Kiowa whispered in the dark. I swear to God—boom-down. Not a word.

45   I've heard this, said Norman Bowker.

A pisser, you know? Still zipping himself up. Zapped while zipping.

All right, fine. That's enough.

Yeah, but you had to see it, the guy just—

I *heard*, man. Cement. So why not shut the fuck *up*?

50   Kiowa shook his head sadly and glanced over at the hole where Lieutenant Jimmy Cross sat watching the night. The air was thick and wet. A warm, dense fog had settled over the paddies and there was the stillness that precedes rain.

After a time Kiowa sighed.

One thing for sure, he said. The Lieutenant's in some deep hurt. I mean that crying jag—the way he was carrying on—it wasn't fake or anything, it was real heavy-duty hurt. The man cares.

Sure, Norman Bowker said.

Say what you want, the man does care.

55   We all got problems.

Not Lavender.

No, I guess not, Bowker said. Do me a favor, though.

Shut up?

That's a smart Indian. Shut up.

60   Shrugging, Kiowa pulled off his boots. He wanted to say more, just to lighten up his sleep, but instead he opened his New Testament and

arranged it beneath his head as a pillow. The fog made things seem hollow and unattached. He tried not to think about Ted Lavender, but then he was thinking how fast it was, no drama, down and dead, and how it was hard to feel anything except surprise. It seemed un-Christian. He wished he could find some great sadness, or even anger, but the emotion wasn't there and he couldn't make it happen. Mostly he felt pleased to be alive. He liked the smell of the New Testament under his cheek, the leather and ink and paper and glue, whatever the chemicals were. He liked hearing the sounds of night. Even his fatigue, it felt fine, the stiff muscles and the prickly awareness of his own body, a floating feeling. He enjoyed not being dead. Lying there, Kiowa admired Lieutenant Jimmy Cross's capacity for grief. He wanted to share the man's pain, he wanted to care as Jimmy Cross cared. And yet when he closed his eyes, all he could think was Boom-down, and all he could feel was the pleasure of having his boots off and the fog curling in around him and the damp soil and the Bible smells and the plush comfort of night.

After a moment Norman Bowker sat up in the dark.

What the hell, he said. You want to talk, *talk*. Tell it to me.

Forget it.

No, man, go on. One thing I hate, it's a silent Indian.

For the most part they carried themselves with poise, a kind of dignity. 65 Now and then, however, there were times of panic, when they squealed or wanted to squeal but couldn't, when they twitched and made moaning sounds and covered their heads and said Dear Jesus and flopped around on the earth and fired their weapons blindly and cringed and sobbed and begged for the noise to stop and went wild and made stupid promises to themselves and to God and to their mothers and fathers, hoping not to die. In different ways, it happened to all of them. Afterward, when the firing ended, they would blink and peek up. They would touch their bodies, feeling shame, then quickly hiding it. They would force themselves to stand. As if in slow motion, frame by frame, the world would take on the old logic—absolute silence, then the wind, then sunlight, then voices. It was the burden of being alive. Awkwardly, the men would reassemble themselves, first in private, then in groups, becoming soldiers again. They would repair the leaks in their eyes. They would check for casualties, call in dust-offs, light cigarettes, try to smile, clear their throats and spit and begin cleaning their weapons. After a time someone would shake his head and say, No lie, I almost shit my pants, and someone else would laugh, which meant it was bad, yes, but the guy had obviously not shit his pants, it wasn't that bad, and in any case nobody would ever do such a thing and then go ahead and talk about it. They would squint into the dense, oppressive sunlight. For a few moments, perhaps, they would fall silent, lighting a joint and tracking its passage from man to man, inhaling, holding in the humiliation. Scary stuff, one of them might say. But then someone else would grin or flick his eyebrows and say, Roger-dodger, almost cut me a new asshole, *almost*.

There were numerous such poses. Some carried themselves with a sort of wistful resignation, others with pride or stiff soldierly discipline or good humor or macho zeal. They were afraid of dying but they were even more afraid to show it.

They found jokes to tell.

They used a hard vocabulary to contain the terrible softness. *Greased*, they'd say. *Offed, lit up,*[4] *zapped while zipping.*[5] It wasn't cruelty, just stage presence. They were actors and the war came at them in 3-D. When someone died, it wasn't quite dying, because in a curious way it seemed scripted, and because they had their lines mostly memorized, irony mixed with tragedy, and because they called it by other names, as if to encyst and destroy the reality of death itself. They kicked corpses. They cut off thumbs. They talked grunt lingo. They told stories about Ted Lavender's supply of tranquilizers, how the poor guy didn't feel a thing, how incredibly tranquil he was.

There's a moral here, said Mitchell Sanders.

70 They were waiting for Lavender's chopper, smoking the dead man's dope.

The moral's pretty obvious, Sanders said, and winked. Stay away from drugs. No joke, they'll ruin your day every time.

Cute, said Henry Dobbins.

Mind-blower, get it? Talk about wiggy—nothing left, just blood and brains.

They made themselves laugh.

75 There it is, they'd say, over and over, as if the repetition itself were an act of poise, a balance between crazy and almost crazy, knowing without going. There it is, which meant be cool, let it ride, because oh yeah, man, you can't change what can't be changed, there it is, there it absolutely and positively and fucking well *is*.

They were tough.

They carried all the emotional baggage of men who might die. Grief, terror, love, longing—these were intangibles, but the intangibles had their own mass and specific gravity, they had tangible weight. They carried shameful memories. They carried the common secret of cowardice barely restrained, the instinct to run or freeze or hide, and in many respects this

---

[4]Offed, lit up: Killed.
[5]zapped while zipping: Killed while urinating.

was the heaviest burden of all, for it could never be put down, it required perfect balance and perfect posture. They carried their reputations. They carried the soldier's greatest fear, which was the fear of blushing. Men killed, and died, because they were embarrassed not to. It was what had brought them to the war in the first place, nothing positive, no dreams of glory or honor, just to avoid the blush of dishonor. They died so as not to die of embarrassment. They crawled into tunnels and walked point and advanced under fire. Each morning, despite the unknowns, they made their legs move. They endured. They kept humping. They did not submit to the obvious alternative, which was simply to close the eyes and fall. So easy, really. Go limp and tumble to the ground and let the muscles unwind and not speak and not budge until your buddies picked you up and lifted you into the chopper that would roar and dip its nose and carry you off to the world. A mere matter of falling, yet no one ever fell. It was not courage, exactly; the object was not valor. Rather, they were too frightened to be cowards.

By and large they carried these things inside, maintaining the masks of composure. They sneered at sick call. They spoke bitterly about guys who had found release by shooting off their own toes or fingers. Pussies, they'd say. Candyasses. It was fierce, mocking talk, with only a trace of envy or awe, but even so, the image played itself out behind their eyes.

They imagined the muzzle against flesh. They imagined the quick, sweet pain, then the evacuation to Japan, then a hospital with warm beds and cute geisha nurses.

They dreamed of freedom birds.   80

At night, on guard, staring into the dark, they were carried away by jumbo jets. They felt the rush of takeoff. *Gone!* they yelled. And then velocity, wings and engines, a smiling stewardess—but it was more than a plane, it was a real bird, a big sleek silver bird with feathers and talons and high screeching. They were flying. The weights fell off, there was nothing to bear. They laughed and held on tight, feeling the cold slap of wind and altitude, soaring, thinking *It's over, I'm gone!*—they were naked, they were light and free—it was all lightness, bright and fast and buoyant, light as light, a helium buzz in the brain, a giddy bubbling in the lungs as they were taken up over the clouds and the war, beyond duty, beyond gravity and mortification and global entanglements—*Sin loi!* they yelled, *I'm sorry, motherfuckers, but I'm out of it, I'm goofed, I'm on a space cruise, I'm gone!*—and it was a restful, disencumbered sensation, just riding the light waves, sailing that big silver freedom bird over the mountains and oceans, over America, over the farms and great sleeping cities and cemeteries and highways and the golden arches of McDonald's. It was flight, a kind of fleeing, a kind of falling, falling higher and higher, spinning off the edge of the earth and beyond the sun and through the vast, silent vacuum where there were no burdens and where everything weighed exactly nothing. *Gone!* they screamed, *I'm sorry but I'm gone!* And so at night, not quite dreaming, they gave themselves over to lightness, they were carried, they were purely borne.

On the morning after Ted Lavender died, First Lieutenant Jimmy Cross crouched at the bottom of his foxhole and burned Martha's letters. Then he burned the two photographs. There was a steady rain falling, which made it difficult, but he used heat tabs and Sterno to build a small fire, screening it with his body, holding the photographs over the tight blue flame with the tips of his fingers.

He realized it was only a gesture. Stupid, he thought. Sentimental, too, but mostly just stupid.

Lavender was dead. You couldn't burn the blame.

85   Besides, the letters were in his head. And even now, without photographs, Lieutenant Cross could see Martha playing volleyball in her white gym shorts and yellow T-shirt. He could see her moving in the rain.

When the fire died out, Lieutenant Cross pulled his poncho over his shoulders and ate breakfast from a can.

There was no great mystery, he decided.

In those burned letters Martha had never mentioned the war, except to say, Jimmy, take care of yourself. She wasn't involved. She signed the letters "Love," but it wasn't love, and all the fine lines and technicalities did not matter.

The morning came up wet and blurry. Everything seemed part of everything else, the fog and Martha and the deepening rain.

90   It was a war, after all.

Half smiling, Lieutenant Jimmy Cross took out his maps. He shook his head hard, as if to clear it, then bent forward and began planning the day's march. In ten minutes, or maybe twenty, he would rouse the men and they would pack up and head west, where the maps showed the country to be green and inviting. They would do what they had always done. The rain might add some weight, but otherwise it would be one more day layered upon all the other days.

He was realistic about it. There was that new hardness in his stomach. No more fantasies, he told himself.

Henceforth, when he thought about Martha, it would be only to think that she belonged elsewhere. He would shut down the daydreams. This was not Mount Sebastian, it was another world, where there were no pretty poems or midterm exams, a place where men died because of carelessness and gross stupidity. Kiowa was right. Boom-down, and you were dead, never partly dead.

95   Briefly, in the rain, Lieutenant Cross saw Martha's gray eyes gazing back at him.

He understood.

It was very sad, he thought. The things men carried inside. The things men did or felt they had to do.

He almost nodded at her, but didn't.

Instead he went back to his maps. He was now determined to perform his duties firmly and without negligence. It wouldn't help Lavender, he knew that, but from this point on he would comport himself as a soldier. He would dispose of his good-luck pebble. Swallow it, maybe, or use Lee Strunk's slingshot, or just drop it along the trail. On the march he would impose strict field discipline. He would be careful to send out flank security, to prevent straggling or bunching up, to keep his troops moving at the proper pace and at the proper interval. He would insist on clean weapons. He would confiscate the remainder of Lavender's dope. Later in the day, perhaps, he would call the men together and speak to them plainly. He would accept the blame for what had happened to Ted Lavender. He would be a man about it. He would look them in the eyes, keeping his chin level, and he would issue the new SOPs in a calm, impersonal tone of voice, an officer's voice, leaving no room for argument or discussion. Commencing immediately, he'd tell them, they would no longer abandon equipment along the route of march. They would police up their acts. They would get their shit together, and keep it together, and maintain it neatly and in good working order.

He would not tolerate laxity. He would show strength, distancing 100 himself.

Among the men there would be grumbling, of course, and maybe worse, because their days would seem longer and their loads heavier, but Lieutenant Cross reminded himself that his obligation was not to be loved but to lead. He would dispense with love; it was not now a factor. And if anyone quarreled or complained, he would simply tighten his lips and arrange his shoulders in the correct command posture. He might give a curt little nod. Or he might not. He might just shrug and say Carry on, then they would saddle up and form into a column and move out toward the villages west of Than Khe.

Reading and Reacting

1. Although the setting and the events described in "The Things They Carried" are dramatic and moving, the story's tone is often flat and emotionless. Give some examples. Why do you think the narrator adopts this kind of tone?

2. Consider the different meanings of the word *carry*, which can refer to burdens abstract or concrete as well as to things carried physically or emotionally, actively or passively. Give one or two examples of each

of the different senses in which O'Brien uses the word. How does his repeated use of the word enrich the story?

3. A striking characteristic of the story's style is its thorough catalogs of the concrete, tangible "things" the soldiers carry. Why do you suppose such detailed lists are included? What does what each man carries tell you about him? In a less literal, more abstract sense, what else do these men "carry"?

4. One stylistic technique O'Brien uses is intentional repetition—of phrases ("they carried"); people's names and identifying details (Martha's virginity, for example); and pieces of equipment. What effect do you think O'Brien hopes to achieve through such repetition? Is he successful?

5. Interspersed among long paragraphs crammed with detail are short one- or two-sentence paragraphs. What function do these brief paragraphs serve?

6. What role does Martha play in the story? Why does Lieutenant Cross burn her letters?

7. In paragraph 68, the narrator says of the soldiers, "They used a hard vocabulary to contain the terrible softness." What do you think he means by this? Do you think this "hard vocabulary" is necessary? How does it affect your feelings about the characters?

8. Describing Lieutenant Cross's new sense of purpose in the story's final paragraph, the narrator uses the phrase "Carry on." Do you think the use of this phrase is linked in any way to the story's other uses of the word *carry*, or do you believe it is unrelated? Explain.

9. **JOURNAL ENTRY** "The Things They Carried" is a story about war. Do you think it is an antiwar story? Why or why not?

10. **CRITICAL PERSPECTIVE** In an essay about war memoirs, Clayton W. Lewis questions O'Brien's decision to present "the nightmare [he] faced in a Vietnam rice paddy" as fiction. Lewis believes that some of O'Brien's stories "dissolve into clever artifice" and, therefore, are not as effective as actual memoirs of the Vietnam experience would be. He concludes that "for all its brilliance and emotional grounding, [the stories do not] satisfy one's appetite to hear what happened rendered as it was experienced and remembered."

Do you think Lewis has a point? Or do you think O'Brien's "artifice" communicates his emotions and experiences more effectively than a straightforward memoir could? Explain your position.

Related Works: from *The Harlem Hellfighters* (p. 104), "Dulce et Decorum Est" (p. 723), "The Soldier" (p. 725), "Facing It" (p. 728), "Terza Rima" (p. 729)

WRITING SUGGESTIONS: Style, Tone, and Language

1. In "The Things They Carried," Tim O'Brien considers his characters' emotional and psychological burdens as well as the physical "things they carry." Applying O'Brien's criteria to "The Yellow Wallpaper" (p. 434), write an essay in which you consider what the narrator "carries" (and what her husband "carries") and why.

2. In all three of this chapter's stories, characters are trapped. Whether trapped by social roles, by circumstance, or by their own limitations, they are unable to escape their destinies. Explain what factors imprison each character; then, consider whether—and how—each might escape.

3. Imagine The Misfit in a prison cell, relating the violent incident at the end of "A Good Man Is Hard to Find" to another prisoner—or to a member of the clergy. Would his tone be boastful? regretful? apologetic? defiant? Would he use the elaborate poetic style he sometimes uses in the story or more straightforward language? Tell his version of the incident in his own words.

4. Both "Araby" and "The Things They Carried" deal, at least in part, with infatuation. Compare and contrast the infatuations described in the two stories. How does the language used by the narrators in the two stories communicate the two characters' fascination and subsequent disillusionment?

CHAPTER 12

SYMBOL, ALLEGORY, AND MYTH

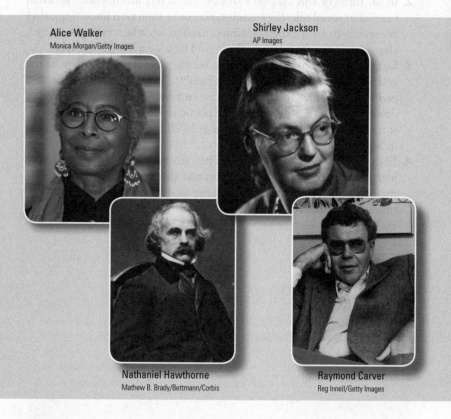

Alice Walker
Monica Morgan/Getty Images

Shirley Jackson
AP Images

Nathaniel Hawthorne
Mathew B. Brady/Bettmann/Corbis

Raymond Carver
Reg Innell/Getty Images

 ## Symbol

A **symbol** is a person, object, action, place, or event that, in addition to its literal meaning, suggests a more complex meaning or range of meanings. **Universal** or **archetypal symbols**, such as the Old Man, the Mother, or the Grim Reaper, are so much a part of human experience that they suggest the same thing to most people. **Conventional symbols** are also likely to suggest the same thing to most people (a rose suggests love, a skull and crossbones

328

denotes poison), provided the people share cultural and social assumptions. For this reason, conventional symbols are often used as a kind of shorthand in films and advertising, where they elicit predictable responses.

A conventional symbol, such as the stars and stripes of the American flag, can evoke powerful feelings of pride and patriotism in a group of people who share certain cultural assumptions, just as the maple leaf and the Union Jack can. Symbols used in works of literature can function in much the same way, enabling writers to convey particular emotions or messages with a high degree of predictability. Thus, spring can be expected to suggest rebirth and promise; autumn, declining years and powers; summer, youth and beauty. Because a writer expects a dark forest to evoke fear, or a rainbow to communicate hope, he or she can be quite confident in using such images to convey a particular idea or mood (provided the audience shares the writer's frame of reference).

Many symbols, however, suggest different things to different people, and different cultures may react differently to the same symbols. (In the United States, for example, an owl suggests wisdom; in India it suggests the opposite.) Thus, symbols enhance meaning, expanding the possibilities for interpretation and for readers' interaction with the text. Because they are so potentially rich, symbols have the power to open up a work of literature.

Literary Symbols

Both universal and conventional symbols can function as **literary symbols**— symbols that take on additional meanings in particular works. For instance, a watch or clock denotes time; as a conventional symbol, it suggests the passing of time; as a literary symbol in a particular work, it might also convey anything from a character's inability to recapture the past to the idea of time running out—or it might suggest something else.

Considering an object's symbolic significance can suggest a variety of ways to interpret a text. For instance, William Faulkner focuses attention on an unseen watch in a pivotal scene in "A Rose for Emily" (p. 143). The narrator first describes Emily Grierson as "a small, fat woman in black, with a thin gold chain descending to her waist and vanishing into her belt." Several sentences later, the narrator notes that Emily's visitors "could hear the invisible watch ticking at the end of the gold chain." Like these visitors, readers are drawn to the unseen watch as it ticks away. Because Emily is portrayed as a woman living in the past, readers can assume that the watch is intended to reinforce the impression that she cannot see that time (the watch) has moved on. The vivid picture of the pale, plump woman in the musty room with the watch invisibly ticking does indeed suggest that she is frozen in time and remains unaware of the progress around her. Thus, the symbol of the watch enriches both the depiction of character and the story's theme.

In "Barn Burning" (p. 256), another Faulkner story, the clock is a more complex symbol. The itinerant Snopes family is without financial security and apparently without a future. The clock the mother carries from shack to shack—"The clock inlaid with mother-of-pearl, which would not run, stopped at some fourteen minutes past two o'clock of a dead and forgotten day and time, which had been [Sarty's] mother's dowry"—is their only possession of value. The fact that the clock no longer works seems at first to suggest that time has run out for the family. On another level, the clock stands in stark contrast to Major de Spain's grand home, with its gold and glitter and Oriental rugs. Knowing that the clock was part of the mother's dowry, and that a dowry suggests a promise, readers may decide that the broken clock symbolizes lost hope. The fact that the mother still clings to the clock, however, could suggest just the opposite: her refusal to give up.

As you read, you should not try to find one exact equivalent for each symbol; that kind of search is reductive and unrewarding. Instead, consider the different meanings a symbol might suggest. Then consider how these various interpretations enrich other elements of the story and the work as a whole.

Recognizing Symbols

When is a clock just a clock, and when is it also a symbol with a meaning (or meanings) beyond its literal significance? If a character waiting for a friend glances once at a watch to check the time, there is probably nothing symbolic about the watch or about the act of looking at it. If, however, the watch keeps appearing again and again in the story, at key moments; if the narrator devotes a good deal of time to describing it; if it is placed in a conspicuous physical location; if characters keep noticing it and commenting on its presence; if it is lost (or found) at a critical moment; if its function in some way parallels the development of plot or character (for instance, if it stops as a relationship ends or when a character dies); if the story's opening or closing paragraph focuses on the timepiece; or if the story is called "The Watch"—the watch most likely has symbolic significance. In other words, considering how an image is used, how often it is used, and when it appears will help you to determine whether or not it functions as a symbol.

Symbols expand the possible meanings of a story, thereby heightening interest and actively involving readers in the text. In "The Lottery" (p. 335), for example, the mysterious black box has symbolic significance. It is mentioned prominently and repeatedly, and it plays a pivotal role in the story's action. Of course, the black box is important on a purely literal level: it functions as a key component of the lottery. But the box has other associations as well, and it is these associations that suggest what its symbolic significance might be.

The black wooden box is very old, a relic of many past lotteries; the narrator observes that it represents tradition. It is also closed and closely guarded, suggesting mystery and uncertainty. It is shabby, "splintered badly along one side...and in places faded or stained," and this state of disrepair could suggest that the ritual it is part of has also deteriorated or that tradition itself has deteriorated. The box is also simple in construction and design, suggesting the primitive (and therefore perhaps outdated) nature of the ritual. Thus, this symbol encourages readers to probe the story for values and ideas, to consider and weigh the suitability of a variety of interpretations. It serves as a "hot spot" that invites questions, and the answers to these questions reinforce and enrich the story's theme.

Allegory

An **allegory** communicates a doctrine, message, or moral principle by making it into a narrative in which the characters personify ideas, concepts, qualities, or other abstractions. Thus, an allegory is a story with two parallel and consistent levels of meaning—one literal and one figurative. The figurative level, which offers some moral or political lesson, is the story's main concern.

Whereas a symbol has multiple symbolic associations as well as a literal meaning, an **allegorical figure**—a character, object, place, or event in the allegory—has just one meaning within an **allegorical framework**, the set of ideas that conveys the allegory's message. (At the simplest level, for instance, one character can stand for good and another can stand for evil.) For this reason, allegorical figures do not open up a text to various interpretations the way symbols do. The allegorical figures are significant only because they represent something beyond their literal meaning in a fixed system. Because the purpose of allegory is to communicate a particular lesson, readers are not encouraged to speculate about the allegory's possible meanings; each element has only one equivalent, which readers must discover if they are to make sense of the story.

Naturally, the better a reader understands the political, religious, and literary assumptions of a writer (as well as the context of the work itself), the easier it will be to recognize the allegorical significance of his or her work. John Bunyan's *The Pilgrim's Progress*, for example, is a famous seventeenth-century allegory based on the Christian doctrine of salvation. In order to appreciate the complexity of Bunyan's work, readers would have to familiarize themselves with this doctrine.

One type of allegory, called a **beast fable**, is a short tale, usually including a moral, in which animals assume human characteristics. Aesop's *Fables* are the best-known examples of beast fables. More recently, contemporary writers have used beast fables to satirize the political and social conditions of our time. In one such tale, "The Gentlemen of the Jungle" by the Kenyan writer Jomo Kenyatta, an elephant is allowed to put his trunk inside a man's hut during a rainstorm. Not content with keeping his trunk dry, the elephant pushes his entire body inside the hut, displacing the man. When the man protests, the elephant takes the matter to the lion, who appoints a Commission of Enquiry to settle the matter. Eventually, the man is forced not only to abandon his hut to the elephant but also to build new huts for all the animals on the Commission. Even so, the jealous animals occupy the man's new hut and begin fighting for space; while they are arguing, the man burns down the hut, animals and all. Like the tales told by Aesop, "The Gentlemen of the Jungle" has a moral: "Peace is costly," says the man as he walks away happily, "but it's worth the expense."

The following passage from Kenyatta's tale reveals how the allegorical figures work within the framework of the allegory:

> The elephant, obeying the command of his master (the lion), got busy with the other ministers to appoint a Commission of Enquiry. The following elders of the jungle were appointed to sit in the Commission: (1) Mr. Rhinoceros; (2) Mr. Buffalo; (3) Mr. Alligator; (4) The Rt. Hon. Mr. Fox to act as chairman; and (5) Mr. Leopard to act as Secretary of the Commission. On seeing the personnel, the man protested and asked if it was not necessary to include in this Commission a member from his side. But he was told that it was impossible, since no one from his side was well enough educated to understand the intricacy of jungle law.

From this excerpt, we can see that each character represents a particular idea. For example, the members of the Commission stand for bureaucratic smugness and inequity, and the man stands for the citizens who are victimized by the government. In order to fully understand the allegorical significance of each figure in this story, of course, readers would have to know something about government bureaucracies, colonialism in Africa, and possibly a specific historical event in Kenya.

Some works contain both symbolic elements *and* allegorical elements, as Nathaniel Hawthorne's "Young Goodman Brown" (p. 367) does. The names of the story's two main characters, "Goodman" and "Faith," suggest that they fit within an allegorical system of some sort: Young Goodman Brown represents a good person who, despite his best efforts, strays from the path of righteousness; his wife, Faith, represents the quality he must hold on to in order to avoid temptation. As characters, they have no significance outside of their allegorical functions. Other elements of the story, however, are not so clear-cut. The older man whom Young Goodman Brown meets in the woods carries a staff that has carved on it "the likeness of a great black snake, so curiously wrought, that it might almost be seen to twist and wriggle itself like a living serpent." This staff, carried by a Satanic figure who represents evil and temptation, suggests the snake in the Garden of Eden, an association that neatly fits into the allegorical framework of the story. Alternatively, however, the staff could suggest the "slippery," ever-changing nature of sin, the difficulty people have in perceiving sin, or even sexuality (which may explain Young Goodman Brown's susceptibility to temptation). This range of possible meanings suggests that the staff functions as a symbol (not an allegorical figure) that enriches Hawthorne's story.

Other stories work entirely on a symbolic level and contain no allegorical figures. "The Lottery," despite its moral overtones, is not an allegory because its characters, events, and objects are not arranged to serve one rigid, didactic purpose. In fact, many different interpretations have been suggested for this story. When it was first published in June 1948 in the *New Yorker*, some readers believed it to be a story about an actual custom or ritual. As author Shirley Jackson reports in her essay "Biography of a Story," even those who recognized it as fiction speculated about its meaning, seeing it as (among other things) an attack on prejudice; a criticism of society's need for a scapegoat; or a treatise on witchcraft, Christian martyrdom, or village gossip. The fact is that an allegorical interpretation will not account for every major character, object, and event in the story.

 Myth

Throughout history, human beings have been makers of myths. For the purpose of this discussion, a **myth** is a story that is central to a culture; it embodies the values on which a culture or society is built. Thus, myths are not synonymous with falsehoods or fairy tales. Rather, they are stories that contain ideas that inform a culture and that give that culture meaning. In this sense, then, both an ancient epic and a contemporary religious text can be considered myths.

Although many myths have to do with religion, myths are not limited to the theological. Myths explain everything from natural phenomena—such as the creation of the world—to the existence of human beings and the beginnings of agriculture. The importance of myths rests on their ability to embody a set of beliefs that unifies both individuals and the society in which they live. By examining myths, we can learn much about our own origins and about our most deeply held beliefs.

One of the most prevalent types of myth is the **creation myth**. Almost every culture has an explanation for how the earth, sun, and stars—not to mention people—came into being. According to the ancient Greeks, for example, the world began as an empty void from which Nyx, a bird with black wings, emerged. She laid a golden egg, and out of it arose Eros, the god of love. The two halves of the eggshell became the earth and the sky, who fell in love with each other and had many children and grandchildren. These offspring became the gods of the Greek pantheon, who eventually created human beings in their own likeness. Each of these gods had a role to play in the creation and maintenance of the world, and their actions—in particular, their constant meddling in the lives of people—comprise the myths of ancient Greece.

In various cultures all over the world, creation myths take different forms. According to the ancient Japanese, for example, the world emerged from a single seed, which grew to form a god who, in turn, created other gods and eventually the islands of Japan and their inhabitants. Several Native American tribes share common beliefs about "sky ancestors," who created the people on the planet.

In Western culture, the most recognizable creation myth appears in Genesis, the first book of the Old Testament. According to Genesis, God created the heavens and the earth as well as all living creatures—including Adam and Eve. Other stories are part of the oral tradition of Judaism and do not appear in Genesis. An example of such a story is the tale of Lilith, which emerged sometime between the eighth and eleventh centuries. According to this Hebrew myth, Lilith, who was created before Eve, was Adam's first wife. However, she refused to be subservient to Adam, and so she left Eden, eventually to be replaced by Eve. Talmudic tradition holds that she later mated with demons and gave birth to a legion of demonic offspring who inhabit the dark places of the earth.

The influence of mythology on literature is profound, and our contemporary understanding of narrative fiction owes a great deal to mythology. In fact, many of the short stories in this anthology contain allusions to myth. Consider, for example, the role of myth in "The Lottery," "Young Goodman Brown," and Raymond Carver's "Cathedral" (p. 353). In each of these short stories, myth is central to the characters' behavior, sensibility, and understanding of the world in which they live.

✔ CHECKLIST Writing about Symbol, Allegory, and Myth

☐ Are any universal symbols used in the work? any conventional symbols? What is their function?

☐ Is any character, place, action, event, or object given unusual prominence or emphasis in the story? If so, does this element seem to have symbolic as well as literal significance?

☐ What possible meanings does each symbol suggest?

☐ How do symbols help to depict the story's characters?

☐ How do symbols help to characterize the story's setting?

☐ How do symbols help to advance the story's plot?

- Does the story have a moral or didactic purpose? What is the message, idea, or moral principle the story seeks to convey? Is the story an allegory?

- What equivalent may be assigned to each allegorical figure in the story?

- What is the allegorical framework of the story?

- Does the story combine allegorical figures and symbols? How do they work together in the story?

- Does the story have any references to myth? If so, what do these references contribute to the story's plot or theme?

Source: © AP Images

SHIRLEY JACKSON (1916–1965) is best known for her restrained tales of horror and the supernatural, most notably her novel *The Haunting of Hill House* (1959) and the short story "The Lottery" (1948). Among her other works are two novels dealing with multiple personalities—*The Bird's Nest* (1954) and *We Have Always Lived in the Castle* (1962)—and two collections of comic tales about her children and family life, *Life among the Savages* (1953) and *Raising Demons* (1957). A posthumous collection of stories, *Just an Ordinary Day* (1997), was published after the discovery of a box of some of Jackson's unpublished papers in a Vermont barn and her heirs' subsequent search for her other uncollected works.

With her husband, literary critic Stanley Edgar Hyman, she settled in the small town of Bennington, Vermont, but was never accepted by the townspeople. "The Lottery" is set in much the same kind of small, parochial town. Despite the story's matter-of-fact tone and familiar setting, its publication in the *New Yorker* provoked a torrent of letters from enraged and shocked readers. In her quiet way, Jackson presented the underside of village life and revealed to readers the dark side of human nature. Future writers of gothic tales recognized their great debt to Jackson. Horror master Stephen King dedicated his book *Firestarter* "to Shirley Jackson, who never had to raise her voice."

Cultural Context "The Lottery" is sometimes seen as a protest against totalitarianism, a form of authoritarian government that permits no individual freedom. In *Eichmann in Jerusalem* (1963), political scientist Hannah Arendt (1906–1975) wrote about totalitarianism as it pertained to Nazi Germany and the Holocaust. Here, she introduced the concept of "the banality of evil," the potential in ordinary people to do evil things. Americans of the post–World War II era saw themselves as "good guys" defending the world against foreign evils. Jackson's story, written scarcely three years after the liberation of Auschwitz, told Americans something they did not want to hear—that the face of human evil could look just like their next-door neighbor.

The Lottery (1948)

The morning of June 27th was clear and sunny, with the fresh warmth of a full-summer day; the flowers were blossoming profusely and the grass was richly green. The people of the village began to gather in the square, between the post office and the bank, around ten o'clock; in some towns there were so many people that the lottery took two days and had to be started on June 26th, but in this village, where there were only about three hundred people, the whole lottery took less than two hours, so it could begin at ten o'clock in the morning and still be through in time to allow the villagers to get home for noon dinner.

The children assembled first, of course. School was recently over for the summer, and the feeling of liberty sat uneasily on most of them; they tended to gather together quietly for a while before they broke into boisterous play, and their talk was still of the classroom and the teacher, of books and reprimands. Bobby Martin had already stuffed his pockets full of stones, and the other boys soon followed his example, selecting the smoothest and roundest stones; Bobby and Harry Jones and Dickie Delacroix—the villagers pronounced this name "Dellacroy"—eventually made a great pile of stones in one corner of the square and guarded it against the raids of the other boys. The girls stood aside, talking among themselves, looking over their shoulders at the boys, and the very small children rolled in the dust or clung to the hands of their older brothers or sisters.

Soon the men began to gather, surveying their own children, speaking of planting and rain, tractors and taxes. They stood together, away from the pile of stones in the corner, and their jokes were quiet and they smiled rather than laughed. The women, wearing faded house dresses and sweaters, came shortly after their menfolk. They greeted one another and exchanged bits of gossip as they went to join their husbands. Soon the women, standing by their husbands, began to call to their children, and the children came reluctantly, having to be called four or five times. Bobby Martin ducked under his mother's grasping hand and ran, laughing, back to the pile of stones. His father spoke up sharply, and Bobby came quickly and took his place between his father and his oldest brother.

The lottery was conducted—as were the square dances, the teenage club, the Halloween program—by Mr. Summers, who had time and energy to devote to civic activities. He was a round-faced, jovial man and he ran the coal business, and people were sorry for him, because he had no children and his wife was a scold. When he arrived in the square, carrying the black wooden box, there was a murmur of conversation among the villagers, and he waved and called, "Little late today, folks." The postmaster, Mr. Graves, followed him, carrying a three-legged stool, and the stool was put in the center of the square and Mr. Summers set the black box down on it. The villagers kept their distance, leaving a space between themselves and the stool, and when Mr. Summers said, "Some of you fellows want to give me a hand?" there was a hesitation before two men, Mr. Martin and his oldest son, Baxter, came forward to hold the box steady on the stool while Mr. Summers stirred up the papers inside it.

The original paraphernalia for the lottery had been lost long ago, and 5 the black box now resting on the stool had been put into use even before Old Man Warner, the oldest man in town, was born. Mr. Summers spoke frequently to the villagers about making a new box, but no one liked to upset even as much tradition as was represented by the black box. There was a story that the present box had been made with some pieces of the box that had preceded it, the one that had been constructed when the first people settled down to make a village here. Every year, after the lottery, Mr. Summers began talking again about a new box, but every year the subject was allowed to fade off without anything's being done. The black box grew shabbier each year; by now it was no longer completely black but splintered badly along one side to show the original wood color, and in some places faded or stained.

Mr. Martin and his oldest son, Baxter, held the black box securely on the stool until Mr. Summers had stirred the papers thoroughly with his hand. Because so much of the ritual had been forgotten or discarded, Mr. Summers had been successful in having slips of paper substituted for the chips of wood that had been used for generations. Chips of wood, Mr. Summers had argued, had been all very well when the village was tiny, but now that the population was more than three hundred and likely to keep on growing, it was necessary to use something that would fit more easily into the black box. The night before the lottery, Mr. Summers and Mr. Graves made up the slips of paper and put them in the box, and it was then taken to the safe of Mr. Summers's coal company and locked up until Mr. Summers was ready to take it to the square next morning. The rest of the year, the box was put away, sometimes one place, sometimes another; it had spent one year in Mr. Graves's barn and another year underfoot in the post office, and sometimes it was set on a shelf in the Martin grocery and left there.

There was a great deal of fussing to be done before Mr. Summers declared the lottery open. There were the lists to make up—of heads of families, heads of households in each family, members of each household in each family. There was the proper swearing-in of Mr. Summers by the postmaster, as the official of the lottery; at one time, some people remembered, there had been a recital of some sort, performed by the official of the lottery, a perfunctory, tuneless chant that had been rattled off duly each year; some people believed that the official of the lottery used to stand just so when he said or sang it, others believed that he was supposed to walk among the people, but years and years ago this part of the ritual had been allowed to lapse. There had been, also, a ritual salute, which the official of the lottery had had to use in addressing each person who came up to draw from the box, but this also had changed with time, until now it was felt necessary only for the official to speak to each person approaching. Mr. Summers was very good at all this; in his clean white shirt and blue jeans, with one hand resting carelessly on the black box, he seemed very proper and important as he talked interminably to Mr. Graves and the Martins.

Just as Mr. Summers finally left off talking and turned to the assembled villagers, Mrs. Hutchinson came hurriedly along the path to the square, her sweater thrown over her shoulders, and slid into place in the back of the crowd. "Clean forgot what day it was," she said to Mrs. Delacroix, who stood next to her, and they both laughed softly. "Thought my old man was out back stacking wood," Mrs. Hutchinson went on, "and then I looked out the window and the kids was gone, and then I remembered it was the twenty-seventh and came a-running." She dried her hands on her apron, and Mrs. Delacroix said, "You're in time, though. They're still talking away up there."

Mrs. Hutchinson craned her neck to see through the crowd and found her husband and children standing near the front. She tapped Mrs. Delacroix on the arm as a farewell and began to make her way through the crowd. The people separated good-humoredly to let her through; two or three people said, in voices just loud enough to be heard across the crowd, "Here comes your Missus, Hutchinson," and "Bill, she made it after all." Mrs. Hutchinson reached her husband, and Mr. Summers, who had been waiting, said cheerfully, "Thought we were going to have to get on without you, Tessie." Mrs. Hutchinson said, grinning, "Wouldn't have me leave m'dishes in the sink, now, would you, Joe?," and soft laughter ran through the crowd as the people stirred back into position after Mrs. Hutchinson's arrival.

10   "Well, now," Mr. Summers said soberly, "guess we better get started, get this over with, so's we can go back to work. Anybody ain't here?"

"Dunbar," several people said. "Dunbar, Dunbar."

Mr. Summers consulted his list. "Clyde Dunbar," he said. "That's right. He's broke his leg, hasn't he? Who's drawing for him?"

"Me, I guess," a woman said, and Mr. Summers turned to look at her. "Wife draws for her husband," Mr. Summers said. "Don't you have a grown boy to do it for you, Janey?" Although Mr. Summers and everyone else in the village knew the answer perfectly well, it was the business of the official of the lottery to ask such questions formally. Mr. Summers waited with an expression of polite interest while Mrs. Dunbar answered.

"Horace's not but sixteen yet," Mrs. Dunbar said regretfully. "Guess I gotta fill in for the old man this year."

"Right," Mr. Summers said. He made a note on the list he was holding. 15 Then he asked, "Watson boy drawing this year?"

A tall boy in the crowd raised his hand. "Here," he said. "I'm drawing for m'mother and me." He blinked his eyes nervously and ducked his head as several voices in the crowd said things like "Good fellow, Jack," and "Glad to see your mother's got a man to do it."

"Well," Mr. Summers said, "guess that's everyone. Old Man Warner make it?"

"Here," a voice said, and Mr. Summers nodded.

A sudden hush fell on the crowd as Mr. Summers cleared his throat and looked at the list. "All ready?" he called. "Now, I'll read the names— heads of families first—and the men come up and take a paper out of the box. Keep the paper folded in your hand without looking at it until everyone has had a turn. Everything clear?"

The people had done it so many times that they only half listened 20 to the directions; most of them were quiet, wetting their lips, not looking around. Then Mr. Summers raised one hand high and said, "Adams." A man disengaged himself from the crowd and came forward. "Hi, Steve," Mr. Summers said, and Mr. Adams said, "Hi, Joe." They grinned at one another humorlessly and nervously. Then Mr. Adams reached into the black box and took out a folded paper. He held it firmly by one corner as he turned and went hastily back to his place in the crowd, where he stood a little apart from his family, not looking down at his hand.

"Allen," Mr. Summers said. "Anderson.... Bentham."

"Seems like there's no time at all between lotteries any more," Mrs. Delacroix said to Mrs. Graves in the back row. "Seems like we got through with the last one only last week."

"Time sure goes fast," Mrs. Graves said.

"Clark.... Delacroix."

"There goes my old man," Mrs. Delacroix said. She held her breath 25 while her husband went forward.

"Dunbar," Mr. Summers said, and Mrs. Dunbar went steadily to the box while one of the women said, "Go on, Janey," and another said, "There she goes."

"We're next," Mrs. Graves said. She watched while Mr. Graves came around from the side of the box, greeted Mr. Summers gravely, and selected a slip of paper from the box. By now, all through the crowd there were men holding the small folded papers in their large hands, turning them over and over nervously. Mrs. Dunbar and her two sons stood together, Mrs. Dunbar holding the slip of paper.

"Harburt.... Hutchinson."

"Get up there, Bill," Mrs. Hutchinson said, and the people near her laughed.

30 "Jones."

"They do say," Mr. Adams said to Old Man Warner, who stood next to him, "that over in the north village they're talking of giving up the lottery."

Old Man Warner snorted. "Pack of crazy fools," he said. "Listening to the young folks, nothing's good enough for *them*. Next thing you know, they'll be wanting to go back to living in caves, nobody work any more, live *that* way for a while. Used to be a saying about 'Lottery in June, corn be heavy soon.' First thing you know, we'd all be eating stewed chick-weed and acorns. There's *always* been a lottery," he added petulantly. "Bad enough to see young Joe Summers up there joking with everybody."

"Some places have already quit lotteries," Mrs. Adams said.

"Nothing but trouble in *that*," Old Man Warner said stoutly. "Pack of young fools."

35 "Martin." And Bobby Martin watched his father go forward. "Overdyke.... Percy."

"I wish they'd hurry," Mrs. Dunbar said to her older son. "I wish they'd hurry."

"They're almost through," her son said.

"You get ready to run tell Dad," Mrs. Dunbar said.

Mr. Summers called his own name and then stepped forward precisely and selected a slip from the box. Then he called, "Warner."

40 "Seventy-seventh year I been in the lottery," Old Man Warner said as he went through the crowd. "Seventy-seventh time."

"Watson." The tall boy came awkwardly through the crowd. Someone said, "Don't be nervous, Jack," and Mr. Summers said, "Take your time, son."

"Zanini."

After that, there was a long pause, a breathless pause, until Mr. Summers, holding his slip of paper in the air, said, "All right, fellows." For a minute, no one moved, and then all the slips of paper were opened. Suddenly, all the women began to speak at once, saying, "Who is it?," "Who's got it?," "Is it the Dunbars?," "Is it the Watsons?" Then the voices began to say, "It's Hutchinson. It's Bill," "Bill Hutchinson's got it."

"Go tell your father," Mrs. Dunbar said to her older son.

45 People began to look around to see the Hutchinsons. Bill Hutchinson was standing quiet, staring down at the paper in his hand. Suddenly, Tessie Hutchinson shouted to Mr. Summers, "You didn't give him time enough to take any paper he wanted. I saw you. It wasn't fair!"

"Be a good sport, Tessie," Mrs. Delacroix called, and Mrs. Graves said, "All of us took the same chance."

"Shut up, Tessie," Bill Hutchinson said.

"Well, everyone," Mr. Summers said, "that was done pretty fast, and now we've got to be hurrying a little more to get done in time." He consulted his next list. "Bill," he said, "you draw for the Hutchinson family. You got any other households in the Hutchinsons?"

"There's Don and Eva," Mrs. Hutchinson yelled, "Make *them* take their chance!"

"Daughters draw with their husbands' families, Tessie," Mr. Summers 50 said gently. "You know that as well as anyone else."

"It wasn't *fair*," Tessie said.

"I guess not, Joe," Bill Hutchinson said regretfully. "My daughter draws with her husband's family, that's only fair. And I've got no other family except the kids."

"Then, as far as drawing for families is concerned, it's you," Mr. Summers said in explanation, "and as far as drawing for households is concerned, that's you, too. Right?"

"Right," Bill Hutchinson said.

"How many kids, Bill?" Mr. Summers asked formally.   55

"Three," Bill Hutchinson said. "There's Bill, Jr., and Nancy, and little Dave. And Tessie and me."

"All right, then," Mr. Summers said. "Harry, you got their tickets back?"

Mr. Graves nodded and held up the slips of paper. "Put them in the box, then," Mr. Summers directed. "Take Bill's and put it in."

"I think we ought to start over," Mrs. Hutchinson said, as quietly as she could. "I tell you it wasn't *fair*. You didn't give him time enough to choose. *Every*body saw that."

Mr. Graves had selected the five slips and put them in the box, and he 60 dropped all the papers but those onto the ground, where the breeze caught them and lifted them off.

"Listen, everybody," Mrs. Hutchinson was saying to the people around her.

"Ready, Bill?" Mr. Summers asked, and Bill Hutchinson, with one quick glance around at his wife and children, nodded.

"Remember," Mr. Summers said, "take the slips and keep them folded until each person has taken one. Harry, you help little Dave." Mr. Graves took the hand of the little boy, who came willingly with him up to the box. "Take a paper out of the box, Davy," Mr. Summers said. Davy put his hand into the box and laughed. "Take just *one* paper," Mr. Summers said. "Harry, you hold it for him." Mr. Graves took the child's hand and removed the folded paper from the tight fist and held it while little Dave stood next to him and looked at him wonderingly.

"Nancy next," Mr. Summers said. Nancy was twelve, and her school friends breathed heavily as she went forward, switching her skirt, and took a slip daintily from the box. "Bill, Jr.," Mr. Summers said, and Billy, his face red and his feet overlarge, nearly knocked the box over as he got a paper out. "Tessie," Mr. Summers said. She hesitated for a minute, looking around defiantly, and then set her lips and went up to the box. She snatched a paper out and held it behind her.

65   "Bill," Mr. Summers said, and Bill Hutchinson reached into the box and felt around, bringing his hand out at last with the slip of paper in it.

The crowd was quiet. A girl whispered, "I hope it's not Nancy," and the sound of the whisper reached the edges of the crowd.

"It's not the way it used to be," Old Man Warner said clearly. "People ain't the way they used to be."

"All right," Mr. Summers said. "Open the papers. Harry, you open little Dave's."

Mr. Graves opened the slip of paper and there was a general sigh through the crowd as he held it up and everyone could see that it was blank. Nancy and Bill, Jr., opened theirs at the same time, and both beamed and laughed, turning around to the crowd and holding their slips of paper above their heads.

70   "Tessie," Mr. Summers said. There was a pause, and then Mr. Summers looked at Bill Hutchinson, and Bill unfolded his paper and showed it. It was blank.

"It's Tessie," Mr. Summers said, and his voice was hushed. "Show us her paper, Bill."

Bill Hutchinson went over to his wife and forced the slip of paper out of her hand. It had a black spot on it, the black spot Mr. Summers had made the night before with the heavy pencil in the coal-company office. Bill Hutchinson held it up, and there was a stir in the crowd.

"All right, folks," Mr. Summers said. "Let's finish quickly."

Although the villagers had forgotten the ritual and lost the original black box, they still remembered to use stones. The pile of stones the boys had made earlier was ready; there were stones on the ground with the blowing scraps of paper that had come out of the box. Mrs. Delacroix selected a stone so large she had to pick it up with both hands and turned to Mrs. Dunbar. "Come on," she said. "Hurry up."

75   Mrs. Dunbar had small stones in both hands, and she said, gasping for breath, "I can't run at all. You'll have to go ahead and I'll catch up with you."

The children had stones already, and someone gave little Davy Hutchinson a few pebbles.

Tessie Hutchinson was in the center of a cleared space by now, and she held her hands out desperately as the villagers moved in on her. "It isn't fair," she said. A stone hit her on the side of the head.

Old Man Warner was saying, "Come on, come on, everyone." Steve Adams was in the front of the crowd of villagers, with Mrs. Graves beside him.

"It isn't fair, it isn't right," Mrs. Hutchinson screamed, and then they were upon her.

Reading and Reacting

1. What possible significance, beyond their literal meaning, might each of the following have:

- The village square
- Mrs. Hutchinson's apron
- Old Man Warner
- The slips of paper
- The black spot

2. "The Lottery" takes place in summer, a conventional symbol that has a positive connotation. What does this setting contribute to the story's plot? to its atmosphere?

3. What, if anything, might the names *Graves, Adams, Summers,* and *Delacroix* signify in the context of this story? Do you think these names are intended to have any special significance? Why or why not?

4. What role do the children play in the ritual? How can you explain their presence in the story? Do they have any symbolic role?

5. What symbolic significance might be found in the way the characters are dressed? in their conversation?

6. In what sense is the story's title ironic?

7. Throughout the story, there is a general atmosphere of excitement. What indication is there of nervousness or apprehension?

8. Early in the story, the boys stuff their pockets with stones, foreshadowing the attack in the story's conclusion. What other examples of foreshadowing can you identify?

9. JOURNAL ENTRY How can a ritual like the lottery continue to be held year after year? Why does no one move to end it? Can you think of a modern-day counterpart to this lottery—a situation in which people continue to act in ways they know to be wrong rather than challenge the status quo? How can you account for such behavior?

10. CRITICAL PERSPECTIVE When "The Lottery" was published in the June 26, 1948, issue of the *New Yorker,* its effect was immediate. The story, as the critic Judy Oppenheimer notes in her book *Private Demons: The Life of Shirley Jackson,* "provoked an unprecedented outpouring of fury, horror, rage, disgust, and intense fascination." As a result, Jackson received

hundreds of letters, which included (among others) the following interpretations of the story:

- The story is an attack on small-town America.
- The story is a parable about the perversion of democracy.
- The story is a criticism of prejudice, particularly anti-Semitism.
- The story has no point at all.

How plausible do you think each of these interpretations is? Which
comes closest to your interpretation of the story? Why?

Related Works: "Young Goodman Brown" (p. 367), "Where Are You Going,
Where Have You Been?" (p. 453), "Patterns" (p. 512), "Ballad of Birmingham" (p. 529), *Nine Ten* (p. 861)

ALICE WALKER (1944–   ) was the youngest of eight
children born to Willie Lee and Minnie Tallulah Grant
Walker, sharecroppers who raised cotton. She left
the rural South to attend Spelman College in Atlanta
(1961–1963) and Sarah Lawrence College in Bronxville,
New York (1963–1965).

In 1967, Walker moved to Mississippi, where
she was supported in the writing of her first novel, *The
Third Life of Grange Copeland* (1970), by a National
Endowment for the Arts grant. Her short story "Everyday Use" was included in *Best American Short Stories
1973* and has been widely anthologized and studied.
Other novels and collections of short stories followed,
including *In Love & Trouble: Stories of Black Women* (1973), *Meridian* (1976), *You Can't Keep
a Good Woman Down* (1981), *The Temple of My Familiar* (1989), *Possessing the Secret of Joy*
(1993), *The Complete Stories* (1994), *By the Light of My Father's Smile* (1998), and *Now Is the
Time to Open Your Heart* (2004). Her latest books include the essay collection *The Cushion in
the Road* (2013) and the poetry collection *The World Will Follow Joy* (2013). Her third novel,
The Color Purple (1982), won the American Book Award and a Pulitzer Prize and was made
into an award-winning movie and a long-running Broadway play.

In the third year of her marriage, Walker took back her maiden name because she wanted
to honor her great-great-great-grandmother who had walked, carrying her two children, from
Virginia to Georgia. Walker's renaming is consistent with one of her goals in writing, which
is to further the process of reconnecting people to their ancestors. She has said that "it is
fatal to see yourself as separate" and that if people can reaffirm the past, they can "make a
different future."

Cultural Context Quilting attained the status of art in Europe in the fourteenth century but
reached its fullest development later in North America. By the end of the eighteenth century,
the American quilt had taken on unique and distinctive features that separated it from quilts
made in other parts of the world. For African Americans, quilting has particular significance.
Some scholars think that during slavery, members of the Underground Railroad used quilts
to send messages. One design, the Log Cabin, was hung outside to mark a house of refuge
for fugitive slaves. Other quilts mapped escape routes out of a plantation or county, often by

marking the stars that would act as a guide to freedom for those escaping at night. After the emancipation of slaves, quilts retained their cultural and historical significance, as the quilt in this story does.

Everyday Use (1973)

For Your Grandmama

I will wait for her in the yard that Maggie and I made so clean and wavy yesterday afternoon. A yard like this is more comfortable than most people know. It is not just a yard. It is like an extended living room. When the hard clay is swept clean as a floor and the fine sand around the edges lined with tiny, irregular grooves, anyone can come and sit and look up into the elm tree and wait for the breezes that never come inside the house.

Maggie will be nervous until after her sister goes: she will stand hopelessly in corners, homely and ashamed of the burn scars down her arms and legs, eying her sister with a mixture of envy and awe. She thinks her sister has held life always in the palm of one hand, that "no" is a word the world never learned to say to her.

You've no doubt seen those TV shows where the child who has "made it" is confronted, as a surprise, by her own mother and father, tottering in weakly from backstage. (A pleasant surprise, of course: What would they do if parent and child came on the show only to curse out and insult each other?) On TV mother and child embrace and smile into each other's faces. Sometimes the mother and father weep, the child wraps them in her arms and leans across the table to tell how she would not have made it without their help. I have seen these programs.

Sometimes I dream a dream in which Dee and I are suddenly brought together on a TV program of this sort. Out of a dark and soft-seated limousine I am ushered into a bright room filled with many people. There I meet a smiling, gray, sporty man like Johnny Carson who shakes my hand and tells me what a fine girl I have. Then we are on the stage and Dee is embracing me with tears in her eyes. She pins on my dress a large orchid, even though she has told me once that she thinks orchids are tacky flowers.

In real life I am a large, big-boned woman with rough, man-working 5 hands. In the winter I wear flannel nightgowns to bed and overalls during the day. I can kill and clean a hog as mercilessly as a man. My fat keeps me hot in zero weather. I can work outside all day, breaking ice to get water for washing; I can eat pork liver cooked over the open fire minutes after it comes steaming from the hog. One winter I knocked a bull calf straight in the brain between the eyes with a sledge hammer and had the meat hung up to chill before nightfall. But of course all this does not show on television. I am the way my daughter would want me to be: a hundred pounds lighter, my skin like an uncooked barley pancake. My hair glistens in the hot bright lights. Johnny Carson has much to do to keep up with my quick and witty tongue.

But that is a mistake. I know even before I wake up. Who ever knew a Johnson with a quick tongue? Who can even imagine me looking a strange white man in the eye? It seems to me I have talked to them always with one foot raised in flight, with my head turned in whichever way is farthest from them. Dee, though. She would always look anyone in the eye. Hesitation was no part of her nature.

"How do I look, Mama?" Maggie says, showing just enough of her thin body enveloped in pink skirt and red blouse for me to know she's there, almost hidden by the door.

"Come out into the yard," I say.

Have you ever seen a lame animal, perhaps a dog run over by some careless person rich enough to own a car, sidle up to someone who is ignorant enough to be kind to him? That is the way my Maggie walks. She has been like this, chin on chest, eyes on ground, feet in shuffle, ever since the fire that burned the other house to the ground.

10   Dee is lighter than Maggie, with nicer hair and a fuller figure. She's a woman now, though sometimes I forget. How long ago was it that the other house burned? Ten, twelve years? Sometimes I can still hear the flames and feel Maggie's arms sticking to me, her hair smoking and her dress falling off her in little black papery flakes. Her eyes seemed stretched open, blazed open by the flames reflected in them. And Dee. I see her standing off under the sweet gum tree she used to dig gum out of; a look of concentration on her face as she watched the last dingy gray board of the house fall in toward the red-hot brick chimney. Why don't you do a dance around the ashes? I'd wanted to ask her. She had hated the house that much.

I used to think she hated Maggie, too. But that was before we raised the money, the church and me, to send her to Augusta to school. She used to read to us without pity; forcing words, lies, other folks' habits, whole lives upon us two, sitting trapped and ignorant underneath her voice. She washed us in a river of make-believe, burned us with a lot of knowledge we didn't necessarily need to know. Pressed us to her with the serious way she read, to shove us away at just the moment, like dimwits, we seemed about to understand.

Dee wanted nice things. A yellow organdy dress to wear to her graduation from high school; black pumps to match a green suit she'd made from an old suit somebody gave me. She was determined to stare down any disaster in her efforts. Her eyelids would not flicker for minutes at a time. Often I fought off the temptation to shake her. At sixteen she had a style of her own, and knew what style was.

I never had an education myself. After second grade the school was closed down. Don't ask me why: in 1927 colored asked fewer questions than they do now. Sometimes Maggie reads to me. She stumbles along good-naturedly but can't see well. She knows she is not bright. Like good looks and money, quickness passed her by. She will marry John Thomas (who has mossy teeth in an earnest face) and then I'll be free to sit here and I guess just sing church songs to myself. Although I never was a good singer. Never could carry a tune. I was always better at a man's job. I used to love to milk till I was hooked in the side in '49. Cows are soothing and slow and don't bother you, unless you try to milk them the wrong way.

I have deliberately turned my back on the house. It is three rooms, just like the one that burned, except the roof is tin; they don't make shingle roofs any more. There are no real windows, just some holes cut in the sides, like the portholes in a ship, but not round and not square, with rawhide holding the shutters up on the outside. This house is in a pasture, too, like the other one. No doubt when Dee sees it she will want to tear it down. She wrote me once that no matter where we "choose" to live, she will manage to come see us. But she will never bring her friends. Maggie and I thought about this and Maggie asked me, "Mama, when did Dee ever *have* any friends?"

She had a few. Furtive boys in pink shirts hanging about on washday 15 after school. Nervous girls who never laughed. Impressed with her they worshiped the well-turned phrase, the cute shape, the scalding humor that erupted like bubbles in lye. She read to them.

When she was courting Jimmy T she didn't have much time to pay to us, but turned all her faultfinding power on him. He *flew* to marry a cheap city girl from a family of ignorant flashy people. She hardly had time to recompose herself.

When she comes I will meet—but there they are!

Maggie attempts to make a dash for the house, in her shuffling way, but I stay her with my hand. "Come back here," I say. And she stops and tries to dig a well in the sand with her toe.

It is hard to see them clearly through the strong sun. But even the first glimpse of leg out of the car tells me it is Dee. Her feet were always neat-looking, as if God himself had shaped them with a certain style. From the other side of the car comes a short, stocky man. Hair is all over his head a foot long and hanging from his chin like a kinky mule tail. I hear Maggie suck in her breath. "Uhnnnh," is what it sounds like. Like when you see the wriggling end of a snake just in front of your foot on the road. "Uhnnnh."

Dee next. A dress down to the ground, in this hot weather. A dress so 20 loud it hurts my eyes. There are yellows and oranges enough to throw back the light of the sun. I feel my whole face warming from the heat waves it throws out. Earrings gold, too, and hanging down to her shoulders. Bracelets dangling and making noises when she moves her arm up to shake the folds of the dress out of her armpits. The dress is loose and flows, and as she walks closer, I like it. I hear Maggie go "Uhnnnh" again. It is her sister's hair. It stands straight up like the wool on a sheep. It is black as night and around the edges are two long pigtails that rope about like small lizards disappearing behind her ears.

"Wa-su-zo-Tean-o!"[1] she says, coming on in that gliding way the dress makes her move. The short stocky fellow with the hair to his navel is all grinning and he follows up with "Asalamalakim,[2] my mother and sister!" He moves to hug Maggie but she falls back, right up against the back of my chair. I feel her trembling there and when I look up I see the perspiration falling off her chin.

"Don't get up," says Dee. Since I am stout it takes something of a push. You can see me trying to move a second or two before I make it. She turns, showing white heels through her sandals, and goes back to the car. Out she peeks next with a Polaroid.[3] She stoops down quickly and lines up picture after picture of me sitting there in front of the house with Maggie cowering behind me. She never takes a shot without making sure the house is included. When a cow comes nibbling around the edge of the yard she snaps it and me and Maggie *and* the house. Then she puts the Polaroid in the back seat of the car, and comes up and kisses me on the forehead.

Meanwhile Asalamalakim is going through motions with Maggie's hand. Maggie's hand is as limp as a fish, and probably as cold, despite the sweat, and she keeps trying to pull it back. It looks like Asalamalakim wants to shake hands but wants to do it fancy. Or maybe he don't know how people shake hands. Anyhow, he soon gives up on Maggie.

"Well," I say. "Dee."

25   "No, Mama," she says. "Not 'Dee,' Wangero Leewanika Kemanjo!"

"What happened to 'Dee'?" I wanted to know.

"She's dead," Wangero said. "I couldn't bear it any longer, being named after the people who oppress me."

"You know as well as me you was named after your aunt Dicie," I said. Dicie is my sister. She named Dee. We called her "Big Dee" after Dee was born.

"But who was *she* named after?" asked Wangero.

30   "I guess after Grandma Dee," I said.

"And who was she named after?" asked Wangero.

"Her mother," I said, and saw Wangero was getting tired. "That's about as far back as I can trace it," I said. Though, in fact, I probably could have carried it back beyond the Civil War through the branches.

---

[1] *Wa-su-zo-Tean-o:* A greeting in Swahili; Dee sounds it out one syllable at a time.

[2] *Asalamalakim:* A greeting in Arabic: "Peace be upon you."

[3] *Polaroid:* A type of camera with self-developing film.

"Well," said Asalamalakim, "there you are."

"Uhnnnh," I heard Maggie say.

"There I was not," I said, "before 'Dicie' cropped up in our family, so 35 why should I try to trace it that far back?"

He just stood there grinning, looking down on me like somebody inspecting a Model A car. Every once in a while he and Wangero sent eye signals over my head.

"How do you pronounce this name?" I asked.

"You don't have to call me by it if you don't want to," said Wangero.

"Why shouldn't I?" I asked. "If that's what you want us to call you, we'll call you."

"I know it might sound awkward at first," said Wangero.   40

"I'll get used to it," I said. "Ream it out again."

Well, soon we got the name out of the way. Asalamalakim had a name twice as long and three times as hard. After I tripped over it two or three times he told me to just call him Hakim-a-barber. I wanted to ask him was he a barber, but I didn't really think he was, so I didn't ask.

"You must belong to those beef-cattle peoples down the road," I said. They said "Asalamalakim" when they met you, too, but they didn't shake hands. Always too busy: feeding the cattle, fixing the fences, putting up salt-lick shelters, throwing down hay. When the white folks poisoned some of the herd the men stayed up all night with rifles in their hands. I walked a mile and a half just to see the sight.

Hakim-a-barber said, "I accept some of their doctrines, but farming and raising cattle is not my style." (They didn't tell me, and I didn't ask, whether Wangero [Dee] had really gone and married him.)

We sat down to eat and right away he said he didn't eat collards and 45 pork was unclean. Wangero, though, went on through the chitlins and corn bread, the greens and everything else. She talked a blue streak over the sweet potatoes. Everything delighted her. Even the fact that we still used the benches her daddy made for the table when we couldn't afford to buy chairs.

"Oh, Mama!" she cried. Then turned to Hakim-a-barber. "I never knew how lovely these benches are. You can feel the rump prints," she said, running her hands underneath her and along the bench. Then she gave a sigh and her hand closed over Grandma Dee's butter dish. "That's it!" she said. "I knew there was something I wanted to ask you if I could have." She jumped up from the table and went over in the corner where the churn stood, the milk in it clabber by now. She looked at the churn and looked at it.

"This churn top is what I need," she said. "Didn't Uncle Buddy whittle it out of a tree you all used to have?"

"Yes," I said.

"Uh huh," she said happily. "And I want the dasher, too."

"Uncle Buddy whittle that, too?" asked the barber.

50   Dee (Wangero) looked up at me.

"Aunt Dee's first husband whittled the dash," said Maggie so low you almost couldn't hear her. "His name was Henry, but they called him Stash."

"Maggie's brain is like an elephant's," Wangero said, laughing. "I can use the churn top as a centerpiece for the alcove table," she said, sliding a plate over the churn, "and I'll think of something artistic to do with the dasher."

When she finished wrapping the dasher the handle stuck out. I took it for a moment in my hands. You didn't even have to look close to see where hands pushing the dasher up and down to make butter had left a kind of sink in the wood. In fact, there were a lot of small sinks; you could see where thumb and fingers had sunk into the wood. It was beautiful light yellow wood, from a tree that grew in the yard where Big Dee and Stash had lived.

55   After dinner Dee (Wangero) went to the trunk at the foot of my bed and started rifling through it. Maggie hung back in the kitchen over the dishpan. Out came Wangero with two quilts. They had been pieced by Grandma Dee and then Big Dee and me had hung them on the quilt frames on the front porch and quilted them. One was in the Lone Star pattern. The other was Walk Around the Mountain. In both of them were scraps of dresses Grandma Dee had worn fifty and more years ago. Bits and pieces of Grandpa Jarrell's Paisley shirts. And one teeny faded blue piece, about the size of a penny matchbox, that was from Great Grandpa Ezra's uniform that he wore in the Civil War.

"Mama," Wangero said sweet as a bird. "Can I have these old quilts?"

I heard something fall in the kitchen, and a minute later the kitchen door slammed.

"Why don't you take one or two of the others?" I asked. "These old things was just done by me and Big Dee from some tops your grandma pieced before she died."

"No," said Wangero. "I don't want those. They are stitched around the borders by machine."

60   "That'll make them last better," I said.

"That's not the point," said Wangero. "These are all pieces of dresses Grandma used to wear. She did all this stitching by hand. Imagine!" She held the quilts securely in her arms, stroking them.

"Some of the pieces, like those lavender ones, come from old clothes her mother handed down to her," I said, moving up to touch the quilts. Dee (Wangero) moved back just enough so that I couldn't reach the quilts. They already belonged to her.

"Imagine!" she breathed again, clutching them closely to her bosom.

"The truth is," I said, "I promised to give them quilts to Maggie, for when she marries John Thomas."

She gasped like a bee had stung her. "Maggie can't appreciate these 65 quilts!" she said. "She'd probably be backward enough to put them to everyday use."

"I reckon she would," I said. "God knows I been saving 'em for long enough with nobody using 'em. I hope she will!" I didn't want to bring up how I had offered Dee (Wangero) a quilt when she went away to college. Then she had told me they were old-fashioned, out of style.

"But, they're *priceless!*" she was saying now, furiously; for she has a temper. "Maggie would put them on the bed and in five years they'd be in rags. Less than that!"

"She can always make some more," I said. "Maggie knows how to quilt."

Dee (Wangero) looked at me with hatred. "You just will not understand. The point is these quilts, *these* quilts!"

"Well," I said, stumped. "What would *you* do with them?" 70

"Hang them," she said. As if that was the only thing you *could* do with quilts.

Maggie by now was standing in the door. I could almost hear the sound her feet made as they scraped over each other.

"She can have them, Mama," she said, like somebody used to never winning anything, or having anything reserved for her. "I can 'member Grandma Dee without the quilts."

I looked at her hard. She had filled her bottom lip with checkerberry snuff and it gave her face a kind of dopey, hangdog look. It was Grandma Dee and Big Dee who taught her how to quilt herself. She stood there with her scarred hands hidden in the folds of her skirt. She looked at her sister with something like fear but she wasn't mad at her. This was Maggie's portion. This was the way she knew God to work.

When I looked at her like that something hit me in the top of my head 75 and ran down to the soles of my feet. Just like when I'm in church and the spirit of God touches me and I get happy and shout. I did something I never had done before: hugged Maggie to me, then dragged her on into the room, snatched the quilts out of Miss Wangero's hands and dumped them into Maggie's lap. Maggie just sat there on my bed with her mouth open.

"Take one or two of the others," I said to Dee.

But she turned without a word and went out to Hakim-a-barber.

"You just don't understand," she said, as Maggie and I came out to the car.

"What don't I understand?" I wanted to know.

80   "Your heritage," she said. And then she turned to Maggie, kissed her, and said, "You ought to try to make something of yourself, too, Maggie. It's really a new day for us. But from the way you and Mama still live you'd never know it."

She put on some sunglasses that hid everything above the tip of her nose and her chin.

Maggie smiled; maybe at the sunglasses. But a real smile, not scared. After we watched the car dust settle I asked Maggie to bring me a dip of snuff. And then the two of us sat there just enjoying, until it was time to go in the house and go to bed.

Reading and Reacting

1. In American culture, what does a patchwork quilt symbolize?
2. What is the literal meaning of the two quilts to Maggie and her mother? to Dee? What symbolic meaning, if any, do they have to Maggie and her mother? Do the quilts have any symbolic meaning to Dee?
3. How does the contrast between the two sisters' appearances, personalities, lifestyles, and feelings about the quilts help to convey the story's theme?
4. What does the name *Wangero* signify to Dee? to her mother and sister? Could the name be considered a symbol? Why or why not?
5. Why do you think Maggie gives the quilts to her sister?
6. What is Dee's opinion of her mother and sister? Do you agree with her assessment?
7. What does the story's title suggest to you? Is it ironic? What other titles would be effective?
8. Discuss the possible meanings, aside from their literal meanings, that each of the following suggest: the family's yard, Maggie's burn scars, the trunk in which the quilts are kept, Dee's Polaroid camera. What symbolic functions, if any, do these items serve in the story?

9. **JOURNAL ENTRY** What objects have the kind of symbolic value to you that the quilts have to Maggie? What gives these objects this value?

10. **CRITICAL PERSPECTIVE** In her article "The Black Woman Artist as Wayward," critic Barbara Christian characterizes "Everyday Use" as a story in which Alice Walker examines the "creative legacy" of ordinary African American women. According to Christian, the story "is about the use and misuse of the concept of heritage. The mother of two daughters, one selfish and stylish, the other scarred and caring, passes on to us its true definition."

What definition of *heritage* does the mother attempt to pass on to her children? How is this definition like or unlike Dee's definition?

Related Works: "Discovering America" (p. 93), "Two Kinds" (p. 471), "Aunt Jennifer's Tigers" (p. 617), "Digging" (p. 706), *Beauty* (p. 831), *Trifles* (p. 867), *Fences* (p. 1270)

RAYMOND CARVER (1938–1988) Is one of the most influential and widely read writers of our time. He fashioned his stories from the stuff of common life uncommonly perceived. He married at nineteen and fathered two children by the time he was twenty; during this period, he also began to write. He received a degree from Humboldt State University and later from the University of Iowa. His first collection of stories, *Will You Please Be Quiet, Please* (1976), was nominated for a National Book Award. Five more collections of stories followed, including *Cathedral* (1983)—nominated for both a Pulitzer Prize and a National Book Critics Circle Award—and *Where I'm Calling From: New and Selected Stories* (1988). Carver was also the author of five books of poetry. In his last years, Carver was praised as the best American short story writer since Ernest Hemingway; novelist Robert Stone called him "a hero of perception." He was made an Honorary Doctor of Letters at the University of Hartford and was inducted into the American Academy and Institute of Arts and Letters.

Cultural Context A cathedral is the principal church of a bishop's diocese. As centers of religious authority, civic pomp, and communal worship, cathedrals began to be built in Europe around the year 1000. They flourished throughout the Middle Ages as the power of the Catholic Church grew. The lavish decoration and dazzling design of these structures were meant not only to celebrate God but also to honor those secular and religious authorities who had financed the construction of the buildings. Cathedrals—especially those built in the Gothic period, between 1200 and 1500—often featured pointed arches, flying buttresses, and high spires designed to lift worshipers' eyes toward heaven. Most of the great cathedrals took several generations to complete, and for this reason, the craftsmen who worked on them had no expectation of seeing them completed. Their reward was to contribute their labors to a project that was so uplifting that it inspired many of them to contribute without conditions or self-interest.

Cathedral (1983)

This blind man, an old friend of my wife's, he was on his way to spend the night. His wife had died. So he was visiting the dead wife's relatives in Connecticut. He called my wife from his in-laws'. Arrangements were made. He would come by train, a five-hour trip, and my wife would meet him at the station. She hadn't seen him since she worked for him one summer in Seattle ten years ago. But she and the blind man had kept in touch. They made tapes and mailed them back and forth. I wasn't enthusiastic about his visit. He was no one I knew. And his being blind bothered me. My idea of blindness came from the movies. In the movies, the blind moved slowly and never laughed. Sometimes they were led by seeing-eye dogs. A blind man in my house was not something I looked forward to.

That summer in Seattle she had needed a job. She didn't have any money. The man she was going to marry at the end of the summer was in officers' training school. He didn't have any money, either. But she was in love with the guy, and he was in love with her, etc. She'd seen something in the paper: HELP WANTED—*Reading to Blind Man*, and a telephone number. She phoned and went over, was hired on the spot. She'd worked with this blind man all summer. She read stuff to him, case studies, reports, that sort of thing. She helped him organize his little office in the county social-service department. They'd become good friends, my wife and the blind man. How do I know these things? She told me. And she told me something else. On her last day in the office, the blind man asked if he could touch her face. She agreed to this. She told me he touched his fingers to every part of her face, her nose—even her neck! She never forgot it. She even tried to write a poem about it. She was always trying to write a poem. She wrote a poem or two every year, usually after something really important had happened to her.

When we first started going out together, she showed me the poem. In the poem, she recalled his fingers and the way they had moved around over her face. In the poem, she talked about what she had felt at the time, about what went through her mind when the blind man touched her nose and lips. I can remember I didn't think much of the poem. Of course, I didn't tell her that. Maybe I just don't understand poetry. I admit it's not the first thing I reach for when I pick up something to read.

Anyway, this man who'd first enjoyed her favors, the officer-to-be, he'd been her childhood sweetheart. So okay. I'm saying that at the end of the summer she let the blind man run his hands over her face, said goodbye to him, married her childhood etc., who was now a commissioned officer, and she moved away from Seattle. But they'd kept in touch, she and the blind man. She made the first contact after a year or so. She called him up one night from an Air Force base in Alabama. She wanted to talk. They talked. He asked her to send a tape and tell him about her life. She did this. She sent the tape. On the tape, she told the blind man about her husband and about their life together in the military. She told the blind man she loved her husband but she didn't like it where they lived and she didn't like it that he was part of the military-industrial thing. She told the blind man she'd written a poem and he was in it. She told him that she was writing a poem about what it was like to be an Air Force officer's wife. The poem wasn't finished yet. She was still writing it. The blind man made a tape. He sent her the tape. She made a tape. This went on for years. My wife's officer was posted to one base and then another. She sent tapes from Moody AFB, McGuire, McConnell, and finally Travis,[1] near Sacramento, where one night she got to feeling lonely and cut off from people she kept losing in that moving-around life. She got to feeling she couldn't go it another step. She went in and swallowed all the pills and capsules in the medicine chest and washed them down with a bottle of gin. Then she got into a hot bath and passed out.

But instead of dying, she got sick. She threw up. Her officer—why 5 should he have a name? he was the childhood sweetheart, and what more does he want?—came home from somewhere, found her, and called the ambulance. In time, she put it all on a tape and sent the tape to the blind man. Over the years, she put all kinds of stuff on tapes and sent the tapes off lickety-split. Next to writing a poem every year, I think it was her chief means of recreation. On one tape, she told the blind man she'd decided to live away from her officer for a time. On another tape, she told him about her divorce. She and I began going out, and of course she told her blind man about it. She told him everything, or so it seemed to me. Once she asked me if I'd like to hear the latest tape from the blind man. This was a year ago. I was on the tape, she said. So I said okay, I'd listen to it. I got us drinks and we settled down in the living room. We made ready to listen. First she inserted the tape into the player and adjusted a couple of dials. Then she pushed a lever. The tape squeaked and someone began to talk in this loud voice. She lowered the volume. After a few minutes of harmless chitchat, I heard my own name in the mouth of this stranger, this blind man I didn't even know! And then this: "From all you've said about him, I can only conclude—" But we were interrupted, a knock at the door, something, and we didn't ever get back to the tape. Maybe it was just as well. I'd heard all I wanted to.

Now this same blind man was coming to sleep in my house.

"Maybe I could take him bowling," I said to my wife. She was at the draining board doing scalloped potatoes. She put down the knife she was using and turned around.

"If you love me," she said, "you can do this for me. If you don't love me, okay. But if you had a friend, any friend, and the friend came to visit, I'd make him feel comfortable." She wiped her hands with the dish towel.

"I don't have any blind friends," I said.

"You don't have *any* friends," she said. "Period. Besides," she said, 10 "goddamn it, his wife's just died! Don't you understand that? The man's lost his wife!"

I didn't answer. She'd told me a little about the blind man's wife. Her name was Beulah. Beulah! That's a name for a colored woman.

"Was his wife a Negro?" I asked.

---

[1] *Moody…Travis:* United States Air Force bases.

"Are you crazy?" my wife said. "Have you just flipped or something?" She picked up a potato. I saw it hit the floor, then roll under the stove. "What's wrong with you?" she said. "Are you drunk?"

"I'm just asking," I said.

15   Right then my wife filled me in with more detail than I cared to know. I made a drink and sat at the kitchen table to listen. Pieces of the story began to fall into place.

Beulah had gone to work for the blind man the summer after my wife had stopped working for him. Pretty soon Beulah and the blind man had themselves a church wedding. It was a little wedding—who'd want to go to such a wedding in the first place?—just the two of them, plus the minister and the minister's wife. But it was a church wedding just the same. It was what Beulah had wanted, he'd said. But even then Beulah must have been carrying the cancer in her glands. After they had been inseparable for eight years—my wife's word, *inseparable*—Beulah's health went into a rapid decline. She died in a Seattle hospital room, the blind man sitting beside the bed and holding on to her hand. They'd married, lived and worked together, slept together—had sex, sure—and then the blind man had to bury her. All this without his having ever seen what the goddamned woman looked like. It was beyond my understanding. Hearing this, I felt sorry for the blind man for a little bit. And then I found myself thinking what a pitiful life this woman must have led. Imagine a woman who could never see herself as she was seen in the eyes of her loved one. A woman who could go on day after day and never receive the smallest compliment from her beloved. A woman whose husband could never read the expression on her face, be it misery or something better. Someone who could wear makeup or not—what difference to him? She could, if she wanted, wear green eye-shadow around one eye, a straight pin in her nostril, yellow slacks, and purple shoes, no matter. And then to slip off into death, the blind man's hand on her hand, his blind eyes streaming tears—I'm imagining now—her last thought maybe this: that he never even knew what she looked like, and she on an express to the grave. Robert was left with a small insurance policy and a half of a twenty-peso Mexican coin. The other half of the coin went into the box with her. Pathetic.

So when the time rolled around, my wife went to the depot to pick him up. With nothing to do but wait—sure, I blamed him for that— I was having a drink and watching the TV when I heard the car pull into the drive. I got up from the sofa with my drink and went to the window to have a look.

I saw my wife laughing as she parked the car. I saw her get out of the car and shut the door. She was still wearing a smile. Just amazing. She went around to the other side of the car to where the blind man was already starting to get out. This blind man, feature this, he was wearing a full beard! A beard on a blind man! Too much, I say. The blind man reached into the backseat and dragged out a suitcase. My wife took his arm, shut the car door, and, talking all the way, moved him down the drive and then up the steps to the front porch. I turned off the TV. I finished my drink, rinsed the glass, dried my hands. Then I went to the door.

My wife said, "I want you to meet Robert. Robert, this is my husband. I've told you all about him." She was beaming. She had this blind man by his coat sleeve.

The blind man let go of his suitcase and up came his hand.   20

I took it. He squeezed hard, held my hand, and then he let it go.

"I feel like we've already met," he boomed.

"Likewise," I said. I didn't know what else to say. Then I said, "Welcome. I've heard a lot about you." We began to move then, a little group, from the porch into the living room, my wife guiding him by the arm. The blind man was carrying his suitcase in his other hand. My wife said things like, "To your left here, Robert. That's right. Now watch it, there's a chair. That's it. Sit down right here. This is the sofa. We just bought this sofa two weeks ago."

I started to say something about the old sofa. I'd liked that old sofa. But I didn't say anything. Then I wanted to say something else, small-talk, about the scenic ride along the Hudson.[2] How going *to* New York, you should sit on the right-hand side of the train, and coming *from* New York, the left-hand side.

"Did you have a good train ride?" I said. "Which side of the train did   25
you sit on, by the way?"

"What a question, which side!" my wife said. "What's it matter which side?" she said.

"I just asked," I said.

"Right side," the blind man said. "I hadn't been on a train in nearly forty years. Not since I was a kid. With my folks. That's been a long time. I'd nearly forgotten the sensation. I have winter in my beard now," he said. "So I've been told, anyway. Do I look distinguished, my dear?" the blind man said to my wife.

"You look distinguished, Robert," she said. "Robert," she said. "Robert, it's just so good to see you."

My wife finally took her eyes off the blind man and looked at me.   30
I had the feeling she didn't like what she saw. I shrugged.

I've never met, or personally known, anyone who was blind. This blind man was late forties, a heavy-set, balding man with stooped shoulders, as

---

[2] *Hudson:* A river in New York State.

if he carried a great weight there. He wore brown slacks, brown shoes, a light-brown shirt, a tie, a sports coat. Spiffy. He also had this full beard. But he didn't use a cane and he didn't wear dark glasses. I'd always thought dark glasses were a must for the blind. Fact was, I wished he had a pair. At first glance, his eyes looked like anyone else's eyes. But if you looked close, there was something different about them. Too much white in the iris, for one thing, and the pupils seemed to move around in the sockets without his knowing it or being able to stop it. Creepy. As I stared at his face, I saw the left pupil turn in toward his nose while the other made an effort to keep in one place. But it was only an effort, for that eye was on the roam without his knowing it or wanting it to be.

I said, "Let me get you a drink. What's your pleasure? We have a little of everything. It's one of our pastimes."

"Bub, I'm a Scotch man myself," he said fast enough in this big voice.

"Right," I said. Bub! "Sure you are. I knew it."

35   He let his fingers touch his suitcase, which was sitting alongside the sofa. He was taking his bearings. I didn't blame him for that.

"I'll move that up to your room," my wife said.

"No, that's fine," the blind man said loudly. "It can go up when I go up."

"A little water with the Scotch?" I said.

"Very little," he said.

40   "I knew it," I said.

He said, "Just a tad. The Irish actor, Barry Fitzgerald? I'm like that fellow. When I drink water, Fitzgerald said, I drink water. When I drink whiskey, I drink whiskey." My wife laughed. The blind man brought his hand up under his beard. He lifted his beard slowly and let it drop.

I did the drinks, three big glasses of Scotch with a splash of water in each. Then we made ourselves comfortable and talked about Robert's travels. First the long flight from the West Coast to Connecticut, we covered that. Then from Connecticut up here by train. We had another drink concerning that leg of the trip.

I remembered having read somewhere that the blind didn't smoke because, as speculation had it, they couldn't see the smoke they exhaled. I thought I knew that much and that much only about blind people. But this blind man smoked his cigarette down to the nubbin and then lit another one. This blind man filled his ashtray and my wife emptied it.

When we sat down at the table for dinner, we had another drink. My wife heaped Robert's plate with cube steak, scalloped potatoes, green beans. I buttered him up two slices of bread. I said, "Here's bread and butter for you." I swallowed some of my drink. "Now let us pray," I said, and the blind man lowered his head. My wife looked at me, her mouth agape. "Pray the phone won't ring and the food doesn't get cold," I said.

We dug in. We ate everything there was to eat on the table. We ate 45 like there was no tomorrow. We didn't talk. We ate. We scarfed. We grazed that table. We were into serious eating. The blind man had right away located his foods, he knew just where everything was on his plate. I watched with admiration as he used his knife and fork on the meat. He'd cut two pieces of meat, fork the meat into his mouth, and then go all out for the scalloped potatoes, the beans next, and then he'd tear off a hunk of buttered bread and eat that. He'd follow this up with a big drink of milk. It didn't seem to bother him to use his fingers once in a while, either.

We finished everything, including half a strawberry pie. For a few moments, we sat as if stunned. Sweat beaded on our faces. Finally, we got up from the table and left the dirty plates. We didn't look back. We took ourselves into the living room and sank into our places again. Robert and my wife sat on the sofa. I took the big chair. We had us two or three more drinks while they talked about the major things that had come to pass for them in the past ten years. For the most part, I just listened. Now and then I joined in. I didn't want him to think I'd left the room, and I didn't want her to think I was feeling left out. They talked of things that had happened to them—to them!—these past ten years. I waited in vain to hear my name on my wife's sweet lips: "And then my dear husband came into my life"—something like that. But I heard nothing of the sort. More talk of Robert. Robert had done a little of everything, it seemed, a regular blind jack-of-all-trades. But most recently he and his wife had had an Amway distributorship, from which, I gathered, they'd earned their living, such as it was. The blind man was also a ham radio operator.[3] He talked in his loud voice about conversations he'd had with fellow operators in Guam, in the Philippines, in Alaska, and even in Tahiti. He said he'd have a lot of friends there if he ever wanted to go visit those places. From time to time, he'd turn his blind face toward me, put his hand under his beard, ask me something. How long had I been in my present position? (Three years.) Did I like my work? (I didn't.) Was I going to stay with it? (What were the options?) Finally, when I thought he was beginning to run down, I got up and turned on the TV.

My wife looked at me with irritation. She was heading toward a boil. Then she looked at the blind man and said, "Robert, do you have a TV?"

The blind man said, "My dear, I have two TVs. I have a color set and a black-and-white thing, an old relic. It's funny, but if I turn the TV on, and I'm always turning it on, I turn on the color set. It's funny, don't you think?"

---

[3] *ham radio operator:* A licensed amateur radio operator.

I didn't know what to say to that. I had absolutely nothing to say to that. No opinion. So I watched the news program and tried to listen to what the announcer was saying.

50 "This is a color TV," the blind man said. "Don't ask me how, but I can tell."

"We traded up a while ago," I said.

The blind man had another taste of his drink. He lifted his beard, sniffed it, and let it fall. He leaned forward on the sofa. He positioned his ashtray on the coffee table, then put the lighter to his cigarette. He leaned back on the sofa and crossed his legs at the ankles.

My wife covered her mouth, and then she yawned. She stretched. She said, "I think I'll go upstairs and put on my robe. I think I'll change into something else. Robert, you make yourself comfortable," she said.

"I'm comfortable," the blind man said.

55 "I want you to feel comfortable in this house," she said.

"I am comfortable," the blind man said.

After she'd left the room, he and I listened to the weather report and then to the sports roundup. By that time, she'd been gone so long I didn't know if she was going to come back. I thought she might have gone to bed. I wished she'd come back downstairs. I didn't want to be left alone with a blind man. I asked him if he wanted another drink, and he said sure. Then I asked if he wanted to smoke some dope with me. I said I'd just rolled a number. I hadn't, but I planned to do so in about two shakes.

"I'll try some with you," he said.

"Damn right," I said. "That's the stuff."

60 I got our drinks and sat down on the sofa with him. Then I rolled us two fat numbers. I lit one and passed it. I brought it to his fingers. He took it and inhaled.

"Hold it as long as you can," I said. I could tell he didn't know the first thing.

My wife came back downstairs wearing her pink robe and her pink slippers.

"What do I smell?" she said.

"We thought we'd have us some cannabis," I said.

65 My wife gave me a savage look. Then she looked at the blind man and said, "Robert, I didn't know you smoked."

He said, "I do now, my dear. There's a first time for everything. But I don't feel anything yet."

"This stuff is pretty mellow," I said. "This stuff is mild. It's dope you can reason with," I said. "It doesn't mess you up."

"Not much it doesn't, bub," he said, and laughed.

My wife sat on the sofa between the blind man and me. I passed her the number. She took it and toked[4] and then passed it back to me. "Which way is this going?" she said. Then she said, "I shouldn't be smoking this. I can hardly keep my eyes open as it is. That dinner did me in. I shouldn't have eaten so much."

"It was the strawberry pie," the blind man said. "That's what did it," he said, and he laughed his big laugh. Then he shook his head.   70

"There's more strawberry pie," I said.

"Do you want some more, Robert?" my wife said.

"Maybe in a little while," he said.

We gave our attention to the TV. My wife yawned again. She said, "Your bed is made up when you feel like going to bed, Robert. I know you must have had a long day. When you're ready to go to bed, say so." She pulled his arm. "Robert?"

He came to and said, "I've had a real nice time. This beats tapes, doesn't it?"   75

I said, "Coming at you," and I put the number between his fingers. He inhaled, held the smoke, and then let it go. It was like he'd been doing it since he was nine years old.

"Thanks, bub," he said. "But I think this is all for me. I think I'm beginning to feel it," he said. He held the burning roach out for my wife.

"Same here," she said. "Ditto. Me, too." She took the roach and passed it to me. "I may just sit here for a while between you two guys with my eyes closed. But don't let me bother you, okay? Either one of you. If it bothers you, say so. Otherwise, I may just sit here with my eyes closed until you're ready to go to bed," she said. "Your bed's made up, Robert, when you're ready. It's right next to our room at the top of the stairs. We'll show you up when you're ready. You wake me up now, you guys, if I fall asleep." She said that and then she closed her eyes and went to sleep.

The news program ended. I got up and changed the channel. I sat back down on the sofa. I wished my wife hadn't pooped out. Her head lay across the back of the sofa, her mouth open. She'd turned so that her robe slipped away from her legs, exposing a juicy thigh. I reached to draw her robe back over her, and it was then that I glanced at the blind man. What the hell! I flipped the robe open again.

"You say when you want some strawberry pie," I said.   80

"I will," he said.

I said, "Are you tired? Do you want me to take you up to your bed? Are you ready to hit the hay?"

---

[4]*toked:* Inhaled.

"Not yet," he said. "No, I'll stay up with you, bub. If that's all right. I'll stay up until you're ready to turn in. We haven't had a chance to talk. Know what I mean? I feel like me and her monopolized the evening." He lifted his beard and he let it fall. He picked up his cigarettes and his lighter.

"That's all right," I said. Then I said, "I'm glad for the company."

85   And I guess I was. Every night I smoked dope and stayed up as long as I could before I fell asleep. My wife and I hardly ever went to bed at the same time. When I did go to sleep, I had these dreams. Sometimes I'd wake up from one of them, my heart going crazy.

Something about the church and the Middle Ages was on the TV. Not your run-of-the-mill TV fare. I wanted to watch something else. I turned to the other channels. But there was nothing on them, either. So I turned back to the first channel and apologized.

"Bub, it's all right," the blind man said. "It's fine with me. Whatever you want to watch is okay. I'm always learning something. Learning never ends. It won't hurt me to learn something tonight. I got ears," he said.

We didn't say anything for a time. He was leaning forward with his head turned at me, his right ear aimed in the direction of the set. Very disconcerting. Now and then his eyelids drooped and then they snapped open again. Now and then he put his fingers into his beard and tugged, like he was thinking about something he was hearing on the television.

On the screen, a group of men wearing cowls was being set upon and tormented by men dressed in skeleton costumes and men dressed as devils. The men dressed as devils wore devil masks, horns, and long tails. This pageant was part of a procession. The Englishman who was narrating the thing said it took place in Spain once a year. I tried to explain to the blind man what was happening.

90   "Skeletons," he said. "I know about skeletons," he said, and nodded.

The TV showed this one cathedral. Then there was a long, slow look at another one. Finally, the picture switched to the famous one in Paris, with its flying buttresses[5] and its spires reaching up to the clouds. The camera pulled away to show the whole of the cathedral rising above the skyline.

There were times when the Englishman who was telling the thing would shut up, would simply let the camera move around the cathedrals. Or else the camera would tour the countryside, men in fields walking behind oxen. I waited as long as I could. Then I felt I had to say something. I said, "They're showing the outside of this cathedral now. Gargoyles. Little statues carved to look like monsters. Now I guess they're in Italy. Yeah, they're in Italy. There's paintings on the walls of this one church."

---

[5] *flying buttresses:* Supports that are often connected to a building or structure by an arch.

"Are those fresco[6] paintings, bub?" he asked, and he sipped from his drink.

I reached for my glass. But it was empty. I tried to remember what I could remember. "You're asking me are those frescoes?" I said. "That's a good question. I don't know."

The camera moved to a cathedral outside Lisbon.[7] The differences in 95 the Portuguese cathedral compared with the French and Italian were not that great. But they were there. Mostly the interior stuff. Then something occurred to me, and I said, "Something has occurred to me. Do you have any idea what a cathedral is? What they look like, that is? Do you follow me? If somebody says cathedral to you, do you have any notion what they're talking about? Do you know the difference between that and a Baptist church, say?"

He let the smoke dribble from his mouth. "I know they took hundreds of workers fifty or a hundred years to build," he said. "I just heard the man say that, of course. I know generations of the same families worked on a cathedral. I heard him say that, too. The men who began their life's work on them, they never lived to see the completion of their work. In that wise, bub, they're no different from the rest of us, right?" He laughed. Then his eyelids drooped again. His head nodded. He seemed to be snoozing. Maybe he was imagining himself in Portugal. The TV was showing another cathedral now. This one was in Germany. The Englishman's voice droned on. "Cathedrals," the blind man said. He sat up and rolled his head back and forth. "If you want the truth, bub, that's about all I know. What I just said. What I heard him say. But maybe you could describe one to me? I wish you'd do it. I'd like that. If you want to know, I really don't have a good idea."

I stared hard at the shot of the cathedral on the TV. How could I even begin to describe it? But say my life depended on it. Say my life was being threatened by an insane guy who said I had to do it or else.

I stared some more at the cathedral before the picture flipped off into the countryside. There was no use. I turned to the blind man and said, "To begin with, they're very tall." I was looking around the room for clues. "They reach way up. Up and up. Toward the sky. They're so big, some of them, they have to have these supports. To help hold them up, so to speak. These supports are called buttresses. They remind me of viaducts,[8] for some reason. But maybe you don't know viaducts, either? Sometimes the

---

[6]*fresco:* Painted plaster.

[7]*Lisbon:* The capital of Portugal.

[8]*viaducts:* Long, elevated roadways.

cathedrals have devils and such carved into the front. Sometimes lords and ladies. Don't ask me why this is," I said.

He was nodding. The whole upper part of his body seemed to be moving back and forth.

100   "I'm not doing so good, am I?" I said.

He stopped nodding and leaned forward on the edge of the sofa. As he listened to me, he was running his fingers through his beard. I wasn't getting through to him, I could see that. But he waited for me to go on just the same. He nodded, like he was trying to encourage me. I tried to think what else to say. "They're really big," I said. "They're massive. They're built of stone. Marble, too, sometimes. In those olden days, when they built cathedrals, men wanted to be close to God. In those olden days, God was an important part of everyone's life. You could tell this from their cathedral-building. I'm sorry," I said, "but it looks like that's the best I can do for you. I'm just no good at it."

"That's all right, bub," the blind man said. "Hey, listen. I hope you don't mind my asking you. Can I ask you something? Let me ask you a simple question, yes or no. I'm just curious and there's no offense. You're my host. But let me ask if you are in any way religious? You don't mind my asking?"

I shook my head. He couldn't see that, though. A wink is the same as a nod to a blind man. "I guess I don't believe in it. In anything. Sometimes it's hard. You know what I'm saying?"

"Sure, I do," he said.

105   "Right," I said.

The Englishman was still holding forth. My wife sighed in her sleep. She drew a long breath and went on with her sleeping.

"You'll have to forgive me," I said. "But I can't tell you what a cathedral looks like. It just isn't in me to do it. I can't do any more than I've done."

The blind man sat very still, his head down, as he listened to me.

I said, "The truth is, cathedrals don't mean anything special to me. Nothing. Cathedrals. They're something to look at on late-night TV. That's all they are."

110   It was then that the blind man cleared his throat. He brought something up. He took a handkerchief from his back pocket. Then he said, "I get it, bub. It's okay. It happens. Don't worry about it," he said. "Hey, listen to me. Will you do me a favor? I got an idea. Why don't you find us some heavy paper? And a pen. We'll do something. We'll draw one together. Get us a pen and some heavy paper. Go on, bub, get the stuff," he said.

So I went upstairs. My legs felt like they didn't have any strength in them. They felt like they did after I'd done some running. In my wife's room, I looked around. I found some ballpoints in a little basket on her table. And then I tried to think where to look for the kind of paper he was talking about.

Downstairs, in the kitchen, I found a shopping bag with onion skins in the bottom of the bag. I emptied the bag and shook it. I brought it into the living room and sat down with it near his legs. I moved some things, smoothed the wrinkles from the bag, spread it out on the coffee table.

The blind man got down from the sofa and sat next to me on the carpet.

He ran his fingers over the paper. He went up and down the sides of the paper. The edges, even the edges. He fingered the corners.

"All right," he said. "All right, let's do her."   115

He found my hand, the hand with the pen. He closed his hand over my hand. "Go ahead, bub, draw," he said. "Draw. You'll see. I'll follow along with you. It'll be okay. Just begin now like I'm telling you. You'll see. Draw," the blind man said.

So I began. First I drew a box that looked like a house. It could have been the house I lived in. Then I put a roof on it. At either end of the roof, I drew spires. Crazy.

"Swell," he said. "Terrific. You're doing fine," he said. "Never thought anything like this could happen in your lifetime, did you, bub? Well, it's a strange life, we all know that. Go on now. Keep it up."

I put in windows with arches. I drew flying buttresses. I hung great doors. I couldn't stop. The TV station went off the air. I put down the pen and closed and opened my fingers. The blind man felt around over the paper. He moved the tips of his fingers over the paper, all over what I had drawn, and he nodded.

"Doing fine," the blind man said.   120

I took up the pen again, and he found my hand. I kept at it. I'm no artist. But I kept drawing just the same.

My wife opened up her eyes and gazed at us. She sat up on the sofa, her robe hanging open. She said, "What are you doing? Tell me, I want to know."

I didn't answer her.

The blind man said, "We're drawing a cathedral. Me and him are working on it. Press hard," he said to me. "That's right. That's good," he said. "Sure. You got it, bub, I can tell. You didn't think you could. But you can, can't you? You're cooking with gas now. You know what I'm saying? We're going to really have us something here in a minute. How's the old arm?" he said. "Put some people in there now. What's a cathedral without people?"

My wife said, "What's going on? Robert, what are you doing? What's 125 going on?"

"It's all right," he said to her. "Close your eyes now," the blind man said to me.

I did it. I closed them just like he said.

"Are they closed?" he said. "Don't fudge."

"They're closed," I said.

130   "Keep them that way," he said. He said, "Don't stop now. Draw."

So we kept on with it. His fingers rode my fingers as my hand went over the paper. It was like nothing else in my life up to now.

Then he said, "I think that's it. I think you got it," he said. "Take a look. What do you think?"

But I had my eyes closed. I thought I'd keep them that way for a little longer. I thought it was something I ought to do.

"Well?" he said. "Are you looking?"

135   My eyes were still closed. I was in my house. I knew that. But I didn't feel like I was inside anything.

"It's really something," I said.

Reading and Reacting

1. Who is the narrator? What do we know about him? Why does the impending visit by the blind man disturb him?

2. At several points in the story, the narrator's wife loses patience with him. What causes her displeasure? What do her reactions reveal about the wife? about the narrator?

3. Why did the narrator's wife leave her first husband? What qualities in the narrator might have led his wife to marry him?

4. Why is the narrator's wife so devoted to the blind man? What does she gain from her relationship with him?

5. According to the narrator, his wife never forgot the blind man's running his fingers over her face. Why is this experience so important to her?

6. Toward the end of the story, the blind man asks the narrator to describe a cathedral. Why is the narrator unable to do so? What does his inability to do so reveal about him?

7. Why does the blind man tell the narrator to close his eyes while he is drawing? What does he hope to teach him? What is the narrator able to "see" with his eyes shut that he cannot see with them open?

8. In paragraph 96, the blind man observes that the men who began work on a cathedral never lived to see it completed. In this way, he says, "they're no different from the rest of us." What does the cathedral symbolize to the blind man? What does it come to symbolize to the narrator?

9. **Journal Entry** The blind man is an old friend of the narrator's wife. Why then does he focus on the narrator? In what way is the narrator's spiritual development the blind man's gift to the narrator's wife?

10. CRITICAL PERSPECTIVE Critic Kirk Nesset, in his discussion of "Cathedral," notes that the narrator becomes more open as the story progresses, and that this coming out is mirrored by the rhetoric of the story. Early on in the story, the narrator feels momentarily "sorry for the blind man," his insulated hardness beginning to soften. As the walls of his resentment noticeably crack, he watches with "admiration" as Robert eats, recognizing Robert's handicap to be "no impairment to his performance at the dinner table. . . . Like Robert, who is on a journey by train, dropping in on friends and relatives, trying to get over the loss of his wife, the narrator is also on a journey, one signaled by signposts in his language and played out by the events of the story he tells."

Do you agree that the narrator becomes more open? If so, can you cite any other instances where the words he chooses reflect this increasing openness?

Related Works: "Gryphon" (p. 172), "Doe Season" (p. 395), "When I Heard the Learn'd Astronomer" (p. 536), "The Value of Education" (p. 549), "On First Looking into Chapman's Homer" (p. 640), "Batter My Heart, Three-Personed God" (p. 756), "God's Grandeur" (p. 769)

Mathew B. Brady/Bettmann/Corbis

NATHANIEL HAWTHORNE (1804–1864) was born in Salem, Massachusetts, the great-great-grandson of a judge who presided over the infamous Salem witch trials. After his sea captain father was killed on a voyage when Hawthorne was four years old, his childhood was one of genteel poverty. An uncle paid for his education at Bowdoin College in Maine, where Hawthorne's friends included a future president of the United States, Franklin Pierce, who in 1853 appointed him U.S. consul in Liverpool, England. Hawthorne published four novels—*The Scarlet Letter* (1850), *The House of the Seven Gables* (1851), *The Blithedale Romance* (1852), and *The Marble Faun* (1860)—and more than one hundred short stories and sketches.

Hawthorne referred to his own work as *romance*. He used this term to mean not an escape from reality but rather a method of confronting "the depths of our common nature" and "the truth of the heart." His stories probe the dark side of human nature and frequently paint a world that is virtuous on the surface but (as Young Goodman Brown comes to believe) "one stain of guilt, one mighty blood spot" beneath. Hawthorne's stories often emphasize the ambiguity of human experience. For example, the reader is left to wonder whether Goodman Brown actually saw a witch's coven or dreamed about the event. For Hawthorne, what is important is Brown's recognition that evil may be found everywhere. "Young Goodman Brown," as Hawthorne's neighbor and friend Herman Melville once said, is a tale "as deep as Dante."

Cultural Context During the five months of the Salem witch trials of 1692, nineteen women and men accused of being witches were executed by hanging. The accusations began when a few young girls claimed they were possessed by the devil and accused three Salem women of witchcraft. As the hysteria grew throughout Massachusetts, the list of the accused grew as well. Eventually, 150 people were imprisoned before the governor dismissed the special witchcraft court and released the remaining twenty-two prisoners. It is in this historical setting that "Young Goodman Brown" takes place.

Young Goodman[1] Brown (1835)

Young Goodman Brown came forth at sunset, into the street of Salem village, but put his head back, after crossing the threshold, to exchange a parting kiss with his young wife. And Faith, as the wife was aptly named, thrust her own pretty head into the street, letting the wind play with the pink ribbons of her cap, while she called to Goodman Brown.

"Dearest heart," whispered she, softly and rather sadly, when her lips were close to his ear, "prithee, put off your journey until sunrise, and sleep in your own bed to-night. A lone woman is troubled with such dreams and such thoughts, that she's afeard of herself, sometimes. Pray, tarry with me this night, dear husband, of all nights in the year!"

"My love and my Faith," replied young Goodman Brown, "of all nights in the year, this one night must I tarry away from thee. My journey, as thou callest it, forth and back again, must needs be done 'twixt now and sunrise. What, my sweet, pretty wife, dost thou doubt me already, and we but three months married!"

"Then God bless you!" said Faith with the pink ribbons, "and may you find all well, when you come back."

5   "Amen!" cried Goodman Brown. "Say thy prayers, dear Faith, and go to bed at dusk, and no harm will come to thee."

So they parted; and the young man pursued his way, until, being about to turn the corner by the meeting-house, he looked back and saw the head of Faith still peeping after him, with a melancholy air, in spite of her pink ribbons.

"Poor little Faith!" thought he, for his heart smote him. "What a wretch am I, to leave her on such an errand! She talks of dreams, too. Methought, as she spoke, there was trouble in her face, as if a dream had warned her what work is to be done to-night. But no, no! 't would kill her to think it. Well; she's a blessed angel on earth; and after this one night, I'll cling to her skirts and follow her to Heaven."

With this excellent resolve for the future, Goodman Brown felt himself justified in making more haste on his present evil purpose. He

---

[1]*Goodman:* A form of address, similar to *Mr.*, meaning "husband."

had taken a dreary road, darkened by all the gloomiest trees of the forest, which barely stood aside to let the narrow path creep through, and closed immediately behind. It was as lonely as could be; and there is this peculiarity in such a solitude, that the traveller knows not who may be concealed by the innumerable trunks and the thick boughs overhead; so that, with lonely footsteps, he may yet be passing through an unseen multitude.

"There may be a devilish Indian behind every tree," said Goodman Brown to himself; and he glanced fearfully behind him, as he added, "What if the devil himself should be at my very elbow!"

His head being turned back, he passed a crook of the road, and 10 looking forward again, beheld the figure of a man, in grave and decent attire, seated at the foot of an old tree. He arose at Goodman Brown's approach, and walked onward, side by side with him.

"You are late, Goodman Brown," said he. "The clock of the Old South[2] was striking, as I came through Boston; and that is full fifteen minutes agone."

"Faith kept me back awhile," replied the young man, with a tremor in his voice, caused by the sudden appearance of his companion, though not wholly unexpected.

It was now deep dusk in the forest, and deepest in that part of it where these two were journeying. As nearly as could be discerned, the second traveller was about fifty years old, apparently in the same rank of life as Goodman Brown, and bearing a considerable resemblance to him, though perhaps more in expression than features. Still, they might have been taken for father and son. And yet, though the elder person was as simply clad as the younger, and as simple in manner too, he had an indescribable air of one who knew the world, and would not have felt abashed at the governor's dinner-table, or in King William's[3] court, were it possible that his affairs should call him thither. But the only thing about him that could be fixed upon as remarkable, was his staff, which bore the likeness of a great black snake, so curiously wrought, that it might almost be seen to twist and wriggle itself like a living serpent. This, of course, must have been an ocular deception, assisted by the uncertain light.

"Come, Goodman Brown!" cried his fellow-traveller, "this is a dull pace for the beginning of a journey. Take my staff, if you are so soon weary."

---

[2]*Old South:* Old South Church in Boston, renowned meeting place for American patriots during the Revolution.

[3]*King William:* William III, king of England from 1689 to 1702.

15   "Friend," said the other, exchanging his slow pace for a full stop, "having kept covenant by meeting thee here, it is my purpose now to return whence I came. I have scruples, touching the matter thou wot'st[4] of."

"Sayest thou so?" replied he of the serpent, smiling apart. "Let us walk on, nevertheless, reasoning as we go, and if I convince thee not, thou shalt turn back. We are but a little way in the forest, yet."

"Too far, too far!" exclaimed the goodman, unconsciously resuming his walk. "My father never went into the woods on such an errand, nor his father before him. We have been a race of honest men and good Christians, since the days of the martyrs. And shall I be the first of the name of Brown that ever took this path and kept—"

"Such company, thou wouldst say," observed the elder person, interrupting his pause. "Well said, Goodman Brown! I have been as well acquainted with your family as with ever a one among the Puritans; and that's no trifle to say. I helped your grandfather, the constable, when he lashed the Quaker woman so smartly through the streets of Salem. And it was I that brought your father a pitch-pine knot, kindled at my own hearth, to set fire to an Indian village, in King Philip's war.[5] They were my good friends, both; and many a pleasant walk have we had along this path, and returned merrily after midnight. I would fain be friends with you, for their sake."

"If it be as thou sayest," replied Goodman Brown, "I marvel they never spoke of these matters. Or, verily, I marvel not, seeing that the least rumor of the sort would have driven them from New England. We are a people of prayer, and good works to boot, and abide no such wickedness."

20   "Wickedness or not," said the traveller with the twisted staff, "I have a very general acquaintance here in New England. The deacons of many a church have drunk the communion wine with me; the selectmen, of divers towns, make me their chairman; and a majority of the Great and General Court are firm supporters of my interest. The governor and I, too—but these are state secrets."

"Can this be so!" cried Goodman Brown, with a stare of amazement at his undisturbed companion. "Howbeit, I have nothing to do with the governor and council; they have their own ways, and are no rule for a simple husbandman like me. But, were I to go on with thee, how should I meet the eye of that good old man, our minister, at Salem village? Oh, his voice would make me tremble, both Sabbath-day and lecture-day!"[6]

---

[4]*wot'st of:* Know of.

[5]*King Philip's war:* A war of Indian resistance led by Metacomet of the Wampanoags, known to the English as "King Philip." The war, intended to halt expansion of English settlers in Massachusetts, collapsed after Metacomet's death in August 1676.

[6]*lecture-day:* The day of the midweek sermon, usually Thursday.

Thus far, the elder traveller had listened with due gravity, but now burst into a fit of irrepressible mirth, shaking himself so violently, that his snakelike staff actually seemed to wriggle in sympathy.

"Ha, ha, ha!" shouted he, again and again; then composing himself, "Well, go on, Goodman Brown, go on; but, prithee, don't kill me with laughing!"

"Well, then, to end the matter at once," said Goodman Brown, considerably nettled, "there is my wife, Faith. It would break her dear little heart; and I'd rather break my own!"

"Nay, if that be the case," answered the other, "e'en go thy ways, Good-   25
man Brown. I would not, for twenty old women like the one hobbling before us, that Faith should come to any harm."

As he spoke, he pointed his staff at a female figure on the path, in whom Goodman Brown recognized a very pious and exemplary dame, who had taught him his catechism in youth, and was still his moral and spiritual adviser, jointly with the minister and Deacon Gookin.

"A marvel, truly, that Goody[7] Cloyse should be so far in the wilderness, at nightfall!" said he. "But, with your leave, friend, I shall take a cut through the woods, until we have left this Christian woman behind. Being a stranger to you, she might ask whom I was consorting with, and whither I was going."

"Be it so," said his fellow-traveller. "Betake you to the woods, and let me keep the path."

Accordingly, the young man turned aside, but took care to watch his companion, who advanced softly along the road, until he had come within a staff's length of the old dame. She, meanwhile, was making the best of her way, with singular speed for so aged a woman, and mumbling some indistinct words, a prayer, doubtless, as she went. The traveller put forth his staff, and touched her withered neck with what seemed the serpent's tail.

"The devil!" screamed the pious old lady.   30

"Then Goody Cloyse knows her old friend?" observed the traveller, confronting her, and leaning on his writhing stick.

"Ah, forsooth, and is it your worship, indeed?" cried the good dame. "Yea, truly is it, and in the very image of my old gossip, Goodman Brown, the grandfather of the silly fellow that now is. But, would your worship believe it? my broomstick hath strangely disappeared, stolen, as I suspect, by that unhanged witch, Goody Cory, and that, too, when I was all anointed with the juice of smallage and cinque-foil and wolf's bane[8]—"

---

[7]*Goody:* A contraction of "Goodwife," a term of politeness used in addressing a woman of humble station. Goody Cloyse, like Goody Cory and Martha Carrier, who appear later in the story, was one of the Salem "witches" sentenced in 1692.

[8]*smallage . . . wolf's bane:* Plants believed to have magical powers. Smallage is wild celery.

"Mingled with fine wheat and the fat of a new-born babe," said the shape of old Goodman Brown.

"Ah, your worship knows the recipe," cried the old lady, cackling aloud. "So, as I was saying, being all ready for the meeting, and no horse to ride on, I made up my mind to foot it; for they tell me there is a nice young man to be taken into communion to-night. But now your good worship will lend me your arm, and we shall be there in a twinkling."

35 "That can hardly be," answered her friend. "I may not spare you my arm, Goody Cloyse, but here is my staff, if you will."

So saying, he threw it down at her feet, where, perhaps, it assumed life, being one of the rods which its owner had formerly lent to the Egyptian Magi. Of this fact, however, Goodman Brown could not take cognizance. He had cast his eyes in astonishment, and looking down again, beheld neither Goody Cloyse nor the serpentine staff, but his fellow-traveller alone, who waited for him as calmly as if nothing had happened.

"That old woman taught me my catechism!" said the young man; and there was a world of meaning in this simple comment.

They continued to walk onward, while the elder traveller exhorted his companion to make good speed and persevere in the path, discoursing so aptly, that his arguments seemed rather to spring up in the bosom of his auditor, than to be suggested by himself. As they went he plucked a branch of maple, to serve for a walking-stick, and began to strip it of the twigs and little boughs, which were wet with evening dew. The moment his fingers touched them, they became strangely withered and dried up, as with a week's sunshine. Thus the pair proceeded, at a good free pace, until suddenly, in a gloomy hollow of the road, Goodman Brown sat himself down on the stump of a tree, and refused to go any farther.

"Friend," said he, stubbornly, "my mind is made up. Not another step will I budge on this errand. What if a wretched old woman do choose to go to the devil, when I thought she was going to Heaven! Is that any reason why I should quit my dear Faith, and go after her?"

40 "You will think better of this by and by," said his acquaintance, composedly. "Sit here and rest yourself awhile; and when you feel like moving again, there is my staff to help you along."

Without more words, he threw his companion the maple stick, and was as speedily out of sight as if he had vanished into the deepening gloom. The young man sat a few moments by the roadside, applauding himself greatly, and thinking with how clear a conscience he should meet the minister, in his morning walk, nor shrink from the eye of good old Deacon Gookin. And what calm sleep would be his, that very night, which was to have been spent so wickedly, but purely and sweetly now, in the arms of Faith! Amidst these pleasant and praiseworthy meditations, Goodman Brown heard the tramp of horses along the road, and deemed it advisable to conceal himself within the verge of the forest, conscious of the guilty purpose that had brought him thither, though now so happily turned from it.

On came the hoof-tramps and the voices of the riders, two grave old voices, conversing soberly as they drew near. These mingled sounds appeared to pass along the road, within a few yards of the young man's hiding-place; but owing, doubtless, to the depth of the gloom, at that particular spot, neither the travellers nor their steeds were visible. Though their figures brushed the small boughs by the wayside, it could not be seen that they intercepted, even for a moment, the faint gleam from the strip of bright sky, athwart which they must have passed. Goodman Brown alternately crouched and stood on tiptoe, pulling aside the branches, and thrusting forth his head as far as he durst, without discerning so much as a shadow. It vexed him the more, because he could have sworn, were such a thing possible, that he recognized the voices of the minister and Deacon Gookin, jogging along quietly, as they were wont to do, when bound to some ordination or ecclesiastical council. While yet within hearing, one of the riders stopped to pluck a switch.

"Of the two, reverend Sir," said the voice like the deacon's, "I had rather miss an ordination dinner than to-night's meeting. They tell me that some of our community are to be here from Falmouth and beyond, and others from Connecticut and Rhode Island; besides several of the Indian powwows, who, after their fashion, know almost as much deviltry as the best of us. Moreover, there is a goodly young woman to be taken into communion."

"Mighty well, Deacon Gookin!" replied the solemn old tones of the minister. "Spur up, or we shall be late. Nothing can be done, you know, until I get on the ground."

The hoofs clattered again, and the voices, talking so strangely in the 45 empty air, passed on through the forest, where no church had ever been gathered, nor solitary Christian prayed. Whither, then, could these holy men be journeying, so deep into the heathen wilderness? Young Goodman Brown caught hold of a tree, for support, being ready to sink down on the ground, faint and over-burthened with the heavy sickness of his heart. He looked up to the sky, doubting whether there really was a Heaven above him. Yet, there was the blue arch, and the stars brightening in it.

"With Heaven above, and Faith below, I will yet stand firm against the devil!" cried Goodman Brown.

While he still gazed upward, into the deep arch of the firmament, and had lifted his hands to pray, a cloud, though no wind was stirring, hurried across the zenith, and hid the brightening stars. The blue sky was still visible, except directly overhead, where this black mass of cloud was sweeping swiftly northward. Aloft in the air, as if from the depths of the cloud, came a confused and doubtful sound of voices. Once, the listener fancied that he could distinguish the accents of townspeople of his own, men and women, both pious and ungodly, many of whom he had met at the communion-table, and had seen others rioting at the tavern. The next moment, so indistinct were the sounds, he doubted whether he had heard aught but the murmur of the old forest, whispering without a wind. Then came a stronger swell of those familiar tones, heard daily in the sunshine, at Salem village, but never, until now, from a cloud at night. There was one voice, of a young woman, uttering lamentations, yet with an uncertain sorrow, and entreating for some favor, which, perhaps, it would grieve her to obtain. And all the unseen multitude, both saints and sinners, seemed to encourage her onward.

"Faith!" shouted Goodman Brown, in a voice of agony and desperation; and the echoes of the forest mocked him, crying—"Faith! Faith!" as if bewildered wretches were seeking her, all through the wilderness.

The cry of grief, rage, and terror was yet piercing the night, when the unhappy husband held his breath for a response. There was a scream, drowned immediately in a louder murmur of voices fading into far-off laughter, as the dark cloud swept away, leaving the clear and silent sky above Goodman Brown. But something fluttered lightly down through the air, and caught on the branch of a tree. The young man seized it and beheld a pink ribbon.

50   "My Faith is gone!" cried he, after one stupefied moment. "There is no good on earth, and sin is but a name. Come, devil! for to thee is this world given."

And maddened with despair, so that he laughed loud and long, did Goodman Brown grasp his staff and set forth again, at such a rate, that he seemed to fly along the forest path, rather than to walk or run. The road grew wilder and drearier, and more faintly traced, and vanished at length, leaving him in the heart of the dark wilderness, still rushing onward, with the instinct that guides mortal man to evil. The whole forest was peopled with frightful sounds: the creaking of the trees, the howling of wild beasts, and the yell of Indians; while, sometimes, the wind tolled like a distant church bell, and sometimes gave a broad roar around the traveller, as if all Nature was laughing him to scorn. But he was himself the chief horror of the scene, and shrank not from its other horrors.

"Ha! ha! ha!" roared Goodman Brown, when the wind laughed at him. "Let us hear which will laugh loudest! Think not to frighten me with your deviltry! Come witch, come wizard, come Indian powwow, come devil himself! and here comes Goodman Brown. You may as well fear him as he fear you!"

In truth, all through the haunted forest, there could be nothing more frightful than the figure of Goodman Brown. On he flew, among the black pines, brandishing his staff with frenzied gestures, now giving vent to an inspiration of horrid blasphemy, and now shouting forth such laughter, as set all the echoes of the forest laughing like demons around him. The fiend in his own shape is less hideous, than when he rages in the breast of man. Thus sped the demoniac on his course, until, quivering among the trees, he saw a red light before him, as when the felled trunks and branches of a clearing have been set on fire, and throw up their lurid blaze against the sky, at the hour of midnight. He paused, in a lull of the tempest that had driven him onward, and heard the swell of what seemed a hymn, rolling solemnly from a distance, with the weight of many voices. He knew the tune. It was a familiar one in the choir of the village meeting-house. The verse died heavily away, and was lengthened by a chorus, not of human voices, but of all the sounds of the benighted wilderness, pealing in awful harmony together. Goodman Brown cried out; and his cry was lost to his own ear, by its unison with the cry of the desert.

In the interval of silence, he stole forward, until the light glared full upon his eyes. At one extremity of an open space, hemmed in by the dark wall of the forest, arose a rock, bearing some rude, natural resemblance either to an altar or a pulpit, and surrounded by four blazing pines, their tops aflame, their stems untouched, like candles at an evening meeting. The mass of foliage, that had overgrown the summit of the rock, was all on fire, blazing high into the night, and fitfully illuminating the whole field. Each pendent twig and leafy festoon was in a blaze. As the red light arose and fell, a numerous congregation alternately shone forth, then disappeared in shadow, and again grew, as it were, out of the darkness, peopling the heart of the solitary woods at once.

"A grave and dark-clad company!" quoth Goodman Brown.   55

In truth, they were such. Among them, quivering to-and-fro, between gloom and splendor, appeared faces that would be seen, next day, at the council-board of the province, and others which, Sabbath after Sabbath, looked devoutly heavenward, and benignantly over the crowded pews, from the holiest pulpits in the land. Some affirm, that the lady of the governor was there. At least, there were high dames well known to her, and wives of honored husbands, and widows a great multitude, and ancient maidens, all of excellent repute, and fair young girls, who trembled lest their mothers should espy them. Either the sudden gleams of light, flashing over the obscure field, bedazzled Goodman Brown, or he recognized a score of the church members of Salem village, famous for their especial sanctity. Good old Deacon Gookin had arrived, and waited at the skirts of that venerable saint, his reverend pastor. But, irreverently consorting with these grave, reputable, and pious people, these elders of the church, these chaste dames and dewy virgins, there were men of dissolute lives and women of spotted fame, wretches given over to all mean and filthy vice, and suspected even of horrid crimes. It was strange to see, that the good shrank not from the wicked, nor were the sinners abashed by the saints. Scattered, also, among their pale-faced enemies, were the Indian priests, or powwows, who had often scared their native forest with more hideous incantations than any known to English witchcraft.

"But, where is Faith?" thought Goodman Brown; and, as hope came into his heart, he trembled.

Another verse of the hymn arose, a slow and mournful strain, such as the pious love, but joined to words which expressed all that our nature can conceive of sin, and darkly hinted at far more. Unfathomable to mere mortals is the lore of fiends. Verse after verse was sung, and still the chorus of the desert swelled between, like the deepest tone of a mighty organ. And, with the final peal of that dreadful anthem, there came a sound, as if the roaring wind, the rushing streams, the howling beasts, and every other voice of the unconverted wilderness were mingling and according with the voice of guilty man, in homage to the prince of all. The four blazing pines threw up a loftier flame, and obscurely discovered shapes and visages of horror on the smoke-wreaths, above the impious assembly. At the same moment, the fire on the rock shot redly forth, and formed a glowing arch above its base, where now appeared a figure. With reverence be it spoken, the apparition bore no slight similitude, both in garb and manner, to some grave divine of the New England churches.

"Bring forth the converts!" cried a voice, that echoed through the field and rolled into the forest.

60   At the word, Goodman Brown stepped forth from the shadow of the trees, and approached the congregation, with whom he felt a loathful brotherhood, by the sympathy of all that was wicked in his heart. He could have well-nigh sworn, that the shape of his own dead father beckoned him to advance, looking downward from a smoke-wreath, while a woman, with dim features of despair, threw out her hand to warn him back. Was it his mother? But he had no power to retreat one step, nor to resist, even in thought, when the minister and good old Deacon Gookin seized his arms, and led him to the blazing rock. Thither came also the slender form of a veiled female, led between Goody Cloyse, that pious teacher of the catechism, and Martha Carrier, who had received the devil's promise to be queen of hell. A rampant hag was she! And there stood the proselytes, beneath the canopy of fire.

"Welcome, my children," said the dark figure, "to the communion of your race! Ye have found, thus young, your nature and your destiny. My children, look behind you!"

They turned; and flashing forth, as it were, in a sheet of flame, the fiend-worshippers were seen; the smile of welcome gleamed darkly on every visage.

"There," resumed the sable form, "are all whom ye have reverenced from youth. Ye deemed them holier than yourselves, and shrank from your own sin, contrasting it with their lives of righteousness and prayerful aspirations heavenward. Yet, here are they all, in my worshipping assembly! This night it shall be granted you to know their secret deeds; how hoary-bearded elders of the church have whispered wanton words to the young maids of their households; how many a woman, eager for widow's weeds, has given her husband a drink at bedtime, and let him sleep his last sleep in her bosom; how beardless youths have made haste to inherit their father's wealth; and how fair damsels—blush not, sweet ones!—have dug little graves in the garden, and bidden me, the sole guest, to an infant's funeral. By the sympathy of your human hearts for sin, ye shall scent out all the places—whether in church, bedchamber, street, field, or forest—where crime has been committed, and shall exult to behold the whole earth one stain of guilt, one mighty blood-spot. Far more than this! It shall be yours to penetrate, in every bosom, the deep mystery of sin, the fountain of all wicked arts, and which inexhaustibly supplies more evil impulses than human power—than my power, at its utmost!—can make manifest in deeds. And now, my children, look upon each other."

They did so; and, by the blaze of the hell-kindled torches, the wretched man beheld his Faith, and the wife her husband, trembling before that unhallowed altar.

"Lo! there ye stand, my children," said the figure, in a deep and solemn 65 tone, almost sad, with its despairing awfulness, as if his once angelic nature could yet mourn for our miserable race. "Depending upon one another's hearts, ye had still hoped that virtue were not all a dream! Now are ye undeceived!—Evil is the nature of mankind. Evil must be your only happiness. Welcome, again, my children, to the communion of your race!"

"Welcome!" repeated the fiend-worshippers, in one cry of despair and triumph.

And there they stood, the only pair, as it seemed, who were yet hesitating on the verge of wickedness, in this dark world. A basin was hollowed, naturally, in the rock. Did it contain water, reddened by the lurid light? or was it blood? or, perchance, a liquid flame? Herein did the Shape of Evil dip his hand, and prepare to lay the mark of baptism upon their foreheads, that they might be partakers of the mystery of sin, more conscious of the secret guilt of others, both in deed and thought, than they could now be of their own. The husband cast one look at his pale wife, and Faith at him. What polluted wretches would the next glance show them to each other, shuddering alike at what they disclosed and what they saw!

"Faith! Faith!" cried the husband. "Look up to Heaven, and resist the Wicked One!"

Whether Faith obeyed, he knew not. Hardly had he spoken, when he found himself amid calm night and solitude, listening to a roar of the wind, which died heavily away through the forest. He staggered against the rock, and felt it chill and damp, while a hanging twig, that had been all on fire, besprinkled his cheek with the coldest dew.

70   The next morning, young Goodman Brown came slowly into the street of Salem village staring around him like a bewildered man. The good old minister was taking a walk along the grave-yard, to get an appetite for breakfast and meditate his sermon, and bestowed a blessing, as he passed, on Goodman Brown. He shrank from the venerable saint, as if to avoid an anathema. Old Deacon Gookin was at domestic worship, and the holy words of his prayer were heard through the open window. "What God doth the wizard pray to?" quoth Goodman Brown. Goody Cloyse, that excellent old Christian, stood in the early sunshine, at her own lattice, catechising a little girl, who had brought her a pint of morning's milk. Goodman Brown snatched away the child, as from the grasp of the fiend himself. Turning the corner by the meeting-house, he spied the head of Faith, with the pink ribbons, gazing anxiously forth, and bursting into such joy at sight of him that she skipt along the street, and almost kissed her husband before the whole village. But Goodman Brown looked sternly and sadly into her face, and passed on without a greeting.

Had Goodman Brown fallen asleep in the forest, and only dreamed a wild dream of a witch-meeting?

Be it so, if you will. But, alas! it was a dream of evil omen for young Goodman Brown. A stern, a sad, a darkly meditative, a distrustful, if not a desperate man did he become, from the night of that fearful dream. On the Sabbath day, when the congregation were singing a holy psalm, he could not listen, because an anthem of sin rushed loudly upon his ear, and drowned all the blessed strain. When the minister spoke from the pulpit, with power and fervid eloquence, and with his hand on the open Bible, of the sacred truths of our religion, and of saint-like lives and triumphant deaths, and of future bliss or misery unutterable, then did Goodman Brown turn pale, dreading lest the roof should thunder down upon the gray blasphemer and his hearers. Often, awaking suddenly at midnight, he shrank from the bosom of Faith, and at morning or eventide, when the family knelt down at prayer, he scowled, and muttered to himself, and gazed sternly at his wife, and turned away. And when he had lived long, and was borne to his grave, a hoary corpse, followed by Faith, an aged woman, and children and grand-children, a goodly procession, besides neighbors not a few, they carved no hopeful verse upon his tombstone; for his dying hour was gloom.

Reading and Reacting

1. Who is the narrator of "Young Goodman Brown"? What advantages does the narrative point of view give the author?

2. What does young Goodman Brown mean when he says "of all nights in the year, this one night must I tarry away from thee" (par. 3)? What

is important about *this* night, and why does Goodman Brown believe he must journey "'twixt now and sunrise"?

3. Is Goodman Brown surprised to encounter the second traveler on the road, or does he seem to expect him? What is the significance of their encounter? What do you make of the fact that the stranger bears a strong resemblance to young Goodman Brown?

4. What sins are the various characters Goodman Brown meets in the woods guilty of committing?

5. "Young Goodman Brown" has two distinct settings: Salem and the woods. What are the differences between these settings? What significance does each setting have in the story?

6. Which figures in the story are allegorical, and which are symbols? On what evidence do you base your conclusions?

7. Why do the people gather in the woods? Why do they attend the ceremony?

8. Explain the change that takes place in young Goodman Brown at the end of the story. Why can he not listen to the singing of holy psalms or to the minister's sermons? What causes him to turn away from Faith and die in gloom?

9. **JOURNAL ENTRY** At the end of the story, the narrator suggests that Goodman Brown might have fallen asleep and imagined his encounter with the witches. Do you think the events in the story are all a dream?

10. **CRITICAL PERSPECTIVE** In *The Power of Blackness*, his classic study of nineteenth-century American writers, Harry Levin observes that Hawthorne had doubts about conventional religion. This, Levin believes, is why all efforts to read an enlightening theological message into Hawthorne's works are "doomed to failure."

    What comment do you think Hawthorne is making in "Young Goodman Brown" about religious faith?

Related Works: "Greasy Lake" (p. 425), "Where Are You Going, Where Have You Been?" (p. 453), "La Belle Dame sans Merci: A Ballad" (p. 771)

WRITING SUGGESTIONS: Symbol, Allegory, and Myth

1. In "Cathedral" and "Young Goodman Brown," certain minor characters offer the possibility of salvation or healing. For example, in "Cathedral," The blind man holds out the possibility of healing to the narrator, and in "Young Goodman Brown," Faith offers her husband salvation from evil. Write an essay in which you examine the symbolic roles these characters play.

2. Strangers figure prominently in "Young Goodman Brown" and "Cathedral." Write an essay in which you discuss the possible symbolic significance of strangers in each story. If you like, you may also discuss Arnold Friend in "Where Are You Going, Where Have You Been?" (p. 453) or The Misfit in "A Good Man Is Hard to Find" (p. 295).

3. Write an essay in which you discuss the use of symbols in "Young Goodman Brown" or Cathedral.

4. If Shirley Jackson had wished to write "The Lottery" as an allegory whose purpose was to expose the evils of Nazi Germany, what revisions would she have had to make to convey the dangers of blind obedience to authority? Consider the story's symbols, the characters (and their names), and the setting.

5. In literary works, objects can function as symbols. In this chapter, for example, the quilt in "Everyday Use" and the box in "The Lottery" take on symbolic significance. Write an essay in which you analyze objects that have symbolic significance in two or three of the stories in this text and discuss how these objects help to convey the main themes of the stories in which they appear.

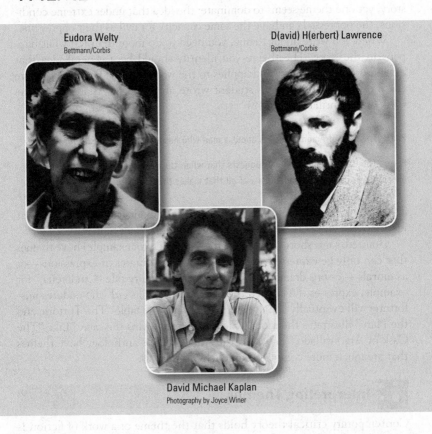

CHAPTER 13

THEME

Eudora Welty
Bettmann/Corbis

D(avid) H(erbert) Lawrence
Bettmann/Corbis

David Michael Kaplan
Photography by Joyce Winer

The **theme** of a work of literature is its central or dominant idea. *Theme* is
not the same as *plot* or *subject*, two terms with which it is sometimes confused. A summary of the **plot** of Tadeusz Borowski's "Silence," a story about
survivors of the Holocaust, could be, "Prisoners are liberated from a concentration camp, and, despite the warnings of the American officer, they kill a
captured German guard." The statement "'Silence' is about freed prisoners
and a guard" could define the **subject** of the story. A statement of the theme

381

of "Silence," however, has to do more than summarize its plot or define its subject; it has to convey the values and ideas expressed by the story.

Many effective stories are complex, expressing more than one theme, and "Silence" is no exception. You could say that "Silence" suggests that human beings have a need for vengeance. You could also say the story demonstrates that silence is sometimes the only response possible when people confront unspeakable horrors. Both these themes—and others—are expressed in the story, yet one theme seems to dominate: the idea that under extreme conditions, the oppressed can have the same capacity for evil as their oppressors.

When you write about theme, you need to do more than tell what happens in the story. The theme you identify should be a general idea that extends beyond the story and applies to the world outside fiction. Compare these two statements that a student wrote about Edgar Allan Poe's "The Cask of Amontillado" (p. 249):

Poe's "The Cask of Amontillado" is about a man who has an obsessive desire for revenge.

Poe's "The Cask of Amontillado" suggests that when the desire for revenge becomes obsessive, it can deprive individuals of all that makes them human.

The first statement merely tells what the story is about; the second statement identifies the story's theme, a general observation about humanity.

Granted, some short works (fairy tales or fables, for example) have themes that can only be expressed as **clichés**—overused phrases or expressions—or as **morals**—lessons dramatized by the work. The fairy tale "Cinderella," for example, expresses the clichéd theme that a virtuous girl who endures misfortune will eventually achieve her just reward; the fable "The Tortoise and the Hare" illustrates the moral "Slow and steady wins the race." Like "The Cask of Amontillado," however, the stories in this anthology have themes that are much more complex than clichés or morals.

Interpreting Themes

Contemporary critical theory holds that the theme of a work of fiction is as much a creation of readers as it is of the writer. Readers' backgrounds, knowledge, values, and beliefs all play a part in determining the theme (or themes) they will identify in a work. Many readers, for example, will realize that David Michael Kaplan's story "Doe Season" (p. 395)—in which the main character goes hunting, kills her first deer, and is forced to confront suffering and death—expresses a conventional **initiation theme**, revealing growing up to be a disillusioning and painful process. Still, different readers bring different perspectives to the story and, in some cases, see different themes.

During a classroom discussion of "Doe Season," a student familiar with hunting saw more than his classmates did in the story's conventional initiation theme. He knew that in many states there really is a doe season. Shorter than the ten-day buck season, it allows hunters to control the size of the deer herd by killing females. This knowledge enabled the student to conclude that by the end of the story the female child's innocence is destroyed, just as the doe is.

Another student pointed out that the participation of Andy—a female who uses a male name—in hunting, a traditional male rite of passage, leads to her killing the deer and to her subsequent disillusionment. It also leads to her decision to abandon her nickname. By contrasting "Andrea" with "Andy," the story reveals the conflict between her "female" nature (illustrated by her compassion) and her desire to emulate the men to whom killing is a sport. This interpretation led the student to conclude that the theme of "Doe Season" is that males and females must, by their natures, have very different outlooks on life.

Other students rejected the negative portrayal of the story's male characters that the preceding interpretation implies. They pointed out that the father is a sympathetic figure who is extremely supportive; he encourages and defends his daughter. He takes her hunting because he loves her, not because he wants to initiate her into life or to hurt her. One student mentioned that Andy's reaction (called *buck fever*) when she sees the doe is common in children who kill their first deer. In light of this information, several students concluded that far from being about irreconcilable male and female differences, "Doe Season" makes a statement about a young girl who is hunting for her own identity and who in the process discovers her mortality. Her father is therefore the agent who enables her to confront the inevitability of death, a fact she must accept if she is going to take her place in the adult world. In this sense, the theme of the story is the idea that in order to mature, a child must come to terms with the reality of death.

Different readers may see different themes in a story, but any interpretation of a theme must make sense in light of what is actually in the story. Evidence from the work, not just your own feelings or assumptions, must support your interpretation, and a single statement by a character is not usually enough in itself to reveal a story's theme. Therefore, you must present a cross-section of examples from the text to support your interpretation of the story's theme. If you say that the theme of James Joyce's "Araby" (p. 288) is that an innocent idealist is inevitably doomed to disillusionment, you have to find examples from the text to support this statement. You could begin with the title, concluding that the word *Araby* suggests idealistic dreams of exotic beauty that the boy tries to find when he goes to a bazaar. You could reinforce your interpretation by pointing out that the unattainable woman is a symbol of all that the boy wants so desperately to find. Finally, you could show how idealism is ultimately crushed by society: at the end of the story, the boy stands alone in the darkness and realizes that his dreams are childish fantasies. Although other readers may have different responses to "Araby," they will find your interpretation reasonable if you support it with enough examples.

 ## Identifying Themes

Every element of a story can shed light on its themes. As you analyze a short story, look for features that reveal and reinforce what you perceive to be the story's most important ideas.

- *The title can often provide insight into the theme or themes of a story.* The title of an F. Scott Fitzgerald story, "Babylon Revisited," emphasizes a major idea in the story—that Paris of the 1920s is like Babylon, the ancient city the Bible singles out as the epitome of evil and corruption. The story's protagonist, Charlie Wales, comes to realize that no matter how much money he lost after the 1929 stock market crash, he lost more—his wife and his daughter—during the boom, when he was in Paris. Charlie's search through his past—his return to "Babylon"—provides new meaning to his life and offers him at least a small bit of hope for the future.

- *Sometimes a narrator's or character's statement can reveal a theme.* For example, at the beginning of Alberto Alvaro Ríos's "The Secret Lion" (p. 466), the first-person narrator says, "I was twelve and in junior high school and something happened that we didn't have a name for, but it was there nonetheless like a lion, and roaring, roaring that way the biggest things do. Everything changed." Although the narrator does not directly announce the story's theme, he suggests that the story will convey the idea that the price children pay for growing up is realizing that everything changes, that nothing stays the way it is.

- *The arrangement of events can suggest a story's theme,* as it does in an Ernest Hemingway story, "The Short Happy Life of Francis Macomber." At the beginning of the story, the title character is a coward who is stuck in an unhappy marriage. As the story progresses, he gradually learns the nature of courage and, finally, finds it in himself. At the moment of his triumph, however, Francis is shot by his wife; his "happy life" is short indeed. The way the events of the story are presented, through foreshadowing and flashbacks, reveals the connection between Macomber's marriage and his behavior as a hunter, and this connection in turn helps to reveal a possible theme: that sometimes courage can be more important than life itself.

- *A story's central conflict can offer clues to its theme.* For example, the main character in "The Yellow Wallpaper" (p. 434), a woman who has recently had a baby, is in conflict with the nineteenth-century society in which she lives. She is suffering from "temporary nervous depression," what doctors today recognize as postpartum depression. Following the practice of the time, her physician has ordered complete bed rest and has instructed her husband to deprive her of all mental and physical stimulation. This harsh treatment leads the narrator to lose her grasp on reality; eventually, she begins to hallucinate. The main conflict of the story is clearly between the woman and her society, controlled by men. This conflict communicates the central theme: that in nineteenth-century America, women are controlled not just by their husbands and the male medical establishment, but also by the society men have created.

- *The point of view of a story can shed light on its theme.* For instance, a writer's use of an unreliable first-person narrator can help to communicate the theme of a story. Thus, Montresor's self-serving first-person account of his crime in "The Cask of Amontillado"—along with his attempts to justify these actions—enables readers to understand the dangers of irrational anger and misplaced ideas about honor. The voice of a third-person narrator can also help to convey a story's theme. For example, the detachment of the narrator in Stephen Crane's Civil War novel *The Red Badge of Courage* reinforces the theme of the novel: that bravery, cowardice, war, and even life itself are insignificant when set beside the indifference of the universe.

- *Quite often a story's symbols—names, places, and objects—can suggest its theme.* For example, the rocking horse in D. H. Lawrence's "The Rocking-Horse Winner" (p. 409) can be seen as a symbol of the boy's desperate desire to remain a child. Interpreted in this way, it reinforces the theme that innocence cannot survive when it confronts adult greed and selfishness. Similarly, Hawthorne's "Young Goodman Brown" (p. 367) uses symbols such as the walking stick, the woods, sunset and night, and the vague shadows to develop one of its central themes: that once a person strays from the path of faith, evil is everywhere.

- *Finally, changes in a character can shed light on the theme or themes of the story.* The main character in Charles Baxter's "Gryphon" (p. 172), for example, eventually comes to realize that the "lies" his substitute teacher tells may be closer to the truth than the "facts" his other teachers present, and his changing attitude toward her helps to communicate the story's central theme about the nature of truth.

✔ **CHECKLIST**   **Writing about Theme**

☐ What is the central theme of the story?

☐ What other themes can you identify?

☐ Does the title of the story suggest a theme?

☐ Does the narrator, or any character, make statements that express or imply a theme?

☐ In what way does the arrangement of events in the story suggest a theme?

☐ In what way does the central conflict of the story suggest a theme?

☐ How does the point of view shed light on the story's central theme?

☐ Do any symbols suggest a theme?

☐ Do any characters in the story change in any significant way? Do these changes convey a particular theme?

Bettmann/Corbis

EUDORA WELTY (1909–2001) was born and raised in Jackson, Mississippi. After attending the Mississippi College for Women, the University of Wisconsin, and Columbia University (where she studied advertising), she returned to Jackson to pursue her long career as a writer, beginning as a journalist. In 1936, she wrote the first of her many short stories, which are gathered in *Collected Stories* (1980). Welty also wrote several novels, including *Delta Wedding* (1946), *Losing Battles* (1970), and the Pulitzer Prize–winning *The Optimist's Daughter* (1972). Her volume of memoirs, *One Writer's Beginnings* (1984), was a best-seller.

One of America's most accomplished writers, Welty focused much of her fiction on life in southern towns and villages peopled with dreamers, eccentrics, and close-knit families. Her sharply observed characters are sometimes presented with great humor, sometimes with poignant lyricism, but always with clarity and sympathy. "Of course any writer is in part all of his characters," she observed. "How otherwise would they be known to him, occur to him, become what they are?" In "A Worn Path," Welty creates a particularly memorable character in the tenacious Phoenix Jackson, and through her she explores a theme that transcends race and region.

Cultural Context   During the 1930s, the years of the Great Depression, poverty and unemployment were widespread but were especially severe in isolated rural areas of the South.

For the black population living in this poor and undeveloped region, difficult economic conditions were made worse by the system of segregation that prevented them from voting, receiving a good education, or enjoying the same rights and privileges as their white counterparts. Hoping to improve their situation, many African American families left the South and moved into northern and midwestern cities where there were better opportunities for education and employment. Others, like the protagonist of this story, remained in the South in an atmosphere of residual racism and oppression.

A Worn Path (1940)

It was December—a bright frozen day in the early morning. Far out in the country there was an old Negro woman with her head tied in a red rag, coming along a path through the pinewoods. Her name was Phoenix Jackson. She was very old and small and she walked slowly in the dark pine shadows, moving a little from side to side in her steps, with the balanced heaviness and lightness of a pendulum in a grandfather clock. She carried a thin, small cane made from an umbrella, and with this she kept tapping the frozen earth in front of her. This made a grave and persistent noise in the still air, that seemed meditative like the chirping of a solitary little bird.

She wore a dark striped dress reaching down to her shoe tops, and an equally long apron of bleached sugar sacks, with a full pocket: all neat and tidy, but every time she took a step she might have fallen over her shoelaces, which dragged from her unlaced shoes. She looked straight ahead. Her eyes were blue with age. Her skin had a pattern all its own of numberless branching wrinkles and as though a whole little tree stood in the middle of her forehead, but a golden color ran underneath, and the two knobs of her cheeks were illumined by a yellow burning under the dark. Under the red rag her hair came down on her neck in the frailest of ringlets, still black, and with an odor like copper.

Now and then there was a quivering in the thicket. Old Phoenix said, "Out of my way, all you foxes, owls, beetles, jack rabbits, coons and wild animals!...Keep out from under these feet, little bob-whites.... Keep the big wild hogs out of my path. Don't let none of those come running my direction. I got a long way." Under her small black-freckled hand her cane, limber as a buggy whip, would switch at the brush as if to rouse up any hiding things.

On she went. The woods were deep and still. The sun made the pine needles almost too bright to look at, up where the wind rocked. The cones dropped as light as feathers. Down in the hollow was the mourning dove—it was not too late for him.

5   The path ran up a hill. "Seem like there is chains about my feet, time I get this far," she said, in the voice of argument old people keep to use with themselves. "Something always take a hold of me on this hill—pleads I should stay."

After she got to the top she turned and gave a full, severe look behind her where she had come. "Up through pines," she said at length. "Now down through oaks."

Her eyes opened their widest, and she started down gently. But before she got to the bottom of the hill a bush caught her dress.

Her fingers were busy and intent, but her skirts were full and long, so that before she could pull them free in one place they were caught in another. It was not possible to allow the dress to tear. "I in the thorny bush," she said. "Thorns, you doing your appointed work. Never want to let folks pass, no sir. Old eyes thought you was a pretty little *green* bush."

Finally, trembling all over, she stood free, and after a moment dared to stoop for her cane.

10   "Sun so high!" she cried, leaning back and looking, while the thick tears went over her eyes. "The time getting all gone here."

At the foot of this hill was a place where a log was laid across the creek. "Now comes the trial," said Phoenix.

Putting her right foot out, she mounted the log and shut her eyes. Lifting her skirt, leveling her cane fiercely before her, like a festival figure in some parade, she began to march across. Then she opened her eyes and she was safe on the other side.

"I wasn't as old as I thought," she said.

15   But she sat down to rest. She spread her skirts on the bank around her and folded her hands over her knees. Up above her was a tree in a pearly cloud of mistletoe. She did not dare to close her eyes, and when a little boy brought her a plate with a slice of marble-cake on it she spoke to him. "That would be acceptable," she said. But when she went to take it there was just her own hand in the air.

So she left that tree, and had to go through a barbed-wire fence. There she had to creep and crawl, spreading her knees and stretching her fingers like a baby trying to climb the steps. But she talked loudly to herself: she could not let her dress be torn now, so late in the day, and she could not pay for having her arm or her leg sawed off if she got caught fast where she was.

At last she was safe through the fence and risen up out in the clearing. Big dead trees, like black men with one arm, were standing in the purple stalks of the withered cotton field. There sat a buzzard.

"Who you watching?"

In the furrow she made her way along.

20   "Glad this not the season for bulls," she said, looking sideways, "and the good Lord made his snakes to curl up and sleep in the winter.

A pleasure I don't see no two-headed snake coming around that tree, where it come once. It took a while to get by him, back in the summer."

She passed through the old cotton and went into a field of dead corn. It whispered and shook and was taller than her head. "Through the maze now," she said, for there was no path.

Then there was something tall, black, and skinny there, moving before her.

At first she took it for a man. It could have been a man dancing in the field. But she stood still and listened, and it did not make a sound. It was as silent as a ghost.

"Ghost," she said sharply, "who be you the ghost of? For I have heard of nary death close by."

But there was no answer—only the ragged dancing in the wind.   25

She shut her eyes, reached out her hand, and touched a sleeve. She found a coat and inside that an emptiness, cold as ice.

"You scarecrow," she said. Her face lighted. "I ought to be shut up for good," she said with laughter. "My senses is gone. I too old. I the oldest people I ever know. Dance, old scarecrow," she said, "while I dancing with you."

She kicked her foot over the furrow, and with mouth drawn down, shook her head once or twice in a little strutting way. Some husks blew down and whirled in streamers about her skirts.

Then she went on, parting her way from side to side with the cane, through the whispering field. At last she came to the end, to a wagon track where the silver grass blew between the red ruts. The quail were walking around like pullets, seeming all dainty and unseen.

"Walk pretty," she said. "This is the easy place. This the easy going."   30

She followed the track, swaying through the quiet bare fields, through the little strings of trees silver in their dead leaves, past cabins silver from weather, with the doors and windows boarded shut, all like old women under a spell sitting there. "I walking in their sleep," she said, nodding her head vigorously.

In a ravine she went where a spring was silently flowing through a hollow log. Old Phoenix bent and drank. "Sweet-gum makes the water sweet," she said, and drank more. "Nobody know who made this well, for it was here when I was born."

The track crossed a swampy part where the moss hung as white as lace from every limb. "Sleep on, alligators, and blow your bubbles." Then the track went into the road.

Deep, deep the road went down between the high green-colored banks. Overhead the live-oaks met, and it was as dark as a cave.

A black dog with a lolling tongue came up out of the weeds by the   35
ditch. She was meditating, and not ready, and when he came at her she

only hit him a little with her cane. Over she went in the ditch, like a little puff of milkweed.

Down there, her senses drifted away. A dream visited her, and she reached her hand up, but nothing reached down and gave her a pull. So she lay there and presently went to talking. "Old woman," she said to herself, "that black dog come up out of the weeds to stall you off, and now there he sitting on his fine tail, smiling at you."

A white man finally came along and found her—a hunter, a young man, with his dog on a chain.

"Well, Granny!" he laughed. "What are you doing there?"

"Lying on my back like a June-bug waiting to be turned over, mister," she said, reaching up her hand.

40   He lifted her up, gave her a swing in the air, and set her down. "Anything broken, Granny?"

"No sir, them old dead weeds is springy enough," said Phoenix, when she had got her breath. "I thank you for your trouble."

"Where do you live, Granny?" he asked, while the two dogs were growling at each other.

"Away back yonder, sir, behind the ridge. You can't even see it from here."

"On your way home?"

45   "No sir, I going to town."

"Why, that's too far! That's as far as I walk when I come out myself, and I get something for my trouble." He patted the stuffed bag he carried, and there hung down a little closed claw. It was one of the bob-whites, with its beak hooked bitterly to show it was dead. "Now you go on home, Granny!"

"I bound to go to town, mister," said Phoenix. "The time come around."

He gave another laugh, filling the whole landscape. "I know you old colored people! Wouldn't miss going to town to see Santa Claus!"

But something held old Phoenix very still. The deep lines in her face went into a fierce and different radiation. Without warning, she had seen with her own eyes a flashing nickel fall out of the man's pocket onto the ground.

50   "How old are you, Granny?" he was saying.

"There is no telling, mister," she said, "no telling."

Then she gave a little cry and clapped her hands and said, "Git on away from here, dog! Look! Look at that dog!" She laughed as if in admiration. "He ain't scared of nobody. He a big black dog." She whispered, "Sic him!"

"Watch me get rid of that cur," said the man. "Sic him, Pete! Sic him!"

Phoenix heard the dogs fighting, and heard the man running and throwing sticks. She even heard a gunshot. But she was slowly bending forward by that time, further and further forward, the lid stretched down over her eyes, as if she were doing this in her sleep. Her chin was lowered almost to her knees. The yellow palm of her hand came out from the fold of her apron. Her fingers slid down and along the ground under the piece of money with the grace and care they would have in lifting an egg from under a setting hen. Then she slowly straightened up, she stood erect, and the nickel was in her apron pocket. A bird flew by. Her lips moved. "God watching me the whole time. I come to stealing."

The man came back, and his own dog panted about them. "Well, 55 I scared him off that time," he said, and then he laughed and lifted his gun and pointed it at Phoenix.

She stood straight and faced him.

"Doesn't the gun scare you?" he said, still pointing it.

"No, sir, I seen plenty go off closer by, in my day, and for less than what I done," she said, holding utterly still.

He smiled, and shouldered the gun. "Well, Granny," he said, "you must be a hundred years old, and scared of nothing. I'd give you a dime if I had any money with me. But you take my advice and stay home, and nothing will happen to you."

"I bound to go on my way, mister," said Phoenix. She inclined her 60 head in the red rag. Then they went in different directions, but she could hear the gun shooting again and again over the hill.

She walked on. The shadows hung from the oak trees to the road like curtains. Then she smelled wood-smoke, and smelled the river, and she saw a steeple and the cabins on their steep steps. Dozens of little black children whirled around her. There ahead was Natchez shining. Bells were ringing. She walked on.

In the paved city it was Christmas time. There were red and green electric lights strung and crisscrossed everywhere, and all turned on in the daytime. Old Phoenix would have been lost if she had not distrusted her eyesight and depended on her feet to know where to take her.

She paused quietly on the sidewalk where people were passing by. A lady came along in the crowd, carrying an armful of red-, green- and silver-wrapped presents; she gave off perfume like the red roses in hot summer, and Phoenix stopped her.

"Please, missy, will you lace up my shoe?" She held up her foot.

"What do you want, Grandma?"   65

"See my shoe," said Phoenix. "Do all right for out in the country, but wouldn't look right to go in a big building."

"Stand still then, Grandma," said the lady. She put her packages down on the sidewalk beside her and laced and tied both shoes tightly.

"Can't lace 'em with a cane," said Phoenix. "Thank you, missy. I doesn't mind asking a nice lady to tie up my shoe, when I gets out on the street."

Moving slowly and from side to side, she went into the big building, and into a tower of steps, where she walked up and around and around until her feet knew to stop.

70   She entered a door, and there she saw nailed up on the wall the document that had been stamped with the gold seal and framed in the gold frame, which matched the dream that was hung up in her head.

"Here I be," she said. There was a fixed and ceremonial stiffness over her body.

"A charity case, I suppose," said an attendant who sat at the desk before her.

But Phoenix only looked above her head. There was sweat on her face, the wrinkles in her face shone like a bright net.

"Speak up, Grandma," the woman said. "What's your name? We must have your history, you know. Have you been here before? What seems to be the trouble with you?"

75   Old Phoenix only gave a twitch to her face as if a fly were bothering her.

"Are you deaf?" cried the attendant.

But then the nurse came in.

"Oh, that's just old Aunt Phoenix," she said. "She doesn't come for herself—she has a little grandson. She makes these trips just as regular as clockwork. She lives away back off the Old Natchez Trace." She bent down. "Well, Aunt Phoenix, why don't you just take a seat? We won't keep you standing after your long trip." She pointed.

The old woman sat down, bolt upright in the chair.

80   "Now, how is the boy?" asked the nurse.

Old Phoenix did not speak.

"I said, how is the boy?"

But Phoenix only waited and stared straight ahead, her face very solemn and withdrawn into rigidity.

"Is his throat any better?" asked the nurse. "Aunt Phoenix, don't you hear me? Is your grandson's throat any better since the last time you came for the medicine?"

85   With her hands on her knees, the old woman waited, silent, erect and motionless, just as if she were in armor.

"You mustn't take up our time this way, Aunt Phoenix," the nurse said. "Tell us quickly about your grandson, and get it over. He isn't dead, is he?"

At last there came a flicker and then a flame of comprehension across her face, and she spoke.

"My grandson. It was my memory had left me. There I sat and forgot why I made my long trip."

"Forgot?" The nurse frowned. "After you came so far?"

90   Then Phoenix was like an old woman begging a dignified forgiveness for waking up frightened in the night. "I never did go to school, I was too

old at the Surrender,"[1] she said in a soft voice. "I'm an old woman without an education. It was my memory fail me. My little grandson, he is just the same, and I forgot it in the coming."

"Throat never heals, does it?" said the nurse, speaking in a loud, sure voice to old Phoenix. By now she had a card with something written on it, a little list. "Yes. Swallowed lye. When was it?—January—two-three years ago—"

Phoenix spoke unasked now. "No, missy, he not dead, he just the same. Every little while his throat begin to close up again, and he not able to swallow. He not get his breath. He not able to help himself. So the time come around, and I go on another trip for the soothing medicine."

"All right. The doctor said as long as you came to get it, you could have it," said the nurse. "But it's an obstinate case."

"My little grandson, he sit up there in the house all wrapped up, wait-ing by himself," Phoenix went on. "We is the only two left in the world. He suffer and it don't seem to put him back at all. He got a sweet look. He going to last. He wear a little patch quilt and peep out holding his mouth open like a little bird. I remembers so plain now. I not going to forget him again, no, the whole enduring time. I could tell him from all the others in creation."

"All right." The nurse was trying to hush her now. She brought her a 95 bottle of medicine. "Charity," she said, making a check mark in a book.

Old Phoenix held the bottle close to her eyes, and then carefully put it into her pocket.

"I thank you," she said.

"It's Christmas time, Grandma," said the attendant. "Could I give you a few pennies out of my purse?"

"Five pennies is a nickel," said Phoenix stiffly.

"Here's a nickel," said the attendant.   100

Phoenix rose carefully and held out her hand. She received the nickel and then fished the other nickel out of her pocket and laid it beside the new one. She stared at her palm closely, with her head on one side.

Then she gave a tap with her cane on the floor.

"This is what come to me to do," she said. "I going to the store and buy my child a little windmill they sells, made out of paper. He going to find it hard to believe there such a thing in the world. I'll march myself back where he waiting, holding it straight up in this hand."

She lifted her free hand, gave a little nod, turned around, and walked out of the doctor's office. Then her slow step began on the stairs, going down.

---

[1] *the Surrender:* The surrender of General Robert E. Lee to General Ulysses S. Grant at the end of the Civil War, April 9, 1865.

Reading and Reacting

1. How does the first paragraph set the scene for the rest of the story? How does it foreshadow the events that will take place later on?

2. Traditionally, a **quest** is a journey in which a knight overcomes a series of obstacles in order to perform a prescribed feat. In what way is Phoenix's journey a quest? What obstacles does she face? What feat must she perform?

3. Because Phoenix is old, she has trouble seeing. What things does she have difficulty seeing? How do her mistakes shed light on her character? How do they contribute to the impact of the story?

4. What is the major theme of this story? What other themes are expressed?

5. A **phoenix** is a mythical bird that would live for five hundred years, be consumed by fire, and then rise from its own ashes. In what way is the name of this creature appropriate for the main character of this story?

6. Phoenix is not intimidated by the man with the gun and has no difficulty asking a white woman to tie her shoe. In spite of her pride and her strength of character, however, Phoenix has no qualms about stealing a nickel or taking charity from the doctor. How do you account for this apparent contradiction?

7. How do the various people Phoenix encounters react to her? Do they treat her with respect? with disdain? Why do you think they react the way they do?

8. In paragraph 90, Phoenix says that she is an old woman without an education. Even so, what knowledge does she seem to have that the other characters lack?

9. JOURNAL ENTRY Could "A Worn Path" be seen as an **allegory**? If so, what might each of the characters represent?

10. CRITICAL PERSPECTIVE Writing about "A Worn Path," Eudora Welty said that the question she was asked most frequently by both students and teachers was whether Phoenix Jackson's grandson was actually dead. Here she attempts to answer this question:

> I had not meant to mystify readers by withholding any fact; it is not a writer's business to tease. The story is told through Phoenix's mind and she undertakes her errand. As the author at one with the character as I tell it, I must assume that the boy is alive. As the reader, you are free to think as you like, of course; the story invites you to believe that no matter what happens, Phoenix for as long as she is able to walk and can hold to her purpose will make her journey.

Do you think Phoenix's grandson is alive or dead? Why?

Related Works: "Miss Brill" (p. 166), "Araby" (p. 288), "Everyday Use" (p. 344), "The Negro Speaks of Rivers" (p. 769)

DAVID MICHAEL KAPLAN (1946–   ) is one of a group of American writers who, along with South American writers such as Gabriel García Márquez of Columbia, are called "magic realists." Magic realists work outside of the borders of traditional fantasy writing, seamlessly interweaving magical elements with detailed, realistically drawn "everyday" settings. These elements, says a reviewer of Kaplan's work, are invoked "to illuminate and underscore heightened moments of reality." The story "Doe Season," which appeared in Kaplan's debut collection, *Comfort* (1987), was included in *Best American Short Stories 1985.* Kaplan's first novel, *Skating in the Dark*, was published in 1991, and his writing text, *Revision: A Creative Approach to Writing and Re-writing Fiction*, was published in 1997. Kaplan teaches fiction writing at Loyola University Chicago.

Interestingly, the stories in *Comfort* break from classic "first-time author" tradition by side-stepping the autobiographical, young-man-comes-of-age theme. Instead, these stories are about young girls—or young women—coming to grips with parents (present or absent) and with loss and searching for ways to resolve their ambivalence about becoming women. In "Doe Season," Andy's surreal encounter with the doe may be a dream, but the beauty and horror of their meeting will affect the rest of her life.

Cultural Context When European settlers first came to America, deer roamed freely from coast to coast, and the settlers hunted them to put meat on the table. Today, deer are hunted in a regulated fashion in order to control their numbers and maintain a balance in their population. Deer hunting has long been viewed as a coming-of-age ritual for young men—and, more recently, for young women first entering adulthood, like the protagonist in this story. It used to be the tradition that a young hunter who missed his first deer had his shirttail cut off; if he succeeded, his face was smeared with the blood of his first kill. Now few hunters observe these initiation rites.

Doe Season (1985)

They were always the same woods, she thought sleepily as they drove through the early morning darkness—deep and immense, covered with yesterday's snowfall, which had frozen overnight. They were the same woods that lay behind her house, *and they stretch all the way to here,* she thought, *for miles and miles, longer than I could walk in a day, or a week even, but they are still the same woods.* The thought made her feel good: it was like thinking of God; it was like thinking of the space between here and the moon; it was like thinking of all the foreign countries from her geography book where even now, Andy knew, people were going to bed, while they—she and her father and Charlie Spoon and Mac, Charlie's

eleven-year-old son—were driving deeper into the Pennsylvania countryside, to go hunting.

They had risen long before dawn. Her mother, yawning and not trying to hide her sleepiness, cooked them eggs and French toast. Her father
smoked a cigarette and flicked ashes into his saucer while Andy listened,
wondering *Why doesn't he come?* and *Won't he ever come?* until at last a car
pulled into the graveled drive and honked. "That will be Charlie Spoon,"
her father said; he always said "Charlie Spoon," even though his real name
was Spreun, because Charlie was, in a sense, shaped like a spoon, with a
large head and a narrow waist and chest.

Andy's mother kissed her and her father and said, "Well, have a good
time" and "Be careful." Soon they were outside in the bitter dark, loading
gear by the back-porch light, their breath steaming. The woods behind
the house were then only a black streak against the wash of night.

Andy dozed in the car and woke to find that it was half light. Mac—
also sleeping—had slid against her. She pushed him away and looked out
the window. Her breath clouded the glass, and she was cold; the car's
heater didn't work right. They were riding over gentle hills, the woods on
both sides now—the same woods, she knew, because she had been watching the whole way, even while she slept. They had been in her dreams,
and she had never lost sight of them.

5   Charlie Spoon was driving. "I don't understand why she's coming," he
said to her father. "How old is she anyway—eight?"

"Nine," her father replied. "She's small for her age."

"So—nine. What's the difference? She'll just add to the noise and get
tired besides."

"No, she won't," her father said. "She can walk me to death. And she'll
bring good luck, you'll see. Animals—I don't know how she does it, but
they come right up to her. We go walking in the woods, and we'll spot
more raccoons and possums and such than I ever see when I'm alone."

Charlie grunted.

10   "Besides, she's not a bad little shot, even if she doesn't hunt yet. She
shoots the .22 real good."

"Popgun," Charlie said, and snorted. "And target shooting ain't deer
hunting."

"Well, she's not gonna be shooting anyway, Charlie," her father said.
"Don't worry. She'll be no bother."

"I still don't know why she's coming," Charlie said.

"Because she wants to, and I want her to. Just like you and Mac. No
difference."

15   Charlie turned onto a side road and after a mile or so slowed down.
"That's it!" he cried. He stopped, backed up, and entered a narrow dirt
road almost hidden by trees. Five hundred yards down, the road ran

parallel to a fenced-in field. Charlie parked in a cleared area deeply rutted by frozen tractor tracks. The gate was locked. *In the spring,* Andy thought, *there will be cows here, and a dog that chases them,* but now the field was unmarked and bare.

"This is it," Charlie Spoon declared. "Me and Mac was up here just two weeks ago, scouting it out, and there's deer. Mac saw the tracks."

"That's right," Mac said.

"Well, we'll just see about that," her father said, putting on his gloves. He turned to Andy. "How you doing, honeybun?"

"Just fine," she said.

Andy shivered and stamped as they unloaded: first the rifles, which   20
they unsheathed and checked, sliding the bolts, sighting through scopes, adjusting the slings; then the gear, their food and tents and sleeping bags and stove stored in four backpacks—three big ones for Charlie Spoon and her father and Mac, and a day pack for her.

"That's about your size," Mac said, to tease her.

She reddened and said, "Mac, I can carry a pack big as yours any day." He laughed and pressed his knee against the back of hers, so that her leg buckled. "Cut it out," she said. She wanted to make an iceball and throw it at him, but she knew that her father and Charlie were anxious to get going, and she didn't want to displease them.

Mac slid under the gate, and they handed the packs over to him. Then they slid under and began walking across the field toward the same woods that ran all the way back to her home, where even now her mother was probably rising again to wash their breakfast dishes and make herself a fresh pot of coffee. *She is there, and we are here:* the thought satisfied Andy. There was no place else she would rather be.

Mac came up beside her. "Over there's Canada," he said, nodding toward the woods.

"Huh!" she said. "Not likely."   25

"I don't mean *right* over there. I mean farther up north. You think I'm dumb?"

Dumb as your father, she thought.

"Look at that," Mac said, pointing to a piece of cow dung lying on a spot scraped bare of snow. "A frozen meadow muffin." He picked it up and sailed it at her. "Catch!"

"Mac!" she yelled. His laugh was as gawky as he was. She walked faster. He seemed different today somehow, bundled in his yellow-and-black-checkered coat, a rifle in hand, his silly floppy hat not quite covering his ears. They all seemed different as she watched them trudge through the snow—Mac and her father and Charlie Spoon—bigger, maybe, as if the cold landscape enlarged rather than diminished them, so that they, the only figures in that landscape, took on size and meaning just by being there. If they weren't there, everything would be quieter, and the woods would be the same as before. *But they are here*, Andy thought, looking behind her at the boot prints in the snow, *and I am too, and so it's all different.*

30   "We'll go down to the cut where we found those deer tracks," Charlie said as they entered the woods. "Maybe we'll get lucky and get a late one coming through."

The woods descended into a gully. The snow was softer and deeper here, so that often Andy sank to her knees. Charlie and Mac worked the top of the gully while she and her father walked along the base some thirty yards behind them. "If they miss the first shot, we'll get the second," her father said, and she nodded as if she had known this all the time. She listened to the crunch of their boots, their breathing, and the drumming of a distant woodpecker. And the crackling. In winter the woods crackled as if everything were straining, ready to snap like dried chicken bones.

We are hunting, Andy thought. The cold air burned her nostrils.

They stopped to make lunch by a rock outcropping that protected them from the wind. Her father heated the bean soup her mother had made for them, and they ate it with bread already stiff from the cold. He and Charlie took a few pulls from a flask of Jim Beam while she scoured the plates with snow and repacked them. Then they all had coffee with sugar and powdered milk, and her father poured her a cup too. "We won't tell your momma," he said, and Mac laughed. Andy held the cup the way her father did, not by the handle but around the rim. The coffee tasted smoky. She felt a little queasy, but she drank it all.

Charlie Spoon picked his teeth with a fingernail. "Now, you might've noticed one thing," he said.

35   "What's that?" her father asked.

"You might've noticed you don't hear no rifles. That's because there ain't no other hunters here. We've got the whole damn woods to ourselves. Now, I ask you—do I know how to find 'em?"

"We haven't seen deer yet, neither."

"Oh, we will," Charlie said, "but not for a while now." He leaned back against the rock. "Deer're sleeping, resting up for the evening feed."

"I seen a deer behind our house once, and it was afternoon," Andy said.

40   "Yeah, honey, but that was *before* deer season," Charlie said, grinning. "They know something now. They're smart that way."

"That's right," Mac said.

Andy looked at her father—had she said something stupid?

"Well, Charlie," he said, "if they know so much, how come so many get themselves shot?"

"Them's the ones that don't *believe* what they know," Charlie replied. The men laughed. Andy hesitated, and then laughed with them.

They moved on, as much to keep warm as to find a deer. The wind 45 became even stronger. Blowing through the treetops, it sounded like the ocean, and once Andy thought she could smell salt air. But that was impossible; the ocean was *hundreds* of miles away, farther than Canada even. She and her parents had gone last summer to stay for a week at a motel on the New Jersey shore. That was the first time she'd seen the ocean, and it frightened her. It was huge and empty, yet always moving. Everything lay hidden. If you walked in it, you couldn't see how deep it was or what might be below; if you swam, something could pull you under and you'd never be seen again. Its musky, rank smell made her think of things dying. Her mother had floated beyond the breakers, calling to her to come in, but Andy wouldn't go farther than a few feet into the surf. Her mother swam and splashed with animal-like delight while her father, smiling shyly, held his white arms above the waist-deep water as if afraid to get them wet. Once a comber rolled over and sent them both tossing, and when her mother tried to stand up, the surf receding behind, Andy saw that her mother's swimsuit top had come off, so that her breasts swayed free, her nipples like two dark eyes. Embarrassed, Andy looked around: except for two women under a yellow umbrella farther up, the beach was empty. Her mother stood up unsteadily, regained her footing. Taking what seemed the longest time, she calmly refixed her top. Andy lay on the beach towel and closed her eyes. The sound of the surf made her head ache.

And now it was winter; the sky was already dimming, not just with the absence of light but with a mist that clung to the hunters' faces like cobwebs. They made camp early. Andy was chilled. When she stood still, she kept wiggling her toes to make sure they were there. Her father rubbed her arms and held her to him briefly, and that felt better. She unpacked the food while the others put up the tents.

"How about rounding us up some firewood, Mac?" Charlie asked.

"I'll do it," Andy said. Charlie looked at her thoughtfully and then handed her the canvas carrier.

There wasn't much wood on the ground, so it took her a while to get a good load. She was about a hundred yards from camp, near a cluster of high, lichen-covered boulders, when she saw through a crack in the rock a buck and two does walking gingerly, almost daintily, through the alder trees. She tried to hush her breathing as they passed not more than twenty yards away. There was nothing she could do. If she yelled, they'd be gone; by the time she got back to camp, they'd be gone. The buck stopped, nostrils quivering, tail up and alert. He looked directly at her. Still she didn't move, not one muscle. He was a beautiful buck, the color of late-turned maple leaves. Unafraid, he lowered his tail, and he and his does silently merged into the trees. Andy walked back to camp and dropped the firewood.

50   "I saw three deer," she said. "A buck and two does."

"Where?" Charlie Spoon cried, looking behind her as if they might have followed her into camp.

"In the woods yonder. They're gone now."

"Well, hell!" Charlie banged his coffee cup against his knee.

"Didn't I say she could find animals?" her father said, grinning.

55   "Too late to go after them," Charlie muttered. "It'll be dark in a quarter hour. Damn!"

"Damn," Mac echoed.

"They just walk right up to her," her father said.

"Well, leastwise this proves there's deer here." Charlie began snapping long branches into shorter ones. "You know, I think I'll stick with you," he told Andy, "since you're so good at finding deer and all. How'd that be?"

"Okay, I guess," Andy murmured. She hoped he was kidding; no way did she want to hunt with Charlie Spoon. Still, she was pleased he had said it.

60   Her father and Charlie took one tent, she and Mac the other. When they were in their sleeping bags, Mac said in the darkness, "I bet you really didn't see no deer, did you?"

She sighed. "I did, Mac. Why would I lie?"

"How big was the buck?"

"Four point. I counted."

Mac snorted.

65   "You just believe what you want, Mac," she said testily.

"Too bad it ain't buck season," he said. "Well, I got to go pee."

"So pee."

She heard him turn in his bag. "You ever see it?" he asked.

"It? What's 'it'?"

70   "It. A pecker."

"Sure," she lied.

"Whose? Your father's?"

She was uncomfortable. "No," she said.

"Well, whose then?"

75   "Oh I don't know! Leave me be, why don't you?"

"Didn't see a deer, didn't see a pecker," Mac said teasingly.

She didn't answer right away. Then she said, "My cousin Lewis. I saw his."

"Well, how old's he?"

"One and a half."

80   "Ha! A baby! A baby's is like a little worm. It ain't a real one at all."

If he says he'll show me his, she thought, *I'll kick him. I'll just get out of my bag and kick him.*

"I went hunting with my daddy and Versh and Danny Simmons last year in buck season," Mac said, "and we got ourselves one. And we hog-dressed the thing. You know what that is, don't you?"

"No," she said. She was confused. What was he talking about now?

"That's when you cut him open and take out all his guts, so the meat don't spoil. Makes him lighter to pack out, too."

She tried to imagine what the deer's guts might look like, pulled from 85 the gaping hole. "What do you do with them?" she said. "The guts?"

"Oh, just leave 'em for the bears."

She ran her finger like a knife blade along her belly.

"When we left them on the ground," Mac said, "they smoked. Like they were cooking."

"Huh," she said.

"They cut off the deer's pecker, too, you know." 90

Andy imagined Lewis's pecker and shuddered. "Mac, you're disgusting."

He laughed. "Well, I gotta go pee." She heard him rustle out of his bag. "Broo!" he cried, flapping his arms. "It's cold!"

He makes so much noise, she thought, *just noise and more noise.*

Her father woke them before first light. He warned them to talk softly and said that they were going to the place where Andy had seen the deer, to try to cut them off on their way back from their night feeding. Andy couldn't shake off her sleep. Stuffing her sleeping bag into its sack seemed to take an hour, and tying her boots was the strangest thing she'd ever done. Charlie Spoon made hot chocolate and oatmeal with raisins. Andy closed her eyes and, between beats of her heart, listened to the breathing of the forest. *When I open my eyes, it will be lighter,* she decided. But when she did, it was still just as dark, except for the swaths of their flashlights and the hissing blue flame of the stove. *There has to be just one moment when it all changes from dark to light,* Andy thought. She had missed it yesterday, in the car; today she would watch more closely.

But when she remembered again, it was already first light and they had 95 moved to the rocks by the deer trail and had set up shooting positions— Mac and Charlie Spoon on the up-trail side, she and her father behind them, some six feet up on a ledge. The day became brighter, the sun piercing the tall pines, raking the hunters, yet providing little warmth. Andy now smelled alder and pine and the slightly rotten odor of rock lichen. She rubbed her hand over the stone and considered that it must be very old, had probably been here before the giant pines, *before anyone was in these woods at all.* A chipmunk sniffed on a nearby branch. She aimed an imaginary rifle and pressed the trigger. The chipmunk froze, then scurried away. Her legs were cramping on the narrow ledge. Her father seemed to doze, one hand in his parka, the other cupped lightly around the rifle. She could smell his scent of old wool and leather. His cheeks were speckled with gray-black whiskers, and he worked his jaws slightly, as if chewing a small piece of gum.

Please let us get a deer, she prayed.

A branch snapped on the other side of the rock face. Her father's hand stiffened on the rifle, startling her—*He hasn't been sleeping at all,* she marveled—and then his jaw relaxed, as did the lines around his eyes, and she heard Charlie Spoon call, "Yo, don't shoot, it's us." He and Mac appeared from around the rock. They stopped beneath the ledge. Charlie solemnly crossed his arms.

"I don't believe we're gonna get any deer here," he said drily.

Andy's father lowered his rifle to Charlie and jumped down from the ledge. Then he reached up for Andy. She dropped into his arms and he set her gently on the ground.

100　　Mac sidled up to her. "I knew you didn't see no deer," he said.

"Just because they don't come when you want 'em to don't mean she didn't see them," her father said.

Still, she felt bad. Her telling about the deer had caused them to spend the morning there, cold and expectant, with nothing to show for it.

They tramped through the woods for another two hours, not caring much about noise. Mac found some deer tracks, and they argued about how old they were. They split up for a while and then rejoined at an old logging road that deer might use, and followed it. The road crossed a stream, which had mostly frozen over but in a few spots still caught leaves and twigs in an icy swirl. They forded it by jumping from rock to rock. The road narrowed after that, and the woods thickened.

They stopped for lunch, heating up Charlie's wife's corn chowder. Andy's father cut squares of applesauce cake with his hunting knife and handed them to her and Mac, who ate his almost daintily. Andy could faintly taste knife oil on the cake. She was tired. She stretched her leg; the muscle that had cramped on the rock still ached.

105　　"Might as well relax," her father said, as if reading her thoughts. "We won't find deer till suppertime."

Charlie Spoon leaned back against his pack and folded his hands across his stomach. "Well, even if we don't get a deer," he said expansively, "it's still great to be out here, breathe some fresh air, clomp around a bit. Get away from the house and the old lady." He winked at Mac, who looked away.

"That's what the woods are all about, anyway," Charlie said. "It's where the women don't want to go." He bowed his head toward Andy. "With your exception, of course, little lady." He helped himself to another piece of applesauce cake.

"She ain't a woman," Mac said.

"Well, she damn well's gonna be," Charlie said. He grinned at her. "Or will you? You're half a boy anyway. You go by a boy's name. What's your real name? Andrea, ain't it?"

"That's right," she said. She hoped that if she didn't look at him, 110 Charlie would stop.

"Well, which do you like? Andy or Andrea?"

"Don't matter," she mumbled. "Either."

"She's always been Andy to me," her father said.

Charlie Spoon was still grinning. "So what are you gonna be, Andrea? A boy or a girl?"

"I'm a girl," she said.   115

"But you want to go hunting and fishing and everything, huh?"

"She can do whatever she likes," her father said.

"Hell, you might as well have just had a boy and be done with it!" Charlie exclaimed.

"That's funny," her father said, and chuckled. "That's just what her momma tells me."

They were looking at her, and she wanted to get away from them all, 120 even from her father, who chose to joke with them.

"I'm going to walk a bit," she said.

She heard them laughing as she walked down the logging trail. She flapped her arms; she whistled. *I don't care how much noise I make*, she thought. Two grouse flew from the underbrush, startling her. A little farther down, the trail ended in a clearing that enlarged into a frozen meadow; beyond it the woods began again. A few moldering posts were all that was left of a fence that had once enclosed the field. The low afternoon sunlight reflected brightly off the snow, so that Andy's eyes hurt. She squinted hard. A gust of wind blew across the field, stinging her face. And then, as if it had been waiting for her, the doe emerged from the trees opposite and stepped cautiously into the field. Andy watched: it stopped and stood quietly for what seemed a long time and then ambled across. It stopped again about seventy yards away and began to browse in a patch of sugar grass uncovered by the wind. Carefully, slowly, never taking her eyes from the doe, Andy walked backward, trying to step into the boot prints she'd already made. When she was far enough back into the woods, she turned and walked faster, her heart racing. *Please let it stay*, she prayed.

"There's doe in the field yonder," she told them.

They got their rifles and hurried down the trail.

"No use," her father said. "We're making too much noise any way you 125 look at it."

"At least we got us the wind in our favor," Charlie Spoon said, breathing heavily.

But the doe was still there, grazing.

"Good Lord," Charlie whispered. He looked at her father. "Well, whose shot?"

"Andy spotted it," her father said in a low voice. "Let her shoot it."

130 "What!" Charlie's eyes widened.

Andy couldn't believe what her father had just said. She'd only shot tin cans and targets; she'd never even fired her father's .30-.30, and she'd never killed anything.

"I can't," she whispered.

"That's right, she can't," Charlie Spoon insisted. "She's not old enough and she don't have a license even if she was!"

"Well, who's to tell?" her father said in a low voice. "Nobody's going to know but us." He looked at her. "Do you want to shoot it, punkin?"

135 *Why doesn't it hear us?* she wondered. *Why doesn't it run away?* "I don't know," she said.

"Well, I'm sure as hell gonna shoot it," Charlie said. Her father grasped Charlie's rifle barrel and held it. His voice was steady.

"Andy's a good shot. It's her deer. She found it, not you. You'd still be sitting on your ass back in camp." He turned to her again. "Now—do you want to shoot it, Andy? Yes or no."

He was looking at her; they were all looking at her. Suddenly she was angry at the deer, who refused to hear them, who wouldn't run away even when it could. "I'll shoot it," she said. Charlie turned away in disgust.

She lay on the ground and pressed the rifle stock against her shoulder bone. The snow was cold through her parka; she smelled oil and wax and damp earth. She pulled off one glove with her teeth. "It sights just like the .22," her father said gently. "Cartridge's already chambered." As she had done so many times before, she sighted down the scope; now the doe was in the reticle. She moved the barrel until the cross hairs lined up. Her father was breathing beside her.

140 "Aim where the chest and legs meet, or a little above, punkin," he was saying calmly. "That's the killing shot."

But now, seeing it in the scope, Andy was hesitant. Her finger weakened on the trigger. Still, she nodded at what her father said and sighted again, the cross hairs lining up in exactly the same spot—the doe had hardly moved, its brownish-gray body outlined starkly against the blue-backed snow. *It doesn't know*, Andy thought. *It just doesn't know*. And as she looked, deer and snow and faraway trees flattened within the circular frame to become like a picture on a calendar, not real, and she felt calm, as if she had been dreaming everything—the day, the deer, the hunt itself. And she, finger on trigger, was only a part of that dream.

"Shoot!" Charlie hissed.

Through the scope she saw the deer look up, ears high and straining.

Charlie groaned, and just as he did, and just at the moment when Andy knew—*knew*—the doe would bound away, as if she could feel its haunches tensing and gathering power, she pulled the trigger. Later she would think, *I felt the recoil, I smelled the smoke, but I don't remember pulling the trigger.* Through the scope the deer seemed to shrink into itself, and then slowly knelt, hind legs first, head raised as if to cry out. It trembled, still straining to keep its head high, as if that alone would save it; failing, it collapsed, shuddered, and lay still.

"Whoee!" Mac cried.   145

"One shot! One shot!" her father yelled, clapping her on the back. Charlie Spoon was shaking his head and smiling dumbly.

"I told you she was a great little shot!" her father said. "I told you!" Mac danced and clapped his hands. She was dazed, not quite understanding what had happened. And then they were crossing the field toward the fallen doe, she walking dreamlike, the men laughing and joking, released now from the tension of silence and anticipation. Suddenly Mac pointed and cried out, "Look at that!"

The doe was rising, legs unsteady. They stared at it, unable to comprehend, and in that moment the doe regained its feet and looked at them, as if it too were trying to understand. Her father whistled softly. Charlie Spoon unslung his rifle and raised it to his shoulder, but the doe was already bounding away. His hurried shot missed, and the deer disappeared into the woods.

"Damn, damn, damn," he moaned.

"I don't believe it," her father said. "That deer was dead."   150

"Dead, hell!" Charlie yelled. "It was gutshot, that's all. Stunned and gutshot. Clean shot, my ass!"

What have I done? Andy thought.

Her father slung his rifle over his shoulder. "Well, let's go. It can't get too far."

"Hell, I've seen deer run ten miles gutshot," Charlie said. He waved his arms. "We may never find her!"

As they crossed the field, Mac came up to her and said in a low voice, 155 "Gutshoot a deer, you'll go to hell."

"Shut up, Mac," she said, her voice cracking. It was a terrible thing she had done, she knew. She couldn't bear to think of the doe in pain and frightened. *Please let it die,* she prayed.

But though they searched all the last hour of daylight, so that they had to recross the field and go up the logging trail in a twilight made even deeper by thick, smoky clouds, they didn't find the doe. They lost its trail almost immediately in the dense stands of alderberry and larch.

"I am cold, and I am tired," Charlie Spoon declared. "And if you ask me, that deer's in another county already."

"No one's asking you, Charlie," her father said.

160 They had a supper of hard salami and ham, bread, and the rest of the applesauce cake. It seemed a bother to heat the coffee, so they had cold chocolate instead. Everyone turned in early.

"We'll find it in the morning, honeybun," her father said, as she went to her tent.

"I don't like to think of it suffering." She was almost in tears.

"It's dead already, punkin. Don't even think about it." He kissed her, his breath sour and his beard rough against her cheek.

Andy was sure she wouldn't get to sleep; the image of the doe falling, falling, then rising again, repeated itself whenever she closed her eyes. Then she heard an owl hoot and realized that it had awakened her, so she must have been asleep after all. She hoped the owl would hush, but instead it hooted louder. She wished her father or Charlie Spoon would wake up and do something about it, but no one moved in the other tent, and suddenly she was afraid that they had all decamped, wanting nothing more to do with her. She whispered, "Mac, Mac," to the sleeping bag where he should be, but no one answered. She tried to find the flashlight she always kept by her side, but couldn't, and she cried in panic, "Mac, are you there?" He mumbled something, and immediately she felt foolish and hoped he wouldn't reply.

165 When she awoke again, everything had changed. The owl was gone, the woods were still, and she sensed light, blue and pale, light where before there had been none. *The moon must have come out*, she thought. And it was warm, too, warmer than it should have been. She got out of her sleeping bag and took off her parka—it was that warm. Mac was asleep, wheezing like an old man. She unzipped the tent and stepped outside.

The woods were more beautiful than she had ever seen them. The moon made everything ice-rimmed glimmer with a crystallized, immanent light, while underneath that ice the branches of trees were as stark as skeletons. She heard a crunching in the snow, the one sound in all that silence, and there, walking down the logging trail into their camp, was the doe. Its body, like everything around her, was silvered with frost and moonlight. It walked past the tent where her father and Charlie Spoon were sleeping and stopped no more than six feet from her. Andy saw that she had shot it, yes, had shot it cleanly, just where she thought she had, the wound a jagged, bloody hole in the doe's chest.

A heart shot, she thought.

The doe stepped closer, so that Andy, if she wished, could have reached out and touched it. It looked at her as if expecting her to do this, and so she did, running her hand, slowly at first, along the rough, matted fur, then down to the edge of the wound, where she stopped. The doe stood still. Hesitantly, Andy felt the edge of the wound. The torn flesh was sticky and warm. The wound parted under her touch. And then, almost without her knowing it, her fingers were within, probing, yet still the doe didn't move. Andy pressed deeper, through flesh and muscle and sinew, until her whole hand and more was inside the wound and she had found the doe's heart, warm and beating. She cupped it gently in her hand. *Alive*, she marveled. *Alive.*

The heart quickened under her touch, becoming warmer and warmer until it was hot enough to burn. In pain, Andy tried to remove her hand, but the wound closed about it and held her fast. Her hand was burning. She cried out in agony, sure they would all hear and come help, but they didn't. And then her hand pulled free, followed by a steaming rush of blood, more blood than she ever could have imagined—it covered her hand and arm, and she saw to her horror that her hand was steaming. She moaned and fell to her knees and plunged her hand into the snow. The doe looked at her gently and then turned and walked back up the trail.

In the morning, when she woke, Andy could still smell the blood, but 170 she felt no pain. She looked at her hand. Even though it appeared unscathed, it felt weak and withered. She couldn't move it freely and was afraid the others would notice. *I will hide it in my jacket pocket*, she decided, *so nobody can see*. She ate the oatmeal that her father cooked and stayed apart from them all. No one spoke to her, and that suited her. A light snow began to fall. It was the last day of their hunting trip. She wanted to be home.

Her father dumped the dregs of his coffee. "Well, let's go look for her," he said.

Again they crossed the field. Andy lagged behind. She averted her eyes from the spot where the doe had fallen, already filling up with snow. Mac and Charlie entered the woods first, followed by her father. Andy remained in the field and considered the smear of gray sky, the nearby flock of crows pecking at unyielding stubble. *I will stay here*, she thought, *and not move for a long while*. But now someone—Mac—was yelling. Her father appeared at the woods' edge and waved for her to come. She ran and pushed through a brake of alderberry and larch. The thick under-brush scratched her face. For a moment she felt lost and looked wildly about. Then, where the brush thinned, she saw them standing quietly in the falling snow. They were staring down at the dead doe. A film covered its upturned eye, and its body was lightly dusted with snow.

"I told you she wouldn't get too far," Andy's father said triumphantly. "We must've just missed her yesterday. Too blind to see."

"We're just damn lucky no animal got to her last night," Charlie muttered.

Her father lifted the doe's foreleg. The wound was blood-clotted, 175 brown, and caked like frozen mud. "Clean shot," he said to Charlie. He grinned. "My little girl."

Then he pulled out his knife, the blade gray as the morning. Mac whispered to Andy, "Now watch this," while Charlie Spoon lifted the doe from behind by its forelegs so that its head rested between his knees, its underside exposed. Her father's knife sliced thickly from chest to belly to crotch, and Andy was running from them, back to the field and across, scattering the crows who cawed and circled angrily. And now they were all calling to her—Charlie Spoon and Mac and her father—crying *Andy, Andy* (but that wasn't her name, she would no longer be called that); yet louder than any of them was the wind blowing through the treetops, like the ocean where her mother floated in green water, also calling *Come in, come in*, while all around her roared the mocking of the terrible, now inevitable, sea.

Reading and Reacting

1. The initiation of a child into adulthood is a common literary theme. In this story, hunting is presented as an initiation rite. In what way is hunting an appropriate coming-of-age ritual?

2. Which characters are in conflict in this story? Which ideas are in conflict? How do these conflicts help to communicate the story's initiation theme?

3. In the story's opening paragraph and elsewhere, Andy finds comfort and reassurance in the idea that the woods are "always the same"; later in the story, she remembers the ocean, "huge and empty, yet always moving. Everything lay hidden . . ." (par. 45). How does the contrast between the woods and the ocean suggest the transition she must make from childhood to adulthood?

4. How do the references to blood support the story's initiation theme? Do they suggest other themes as well?

5. Throughout the story, references are made to Andy's ability to inspire the trust of animals. As her father says, "Animals—I don't know how she does it, but they come right up to her" (par. 8). How does his comment foreshadow later events?

6. Why does Andy pray that she and the others will get a deer? What makes her change her mind? How does the change in Andy's character help to convey the story's theme?

7. Andy's mother is not an active participant in the story's events. Still, she is important to the story. Why is her role important? How does paragraph 45 reveal the importance of the mother's role?

8. What has Andy learned as a result of her experience? What else do you think she still has to learn?

9. JOURNAL ENTRY How would the story be different if Andy were a boy? What would be the same?

10. CRITICAL PERSPECTIVE In a review of *Comfort*, the book in which "Doe Season" appears, Susan Wood makes the following observation:

> The dozen or so stories in David Michael Kaplan's affecting first collection share a common focus on the extraordinary moments of recognition in ordinary lives. He is at his best suggesting how such moments may alter, for better or for worse, our relationships with those to whom we are most deeply bound—children, parents, lovers—in love and guilt.

At what point does "the extraordinary moment of recognition" occur in "Doe Season"? How does this moment alter Andy's relationship with both her parents?

Related Works: "Snow" (p. 82), from *Persepolis* (p. 111), "A&P" (p. 160), "The Girl with Bangs" (p. 187), "Greasy Lake" (p. 425), "The Lamb" (p. 739)

Source: © Bettmann/CORBIS

D(AVID) H(ERBERT) LAWRENCE (1885–1930) was born in Nottinghamshire, England, the son of a coal miner and a schoolteacher. Determined to escape the harsh life of a miner, Lawrence taught for several years after graduating from high school. He soon began writing fiction and established himself in London literary circles.

During World War I, Lawrence and his wife were suspected of treason because of his pacifism and her connection to German aristocracy. Because Lawrence suffered from tuberculosis, he and his wife left England after the armistice in search of a healthier climate. They traveled in Australia, France, Italy, Mexico, and the United States throughout their lives.

Lawrence is recognized for his impassioned portrayal of our unconscious and instinctive natures. In his novel *Lady Chatterley's Lover* (1928), he attempted to incorporate explicit sexuality into English fiction, and the book was banned for years in Britain and the United States. His other novels include *Sons and Lovers* (1913), *The Rainbow* (1915), *Women in Love* (1921), and *The Plumed Serpent* (1926). Lawrence was also a gifted poet, essayist, travel writer, and short story writer, and his work strongly influenced other writers.

Lawrence's fascination with the struggle between the unconscious and the intellect is revealed in his short story "The Rocking-Horse Winner" (1920). Lawrence sets his story in a house full of secrets and weaves symbolism with elements of the fairy tale and the gothic to produce a tale that has often been the subject of literary debate.

Cultural Context Horse racing in England has a long history, beginning with casual competitions organized by Roman soldiers in Yorkshire in A.D. 200. The first recorded horse race was run during the reign of Henry II in 1174. Today, horses can be raced over fences or hurdles (National Hunt Racing) or over unobstructed distances (flat racing). There are also cross-country races from point to point, which are called steeplechases. A derby, like the one mentioned in this story, usually denotes a race in which three-year-old horses compete. The name *derby* is derived from the Epsom Derby, which is still run at the Epsom racecourse and is named for Edward Smith Stanley, the twelfth Earl of Derby.

The Rocking-Horse Winner (1920)

There was a woman who was beautiful, who started with all the advantages, yet she had no luck. She married for love, and the love turned to dust. She had bonny children, yet she felt they had been thrust upon her, and she could not love them. They looked at her coldly, as if they were finding fault with her. And hurriedly she felt she must cover up some fault in herself. Yet what it was that she must cover up she never knew. Nevertheless, when her children were present, she always felt the centre of her heart go hard. This troubled her, and in her manner she was all the more gentle and anxious for her children, as if she loved them very much. Only she herself knew that at the centre of her heart was a hard little place that could not feel love, no, not for anybody. Everybody else said of her: "She is such a good mother. She adores her children." Only she herself, and her children themselves, knew it was not so. They read it in each other's eyes.

There were a boy and two little girls. They lived in a pleasant house, with a garden, and they had discreet servants, and felt themselves superior to anyone in the neighbourhood.

Although they lived in style, they felt always an anxiety in the house. There was never enough money. The mother had a small income, and the father had a small income, but not nearly enough for the social position which they had to keep up. The father went into town to some office. But though he had good prospects, these prospects never materialised. There was always the grinding sense of the shortage of money, though the style was always kept up.

At last the mother said: "I will see if *I* can't make something." But she did not know where to begin. She racked her brains, and tried this thing and the other, but could not find anything successful. The failure made deep lines come into her face. Her children were growing up, they would have to go to school. There must be more money, there must be more money. The father, who was always very handsome and expensive in his tastes, seemed as if he never *would* be able to do anything worth doing. And the mother, who had a great belief in herself, did not succeed any better, and her tastes were just as expensive.

And so the house came to be haunted by the unspoken phrase: *There*   5
must be more money! There must be more money! The children could hear
it all the time, though nobody said it aloud. They heard it at Christmas,
when the expensive and splendid toys filled the nursery. Behind the shining modern rocking-horse, behind the smart doll's house, a voice would
start whispering: "There *must* be more money! There *must* be more
money!" And the children would stop playing, to listen for a moment.
They would look into each other's eyes, to see if they had all heard. And
each one saw in the eyes of the other two that they too had heard. "There
must be more money! There *must* be more money!"

It came whispering from the springs of the still-swaying rocking-
horse, and even the horse, bending his wooden, champing head, heard
it. The big doll, sitting so pink and smirking in her new pram, could hear
it quite plainly, and seemed to be smirking all the more self-consciously
because of it. The foolish puppy, too, that took the place of the teddy-
bear, he was looking so extraordinarily foolish for no other reason but
that he heard the secret whisper all over the house: "There *must* be more
money!"

Yet nobody ever said it aloud. The whisper was everywhere, and therefore no one spoke it. Just as no one ever says: "We are breathing!" in spite
of the fact that breath is coming and going all the time.

"Mother," said the boy Paul one day, "why don't we keep a car of our
own? Why do we always use uncle's, or else a taxi?"

"Because we're the poor members of the family," said the mother.

"But why *are* we, mother?"   10

"Well—I suppose," she said slowly and bitterly, "it's because your
father has no luck."

The boy was silent for some time.

"Is luck money, mother?" he asked, rather timidly.

"No, Paul. Not quite. It's what causes you to have money."

"Oh!" said Paul vaguely. "I thought when Uncle Oscar said *filthy*   15
lucker, it meant money."

"*Filthy lucre*[1] does mean money," said the mother. "But it's lucre, not
luck."

"Oh!" said the boy. "Then what *is* luck, mother?"

"It's what causes you to have money. If you're lucky you have money.
That's why it's better to be born lucky than rich. If you're rich, you may
lose your money. But if you're lucky, you will always get more money."

"Oh! Will you? And is father not lucky?"

"Very unlucky, I should say," she said bitterly.   20

[1]filthy lucre: An expression originating from Titus 1.11 in the Bible, meaning money acquired through
deceit.

The boy watched her with unsure eyes.

"Why?" he asked.

"I don't know. Nobody ever knows why one person is lucky and another unlucky."

"Don't they? Nobody at all? Does *nobody* know?"

25   "Perhaps God. But He never tells."

"He ought to, then. And aren't you lucky either, mother?"

"I can't be, if I married an unlucky husband."

"But by yourself, aren't you?"

"I used to think I was, before I married. Now I think I am very unlucky indeed."

30   "Why?"

"Well—never mind! Perhaps I'm not really," she said.

The child looked at her to see if she meant it. But he saw, by the lines of her mouth, that she was only trying to hide something from him.

"Well, anyhow," he said stoutly, "I'm a lucky person."

"Why?" said his mother, with a sudden laugh.

35   He stared at her. He didn't even know why he had said it.

"God told me," he asserted, brazening it out.

"I hope He did, dear!" she said, again with a laugh, but rather bitter.

"He did, mother!"

"Excellent!" said the mother, using one of her husband's exclamations.

40   The boy saw she did not believe him; or rather, that she paid no attention to his assertion. This angered him somewhat, and made him want to compel her attention.

He went off by himself, vaguely, in a childish way, seeking for the clue to "luck." Absorbed, taking no heed of other people, he went about with a sort of stealth, seeking inwardly for luck. He wanted luck, he wanted it, he wanted it. When the two girls were playing dolls in the nursery, he would sit on his big rocking-horse, charging madly into space, with a frenzy that made the little girls peer at him uneasily. Wildly the horse careered, the waving dark hair of the boy tossed, his eyes had a strange glare in them. The little girls dared not speak to him.

When he had ridden to the end of his mad little journey, he climbed down and stood in front of his rocking-horse, staring fixedly into its lowered face. Its red mouth was slightly open, its big eye was wide and glassy-bright.

"Now!" he would silently command the snorting steed. "Now, take me to where there is luck! Now take me!"

And he would slash the horse on the neck with the little whip he had asked Uncle Oscar for. He *knew* the horse could take him to where there was luck, if only he forced it. So he would mount again and start on his furious ride, hoping at last to get there. He knew he could get there.

"You'll break your horse, Paul!" said the nurse.   45

"He's always riding like that! I wish he'd leave off!" said his elder sister Joan.

But he only glared down on them in silence. Nurse gave him up. She could make nothing of him. Anyhow, he was growing beyond her.

One day his mother and his Uncle Oscar came in when he was on one of his furious rides. He did not speak to them.

"Hallo, you young jockey! Riding a winner?" said his uncle.

"Aren't you growing too big for a rocking-horse? You're not a very   50 little boy any longer, you know," said his mother.

But Paul only gave a blue glare from his big, rather close-set eyes. He would speak to nobody when he was in full tilt. His mother watched him with an anxious expression on her face.

At last he suddenly stopped forcing his horse into the mechanical gallop and slid down.

"Well, I got there!" he announced fiercely, his blue eyes still flaring, and his sturdy long legs straddling apart.

"Where did you get to?" asked his mother.

"Where I wanted to go," he flared back at her.   55

"That's right, son!" said Uncle Oscar. "Don't you stop till you get there. What's the horse's name?"

"He doesn't have a name," said the boy.

"Gets on without all right?" asked the uncle.

"Well, he has different names. He was called Sansovino last week."

"Sansovino, eh? Won the Ascot.[2] How did you know this name?"   60

"He always talks about horse-races with Bassett," said Joan.

The uncle was delighted to find that his small nephew was posted with all the racing news. Bassett, the young gardener, who had been wounded in the left foot in the war and had got his present job through Oscar Cresswell, whose batman[3] he had been, was a perfect blade of the "turf." He lived in the racing events, and the small boy lived with him.

Oscar Cresswell got it all from Bassett.

"Master Paul comes and asks me, so I can't do more than tell him, sir," said Bassett, his face terribly serious, as if he were speaking of religious matters.

"And does he ever put anything on a horse he fancies?"   65

"Well—I don't want to give him away—he's a young sport, a fine sport, sir. Would you mind asking him himself? He sort of takes a pleasure in it, and perhaps he'd feel I was giving him away, sir, if you don't mind."

Bassett was serious as a church.

---

[2] *the Ascot:* The annual horse race at Ascot Heath in England.
[3] *batman:* A British military officer's personal assistant.

The uncle went back to his nephew and took him off for a ride in the car.

"Say, Paul, old man, do you ever put anything on a horse?" the uncle asked.

70 The boy watched the handsome man closely.

"Why, do you think I oughtn't to?" he parried.

"Not a bit of it! I thought perhaps you might give me a tip for the Lincoln."[4]

The car sped on into the country, going down to Uncle Oscar's place in Hampshire.

75 "Honour bright?" said the nephew.

"Honour bright, son!" said the uncle.

"Well, then, Daffodil."

"Daffodil! I doubt it, sonny. What about Mirza?"

"I only know the winner," said the boy. "That's Daffodil."

"Daffodil, eh?"

80 There was a pause. Daffodil was an obscure horse comparatively.

"Uncle!"

"Yes, son?"

"You won't let it go any further, will you? I promised Bassett."

"Bassett be damned, old man! What's he got to do with it?"

85 "We're partners. We've been partners from the first. Uncle, he lent me my first five shillings, which I lost. I promised him, honour bright, it was only between me and him; only you gave me that ten-shilling note I started winning with, so I thought you were lucky. You won't let it go any further, will you?"

The boy gazed at his uncle from those big, hot, blue eyes, set rather close together. The uncle stirred and laughed uneasily.

"Right you are, son! I'll keep your tip private. Daffodil, eh? How much are you putting on him?"

"All except twenty pounds," said the boy. "I keep that in reserve."

The uncle thought it a good joke.

90 "You keep twenty pounds in reserve, do you, you young romancer? What are you betting, then?"

"I'm betting three hundred," said the boy gravely. "But it's between you and me, Uncle Oscar! Honour bright?"

The uncle burst into a roar of laughter.

"It's between you and me all right, you young Nat Gould,"[5] he said, laughing. "But where's your three hundred?"

---

[4]*the Lincoln:* The Lincolnshire Handicap, a horse race.

[5]*Nat Gould:* Nathaniel Gould (1857–1919), British journalist and writer known for his stories about horse racing.

"Bassett keeps it for me. We're partners."

"You are, are you! And what is Bassett putting on Daffodil?" 95

"He won't go quite as high as I do, I expect. Perhaps he'll go a hundred and fifty."

"What, pennies?" laughed the uncle.

"Pounds," said the child, with a surprised look at his uncle. "Bassett keeps a bigger reserve than I do."

Between wonder and amusement Uncle Oscar was silent. He pursued the matter no further, but he determined to take his nephew with him to the Lincoln races.

"Now, son," he said, "I'm putting twenty on Mirza, and I'll put five on 100 for you on any horse you fancy. What's your pick?"

"Daffodil, uncle."

"No, not the fiver on Daffodil!"

"I should if it was my own fiver," said the child.

"Good! Good! Right you are! A fiver for me and a fiver for you on Daffodil."

The child had never been to a race-meeting before, and his eyes were 105 blue fire. He pursed his mouth tight and watched. A Frenchman just in front had put his money on Lancelot. Wild with excitement, he flayed his arms up and down, yelling *"Lancelot! Lancelot!"* in his French accent.

Daffodil came in first, Lancelot second, Mirza third. The child, flushed and with eyes blazing, was curiously serene. His uncle brought him four five-pound notes, four to one.

"What am I to do with these?" he cried, waving them before the boy's eyes.

"I suppose we'll talk to Bassett," said the boy. "I expect I have fifteen hundred now; and twenty in reserve; and this twenty."

His uncle studied him for some moments.

"Look here, son!" he said. "You're not serious about Bassett and that 110 fifteen hundred, are you?"

"Yes, I am. But it's between you and me, uncle. Honour bright?"

"Honour bright all right, son! But I must talk to Bassett."

"If you'd like to be a partner, uncle, with Bassett and me, we could all be partners. Only, you'd have to promise, honour bright, uncle, not to let it go beyond us three. Bassett and I are lucky, and you must be lucky, because it was your ten shillings I started winning with. . . ."

Uncle Oscar took both Bassett and Paul into Richmond Park for an afternoon, and there they talked.

"It's like this, you see, sir," Bassett said. "Master Paul would get me 115 talking about racing events, spinning yarns, you know, sir. And he was always keen on knowing if I'd made or if I'd lost. It's about a year since, now, that I put five shillings on Blush of Dawn for him: and we lost.

Then the luck turned, with that ten shillings he had from you: that we put on Singhalese. And since that time, it's been pretty steady, all things considering. What do you say, Master Paul?"

"We're all right when we're sure," said Paul. "It's when we're not quite sure that we go down."

"Oh, but we're careful then," said Bassett.

"But when are you *sure?*" smiled Uncle Oscar.

"It's Master Paul, sir," said Bassett in a secret, religious voice. "It's as if he had it from heaven. Like Daffodil, now, for the Lincoln. That was as sure as eggs."

120   "Did you put anything on Daffodil?" asked Oscar Cresswell.

"Yes, sir. I made my bit."

"And my nephew?"

Bassett was obstinately silent, looking at Paul.

"I made twelve hundred, didn't I, Bassett? I told uncle I was putting three hundred on Daffodil."

125   "That's right," said Bassett, nodding.

"But where's the money?" asked the uncle.

"I keep it safe locked up, sir. Master Paul can have it any minute he likes to ask for it."

"What, fifteen hundred pounds?"

"And twenty! And *forty,* that is, with the twenty he made on the course."

130   "It's amazing!" said the uncle.

"If Master Paul offers you to be partners, sir, I would, if I were you: if you'll excuse me," said Bassett.

Oscar Cresswell thought about it.

"I'll see the money," he said.

They drove home again, and, sure enough, Bassett came round to the garden-house with fifteen hundred pounds in notes. The twenty pounds reserve was left with Joe Glee, in the Turf Commission deposit.

135   "You see, it's all right, uncle, when I'm *sure!* Then we go strong, for all we're worth. Don't we, Bassett?"

"We do that, Master Paul."

"And when are you sure?" said the uncle, laughing.

"Oh, well, sometimes I'm *absolutely* sure, like about Daffodil," said the boy; "and sometimes I have an idea; and sometimes I haven't even an idea, have I, Bassett? Then we're careful, because we mostly go down."

"You do, do you! And when you're sure, like about Daffodil, what makes you sure, sonny?"

140   "Oh, well, I don't know," said the boy uneasily. "I'm sure, you know, uncle; that's all."

"It's as if he had it from heaven, sir," Bassett reiterated.

"I should say so!" said the uncle.

But he became a partner. And when the Leger[6] was coming on Paul was "sure" about Lively Spark, which was a quite inconsiderable horse. The boy insisted on putting a thousand on the horse, Bassett went for five hundred, and Oscar Cresswell two hundred. Lively Spark came in first, and the betting had been ten to one against him. Paul had made ten thousand.

"You see," he said, "I was absolutely sure of him."

Even Oscar Cresswell had cleared two thousand.   145

"Look here, son," he said, "this sort of thing makes me nervous."

"It needn't, uncle! Perhaps I shan't be sure again for a long time."

"But what are you going to do with your money?" asked the uncle.

"Of course," said the boy, "I started it for mother. She said she had no luck, because father is unlucky, so I thought if *I* was lucky, it might stop whispering."

"What might stop whispering?"   150

"Our house. I *hate* our house for whispering."

"What does it whisper?"

"Why—why"—the boy fidgeted—"why, I don't know. But it's always short of money, you know, uncle."

"I know it, son, I know it."

"You know people send mother writs,[7] don't you, uncle?"   155

"I'm afraid I do," said the uncle.

"And then the house whispers, like people laughing at you behind your back. It's awful, that is! I thought if I was lucky . . ."

"You might stop it," added the uncle.

The boy watched him with big blue eyes, that had an uncanny cold fire in them, and he said never a word.

"Well, then!" said the uncle. "What are we doing?"   160

"I shouldn't like mother to know I was lucky," said the boy.

"Why not, son?"

"She'd stop me."

"I don't think she would."

"Oh!"—and the boy writhed in an odd way—"I *don't* want her to 165 know, uncle."

"All right, son! We'll manage it without her knowing."

They managed it very easily. Paul, at the other's suggestion, handed over five thousand pounds to his uncle, who deposited it with the family lawyer, who was then to inform Paul's mother that a relative had put five

---

[6] *the Leger:* The St. Leger Stakes, a horse race.

[7] *writs:* Letters from creditors requesting payment.

thousand pounds into his hands, which sum was to be paid out a thousand pounds at a time, on the mother's birthday, for the next five years.

"So she'll have a birthday present of a thousand pounds for five successive years," said Uncle Oscar. "I hope it won't make it all the harder for her later."

Paul's mother had her birthday in November. The house had been "whispering" worse than ever lately, and, even in spite of his luck, Paul could not bear up against it. He was very anxious to see the effect of the birthday letter, telling his mother about the thousand pounds.

170   When there were no visitors, Paul now took his meals with his parents, as he was beyond the nursery control. His mother went into town nearly every day. She had discovered that she had an odd knack of sketching furs and dress materials, so she worked secretly in the studio of a friend who was the chief "artist" for the leading drapers. She drew the figures of ladies in furs and ladies in silk and sequins for the newspaper advertisements. This young woman artist earned several thousand pounds a year, but Paul's mother only made several hundreds, and she was again dissatisfied. She so wanted to be first in something, and she did not succeed, even in making sketches for drapery advertisements.

She was down to breakfast on the morning of her birthday. Paul watched her face as she read her letters. He knew the lawyer's letter. As his mother read it, her face hardened and became more expressionless. Then a cold, determined look came on her mouth. She hid the letter under the pile of others, and said not a word about it.

"Didn't you have anything nice in the post for your birthday, mother?" said Paul.

"Quite moderately nice," she said, her voice cold and absent.

She went away to town without saying more.

175   But in the afternoon Uncle Oscar appeared. He said Paul's mother had had a long interview with the lawyer, asking if the whole five thousand could not be advanced at once, as she was in debt.

"What do you think, uncle?" asked the boy.

"I leave it to you, son."

"Oh, let her have it, then! We can get some more with the other," said the boy.

"A bird in the hand is worth two in the bush, laddie!" said Uncle Oscar.

180   "But I'm sure to *know* for the Grand National; or the Lincolnshire; or else the Derby.[8] I'm sure to know for *one* of them," said Paul.

---

[8]*Grand National . . . Derby:* Famous British horse races. The Grand National is run at Aintree; the Derby, at Epsom Downs.

So Uncle Oscar signed the agreement, and Paul's mother touched the whole five thousand. Then something very curious happened. The voices in the house suddenly went mad, like a chorus of frogs on a spring evening. There was certain new furnishings, and Paul had a tutor. He was *really* going to Eton, his father's school, in the following autumn. There were flowers in the winter, and a blossoming of the luxury Paul's mother had been used to. And yet the voices in the house, behind the sprays of mimosa and almond-blossom, and from under the piles of iridescent cushions, simply trilled and screamed in a sort of ecstasy: "There *must* be more money! Oh-h-h; there *must* be more money. Oh, now, now-w! Now-w-w—there *must* be more money!—more than ever! More than ever!"

It frightened Paul terribly. He studied away at his Latin and Greek with his tutor. But his intense hours were spent with Bassett. The Grand National had gone by: he had not "known," and had lost a hundred pounds. Summer was at hand. He was in agony for the Lincoln. But even for the Lincoln he didn't "know," and he lost fifty pounds. He became wild-eyed and strange, as if something were going to explode in him.

"Let it alone, son! Don't you bother about it!" urged Uncle Oscar. But it was as if the boy couldn't really hear what his uncle was saying.

"I've got to know for the Derby! I've got to know for the Derby!" the child reiterated, his big blue eyes blazing with a sort of madness.

His mother noticed how overwrought he was.   185

"You'd better go to the seaside. Wouldn't you like to go now to the seaside, instead of waiting? I think you'd better," she said, looking down at him anxiously, her heart curiously heavy because of him.

But the child lifted his uncanny blue eyes.

"I couldn't possibly go before the Derby, mother!" he said. "I couldn't possibly!"

"Why not?" she said, her voice becoming heavy when she was opposed. "Why not? You can still go from the seaside to see the Derby with your Uncle Oscar, if that's what you wish. No need for you to wait here. Besides, I think you care too much about these races. It's a bad sign. My family has been a gambling family, and you won't know till you grow up how much damage it has done. But it has done damage. I shall have to send Bassett away, and ask Uncle Oscar not to talk racing to you, unless you promise to be reasonable about it: go away to the seaside and forget it. You're all nerves!"

"I'll do what you like, mother, so long as you don't send me away till 190 after the Derby," the boy said.

"Send you away from where? Just from this house?"

"Yes," he said, gazing at her.

"Why, you curious child, what makes you care about this house so much, suddenly? I never knew you loved it."

He gazed at her without speaking. He had a secret within a secret, something he had not divulged, even to Bassett or to his Uncle Oscar.

195   But his mother, after standing undecided and a little bit sullen for some moments, said:

"Very well, then! Don't go to the seaside till after the Derby, if you don't wish it. But promise me you won't let your nerves go to pieces. Promise you won't think so much about horse-racing and *events*, as you call them!"

"Oh no," said the boy casually. "I won't think much about them, mother. You needn't worry. I wouldn't worry, mother, if I were you."

"If you were me and I were you," said his mother, "I wonder what we *should* do!"

"But you know you needn't worry, mother, don't you?" the boy repeated.

200   "I should be awfully glad to know it," she said wearily.

"Oh, well, you *can*, you know. I mean, you *ought* to know you needn't worry," he insisted.

"Ought I? Then I'll see about it," she said.

Paul's secret of secrets was his wooden horse, that which had no name. Since he was emancipated from a nurse and a nursery-governess, he had had his rocking-horse removed to his own bedroom at the top of the house.

"Surely you're too big for a rocking-horse!" his mother had remonstrated.

205   "Well, you see, mother, till I can have a *real* horse, I like to have *some* sort of animal about," had been his quaint answer.

"Do you feel he keeps you company?" she laughed.

"Oh yes! He's very good, he always keeps me company, when I'm there," said Paul.

So the horse, rather shabby, stood in an arrested prance in the boy's bedroom.

The Derby was drawing near, and the boy grew more and more tense. He hardly heard what was spoken to him, he was very frail, and his eyes were really uncanny. His mother had sudden strange seizures of uneasiness about him. Sometimes, for half an hour, she would feel a sudden anxiety about him that was almost anguish. She wanted to rush to him at once, and know he was safe.

210   Two nights before the Derby, she was at a big party in town, when one of her rushes of anxiety about her boy, her firstborn, gripped her heart till she could hardly speak. She fought with the feeling, might and main, for she believed in common sense. But it was too strong. She had to leave the dance and go downstairs to telephone to the country. The children's nursery-governess was terribly surprised and startled at being rung up in the night.

"Are the children all right, Miss Wilmot?"

"Oh yes, they are quite all right."

"Master Paul? Is he all right?"

"He went to bed as right as a trivet. Shall I run up and look at him?"

"No," said Paul's mother reluctantly. "No! Don't trouble. It's all right. 215 Don't sit up. We shall be home fairly soon." She did not want her son's privacy intruded upon.

"Very good," said the governess.

It was about one o'clock when Paul's mother and father drove up to their house. All was still. Paul's mother went to her room and slipped off her white fur cloak. She had told her maid not to wait up for her. She heard her husband downstairs, mixing a whisky and soda.

And then, because of the strange anxiety at her heart, she stole upstairs to her son's room. Noiselessly she went along the upper corridor. Was there a faint noise? What was it?

She stood, with arrested muscles, outside his door, listening. There was a strange, heavy, and yet not loud noise. Her heart stood still. It was a soundless noise, yet rushing and powerful. Something huge, in violent, hushed motion. What was it? What in God's name was it? She ought to know. She felt that she knew the noise. She knew what it was.

Yet she could not place it. She couldn't say what it was. And on and 220 on it went, like a madness.

Softly, frozen with anxiety and fear, she turned the door-handle.

The room was dark. Yet in the space near the window, she heard and saw something plunging to and fro. She gazed in fear and amazement.

Then suddenly she switched on the light, and saw her son, in his green pyjamas, madly surging on the rocking-horse. The blaze of light suddenly lit him up, as he urged the wooden horse, and lit her up, as she stood, blonde, in her dress of pale green and crystal, in the doorway.

"Paul!" she cried. "Whatever are you doing?"

"It's Malabar!" he screamed in a powerful, strange voice. "It's 225 Malabar!"

His eyes blazed at her for one strange and senseless second, as he ceased urging his wooden horse. Then he fell with a crash to the ground, and she, all her tormented motherhood flooding upon her, rushed to gather him up.

But he was unconscious, and unconscious he remained, with some brain-fever. He talked and tossed, and his mother sat stonily by his side.

"Malabar! It's Malabar! Bassett, Bassett, I *know*! It's Malabar!"

So the child cried, trying to get up and urge the rocking-horse that gave him his inspiration.

"What does he mean by Malabar?" asked the heart-frozen mother.   230

"I don't know," said the father stonily.

"What does he mean by Malabar?" she asked her brother Oscar.

"It's one of the horses running for the Derby," was the answer.

And, in spite of himself, Oscar Cresswell spoke to Bassett, and himself put a thousand on Malabar: at fourteen to one.

235   The third day of the illness was critical: they were waiting for a change. The boy, with his rather long, curly hair, was tossing ceaselessly on the pillow. He neither slept nor regained consciousness, and his eyes were like blue stones. His mother sat, feeling her heart had gone, turned actually into a stone.

In the evening, Oscar Cresswell did not come, but Bassett sent a message, saying could he come up for one moment, just one moment? Paul's mother was very angry at the intrusion, but on second thought she agreed. The boy was the same. Perhaps Bassett might bring him to consciousness.

The gardener, a shortish fellow with a little brown moustache and sharp little brown eyes, tiptoed into the room, touched his imaginary cap to Paul's mother, and stole to the bedside, staring with glittering, smallish eyes at the tossing, dying child.

"Master Paul!" he whispered. "Master Paul! Malabar came in first all right, a clean win. I did as you told me. You've made over seventy thousand pounds, you have; you've got over eighty thousand. Malabar came in all right, Master Paul."

"Malabar! Malabar! Did I say Malabar, mother? Did I say Malabar? Do you think I'm lucky, mother? I knew Malabar, didn't I? Over eighty thousand pounds! I call that lucky, don't you, mother? Over eighty thousand pounds! I knew, didn't I know I knew? Malabar came in all right. If I ride my horse till I'm sure, then I tell you, Bassett, you can go as high as you like. Did you go for all you were worth, Bassett?"

240   "I went a thousand on it, Master Paul."

"I never told you, mother, that if I can ride my horse, and *get there*, then I'm absolutely sure—oh, absolutely! Mother, did I ever tell you? I *am* lucky!"

"No, you never did," said his mother.

But the boy died in the night.

And even as he lay dead, his mother heard her brother's voice saying to her: "My God, Hester, you're eighty-odd thousand to the good, and a poor devil of a son to the bad. But, poor devil, poor devil, he's best gone out of a life where he rides his rocking-horse to find a winner."

Reading and Reacting

1. From what point of view is "The Rocking-Horse Winner" told? How does this point of view help to communicate the story's theme?

2. In what ways is "The Rocking-Horse Winner" like a fairy tale? How is it different?

3. Many fairy tales involve a hero who goes on a journey to search for something of great value. What journey does Paul go on? What thing of value does he search for? Is he successful?

4. In paragraph 5, the narrator says that the house is "haunted by the unspoken phrase: '*There must be more money!*'" In what way does this phrase "haunt" the house?

5. How would you characterize Paul's parents? his uncle? Bassett? Are they weak? evil? What motivates them?

6. Beginning in paragraph 11, Paul's mother attempts to define the word *luck*. According to her definition, is Paul lucky?

7. In what ways does Paul behave like other children? In what ways is he different? How do you account for these differences? How old do you think Paul is? Why is his age significant?

8. The rocking horse is an important literary **symbol** in the story. What possible meanings might the rocking horse suggest? In what ways does this symbol reinforce the story's theme?

9. What secrets do the various characters keep from one another? Why do they keep them? What do these secrets suggest about the story's theme?

10. How does Paul know who the winners will be? Does the rocking horse really tell him? Does he get his information "from heaven" as Bassett suggests (par. 119)? Or does he just guess?

11. **JOURNAL ENTRY** In your opinion, who or what is responsible for Paul's death?

12. **CRITICAL PERSPECTIVE** In a letter dated January 17, 1913, Lawrence wrote the following:

> My great religion is a belief in the blood, the flesh, as being wiser than the intellect. We can go wrong in our minds. But what our blood feels and believes and says, is always true. The intellect is only a bit and a bridle. What do I care about knowledge. All I want is to answer to my blood, direct, without fribbling intervention of mind, or moral, or what-not.

How does Lawrence's portrayal of Paul in "The Rocking-Horse Winner" support his belief in "the blood . . . being wiser than the intellect"? How does Lawrence remain true in this story to his metaphor of the intellect as "a bit and a bridle"?

Related Works: "Gretel in Darkness" (p. 501), "Suicide Note" (p. 507), "Birches" (p. 715), *Death of a Salesman* (p. 960)

WRITING SUGGESTIONS: Theme

1. Both Paul in "The Rocking-Horse Winner" and Andy in "Doe Season" experience traumatic events that, as children, they cannot fully understand or interpret what they see. Write an essay in which you examine the limited nature of each character's view of events. Then discuss how this limited view helps each author develop the main theme of his story.
2. Both "The Rocking-Horse Winner" and "A Worn Path" deal with characters who make journeys. What is the significance of each journey? How do the protagonists of these two stories overcome the obstacles they encounter? In what sense are these journeys symbolic as well as actual?
3. Like "Doe Season," the following poem focuses on a child's experience with hunting. Write an essay in which you contrast its central theme with the central theme of "Doe Season."

ROBERT HUFF (1924–1993)

Rainbow[1]

After the shot the driven feathers rock
In the air and are by sunlight trapped.
Their moment of descent is eloquent.
It is the rainbow echo of a bird
Whose thunder, stopped, puts in my daughter's eyes   5
A question mark. She does not see the rainbow,
And the folding bird-fall was for her too quick.
It is about the stillness of the bird
Her eyes are asking. She is three years old;
Has cut her fingers; found blood tastes of salt;   10
But she has never witnessed quiet blood,
Nor ever seen before the peace of death.
I say: "The feathers—Look!" but she is torn
And wretched and draws back. And I am glad
That I have wounded her, have winged her heart,   15
And that she goes beyond my fathering.

---

[1]Publication date is not available.

CHAPTER 14

FICTION FOR FURTHER READING

T. CORAGHESSAN BOYLE (1948–)

Greasy Lake (1985)

It's about a mile down on the dark side of Route 88.

—*Bruce Springsteen*

There was a time when courtesy and winning ways went out of style, when it was good to be bad, when you cultivated decadence like a taste. We were all dangerous characters then. We wore torn-up leather jackets, slouched around with toothpicks in our mouths, sniffed glue and ether and what somebody claimed was cocaine. When we wheeled our parents' whining station wagons out into the street we left a patch of rubber half a block long. We drank gin and grape juice, Tango, Thunderbird, and Bali Hai. We were nineteen. We were bad. We read André Gide[1] and struck elaborate poses to show that we didn't give a shit about anything. At night, we went up to Greasy Lake.

Through the center of town, up the strip, past the housing developments and shopping malls, street lights giving way to the thin streaming illumination of the headlights, trees crowding the asphalt in a black unbroken wall: that was the way out to Greasy Lake. The Indians had called it Wakan, a reference to the clarity of its waters. Now it was fetid and murky, the mud banks glittering with broken glass and strewn with beer cans and the charred remains of bonfires. There was a single ravaged island a hundred yards from shore, so stripped of vegetation it looked as if the air force had strafed it. We went up to the lake because everyone went there, because we wanted to snuff the rich scent of possibility on the breeze, watch a girl take off her clothes and plunge into the festering

---

[1]*André Gide:* French novelist and critic (1869–1951) whose work—much of it semiautobiographical—examines the conflict between desire and discipline and shows individuals battling conventional morality.

murk, drink beer, smoke pot, howl at the stars, savor the incongruous full-throated roar of rock and roll against the primeval susurrus[2] of frogs and crickets. This was nature.

I was there one night, late, in the company of two dangerous characters. Digby wore a gold star in his right ear and allowed his father to pay his tuition at Cornell; Jeff was thinking of quitting school to become a painter/musician/head-shop proprietor. They were both expert in the social graces, quick with a sneer, able to manage a Ford with lousy shocks over a rutted and gutted blacktop road at eighty-five while rolling a joint as compact as a Tootsie Roll Pop stick. They could lounge against a bank of booming speakers and trade "man"s with the best of them or roll out across the dance floor as if their joints worked on bearings. They were slick and quick and they wore their mirror shades at breakfast and dinner, in the shower, in closets and caves. In short, they were bad.

I drove. Digby pounded the dashboard and shouted along with Toots & the Maytals while Jeff hung his head out the window and streaked the side of my mother's Bel Air with vomit. It was early June, the air soft as a hand on your cheek, the third night of summer vacation. The first two nights we'd been out till dawn, looking for something we never found. On this, the third night, we'd cruised the strip sixty-seven times, been in and out of every bar and club we could think of in a twenty-mile radius, stopped twice for bucket chicken and forty-cent hamburgers, debated going to a party at the house of a girl Jeff's sister knew, and chucked two dozen raw eggs at mailboxes and hitchhikers. It was 2:00 A.M.; the bars were closing. There was nothing to do but take a bottle of lemon-flavored gin up to Greasy Lake.

5   The taillights of a single car winked at us as we swung into the dirt lot with its tufts of weed and washboard corrugations; '57 Chevy, mint, metallic blue. On the far side of the lot, like the exoskeleton of some gaunt chrome insect, a chopper leaned against its kickstand. And that was it for excitement: some junkie half-wit biker and a car freak pumping his girlfriend. Whatever it was we were looking for, we weren't about to find it at Greasy Lake. Not that night.

But then all of a sudden Digby was fighting for the wheel. "Hey, that's Tony Lovett's car! Hey!" he shouted, while I stabbed at the brake pedal and the Bel Air nosed up to the gleaming bumper of the parked Chevy. Digby leaned on the horn, laughing, and instructed me to put my brights on. I flicked on the brights. This was hilarious. A joke. Tony would experience premature withdrawal and expect to be confronted by grim-looking state troopers with flashlights. We hit the horn, strobed the lights, and

---

[2]*susurrus:* A whispering or rustling sound.

then jumped out of the car to press our witty faces to Tony's windows; for all we knew we might even catch a glimpse of some little fox's tit, and then we could slap backs with red-faced Tony, roughhouse a little, and go on to new heights of adventure and daring.

The first mistake, the one that opened the whole floodgate, was losing my grip on the keys. In the excitement, leaping from the car with the gin in one hand and a roach clip in the other, I spilled them in the grass—in the dark, rank, mysterious nighttime grass of Greasy Lake. This was a tactical error, as damaging and irreversible in its way as Westmoreland's decision to dig in at Khe Sanh.[3] I felt it like a jab of intuition, and I stopped there by the open door, peering vaguely into the night that puddled up round my feet.

The second mistake—and this was inextricably bound up with the first—was identifying the car as Tony Lovett's. Even before the very bad character in greasy jeans and engineer boots ripped out of the driver's door, I began to realize that this chrome blue was much lighter than the robin's-egg of Tony's car, and that Tony's car didn't have rear-mounted speakers. Judging from their expressions, Digby and Jeff were privately groping toward the same inevitable and unsettling conclusion as I was.

In any case, there was no reasoning with this bad greasy character— clearly he was a man of action. The first lusty Rockette[4] kick of his steel-toed boot caught me under the chin, chipped my favorite tooth, and left me sprawled in the dirt. Like a fool, I'd gone down on one knee to comb the stiff hacked grass for the keys, my mind making connections in the most dragged-out, testudineous[5] way, knowing that things had gone wrong, that I was in a lot of trouble, and that the lost ignition key was my grail and my salvation. The three or four succeeding blows were mainly absorbed by my right buttock and the tough piece of bone at the base of my spine.

Meanwhile, Digby vaulted the kissing bumpers and delivered a savage   10 kung-fu blow to the greasy character's collarbone. Digby had just finished a course in martial arts for phys-ed credit and had spent the better part of the past two nights telling us apocryphal tales of Bruce Lee types and of the raw power invested in lightning blows shot from coiled wrists, ankles, and elbows. The greasy character was unimpressed. He merely backed off

---

[3]*Khe Sanh:* In late 1967, North Vietnamese and Viet Cong forces mounted a strong attack against American troops at Khe Sanh, thereby causing General William C. Westmoreland, commander of United States forces in Vietnam, to "dig in" to defend an area of relatively little tactical importance.

[4]*Rockette:* The reference is to the Rockettes, a dance troupe at New York's Radio City Music Hall noted for precision and cancan-like high kicks.

[5]*testudineous:* Slow, like the pace of a tortoise.

a step, his face like a Toltec mask, and laid Digby out with a single whistling roundhouse blow...but by now Jeff had got into the act, and I was beginning to extricate myself from the dirt, a tinny compound of shock, rage, and impotence wadded in my throat.

Jeff was on the guy's back, biting at his ear. Digby was on the ground, cursing. I went for the tire iron I kept under the driver's seat. I kept it there because bad characters always keep tire irons under the driver's seat, for just such an occasion as this. Never mind that I hadn't been involved in a fight since sixth grade, when a kid with a sleepy eye and two streams of mucus depending from his nostrils hit me in the knee with a Louisville slugger,[6] never mind that I'd touched the tire iron exactly twice before, to change tires: it was there. And I went for it.

I was terrified. Blood was beating in my ears, my hands were shaking, my heart turning over like a dirtbike in the wrong gear. My antagonist was shirtless, and a single cord of muscle flashed across his chest as he bent forward to peel Jeff from his back like a wet overcoat. "Motherfucker," he spat, over and over, and I was aware in that instant that all four of us—Digby, Jeff, and myself included—were chanting "motherfucker, motherfucker," as if it were a battle cry. (What happened next? the detective asks the murderer from beneath the turned-down brim of his porkpie hat. I don't know, the murderer says, something came over me. Exactly.)

Digby poked the flat of his hand in the bad character's face and I came at him like a kamikaze, mindless, raging, stung with humiliation—the whole thing, from the initial boot in the chin to this murderous primal instant involving no more than sixty hyperventilating, gland-flooding seconds—I came at him and brought the tire iron down across his ear. The effect was instantaneous, astonishing. He was a stunt man and this was Hollywood, he was a big grimacing toothy balloon and I was a man with a straight pin. He collapsed. Wet his pants. Went loose in his boots.

A single second, big as a zeppelin, floated by. We were standing over him in a circle, gritting our teeth, jerking our necks, our limbs and hands and feet twitching with glandular discharges. No one said anything. We just stared down at the guy, the car freak, the lover, the bad greasy character laid low. Digby looked at me; so did Jeff. I was still holding the tire iron, a tuft of hair clinging to the crook like dandelion fluff, like down. Rattled, I dropped it in the dirt, already envisioning the headlines, the pitted faces of the police inquisitors, the gleam of handcuffs, clank of bars, the big black shadows rising from the back of the cell...when suddenly a raw torn shriek cut through me like all the juice in all the electric chairs in the country.

---

[6]*Louisville slugger:* A popular brand of baseball bat.

It was the fox. She was short, barefoot, dressed in panties and a man's 15
shirt. "Animals!" she screamed, running at us with her fists clenched and
wisps of blow-dried hair in her face. There was a silver chain round her
ankle, and her toenails flashed in the glare of the headlights. I think it
was the toenails that did it. Sure, the gin and the cannabis and even the
Kentucky Fried may have had a hand in it, but it was the sight of those
flaming toes that set us off—the toad emerging from the loaf in *Virgin
Spring*,[7] lipstick smeared on a child: she was already tainted. We were
on her like Bergman's deranged brothers—see no evil, hear none, speak
none—panting, wheezing, tearing at her clothes, grabbing for flesh. We
were bad characters, and we were scared and hot and three steps over the
line—anything could have happened.

It didn't.

Before we could pin her to the hood of the car, our eyes masked
with lust and greed and the purest primal badness, a pair of headlights
swung into the lot. There we were, dirty, bloody, guilty, dissociated
from humanity and civilization, the first of the Ur-crimes[8] behind us, the
second in progress, shreds of nylon panty and spandex brassiere dangling
from our fingers, our flies open, lips licked—there we were, caught in
the spotlight. Nailed.

We bolted. First for the car, and then, realizing we had no way of starting it, for the woods. I thought nothing. I thought escape. The headlights
came at me like accusing fingers. I was gone.

Ram-bam-bam, across the parking lot, past the chopper and into the
feculent undergrowth at the lake's edge, insects flying up in my face,
weeds whipping, frogs and snakes and red-eyed turtles splashing off into
the night: I was already ankle-deep in muck and tepid water and still
going strong. Behind me, the girl's screams rose in intensity, disconsolate,
incriminating, the screams of the Sabine women,[9] the Christian martyrs,
Anne Frank[10] dragged from the garret. I kept going, pursued by those cries,
imagining cops and bloodhounds. The water was up to my knees when
I realized what I was doing: I was going to swim for it. Swim the breadth
of Greasy Lake and hide myself in the thick clot of woods on the far side.
They'd never find me there.

---

[7]*Virgin Spring:* A film by Swedish director Ingmar Bergman.

[8]*Ur-crimes:* Primitive crimes.

[9]*Sabine women:* According to legend, members of an ancient Italian tribe abducted by Romans who
took them for wives. The "Rape of the Sabine Women" has been depicted by various artists, most
notably by seventeenth-century French painter Nicolas Poussin.

[10]*Anne Frank:* German Jewish girl (1929–1945) whose family hid in an attic in Amsterdam during the
Nazi occupation of the Netherlands. Frank, who along with her family was discovered by storm troopers
and sent to die at the concentration camp at Belsen, is famous for her diary, which recounts her days in
hiding. A new version of the diary containing five missing pages surfaced in 1998.

20   I was breathing in sobs, in gasps. The water lapped at my waist as I looked out over the moon-burnished ripples, the mats of algae that clung to the surface like scabs. Digby and Jeff had vanished. I paused. Listened. The girl was quieter now, screams tapering to sobs, but there were male voices, angry, excited, and the high-pitched ticking of the second car's engine. I waded deeper, stealthy, hunted, the ooze sucking at my sneakers. As I was about to take the plunge—at the very instant I dropped my shoulder for the first slashing stroke—I blundered into something. Something unspeakable, obscene, something soft, wet, moss-grown. A patch of weed? A log? When I reached out to touch it, it gave like a rubber duck, it gave like flesh.

In one of those nasty little epiphanies for which we are prepared by films and TV and childhood visits to the funeral home to ponder the shrunken painted forms of dead grandparents, I understood what it was that bobbed there so inadmissibly in the dark. Understood, and stumbled back in horror and revulsion, my mind yanked in six different directions (I was nineteen, a mere child, an infant, and here in the space of five minutes I'd struck down one greasy character and blundered into the waterlogged carcass of a second), thinking, The keys, the keys, why did I have to go and lose the keys? I stumbled back, but the muck took hold of my feet—a sneaker snagged, balance lost—and suddenly I was pitching face forward into the buoyant black mass, throwing out my hands in desperation while simultaneously conjuring the image of reeking frogs and muskrats revolving in slicks of their own deliquescing[11] juices. AAAAArrrgh! I shot from the water like a torpedo, the dead man rotating to expose a mossy beard and eyes cold as the moon. I must have shouted out, thrashing around in the weeds, because the voices behind me suddenly became animated.

"What was that?"

"It's them, it's them: they tried to, tried to ...*rape* me!" Sobs.

A man's voice, flat Midwestern accent. "You sons a bitches, we'll kill you!"

25   Frogs, crickets.

Then another voice, harsh, *r*-less, Lower East Side: "Motherfucker!" I recognized the verbal virtuosity of the bad greasy character in the engineer boots. Tooth chipped, sneakers gone, coated in mud and slime and worse, crouching breathless in the weeds waiting to have my ass thoroughly and definitively kicked and fresh from the hideous stinking embrace of a three-days-dead-corpse, I suddenly felt a rush of joy and vindication: the son of a bitch was alive! Just as quickly, my bowels

---

[11]*deliquescing:* Melting.

turned to ice. "Come on out of there, you pansy mothers!" the bad greasy character was screaming. He shouted curses till he was out of breath.

The crickets started up again, then the frogs. I held my breath. All at once there was a sound in the reeds, a swishing, a splash: thunk-a-thunk. They were throwing rocks. The frogs fell silent. I cradled my head. Swish, swish, thunk-a-thunk. A wedge of feldspar the size of a cue ball glanced off my knee. I bit my finger.

It was then that they turned to the car. I heard a door slam, a curse, and then the sound of the headlights shattering—almost a good-natured sound, celebratory, like corks popping from the necks of bottles. This was succeeded by the dull booming of the fenders, metal on metal, and then the icy crash of the windshield. I inched forward, elbows and knees, my belly pressed to the muck, thinking of guerrillas and commandos and *The Naked and the Dead*.[12] I parted the weeds and squinted the length of the parking lot.

The second car—it was a Trans-Am—was still running, its high beams washing the scene in a lurid stagy light. Tire iron flailing, the greasy bad character was laying into the side of my mother's Bel Air like an avenging demon, his shadow riding up the trunks of the trees. Whomp. Whomp. Whomp-whomp. The other two guys—blond types, in fraternity jackets—were helping out with tree branches and skull-sized boulders. One of them was gathering up bottles, rocks, muck, candy wrappers, used condoms, pop-tops, and other refuse and pitching it through the window on the driver's side. I could see the fox, a white bulb behind the windshield of the '57 Chevy. "Bobbie," she whined over the thumping, "come on." The greasy character paused a moment, took one good swipe at the left taillight, and then heaved the tire iron halfway across the lake. Then he fired up the '57 and was gone.

Blond head nodded at blond head. One said something to the other, 30 too low for me to catch. They were no doubt thinking that in helping to annihilate my mother's car they'd committed a fairly rash act, and thinking too that there were three bad characters connected with that very car watching them from the woods. Perhaps other possibilities occurred to them as well—police, jail cells, justices of the peace, reparations, lawyers, irate parents, fraternal censure. Whatever they were thinking, they suddenly dropped branches, bottles, and rocks and sprang for their car in unison, as if they'd choreographed it. Five seconds. That's all it took. The engine shrieked, the tires squealed, a cloud of dust rose from the rutted lot and then settled back on darkness.

---

[12]The Naked and the Dead: A popular and critically praised 1948 novel by Norman Mailer depicting Army life among U.S. soldiers during World War II.

I don't know how long I lay there, the bad breath of decay all around me, my jacket heavy as a bear, the primordial ooze subtly reconstituting itself to accommodate my upper thighs and testicles. My jaws ached, my knee throbbed, my coccyx[13] was on fire. I contemplated suicide, wondered if I'd need bridgework, scraped the recesses of my brain for some sort of excuse to give my parents—a tree had fallen on the car, I was blindsided by a bread truck, hit and run, vandals had got to it while we were playing chess at Digby's. Then I thought of the dead man. He was probably the only person on the planet worse off than I was. I thought about him, fog on the lake, insects chirring eerily, and felt the tug of fear, felt the darkness opening up inside me like a set of jaws. Who was he, I wondered, this victim of time and circumstance bobbing sorrowfully in the lake at my back. The owner of the chopper, no doubt, a bad older character come to this. Shot during a murky drug deal, drowned while drunkenly frolicking in the lake. Another headline. My car was wrecked; he was dead.

When the eastern half of the sky went from black to cobalt and the trees began to separate themselves from the shadows, I pushed myself up from the mud and stepped out into the open. By now the birds had begun to take over for the crickets, and dew lay slick on the leaves. There was a smell in the air, raw and sweet at the same time, the smell of the sun firing buds and opening blossoms. I contemplated the car. It lay there like a wreck along the highway, like a steel sculpture left over from a vanished civilization. Everything was still. This was nature.

I was circling the car, as dazed and bedraggled as the sole survivor of an air blitz, when Digby and Jeff emerged from the trees behind me. Digby's face was crosshatched with smears of dirt; Jeff's jacket was gone and his shirt was torn across the shoulder. They slouched across the lot, looking sheepish, and silently came up beside me to gape at the ravaged automobile. No one said a word. After a while Jeff swung open the driver's door and began to scoop the broken glass and garbage off the seat. I looked at Digby. He shrugged. "At least they didn't slash the tires," he said.

It was true: the tires were intact. There was no windshield, the headlights were staved in, and the body looked as if it had been sledgehammered for a quarter a shot at the county fair, but the tires were inflated to regulation pressure. The car was drivable. In silence, all three of us bent to scrape the mud and shattered glass from the interior. I said nothing about the biker. When we were finished, I reached in my pocket for the keys, experienced a nasty stab of recollection, cursed myself, and turned to search the grass. I spotted them almost immediately, no more than five feet from the open door, glinting like jewels in the first tapering shaft of

---

[13]*coccyx:* Tailbone.

sunlight. There was no reason to get philosophical about it: I eased into the seat and turned the engine over.

It was at that precise moment that the silver Mustang with the flame 35 decals rumbled into the lot. All three of us froze; then Digby and Jeff slid into the car and slammed the door. We watched as the Mustang rocked and bobbed across the ruts and finally jerked to a halt beside the forlorn chopper at the far end of the lot. "Let's go," Digby said. I hesitated, the Bel Air wheezing beneath me.

Two girls emerged from the Mustang. Tight jeans, stiletto heels, hair like frozen fur. They bent over the motorcycle, paced back and forth aimlessly, glanced once or twice at us, and then ambled over to where the reeds sprang up in a green fence round the perimeter of the lake. One of them cupped her hands to her mouth. "Al," she called, "Hey, Al!"

"Come on," Digby hissed. "Let's get out of here."

But it was too late. The second girl was picking her way across the lot, unsteady on her heels, looking up at us and then away. She was older—twenty-five or six—and as she came closer we could see there was something wrong with her: she was stoned or drunk, lurching now and waving her arms for balance. I gripped the steering wheel as if it were the ejection lever of a flaming jet, and Digby spat out my name, twice, terse and impatient.

"Hi," the girl said.

We looked at her like zombies, like war veterans, like deaf-and-dumb 40 pencil peddlers.

She smiled, her lips cracked and dry. "Listen," she said, bending from the waist to look in the window, "you guys seen Al?" Her pupils were pinpoints, her eyes glass. She jerked her neck. "That's his bike over there—Al's. You seen him?"

Al. I didn't know what to say. I wanted to get out of the car and retch, I wanted to go home to my parents' house and crawl into bed. Digby poked me in the ribs. "We haven't seen anybody," I said.

The girl seemed to consider this, reaching out a slim veiny arm to brace herself against the car. "No matter," she said, slurring the *t*'s, "he'll turn up." And then, as if she'd just taken stock of the whole scene—the ravaged car and our battered faces, the desolation of the place—she said: "Hey, you guys look like some pretty bad characters—been fightin', huh?" We stared straight ahead, rigid as catatonics. She was fumbling in her pocket and muttering something. Finally she held out a handful of tablets in glassine wrappers: "Hey, you want to party, you want to do some of these with me and Sarah?"

I just looked at her. I thought I was going to cry. Digby broke the silence. "No, thanks," he said, leaning over me. "Some other time."

I put the car in gear and it inched forward with a groan, shaking off 45 pellets of glass like an old dog shedding water after a bath, heaving over the ruts on its worn springs, creeping toward the highway. There was a sheen of sun on the lake. I looked back. The girl was still standing there, watching us, her shoulders slumped, hand outstretched.

*   *   *

CHARLOTTE PERKINS GILMAN (1860–1935)

The Yellow Wallpaper (1892)

It is very seldom that mere ordinary people like John and myself secure ancestral halls for the summer.

A colonial mansion, a hereditary estate, I would say a haunted house, and reach the height of romantic felicity—but that would be asking too much of fate!

Still I will proudly declare that there is something queer about it.

Else, why should it be let so cheaply? And why have stood so long untenanted?

5   John laughs at me, of course, but one expects that in marriage.

John is practical in the extreme. He has no patience with faith, an intense horror of superstition, and he scoffs openly at any talk of things not to be felt and seen and put down in figures.

John is a physician, and *perhaps*—(I would not say it to a living soul, of course, but this is dead paper and a great relief to my mind—) *perhaps* that is one reason I do not get well faster.

You see he does not believe I am sick!

And what can one do?

10   If a physician of high standing, and one's own husband, assures friends and relatives that there is really nothing the matter with one but temporary nervous depression—a slight hysterical tendency—what is one to do?

My brother is also a physician, and also of high standing, and he says the same thing.

So I take phosphates or phosphites[1]—whichever it is, and tonics, and journeys, and air, and exercise, and am absolutely forbidden to "work" until I am well again.

Personally, I disagree with their ideas.

Personally, I believe that congenial work, with excitement and change, would do me good.

---

[1] *phosphates or phosphites:* Both terms refer to salts of phosphorous acid. The narrator, however, means "phosphate," a carbonated beverage of water, flavoring, and a small amount of phosphoric acid.

But what is one to do?   15

I did write for a while in spite of them; but it *does* exhaust me a good deal—having to be so sly about it, or else meet with heavy opposition.

I sometimes fancy that in my condition if I had less opposition and more society and stimulus—but John says the very worst thing I can do is to think about my condition, and I confess it always makes me feel bad.

So I will let it alone and talk about the house.

The most beautiful place! It is quite alone, standing well back from the road, quite three miles from the village. It makes me think of English places that you read about, for there are hedges and walls and gates that lock, and lots of separate little houses for the gardeners and people.

There is a *delicious* garden! I never saw such a garden—large and shady,   20 full of box-bordered paths, and lined with long grape-covered arbors with seats under them.

There were greenhouses, too, but they are all broken now.

There was some legal trouble, I believe, something about the heirs and co-heirs; anyhow, the place has been empty for years.

That spoils my ghostliness, I am afraid, but I don't care—there is something strange about the house—I can feel it.

I even said so to John one moonlight evening, but he said what I felt was a *draught*, and shut the window.

I get unreasonably angry with John sometimes. I'm sure I never used to   25 be so sensitive. I think it is due to this nervous condition.

But John says if I feel so, I shall neglect proper self-control; so I take pains to control myself—before him, at least, and that makes me very tired.

I don't like our room a bit. I wanted one downstairs that opened on the piazza and had roses all over the window, and such pretty old-fashioned chintz hangings! But John would not hear of it.

He said there was only one window and not room for two beds, and no near room for him if he took another.

He is very careful and loving, and hardly lets me stir without special direction.

I have a schedule prescription for each hour in the day; he takes all   30 care from me, and so I feel basely ungrateful not to value it more.

He said we came here solely on my account, that I was to have perfect rest and all the air I could get. "Your exercise depends on your strength, my dear," said he, "and your food somewhat on your appetite; but air you can absorb all the time." So we took the nursery at the top of the house.

It is a big, airy room, the whole floor nearly, with windows that look all ways, and air and sunshine galore. It was nursery first and then playroom and gymnasium, I should judge; for the windows are barred for little children, and there are rings and things in the walls.

The paint and paper look as if a boys' school had used it. It is stripped off—the paper—in great patches all around the head of my bed, about as far as I can reach, and in a great place on the other side of the room low down. I never saw a worse paper in my life.

One of those sprawling flamboyant patterns committing every artistic sin.

35   It is dull enough to confuse the eye in following, pronounced enough to constantly irritate and provoke study, and when you follow the lame uncertain curves for a little distance they suddenly commit suicide—plunge off at outrageous angles, destroy themselves in unheard of contradictions.

The color is repellent, almost revolting; a smouldering unclean yellow, strangely faded by the slow-turning sunlight.

It is a dull yet lurid orange in some places, a sickly sulphur tint in others.

No wonder the children hated it! I should hate it myself if I had to live in this room long.

There comes John, and I must put this away,—he hates to have me write a word.

*   *   *

40   We have been here two weeks, and I haven't felt like writing before, since that first day.

I am sitting by the window now, up in this atrocious nursery, and there is nothing to hinder my writing as much as I please, save lack of strength.

John is away all day, and even some nights when his cases are serious.

I am glad my case is not serious!

But these nervous troubles are dreadfully depressing.

45   John does not know how much I really suffer. He knows there is no *reason* to suffer, and that satisfies him.

Of course it is only nervousness. It does weigh on me so not to do my duty in any way!

I meant to be such a help to John, such a real rest and comfort, and here I am a comparative burden already!

Nobody would believe what an effort it is to do what little I am able,— to dress and entertain, and order things.

It is fortunate Mary is so good with the baby. Such a dear baby!

50   And yet I *cannot* be with him, it makes me so nervous.

I suppose John never was nervous in his life. He laughs at me so about this wallpaper!

At first he meant to repaper the room, but afterwards he said that I was letting it get the better of me, and that nothing was worse for a nervous patient than to give way to such fancies.

He said that after the wallpaper was changed it would be the heavy bedstead, and then the barred windows, and then that gate at the head of the stairs, and so on.

"You know the place is doing you good," he said, "and really, dear, I don't care to renovate the house just for a three months' rental."

"Then do let us go downstairs," I said, "there are such pretty rooms 55 there."

Then he took me in his arms and called me a blessed little goose, and said he would go down cellar, if I wished, and have it whitewashed into the bargain.

But he is right enough about the beds and windows and things.

It is an airy and comfortable room as any one need wish, and, of course, I would not be so silly as to make him uncomfortable just for a whim.

I'm really getting quite fond of the big room, all but that horrid paper.

Out of one window I can see the garden, those mysterious deep-shaded 60 arbors, the riotous old-fashioned flowers, and bushes and gnarly trees.

Out of another I get a lovely view of the bay and a little private wharf belonging to the estate. There is a beautiful shaded lane that runs down there from the house. I always fancy I see people walking in these numerous paths and arbors, but John has cautioned me not to give way to fancy in the least. He says that with my imaginative power and habit of story-making, a nervous weakness like mine is sure to lead to all manner of excited fancies, and that I ought to use my will and good sense to check the tendency. So I try.

I think sometimes that if I were only well enough to write a little it would relieve the press of ideas and rest me.

But I find I get pretty tired when I try.

It is so discouraging not to have any advice and companionship about my work. When I get really well, John says we will ask Cousin Henry and Julia down for a long visit; but he says he would as soon put fireworks in my pillow-case as to let me have those stimulating people about now.

I wish I could get well faster.   65

But I must not think about that. This paper looks to me as if it *knew* what a vicious influence it had!

There is a recurrent spot where the pattern lolls like a broken neck and two bulbous eyes stare at you upside down.

I get positively angry with the impertinence of it and the everlasting-ness. Up and down and sideways they crawl, and those absurd, unblinking eyes are everywhere. There is one place where two breadths didn't match, and the eyes go all up and down the line, one a little higher than the other.

I never saw so much expression in an inanimate thing before, and we all know how much expression they have! I used to lie awake as a child and get more entertainment and terror out of blank walls and plain furniture than most children could find in a toy-store.

70   I remember what a kindly wink the knobs of our big, old bureau used to have, and there was one chair that always seemed like a strong friend.

I used to feel that if any of the other things looked too fierce I could always hop into that chair and be safe.

The furniture in this room is no worse than inharmonious, however, for we had to bring it all from downstairs. I suppose when this was used as a playroom they had to take the nursery things out, and no wonder! I never saw such ravages as the children have made here.

The wallpaper, as I said before, is torn off in spots, and it sticketh closer than a brother—they must have had perseverance as well as hatred.

Then the floor is scratched and gouged and splintered, the plaster itself is dug out here and there, and this great heavy bed which is all we found in the room, looks as if it had been through the wars.

75   But I don't mind it a bit—only the paper.

There comes John's sister. Such a dear girl as she is, and so careful of me! I must not let her find me writing.

She is a perfect and enthusiastic housekeeper, and hopes for no better profession. I verily believe she thinks it is the writing which made me sick!

But I can write when she is out, and see her a long way off from these windows.

There is one that commands the road, a lovely shaded winding road, and one that just looks off over the country. A lovely country, too, full of great elms and velvet meadows.

80   This wallpaper has a kind of sub-pattern in a different shade, a particularly irritating one, for you can only see it in certain lights, and not clearly then.

But in the places where it isn't faded and where the sun is just so—I can see a strange, provoking, formless sort of figure, that seems to skulk about behind that silly and conspicuous front design.

There's sister on the stairs!

*   *   *

Well, the Fourth of July is over! The people are all gone and I am tired out. John thought it might do me good to see a little company, so we just had mother and Nellie and the children down for a week.

Of course I didn't do a thing. Jennie sees to everything now.

85   But it tired me all the same.

John says if I don't pick up faster he shall send me to Weir Mitchell[2] in the fall.

---

[2] *Weir Mitchell:* Silas Weir Mitchell (1829–1914), a Philadelphia neurologist-psychologist who introduced the "rest cure" for nervous diseases.

But I don't want to go there at all. I had a friend who was in his hands once, and she says he is just like John and my brother, only more so!

Besides, it is such an undertaking to go so far.

I don't feel as if it was worth while to turn my hand over for anything, and I'm getting dreadfully fretful and querulous.

I cry at nothing, and cry most of the time.   90

Of course I don't when John is here, or anybody else, but when I am alone.

And I am alone a good deal just now. John is kept in town very often by serious cases, and Jennie is good and lets me alone when I want her to.

So I walk a little in the garden or down that lovely lane, sit on the porch under the roses, and lie down up here a good deal.

I'm getting really fond of the room in spite of the wallpaper. Perhaps *because* of the wallpaper.

It dwells in my mind so!   95

I lie here on this great immovable bed—it is nailed down, I believe— and follow that pattern about by the hour. It is as good as gymnastics, I assure you. I start, we'll say, at the bottom, down in the corner over there where it has not been touched, and I determine for the thousandth time that I *will* follow that pointless pattern to some sort of a conclusion.

I know a little of the principle of design, and I know this thing was not arranged on any laws of radiation, or alternation, or repetition, or symmetry, or anything else that I ever heard of.

It is repeated, of course, by the breadths, but not otherwise.

Looked at in one way each breadth stands alone, the bloated curves and flourishes—a kind of "debased Romanesque" with *delirium tremens*[3] go waddling up and down in isolated columns of fatuity.

But, on the other hand, they connect diagonally, and the sprawling   100 outlines run off in great slanting waves of optic horror, like a lot of wallowing seaweeds in full chase.

The whole thing goes horizontally, too, at least it seems so, and I exhaust myself in trying to distinguish the order of its going in that direction.

They have used a horizontal breadth for a frieze, and that adds wonderfully to the confusion.

There is one end of the room where it is almost intact, and there, when the crosslights fade and the low sun shines directly upon it, I can almost fancy radiation after all,—the interminable grotesques seems to form around a common center and rush off in headlong plunges of equal distraction.

It makes me tired to follow it. I will take a nap I guess.

---

[3]*delirium tremens:* Mental confusion caused by alcohol poisoning and characterized by physical tremors and hallucinations.

105 I don't know why I should write this.

I don't want to.

I don't feel able.

And I know John would think it absurd. But I *must* say what I feel and think in some way—it is such a relief!

But the effort is getting to be greater than the relief.

110 Half the time now I am awfully lazy, and lie down ever so much.

John says I mustn't lose my strength, and has me take cod liver oil and lots of tonics and things, to say nothing of ale and wine and rare meat.

Dear John! He loves me very dearly, and hates to have me sick. I tried to have a real earnest reasonable talk with him the other day, and tell him how I wish he would let me go and make a visit to Cousin Henry and Julia.

But he said I wasn't able to go, nor able to stand it after I got there; and I did not make out a very good case for myself, for I was crying before I had finished.

It is getting to be a great effort for me to think straight. Just this nervous weakness I suppose.

115 And dear John gathered me up in his arms, and just carried me upstairs and laid me on the bed, and sat by me and read to me till it tired my head.

He said I was his darling and his comfort and all he had, and that I must take care of myself for his sake, and keep well.

He says no one but myself can help me out of it, that I must use my will and self-control and not let any silly fancies run away with me.

There's one comfort, the baby is well and happy, and does not have to occupy this nursery with the horrid wallpaper.

If we had not used it, that blessed child would have! What a fortunate escape! Why, I wouldn't have a child of mine, an impressionable little thing, live in such a room for worlds.

120 I never thought of it before, but it is lucky that John kept me here after all, I can stand it so much easier than a baby, you see.

Of course I never mention it to them any more—I am too wise,—but I keep watch of it all the same.

There are things in that paper that nobody knows but me, or ever will.

Behind that outside pattern the dim shapes get clearer every day.

It is always the same shape, only very numerous.

125 And it is like a woman stooping down and creeping about behind that pattern. I don't like it a bit. I wonder—I begin to think—I wish John would take me away from here!

It is so hard to talk with John about my case, because he is so wise, and because he loves me so.

But I tried it last night.

It was moonlight. The moon shines in all around just as the sun does.

I hate to see it sometimes, it creeps so slowly, and always comes in by one window or another.

John was asleep and I hated to waken him, so I kept still and watched 130 the moonlight on that undulating wallpaper till I felt creepy.

The faint figure behind seemed to shake the pattern, just as if she wanted to get out.

I got up softly and went to feel and see if the paper *did* move, and when I came back John was awake.

"What is it, little girl?" he said. "Don't go walking about like that— you'll get cold."

I thought it was a good time to talk, so I told him that I really was not gaining here, and that I wished he would take me away.

"Why, darling!" said he, "our lease will be up in three weeks, and I 135 can't see how to leave before.

"The repairs are not done at home, and I cannot possibly leave town just now. Of course if you were in any danger, I could and would, but you really are better, dear, whether you can see it or not. I am a doctor, dear, and I know. You are gaining flesh and color, your appetite is better, I feel really much easier about you."

"I don't weigh a bit more," said I, "nor as much; and my appetite may be better in the evening when you are here, but it is worse in the morning when you are away!"

"Bless her little heart!" said he with a big hug, "she shall be as sick as she pleases! But now let's improve the shining hours by going to sleep, and talk about it in the morning!"

"And you won't go away?" I asked gloomily.

"Why, how can I, dear? It is only three weeks more and then we will 140 take a nice little trip of a few days while Jennie is getting the house ready. Really dear you are better!"

"Better in body perhaps—" I began, and stopped short, for he sat up straight and looked at me with such a stern, reproachful look that I could not say another word.

"My darling," said he, "I beg of you, for my sake and for our child's sake, as well as for your own, that you will never for one instant let that idea enter your mind! There is nothing so dangerous, so fascinating, to a temperament like yours. It is a false and foolish fancy. Can you not trust me as a physician when I tell you so?"

So of course I said no more on that score, and we went to sleep before long. He thought I was asleep first, but I wasn't, and lay there for hours trying to decide whether that front pattern and the back pattern really did move together or separately.

On a pattern like this, by daylight, there is a lack of sequence, a defiance of law, that is a constant irritant to a normal mind.

145 The color is hideous enough, and unreliable enough, and infuriating enough, but the pattern is torturing.

You think you have mastered it, but just as you get well underway in following, it turns back-somersault and there you are. It slaps you in the face, knocks you down, and tramples upon you. It is like a bad dream.

The outside pattern is a florid arabesque, reminding one of a fungus. If you can imagine a toadstool in joints, an interminable string of toadstools, budding and sprouting in endless convolutions—why, that is something like it.

That is, sometimes!

There is one marked peculiarity about this paper, a thing nobody seems to notice but myself, and that is that it changes as the light changes.

150 When the sun shoots in through the east window—I always watch for that first long, straight ray—it changes so quickly that I never can quite believe it.

That is why I watch it always.

By moonlight—the moon shines in all night when there is a moon—I wouldn't know it was the same paper.

At night in any kind of light, in twilight, candlelight, lamplight, and worst of all by moonlight, it becomes bars! The outside pattern I mean, and the woman behind it is as plain as can be.

I didn't realize for a long time what the thing was that showed behind, that dim sub-pattern, but now I am quite sure it is a woman.

155 By daylight she is subdued, quiet. I fancy it is the pattern that keeps her so still. It is so puzzling. It keeps me quiet by the hour.

I lie down ever so much now. John says it is good for me, and to sleep all I can.

Indeed he started the habit by making me lie down for an hour after each meal.

It is a very bad habit I am convinced, for you see I don't sleep.

And that cultivates deceit, for I don't tell them I'm awake—O no!

160 The fact is I am getting a little afraid of John.

He seems very queer sometimes, and even Jennie has an inexplicable look.

It strikes me occasionally, just as a scientific hypothesis,—that perhaps it is the paper!

I have watched John when he did not know I was looking, and come into the room suddenly on the most innocent excuses, and I've caught him several times *looking at the paper!* And Jennie too. I caught Jennie with her hand on it once.

She didn't know I was in the room, and when I asked her in a quiet, a very quiet voice, with the most restrained manner possible, what she was doing with the paper—she turned around as if she had been caught stealing, and looked quite angry—asked me why I should frighten her so!

Then she said that the paper stained everything it touched, that she had found yellow smooches on all my clothes and John's, and she wished we would be more careful!

Did not that sound innocent? But I know she was studying that pattern, and I am determined that nobody shall find it out but myself!

Life is very much more exciting now than it used to be. You see I have something more to expect, to look forward to, to watch. I really do eat better, and am more quiet than I was.

John is so pleased to see me improve! He laughed a little the other day, and said I seemed to be flourishing in spite of my wallpaper.

I turned it off with a laugh. I had no intention of telling him it was *because* of the wallpaper—he would make fun of me. He might even want to take me away.

I don't want to leave now until I have found it out. There is a week more, and I think that will be enough.

I'm feeling ever so much better! I don't sleep much at night, for it is so interesting to watch developments; but I sleep a good deal in the daytime.

In the daytime it is tiresome and perplexing.

There are always new shoots on the fungus, and new shades of yellow all over it. I cannot keep count of them, though I have tried conscientiously.

It is the strangest yellow, that wallpaper! It makes me think of all the yellow things I ever saw—not beautiful ones like buttercups, but old foul, bad yellow things.

But there is something else about that paper—the smell! I noticed it the moment we came into the room, but with so much air and sun it was not bad. Now we have had a week of fog and rain, and whether the windows are open or not, the smell is here.

It creeps all over the house.

I find it hovering in the dining-room, skulking in the parlor, hiding in the hall, lying in wait for me on the stairs.

It gets into my hair.

Even when I go to ride, if I turn my head suddenly and surprise it— there is that smell!

Such a peculiar odor, too! I have spent hours in trying to analyze it, to find what it smelled like.

It is not bad—at first, and very gentle, but quite the subtlest, most enduring odor I ever met.

In this damp weather it is awful, I wake up in the night and find it hanging over me.

It used to disturb me at first. I thought seriously of burning the house—to reach the smell.

But now I am used to it. The only thing I can think of that it is like is the *color* of the paper! A yellow smell.

185   There is a very funny mark on this wall, low down, near the mopboard. A streak that runs round the room. It goes behind every piece of furniture, except the bed, a long, straight, even *smooch*, as if it had been rubbed over and over.

I wonder how it was done and who did it, and what they did it for. Round and round and round—round and round and round!—it makes me dizzy!

I really have discovered something at last.

Through watching so much at night, when it changes so, I have finally found out.

The front pattern *does* move—and no wonder! The woman behind shakes it!

190   Sometimes I think there are a great many women behind, and sometimes only one, and she crawls around fast, and her crawling shakes it all over.

Then in the very bright spots she keeps still, and in the very shady spots she just takes hold of the bars and shakes them hard.

And she is all the time trying to climb through. But nobody could climb through that pattern—it strangles so; I think that is why it has so many heads.

They get through, and then the pattern strangles them off and turns them upside down, and makes their eyes white!

If those heads were covered or taken off it would not be half so bad.

195   I think that woman gets out in the daytime!

And I'll tell you why—privately—I've seen her!

I can see her out of every one of my windows!

It is the same woman, I know, for she is always creeping, and most women do not creep by daylight.

I see her in that long shaded lane, creeping up and down. I see her in those dark grape arbors, creeping all around the garden.

200   I see her on that long road under the trees, creeping along, and when a carriage comes she hides under the blackberry vines.

I don't blame her a bit. It must be very humiliating to be caught creeping by daylight!

I always lock the door when I creep by daylight. I can't do it at night, for I know John would suspect something at once.

And John is so queer now, that I don't want to irritate him. I wish he would take another room! Besides, I don't want anybody to get that woman out at night but myself.

I often wonder if I could see her out of all the windows at once.

But, turn as fast as I can, I can only see out of one at one time.   205

And though I always see her, she *may* be able to creep faster than I can turn!

I have watched her sometimes away off in the open country, creeping as fast as a cloud shadow in a high wind.

If only that top pattern could be gotten off from the under one! I mean to try it, little by little.

I have found out another funny thing, but I shan't tell it this time! It does not do to trust people too much.

There are only two more days to get this paper off, and I believe John 210 is beginning to notice. I don't like the look in his eyes.

And I heard him ask Jennie a lot of professional questions about me. She had a very good report to give.

She said I slept a good deal in the daytime.

John knows I don't sleep very well at night, for all I'm so quiet!

He asked me all sorts of questions, too, and pretended to be very loving and kind.

As if I couldn't see through him!   215

Still, I don't wonder he acts so, sleeping under this paper for three months.

It only interests me, but I feel sure John and Jennie are secretly affected by it.

*   *   *

Hurrah! This is the last day, but it is enough. John is to stay in town over night, and won't be out until this evening.

Jennie wanted to sleep with me—the sly thing! But I told her I should undoubtedly rest better for a night all alone.

That was clever, for really I wasn't alone a bit! As soon as it was 220 moon-light and that poor thing began to crawl and shake the pattern, I got up and ran to help her.

I pulled and she shook, I shook and she pulled, and before morning we had peeled off yards of that paper.

A strip about as high as my head and half around the room.

And then when the sun came and that awful pattern began to laugh at me, I declared I would finish it to-day!

We go away to-morrow, and they are moving all my furniture down again to leave things as they were before.

225   Jennie looked at the wall in amazement, but I told her merrily that I did it out of pure spite at the vicious thing.

She laughed and said she wouldn't mind doing it herself, but I must not get tired.

How she betrayed herself that time!

But I am here, and no person touches this paper but me,—not *alive!*

She tried to get me out of the room—it was too patent! But I said it was so quiet and empty and clean now that I believed I would lie down again and sleep all I could; and not to wake me even for dinner—I would call when I woke.

230   So now she is gone, and the servants are gone, and the things are gone, and there is nothing left but that great bedstead nailed down, with the canvas mattress we found on it.

We shall sleep downstairs to-night, and take the boat home tomorrow.

I quite enjoy the room, now it is bare again.

How those children did tear about here!

This bedstead is fairly gnawed!

235   But I must get to work.

I have locked the door and thrown the key down into the front path.

I don't want to go out, and I don't want to have anybody come in, till John comes.

I want to astonish him.

I've got a rope up here that even Jennie did not find. If that woman does get out, and tries to get away, I can tie her!

240   But I forgot I could not reach far without anything to stand on!

This bed will *not* move!

I tried to lift and push it until I was lame, and then I got so angry I bit off a little piece at one corner—but it hurt my teeth.

Then I peeled off all the paper I could reach standing on the floor. It sticks horribly and the pattern just enjoys it! All those strangled heads and bulbous eyes and waddling fungus growths just shriek with derision!

I am getting angry enough to do something desperate. To jump out of the window would be admirable exercise, but the bars are too strong even to try.

245   Besides I wouldn't do it. Of course not. I know well enough that a step like that is improper and might be misconstrued.

I don't like to *look* out of the windows even—there are so many of those creeping women, and they creep so fast.

I wonder if they come out of that wallpaper as I did?

But I am securely fastened now by my well-hidden rope—you don't get *me* out in the road there!

I suppose I shall have to get back behind the pattern when it comes night, and that is hard!

It is so pleasant to be out in this great room and creep around as 250 I please!

I don't want to go outside. I won't, even if Jennie asks me to.

For outside you have to creep on the ground, and everything is green instead of yellow.

But here I can creep smoothly on the floor, and my shoulder just fits in that long smooch around the wall, so I cannot lose my way.

Why there's John at the door!

It is no use, young man, you can't open it! 255

How he does call and pound!

Now he's crying for an axe.

It would be a shame to break down that beautiful door!

"John dear!" said I in the gentlest voice, "the key is down by the front steps, under a plantain leaf!"

That silenced him for a few moments. 260

Then he said—very quietly indeed, "Open the door, my darling!"

"I can't," said I. "The key is down by the front door under a plantain leaf!"

And then I said it again, several times, very gently and slowly, and said it so often that he had to go and see, and he got it of course, and came in. He stopped short by the door.

"What is the matter?" he cried. "For God's sake, what are you doing!"

I kept on creeping just the same, but I looked at him over my shoulder. 265

"I've got out at last," said I, "in spite of you and Jane. And I've pulled off most of the paper, so you can't put me back!"

Now why should that man have fainted? But he did, and right across my path by the wall, so that I had to creep over him every time!

*   *   *

LORRIE MOORE (1957–)

Referential (2012)

Mania. For the third time in three years they talked in a frantic way about what would be a suitable birthday present for her deranged son. There was so little they were actually allowed to bring: almost everything could be transformed into a weapon and so most items had to be left at the front desk, and then, if requested, brought in later by a big blond aide, who would look the objects over beforehand for their wounding possibilities. Pete had bought a basket of jams, but they were in glass jars, and so not allowed. "I forgot about that," he said. They were arranged in colour from brightest marmalade to cloudberry to fig, as if they contained the urine tests of an increasingly ill person, and so she thought, *Just as well they will be confiscated.* They would find something else to bring.

By the time her son was twelve, and had begun his dazed and spell-bound muttering, no longer brushing his teeth, Pete had been in their lives for four years, and now it was four years after that. The love they had for Pete was long and winding, not without hidden turns, but without any real halts. They thought of him as a kind of stepfather. Perhaps all three of them had gotten old together, although it showed mostly on her, the mother, with her black shirtdresses worn for slimming and her now greying hair undyed and often pinned up with strands hanging down like Spanish moss. Once her son had been stripped and gowned and placed in the facility, she, too, removed her necklaces, earrings, scarves—all her prosthetic devices, she said to Pete, trying to amuse—and put them in a latched accordion file under her bed. She was not allowed to wear them when visiting so she would no longer wear them at all, a kind of solidarity with her child, a kind of new widowhood on top of the widowhood she already possessed. Unlike other women her age (who tried too hard with lurid lingerie and flashing jewellery), she now felt that sort of effort was ludicrous, and she went out into the world like an Amish woman, or per-haps, even worse, as when the unforgiving light of spring hit her face, an Amish man. If she were going to be old, let her be a full-fledged citizen of the old country! "To me you always look so beautiful," Pete no longer said.

Pete had lost his job in the new economic downturn. At one point he had been poised to live with her, but her child's deepening troubles had caused him to pull back—he believed he loved her but could not find the large space he needed for himself in her life or in her house (and did not blame her son, or did he?). He eyed with somewhat visible covetousness and sour remarks the front room that her son, when home, lived in with large blankets and empty ice-cream pints, an Xbox, and DVDs.

She no longer knew where Pete went, sometimes for weeks at a time. She thought it an act of vigilance and attachment that she would not ask, would try not to care. She once grew so hungry for touch she went to the Stressed Tress salon around the corner just to have her hair washed. The few times she had flown to Buffalo to see her brother and his family, at airport security she had chosen the pat-downs and the wandings rather than the scanning machine.

5   "Where is Pete?" her son cried out at visits she made alone, his face scarlet with acne, swollen and wide with the effects of medications that had been changed then changed again, and she said Pete was busy today, but soon, soon, maybe next week. A maternal vertigo beset her, the room circled, and the cutting scars on her son's arms sometimes seemed to spell

out Pete's name in the thin lines there, the loss of fathers etched primitively in an algebra of skin. In the carousel spin of the room, the white webbed lines resembled coarse campfire writing, as when young people used to stiffly carve the words peace and f--- in park picnic tables and trees, the C three-quarters of a square. Mutilation was a language. And vice versa. The cutting endeared her boy to the girls, who were all cutters themselves and seldom saw a boy who was one as well, and so in the group sessions he became popular, which he seemed neither to mind nor perhaps really to notice. When no one was looking he cut the bottoms of his feet with crisp paper from crafts hour. He also pretended to read the girls' soles like palms, announcing the arrival of strangers and the progress toward romance—"toemances!" he called them—and detours, sometimes glimpsing his own fate in the words they had cut there.

Now she and Pete went to see her son without the jams but with a soft deckle-edged book about Daniel Boone, which was allowed, even if her son would believe it contained messages for him, believe that although it was a story about a long-ago person it was also the story of his own sorrow and heroism in the face of every manner of wilderness and defeat and abduction and that his own life could be draped over the book, which was noble armature for the revelation of tales of *him*. There would be clues in the words on pages with numbers that added up to his age: 97, 88, 466. There were other veiled references to his existence. There always were.

They sat at the visitors' table together and her son set the book aside and did try to smile at both of them. There was still sweetness in his eyes, the sweetness he was born with, even if fury could dart in a scattershot fashion across them. Someone had cut his tawny hair—or at least had tried. Perhaps the staff person did not want the scissors near him for a prolonged period and had snipped quickly, then leaped away, then approached again, grabbed and snipped, then jumped back. At least that's what it looked like. It was wavy hair and had to be cut carefully. Now it no longer cascaded down but was close to his head, springing out at angles that seemed to matter to no one but a mother.

"So where have you been?" her son asked Pete, giving him a hard stare.

"Good question," said Pete, as if praising the thing would make it go away. How could people be mentally well in such a world?

"Do you miss us?" the boy asked. 10

Pete did not answer.

"Do you think of me when you look at the black capillaries of the trees at night?"

"I suppose I do." Pete stared back at him, so as not to shift in his seat. "I am always hoping you are OK and that they treat you well here."

"Do you think of my mom when staring up at the clouds and all they hold?"

15   Pete fell quiet again.

Her son continued, studying Pete. "Have you ever watched how sparrows can kill the offspring of others? Baby wrens, for instance? I've been watching out the windows. Did you know that sparrows can swoop into the wrens' house and pluck out the fledglings from their nests and hurl them to the ground with a force you would not think possible for a sparrow? Even a homicidal sparrow?"

"Nature can be cruel," said Pete.

"Nature can be one big horror movie! But murder is not something one would expect—from a sparrow. All things can be found in the world—but usually you have to look for them. You have to look! For instance, you have to look for us! We are sort of hidden but sort of not. We can be found. If you look in the obvious places, we can be found. We haven't disappeared, even if you want us to, we are there to—"

"That's enough," she said to her son, who turned to her with a change of expression.

20   "There's supposed to be cake this afternoon for someone's birthday," he said.

"That will be nice!" she said, smiling back.

"No candles, of course. Or forks. We will just have to grab the frosting and mash it into our eyes for blinding. Do you ever think about how at that moment of the candles time stands still, even as the moments carry away the smoke? It's like the fire of burning love. Do you ever wonder why so many people have things they don't deserve but how absurd all those things are to begin with? Do you really think a wish can come true if you never ever ever ever ever ever tell it to anyone?"

On the ride home she and Pete did not exchange a word, and every time she looked at his ageing hands, clasped arthritically around the steering wheel, the familiar thumbs slung low in their slightly simian way, she would understand anew the desperate place they both were in, though the desperations were separate, not joined, and her eyes would then feel the stabbing pressure of tears. The last time her son had tried to do it, his method had been, in the doctor's words, morbidly ingenious. He might have succeeded but a fellow patient, a girl from group, had stopped him at the last minute. There had been blood to be mopped. Once her son had only wanted a distracting pain, but then soon he had wanted to tear a hole in himself and flee through it. Life was full of spies and preoccupying espionage. Yet the spies sometimes would flee as well and someone might have to go after them in order, paradoxically, to escape them altogether, over the rolling fields of living dream, into the early morning mountains of dawning signification.

There was a storm in front and lightning did its quick, purposeful zigzag between and in the clouds. She did not need such stark illustration that horizons could be shattered, filled with messages, broken codes, yet there it was. A spring snow began to fall with the lightning still cracking, and Pete put the windshield wipers on so that they both could peer through the cleared semicircles at the darkening road before them. She knew that the world was not created to speak just to her, and yet, as with her son, sometimes things did. The fruit trees had bloomed early, for instance, and the orchards they passed were pink, but the early warmth precluded bees, and so there would be little fruit. Most of the dangling blossoms would fall in this very storm.

When they arrived at her house and went in, Pete glanced at himself 25 in the hallway mirror. Perhaps he needed assurance that he was alive and not the ghost he seemed.

"Would you like a drink?" she asked, hoping he would stay. "I have some good vodka. I could make you a nice White Russian!"

"Just vodka," he said reluctantly. "Straight."

She opened the freezer to find the vodka, and when she closed it again, she stood waiting there for a moment, looking at the photos she'd attached with magnets to the refrigerator. As a baby her son had looked happier than most babies. As a six-year-old he was still smiling and hamming it up, his arms and legs shooting out like starbursts, his perfectly gapped teeth flashing, his hair curling in honeyed coils. At ten his expression was already vaguely brooding and fearful, though there was light in his eyes, his lovely cousins beside him. There he was a plumpish teenager, his arm around Pete. And there in the corner he was an infant again, held by his dignified, handsome father, whom her son did not recall because he had died so long ago. All this had to be accepted. Living did not mean one joy piled upon another. It was merely the hope for less pain, hope played like a playing card upon another hope, a wish for kindnesses and mercies to emerge like kings and queens in an unexpected change of the game. One could hold the cards oneself or not: they would land the same regardless. Tenderness did not enter except in a damaged way and by luck.

"You don't want ice?"

"No," said Pete. "No thank you."   30

She placed two glasses of vodka on the kitchen table and there they sat.

"Perhaps this will help you sleep," she said.

"Don't know if anything can do that," he said, with a swig. Insomnia plagued him.

"I am going to bring him home tomorrow," she said. "He needs his home back, his house, his room. He is no danger to anyone."

Pete drank some more, sipping noisily. She could see he wanted no 35 part of this, but she felt she had no choice but to proceed. "Perhaps you could help. He looks up to you."

"Help how?" asked Pete with a flash of anger. There was the clink of his glass on the table.

"We could each spend part of the night near him," she said.

The telephone rang. The Radio Shack wall phone brought almost nothing but bad news, and so its ringing sound, especially in the evening, always startled her. She repressed a shudder but still her shoulders hunched and curved. She stood.

"Hello?" she said, answering it on the third ring, her heart pounding. But the person on the other end hung up. She sat back down. "I guess it was a wrong number," she said, adding, "Perhaps you would like more vodka."

40   "Only a little. Then I should go."

She poured him more. She had said what she'd wanted to say and did not want to have to persuade him. She would wait for him to step forward with the right words. Unlike some of her meaner friends, who kept warning her, she believed there was a deep good side of him and she was always patient for it. What else could she be?

The phone rang again.

"Probably telemarketers," he said.

"I hate them," she said. "Hello?" she said more loudly into the receiver.

45   This time when the caller hung up she glanced at the number on the phone, in the lit panel where the caller ID was supposed to reveal it.

She sat back down and poured herself more vodka. "Someone is calling here from your apartment," she said.

He threw back the rest of his vodka. "I should go," he said and got up and headed for the door. She followed him. At the door she watched him grasp the front knob and twist it firmly. He opened the door wide, blocking the mirror.

"Good night," he said. His expression had already forwarded itself to someplace far away.

She threw her arms around him to kiss him, but he turned his head abruptly so her mouth landed on his ear. She remembered he had done this evasive move eight years ago, at the beginning, when they had first met, and he was in a condition of romantic overlap.

50   "Thank you for coming with me," she said.

"You're welcome," he replied, then hurried down the steps to his car, which was parked at the curb out front. She did not attempt to walk him to it. She closed the door and locked it, as the telephone began to ring again. She turned off all the lights, including the porches'.

She went into the kitchen. She had not really been able to read the caller ID without reading glasses, and had invented the part about its being Pete's number, though he had made it the truth anyway, which was the black magic of lies, good guesses, and nimble bluffs. Now she braced herself. She planted her feet. "Hello?" she said, answering on the fifth ring. The plastic panel where the number should show was clouded as if by a scrim, a page of onionskin over the onion—or rather, over a picture of an onion. One depiction on top of another.

"Good evening," she said again loudly. What would burst forth? A monkey's paw. A lady. A tiger.

But there was nothing at all.

*　　*　　*

JOYCE CAROL OATES (1938–   )

Where Are You Going, Where Have You Been? (1966)

For Bob Dylan

Her name was Connie. She was fifteen and she had a quick nervous giggling habit of craning her neck to glance into mirrors, or checking other people's faces to make sure her own was all right. Her mother, who noticed everything and knew everything and who hadn't much reason any longer to look at her own face, always scolded Connie about it. "Stop gawking at yourself, who are you? You think you're so pretty?" she would say. Connie would raise her eye-brows at these familiar complaints and look right through her mother, into a shadowy vision of herself as she was right at that moment: she knew she was pretty and that was everything. Her mother had been pretty once too, if you could believe those old snapshots in the album, but now her looks were gone and that was why she was always after Connie.

"Why don't you keep your room clean like your sister? How've you got your hair fixed—what the hell stinks? Hair spray? You don't see your sister using that junk."

Her sister June was twenty-four and still lived at home. She was a secretary in the high school Connie attended, and if that wasn't bad enough—with her in the same building—she was so plain and chunky and steady that Connie had to hear her praised all the time by her mother and her mother's sisters. June did this, June did that, she saved money and helped clean the house and cooked and Connie couldn't do a thing, her mind was all filled with trashy daydreams. Their father was away at work most of the time and when he came home he wanted supper and he read the newspaper at supper and after supper he went to bed. He didn't bother talking much to them, but around his bent head Connie's mother kept picking at her until Connie wished her mother was dead and she herself was dead and it was all over. "She makes me want to throw up sometimes," she complained to her friends. She had a high, breathless, amused voice which made everything she said sound a little forced, whether it was sincere or not.

There was one good thing: June went places with girl friends of hers, girls who were just as plain and steady as she, and so when Connie wanted to do that her mother had no objections. The father of Connie's best girl friend drove the girls the three miles to town and left them off at a shopping plaza, so that they could walk through the stores or go to a movie, and when he came to pick them up again at eleven he never bothered to ask what they had done.

5   They must have been familiar sights, walking around that shopping plaza in their shorts and flat ballerina slippers that always scuffed the sidewalk, with charm bracelets jingling on their thin wrists; they would lean together to whisper and laugh secretly if someone passed by who amused or interested them. Connie had long dark blond hair that drew anyone's eye to it, and she wore part of it pulled up on her head and puffed out and the rest of it she let fall down her back. She wore a pull-over jersey blouse that looked one way when she was at home and another way when she was away from home. Everything about her had two sides to it, one for home and one for anywhere that was not home: her walk that could be childlike and bobbing, or languid enough to make anyone think she was hearing music in her head, her mouth which was pale and smirking most of the time, but bright and pink on these evenings out, her laugh which was cynical and drawling at home—"Ha, ha, very funny"—but high-pitched and nervous anywhere else, like the jingling of the charms on her bracelet.

Sometimes they did go shopping or to a movie, but sometimes they went across the highway, ducking fast across the busy road, to a drive-in restaurant where older kids hung out. The restaurant was shaped like a big bottle, though squatter than a real bottle, and on its cap was a revolving figure of a grinning boy who held a hamburger aloft. One night in midsummer they ran across, breathless with daring, and right away someone leaned out a car window and invited them over, but it was just a boy from high school they didn't like. It made them feel good to be able to ignore him. They went up through the maze of parked and cruising cars to the bright-lit, fly-infested restaurant, their faces pleased and expectant as if they were entering a sacred building that loomed out of the night to give them what haven and what blessing they yearned for. They sat at the counter and crossed their legs at the ankles, their thin shoulders rigid with excitement, and listened to the music that made everything so good: the music was always in the background like music at a church service, it was something to depend upon.

A boy named Eddie came in to talk with them. He sat backwards on his stool, turning himself jerkily around in semi-circles and then stopping and turning again, and after a while he asked Connie if she would like something to eat. She said she did and so she tapped her friend's arm on her way out—her friend pulled her face up into a brave droll look—and Connie said she would meet her at eleven, across the way. "I just hate to leave her like that," Connie said earnestly, but the boy said that she wouldn't be alone for long. So they went out to his car and on the way Connie couldn't help but let her eyes wander over the windshields and faces all around her, her face gleaming with a joy that had nothing to do with Eddie or even this place; it might have been the music. She drew her shoulders up and sucked in her breath with the pure pleasure of being alive, and just at that moment she happened to glance at a face just a few feet from hers. It was a boy with shaggy black hair, in a convertible jalopy painted gold. He stared at her and then his lips widened into a grin. Connie slit her eyes at him and turned away, but she couldn't help glancing back and there he was still watching her. He wagged a finger and laughed and said, "Gonna get you, baby," and Connie turned away again without Eddie noticing anything.

She spent three hours with him, at the restaurant where they ate hamburgers and drank Cokes in wax cups that were always sweating, and then down an alley a mile or so away, and when he left her off at five to eleven only the movie house was still open at the plaza. Her girl friend was there, talking with a boy. When Connie came up the two girls smiled at each other and Connie said, "How was the movie?" and the girl said, "You should know." They rode off with the girl's father, sleepy and pleased, and Connie couldn't help but look at the darkened shopping plaza with its big empty parking lot and its signs that were faded and ghostly now, and over at the drive-in restaurant where cars were still circling tirelessly. She couldn't hear the music at this distance.

Next morning June asked her how the movie was and Connie said, "So-so."

She and that girl and occasionally another girl went out several 10 times a week that way, and the rest of the time Connie spent around the house—it was summer vacation—getting in her mother's way and thinking, dreaming, about the boys she met. But all the boys fell back and dissolved into a single face that was not even a face, but an idea, a feeling, mixed up with the urgent insistent pounding of the music and the humid night air of July. Connie's mother kept dragging her back to the daylight by finding things for her to do or saying, suddenly, "What's this about the Pettinger girl?"

And Connie would say nervously, "Oh, her. That dope." She always drew thick clear lines between herself and such girls, and her mother was simple and kindly enough to believe her. Her mother was so simple, Connie thought, that it was maybe cruel to fool her so much. Her mother went scuffling around the house in old bedroom slippers and complained over the telephone to one sister about the other, then the other called up and the two of them complained about the third one. If June's name was mentioned her mother's tone was approving, and if Connie's name was mentioned it was disapproving. This did not really mean she disliked

Connie and actually Connie thought that her mother preferred her to June because she was prettier, but the two of them kept up a pretense of exasperation, a sense that they were tugging and struggling over something of little value to either of them. Sometimes, over coffee, they were almost friends, but something would come up—some vexation that was like a fly buzzing suddenly around their heads—and their faces went hard with contempt.

One Sunday Connie got up at eleven—none of them bothered with church—and washed her hair so that it could dry all day long, in the sun. Her parents and sister were going to a barbecue at an aunt's house and Connie said no, she wasn't interested, rolling her eyes to let her mother know just what she thought of it. "Stay home alone then," her mother said sharply. Connie sat out back in a lawn chair and watched them drive away, her father quiet and bald, hunched around so that he could back the car out, her mother with a look that was still angry and not at all softened through the windshield, and in the back seat poor old June all dressed up as if she didn't know what a barbecue was, with all the running yelling kids and the flies. Connie sat with her eyes closed in the sun, dreaming and dazed with the warmth about her as if this were a kind of love, the caresses of love, and her mind slipped over onto thoughts of the boy she had been with the night before and how nice he had been, how sweet it always was, not the way someone like June would suppose but sweet, gentle, the way it was in movies and promised in songs; and when she opened her eyes she hardly knew where she was, the back yard ran off into weeds and a fence-line of trees and behind it the sky was perfectly blue and still. The asbestos "ranch house" that was now three years old startled her—it looked small. She shook her head as if to get awake.

It was too hot. She went inside the house and turned on the radio to drown out the quiet. She sat on the edge of her bed, barefoot, and listened for an hour and a half to a program called XYZ Sunday Jamboree, record after record of hard, fast, shrieking songs she sang along with, interspersed by exclamations from "Bobby King": "An' look here you girls at Napoleon's—Son and Charley want you to pay real close attention to this song coming up!"

And Connie paid close attention herself, bathed in a glow of slow-pulsed joy that seemed to rise mysteriously out of the music itself and lay languidly about the airless little room, breathed in and breathed out with each gentle rise and fall of her chest.

15　　After a while she heard a car coming up the drive. She sat up at once, startled, because it couldn't be her father so soon. The gravel kept crunching all the way in from the road—the driveway was long—and Connie ran to the window. It was a car she didn't know. It was an open jalopy, painted a bright gold that caught the sunlight opaquely. Her heart began to pound and her fingers snatched at her hair, checking it, and she whispered "Christ. Christ," wondering how bad she looked. The car came to a stop at the side door and the horn sounded four short taps as if this were a signal Connie knew.

She went into the kitchen and approached the door slowly, then hung out the screen door, her bare toes curling down off the step. There were two boys in the car and now she recognized the driver: he had shaggy, shabby black hair that looked crazy as a wig and he was grinning at her.

"I ain't late, am I?" he said.

"Who the hell do you think you are?" Connie said.

"Toldja I'd be out, didn't I?"

"I don't even know who you are." 20

She spoke sullenly, careful to show no interest or pleasure, and he spoke in a fast bright monotone. Connie looked past him to the other boy, taking her time. He had fair brown hair, with a lock that fell onto his forehead. His sideburns gave him a fierce, embarrassed look, but so far he hadn't even bothered to glance at her. Both boys wore sunglasses. The driver's glasses were metallic and mirrored everything in miniature.

"You wanta come for a ride?" he said.

Connie smirked and let her hair fall loose over one shoulder.

"Don'tcha like my car? New paint job," he said. "Hey."

"What?" 25

"You're cute."

She pretended to fidget, chasing flies away from the door.

"Don'tcha believe me, or what?" he said.

"Look, I don't even know who you are," Connie said in disgust.

"Hey, Ellie's got a radio, see. Mine's broke down." He lifted his 30 friend's arm and showed her the little transistor the boy was holding, and now Connie began to hear the music. It was the same program that was playing inside the house.

"Bobby King?" she said.

"I listen to him all the time. I think he's great."

"He's kind of great," Connie said reluctantly.

"Listen, that guy's *great*. He knows where the action is."

Connie blushed a little, because the glasses made it impossible for 35 her to see just what this boy was looking at. She couldn't decide if she liked him or if he was just a jerk, and so she dawdled in the doorway and wouldn't come down or go back inside. She said, "What's all that stuff painted on your car?"

"Can'tcha read it?" He opened the door very carefully, as if he was afraid it might fall off. He slid out just as carefully, planting his feet firmly on the ground, the tiny metallic world in his glasses slowing down like gelatine hardening and in the midst of it Connie's bright green blouse. "This here is my name, to begin with," he said. ARNOLD FRIEND was written in tarlike black letters on the side, with a drawing of a round grinning face that reminded Connie of a pumpkin, except it wore sunglasses.

"I wanta introduce myself, I'm Arnold Friend and that's my real name and I'm gonna be your friend, honey, and inside the car's Ellie Oscar, he's kinda shy." Ellie brought his transistor radio up to his shoulder and balanced it there. "Now these numbers are a secret code, honey," Arnold Friend explained. He read off the numbers 33, 19, 17 and raised his eyebrows at her to see what she thought of that, but she didn't think much of it. The left rear fender had been smashed and around it was written, on the gleaming gold background: DONE BY CRAZY WOMAN DRIVER. Connie had to laugh at that. Arnold Friend was pleased at her laughter and looked up at her. "Around the other side's a lot more—you wanta come and see them?"

"No."

"Why not?"

"Why should I?"

40 "Don'tcha wanta see what's on the car? Don'tcha wanta go for a ride?"

"I don't know."

"Why not?"

"I got things to do."

"Like what?"

45 "Things."

He laughed as if she had said something funny. He slapped his thighs. He was standing in a strange way, leaning back against the car as if he were balancing himself. He wasn't tall, only an inch or so taller than she would be if she came down to him. Connie liked the way he was dressed, which was the way all of them dressed: tight faded jeans stuffed into black, scuffed boots, a belt that pulled his waist in and showed how lean he was, and a white pull-over shirt that was a little soiled and showed the hard small muscles of his arms and shoulders. He looked as if he probably did hard work, lifting and carrying things. Even his neck looked muscular. And his face was a familiar face, somehow: the jaw and chin and cheeks slightly darkened, because he hadn't shaved for a day or two, and the nose long and hawk-like, sniffing as if she were a treat he was going to gobble up and it was all a joke.

"Connie, you ain't telling the truth. This is your day set aside for a ride with me and you know it," he said, still laughing. The way he straightened and recovered from his fit of laughing showed that it had been all fake.

"How do you know what my name is?" she said suspiciously.

"It's Connie."

50 "Maybe and maybe not."

"I know my Connie," he said, wagging his finger. Now she remembered him even better, back at the restaurant, and her cheeks warmed at the thought of how she sucked in her breath just at the moment she passed him—how she must have looked to him. And he had remembered her.

"Ellie and I come out here especially for you," he said. "Ellie can sit in back. How about it?"

"Where?"

"Where what?"

"Where're we going?"

He looked at her. He took off the sunglasses and she saw how pale the 55 skin around his eyes was, like holes that were not in shadow but instead in light. His eyes were chips of broken glass that catch the light in an amiable way. He smiled. It was as if the idea of going for a ride somewhere, to some place, was a new idea to him.

"Just for a ride, Connie sweetheart."

"I never said my name was Connie," she said.

"But I know what it is. I know your name and all about you, lots of things," Arnold Friend said. He had not moved yet but stood still leaning back against the side of his jalopy. "I took a special interest in you, such a pretty girl, and found out all about you like I know your parents and sister are gone somewheres and I know where and how long they're going to be gone, and I know who you were with last night, and your best girl friend's name is Betty. Right?"

He spoke in a simple lilting voice, exactly as if he were reciting the words to a song. His smile assured her that everything was fine. In the car Ellie turned up the volume on his radio and did not bother to look around at them.

"Ellie can sit in the back seat," Arnold Friend said. He indicated his 60 friend with a casual jerk of his chin, as if Ellie did not count and she should not bother with him.

"How'd you find out all that stuff?" Connie said.

"Listen: Betty Schultz and Tony Fitch and Jimmy Pettinger and Nancy Pettinger," he said, in a chant. "Raymond Stanley and Bob Hutter—"

"Do you know all those kids?"

"I know everybody."

"Look, you're kidding. You're not from around here."   65

"Sure."

"But—how come we never saw you before?"

"Sure you saw me before," he said. He looked down at his boots, as if he were a little offended. "You just don't remember."

"I guess I'd remember you," Connie said.

"Yeah?" He looked up at this, beaming. He was pleased. He began 70 to mark time with the music from Ellie's radio, tapping his fists lightly together. Connie looked away from his smile to the car, which was painted so bright it almost hurt her eyes to look at it. She looked at that name, ARNOLD FRIEND. And up at the front fender was an expression that was familiar—MAN THE FLYING SAUCERS. It was an expression kids had used the year before, but didn't use this year. She looked at it for a while as if the words meant something to her that she did not yet know.

"What're you thinking about? Huh?" Arnold Friend demanded. "Not worried about your hair blowing around in the car, are you?"

"No."

"Think I maybe can't drive good?"

"How do I know?"

75   "You're a hard girl to handle. How come?" he said. "Don't you know I'm your friend? Didn't you see me put my sign in the air when you walked by?"

"What sign?"

"My sign." And he drew an X in the air, leaning out toward her. They were maybe ten feet apart. After his hand fell back to his side the X was still in the air, almost visible. Connie let the screen door close and stood perfectly still inside it, listening to the music from her radio and the boy's blend together. She stared at Arnold Friend. He stood there so stiffly relaxed, pretending to be relaxed, with one hand idly on the door handle as if he were keeping himself up that way and had no intention of ever moving again. She recognized most things about him, the tight jeans that showed his thighs and buttocks and the greasy leather boots and the tight shirt, and even that slippery friendly smile of his, that sleepy dreamy smile that all the boys used to get across ideas they didn't want to put into words. She recognized all this and also the singsong way he talked, slightly mocking, kidding, but serious and a little melancholy, and she recognized the way he tapped one fist against the other in homage to the perpetual music behind him. But all these things did not come together.

She said suddenly, "Hey, how old are you?"

His smile faded. She could see then that he wasn't a kid, he was much older—thirty, maybe more. At this knowledge her heart began to pound faster.

80   "That's a crazy thing to ask. Can'tcha see I'm your own age?"

"Like hell you are."

"Or maybe a coupla years older, I'm eighteen."

"Eighteen?" she said doubtfully.

He grinned to reassure her and lines appeared at the corners of his mouth. His teeth were big and white. He grinned so broadly his eyes became slits and she saw how thick the lashes were, thick and black as if painted with a black tarlike material. Then he seemed to become embarrassed, abruptly, and looked over his shoulder at Ellie. "*Him*, he's crazy," he said. "Ain't he a riot, he's a nut, a real character." Ellie was still listening to the music. His sunglasses told nothing about what he was thinking. He wore a bright orange shirt unbuttoned halfway to show his chest, which was a pale, bluish chest and not muscular like Arnold Friend's. His shirt collar was turned up all around and the very tips of the collar pointed out past his chin as if they were protecting him. He was pressing the transistor radio up against his ear and sat there in a kind of daze, right in the sun.

"He's kinda strange," Connie said.   85

"Hey, she says you're kinda strange! Kinda strange!" Arnold Friend cried. He pounded on the car to get Ellie's attention. Ellie turned for the first time and Connie saw with shock that he wasn't a kid either—he had a fair, hairless face, cheeks reddened slightly as if the veins grew too close to the surface of his skin, the face of a forty-year-old baby. Connie felt a wave of dizziness rise in her at this sight and she stared at him as if waiting for something to change the shock of the moment, make it all right again. Ellie's lips kept shaping words, mumbling along with the words blasting in his ear.

"Maybe you two better go away," Connie said faintly.

"What? How come?" Arnold Friend cried. "We come out here to take you for a ride. It's Sunday." He had the voice of the man on the radio now. It was the same voice, Connie thought. "Don'tcha know it's Sunday all day and honey, no matter who you were with last night today you're with Arnold Friend and don't you forget it!—Maybe you better step out here," he said, and this last was in a different voice. It was a little flatter, as if the heat was finally getting to him.

"No. I got things to do."

"Hey."   90

"You two better leave."

"We ain't leaving until you come with us."

"Like hell I am—"

"Connie, don't fool around with me. I mean, I mean, don't fool *around*," he said, shaking his head. He laughed incredulously. He placed his sunglasses on top of his head, carefully, as if he were indeed wearing a wig, and brought the stems down behind his ears. Connie stared at him, another wave of dizziness and fear rising in her so that for a moment he wasn't even in focus but was just a blur, standing there against his gold car, and she had the idea that he had driven up the driveway all right but had come from nowhere before that and belonged nowhere and that everything about him and even about the music that was so familiar to her was only half real.

"If my father comes and sees you—"   95

"He ain't coming. He's at a barbecue."

"How do you know that?"

"Aunt Tillie's. Right now they're—uh—they're drinking. Sitting around," he said vaguely, squinting as if he were staring all the way to town and over to Aunt Tillie's backyard. Then the vision seemed to get clear and he nodded energetically. "Yeah. Sitting around. There's your sister in a blue dress, huh? And high heels, the poor sad bitch—nothing like you sweetheart! And your mother's helping some fat woman with the corn, they're cleaning the corn—husking the corn—"

"What fat woman?" Connie cried.

100 "How do I know what fat woman. I don't know every goddam fat woman in the world!" Arnold Friend laughed.

"Oh, that's Mrs. Hornby.... Who invited her?" Connie said. She felt a little light-headed. Her breath was coming quickly.

"She's too fat. I don't like them fat. I like them the way you are, honey," he said, smiling sleepily at her. They stared at each other for a while, through the screen door. He said softly, "Now what you're going to do is this: you're going to come out that door. You're going to sit up front with me and Ellie's going to sit in the back, the hell with Ellie, right? This isn't Ellie's date. You're my date. I'm your lover, honey."

"What? You're crazy—"

"Yes, I'm your lover. You don't know what that is but you will," he said. "I know that too. I know all about you. But look: it's real nice and you couldn't ask for nobody better than me, or more polite. I always keep my word. I'll tell you how it is, I'm always nice at first, the first time. I'll hold you so tight you won't think you have to try to get away or pretend anything because you'll know you can't. And I'll come inside you where it's all secret and you'll give in to me and you'll love me—"

105 "Shut up! You're crazy!" Connie said. She backed away from the door. She put her hands against her ears as if she'd heard something terrible, something not meant for her. "People don't talk like that, you're crazy," she muttered. Her heart was almost too big now for her chest and its pumping made sweat break out all over her. She looked out to see Arnold Friend pause and then take a step toward the porch lurching. He almost fell. But, like a clever drunken man, he managed to catch his balance. He wobbled in his high boots and grabbed hold of one of the porch posts.

"Honey?" he said. "You still listening?"

"Get the hell out of here!"

"Be nice, honey. Listen."

"I'm going to call the police—"

110 He wobbled again and out of the side of his mouth came a fast spat curse, an aside not meant for her to hear. But even this "Christ!" sounded forced. Then he began to smile again. She watched this smile come, awkward as if he were smiling from inside a mask. His whole face was a mask, she thought wildly, tanned down onto his throat but then running out as if he had plastered makeup on his face but had forgotten about his throat.

"Honey—? Listen, here's how it is. I always tell the truth and I promise you this: I ain't coming in that house after you."

"You better not! I'm going to call the police if you—if you don't—"

"Honey," he said, talking right through her voice, "honey, I'm not coming in there but you are coming out here. You know why?"

She was panting. The kitchen looked like a place she had never seen before, some room she had run inside but which wasn't good enough, wasn't going to help her. The kitchen window had never had a curtain, after three years, and there were dishes in the sink for her to do—probably—and if you ran your hand across the table you'd probably feel something sticky there.

"You listening, honey? Hey?"   115

"—going to call the police—"

"Soon as you touch the phone I don't need to keep my promise and can come inside. You won't want that."

She rushed forward and tried to lock the door. Her fingers were shaking. "But why lock it," Arnold Friend said gently, talking right into her face. "It's just a screen door. It's just nothing." One of his boots was at a strange angle, as if his foot wasn't in it. It pointed out to the left, bent at the ankle. "I mean, anybody can break through a screen door and glass and wood and iron or anything else if he needs to, anybody at all and specially Arnold Friend. If the place got lit up with a fire honey you'd come running out into my arms, right into my arms and safe at home—like you knew I was your lover and'd stopped fooling around. I don't mind a nice shy girl but I don't like no fooling around." Part of those words were spoken with a slight rhythmic lilt, and Connie somehow recognized them—the echo of a song from last year, about a girl rushing into her boy friend's arms and coming home again—

Connie stood barefoot on the linoleum floor, staring at him. "What do you want?" she whispered.

"I want you," he said.   120

"What?"

"Seen you that night and thought, that's the one, yes sir. I never needed to look any more."

"But my father's coming back. He's coming to get me. I had to wash my hair first—" She spoke in a dry, rapid voice, hardly raising it for him to hear.

"No, your daddy is not coming and yes, you had to wash your hair and you washed it for me. It's nice and shining and all for me, I thank you, sweetheart," he said, with a mock bow, but again he almost lost his balance. He had to bend and adjust his boots. Evidently his feet did not go all the way down; the boots must have been stuffed with something so that he would seem taller. Connie stared out at him and behind him Ellie in the car, who seemed to be looking off toward Connie's right, into nothing. This Ellie said, pulling the words out of the air one after another as if he were just discovering them, "You want me to pull out the phone?"

"Shut your mouth and keep it shut," Arnold Friend said, his face red 125 from bending over or maybe from embarrassment because Connie had seen his boots. "This ain't none of your business."

"What—what are you doing? What do you want?" Connie said. "If I call the police they'll get you, they'll arrest you—"

"Promise was not to come in unless you touch that phone, and I'll keep that promise," he said. He resumed his erect position and tried to force his shoulders back. He sounded like a hero in a movie, declaring something important. He spoke too loudly and it was as if he were speaking to someone behind Connie. "I ain't made plans for coming in that house where I don't belong but just for you to come out to me, the way you should. Don't you know who I am?"

"You're crazy," she whispered. She backed away from the door but did not want to go into another part of the house, as if this would give him permission to come through the door. "What do you.... You're crazy, you..."

"Huh? What're you saying, honey?"

130   Her eyes darted everywhere in the kitchen. She could not remember what it was, this room.

"This is how it is, honey: you come out and we'll drive away, have a nice ride. But if you don't come out we're gonna wait till your people come home and then they're all going to get it."

"You want that telephone pulled out?" Ellie said. He held the radio away from his ear and grimaced, as if without the radio the air was too much for him.

"I toldja shut up, Ellie," Arnold Friend said, "you're deaf, get a hearing aid, right? Fix yourself up. This little girl's no trouble and's gonna be nice to me, so Ellie keep to yourself, this ain't your date—right? Don't hem in on me. Don't hog. Don't crush. Don't bird dog. Don't trail me," he said in a rapid meaningless voice, as if he were running through all the expressions he'd learned but was no longer sure which one of them was in style, then rushing on to new ones, making them up with his eyes closed, "Don't crawl under my fence, don't squeeze in my chipmunk hole, don't sniff my glue, suck my popsicle, keep your own greasy fingers on yourself!" He shaded his eyes and peered in at Connie, who was backed against the kitchen table. "Don't mind him honey he's just a creep. He's a dope. Right? I'm the boy for you and like I said you come out here nice like a lady and give me your hand, and nobody else gets hurt, I mean, your nice old bald-headed daddy and your mummy and your sister in her high heels. Because listen: why bring them in this?"

"Leave me alone," Connie whispered.

135   "Hey, you know that old woman down the road, the one with the chickens and stuff—you know her?"

"She's dead!"

"Dead? What? You know her?" Arnold Friend said.

"She's dead—"

"Don't you like her?"

"She's dead—she's—she isn't here any more—"   140

"But don't you like her, I mean, you got something against her? Some grudge or something?" Then his voice dipped as if he were conscious of a rudeness. He touched the sunglasses perched on top of his head as if to make sure they were still there. "Now you be a good girl."

"What are you going to do?"

"Just two things, or maybe three," Arnold Friend said. "But I promise it won't last long and you'll like me that way you get to like people you're close to. You will. It's all over for you here, so come on out. You don't want your people in any trouble, do you?"

She turned and bumped against a chair or something, hurting her leg, but she ran into the back room and picked up the telephone. Something roared in her ear, a tiny roaring, and she was so sick with fear that she could do nothing but listen to it—the telephone was clammy and very heavy and her fingers groped down to the dial but were too weak to touch it. She began to scream into the phone, into the roaring. She cried out, she cried for her mother, she felt her breath start jerking back and forth in her lungs as if it were something Arnold Friend were stabbing her with again and again with no tenderness. A noisy sorrowful wailing rose all about her and she was locked inside it the way she was locked inside the house.

After a while she could hear again. She was sitting on the floor with   145
her wet back against the wall.

Arnold Friend was saying from the door, "That's a good girl. Put the phone back."

She kicked the phone away from her.

"No, honey. Pick it up. Put it back right."

She picked it up and put it back. The dial tone stopped.

"That's a good girl. Now you come outside."   150

She was hollow with what had been fear, but what was now just an emptiness. All that screaming had blasted it out of her. She sat, one leg cramped under her, and deep inside her brain was something like a pin-point of light that kept going and would not let her relax. She thought, I'm not going to see my mother again. She thought, I'm not going to sleep in my bed again. Her bright green blouse was all wet.

Arnold Friend said, in a gentle-loud voice that was like a stage voice, "The place where you came from ain't there any more, and where you had in mind to go is cancelled out. This place you are now—inside your daddy's house—is nothing but a cardboard box I can knock down any time. You know that and always did know it. You hear me?"

She thought, I have got to think. I have to know what to do.

"We'll go out to a nice field, out in the country here where it smells so nice and it's sunny," Arnold Friend said. "I'll have my arms around you so you won't need to try to get away and I'll show you what love is like, what it does. The hell with this house! It looks solid all right," he said. He ran a fingernail down the screen and the noise did not make Connie shiver, as it would have the day before. "Now put your hand on your heart, honey. Feel that? That feels solid too but we know better, be nice to me, be sweet like you can because what else is there for a girl like you but to be sweet and pretty and give in?—and get away before her people come back?"

155   She felt her pounding heart. Her hand seemed to enclose it. She thought for the first time in her life that it was nothing that was hers, that belonged to her, but just a pounding, living thing inside this body that wasn't really hers either.

"You don't want them to get hurt," Arnold Friend went on. "Now get up, honey. Get up all by yourself."

She stood.

"Now turn this way. That's right. Come over here to me—Ellie, put that away, didn't I tell you? You dope. You miserable creepy dope," Arnold Friend said. His words were not angry but only part of an incantation. The incantation was kindly. "Now come out through the kitchen to me honey and let's see a smile, try it, you're a brave sweet little girl and now they're eating corn and hotdogs cooked to bursting over an outdoor fire, and they don't know one thing about you and never did and honey you're better than them because not a one of them would have done this for you."

Connie felt the linoleum under her feet; it was cool. She brushed her hair back out of her eyes. Arnold Friend let go of the post tentatively and opened his arms for her, his elbows pointing in toward each other and his wrists limp, to show that this was an embarrassed embrace and a little mocking, he didn't want to make her self-conscious.

160   She put out her hand against the screen. She watched herself push the door slowly open as if she were safe back somewhere in the other doorway, watching this body and this head of long hair moving out into the sunlight where Arnold Friend waited.

"My sweet little blue-eyed girl," he said, in a half-sung sigh that had nothing to do with her brown eyes but was taken up just the same by the vast sunlit reaches of the land behind him and on all sides of him, so much land that Connie had never seen before and did not recognize except to know that she was going to it.

*   *   *

ALBERTO ALVARO RÍOS (1952–   )

The Secret Lion (1984)

I was twelve and in junior high school and something happened that we didn't have a name for, but it was there nonetheless like a lion, and roaring, roaring that way the biggest things do. Everything changed. Just that.

Like the rug, the one that gets pulled—or better, like the tablecloth those magicians pull where the stuff on the table stays the same but the gasp! from the audience makes the staying-the-same part not matter. Like that.

What happened was there were teachers now, not just one teacher, teach-erz, and we felt personally abandoned somehow. When a person had all these teachers now, he didn't get taken care of the same way, even though six was more than one. Arithmetic went out the door when we walked in. And we saw girls now, but they weren't the same girls we used to know because we couldn't talk to them anymore, not the same way we used to, certainly not to Sandy, even though she was my neighbor, too. Not even to her. She just played the piano all the time. And there were words, oh there were words in junior high school, and we wanted to know what they were, and how a person did them—that's what school was supposed to be for. Only, in junior high school, school wasn't school, everything was backward-like. If you went up to a teacher and said the word to try and find out what it meant you got in trouble for saying it. So we didn't. And we figured it must have been that way about other stuff, too, so we never said anything about anything—we weren't stupid.

But my friend Sergio and I, we solved junior high school. We would come home from school on the bus, put our books away, change shoes, and go across the highway to the arroyo. It was the one place we were not supposed to go. So we did. This was, after all, what junior high had at least shown us. It was our river, though, our personal Mississippi, our friend from long back, and it was full of stories and all the branch forts we had built in it when we were still the Vikings of America, with our own symbol, which we had carved everywhere, even in the sand, which let the water take it. That was good, we had decided; whoever was at the end of this river would know about us.

At the very very top of our growing lungs, what we would do down there was shout every dirty word we could think of, in every combination we could come up with, and we would yell about girls, and all the things we wanted to do with them, as loud as we could—we didn't know what we wanted to do with them, just things—and we would yell about teachers, and how we loved some of them, like Miss Crevelone, and how we wanted to dissect some of them, making signs of the cross, like priests, and we would yell this stuff over and over because it felt good, we couldn't explain why, it just felt good and for the first time in our lives there was nobody to tell us we couldn't. So we did.

One Thursday we were walking along shouting this way, and the rail- 5 road, the Southern Pacific, which ran above and along the far side of the arroyo, had dropped a grinding ball down there, which was, we found out later, a cannonball thing used in mining. A bunch of them were put in a big vat which turned around and crushed the ore. One had been dropped, or thrown—what do caboose men do when they get bored—but it got down there regardless and as we were walking along yelling about one girl or another, a particular Claudia, we found it, one of these things, looked at it, picked it up, and got very very excited, and held it and passed it back and forth, and we were saying "Guythisis, this is, geeGuythis…": we had this perception about nature then, that nature is imperfect and that round things are perfect: we said "GuyGodthis is perfect, thisisthis is perfect, it's round, round and heavy, it'sit's the best thing we'veeverseen. Whatisit?" We didn't know. We just knew it was great. We just, whatever, we played with it, held it some more.

And then we had to decide what to do with it. We knew, because of a lot of things, that if we were going to take this and show it to anybody, this discovery, this best thing, was going to be taken away from us. That's the way it works with little kids, like all the polished quartz, the tons of it we had collected piece by piece over the years. Junior high kids too. If we took it home, my mother, we knew, was going to look at it and say "throw that dirty thing in the, get rid of it." Simple like, like that. "But ma it's the best thing I" "Getridofit." Simple.

So we didn't. Take it home. Instead, we came up with the answer. We dug a hole and buried it. And we marked it secretly. Lots of secret signs. And came back the next week to dig it up and, we didn't know, pass it around some more or something, but we didn't find it. We dug up that whole bank, and we never found it again. We tried.

Sergio and I talked about that ball or whatever it was when we couldn't find it. All we used were small words, neat, good. Kid words. What we were really saying, but didn't know the words, was how much that ball was like that place, that whole arroyo: couldn't tell anybody about it, didn't understand what it was, didn't have a name for it. It just felt good. It was just perfect in the way it was that place, that whole going to that place, that whole junior high school lion. It was just iron-heavy, it had no name, it felt good or not, we couldn't take it home to show our mothers, and once we buried it, it was gone forever.

The ball was gone, like the first reasons we had come to that arroyo years earlier, like the first time we had seen the arroyo, it was gone like everything else that had been taken away. This was not our first lesson. We stopped going to the arroyo after not finding the thing, the same way we had stopped going there years earlier and headed for the mountains. Nature seemed to keep pushing us around one way or another, teaching us the same thing every place we ended up. Nature's gang was tough that way, teaching us stuff.

10   When we were young we moved away from town, me and my family. Sergio's was already out there. Out in the wilds. Or at least the new place seemed like the wilds since everything looks bigger the smaller a man is. I was five, I guess, and we had moved three miles north of Nogales where

we had lived, three miles north of the Mexican border. We looked across the highway in one direction and there was the arroyo; hills stood up in the other direction. Mountains, for a small man.

When the first summer came the very first place we went to was of course the one place we weren't supposed to go, the arroyo. We went down in there and found water running, summer rain water mostly, and we went swimming. But every third or fourth or fifth day, the sewage treatment plant that was, we found out, upstream, would release whatever it was that it released, and we would never know exactly what day that was, and a person really couldn't tell right off by looking at the water, not every time, not so a person could get out in time. So, we went swimming that summer and some days we had a lot of fun. Some days we didn't. We found a thousand ways to explain what happened on those other days, constructing elaborate stories about the neighborhood dogs, and hadn't she, my mother, miscalculated her step before, too? But she knew something was up because we'd come running into the house those days, wanting to take a shower, even—if this can be imagined—in the middle of the day.

That was the first time we stopped going to the arroyo. It taught us to look the other way. We decided, as the second side of summer came, we wanted to go into the mountains. They were still mountains then. We went running in one summer Thursday morning, my friend Sergio and I, into my mother's kitchen, and said, well, what'zin, what'zin those hills over there—we used her word so she'd understand us—and she said nothingdon'tworryaboutit. So we went out, and we weren't dumb, we thought with our eyes to each other, ohhoshe'stryingtokeepsomething-fromus. We knew adults.

We had read the books, after all; we knew about bridges and castles and wildtreacherousraging alligatormouth rivers. We wanted them. So we were going to go out and get them. We went back that morning into that kitchen and we said, "We're going out there, we're going into the hills, we're going away for three days, don't worry." She said, "All right."

"You know," I said to Sergio, "if we're going to go away for three days, well, we ought to at least pack a lunch."

But we were two young boys with no patience for what we thought at 15 the time was mom-stuff: making sa-and-wiches. My mother didn't offer. So we got out little kid knapsacks that my mother had sewn for us, and into them we put the jar of mustard. A loaf of bread. Knivesforksplates, bottles of Coke, a can opener. This was lunch for the two of us. And we were weighed down, humped over to be strong enough to carry this stuff. But we started walking anyway, into the hills. We were going to eat berries and stuff otherwise. "Goodbye." My mom said that.

After the first hill we were dead. But we walked. My mother could still see us. And we kept walking. We walked until we got to where the sun is straight overhead, noon. That place. Where that is doesn't matter; it's time to eat. The truth is we weren't anywhere close to that place. We just agreed that the sun was overhead and that it was time to eat, and by tilting our heads a little we could make that the truth.

"We really ought to start looking for a place to eat."

"Yeah. Let's look for a good place to eat." We went back and forth saying that for fifteen minutes, making it lunchtime because that's what we always said back and forth before lunchtimes at home. "Yeah, I'm hungry all right." I nodded my head. "Yeah, I'm hungry all right too. I'm hungry." He nodded his head. I nodded my head back. After a good deal more nodding, we were ready, just as we came over a little hill. We hadn't found the mountains yet. This was a little hill.

And on the other side of this hill we found heaven.

20   It was just what we thought it would be.

Perfect. Heaven was green, like nothing else in Arizona. And it wasn't a cemetery or like that because we had seen cemeteries and they had gravestones and stuff and this didn't. This was perfect, had trees, lots of trees, had birds, like we had never seen before. It was like *The Wizard of Oz*, like when they got to Oz and everything was so green, so emerald, they had to wear those glasses, and we ran just like them, laughing, laughing that way we did that moment, and we went running down to this clearing in it all, hitting each other that good way we did.

We got down there, we kept laughing, we kept hitting each other, we unpacked our stuff, and we started acting "rich." We knew all about how to do that, like blowing on our nails, then rubbing them on our chests for the shine. We made our sandwiches, opened our Cokes, got out the rest of the stuff, the salt and pepper shakers. I found this particular hole and I put my Coke right into it, a perfect fit, and I called it my Coke-holder. I got down next to it on my back, because everyone knows that rich people eat lying down, and I got my sandwich in one hand and put my other arm around the Coke in its holder. When I wanted a drink, I lifted my neck a little, put out my lips, and tipped my Coke a little with the crook of my elbow. Ah.

We were there, lying down, eating our sandwiches, laughing, throwing bread at each other and out for the birds. This was heaven. We were laughing and we couldn't believe it. My mother was keeping something from us, ah ha, but we had found her out. We even found water over at the side of the clearing to wash our plates with—we had brought plates. Sergio started washing his plates when he was done, and I was being rich with my Coke, and this day in summer was right.

When suddenly these two men came, from around a corner of trees and the tallest grass we had ever seen. They had bags on their backs, leather bags, bags and sticks.

We didn't know what clubs were, but I learned later, like I learned 25 about the grinding balls. The two men yelled at us. Most specifically, one wanted me to take my Coke out of my Coke-holder so he could sink his golf ball into it.

Something got taken away from us that moment. Heaven. We grew up a little bit, and couldn't go backward. We learned. No one had ever told us about golf. They had told us about heaven. And it went away. We got golf in exchange.

We went back to the arroyo for the rest of that summer, and tried to have fun the best we could. We learned to be ready for finding the grinding ball. We loved it, and when we buried it we knew what would happen. The truth is, we didn't look so hard for it. We were two boys and twelve summers then, and not stupid. Things get taken away.

We buried it because it was perfect. We didn't tell my mother, but together it was all we talked about, till we forgot. It was the lion.

*   *   *

AMY TAN (1952–   )

Two Kinds (1989)

My mother believed you could be anything you wanted to be in America. You could open a restaurant. You could work for the government and get good retirement. You could buy a house with almost no money down. You could become rich. You could become instantly famous.

"Of course you can be prodigy, too," my mother told me when I was nine. "You can be best anything. What does Auntie Lindo know? Her daughter, she is only best tricky."

America was where all my mother's hopes lay. She had come here in 1949 after losing everything in China: her mother and father, her family home, her first husband, and two daughters, twin baby girls. But she never looked back with regret. There were so many ways for things to get better.

We didn't immediately pick the right kind of prodigy. At first my mother thought I could be a Chinese Shirley Temple. We'd watch Shirley's old movies on TV as though they were training films. My mother would poke my arm and say, "Ni kan"—You watch. And I would see Shirley tapping her feet, or singing a sailor song, or pursing her lips into a very round O while saying, "Oh my goodness."

"Ni kan," said my mother as Shirley's eyes flooded with tears. "You 5 already know how. Don't need talent for crying!"

Soon after my mother got this idea about Shirley Temple, she took me to a beauty training school in the Mission district and put me in the hands of a student who could barely hold the scissors without shaking. Instead of getting big fat curls, I emerged with an uneven mass of crinkly black fuzz. My mother dragged me off to the bathroom and tried to wet down my hair.

"You look like Negro Chinese," she lamented, as if I had done this on purpose.

The instructor of the beauty training school had to lop off these soggy clumps to make my hair even again. "Peter Pan is very popular these days," the instructor assured my mother. I now had hair the length of a boy's, with straight-across bangs that hung at a slant two inches above my eyebrows. I liked the haircut and it made me actually look forward to my future fame.

In fact, in the beginning, I was just as excited as my mother, maybe even more so. I pictured this prodigy part of me as many different images, trying each one on for size. I was a dainty ballerina girl standing by the curtains, waiting to hear the right music that would send me floating on my tiptoes. I was like the Christ child lifted out of the straw manger, crying with holy indignity. I was Cinderella stepping from her pumpkin carriage with sparkly cartoon music filling the air.

10   In all of my imaginings, I was filled with a sense that I would soon become *perfect*. My mother and father would adore me. I would be beyond reproach. I would never feel the need to sulk for anything.

But sometimes the prodigy in me became impatient. "If you don't hurry up and get me out of here, I'm disappearing for good," it warned. "And then you'll always be nothing."

Every night after dinner, my mother and I would sit at the Formica kitchen table. She would present new tests, taking her examples from stories of amazing children she had read in *Ripley's Believe It or Not*, or *Good Housekeeping, Reader's Digest*, and a dozen other magazines she kept in a pile in our bathroom. My mother got these magazines from people whose houses she cleaned. And since she cleaned many houses each week, we had a great assortment. She would look through them all, searching for stories about remarkable children.

The first night she brought out a story about a three-year-old boy who knew the capitals of all the states and even most of the European countries. A teacher was quoted as saying the little boy could also pronounce the names of the foreign cities correctly.

"What's the capital of Finland?" my mother asked me, looking at the magazine story.

15   All I knew was the capital of California, because Sacramento was the name of the street we lived on in Chinatown. "Nairobi!" I guessed, saying the most foreign word I could think of. She checked to see if that was possibly one way to pronounce "Helsinki" before showing me the answer.

The tests got harder—multiplying numbers in my head, finding the queen of hearts in a deck of cards, trying to stand on my head without using my hands, predicting the daily temperatures in Los Angeles, New York, and London.

One night I had to look at a page from the Bible for three minutes and then report everything I could remember. "Now Jehoshaphat had riches and honor in abundance and...that's all I remember, Ma," I said.

And after seeing my mother's disappointed face once again, something inside of me began to die. I hated the tests, the raised hopes and failed expectations. Before going to bed that night, I looked in the mirror above the bathroom sink and when I saw only my face staring back—and that it would always be this ordinary face—I began to cry. Such a sad, ugly girl! I made high-pitched noises like a crazed animal, trying to scratch out the face in the mirror.

And then I saw what seemed to be the prodigy side of me—because I had never seen that face before. I looked at my reflection, blinking so I could see more clearly. The girl staring back at me was angry, powerful. This girl and I were the same. I had new thoughts, willful thoughts, or rather thoughts filled with lots of won'ts. I won't let her change me, I promised myself. I won't be what I'm not.

So now on nights when my mother presented her tests, I performed 20 listlessly, my head propped on one arm. I pretended to be bored. And I was. I got so bored I started counting the bellows of the foghorns out on the bay while my mother drilled me in other areas. The sound was comforting and reminded me of the cow jumping over the moon. And the next day, I played a game with myself, seeing if my mother would give up on me before eight bellows. After a while I usually counted only one, maybe two bellows at most. At last she was beginning to give up hope.

Two or three months had gone by without any mention of my being a prodigy again. And then one day my mother was watching *The Ed Sullivan Show* on TV. The TV was old and the sound kept shorting out. Every time my mother got halfway up from the sofa to adjust the set, the sound would go back on and Ed would be talking. As soon as she sat down, Ed would go silent again. She got up, the TV broke into loud piano music. She sat down. Silence. Up and down, back and forth, quiet and loud. It was like a stiff embraceless dance between her and the TV set. Finally she stood by the set with her hand on the sound dial.

She seemed entranced by the music, a little frenzied piano piece with this mesmerizing quality, sort of quick passages and then teasing lilting ones before it returned to the quick playful parts.

"*Ni kan*," my mother said, calling me over with hurried hand gestures, "Look here."

I could see why my mother was fascinated by the music. It was being pounded out by a little Chinese girl, about nine years old, with a Peter Pan haircut. The girl had the sauciness of a Shirley Temple. She was proudly modest like a proper Chinese child. And she also did this fancy sweep of a curtsy, so that the fluffy skirt of her white dress cascaded slowly to the floor like the petals of a large carnation.

25   In spite of these warning signs, I wasn't worried. Our family had no piano and we couldn't afford to buy one, let alone reams of sheet music and piano lessons. So I could be generous in my comments when my mother bad-mouthed the little girl on TV.

"Play note right, but doesn't sound good! No singing sound," complained my mother.

"What are you picking on her for?" I said carelessly. "She's pretty good. Maybe she's not the best, but she's trying hard." I knew almost immediately I would be sorry I said that.

"Just like you," she said. "Not the best. Because you not trying." She gave a little huff as she let go of the sound dial and sat down on the sofa.

The little Chinese girl sat down also to play an encore of "Anitra's Dance" by Grieg. I remember the song, because later on I had to learn how to play it.

30   Three days after watching *The Ed Sullivan Show*, my mother told me what my schedule would be for piano lessons and piano practice. She had talked to Mr. Chong, who lived on the first floor of our apartment building. Mr. Chong was a retired piano teacher and my mother had traded housecleaning services for weekly lessons and a piano for me to practice on every day, two hours a day, from four until six.

When my mother told me this, I felt as though I had been sent to hell. I whined and then kicked my foot a little when I couldn't stand it anymore.

"Why don't you like me the way I am? I'm *not* a genius! I can't play the piano. And even if I could, I wouldn't go on TV if you paid me a million dollars!" I cried.

My mother slapped me. "Who ask you be genius?" she shouted. "Only ask you be your best. For you sake. You think I want you be genius? Hnnh! What for! Who ask you!"

"So ungrateful," I heard her mutter in Chinese. "If she had as much talent as she has temper, she would be famous now."

35   Mr. Chong, whom I secretly nicknamed Old Chong, was very strange, always tapping his fingers to the silent music of an invisible orchestra. He looked ancient in my eyes. He had lost most of the hair on top of his head and he wore thick glasses and had eyes that always looked tired and sleepy. But he must have been younger than I thought, since he lived with his mother and was not yet married.

I met Old Lady Chong once and that was enough. She had this peculiar smell like a baby that had done something in its pants. And her
fingers felt like a dead person's, like an old peach I once found in the
back of the refrigerator; the skin just slid off the meat when I picked it up.

I soon found out why Old Chong had retired from teaching piano. He
was deaf. "Like Beethoven!" he shouted to me. "We're both listening only
in our head!" And he would start to conduct his frantic silent sonatas.

Our lessons went like this. He would open the book and point to different things, explaining their purpose: "Key! Treble! Bass! No sharps or
flats! So this is C major! Listen now and play after me!"

And then he would play the C scale a few times, a simple chord, and
then, as if inspired by an old, unreachable itch, he gradually added more
notes and running trills and a pounding bass until the music was really
something quite grand.

I would play after him, the simple scale, the simple chord, and then 40
I just played some nonsense that sounded like a cat running up and down
on top of garbage cans. Old Chong smiled and applauded and then said,
"Very good! But now you must learn to keep time!"

So that's how I discovered that Old Chong's eyes were too slow
to keep up with the wrong notes I was playing. He went through the
motions in half-time. To help me keep rhythm, he stood behind me,
pushing down on my right shoulder for every beat. He balanced pennies
on top of my wrists so I would keep them still as I slowly played scales
and arpeggios. He had me curve my hand around an apple and keep that
shape when playing chords. He marched stiffly to show me how to make
each finger dance up and down, staccato like an obedient little soldier.

He taught me all these things, and that was how I also learned I could
be lazy and get away with mistakes, lots of mistakes. If I hit the wrong
notes because I hadn't practiced enough, I never corrected myself. I
just kept playing in rhythm. And Old Chong kept conducting his own
private reverie.

So maybe I never really gave myself a fair chance. I did pick up the
basics pretty quickly, and I might have become a good pianist at that
young age. But I was so determined not to try, not to be anybody different that I learned to play only the most ear-splitting preludes, the most
discordant hymns.

Over the next year, I practiced like this, dutifully in my own way. And
then one day I heard my mother and her friend Lindo Jong both talking
in a loud bragging tone of voice so others could hear. It was after church,
and I was leaning against the brick wall wearing a dress with stiff white
petticoats. Auntie Lindo's daughter, Waverly, who was about my age,
was standing farther down the wall about five feet away. We had grown
up together and shared all the closeness of two sisters squabbling over

crayons and dolls. In other words, for the most part, we hated each other. I thought she was snotty. Waverly Jong had gained a certain amount of fame as "Chinatown's Littlest Chinese Chess Champion."

45   "She bring home too many trophy," lamented Auntie Lindo that Sunday. "All day she play chess. All day I have no time do nothing but dust off her winnings." She threw a scolding look at Waverly, who pretended not to see her.

"You lucky you don't have this problem," said Auntie Lindo with a sigh to my mother.

And my mother squared her shoulders and bragged: "Our problem worser than yours. If we ask Jing-mei wash dish, she hear nothing but music. It's like you can't stop this natural talent."

And right then, I was determined to put a stop to her foolish pride.

A few weeks later, Old Chong and my mother conspired to have me play in a talent show which would be held in the church hall. By then, my parents had saved up enough to buy me a secondhand piano, a black Wurlitzer spinet with a scarred bench. It was the showpiece of our living room.

50   For the talent show, I was to play a piece called "Pleading Child" from Schumann's *Scenes from Childhood*. It was a simple, moody piece that sounded more difficult than it was. I was supposed to memorize the whole thing, playing the repeat parts twice to make the piece sound longer. But I dawdled over it, playing a few bars and then cheating, looking up to see what notes followed. I never really listened to what I was playing. I daydreamed about being somewhere else, about being someone else.

The part I liked to practice best was the fancy curtsy: right foot out, touch the rose on the carpet with a pointed foot, sweep to the side, left leg bends, look up and smile.

My parents invited all the couples from the Joy Luck Club[1] to witness my debut. Auntie Lindo and Uncle Tin were there. Waverly and her two older brothers had also come. The first two rows were filled with children both younger and older than I was. The littlest ones got to go first. They recited simple nursery rhymes, squawked out tunes on miniature violins, twirled Hula Hoops, pranced in pink ballet tutus, and when they bowed or curtsied, the audience would sigh in unison, "Awww," and then clap enthusiastically.

When my turn came, I was very confident. I remember my childish excitement. It was as if I knew, without a doubt, that the prodigy side of me really did exist. I had no fear whatsoever, no nervousness. I remember thinking to myself, This is it! This is it! I looked out over the audience,

---

[1] *Joy Luck Club:* A name denoting the mother's circle of friends, all of whom were Chinese immigrants to the United States.

at my mother's blank face, my father's yawn, Auntie Lindo's stiff-lipped smile, Waverly's sulky expression. I had on a white dress layered with sheets of lace, and a pink bow in my Peter Pan haircut. As I sat down I envisioned people jumping to their feet and Ed Sullivan rushing up to introduce me to everyone on TV.

And I started to play. It was so beautiful. I was so caught up in how lovely I looked that at first I didn't worry how I would sound. So it was a surprise to me when I hit the first wrong note and I realized something didn't sound quite right. And then I hit another and another followed that. A chill started at the top of my head and began to trickle down. Yet I couldn't stop playing, as though my hands were bewitched. I kept thinking my fingers would adjust themselves back, like a train switching to the right track. I played this strange jumble through two repeats, the sour notes staying with me all the way to the end.

When I stood up, I discovered my legs were shaking. Maybe I had just 55 been nervous and the audience, like Old Chong, had seen me go through the right motions and had not heard anything wrong at all. I swept my right foot out, went down on my knee, looked up and smiled. The room was quiet, except for Old Chong, who was beaming and shouting, "Bravo! Bravo! Well done!" But then I saw my mother's face, her stricken face. The audience clapped weakly, and as I walked back to my chair, with my whole face quivering as I tried not to cry, I heard a little boy whisper loudly to his mother, "That was awful," and the mother whispered back, "Well, she certainly tried."

And now I realized how many people were in the audience, the whole world it seemed. I was aware of eyes burning into my back. I felt the shame of my mother and father as they sat stiffly throughout the rest of the show.

We could have escaped during intermission. Pride and some strange sense of honor must have anchored my parents to their chairs. And so we watched it all: the eighteen-year-old boy with a fake mustache who did a magic show and juggled flaming hoops while riding a unicycle. The breasted girl with white makeup who sang from *Madama Butterfly* and got honorable mention. And the eleven-year-old boy who won first prize playing a tricky violin song that sounded like a busy bee.

After the show, the Hsus, the Jongs, and the St. Clairs from the Joy Luck Club came up to my mother and father.

"Lots of talented kids," Auntie Lindo said vaguely, smiling broadly.

"That was somethin' else," said my father, and I wondered if he was 60 referring to me in a humorous way, or whether he even remembered what I had done.

Waverly looked at me and shrugged her shoulders. "You aren't a genius like me," she said matter-of-factly. And if I hadn't felt so bad, I would have pulled her braids and punched her stomach.

But my mother's expression was what devastated me: a quiet, blank look that said she had lost everything. I felt the same way, and it seemed as if everybody were now coming up, like gawkers at the scene of an accident, to see what parts were actually missing. When we got on the bus to go home, my father was humming the busy-bee tune and my mother was silent. I kept thinking she wanted to wait until we got home before shouting at me. But when my father unlocked the door to our apartment, my mother walked in and then went to the back, into the bedroom. No accusations. No blame. And in a way, I felt disappointed. I had been waiting for her to start shouting, so I could shout back and cry and blame her for all my misery.

I assumed my talent-show fiasco meant I never had to play the piano again. But two days later, after school, my mother came out of the kitchen and saw me watching TV.

"Four clock," she reminded me as if it were any other day. I was stunned, as though she were asking me to go through the talent-show torture again. I wedged myself more tightly in front of the TV.

65   "Turn off TV," she called from the kitchen five minutes later.

I didn't budge. And then I decided. I didn't have to do what my mother said anymore. I wasn't her slave. This wasn't China. I had listened to her before and look what happened. She was the stupid one.

She came out from the kitchen and stood in the arched entryway of the living room. "Four clock," she said once again, louder.

"I'm not going to play anymore," I said nonchalantly. "Why should I? I'm not a genius."

She walked over and stood in front of the TV. I saw her chest was heaving up and down in an angry way.

70   "No!" I said, and I now felt stronger, as if my true self had finally emerged. So this was what had been inside me all along.

"No! I won't!" I screamed.

She yanked me by the arm, pulled me off the floor, snapped off the TV. She was frighteningly strong, half pulling, half carrying me toward the piano as I kicked the throw rugs under my feet. She lifted me up and onto the hard bench. I was sobbing by now, looking at her bitterly. Her chest was heaving even more and her mouth was open, smiling crazily as if she were pleased I was crying.

"You want me to be someone that I'm not!" I sobbed. "I'll never be the kind of daughter you want me to be!"

"Only two kinds of daughters," she shouted in Chinese. "Those who are obedient and those who follow their own mind! Only one kind of daughter can live in this house. Obedient daughter!"

75   "Then I wish I wasn't your daughter. I wish you weren't my mother," I shouted. As I said these things I got scared. It felt like worms and toads

and slimy things crawling out of my chest, but it also felt good, as if this awful side of me had surfaced, at last.

"Too late change this," said my mother shrilly.

And I could sense her anger rising to its breaking point. I wanted to see it spill over. And that's when I remembered the babies she had lost in China, the ones we never talked about. "Then I wish I'd never been born!" I shouted. "I wish I were dead! Like them."

It was as if I had said the magic words. Alakazam!—and her face went blank, her mouth closed, her arms went slack, and she backed out of the room, stunned, as if she were blowing away like a small brown leaf, thin, brittle, lifeless.

It was not the only disappointment my mother felt in me. In the years that followed, I failed her so many times, each time asserting my own will, my right to fall short of expectations. I didn't get straight As. I didn't become class president. I didn't get into Stanford. I dropped out of college.

For unlike my mother, I did not believe I could be anything I wanted   80
to be. I could only be me.

And for all those years, we never talked about the disaster at the recital or my terrible accusations afterward at the piano bench. All that remained unchecked, like a betrayal that was now unspeakable. So I never found a way to ask her why she had hoped for something so large that failure was inevitable.

And even worse, I never asked her what frightened me the most: Why had she given up hope?

For after our struggle at the piano, she never mentioned my playing again. The lessons stopped. The lid to the piano was closed, shutting out the dust, my misery, and her dreams.

So she surprised me. A few years ago, she offered to give me the piano, for my thirtieth birthday. I had not played in all those years. I saw the offer as a sign of forgiveness, a tremendous burden removed.

"Are you sure?" I asked shyly. "I mean, won't you and Dad miss it?"   85

"No, this your piano," she said firmly. "Always your piano. You only one can play."

"Well, I probably can't play anymore," I said. "It's been years."

"You pick up fast," said my mother, as if she knew this was certain. "You have natural talent. You could been genius if you want to."

"No I couldn't."

"You just not trying," said my mother. And she was neither angry nor   90
sad. She said it as if to announce a fact that could never be disproved. "Take it," she said.

But I didn't at first. It was enough that she had offered it to me. And after that, every time I saw it in my parents' living room, standing in front of the bay windows, it made me feel proud, as if it were a shiny trophy I had won back.

Last week I sent a tuner over to my parents' apartment and had the piano reconditioned, for purely sentimental reasons. My mother had died a few months before and I had been getting things in order for my father, a little bit at a time. I put the jewelry in special silk pouches. The sweaters she had knitted in yellow, pink, bright orange—all the colors I hated—I put those in moth-proof boxes. I found some old Chinese silk dresses, the kind with little slits up the sides. I rubbed the old silk against my skin, then wrapped them in tissue and decided to take them home with me.

After I had the piano tuned, I opened the lid and touched the keys. It sounded even richer than I remembered. Really, it was a very good piano. Inside the bench were the same exercise notes with handwritten scales, the same secondhand music books with their covers held together with yellow tape.

I opened up the Schumann book to the dark little piece I had played at the recital. It was on the left-hand side of the page, "Pleading Child." It looked more difficult than I remembered. I played a few bars, surprised at how easily the notes came back to me.

95   And for the first time, or so it seemed, I noticed the piece on the right-hand side. It was called "Perfectly Contented." I tried to play this one as well. It had a lighter melody but the same flowing rhythm and turned out to be quite easy. "Pleading Child" was shorter but slower; "Perfectly Contented" was longer, but faster. And after I played them both a few times, I realized they were two halves of the same song.

*   *   *

TOBIAS WOLFF (1945–   )

Bullet in the Brain (1996)

Anders couldn't get to the bank until just before it closed, so of course the line was endless and he got stuck behind two women whose loud, stupid conversation put him in a murderous temper. He was never in the best of tempers anyway, Anders—a book critic known for the weary, elegant savagery with which he dispatched almost everything he reviewed.

With the line still doubled around the rope, one of the tellers stuck a "POSITION CLOSED" sign in her window and walked to the back of the bank, where she leaned against a desk and began to pass the time with a man shuffling papers. The women in front of Anders broke off their conversation and watched the teller with hatred. "Oh, that's nice," one of them said. She turned to Anders and added, confident of his accord, "One of those little human touches that keep us coming back for more."

Anders had conceived his own towering hatred of the teller, but he immediately turned it on the presumptuous crybaby in front of him. "Damned unfair," he said. "Tragic, really. If they're not chopping off the wrong leg, or bombing your ancestral village, they're closing their positions."

She stood her ground. "I didn't say it was tragic," she said. "I just think it's a pretty lousy way to treat your customers."

"Unforgivable," Anders said. "Heaven will take note."   5

She sucked in her cheeks but stared past him and said nothing. Anders saw that the other woman, her friend, was looking in the same direction. And then the tellers stopped what they were doing, and the customers slowly turned, and silence came over the bank. Two men wearing black ski masks and blue business suits were standing to the side of the door. One of them had a pistol pressed against the guard's neck. The guard's eyes were closed, and his lips were moving. The other man had a sawed-off shotgun. "Keep your big mouth shut!" the man with the pistol said, though no one had spoken a word. "One of you tellers hits the alarm, you're all dead meat. Got it?"

The tellers nodded.

"Oh, bravo," Anders said. "*Dead meat*." He turned to the woman in front of him. "Great script, eh? The stern, brass-knuckled poetry of the dangerous classes."

She looked at him with drowning eyes.

The man with the shotgun pushed the guard to his knees. He handed 10 up the shotgun to his partner and yanked the guard's wrists up behind his back and locked them together with a pair of handcuffs. He toppled him onto the floor with a kick between the shoulder blades. Then he took his shotgun back and went over to the security gate at the end of the counter. He was short and heavy and moved with peculiar slowness, even torpor. "Buzz him in," his partner said. The man with the shotgun opened the gate and sauntered along the line of tellers, handing each of them a Hefty bag. When he came to the empty position he looked over at the man with the pistol, who said, "Whose slot is that?"

Anders watched the teller. She put her hand to her throat and turned to the man she'd been talking to. He nodded. "Mine," she said.

"Then get your ugly ass in gear and fill that bag."

"There you go," Anders said to the woman in front of him. "Justice is done."

"Hey! Bright Boy! Did I tell you to talk?"

"No," Anders said.   15

"Then shut your trap."

"Did you hear that?" Anders said. "'Bright boy.' Right out of 'The Killers'."

"Please be quiet," the woman said.

"Hey, you deaf or what?" The man with the pistol walked over to Anders. He poked the weapon into Anders' gut. "You think I'm playing games?"

20   "No," Anders said, but the barrel tickled like a stiff finger and he had to fight back the titters. He did this by making himself stare into the man's eyes, which were clearly visible behind the holes in the mask: pale blue, and rawly red-rimmed. The man's left eyelid kept twitching. He breathed out a piercing, ammoniac smell that shocked Anders more than anything that had happened, and he was beginning to develop a sense of unease when the man prodded him again with the pistol.

"You like me, bright boy?" he said. "You want to suck my dick?"

"No," Anders said.

"Then stop looking at me."

Anders fixed his gaze on the man's shiny wing-tip shoes.

25   "Not down there. Up there." He stuck the pistol under Anders' chin and pushed it upward until Anders was looking at the ceiling.

Anders had never paid much attention to that part of the bank, a pompous old building with marble floors and counters and pillars, and gilt scrollwork over the tellers' cages. The domed ceiling had been decorated with mythological figures whose fleshy, toga-draped ugliness Anders had taken in at a glance many years earlier and afterward declined to notice. Now he had no choice but to scrutinize the painter's work. It was even worse than he remembered, and all of it executed with the utmost gravity. The artist had a few tricks up his sleeve and used them again and again—a certain rosy blush on the underside of the clouds, a coy backward glance on the faces of the cupids and fauns. The ceiling was crowded with various dramas, but the one that caught Anders' eye was Zeus and Europa[1]—portrayed, in this rendition, as a bull ogling a cow from behind a haystack. To make the cow sexy, the painter had canted her hips suggestively and given her long, droopy eyelashes through which she gazed back at the bull with sultry welcome. The bull wore a smirk and his eyebrows were arched. If there'd been a bubble coming out of his mouth, it would have said, "Hubba hubba."

"What's so funny, bright boy?"

"Nothing."

"You think I'm comical? You think I'm some kind of clown?"

30   "No."

---

[1]*Zeus and Europa:* According to Greek mythology, the god Zeus, as a white bull, seduced Europa, who in turn gave birth to three sons.

"You think you can fuck with me?"

"No."

"Fuck with me again, you're history. *Capiche?*"[2]

Anders burst out laughing. He covered his mouth with both hands and said, "I'm sorry, I'm sorry," then snorted helplessly through his fingers and said, "*Capiche*—oh, God, capiche," and at that the man with the pistol raised the pistol and shot Anders right in the head.

The bullet smashed Anders' skull and ploughed through his brain and exited behind his right ear, scattering shards of bone into the cerebral cortex, the corpus callosum, back toward the basal ganglia, and down into the thalamus. But before all this occurred, the first appearance of the bullet in the cerebrum set off a cracking chain of ion transports and neuro-transmissions. Because of their peculiar origin these traced a peculiar pattern, flukishly calling to life a summer afternoon some forty years past, and long since lost to memory. After striking the cranium the bullet was moving at 900 feet per second, a pathetically sluggish, glacial pace compared to the synaptic lightning that flashed around it. Once in the brain, that is, the bullet came under the mediation of brain time, which gave Anders plenty of leisure to contemplate the scene that, in a phrase he would have abhorred, "passed before his eyes."

It is worth noting what Anders did not remember, given what he did remember. He did not remember his first lover, Sherry, or what he had most madly loved about her, before it came to irritate him—her unembarrassed carnality, and especially the cordial way she had with his unit, which she called Mr. Mole, as in, "Uh-oh, looks like Mr. Mole wants to play," and "Let's hide Mr. Mole!" Anders did not remember his wife, whom he had also loved before she exhausted him with her predictability, or his daughter, now a sullen professor of economics at Dartmouth. He did not remember standing just outside his daughter's door as she lectured her bear about his naughtiness and described the truly appalling punishments Paws would receive unless he changed his ways. He did not remember a single line of the hundreds of poems he had committed to memory in his youth so that he could give himself the shivers at will—not "Silent, upon a peak in Darien," or "My God, I heard this day," or "All my pretty ones? Did you say all? O hell-kite! All?" None of these did he remember; not one. Anders did not remember his dying mother saying of his father, "I should have stabbed him in his sleep."

He did not remember Professor Josephs telling his class how Athenian prisoners in Sicily had been released if they could recite Aeschylus,[3] and

35

[2]*Capiche?*: Americanized spelling of *capisci,* Italian for "Do You Understand?"

[3]*Aeschylus:* Greek tragic dramatist (525/524 B.C.–456/455 B.C.).

then reciting Aeschylus himself, right there, in the Greek. Anders did not remember how his eyes had burned at those sounds. He did not remember the surprise of seeing a college classmate's name on the jacket of a novel not long after they graduated, or the respect he had felt after reading the book. He did not remember the pleasure of giving respect.

Nor did Anders remember seeing a woman leap to her death from the building opposite his own just days after his daughter was born. He did not remember shouting, "Lord have mercy!" He did not remember deliberately crashing his father's car into a tree, or having his ribs kicked in by three policemen at an anti-war rally, or waking himself up with laughter. He did not remember when he began to regard the heap of books on his desk with boredom and dread, or when he grew angry at writers for writing them. He did not remember when everything began to remind him of something else.

This is what he remembered. Heat. A baseball field. Yellow grass, the whirr of insects, himself leaning against a tree as the boys of the neighborhood gather for a pickup game. He looks on as the others argue the relative genius of Mantle and Mays.[4] They have been worrying this subject all summer, and it has become tedious to Anders: an oppression, like the heat.

40   Then the last two boys arrive, Coyle and a cousin of his from Mississippi. Anders has never met Coyle's cousin before and will never see him again. He says hi with the rest but takes no further notice of him until they've chosen sides and someone asks the cousin what position he wants to play. "Shortstop," the boy says. "Short's the best position they is." Anders turns and looks at him. He wants to hear Coyle's cousin repeat what he's just said, but he knows better than to ask. The others will think he's being a jerk, ragging the kid for his grammar. But that isn't it, not at all—it's that Anders is strangely roused, elated, by those final two words, their pure unexpectedness and their music. He takes the field in a trance, repeating them to himself.

The bullet is already in the brain; it won't be outrun forever, or charmed to a halt. In the end it will do its work and leave the troubled skull behind, dragging its comet's tail of memory and hope and talent and love into the marble hall of commerce. That can't be helped. But for now Anders can still make time. Time for the shadows to lengthen on the grass, time for the tethered dog to bark at the flying ball, time for the boy in right field to smack his sweat-blackened mitt and softly chant, *They is, they is, they is.*

---

[4]*Mantle and Mays:* American professional baseball players Mickey Mantle (1931–1995) and Willie Mays (1931–   ).

3| POETRY

UNDERSTANDING POETRY

MARIANNE MOORE (1887–1972)

Poetry (1921)

I, too, dislike it: there are things that are
    important beyond all this fiddle.
  Reading it, however, with a perfect contempt
    for it, one
discovers in it after all, a place for the genuine.
    Hands that can grasp, eyes
    that can dilate, hair that can rise   5
      if it must, these things are important not
      because a

high-sounding interpretation can be put upon them but because
they are useful. When they become so derivative as to become
unintelligible, the same thing may be said for all of us, that we
do not admire what   10
we cannot understand: the bat
    holding on upside down or in quest of something to

eat, elephants pushing, a wild horse taking a roll, a tireless wolf under
a tree, the immovable critic twitching his skin like a horse that
feels a flea, the base-
    ball fan, the statistician—   15
      nor is it valid
      to discriminate against "business documents and
school-books";[1] all these phenomena are important. One must
    make a distinction

---

[1] *"business documents and school-books":* Moore quotes the *Diaries of Tolstoy* (New York, 1917): "Where
the boundary between prose and poetry lies, I shall never be able to understand…. Poetry is verse; prose
is not verse. Or else poetry is everything with the exception of business documents and school books."

however: when dragged into prominence by half poets, the
    result is not poetry,
nor till the poets among us can be   20
    "literalists of
the imagination"[2]—above
        insolence and triviality and can present

for inspection, "imaginary gardens with real toads in them,"[3]
    shall we have
it. In the meantime, if you demand on the one hand,   25
the raw material of poetry in
    all its rawness and
    that which is on the other hand
        genuine, you are interested in poetry.

PAMELA SPIRO WAGNER (1952–   )

How to Read a Poem: Beginner's Manual*

First, forget everything you have learned,
that poetry is difficult,
that it cannot be appreciated by the likes of you,
with your high school equivalency diploma,
your steel-tipped boots,   5
or your white-collar misunderstandings.

Do not assume meanings hidden from you:
the best poems mean what they say and say it.

To read poetry requires only courage
enough to leap from the edge   10
and trust.

---

[2] *"literalists of the imagination"*: A reference (given by Moore) to W. B. Yeats's "William Blake and His Illustrations" (in *Ideas of Good and Evil*, 1903): "The limitation of his view was from the very intensity of his vision; he was a too literal realist of the imagination as others are of nature; and because he believed that the figures seen by the mind's eye, when exalted by inspiration, were 'external existences,' symbols of divine essences, he hated every grace of style that might obscure their lineaments."

[3] *"imaginary gardens with real toads in them"*: Moore places these words in quotations, but the source is unknown.

*Publication date is unavailable.

Treat a poem like dirt,
humus rich and heavy from the garden.
Later it will become the fat tomatoes
and golden squash piled high upon your kitchen table.   15

Poetry demands surrender,
language saying what is true,
doing holy things to the ordinary.

Read just one poem a day.
Someday a book of poems may open in your hands   20
like a daffodil offering its cup
to the sun.

When you can name five poets
without including Bob Dylan,
when you exceed your quota   25
and don't even notice,
close this manual.

Congratulations.
You can now read poetry.

Origins of Modern Poetry

The history of poetry begins where the history of all literature begins—with the **oral tradition,** information passed down from one generation to another by word of mouth. In a time before literacy and the printing press, the oral tradition was relied on as a way of preserving stories, histories, values, and beliefs. These stories were usually put into the form of rhyming poems, with repeated words and sounds used to make the poems easier to memorize and remember.

These extended narratives were eventually transcribed as **epics**—long poems depicting the actions of heroic figures who determine the fate of a nation or of an entire race. Early epics include Homer's *Iliad* and *Odyssey*, the *Epic of Gilgamesh*, the *Bhagavad Gita*, and Virgil's *Aeneid*. Early poetry can also be found in various religious texts, including ancient Hindu holy books like the Upanishads; sections of the Bible, including the Song of Solomon; and the Koran.

During the **Anglo-Saxon era** (late sixth to mid-eleventh centuries), poetry flourished as a literary form. Unfortunately, only about 30,000 lines of poetry survive from this period. Those poems that did survive are marked by violence, carnage, and heroic deeds as well as Pagan and Christian themes. The major texts of this time include *Beowulf*, *The Battle of Maldon*, and *The Dream of the Rood*, which is one of the earliest Christian poems. The theme of Christian morality in poetry continued into the Middle Ages with poems such as William Langland's *Piers Plowman*, which consists of three religious dream visions, and Chaucer's *Canterbury Tales*, a collection of narrative poems told by pilgrims as they travel to Canterbury, England. Using a slightly different approach to similar subject matter, Dante Alighieri wrote the Italian epic poem *The Divine Comedy*, which depicts an imaginary journey through hell, purgatory, and heaven. In France, the **troubadours**, poets of the Provençal region, wrote complex lyric poems about courtly love.

The next major literary period, the **Renaissance** (late fourteenth to mid-sixteenth centuries), witnessed the rebirth of science, philosophy, and the classical arts. Perhaps the most important writer of this period was William Shakespeare. A prolific poet, Shakespeare also wrote plays in verse, continuing in the tradition of the ancient Greek tragedian Sophocles and the ancient Roman playwright Seneca. Other notable writers of the Renaissance included Sir Philip Sidney, Christopher Marlowe, and Edmund Spenser.

During the seventeenth century, several literary movements emerged that contributed to poetry's growing prevalence and influence. John Milton continued the tradition of Christian poetry with his epic *Paradise Lost*, which told the tale of Adam and Eve's exile from the Garden of Eden. The **metaphysical**

Illustration of Trojan horse from Virgil's *Aenied*
Source: © Bettman/Corbis

Image depicting the pilgrims from Geoffrey Chaucer's *The Canterbury Tales*
Source: Roy 18 D II f.148 Lydgate and the Canterbury Pilgrims Leaving Canterbury from the 'Troy Book and the Siege of Thebes' by John Lydgate (c.1370–c.1451) 1412–22 (vellum) (detail of 8063), English School, (15th century) / British Library, London, UK / © British Library Board. All Rights Reserved / Bridgeman Images

poets (John Donne, Andrew Marvell, and George Herbert) used elaborate figures of speech and favored intellect over emotions in their writing. Their poems were characterized by reason, complex comparisons and allusions, and paradoxes, and they introduced the **meditative poem** (a poem that abstractly ponders a concept or idea) into the literary world.

In the early eighteenth century, British poets (such as Alexander Pope and Samuel Johnson) wrote poems, biographies, and literary criticism. Toward the end of the eighteenth century, the movement known as

Illuminated manuscript (fifteenth century) from Dante's *Divine Comedy* depicting Dante and Virgil in Hell

Alfredo Dagli Orti/The Art Archive/Corbis

Romanticism began. Romantic poetry was marked by heightened emotion and sentiment; a strong sense of individualism; a fascination with nature, the Middle Ages, and mysticism; a rebellion against social and political norms;

John Martin's painting *The Bard* (1817) illustrating the mystical view of nature characteristic of Romanticism

The Bard, c.1817 (oil on canvas), Martin, John (1789–1854) / Yale Center for British Art, Paul Mellon Collection, USA / Paul Mellon Collection / Bridgeman Images

Illuminated manuscript from William Blake's "The Tyger"

Source: ©Fitzwilliam Museum, University of Cambridge, UK/ Bridgeman Art Library and a return to first-person lyric poems. The early British Romantics included Samuel Taylor Coleridge, William Wordsworth, and William Blake. This generation was followed by the later Romantics, including Percy Bysshe Shelley, John Keats, and George Gordon, Lord Byron. American Romantics (called **transcendentalists**) included Henry David Thoreau, Ralph Waldo Emerson, and Walt Whitman.

The nineteenth century was marked by yet another shift in poetic consciousness. This time, poets moved away from the contemplation of the self within nature that characterized Romanticism and returned to a more elevated sense of rhetoric and subject matter. Notable

Undated engraving illustrating Edgar Allan Poe's "The Raven"
Source: ©Bettmann/CORBIS

British poets included Matthew Arnold, Robert Browning, Elizabeth Barrett Browning, and Alfred, Lord Tennyson. American poets of the this period included Edgar Allan Poe, Henry Wadsworth Longfellow, Emily Dickinson, and Phillis Wheatley, a slave who became the first African American poet.

The twentieth century had perhaps the largest number of literary movements to date, with each one reflecting its predecessors and influencing future generations of poets. In the early twentieth century, a literary movement that became known as **modernism** developed. As writers responded to the increasing complexity of a changing world, the overarching sentiment of modernism was that the "old ways" would no longer suffice in a world that had changed almost overnight as a result of the rise of industrialization and urbanization, as well as the devastation of World War I. Key modernist poets included W. H. Auden, William Butler Yeats, Ezra Pound, and T. S. Eliot, whose epic poem *The Waste Land* expressed the fragmentation of consciousness in the modern world.

After World War I, poets began to challenge the prevailing ideas of subject matter and form. Ezra Pound, along with Amy Lowell and other poets, founded **imagism**, a poetic movement that emphasized free verse and the writer's response to a visual scene or an object. William Carlos Williams wrote poems that were often deceptively simple, while the poetry of Wallace Stevens was often opaque and difficult to grasp. Dylan Thomas and E. E. Cummings also experimented with form, with Cummings intentionally manipulating the accepted constructs of grammar, syntax, and punctuation.

In the 1920s, the United States experienced the **Harlem Renaissance**. This rebirth of arts and culture was centered in Harlem, an area in New

York City where, by the mid-1920s, the African American population had reached 150,000. Harlem was teeming with creativity, especially in music (jazz and blues), literature, art, and drama. The poets who were part of the Harlem Renaissance—including Langston Hughes, Countee Cullen, James Weldon Johnson, and Jean Toomer—chose diverse subject matter and styles, but they were united in their celebration of African American culture.

In the early 1930s, a group of poets gathered at a college in Black Mountain, North Carolina, with the aim of teaching and writing about poetry in a new way. The **Black Mountain poets**, as they were called, stressed the process of writing poetry rather than the finished poem. Notable poets in this group included Robert Creeley, Denise Levertov, and Charles Olson. Meanwhile, in Latin America, poetry was growing in importance, with poets such as Pablo Neruda experimenting with subject matter, language, form, and imagery.

In the late 1940s, in the aftermath of World War II, a group of disillusioned American poets turned to eastern mysticism and newly available hallucinogenic drugs to achieve higher consciousness. They became known as the **Beat poets**, and their work was known for social and political criti-

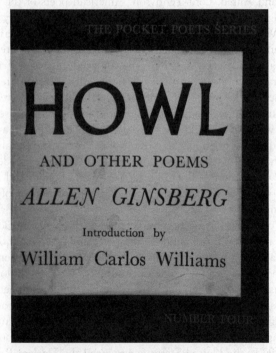

Cover of the first edition of *Howl,* published by City Lights
Books in 1956
1956 by City Light Books

cism that challenged the established norms of the time. These poets included Allen Ginsberg, whose long poem *Howl* became an unofficial anthem of the revolutionary 1960s, and Lawrence Ferlinghetti.

Up until the late 1950s, subject matter in American poetry was largely impersonal, concentrating chiefly on symbols, ideas, and politics. This changed when a group of poets—including Robert Lowell, Anne Sexton, W. D. Snodgrass, and Sylvia Plath—began to write **confessional poems** about their own personal experiences, emotions, triumphs, and tragedies (including mental illness and attempted suicide). Although there was considerable backlash against these poets from writers who thought that such highly personal subjects were not suitable for poetry, contemporary poets such as Sharon Olds continue to write confessional poetry.

The early 1960s witnessed the rise of the **Black Arts Movement**, which had its roots in the ideas of the civil rights struggle, Malcolm X and the Nation of Islam, and the Black Power Movement. The Black Arts poets wrote political works that addressed the sociopolitical and cultural context of African American life. Notable authors in this group included Amiri Baraka, Gwendolyn Brooks, Jayne Cortez, and Etheridge Knight.

The next major literary movement in poetry had its beginnings in the mid to late 1980s with slam poetry. **Slam poetry**, with origins in the oral tradition, was influenced by the Beat poets, who stressed the live performance of poems. In a **slam**, poets compete either individually or in teams before an audience, which serves as the judge. (The structure of a traditional poetry slam was created by Marc Smith, a poet and construction worker, in 1986.) Slam poetry is concerned with current events and social and political themes, and often the winning poet is the one who best combines enthusiasm,

Staceyann Chin, acclaimed slam poet and the star of
Def Poetry Jam on Broadway
Richard Termine/The New York Times/Redux

presentation, and attitude with contemporary subject matter. A home base for slam poetry is the Nyuorican Poets Café in New York City, which has become a forum for poetry, music, video, and theater. Notable slam poets past and present include Miguel Piñero, Maggie Estep, Jeffrey McDaniel, and Bob Holman.

A spinoff of slam poetry is the **spoken word** movement, which, unlike slam poetry, is a rehearsed performance. Spoken word performances have captivated a broad audience due in part to television shows such as HBO's *Def Poetry Jam* (2002–2007). **Hip-hop** and **rap**, musical forms whose lyrics rely heavily on rhyme, alliteration, assonance, consonance, and other poetic devices, also owe a debt to slam poetry and the spoken word movement.

Contemporary poetry is an extremely diverse genre whose practitioners have been influenced by many of the literary movements discussed above. Some contemporary poets embrace narrative poetry; others favor the lyric. Some write free verse; others experiment with traditional forms like the **sonnet** or the **villanelle**. Still others write **concrete poetry**, which uses words as well as varying type sizes and type fonts to form pictures on a page, or other forms of **visual poetry**.

With the advent of digital media, new forms of poetry have emerged that use multimedia elements to create texts. Not just words, but also sound, images, and video combine to create new poetic forms and new levels of aesthetic experience. For example, **hypertext poetry** has links to other texts (or visuals) that are available electronically. These links can appear all at once on the screen, or they can be revealed gradually, creating multiple levels of meaning. **Kinetic poetry** is a form in which letters (or words) drift around the screen, gradually coalescing to form phrases, lines, and possibly entire poems. **Interactive poetry** depends on readers contributing content that enhances and possibly determines the meaning of the poem. **Code poetry** is programming code expressed as poetry. The most famous code poem is "Black Perl," which is written in Perl programming language. These and other forms of digital poetry use digital technology to challenge and expand the notion of what poetry is and should be.

Defining Poetry

Throughout history and across national and cultural boundaries, poetry has occupied an important place. In ancient China and Japan, for example, poetry was prized above all else. One story tells of a samurai warrior who, when defeated, asked for a pen and paper. Thinking that he wanted to write a will before being executed, his captor granted his wish. Instead of writing a will, however, the warrior wrote a farewell poem that so moved his captor that he immediately released him.

To the ancient Greeks and Romans, poetry was the medium of spiritual and philosophical expression. Today, throughout the world, poetry continues to delight and to inspire. For many people in countless places, poetry is the language of the emotions, the medium of expression they use when they speak from the heart.

But what exactly *is* poetry? Is it, as Pamela Spiro Wagner says, "language saying what is true / doing holy things to the ordinary" (p. 488)? Or is a poem simply what Marianne Moore (p. 486) calls "all this fiddle"?

One way of defining poetry is to examine how it is different from other forms of literature, such as fiction or drama. The first and most important element of poetry that distinguishes it from other genres is its **form**. Unlike prose, which is written from margin to margin, poetry is made up of individual **lines**. A poetic line begins and ends where the poet chooses: it can start at the left margin or halfway across the page, and it can end at the right margin or after only a word or two. A poet chooses when to stop, or break, the line according to his or her sense of rhythm and meter.

Poets also use the **sound** of the words themselves, alone and in conjunction with the other words of the poem, to create a sense of rhythm and melody. **Alliteration** (the repetition of initial consonant sounds in consecutive or neighboring words), **assonance** (the repetition of vowel sounds), and **consonance** (the repetition of consonant sounds within words) are three devices commonly used by poets to help create the music of a poem. Poets can also use **rhyme** (either at the ends of lines or within the lines themselves), which contributes to the pattern of sounds in a poem.

In addition, poets are more likely than writers of other kinds of literature to rely on **imagery**, words or phrases that describe the senses. These vivid descriptions or details help the reader to connect with the poet's ideas in a tangible way. Poets also make extensive use of **figurative language**, including metaphors and similes, to convey their ideas and to help their readers access these ideas.

Another way of defining poetry is to examine our assumptions about it. Different readers, different poets, different generations of readers and poets, and different cultures often have different expectations about poetry. As a result, they have varying assumptions about what poetry should be, and these assumptions raise questions. Must poetry be written to delight or inspire, or can a poem have a political or social message? Must a poem's theme be conveyed subtly, embellished with imaginatively chosen sounds and words, or can it be explicit and straightforward? Such questions, which have been debated by literary critics as well as by poets for many years, have no easy answers—and perhaps no answers at all. A **haiku**—a short poem, rich in imagery, adhering to a rigid formal structure—is certainly poetry. To some Western readers, however, a haiku might seem too plain or understated to be "poetic." Still, most of these readers would agree that the following lines qualify as poetry.

WILLIAM SHAKESPEARE (1564–1616)

That time of year thou mayst in me behold (1609)

That time of year thou mayst in me behold
When yellow leaves, or none, or few, do hang
Upon those boughs which shake against the cold,
Bare ruined choirs, where late the sweet birds sang.
In me thou see'st the twilight of such day   5
As after sunset fadeth in the West,
Which by and by black night doth take away,
Death's second self that seals up all in rest.
In me thou see'st the glowing of such fire,
That on the ashes of his youth doth lie,   10
As the deathbed whereon it must expire,
Consumed with that which it was nourished by.
  This thou perceiv'st, which makes thy love more strong,
  To love that well which thou must leave ere long.

This poem includes many of the characteristics that Western readers commonly associate with poetry. For instance, its lines have a regular pattern of rhyme and meter that identifies it as a **sonnet**. The poem also develops a complex network of related images and figures of speech that compare the lost youth of the aging speaker to the sunset and to autumn. Finally, the pair of rhyming lines at the end of the poem expresses a familiar poetic theme: the lovers' realization that they must eventually die makes their love stronger.

Although most readers would classify Shakespeare's sonnet as a poem, they might be less certain about the following lines.

E. E. CUMMINGS (1894–1962)

l(a (1923)

l(a

le

af

fa

ll

s)

one

l

iness

Unlike Shakespeare's poem, "l(a" does not seem to have any of the characteristics normally associated with poetry. It has no meter, rhyme, or imagery. It has no repeated sounds and no figures of speech. It cannot even be read aloud because its "lines" are fragments of words. In spite of its odd appearance, however, "l(a" does communicate a conventional poetic theme.

When reconstructed, the words Cummings broke apart have the following appearance: "l (a leaf falls) one l iness." In a sense, this poem is a complex visual and verbal pun. If the parenthetical insertion "(a leaf falls)" is removed, the remaining letters spell "loneliness." Moreover, the form of the letter *l* in loneliness suggests the number *1*—which, in turn, suggests the loneliness and isolation of the individual, as reflected in nature (the single leaf). Like Shakespeare, Cummings uses an image of a leaf to express his ideas about life and human experience. At the same time, by breaking words into bits and pieces, Cummings suggests the flexibility of language and conveys the need to break out of customary ways of using words to define experience.

As these two poems illustrate, defining what a poem is (and what it is not) can be difficult. Poems can rhyme or not rhyme. They can be divided into stanzas and have a distinct form, or they can flow freely and have no discernable form. These and other choices are what many poets find alluring about the process of writing poetry. As a form, poetry is compact and concise, and choosing the right words to convey ideas is a challenge. As a literary genre, it offers room for experimentation while at the same time remaining firmly grounded in a literary tradition that stretches back through time to antiquity.

 ## Recognizing Kinds of Poetry

Most poems are either **narrative** poems, which recount a story, or **lyric** poems, which communicate a speaker's mood, feelings, or state of mind.

Narrative Poetry

Although any brief poem that tells a story, such as Edwin Arlington Robinson's "Richard Cory" (p. 783), may be considered a narrative poem, the two most familiar forms of narrative poetry are the *epic* and the *ballad.*

Epics are narrative poems that recount the accomplishments of heroic figures, typically including expansive settings, superhuman feats, and gods and supernatural beings. The language of epic poems tends to be formal, even elevated, and often quite elaborate. In ancient times, epics were handed down orally; more recently, poets have written literary epics, such as John Milton's *Paradise Lost* (1667) and Nobel Prize–winning poet Derek Walcott's *Omeros* (1990), that follow many of the same conventions.

The **ballad** is another type of narrative poetry with roots in an oral tradition. Originally intended to be sung, a ballad uses repeated words and phrases, including a refrain, to advance its story. Some—but not all—ballads use the **ballad stanza**. For an example of a traditional ballad in this book, see "Bonny Barbara Allan" (p. 734). Dudley Randall's "Ballad of Birmingham" (p. 529) is an example of a contemporary ballad.

Lyric Poetry

Like narrative poems, lyric poems take various forms.

An **elegy** is a poem in which a poet mourns the death of a specific person (or persons), as in "To an Athlete Dying Young" (p. 557).

An **ode** is a long lyric poem, formal and serious in style, tone, and subject matter. An ode typically has a fairly complex stanzaic pattern, such as the **terza rima** used by Percy Bysshe Shelley in "Ode to the West Wind" (p. 786). Another ode in this text is John Keats's "Ode on a Grecian Urn" (p. 773).

An **aubade** is a poem about morning, usually celebrating the coming of dawn. For example, see Bill Coyle's "Aubade" (p. 750).

An **occasional poem** is written to celebrate a particular event or occasion. An example is Billy Collins's 2002 poem "The Names," read before a joint session of Congress to commemorate the first anniversary of the terrorist attacks on the World Trade Center.

A **meditation** is a lyric poem that focuses on a physical object, using this object as a vehicle for considering larger issues. Edmund Waller's seventeenth-century poem "Go, lovely rose" is a meditation.

A **pastoral**—for example, Christopher Marlowe's "The Passionate Shepherd to His Love" (p. 777)—is a lyric poem that celebrates the simple, idyllic pleasures of country life.

A **dramatic monologue** is a poem whose speaker addresses one or more silent listeners, often revealing much more than he or she intends. Robert Browning's "My Last Duchess" (p. 503) and "Porphyria's Lover" (p. 520) and Alfred Lord Tennyson's "Ulysses" (p. 790) are dramatic monologues.

As you read the poems in this text, you will encounter works with a wide variety of forms, styles, and themes. Some you will find appealing, amusing, uplifting, or moving; others may strike you as puzzling, intimidating, or depressing. But regardless of your critical reaction to the poems, one thing is certain: if you take the time to connect with the lines you are reading, you will come away from them thinking not just about the images and ideas they express but also about yourself and your world.

CHAPTER 16

VOICE

Langston Hughes
Library of Congress Prints and Photographs
Division[LC-USZ62-43605]

Robert Browning
AP Images

Loüise Glück
Robin Marchant/Getty Images

Janice Mirikitani
David Paul Morris/ Getty Images
Entertainment/Getty Images

Source: ©Bettmann/Corbis

EMILY DICKINSON (1830–1886)

I'm nobody! Who are you? (1891)

I'm nobody! Who are you?
Are you—Nobody—Too?
Then there's a pair of us?
Don't tell! they'd advertise—you know!

How dreary—to be—Somebody!   5
How public—like a Frog—
To tell one's name—the livelong June—
To an admiring Bog!

 ## The Speaker in the Poem

When they read a work of fiction, readers must decide whether the narrator is sophisticated or unsophisticated, trustworthy or untrustworthy, innocent or experienced. Just as fiction depends on a narrator, poetry depends on a **speaker** who describes events, feelings, and ideas to readers. Finding out as much as possible about this speaker can help readers to interpret a poem. For example, the speaker in Emily Dickinson's "I'm nobody! Who are you?" seems at first to be not just self-effacing but also playful, even flirtatious. As the poem continues, however, the speaker becomes more complex. In the first stanza, she reveals her private self—internal, isolated, with little desire to be well known; in the second stanza, she expresses disdain for those who seek to become "somebody," whom she sees as self-centered, self-promoting, and inevitably superficial. Far from being defeated by her isolation, the speaker rejects fame and celebrates her status as a "nobody."

One question readers might ask about "I'm nobody! Who are you?" is how close the speaker's voice is to the poet's. Readers who conclude that the poem is about the conflict between a poet's public and private selves may be tempted to see the speaker and the poet as one. But this is not necessarily the case. Like the narrator of a short story, the speaker of a poem is a **persona**, or mask, that the poet puts on. Granted, in some poems little distance exists between the poet and the speaker. Without hard evidence to support a link between speaker and poet, however, readers should not simply assume they are one and the same.

In many cases, the speaker is quite different from the poet—even when the speaker's voice conveys the attitude of the poet, either directly or indirectly. In the 1789 poem "The Chimney Sweeper" (p. 738), for example, William Blake assumes the voice of a child to criticize the system of child labor that existed in eighteenth-century England. Even though the child speaker does not understand the economic and social forces that cause his misery, readers sense the poet's anger as the trusting speaker describes the appalling conditions under which he works. The poet's indignation is especially apparent in the biting irony of the last line, in which the victimized speaker echoes the moral precepts of the time by innocently assuring readers that if all people do their duty, "they need not fear harm."

Sometimes the poem's speaker is anonymous. In such cases—as in William Carlos Williams's "Red Wheelbarrow" (p. 563), for instance—the first-person voice is absent, and the speaker remains outside the poem. At other times, the speaker has a set identity—a king, a beggar, a highwayman, a sheriff, a husband, a wife, a rich man, a murderer, a child, a mythical figure, an explorer, a teacher, a faithless lover, a saint—or even a flower, an animal, or a clod of earth. Whatever the case, the speaker is not the poet but rather a creation that the poet uses to convey his or her ideas. (For this reason, poems by a single poet may have very different voices. Compare Sylvia Plath's bitter and sardonic poem "Daddy" [p. 589] with her nurturing and celebratory work "Morning Song" [p. 517], for example.)

Sometimes a poem's title tells readers that the poet is assuming a particular persona. In the following poem, for example, the title identifies the speaker as a fictional character, Gretel from the fairy tale "Hansel and Gretel."

LOUISE GLÜCK (1943–   )

Gretel in Darkness (1971)

This is the world we wanted.
All who would have seen us dead
are dead. I hear the witch's cry
break in the moonlight through a sheet
of sugar: God rewards.   5
Her tongue shrivels into gas....
Now, far from women's arms
And memory of women, in our father's hut
we sleep, are never hungry.
Why do I not forget?   10
My father bars the door, bars harm
from this house, and it is years.

No one remembers. Even you, my brother,
summer afternoons you look at me as though
you meant to leave,   15
as though it never happened.
But I killed for you. I see armed firs,
the spires of that gleaming kiln—

Nights I turn to you to hold me
but you are not there.   20
Am I alone? Spies
hiss in the stillness, Hansel
we are there still, and it is real, real,
that black forest, and the fire in earnest.

Illustration of "Hansel and Gretel" (1930)
AP Images

The speaker in this poem comments on her life after her encounter with the witch in the forest. Speaking to her brother, Gretel observes that they now live in the world they wanted: they live with their father in his hut, and the witch and the wicked stepmother are dead. Even so, the memory of the events in the forest haunts Gretel and makes it impossible for her to live "happily ever after."

By assuming the persona of Gretel, the poet is able to convey some interesting and complex ideas. On one level, Gretel represents any person who has lived through a traumatic experience. Memories of the event keep breaking through into the present, frustrating her attempts to reestablish her belief in the goodness of the world. The voice we hear is sad, alone, and frightened: "Nights I turn to you to hold me," she says, "but you are not there." Although the murder Gretel committed for her brother was justified, it seems to haunt her. "No one remembers," laments Gretel, not even her brother. At some level, she realizes that by killing the witch she has killed a part of herself, perhaps the part of women that men fear and consequently transform into witches and wicked stepmothers. The world that is left after the killing is her father's and her brother's, not her own, and she is now alone haunted by the memories of the black forest. In this sense, Gretel—"Now, far from women's arms / And memory of women"—may be the voice of all victimized women who, because of men, act against their own best interests—and regret it.

As "Gretel in Darkness" illustrates, a title can identify a poem's speaker, but the speaker's words can provide even more information. In the next poem, the first line of each stanza establishes the identity of the speaker—and defines his perspective.

LANGSTON HUGHES (1902–1967)

Negro (1926)

I am a Negro:
   Black as the night is black,
   Black like the depths of my Africa.

I've been a slave:
   Caesar told me to keep his door-steps clean.   5
   I brushed the boots of Washington.

I've been a worker:
   Under my hand the pyramids arose.
   I made mortar for the Woolworth Building.

I've been a singer: 10
   All the way from Africa to Georgia
   I carried my sorrow songs.
   I made ragtime.

I've been a victim:
   The Belgians cut off my hands in the Congo.   15
   They lynch me still in Mississippi.

I am a Negro:
   Black as the night is black,
   Black like the depths of my Africa.

Here the speaker, identifying himself as "a Negro," assumes each of the roles African Americans have historically played in Western society—slave, worker, singer, and victim. By so doing, he gives voice to his ancestors who, by being forced to serve others, were deprived of their identities. By presenting not only their suffering but also their accomplishments, the speaker asserts his pride in being black. The speaker also implies that the suffering of black people has been caused by economic exploitation: Romans, Egyptians, Belgians, and Americans all used black labor to help build their societies. In this context, the speaker's implied warning is clear: except for the United States, all the societies that have exploited blacks have declined, and long after the fall of those empires, black people still endure.

In each of the preceding poems, the speaker is alone. The following poem, a **dramatic monologue**, presents a more complex situation in which the poet creates a complete dramatic scene. The speaker is developed as a character whose distinctive personality is revealed through his words as he addresses a silent listener.

ROBERT BROWNING (1812–1889)

My Last Duchess (1842)

Ferrara

That's my last Duchess painted on the wall,
Looking as if she were alive. I call
That piece a wonder, now: Frà Pandolf's[1] hands
Worked busily a day, and there she stands.
Will't please you sit and look at her? I said   5

---

[1] *Frà Pandolf:* "Brother" Pandolf, a fictive painter.

"Frà Pandolf" by design, for never read
Strangers like you that pictured countenance,
The depth and passion of its earnest glance,
But to myself they turned (since none puts by
The curtain I have drawn for you, but I)   10
And seemed as they would ask me, if they durst,
How such a glance came there; so, not the first
Are you to turn and ask thus. Sir, 'twas not
Her husband's presence only, called that spot
Of joy into the Duchess' cheek: perhaps   15
Frà Pandolf chanced to say "Her mantle laps
Over my lady's wrist too much," or "Paint
Must never hope to reproduce the faint
Half-flush that dies along her throat": such stuff
Was courtesy, she thought, and cause enough   20
For calling up that spot of joy. She had
A heart—how shall I say?—too soon made glad,
Too easily impressed; she liked whate'er
She looked on, and her looks went everywhere.
Sir, 'twas all one! My favor at her breast,   25
The dropping of the daylight in the West,
The bough of cherries some officious fool
Broke in the orchard for her, the white mule
She rode with round the terrace—all and each
Would draw from her alike the approving speech,   30
Or blush, at least. She thanked men—good! but thanked
Somehow—I know not how—as if she ranked
My gift of a nine-hundred-years-old name
With anybody's gift. Who'd stoop to blame
This sort of trifling? Even had you skill   35
In speech—(which I have not)—to make your will
Quite clear to such an one, and say, "Just this
Or that in you disgusts me; here you miss,
Or there exceed the mark"—and if she let
Herself be lessoned so, nor plainly set   40
Her wits to yours, forsooth, and made excuse
—E'en then would be some stooping; and I choose
Never to stoop. Oh sir, she smiled, no doubt,
Whene'er I passed her; but who passed without
Much the same smile? This grew; I gave commands;   45
Then all smiles stopped together. There she stands
As if alive. Will't please you rise? We'll meet
The company below, then. I repeat,

The Count your master's known munificence
Is ample warrant that no just pretense 50
Of mine for dowry will be disallowed;
Though his fair daughter's self, as I avowed
At starting, is my object. Nay, we'll go
Together down, sir. Notice Neptune,[2] though,
Taming a sea horse, thought a rarity, 55
Which Claus of Innsbruck[3] cast in bronze for me!

Art gallery similar to setting of "My Last Duchess"
The King's Closet, Windsor Castle, from 'Royal Residences', engraved by William James Bennett
(1769–1844), published by William Henry Pyne (1769–1843), 1816, Wild, Charles (1781–1835)
(after) / Private Collection / The Stapleton Collection / Bridgeman Images

The speaker in "My Last Duchess" is most likely Alfonso II, duke of Ferrara,
Italy, whose young wife, Lucrezia, died in 1561 after only three years of marriage. Shortly after her death, the duke began negotiations to marry again.
When the poem opens, the duke is showing a portrait of his late wife to an
emissary of an unnamed count who is there to arrange a marriage between
the duke and the count's daughter. The duke remarks that the artist, Frà
Pandolf, has caught a certain look on the duchess's face. This look aroused
the jealousy of the duke, who thought that it should have been for him alone.
Eventually, the duke could tolerate the situation no longer; he "gave commands," and "all smiles stopped together."

---

[2] *Neptune:* In Roman mythology, the god of the sea.

[3] *Claus of Innsbruck:* A fictive—or unidentified—sculptor. The count of Tyrol's capital was at Innsbrück,
Austria.

Though silent, the listener plays a subtle but important role in the poem: his presence establishes the dramatic situation that allows the character of the duke to be revealed. The duke tells his story to communicate to the emissary exactly what he expects from his prospective bride and from her father. As he speaks, the duke provides only the information that he wants the emissary to take back to his master, the count. Although the duke appears vain and superficial, he is actually extraordinarily shrewd. Throughout the poem, he turns the conversation to his own ends and gains the advantage through flattery and false modesty. The success of the poem lies in the poet's ability to develop the voice of this complex character, who embodies both superficial elegance and shocking cruelty.

FURTHER READING: The Speaker in the Poem

LESLIE MARMON SILKO (1948–   )

Where Mountain Lion Lay Down with Deer (1973)

I climb the black rock mountain
   stepping from day to day
               silently.
I smell the wind for my ancestors
     pale blue leaves
       crushed wild mountain smell.   5
Returning
   up the gray stone cliff
   where I descended
     a thousand years ago.   10
Returning to faded black stone.
   where mountain lion lay down with deer.
It is better to stay up here
         watching wind's reflection
         in tall yellow flowers.   15
The old ones who remember me are gone
     the old songs are all forgotten
and the story of my birth.
How I danced in snow-frost moonlight
      distant stars to the end of the Earth,   20
How I swam away
       in freezing mountain water
      narrow mossy canyon tumbling down
      out of the mountain

out of the deep canyon stone   25
down
   the memory
     spilling out
     into the world.

Reading and Reacting

1. Who is speaking in line 4? in line 9? Can you explain this shift?

2. From where is the speaker returning? What is she trying to recover?

3. JOURNAL ENTRY Is it important to know that the poet is Native American? How does this information affect your interpretation of the poem?

4. CRITICAL PERSPECTIVE In her 1983 essay "Answering the Deer," poet and critic Paula Gunn Allen observes that the possibility of cultural extinction is a reality Native Americans must face. Native American women writers, says Allen, face this fact directly but with a kind of hope:

> The sense of hope...comes about when one has faced ultimate disaster time and time again over the ages and has emerged...stronger and more certain of the endurance of the people, the spirits, and the land from which they both arise and which informs both with life. Transformation, or more directly, metamorphosis, is the oldest tribal ceremonial theme....And it comes once again into use within American Indian poetry of extinction and regeneration that is ultimately the only poetry any contemporary Indian woman can write.

Does Silko's poem address the issue of cultural extinction and the possibility of regeneration or metamorphosis? How?

Related Works: "This Is What It Means to Say Phoenix, Arizona" (p. 205), "Two Kinds" (p. 471), "We Wear the Mask" (p. 550)

JANICE MIRIKITANI (1942–   )

Suicide Note (1987)

> *...An Asian American college student was reported to have jumped to her death from her dormitory window. Her body was found two days later under a deep cover of snow. Her suicide note contained an apology to her parents for having received less than a perfect four point grade average....*

How many notes written...
ink smeared like birdprints in snow.

not good enough   not pretty enough   not smart enough
dear mother and father.
I apologize   5
for disappointing you.
I've worked very hard,
        not good enough
harder, perhaps to please you.
If only I were a son, shoulders broad   10
as the sunset threading through pine,
I would see the light in my mother's
eyes, or the golden pride reflected
in my father's dream
of my wide, male hands worthy of work   15
and comfort.
I would swagger through life
muscled and bold and assured,
drawing praises to me
like currents in the bed of wind, virile   20
with confidence.
    not good enough   not strong enough   not good enough

I apologize.
Tasks do not come easily.
Each failure, a glacier.   25
Each disapproval, a bootprint.
Each disappointment,
ice above my river.
So I have worked hard.
        not good enough   30
My sacrifice I will drop
bone by bone, perched
on the ledge of my womanhood,
fragile as wings.
        not strong enough   35
It is snowing steadily
surely not good weather
for flying—this sparrow
sillied and dizzied by the wind
on the edge.   40
        not smart enough
I make this ledge my altar
to offer penance.
This air will not hold me,
the snow burdens my crippled wings,   45

my tears drop like bitter cloth
softly into the gutter below.
    not good enough   not strong enough   not smart enough
        Choices thin as shaved
        ice. Notes shredded   50
        drift like snow
on my broken body,
cover me like whispers
of sorries
sorries.   55
Perhaps when they find me
they will bury
my bird bones beneath
a sturdy pine
and scatter my feathers like   60
unspoken song
over this white and cold and silent
breast of earth.

Reading and Reacting

1. This poem is a suicide note that contains an apology. Why does the speaker feel she must apologize? Do you agree that she needs to apologize?

2. What attitude does the speaker convey toward her parents?

3. **JOURNAL ENTRY** Is the college student who speaks in this poem a stranger to you, or is her voice in any way like that of students you know?

4. **CRITICAL PERSPECTIVE** In her essay "Reading Asian American Poetry," Juliana Chang discusses the reasons why Asian American prose, both fiction and nonfiction, has received more critical attention than Asian American poetry. In particular, she points to "the critical perception that poetry is to prose precisely as the private and individual are to the public and the social, and that the poetic therefore has less social relevance." Chang continues, "Anecdotally, I have heard consistently that poetry is considered 'difficult,' that readers often experience an anxiety over being equipped with the right 'key' to decipher a complex of images and patterns in order to gain access to a 'hidden,' and therefore private, meaning."

Do you feel that "Suicide Note" has social relevance? Does the poem seem accessible or difficult? Does its meaning seem "hidden" in any way?

Related Works: "The Rocking-Horse Winner" (p. 409), "The Value of Education" (p. 549), "Dreams of Suicide" (p. 684), "Death Be Not Proud" (p. 757), *The Cuban Swimmer* (p. 1166)

The Tone of the Poem

The **tone** of a poem conveys the speaker's attitude toward his or her subject or audience. In speech, this attitude can be conveyed easily: stressing a word in a sentence can modify or color a statement. For example, the statement "Of course, you would want to go to that restaurant" is quite straightforward, but changing the emphasis to "Of course *you* would want to go to *that* restaurant" transforms a neutral statement into a sarcastic one. For poets, however, conveying a particular tone to readers poses a challenge because readers rarely hear poets' spoken voices. Instead, poets indicate tone by using rhyme, meter, word choice, sentence structure, figures of speech, and imagery.

The range of possible tones is wide. For example, a poem's speaker may be joyful, sad, playful, serious, comic, intimate, formal, relaxed, condescending, or ironic. In the following poem, notice the speaker's detached, almost irreverent attitude toward his subject.

ROBERT FROST (1874–1963)

Fire and Ice (1923)

Some say the world will end in fire,
Some say in ice.
From what I've tasted of desire
I hold with those who favor fire.
But if it had to perish twice,   5
I think I know enough of hate
To say that for destruction ice
Is also great
And would suffice.

Here the speaker uses word choice, rhyme, and especially **understatement** to comment on the human condition. The conciseness as well as the simple, regular meter and rhyme suggest an **epigram**—a short poem that makes a pointed comment in an unusually clear, and often witty, manner. This pointedness is consistent with the speaker's glib, unemotional tone, as is the last line's wry understatement that ice "would suffice." The contrast between the poem's serious message—that hatred and indifference are equally destructive—and its informal style and offhand tone complement the speaker's detached, almost smug, posture.

Sometimes shifts in tone reveal changes in the speaker's attitude. In the next poem, subtle shifts in tone reveal a change in the speaker's attitude toward war.

THOMAS HARDY (1840–1928)

The Man He Killed (1902)

"Had he and I but met
By some old ancient inn,
We should have sat us down to wet
Right many a nipperkin![1]

"But ranged as infantry,   5
And staring face to face,
I shot at him as he at me,
And killed him in his place.

"I shot him dead because—
Because he was my foe,   10
Just so: my foe of course he was;
That's clear enough; although

"He thought he'd 'list,[2] perhaps,
Off-hand-like—just as I—
Was out of work—had sold his traps—   15
No other reason why.

"Yes; quaint and curious war is!
You shoot a fellow down
You'd treat if met where any bar is,
Or help to half-a crown."[3]   45

British infantry fighting in South Africa during the Boer War

---

[1] *nipperkin:* A small container of liquor.

[2] *'list:* Enlist.

[3] *crown:* A unit of British currency.

The speaker in this poem is a soldier relating a wartime experience. Quotation marks indicate that he is engaged in conversation—perhaps in a pub—and his dialect indicates that he is a member of the English working class. For him, at least at first, the object of war is simple: kill or be killed. To Hardy, this speaker represents all men who are thrust into a war without understanding its underlying social, economic, or ideological causes. In this sense, the speaker and his enemy are both victims of forces beyond their comprehension or control.

The tone of "The Man He Killed" changes as the speaker tells his story. In the first two stanzas, sentences are smooth and unbroken, establishing the speaker's matter-of-fact tone and reflecting his confidence that he has done what he had to do. In the third and fourth stanzas, broken syntax reflects the narrator's increasingly disturbed state of mind as he tells about the man he killed. The poem's singsong meter and regular rhyme scheme (*met/wet, inn/nipperkin*) suggest that the speaker is struggling to maintain his composure; the smooth sentence structure of the last stanza and the use of a cliché ("Yes; quaint and curious war is!") indicate that the speaker is trying to trivialize an incident that has seriously traumatized him.

Sometimes a poem's tone can establish an ironic contrast between the speaker and his or her subject. The speaker's abrupt change of tone at the end of the next poem establishes such a contrast.

AMY LOWELL (1874–1925)

Patterns (1915)

I walk down the garden-paths,
And all the daffodils
Are blowing, and the bright blue squills.
I walk down the patterned garden-paths
In my stiff, brocaded gown.   5
With my powdered hair and jewelled fan,
I too am a rare
Pattern. As I wander down
The garden-paths.

My dress is richly figured,   10
And the train
Makes a pink and silver stain
On the gravel, and the thrift
Of the borders.
Just a plate of current fashion   15
Tripping by in high-heeled, ribboned shoes.

Not a softness anywhere about me,
Only whalebone[1] and brocade.
And I sink on a seat in the shade
Of a lime tree. For my passion   20
Wars against the stiff brocade.
The daffodils and squills
Flutter in the breeze
As they please.
And I weep;   25
For the lime-tree is in blossom
And one small flower has dropped upon my bosom.

And the plashing of waterdrops
In the marble fountain
Comes down the garden-paths.   30
The dripping never stops.
Underneath my stiffened gown
Is the softness of a woman bathing in a marble basin,
A basin in the midst of hedges grown
So thick, she cannot see her lover hiding,   35
But she guesses he is near,
And the sliding of the water
Seems the stroking of a dear
Hand upon her.
What is Summer in a fine brocaded gown!   40
I should like to see it lying in a heap upon the ground.
All the pink and silver crumpled up on the ground.

I would be the pink and silver as I ran along the paths,
And he would stumble after,
Bewildered by my laughter.   45
I should see the sun flashing from his sword-hilt and buckles
    on his shoes.
I would choose
To lead him in a maze along the patterned paths,
A bright and laughing maze for my heavy-booted lover.
Till he caught me in the shade,   50
And the buttons of his waistcoat bruised my body as
    he clasped me,
Aching, melting, unafraid.
With the shadows of the leaves and the sundrops,

---

[1] *whalebone:* The type of bone used to stiffen corsets.

And the plopping of the waterdrops,
All about us in the open afternoon—   55
I am very like to swoon
With the weight of this brocade,
For the sun sifts through the shade.

Underneath the fallen blossom
In my bosom,
Is a letter I have hid.   60
It was brought to me this morning by a rider from the Duke.
Madam, we regret to inform you that Lord Hartwell
Died in action Thursday se'nnight.[2]
As I read it in the white, morning sunlight,   65
The letters squirmed like snakes.
"Any answer, Madam," said my footman.
"No," I told him.
"See that the messenger takes some refreshment.
No, no answer."   70
And I walked into the garden,
Up and down the patterned paths,
In my stiff, correct brocade.
The blue and yellow flowers stood up proudly in the sun,
Each one.   75
I stood upright too,
Held rigid to the pattern
By the stiffness of my gown.
Up and down I walked.
Up and down.   80
In a month he would have been my husband.
In a month, here, underneath this lime,
We would have broken the pattern;
He for me, and I for him,
He as Colonel, I as Lady,   85
On this shady seat.
He had a whim
That sunlight carried blessing.
And I answered, "It shall be as you have said."
Now he is dead.   90

---

[2] *se'nnight:* "Seven night," or a week ago Thursday.

In Summer and in Winter I shall walk
Up and down
The patterned garden-paths
In my stiff, brocaded gown.
The squills and daffodils   95
Will give place to pillared roses, and to asters, and to snow.
I shall go
Up and down,
In my gown.
Gorgeously arrayed,   100
Boned and stayed.
And the softness of my body will be guarded from embrace
By each button, hook, and lace.
For the man who should loose me is dead,
Fighting with the Duke in Flanders,[3]   105
In a pattern called a war.
Christ! What are patterns for?

The speaker begins by describing herself walking down garden paths. She wears a stiff brocaded gown, has powdered hair, and carries a jeweled fan. By her own admission, she is "a plate of current fashion." Although her tone is controlled, she is preoccupied by sensual thoughts. Beneath her "stiffened gown / Is the softness of a woman bathing in a marble basin," and the "sliding of the water" in a fountain reminds the speaker of the stroking of her lover's hand. She imagines herself shedding her brocaded gown and running with her lover along the maze of "patterned paths." The sensuality of the speaker's thoughts stands in ironic contrast to the images of stiffness and control that dominate the poem: her passion "Wars against the stiff brocade." She is also full of repressed rage. She knows that her lover has been killed, and she realizes the meaninglessness of the patterns of her life, patterns to which she has conformed, just as her lover conformed by going to war. Throughout the poem, the speaker's tone reflects her barely contained anger and frustration. In the last line, when she finally lets out her rage, the poem's point about the senselessness of conformity and war becomes apparent.

----

[3]*Flanders:* A region in northwestern Europe, including part of northern France and western Belgium. Flanders was a site of prolonged fighting during World War I.

FURTHER READING: The Tone of the Poem

WILLIAM WORDSWORTH (1770–1850)

The World Is Too Much with Us (1807)

The world is too much with us; late and soon,
Getting and spending, we lay waste our powers;
Little we see in Nature that is ours;
We have given our hearts away, a sordid boon!
This Sea that bares her bosom to the moon;   5
The winds that will be howling at all hours,
And are up-gathered now like sleeping flowers;
For this, for everything, we are out of tune;
It moves us not. Great God! I'd rather be
A Pagan suckled in a creed outworn;   10
So might I, standing on this pleasant lea,
Have glimpses that would make me less forlorn;
Have sight of Proteus[1] rising from the sea;
Or hear old Triton[2] blow his wreathèd horn.

Triton blowing his horn (detail from Trevi fountain, Rome)
sootra/Shutterstock.com

Reading and Reacting

1. What is the speaker's attitude toward the contemporary world? How is this attitude revealed through the poem's tone?

2. This poem is a **sonnet**, a highly structured traditional form. How do the regular meter and rhyme scheme help to establish the poem's tone?

3. JOURNAL ENTRY Imagine that you are a modern-day environmentalist, labor organizer, or corporate executive. Write a response to the sentiments expressed in this poem.

4. CRITICAL PERSPECTIVE In his 1972 essay "Two Roads to Wordsworth," M. H. Abrams notes that critics have tended to view Wordsworth in one of two ways:

> One Wordsworth is simple, elemental, forthright, the other is complex, paradoxical, problematic; one is an affirmative poet of life, love, and joy, the other is an equivocal or self-divided poet whose affirmations are implicitly

---

[1] *Proteus:* Sometimes said to be Poseidon's son, this Greek sea-god had the ability to change shape at will and to tell the future.

[2] *Triton:* The trumpeter of the sea, this sea-god is usually pictured blowing on a conch shell. Triton was the son of Poseidon, ruler of the sea.

qualified... by a pervasive sense of morality and an ever-incipient despair of life;... one is the Wordsworth of light, the other the Wordsworth of [shadow], or even darkness.

Does your reading of "The World Is Too Much with Us" support one of these versions of Wordsworth over the other? Which one? Why?

Related Works: "The Rocking-Horse Winner" (p. 409), "The Road Not Taken" (p. 624), "The Peace of Wild Things" (p. 717), "Dover Beach" (p. 737), "The Lake Isle of Innisfree" (p. 798)

SYLVIA PLATH (1932–1963)

Morning Song (1962)

Love set you going like a fat gold watch.
The midwife slapped your footsoles, and your bald cry
Took its place among the elements.

Our voices echo, magnifying your arrival. New statue.
In a drafty museum, your nakedness   5
Shadows our safety. We stand round blankly as walls.

I'm no more your mother
Than the cloud that distills a mirror to reflect its own slow
Effacement at the wind's hand.

All night your moth-breath   10
Flickers among the flat pink roses. I wake to listen:
A far sea moves in my ear.

One cry, and I stumble from bed, cow-heavy and floral
In my Victorian nightgown.
Your mouth opens clean as a cat's. The window square   15

Whitens and swallows its dull stars. And now you try
Your handful of notes;
The clear vowels rise like balloons.

Reading and Reacting

1. Who is the speaker? To whom is she speaking? What does the poem reveal about her?
2. What is the poem's subject? What attitudes about this subject do you suppose the poet expects her readers to have?
3. How is the tone of the first stanza different from that of the third? How does the tone of each stanza reflect its content?

4. **JOURNAL ENTRY** In what sense does this poem reinforce traditional ideas about motherhood? How does it challenge them?

5. **CRITICAL PERSPECTIVE** Sylvia Plath's life, which ended in suicide, was marked by emotional turbulence and instability. As Anne Stevenson observes in *Bitter Fame*, her 1988 biography of Plath, in the weeks immediately preceding the composition of "Morning Song" a fit of rage over her husband's supposed infidelity caused Plath to destroy many of his books and poetic works in progress. Then, only a few days later, she suffered a miscarriage. According to Stevenson, "Morning Song" is about sleepless nights and surely reflects Plath's depression. However, in a 1991 biography, *Rough Magic*, Paul Alexander says, "Beautiful, simple, touching, 'Morning Song' was Plath's—then—definitive statement of motherhood."

   Which biographer's assessment of the poem do you think makes more sense? Why?

Related Works: "The Yellow Wallpaper" (p. 434), "Metaphors" (p. 582), "Daddy" (p. 589), "Those Winter Sundays" (p. 705)

Gather Ye Rosebuds While Ye May (1909 oil painting)
'Gather Ye Rosebuds While Ye May', 1909 (oil on canvas), Waterhouse, John William (1849–1917) / Private Collection / Photo © Odon Wagner Gallery, Toronto, Canada / Bridgeman Images

ROBERT HERRICK (1591–1674)

To the Virgins, to Make Much of Time (1646)

Gather ye rosebuds while ye may,
Old Time is still a-flying;
And this same flower that smiles today,
Tomorrow will be dying.

The glorious lamp of heaven, the sun,   5
The higher he's a-getting,
The sooner will his race be run,
And nearer he's to setting.

That age is best which is the first,
When youth and blood are warmer;   10
But being spent, the worse, and worst
Times still succeed the former.

Then be not coy, but use your time,
And while ye may, go marry;
For having lost but once your prime,   15
You may forever tarry.

Reading and Reacting

1. How would you characterize the speaker? Do you think he expects his listeners to share his views? How might his expectations affect his tone?

2. This poem is developed like an argument. What is the speaker's main point? How does he support it?

3. What effect does the poem's use of rhyme have on its tone?

4. JOURNAL ENTRY Whose side are you on—the speaker's or those he addresses?

5. CRITICAL PERSPECTIVE Critic Roger Rollin offers the following reading of the final stanza of "To the Virgins, to Make Much of Time":

> This last stanza makes it clear enough that to the speaker young women are coy by [custom or choice] rather than by nature. Their receptivity to love is under their control. The delaying tactics that social custom prescribes for them are self-defeating, threatening to waste life's most precious commodities—time, youth, and love.

Does Rollin's interpretation seem plausible to you? What evidence do you find in the final stanza, or elsewhere in the poem, that the virgins addressed are not naturally "coy" but rather are constrained by social convention?

Related Works: "Love and Other Catastrophes: A Mix Tape" (p. 84), "The Passionate Shepherd to His Love" (p. 777), *The Brute* (p. 814), *The Date* (p. 1160)

 ## Irony

Just as in fiction and drama, **irony** occurs in poetry when a discrepancy exists between two levels of meaning or experience. Consider the tone of the following lines by Stephen Crane:

> Do not weep, maiden, for war is kind.
> Because your lover threw wild hands toward the sky
> And the afrightened steed ran on alone,
> Do not weep.
> War is kind.

Surely the speaker in this poem does not intend his words to be taken literally. How can war be "kind"? Isn't war exactly the opposite of "kind"? By making this ironic statement, the speaker actually conveys the opposite idea: war is a cruel, mindless exercise of violence.

Skillfully used, irony enables a poet to make a pointed comment about a situation or to manipulate a reader's emotions. Implicit in irony is the writer's assumption that readers will not be misled by the literal meaning of a statement. In order for irony to work, readers must recognize the disparity between what is said and what is meant, or between what a speaker thinks is occurring and what readers know to be occurring.

One kind of irony that appears in poetry is **dramatic irony**, which occurs when a speaker believes one thing and readers realize something else. In the following poem, the poet uses a deranged speaker to tell a story that is filled with irony.

ROBERT BROWNING (1812–1889)

Porphyria's Lover (1836)

The rain set early in to-night,
　The sullen wind was soon awake,
It tore the elm-tops down for spite,
　And did its worst to vex the lake:
　I listened with heart fit to break.   5
When glided in Porphyria; straight
　She shut the cold out and the storm,
And kneeled and made the cheerless grate
　Blaze up, and all the cottage warm;
　Which done, she rose, and from her form   10
Withdrew the dripping cloak and shawl,
　And laid her soiled gloves by, untied
Her hat and let the damp hair fall,
　And, last, she sat down by my side
　And called me. When no voice replied,   15
She put my arm about her waist,
　And made her smooth white shoulder bare,
And all her yellow hair displaced,
　And, stooping, made my cheek lie there,
　And spread, o'er all, her yellow hair,   20
Murmuring how she loved me—she
　Too weak, for all her heart's endeavour,
To set its struggling passion free
　From pride, and vainer ties dissever,
　And give herself to me for ever.   25
But passion sometimes would prevail,
　Nor could to-night's gay feast restrain
A sudden thought of one so pale
　For love of her, and all in vain:
　So, she was come through wind and rain.   30

Be sure I looked up at her eyes
    Happy and proud; at last I knew
Porphyria worshipped me; surprise
    Made my heart swell, and still it grew
    While I debated what to do.   35
That moment she was mine, mine, fair,
    Perfectly pure and good: I found
A thing to do, and all her hair
    In one long yellow string I wound
    Three times her little throat around,   40
And strangled her. No pain felt she;
    I am quite sure she felt no pain.
As a shut bud that holds a bee,
    I warily oped her lids: again
    Laughed the blue eyes without a stain.   45
And I untightened next the tress
    About her neck; her cheek once more
Blushed bright beneath my burning kiss:
    I propped her head up as before,
    Only, this time my shoulder bore   50
Her head, which droops upon it still:
    The smiling rosy little head,
So glad it has its utmost will,
    That all it scorned at once is fled,
    And I, its love, am gained instead!   55
Porphyria's love: she guessed not how
    Her darling one wish would be heard.
And thus we sit together now,
    And all night long we have not stirred,
    And yet God has not said a word!   60

Like Browning's "My Last Duchess" (p. 503), this poem is a **dramatic monologue**, a poem that assumes an implied listener as well as a speaker. The speaker recounts his story in a straightforward manner, seemingly unaware of the horror of his tale. In fact, much of the effect of this poem comes from the speaker's telling his tale of murder in a flat, unemotional tone—and from readers' gradual realization that the speaker is mad.

The irony of the poem, as well as its title, becomes apparent as the monologue progresses. At first, the speaker fears that Porphyria is too weak to free herself from pride and vanity to love him. As he looks into her eyes, however, he comes to believe that she worships him. The moment the speaker realizes that Porphyria loves him, he feels compelled to kill her and keep her his forever. According to him, she is at this point "mine, mine, fair, / Perfectly pure and good," and he believes that by murdering her, he actually fulfills "Her darling one wish"—to stay with him forever. As he attempts to justify his actions, the speaker reveals himself to be a deluded psychopathic killer.

Another kind of irony is **situational irony**, which occurs when the situation itself contradicts readers' expectations. For example, in "Porphyria's Lover" the meeting of two lovers ironically results not in joy and passion but in murder.

In the next poem, the situation also creates irony.

The Granger Collection, NYC

PERCY BYSSHE SHELLEY (1792–1822)

Ozymandias[1] (1818)

I met a traveler from an antique land
Who said: Two vast and trunkless legs of stone
Stand in the desert. Near them, on the sand,
Half sunk, a shattered visage lies, whose frown,
And wrinkled lip, and sneer of cold command,   5
Tell that its sculptor well those passions read
Which yet survive, stamped on these lifeless
    things,
The hand that mocked them, and the heart
    that fed;
And on the pedestal these words appear:
"My name is Ozymandias, king of kings: 10
Look on my works, ye Mighty, and despair!"
Nothing beside remains. Round the decay
Of that colossal wreck, boundless and bare
The lone and level sands stretch far away.

The speaker in "Ozymandias" recounts a tale about a colossal statue that lies shattered in the desert. Its head lies separated from the trunk, and the face has a wrinkled lip and a "sneer of cold command." On the pedestal of the monument are words exhorting all those who pass: "Look on my works, ye Mighty, and despair!" The situational irony of the poem has its source in the contrast between the "colossal wreck" and the boastful inscription on its base: Ozymandias is a monument to the vanity of those who mistakenly think they can withstand the ravages of time.

Perhaps the most common kind of irony found in poetry is **verbal irony**, which is created when words say one thing but mean another, often exactly

---

[1] *Ozymandias:* The Greek name for Ramses II, ruler of Egypt in the thirteenth century B.C.

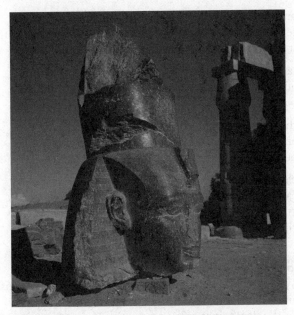

Head of Ramses II, possible inspiration for "Ozymandias"
© Roger Wood/CORBIS

the opposite. When verbal irony is particularly biting, it is called **sarcasm**—for example, Stephen Crane's use of the word *kind* in his antiwar poem "War Is Kind." In speech, verbal irony is easy to detect through the speaker's change in tone or emphasis. In writing, when these signals are absent, verbal irony becomes more difficult to convey. Poets must depend on the context of a remark or on the contrast between a word and other images in the poem to create irony.

FURTHER READING: Irony

SHERMAN ALEXIE (1966–   )

Evolution (1992)

Buffalo Bill[1] opens a pawn shop on the reservation
right across the border from the liquor store
and he stays open 24 hours a day, 7 days a week

---

[1] *Buffalo Bill:* Nickname of William Frederick Cody (1846–1917), soldier, showman, and hunter.

and the Indians come running in with jewelry
television sets, a VCR, a full-length beaded buckskin outfit   5
it took Inez Muse 12 years to finish. Buffalo Bill

takes everything the Indians have to offer, keeps it
all catalogued and filed in a storage room. The Indians
pawn their hands, saving the thumbs for last, they pawn

their skeletons, falling endlessly from the skin   10
and when the last Indian has pawned everything
but his heart, Buffalo Bill takes that for twenty bucks

closes up the pawn shop, paints a new sign over the old
calls his venture THE MUSEUM OF NATIVE AMERICAN
CULTURES
charges the Indians five bucks a head to enter.   15

Reading and Reacting

1. In this poem, what is Buffalo Bill's relationship with the Indians? Why do you think Alexie introduces this historical figure?

2. What is the significance of the poem's title? Is it ironic in any way?

3. Identify several examples of irony in this poem. What different kinds of irony are present?

4. **JOURNAL ENTRY** What point do you think the speaker is making about American culture? about Native American culture?

5. **CRITICAL PERSPECTIVE** In an essay on Sherman Alexie's poetry, critic Jennifer Gillan notes that Alexie is "a Spokane/Coeur d'Alene Indian from Washington State" and goes on to discuss the ways in which this fact informs his work:

> From a tribe neither Plains nor Pueblo, which few would associate with the Hollywood version of American Indians, Alexie wonders whether his people ever had access to the authenticity all America seems to associate with Indians. Alienated from their American Indian culture as well as from America, the characters in Alexie's poetry and prose collections want to believe in the wisdom of old Indian prophets, want to return to the "old ways," but know that doing so will just trap them inside another clichéd Hollywood narrative.

In what sense, if any, are the Indians portrayed in "Evolution" "trapped"? Are they "alienated" from both their own culture and the broader American culture?

Related Works: "This Is What It Means to Say Phoenix, Arizona" (p. 205), "Where Mountain Lion Lay Down with Deer" (p. 506), "The English Canon" (p. 548), "Buffalo Bill's" (p. 750), "Indian Boarding School: The Runaways" (p. 763), *The Cuban Swimmer* (p. 1166)

SANDRA M. CASTILLO (1962–   )

Castro[1] Moves into the Havana Hilton[*]

"History always dresses us for the wrong occasions."
                                        —Ricardo Pau-Llosa

Camera Obscura[2]

The afternoon lightening his shadow,
Fidel descends from the mountains,
the clean-shaven lawyer turned guerilla,
his eyes focused on infinity,
El Jefe Máximo con sus Barbudos,[3]   5
rebels with rosary beads
on their 600-mile procession across the island
with campesinos[4] on horseback, flatbed trucks, tanks,
a new year's journey down the oldest roads
towards betrayal.   10

Ambient light.[5] *Available light*[6]

Light inside of them,
nameless isleños[7] line El Malecón[8] to touch Fidel,
already defining himself in black and white.
The dramatic sky moving in for the close-up
that will frame his all-night oratory,   15
he turns to the crowd,
variations on an enigma,
waving from his pulpit with rehearsed eloquence,
a dove on his shoulder.

This is a photograph. This is not a sign.   20

---

[*]Publication date unavailable.
[1]*Castro:* Fidel Castro (1962–   ), head of the Cuban government from 1959 to 2008.
[2]Camera Obscura: A simple device for projecting images.
[3]*El Jefe Máximo con sus Barbudos:* Spanish for "the big boss with his bearded companions."
[4]*campesinos:* Spanish for "farmers."
[5]Ambient light: A photographic term meaning either the natural light available in a given setting, or the minimal light from a single source provided by a photographer.
[6]Available light: A photographic term meaning the natural light available in a given setting.
[7]*isleños:* Spanish for "islanders."
[8]*El Malecón:* A long, wide street in Havana, Cuba.

Flash-on camera. Celebrity portraits.

1. Fidel on a balcony across the street
    from Grand Central Station,
    an American flag above his head,
    New York, 1959.

2. Fidel made small by the Lincoln Memorial,   25
    Washington D.C., 1959.

3. Fidel learning to ski,
    a minor black ball against a white landscape,
    Russia, 1962.

4. Fidel and shotgun,   30
    hunting with Nikita,[9]
    Russia, 1962.

Circles of Confusion

Beyond photographs,
Havana is looted and burned.
Women weep at out wailing wall,   35
El Paredón,[10] where traitors are taken,
and television cameras shoot
the executions, this blood soup,
the paradoxes of our lives,
three years before I am born.   40

Photoflood[11]

But it is late afternoon,
and a shower of confetti and serpentine[12]
falls from every floor of the Havana Hilton,
where history is a giant piñata,
where at midnight, Fidel will be photographed   45
eating a ham sandwich.

---

[9]*Nikita:* Nikita Khrushchev (1894–1971), leader of the Soviet Union from 1953 to 1964.

[10]*El Paredón:* A wall in Havana where executions were carried out.

[11]Photoflood: An extremely bright floodlight used in photography and cinematography.

[12]*serpentine:* A coiled type of party streamer.

Fidel Castro in New York, April 1959.

Reading and Reacting

1. The Havana Hilton was built in 1957. The majority of the hotel was owned by Meyer Lansky, a major organized crime figure, who paid the Cuban dictator, Fulgencio Batista, a share of the profits. When Fidel Castro overthrew Batista in 1959, Castro made the hotel his headquarters. Why do you think Castillo chooses to focus on this hotel? What point do you think that she is trying to make?

2. In the section of the poem entitled "Flash-on camera. Celebrity portraits," Castillo describes four pictures of Castro along with the dates they were taken. What do these pictures show about Castro?

3. What does Castillo mean when she says that at the Havana Hilton "history is a giant piñata"?

4. **JOURNAL ENTRY** What is Castillo's attitude toward Castro? How can you tell?

Related Works: from *Persepolis* (p. 111), "Hitler's First Photograph" (p. 530), *The Cuban Swimmer* (p. 1166)

AGHA SHAHID ALI (1949–2001)

The Wolf's Postscript to "Little Red Riding Hood"*

> First, grant me my sense of history:
> I did it for posterity,
> for kindergarten teachers
> and a clear moral:
> Little girls shouldn't wander off   5

---

*Publication date unavailable.

in search of strange flowers,
and they mustn't speak to strangers.

And then grant me my generous sense of plot:
Couldn't I have gobbled her up
right there in the jungle?   10
Why did I ask her where her grandma lived?
As if I, a forest-dweller,
didn't know of the cottage
under the three oak trees
and the old woman lived there   15
all alone?
As if I couldn't have swallowed her years before?

And you may call me the Big Bad Wolf,
now my only reputation.
But I was no child-molester   20
though you'll agree she was pretty.

And the huntsman:
Was I sleeping while he snipped
my thick black fur
and filled me with garbage and stones?   25
I ran with that weight and fell down,
simply so children could laugh
at the noise of the stones
cutting through my belly,
at the garbage spilling out   30
with a perfect sense of timing,
just when the tale
should have come to an end.

Reading and Reacting

1. How does Ali portray the Big Bad Wolf? How is this characterization different from the one in the classic fairy tale "Little Red Riding
   Hood"?
2. How would you describe the tone of this poem? How does Ali create
   this tone?
3. The wolf says that he "did it for posterity" and "for kindergarten teachers."
   What does he mean?
4. Why does the wolf think that he needs to add a postscript to "Little Red
   Riding Hood"?
5. **JOURNAL ENTRY** What "clear moral" does the poem have? In what sense is
   this moral ironic?

Related Works: "Gretel in Darkness" (p. 501), "Porphyria's Lover" (p. 520), "The Chimney Sweeper" (p. 738), *Beauty* (p. 831)

DUDLEY RANDALL (1914–2000)

Ballad of Birmingham (1969)

(On the bombing of a church in Birmingham, Alabama, 1963)

"Mother dear, may I go downtown
Instead of out to play,
And march the streets of Birmingham
In a Freedom March today?"
"No, baby, no, you may not go,   5
For the dogs are fierce and wild,
And clubs and hoses, guns and jails
Aren't good for a little child."

"But, mother, I won't be alone.
Other children will go with me,   10
And march the streets of Birmingham
To make our country free."

"No, baby, no, you may not go,
For I fear those guns will fire.
But you may go to church instead   15
And sing in the children's choir."

She has combed and brushed her night-dark hair,
And bathed rose petal sweet,
And drawn white gloves on her small brown hands,
And white shoes on her feet.   20

The mother smiled to know her child
Was in the sacred place,
But that smile was the last smile
To come upon her face.

For when she heard the explosion,   25
Her eyes grew wet and wild.
She raced through the streets of Birmingham
Calling for her child.

She clawed through bits of glass and brick,
Then lifted out a shoe.   30
"O, here's the shoe my baby wore,
But, baby, where are you?"

Reading and Reacting

1. Who are the speakers in the poem? How do their tones differ?
2. What kinds of irony are present in the poem? Give examples of each kind you identify.
3. What point do you think the poem makes about violence? about racial hatred? about the civil rights struggle?
4. This poem is a **ballad**, a form of poetry traditionally written to be sung or recited. Ballads typically repeat words and phrases and have regular meter and rhyme. How do the regular rhyme, repeated words, and singsong meter affect the poem's tone?

5. JOURNAL ENTRY This poem was written in response to the 1963 bombing of the 16th Street Baptist Church in Birmingham, Alabama, a bomb that killed four African American children. How does this historical background help you to understand the irony of the poem?

6. CRITICAL PERSPECTIVE Speaking of "Ballad of Birmingham," critic James Sullivan says, "This poem uses the ballad convention of the innocent questioner and the wiser respondent (the pattern of, for example, 'Lord Randall' and 'La Belle Dame sans Merci' [p. 771]), but it changes the object of knowledge from fate to racial politics. The child is the conventional innocent, while the mother understands the violence of this political moment."

   How does Randall's use of these ballad conventions help him create irony?

Related Works: "Bonny Barbara Allan" (p. 734), "If We Must Die" (p. 778), *Fences* (p. 1270)

Adolph Hitler as a baby
The Granger Collection, NYC

WISLAWA SZYMBORSKA (1923–   )

Hitler's First Photograph (1986)

And who's this little fellow in his itty-bitty robe?
That's tiny baby Adolf, the Hitler's little boy!
Will he grow up to be an LL.D.?[1]
Or a tenor in Vienna's Opera House?
Whose teensy hand is this, whose little ear and   5
    eye and nose?
Whose tummy full of milk, we just don't know:
printer's, doctor's, merchant's, priest's?
Where will those tootsy-wootsies finally wander?

---

[1] *LL.D.: Legum Doctor,* or Doctor of Law.

To garden, to school, to an office, to a bride,
maybe to the Burgermeister's[2] daughter?   10

Precious little angel, mommy's sunshine, honeybun,
while he was being born a year ago,
there was no dearth of signs on the earth and in the sky:
spring sun, geraniums in windows,
the organ-grinder's music in the yard,   15
a lucky fortune wrapped in rosy paper,
then just before the labor his mother's fateful dream:
a dove seen in dream means joyful news,
if it is caught, a long-awaited guest will come.
Knock knock, who's there, it's Adolf's heartchen[3] knocking.   20

A little pacifier, diaper, rattle, bib,
our bouncing boy, thank God and knock on wood, is well,
looks just like his folks, like a kitten in a basket,
like the tots in every other family album.
Shush, let's not start crying, sugar,   25
the camera will click from under that black hood.

The Klinger Atelier,[4] Grabenstrasse,[5] Braunau,[6]
and Braunau is small but worthy town,
honest businesses, obliging neighbors,
smell of yeast dough, of gray soap.   30
No one hears howling dogs, or fate's footsteps.
A history teacher loosens his collar
and yawns over homework.

Reading and Reacting

1. What attitude toward her subject does the speaker expect readers to have? How do you know? How much information about Hitler does she expect readers to know?
2. Throughout the poem, the speaker speaks to baby Hitler as she would to any other baby. How do words like "angel," sunshine," "honeybun," and "sugar" create irony in the poem?
3. What does the speaker mean in line 31 of the poem when she says, "No one hears howling dogs, or fate's footsteps"?

---

[2] *Burgermeister:* An executive of a town in Germany.
[3] *heartchen:* A partial translation of a German word meaning "little heart."
[4] *Klinger Atelier:* Painting of Max Klinger's artist's studio.
[5] *Grabenstrasse:* Street in Austria.
[6] *Braunau:* Birthplace of Hitler in Austria-Hungary.

4. Why does the poem end with the image of a history teacher loosening his tie and yawning? What effect does this image have on you?

5. JOURNAL ENTRY What point do you think Szymborska is making in this poem? How does irony help her make this point?

6. CRITICAL PERSPECTIVE Speaking of "Hitler's First Photograph," critic Alan Reid makes this observation:

> "Hitler's First Photograph" is one of the most chilling poetic inspections of the psychopathological phenomena associated with its namesake and Nazism ever written. By describing Hitler in his first year of life from the perspective of his parents (any parents), [Szymborska] jolts us out of our complacency around the question of how this could have happened. . . . She prods us to question whether the signs were there and, if they were not, to ask what gives rise to such abominations and to recognize the need to be vigilant.

Do you agree with Reid's assessment of the poem? Why or why not?

Related Works: "I Stand Here Ironing" (p. 217), "Young Goodman Brown" (p. 367), "What Shall I Give My Children?" (p. 553), "The Lamb" (p. 739), "Daddy" (p. 589), "Those Winter Sundays" (p. 705)

✔ CHECKLIST   Writing about Voice

The Speaker in the Poem

☐ What do we know about the speaker?

☐ Is the speaker anonymous, or does he or she have a particular identity?

☐ How does assuming a particular persona help the poet to convey his or her ideas?

☐ Does the title give readers any information about the speaker's identity?

☐ How does word choice provide information about the speaker?

☐ Does the speaker make any direct statements to readers that help establish his or her identity or character?

☐ Does the speaker address anyone? How can you tell? How does the presence of a listener affect the speaker?

The Tone of the Poem

☐ What is the speaker's attitude toward his or her subject?

- How do word choice, rhyme, meter, sentence structure, figures of speech, and imagery help to convey the attitude of the speaker?

- Is the poem's tone consistent? How do shifts in tone reveal the changing mood or attitude of the speaker?

Irony
- Does the poem include dramatic irony? situational irony? verbal irony?

WRITING SUGGESTIONS: Voice

1. The poet Robert Frost once said that he wanted to write "poetry that talked." According to Frost, "whenever I write a line it is because that line has already been spoken clearly by a voice within my mind, an audible voice." Choose some poems in this chapter (or from elsewhere in the book) that you consider "poetry that talks." Then, write an essay about how successful they are in communicating "an audible voice."

2. Compare the speakers' voices in "Patterns" (p. 512), and "Gretel in Darkness" (p. 501). How are their attitudes toward men similar? How are they different?

3. The theme of Herrick's poem "To the Virgins, to Make Much of Time" (p. 518) is known as **carpe diem**, or "seize the day." Read Andrew Marvell's "To His Coy Mistress" (p. 594), which has the same theme, and compare its tone with that of "To the Virgins, to Make Much of Time."

4. Because the speaker and the poet are not the same, poems by the same author can have different voices. Compare the voices of several poems by one poet—for example, Sylvia Plath, W. H. Auden, Robert Frost, or William Blake—whose works are included in this anthology.

CHAPTER 17

WORD CHOICE, WORD ORDER

Adrienne Rich
AP Images/Chuck Knoblock

Margaret Atwood
AP Images/Dave Thomson

E. E. Cummings
Pictorial Press Ltd/Alamy

Gwendolyn Brooks
Bill Tague

Durfy-Marie Arnoult/WireImage/Getty Images

BOB HOLMAN (1948–)

Beautiful (2002)

January 3, 2002

Dear Bob,
You are not allowed to use
the word "beautiful" in a poem
this year.

Signed,
The Rest of the World
Except for You

Words identify and name, characterize and distinguish, compare and contrast. Words describe, limit, and embellish; words locate and measure. Even though words may be elusive and uncertain and changeable, a single word—such as Holman's "beautiful" in the poem on the preceding page—can also be meaningful. In poetry, as in love and in politics, words matter.

Beyond the quantitative—how many words, how many letters and syllables—is a much more important consideration: the *quality* of words. Which words are chosen, and why? Why are certain words placed next to others? What does a word suggest in a particular context? How are the words arranged? What exactly constitutes the "right word"?

Word Choice

In poetry, even more than in fiction or drama, words are the focus—sometimes even the true subject—of a work. For this reason, the choice of one word over another can be crucial. Because poems are brief, they must compress many ideas into just a few lines; poets know how much weight each individual word carries, so they choose with great care, trying to select words that imply more than they state.

In general, poets (like prose writers) select words because they communicate particular ideas. However, poets may also choose words for their sound. For instance, a word may echo another word's sound, and such repetition may place emphasis on both words; a word may rhyme with another word and therefore be needed to preserve the poem's rhyme scheme; or a word may have a certain combination of stressed and unstressed syllables needed to maintain the poem's metrical pattern. Occasionally, a poet may even choose a word because of how it looks on the page.

At the same time, poets may choose words for their degree of concreteness or abstraction, specificity or generality. A **concrete word** refers to an item that is a perceivable, tangible entity—for example, a kiss or a flag. An **abstract word** refers to an intangible idea, condition, or quality, something that cannot be perceived by the senses—love or patriotism, for instance. **Specific words** refer to particular items; **general words** refer to entire classes or groups of items. The following sequence illustrates the movement from general to specific.

Poem
↓
closed form poem
↓
sonnet
↓
seventeenth-century sonnet
↓

Elizabethan sonnet

↓

sonnet by Shakespeare

↓

"My mistress' eyes are nothing like the sun"

Sometimes a poet wants a precise word, one that is both specific and concrete. At other times, a poet might prefer general or abstract language, which may allow for more subtlety—or even for intentional ambiguity.

Finally, a word may be chosen for its **connotation**—what it suggests. Every word has one or more **denotations**—what it signifies without emotional associations, judgments, or opinions. The word *family*, for example, denotes "a group of related things or people." Connotation is a more complex matter; after all, a single word may have many different associations. In general terms, a word may have a connotation that is positive, neutral, or negative. Thus, *family* may have a positive connotation when it describes a group of loving relatives, a neutral connotation when it describes a biological category, and an ironically negative connotation when it describes an organized crime family. Beyond this distinction, *family*, like any other word, may have a variety of emotional and social associations, suggesting loyalty, warmth, home, security, or duty. In fact, many words have somewhat different meanings in different contexts. When poets choose words, then, they must consider what a particular word may suggest to readers as well as what it denotes.

In the poem that follows, the poet chooses words for their sounds and for their relationships to other words as well as for their connotations.

WALT WHITMAN   (1819–1892)

When I Heard the Learn'd Astronomer (1865)

When I heard the learn'd astronomer,
When the proofs, the figures, were ranged in columns before me,
When I was shown the charts and diagrams, to add, divide, and
    measure them,
When I sitting heard the astronomer where he lectured with much
    applause in the lecture-room,
How soon unaccountable I became tired and sick,   5
Till rising and gliding out I wander'd off by myself,
In the mystical moist night-air, and from time to time,
Look'd up in perfect silence at the stars.

This poem might be paraphrased as follows: "When I grew restless listening to an astronomy lecture, I went outside, where I found I learned more just by looking at the stars than I had learned inside." However, the paraphrase is obviously neither as rich nor as complex as the poem. Through careful use of diction, Whitman establishes a dichotomy that supports the poem's central theme about the relative merits of two ways of learning.

The poem can be divided into two groups of four lines each. The first four lines, unified by the repetition of "When," introduce the astronomer and his tools: "proofs," "figures," and "charts and diagrams" to be added, divided, or measured. In this section of the poem, the speaker is passive: he sits and listens ("I heard"; "I was shown"; "I sitting heard"). The repetition of "When" reinforces the dry monotony of the lecture. In the next four lines, the choice of words signals the change in the speaker's actions and reactions. The confined lecture hall is replaced by "the mystical moist night-air," and the dry lecture and the applause give way to "perfect silence"; instead of sitting passively, the speaker becomes active (he rises, glides, wanders); instead of listening, he looks. The mood of the first half of the poem is restrained: the language is concrete and physical, and the speaker is passively receiving information from a "learn'd" authority. The rest of the poem, celebrating intuitive knowledge and feelings, is more abstract, freer. Throughout the poem, the lecture hall is set in sharp contrast to the natural world outside its walls.

After considering the poem as a whole, readers should not find it hard to understand why the poet selected certain words. Whitman's use of "lectured" in line 4 rather than a more neutral word like "spoke" is appropriate both because it suggests formality and distance and because it echoes "lecture-room" in the same line. The word "sick" in line 5 is striking because it connotes physical as well as emotional distress, more effectively conveying the extent of the speaker's discomfort than "bored" or "restless" would. "Rising" and "gliding" (line 6) are used rather than "standing" and "walking out" both because of the way their stressed vowel sounds echo each other (and echo "time to time" in the next line) and because of their connotation of dreaminess, which is consistent with "wander'd" (line 6) and "mystical" (line 7). The word "moist" (line 7) is chosen not only because its consonant sounds echo the *m* and *st* sounds in "mystical," but also because it establishes a contrast with the dry, airless lecture hall. Finally, line 8's "perfect silence" is a better choice than a reasonable substitute like "complete silence" or "total silence," either of which would suggest the degree of the silence but not its quality.

FURTHER READING: Word Choice

RHINA ESPAILLAT (1932–   )

Bilingual/Bilingüe (1998)

My father liked them separate, one there,
one here (allá y aquí), as if aware

that words might cut in two his daughter's heart
(el corazón) and lock the alien part

to what he was—his memory, his name   5
(su nombre)—with a key he could not claim.
"English outside this door, Spanish inside,"
he said, "y basta."[1] But who can divide

the world, the word (mundo y palabra) from
any child? I knew how to be dumb   10

and stubborn (testaruda); late, in bed,
I hoarded secret syllables I read

until my tongue (mi lengua) learned to run
where his stumbled. And still the heart was one.

I like to think he knew that, even when,   15
proud (orgulloso) of his daughter's pen,

he stood outside mis versos,[2] half in fear
of words he loved but wanted not to hear.

Reading and Reacting

1. Why do you think the poet includes parenthetical Spanish translations in this poem? Are they necessary? Why do you think the Spanish words "y basta" (line 8) and "mis versos" (line 17) are not translated as the others are?

2. Some of the words in this poem might be seen as having more than one connotation. Consider, for example, "alien" (line 4), "word" (line 9), "dumb" (line 10), and "syllables" (line 12). What meanings could each of these words have? Which meaning do you think the poet intended them to have?

3. What is the relationship between "the word" and "the world" in this poem?

4. **JOURNAL ENTRY** What is the father's fear? Do you think this fear is justified? Why do you think he doesn't want to hear his daughter's words?

Related Works: "The Secret Lion" (p. 466), "Two Kinds" (p. 471), "Baca Grande" (p. 545), "Find Work" (p. 645)

ADRIENNE RICH (1929–   )

Living in Sin (1955)

She had thought the studio would keep itself,
no dust upon the furniture of love.
Half heresy, to wish the taps less vocal,
the panes relieved of grime. A plate of pears,
a piano with a Persian shawl, a cat   5

AP Images/Chuck Knoblock

---

[1] *"y basta.":* and enough.
[2] *mis versos:* my poems.

stalking the picturesque amusing mouse
had risen at his urging.
Not that at five each separate stair would writhe
under the milkman's tramp; that morning light
so coldly would delineate the scraps   10
of last night's cheese and three sepulchral bottles;
that on the kitchen shelf among the saucers
a pair of beetle-eyes would fix her own—
envoy from some black village in the mouldings . . .
Meanwhile, he, with a yawn,   15
sounded a dozen notes upon the keyboard,
declared it out of tune, shrugged at the mirror,
rubbed at his beard, went out for cigarettes;
while she, jeered by the minor demons,
pulled back the sheets and made the bed and found   20
a towel to dust the table-top,
and let the coffee-pot boil over on the stove.
By evening she was back in love again,
though not so wholly but throughout the night
she woke sometimes to feel the daylight coming   25
like a relentless milkman up the stairs.

1950s milkman making delivery
Philip Gendreau/© Bettmann/Corbis

Reading and Reacting

1. How might the poem's impact change if each of these words were deleted: "Persian" (line 5), "picturesque" (line 6), "sepulchral" (line 11), "minor" (line 19), "sometimes" (line 25)?

2. What words in the poem have strongly negative connotations? What do these words suggest about the relationship the poem describes? How does the image of the "relentless milkman" (line 26) sum up this relationship?

3. This poem, about a woman in love, uses very few words conventionally associated with love poems. Instead, many of its words denote the everyday routine of housekeeping. Give examples of such words. Why do you think they are used?

4. **JOURNAL ENTRY** What connotations does the title have? What other phrases have similar denotative meanings? How do their connotations differ? Why do you think Rich chose the title "Living in Sin"?

5. **CRITICAL PERSPECTIVE** In "Her Cargo: Adrienne Rich and the Common Language," a 1979 essay examining the poet's work over almost thirty years, Alicia Ostriker offers the following analysis of Rich's early poems, including "Living in Sin":

> They seem about to state explicitly... a connection between feminine subordination in male-dominated middle-class relationships, and emotionally lethal inarticulateness for both sexes. But the poetry... is minor because it is polite. It illustrates symptoms but does not probe sources. There is no disputing the ideas of the predecessors, and Adrienne Rich at this point is a cautious good poet in the sense of being a good girl, a quality noted with approval by her reviewers.

Does your reading of "Living in Sin" support Ostriker's characterization of the poem as "polite" and "cautious"? Do you think Rich is "being a good girl"?

Related Works: "Hills Like White Elephants" (p. 74), "Love and Other Catastrophies: A Mix Tape" (p. 84), "The Storm" (p. 199), "What lips my lips have kissed" (p. 720)

E. E. CUMMINGS (1894–1962)

in Just-[1] (1923)

in Just-
spring when the world is mud-
luscious the little
lame balloonman
whistles   far   and wee   5

---

[1] *in Just-:* This poem is also known as "Chansons Innocentes I."

and eddieandbill come
running from marbles and
piracies and it's
spring
when the world is puddle-wonderful   10
the queer
old balloonman whistles
far   and   wee

and bettyandisbel come dancing

from hop-scotch and jump-rope and   15
it's
spring
and
  the
    goat-footed   20
balloonMan whistles
far
and
wee

Reading and Reacting

1. In this poem, Cummings coins a number of words that he uses to modify other words. Identify these coinages. What other, more conventional, words could be used in their place? What does Cummings accomplish by using the coined words instead?

2. What do you think Cummings means by "far and wee" in lines 5, 13, and 22–24? Why do you think he arranges these three words in a different way on the page each time he uses them?

3. **Journal Entry** Evaluate this poem. Do you like it? Is it memorable? moving? Or is it just clever?

4. **Critical Perspective** In "Latter-Day Notes on E. E. Cummings' Language" (1955), Robert E. Maurer suggests that Cummings often coined new words in the same way that children do: for example, "by adding the normal *-er* or *-est* (*beautifuler, chiefest*), or stepping up the power of a word such as *last*, which is already superlative, and saying *lastest*," creating words such as *givingest* and *whirlingest*. In addition to "combining two or more words to form a single new one . . . to give an effect of wholeness, of one quality" (for example, *yellowgreen*), "in the simplest of his word coinages, he merely creates a new word by analogy as a child would without adding any shade of meaning other than that inherent in the prefix or suffix he utilizes, as in the words

unstrength and *untimid*...." Many early reviewers, Maurer notes, criticized such coinages because they "convey a thrill but not a precise impression," a criticism also leveled at Cummings's poetry more broadly. Consider the coinages in "in Just-." Do you agree that many do not add "shades of meaning" or provide a "precise impression"? Or, do you find that the coinages contribute to the poem in a meaningful way?

Related Works: "The Secret Lion" (p. 466), "anyone lived in a pretty how town" (p. 555), "Constantly Risking Absurdity" (p. 578), "Jabberwocky" (p. 629), "the sky was can dy" (p. 662)

FRANCISCO X. ALARCÓN (1954–   )

"Mexican" Is Not a Noun (2002)

> to forty-six UC Santa Cruz students and
> seven faculty arrested in Watsonville for
> showing solidarity with two thousand
> striking cannery workers who were mostly
> Mexican women, October 27, 1985

"Mexican"
is not
a noun
or an
adjective   5

"Mexican"
is a life
long
low-paying
job   10

a check
mark on
a welfare
police
form   15

more than
a word
a nail in
the soul
but   20

it hurts
it points
it dreams
it offends
it cries   25

it moves
it strikes
it burns
just like
a verb   30

Reading and Reacting

1. According to the speaker, the word *Mexican* is "not / a noun / or an / adjective" (lines 3–5). What part of speech does he see it as? Why?

2. What is gained by isolating the word *Mexican* on its own line in lines 1 and 6? by repeating the word?

3. In what sense is the word *Mexican* "a nail in / the soul" (18–19)? Why is it "more than / a word" (16–17)?

4. JOURNAL ENTRY Write a paragraph in which you define the word *Mexican* by elaborating on the speaker's characterizations.

Related Works: "The Secret Lion" (p. 466), "Reapers" (p. 571), "The Carpet Factory" (p. 643), "La Migra" (p. 778)

Levels of Diction

The diction of a poem may be formal or informal or fall anywhere in between, depending on the identity of the speaker and on the speaker's attitude toward the reader and toward his or her subject. At one extreme, very formal poems can seem lofty and dignified, far removed in style and vocabulary from everyday speech. At the other extreme, highly informal poems can be full of jargon, regionalisms, and slang. Many poems, of course, use language that falls somewhere between formal and informal diction.

Formal diction is characterized by a learned vocabulary and grammatically correct forms. In general, formal diction does not include colloquialisms, such as contractions and shortened word forms (*phone* for *telephone*). As the following poem illustrates, a speaker who uses formal diction can sound aloof and impersonal.

AP Images/Dave Thomson

MARGARET ATWOOD (1939–)

The City Planners (1966)

Cruising these residential Sunday
streets in dry August sunlight:
what offends us is
the sanities:
the houses in pedantic rows, the planted   5
sanitary trees, assert
levelness of surface like a rebuke
to the dent in our car door.
No shouting here, or
shatter of glass; nothing more abrupt   10
than the rational whine of a power mower
cutting a straight swath in the discouraged grass.

But though the driveways neatly
sidestep hysteria
by being even, the roofs all display   15
the same slant of avoidance to the hot sky,
certain things:
the smell of spilled oil a faint

sickness lingering in the garages,
a splash of paint on brick surprising as a bruise,   20
a plastic hose poised in a vicious

coil; even the too-fixed stare of the wide windows
give momentary access to
the landscape behind or under
the future cracks in the plaster   25

when the houses, capsized, will slide
obliquely into the clay seas, gradual as glaciers
that right now nobody notices.

That is where the City Planners
with the insane faces of political conspirators   30
are scattered over unsurveyed
territories, concealed from each other,
each in his own private blizzard;

guessing directions, they sketch
transitory lines rigid as wooden borders   35
on a wall in the white vanishing air

tracing the panic of suburb
order in a bland madness of snows.

1950s suburban housing development
Masterfile

Atwood's speaker is clearly concerned about the poem's central issue, but rather than use *I*, the poem uses the first-person plural (*us*) to convey some degree of emotional detachment. Although phrases such as "sickness lingering in the garages" and "insane faces of political conspirators" clearly communicate the speaker's disapproval, formal words—"pedantic," "rebuke," "display," "poised," "obliquely," "conspirators," "transitory"—help her to maintain her distance. Both the speaker herself and her attack on the misguided city planners gain credibility through her balanced, measured tone and through her use of language that is as formal and "professional" as theirs.

Informal diction is the language closest to everyday conversation. It includes **colloquialisms**—contractions, shortened word forms, and the like—and may also include slang, regional expressions, and even nonstandard words.

In the poem that follows, the speaker uses informal diction to highlight the contrast between James Baca, a law student speaking to the graduating class of his old high school, and the graduating seniors.

JIM SAGEL (1947–1998)

Baca Grande[1] (1982)

> *Una vaca se topó con un ratón y le dice:*
> *"Tú—¿tan chiquito y con bigote?" Y le responde el ratón:*
> *"Y tú tan grandota—¿y sin brassiere?"* [2]

---

[1] *Baca Grande: Baca* is both a phonetic spelling of the Spanish word *vaca* (cow) and the last name of one of the poem's characters. *Grande* means "large."

[2] *Una ... brassiere?:* A cow ran into a rat and said: "You—so small and with a moustache?" The rat responded: "And you—so big and without a bra?"

It was nearly a miracle
James Baca remembered anyone at all
from the old hometown gang
having been two years at Yale
    no less   5
and halfway through law school
at the University of California at Irvine
They hardly recognized him either
in his three-piece grey business suit
and surfer-swirl haircut   10
with just the menacing hint
of a tightly trimmed Zapata moustache
    for cultural balance
and relevance

He had come to deliver the keynote address   15
to the graduating class of 80
at his old alma mater
and show off his well-trained lips
which laboriously parted
    each Kennedyish "R"   20
and drilled the first person pronoun
through the microphone
like an oil bit
with the slick, elegantly honed phrases
that slid so smoothly   25
off his meticulously bleached
    tongue
He talked Big Bucks
with astronautish fervor and if he
    the former bootstrapless James A. Baca   30
could dazzle the ass
off the universe
then even you
    yes you

Joey Martinez toying with your yellow   35
    tassle
and staring dumbly into space
could emulate Mr. Baca someday
    possibly
well   40
there was of course

such a thing
as being an outrageously successful
gas station attendant too
   let us never forget   45
it doesn't really matter what you do
so long as you excel
   James said
never believing a word
of it   50
for he had already risen
   as high as they go

Wasn't nobody else
from this deprived environment
who'd ever jumped   55
   straight out of college
into the Governor's office
and maybe one day
he'd sit in that big chair
   himself   60
and when he did
he'd forget this damned town
and all the petty little people
in it
once and for all   65

That much he promised himself

"Baca Grande" uses numerous colloquialisms, including contractions; conversational placeholders, such as "no less" and "well"; shortened word forms, such as "gas"; slang terms, such as "Big Bucks"; whimsical coinages ("Kennedyish," "astronautish," "bootstrapless"); nonstandard grammatical constructions, such as "Wasn't nobody else"; and even profanity. The level of language is perfectly appropriate for the poem's speaker, one of the students Baca addresses—suspicious, streetwise, and unimpressed by Baca's "three-piece grey business suit" and "surfer-swirl haircut." In fact, the informal diction is a key element in the poem, expressing the gap between the slick James Baca, with "his well-trained lips / which laboriously parted / each Kennedyish 'R'" and members of his audience, with their unpretentious, forthright speech—and also the gap between Baca as he is today and the student he once was. In this sense, "Baca Grande" is as much a linguistic commentary as a social one.

FURTHER READING: Levels of Diction

ADRIENNE SU (1967–   )

The English Canon[1] (2000)

It's not that the first speakers left out women
Unless they were goddesses, harlots, or impossible loves
Seen from afar, often while bathing,

And it's not that the only parts my grandfathers
   could have played
Were as extras in Xanadu[2]   5
Nor that it gives no instructions for shopping or cooking.

The trouble is, I've spent my life
Getting over the lyrics
That taught me to brush my hair till it's gleaming,

Stay slim, dress tastefully, and not speak of sex,   10
Death, violence, or the desire for any of them,
And to let men do the talking and warring

And bringing of the news. I know a girl's got to protest
These days, but she also has to make money
And do her share of journalism and combat,   15

And she has to know from the gut whom to trust,
Because what do her teachers know, living in books,
And what does she know, starting from scratch?

Reading and Reacting

1. What criticisms does the speaker have of the traditional English literary canon?
2. List the words and expressions that identify this poem's diction as informal. Given the poem's subject and theme, do you think this informal language (and the speaker's use of contractions) is a strength or a weakness?

---

[1] *English Canon:* Those works in English traditionally thought worthy of study.

[2] *Xanadu:* The summer capital of the emperor Kublai Kahn; also the setting for the poem "Kubla Khan" (p. 747) by the English poet Samuel Taylor Coleridge.

3. What does the speaker mean when she says, "The trouble is, I've spent my life / Getting over the lyrics" (7–8)?

4. JOURNAL ENTRY Reread the poem's last two lines. What does the speaker know that her teachers do not know? What do her teachers know that she does not know?

5. CRITICAL PERSPECTIVE In her essay "Teaching Literature: Canon, Controversy, and the Literary Anthology," Barbara Mujica discusses the way in which literary anthologies (like this one) naturally tend to create lists of works, known as **canons**, that are considered to be of especially high quality:

> "Anthology". . . is from the Greek word for "collection of flowers," a term implying selection. The very format of an anthology prompts canon formation . . . Anthologies convey the notion of evolution (the succession of literary movements) and hierarchy (the recognition of masterpieces). They create and reform canons, establish literary reputations, and help institutionalize the national culture, which they reflect.

How would you characterize the attitude of the speaker in "The English Canon" toward the process that Mujica describes? What is your own attitude toward the idea of canons in literature? Do you think some works can be said to be indisputably better than others?

Related Works: "Gryphon" (p. 172), "The Secretary Chant" (p. 584), "Aristotle" (p. 685), "Theme for English B" (p. 770)

MARK HALLIDAY (1949–   )

The Value of Education (2000)

I go now to the library. When I sit in the library
I am not illegally dumping bags of kitchen garbage
in the dumpster behind Clippinger Laboratory,
and a very pissed-off worker at Facilities Management
is not picking through my garbage and finding   5
several yogurt-stained and tomato-sauce-stained envelopes
with my name and address on them.
When I sit in the library,
I might doze off a little,
and what I read might not penetrate my head   10
which is mostly porridge in a bowl of bone.
However, when I sit there trying to read

I am not, you see, somewhere else being a hapless ass.
I am not leaning on the refrigerator
in the apartment of a young female colleague   15
chatting with oily pep
because I imagine she may suddenly decide to
do sex with me while her boyfriend is on a trip.
Instead I am in the library! Sitting still!
No one in town is approaching my chair   20
with a summons, or a bill, or a huge fist.
This is good. You may say,
"But this is merely a negative definition of
the value of education." Maybe so,
but would you be able to say that   25
if you hadn't been to the library?

Reading and Reacting

1. Who is the speaker? What does he reveal about himself? Whom might he be addressing?

2. How is the speaker's life outside the library different from the life he leads inside the library?

3. In lines 23–24, the speaker imagines a challenge to his comments. Do you think this challenge is valid? What do you think of the speaker's reply?

4. What phrases are repeated in this poem? Why?

5. **JOURNAL ENTRY** What argument is the speaker making for the benefits of the library (and for the value of education)? Is he joking, or is he serious?

Related Works: "Gryphon" (p. 172), "When I Heard the Learn'd Astronomer" (p. 536), "Why I Went to College" (p. 655)

PAUL LAURENCE DUNBAR (1872–1906)

We Wear the Mask (1896)

We wear the mask that grins and lies,
It hides our cheeks and shades our eyes—
This debt we pay to human guile;
With torn and bleeding hearts we smile,
And mouth with myriad subtleties.   5

Why should the world be over-wise,
In counting all our tears and sighs?
Nay, let them only see us, while
    We wear the mask.

We smile, but, O great Christ, our cries   10

To thee from tortured souls arise.
We sing, but oh the clay is vile
Beneath our feet, and long the mile;
But let the world dream otherwise,
    We wear the mask!   15

Reading and Reacting

1. Which of the following words and phrases do you see as formal? Why?
- "human guile" (line 3)
- "torn and bleeding hearts" (4)
- "myriad subtleties" (5)
- "over-wise" (6)
- "tortured souls" (11)
- "vile" (12)

2. Some choices of words and phrases listed in question 1 are determined at least in part by the poem's rhyme scheme and metrical pattern. If rhyme and meter were not an issue, what other words and phrases could you substitute for those listed? How would your substitutions change the poem's level of diction?

3. Do you think the poem's meter and rhyme make it seem more or less formal? Explain.

4. Given the poem's subject matter, is its relatively formal level of diction appropriate? Why or why not?

5. JOURNAL ENTRY What exactly is the mask to which the speaker refers? Who is the "we" who wears this mask? (Note that Dunbar is an African American poet writing in the late nineteenth century.)

6. CRITICAL PERSPECTIVE In his book *Paul Laurence Dunbar*, Peter Revell explains that "'We Wear the Mask' itself is 'masked'" in its hidden references to race. How does the poem's diction help to mask its message?

Related Works: from *The Harlem Hellfighters* (p. 104), "Big Black Good Man" (p. 236), "Negro" (p. 502), "Yet Do I Marvel" (p. 690)

Source: ©Bill Tague

GWENDOLYN BROOKS (1917–2000)

We Real Cool (1959)

The Pool Players.
Seven at the Golden Shovel.

We real cool. We
Left School. We

Lurk late. We
Strike straight. We

Sing sin. We   5
Thin gin. We

Jazz June. We
Die soon.

Reading and Reacting

1. What elements of nonstandard English grammar appear in this poem? How does the use of such language affect your attitude toward the speaker?
2. Every word in this poem is a single syllable. Why?
3. Why do you think the poet begins with "We" only in the first line instead of isolating each complete sentence on its own line? How does this strategy change the poem's impact?

4. **JOURNAL ENTRY** Write a prose version of this poem, adding words, phrases, and sentences to expand the poem into a paragraph.

5. **CRITICAL PERSPECTIVE** In *Gwendolyn Brooks: Poetry and the Heroic Voice*, critic D. H. Malhem writes of "We Real Cool," "Despite presentation in the voice of the gang, this is a maternal poem, gently scolding yet deeply sorrowing for the hopelessness of the boys."

   Do you agree with Malhem that the speaker's attitude is "maternal"?

Related Works: "Greasy Lake" (p. 425), "Where Are You Going, Where Have You Been?" (p. 453), "Why I Went to College" (p. 655)

Players in a pool hall (1950s)
Mac Gramlich/Hulton Archive/Getty Images

GWENDOLYN BROOKS   (1917–2000)

What Shall I Give My Children?   (1949)

What shall I give my children? who are poor,
Who are adjudged the leastwise of the land,
Who are my sweetest lepers, who demand
No velvet and no velvety velour;
But who have begged me for a brisk contour,   5
Crying that they are quasi, contraband
Because unfinished, graven by a hand
Less than angelic, admirable or sure.
My hand is stuffed with mode, design, device.
But I lack access to my proper stone.   10
And plenitude of plan shall not suffice
Nor grief nor love shall be enough alone
To ratify my little halves who bear
Across an autumn freezing everywhere.

Reading and Reacting

1. Unlike "We Real Cool" (p. 551), also by Gwendolyn Brooks, this sonnet's diction is quite formal. Given the subject of each poem, do the poet's decisions about level of diction make sense to you?

2. Which words in this poem do you see as elevated—that is, not likely to be used in conversation?

3. Apart from individual words, what else strikes you as formal about this poem?

4. JOURNAL ENTRY Consulting a dictionary if necessary, write down a synonym for each of the formal words you identified in question 2. Then, write out three or four lines of this poem in more conversational language.

Related Work: "We Real Cool" (p. 551)

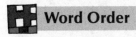 **Word Order**

The order in which words are arranged in a poem is as important as the choice of words. Because English sentences nearly always have a subject-verb-object sequence, with adjectives preceding the nouns they modify, a departure from this order calls attention to itself. Thus, poets can use readers' expectations about word order to their advantage.

For example, poets often manipulate word order to place emphasis on a word. Sometimes they achieve this emphasis by using a very unconventional sequence; sometimes they simply place the word first or last in a line or place it in a stressed position in the line. Poets may also choose a particular word order to make two related—or startlingly unrelated—words fall in adjacent or parallel positions, calling attention to the similarity (or the difference) between them. In other cases, poets may manipulate syntax to preserve a poem's rhyme or meter or to highlight sound correspondences that might otherwise not be noticeable. Finally, irregular syntax may be used throughout a poem to reveal a speaker's mood—for example, to give a playful quality to a poem or to suggest a speaker's disoriented state.

In the poem that follows, word order frequently departs from conventional English syntax.

EDMUND SPENSER (1552–1599)

One day I wrote her name upon the strand (1595)

One day I wrote her name upon the strand,[1]
But came the waves and washed it away:
Again I wrote it with a second hand,
But came the tide and made my pains his prey.
"Vain man," said she, "that doest in vain assay,   5
A mortal thing so to immortalize,
For I myself shall like to this decay,
And eek [2] my name be wiped out likewise."
"Not so," quod[3] I, "let baser things devise,
To die in dust, but you shall live by fame: 10
My verse your virtues rare shall eternize,
And in the heavens write your glorious name.
Where whenas death shall all the world subdue,
Our love shall live, and later life renew."

"One day I wrote her name upon the strand," a sonnet, has a fixed metrical pattern and rhyme scheme. To accommodate the sonnet's rhyme and meter, Spenser makes a number of adjustments in syntax. For example, to make sure certain rhyming words fall at the ends of lines, the poet sometimes moves words out of their conventional order, as the following three comparisons illustrate.

---

[1] *strand:* Beach.
[2] *eek:* Also, indeed.
[3] *quod:* Said.

Conventional Word Order	Inverted Sequence
"'Vain man,' she said, 'that doest *assay in vain.*'"	"'Vain man,' said she, 'that doest *in vain assay.*'" ("Assay" appears at end of line 5, to rhyme with line 7's "decay.")
"My verse shall *eternize your rare virtues.*"	"My verse *your virtues rare shall eternize.*" ("Eternize" appears at end of line 11 to rhyme with line 9's "devise.")
"Where whenas death shall *subdue all the world,* / Our love shall live, and *later renew life.*"	"Where whenas death shall *all the world subdue,* / Our love shall live, and *later life renew.*" (Rhyming words "subdue" and "renew" are placed at ends of lines.)

To make sure the metrical pattern stresses certain words, the poet occasionally moves a word out of conventional order and places it in a stressed position. The following comparison illustrates this technique.

Conventional Word Order	Inverted Sequence
"But *the waves came* and washed it away."	"But *came the waves* and washed it away." (Stress in line 2 falls on "waves" rather than on "the.")

As the above comparisons show, Spenser's adjustments in syntax are motivated at least in part by a desire to preserve his sonnet's rhyme and meter.

The next poem does more than simply invert word order; it presents an intentionally disordered syntax.

E. E. CUMMINGS (1894–1962)

anyone lived in a pretty how town (1940)

anyone lived in a pretty how town
(with up so floating many bells down)
spring summer autumn winter
he sang his didn't he danced his did.

Women and men (both little and small)   5
cared for anyone not at all
they sowed their isn't they reaped their same
sun moon stars rain

children guessed (but only a few
and down they forgot as up they grew   10
autumn winter spring summer)
that noone loved him more by more

when by now and tree by leaf
she laughed his joy she cried his grief
bird by snow and stir by still   15
anyone's any was all to her

someones married their everyones
laughed their cryings and did their dance
(sleep wake hope and then) they
said their nevers they slept their dream   20

stars rain sun moon
(and only the snow can begin to explain
how children are apt to forget to remember
with up so floating many bells down)

one day anyone died i guess   25
(and noone stooped to kiss his face)
busy folk buried them side by side
little by little and was by was

all by all and deep by deep   30
and more by more they dream their sleep
noone and anyone earth by april
wish by spirit and if by yes.

Women and men (both dong and ding)
summer autumn winter spring
reaped their sowing and went their came   35
sun moon stars rain

Cummings, like Spenser, sometimes manipulates syntax in response to the demands of rhyme and meter—for example, in line 10. But Cummings goes much further, using unconventional syntax as part of a scheme that includes other unusual elements of the poem, such as its unexpected departures from the musical metrical pattern (for example, in lines 3 and 8) and from the rhyme scheme (for example, in lines 3 and 4) and its use of various parts of speech in unfamiliar contexts. Together, these techniques give the poem a playful quality. The refreshing disorder of the syntax (for instance, in lines 1–2, 10, and 24) adds to the poem's whimsical effect.

FURTHER READING: Word Order

A. E. HOUSMAN (1859–1936)

To an Athlete Dying Young (1896)

The time you won your town the race
We chaired you through the market-place;
Man and boy stood cheering by,
And home we brought you shoulder-high.

Today, the road all runners come,   5
Shoulder-high we bring you home,
And set you at your threshold down,
Townsman of a stiller town.

Smart lad, to slip betimes away
From fields where glory does not stay,   10
And early though the laurel grows
It withers quicker than the rose.

Eyes the shady night has shut
Cannot see the record cut,
And silence sounds no worse than cheers   15
After earth has stopped the ears.

Now you will not swell the rout
Of lads that wore their honors out,
Runners whom renown outran
And the name died before the man.   20

So set, before its echoes fade,
The fleet foot on the sill of shade,
And hold to the low lintel up
The still-defended challenge-cup.

And round that early-laureled head   20
Will flock to gaze the strengthless dead,
And find unwithered on its curls
The garland briefer than a girl's.

Reading and Reacting

1. Where does the poem's meter or rhyme scheme require the poet to depart from conventional syntax?
2. Edit the poem so its word order is more conventional. Do your changes improve the poem?

3. JOURNAL ENTRY Who do you think the speaker might be? What might his relationship to the athlete be?

Related Works: "To the Virgins, to Make Much of Time" (p. 518), "Nothing Gold Can Stay" (p. 569)

✔ **CHECKLIST**   **Writing about Word Choice and Word Order**

Word Choice

☐ Which words are of key importance in the poem? What is the denotative meaning of each of these key words?

☐ Which key words have neutral connotations? Which have negative connotations? Which have positive connotations? Beyond its literal meaning, what does each word suggest?

☐ Why is each word chosen instead of a synonym? (For example, is the word chosen for its sound? its connotation? its relationship to other words in the poem? its contribution to the poem's metrical pattern?)

☐ What other words could be effectively used in place of words now in the poem? How would substitutions change the poem's meaning?

☐ Are any words repeated? Why?

Levels of Diction

☐ How would you characterize the poem's level of diction? Why is this level of diction used? Is it appropriate?

☐ Does the poem mix different levels of diction? If so, why?

Word Order

☐ Is the poem's word order conventional, or are words arranged in unexpected order?

☐ What is the purpose of the unusual word order? (For example, does it preserve the poem's meter or rhyme scheme? Does it highlight particular sound correspondences? Does it place emphasis on a particular word or phrase? Does it reflect the speaker's mood?)

☐ How would the poem's impact change if conventional syntax were used?

WRITING SUGGESTIONS: Word Choice, Word Order

1. Reread the two poems in this chapter by E. E. Cummings—"in Just-" (p. 540) and "anyone lived in a pretty how town" (p. 555). If you like, you may also read one or two additional poems in this book by Cummings. Do you believe Cummings chose words primarily for their sound? for their appearance on the page? What other factors might have influenced his choices?

2. The tone of "We Real Cool" (p. 551) is flat and unemotional; the problem on which it focuses, however, is serious. Expand this concise poem into a few paragraphs that retain the poem's informal, colloquial tone but use more detailed, more emotional language to communicate the hopeless situation of the speaker and his friends. Include dialogue as well as narrative.

3. Reread "Living in Sin" (p. 538) and "The English Canon" (p. 548), and choose one or two other poems in this book whose speaker is a woman. Compare the speakers' levels of diction and choice of words. What does their language reveal about their lives?

4. Analyze the choice of words and the level of diction in several poems in this book that express social or political criticism. Poems that might work well include Claude McKay's "If We Must Die" (p. 778) and Louise Erdrich's "Indian Boarding School: The Runaways" (p. 763).

CHAPTER 18

IMAGERY

William Shakespeare
Bettmann/CORBIS

Ezra Pound
AP Images

William Carlos Williams
John D. Schiff/Bettmann/Corbis

Steven Flanders

JANE FLANDERS (1940–2001)

Cloud Painter (1984)

Suggested by the life and art of John Constable[1]

At first, as you know, the sky is incidental—
a drape, a backdrop for trees and steeples.
Here an oak clutches a rock (already he works
    outdoors),
a wall buckles but does not break,
water pearls through a lock, a haywain[2] trembles.   5

The pleasures of landscape are endless. What we see
around us should be enough.
Horizons are typically high and far away.

---

[1] *John Constable:* British painter (1776–1837) noted for his landscapes.
[2] *haywain:* An open horse-drawn wagon for carrying hay.

Still, clouds let us drift and remember. He is, after all,
a miller's son, used to trying   10
to read the future in the sky, seeing instead
ships, horses, instruments of flight.
Is that his mother's wash flapping on the line?
His schoolbook, smudged, illegible?

In this period the sky becomes significant.   15
Cloud forms are technically correct—mares' tails,
sheep-in-the-meadow, thunderheads.
You can almost tell which scenes have been interrupted
by summer showers.

Now his young wife dies.   20
His landscapes achieve belated success.
He is invited to join the Academy. I forget
whether he accepts or not.

In any case, the literal forms give way
to something spectral, nameless. His palette shrinks   25
to gray, blue, white—the colors of charity.

Horizons sink and fade,
trees draw back till they are little more than frames,
then they too disappear.

Finally the canvas itself begins to vibrate   30
with waning light,
as if the wind could paint.
And we too, at last, stare into a space
which tells us nothing,
except that the world can vanish along with our need for it.   35

Because the purpose of poetry—and, for that matter, of all literature—is to expand the perception of readers, poets appeal to the senses. In "Cloud Painter," Jane Flanders uses **images**, such as the mother's wash on the line and the smudged schoolbook, to enable readers to visualize particular scenes in John Constable's early paintings. (For additional poems written in response to works of art, see the "Poetry Sampler: Poetry and Art," p. PS1). Clouds are described so readers can picture them—"mares' tails, / sheep-in-the-meadow, thunderheads." Thus, "Cloud Painter" is not only about the work of John Constable but also about the ability of an artist—poet or painter—to call up images in the minds of an audience. To achieve this end, a poet uses **imagery**, language that evokes a physical sensation produced by one or more of the five senses—sight, hearing, taste, touch, smell.

John Constable (1776–1837). *Landscape, Noon, The Haywain*. 1821. Oil on canvas, 130½ × 185½ cm. London, National Gallery.

The Hay Wain, 1821 (oil on canvas), Constable, John (1776–1837) / National Gallery, London, UK / Bridgeman Images

Although the effect can be complex, the way images work is simple: when you read the word *red*, your memory of the various red things that you have seen determines how you picture the image. In addition, the word *red* may have **connotations**—emotional associations that define your response. A red sunset, for example, can have a positive connotation or a negative one, depending on whether it is associated with the end of a perfect day or with air pollution. By choosing images carefully, poets not only create pictures in a reader's mind but also create a great number of imaginative associations. These associations help poets to establish the **atmosphere** or **mood** of the poem. The image of softly falling snow in "Stopping by Woods on a Snowy Evening" (p. 765), for example, creates a quiet, almost mystical mood.

Readers come to a poem with their own unique experiences, so an image in a poem does not suggest exactly the same thing to all readers. In "Cloud Painter," for example, the poet presents the image of an oak tree clutching a rock. Although most readers will probably see a picture that is generally consistent with the one the poet sees, no two images will be identical. Every reader will have his or her own distinct mental image of a tree clinging to a rock; some images will be remembered experiences, whereas others will be imaginative creations. Some readers may even be familiar enough with the work of the painter John Constable to visualize a particular tree clinging to a particular rock in one of his paintings. By conveying what the poet imagines, images open readers' minds to perceptions and associations different from—and possibly more original and complex than—their own.

One advantage of imagery is its extreme economy. A few carefully chosen words enable poets to evoke a range of emotions and reactions. In the following poem, William Carlos Williams uses simple visual images to create a rich and compelling picture.

John D. Schiff/© Bettmann/Corbis

WILLIAM CARLOS WILLIAMS (1883–1963)

Red Wheelbarrow (1923)

so much depends
upon

a red wheel
barrow

glazed with rain   5
water

beside the white
chickens

What is immediately apparent in this poem is its verbal economy. The poet does not tell readers what the barnyard smells like or what sounds the animals make. In fact, he does not present a detailed picture of the scene. How large is the wheelbarrow? What is its condition? How many chickens are in the barnyard? In this poem, the answers to these questions are not important.

Even without answering these questions, the poet is able to use simple imagery to create a scene on which, he says, "so much depends." The wheelbarrow establishes a momentary connection between the poet and his world. Like a still-life painting, the red wheelbarrow beside the white chickens gives order to a world that is full of seemingly unrelated objects. In this poem, the poet suggests that our ability to perceive the objects of this world gives our lives meaning and that our ability to convey our perceptions to others is central to our lives as well as to poetry.

Images enable poets to present ideas that would be difficult to convey in any other way. One look at a dictionary will illustrate that concepts such as *beauty* and *mystery* are so abstract that they are difficult to define, let alone to discuss in specific terms. However, by choosing an image or a series of images to embody these ideas, poets can effectively make their feelings known, as Ezra Pound does in the two-line poem that follows.

AP Images

EZRA POUND (1885–1972)

In a Station of the Metro (1916)

The apparition of these faces in the crowd;
Petals on a wet, black bough.

This poem is almost impossible to paraphrase because the information it communicates is less important than the feelings associated with this information. The poem's title indicates that the first line is meant to suggest a group of people standing in a station of the Paris subway. The scene, however, is presented not as a clear picture but as an "apparition," suggesting that it is unexpected or even dreamlike. In contrast with the image of the subway platform is the image of the people's faces as flower petals on the dark branch of a tree. Thus, the subway platform—dark, cold, wet, subterranean (associated with baseness, death, and hell)—is juxtaposed with flower petals—delicate, pale, radiant, lovely (associated with the ideal, life, and heaven). These contrasting images, presented without comment, bear the entire weight of the poem.

Although images can be strikingly visual, they can also appeal to the senses of hearing, smell, taste, and touch. The following poem uses images of sound and taste as well as sight.

Paris Metro station platform
Hulton Archive/ Archive Photos/Getty Images

GARY SNYDER (1930–   )

Some Good Things to Be Said for the Iron Age (1970)

A ringing tire iron
   dropped on the pavement
Whang of a saw
brusht on limbs
the taste   5
of rust

Here Snyder presents two commonplace aural images: the ringing of a tire iron and the sound of a saw. These somewhat ordinary images gain power, however, through their visual isolation on separate lines in the poem. Together they produce a harsh and jarring chord that creates a sense of uneasiness in the reader. This poem does more than present sensory images, though; it also conveys the speaker's interpretations of these images. The last two lines imply not only that the time in which we live (the Iron Age) is base and mundane, but also that it is declining, decaying into an age of rust. The title of the poem makes an ironic comment, suggesting that compared to the time that is approaching, the age of iron may be "good." Thus, in the mind of the poet, ordinary events gain added significance, and images that spring from everyday experience become sources of insight.

    Much visual imagery is **static**, freezing the moment and thereby giving it the timeless quality of painting or sculpture. ("Red Wheelbarrow" presents such a tableau, and so does "In a Station of the Metro.") In contrast, some imagery is **kinetic**, conveying a sense of motion or change.

WILLIAM CARLOS WILLIAMS (1883–1963)

The Great Figure (1938)

Among the rain
and lights
I saw the figure 5
in gold
on a red   5
firetruck
moving
tense
unheeded
to gong clangs   10

siren howls
and wheels rumbling
through the dark city.

Commenting on "The Great Figure" in his autobiography, Williams explained that while walking in New York, he heard the sound of a fire engine. As he turned the corner, he saw a golden figure 5 on a red background speed by. The impression was so forceful that he immediately jotted down a poem about it. In the poem, Williams attempts to recreate the sensation the figure 5 made as it moved into his consciousness. The poet presents images in the order in which he perceived them: first the 5, and then the red fire truck howling and clanging into the darkness. Thus, "The Great Figure" uses images of sight, sound, and movement to convey the poet's experience. The American painter Charles Demuth was fascinated by the poem. Working closely with Williams, he attempted to capture the poem's kinetic energy in a painting.

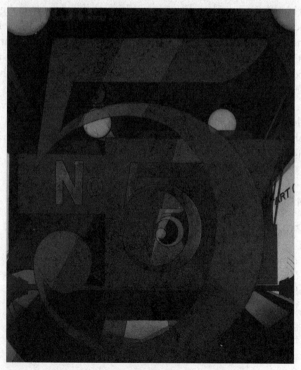

Charles Henry Demuth (1883–1935). *The Figure 5 in Gold.* Oil on composition board, 36 × 29¾ in.
The Metropolitan Museum of Art/ Image source/ Art Resource, NY

■ NOTE A special use of imagery, called **synesthesia**, occurs when one sense is described in terms of another sense—for instance, when a sound is described with color. When people say they are feeling *blue* or describe music as *hot* or *smooth*, they are using synesthesia.

FURTHER READING: Imagery

F. J. BERGMANN (1954–   )

An Apology (2003)

Forgive me
for backing over
and smashing
your red wheelbarrow.

It was raining   5
and the rear wiper
does not work on
my new plum-colored SUV.

I am also sorry
about the white   10
chickens.

Reading and Reacting

1. A **parody** is a literary work that imitates the style of another work for comic effect or ridicule. Bergmann's "An Apology" is a parody of William Carlos Williams's "Red Wheelbarrow" (p. 563). Why do you think Bergmann chose this poem to parody?

2. What aspects of "Red Wheelbarrow" does Bergmann parody? Do you think these elements deserve to be parodied, or do you think Bergmann's parody is unjustified or unfair?

3. Do you think Bergmann's purpose is to ridicule "Red Wheelbarrow" or just to amuse his readers? Explain.

4. **JOURNAL ENTRY** Write a parody of another poem in this book. Make sure you decide in advance what elements of the poem you want to parody.

5. **CRITICAL PERSPECTIVE** Blogger and critic Kerry Michael Wood observes that some readers think that critics have read too much into "The Red Wheelbarrow." According to him, however, "The Red Wheelbarrow"

is a "sparkling gem" of the Imagist school of poetry that "insisted on 'no ideas but in things.'"

Do you agree or disagree with Wood's assessment? Explain.

Related Works: "Red Wheelbarrow" (p. 563), "My mistress' eyes are nothing like the sun" (p. 572)

HART CRANE (1899–1932)

Echoes (1917)

1
Slivers of rain upon the pane,
Jade-green with sunlight, melt and flow
Upward again:—they leave no stain
Of all the storm an hour ago.

2
Over the hill a last cloud dips   5
And disappears, and I should go
As silently but that your lips
Are warmed with a redder glow.

3
Fresh and fragile, your arms now
Are circles of cool roses,—so . . .   10
In opal pools beneath your brow
I dream we quarreled long, long ago.

Reading and Reacting

1. What images does Crane use to describe the storm? What qualities of the storm does he stress?
2. "Echoes" consists of three stanzas. What ideas are presented in each stanza?
3. What do you think the poem's title means? In what sense does this poem deal with echoes?
4. How does the poem's last line suggest what happened before the storm? Is the speaker referring to a literal storm or to something else?
5. **Journal Entry** Crane uses a metaphor in stanza 3. Find this metaphor and explain its significance.

Related Works: "Love and Other Catastrophes: A Mix Tape" (p. 84), "The Storm" (p. 199), "Porphyria's Lover" (p. 520), "To His Coy Mistress" (p. 594), "Four Haiku" (p. 657), "Parting at Morning" (p. 719)

LOLA RIDGE (1873–1941)

Wall Street at Night (1920)

Long vast shapes . . . cooled and flushed through with darkness . . .
Lidless windows
Glazed with a flashy luster
From some little pert café chirping up like a sparrow.
And down among iron guts   5
Piled silver
Throwing gray spatter of light . . . pale without heat . . .
Like the pallor[1] of dead bodies.

Reading and Reacting

1. What are the "long vast shapes" that the speaker mentions in line 1?
2. Find examples of similes, metaphors, and personification. How do these figures of speech reinforce the poem's theme?
3. What possible meanings could the poem's title have?

4. **JOURNAL ENTRY** This poem was written in 1893, a year when there was a serious economic depression in the United States. What images in "Wall Street at Night" suggest this economic turmoil?

Related Works: "Discovering America" (p. 93), "A Worn Path" (p. 386), "The World Is Too Much with Us" (p. 516), "The City Planners" (p. 544)

ROBERT FROST (1874–1963)

Nothing Gold Can Stay (1923)

Nature's first green is gold,
Her hardest hue to hold.
Her early leaf's a flower;
But only so an hour.
Then leaf subsides to leaf.   5
So Eden sank to grief.
So dawn goes down to day.
Nothing gold can stay.

---

[1] *pallor:* Paleness.

Painting of the Garden of Eden
© SuperStock

Reading and Reacting

1. What central idea does this poem express?

2. What do you think the first line of the poem means? In what sense is this line ironic?

3. What is the significance of the colors green and gold in this poem? What do these colors have to do with "Eden" and "dawn"?

4. JOURNAL ENTRY How do the various images in the poem prepare readers for the last line? Do you think the title spoils the impact of the last line?

5. CRITICAL PERSPECTIVE In "The Figure a Poem Means," the introduction to the first edition of his *Collected Poems* (1930), Frost laid out a theory of poetry:

> It begins in delight, it inclines to the impulse, it assumes direction with the first line laid down, it runs a course of lucky events, and ends in a clarification of life—not necessarily a great clarification . . . but a momentary stay against confusion. . . . Like a piece of ice on a hot stove the poem must ride on its own melting. . . . Read it a hundred times: it will forever keep its freshness as a metal keeps its fragrance. It can never lose its sense of a meaning that once unfolded by surprise as it went.

Explain how Frost's remarks apply to "Nothing Gold Can Stay."

Related Works: "Araby" (p. 288), "Greasy Lake" (p. 425), "The Secret Lion" (p. 466), "Shall I compare thee to a summer's day?" (p. 575), "God's Grandeur" (p. 769)

JEAN TOOMER (1894–1967)

Reapers (1923)

Black reapers with the sound of steel on stones
Are sharpening scythes. I see them place the hones¹
In their hip-pockets as a thing that's done,
And start their silent swinging, one by one.
Black horses drive a mower through the weeds,   5
And there, a field rat, startled, squealing bleeds,
His belly close to ground. I see the blade,
Blood-stained, continue cutting weeds and shade.

Reading and Reacting

1. What determines the order in which the speaker arranges the images in this poem? At what point does he comment on these images?
2. The first four lines of the poem seem to suggest that the workers are content. What image contradicts this impression? How does it do so?
3. What ideas are traditionally associated with the image of the reaper? the scythe? the harvest? (To answer these questions, you may want to consult a reference source, such as <http://www.symbols.com>.) In what way does the speaker rely on these conventional associations to help him convey his ideas? Can you appreciate the poem without understanding these associations?
4. **JOURNAL ENTRY** Who do you think the speaker might be? Why?
5. **CRITICAL PERSPECTIVE** As Brian Joseph Benson and Mabel Mayle Dillard point out in their 1980 study *Jean Toomer*, the poet disagreed with some other artists of the Harlem Renaissance, choosing not to focus on "Negro" themes for a primarily black audience but rather to try to make his work universal in scope.
   Do you think he has achieved this goal in "Reapers"?

Related Works: "A Worn Path" (p. 386), "The Negro Speaks of Rivers" (p. 769), "Because I could not stop for Death—" (p. 752)

---

¹*hones:* Stones used to sharpen cutting instruments.

FREDERICK MORGAN (1922–2004)

The Busses (1995)

From our corner window
rainy winter mornings
nudging their way down Park
moistly glowing, puddled by the rain.

Stopping at doorways here and there   5
where children climb aboard
they merge into the traffic's flow
and dwindle from our sight.

We watch—then turn away,
and when in changing light   10
we look again, we see a stream
dark and serene in China,
down which sleek goldfish dart and gleam.

Reading and Reacting

1. Who is the speaker? Why do you think he uses the first-person plural pronoun *we*?
2. What words in the poem rhyme? What ideas do these rhyming words emphasize?
3. In the first two stanzas of the poem, the speaker describes school busses picking up children—probably along Park Avenue in New York City. In the third stanza, the imagery abruptly changes. How does this change expand the poem's meaning?
4. **JOURNAL ENTRY** What point is this poem making? How does the image in the last stanza help make this point?

Related Works: "How to Talk to Girls at Parties" (p. 131), "The Secret Lion" (p. 466), "Red Wheelbarrow" (p. 563), "In a Station of the Metro" (p. 564), "For Once, Then, Something" (p. 672), "Cézanne's Ports" (p. PS4)

WILLIAM SHAKESPEARE (1564–1616)

My mistress' eyes are nothing like the sun (1609)

My mistress' eyes are nothing like the sun;
Coral is far more red than her lips' red;

If snow be white, why then her breasts are dun;
If hairs be wires, black wires grow on her head.
I have seen roses damasked red and white,   5
But no such roses see I in her cheeks;
And in some perfumes is there more delight
Than in the breath that from my mistress reeks.
I love to hear her speak, yet well I know
That music hath a far more pleasing sound;   10
I grant I never saw a goddess go:
My mistress, when she walks, treads on the ground.
    And yet, by heaven, I think my love as rare
    As any she, belied with false compare.

Red and white damasked rose
RMN-Grand Palais / Art Resource, NY

Reading and Reacting

1. What point does Shakespeare make in the first twelve lines of his sonnet?
2. What point does the rhymed couplet at the end of the poem make?
3. How is Shakespeare's imagery like and unlike that of traditional love poems? For example, how is the imagery in this poem different from that in Elizabeth Barrett Browning's "How Do I Love Thee?" (p. 719).
4. **JOURNAL ENTRY** How do you think the woman to whom the poem is addressed will react?
5. **CRITICAL PERSPECTIVE** During the Renaissance, poets commonly used the "Petrarchan conceit" to praise their lovers. In this type of metaphor, the author draws elaborate comparisons between his beloved and one or more dissimilar things. According to critic Felicia Jean Steele, "Traditional readings of Shakespeare's Sonnet 130 argue that Shakespeare cunningly employs Petrarchan imagery while deliberately undermining it."

   How does this poem use the Petrarchan conceit? How does it undercut this convention?

Related Works: "A&P" (p. 160), "The Storm" (p. 199), "General Review of the Sex Situation" (p. 721), *The Brute* (p. 814)

> ✔ **CHECKLIST   Writing about Imagery**
>
> ▪ Do the images in the poem appeal to the sense of sight? hearing? taste? touch? smell?
>
> ▪ Does the poem depend on a single image or on several different images?
>
> ▪ Does the poem depend on a group of related images?
>
> ▪ What details make the images memorable?
>
> ▪ What mood do the images create?
>
> ▪ Are the images static or kinetic?
>
> ▪ How do the poem's images help to convey its theme?
>
> ▪ How effective are the images? How do they enhance your enjoyment of the poem?

WRITING SUGGESTIONS: Imagery

1. Read the definition of **haiku** on page 656. How are short poems such as "Some Good Things to Be Said for the Iron Age" (p. 565) and "In a Station of the Metro" (p. 564) like and unlike haiku?

2. After rereading "Cloud Painter" (p. 560) and "The Great Figure" (p. 565), read "Musée des Beaux Arts" (p. 696), and study the corresponding paintings *Landscape, Noon, the Haywain* (p. 562), *The Figure 5 in Gold* (p. 566), and *Landscape with the Fall of Icarus* (p. 697). Then, write an essay in which you draw some conclusions about the differences between artistic and poetic images. If you like, you may also consider the pictures and poems in the Poetry Sampler: Poetry and Art, PS1–PS8.

3. Analyze the role of imagery in the depiction of the parent/child relationships in "My Papa's Waltz" (p. 705) and "Digging" (p. 706). How does each poem's imagery convey the nature of the relationship it describes?

4. Write an essay in which you discuss the color imagery in "Nothing Gold Can Stay" (p. 569). In what way does color reinforce the theme of the poems?

CHAPTER 19

FIGURES OF SPEECH

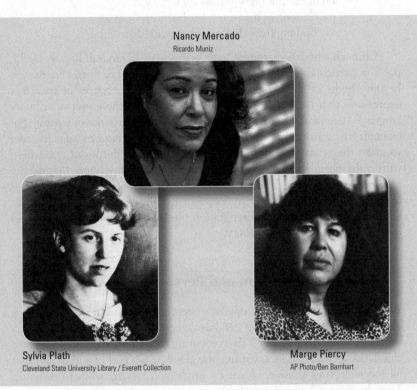

Nancy Mercado
Ricardo Muniz

Sylvia Plath
Cleveland State University Library / Everett Collection

Marge Piercy
AP Photo/Ben Barnhart

WILLIAM SHAKESPEARE (1564–1616)

Shall I compare thee to a summer's day? (1609)

Source: ©Bettmann/Corbis

Shall I compare thee to a summer's day?
Thou art more lovely and more temperate.
Rough winds do shake the darling buds of May,
And summer's lease hath all too short a date.

575

Sometime too hot the eye of heaven shines,   5
And often is his gold complexion dimmed;
And every fair from fair sometimes declines,
By chance, or nature's changing course, untrimmed.
But thy eternal summer shall not fade,
Nor lose possession of that fair thou ow'st;[1]   10
Nor shall death brag thou wand'rest in his shade,
When in eternal lines to time thou grow'st.
        So long as men can breathe or eyes can see,
        So long lives this, and this gives life to thee.

 Although writers experiment with language in all kinds of literary works, poets in particular recognize the power of a figure of speech to take readers beyond the literal meaning of a word. For this reason, **figures of speech**—expressions that use words to achieve effects beyond the power of ordinary language—are more prominent in poetry than in other kinds of writing. For example, the sonnet above compares a loved one to a summer's day in order to make the point that, unlike the fleeting summer, the loved one will—within the poem—remain forever young. But this sonnet goes beyond the obvious equation (loved one = summer's day): the speaker's assertion that his loved one will live forever in his poem actually says more about his confidence in his own talent and reputation (and about the power of language) than about the loved one's beauty.

 ## Simile, Metaphor, and Personification

When William Wordsworth opens a poem with "I wandered lonely as a cloud" (p. 712), he conveys a good deal more than he would if he simply began, "I wandered, lonely." By comparing himself in his loneliness to a cloud, the speaker suggests that like the cloud he is a part of nature and that he too is drifting, passive, blown by winds, and lacking will or substance. Thus, by using a figure of speech, the poet can suggest a wide variety of feelings and associations in very few words.

 The phrase "I wandered lonely as a cloud" is a **simile**, a comparison between two unlike items that uses *like* or *as*. When an imaginative comparison between two unlike items does not use *like* or *as*—that is, when it says "a *is* b" rather than "a is *like* b"—it is a **metaphor**.

 Accordingly, when the speaker in Adrienne Rich's "Living in Sin" (p. 538) speaks of "daylight coming / like a relentless milkman up the stairs," she is using a strikingly original simile to suggest that daylight brings not the conventional associations of promise and awakening but rather a stale, never-ending

---

[1] *that fair thou ow'st:* That beauty you possess.

routine that is greeted without enthusiasm. This idea is consistent with the rest of the poem, an account of an unfulfilling relationship. However, when the speaker in the Audre Lorde poem on page 579 says, "Rooming houses are old women," she uses a metaphor, equating two elements to stress their common associations with emptiness, transience, and hopelessness. At the same time, by identifying rooming houses as old women, Lorde is using **personification**, a special kind of comparison, closely related to metaphor, that gives life or human characteristics to inanimate objects or abstract ideas.

Sometimes, as in Wordsworth's "I wandered lonely as a cloud," a single brief simile or metaphor can be appreciated for what it communicates on its own. At other times, however, a simile or metaphor may be one of several related figures of speech that work together to convey a poem's meaning. The following poem, for example, presents a series of related similes. Together, they suggest the depth of the problem the poem explores in a manner that each individual simile could not do on its own.

Harlem street scene, 1957
AP Images/Robert Kradin

LANGSTON HUGHES (1902–1967)

Harlem (1951)

What happens to a dream deferred?

Does it dry up
like a raisin in the sun?
Or fester like a sore—
And then run?   5
Does it stink like rotten meat?
Or crust and sugar over—
like a syrupy sweet?

Maybe it just sags
like a heavy load.   10

Or does it explode?

The dream to which Hughes alludes in this poem is the dream of racial equality. It is also the American Dream—and, by extension, any important unrealized dream. His speaker offers six tentative answers to the question asked in the poem's first line, and five of the six are presented as similes. As the poem unfolds, the speaker considers different alternatives: the dream can shrivel up and die, fester, decay, crust over—or sag under the weight of the burden those who hold the dream must carry. In each case, the speaker transforms an abstract entity—a dream—into a concrete item—a raisin in the sun, a sore, rotten meat, syrupy candy, a heavy load. The final line, italicized for emphasis, gains power less from what it says than from what it leaves unsaid. Unlike the other alternatives explored in the poem, *"Or does it explode?"* is not presented as a simile. Nevertheless, because of the pattern of figurative language the poem has established, readers can supply the other, unspoken half of the comparison: "… like a bomb."

Sometimes a single extended simile or extended metaphor is developed throughout a poem. The following poem develops an **extended simile**, comparing a poet to an acrobat.

LAWRENCE FERLINGHETTI (1919–   )

Constantly Risking Absurdity (1958)

Constantly risking absurdity
              and death
   whenever he performs
        above the heads
            of his audience   5
  the poet like an acrobat
         climbs on rime
         to a high wire of his own making
  and balancing on eyebeams
         above a sea of faces   10
      paces his way
        to the other side of day
    performing entrechats
        and sleight-of-foot tricks
 and other high theatrics   15
        and all without mistaking
      any thing
        for what it may not be

     For he's the super realist
         who must perforce perceive   20
      taut truth
        before the taking of each stance or step
 in his supposed advance
        toward that still higher perch
 where Beauty stands and waits   25
        with gravity
         to start her death-defying leap
 And he
     a little charleychaplin man
        who may or may not catch   30
 her fair eternal form
       spreadeagled in the empty air
  of existence

In his extended comparison of a poet and an acrobat, Ferlinghetti characterizes the poet as a circus performer, at once swinging recklessly on a trapeze and balancing carefully on a tightrope.

What the poem suggests is that the poet, like an acrobat, works hard at his craft but manages to make it all look easy. Something of an exhibitionist, the poet is innovative and creative, taking impossible chances yet also building on traditional skills in his quest for truth and beauty. Moreover, like an acrobat, the poet is balanced "on eyebeams / above a sea of faces," for he too depends on audience reaction to help him keep his performance focused. The poet may be "the super realist," but he also has plenty of playful tricks up his sleeve: "entrechats / and sleight-of-foot tricks / and other high theatrics," including puns ("above the heads / of his audience"), unexpected rhyme ("climbs on rime"), alliteration ("taut truth"), coinages ("a little charleychaplin man"), and all the other linguistic acrobatics available to poets. (Even the arrangement of the poem's lines on the page suggests the acrobatics it describes.) Like these tricks, the poem's central simile is a whimsical one, perhaps suggesting that Ferlinghetti is poking fun at poets who take their craft too seriously. In any case, the simile helps him to illustrate the acrobatic possibilities of language in a fresh and original manner.

The following poem develops an **extended metaphor**, personifying rooming houses as old women.

AUDRE LORDE (1934–1992)

Rooming houses are old women (1968)

Rooming houses are old women
rocking dark windows into their whens
waiting incomplete circles
rocking
rent office to stoop to   5
community bathrooms to gas rings and
under-bed boxes of once useful garbage
city issued with a twice monthly check
and the young men next door
with their loud midnight parties   10
and fishy rings left in the bathtub
no longer arouse them
from midnight to mealtime no stops inbetween
light breaking to pass through jumbled up windows
and who was it who married the widow that Buzzie's   15
    son messed with?

> To Welfare and insult form the slow shuffle
> from dayswork to shopping bags
> heavy with leftovers
> Rooming houses
> are old women waiting   20
> searching
> through darkening windows
> the end or beginning of agony
> old women seen through half-ajar doors
> hoping   25
> they are not waiting
> but being
> the entrance to somewhere
> unknown and desired
> but not new.   30

So closely does Lorde equate rooming houses and old women in this poem that at times it is difficult to tell which of the two is actually the poem's subject. Despite the poem's assertion, rooming houses are *not* old women; however, they are *comparable to* the old women who live there because their walls enclose a lifetime of disappointments as well as the physical detritus of life. Like the old women, rooming houses are in decline, rocking away their remaining years. And, like the houses they inhabit, these women's boundaries are fixed—"rent office to stoop to / community bathrooms to gas rings"—and their hopes and expectations are few. They are surrounded by other people's loud parties, but their own lives have been reduced to a "slow shuffle" to nowhere, a hopeless, frightened—and perhaps pointless—"waiting / searching." Over time, the women and the places in which they live have become one. By using an unexpected comparison between two seemingly unrelated entities, the poem illuminates both the essence of the rooming houses and the essence of their elderly occupants.

FURTHER READING: Simile, Metaphor, and Personification

ROBERT BURNS (1759–1796)

Oh, my love is like a red, red rose (1796)

> Oh, my love is like a red, red rose
>   That's newly sprung in June;
> My love is like the melody
>   That's sweetly played in tune.

So fair art thou, my bonny lass,   5
   So deep in love am I;
And I will love thee still, my dear,
   Till a' the seas gang[1] dry.

Till a' the seas gang dry, my dear,
   And the rocks melt wi' the sun;   10
And I will love thee still, my dear,
   While the sands o' life shall run.

And fare thee weel, my only love!
   And fare thee weel awhile!
And I will come again, my love   15
   Though it were ten thousand mile.

Reading and Reacting

1. Why does the speaker compare his love to a rose? What other simile is used in the poem? For what purpose is it used?

2. Why do you suppose Burns begins his poem with similes? Would moving them to the end change the poem's impact?

3. Where does the speaker seem to exaggerate the extent of his love? Why does he exaggerate? Do you think this exaggeration weakens the poem? Explain.

4. **JOURNAL ENTRY** Create ten original similes that begin with, "My love is like _____."

Related Works: "Araby" (p. 288), "Baca Grande" (p. 545), "My mistress' eyes are nothing like the sun" (p. 572), "To His Coy Mistress" (p. 594), "How Do I Love Thee?" (p. 719), *The Brute* (p. 814)

AP Images/Jacques Brinon

N. SCOTT MOMADAY (1934–   )

Simile (1974)

What did we say to each other
that now we are as the deer
who walk in single file
with heads high
with ears forward   5

---

[1]*gang:* Go.

with eyes watchful
with hooves always placed on firm ground
in whose limbs there is latent flight

Reading and Reacting

1. In what sense are the speaker and the person he is speaking to like the deer he describes in this extended simile? In what sense are their limbs in "latent flight" (line 8)?
2. Without using similes or metaphors, paraphrase this poem.
3. This entire poem consists of a single sentence, but it has no punctuation. Do you see this as a problem? What punctuation marks, if any, would you add? Why?
4. JOURNAL ENTRY What do you suppose the speaker and the person he addresses might have said to each other to inspire the feelings described in this poem?

Related Work: "Let me not to the marriage of true minds" (p. 785)

SYLVIA PLATH (1932–1963)

Metaphors (1960)

I'm a riddle in nine syllables,
An elephant, a ponderous house,
A melon strolling on two tendrils.
O red fruit, ivory, fine timbers!
This loaf's big with its yeasty rising.   5
Money's new-minted in this fat purse.
I'm a means, a stage, a cow in calf.
I've eaten a bag of green apples,
Boarded the train there's no getting off.

Reading and Reacting

1. The speaker in this poem is a pregnant woman. Do all the metaphors she uses to characterize herself seem appropriate? For instance, in what sense is the speaker "a means, a stage" (line 7)?
2. If you were going to expand this poem, what other metaphors (or similes) would you add?
3. What are the "nine syllables" to which the speaker refers in the poem's first line? What significance does the number *nine* have in terms of the poem's subject? in terms of its form?

4. JOURNAL ENTRY Would you say the speaker has a positive, negative, or neutral attitude toward her pregnancy? Which metaphors give you this impression?

Related Work: "I Stand Here Ironing" (p. 217)

RANDALL JARRELL (1914–1965)

The Death of the Ball Turret Gunner[1] (1945)

From my mother's sleep I fell into the State
And I hunched in its belly till my wet fur froze.
Six miles from earth, loosed from its dream of life,
I woke to black flak and the nightmare fighters.
When I died they washed me out of the turret with a hose.   5

Gunner in ball turret
Source: ©Cape Canaveral Hangar, United States Air Force

Reading and Reacting

1. Who is the speaker? To what does he compare himself in the poem's first two lines? What words establish this comparison?
2. Contrast the speaker's actual identity with the one he creates for himself in lines 1–2. What elements of his actual situation do you think lead him to characterize himself as he does in these lines?

---

[1]*Ball turret gunner:* World War II machine gunner positioned upside-down in a plexiglass sphere in the belly of a bomber.

3. **JOURNAL ENTRY** Both this poem and "Dulce et Decorum Est" (p. 723) use figures of speech to describe the horrors of war. Which poem has a greater impact on you? How does the poem's figurative language contribute to this impact?

4. **CRITICAL PERSPECTIVE** In a 1974 article, Frances Ferguson criticizes "The Death of the Ball Turret Gunner," arguing that the poem "thoroughly manifests the lack of a middle between the gunner's birth and his death.... Because the poem presents a man who seems to have lived in order to die, we forget the fiction that he must have lived." However, in a 1978 explication, Patrick J. Horner writes that the "manipulation of time reveals the stunning brevity of the gunner's waking life and the State's total disregard for that phenomenon.... Because of the telescoping of time, [the poem] resonates with powerful feeling."

  With which critic do you agree? Do you see the "lack of a middle" as a positive or negative quality of this poem?

Related Works: "The Things They Carried" (p. 310), "The Soldier" (p. 725), from *In Time of War* (p. 727), "Terza Rima" (p. 729)

MARGE PIERCY (1936–   )

The Secretary Chant (1973)

My hips are a desk.
From my ears hang
chains of paper clips.
Rubber bands form my hair.
My breasts are wells of mimeograph ink.   5
My feet bear casters.
Buzz. Click.
My head is a badly organized file.
My head is a switchboard
where crossed lines crackle.   10
Press my fingers
and in my eyes appear
credit and debit.
Zing. Tinkle.
My navel is a reject button.   15
From my mouth issue canceled reams.
Swollen, heavy, rectangular
I am about to be delivered
of a baby

Xerox machine.   20
File me under W
because I wonce
was
a woman.

Secretaries in typing pool, 1956
© TopFoto / The Image Works

Reading and Reacting

1. Examine each of the poem's figures of speech. Do they all make reasonable comparisons, or are some far-fetched or hard to visualize? Explain
   the relationship between the secretary and each item with which she is
   compared.

2. **JOURNAL ENTRY** Using as many metaphors and similes as you can, write a
   "chant" about a job you have held.

3. **CRITICAL PERSPECTIVE** In a review of a recent collection of Piercy's poetry,
   critic Sandra Gilbert notes instances of "a kind of bombast" (pompous
   language) and remarks, "As most poets realize, political verse is almost
   the hardest kind to write."

   In what sense can "The Secretary Chant" be seen as "political verse"?
   Do you think Piercy successfully achieves her political purpose, or does
   she undercut it with "bombast"?

Related Works: "A&P" (p. 160), "The Carpet Factory" (p. 643), *Applicant*
(p. 840)

JOHN DONNE (1572–1631)

A Valediction: Forbidding Mourning (1611)

As virtuous men pass mildly away,
    And whisper to their souls to go,
Whilst some of their sad friends do say
    The breath goes now, and some say no:

So let us melt, and make no noise,   5
    No tear-floods, nor sigh-tempests move;
'Twere profanation of our joys
    To tell the laity[1] our love.

Moving of th' earth brings harms and fears;
    Men reckon what it did and meant;   10
But trepidation of the spheres,
    Though greater far, is innocent.

Dull sublunary lovers' love
    (Whose soul is sense) cannot admit
Absence, because it doth remove   15
    Those things which elemented it.

But we, by a love so much refined
    That ourselves know not what it is,
Inter-assurèd of the mind,
    Care less, eyes, lips, and hands to miss.   20

Our two souls, therefore, which are one,
    Though I must go, endure not yet
A breach, but an expansion,
    Like gold to airy thinness beat.

If they be two, they are two so   25
    As stiff twin compasses[2] are two:
Thy soul, the fixed foot, makes no show
    To move, but doth, if th' other do.

And though it in the center sit,
    Yet when the other far doth roam,   30
It leans and harkens after it,
    And grows erect as that comes home.

---

[1] *laity:* Here, "common people."

[2] *compasses:* V-shaped instruments used for drawing circles.

Such wilt thou be to me, who must,
  Like th' other foot, obliquely run;
Thy firmness makes my circle just,[3]   35
  And makes me end where I begun.

A TRADE-MARK.

Engraving of compass

Reading and Reacting

1. Beginning with line 25, the poem develops an extended metaphor that compares the speaker and his loved one to "twin compasses" (line 26), attached yet separate. Why is the compass (pictured above) an especially apt metaphor? What physical characteristics of the compass does the poet emphasize?

2. The poem uses other figures of speech to characterize both the lovers' union and their separation. To what other events does the speaker compare his separation from his loved one? To what other elements does he compare their attachment? Do you think these comparisons make sense?

---

[3] *just:* Perfect.

3. JOURNAL ENTRY To what other object could Donne have compared his loved one and himself? Explain the logic of the extended metaphor you suggest.

4. CRITICAL PERSPECTIVE In *John Donne and the Metaphysical Poets* (1970), Judah Stampfer writes of this poem's "thin, dry texture, its stanzas of pinched music," noting that its form "has too clipped a brevity to qualify as a song" and that its "music wobbles on a dry, measured beat." Yet, he argues, "the poem comes choked with emotional power" because "the speaker reads as a naturally reticent man, leaving his beloved in uncertainty and deep trouble." Stampfer concludes, "Easy self-expression here would be self-indulgent, if not reprehensible.... For all his careful dignity, we feel a heart is breaking here."

Do you find such emotional power in this highly intellectual poem?

Related Works: "To My Dear and Loving Husband" (p. 593), "How Do I Love Thee?" (p. 719), *A Doll House* (p. 881) *Post-its* (p. 955)

Hyperbole and Understatement

Two additional kinds of figurative language, *hyperbole* and *understatement*, also give poets opportunities to suggest meaning beyond the literal level of language.

Hyperbole is intentional exaggeration—saying more than is actually meant. In the poem "Oh, my love is like a red, red rose" (p. 580), when the speaker says that he will love his lady until all the seas go dry, he is using hyperbole.

Understatement is the opposite—saying less than is meant. When the speaker in the poem "Fire and Ice" (p. 510), weighing two equally grim alternatives for the end of the world, says that "for destruction ice / Is also great / And would suffice," he is using understatement. In both cases, the poets expect their readers to understand that their words are not to be taken literally.

By using hyperbole and understatement, poets enhance the impact of their poems. For example, poets can use hyperbole to convey exaggerated anger or graphic images of horror—and to ridicule and satirize as well as to inflame and shock. With understatement, poets can convey the same kind of powerful emotions subtly, without artifice or embellishment, thereby leading readers to read more closely than they might otherwise.

The emotionally charged poem that follows uses hyperbole to convey anger and bitterness that seem almost beyond the power of words.

© Cleveland State University Library / Everett Collection

SYLVIA PLATH (1932–1963)

Daddy (1965)

You do not do, you do not do
Any more, black shoe
In which I have lived like a foot
For thirty years, poor and white,
Barely daring to breathe or Achoo.   5

Daddy, I have had to kill you.
You died before I had time—
Marble-heavy, a bag full of God,
Ghastly statue with one grey toe
Big as a Frisco seal   10

And a head in the freakish Atlantic
Where it pours bean green over blue
In the waters off beautiful Nauset.
I used to pray to recover you.
Ach, du.[1]   15

In the German tongue, in the Polish town[2]
Scraped flat by the roller
Of wars, wars, wars.
But the name of the town is common.
My Polack friend   20

Says there are a dozen or two.
So I never could tell where you
Put your foot, your root,
I never could talk to you.
The tongue stuck in my jaw.   25

It stuck in a barb wire snare.
Ich, ich, ich, ich,[3]
I could hardly speak.
I thought every German was you.
And the language obscene   30

An engine, an engine
Chuffing me off like a Jew.

[1] *Ach, du:* "Ah, you" (German).
[2] *Polish town:* Grabôw, where Plath's father was born.
[3] *ich:* "I" (German).

A Jew to Dachau, Auschwitz, Belsen.[4]
I began to talk like a Jew.
I think I may well be a Jew.   35

The snows of the Tyrol, the clear beer of Vienna
Are not very pure or true.
With my gypsy ancestress and my weird luck
And my Taroc pack and my Taroc pack
I may be a bit of a Jew.   40

I have always been scared of *you*,
With your Luftwaffe,[5] your gobbledygoo.
And your neat moustache
And your Aryan eye, bright blue.
Panzer[6]-man, panzer-man, O You—   45

Not God but a swastika
So black no sky could squeak through.
Every woman adores a Fascist,
The boot in the face, the brute
Brute heart of a brute like you.   50

You stand at the blackboard, daddy,
In the picture I have of you,
A cleft in your chin instead of your foot
But no less a devil for that, no not
Any less the black man who   55

Bit my pretty red heart in two.
I was ten when they buried you.
At twenty I tried to die
And get back, back, back to you.
I thought even the bones would do.   60

But they pulled me out of the sack,
And they stuck me together with glue.
And then I knew what to do.
I made a model of you,
A man in black with a Meinkampf[7] look   65

And a love of the rack and the screw.
And I said I do, I do.

---

[4] *Dachau, Auschwitz, Belsen:* Nazi concentration camps.

[5] *Luftwaffe:* The German air force.

[6] *Panzer:* Protected by armor. The Panzer division was the German armored division.

[7] *Meinkampf: Mein Kampf* (My Struggle) is Adolf Hitler's autobiography.

So daddy, I'm finally through.
The black telephone's off at the root,
The voices just can't worm through.   70

If I've killed one man, I've killed two—
The vampire who said he was you
And drank my blood for a year,
Seven years, if you want to know.
Daddy, you can lie back now.   75

There's a stake in your fat black heart
And the villagers never liked you.
They are dancing and stamping on you.
They always *knew* it was you.
Daddy, daddy, you bastard, I'm through.   80

Nazi poster, 1941
Hulton Archive/Archive Photos/Getty Images

In her anger and frustration, the speaker sees herself as a helpless victim—a foot entrapped in a shoe, a Jew in a concentration camp—of her father's (and, later, her husband's) absolute tyranny. Thus, her hated father is characterized as a "black shoe," "a bag full of God," a "Ghastly statue," and, eventually, a Nazi, a torturer, the devil, a vampire. The poem "Daddy" is widely accepted by scholars as autobiographical, and the fact that Plath's own father was actually neither a Nazi nor a sadist (nor, obviously, the devil or a vampire) makes it clear that the figures of speech in the poem are wildly exaggerated. Even so, they may convey the poet's true feelings toward her father—and, perhaps, toward the patriarchal society in which she lived.

Plath uses hyperbole to communicate these emotions to readers who she knows cannot possibly feel the way she does. Her purpose, therefore, is not only to shock but also to enlighten, to persuade, and perhaps even to empower her readers. Throughout the poem, the inflammatory language is set in ironic opposition to the childish, affectionate term "Daddy"—most strikingly in the last line's choked out "Daddy, daddy, you bastard, I'm through." The result of the exaggerated rhetoric is a poem that is vivid and shocking. And, although some might believe that Plath's almost wild exaggeration undermines the poem's impact, others would argue that the powerful language is necessary to convey the extent of the speaker's rage.

Like "Daddy," the following poem describes a situation whose emotional impact is devastating. In this case, however, the poet does not use highly charged language; instead, she uses understatement, presenting her imagined scenario without embellishment.

EDNA ST. VINCENT MILLAY (1892–1950)

If I should learn, in some quite casual way (1931)

If I should learn, in some quite casual way,
That you were gone, not to return again—
Read from the back-page of a paper, say,
Held by a neighbor in a subway train,
How at a corner of this avenue   5
And such a street (so are the papers filled)
A hurrying man—who happened to be you—
At noon today had happened to be killed,
I should not cry aloud—could not cry
Aloud, or wring my hands in such a place—   10
I should but watch the station lights rush by
With a more careful interest on my face,
Or raise my eyes and read with greater care
Where to store furs and how to treat the hair.

Although this poem's speaker imagines a tragic scenario—receiving the news of her lover's death—her language is restrained. In the poem's first eight lines, words and expressions like "quite casual" (1), "say" (3), "this avenue / And such a street" (5–6), and "happened to be" (7, 8) convey a sense of randomness. The speaker's voice is detached and passive. In the remaining six lines, which describe her reaction to the news, she calmly explains her unwillingness to make a scene, telling what she will not do—"cry / Aloud, or wring my hands…" (9–10)—and expressing her determination to adopt an air of studied interest in the subway car's trivial advertisements. The poem's language and tone are consistently flat and unemotional, conveying a sense of detachment and resignation.

FURTHER READING: Hyperbole and Understatement

ANNE BRADSTREET (1612–1672)

To My Dear and Loving Husband (1678)

If ever two were one, then surely we.
If ever man were lov'd by wife, then thee;
If ever wife was happy in a man,
Compare with me ye women if you can.
I prize thy love more than whole Mines of gold,   5
Or all the riches that the East doth hold.
My love is such that Rivers cannot quench,
Nor ought but love from thee, give recompense.
Thy love is such I can no way repay,
The heavens reward thee manifold I pray.   10
Then while we live, in love let's so persever,
That when we live no more, we may live ever.

Reading and Reacting

1. Review the claims the poem's speaker makes about her love in lines 5–8. Are such exaggerated declarations of love necessary, or would the rest of the poem be sufficient to convey the extent of her devotion to her husband?

2. **JOURNAL ENTRY** Compare this poem's declarations of love to those of John Donne's speaker in "A Valediction: Forbidding Mourning" (p. 586). Which speaker do you find more convincing? Why?

Related Works: "A Rose for Emily" (p. 143), "How Do I Love Thee?" (p. 719), "Let me not to the marriage of true minds" (p. 785)

ANDREW MARVELL (1621–1678)

To His Coy Mistress (1681)

Had we but world enough and time,
This coyness, lady, were no crime.
We would sit down and think which way
To walk, and pass our long love's day.
Thou by the Indian Ganges' side   5
Should'st rubies find; I by the tide
Of Humber[1] would complain. I would
Love you ten years before the Flood,
And you should, if you please, refuse
Till the conversion of the Jews.   10
My vegetable love should grow
Vaster than empires, and more slow.
An hundred years should go to praise
Thine eyes, and on thy forehead gaze,
Two hundred to adore each breast,   15
But thirty thousand to the rest.
An age at least to every part,
And the last age should show your heart.
For, lady, you deserve this state,
Nor would I love at lower rate.   20
    But at my back I always hear
Time's wingèd chariot hurrying near,
And yonder all before us lie
Deserts of vast eternity.
Thy beauty shall no more be found,   25
Nor in thy marble vault shall sound
My echoing song; then worms shall try
That long preserved virginity,
And your quaint honor turn to dust,
And into ashes all my lust.   30
The grave's a fine and private place,
But none, I think, do there embrace.
    Now therefore, while the youthful hue
Sits on thy skin like morning glew[2]
And while thy willing soul transpires   35
At every pore with instant fires,

Winged horses pulling chariot
Helene Rogers /Art Directors & TRIP / Alamy

---

[1] *Humber:* An estuary on the east coast of England.
[2] *glew:* Dew.

Now let us sport us while we may;
And now, like amorous birds of prey,
Rather at once our time devour
Than languish in his slow-chapped³ power.   40
Let us roll all our strength and all
Our sweetness up into one ball
And tear our pleasures with rough strife
Thorough the iron gates of life.
Thus, though we cannot make our sun   45
Stand still, yet we will make him run.

Reading and Reacting

1. In this poem, Marvell's speaker sets out to convince a reluctant woman to become his lover. In order to make his case more persuasive, he uses hyperbole, exaggerating time periods, sizes, spaces, and the possible fate of the woman if she refuses him. Identify as many examples of hyperbole as you can.

2. The tone of "To His Coy Mistress" is more whimsical than serious. Given this tone, what do you see as the purpose of Marvell's use of hyperbole?

3. JOURNAL ENTRY Using contemporary prose, paraphrase the first four lines of the poem. Then, beginning with the word *However*, compose a few new sentences of prose, continuing the argument Marvell's speaker makes.

4. CRITICAL PERSPECTIVE In her essay "Andrew Marvell's 'To His Coy Mistress': A Feminist Reading," critic Margaret Wald presents the following analysis of the poem:

> Andrew Marvell's speaker in "To His Coy Mistress" invokes Petrarchan convention, a poetic mode originating in the fourteenth century in which a male lover uses exaggerated metaphors to appeal to his female beloved. Yet Marvell alludes to such excessive—and disempowering—pining only to defy this tradition of unrequited love. Instead of respectful adulation, he offers lustful invitation; rather than anticipating rejection, he assumes sexual dominion over the eponymous "mistress." The poem is as much a celebration of his rhetorical mastery as it is of his physical conquest.

In what sense is the speaker in this poem celebrating his beloved? In what sense is he celebrating himself? Is his portrayal of his loved one entirely positive? Which elements, if any, are negative?

Related Works: "Where Are You Going, Where Have You Been?" (p. 453), "To the Virgins, to Make Much of Time" (p. 518), "The Passionate Shepherd to His Love" (p. 777), *The Brute* (p. 814)

---

³*slow-chapped:* Slowly crushing.

ROBERT FROST (1874–1963)

"Out, Out—" (1916)

The buzz saw snarled and rattled in the yard
And made dust and dropped stove-length sticks of wood,
Sweet-scented stuff when the breeze drew across it.
And from there those that lifted eyes could count
Five mountain ranges one behind the other   5
Under the sunset far into Vermont.
And the saw snarled and rattled, snarled and rattled,
As it ran light, or had to bear a load.
And nothing happened: day was all but done.
Call it a day, I wish they might have said   10
To please the boy by giving him the half hour
That a boy counts so much when saved from work.
His sister stood beside them in her apron
To tell them "Supper." At the word, the saw,
As if to prove saws knew what supper meant,   15
Leaped out at the boy's hand, or seemed to leap—
He must have given the hand. However it was,
Neither refused the meeting. But the hand!
The boy's first outcry was a rueful laugh,
As he swung toward them holding up the hand   20
Half in appeal, but half as if to keep
The life from spilling. Then the boy saw all—
Since he was old enough to know, big boy
Doing a man's work, though a child at heart—
He saw all spoiled. "Don't let him cut my hand off—   25
The doctor, when he comes. Don't let him, sister!"
So. But the hand was gone already.
The doctor put him in the dark of ether.
He lay and puffed his lips out with his breath.
And then—the watcher at his pulse took fright.   30
No one believed. They listened at his heart.
Little—less—nothing!—and that ended it.
No more to build on there. And they, since they
Were not the one dead, turned to their affairs.

Reading and Reacting

1. The poem's title is an **allusion** to a passage in Shakespeare's *Macbeth* (5.5.23–28) that addresses the brevity and meaninglessness of life in very emotional terms:

> Out, out brief candle!
> Life's but a walking shadow, a poor player,
> That struts and frets his hour upon the stage
> And then is heard no more. It is a tale
> Told by an idiot, full of sound and fury,
> Signifying nothing.

What idea do you think Frost wants to convey through the title "Out, Out—"?

2. Explain why each of the following qualifies as understatement:

- "Neither refused the meeting." (line 18)
- "He saw all spoiled." (line 25)
- "—and that ended it." (line 32)
- "No more to build on there." (line 33)

Can you identify any other examples of understatement in the poem?

3. JOURNAL ENTRY Do you think the poem's impact is strengthened or weakened by its understated tone?

4. CRITICAL PERSPECTIVE In an essay on Frost in his book *Affirming Limits*, poet and critic Robert Pack focuses on the single word "So" in line 27 of "Out, Out—":

> For a moment, his narration is reduced to the impotent word "So," and in that minimal word all his restrained grief is held.... That "So" is the narrator's cry of bearing witness to a story that must be what it is in a scene he cannot enter. He cannot rescue or protect the boy.... In the poem's sense of human helplessness in an indifferent universe, we are all "watchers," and what we see is death without redemption, "signifying nothing." So. So? So! How shall we read that enigmatic word?

How do you read this "enigmatic word"? Why?

Related Works: "The Lottery" (p. 335), "The Death of the Ball Turret Gunner" (p. 583), "Terza Rima" (p. 729)

COUNTEE CULLEN (1903–1946)

Incident (1925)

Once riding in old Baltimore,
Heart-filled, head-filled with glee;
I saw a Baltimorean
Keep looking straight at me.

Now I was eight and very small,   5
And he was no whit bigger,

And so I smiled, but he poked out
His tongue, and called me, "Nigger."

I saw the whole of Baltimore
From May until December;   10
Of all the things that happened there
That's all that I remember.

Reading and Reacting

1. This poem's last two lines are extremely understated. What words or lines in the poem are *not* understated? Does this use of both direct and understated language make sense? Explain.

2. What do you think the speaker might be referring to by "all the things that happened" in Baltimore (11)? Why?

3. **JOURNAL ENTRY** Retell the events of this poem in a paragraph, paraphrasing lines 1–10 but quoting the last two lines exactly. Include a few sentences that reveal the speaker's emotions.

4. **CRITICAL PERSPECTIVE** According to critic Jervis Anderson, Countee Cullen, although one of the most prominent African American poets of his time, placed relatively little emphasis in his work on race and racial politics:

> Cullen did not, could not, avoid entirely the question of race. But his view of himself as a poet did not permit him to make that question his main subject.... Usually, Cullen engaged the race problem obliquely—at times with deft jabs and glancing blows. . . at times with understated amusement, as in "Incident."

Do you agree with Anderson that in "Incident," Cullen deals with race with "understated amusement." What evidence for or against this interpretation do you see in the poem?

Related Works: "Big Black Good Man" (p. 236), "Negro" (p. 502), "Ethel's Sestina" (p. 649), "Yet Do I Marvel" (p. 690), "If We Must Die" (p. 778)

MARGARET ATWOOD (1939–   )

You fit into me   (1971)

you fit into me
like a hook into an eye

a fish hook
an open eye

Reading and Reacting

1. What positive connotations does Atwood expect readers to associate with the phrase "you fit into me"? What does the speaker seem at first to mean by "like a hook into an eye" in line 2?

2. The speaker's shift to the brutal suggestions of lines 3 and 4 is calculated to shock readers. Does the use of hyperbole here have another purpose in the context of the poem? Explain.

3. JOURNAL ENTRY Do you find this poem unsettling? Do you think it is serious or just a joke?

Related Works: "Hills Like White Elephants" (p. 74), "Love and Other Catastrophes: A Mix Tape" (p. 84), "Daddy" (p. 589), *A Doll House* (p. 881)

 Metonymy and Synecdoche

Metonymy and synecdoche are two related figures of speech. **Metonymy** is the substitution of the name of one thing for the name of another thing that most readers associate with the first—for example, using *hired gun* to mean "paid assassin" or *suits* to mean "business executives." A specific kind of metonymy, called **synecdoche**, is the substitution of a part for the whole (for example, using *wheels* to refer to an automobile or *bread*—as in "Give us this day our daily bread"—to mean "food") or the whole for a part (for example, using *the law* to refer to a police officer).

With metonymy and synecdoche, instead of describing something by saying it is like something else (as in simile) or by equating it with something else (as in metaphor), writers can characterize an object or concept by using a term that evokes it. The following poem illustrates the use of synecdoche.

RICHARD LOVELACE (1618–1658)

To Lucasta Going to the Wars (1649)

Tell me not, Sweet, I am unkind
    That from the nunnery
Of thy chaste breast and quiet mind,
    To war and arms I fly.

True, a new mistress now I chase,   5
    The first foe in the field;
And with a stronger faith embrace
    A sword, a horse, a shield.

Yet this inconstancy is such
        As you too shall adore;   10
I could not love thee, Dear, so much,
        Loved I not Honor more.

Prince Rupert's cavalry charging at Edgehill, 1642
The Print Collector / HIP / The Image Works

Here, Lovelace's use of synecdoche allows him to condense a number of complex ideas into a very few words. In line 3, when the speaker says that he is flying from his loved one's "chaste breast and quiet mind," he is using "breast" and "mind" to stand for all his loved one's physical and intellectual attributes. In line 8, when he says that he is embracing "A sword, a horse, a shield," he is using these three items to represent the trappings of war—and, thus, to represent war itself.

 ## Apostrophe

With **apostrophe**, a poem's speaker addresses an absent person or thing—for example, a historical or literary figure or even an inanimate object or an abstract concept.

In the following poem, the speaker addresses the Twin Towers of the World Trade Center, destroyed in the terrorist attacks of September 11, 2001.

NANCY MERCADO (1959–   )

Going to Work (2001)

On their daily trips
Commuters shed tears now
Use American flags
Like veiled women
To hide their sorrows   5
Rush to buy throwaway cameras
To capture your twin ghosts

Frantically I too
Purchase your memory
On postcards & coffee mugs   10
In New York City souvenir shops
Afraid I'll forget your facade
Forget my hallowed Sunday
Morning PATH Train rides
My subway travels through   15
The center of your belly
Day after day

Afraid I'll forget your powers
To transform helicopters
Into ladybugs gliding in the air   20
To turn New York City
Into a breathing map
To display the curvature
Of our world

In "Going to Work," the poem's speaker describes her reactions in the aftermath of the September 11th attacks and remembers how, before the towers were destroyed, she traveled to work on the PATH (Port Authority Trans-Hudson) train that ran beneath them. Now, she says, commuters "Rush to buy throwaway cameras / To capture your twin ghosts." She continues, "Frantically I too / Purchase your memory" in the form of souvenirs. In the speaker's mind, the towers loom large; despite her fears, there is little danger of her forgetting them. In their remembered size and power, they still "display the curvature / Of our world."

FURTHER READING: Apostrophe

JOHN KEATS (1795–1821)

Ode to a Nightingale (1819)

I

My heart aches, and a drowsy numbness pains
  My sense, as though of hemlock[1] I had drunk,
Or emptied some dull opiate[2] to the drains
  One minute past, and Lethe[3]-wards had sunk:
'Tis not through envy of thy happy lot.   5
  But being too happy in thine happiness,—
    That thou, light-wingèd Dryad[4] of the trees,
      In some melodious plot
Of beechen[5] green, and shadows numberless,
  Singest of summer in full-throated ease.   10

II

O for a draught[6] of vintage! that hath been
  Cool'd a long age in the deep-delvèd[7] earth,
Tasting of Flora[8] and the country-green,
  Dance, and Provençal[9] song, and sunburnt mirth!
O for a beaker full of the warm South!   15
  Full of the true, the blushful Hippocrene,[10]
    With beaded bubbles winking at the brim,
      And purple-stainèd mouth;
That I might drink, and leave the world unseen,
  And with thee fade away into the forest dim: 20

III

Fade far away, dissolve, and quite forget
  What thou among the leaves hast never known,
The weariness, the fever, and the fret
  Here, where men sit and hear each other groan;

---

[1] *hemlock:* A medicinal plant used as a sedative or, in higher doses, a deadly poison.

[2] *opiate:* A medicine containing opium, a substance derived from poppies, which aids sleep and relieves pain.

[3] *Lethe:* In Greek mythology, a river in Hades, the land of the dead. Those who drank its water lost all memory of the past.

[4] *Dryad:* A spirit believed to inhabit trees.

[5] *beechen:* Of or relating to a beech tree.

[6] *draught:* A large sip of liquid.

[7] *deep-delvèd:* Excavated.

[8] *Flora:* In Roman mythology, the goddess of flowers.

[9] *Provençal:* From Provence, a region of southern France.

[10] *Hippocrene:* A fountain on Mt. Helicon, in Greece, considered sacred to the Muses.

Where palsy shakes a few, sad, last grey hairs,   25
　　Where youth grows pale, and spectre-thin, and dies;
　　　Where but to think is to be full of sorrow
　　　　And leaden-eyed despairs,
　　Where beauty cannot keep her lustrous eyes,
　　　Or new Love pine at them beyond to-morrow.   30

IV

Away! away! for I will fly to thee,
　　Not charioted by Bacchus[11] and his pards,[12]
But on the viewless wings of Poesy,
　　Though the dull brain perplexes and retards:
Already with thee! tender is the night,   35
　　And haply the Queen-Moon is on her throne,
　　　Cluster'd around by all her starry Fays;[13]
　　　　But here there is no light,
Save what from heaven is with the breezes blown
　　Through verdurous[14] glooms and winding mossy ways.   40

V

I cannot see what flowers are at my feet,
　　Nor what soft incense hangs upon the boughs,
But, in embalmèd darkness, guess each sweet
　　Wherewith the seasonable month endows
The grass, the thicket, and the fruit-tree wild;   45
　　White hawthorn, and the pastoral eglantine;[15]
　　　Fast-fading violets cover'd up in leaves;
　　　　And mid-May's eldest child,
The coming musk-rose, full of dewy wine,
　　The murmurous haunt of flies on summer eves.   50

VI

Darkling I listen; and, for many a time
　　I have been half in love with easeful Death,
Call'd him soft names in many a musèd rhyme,
　　To take into the air my quiet breath;
Now more than ever seems it rich to die,   55
　　To cease upon the midnight with no pain,
　　　While thou art pouring forth the soul abroad
　　　　In such an ecstasy!
Still wouldst thou sing, and I have ears in vain—
　　To thy high requiem become a sod.   60

---

[11] *Bacchus:* The god of wine.
[12] *pards:* Leopards or panthers.
[13] *Fays:* Fairies.
[14] *verdurous:* Green with vegetation.
[15] *eglantine:* A plant also known as the sweet-briar.

VII

Thou wast not born for death, immortal Bird!
　No hungry generations tread thee down;
The voice I hear this passing night was heard
　In ancient days by emperor and clown:
Perhaps the self-same song that found a path　　　　　　　　65
　　Through the sad heart of Ruth, when, sick for home,
　　　She stood in tears amid the alien corn;[16]
　　　　The same that ofttimes hath
Charm'd magic casements,[17] opening on the foam
Of perilous seas, in faery lands forlorn.[18]　　　　　　　　70

VIII

Forlorn! the very word is like a bell
　To toll me back from thee to my sole self!
Adieu! the fancy cannot cheat so well
　As she is famed to do, deceiving elf.
Adieu![19] adieu! the plaintive anthem fades　　　　　　　　75
　　Past the near meadows, over the still stream,
　　Up the hill-side; and now 'tis buried deep
　　　In the next valley-glades:
Was it a vision, or a waking dream?
　　Fled is that music:—Do I wake or sleep?

Le Rossignol de France.

Lithograph of nightingale, c. 1830
The Nightingale of France, c.1830 (colour litho), Oudart, Paul
Louis (b.1796) (after) / Bibliotheque des Arts Decoratifs, Paris,
France / Archives Charmet / Bridgeman Images

---

[16]*corn:* Grain.
[17]*casements:* Windows.
[18]*forlorn:* Lost.
[19]*Adieu:* Farewell.

Reading and Reacting

1. Where does the speaker first address the nightingale? Where else does he speak directly to the nightingale?

2. In lines 19–20, the speaker expresses his desire to "leave the world unseen, / And with thee fade away into the forest dim...." Why does he want to "fade away"? What is it about the "forest dim" that attracts him? Give some examples from the poem to contrast the speaker's world with the world of the nightingale.

3. What is it that the speaker admires about the nightingale? In what sense does he see the nightingale as superior to human beings?

4. **JOURNAL ENTRY** If you were to write an **ode**—a long, serious, and formal poem—to a creature or an object, what would you choose as your subject? Why? How do you see your own world as different from (and inferior to) the world of your subject?

Related Works: "Young Goodman Brown" (p. 367), "The World Is Too Much with Us" (p. 516), "Death Be Not Proud" (p. 757)

ALLEN GINSBERG (1926–1997)

A Supermarket in California (1956)

What thoughts I have of you tonight, Walt Whitman,[1] for I walked down the sidestreets under the trees with a headache self-conscious looking at the full moon.

In my hungry fatigue, and shopping for images, I went into the neon fruit supermarket, dreaming of your enumerations!

What peaches and what penumbras! Whole families shopping at night! Aisles full of husbands! Wives in the avocados, babies in the tomatoes!—and you, Garcia Lorca,[2] what were you doing down by the watermelons?

I saw you, Walt Whitman, childless, lonely old grubber, poking among the meats in the refrigerator and eyeing the grocery boys.[3]

I heard you asking questions of each: Who killed the pork chops?   5
What price bananas? Are you my Angel?

---

[1] *Walt Whitman:* American poet (1819–1892) whose poems frequently praise the commonplace and often contain lengthy "enumerations."

[2] *Federico Garcia Lorca:* Spanish poet and dramatist (1899–1936).

[3] *eyeing the grocery boys:* Whitman's sexual orientation is the subject of much debate. Ginsberg is suggesting here that Whitman was homosexual.

I wandered in and out of the brilliant stacks of cans following you, and followed in my imagination by the store detective.

We strode down the open corridors together in our solitary fancy tasting artichokes, possessing every frozen delicacy, and never passing the cashier.

Where are we going, Walt Whitman? The doors close in an hour. Which way does your beard point tonight?

(I touch your book[4] and dream of our odyssey in the supermarket and feel absurd.)

Will we walk all night through solitary streets? The trees add   10
shade to shade, lights out in the houses, we'll both be lonely.

Will we stroll dreaming of the lost America of love past blue automobiles in driveways, home to our silent cottage?

Ah, dear father, graybeard, lonely old courage-teacher, what America did you have when Charon[5] quit poling his ferry and you got out on a smoking bank and stood watching the boat disappear on the black waters of Lethe?[6]

Reading and Reacting

1. In this poem, Ginsberg's speaker wanders through the aisles of a super-market, speaking to the nineteenth-century American poet Walt Whit-man and asking Whitman a series of questions. Why do you think the speaker addresses Whitman? What kind of answers do you think he is looking for?

2. In paragraph 2, the speaker says he is "shopping for images." What does he mean? Why does he look for these images in a supermarket? Does he find them?

3. Is this poem about supermarkets? about Walt Whitman? about poetry? about love? about America? What do you see as its primary theme? Why?

4. **JOURNAL ENTRY** Does the incongruous image of the respected poet "poking / among the meats" (paragraph 4) in the supermarket strengthen the poem's impact, or does it undercut any serious "message" the poem might have? Explain.

5. **CRITICAL PERSPECTIVE** The critic Leslie Fiedler discusses some of the ways in which Ginsberg's style resembles that of Walt Whitman:

---

[4]*your book: Leaves of Grass.*

[5]*Charon:* In Greek mythology, the ferryman who transported the dead over the river Styx to Hades.

[6]*Lethe:* In Greek mythology, the river of forgetfulness (one of five rivers in Hades).

Everything about Ginsberg is... blatantly Whitmanian: his meter is resolutely anti-iambic, his line groupings stubbornly anti-stanzaic, his diction aggressively colloquial and American, his voice public.

Does this characterization apply to "A Supermarket in California"? If so, how?

Related Works: "A&P" (p. 160), "Chicago" (p. 660), *from* "Out of the Cradle Endlessly Rocking" (p. 663), "Defending Walt Whitman" (p. 732), "I Hear America Singing" (p. 795), *from* "Song of Myself" (p. 796), *The Cuban Swimmer* (p. 1166)

✔ CHECKLIST   Writing about Figures of Speech

- What figures of speech are used in the poem? Identify any examples of simile, metaphor, personification, hyperbole, understatement, metonymy, synecdoche, and apostrophe.

- What two elements are being compared in each use of simile, metaphor, and personification? What characteristics are shared by the two items being compared?

- Does the poet use hyperbole? Why? For example, is it used to move or to shock readers, or is its use intended to produce a humorous or satirical effect? Would more understated language be more effective?

- Does the poet use understatement? For what purpose? Would more emotionally charged language be more effective?

- If the poem includes metonymy or synecdoche, what term is being substituted for another? To what object or concept does the term refer?

- If the poem includes apostrophe, whom or what does the speaker address? What does the use of apostrophe accomplish?

- How do figures of speech contribute to the impact of the poem as a whole?

WRITING SUGGESTIONS: Figures of Speech

1. Various figures of speech are often used to describe characters in literary works. Choose two or three works that focus on a single character—for example, "A Rose for Emily" (p. 143), "Miss Brill" (p. 166), "Gryphon" (p. 172), or "Richard Cory" (p. 783)—and explain how figures of speech are used to characterize each work's central figure. If you like, you may write about works that focus on real (rather than fictional) people.

2. Write an essay in which you discuss the different ways poets use figures of speech to examine the nature of poetry itself. What kinds of figures of speech do poets use to describe their craft? (You might begin by reading the two poems about poetry that open Chapter 15.)

3. Write a letter (or a poem) replying to the speaker in the poem by Marvell, Bradstreet, Donne, or Burns that appears in this chapter. Use figures of speech to express the depth of your love and the extent of your devotion.

4. Choose three or four poems that have a common subject—for example, love or nature—and write an essay in which you draw some general conclusions about the relative effectiveness of the poems' use of figures of speech to examine that subject. (If you like, you may focus on the poems clustered under the heads "Poems about Parents," "Poems about Nature," "Poems about Love," and "Poems about War" in Chapter 23.)

5. Select a poem and a short story that deal with the same subject, and write an essay in which you compare their use of figures of speech.

CHAPTER 20

SOUND

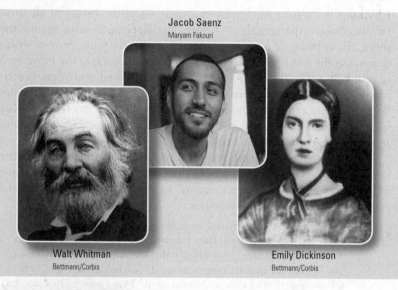

Jacob Saenz
Maryam Fakouri

Walt Whitman
Bettmann/Corbis

Emily Dickinson
Bettmann/Corbis

Detail of vase showing Achilles killing Hector

© The Trustees of the British Museum / Art Resource, NY

WALT WHITMAN (1819–1892)

Had I the Choice*

Had I the choice to tally greatest bards,
To limn[1] their portraits, stately, beautiful, and
    emulate at will,
Homer with all his wars and warriors—Hector,
    Achilles, Ajax,
Or Shakespeare's woe-entangled Hamlet, Lear,
    Othello—Tennyson's fair ladies,
Meter or wit the best, or choice conceit to
    wield in perfect   5
    rhyme, delight of singers;

*Publication date is not available.

[1] *limn:* To draw, depict.

These, these, O sea, all these I'd gladly barter,
Would you the undulation of one wave, its trick to me transfer,
Or breathe one breath of yours upon my verse,
And leave its odor there.

 ## Rhythm

Rhythm—the regular recurrence of sounds—is at the center of all natural phenomena: the beating of a heart, the lapping of waves against the shore, the croaking of frogs on a summer's night, the whispering of wheat swaying in the wind. Even mechanical phenomena, such as the movement of rush-hour traffic through a city's streets, have a kind of rhythm. Poetry, which explores these phenomena, often tries to reflect the same rhythms. Walt Whitman expresses this idea in "Had I the Choice" when he says that he would gladly trade the "perfect rhyme" of Shakespeare for the ability to reproduce "the undulation of one wave" in his verse.

Public speakers frequently repeat key words and phrases to create rhythm. In his "I Have a Dream" speech, for example, Martin Luther King Jr. repeats the phrase "I have a dream" to create a rhythm that ties the central section of the speech together:

> I say to you today, my friends, even though we face the difficulties of today and tomorrow, <u>I still have a dream.</u> It is a dream deeply rooted in the American dream. <u>I have a dream</u> that one day this nation will rise up and live out the true meaning of its creed: "We hold these truths to be self-evident, that all men are created equal." <u>I have a dream</u> that one day, on the red hills of Georgia, sons of former slaves and the sons of former slave owners will be able to sit down together at the table of brotherhood. <u>I have a dream</u> that one day even the state of Mississippi, a state sweltering with the heat of injustice, sweltering with the heat of oppression, will be transformed into an oasis of freedom and justice. <u>I have a dream</u> that my four little children will one day live in a nation where they will not be judged by the color of their skin, but by the content of their character.

Poets too create rhythm by using repeated words and phrases, as Gwendolyn Brooks does in the poem that follows.

GWENDOLYN BROOKS (1917–2000)

Sadie and Maud (1945)

Maud went to college.
Sadie stayed at home.
Sadie scraped life
With a fine-tooth comb.

She didn't leave a tangle in.   5
Her comb found every strand.
Sadie was one of the livingest chits
In all the land.

Sadie bore two babies
Under her maiden name.   10
Maud and Ma and Papa
Nearly died of shame.

When Sadie said her last so-long
Her girls struck out from home.
(Sadie had left as heritage   15
Her fine-tooth comb.)

Maud, who went to college,
Is a thin brown mouse.
She is living all alone
In this old house.   20

Much of the force of this poem comes from the repeated words "Sadie" and "Maud," which shift the focus from one subject to the other and back again ("Maud went to college / Sadie stayed home"). The poem's singsong rhythm recalls the rhymes children recite when jumping rope. This evocation of carefree childhood is ironically contrasted with the adult realities that both Sadie and Maud face as they grow up: Sadie stays at home and has two children out of wedlock; Maud goes to college and ends up "a thin brown mouse." The speaker implies that the alternatives Sadie and Maud represent are both undesirable. Although Sadie "scraped life / with a fine-tooth comb," she dies young and leaves nothing to her girls but her desire to experience life. Maud, who graduated from college, shuts out life and cuts herself off from her roots.

Just as the repetition of words and phrases can create rhythm, so can the appearance of words on the printed page. How a poem looks is especially important in **open form poetry** (see p. 660), which dispenses with traditional patterns of versification. In the following excerpt from "The Moon Is Hiding In" by E. E. Cummings, for example, an unusual arrangement of words forces readers to slow down and then to speed up, creating a rhythm that emphasizes a key phrase—"The / lily":

the moon is hiding
in her hair.
The
lily
of heaven
full of all dreams,
draws down.

Meter

Although rhythm can be affected by the regular repetition of words and phrases or by the arrangement of words into lines, poetic rhythm is largely created by **meter**, the recurrence of regular units of stressed and unstressed syllables. A **stress** (or accent) occurs when one syllable is emphasized more than another, unstressed, syllable: *fór* • *ceps, bá* • *sic, il* • *lú* • *sion, ma* • *lár* • *i* • *a*. In a poem, even one-syllable words can be stressed to create a particular effect. For example, in Elizabeth Barrett Browning's line "How do I love thee? Let me count the ways," the metrical pattern that places stress on "love" creates one meaning; stressing "I" would create another.

Scansion is the analysis of patterns of stressed and unstressed syllables within a line. The most common method of poetic notation indicates stressed syllables with a ′ and unstressed syllables with a ˘. Although scanning lines gives readers the "beat" of the poem, scansion only generally suggests the sound of spoken language, which contains an infinite variety of stresses. By providing a graphic representation of the stressed and unstressed syllables of a poem, scansion aids understanding, but it is no substitute for reading the poem aloud and experimenting with various patterns of emphasis.

The basic unit of meter is a **foot**—a group of syllables with a fixed pattern of stressed and unstressed syllables. The chart that follows illustrates the most common types of metrical feet in English and American verse.

<u>Foot</u>	<u>Stress Pattern</u>	<u>Example</u>
Iamb	˘′	They pace | in sleek | chi val | ric cer | tain ty (Adrienne Rich)
Trochee	′˘	Thou, when | thou re | turn'st, wilt | tell me. (John Donne)
Anapest	˘˘′	With a hey, | and a ho, | and a hey | no ni no (William Shakespeare)
Dactyl	′˘˘	Constantly | risking ab | surdity (Lawrence Ferlinghetti)

Iambic and *anapestic* meters are called **rising meters** because they progress from unstressed to stressed syllables. *Trochaic* and *dactylic* meters are called **falling meters** because they progress from stressed to unstressed syllables.

The following types of metrical feet, less common than those listed above, are used to add emphasis or to provide variety rather than to create the dominant meter of a poem.

Foot	Stress Pattern	Example
Spondee	′ ′	Pomp, pride | and circumstance of glorious war! (William Shakespeare)
Pyrrhic	˘˘	A horse! a horse! My king | dom for | a horse! (William Shakespeare)

A metric line of poetry is measured by the number of feet it contains.

Monometer	one foot	**Pentameter**	five feet
Dimeter	two feet	**Hexameter**	six feet
Trimeter	three feet	**Heptameter**	seven feet
Tetrameter	four feet	**Octameter**	eight feet

The name for a metrical pattern of a line of verse identifies the name of the foot used and the number of feet the line contains. For example, the most common foot in English poetry is the **iamb**, most often occurring in lines of three or five feet.

Metrical Pattern	Example
Iambic trimeter	Eight hun | dred of | the brave (William Cowper)
Iambic pentameter	O, how | much more | doth beau | ty beau | teous seem (William Shakespeare)

Because **iambic pentameter** is so well suited to the rhythms of English speech, writers frequently use it in plays and poems. Shakespeare's plays, for example, are written in unrhymed lines of iambic pentameter called **blank verse** (see pp. 635–36).

Many other metrical combinations are also possible; a few are illustrated below.

Metrical Pattern	Example
Trochaic trimeter	Like a | high-born | maiden (Percy Bysshe Shelley)
Anapestic tetrameter	The As sy | rian came down | like the wolf | on the fold (Lord Byron)
Dactylic hexameter	Maid en most | beau ti ful | moth er most | boun ti ful, | la dy of | lands, (A. C. Swinburne)
Iambic heptameter	The yel | low fog | that rubs | its back | up on | the win | dow-panes (T. S. Eliot)

Scansion can be an extremely technical process, and when readers become bogged down with anapests and dactyls, they can easily forget that poetic scansion is not an end in itself. Meter should be appropriate for the ideas expressed by the poem, and it should help to create a suitable tone. A light, skipping rhythm, for example, would be inappropriate for an **elegy**, and a slow, heavy rhythm would surely be out of place in an **epigram** or a limerick. The following lines of a poem by Samuel Taylor Coleridge illustrate the uses of different types of metrical feet:

> Trochee trips from long to short;
>
> From long to long in solemn sort
>
> Slow Spondee stalks; strong foot! yet ill able
>
> Ever to come up with Dactyl trisyllable.
>
> Iambics march from short to long—   5
>
> With a leap and a bound the swift Anapests throng;

One syllable long, with one short at each side,
Amphibrachys hastes with a stately stride—
First and last being long, middle short, Amphimacer
Strikes his thundering hoofs like a proud high-bred Racer.   10

A poet may use one kind of meter—iambic meter, for example—throughout a poem, but may occasionally vary line length to relieve monotony or to accommodate the poem's meaning or emphasis. In the following poem, the poet uses iambic lines of different lengths.

© Bettmann/Corbis

EMILY DICKINSON (1830–1886)

I like to see it lap the Miles— (1891)

I like to see it lap the Miles—
And lick the Valleys up—
And stop to feed itself at Tanks—
And then—prodigious step

Around a Pile of Mountains—   5
And supercilious peer
In Shanties—by the sides of Roads—
And then a Quarry pare

To fit its Ribs
And crawl between   10
Complaining all the while
In horrid—hooting stanza—
Then chase itself down Hill—

And neigh like Boanerges[1]—
Then—punctual as a Star   15
Stop—docile and omnipotent
At its own stable door—

Dickinson's poem is a single sentence that, except for some pauses, stretches unbroken from beginning to end. Iambic lines of varying lengths actually suggest the movements of the train that the poet describes. Lines of iambic tetrameter, such as the first, give readers a sense of the train's steady,

---

[1]*Boanerges:* A vociferous preacher and orator. Also, the name, meaning "son of thunder," Jesus gave to apostles John and James because of their fiery zeal.

rhythmic movement across a flat landscape, and shorter lines ("To fit its Ribs / And crawl between") suggest the train's slowing motion. Beginning with two iambic dimeter lines and progressing to iambic trimeter lines, the third stanza increases in speed just like the train that is racing downhill "In horrid—hooting stanza—."

When a poet uses more than one type of metrical foot, any variation in a metrical pattern—the substitution of a trochee for an iamb, for instance—immediately calls attention to itself. For example, in line 16 of "I like to see it lap the Miles," the poet departs from iambic meter by placing unexpected stress on the first word, *stop*. By emphasizing this word, the poet brings the flow of the poem to an abrupt halt, suggesting the jolt riders experience when a train comes to a stop.

Another way of varying the meter of a poem is to introduce a pause known as a **caesura**—a Latin word meaning "a cutting"—within a line. When scanning a poem, you indicate a caesura with two parallel lines: ‖. Unless a line of poetry is extremely short, it probably will contain a caesura.

A caesura occurs after a punctuation mark or at a natural break in phrasing:

> How do I love thee? ‖ Let me count the ways.
> **Elizabeth Barrett Browning**

> Two loves I have ‖ of comfort and despair.
> **William Shakespeare**

> High on a throne of royal state, ‖ which far
> Outshone the wealth of Ormus ‖ and of Ind
> **John Milton**

Sometimes more than one caesura occurs in a single line:

> 'Tis good. ‖ Go to the gate. ‖ Somebody knocks.
> **William Shakespeare**

Although the end of a line may mark the end of a metrical unit, it does not always coincide with the end of a sentence. Lines that have distinct pauses at the end—usually signaled by punctuation—are called **end-stopped lines**. Lines that do not end with strong pauses are called **run-on lines**. (Sometimes the term **enjambment** is used to describe run-on lines.) End-stopped lines can sometimes seem formal, or even forced, because their length is rigidly dictated by the poem's meter, rhythm, and rhyme scheme. In the following excerpt from John Keats's "La Belle Dame sans Merci" (p. 771), for example, rhythm, meter, and rhyme dictate the pauses that occur at the ends of the lines:

> O, what can ail thee, knight-at-arms,
>   Alone and palely loitering?

The sedge has wither'd from the lake,
  And no birds sing.

In contrast to end-stopped lines, run-on lines often seem more natural. Because their ending points are determined by the rhythms of speech and by the meaning and emphasis the poet wishes to convey rather than by meter and rhyme, run-on lines are suited to the open form of much modern poetry. In the following lines from the poem "We Have Come Home," by Lenrie Peters, run-on lines give readers the sense of spoken language:

We have come home
From the bloodless war
With sunken hearts
Our boots full of pride—
From the true massacre of the soul
When we have asked
"What does it cost
To be loved and left alone?"

Rather than relying exclusively on end-stopped or run-on lines, poets often use a combination of the two to produce the effects they want.

FURTHER READING: Rhythm and Meter

ADRIENNE RICH (1929–   )

Aunt Jennifer's Tigers (1951)

Aunt Jennifer's tigers prance across a screen,
Bright topaz denizens of a world of green.
They do not fear the men beneath the tree;
They pace in sleek chivalric certainty.[1]

Aunt Jennifer's fingers fluttering through her wool   5
Find even the ivory needle hard to pull.
The massive weight of Uncle's wedding band
Sits heavily upon Aunt Jennifer's hand.

When Aunt is dead, her terrified hands will lie
Still ringed with ordeals she was mastered by.   10
The tigers in the panel that she made
Will go on prancing, proud and unafraid.

---

[1]*chivalric certainty:* With pride and honor.

Reading and Reacting

1. What is the dominant metrical pattern of the poem? How does the meter enhance the contrast the poem develops?

2. The lines in the first stanza are end-stopped, and those in the second and third stanzas combine end-stopped and run-on lines. What does the poet achieve by varying the rhythm?

3. What ideas do the caesuras in the first and fourth lines of the last stanza emphasize?

4. **JOURNAL ENTRY** What is the speaker's opinion of Aunt Jennifer's marriage? Do you think she is commenting on this particular marriage or on marriage in general?

5. **CRITICAL PERSPECTIVE** In *The Aesthetics of Power*, Claire Keyes writes of this poem that although it is formally beautiful, almost perfect, its voice creates problems:

> [T]he tone seldom approaches intimacy, the speaker seeming fairly detached from the fate of Aunt Jennifer....The dominant voice of the poem asserts the traditional theme that art outlives the person who produces it....The speaker is almost callous in her disregard for Aunt's death....Who cares that Aunt Jennifer dies? The speaker does not seem to; she gets caught up in those gorgeous tigers....Here lies the dominant voice: Aunt is not compelling; her creation is.

Do you agree with Keyes's interpretation of the poem?

Related Works: "Miss Brill" (p. 166), "Everyday Use" (p. 344), "Rooming houses are old women" (p. 579)

THOMAS LUX (1946–   )

A Little Tooth (1989)

Your baby grows a tooth, then two,
and four, and five, then she wants some meat
directly from bone. It's all
over: she'll learn some words she'll fall
in love with cretins, dolts, a sweets   5
talker on his way to jail. And you,

your wife, get old, flyblown, and rue
nothing. You did, you loved, your feet
are sore. It's dusk. Your daughter's tall.

Reading and Reacting

1. This poem was selected to be featured in the New York City's "Poetry in Motion" program, which posts poems in public busses and trains. What qualities make "A Little Tooth" suitable for this program?

2. What is the dominant metrical pattern of this poem? Do you think this meter is an appropriate choice here? Explain.

3. Where in the poem does Lux use caesuras? What effect do these pauses have?

4. JOURNAL ENTRY "A Little Tooth" is characterized by its extreme compression. What ideas does the poem express? Does the poem effectively communicate these ideas, or does it try to do too much in too few lines?

5. CRITICAL PERSPECTIVE Writing about Thomas Lux's work in the journal *Poetry*, Peter Campion makes the following observation:

> The problem is not simply that Lux knows the course his poems will take before he begins, though this probably contributes. It's that he writes from above his material. Reading Lux you rarely sense a consciousness moving down in the lines themselves. The poems are set speeches: their odd images or turns of phrase glimmer for moments then disappear as Lux glides on toward his desired effect.

Do you feel that Campion's criticisms apply to "A Little Tooth"? Why or why not?

Related Works: "Everyday Use" (p. 344), "Doe Season" (p. 395), "Where Are You Going, Where Have You Been?" (p. 453), "Sadie and Maud" (p. 610), "Aristotle" (p. 685)

LEWIS CARROLL (1832–1898)

A Boat Beneath a Sunny Sky (1872)

A boat beneath a sunny sky,
Lingering onward dreamily
In an evening of July—

Children three that nestle near,
Eager eye and willing ear,   5
Pleased a simple tale to hear—

Long has paled that sunny sky:
Echoes fade and memories die:
Autumn frosts have slain July.

Still she haunts me, phantomwise,   10
Alice moving under skies
Never seen by waking eyes.

Children yet, the tale to hear,
Eager eye and willing ear,
Lovingly shall nestle near.   15

In a Wonderland they lie,
Dreaming as the days go by,
Dreaming as the summers die:

Ever drifting down the stream—
Lingering in the golden gleam—   20
Life, what is it but a dream?

Reading and Reacting

1. Lewis Carroll (whose real name was Charles Lutwidge Dodgson) took three young sisters (including Alice Pleasance Liddell) on a boat trip in 1862. As he rowed, he told them a story of a girl named Alice, who follows a rabbit down a rabbit hole to Wonderland. The girls—especially Alice—were so enchanted by the story, that they asked Carroll to write it down. Eventually, this story became *Alice's Adventures in Wonderland.* What specific references to this boat trip are in the poem?

2. What is the poem's primary metrical pattern? How does this pattern help establish the poem's mood?

3. Where in the poem are caesuras used? What effect does each of these pauses have?

4. What point is Carroll making about childhood? about Wonderland? What do you think Carroll means in the poem's last line: "Life, what is it but a dream?"

5. **JOURNAL ENTRY** "A Boat Beneath a Sunny Sky" is an **acrostic poem**; that is, the first letter of each line spells out a word—in this case, *Alice Pleasance Liddell.* Is this technique just a clever device, or does it somehow add to the poem? Explain.

Related Works: "Encounters with Unexpected Animals" (p. 90), "A&P" (p. 160), "Gretel in Darkness" (p. 501), "What Shall I Give My Children?" (p. 553), "One day I wrote her name upon the strand" (p. 554), "Where the Sidewalk Ends" (p. 626), "Jabberwocky" (p. 629)

Alliteration and Assonance

Just as poetry depends on rhythm, it also depends on the sounds of individual words. An effect pleasing to the ear, such as "Did he who made the Lamb make thee?" from William Blake's "The Tyger" (p. 740), is called **euphony**. A jarring or discordant effect, such as "The vorpal blade went snicker-snack!" from Lewis Carroll's "Jabberwocky" (p. 629), is called **cacophony**.

One of the earliest, and perhaps the most primitive, methods of enhancing sound is **onomatopoeia**, which occurs when the sound of a word echoes its meaning, as it does in common words such as *bang, crash,* and *hiss.* Poets make broad application of this technique by using combinations of words that suggest a correspondence between sound and meaning, as Edgar Allan Poe does in these lines from his poem "The Bells":

> Yet the ear, it fully knows,
>   By the twanging
>   And the clanging,
>   How the danger ebbs and flows;
> Yet the ear distinctly tells,
>   In the jangling
>   And the wrangling
>   How the danger sinks and swells
> By the sinking or the swelling in the anger of the bells—
>   Of the bells,—
>   Of the bells, bells, bells, bells....

Poe's primary objective in this poem is to re-create the sound of ringing bells. Although he succeeds, the aural effect throughout the 113-line poem is extremely tedious. A more subtle use of onomatopoetic words appears in the following passage from *An Essay on Criticism* by Alexander Pope:

> Soft is the strain when Zephyr gently blows,
> And the smooth stream in smoother numbers flows;
> But when the loud surges lash the sounding shore,
> The hoarse, rough verse should like the torrent roar:
> When Ajax strives some rock's vast weight to throw,
> The line too Labors, and the words move slow.

After earlier admonishing readers that sound must echo sense, Pope uses onomatopoetic words such as *lash* and *roar* to convey the fury of the sea, and he uses repeated consonants to echo the sounds these words suggest. Notice, for example, how the *s* and *m* sounds suggest the gently blowing Zephyr and the flowing of the smooth stream and how the series of *r* sounds echoes the torrent's roar.

Alliteration—the repetition of consonant sounds in consecutive or neighboring words, usually at the beginning of words—is another device used to enhance sound in a poem. Both Poe ("<u>s</u>inks and <u>s</u>wells") and Pope ("<u>s</u>mooth <u>s</u>tream") make use of alliteration in the preceding excerpts.

Assonance—the repetition of the same or similar vowel sounds, especially in stressed syllables—can also enrich a poem. When used effectively, assonance can create both mood and tone in a subtle, musical way. Consider, for example, the use of assonance in the following lines from Dylan Thomas's "Do not go gentle into that good night": "Old age should burn and rave at close of day; / Rage, rage, against the dying of the light."

Sometimes assonance unifies an entire poem. In the following poem, assonance emphasizes the thematic connections among words and thus links the poem's ideas.

ROBERT HERRICK (1591–1674)

Delight in Disorder (1648)

A sweet disorder in the dress
Kindles in clothes a wantonness.
A lawn[1] about the shoulders thrown
Into a fine distractión;
An erring lace, which here and there   5
Enthralls the crimson stomacher;[2]
A cuff neglectful, and thereby
Ribbons to flow confusedly;
A winning wave, deserving note,
In the tempestuous petticoat;   10
A careless shoestring, in whose tie
I see a wild civility;
Do more bewitch me than when art
Is too precise in every part.

Repeated vowel sounds extend throughout this poem—for instance, "sh<u>ou</u>lders" and "thr<u>ow</u>n" in line 3; and "t<u>ie</u>," "w<u>i</u>ld," and "prec<u>i</u>se" in lines 11, 12, and 14. Using alliteration as well as assonance, Herrick subtly links

---

[1] *lawn:* A shawl made of fine fabric.
[2] *stomacher:* A heavily embroidered garment worn by females over the chest and stomach.

certain words—"tem<u>pes</u>tuous pet<u>ti</u>coat," for example. By connecting these words, he calls attention to the pattern of imagery that helps to convey the poem's theme.

 ## Rhyme

In addition to alliteration and assonance, poets create sound patterns with **rhyme**—the use of matching sounds in two or more words: "tight" and "might"; "born" and "horn"; "sleep" and "deep." For a rhyme to be **perfect**, final vowel and consonant sounds must be the same, as they are in each of the preceding examples. **Imperfect rhyme** (also called *near rhyme, slant rhyme, approximate rhyme,* or **consonance**) occurs when the final consonant sounds in two words are the same but the preceding vowel sounds are different— "learn" / "barn" or "pads" / "lids," for example. Finally, **eye rhyme** occurs when two words look as if they should rhyme but do not—for example, "watch" and "catch."

Rhyme can also be classified according to the position of the rhyming syllables in a line of verse. The most common type of rhyme is **end rhyme**, which occurs at the end of a line:

> Tyger! Tyger! burning <u>bright</u>
> In the forests of the <u>night</u>
> **William Blake**, "The Tyger"

Internal rhyme occurs within a line:

> The Sun came up upon the left,
> Out of the <u>sea</u> came <u>he</u>!
> And he shone <u>bright</u> and on the <u>right</u>
> Went down into the sea.
> **Samuel Taylor Coleridge**, "The Rime of the Ancient Mariner"

Beginning rhyme occurs at the beginning of a line:

> Red river, red river,
> <u>Slow</u> flow heat is silence
> <u>No</u> will is still as a river
> **T. S. Eliot**, "Virginia"

Rhyme can also be classified according to the number of syllables that correspond. **Masculine rhyme** (also called **rising rhyme**) occurs when single syllables correspond ("can" / "ran"; "descend" / "contend"). **Feminine rhyme** (also called **double rhyme** or **falling rhyme**) occurs when two syllables, a stressed one followed by an unstressed one, correspond ("ocean" / "motion";

"leaping" / "sleeping"). **Triple rhyme** occurs when three syllables correspond. Less common than the other two, triple rhyme is often used for humorous or satiric purposes, as in the following lines from the long poem *Don Juan* by Lord Byron:

> Sagest of women, even of widows, she
> Resolved that Juan should be quite a <u>paragon</u>,
> And worthy of the noblest pedigree:
> (His sire of Castile, his dam from <u>Aragon</u>).

The conventional way to describe a poem's rhyme scheme is to chart rhyming sounds that appear at the ends of lines. The sound that ends the first line is designated *a*, and all subsequent lines that end in that sound are also labeled *a*. The next sound to appear at the end of a line is designated *b*, and all other lines whose last sounds rhyme with it are also designated *b*—and so on through the alphabet. The lines of the poem that follows are labeled in this manner.

ROBERT FROST (1874–1963)

The Road Not Taken (1915)

Two roads diverged in a yellow wood,	a	
And sorry I could not travel both	b	
And be one traveler, long I stood	a	
And looked down one as far as I could	a	
To where it bent in the undergrowth;	b	5
Then took the other, as just as fair	c	
And having perhaps the better claim,	d	
Because it was grassy and wanted wear;	c	
Though as for that, the passing there	c	
Had worn them really about the same,	d	10
And both that morning equally lay	e	
In leaves no step had trodden black	f	
Oh, I kept the first for another day!	e	
Yet knowing how way leads on to way,	e	
I doubted if I should ever come back.	f	15
I shall be telling this with a sigh	g	
Somewhere ages and ages hence:	h	
two roads diverged in a wood, and I—	g	
I took the one less traveled by,	g	
And that has made all the difference.	h	20

The rhyme scheme of the four five-line stanzas in "The Road Not Taken" is the same in each stanza: *abaab, cdccd*, and so on. Except for the last line of the poem, all the rhymes are masculine. Despite its regular rhyme scheme, the poem sounds conversational, as if someone is speaking it without any effort or planning. The beauty of this poem comes from Frost's subtle use of rhyme, which makes the lines flow together, and from the alternating rhymes, which suggest the divergent roads that confront the speaker.

FURTHER READING: Alliteration, Assonance, and Rhyme

John Constable, *Summer Evening Near East Bergholt,* Suffolk (1806–09)
V&A Images, London / Art Resource, NY

GERARD MANLEY HOPKINS (1844–1889)

Pied Beauty (1918)

Glory be to God for dappled things—
    For skies of couple-color as a brinded[1] cow;
        For rose-moles all in stipple upon trout that swim;
Fresh-firecoal chestnut-falls; finches' wings;
    Landscape plotted and pieced—fold, fallow, and plow;   5
        And áll trádes, their gear and tackle and trim.[2]

---

[1] *brinded:* Brindled (streaked).

[2] *trim:* Equipment.

> All things counter, original, spare, strange;
>   Whatever is fickle, freckled (who knows how?)
>   With swift, slow; sweet, sour; adazzle, dim;
>   He fathers-forth whose beauty is past change: 10
>   Praise him.

Reading and Reacting

1. Identify examples of onomatopoeia, alliteration, assonance, imperfect rhyme, and perfect rhyme. Do you think all these techniques are essential to the poem? Are any of them annoying or distracting?

2. What is the central idea of this poem? How do the sounds of the poem help to communicate this idea?

3. Identify examples of masculine and feminine rhyme.

4. **JOURNAL ENTRY** Hopkins uses both pleasing and discordant sounds in his poem. Identify uses of euphony and cacophony, and explain how these techniques affect your reactions to the poem.

5. **CRITICAL PERSPECTIVE** In her essay "The Allegory of Form in Hopkins's Religious Sonnets," Jennifer A. Wagner discusses the ways in which Gerard Manley Hopkins saw relationships between what his poems were saying and how they expressed it:

> Hopkins's most profound perception with regard to the form lies precisely in his demand for the conventional integrity of the sonnet, in his "dogmatic" (his word) insistence on the division of the octave and sestet—and in his recognition of the revisionary movement in the sonnet structure.... For Hopkins the play between octave and sestet is not incidental; it creates a "turn" that becomes a trope of limitation or reduction.

Since "Pied Beauty" is what is known as a "curtal," or shortened, sonnet, it is not divided into sections of eight and six lines (the "octet" and "sestet" that Wagner mentions). Still, there is a turn, or change of emphasis, between the poem's two parts. How does the poem change after that turn occurs?

Related Works: "Cathedral" (p. 353), "I wandered lonely as a cloud" (p. 712), "Loveliest of Trees" (p. 714), "Batter My Heart, Three-Personed God" (p. 756), *Beauty* (p. 831)

SHEL SILVERSTEIN (1930–1999)

Where the Sidewalk Ends (1974)

There is a place where the sidewalk ends
And before the street begins,

And there the grass grows soft and white,
And there the sun burns crimson bright,
And there the moon-bird rests from his flight,   5
To cool in the peppermint wind.

Let us leave this place where the smoke blows black
And the dark street winds and bends.
Past the pits where the asphalt flowers grow
We shall walk with a walk that is measured and slow,   10
And watch where the chalk-white arrows go
To the place where the sidewalk ends.

Yes we'll walk with a walk that is measured and slow,
And we'll go where the chalk-white arrows go,
For the children, they mark, and the children, they know   15
The place where the sidewalk ends.

Reading and Reacting

1. Describe the rhyme scheme of this poem. How does the rhyme scheme contribute to the poem's overall effect?
2. What words does the poem repeat? What ideas does this repetition emphasize?
3. Where does the poem use alliteration and assonance? Do the alliteration and assonance contribute something vital to the poem, or are they just a distraction?

4. **JOURNAL ENTRY** Silverstein is primarily known as a children's poet. What message does "Where the Sidewalk Ends" have for children? What message do you think it has for adults?

Related Works: "Gryphon" (p. 172), "A Boat Beneath a Sunny Sky" (p. 619), "The Lamb" (p. 739)

Maryam Fakouri

JACOB SAENZ

Evolution of My Block (2010)

As a boy I bicycled the block
w/a brown mop top falling
into a tail bleached blond,

gold-like under golden light,
like colors of Noble Knights   5
'banging on corners, unconcerned

w/the colors I bore—a shorty
too small to war with, too brown
to be down for the block.

White Knights became brown   10
Kings still showing black & gold
on corners now crowned,

the block a branch branded
w/la corona graffitied on
garage doors by the pawns.   15

As a teen, I could've beamed
the crown, walked in w/out
the beat down custom,

warred w/my cousin
who claimed Two-Six,   20
the set on the next block

decked in black & beige.
But I preferred games to gangs,
books to crooks wearing hats

crooked to the left or right   25
fighting for a plot, a block
to spot & mark w/blood

of boys who knew no better
way to grow up than throw up
the crown & be down for whatever.   30

Reading and Reacting

1. Identify several different kinds of rhyme in this poem. Then, find examples of alliteration and assonance.
2. What image does the poem create? How do rhyme, alliteration, and assonance help Saenz convey this image?
3. What words are repeated throughout the poem? What is the purpose of this repetition?
4. Explain the poem's title. How has the speaker's block "evolved"?
5. **JOURNAL ENTRY** How is the speaker different from the other boys on his block? How do you account for these differences?

Related Works: "Greasy Lake" (p. 425), "The Secret Lion" (p. 466), "The United Fruit Co." (p. 780), *The Cuban Swimmer* (p. 1166)

Illustration of Jabberwock from *Alice in Wonderland*
© Mary Evans Picture Library / Alamy

LEWIS CARROLL (1832–1898)

Jabberwocky (1871)

'Twas brillig, and the slithy toves
   Did gyre and gimble in the wabe:
All mimsy were the borogoves,
   And the mome raths outgrabe.

"Beware the Jabberwock, my son!   5
   The jaws that bite, the claws that catch!
Beware the Jubjub bird, and shun
   The frumious Bandersnatch!"

He took his vorpal sword in hand;
   Long time the manxome foe he
   sought—   10
So rested he by the Tumtum tree
   And stood awhile in thought.

And, as in uffish thought he stood,
   The Jabberwock, with eyes of flame,
Came whiffling through the tulgey wood,   15
   And burbled as it came!

One, two! One, two! And through and
   through
The vorpal blade went snicker-snack!
He left it dead, and with its head
   He went galumphing back.   20

"And hast thou slain the Jabberwock?
   Come to my arms, my beamish boy!
O frabjous day! Callooh, Callay!"
   He chortled in his joy.

'Twas brillig, and the slithy toves   25
   Did gyre and gimble in the wabe:
All mimsy were the borogoves,
   And the mome raths outgrabe.

Reading and Reacting

1. Many words in this poem may be unfamiliar to you. Are they actual words? Use a dictionary to check before you dismiss any. Do some words that do not appear in the dictionary nevertheless seem to have meaning in the context of the poem? Explain.

2. This poem contains many examples of onomatopoeia. What meanings does the sound of each of these words suggest?

3. JOURNAL ENTRY Summarize the story the poem tells. In what sense is this poem a story of a young man's initiation into adulthood?

4. CRITICAL PERSPECTIVE According to Humpty Dumpty in Carroll's *Alice in Wonderland*, the nonsense words in the poem are **portmanteau words** (that is, words whose form and meaning are derived from two other distinct words—as *smog* is a portmanteau of *smoke* and *fog*). Critic Elizabeth Sewell, however, rejects this explanation: "*[F]rumious*, for instance, is not a word, and does not have two meanings packed up in it; it is a group of letters without any meaning at all.... [I]t looks like other words, and almost certainly more than two."

Which nonsense words in the poem seem to you to be portmanteau words, and which do not? Can you suggest possible sources for the words that are not portmanteau words?

Related Works: "A&P" (p. 160), "Gryphon" (p. 172), "The Secret Lion" (p. 466), "To Lucasta Going to the Wars" (p. 599), "A Boat Beneath a Sunny Sky" (p. 619), "Ulysses" (p. 790)

✔ CHECKLIST   Writing about Sound

Rhythm and Meter
- Does the poem contain repeated words and phrases? If so, how do they help to create rhythm?

- Does the poem use one kind of meter throughout, or does the meter vary from line to line?

- How does the meter contribute to the overall effect of the poem?

- Where do caesuras appear? What effect do they have?

- Are the lines of the poem end-stopped, run-on, or a combination of the two? What effects are created by the presence or absence of pauses at the ends of lines?

Alliteration, Assonance, and Rhyme
- Does the poem include alliteration or assonance?

- Does the poem have a regular rhyme scheme?

> ▢ Does the poem use internal rhyme? beginning rhyme?
>
> ▢ Does the poem include examples of masculine, feminine, or triple rhyme?
>
> ▢ How does rhyme unify the poem?
>
> ▢ How does rhyme reinforce the poem's ideas?

WRITING SUGGESTIONS: Sound

1. William Blake's "The Tyger" appeared in a collection entitled *Songs of Experience.* Compare this poem (p. 740) to "The Lamb" (p. 739), which appeared in a collection called *Songs of Innocence.* In what sense are the speakers in these two poems either "innocent" or "experienced"? How does sound help to convey the voice of the speakers in these two poems?

2. "Sadie and Maud" (p. 610), like "My Papa's Waltz" (p. 705) and "Daddy" (p. 589), communicates the speaker's attitude toward home and family. How does the presence or absence of rhyme in these poems help to convey the speakers' attitudes?

3. Robert Frost once said that writing **free verse** poems, which have no fixed metrical pattern, is like playing tennis without a net. What do you think he meant? Do you agree? After reading "Out, Out—" (p. 596), "Stopping by Woods on a Snowy Evening" (p. 765), and "The Road Not Taken" (p. 624), write an essay in which you discuss Frost's use of meter.

4. Select two or three contemporary poems that have no end rhyme. Write an essay in which you discuss what these poets gain and lose by not using end rhyme.

5. Prose writers as well as poets use assonance and alliteration. Choose two or three a passages of prose—from "Araby" (p. 288), "Barn Burning" (p. 256), or "The Things They Carried" (p. 310), for example—and discuss their use of assonance and alliteration. Where are these techniques used? How do they help the writer create a mood?

FORM

Alberto Alvaro Ríos
Courtesy of Alberto Avaro Ríos

Carl Sandburg
Bettmann/Corbis

Elizabeth Bishop
The Granger Collection, NYC

JOHN KEATS (1795–1821)

On the Sonnet (1819)

If by dull rhymes our English must be chained,
And like Andromeda,[1] the sonnet sweet
Fettered, in spite of painéd loveliness,
Let us find, if we must be constrained,
Sandals more interwoven and complete   5
To fit the naked foot of Poesy:

---

[1] *Andromeda:* In Greek mythology, an Ethiopian princess chained to a rock to appease a sea monster.

Let us inspect the lyre, and weigh the stress
Of every chord, and see what may be gained
By ear industrious, and attention meet;
Misers of sound and syllable, no less   10
Than Midas[2] of his coinage, let us be
Jealous of dead leaves in the bay-wreath crown;
So, if we may not let the Muse be free,
She will be bound with garlands of her own.

Andromeda in Chains
Alinari Archives/Corbis

*   *   *

The **form** of a literary work is its structure or shape, the way its elements fit together to form a whole; **poetic form** is the design of a poem described in terms of rhyme, meter, and stanzaic pattern.

---

[2]*Midas:* A legendary king of Phrygia whose wish that everything he touched would turn to gold was granted by the god Dionysus.

Until the twentieth century, most poetry was written in **closed form** (sometimes called **fixed form**), characterized by regular patterns of meter, rhyme, line length, and stanzaic divisions. Early poems that were passed down orally—epics and ballads, for example—relied on regular form to facilitate memorization. Even after poems began to be written down, poets tended to favor regular patterns. In fact, until relatively recently, regular form was what distinguished poetry from prose. Of course, strict adherence to regular patterns sometimes produced poems that were, in John Keats's words, "chained" by "dull rhymes" and "fettered" by the rules governing a particular form (p. 632). But rather than feeling "constrained" by form, many poets have experimented with imagery, figures of speech, allusion, and other techniques, moving away from rigid patterns of rhyme and meter and thus stretching closed form to its limits.

As they sought new ways in which to express themselves, poets also borrowed forms from other cultures, adapting them to the demands of their own languages. English and American poets, for example, adopted (and still use) early French forms, such as the **villanelle** and the **sestina**, and early Italian forms, such as the **Petrarchan** **sonnet** and terza rima. The nineteenth-century American poet Henry Wadsworth Longfellow studied Icelandic epics; the twentieth-century poet Ezra Pound studied the works of French troubadours; and Pound and other twentieth-century American poets, such as Richard Wright and Carolyn Kizer, were inspired by Japanese haiku. Other American poets, such as Vachel Lindsay, Langston Hughes, and Maya Angelou, looked closer to home—to the rhythms of blues, jazz, and spirituals—for inspiration.

As time went on, more and more poets moved away from closed form to experiment with **open form** poetry (sometimes called **free verse** or *vers libre*), varying line length within a poem, dispensing with meter and stanzaic divisions, breaking lines in unexpected places, and even abandoning any semblance of formal structure. In English, nineteenth-century poets—such as William Blake and Matthew Arnold—experimented with lines of irregular meter and length, and Walt Whitman wrote **prose poems**, poems whose lines extend from the left to the right margin, with no line breaks, so that they look like prose. (Well before this time, Asian poetry and some biblical passages had used a type of free verse.) In nineteenth-century France, symbolist poets, such as Baudelaire, Rimbaud, Verlaine, and Mallarmé, also used free verse. In the early twentieth century, a group of American poets— including Ezra Pound, William Carlos Williams, and Amy Lowell—who were associated with a movement known as **imagism** wrote poetry that dispensed with traditional principles of English versification, creating new rhythms and meters.

Although much contemporary English and American poetry is composed in open form, many poets also continue to write in closed form—even in very traditional, highly structured patterns. Still, new forms, and new variations of old forms, are being created all the time. And, because contemporary poets do not necessarily feel bound by rules or restrictions about what constitutes "acceptable" poetic form, they experiment freely, trying to discover the form that best suits the poem's purpose, subject, language, and theme.

 ## Closed Form

A **closed form** poem has an identifiable, repeated pattern, with lines of similar length arranged in groups of two, three, four, or more. A closed form poem also tends to rely on a regular metrical pattern and rhyme scheme.

Despite what its name suggests, closed form poetry does not have to be confining or conservative. In fact, contemporary poets often experiment with closed form—for example, by using characteristics of open form poetry (such as lines of varying length) within a closed form. Sometimes poets move back and forth within a single poem from open to closed to open form; sometimes (like their eighteenth-century counterparts) they combine different stanzaic forms (stanzas of two and three lines, for example) within a single poem.

Even when poets work within a traditional closed form, such as a sonnet, sestina, or villanelle, they can break new ground. For example, they can write a sonnet with an unexpected meter or rhyme scheme (or with no consistent pattern of rhyme or meter at all), add an extra line or even extra stanzas to a traditional sonnet form, combine two different traditional sonnet forms in a single poem, or write an abbreviated version of a sestina or villanelle. In other words, poets can use traditional forms as building blocks, combining them in innovative ways to create new patterns and new forms.

Sometimes a pattern (such as **blank verse**) simply determines the meter of a poem's individual lines. At other times, the pattern extends to the level of the **stanza**, with lines arranged into groups (**couplets**, **quatrains**, and so on). At still other times, as in the case of traditional closed forms like sonnets, a poetic pattern gives shape to an entire poem.

Blank Verse

Blank verse is unrhymed poetry with each line written in a pattern of five stressed and five unstressed syllables called **iambic pentameter** (see p. 613).

Many passages from Shakespeare's plays, such as the following lines from *Hamlet*, are written in blank verse:

> To sleep! perchance to dream:—ay, there's the rub;
> For in that sleep of death what dreams may come,
> When we have shuffled off this mortal coil,
> Must give us pause: there's the respect
> That makes calamity of so long life

Stanza

A **stanza** is a group of two or more lines with the same metrical pattern—and often with a regular rhyme scheme as well—separated by blank space from other such groups of lines. Stanzas in poetry are like paragraphs in prose: they group related ideas into units.

A two-line stanza with rhyming lines of similar length and meter is called a **couplet.** The **heroic couplet,** first used by Chaucer and later very popular throughout the eighteenth century, consists of two rhymed lines of iambic pentameter, with a weak pause after the first line and a strong pause after the second. The following example, from Alexander Pope's *An Essay on Criticism*, is a heroic couplet:

> True ease in writing comes from art, not chance,
> As those move easiest who have learned to dance.

A three-line stanza with lines of similar length and a set rhyme scheme is called a **tercet.** Percy Bysshe Shelley's "Ode to the West Wind" (p. 786) is built largely of tercets:

> O wild West Wind, thou breath of Autumn's being,
> Thou, from whose unseen presence the leaves dead
> Are driven, like ghosts from an enchanter fleeing,
>
> Yellow, and black, and pale, and hectic red,
> Pestilence-stricken multitudes: O Thou,
> Who chariotest to their dark wintry bed

Although in many tercets all three lines rhyme, "Ode to the West Wind" uses a special rhyme scheme, also used by Dante, called **terza rima.** This rhyme scheme (*aba, bcb, cdc, ded,* and so on) creates an interlocking series of stanzas: line 2's *dead* looks ahead to the rhyming words *red* and *bed*, which close lines 4 and 6, and the pattern continues throughout the poem. Robert Frost's 1928 poem "Acquainted with the Night" is a contemporary example of terza rima.

A four-line stanza with lines of similar length and a set rhyme scheme is called a **quatrain**. The quatrain, the most widely used and versatile unit in English and American poetry, is used by William Wordsworth in the following excerpt from "She dwelt among the untrodden ways":

> A violet by a mossy stone
> Half hidden from the eye!
> —Fair as a star, when only one
> Is shining in the sky.

Quatrains are frequently used by contemporary poets as well—for instance, in Theodore Roethke's "My Papa's Waltz" (p. 705) and Adrienne Rich's "Aunt Jennifer's Tigers" (p. 617).

One special kind of quatrain, called the **ballad stanza**, alternates lines of eight and six syllables; typically, only the second and fourth lines rhyme. The following lines from the traditional Scottish ballad "Sir Patrick Spence" illustrate the ballad stanza:

> The king sits in Dumferling toune,
> Drinking the blude-reid wine:
> "O whar will I get guid sailor
> To sail this schip of mine?"

Common measure, a four-line stanzaic pattern closely related to the ballad stanza, is used in hymns as well as in poetry. It differs from the ballad stanza in that its rhyme scheme is *abab* rather than *abcb*.

Other stanzaic forms include **rhyme royal**, a seven-line stanza (*ababbcc*) set in iambic pentameter, used in Sir Thomas Wyatt's sixteenth-century poem "They Flee from Me That Sometimes Did Me Seke" as well as in Theodore Roethke's twentieth-century "I Knew a Woman"; **ottava rima**, an eight-line stanza (*abababcc*) set in iambic pentameter; and the **Spenserian stanza**, a nine-line form (*ababbcbcc*) whose first eight lines are set in iambic pentameter and whose last line is in iambic hexameter. The Romantic poets John Keats and Percy Bysshe Shelley were among those who used the Spenserian stanza. (See Chapter 20 for definitions and examples of various metrical patterns.)

The Sonnet

Perhaps the most familiar kind of traditional closed form poem written in English is the **sonnet**, a fourteen-line poem with a distinctive rhyme scheme and metrical pattern. The English or **Shakespearean sonnet**, which consists of fourteen lines divided into three quatrains and a concluding couplet, is written in iambic pentameter and follows the rhyme scheme *abab cdcd efef gg*. The **Petrarchan sonnet**, popularized in the fourteenth century by the Italian poet Francesco Petrarch, also consists of fourteen lines of iambic pentameter, but these lines are divided into an eight-line unit called an **octave** and a six-line unit (composed of two tercets) called a **sestet**. The rhyme scheme of the octave is *abba abba*; the rhyme scheme of the sestet is *cde cde*.

The conventional structures of these sonnet forms reflect the arrangement of ideas within the poem. In the Shakespearean sonnet, the poet typically presents three "paragraphs" of related thoughts, introducing an idea in the first quatrain, developing it in the two remaining quatrains, and summing up in a succinct closing couplet. In the Petrarchan sonnet, the octave introduces a problem that is resolved in the sestet. (Many Shakespearean sonnets also have a problem–solution structure.) Some poets vary the traditional patterns somewhat to suit the poem's language or ideas. For example, they may depart from the pattern to sidestep a forced rhyme or unnatural stress on a syllable, or they may shift from problem to solution in a place other than between octave and sestet.

The following poem is a traditional English sonnet.

WILLIAM SHAKESPEARE (1564–1616)

When, in disgrace with Fortune and men's eyes (1609)

When, in disgrace with Fortune and men's eyes,
I all alone beweep my outcast state,
And trouble deaf heaven with my bootless[1] cries,
And look upon myself and curse my fate,
Wishing me like to one more rich in hope,   5
Featured like him, like him with friends possessed,
Desiring this man's art, and that man's scope,
With what I most enjoy contented least,
Yet in these thoughts myself almost despising,
Haply[2] I think on thee, and then my state,   10
Like to the lark at break of day arising
From sullen earth, sings hymns at heaven's gate;
For thy sweet love rememb'red such wealth brings
That then I scorn to change my state with kings.

---

[1] *bootless:* Futile.
[2] *Haply:* Luckily.

Goddess of Fortune turning wheel
©Charles Walker / Topfoto / The Image Works

Shakespeare's sonnet is written in iambic pentameter and has a conventional rhyme scheme: *abab* (eyes-state-cries-fate), *cdcd* (hope-possessed-scope-least), *efef* (despising-state-arising-gate), *gg* (brings-kings). In this poem, in which the speaker explains how thoughts of his loved one can rescue him from despair, each quatrain is unified by subject matter as well as by rhyme.

In the first quatrain, the speaker presents his problem: he is down on his luck and out of favor with his peers, isolated in self-pity and cursing his fate. In the second quatrain, he develops this idea further: he is envious of others and dissatisfied with things that usually please him. In the third quatrain, the focus shifts. The first two quatrains have developed a dependent clause ("When . . .") that introduces a problem, and now line 9 begins to present the solution. In the third quatrain, the speaker explains how, in the midst of his despair and self-hatred, he thinks of his loved one, and his spirits soar. The closing couplet sums up the mood transformation the poem describes and explains its significance: when the speaker realizes the emotional riches his loved one gives him, he is no longer envious of others.

FURTHER READING: The Sonnet

JOHN KEATS (1795–1821)

On First Looking into Chapman's Homer[1] (1816)

Much have I traveled in the realms of gold,
    And many goodly states and kingdoms seen;
    Round many western islands have I been
Which bards in fealty to Apollo[2] hold.
Oft of one wide expanse had I been told   5
    That deep-browed Homer ruled as his demesne,[3]
    Yet did I never breathe its pure serene[4]
Till I heard Chapman speak out loud and bold.
Then felt I like some watcher of the skies
    When a new planet swims into his ken;   10
Or like stout Cortez[5] when with eagle eyes
    He stared at the Pacific—and all his men
Looked at each other with a wild surmise—
    Silent, upon a peak in Darien.[6]

[1] *Chapman's Homer:* The translation of Homer's works by Elizabethan poet George Chapman.

[2] *Apollo:* Greek god of light, truth, reason, male beauty; associated with music and poetry.

[3] *demesne:* Realm, domain.

[4] *serene:* Air, atmosphere.

[5] *Cortez:* It was Vasco de Balboa (not Hernando Cortez as Keats suggests) who first saw the Pacific Ocean, from "a peak in Darien."

[6] *Darien:* Former name of the Isthmus of Panama.

Bust of Homer
Portrait bust of Homer (marble), Greek, (9th century BC) /
Private Collection / Photo © Boltin Picture Library /
Bridgeman Images

Reading and Reacting

1. Is this a Petrarchan or a Shakespearean sonnet? Explain.

2. **JOURNAL ENTRY** The sestet's change of focus is introduced with the word *Then* in line 9. How does the mood of the sestet differ from the mood of the octave? How does the language differ?

3. **CRITICAL PERSPECTIVE** As Keats's biographer Aileen Ward observes, Homer's epic tales of gods and heroes were known to most readers of Keats's day only in a very formal eighteenth-century translation by Alexander Pope. Here is Pope's description of Ulysses escaping from a shipwreck:

> his knees no more
> Perform'd their office, or his weight upheld:
> His swoln heart heav'd, his bloated body swell'd:
> From mouth to nose the briny torrent ran,
> And lost in lassitude lay all the man,
> Deprived of voice, of motion, and of breath,
> The soul scarce waking in the arms of death . . .

In a rare 1616 edition of Chapman's translation, Keats discovered a very different poem:

> both knees falt'ring, both
> His strong hands hanging down, and all with froth
> His cheeks and nostrils flowing, voice and breath

> Spent to all use, and down he sank to death.
> The sea had soak'd his heart through. . . .

This, as Ward notes, was "poetry of a kind that had not been written in England for two hundred years."

Can you understand why Keats was so moved by Chapman's translation? Do you think Keats's own poem seems closer in its form and language to Pope or to Chapman?

Related Works: "Snow" (p. 82), "Gryphon" (p. 172), "Araby" (p. 288), "When I Heard the Learn'd Astronomer" (p. 536), *Trifles* (p. 867)

EDNA ST. VINCENT MILLAY (1892–1950)

Love is not all (1931)

Love is not all: it is not meat nor drink
Nor slumber nor a roof against the rain;
Nor yet a floating spar to men that sink
And rise and sink and rise and sink again;
Love can not fill the thickened lung with breath,   5
Nor clean the blood, nor set the fractured bone;
Yet many a man is making friends with death
Even as I speak, for lack of love alone.
It well may be that in a difficult hour,
Pinned down by pain and moaning for release,   10
Or nagged by want past resolution's power,
I might be driven to sell your love for peace,
Or trade the memory of this night for food.
It well may be. I do not think I would.

Reading and Reacting

1. Describe the poem's rhyme scheme. Is it a Petrarchan or a Shakespearean sonnet?

2. Does this poem have a problem–solution structure, or is there some other thematic distinction between its octave and its sestet?

3. Why are the words "It well may be" repeated in lines 9 and 14?

4. **Journal Entry** The poem's first six lines list all the things that love is *not* and what it *cannot* do. Why do you think the poet chose not to enumerate what love *is* and what it *can* do?

5. **Critical Perspective** In an essay on Edna St. Vincent Millay's love sonnets, poet and critic Anna Evans notes the ways in which Millay's unconventional lifestyle provided material for her poetry:

Some of Millay's finest sonnets written during her marriage are presumed to be addressed to her younger poet lover George Dillon, who became part of a ménage a trois in the Millay household . . . The narrator of "Love is not all: it is not meat or drink" demonstrates Millay's newest philosophy of romantic love. There is no doubt that the speaker is expressing love for the object of the poem, yet there is no commitment, the love is spoken of already almost as of something in the past, and the poem lacks an absolute conviction of permanence.

What evidence can you find in the poem to support Evans's claims that there is no romantic "commitment," and that the speaker "lacks an absolute conviction of permanence"?

Related Works: "Love and Other Catastrophes: A Mix Tape" (p. 84), "If I should learn, in some quite casual way" (p. 592), "When, in disgrace with Fortune and men's eyes" (p. 638), "How Do I Love Thee?" (p. 719), "What lips my lips have kissed" (p. 720), "General Review of the Sex Situation" (p. 721)

LYNN AARTI CHANDHOK (1963–   )

The Carpet Factory (2001)

A wood shack on the riverbank. Inside,
through dust-filled shafts of light, bright colors rise
and drown the warps, transforming their brown threads
to poppy fields, the Tree of Life, a wide
sun hemmed by cartwheeled tulips, fountainheads   5
that spew blue waterfalls of peacock eyes.

With furious fingers mothlike at the weft,
the children tie and cut and tie and cut
and tamp the knots down, turning blade to gavel.
Each pull's a dust-cloud *plink*—bereft   10
of music. Toothless men spit betelnut
in blood-red stains. Everywhere, reds unravel.

The bended limbs of saplings twist and part
and weave into the prayer rug's pale silk heart.

Reading and Reacting

1. Look carefully at this poem's rhyme scheme and at the way its lines are divided into stanzas. Is it more like a Shakespearean or a Petrarchan sonnet? Explain.

2. This poem uses color imagery to describe a prayer rug. Identify the references to color. Do they all describe the rug?

3. What point does this poem make about the carpet factory? How does the closing couplet sum up this point?

4. **JOURNAL ENTRY** How are the descriptions of the factory—and of its child laborers—different from the descriptions of the carpets produced there?

5. **CRITICAL PERSPECTIVE** Reviewing Lynn Aarti Chandhok's book *The View from Zero Bridge*, Patty Paine focuses on the poem "The Carpet Factory":

> This poem itself is meticulously crafted and beautifully realized. The form and the content merge seamless . . . One can see the slants of light, the children's fingers darting at the weft, hear the plink and watch the blood-red spittle seep into the ground. By taking such care with her images, the poet has created an intimacy and familiarity that transports the reader into a world that is fully formed . . . The specter of child labor hovers over "The Carpet Factory," and Chandhok confronts the issue through imagery rather than polemics.

Given its focus on the issue of child labor, do you see this poem as social protest? Or, do you see the poem's content as less important than its form and imagery? How does Paine's reading of the poem affect your own interpretation of it? Do the poem's "form and content merge seamlessly"?

Related Works: "Girl" (p. 95), "Gretel in Darkness" (p. 501), "The Secretary Chant" (p. 584), "Aunt Jennifer's Tigers" (p. 617), "Indian Boarding School: The Runaways" (p. 763), *Trifles* (p. 867)

GWENDOLYN BROOKS (1917–2000)

First Fight. Then Fiddle (1949)

First fight. Then fiddle. Ply the slipping string
With feathery sorcery; muzzle the note
With hurting love; the music that they wrote
Bewitch, bewilder. Qualify to sing
Threadwise. Devise no salt, no hempen thing   5
For the dear instrument to bear. Devote
The bow to silks and honey. Be remote
A while from malice and from murdering.
But first to arms, to armor. Carry hate
In front of you and harmony behind.   10
Be deaf to music and to beauty blind.
Win war. Rise bloody, maybe not too late
For having first to civilize a space
Wherein to play your violin with grace.

Reading and Reacting

1. What is the subject of Brooks's poem?
2. Explain the poem's rhyme scheme. Is this rhyme scheme an essential element of the poem? Would the poem be equally effective if it did not include end rhyme? Why or why not?
3. Study the poem's use of capitalization and punctuation carefully. Why do you think Brooks chooses to end many of her sentences in midline? How do her decisions determine how you read the poem?

4. **JOURNAL ENTRY** What do you think Brooks means by "fight" and "fiddle"?

Related Work: "The Soldier" (p. 725)

RHINA ESPAILLAT (1932–   )

"Find Work" (1999)

> *I tie my Hat—I crease my Shawl—*
> *Life's little duties do—precisely*
> *As the very least*
> *Were infinite—to me—*
> *—Emily Dickinson, #443*

My mother's mother, widowed very young
of her first love, and of that love's first fruit,
moved through her father's farm, her country tongue
and country heart anaesthetized and mute
with labor. So her kind was taught to do—   5
"Find work," she would reply to every grief—
and her one dictum, whether false or true,
tolled heavy with her passionate belief.
Widowed again, with children, in her prime,
she spoke so little it was hard to bear   10
so much composure, such a truce with time
spent in the lifelong practice of despair.
But I recall her floors, scrubbed white as bone,
her dishes, and how painfully they shone.

Reading and Reacting

1. Explain the meaning of each of the following in the context of the poem:
   - "that love's first fruit" (line 2)
   - "her kind" (5)
   - "truce with time" (11)

2. Why does the poet choose the words "anaesthetized" (4) and "painfully" (14)? What other words would work with the poem's content and meter?

3. Why do you think the poet introduces the poem with lines from Emily Dickinson? How are these lines related to the poem's content?

4. JOURNAL ENTRY Do you think the sonnet form suits this poem's subject matter? Why or why not?

Related Works: "I Stand Here Ironing" (p. 217), "A Worn Path" (p. 386), "Mexican Almuerzo in New England" (p. 666), "Dusting" (p. 706), "Not Waving but Drowning" (p. 788), *Trifles* (p. 867)

The Sestina

The **sestina**, introduced in thirteenth-century France, is composed of six six-line stanzas and a three-line conclusion called an **envoi**. The sestina does not require end rhyme; however, it requires that each line end with one of six key words, which are repeated throughout the poem in a fixed order. The alternation of these six words in different positions—but always at the ends of lines—in each of the poem's six stanzas creates a rhythmic verbal pattern that unifies the poem, as the key words do in the poem that follows.

ALBERTO ALVARO RÍOS (1952–)

Nani (1982)

Sitting at her table, she serves
the sopa de arroz[1] to me
instinctively, and I watch her,
the absolute mamá, and eat words
I might have had to say more   5
out of embarrassment. To speak,
now-foreign words I used to speak,
too, dribble down her mouth as she serves
me albóndigas.[2] No more
than a third are easy to me.   10
By the stove she does something with words
and looks at me only with her
back. I am full. I tell her
I taste the mint, and watch her speak

---

[1] *sopa de arroz:* Rice soup.
[2] *albóndigas:* Meatballs.

smiles at the stove. All my words   15
make her smile. Nani never serves
herself, she only watches me
with her skin, her hair. I ask for more.
I watch the mamá warming more
tortillas for me. I watch her   20
fingers in the flame for me.
Near her mouth, I see a wrinkle speak
of a man whose body serves
the ants like she serves me, then more words
from more wrinkles about children, words   25
about this and that, flowing more
easily from these other mouths. Each serves
as a tremendous string around her,
holding her together. They speak
nani was this and that to me   30
and I wonder just how much of me
will die with her, what were the words
I could have been, was. Her insides speak
through a hundred wrinkles, now, more
than she can bear, steel around her,   35
shouting, then, What is this thing she serves?

She asks me if I want more.
I own no words to stop her.
Even before I speak, she serves.

In many respects, Ríos's poem closely follows the form of the traditional
sestina. For instance, it interweaves six key words—"serves," "me," "her,"
"words," "more," and "speak"—through six groups of six lines each, rearranging the order in which the words appear so that the first line of each group
of six lines ends with the same key word that also ended the preceding group
of lines. The poem repeats the key words in exactly the order prescribed:
abcdef, faebdc, cfdabe, and so on. In addition, the sestina closes with a three-
line envoi that includes all six of the poem's key words, three at the ends of
lines and three within the lines. Despite this generally strict adherence to the
sestina form, Ríos departs from the form by grouping his six sets of six lines
not into six separate stanzas but rather into two eighteen-line stanzas.

The sestina form suits Ríos's subject matter. The focus of the poem, on
the verbal and nonverbal interaction between the poem's "me" and "her,"
is reinforced by each of the related words. "Nani" is a poem about communication, and the key words return to probe this theme again and again.
Throughout the poem, these repeated words help to create a fluid, melodic,
and tightly woven work.

FURTHER READING: The Sestina

ELIZABETH BISHOP (1911–1979)

Sestina (1965)

September rain falls on the house.
In the failing light, the old grandmother
sits in the kitchen with the child
beside the Little Marvel Stove,
reading the jokes from the almanac,   5
laughing and talking to hide her tears.

She thinks that her equinoctial tears
and the rain that beats on the roof of the house
were both foretold by the almanac,
but only known to a grandmother.   10
The iron kettle sings on the stove.
She cuts some bread and says to the child,

It's time for tea now; but the child
is watching the teakettle's small hard tears
dance like mad on the hot black stove,   15
the way the rain must dance on the house.
Tidying up, the old grandmother
hangs up the clever almanac

on its string. Birdlike, the almanac
hovers half open above the child,   20
hovers above the old grandmother
and her teacup full of dark brown tears.
She shivers and says she thinks the house
feels chilly, and puts more wood in the stove.

It was to be, says the Marvel Stove.   25
I know what I know, says the almanac.
With crayons the child draws a rigid house
and a winding pathway. Then the child
puts in a man with buttons like tears
and shows it proudly to the grandmother.   30

But secretly, while the grandmother
busies herself about the stove,
the little moons fall down like tears
from between the pages of the almanac
into the flower bed the child   35
has carefully placed in the front of the house.

Time to plant tears, says the almanac.
The grandmother sings to the marvellous stove
and the child draws another inscrutable house.

Reading and Reacting

1. Does the poet's adherence to the traditional sestina form create any problems? For example, do you think word order seems forced at any point?

2. Consider the adjectives used in this poem. Which of them are unexpected? What is the effect of these surprising choices? Do you find them distracting, or do you think they strengthen the poem?

3. **JOURNAL ENTRY** What are the poem's six key words? How are these words related to the poem's theme?

4. **CRITICAL PERSPECTIVE** In his essay "Elizabeth Bishop's Surrealist Inheritance," Richard Mullen writes the following:

> Some of the enchanted mystery which permeates Elizabeth Bishop's poetry arises from her preoccupation with dreams, sleep, and the borders between sleeping and waking. Her poems contain much of the magic, uncanniness and displacement associated with the works of the surrealists, for she too explores the workings of the unconscious and the interplay between conscious perception and dream.

What examples can you find in "Sestina" of "the enchanted mystery" to which Mullen refers? In what ways is the poem dreamlike?

Related Works: "Nani" (p. 646), "My Papa's Waltz" (p. 705)

PATRICIA SMITH (1955–   )

Ethel's Sestina (2006)

Ethel Freeman's body sat for days in her wheelchair outside the New Orleans Convention Center. Her son Herbert, who has assured his mother that help was on the way, was forced to leave her there once she died.

Gon' be obedient in this there chair,
gon's bide my time, fanning against this sun.
I ask my boy, and all he says is *Wait.*
He wipes my brow with steam, says I should sleep.
I trust his every word. Herbert my son.   5
I believe him when he says help gon' come

Been so long since all these suffrin' folks come
to this place. Now on the ground 'round my chair,
they sweat in my shade, keep asking my son
could that be a bus they see. It's the sun   10
foolin' them, shining much too loud for sleep,
making us hear engines, wheels. Not yet. Wait.

Lawd, some folks prayin' for rain while they wait,
forgetting what rain can do. When it come,
it smashes living flat, wakes you from sleep,   15
eats streets, washes you clean out of the chair
you be sittin' in. Best to praise this sun,
shinin' its dry shine *Lawd have mercy, son.*

Is it coming? Such a strong man, my son.
Can't help but believe when he tells us, *Wait.*   20
Wait some more. Wish some trees would block this sun.
We wait. Ain't no white men or buses come,
but look—see that there? Get me out this chair,
help me stand on up. No time for sleepin',

cause look what's rumbling this way. If you sleep   25
you gon' miss it. *Look there,* I tell my son.
He don't hear. I'm 'bout to get out this chair,
but the ghost in my legs tells me to wait,
wait for the salvation that's sho to come.
I see my savior's face 'longside that sun.   30

Nobody sees me running toward the sun.
Lawd, they think I done gone and fell asleep.
They don't hear *Come.*

Come.   35
Come.
Come.
Come.
Come.
Come.

Ain't but one power make me leave my son.   40
I can't wait, Herbert. Lawd knows I can't wait.
Don't cry, boy, I ain't in that chair no more.

Wish you coulda come on this journey, son,
seen that ol' sweet sun lift me out of sleep.
Didn't have to wait. And see my golden chair?   45

People waiting for help outside the New Orleans Convention Center
after Hurricane Katrina in 2005

Reading and Reacting

1. What six key words are repeated in this poem? What other words are repeated? Why?

2. Where does this sestina depart from its required form? Is this departure justified by the poem's theme or subject matter? Does it strengthen or weaken the poem's impact?

3. **JOURNAL ENTRY** Write a few sentences—or a few lines of poetry—from Herbert's point of view, expressing what you think he would like to tell his mother.

4. **CRITICAL PERSPECTIVE** In an interview with Cherryl Floyd-Miller for the Webzine *Torch*, Patricia Smith talked about the qualities of a good "persona poem":

> I think the persona poem moves us out of our space, moves us out of our comfort zone where we're almost forced to take a really hard look at another life. Whether it be something you're just doing for the fun of it, like, you know, wow, what's it like to be Little Richard for a day, or you're sitting next to some woman who is clutching like twenty bags or something on the subway, you know that her whole life is in those bags, and you realize just how close everyone's life is to your own.

Does "Ethel's Sestina" take you "out of [your] comfort zone"? Does it make you "realize just how close everyone's life is to your own"?

Related Works: "Girl" (p. 95), "Everyday Use" (p. 344), "Incident" (p. 597), "Do not go gentle into that good night" (p. 710), *Fences* (p. 1270)

The Villanelle

The **villanelle**, first introduced in France during the Middle Ages, is a nineteen-line poem composed of five tercets and a concluding quatrain; its rhyme scheme is *aba aba aba aba aba abaa*. Two different lines are systematically repeated in the poem: line 1 appears again in lines 6, 12, and 18, and line 3 reappears as lines 9, 15, and 19. Thus, each tercet concludes with an exact (or close) duplication of either line 1 or line 3, and the final quatrain concludes by repeating both line 1 and line 3.

Earth Mother, **painting of Mother Nature by Sir Edward Burne-Jones, 1882**

Earth Mother, 1882 (encaustic on panel), Burne-Jones, Sir Edward Coley (1833-98) / Worcester Art Museum, Massachusetts, USA / Bridgeman Images

THEODORE ROETHKE (1908–1963)

The Waking (1953)

I wake to sleep, and take my waking slow.
I feel my fate in what I cannot fear.
I learn by going where I have to go.

We think by feeling. What is there to know?
I hear my being dance from ear to ear.   5
I wake to sleep, and take my waking slow.

Of those so close beside me, which are you?
God bless the Ground! I shall walk softly there,
And learn by going where I have to go.

Light takes the Tree; but who can tell us how?   10
The lowly worm climbs up a winding stair;
I wake to sleep, and take my waking slow.

Great Nature has another thing to do
To you and me; so take the lively air,
And, lovely, learn by going where to go.   15

This shaking keeps me steady. I should know.
What falls away is always. And is near.
I wake to sleep, and take my waking slow.
I learn by going where I have to go.

"The Waking," like all villanelles, closely intertwines threads of sounds and words. The repeated lines and the very regular rhyme and meter give the poem a monotonous, almost hypnotic, rhythm. This poem uses end rhyme and repeats entire lines. It also makes extensive use of alliteration ("I feel my fate in what I cannot fear") and internal rhyme ("I hear my being dance from ear to ear"; "I wake to sleep and take my waking slow"). The result is a tightly constructed poem of overlapping sounds and images.

DEBORAH PAREDEZ (1970–   )

Wife's Disaster Manual (2012)

When the forsaken city starts to burn,
after the men and children have fled,
stand still, silent as prey, and slowly turn

back. Behold the curse. Stay and mourn
the collapsing doorways, the unbroken bread   5
in the forsaken city starting to burn.

Don't flinch. Don't join in.
Resist the righteous scurry and instead
stand still, silent as prey. Slowly turn

your thoughts away from escape: the iron   10
gates unlatched, the responsibilities shed.
When the forsaken city starts to burn,

surrender to your calling, show concern
for those who remain. Come to a dead
standstill. Silent as prey, slowly turn   15

into something essential. Learn
the names of the fallen. Refuse to run ahead
when the forsaken city starts to burn.
Stand still and silent. Pray. Return.

Reading and Reacting

1. This poem is a series of commands. To whom are these commands addressed? What reaction do you think the speaker expects?
2. What does the word *forsaken* mean? What is the "forsaken city"?
3. What two lines are repeated in this villanelle? What is the poem's rhyme scheme? Does it depart form the traditional structure of the villanelle in any respects? Explain.

4. **JOURNAL ENTRY** What do you think this poem is about? What makes you think so?

Related Works: "Fire and Ice" (p. 510), "The World Is Too Much with Us" (p. 516), "Going to Work" (p. 601), "Aristotle" (p. 685), "The End and the Beginning" (p. 729)

The Epigram

Originally, an epigram was an inscription carved in stone on a monument or statue. As a literary form, an **epigram** is a very brief poem that makes a pointed, often sarcastic, comment in a surprising twist at the end. In a sense, it is a poem with a punch line. Although some epigrams rhyme, others do not. Many are only two lines long, but others are somewhat longer. What they have in common is their economy of language and their tone.

FURTHER READING: The Epigram

SAMUEL TAYLOR COLERIDGE (1772–1834)

What Is an Epigram? (1802)

What is an epigram? a dwarfish whole,
Its body brevity, and wit its soul.

DOROTHY PARKER (1893–1967)

News Item (1937)

Men seldom make passes
At girls who wear glasses.

CAROL ANN DUFFY (1955–   )

Mrs. Darwin (2001)

7 April 1852
Went to the Zoo.
I said to Him—
Something about that Chimpanzee over there reminds me of you.

Reading and Reacting

1. Explain the point made in each of the epigrams above.
2. Evaluate each poem. What qualities do you conclude make an epigram effective?

3. JOURNAL ENTRY In what respects are short-short stories (see Chapter 5) and ten-minute plays (see Chapter 26) like epigrams?

4. CRITICAL PERSPECTIVE In "Making Love Modern: Dorothy Parker and Her Public," Nina Miller explains why Dorothy Parker's poetry achieved its considerable popularity during the 1920s:

> Sophistication—that highly prized commodity which was to define the Jazz Age—meant cynicism and a barbed wit, and women like Parker were perfectly situated to dominate this discourse. In the twenties, as a wisecracking member of the celebrated Algonquin Round Table, Parker would be at the cutting edge of a mannered and satirical wittiness, one which determined the shape of her poetry in important ways.

What is it that makes "News Item" witty? If it is satirical, what attitudes in society does it satirize?

Related Works: "Love and Other Catastrophes: A Mix Tape" (p. 84), "Fire and Ice" (p. 510), "You fit into me" (p. 598), "Shakespearean Sonnet" (p. 688), "General Review of the Sex Situation" (p. 721), *Nine Ten* (p. 861)

MARTÍN ESPADA (1957–   )

Why I Went to College (2000)

If you don't,
my father said,
you better learn
to eat soup
through a straw,   5
'cause I'm gonna
break your jaw

Reading and Reacting

1. How is "Why I Went to College" different from the three epigrams on page 654? How is it similar to them?
2. What function does the poem's title serve? Is it the epigram's "punch line," or does it serve another purpose?
3. What can you infer about the speaker's father from this poem? Why, for example, do you think he wants his son to go to college?
4. **JOURNAL ENTRY** Exactly why did the speaker go to college? Expand this short poem into a paragraph written from the speaker's point of view.

Related Works: "Baca Grande" (p. 545), "My Papa's Waltz" (p. 705), "'Faith' is a fine invention" (p. 752)

A. R. AMMONS (1926–2001)

Both Ways (1990)

One can't
have it
both ways
and both

ways is   5
the only

way I
want it.

Reading and Reacting

1. Is this poem actually an epigram, or is it just a short poem? Explain your conclusion.

2. Why do you think the speaker uses "one" in line 1 and "I" in line 7? Try substituting other pronouns for these two. How do your substitutions change the poem's meaning?

3. **JOURNAL ENTRY** Write three original epigrams: one about love, one about school or work, and one about a social or political issue.

4. **CRITICAL PERSPECTIVE** In reviewing *The Really Short Poems of A. R. Ammons,* poet and critic Fred Chappell criticizes some of the individual poems as trivial or even confusing but then goes on to add the following:

   [A]t his best [Ammons] is incomparable. No one else is so cheerfully quirky, so slyly sensible, so oxymoronically accurate. Most of us think in clichés, I'm afraid, but Ammons appears to think in reversed clichés; it's hard to believe he ever met a thought he didn't want to stand on its head. When he has done so, the effect may be merely clumsy. But it may also be utterly fresh and original, witty, unexpected, serious, and even profound.

   Is "Both Ways" an example of one of the "reversed clichés" that Chappell discusses? Is the poem "witty"? Could it be considered "serious, and even profound"?

Related Works: "The Story of an Hour" (p. 127), "Two Kinds" (p. 471), "The Road Not Taken" (p. 624), *Beauty* (p. 831)

Haiku

Like an epigram, a haiku compresses words into a very small package. Unlike an epigram, however, a haiku focuses on an image, not an idea. A traditional

Japanese form, the **haiku** is a brief unrhymed poem that presents the essence of some aspect of nature, concentrating a vivid image in three lines. Although in the strictest sense a haiku consists of seventeen syllables divided into three lines of five, seven, and five syllables, respectively, not all poets conform to this rigid structure.

The following poem is a translation of a classic Japanese haiku by Matsuo Bashō:

> Silent and still: then
> Even sinking into the rocks,
> The cicada's screech.

Notice that this poem conforms to the haiku's three-line structure and traditional subject matter, vividly depicting a natural scene without comment or analysis.

FURTHER READING: Haiku

MATSUO BASHŌ (1644–1694)

Four Haiku*

Translated by Geoffrey Bownas and Anthony Thwaite

Spring:
A hill without a name
Veiled in morning mist.

The beginning of autumn:
Sea and emerald paddy   5
Both the same green.

The winds of autumn
Blow: yet still green
The chestnut husks.

A flash of lightning: 10
Into the gloom
Goes the heron's cry.

Reading and Reacting

1. Haiku are admired for their extreme economy and their striking images. What are the central images in each of Bashō's haiku? To what senses do these images appeal?

---

*Publication date is not available.

2. In another poem, Bashō says that art begins with "The depths of the country / and a rice-planting song." What do you think he means? How do these four haiku exemplify this idea?

3. Do you think the conciseness of these poems increases or decreases the impact of their images? Explain.

4. Journal Entry "In a Station of the Metro" (p. 564) is Ezra Pound's version of a haiku. How successful do you think his poem is as a haiku? Do you think a longer poem could have conveyed the images more effectively?

Related Works: "Where Mountain Lion Lay Down with Deer" (p. 506), "Some Good Things to Be Said for the Iron Age" (p. 565), "the sky was can dy" (p. 662), "Fog" (p. 714), "Birches" (p. 715), "Meeting at Night" (p. 719)

JACK KEROUAC (1922–1969)

American Haiku*

Early morning yellow flowers,
thinking about
the drunkards of Mexico.

No telegram today
only more leaves   5
fell.

Nightfall,
boy smashing dandelions
with a stick.

Holding up my   10
purring cat to the moon
I sighed.

Drunk as a hoot owl,
writing letters
by thunderstorm.   15

Empty baseball field
a robin
hops along the bench.

All day long
wearing a hat   20
that wasn't on my head.

*Publication date is not available.

Crossing the football field
coming home from work—
the lonely businessman.

After the shower   25
among the drenched roses
the bird thrashing in the bath.

Snap your finger
stop the world—
rain falls harder.   30

Nightfall,
too dark to read the page
too cold.

Following each other
my cats stop   35
when it thunders.

Wash hung out
by moonlight
Friday night in May.

The bottoms of my shoes   40
are clean
from walking in the rain.

Glow worm
sleeping on this flower—
your light's on.   45

Reading and Reacting

1. How are these haiku different from those by Matsuo Bashō (p. 657)? Do
they fit the definition of *haiku* on page 657?

2. What, if anything, makes these poems "American"? Is it their language?
their subject matter? something else?

3. JOURNAL ENTRY Try writing a few "American haiku" of your own. Then,
evaluate the success of your efforts. What problems did you encounter?

4. CRITICAL PERSPECTIVE Writing about his experiments with haiku, Jack
Kerouac said, "Above all, a Haiku must be very simple and free of all
poetic trickery and make a little picture and yet be as airy and graceful as
a Vivaldi Pastorella."
Do you think Kerouac's haiku satisfy these conditions?

Related Works: "Love and Other Catastrophes: A Mix Tape" (p. 84),
"Chicago" (p. 660), *from* "Song of Myself" (p. 796)

Open Form

Although an **open form** poem may make occasional use of rhyme and meter, it has no familiar pattern or design: no conventional stanzaic divisions, no consistent metrical pattern or line length, no repeated rhyme scheme. Still, open form poetry is not necessarily shapeless, untidy, or randomly ordered. All poems have form, and the form of a poem may be determined by factors such as repeated sounds, the appearance of words on the printed page, or pauses in natural speech as well as by a conventional metrical pattern or rhyme scheme.

Open form poetry invites readers to participate in the creative process, to discover the relationship between form and meaning. In fact, some modern poets believe that only open form offers them freedom to express their ideas or that the subject matter or mood of their poetry demands a relaxed, experimental approach to form. For example, when Lawrence Ferlinghetti portrays the poet as an acrobat who "climbs on rime" (p. 578), he constructs his poem in a way that is consistent with the poet/acrobat's willingness to take risks. Thus, the poem's idiosyncratic form supports its ideas about the limitless possibilities of poetry and the poet as experimenter.

Without a conventional pattern, however, poets must create forms that suit their needs, and they must continue to shape and reshape the look of the poem on the page as they revise its words. Thus, open form is a challenge, but it is also a way for poets to experiment with fresh arrangements of words and new juxtapositions of ideas, as Carl Sandburg does in the following poem.

Source: ©Bettmann/Corbis

CARL SANDBURG (1878–1967)

Chicago (1914)

Hog Butcher for the World,
Tool Maker, Stacker of Wheat,
Player with Railroads and the Nation's Freight
Handler;
Stormy, husky, brawling,
City of the Big Shoulders: 5
They tell me you are wicked and I believe them, for
     I have seen your painted women under the gas
     lamps
          luring the farm boys.
And they tell me you are crooked and I answer: Yes,
     it is true
     I have seen the gunman kill and go free to kill again.
And they tell me you are brutal and my reply is: On the
     faces of
women and children I have seen the marks of wanton
     hunger.

And having answered so I turn once more to those who sneer at
   this my city, and I give them back the sneer and say to them:
Come and show me another city with lifted head singing so
   proud to be alive and coarse and strong and cunning.   10
Flinging magnetic curses amid the toil of piling job on job,
   here is a tall bold slugger set vivid against the little soft cities;
Fierce as a dog with tongue lapping for action, cunning as a
   savage pitted against the wilderness,
      Bareheaded,
      Shoveling,
      Wrecking,   15
      Planning,
      Building, breaking, rebuilding,
Under the smoke, dust all over his mouth, laughing with white
   teeth,
Under the terrible burden of destiny laughing as a young man
   laughs,
Laughing even as an ignorant fighter laughs who has never
   lost a battle,   20
Bragging and laughing that under his wrist is the pulse,
   and under his ribs the heart of the people,
              Laughing!
Laughing the stormy, husky, brawling laughter of Youth,
   half-naked, sweating, proud to be Hog Butcher, Tool Maker,
   Stacker of Wheat, Player with Railroads and Freight Handler to
   the Nation.

Chicago street scene, 1925
© Hulton-Deutsch Collection/CORBIS

"Chicago" uses capitalization and punctuation conventionally, and it generally (though not always) arranges words in lines in a way that is consistent with the natural divisions of phrases and sentences. However, the poem is not divided into stanzas, and its lines vary widely in length—from a single word isolated on a line to a line crowded with words—and follow no particular metrical pattern. Instead, its form is created through its pattern of alternating sections of long and short lines; through its repeated words and phrases ("They tell me" in lines 6–8, "under" in lines 18–19, and "laughing" in lines 18–23, for example); through **alliteration** (for instance, "slugger set vivid against the little soft cities" in line 11); and, most of all, through the piling up of words and images into catalogs in lines 1–5, 13–17, and 22.

In order to understand Sandburg's reasons for choosing such a form, readers need to consider the poem's subject matter and theme. "Chicago" celebrates the scope and power of a "Stormy, husky, brawling" city, one that is exuberant and outgoing, not sedate and civilized. Chicago is a city that does not follow anyone else's rules; it is, after all, "Bareheaded, / Shoveling, / Wrecking, / Planning, / Building, breaking, rebuilding," constantly active, in flux, on the move, "proud to be alive." "Fierce as a dog . . . cunning as a savage," the city is characterized as, among other things, a worker, a fighter, and a harborer of "painted women" and killers and hungry women and children. Just as Chicago itself does not conform to the rules, the poem departs from the orderly confines of stanzaic form and measured rhyme and meter, a kind of form that is, after all, better suited to "the little soft cities" than to the "tall bold slugger" that is Chicago.

Of course, open form poetry does not have to look like Sandburg's prose poem. The following poem, an extreme example of open form, looks almost as if it has spilled out of a box of words.

E. E. CUMMINGS (1894–1962)

the sky was can dy (1925)

the
    sky
       was
can dy lu
minous   5
      edible
spry
    pinks shy
lemons
greens   coo l choc   10
olate
s.

```
un der,
    a  lo
co                          15
mo
    tive     s pout
              ing
               vi
                o      20
              lets
```

Like many of Cummings's poems, this one seems ready to skip off the page. Its irregular line length and its unconventional capitalization, punctuation, and word divisions immediately draw readers' attention to its form. Despite these oddities, and despite the absence of orderly rhyme and meter, the poem does have its conventional elements.

A closer examination reveals that the poem's theme—the beauty of the sky—is quite conventional; that the poem is divided, though somewhat crudely, into two sections; and that the poet does use some rhyme— "spry" and "shy," for example. However, Cummings's sky is described not in traditional terms but rather as something "edible," not only in terms of color but of flavor as well. The breaks within words ("can dy lu / minous"; "coo l choc / olate / s") seem to expand the words' possibilities, visually stretching them to the limit, extending their taste and visual image over several lines and, in the case of the poem's last two words, visually reinforcing the picture the words describe. In addition, the isolation of syllables exposes hidden rhyme, as in "lo / co / mo" and "lu" / "coo." Thus, by using open form, Cummings illustrates the capacity of a poem to move beyond the traditional boundaries set by words and lines.

FURTHER READING: Open Form

WALT WHITMAN (1819–1892)

from "Out of the Cradle Endlessly Rocking" (1881)

Out of the cradle endlessly rocking,
Out of the mocking-bird's throat, the musical shuttle,
Out of the Ninth-month[1] midnight,
Over the sterile sands and the fields beyond, where the child
      leaving his bed wander'd alone, bareheaded, barefoot,

---

[1] *Ninth-month:* The Quaker designation for September; in context, an allusion to the human birth cycle.

Down from the shower'd halo,   5
Up from the mystic play of shadows twining and twisting as if
    they were alive,
Out from the patches of briers and blackberries,
From the memories of the bird that chanted to me,
From your memories sad brother, from the fitful risings and
    fallings I heard,
From under that yellow half-moon late-risen and swollen as if
    with tears,   10
From those beginning notes of yearning and love there in the
    mist,
From the thousand responses of my heart never to cease,
From the myriad thence-arous'd words,
From the word stronger and more delicious than any,
From such as now they start the scene revisiting,   15
As a flock, twittering, rising, or overhead passing,
Borne hither, ere all eludes me, hurriedly,
A man, yet by these tears a little boy again,
Throwing myself on the sand, confronting the waves,
I, chanter of pains and joys, uniter of here and hereafter,   20
Taking all hints to use them, but swiftly leaping beyond them,
A reminiscence sing.

Reading and Reacting

1. This excerpt, the first twenty-two lines of a poem nearly two hundred
lines long, has no regular metrical pattern or rhyme scheme. What gives
it its form?

2. How might you explain why the poem's lines vary in length?

3. JOURNAL ENTRY Compare this excerpt with the excerpt from Whitman's
"Song of Myself" (p. 796). In what respects are the forms of the two
poems similar?

Related Works: "Chicago" (p. 660), "Defending Walt Whitman" (p. 732),
from "Song of Myself" (p. 796)

WILLIAM CARLOS WILLIAMS (1883–1963)

Spring and All (1923)

By the road to the contagious hospital
under the surge of the blue

mottled clouds driven from the
northeast—a cold wind. Beyond, the
waste of broad, muddy fields   5
brown with dried weeds, standing and fallen

patches of standing water
the scattering of tall trees

All along the road the reddish
purplish, forked, upstanding, twiggy   10
stuff of bushes and small trees
with dead, brown leaves under them
leafless vines—

Lifeless in appearance, sluggish
dazed spring approaches—   15

They enter the new world naked,
cold, uncertain of all
save that they enter. All about them
the cold, familiar wind—

Now the grass, tomorrow
the stiff curl of wildcarrot leaf   20
One by one objects are defined—
It quickens: clarity, outline of leaf

But now the stark dignity of
entrance—Still, the profound change   25
has come upon them: rooted, they
grip down and begin to awaken

Contagious Hospital, Brookline, MA, 1909
© Brookline Historical Society, Brookline, Massachussetts

Reading and Reacting

1. Although this poem is written in free verse and lacks a definite pattern of meter or rhyme, it includes some characteristics of closed form poetry. Explain.
2. What does Williams accomplish by visually isolating lines 7–8 and lines 14–15?
3. "Spring and All" includes assonance, alliteration, and repetition. Give several examples of each technique, and explain what each adds to the poem.
4. **JOURNAL ENTRY** What do you think the word *All* means in the poem's title?
5. **CRITICAL PERSPECTIVE** According to critic Bonnie Costello, "Williams thought about the creative process in painters' terms, and he asks us to experience the work as we might experience a modern painting. His great achievement was to bring some of its qualities into poetry."

    Consider the images Williams uses in this poem. In what ways is this poem like a painting? Which images are conveyed in "painters' terms"? How does he use these images to create meaning in the poem?

Related Works: "l(a" (p. 496), "Pied Beauty" (p. 625), "I wandered lonely as a cloud" (p. 712), "Monet's *Waterlillies*" (PS5)

RICHARD BLANCO (1968–   )

Mexican Almuerzo in New England (2002)

Word is praise for Marina, up past 3:00 a.m. the night before her
flight, preparing and packing the *platos tradicionales* she's now
heating up in the oven while the *tortillas* steam like full moons
on the stovetop. Dish by dish she tries to recreate Mexico in her
son's New England kitchen, taste-testing *el mole* from the pot,   5
stirring everything: *el chorizo-con-papas, el picadillo, el guacamole.*
The spirals of her stirs match the spirals in her eyes, the scented
steam coils around her like incense, suffusing the air with her folk-
lore. She loves Alfredo, as she loves all her sons, as she loves all
things: *seashells, cacti, plumes, artichokes.* Her hand waves us to   10
circle around the kitchen island, where she demonstrates how to
fold tacos for the *gringo* guests, explaining what is *hot* and what is
not, trying to describe tastes with English words she cannot savor.
As we eat, she apologizes: *not as good as at home, pero bueno. . .* It is

the best she can do in this strange kitchen which Sele has tried   15
to disguise with *papel picado* banners of colored tissue paper
displaying our names in piñata pink, maíz yellow, and Guadalupe
green–strung across the lintels of the patio filled with talk of an
early spring and *do you remembers* that leave an after-taste even
the *flan* and *café negro* don't cleanse. Marina has finished. She   20
sleeps in the guest room while Alfredo's paintings confess in
the living room, while the papier-mâché skeletons giggle on the
shelves, and shadows lean on the porch with rain about to fall.
Tomorrow our names will be taken down and Marina will leave
with her empty clay pots, feeling as she feels all things: *velvet,*   25
branches, honey, stones. Feeling what we all feel: home is a forgotten recipe, a spice we can find nowhere, a taste we can never
reproduce, exactly.

Reading and Reacting

1. What does the word *almuerzo* mean? Translate all the Spanish words in this poem. Which meanings are essential to your understanding of the poem, and which are not? Why?
2. Blanco, who is of Cuban heritage, says that he wrote this poem "in homage" to a Mexican American family and its matriarch, Marina. What does *homage* mean? In what sense is this poem written "in homage"?
3. Does the form of this prose poem suit its subject matter? Why or why not?
4. At the end of the poem, the speaker says that Marina feels "what we all feel: ome is a forgotten recipe, a spice we can find nowhere, a taste we can never reproduce, exactly." What does he mean? Do you see this as a pessimistic sentiment? Explain.

5. **Journal Entry** Rewrite this poem so its lines look like lines of poetry. Or, rewrite the poem as a short-short story divided into paragraphs. How does your rewrite change the poem? Is it an improvement?

Related Works: "Pilón" (p. 85), "Bilingual/Bilingue" (p. 537), "Dusting" (p. 706), "Papa's Bridge" (p. 709), "Mosul" (p. 728)

CLAIRE LEE (1997–   )

Living in Numbers (2013)

Sunday, August 22, 2010:
Number of times I've woken up after

oversleeping and sprung out of bed like a ninja: 959
Number of broken bones: 3
Number of scars, physical: 4; emotional: 947
Number of funerals attended: 7   5
Number of friends, Facebook: 744, real: 9
Number of cavities filled: 0

Percentage of people I can stand in the world: 3.5
Number of times I've laughed so hard my sides would bruise: 2,972
Number of times I've wanted to bawl my eyes out: 320   10
Number of things I regret: 11
Number of things I know: 918,394

Monday, August 23, 2010:
Number of times I've woken up after oversleeping and sprung out
of bed like a ninja: 960
Number of broken bones: 3
Number of scars, physical: 4; emotional: 1,293   15
Number of funerals attended: 7
Number of friends, Facebook: 800, real: 7
Number of cavities filled: 0

Percentage of people I can stand in the world: 3.4
Number of times I've laughed so hard my sides would bruise: 2,973   20
Number of times I've wanted to bawl my eyes out: 321
Number of things I regret: 13
Number of things I know: 918,390

Reading and Reacting

1. This poem's lines vary in length, and it is not divided into conventional
   stanzas; it also lacks a regular rhyme scheme and metrical pattern. What
   elements give it its form?
2. In what sense is the poem's speaker "living in numbers"? What function
   do the numbers serve in her life?

3. **JOURNAL ENTRY** What do you know about the life of this poem's speaker?
   What don't you know?

Related Works: "Love and Other Catastrophes: A Mix Tape" (p. 84), "Referential" (p. 447), "Suicide Note" (p. 507)

✔ **CHECKLIST   Writing about Form**

▢ Is the poem written in open or closed form? On what characteristics do you base your conclusion?

▢ Why did the poet choose open or closed form? For example, is the poem's form consistent with its subject matter, tone, or theme? Is it determined by the conventions of the historical period in which it was written?

▢ If the poem is arranged in closed form, does the pattern apply to single lines, to groups of lines, or to the entire poem? What factors determine the breaks between groups of lines?

▢ Is the poem a sonnet? a sestina? a villanelle? an epigram? a haiku? How do the traditional form's conventions suit the poet's language and theme? Does the poem follow the rules of the form at all times, or does it break any new ground?

▢ If the poem is arranged in open form, what determines the breaks at the ends of lines?

▢ Are certain words or phrases isolated on lines? Why?

▢ How do elements such as assonance, alliteration, rhyme, and repetition of words give the poem form?

▢ What use does the poet make of punctuation and capitalization? of white space on the page?

▢ Is the poem a prose poem? How does this form support the poem's subject matter?

▢ Is the poem a concrete poem? How does the poet use the visual shape of the poem to convey meaning?

WRITING SUGGESTIONS: Form

1. Reread the definitions of closed form and open form in this chapter. Based on these definitions, do you think concrete poems are "open" or "closed"? Explain your position in a short essay, supporting your thesis with specific references to the concrete poems in this chapter.

2. Some poets—for example, Emily Dickinson and Robert Frost—write both open and closed form poems. Choose one open and one closed form poem by a single poet, and analyze the two poems, explaining the poet's possible reasons for choosing each type of form.

3. Do you see complex forms, such as the villanelle and the sestina, as exercises or even merely as opportunities for poets to show off their skills—or do you believe the special demands of the forms add something valuable to a poem? To help you answer this question, read Dylan Thomas's "Do not go gentle into that good night" (p. 710) and Elizabeth Bishop's "Sestina" (p. 648).

4. Look through the other poetry chapters in this book, and find a prose poem. Write an essay in which you consider why the form seems suitable for the poem you have chosen. Is there a particular kind of subject matter that seems especially appropriate for a prose poem?

CHAPTER 22

SYMBOL, ALLEGORY, ALLUSION, MYTH

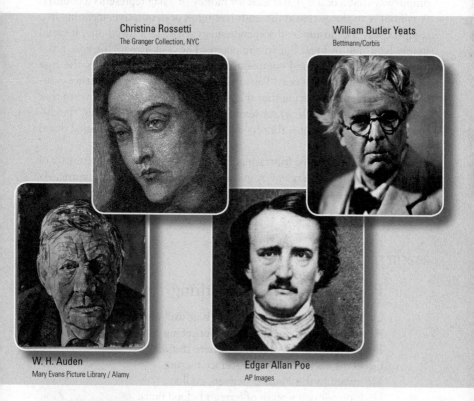

Christina Rossetti
The Granger Collection, NYC

William Butler Yeats
Bettmann/Corbis

W. H. Auden
Mary Evans Picture Library / Alamy

Edgar Allan Poe
AP Images

Bettmann/Corbis

WILLIAM BLAKE (1757–1827)

The Sick Rose (1794)

O Rose thou art sick.
The invisible worm
That flies in the night,
In the howling storm:

Has found out thy bed
Of crimson joy: 5
And his dark secret love
Does thy life destroy.

 ## Symbol

A **symbol** is an idea or image that suggests something else—but not in the simple way that a dollar sign stands for money or a flag represents a country. A symbol is an image that transcends its literal, or denotative, meaning in a complex way. For instance, if someone gives a rose to a loved one, it could simply be a sign of love. But in the poem "The Sick Rose," the rose has a range of contradictory and complementary meanings. What does the rose represent? Beauty? Perfection? Passion? Something else? Blake further complicates the matter by saying that the rose is "sick," infected by a worm that could symbolize death, decay, or sexuality. As this poem illustrates, the distinctive trait of a symbol is that its meaning cannot easily be pinned down or defined.

Such ambiguity can be frustrating, but it is precisely this characteristic of a symbol that enriches a poem by giving it additional layers of meaning. As Robert Frost has said, a symbol is a little thing that touches a larger thing. In the poem of his that follows, the central symbol does just this.

ROBERT FROST (1874–1963)

For Once, Then, Something (1923)

Others taunt me with having knelt at well-curbs
Always wrong to the light, so never seeing
Deeper down in the well than where the water
Gives me back in a shining surface picture
Me myself in the summer heaven, godlike,   5
Looking out of a wreath of fern and cloud puffs.
Once, when trying with chin against a well-curb,
I discerned, as I thought, beyond the picture,
Through the picture, a something white, uncertain,
Something more of the depths—and then I lost it.   10
Water came to rebuke the too clear water.
One drop fell from a fern, and lo, a ripple
Shook whatever it was lay there at bottom,
Blurred it, blotted it out. What was that whiteness?
Truth? A pebble of quartz? For once, then, something.   15

The central symbol in this poem is the "something" that the speaker thinks he sees at the bottom of a well. Traditionally, the act of looking down a well suggests a search for truth. In this poem, the speaker says that he always seems to look down the well at the wrong angle, so that all he can see is his own reflection—the surface, not the depths. Once, however, the speaker thought he saw something "beyond the picture," something "white, uncertain," but the image remained indistinct, disappearing when a drop of water from a fern caused the water to ripple. The poem ends with the speaker questioning the significance of what he saw. Like a reader encountering a symbol, the speaker is left trying to come to terms with images that cannot be clearly perceived and associations that cannot be readily understood. In light of the elusive nature of truth, all the speaker can do is ask questions that have no definite answers.

Symbols that appear in poetic works can be *conventional* or *universal*. **Conventional symbols** are those recognized by people who share certain cultural and social assumptions. For example, national flags evoke a general and agreed-upon response in most people of a particular country and—for better or for worse—American children have for years perceived the golden arches of McDonald's as a symbol of food and fun. **Universal symbols** are those likely to be recognized by people regardless of their culture. In 1890, the noted Scottish anthropologist Sir James George Frazer wrote the first version of his work *The Golden Bough*, in which he identified parallels between the rites and beliefs of early pagan cultures and those of Christianity. Fascinated by Frazer's work, the psychologist Carl Jung sought to explain these parallels by formulating a theory of **archetypes**, which held that certain images or ideas reside in the subconscious of all people. According to Jung, archetypal symbols include water, symbolizing rebirth; spring, symbolizing growth; and winter, symbolizing death.

Sometimes symbols that appear in poems can be obscure or highly idiosyncratic. William Blake is one of many poets (William Butler Yeats is another) whose works combine symbols from different cultural, theological, and philosophical sources to form complex networks of personal symbolic associations. To Blake, for example, the scientist Isaac Newton represents the tendency of scientists to quantify experience while ignoring the beauty and mystery of nature. Readers cannot begin to understand his use of Newton as a symbol until they have read a number of Blake's more difficult poems.

How do you know when an idea or image in a poem is a symbol? At what point do you decide that a particular object or idea goes beyond the literal level and takes on symbolic significance? When is a rose more than a rose or a well more than a well? Frequently you can recognize a symbol by its prominence or repetition. In "For Once, Then, Something," for example, the well is introduced in the first line of the poem, and it is the poem's focal point; in "The Sick Rose," the importance of the rose is emphasized by the title.

It is not enough, however, to identify an image or idea that seems to suggest something else. Your decision that a particular item has symbolic significance must be supported by the details of the poem and make sense in light of the ideas the poem develops. In the following poem, the symbolic significance of the volcano helps readers to understand the poem's central theme.

Eruption of Mt. Etna (Sicily), 2001
© Reuters/CORBIS

EMILY DICKINSON (1830–1886)

Volcanoes be in Sicily (1914)

Volcanoes be in Sicily
And South America
I judge from my Geography—
Volcanoes nearer here
A Lava step at any time   5
Am I inclined to climb—
A Crater I may contemplate
Vesuvius at Home.

This poem opens with a statement of fact: volcanoes are located in Sicily and South America. In line 3, however, the speaker introduces the improbable idea that volcanoes are located near where she is at the moment. Readers familiar with Dickinson know that her poems are highly autobiographical and that she lived in Amherst, Massachusetts, where there are no volcanoes. This information leads readers to suspect that they should not take the speaker's observation literally and that in the context of the poem volcanoes may have symbolic significance. But what do volcanoes suggest here?

On the one hand, volcanoes represent the awesome creative power of nature; on the other hand, they suggest its destructiveness. The speaker's contemplation of the crater of Vesuvius—the volcano that buried the ancient Roman city of Pompeii in A.D. 79—is therefore filled with contradictory associations. Because Dickinson was a recluse, volcanoes—active, destructive, unpredictable, and dangerous—may be seen as symbolic of everything she fears in the outside world—and, perhaps, within herself. Volcanoes may even suggest her own creative power, which, like a volcano, is something to be feared as well as contemplated. Dickinson seems to have a voyeur's attraction to danger and power, but she also fears them. For this reason, Dickinson keeps real volcanoes at a distance but uses her imagination to visit a symbolic, but no less terrifying, "Vesuvius at Home."

FURTHER READING: Symbol

EDGAR ALLAN POE (1809–1849)

The Raven (1844)

Once upon a midnight dreary, while I pondered,
    weak and weary,
Over many a quaint and curious volume of forgot
    ten lore,
While I nodded, nearly napping, suddenly there
    came a tapping,
As of some one gently rapping, rapping at my chamber door.
"'Tis some visitor," I muttered, "tapping at my chamber door—   5
              Only this, and nothing more."

Ah, distinctly I remember it was in the bleak December,
And each separate dying ember wrought its ghost upon the floor.
Eagerly I wished the morrow;—vainly I had sought to borrow
From my books surcease of sorrow—sorrow for the lost Lenore—   10
For the rare and radiant maiden whom the angels name Lenore—
              Nameless here for evermore.

And the silken sad uncertain rustling of each purple curtain
Thrilled me—filled me with fantastic terrors never felt before;
so that now, to still the beating of my heart, I stood repeating   15
"'Tis some visitor entreating entrance at my chamber door;—
Some late visitor entreating entrance at my chamber door;
              This it is, and nothing more."

Presently my soul grew stronger; hesitating then no longer,
"Sir," said I, "or Madam, truly your forgiveness I implore;   20
But the fact is I was napping, and so gently you came rapping,
And so faintly you came tapping, tapping at my chamber door,
That I scarce was sure I heard you"—here I opened wide the door;—
              Darkness there, and nothing more.

Deep into that darkness peering, long I stood there wondering,
    fearing,   25
Doubting, dreaming dreams no mortal ever dared to dream before;
But the silence was unbroken, and the darkness gave no token,

And the only word there spoken was the whispered word,
   "Lenore!"
This I whispered, and an echo murmured back the word,
   "Lenore!"—
       Merely this, and nothing more. 30

Back into the chamber turning, all my soul within me burning,
Soon I heard again a tapping somewhat louder than before.
"Surely," said I, "surely that is something at my window lattice;
Let me see, then, what thereat is, and this mystery explore—
Let my heart be still a moment and this mystery explore;— 35
       'Tis the wind and nothing more!"

Open here I flung the shutter, when, with many a flirt and flutter,
In there stepped a stately raven of the saintly days of yore;
Not the least obeisance made he; not an instant stopped or stayed he;
But, with mien of lord or lady, perched above my chamber door— 40
Perched upon a bust of Pallas[1] just above my chamber door—
       Perched, and sat, and nothing more.

Then this ebony bird beguiling my sad fancy into smiling,
By the grave and stern decorum of the countenance it wore,
"Though thy crest be shorn and shaven, thou," I said, "art sure no
   craven, 45
Ghastly grim and ancient raven wandering from the Nightly shore—
Tell me what thy lordly name is on the Night's Plutonian[2] shore!"
       Quoth the raven, "Nevermore."

Much I marvelled this ungainly fowl to hear discourse so plainly,
Though its answer little meaning—little relevancy bore, 50
For we cannot help agreeing that no living human being
Ever yet was blessed with seeing bird above his chamber door—
Bird or beat upon the sculptured bust above his chamber door,
       With such name as "Nevermore."

But the raven, sitting lonely on the placid bust, spoke only 55
That one word, as if his soul in that one word he did outpour.
Nothing farther then he uttered—not a feather then he fluttered—
Till I scarcely more than muttered "Other friends have flown
   before—
On the morrow *he* will leave me, as my hopes have flown before."
       Then the bird said "Nevermore." 60

---

[1] *Pallas:* Athena, Greek goddess of wisdom.

[2] *Plutonian:* Dark; Pluto was the Greek god of the dead and ruler of the underworld.

Startled at the stillness broken by reply so aptly spoken,
"Doubtless," said I, "what it utters is its only stock and store
Caught from some unhappy master whom unmerciful Disaster
Followed fast and followed faster till his songs one burden bore—
Till the dirges of his Hope that melancholy burden bore   65
                Of 'Never—nevermore.'"

But the raven still beguiling all my sad soul into smiling,
Straight I wheeled a cushioned seat in front of bird and bust and
    door;
Then, upon the velvet sinking, I betook myself to linking
Fancy unto fancy, thinking what this ominous bird of yore—   70
What this grim, ungainly, ghastly, gaunt, and ominous bird of yore
                Meant in croaking "Nevermore."

This I sat engaged in guessing, but no syllable expressing
To the fowl whose fiery eyes now burned into my bosom's core;
This and more I sat divining, with my head at ease reclining   75
On the cushion's velvet lining that the lamplight gloated o'er,
But whose velvet violet lining with the lamplight gloating o'er,
            she shall press, ah, nevermore!

Then, methought, the air grew denser, perfumed from an unseen
    censer
Swung by angels whose faint foot-falls tinkled on the tufted floor.   80
"Wretch," I cried, "thy God hath lent thee—by these angels he
    hath sent thee
Respite—respite and nepenthe[3] from thy memories of Lenore!
Quaff, oh quaff this kind nepenthe and forget this lost Lenore!"
            Quoth the raven, "Nevermore."

"Prophet!" said I, "thing of evil!—prophet still, if bird or devil!—   85
Whether Tempter sent, or whether tempest tossed thee here
    ashore,
Desolate, yet all undaunted, on this desert land enchanted—
On this home by Horror haunted—tell me truly, I implore—
Is there—*is* there balm in Gilead?[4]—tell me—tell me, I implore!"
            Quoth the raven, "Nevermore."   90

"Prophet!" said I, "thing of evil—prophet still, if bird or devil!
By that Heaven that bends above us—by that God we both
    adore—

---

[3] *nepenthe:* A drug mentioned in the *Odessy* as a remedy for grief.
[4] *Gilead:* A region mentioned in the Bible; noted for its soothing ointments.

Tell this soul with sorrow laden if, within the distant Aidenn,[5]
It shall clasp a sainted maiden whom the angels name Lenore—
Clasp a rare and radiant maiden whom the angels name Lenore."   95
                    Quoth the raven, "Nevermore."

"Be that word our sign of parting, bird or fiend!" I shrieked
    upstarting—
"Get thee back into the tempest and the Night's Plutonian shore!
Leave no black plume as a token of that lie thy soul hath spoken!
Leave my loneliness unbroken!—quit the bust above my door!   100
Take thy beak from out my heart, and take thy form from off my
    door!"
                    Quoth the raven, "Nevermore."

And the raven, never flitting, still is sitting, still is sitting
On the pallid bust of Pallas just above my chamber door;
And his eyes have all the seeming of a demon's that is dreaming,   105
And the lamp-light o'er him streaming throws his shadow on the
    floor;
And my soul from out that shadow that lies floating on the floor
                    Shall be lifted—nevermore!

Raven
Ivan Bliznetsov/Dreamstime.com

[5]*Aidenn:* A variation of Eden, the home of Adam and Eve.

Reading and Reacting

1. Who is the speaker in the poem? What is his state of mind? How does the raven mirror the speaker's mental state?

2. "The Raven" contains a good deal of alliteration. Identify some examples. How does this use of repeated initial consonant sounds help to convey the mood of the poem?

3. The speaker refers to the raven in a number of different ways. At one point, it is simply "an ebony bird" (line 42); at another, it is a "prophet" and "a thing of evil" (85). How else does the speaker characterize the raven?

4. **JOURNAL ENTRY** What is the symbolic significance of the raven? Of the repeated word "nevermore"? Of the bust of Pallas, the ancient Greek god of wisdom?

5. **CRITICAL PERSPECTIVE** According to Christoffer Nilsson, who maintains a website dedicated to the works of Poe, "The Raven" was composed with almost mathematical precision. When writing the stanza in which the interrogation of the raven reaches its climax (third stanza from the end), Poe wanted to make certain that no preceding stanza would "surpass this in rhythmical effect":

> Poe then worked backwards from this stanza and used the word "Nevermore" in many different ways, so that even with the repetition of this word, it would not prove to be monotonous. Poe builds the tension in this poem up, stanza by stanza, but after the climaxing stanza he tears the whole thing down, and lets the narrator know that there is no meaning in searching for a moral in the raven's "nevermore."

Do you agree with Nilsson that it makes no sense to look for a moral in the raven's "nevermore"? What kind of moral, if any, do you think "Nevermore" implies for the speaker?

Related Works: "Rooming houses are old women" (p. 579), "Ode to a Nightingale" (p. 602), "The Tyger" (p. 740), *Hamlet* (p. 789)

VIRGIL SUÁREZ (1962–   )

Isla (2000)

In Los Angeles I grew up watching *The Three Stooges,*
The Little Rascals, Speed Racer, and the Godzilla movies,

those my mother called *"Los monstruos,"* and though I didn't
yet speak English, I understood why such a creature would,

upon being woken up from its centuries-long slumber, rise   5
and destroy Tokyo's buildings, cars, people—I understood

by the age of twelve what it meant to be unwanted, exiled,
how you move from one country to another where nobody

wants you, nobody knows you, and I sat in front of the TV,
transfixed by the snow-fizz on our old black and white,   10

and when Godzilla bellows his eardrum-crushing growl,
I screamed back, this victory-holler from one so rejected

and cursed to another. When the monster whipped its tail
and destroyed, I threw a pillow across my room; each time

my mother stormed into the room and asked me what,   15
what I thought I was doing throwing things at the walls.

"¡Ese monstruo, esa isla!" she'd say. That monster, that island,
and I knew she wasn't talking about the movie. She meant

her country, mine, that island in the Caribbean we left behind,
itself a reptile-looking mass on each map, on my globe,   20

a crocodile-like creature rising again, eating us so completely.
                                                    —*for Jarret Keene*

Reading and Reacting

1. What specific elements in the poem make you think that the island is a symbol?

2. Why does the speaker discuss Godzilla? What relation does Godzilla have to Cuba—the island the speaker "left behind"?

3. What does the island symbolize to the speaker? to his mother? to you?

4. **Journal Entry** The speaker uses Spanish in two places (as well as the title) in the poem. Why? What would be lost if these phrases were written in English?

Related Works: "Sticks" (p. 99), "New York Day Women" (p. 273), "Metaphors" (p. 582), "Mexican Almuerzo in New England" (p. 666), "Papa's Bridge" (p. 709), "I Hear America Singing" (p. 795), *The Cuban Swimmer* (p. 1166)

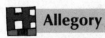 ## Allegory

Allegory is a form of narrative that conveys a message or doctrine (usually moral or political) by using people, places, or things to stand for abstract ideas. **Allegorical figures**, each with a strict equivalent, form an **allegorical framework**, a set of ideas that conveys the allegory's message or lesson. Thus, the allegory takes place on two levels: a **literal level** that tells a story and a **figurative level** on which the allegorical figures in the story stand for ideas, concepts, and other qualities.

Like symbols, allegorical figures suggest other things. But unlike symbols, which have a range of possible meanings, allegorical figures can always be assigned specific meanings. (Because writers use allegory to instruct, they gain nothing by hiding its significance.) Thus, symbols open up possibilities for interpretation, whereas allegories tend to restrict possibilities.

Quite often an allegory involves a journey or an adventure, as in the case of Dante's *Divine Comedy*, which traces a journey through Hell, Purgatory, and Heaven. Within an allegory, everything can have meaning: the road on which the characters walk, the people they encounter, or a phrase that one of them repeats throughout the journey. Once you understand the allegorical framework, your main task is to see how the various elements fit within this system. Some allegorical poems can be relatively straightforward, but others can be so complicated that it takes a great deal of effort to unlock their meaning. In the following poem, a journey is central to the allegory.

CHRISTINA ROSSETTI (1830–1894)

Uphill (1861)

Does the road wind up-hill all the way?
    Yes, to the very end.
Will the day's journey take the whole long day?
    From morn to night, my friend.

But is there for the night a resting-place?   5
    A roof for when the slow dark hours begin.
May not the darkness hide it from my face?
    You cannot miss that inn.

Shall I meet other wayfarers at night?
    Those who have gone before.   10
Then must I knock, or call when just in sight?
    They will not keep you standing at that door.

Shall I find comfort, travel-sore and weak?
    Of labor you shall find the sum.
Will there be beds for me and all who seek?   15
    Yea, beds for all who come.

"Uphill" uses a question-and-answer structure to describe a journey along an uphill road. Like the one described in John Bunyan's seventeenth-century allegory *The Pilgrim's Progress*, this is a spiritual journey, one that suggests the

The Pilgrims going up the hill Difficulty.

Illustration from 1776 printing of *The Pilgrim's
Progress*
© Lebrecht / The Image Works

challenges a person faces throughout life. The day-and-night duration of the
journey stands for life and death, and the inn at the end of the road stands
for the grave, the final resting place.

FURTHER READING: Allegory

CARL DENNIS (1939–   )

At the Border   (2004)

At the border between the past and the future
No sign on a post warns you that your passport
Won't let you return to your native land
As a citizen, just as a tourist
Who won't be allowed to fraternize with the locals.   5

No guard steps out of a booth to explain
You can't bring gifts back, however modest,

Can't even pass a note to a few friends
That suggests what worries of theirs are misguided,
What expectations too ambitious.   10

Are you sure you're ready to leave,
To cross the bridge that begins
Under a clear sky and ends in fog?
But look, you've started across already
And it's one-lane wide, with no room for U-turns.   15

No time even to pause as drivers behind you
Lean on their horns, those who've convinced themselves
Their home awaits them on the other side.

Reading and Reacting

1. On one level, this poem is about a trip. What details suggest that the poem is about something more?

2. In this poem, the border separates the past and the future. Why does the speaker call the distance between the past and the future a border?

3. What is the allegorical significance of each of the following items?

- The passport
- The bridge
- The guard
- The fog
- The one-lane road
- The drivers

4. JOURNAL ENTRY How does this poem describe the past? How is the past different from the future?

5. CRITICAL PERSPECTIVE In a review of "At the Border," poet Robert Pinsky makes the following observation:

> Dennis gives a dreamy urgency to his compact allegory. . . . The feeling is not gloomy, but a gentle and haunted metaphysical teasing. Unornamented and intimate, the poem's even voice describes the humdrum details of tourism— the passport, the bridge, the guard, the traffic—as emblems of a perpetual journey from one misty idea of home to another—one behind, beyond return and the other envisioned ahead, but receding into the fog.

What is the "perpetual journey" to which Pinsky refers? Do you agree that the poem has "a dreamy urgency"?

Related Works: "Young Goodman Brown" (p. 367), "A Worn Path" (p. 386), "The Secret Lion" (p. 466), "Rooming houses are old women" (p. 579), "Uphill" (p. 681)

Allusion

An **allusion** is a brief reference to a person, place, or event (fictional or actual) that readers are expected to recognize. Like symbols and allegories, allusions enrich a work by introducing associations from another context.

Although most poets expect readers to recognize their references, some use allusions to exclude certain readers from their work. In his 1922 poem "The Waste Land," for example, T. S. Eliot alludes to historical events, ancient languages, and obscure literary works. He even includes a set of notes to accompany his poem, but they do little more than complicate an already difficult text. (As you might expect, initial critical response to this poem was mixed: some critics said that it was a work of genius, while others thought that it was arcane and pretentious.)

In a sense, allusions favor those readers who have the background or knowledge to recognize them and excludes those who do not. At one time, writers could expect educated readers to recognize allusions to the Bible and to Greek and Roman classics. For example, when Christopher Marlowe referred to "Olympus' top" in his sixteenth-century play *Doctor Faustus*, he expected his readers to know that he was alluding to Mount Olympus, the home of the gods in Greek mythology. Today, this assumption is not valid, but with the advent of search engines such as *Google*, interpreting an allusion requires nothing more than entering a keyword (or keywords) into a Web browser. If, when reading a poem, you come across a reference to which you are not familiar, take the time to look it up. Your understanding and appreciation of a poem will be enhanced by your ability to interpret an unfamiliar reference.

Allusions can come from any source: history, the arts, other works of literature, the Bible, current events, or even the personal life of the poet. Notice how the following poem uses allusions to prominent literary figures as well as to myth to develop its theme.

WILLIAM MEREDITH (1919–2007)

Dreams of Suicide (1980)

(in sorrowful memory of Ernest Hemingway, Sylvia Plath, and John Berryman)

I

I reach for the awkward shotgun not to disarm
you, but to feel the metal horn,
furred with the downy membrane of dream.
More surely than the unicorn,
you are the mythical beast.   5

II

Or I am sniffing an oven. On all fours
I am imitating a totemic animal
but she is not my totem or the totem
of my people, this is not my magic oven.

III

If I hold you tight by the ankles,   10
still you fly upward from the iron railing.
Your father made these wings,
after he made his own, and now from beyond
he tells you *fly down*, in the voice
my own father might say *walk, boy*.   15

This poem is dedicated to the memory of three writers who committed suicide. In each stanza, the speaker envisions in a dream the death of one of
the writers. In the first stanza, he dreams of Ernest Hemingway, who killed
himself with a shotgun. The speaker grasps the "metal horn" of Hemingway's
shotgun and transforms Hemingway into a mythical beast who, like a unicorn, represents the rare, unique talent of the artist. In the second stanza, the
speaker dreams of Sylvia Plath, who asphyxiated herself in a gas oven. He
sees himself, like Plath, on his knees imitating an animal sniffing an oven.
In the third stanza, the speaker dreams of John Berryman, who leaped to his
death. Berryman is characterized as Icarus, a mythological figure who, along
with his father Daedalus, fled Crete by building wings made of feathers and
wax. Together they flew away; however, ignoring his father's warning, Icarus
flew so close to the sun that the wax melted, and he fell to his death in the
sea. In this poem, then, the speaker uses allusions to make a point about the
difficult lives of writers—and, perhaps, to convey his own empathy for those
who could not survive the struggle to reconcile art and life.

FURTHER READING: Allusion

BILLY COLLINS (1941–)

Aristotle[1] (1998)

This is the beginning.
Almost anything can happen.
This is where you find
the creation of light, a fish wriggling onto land,

---

[1] *Aristotle:* Greek philosopher (384–322 BC).

the first word of Paradise Lost[2] on an empty page.   5
Think of an egg, the letter A,
a woman ironing on a bare stage as the heavy curtain rises.
This is the very beginning.
The first-person narrator introduces himself,
tells us about his lineage.   10
The mezzo-soprano[3] stands in the wings.
Here the climbers are studying a map
or pulling on their long woolen socks.
This is early on, years before the Ark, dawn.
The profile of an animal is being smeared   15
on the wall of a cave,
and you have not yet learned to crawl.
This is the opening, the gambit,
a pawn moving forward an inch.
This is your first night with her, your first night without her   20
This is the first part
where the wheels begin to turn,
where the elevator begins its ascent,
before the doors lurch apart.

This is the middle.   25
Things have had time to get complicated,
messy, really. Nothing is simple anymore.
Cities have sprouted up along the rivers
teeming with people at cross-purposes—
a million schemes, a million wild looks.   30
Disappointment unshoulders his knapsack
here and pitches his ragged tent.
This is the sticky part where the plot congeals,
where the action suddenly reverses
or swerves off in an outrageous direction.   35
Here the narrator devotes a long paragraph
to why Miriam does not want Edward's child.
Someone hides a letter under a pillow.
Here the aria[4] rises to a pitch,
a song of betrayal, salted with revenge,   40
And the climbing party is stuck on a ledge

---

[2] *Paradise Lost:* Epic poem by John Milton (1608–1674).

[3] *mezzo-soprano:* Meaning "middle soprano," a type of female opera singer.

[4] *aria:* A musical piece for one voice, often performed in the context of an opera.

halfway up the mountain.
This is the bridge, the painful modulation.
This is the thick of things.
So much is crowded into the middle—   45
the guitars of Spain, piles of ripe avocados,
Russian uniforms, noisy parties,
lakeside kisses, arguments heard through a wall
too much to name, too much to think about.

And this is the end,   50
the car running out of road,
the river losing its name in an ocean,
the long nose of the photographed horse
touching the white electronic line.
This is the colophon,[5] the last elephant in the parade,   55
the empty wheelchair, and pigeons floating down in the evening.
Here the stage is littered with bodies,
the narrator leads the characters to their cells,
and the climbers are in their graves.
It is me hitting the period   60
and you closing the book.
It is Sylvia Plath[6] in the kitchen
and St. Clement[7] with an anchor around his neck.
This is the final bit
thinning away to nothing.   65
This is the end, according to Aristotle,
what we have all been waiting for,
what everything comes down to,
the destination we cannot help imagining,
a streak of light in the sky,   70
a hat on a peg, and outside the cabin, falling leaves.

Reading and Reacting

1. According to Aristotle, the plot of a tragedy must be "whole"—it must
   have a beginning, a middle, and an end. Do you think the poem's title is
   appropriate? Explain.
2. In what sense is this poem a tragedy? In what sense is it not?

---

[5]*colophon:* The finishing touch.

[6]*Sylvia Plath:* American poet (1932–1963) who committed suicide by inhaling the gas from her oven.

[7]*St. Clement:* First of the Apostolic Fathers and Pope of Rome from 88 to 97 AD or from 92 to 101 AD, Clement
was supposedly martyred by being tied to an anchor and thrown into the sea.

3. What allusions does the speaker make in the last stanza? What is the significance of these allusions?

4. **JOURNAL ENTRY** Does Collins expect readers to be familiar with his allusions? Do you think he expects too much of readers? Or, do you think the effort is worth the gain?

5. **CRITICAL PERSPECTIVE** Critic John Taylor praises the work of Billy Collins in the following terms:

> Rarely has anyone written poems that appear so transparent on the surface yet become so ambiguous, thought-provoking or simply wise once the reader has peered into the depths. Collins's pellucid style greatly facilitates this kind of meditative peering into the unknown, yet this clarity is hard-won. It takes a sure hand indeed to guide readers so often and respectfully into an unobstructed communion with reverie, drollery, gentle mischievousness, or a subdued but genuine joy.

Do you think this description applies to the poem "Aristotle"? For example, is "Aristotle" "transparent on the surface"? Is it in any way "ambiguous"? Which aspects of the poem might be considered "wise" or "thought-provoking"?

Related Works: "Love and Other Catastrophes: A Mix Tape" (p. 84), "Araby" (p. 288), "The Things They Carried" (p. 310), "My Last Duchess" (p. 503), "Daddy" (p. 589), *Oedipus the King* (p. 1182)

R. S. GWYNN (1948–)

Shakespearean Sonnet (2005)

(With a first line taken from the TV listings)

A man is haunted by his father's ghost.
A boy and girl love while their families fight.
A Scottish king is murdered by his host.
Two couples get lost on a summer night.
A hunchback murders all who block his way.   5
A ruler's rivals plot against his life.
A fat man and a prince make rebels pay.
A noble Moor has doubts about his wife.
An English king decides to conquer France.
A duke learns that his best friend is a she,   10
A forest sets the scene for this romance.
An old man and his daughters disagree.
A Roman leader makes a big mistake.
A sexy queen is bitten by a snake.

Reading and Reacting

1. Why does Gwynn write his poem in the form of a Shakespearean sonnet?

2. Each line of the poem summarizes the plot of a Shakespeare play in the form of a TV listing. What do you think Gwynn hopes to accomplish with these summaries?

3. Where does Gwynn use alliteration? At what point does he use irony?

4. JOURNAL ENTRY Try to identify all the plays Gwynn alludes to in his poem.

5. CRITICAL PERSPECTIVE According to critic Bruce Bawer, R. S. Gwynn's recurrent theme is "the decay of Western civilization—trash culture, fashionable politics, education made E-Z—and the enduring faults, frailties, fallacies, foibles, and fraudulencies of the human comedy." In what sense, if any, do you think "Shakespearean Sonnet" is about "the decay of Western civilization"?

Related Works: "Cathedral" (p. 353), "The English Canon" (p. 548), "An Apology" (p. 567), "Shall I compare thee to a summer's day?" (p. 575), "When, in disgrace with Fortune and men's eyes" (p. 638), *Hamlet* (p. 789)

 Myth

A **myth** is a narrative that embodies—and in some cases helps to explain—the religious, philosophical, moral, and political values of a culture. Using gods and supernatural beings, myths try to make sense of occurrences in the natural world. (The term *myth* can also refer to a private belief system devised by an individual poet as well as to any fully realized fictitious setting in which a literary work takes place, such as the myths of William Faulkner's Yoknapatawpha County or of novelist Lawrence Durrell's Alexandria.) Contrary to popular usage, *myth* does not mean "falsehood." In the broadest sense, myths are stories—usually whole groups of stories—that can be true or partly true as well as false; regardless of their degree of accuracy, however, myths frequently express the deepest beliefs of a culture. According to this definition, the *Iliad* and the *Odyssey*, the Koran, and the Old and New Testaments can all be referred to as myths.

The mythologist Joseph Campbell observed that myths contain truths that link people together, whether they live today or lived 2,500 years ago. Myths attempt to explain phenomena that human beings care about, regardless of when and where they live. It is not surprising, then, that myths frequently contain **archetypal images**—images that cut across cultural and racial boundaries and touch us at a very deep level. Many Greek myths illustrate this power. For example, when Orpheus descends into Hades to rescue his wife, Eurydice, he acts out the universal human desire to transcend death; and when Telemachus sets out in search of his father, Odysseus, he reminds readers that we are all lost children searching for parents. When Icarus ignores his father and flies too near the sun and when Pandora cannot resist looking into a box that she has been told not to open, we are reminded of the human weaknesses we all share.

When poets use myths, they are making allusions. They expect readers to bring to the poem the cultural, emotional, and ethical context of the myths to which they are alluding. At one time, when all educated individuals studied the Greek and Latin classics as well as the Bible and other religious texts, poets could safely assume that readers would recognize the mythological allusions they made. Today, many readers are unable to understand the full significance of an allusion or its application within a poem. Many of the poems in this anthology are accompanied by notes, but these may not provide all the information you will need to understand the full significance of each mythological allusion. Occasionally, you may have to look elsewhere for answers, turning to dictionaries, encyclopedias, online information sites such as <http://www.answers.com>, or collections of myths such as the *New Larousse Encyclopedia of Mythology* or *Bulfinch's Mythology*.

Sometimes a poet alludes to a myth in a title; sometimes references to various myths appear throughout a poem; at other times, an entire poem focuses on a single myth. In each case, as in the following poem, the use of myth helps to develop the poem's theme.

COUNTEE CULLEN (1903–1946)

Yet Do I Marvel (1925)

I doubt not God is good, well-meaning, kind,
And did He stoop to quibble could tell why
The little buried mole continues blind,
Why flesh that mirrors Him must some day die,
Make plain the reason tortured Tantalus
Is baited by the fickle fruit, declare   5
If merely brute caprice dooms Sisyphus
To struggle up a never-ending stair.
Inscrutable His ways are, and immune
To catechism by a mind too strewn   10
With petty cares to slightly understand
What awful brain compels His awful hand.
Yet do I marvel at this curious thing:
To make a poet black, and bid him sing!

Engraving of Tantalus reaching for fruit
©The Print Collector / HIP / The Image Works

The speaker begins by affirming his belief in the benevolence of God but then questions why God engages in what appear to be capricious acts. As part of his catalog of questions, the speaker alludes to Tantalus and Sisyphus, two figures from Greek mythology. Tantalus was a king who was condemned to Hades for his crimes. There, he was forced to stand in a pool of water up to his chin. Overhead hung a tree branch laden with fruit. When Tantalus got thirsty and tried to drink, the level of the water dropped, and when he got hungry and reached for fruit, it moved just out of reach. Thus, Tantalus was doomed to be near what he most desired but forever unable to obtain it. Sisyphus also was condemned to Hades. For his disrespect of Zeus, he was sentenced to endless toil. Every day, Sisyphus pushed a boulder up a steep hill. Every time he neared the top, the boulder rolled back down the hill, and Sisyphus had to begin again. Like Tantalus, the speaker in "Yet Do I Marvel" cannot have what he wants; like Sisyphus, he is forced to toil in vain. He wonders why a well-meaning God would "make a poet black, and bid him sing" in a racist society that does not listen to his voice. Thus, the poet's two allusions to Greek mythology enrich the poem by connecting the suffering of the speaker to a universal drama that has been acted out again and again.

FURTHER READING: Myth

MAY SWENSON (1919–1989)

The Centaur (1955)

The summer that I was ten—
Can it be there was only one
summer that I was ten?

It must have been a long one then—
each day I'd go out to choose   5
a fresh horse from my stable

which was a willow grove
down by the old canal.
I'd go on my two bare feet.

But when, with my brother's jack-knife,   10
I had cut me a long limber horse
with a good thick knob for a head,

and peeled him slick and clean
except a few leaves for the tail,
and cinched my brother's belt   15

around his head for a rein,
I'd straddle and canter[1] him fast
up the grass bank to the path,

trot along in the lovely dust
that talcumed over his hoofs,   20
hiding my toes, and turning

his feet to swift half-moons.
The willow knob with the strap
jouncing between my thighs

was the pommel[2] and yet the poll[3]   25
of my nickering[4] pony's head.
My head and my neck were mine,

---

[1] *canter:* A horse's style of walking (faster than a trot, but slower than a gallop).
[2] *pommel:* The raised part at the front of a horse's saddle.
[3] *poll:* The back of a horse's skull.
[4] *nickering:* Neighing or whinnying softly.

yet they were shaped like a horse.
My hair flopped to the side
like the mane of a horse in the wind.   30

My forelock swung in my eyes,
my neck arched and I snorted.
I shied and skittered and reared,

stopped and raised my knees,
pawed at the ground and quivered.   35
My teeth bared as we wheeled

and swished through the dust again.
I was the horse and the rider,
and the leather I slapped to his rump

spanked my own behind.   40
Doubled, my two hoofs beat
a gallop along the bank,

the wind twanged in my mane,
my mouth squared to the bit.
And yet I sat on my steed   45

quiet, negligent riding,
my toes standing the stirrups,
my thighs hugging his ribs.

At a walk we drew up to the porch.
I tethered him to a paling.[5]   50
Dismounting, I smoothed my skirt

and entered the dusky hall.
My feet on the clean linoleum
left ghostly toes in the hall.

Where have you been? said my mother.   55
Been riding, I said from the sink,
and filled me a glass of water.

What's that in your pocket? she said.
Just my knife. It weighted my pocket
and stretched my dress awry.   60

Go tie back your hair, said my mother,
and Why is your mouth all green?
Rob Roy,[6] he pulled some clover
as we crossed the field, I told her.

---

[5]*paling:* One of the vertical wooden pieces making up a fence.
[6]*Rob Roy:* One of the horses in the 1877 novel *Black Beauty.*

Statue of a centaur

Reading and Reacting

1. In Greek mythology, centaurs were a primitive tribe of half-horse half-men, who lived in the mountains and forests. What do they represent to the speaker in the poem?

2. On the surface, the poem describes a child's fantasy of riding a stick horse. What else does it suggest?

3. As the poem progresses, the child speaker becomes more and more like a horse. Find some images that convey this transformation.

4. **Journal Entry** "The Centaur" begins with an adult speaker reminiscing about events that took place when she was ten. Why do you think these events are so important to her?

5. **Critical Perspective** *Poetry* reviewer William Stafford remarked that Swenson's work has a constant, cumulative impact on readers. How does this comment apply to "The Centaur"?

Related Works: "Gryphon" (p. 172), "Young Goodman Brown" (p. 367), "Go Down, Moses" (p. 736), "The Negro Speaks of Rivers" (p. 769), "The Nymph's Reply to the Shepherd" (p. 782), "Ulysses" (p. 790), "The Second Coming" (p. 800)

Source: ©Bettmann/Corbis

WILLIAM BUTLER YEATS (1865–1939)

Leda and the Swan (1924)

A sudden blow: the great wings beating still
Above the staggering girl, her thighs caressed
By the dark webs, her nape caught in his bill,
He holds her helpless breast upon his breast.   5

How can those terrified vague fingers push
The feathered glory from her loosening thighs?
And how can body, laid in that white rush,
But feel the strange heart beating where it lies?

A shudder in the loins engenders there
The broken wall, the burning roof and tower   10
And Agamemnon dead.
                                  Being so caught up,
So mastered by the brute blood of the air,
Did she put on his knowledge with his power
Before the indifferent beak could let her drop?   15

Peter Paul Rubens, *Leda and the Swan*, 1598
bpk, Berlin / Art Resource, NY

Reading and Reacting

1. What event is described in this poem? What is the mythological significance of this event?

2. How is Leda portrayed? Why is the swan described as a "feathered glory" (line 6)? Why in the poem's last line is Leda dropped by his "indifferent beak"?

3. The third stanza refers to the Trojan War, which was indirectly caused by the event described in the poem. How does the allusion to the Trojan War help develop the theme of the poem?

4. JOURNAL ENTRY Does the poem answer the question asked in its last two lines? Explain.

5. CRITICAL PERSPECTIVE According to Richard Ellmann, this poem deals with "transcendence of opposites." The bird's "rape of the human, the coupling of god and woman, the moment at which one epoch ended and another began ... in the act which included all these Yeats had the violent symbol for the transcendence of opposites which he needed."

What opposite or contrary forces exist in the myth of Leda and the swan? Do you think the poem implies that these forces can be reconciled?

Related Works: "Greasy Lake" (p. 425), "Where Are You Going, Where Have You Been?" (p. 453), "The Second Coming" (p. 800)

W. H. AUDEN (1907–1973)

Musée des Beaux Arts (1940)

About suffering they were never wrong,
The Old Masters: how well they understood
Its human position; how it takes place
While someone else is eating or opening a
    window or just walking dully along
How, when the aged are reverently, passionately
    waiting   5
For the miraculous birth, there always must be
Children who did not specially want it to
    happen, skating
On a pond at the edge of the wood:
They never forgot
That even the dreadful martyrdom must run its
    course   10
Anyhow in a corner, some untidy spot

Where the dogs go on with their doggy life and the torturer's horse
Scratches its innocent behind on a tree.
In Brueghel's *Icarus*, for instance: how everything turns away
Quite leisurely from the disaster; the ploughman may   15
Have heard the splash, the forsaken cry,
But for him it was not an important failure; the sun shone
As it had to on the white legs disappearing into the green
Water; and the expensive delicate ship that must have seen
Something amazing, a boy falling out of the sky,   20
Had somewhere to get to and sailed calmly on.

Brueghel, Pieter the Elder (1525?–1569). *Landscape with the Fall of Icarus*
Scala / Art Resource, NY

Reading and Reacting

1. Reread the summary of the myth of Icarus on page 685. What does
Auden's interpretation of this myth contributed to the poem?

2. What point does the poet make by referring to the "Old Masters" (line 2)?

3. JOURNAL ENTRY Brueghel's painting *Landscape with the Fall of Icarus* is
shown above. How does looking at this painting help you to understand
the poem? To what specific details in the painting does the poet refer?

Related Works: "The Lottery" (p. 335), "One day I wrote her name upon the
strand" (p. 554), "Shall I compare thee to a summer's day?" (p. 575), "Not
Waving but Drowning" (p. 788), "The Second Coming" (p. 800)

© AP Photo

T. S. ELIOT (1888–1965)

Journey of the Magi[1] (1927)

"A cold coming we had of it,
Just the worst time of the year
For a journey, and such a long journey:
The ways deep and the weather sharp,
The very dead of winter."*   5
And the camels galled, sore-footed, refractory,
Lying down in the melting snow.
There were times we regretted
The summer palaces on slopes, the terraces,
And the silken girls bringing sherbet.   10
Then the camel men cursing and grumbling
And running away, and wanting their liquor and
    women,
And the night-fires going out, and the lack of shelters,
And the cities hostile and the towns unfriendly
And the villages dirty and charging high prices: 15
A hard time we had of it.
At the end we preferred to travel all night,
Sleeping in snatches,
With the voices singing in our ears, saying
That this was all folly.   20
Then at dawn we came down to a temperate valley,
Wet, below the snow line, smelling of vegetation;
With a running stream and a water-mill beating
    the darkness,
And three trees[2] on the low sky,
And an old white horse[3] galloped away in the
    meadow.   25
Then we came to a tavern with vine-leaves over
    the lintel,
Six hands at an open door dicing for pieces of silver,[4]
And feet kicking the empty wine-skins.
But there was no information, and so we continued

---

[1] *Magi:* The three wise men who ventured east to pay tribute to the infant Jesus (see Matthew 12.1–12)

*The five quoted lines are adapted from a passage in a 1622 Christmas Day sermon by Bishop Lancelot Andrewes.

[2] *three trees:* The three crosses at Calvary (see Luke 23.32–33).

[3] *white horse:* The horse ridden by the conquering Christ in Revelation 19.11–16.

[4] *dicing . . . silver:* Echoes the soldiers dicing for Christ's garments, as well as his betrayal by Judas Iscariot for thirty pieces of silver (see Matthew 27.35 and 26.14–16).

And arrived at evening, not a moment too soon   30
Finding the place; it was (you may say) satisfactory.
All this was a long time ago, I remember,
And I would do it again, but set down
This set down
This: were we led all that way for   35
Birth or Death? There was a Birth, certainly,
We had evidence and no doubt. I had seen birth and death,
But had thought they were different; this Birth was
Hard and bitter agony for us, like Death, our death.
We returned to our places, these Kingdoms,   40
But no longer at ease here, in the old dispensation,
With an alien people clutching their gods.
I should be glad of another death.

Adoration of the Magi by Lavinia
Adoration of the Magi (w/c), Hamer, Lavinia (Contemporary
Artist) / Private Collection / Bridgeman Images

Reading and Reacting

1. The speaker in this poem is one of the three wise men who came to pay tribute to the infant Jesus. In what way are his recollections unexpected? How would you have expected him to react to the birth of Jesus?

2. In what way do the mythical references in the poem allude to future events? Do you need to understand these allusions in order to appreciate the poem?

3. What does the speaker mean in line 41 when he says that the three wise men were "no longer at ease here, in the old dispensation"? What has changed for them? Why does the speaker say that he would be glad for "another death" (line 43)?

4. **JOURNAL ENTRY** How is this poem similar to and different from the story of the three wise men told in the New Testament (Matthew 2.1–18)?

5. **CRITICAL PERSPECTIVE** In an analysis of "Journey of the Magi," poet and critic Anthony Hecht discusses the most common interpretation of the poem, pointing to "a consensus of critical feeling about the tone of the conclusion of this poem, which, it is said, appears to border on despair and exhaustion of hope." Hecht, however, suspects that something more subtle is going on—namely, that Eliot is using the speaker of the poem to express his own imperfect acceptance of Christianity:

> Again, if I am right about this, the poem might have a deeply personal mean-ing for Eliot himself, and might represent a kind of "confession," an acknowl-edgment that he had not yet perfectly embraced the fate to which he nomi-nally adhered, that his imperfect spiritual status was, like the Magus's, that of a person whose faith was incomplete.

Which of the two interpretations given above seems more plausible to you? Is the speaker of the poem wrestling with an incomplete faith, or is he experiencing "despair and exhaustion of hope"?

Related Works: "Araby" (p. 288), "Cathedral" (p. 353), "The World Is Too Much with Us" (p. 516), "On First Looking into Chapman's Homer" (p. 640), "Do not go gentle into that good night" (p. 710), "The Love Song of J. Alfred Prufrock" (p. 759)

✔ **CHECKLIST**   Writing about Symbol, Allegory, Allusion, Myth

Symbol

☐ Are there any symbols in the poem? What leads you to believe they are symbols?

☐ Are these symbols conventional?

☐ Are they universal or archetypal?

☐ Are any symbols obscure or highly idiosyncratic?

☐ What is the literal meaning of each symbol in the context of the poem?

☐ Beyond its literal meaning, what else could each symbol suggest?

☐ How does your interpretation of each symbol enhance your under-standing of the poem?

Allegory

☐ Is the poem an allegory?

☐ Are there any allegorical figures within the poem? How can you tell?

░ What do the allegorical figures signify on a literal level?

░ What lesson does the allegory illustrate?

Allusion

░ Are there any allusions in the poem?

░ Do you recognize the names, places, historical events, or literary works to which the poet alludes?

░ In what way does each allusion deepen the poem's meaning? Does any allusion interfere with your understanding or enjoyment of the poem? If so, how?

░ Would the poem be more effective without a particular allusion?

Myth

░ What myths or mythological figures are alluded to?

░ How does the poem use myth to convey its meaning?

░ How faithful is the poem to the myth? Does the poet add material to the myth? Are any details from the original myth omitted? Is any information distorted? Why?

WRITING SUGGESTIONS: Symbol, Allegory, Allusion, Myth

1. Read "Aunt Jennifer's Tigers" (p. 617), and "Living in Sin" (p. 538) by Adrienne Rich. Then write an essay in which you discuss the similarities and differences in Rich's use of symbols in these poems.

2. Many popular songs make use of allusion. Choose one or two popular songs that you know well, and analyze their use of allusion, paying particular attention to whether the allusions expand the impact and meaning of the song or create barriers to listeners' understanding.

3. Read the Emily Dickinson poem "Because I could not stop for Death—" (p. 752), and then write an interpretation of the poem, identifying its allegorical figures.

4. What applications do the lessons of myth have for life today? Analyze a poem in which myth is central, and then discuss how you might use myth to make generalizations about your own life.

CHAPTER 23

DISCOVERING THEMES IN POETRY

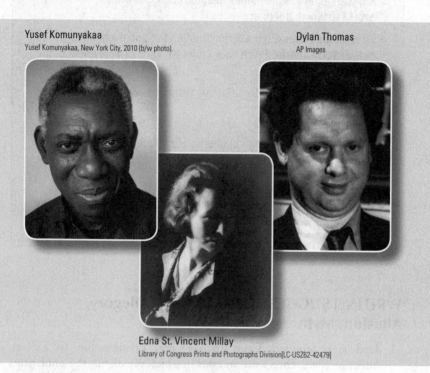

Yusef Komunyakaa
Yusef Komunyakaa, New York City, 2010 (b/w photo).

Dylan Thomas
AP Images

Edna St. Vincent Millay
Library of Congress Prints and Photographs Division[LC-USZ62-42479]

© Hulton-Deutsch Collection/CORBIS

ROBERT HERRICK (1591–1674)

The Argument of His Book (1648)

I sing of brooks, of blossoms, birds, and bowers,
Of April, May, of June, and July-flowers;
I sing of May-poles, hock-carts, wassails, wakes,
Of bridegrooms, brides and of their bridal-cakes;
I write of youth, of love, and have access   5
By these to sing of cleanly wantonness;
I sing of dews, of rains, and piece by piece

702

Of balm, of oil, of spice and ambergris;
I sing of times trans-shifting, and I write
How roses first came red and lilies white;   10
I write of groves, of twilights, and I sing
The court of Mab,[1] and of the fairy king;
I write of Hell; I sing (and ever shall)
Of Heaven, and hope to have it after all.

Dance around Maypole
Hulton Archive/Getty Images

As the poem above makes clear, a poem can be about anything, from the mysteries of the universe to poetry itself. Although no subject is really inappropriate for poetic treatment, certain conventional subjects—family, nature, love, war, death, the folly of human desires, and the inevitability of growing old—recur frequently.

A poem's theme, however, is more than its subject. In general terms, *theme* refers to the ideas that the poet explores, the concerns that the poem examines. More specifically, a poem's **theme** is its main point or idea. Poems "about death," for example, may examine the difficulty of facing one's own mortality, eulogize a friend, assert the need for the acceptance of life's cycles, or cry out against death's inevitability. Such poems may also explore the **carpe diem** theme—the belief that life is brief, so we must "seize the day."

[1] *Mab:* Queen of the fairies.

In order to understand the theme of a poem, readers should consider its form, voice, tone, language, images, allusions, sound—all of its individual elements. Together, these elements communicate the ideas that are important in the poem. Keep in mind, however, that a poem may not mean the same thing to every reader. Different readers will bring different backgrounds, attitudes, and experiences to a poem and will therefore see things in various ways. Moreover, various poets may approach the same subject in drastically different ways, emphasizing different elements as they view the subject matter from their own unique perspectives. Ultimately, there are as many different themes, and ways to approach these themes, as there are writers (and readers) of poetry.

 ## Poems about Parents

Although a poet's individual experience may be vastly different from the experiences of his or her readers, certain ideas seem universal in poems about parents. On the one hand, such poems can express positive sentiments: love, joy, wistfulness, nostalgia, and gratitude for childhood's happy memories and a parent's unconditional love. On the other hand, they may express negative emotions: detachment, frustration, resentment, regret, or even anger. When they write about parents, poets may be emotionally engaged or distant, curious or apathetic, remorseful or grateful; they may idealize parents or attack them. Regardless of the particulars of the poem's specific theme, however, virtually all poems about parents address one basic concept: the influence of a parent over his or her child.

For as long as poets have been writing poetry, their personal experiences (and childhoods) have influenced their subject matter and their poems. In American poetry, poems about parents became more common with the advent of **confessionalism**, a movement in the mid 1950s in which poets began to write subjective verse about their personal experiences. Poems in Robert Lowell's *Life Studies* and W. D. Snodgrass's *Heart's Needle* both addressed the positive and negative aspects of the poets' families (including their parents and children), thus opening the door for an influx of poems about similar themes. Poems by Sylvia Plath and Anne Sexton dealt with previously taboo subjects such as abortion, suicide, and mental illness. Though confessional poets often adapted or fictionalized their experiences when putting them into verse, the line between art and life could be thin, sometimes dangerously so: both Plath and Sexton committed suicide.

The poems in this section all deal with issues related to parents and family, but their styles, voices, and focuses are very different. Sometimes the speakers' voices express ambivalence, communicating conventional sentiments of love and admiration alongside perplexity, frustration, and even anger. This ambivalence is apparent in Theodore Roethke's "My Papa's

Waltz" (p. 705), Robert Hayden's "Those Winter Sundays" (p. 705), and Julia Alvarez's "Dusting" (p. 706) as adult speakers struggle to make peace with their parents' long-ago behavior. In Seamus Heaney's "Digging" (p. 706), the speaker is more positive, finding traits in his father (and grandfather) that he would like to emulate. Mitsuye Yamada's "The Night Before Goodbye" (p. 707) considers a mother's quiet sacrifice, and Richard Blanco's "Papa's Bridge" (p. 709) focuses on a symbol that connects father and son. Finally, Andrew Hudgins's "Elegy for My Father, Who Is Not Dead" (p. 710) and Dylan Thomas's "Do not go gentle into that good night" (p. 710) examine the speakers' emotional reactions to the idea of their parents' deaths.

THEODORE ROETHKE (1908–1963)

Source: ©Bettmann/Corbis

My Papa's Waltz (1948)

The whiskey on your breath
Could make a small boy dizzy;
But I hung on like death:
Such waltzing was not easy.

We romped until the pans   5
Slid from the kitchen shelf;
My mother's countenance
Could not unfrown itself.

The hand that held my wrist
Was battered on one knuckle;   10
At every step you missed
My right ear scraped a buckle.

You beat time on my head
With a palm caked hard by dirt,
Then waltzed me off to bed   15
Still clinging to your shirt.

ROBERT HAYDEN (1913–1980)

Oscar White/Pach Brothers/Corbis

Those Winter Sundays (1962)

Sundays too my father got up early
and put his clothes on in the blueblack cold,
then with cracked hands that ached
from labor in the weekday weather made
banked fires blaze. No one ever thanked him.   5

I'd wake and hear the cold splintering,
breaking.
When the rooms were warm, he'd call,
and slowly I would rise and dress,
fearing the chronic angers of that house,

Speaking indifferently to him,   10
who had driven out the cold
and polished my good shoes as well.
What did I know, what did I know
of love's austere and lonely offices?

JULIA ALVAREZ (1950–   )

Dusting (1996)

Each morning I wrote my name
On the dusty cabinet, then crossed
The dining table in script, scrawled
In capitals on the backs of chairs,
Practicing signatures like scales   5
While mother followed, squirting
Linseed from a burping can
Into a crumpled-up flannel.

She erased my fingerprints
From the bookshelf and rocker,   10
Polished mirrors on the desk
Scribbled with my alphabets.
My name was swallowed in the towel
With which she jeweled the table tops.
The grain surfaced in the oak   15
And the pine grew luminous.
But I refused with every mark
To be like her, anonymous.

Jeff Morgan 12 / Alamy

SEAMUS HEANEY (1939–2013)

Digging (1966)

Between my finger and my thumb
The squat pen rests; snug as a gun.

Under my window, a clean rasping sound
When the spade sinks into gravelly ground:
My father, digging. I look down   5

Till his straining rump among the flowerbeds
Bends low, comes up twenty years away
Stooping in rhythm through potato drills
Where he was digging.

The coarse boot nestled on the lug, the shaft   10
Against the inside knee was levered firmly.
He rooted out tall tops, buried the bright edge deep
To scatter new potatoes that we picked
Loving their cool hardness in our hands.

By God, the old man could handle a spade.   15
Just like his old man.

My grandfather cut more turf in a day
Than any other man on Toner's bog.
Once I carried him milk in a bottle
Corked sloppily with paper. He straightened up   20
To drink it, then fell to right away

Nicking and slicing neatly, heaving sods
Over his shoulder, going down and down
For the good turf. Digging.

The cold smell of potato mould, the squelch and slap   25
Of soggy peat, the curt cuts of an edge
Through living roots awaken in my head.
But I've no spade to follow men like them.

Between my finger and my thumb
The squat pen rests.   30
I'll dig with it.

MITSUYE YAMADA (1923–   )

The Night Before Goodbye (1976)

Mama is mending
my underwear
while my brothers sleep.
Her husband taken away by the FBI
one son lured away by the Army   5
now another son and daughter
lusting for the free world outside.
She must let go.

The war goes on.
She will take one still small son   10
and join Papa in internment[1]
to make a family.
Still sewing
squinting in the dim light
in room C barrack 4 block 4   15
she whispers
Remember
keep your underwear
in good repair
in case of accident   20
don't bring shame
on us.

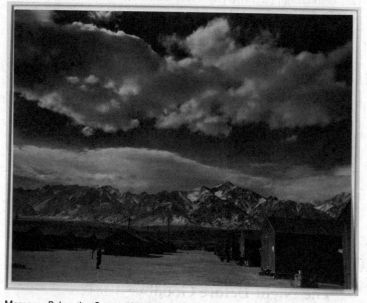

Manzanar Relocation Center, 1943
Ansel Adams's Photographs of Japanese-American Internment at Manzanar, Library of Congress,
#LC-DIG-ppprs-00284

---

[1]*internment:* Shortly after the attack on Pearl Harbor, President Roosevelt ordered that all people of Japanese ancestry—even American citizens—be removed from the West Coast. About 112,000 people were relocated to "internment camps," where they remained until after the war's end.

RICHARD BLANCO (1968–   )

Papa's Bridge (1998)

Morning, driving west again, away from the sun
rising in the slit of the rearview mirror, as I climb
on slabs of concrete and steel bent into a bridge
arcing with all its parabolic[1] y-squared splendor.
I rise to meet the shimmering faces of buildings   5
above tree tops meshed into a calico[2] of greens,
forgetting the river below runs, insists on running
and scouring the earth, moving it grain by grain.

And for a few inclined seconds every morning
I am twelve years old with my father standing   10
at the tenth floor window of his hospital room,
gazing at this same bridge like a mammoth bone
aching with the gravity of its own dense weight.
The glass dosed by a tepid[3] light reviving the city
as I watched and read his sleeping, wondering   15
if he could even dream in such dreamless white:

Was he falling? Was he flying? Who was he, who
was I underneath his eyes, flitting like the birds
across the rooftops and early stars wasting away,
the rush-hour cars pushing through the avenues   20
like the tiny blood cells through his vein, the I.V.
spiraling down like a string of clear licorice feeding
his forearm, bruised pearl and lavender, colors
of the morning haze and the pills on his tongue.

The stitches healed, while the room kept sterile   25
with the usual silence between us. For three days
I served him water or juice in wilting paper cups,
flipped through muted soap operas and game shows,
and filled out the menu cards stamped *Bland Diet.*
For three nights I wedged flat and strange pillows   30
around his body like a fallen S shaped by the bed
and mortared in place by layers of stiff percale.[4]

---

[1]*parabolic:* Having a curved, bowl-like surface.
[2]*calico:* Patchwork.
[3]*tepid:* Weak or lukewarm.
[4]*percale:* Close-woven cotton fabric.

When he was ordered to walk, I took his hand,
together we stepped to the window and he spoke
—*You'll know how to build bridges like that someday*—   35
today, I cross this city, this bridge, still spanning
the silent distance between us with the memory
of a father and son holding hands, secretly in love.

ANDREW HUDGINS (1951–   )

Elegy for My Father, Who Is Not Dead (1987)

One day I'll lift the telephone
and be told my father's dead. He's ready.
In the sureness of his faith, he talks
about the world beyond this world
as though his reservations have   5
been made. I think he wants to go,
a little bit - a new desire
to travel building up, an itch
to see fresh worlds. Or older ones.
He thinks that when I follow him   10
he'll wrap me in his arms and laugh,
they way he did when I arrived
on earth. I do not think he's right.
He's ready. I am not. I can't
just say goodbye as cheerfully   15
as if he were embarking on a trip
to make my later trip go well.
I see myself on deck, convinced
his ship's gone down, while he's convinced
I'll see him standing on the dock   20
and waving, shouting, Welcome back.

DYLAN THOMAS (1914–1953)

Do not go gentle into that good night* (1952)

Do not go gentle into that good night,
Old age should burn and rave at close of day;
Rage, rage against the dying of the light.

AP Images

*This poem was written during the last illness of the poet's father.

Though wise men at their end know dark is right,
Because their words had forked no lightning they   5
Do not go gentle into that good night.

Good men, the last wave by, crying how bright
Their frail deeds might have danced in a green bay,
Rage, rage against the dying of the light.

Wild men who caught and sang the sun in flight,   10
And learn, too late, they grieved it on its way,
Do not go gentle into that good night.

Grave men, near death, who see with blinding sight
Blind eyes could blaze like meteors and be gay,
Rage, rage against the dying of the light.   15

And you, my father, there on the sad height,
Curse, bless, me now with your fierce tears, I pray,
Do not go gentle into that good night.
Rage, rage against the dying of the light.

Reading and Reacting: Poems about Parents

1. What is each speaker's attitude toward his or her parent?
2. Which words, images, and figures of speech in each poem have positive associations? Which create a negative impression?
3. How would you characterize each poem's tone? For example, is the tone sentimental? playful? angry? resentful? regretful? admiring?
4. What problems are explored in each poem?
5. What does each poem say about the parent? What does each poem reveal about the child?
6. What is each poem's central theme?

Related Works: "I Stand Here Ironing" (p. 217), "New York Day Women" (p. 273), "Two Kinds" (p. 471), "Daddy" (p. 589), *Fences* (p. 1270)

 Poems about Nature

In his 1913 poem "Trees," the American poet Joyce Kilmer neatly summarized the symbiotic relationship that exists between poetry and nature: "I think that I shall never see/A poem lovely as a tree." Poets have always found inspiration in the beauty, majesty, and grandeur of the natural world; in fact, some forms of poetry are dedicated solely to the subject of nature. For example, a **pastoral** is a literary form that deals nostalgically with a simple rural life. Many of the early Greek and Roman pastorals were about shepherds who passed the time writing about love while watching their flocks. In these poems, the shepherd's life is idealized; thus, the pastoral tradition celebrates simple times and the beauty of the rural life. Similarly, an **idyll**, a short work in verse or prose (or a painting or a piece of music), depicts simple pastoral or rural scenes, often in idealized terms.

Certain literary movements also focused on the subject of nature. For the **romantic poets**, nature was a source of inspiration, authenticity, and spiritual refreshment, qualities they by and large saw as lacking in the lives of Europeans—both the educated classes and those working in the mills and factories that came with industrialization. Later, the American **transcendentalists**, including Ralph Waldo Emerson and Henry David Thoreau, examined the relationships between philosophy, religion, and nature. In *Walden*, for example, Thoreau wrote about the pleasures and rewards of withdrawing from mainstream life in order to live simply in the woods.

Although all poems about nature deal with the same general subject, their approaches, and their focuses, can differ greatly. Poems "about nature" may focus on the seasons, the weather, mountains or the sea, birds or animals, or trees and flowers. They may praise the beauty of nature, assert the superiority of its simplest creatures, consider nature's evanescence, or mourn its destruction. In this section, romantic poet William Wordsworth's "I wandered lonely as a cloud" (below) extols the virtue of nature and the value of immersing oneself in its beauty, while in "The Windhover" (p. 713), Gerard Manley Hopkins celebrates the divinity of God's natural kingdom, and in "Loveliest of Trees" (p. 714), A. E. Housman's speaker acknowledges the importance of appreciating nature's simple beauty while he still has time. Some poems about nature focus on a single image. For example, in Carl Sandburg's "Fog" (p. 714), the speaker focuses on the image of fog hanging over the city. Other nature poems convey the pull of memory, as in Robert Frost's "Birches" (p. 715), where the speaker recalls the childhood pleasure of climbing trees and longs for the simplicity of those times. Both Denise Levertov's "Living" (p. 716) and Wendell Berry's "The Peace of Wild Things" (p. 717) express a oneness with nature and its creatures. Finally, Carl Sandburg's bittersweet "Autumn Movement" (p. 717) examines the idea that "no beautiful thing lasts."

WILLIAM WORDSWORTH (1770–1850)

I wandered lonely as a cloud (1807)

I wandered lonely as a cloud
    That floats on high o'er vales and hills,
When all at once I saw a crowd,
    A host, of golden daffodils,
Beside the lake, beneath the trees,   5
Fluttering and dancing in the breeze.

Continuous as the stars that shine
    And twinkle on the milky way,
They stretched in never-ending line
    Along the margin of a bay: 10
Ten thousand saw I at a glance,
Tossing their heads in sprightly dance.

The waves beside them danced; but they
    Out-did the sparkling waves in glee;
A poet could not but be gay,   15
    In such a jocund company;
I gazed—and gazed—but little thought
What wealth the show to me had brought:

For oft, when on my couch I lie
    In vacant or in pensive mood,   20
They flash upon that inward eye
    Which is the bliss of solitude;
And then my heart with pleasure fills,
And dances with the daffodils.

GERARD MANLEY HOPKINS (1844–1889)

The Windhover[1] (1877)

To Christ Our Lord

I caught this morning morning's minion,[2] kingdom
    of daylight's dauphin, dapple-dawn-drawn
        Falcon, in his riding
    Of the rolling level underneath him steady air,
        and striding
High there, how he rung upon the rein[3] of a
    wimpling[4] wing
In his ecstasy! then off, off forth on swing,   5
    As a skate's heel sweeps smooth on a bow-bend:
        the hurl and gliding

---

[1] *Windhover:* A kestrel, a European falcon able to hover in the air with its head to the wind.

[2] *minion:* Favorite.

[3] *rung upon the rein:* A horse is "rung upon the rein" when it circles at the end of a long rein held by the trainer.

[4] *wimpling:* Rippling.

Rebuffed the big wind. My heart in hiding
Stirred for a bird,—the achieve of, the mastery of the thing!

Brute beauty and valor and act, oh, air, pride, plume, here
    Buckle! and the fire that breaks from thee then, a billion   10
Times told lovelier, more dangerous, O my chevalier!

No wonder of it: shéer plód, makes plow down sillion[5]
Shine, and blue-bleak embers, ah my dear,
    Fall, gall themselves, and gash gold-vermilion.

A. E. HOUSMAN (1859–1936)

Loveliest of Trees (1896)

Loveliest of trees, the cherry now
Is hung with bloom along the bough,
And stands about the woodland ride
Wearing white for Eastertide.

Now, of my threescore years and ten,   5
Twenty will not come again,
And take from seventy springs a score,
It only leaves me fifty more.

And since to look at things in bloom
Fifty springs are little room,   10
About the woodlands I will go
To see the cherry hung with snow.

CARL SANDBURG (1878–1967)

Fog (1961)

The fog comes
on little cat feet.

It sits looking
over harbor and city
on silent haunches   5
and then moves on.

---

[5]*sillion:* The ridge between two furrows.

Source: ©Bettmann/Corbis

ROBERT FROST (1874–1963)

Birches (1915)

When I see birches bend to left and right
Across the lines of straighter darker trees,
I like to think some boy's been swinging them.
But swinging doesn't bend them down to stay
As ice-storms do. Often you must have seen them   5
Loaded with ice a sunny winter morning
After a rain. They click upon themselves
As the breeze rises, and turn many-colored
As the stir cracks and crazes their enamel.
Soon the sun's warmth makes them shed crystal shells   10
Shattering and avalanching on the snow-crust—
Such heaps of broken glass to sweep away
You'd think the inner dome of heaven had fallen.
They are dragged to the withered bracken by the load,
And they seem not to break; though once they are bowed 15
So low for long, they never right themselves:
You may see their trunks arching in the woods
Years afterwards, trailing their leaves on the ground
Like girls on hands and knees that throw their hair
Before them over their heads to dry in the sun.   20
But I was going to say when Truth broke in
With all her matter-of-fact about the ice-storm
I should prefer to have some boy bend them
As he went out and in to fetch the cows—
Some boy too far from town to learn baseball,   25
Whose only play was what he found himself,
Summer or winter, and could play alone.
One by one he subdued his father's trees
By riding them down over and over again
Until he took the stiffness out of them,   30
And not one but hung limp, not one was left
For him to conquer. He learned all there was
To learn about not launching out too soon
And so not carrying the tree away
Clear to the ground. He always kept his poise   35
To the top branches, climbing carefully
With the same pains you use to fill a cup
Up to the brim, and even above the brim.

Then he flung outward, feet first, with a swish,
Kicking his way down through the air to the ground.   40
So was I once myself a swinger of birches.
And so I dream of going back to be.
It's when I'm weary of considerations,
And life is too much like a pathless wood
Where your face burns and tickles with the cobwebs   45
Broken across it, and one eye is weeping
From a twig's having lashed across it open.
I'd like to get away from earth awhile
And then come back to it and begin over.
May no fate willfully misunderstand me   50
And half grant what I wish and snatch me away
Not to return. Earth's the right place for love:
I don't know where it's likely to go better.
I'd like to go by climbing a birch tree,
And climb black branches up a snow-white trunk   55
Toward Heaven, till the tree could bear no more,
But dipped its top and set me down again.
That would be good both going and coming back.
One could do worse than be a swinger of birches.

DENISE LEVERTOV (1923–1997)

Living (1967)

The fire in leaf and grass
so green it seems
each summer the last summer.

The wind blowing, the leaves
shivering in the sun,   5
each day the last day.

A red salamander
so cold and so
easy to catch, dreamily

moves his delicate feet   10
and long tail. I hold
my hand open for him to go.

Each minute the last minute.

WENDELL BERRY (1934–   )

The Peace of Wild Things (1968)

When despair for the world grows in me
and I wake in the night at the least sound
in fear of what my life and my children's lives may be,
I go and lie down where the wood drake[1]
rests in his beauty on the water, and the great heron feeds.   5
I come into the peace of wild things
who do not tax their lives with forethought
of grief. I come into the presence of still water.
And I feel above me the day-blind stars
waiting with their light. For a time   10
I rest in the grace of the world, and am free.

CARL SANDBURG (1939–2013)

Autumn Movement (1918)

I cried over beautiful things knowing no beautiful thing lasts.

The field of cornflower yellow is a scarf at the neck of the
copper sunburned woman, the mother of the year, the taker
of seeds.

The northwest wind comes and the yellow is torn full of holes,
new beautiful things come in the first spit of snow on the
northwest wind, and the old things go, not one lasts.

Reading and Reacting: Poems about Nature

1. What aspect of nature does the poem focus on?
2. What is the speaker's attitude toward nature? For example, is nature seen as a benevolent, comforting, threatening, awe-inspiring, or overwhelming force?
3. Which words, images, and figures of speech in the poem have positive associations? Which create a negative impression of nature?
4. How would you characterize each poem's tone? For example, is the speaker hopeful? thoughtful? humbled? frightened?

---

[1] *wood drake:* A male wood duck, a species inhabiting North American forested areas.

5. Is the natural world the poem's true subject, or is it just the setting? Explain.

6. What is each poem's central theme?

Related Works: "Snow" (p. 82), "Doe Season" (p. 395), "Greasy Lake" (p. 425), "Nothing Gold Can Stay" (p. 569), "Four Haiku" (p. 657), "Cézanne's Ports" (p. PS4)

 ## Poems about Love

Since the earliest times, romantic love has been one of the great themes of poetry. In the European tradition, Sappho, whose works exist largely in fragments, is one of the early classic Greek poets. Even more influential, in part because most of their works survived, were the Romans Catullus and Ovid. Although the Bible may strike some as an unlikely place to find love poetry, the *Song of Songs* is just that (although it is also commonly interpreted as an allegory of the love between God and his people). In *La Vita Nuova* (*The New Life*), Dante wrote about the life-changing effect of his meeting with Beatrice, a beautiful young woman who was to die young. It is this same Beatrice with whose help Dante embarks on his journey from hell to heaven in *The Divine Comedy*.

Love has played an equally important part in English poetry. During the Middle Ages, poems such as *Sir Gawain and the Green Knight* and *Le Morte d'Arthur* employed the conventions of "courtly love," in which a protagonist performs gallant deeds to win the hand of a fair maiden. Examples of Renaissance love poems include many of the sonnets of William Shakespeare and Edmund Spenser as well as Christopher Marlowe's "The Passionate Shepherd to His Love" (p. 777), which was answered by Sir Walter Raleigh's "The Nymph's Reply to the Shepherd" (p. 782).

Although the Renaissance may arguably be considered the high point of love poetry in English, the tradition has continued to the present day. Increased opportunities for women to read, write, and publish poetry have brought new perspectives to what was once a male-dominated field. **Confessional poetry** has allowed a more direct, frank discussion of love. And, of course, love songs today are as much in fashion as they were in the time of Shakespeare, Dante, or Sappho—and heard by more people than ever.

In each of the poems in this section, the poets address the subject of love in their own unique ways. Husband and wife Robert Browning and Elizabeth Barrett Browning are represented by the traditional love poems "Meeting at Night" (p. 719), "Parting at Morning" (p. 719), and "How Do I Love Thee?" (p. 719), which is one of the most frequently quoted poems in the English language.

In Edna St. Vincent Millay's "What lips my lips have kissed" (p. 720), the speaker reminisces about her past lovers with a mixture of nostalgia and wistfulness, and the speaker in Jehanne Dubrow's "Before the Deployment" (p. 720) re–lives her soldier–lover's departure. On a lighter note, Leigh Hunt's "Jenny Kissed Me" (p. 721) expresses the joy a kiss can bring, and Dorothy Parker's "General Review of the Sex Situation" (p. 721) is a tongue-in-cheek comment on the differences between the sexes.

ROBERT BROWNING (1812–1889)

Meeting at Night (1845)

The gray sea and the long black land;
And the yellow half-moon large and low;
And the startled little waves that leap
In fiery ringlets from their sleep,
As I gain the cove with pushing prow,   5
And quench its speed i' the slushy sand.

Then a mile of warm sea-scented beach;
Three fields to cross till a farm appears;
A tap at the pane, the quick sharp scratch
And blue spurt of a lighted match,   10
And a voice less loud, through its joys and fears,
Than the two hearts beating each to each!

Parting at Morning (1845)

Round the cape of a sudden came the sea,
And the sun looked over the mountain's rim:
And straight was a path of gold for him,
And the need of a world of men for me.

ELIZABETH BARRETT BROWNING (1806–1861)

How Do I Love Thee? (1850)

How do I love thee? Let me count the ways.
I love thee to the depth and breadth and height
My soul can reach, when feeling out of sight

For the ends of being and ideal grace.
I love thee to the level of every day's   5
Most quiet need, by sun and candle-light.
I love thee freely, as men strive for right.
I love thee purely, as they turn from praise.
I love thee with the passion put to use
In my old griefs, and with my childhood's faith.   10
I love thee with a love I seemed to lose
With my lost saints. I love thee with the breath,
Smiles, tears, of all my life; and, if God choose,
I shall but love thee better after death.

Library of Congress Prints and Photographs
Division[LC-USZ62-42479]

EDNA ST. VINCENT MILLAY (1892–1950)

What lips my lips have kissed (1923)

What lips my lips have kissed, and where,
    and why,
I have forgotten, and what arms have lain
Under my head till morning; but the rain
Is full of ghosts tonight, that tap and sigh
Upon the glass and listen for reply,   5
And in my heart there stirs a quiet pain
For unremembered lads that not again
Will turn to me at midnight with a cry.
Thus in the winter stands the lonely tree,
Nor knows what birds have vanished one   10
    by one,
Yet knows its boughs more silent than before:
I cannot say what loves have come and gone,
I only know that summer sang in me
A little while, that in me sings no more.

JEHANNE DUBROW (1975–   )

Before the Deployment (2010)

He kisses me before he goes. While I,
still dozing, half-asleep, laugh and rub my face

against the sueded surface of the sheets,
thinking it's him I touch, his skin beneath

my hands, my body curving in to meet   5
his body there. I never hear him leave.

But I believe he shuts the bedroom door,
as though unsure if he should change his mind,

pull off his boots, crawl beneath the blankets
left behind, his hand a heat against my breast,   10

our heart rates slowing into rest. Perhaps
all good-byes should whisper like a piece of silk—

and then the quick surprise of waking, alone
except for the citrus ghost of his cologne.

LEIGH HUNT (1784–1859)

Jenny Kissed Me (1838)

Jenny kissed me when we met,
Jumping from the chair she sat in.
Time, you thief! who love to get
Sweets into your list, put that in.
Say I'm weary, say I'm sad;   5
Say that health and wealth have missed me;
Say I'm growing old, but add—
Jenny kissed me!

DOROTHY PARKER (1893–1967)

General Review of the
Sex Situation (1933)

Woman wants monogamy;
Man delights in novelty.
Love is woman's moon and sun;
Man has other forms of fun.

Woman lives but in her lord;   5
Count to ten, and man is bored.
With this the gist and sum of it,
What earthly good can come of it?

Reading and Reacting: Poems about Love

1. What general ideas about love are expressed in each poem?

2. What conventional images and figures of speech are used to express feelings of love?

3. Does any poet use any unexpected (or even shocking) images or figures of speech?

4. How would you characterize the tone of each poem? For example, is the tone happy? sad? celebratory? regretful? ambivalent?

5. What does each poem reveal about the speaker? about the person to whom the poem is addressed?

6. What is each poem's central theme?

Related Works: "Hills Like White Elephants" (p. 74), "Love and Other Catastrophes: A Mix Tape" (p. 84), "The Storm" (p. 199), "Living in Sin" (p. 538), "My mistress' eyes are nothing like the sun" (p. 572), "Shall I compare thee to a summer's day?" (p. 575), "A Valediction: Forbidding Mourning" (p. 586), "To My Dear and Loving Husband" (p. 593), "You fit into me" (p. 598), *The Brute* (p. 814)

 Poems about War

In poetry, war is as ancient a theme as love and nature. In fact, the earliest poems, including Homer's *Iliad* and *Odyssey* and Virgil's *Aeneid*, have at their centers epic battles and struggles. These poems were created in metered verse so they could be remembered and passed down from one generation to the next. Portions of them would be recited at public gatherings and festivals, making them analogous to the war movies of today. Epic poems reflected the belief that war could be a noble and glorious endeavor, and they often glorified the heroes of the wars and battles they described. Even in the earliest of these poems, however, there is a sense of the futility and devastation that war brings with it; for example, in the *Iliad*, many of the Greeks laying siege to the city of Troy are sick of the war and want to go home. In the *Aeneid*, the scene where Aeneas witnesses the destruction of his native Troy by the Greeks, and by the gods aiding them, is one of the most moving in literature.

In modern times, poets have tended to concentrate on the horrors of war, no doubt in part because technology has allowed armies to do more damage more quickly than ever before. World War I, which saw the first widespread use of aircraft, poison gas, and machine guns in warfare, marked a turning point in war and in poetic responses to it. One of the best-known poems to come out of this war is "Dulce et Decorum Est" (p. 723), written toward the end of the war by Wilfred Owen, a soldier who was killed on the Western Front in 1918. The poem, which was not published until after

Owen's death, includes graphic images and ends with a bitterly ironic quotation that summarizes the mentality that fuels war: "It is sweet and fitting to die for one's country." In "Atrocities" (p. 724), Siegfried Sassoon, a contemporary of Owen's, offers a similarly cynical look at war (and warriors).

Of course, not all poems about war are poems of protest. For example, "The Soldier," by Rupert Brooke (p. 725), a contemporary of both Owen's and Sassoon's, celebrates the nobility of fighting for the sake of one's beloved country; Joel McCrea's classic "In Flanders Fields" (p. 725) mourns the inevitable losses war brings yet expresses the sentiment that the fight must go on; and Radiohead's lyrics "Harry Patch (in Memory of)" (p. 726) honor the death of the last surviving British soldier of World War I.

Modern poems about war do not always focus on soldiers. Thus, although Henry Reed's "Naming of Parts" (p. 726) focuses on the grim realities of a soldier's training for war, W. H. Auden's poem from "In Time of War" (p. 727) examines the evils of the Nanking Massacre and the Dachau concentration camp.

In the post–World War II years, enemies were not as clearly defined as they had been in the past. The war in Vietnam unfolded before the American people on their television screens and, as a result, many Americans (including American soldiers) came to question the war and its goals. This attempt to come to terms with the war and its aftermath carried over into poems about the war, as seen in Yusef Komunyakaa's "Facing It" (p. 728), in which a Vietnam veteran visits the Vietnam War Memorial in Washington D.C.

The post-Vietnam years have seen troops from various nations take part in conflicts around the globe—conflicts whose costs have been high and whose goals have not always been as clear-cut as they were in past conflicts. Writing about the Iraq war in his prose poem "Mosul" (p. 728), David Hernandez focuses on the physical realities of war. Finally, Richard Wilbur's "Terza Rima" (p. 729) comments on the difficulty of expressing the horrors of war, and Wislawa Szymborska's "The End and the Beginning" (p. 729) addresses the problem of cleaning up the damage left behind.

WILFRED OWEN (1893–1918)

Dulce et Decorum Est[1] (1920)

Bent double, like old beggars under sacks,
Knock-kneed, coughing like hags, we cursed through sludge,
Till on the haunting flares we turned our backs
And towards our distant rest began to trudge.
Men marched asleep. Many had lost their boots   5

---

[1]*Dulce et Decorum Est:* The title and last two lines are from Horace, *Odes* 3.2: "Sweet and fitting it is to die for one's country."

But limped on, blood-shod. All went lame; all blind;
Drunk with fatigue; deaf even to the hoots
Of tired, outstripped Five-Nines[2] that dropped behind.

Gas! GAS Quick, boys!—An ecstasy of fumbling,
Fitting the clumsy helmets just in time;   10
But someone still was yelling out and stumbling
And flound'ring like a man in fire or lime...
Dim, through the misty panes and thick green light,
As under a green sea, I saw him drowning.
In all my dreams, before my helpless sight,   15
He plunges at me, guttering, choking, drowning.
If in some smothering dreams you too could pace
Behind the wagon that we flung him in,
And watch the white eyes writhing in his face,
His hanging face, like a devil's sick of sin;   20
If you could hear, at every jolt, the blood
Come gargling from the froth-corrupted lungs,
Obscene as cancer, bitter as the cud
Of vile, incurable sores on innocent tongues,—
My friend, you would not tell with such high zest   25
To children ardent for some desperate glory,
The old Lie: Dulce et decorum est
Pro patria mori.

SIEGFRIED SASSOON (1886–1967)

Atrocities (1919)

You told me, in your drunken-boasting mood,
How once you butchered prisoners. That was good!
I'm sure you felt no pity while they stood
Patient and cowed and scared, as prisoners should.

How did you do them in? Come, don't be shy: 5
You know I love to hear how Germans die,
Downstairs in dug-outs. 'Camerad! they cry;
Then squeal like stoats when bombs begin to fly.

And you? I know your record. You went sick
When orders looked unwholesome: then, with trick   10
And lie, you wangled home. And here you are,
Still talking big and boozing in a bar.

---

[2]*Five-Nines:* Shells that explode on impact and release poison gas.

British soldier, WWI
©SSPL / The Image Works

RUPERT BROOKE (1887–1915)

The Soldier (1915)

If I should die, think only this of me;
    That there's some corner of a foreign field
That is forever England. There shall be
    In that rich earth a richer dust concealed;
A dust whom England bore, shaped, made aware,   5
    Gave, once, her flowers to love, her ways to roam,
A body of England's breathing English air,
Washed by the rivers, blest by suns of home.
And think, this heart, all evil shed away,
    A pulse in the eternal mind, no less   10
        Gives somewhere back the thoughts by England given;
Her sights and sounds; dreams happy as her day;
    And laughter, learnt of friends; and gentleness,
        In hearts at peace, under an English heaven.

JOHN MCCRAE (1872–1918)

In Flanders[1] Fields (1915)

In Flanders fields the poppies blow
Between the crosses row on row,
That mark our place; and in the sky
The larks, still bravely singing, fly
Scarce heard amid the guns below.   5

We are the Dead. Short days ago
We lived, felt dawn, saw sunset glow,
Loved and were loved, and now we lie
In Flanders fields.

Take up our quarrel with the foe: 10
To you from failing hands we throw
The torch; be yours to hold it high.
If ye break faith with us who die
We shall not sleep, though poppies grow
In Flanders fields.   15

---

[1] *Flanders:* The Dutch-speaking region of Belgium, where some of the bloodiest battles of World War I were fought.

RADIOHEAD

Harry Patch (in Memory of) (2009)

"i am the only one that got through
the others died where ever they fell
it was an ambush
they came up from all sides
give your leaders each a gun and then let them fight it out   5
    themselves
i've seen devils coming up from the ground
i've seen hell upon this earth
the next will be chemical but they will never learn"

HENRY REED (1914–1986)

Naming of Parts (1946)

Today we have naming of parts. Yesterday,
We had daily cleaning. And tomorrow morning,
We shall have what to do after firing. But today,
Today we have naming of parts. Japonica[1]
Glistens like coral in all of the neighboring gardens,   5
    And today we have naming of parts

This is the lower sling swivel. And this
Is the upper sling swivel, whose use you will see,
When you are given your slings. And this is the piling swivel,
Which in your case you have not got. The branches   10
Hold in the gardens their silent, eloquent gestures,
    Which in our case we have not got.

This is the safety-catch, which is always released
With an easy flick of the thumb. And please do not let me
See anyone using his finger. You can do it quite easy   15
If you have any strength in your thumb. The blossoms
Are fragile and motionless, never letting anyone see
    Any of them using their finger.

---

[1]*Japonica:* A shrub having waxy flowers in a variety of colors.

And this you can see is the bolt. The purpose of this
Is to open the breech, as you see. We can slide it 20
Rapidly backwards and forwards: we call this
Easing the spring. And rapidly backwards and forwards
The early bees are assaulting and fumbling the flowers:
> They call it easing the Spring.

They call it easing the Spring: it is perfectly easy 25
If you have any strength in your thumb: like the bolt,
And the breech, and the cocking-piece, and the point
> of balance,
Which in our case we have not got; and the almond-blossom
Silent in all of the gardens and the bees going backwards and
> forwards,
> For today we have the naming of parts. 30

W. H. AUDEN (1907–1973)

from "In Time of War" (1939)

XVI

Here war is simple like a monument:
A telephone is speaking to a man;
Flags on a map assert that troops were sent;
A boy brings milk in bowls. There is a plan

For living men in terror of their lives, 5
Who thirst at nine who were to thirst at noon,
And can be lost and are, and miss their wives,
And, unlike an idea, can die too soon.

But ideas can be true although men die,
And we can watch a thousand faces 10
Made active by one lie:

And maps can really point to places
Where life is evil now:
Nanking[1] Dachau.[2]

---

[1] *Nanking:* A city in China where, in 1937, massacres and rapes were committed on a massive scale by the Japanese Imperial Army.

[2] *Dachau:* A concentration camp in Germany, opened in 1933 and liberated by American forces in 1945.

Yusef Komunyakaa, New York City, 2010 (b/w photo)./© Chris Felver / The Bridgeman Art Library

YUSEF KOMUNYAKAA (1947–   )

Facing It (1988)

My black face fades,
hiding inside the black granite.
I said I wouldn't,
dammit: No tears.
I'm stone. I'm flesh.   5
My clouded reflection eyes me
like a bird of prey, the profile of night
slanted against morning. I turn
this way—the stone lets me go.
I turn that way—I'm inside   10
the Vietnam Veterans Memorial
again, depending on the light
to make a difference.
I go down the 58,022 names,
half-expecting to find   15
my own in letters like smoke.
I touch the name Andrew Johnson;
I see the booby trap's white flash.
Names shimmer on a woman's blouse
but when she walks away   20
the names stay on the wall.
Brushstrokes flash, a red bird's
wings cutting across my stare.
The sky. A plane in the sky.
A white vet's image floats   25
closer to me, then his pale eyes
look through mine. I'm a window.
He's lost his right arm
inside the stone. In the black mirror
a woman's trying to erase names: 30
No, she's brushing a boy's hair.

Hand tracing names of the dead on
the Vietnam War Memorial.
AP Images/Dennis Cook

DAVID HERNANDEZ (1971–   )

Mosul[1] (2011)

The donkey. The donkey pulling the cart.
The caravan of dust. The cart made of plywood,

---

[1] *Mosul:* The second largest city in Iraq.

of crossbeam and junkyard tires. The donkey
made of donkey. The long face. The long ears.
The curled lashes. The obsidian eyes blinking 5
in the dust. The cart rolling, cracking the knuckles
of pebbles. The dust. The blanket over the cart.
The hidden mortar shells. The veins of wires.
The remote device. The red light. The donkey
trotting. The blue sky. The rolling cart. The dust 10
smudging the blue sky. The silent bell of the sun.
The Humvee. The soldiers. The dust-colored
uniforms. The boy from Montgomery, the boy
from Little Falls. The donkey cart approaching.
The dust. The laughter on their lips. The dust 15
on their lips. The moment before the moment.
The shockwave. The dust. The dust. The dust.

RICHARD WILBUR (1921–   )

Terza Rima[1] (2008)

In this great form, as Dante proved in Hell,
There is no dreadful thing that can't be said
In passing. Here, for instance, one could tell

How our jeep skidded sideways toward the dead
Enemy soldier with the staring eyes, 5
Bumping a little as it struck his head,

And then flew on, as if toward Paradise.

WISLAWA SZYMBORSKA (1923–2012)

The End and the Beginning (1993)

After every war
someone has to clean up.
Things won't
straighten themselves up, after all.

---

[1] *Terza Rima:* The interlocking rhyme scheme that Dante Alighieri devised for his *Divine Comedy*, the first third of which deals with hell.

Someone has to push the rubble
to the side of the road.
so the corpse-filled wagons
can pass.

Someone has to get mired
in scum and ashes,
sofa springs,
splintered glass,
and bloody rags.

Someone has to drag in a girder
to prop up a wall,
Someone has to glaze a window,
rehang a door.

Photogenic it's not,
and takes years.
All the cameras have left
for another war.

We'll need the bridges back,
and new railway stations.
Sleeves will go ragged
from rolling them up.
Someone, broom in hand,
still recalls the way it was.

Someone else listens
and nods with unsevered head.
But already there are those nearby
starting to mill about
who will find it dull.

From out of the bushes
sometimes someone still unearths
rusted-out arguments
and carries them to the garbage pile.

Those who knew
what was going on here
must make way for
those who know little.
And less than little.
And finally as little as nothing.

In the grass that has overgrown
causes and effects,
someone must be stretched out   45
blade of grass in his mouth
gazing at the clouds.

Reading and Reacting: Poems about War

1. What is each speaker's attitude toward war? Does the speaker seem to be focusing on a particular war or on war in general?
2. What conventional images and figures of speech does each poem use to express its ideas about war?
3. Do any of the poems use unusual, unexpected, or shocking images or figures of speech?
4. How would you describe each poem's tone? For example, is the tone angry? cynical? sad? disillusioned? resigned?
5. How does each poem's form help to communicate the speaker's attitude toward war?
6. What is each poem's central theme?

Related Works: "The Things They Carried" (p. 310), "The Man He Killed" (p. 511), "Patterns" (p. 512), "The Death of the Ball Turret Gunner" (p. 583), *Nine Ten* (p. 861)

WRITING SUGGESTIONS: Discovering Themes in Poetry

1. Compare any two poems in this chapter about parents, nature, love, or war.
2. Write an **explication** of one of the poems in this chapter.
3. Write an essay in which you compare one of the poems in this chapter to a short story or play on the same general subject. (For possible topics, consult the Related Works list that follows each group of poems.)
4. Some poets write multiple poems on the same general subject. For example, Shakespeare wrote many love poems, and Robert Frost wrote a number of poems about nature. Choose two poems by a single poet that explore the same subject, and compare and contrast the two poems' treatment of this subject.
5. A number of poems in this book focus on the theme of poetry itself. Choose three poems that explore this theme, and write an essay that compares the poems' ideas about reading and writing poetry.

CHAPTER 24

POETRY FOR FURTHER READING

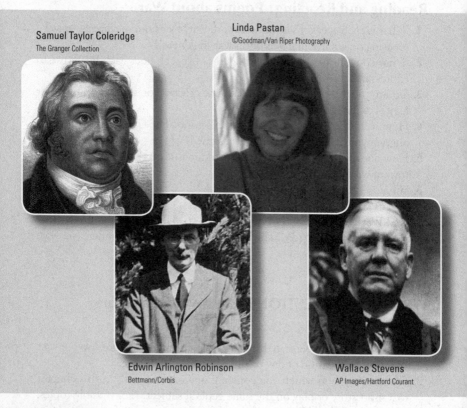

Samuel Taylor Coleridge
The Granger Collection

Linda Pastan
©Goodman/Van Riper Photography

Edwin Arlington Robinson
Bettmann/Corbis

Wallace Stevens
AP Images/Hartford Courant

J. Vespa/WireImage/Getty Images

SHERMAN J. ALEXIE (1966–   )

Defending Walt Whitman (1996)

Basketball is like this for young Indian boys, all arms and legs
and serious stomach muscles. Every body is brown!
These are the twentieth-century warriors who will never kill,
although a few sat quietly in the deserts of Kuwait,
waiting for orders to do something, do something.   5

God, there is nothing as beautiful as a jump shot
on a reservation summer basketball court
where the ball is moist with sweat
and makes a sound when it swishes through the net
that causes Walt Whitman to weep because it is so perfect.   10

There are veterans of foreign wars here,
whose bodies are still dominated
by collarbones and knees, whose bodies still respond
in the ways that bodies are supposed to respond when we
      are young.

Every body is brown! Look there, that boy can run   15
up and down this court forever. He can leap for a rebound
with his back arched like a salmon, all meat and bone
synchronized, magnetic, as if the court were a river,
as if the rim were a dam, as if the air were a ladder
leading the Indian boy toward home.   20

Some of the Indian boys still wear their military haircuts
while a few have let their hair grow back.
It will never be the same as it was before!
One Indian boy has never cut his hair, not once, and he braids it
into wild patterns that do not measure anything.   25
He is just a boy with too much time on his hands.
Look at him. He wants to play this game in bare feet.

God, the sun is so bright! There is no place like this.
Walt Whitman stretches his calf muscles
on the sidelines. He has the next game.   30
His huge beard is ridiculous on the reservation.
Some body throws a crazy pass and Walt Whitman catches it
      with quick hands.
He brings the ball close to his nose
and breathes in all of its smells: leather, brown skin, sweat,
      black hair,
burning oil, twisted ankle, long drink of warm water,   35
gunpowder, pine tree. Walt Whitman squeezes the ball tightly.
He wants to run. He hardly has the patience to wait for his turn.
"What's the score?" he asks. He asks, "What's the score?"

Basketball is like this for Walt Whitman. He watches these
      Indian boys
as if they were the last bodies on earth. Every body is brown!   40
Walt Whitman shakes because he believes in God.

Walt Whitman dreams of the Indian boy who will
   defend him,
trapping him in the corner, all flailing arms and legs
and legendary stomach muscles. Walt Whitman shakes
because he believes in God. Walt Whitman dreams   45
of the first jump shot he will take, the ball arcing clumsily
from his fingers, striking the rim so hard that it sparks.
Walt Whitman shakes because he believes in God.
Walt Whitman closes his eyes. He is a small man and his beard
is ludicrous on the reservation, absolutely insane.   50
His beard makes the Indian boys laugh righteously. His beard
   frightens
the smallest Indian boys. His beard tickles the skin
of the Indian boys who dribble past him. His beard, his beard!

God, there is beauty in every body. Walt Whitman stands
at center court while the Indian boys run from basket to   55
   basket.
Walt Whitman cannot tell the difference between
offense and defense. He does not care if he touches
   the ball.
Half of the Indian boys wear T-shirts damp with sweat
and the other half are barebacked, skin slick and shiny.
There is no place like this. Walt Whitman smiles.   60
Walt Whitman shakes. This game belongs to him.

ANONYMOUS

Bonny Barbara Allan

(Traditional Scottish ballad)

It was in and about the Martinmas[1] time,
   When the green leaves were afalling,
That Sir John Graeme, in the West Country,
   Fell in love with Barbara Allan.

He sent his men down through the town,   5
   To the place where she was dwelling;

---

[1]*Martinmas:* Saint Martin's Day, November 11.

"O haste and come to my master dear,
  Gin² ye be Barbara Allan."

O hooly,³ hooly rose she up,
  To the place where he was lying,   10
And when she drew the curtain by:
  "Young man, I think you're dying."

"O it's I'm sick, and very, very sick,
  And 'tis a' for Barbara Allan."—
"O the better for me ye's never be,   15
  Tho your heart's blood were aspilling.

"O dinna ye mind,⁴ young man," said she,
  "When ye was in the tavern adrinking,
That ye made the health gae round and round,
  And slighted Barbara Allan?"   20

He turned his face unto the wall,
  And death was with him dealing:
"Adieu, adieu, my dear friends all,
  And be kind to Barbara Allan."

And slowly, slowly raise she up,   25
  And slowly, slowly left him,
And sighing said she could not stay,
  Since death of life had reft him.

She had not gane a mile but twa,⁵
  When she heard the dead-bell ringing,   30
And every jow⁶ that the dead-bell geid,
  It cried, "Woe to Barbara Allan!"

"O mother, mother, make my bed!
  O make it saft and narrow!
Since my love died for me today,   35
  I'll die for him tomorrow."

---

²*Gin:* If.
³*hooly:* Slowly.
⁴*O dinna ye mind:* Don't you remember?
⁵*twa:* Two.
⁶*jow:* Stroke.

ANONYMOUS

Go Down, Moses*

Go down, Moses,
Way down in Egyptland
Tell old Pharaoh
To let my people go.

When Israel was in Egyptland   5
Let my people go
Oppressed so hard they could not stand
Let my people go.

Go down, Moses,
Way down in Egyptland   10
Tell old Pharaoh
"Let my people go."

"Thus saith the Lord," bold Moses said,
"Let my people go;
If not I'll smite your first-born dead   15
Let my people go.

"No more shall they in bondage toil,
Let my people go;
Let them come out with Egypt's spoil,
Let my people go."   20

The Lord told Moses what to do
Let my people go;
To lead the children of Israel through,
Let my people go.

Go down, Moses,   25
Way down in Egyptland,
Tell old Pharaoh,
"Let my people go!"

---

*Music, especially religious songs, or "spirituals," was one of the few means of expression permitted for slaves. Many of these spirituals contained coded messages conveying antislavery sentiments or even directions on how to use the Underground Railroad. For example, the spiritual "Wade in the Water" seemed, on the surface, to be about crossing the River Jordan to reach the Promised Land. But its lyrics contained vital information, including the idea that crossing streams was a good way for runaway slaves to cover their scent and thus to lose the bloodhounds used to track them.

MATTHEW ARNOLD (1822–1888)

Dover Beach (1867)

The sea is calm tonight.
The tide is full, the moon lies fair
Upon the straits;—on the French coast the light
Gleams and is gone; the cliffs of England stand,
Glimmering and vast, out in the tranquil bay.   5
Come to the window, sweet is the night-air!
Only, from the long line of spray
Where the sea meets the moon-blanched[1] land,
Listen! you hear the grating roar
Of pebbles which the waves draw back, and fling,   10
At their return, up the high strand,[2]
Begin, and cease, and then again begin,
With tremulous cadence slow, and bring
The eternal note of sadness in.

Sophocles[3] long ago   15
Heard it on the Aegean,[4] and it brought
Into his mind the turbid ebb and flow
Of human misery; we
Find also in the sound a thought,
Hearing it by this distant northern sea.   20

The Sea of Faith
Was once, too, at the full, and round earth's shore
Lay like the folds of a bright girdle furled.
But now I only hear
Its melancholy, long, withdrawing roar,   25
Retreating, to the breath
Of the night-wind, down the vast edges drear
And naked shingles[5] of the world.

---

[1] *moon-blanched:* Whitened by moonlight.
[2] *strand:* Beach.
[3] *Sophocles:* Greek playwright (496–406 B.C.), author of tragedies such as *Oedipus the King* and *Antigone*.
[4] *Aegean:* Sea between Greece and Turkey.
[5] *shingles:* Gravel beaches.

Ah, love, let us be true
To one another! for the world, which seems   30
To lie before us like a land of dreams,
So various, so beautiful, so new,
Hath really neither joy, nor love, nor light,
Nor certitude, nor peace, nor help for pain;
And we are here as on a darkling⁶ plain   35
Swept with confused alarms of struggle and flight,
Where ignorant armies clash by night.

WILLIAM BLAKE (1757–1827)

The Chimney Sweeper¹ (1789)

When my mother died I was very young,
And my father sold me while yet my tongue
Could scarcely cry "'weep! 'weep! 'weep! 'weep!"
So your chimneys I sweep, and in soot I sleep.

There's little Tom Dacre, who cried when his head,   5
That curled like a lamb's back, was shaved: so I said
"Hush, Tom! never mind it, for when your head's bare
You know that the soot cannot spoil your white hair."

And so he was quiet, and that very night,
As Tom was a-sleeping, he had such a sight!   10
That thousands of sweepers, Dick, Joe, Ned, and Jack,
Were all of them locked up in coffins of black.

And by came an Angel who had a bright key,
And he opened the coffins and set them all free;
Then down a green plain leaping, laughing, they run,   15
And wash in a river, and shine in the sun.

Then naked and white, all their bags left behind,
They rise upon clouds and sport in the wind;
And the Angel told Tom, if he'd be a good boy,
He'd have God for his father, and never want joy.   20

---

⁶*darkling:* Darkening.

¹During the eighteenth and early nineteenth centuries, orphans as young as four years old were apprenticed to chimney sweepers.

And so Tom awoke; and we rose in the dark,
And got with our bags and our brushes to work.
Though the morning was cold, Tom was happy and warm;
So if all do their duty they need not fear harm.

WILLIAM BLAKE (1757–1827)

The Lamb (1789)

Little Lamb, who made thee?
  Dost thou know who made thee?
Gave thee life & bid thee feed,
By the stream & o'er the mead;
Gave thee clothing of delight,   5
Softest clothing wooly bright;
Gave thee such a tender voice,
Making all the vales rejoice!
  Little Lamb who made thee?
  Dost thou know who made thee?   10

  Little Lamb I'll tell thee,
  Little Lamb I'll tell thee!
He is calléd by thy name,
For he calls himself a Lamb:
He is meek & he is mild,   15
He became a little child:
I a child & thou a lamb,
We are calléd by his name.
  Little Lamb God bless thee.
  Little Lamb God bless thee.   20

WILLIAM BLAKE (1757–1827)

London (1794)

I wander through each chartered street,
Near where the chartered Thames does flow,
And mark in every face I meet
Marks of weakness, marks of woe.

In every cry of every man,   5
In every infant's cry of fear,
In every voice, in every ban,
The mind-forged manacles I hear.

How the chimney-sweeper's cry
Every black'ning church appalls;   10
And the hapless soldier's sigh
Runs in blood down palace walls.

But most through midnight streets I hear
How the youthful harlot's curse
Blasts the new born infant's tear,   15
And blights with plagues the marriage hearse.

WILLIAM BLAKE (1757–1827)

To see a World in a Grain of Sand (1803)

To see a World in a Grain of Sand
And a Heaven in a Wild Flower,
Hold Infinity in the palm of your hand
And Eternity in an hour.

WILLIAM BLAKE (1757–1827)

The Tyger (1794)

Tyger! Tyger! burning bright
In the forests of the night,
What immortal hand or eye
Could frame thy fearful symmetry?

In what distant deeps or skies   5
Burnt the fire of thine eyes?
On what wings dare he aspire?
What the hand dare seize the fire?

And what shoulder, and what art,
Could twist the sinews of thy heart?   10
And when thy heart began to beat,
What dread hand? and what dread feet?

What the hammer? what the chain?
In what furnace was thy brain?
What the anvil? what dread grasp   15
Dare its deadly terrors clasp?

When the stars threw down their spears,
And watered heaven with their tears,

Did he smile his work to see?
Did he who made the Lamb make thee?   20

Tyger! Tyger! burning bright
In the forests of the night,
What immortal hand or eye
Dare frame thy fearful symmetry?

ELIZABETH BRADFIELD

Why They Went*

> *that men might learn what the world is like at the*
> *spot where the sun does not decline in the heavens.*
> —Apsley Cherry-Garrard

Frost bitten. Snow blind. Hungry. Craving
fresh pie and hot toddies,[1] a whole roasted
unflippered thing to carve. Craving a bed
that had, an hour before entering,
been warmed with a stone from the hearth.   5

Always back to Eden—to the time when we knew
with certainty that something watched and loved us.
That the very air was miraculous and ours.
That all we had to do was show up.

The sun rolled along the horizon. The light never   10
    left them.
The air from their warm mouths became diamonds.
And they longed for everything they did not have.
And they came home and longed again.

ANNE BRADSTREET (1612–1672)

The Author to Her Book[1] (1678)

Thou ill-formed offspring of my feeble brain,
Who after birth did'st by my side remain,

---

*Publication date unavailable.

[1] *hot toddies:* Alcoholic drinks consisting of liquor, hot water, sugar, and spices.

[1] *Her Book:* Bradstreet addresses *The Tenth Muse,* a collection of her poetry published without her consent in 1650.

Till snatched from thence by friends, less wise than true,
Who thee abroad exposed to public view;
Made thee in rags, halting, to the press to trudge,   5
Where errors were not lessened, all may judge.
At thy return my blushing was not small,
My rambling brat (in print) should mother call;
I cast thee by as one unfit for light,
Thy visage was so irksome in my sight   10
Yet being mine own, at length affection would
Thy blemishes amend, if so I could:
I washed thy face, but more defects I saw,
And rubbing off a spot, still made a flaw.
I stretched thy joints to make thee even feet,[2]   15
Yet still thou run'st more hobbling than is meet;[3]
In better dress to trim thee was my mind,
But nought save homespun cloth in the house I find.
In this array, 'mongst vulgars[4] may'st thou roam;
In critics' hands beware thou dost not come;   20
And take thy way where yet thou are not known.
If for thy Father asked, say thou had'st none;
And for thy Mother, she alas is poor,
Which caused her thus to send thee out of door.

GWENDOLYN BROOKS (1917–2000)

The *Chicago Defender*[1] Sends a Man to Little Rock (1960)

Fall, 1957[2]

In Little Rock the people bear
Babes, and comb and part their hair

---

[2]*even feet:* Metrical feet.

[3]*meet:* Appropriate or decorous.

[4]*vulgars:* Common people.

[1]Chicago Defender: A weekly newspaper for African American readers.

[2]*Fall, 1957:* When black students first entered the public high school in Little Rock, Arkansas, in 1957, the city erupted in race riots protesting desegregation.

And watch the want ads, put repair
To roof and latch. While wheat toast burns
A woman waters multiferns.   5

Time upholds or overturns
The many, tight, and small concerns.

In Little Rock the people sing
Sunday hymns like anything,
Through Sunday pomp and polishing.   10

And after testament and tunes,
Some soften Sunday afternoons
With lemon tea and Lorna Doones.

I forecast
And I believe   15
Come Christmas Little Rock will cleave
To Christmas tree and trifle, weave,
From laugh and tinsel, texture fast.

In Little Rock is baseball; Barcarolle.[3]
That hotness in July...the uniformed figures raw and   20
    implacable
And not intellectual,
Batting the hotness or clawing the suffering dust.
The Open Air Concert, on the special twilight green....
When Beethoven is brutal or whispers to lady-like air.
Blanket-sitters are solemn, as Johann troubles to lean   25
To tell them what to mean....

There is love, too, in Little Rock. Soft women softly
Opening themselves in kindness,
Or, pitying one's blindness,
Awaiting one's pleasure   30
In azure
Glory with anguished rose at the root....
To wash away old semi-discomfitures.
They re-teach purple and unsullen blue.
The wispy soils go. And uncertain   35
Half-havings have they clarified to sures.

In Little Rock they know
Not answering the telephone is a way of rejecting life,

---

[3]*Barcarolle:* A Venetian gondolier's song, or a song suggesting the rhythm of rowing.

That it is our business to be bothered, is our business
To cherish bores or boredom, be polite   40
To lies and love and many-faceted fuzziness.

I scratch my head, massage the hate-I-had.
I blink across my prim and pencilled pad.
The saga I was sent for is not down.
Because there is a puzzle in this town.   45
The biggest News I do not dare
Telegraph to the Editor's chair:
"They are like people everywhere."

The angry Editor would reply
In hundred harryings of Why.   50

And true, they are hurling spittle, rock,
Garbage and fruit in Little Rock.
And I saw coiling storm a-writhe
On bright madonnas. And a scythe
Of men harassing brownish girls.   55
(The bows and barrettes in the curls
And braids declined away from joy.)

I saw a bleeding brownish boy....

The lariat lynch-wish I deplored.

The loveliest lynchee was our Lord.   60

GWENDOLYN BROOKS (1917–2000)

Medgar Evers[1] (1964)

For Charles Evers[2]

The man whose height his fear improved he
arranged to fear no further. The raw
intoxicated time was time for better birth or a final death.

Old styles, old tempos, all the engagement of
the day—the sedate, the regulated fray—   5

---

the antique light, the Moral rose, old gusts,
tight whistlings from the past, the mothballs
in the Love at last our man forswore.

Medgar Evers annoyed confetti and assorted
brands of businessmen's eyes.   10

The shows came down: to maxims and surprise.
And palsy.

Roaring no rapt arise-ye to the dead, he
leaned across tomorrow. People said that
he was holding clean globes in his hands.   15

CHARLES BUKOWSKI (1920–1994)

so you want to be a writer?*

if it doesn't come bursting out of you
in spite of everything,
don't do it.
unless it comes unasked out of your
heart and your mind and your mouth   5
and your gut,
don't do it.
if you have to sit for hours
staring at your computer screen
or hunched over your   10
typewriter
searching for words,
don't do it.
if you're doing it for money or
fame,   15
don't do it.
if you're doing it because you want
women in your bed,
don't do it.
if you have to sit there and   20
rewrite it again and again,
don't do it.
if it's hard work just thinking about doing it,
don't do it.

---

*Publication date not available.

if you're trying to write like somebody   25
else,
forget about it.

if you have to wait for it to roar out of
you,
then wait patiently.   30
if it never does roar out of you,
do something else.

if you first have to read it to your wife
or your girlfriend or your boyfriend
or your parents or to anybody at all,   35
you're not ready.

don't be like so many writers,
don't be like so many thousands of
people who call themselves writers,
don't be dull and boring and   40
pretentious, don't be consumed with self-
love.
the libraries of the world have
yawned themselves to
sleep   45
over your kind.
don't add to that.
don't do it.
unless it comes out of
your soul like a rocket,   50
unless being still would
drive you to madness or
suicide or murder,
don't do it.
unless the sun inside you is   55
burning your gut,
don't do it.

when it is truly time,
and if you have been chosen,
it will do it by   60
itself and it will keep on doing it
until you die or it dies in you.

there is no other way.

and there never was.

GEORGE GORDON, LORD BYRON (1788–1824)

She Walks in Beauty (1815)

1

She walks in beauty, like the night
  Of cloudless climes and starry skies;
And all that's best of dark and bright
  Meet in her aspect and her eyes:
Thus mellowed to that tender light   5
  Which heaven to gaudy day denies.

2

One shade the more, one ray the less,
  Had half impaired the nameless grace
Which waves in every raven tress,
  Or softly lightens o'er her face;   10
Where thoughts serenely sweet express
  How pure, how dear their dwelling place.

3

And on that cheek, and o'er that brow,
  So soft, so calm, yet eloquent,
The smiles that win, the tints that glow,   15
  But tell of days in goodness spent,
A mind at peace with all below,
  A heart whose love is innocent!

SAMUEL TAYLOR COLERIDGE (1772–1834)

Kubla Khan[1] (1797, 1798)

Or, a Vision in a Dream. A Fragment.

In Xanadu did Kubla Khan
A stately pleasure-dome decree:
Where Alph,[2] the sacred river, ran
Through caverns measureless to man
Down to a sunless sea.   5

---

[1] *Kubla Khan:* Coleridge mythologizes the actual Kublai Khan, a thirteenth-century Mongol emperor, as well as the Chinese city of Xanadu.

[2] *Alph:* Probably derived from the Greek river Alpheus, whose waters, according to legend, rose from the Ionian Sea in Sicily as the fountain of Arethusa.

So twice five miles of fertile ground
With walls and towers were girdled round;
And there were gardens bright with sinuous rills,
Where blossomed many an incense-bearing tree;
And here were forests ancient as the hills,   10
Enfolding sunny spots of greenery.

But oh! that deep romantic chasm which slanted
Down the green hill athwart a cedarn cover!
A savage place! as holy and enchanted
As e'er beneath a waning moon was haunted   15
By woman wailing for her demon-lover!
And from this chasm, with ceaseless turmoil seething,
As if this earth in fast thick pants were breathing,
A mighty fountain momently was forced:
Amid whose swift half-intermitted burst   20
Huge fragments vaulted like rebounding hail,
Or chaffy grain beneath the thresher's flail:
And 'mid these dancing rocks at once and ever
It flung up momently the sacred river.
Five miles meandering with a mazy motion   25
Through wood and dale the sacred river ran,
Then reached the caverns measureless to man,
And sank in tumult to a lifeless ocean:
And 'mid this tumult Kubla heard from far
Ancestral voices prophesying war!   30

   The shadow of the dome of pleasure
   Floated midway on the waves;
   Where was heard the mingled measure
   From the fountain and the caves.
It was a miracle of rare device,   35
A sunny pleasure-dome with caves of ice!

   A damsel with a dulcimer
   In a vision once I saw:
   It was an Abyssinian maid,
   And on her dulcimer she played,   40
   Singing of Mount Abora.[3]

---

[3]*Mount Abora:* Some scholars see a reminiscence here of John Milton's *Paradise Lost* 4.280–82: "where
Abassin kings their issue guard / Mount Amara, though this by some supposed / True Paradise under the
Ethiop Line."

Could I revive within me
Her symphony and song,
  To such a deep delight 'twould win me,
That with music loud and long,   45
I would build that dome in air,
That sunny dome! those caves of ice!
And all who heard should see them there,
And all should cry, Beware! Beware!
His flashing eyes, his floating hair   50
Weave a circle round him thrice,[4]
And close your eyes with holy dread,
For he on honey-dew hath fed,
And drunk the milk of Paradise.

BILLY COLLINS (1941–   )

Introduction to Poetry (1988)

I ask them to take a poem
and hold it up to the light
like a color slide

or press an ear against its hive.

I say drop a mouse into a poem   5
and watch him probe his way out,

or walk inside the poem's room
and feel the walls for a light switch.

I want them to waterski
across the surface of a poem   10
waving at the author's name on the shore.

But all they want to do
is tie the poem to a chair with rope
and torture a confession out of it.

They begin beating it with a hose   15
to find out what it really means.

---

[4]*Weave . . . thrice:* A magic ritual to keep away intruding spirits.

BILL COYLE (1968–   )

Aubade[1] (2005)

On a dead street
in a high wall
a wooden gate
I don't recall

ever seeing open   5
is today
and I who happen
to pass this way

in passing glimpse
a garden lit   10
by dark lamps
at the heart of it.

E. E. CUMMINGS (1894–1962)

Buffalo Bill 's (1923)

Buffalo Bill 's
defunct
      who used to
      ride a watersmooth-silver
               stallion   5
and break onetwothreefourfive pigeonsjustlikethat
                      Jesus
he was a handsome man
               and what i want to know is
how do you like your blueeyed boy   10
Mister Death

E. E. CUMMINGS (1894–1962)

next to of course god america i (1926)

"next to of course god america i
love you land of the pilgrims' and so forth oh
say can you see by the dawn's early my

---

[1] *Aubade:* A song for the morning.

country 'tis of centuries come and go
and are no more what of it we should worry   5
in every language even deafanddumb
thy sons acclaim your glorious name by gorry
by jingo by gee by gosh by gum
why talk of beauty what could be more beauti-
ful than these heroic happy dead   10
who rushed like lions to the roaring slaughter
they did not stop to think they died instead
then shall the voice of liberty be mute?"

He spoke. And drank rapidly a glass of water

JIM DANIELS (1956–   )

Short-Order Cook (1985)

An average joe comes in
and orders thirty cheeseburgers and thirty fries.

I wait for him to pay before I start cooking.
He pays.
He ain't no average joe.   5

The grill is just big enough for ten rows of three.
I slap the burgers down
throw two buckets of fries in the deep frier
and they pop pop, spit spit...
pssss...   10
The counter girls laugh.
I concentrate.
It is the crucial point—
they are ready for the cheese:
my fingers shake as I tear off slices   15
toss them on the burgers/fries done/dump
refill buckets/burgers ready/flip into buns/
beat that melting cheese/wrap burgers in plastic/
into paper bags/fried done/dump/fill thirty bags/
bring them to the counter/wipe sweat on sleeve   20
and smile at the counter girls.
I puff my chest out and bellow:
Thirty cheeseburgers! Thirty fries!
I grab a handful of ice, toss it in my mouth
do a little dance and walk back to the grill.   25
Pressure, responsibility, success.
Thirty cheeseburgers, thirty fries.

EMILY DICKINSON (1830–1886)

Because I could not stop for Death— (1863)

Because I could not stop for Death—
He kindly stopped for me—
The Carriage held but just Ourselves—
And Immortality.

We slowly drove—He knew no haste   5
And I had put away
My labor and my leisure too,
For His Civility—

We passed the School, where Children strove
At Recess—in the Ring—   10
We passed the Fields of Gazing Grain—
We passed the Setting Sun—

Or rather—He passed Us—
The Dews drew quivering and chill—
For only Gossamer, my Gown—   15
My Tippet[1]—only Tulle—

We passed before a House that seemed
A Swelling of the Ground—
The Roof was scarcely visible—
The Cornice—in the Ground—   20

Since then—'tis Centuries—and yet
Feels shorter than the Day
I first surmised the Horses' Heads
Were toward Eternity—

EMILY DICKINSON (1830–1886)

"Faith" is a fine invention (1860)

"Faith" is a fine invention
When Gentlemen can *see*—
But *Microscopes* are prudent
In an Emergency.

---

[1] *Tippet:* A short cape or scarf.

EMILY DICKINSON (1830–1886)

"Hope" is the thing with feathers— (1861)

"Hope" is the thing with feathers—
That perches in the soul—
And sings the tune without the words—
And never stops—at all—

And sweetest—in the Gale—is heard—   5
And sore must be the storm—
That could abash the little Bird—
That kept so many warm—

I've heard it in the chillest land—
And on the strangest Sea—   10
Yet, never, in Extremity,
It asked a crumb—of Me.

EMILY DICKINSON (1830–1886)

I heard a Fly buzz—when I died— (1862)

I heard a Fly buzz—when I died—
The Stillness in the Room
Was like the Stillness in the Air—
Between the Heaves of Storm—

The Eyes around—had wrung them dry—   5
And Breaths were gathering firm
For that last Onset—when the King
Be witnessed—in the Room—

I willed my Keepsakes—Signed away
What portion of me be   10
Assignable—and then it was
There interposed a Fly—

With Blue—uncertain stumbling Buzz—
Between the light—and me—
And then the Windows failed—and then   15
I could not see to see—

EMILY DICKINSON (1830–1886)

Much Madness is divinest Sense— (1862)

Much Madness is divinest Sense—
To a discerning Eye—
Much Sense—the starkest Madness—
'Tis the Majority
In this, as All, prevail—   5

Assent—and you are sane—
Demur—you're straightway dangerous—
And handled with a Chain—

EMILY DICKINSON (1830–1886)

My Life had stood—a Loaded Gun (c. 1863)

My Life had stood—a Loaded Gun—
In Corners—till a Day
The Owner passed—identified—
And carried Me away—

And now We roam in Sovereign Woods—   5
And now We hunt the Doe—
And every time I speak for Him—
The Mountains straight reply—

And do I smile, such cordial light
Upon the Valley glow—   10
It is as a Vesuvian[1] face
Had let its pleasure through—

And when at Night—Our good Day done—
I guard My Master's Head—
'Tis better than the Eider-Duck's[2]   15
Deep Pillow—to have shared—

---

[1] *Vesuvian:* The volcano Mount Vesuvius erupted in A.D. 79, destroying the city of Pompeii.
[2] *Eider-Duck's:* Eider ducks produce a soft down (eiderdown) used as pillow stuffing.

To foe of His—I'm deadly foe—
None stir the second time—
On whom I lay a Yellow Eye—
Or an emphatic Thumb—   20

Though I than He—may longer live
He longer must—than I—
For I have but the power to kill,
Without—the power to die—

EMILY DICKINSON (1830–1886)

The Soul selects her own Society— (1862)

The Soul selects her own Society—
Then—shuts the Door—
To her divine Majority—
Present no more—

Unmoved—she notes the Chariots—pausing—   5
At her low Gate—
Unmoved—an Emperor be kneeling
Upon her Mat—

I've known her—from an ample nation—
Choose One—   10
Then—close the Valves of her attention—
Like Stone—

EMILY DICKINSON (1830–1886)

There is no Frigate like a Book (1873)

There is no Frigate like a Book
To take us Lands away
Nor any Coursers like a Page
Of prancing Poetry—
This Traverse may the poorest take   5
Without oppress of Toll—
How frugal is the Chariot
That bears the Human soul.

EMILY DICKINSON (1830–1886)

There's a certain Slant of light (c. 1861)

There's a certain Slant of light,
Winter Afternoons—
That oppresses, like the Heft
Of Cathedral Tunes—

Heavenly Hurt, it gives us—   5
We can find no scar,
But internal difference,
Where the Meanings, are—

None may teach it—Any—
'Tis the Seal Despair—   10
An imperial affliction
Sent us of the Air—

When it comes, the landscape listens—
Shadows—hold their breath—
When it goes, 'tis like the Distance   15
On the look of Death—

EMILY DICKINSON (1830–1886)

This is my letter to the World (1862)

This is my letter to the World
That never wrote to Me—
The simple News that Nature told—
With tender Majesty

Her Message is committed   5
To Hands I cannot see
For love of Her—Sweet—countrymen—
Judge tenderly—of Me

JOHN DONNE (1572–1631)

Batter My Heart, Three-Personed God (c. 1610)

Batter my heart, three-personed God, for You
As yet but knock, breathe, shine, and seek to mend.
That I may rise and stand, o'erthrow me, and bend

Your force to break, blow, burn, and make me new.
I, like an usurped town to another due,   5
Labor to admit You, but Oh! to no end.
Reason, Your viceroy in me, me should defend,
But is captived, and proves weak or untrue.
Yet dearly I love You, and would be lovèd fain,
But am betrothed unto Your enemy;   10
Divorce me, untie or break that knot again;
Take me to You, imprison me, for I,
Except You enthrall me, never shall be free,
Nor ever chaste, except You ravish me.

JOHN DONNE (1572–1631)

Death Be Not Proud (c. 1610)

Death be not proud, though some have callèd thee
Mighty and dreadful, for thou art not so;
For those whom thou think'st thou dost overthrow
Die not, poor death, nor yet canst thou kill me.
From rest and sleep, which but thy pictures be,   5
Much pleasure, then from thee much more must flow,
And soonest our best men with thee do go,
Rest of their bones, and soul's delivery.
Thou art slave to fate, chance, kings, and desperate men,
And dost with poison, war, and sickness dwell,   10
And poppy, or charms can make us sleep as well,
And better than thy stroke; why swell'st thou then?
One short sleep past, we wake eternally,
And death shall be no more; death, thou shalt die.

JOHN DONNE (1572–1631)

The Flea (1633)

Mark but this flea, and mark in this[1]
How little that which thou deny'st me is;

---

[1] *mark in this:* Note the moral lesson in it.

It sucked me first, and now sucks thee,
And in this flea our two bloods mingled be;
Thou know'st that this cannot be said   5
A sin, nor shame, nor loss of maidenhead,
    Yet this enjoys before it woo,
    And pampered swells with one blood made of two,
    And this, alas, is more than we would do.[2]

Oh stay, three lives in one flea spare,   10
Where we almost, yea more than, married are.
This flea is you and I, and this
Our marriage bed, and marriage temple is;
Though parents grudge, and you, we're met
And cloistered in these living walls of jet.   15
    Though use make you apt to kill me,
    Let not to that, self-murder added be,
    And sacrilege, three sins in killing three.

Cruel and sudden, hast thou since
Purpled thy nail in blood of innocence?   20
Wherein could this flea guilty be,
Except in that drop which it sucked from thee?
Yet thou triumph'st, and say'st that thou
Find'st not thyself, nor me, the weaker now;
    'Tis true; then learn how false, fears be;   25
    Just so much honor, when thou yield'st to me,
    Will waste, as this flea's death took life from thee.

DENISE DUHAMEL (1961–   )

Buddhist Barbie*

In the 5th century B.C.
an Indian philosopher
Gautama teaches "All is emptiness"
and "There is no self."
In the 20th century A.D.   5
Barbie agrees, but wonders how a man
with such a belly could pose,
smiling, and without a shirt.

---

[2] *more than we would do:* If we do not join our blood.

*Publication date not available.

T. S. ELIOT (1888–1965)

The Love Song of J. Alfred Prufrock (1917)

S'io credessi che mia risposta fosse
A persona che mai tornasse al mondo,
Questa fiamma staria senza piu scosse.
Ma perciocche giammai di questo fondo
Non torno vivo alcun, s'i'odo il vero,
Senza tema d'infamia ti rispondo.[1]

Let us go then, you and I,
When the evening is spread out against the sky
Like a patient etherized upon a table;
Let us go, through certain half-deserted streets,
The muttering retreats   5
Of restless nights in one-night cheap hotels
And sawdust restaurants with oyster-shells:
Streets that follow like a tedious argument
Of insidious intent
To lead you to an overwhelming question . . .   10
Oh, do not ask, "What is it?"
Let us go and make our visit.

In the room the women come and go
Talking of Michelangelo.

The yellow fog that rubs its back upon the window-panes,   15
The yellow smoke that rubs its muzzle on the window-panes
Licked its tongue into the corners of the evening,
Lingered upon the pools that stand in drains,
Let fall upon its back the soot that falls from chimneys,
Slipped by the terrace, made a sudden leap,   20
And seeing that it was a soft October night,
Curled once about the house, and fell asleep.

And indeed there will be time
For the yellow smoke that slides along the street,

---

[1]*S'io . . . rispondo:* The epigraph is from Dante's *Inferno*, Canto 27. In response to the poet's question about his identity, Guido da Montefelto, who for his sin of fraud must spend eternity wrapped in flames, replies: "If I thought that I was speaking to someone who could go back to the world, this flame would shake me no more. But since from this place nobody ever returns alive, if what I hear is true, I answer you without fear of infamy."

Rubbing its back upon the window-panes;   25
There will be time, there will be time
To prepare a face to meet the faces that you meet;
There will be time to murder and create,
And time for all the works and days[2] of hands
That lift and drop a question on your plate;   30
Time for you and time for me,
And time yet for a hundred indecisions,
And for a hundred visions and revisions,
Before the taking of a toast and tea.

In the room the women come and go   35
Talking of Michelangelo.

And indeed there will be time
To wonder, "Do I dare?" and, "Do I dare?"
Time to turn back and descend the stair,
With a bald spot in the middle of my hair—   40
(They will say: "How his hair is growing thin!")
My morning coat, my collar mounting firmly to the chin,
My necktie rich and modest, but asserted by a simple pin—
(They will say: "But how his arms and legs are thin!")
Do I dare   45
Disturb the universe?
In a minute there is time
For decisions and revisions which a minute will reverse.

For I have known them all already, known them all—
Have known the evenings, mornings, afternoons,   50
I have measured out my life with coffee spoons;
I know the voices dying with a dying fall[3]
Beneath the music from a farther room.
    So how should I presume?

And I have known the eyes already, known them all—   55
The eyes that fix you in a formulated phrase,
And when I am formulated, sprawling on a pin,
When I am pinned and wriggling on the wall,

---

[2]*works and days: Works and Days,* by the eighth-century B.C. Greek poet Hesiod, is a poem that celebrates farm life.

[3]*dying fall:* An allusion to Orsino's speech in *Twelfth Night* (1.1): "That strain again! It had a dying fall."

Then how should I begin
To spit out all the butt-ends of my days and ways?   60
     And how should I presume?

And I have known the arms already, known them all—
Arms that are braceleted and white and bare
(But in the lamplight, downed with light brown hair!)
Is it perfume from a dress   65
That makes me so digress?
Arms that lie along a table, or wrap about a shawl.
     And should I then presume?
     And how should I begin?

                    *   *   *

Shall I say, I have gone at dusk through narrow streets   70
And watched the smoke that rises from the pipes
Of lonely men in shirt-sleeves, leaning out of windows? . . .

I should have been a pair of ragged claws
Scuttling across the floors of silent seas.

                    *   *   *

And the afternoon, the evening, sleeps so peacefully!   75
Smoothed by long fingers,
Asleep . . . tired . . . or it malingers,
Stretched on the floor, here beside you and me.
Should I, after tea and cakes and ices,
Have the strength to force the moment to its crisis?   80
But though I have wept and fasted, wept and prayed,
Though I have seen my head (grown slightly bald) brought in
     upon a platter,[4]
I am no prophet—and here's no great matter;
I have seen the moment of my greatness flicker,
And I have seen the eternal Footman[5] hold my coat, and   85
     snicker,
And in short, I was afraid.
And would it have been worth it, after all,
After the cups, the marmalade, the tea,

---

[4]*head . . . platter:* Like John the Baptist, who was beheaded by King Herod (see Matthew 14.3–11).
[5]*eternal Footman:* Perhaps death or fate.

Among the porcelain, among some talk of you and me,
Would it have been worth while,   90
To have bitten off the matter with a smile,
To have squeezed the universe into a ball
To roll it toward some overwhelming question,
To say: "I am Lazarus,[6] come from the dead,
Come back to tell you all, I shall tell you all"—   95
If one, settling a pillow by her head,
　　Should say: "That is not what I meant at all.
　　That is not it, at all."

And would it have been worth it, after all,
Would it have been worth while,   100
After the sunsets and the dooryards and the sprinkled
　　streets,
After the novels, after the teacups, after the skirts that trail
　　along the floor—
And this, and so much more?—
It is impossible to say just what I mean!
But as if a magic lantern threw the nerves in patterns on a   105
　　screen:
Would it have been worth while
If one, settling a pillow or throwing off a shawl,
And turning toward the window, should say:
　　"That is not it at all,
　　That is not what I meant, at all."   110

　　　　　　　　*　　　*　　　*

No! I am not Prince Hamlet, nor was meant to be;
Am an attendant lord, one that will do
To swell a progress,[7] start a scene or two,
Advise the prince; no doubt, an easy tool,
Deferential, glad to be of use,   115
Politic, cautious, and meticulous;
Full of high sentence,[8] but a bit obtuse;
At times, indeed, almost ridiculous—
Almost, at times, the Fool.

---

[6]*Lazarus:* A man whom Christ raised from the dead (see John 11.1–44).
[7]*a progress:* Here, in the Elizabethan sense of a royal journey.
[8]*sentence:* Opinions.

I grow old . . . I grow old . . .   120
I shall wear the bottoms of my trousers rolled.

Shall I part my hair behind? Do I dare to eat a peach?
I shall wear white flannel trousers, and walk upon the beach.
I have heard the mermaids singing, each to each.

I do not think that they will sing to me.   125

I have seen them riding seaward on the waves
Combing the white hair of the waves blown back
When the wind blows the water white and black.

We have lingered in the chambers of the sea
By sea-girls wreathed with seaweed red and brown   130
Till human voices wake us, and we drown.

LOUISE ERDRICH (1954–   )

Indian Boarding School: The Runaways (1984)

Home's the place we head for in our sleep.
Boxcars stumbling north in dreams
don't wait for us. We catch them on the run.
The rails, old lacerations that we love,
shoot parallel across the face and break   5
just under Turtle Mountains.[1] Riding scars
you can't get lost. Home is the place they cross.

The lame guard strikes a match and makes the dark
less tolerant. We watch through cracks in boards
as the land starts rolling, rolling till it hurts   10
to be here, cold in regulation clothes.
We know the sheriff's waiting at midrun
to take us back. His car is dumb and warm.
The highway doesn't rock, it only hums
like a wing of long insults. The worn-down welts   15
of ancient punishments lead back and forth.

All runaways wear dresses, long green ones,
the color you would think shame was. We scrub
the sidewalks down because it's shameful work.
Our brushes cut the stone in watered arcs   20

---

[1] *Turtle Mountains:* Erdrich is a descendant of the Turtle Mountain band of the Chippewa.

and in the soak frail outlines shiver clear
a moment, things us kids pressed on the dark
face before it hardened, pale, remembering
delicate old injuries, the spines of names and leaves.

MARTÍN ESPADA (1957–   )

The Community College Revises Its Curriculum in Response to Changing Demographics (2000)

SPA 100 Conversational Spanish
2 credits

The course
is especially concerned
with giving police
the ability
to express themselves   5
tersely
in matters of interest
to them

ROBERT FROST (1874–1963)

Mending Wall (1914)

Something there is that doesn't love a wall,
That sends the frozen-ground-swell under it,
And spills the upper boulders in the sun;
And makes gaps even two can pass abreast.
The work of hunters is another thing: 5
I have come after them and made repair
Where they have left not one stone on a stone,
But they would have the rabbit out of hiding,
To please the yelping dogs. The gaps I mean,
No one has seen them made or heard them made,   10
But at spring mending-time we find them there.
I let my neighbor know beyond the hill;
And on a day we meet to walk the line
And set the wall between us once again.

We keep the wall between us as we go. 15
To each the boulders that have fallen to each.
And some are loaves and some so nearly balls
We have to use a spell to make them balance:
"Stay where you are until our backs are turned!"
We wear our fingers rough with handling them. 20
Oh, just another kind of outdoor game,
One on a side. It comes to little more:
There where it is we do not need the wall:
He is all pine and I am apple orchard.
My apple trees will never get across 25
And eat the cones under his pines, I tell him.
He only says, "Good fences make good neighbors."
Spring is the mischief in me, and I wonder
If I could put a notion in his head:
"Why do they make good neighbors? Isn't it 30
Where there are cows? But here there are no cows.
Before I built a wall I'd ask to know
What I was walling in or walling out,
And to whom I was like to give offense.
Something there is that doesn't love a wall, 35
That wants it down." I could say "Elves" to him,
But it's not elves exactly, and I'd rather
He said it for himself. I see him there
Bringing a stone grasped firmly by the top
In each hand, like an old-stone savage armed. 40
He moves in darkness as it seems to me,
Not of woods only and the shade of trees.
He will not go behind his father's saying,
And he likes having thought of it so well
He says again, "Good fences make good neighbors." 45

ROBERT FROST (1874–1963)

Stopping by Woods on a Snowy Evening (1923)

Whose woods these are I think I know.
His house is in the village though;
He will not see me stopping here
To watch his woods fill up with snow.

My little horse must think it queer 5
To stop without a farmhouse near

Between the woods and frozen lake
The darkest evening of the year.

He gives his harness bells a shake
To ask if there is some mistake.   10
The only other sound's the sweep
Of easy wind and downy flake.

The woods are lovely, dark and deep,
But I have promises to keep,
And miles to go before I sleep,   15
And miles to go before I sleep.

THOMAS HARDY (1840–1928)

The Convergence of the Twain (1912)

(Lines on the loss of the "Titanic")

I

In a solitude of the sea
Deep from human vanity,
And the Pride of Life that planned her, stilly couches she.

II

Steel chambers, late the pyres[1]
Of her salamandrine fires,[2]   5
Cold currents thrid,[3] and turn to rhythmic tidal lyres.

III

Over the mirrors meant
To glass the opulent
The sea-worm crawls—grotesque, slimed, dumb, indifferent.

IV

Jewels in joy designed
To ravish the sensuous mind   10
Lie lightless, all their sparkles bleared and black and blind.

---

[1] *pyres:* Funeral pyres; piles of wood on which corpses were burned in ancient rites.

[2] *salamandrine fires:* An allusion to the old belief that salamanders could live in fire.

[3] *thrid:* Thread (archaic verb form).

V

Dim moon-eyed fishes near
Gaze at the gilded gear
And query: "What does this vaingloriousness down here?"...   15

VI

Well: while was fashioning
This creature of cleaving wing,
The Immanent[4] Will that stirs and urges everything

VII

Prepared a sinister mate
For her—so gaily great—   20
A Shape of Ice, for the time far and dissociate.

VIII

And as the smart ship grew
In stature, grace, and hue,
In shadowy silent distance grew the Iceberg too.

IX

Alien they seemed to be: 25
No mortal eye could see
The intimate welding of their later history,

X

Or sign that they were bent
By paths coincident
On being anon[5] twin halves of one august[6] event,   30

XI

Till the Spinner of the Years
Said "Now!" And each one hears,
And consummation comes, and jars two hemispheres.

SEAMUS HEANEY (1939–2013)

Mid-Term Break (1966)

I sat all morning in the college sick bay
Counting bells knelling classes to a close.
At two o'clock our neighbors drove me home.

---

[4]*Immanent:* Inherent, dwelling within.

[5]*anon:* Soon.

[6]*august:* Awe-inspiring, majestic.

In the porch I met my father crying—
He had always taken funerals in his stride—   5
And Big Jim Evans saying it was a hard blow.

The baby cooed and laughed and rocked the pram
When I came in, and I was embarrassed
By old men standing up to shake my hand

And tell me they were "sorry for my trouble,"   10
Whispers informed strangers I was the eldest,
Away at school, as my mother held my hand

In hers and coughed out angry tearless sighs.
At ten o'clock the ambulance arrived
With the corpse, stanched and bandaged by the nurses.   15

Next morning I went up into the room. Snowdrops
And candles soothed the bedside; I saw him
For the first time in six weeks. Paler now,

Wearing a poppy bruise on his left temple,
He lay in the four foot box as in his cot.   20
No gaudy scars, the bumper knocked him clear.

A four foot box, a foot for every year.

WILLIAM ERNEST HENLEY (1849–1903)

Invictus (1888)

Out of the night that covers me,
Black as the Pit from pole to pole,
I thank whatever gods may be
For my unconquerable soul.

In the fell clutch of circumstance   5
I have not winced nor cried aloud.
Under the bludgeonings of chance
My head is bloody, but unbowed.

Beyond this place of wrath and tears
Looms but the Horror of the shade,   10
And yet the menace of the years
Finds, and shall find, me unafraid.

It matters not how strait the gate,
How charged with punishments the scroll.
I am the master of my fate: 15
I am the captain of my soul.

GERARD MANLEY HOPKINS (1844–1889)

God's Grandeur (1877)

The world is charged with the grandeur of God.
   It will flame out, like shining from shook foil;
   It gathers to a greatness, like the ooze of oil
Crushed. Why do men then now not reck his rod?
Generations have trod, have trod, have trod;   5
   And all is seared with trade; bleared, smeared with toil;
   And wears man's smudge and shares man's smell: the soil
Is bare now, nor can foot feel, being shod.

And for all this, nature is never spent;
   There lives the dearest freshness deep down things;   10
And though the last lights off the black West went
   Oh, morning, at the brown brink eastward, springs—
Because the Holy Ghost over the bent
   World broods with warm breast and with ah! bright wings.

LANGSTON HUGHES (1902–1967)

The Negro Speaks of Rivers (1921)

I've known rivers:
I've known rivers ancient as the world and old as the flow of
   human blood in human veins.

My soul has grown deep like the rivers.

I bathed in the Euphrates[1] when dawns were young.
I built my hut near the Congo[2] and it lulled me to sleep.   5
I looked upon the Nile and raised the pyramids above it.
I heard the singing of the Mississippi when Abe Lincoln went
   down to New Orleans, and I've seen its muddy bosom turn
   all golden in the sunset.

I've known rivers:
Ancient, dusky rivers.

My soul has grown deep like the rivers.   10

---

[1] *Euphrates:* Major river of southwest Asia; with the Tigris, the Euphrates forms a valley sometimes referred to as the "cradle of civilization."

[2] *Congo:* River in equatorial Africa, the continent's second longest.

LANGSTON HUGHES (1902–1967)

Theme for English B (1949)

The instructor said,

> Go home and write
> a page tonight.
> And let that page come out of you—
> Then, it will be true.   5

I wonder if it's that simple?
I am twenty-two, colored, born in Winston-Salem.
I went to school there, then Durham, then here
to this college on the hill above Harlem.
I am the only colored student in my class.   10
The steps from the hill lead down into Harlem,
through a park, then I cross St. Nicholas,
Eighth Avenue, Seventh, and I come to the Y,
the Harlem Branch Y, where I take the elevator
up to my room, sit down and write this page: 15

It's not easy to know what is true for you or me
at twenty-two, my age. But I guess I'm what
I feel and see and hear, Harlem, I hear you:
hear you, hear me—we two—you, me, talk on this page.
(I hear New York, too) Me—who?   20
Well, I like to eat, sleep, drink, and be in love.
I like to work, read, learn, and understand life.
I like a pipe for a Christmas present,
or records—Bessie,[1] bop,[2] or Bach.
I guess being colored doesn't make me *not* like   25
the same things other folks like who are other races.
So will my page be colored that I write?
Being me, it will not be white.
But it will be
a part of you, instructor.   30
You are white—
yet a part of me, as I am a part of you.
That's American.

---

[1] *Bessie:* Bessie Smith (1894–1937), blues singer.
[2] *bop:* Short for "bebop," a jazz style developed in the early 1940s by Charlie Parker, Dizzy Gillespie, and others.

Sometimes perhaps you don't want to be a part of me.
Nor do I often want to be a part of you.   35
But we are, that's true!
As I learn from you,
I guess you learn from me—
although you're older—and white—
and somewhat more free.   40

This is my page for English B.

JOHN KEATS (1795–1821)

La Belle Dame sans Merci: A Ballad[1] (1819, 1820)

1

O what can ail thee, knight at arms,
    Alone and palely loitering?
The sedge has wither'd from the lake,
    And no birds sing.

2

O what can ail thee, knight at arms,   5
    So haggard and so woe-begone?
The squirrel's granary is full,
    And the harvest's done.

3

I see a lily on thy brow
    With anguish moist and fever dew,   10
And on thy cheeks a fading rose
    Fast withereth too.

4

I met a lady in the meads,
    Full beautiful, a fairy's child;
Her hair was long, her foot was light,   15
    And her eyes were wild.

---

[1] "*La Belle Dame sans Merci*": The title, which means "The Lovely Lady without Pity," was taken from a medieval poem by Alain Chartier.

5

I made a garland for her head,
 And bracelets too, and fragrant zone;[2]
She look'd at me as she did love,
 And made sweet moan. 20

6

I set her on my pacing steed,
 And nothing else saw all day long,
For sidelong would she bend, and sing
 A fairy's song.

7

She found me roots of relish sweet, 25
 And honey wild, and manna dew,
And sure in language strange she said—
 I love thee true.

8

She took me to her elfin grot,[3]
 And there she wept, and sigh'd full sore, 30
And there I shut her wild wild eyes
 With kisses four.

9

And there she lullèd me asleep,
 And there I dream'd—Ah! woe betide!
The latest[4] dream I ever dream'd 35
 On the cold hill's side.

10

I saw pale kings, and princes too,
 Pale warriors, death pale were they all;
They cried—"La belle dame sans merci
 Hath thee in thrall!" 40

---

[2]*fragrant zone:* Belt.
[3]*grot:* Grotto.
[4]*latest:* Last.

11

I saw their starv'd lips in the gloam[5]
  With horrid warning gapèd wide,
And I awoke and found me here
    On the cold hill's side.

12

And this is why I sojourn here,   45
  Alone and palely loitering,
Though the sedge is wither'd from the lake,
    And no birds sing.

JOHN KEATS (1795–1821)

Ode on a Grecian Urn (1819)

1

Thou still unravish'd bride of quietness,
  Thou foster-child of silence and slow time,
Sylvan[1] historian, who canst thus express
A flowery tale more sweetly than our rhyme:
  What leaf-fring'd legend haunts about thy shape 5
    Of deities or mortals, or of both,
      In Tempe[2] or the dales of Arcady?[3]
    What men or gods are these? What maidens loth?
  What mad pursuit? What struggle to escape?
  What pipes and timbrels? What wild ecstasy?   10

2

Heard melodies are sweet, but those unheard
  Are sweeter; therefore, ye soft pipes, play on;
Not to the sensual ear, but, more endear'd,
  Pipe to the spirit ditties of no tone:
Fair youth, beneath the trees, thou canst not leave 15
  Thy song, nor ever can those trees be bare;
    Bold lover, never, never canst thou kiss,

Sketch by John Keats of the Sosibios Vase that may have inspired "Ode on a Grecian Urn."
Keats-Shelley House, Rome, Italy

---

[5]*gloam:* Twilight.

[1]*Sylvan:* Pertaining to woods or forests.

[2]*Tempe:* A beautiful valley in Greece.

[3]*Arcady:* The valleys of Arcadia, a mountainous region on the Greek peninsula. Like Tempe, they represent a rustic pastoral ideal.

Though winning near the goal—yet, do not grieve;
　　She cannot fade, though thou hast not thy bliss,
　For ever wilt thou love, and she be fair!　　　　　　　20

3

Ah, happy, happy boughs! that cannot shed
　Your leaves, nor ever bid the spring adieu;
And, happy melodist, unwearied,
　For ever piping songs for ever new;
More happy love! more happy, happy love!　　　　　　　25
　For ever warm and still to be enjoy'd,
　　For ever panting, and for ever young;
All breathing human passion far above,
　That leaves a heart high-sorrowful and cloy'd,
　A burning forehead, and a parching tongue.　　　　　　30

4

Who are these coming to the sacrifice?
　To what green altar, O mysterious priest,
Lead'st thou that heifer lowing at the skies,
　And all her silken flanks with garlands drest?
What little town by river or sea shore,　　　　　　　35
　Or mountain-built with peaceful citadel,
　　Is emptied of this folk, this pious morn?
And, little town, thy streets for evermore
　Will silent be; and not a soul to tell
　Why thou art desolate, can e'er return.　　　　　　　40

5

O Attic[4] shape! Fair attitude! with brede[5]
　Of marble men and maidens overwrought,[6]
With forest branches and the trodden weed;
　Thou, silent form, dost tease us out of thought
As doth eternity: Cold Pastoral!　　　　　　　45
　When old age shall this generation waste,
　　Thou shalt remain, in midst of other woe
Than ours, a friend to man, to whom thou say'st,
　"Beauty is truth, truth beauty,"—that is all
　Ye know on earth, and all ye need to know.　　　　　　　50

---

[4]*Attic:* Characteristic of Athens or Athenians.
[5]*brede:* Braid.
[6]*overwrought:* Elaborately ornamented.

JOHN KEATS (1795–1821)

When I Have Fears (1818)

When I have fears that I may cease to be
  Before my pen has gleaned my teeming brain,
Before high-piléd books, in charact'ry,[1]
  Hold like rich garners the full-ripened grain;
When I behold, upon the night's starred face,   5
  Huge cloudy symbols of a high romance,
And think that I may never live to trace
  Their shadows, with the magic hand of chance;
And when I feel, fair creature of an hour,
  That I shall never look upon thee more,   10
Never have relish in the faery power
  Of unreflecting love!—then on the shore
Of the wide world I stand alone, and think
Till Love and Fame to nothingness do sink.

LAM THI MY DA (1949–   )

Bomb Crater Sky (2005)

Translated by Martha Collins and Thuy Dinh

They say that you, a road builder
Had such love for our country
You rushed out and waved your torch
To call the bombs down on yourself
And save the road for the troops   5

As my unit passed on that worn road
The bomb crater reminded us of your story
Your grave is radiant with bright-colored stones
Piled high with love for you, a young girl

As I looked in the bomb crater where you died   10
The rain water became a patch of sky
Our country is kind
Water from the sky washes pain away

Now you lie down deep in the earth
As the sky lay down in that earthen crater   15

---

[1]*charact'ry:* Print.

At night your soul sheds light
Like the dazzling stars
Did your soft white skin
Become a bank of white clouds?

By day I pass under a sun-flooded sky   20
And it is your sky
And that anxious, wakeful disc
Is it the sun, or is it your heart
Lighting my way
As I walk down the long road?   25

The name of the road is your name
Your death is a young girl's patch of blue sky
My soul is lit by your life

And my friends, who never saw you
Each has a different image of your face   30

ARCHIBALD MACLEISH (1892–1982)

Ars Poetica[1] (1926)

A poem should be palpable and mute
As a globed fruit,

Dumb
As old medallions to the thumb,

Silent as the sleeve-worn stone   5
Of casement ledges where the moss has grown—

A poem should be wordless
As the flight of birds.

A poem should be motionless in time
As the moon climbs,   10

Leaving, as the moon releases
Twig by twig the night-entangled trees,

Leaving, as the moon behind the winter leaves,
Memory by memory the mind—

A poem should be motionless in time   15
As the moon climbs.

---

[1]*Ars Poetica:* "The Art of Poetry" (Latin).

A poem should be equal to:
Not true.

For all the history of grief
An empty doorway and a maple leaf.   20

For love
The leaning grasses and two lights above the sea—

A poem should not mean
But be.

CHRISTOPHER MARLOWE (1564–1593)

The Passionate Shepherd to His Love (1600)

Come live with me and be my love,
And we will all the pleasures prove
That valleys, groves, hills, and fields,
Woods, or steepy mountain yields.

And we will sit upon the rocks,   5
Seeing the shepherds feed their flocks
By shallow rivers, to whose falls
Melodious birds sing madrigals.

And I will make thee beds of roses
And a thousand fragrant posies,   10
A cap of flowers and a kirtle[1]
Embroidered all with leaves of myrtle;

A gown made of the finest wool
Which from our pretty lambs we pull;
Fair-linèd slippers for the cold,   15
With buckles of the purest gold;

A belt of straw and ivy buds,
With coral clasps and amber studs.
And if these pleasures may thee move,
Come live with me and be my love.   20

The shepherds' swains shall dance and sing
For thy delight each May morning.
If these delights thy mind may move,
Then live with me and be my love.

---

[1] *kirtle:* Skirt.

CLAUDE MCKAY (1890–1948)

If We Must Die (1922)

If we must die, let it not be like hogs
Hunted and penned in an inglorious spot,
While round us bark the mad and hungry dogs,
Making their mock at our accursed lot.
If we must die, O let us nobly die,   5
So that our precious blood may not be shed
In vain; then even the monsters we defy
Shall be constrained to honor us though dead!
O kinsmen! we must meet the common foe!
Though far outnumbered let us show us brave,   10
And for their thousand blows deal one deathblow!
What though before us lies the open grave?
Like men we'll face the murderous, cowardly pack,
Pressed to the wall, dying, but fighting back!

PAT MORA (1942–   )

La Migra[1] (1993)

I

Let's play La Migra
I'll be the Border Patrol.
You be the Mexican maid.
I get the badge and sunglasses.
You can hide and run,   5
but you can't get away
because I have a jeep.
I can take you wherever
I want, but don't ask
questions because   10
I don't speak Spanish.
I can touch you wherever
I want but don't complain
too much because I've got
boots and kick—if I have to,   15
and I have handcuffs.

---

[1] *La Migra:* Mexican slang for U.S. border patrol.

Oh, and a gun.
Get ready, get set, run.

II

Let's play La Migra
You be the Border Patrol.   20
I'll be the Mexican woman.
Your jeep has a flat,
and you have been spotted
by the sun.
All you have is heavy: hat   25
glasses, badge, shoes, gun.
I know this desert,
where to rest,
where to drink.
Oh, I am not alone.   30
You hear us singing
and laughing with the wind,
Agua dulce brota aqui,
aqui, aqui[2] but since you
can't speak Spanish,   35
you do not understand.
Get ready.

PABLO NERUDA (1904–1973)

Tonight I Can Write (1924)

Translated by W. S. Merwin

Tonight I can write the saddest lines.

Write, for example, 'The night is starry
and the stars are blue and shiver in the distance.'

The night wind revolves in the sky and sings.

Tonight I can write the saddest lines.   5
I loved her, and sometimes she loved me too.

Through nights like this one I held her in my arms.
I kissed her again and again under the endless sky.

She loved me, sometimes I loved her too.
How could one not have loved her great still eyes.   10

---

[2]*Agua…aqui:* Sweet water springs here, here, here.

Tonight I can write the saddest lines.
To think that I do not have her. To feel that I have lost her,

To hear the immense night, still more immense without her,
And the verse falls to the soul like dew to the pasture.

What does it matter that my love could not keep her.   15
The night is starry and she is not with me.

This is all. In the distance someone is singing. In the distance.
My soul is not satisfied that it has lost her.

My sight tries to find her as though to bring her closer.
My heart looks for her, and she is not with me.   20

The same night whitening the same trees.
We, of that time, are no longer the same.

I no longer love her, that's certain, but how I loved her.
My voice tried to find the wind to touch her hearing.

Another's. She will be another's. As she was before my kisses.   25
Her voice, her bright body. Her infinite eyes.

I no longer love her, that's certain, but maybe I love her.
Love is so short, forgetting is so long.

Because through nights like this one I held her in my arms
my soul is not satisfied that it has lost her.   30

Though this be the last pain that she makes me suffer
And these the last verses that I write for her.

PABLO NERUDA (1904–1973)

The United Fruit Co.¹ (1950)

Translated by Robert Bly

When the trumpet sounded, it was
all prepared on the earth,
and Jehovah parceled out the earth
to Coca-Cola, Inc., Anaconda,
Ford Motors, and other entities: 5

---

¹*United Fruit Co.:* Incorporated in New Jersey in 1899 by Andrew Preston and Minor C. Keith, United Fruit
became a major force in growing, transporting, and merchandising Latin American produce, especially
bananas. The company is notorious for its involvement in politics, and as a result its name came to represent "Yankee" imperialism and oppression.

The Fruit Company, Inc.
reserved for itself the most succulent,
the central coast of my own land,
the delicate waist of America.
It rechristened its territories   10
as the "Banana Republics"
and over the sleeping dead,
over the restless heroes
who brought about the greatness,
the liberty and the flags,   15
it established the comic opera:
abolished the independencies,
presented crowns of Caesar,
unsheathed envy, attracted
the dictatorship of the flies,   20
Trujillo flies, Tacho flies,
Carias flies, Martinez flies,
Ubico flies,[2] damp flies
of modest blood and marmalade,
drunken flies who zoom   25
over the ordinary graves,
circus flies, wise flies
well trained in tyranny.

Among the bloodthirsty flies
the Fruit Company lands its ships,   30
taking off the coffee and the fruit;
the treasure of our submerged
territories flows as though
on plates into the ships.

Meanwhile Indians are falling   35
into the sugared chasms
of the harbors, wrapped
for burial in the mist of the dawn:
a body rolls, a thing
that has no name, a fallen cipher,   40
a cluster of dead fruit
thrown down on the dump.

---

[2] *Trujillo, Tacho, Carias, Martinez, Ubico:* Political dictators.

LINDA PASTAN (1932–   )

Ethics (1980)

In ethics class so many years ago
our teacher asked this question every fall:
if there were a fire in a museum
which would you save, a Rembrandt painting
or an old woman who hadn't many   5
years left anyhow? Restless on hard chairs
caring little for pictures or old age
we'd opt one year for life, the next for art
and always half-heartedly. Sometimes
the woman borrowed my grandmother's face   10
leaving her usual kitchen to wander
some drafty, half imagined museum.
One year, feeling clever, I replied
why not let the woman decide herself?
Linda, the teacher would report, eschews   15
the burdens of responsibility.
This fall in a real museum I stand
before a real Rembrandt, old woman,
or nearly so, myself. The colors
within this frame are darker than autumn,   20
darker even than winter—the browns of earth,
though earth's most radiant elements burn
through the canvas. I know now that woman
and painting and season are almost one
and all beyond saving by children.   25

SIR WALTER RALEIGH (1552–1618)

The Nymph's Reply
to the Shepherd (1600)

If all the world and love were young,
And truth in every shepherd's tongue,
These pretty pleasures might me move
To live with thee and be thy love.

Time drives the flocks from field to fold,   5
When rivers rage and rocks grow cold;
And Philomel[1] becometh dumb;
The rest complains of cares to come.

The flowers do fade, and wanton fields
To wayward winter reckoning yields: 10
A honey tongue, a heart of gall,
Is fancy's spring, but sorrow's fall.

Thy gowns, thy shoes, thy beds of roses,
Thy cap, thy kirtle, and thy posies
Soon break, soon wither, soon forgotten,   15
In folly ripe, in reason rotten.

Thy belt of straw and ivy buds,
Thy coral clasps and amber studs.
All these in me no means can move
To come to thee and be thy love.   20

But could youth last, and love still breed,
Had joys no date, nor age no need,
Then these delights my mind might move
To live with thee and be thy love.

Bettmann/Corbis

EDWIN ARLINGTON ROBINSON (1869–1935)

Richard Cory (1897)

Whenever Richard Cory went down town,
We people on the pavement looked at him:
He was a gentleman from sole to crown,
Clean favored, and imperially slim.

And he was always quietly arrayed,   5
And he was always human when he talked;
But still he fluttered pulses when he said,
"Good-morning," and he glittered when he walked.

And he was rich—yes, richer than a king—
And admirably schooled in every grace: 10

---

[1] *Philomel:* The nightingale.

In fine, we thought that he was everything
To make us wish that we were in his place.

So on we worked, and waited for the light,
And went without the meat, and cursed the bread;
And Richard Cory, one calm summer night,   15
Went home and put a bullet through his head.

CYNTHIA RYLANT (1954–   )

God Went to Beauty School (2003)

He went there to learn how
to give a good perm
and ended up just crazy
about nails
so He opened up His own shop.   5
"Nails by Jim" He called it.
He was afraid to call it
Nails by God.
He was sure people would
think He was being   10
disrespectful and using
His own name in vain
and nobody would tip.
He got into nails, of course,
because He'd always loved   15
hands—
hands were some of the best things
He'd ever done
and this way He could just
hold one in His   20
and admire those delicate
bones just above the knuckles,
delicate as birds' wings,
and after He'd done that
awhile,   25
He could paint all the nails
any color He wanted,
then say,
"Beautiful,"
and mean it.   30

WILLIAM SHAKESPEARE (1564–1616)

Let me not to the marriage of true minds (1609)

Let me not to the marriage of true minds
Admit impediments.[1] Love is not love
Which alters when it alteration finds,
Or bends with the remover to remove:
Oh, no! it is an ever-fixéd mark,   5
That looks on tempests and is never shaken;
It is the star to every wandering bark,
Whose worth's unknown, although his height be taken.[2]
Love's not Time's fool,[3] though rosy lips and cheeks
Within his bending sickle's compass come;   10
Love alters not with his brief hours and weeks,
But bears it out even to the edge of doom.[4]
    If this be error and upon me proved,
    I never writ, nor no man ever loved.

WILLIAM SHAKESPEARE (1564–1616)

Not marble, nor the gilded monuments (1609)

Not marble, nor the gilded monuments
Of princes, shall outlive this powerful rhyme;
But you shall shine more bright in these contents
Than unswept stone, besmeared with sluttish time.
When wasteful war shall statues overturn,   5
And broils root out the work of masonry,
Nor Mars[1] his sword nor war's quick fire shall burn
The living record of your memory.
'Gainst death and all-oblivious enmity
Shall you pace forth; your praise shall still find room   10

---

[1] *Admit impediments:* A reference to "The Order of Solemnization of Matrimony" in the Anglican Book of Common Prayer: "I require that if either of you know any impediments why ye may not be lawfully joined together in Matrimony, ye do now confess it."

[2] *Whose worth's... taken:* Although the altitude of a star may be measured, its worth is unknowable.

[3] *Love's not Time's fool:* Love is not mocked by Time.

[4] *doom:* Doomsday.

[1] *Mars:* The Roman god of war.

Even in the eyes of all posterity
That wear this world out to the ending doom.
   So, till the judgment that yourself arise,
   You live in this, and dwell in lovers' eyes.

PERCY BYSSHE SHELLEY (1792–1822)

Ode to the West Wind (1820)

I

O wild West Wind, thou breath of Autumn's being,
Thou, from whose unseen presence the leaves dead
Are driven, like ghosts from an enchanter fleeing,

Yellow, and black, and pale, and hectic red,[1]
Pestilence-stricken multitudes: O Thou,   5
Who chariotest to their dark wintry bed

The winged seeds, where they lie cold and low,
Each like a corpse within its grave, until
Thine azure sister of the Spring[2] shall blow

Her clarion o'er the dreaming earth, and fill   10
(Driving sweet buds like flocks to feed in air)
With living hues and odours plain and hill:
Wild Spirit, which art moving everywhere;
Destroyer and Preserver; hear, O hear!

II

Thou on whose stream, mid the steep sky's commotion,   15
Loose clouds like Earth's decaying leaves are shed,
Shook from the tangled boughs of Heaven and Ocean,

Angels of rain and lightning: there are spread
On the blue surface of thine aery surge,
Like the bright hair uplifted from the head   20

Of some fierce Maenad,[3] even from the dim verge
Of the horizon to the zenith's height,
The locks of the approaching storm. Thou Dirge

---

[1] *Yellow...hectic red:* A reference to a tubercular fever that produces flushed cheeks.

[2] *azure...Spring:* The west wind of the spring.

[3] *Maenad:* A female votary who danced wildly in ceremonies for Dionysus (or Bacchus), Greek god of wine and vegetation, who according to legend died in the fall and was reborn in the spring.

Of the dying year, to which this closing night
Will be the dome of a vast sepulchre,   25
Vaulted with all thy congregated might

Of vapours, from whose solid atmosphere
Black rain and fire and hail will burst: O hear!

III

Thou who didst waken from his summer dreams
The blue Mediterranean, where he lay,   30
Lulled by the coil of his crystalline streams,

Beside a pumice isle in Baiae's bay,[4]
And saw in sleep old palaces and towers
Quivering within the wave's intenser day,

All overgrown with azure moss and flowers   35
So sweet, the sense faints picturing them! Thou
For whose path the Atlantic's level powers

Cleave themselves into chasms, while far below
The sea-blooms and the oozy woods which wear
The sapless foliage of the ocean, know   40

Thy voice, and suddenly grow grey with fear,
And tremble and despoil themselves: O hear!

IV

If I were a dead leaf thou mightest bear;
If I were a swift cloud to fly with thee;
A wave to pant beneath thy power, and share   45

The impulse of thy strength, only less free
Than thou, O Uncontrollable! If even
I were as in my boyhood, and could be

The comrade of thy wanderings over Heaven,
As then, when to outstrip thy skiey speed   50
Scarce seemed a vision; I would ne'er have striven

As thus with thee in prayer in my sore need,
Oh! lift me as a wave, a leaf, a cloud!
I fall upon the thorns of life! I bleed!

---

[4]*Baiae's bay:* A bay in the Mediterranean Sea, west of Naples. It was known for the opulent villas built by Roman emperors along its shores.

A heavy weight of hours has chained and bowed   55
One too like thee: tameless, and swift, and proud.

                                        V

Make me thy lyre,[5] even as the forest is:
What if my leaves are falling like its own!
The tumult of thy mighty harmonies

Will take from both a deep, autumnal tone,   60
Sweet though in sadness. Be thou, Spirit fierce,
My spirit! Be thou me, impetuous one!

Drive my dead thoughts over the universe
Like withered leaves to quicken a new birth!
And, by the incantation of this verse,   65

Scatter, as from an unextinguished hearth
Ashes and sparks, my words among mankind!
Be through my lips to unawakened Earth

The trumpet of a prophecy! O Wind,
If Winter comes, can Spring be far behind?   70

STEVIE SMITH (1902–1971)

Not Waving but Drowning (1957)

Nobody heard him, the dead man,
But still he lay moaning:
I was much further out than you thought
And not waving but drowning.

Poor chap, he always loved larking   5
And now he's dead
It must have been too cold for him his heart gave way,
They said.

Oh, no no no, it was too cold always
(Still the dead one lay moaning)   10
I was much too far out all my life
And not waving but drowning.

---

[5]*lyre:* An Aeolian harp, a stringed instrument that produces musical sounds when exposed to the wind.

WOLE SOYINKA (1934–   )

Hamlet (1972)

He stilled his doubts, they rose to halt and lame
A resolution on the rack. Passion's flame
Was doused in fear of error, his mind's unease
Bred indulgence to the state's disease
Ghosts embowelled his earth; he clung to rails   5
In a gallery of abstractions, dissecting tales
As "told by an idiot." Passionless he set a stage
Of passion for the guilt he would engage.

Justice despaired. The turn and turn abouts
Of reason danced default to duty's counterpoint   10
Till treachery scratched the slate of primal clay
Then Metaphysics waived a thought's delay—
It took the salt in the wound, the "point
Envenom'd too" to steel the prince of doubts.

WALLACE STEVENS (1879–1955)

Anecdote of the Jar (1923)

I placed a jar in Tennessee,
And round it was, upon a hill.
It made the slovenly wilderness
Surround that hill.

The wilderness rose up to it,   5
And sprawled around, no longer wild.
The jar was round upon the ground
And tall and of a port in air.

It took dominion everywhere.
The jar was gray and bare.   10
It did not give of bird or bush,
Like nothing else in Tennessee.

WALLACE STEVENS (1879–1955)

The Emperor of Ice-Cream (1923)

Call the roller of big cigars,
The muscular one, and bid him whip
In kitchen cups concupiscent curds.
Let the wenches dawdle in such dress
As they are used to wear, and let the boys   5
Bring flowers in last month's newspapers.
Let be be finale of seem.
The only emperor is the emperor of ice-cream.

Take from the dresser of deal,[1]
Lacking the three glass knobs, that sheet   10
On which she embroidered fantails[2] once
And spread it so as to cover her face.
If her horny feet protrude, they come
To show how cold she is, and dumb.
Let the lamp affix its beam.   15
The only emperor is the emperor of ice-cream.

ALFRED, LORD TENNYSON (1809–1892)

Ulysses[1] (1833)

It little profits that an idle king,
By this still hearth, among these barren crags,
Matched with an agèd wife, I mete and dole
Unequal laws unto a savage race
That hoard, and sleep, and feed, and know   5
      not me.
      I cannot rest from travel; I will drink
Life to the lees. All times I have enjoyed
Greatly, have suffered greatly, both with those

---

[1] *deal:* Fir or pine wood.

[2] *fantails:* According to Stevens, "the word fantails does not mean fans, but fantail pigeons."

[1] *Ulysses:* A legendary Greek king of Ithaca and hero of Homer's *Odyssey,* Ulysses (or Odysseus) is noted for his daring and cunning. After his many adventures—including encounters with the Cyclops, the cannibalistic Laestrygones, and the enchantress Circe—Ulysses returned home to his faithful wife, Penelope. Tennyson portrays an older Ulysses pondering his situation.

That loved me, and alone; on shore, and when
Through scudding drifts the rainy Hyades[2]   10
Vexed the dim sea. I am become a name;
For always roaming with a hungry heart
Much have I seen and known—cities of men
And manners, climates, councils, governments,
Myself not least, but honored of them all—   15
And drunk delight of battle with my peers,
Far on the ringing plains of windy Troy.[3]
I am a part of all that I have met;
Yet all experience is an arch wherethrough
Gleams that untraveled world whose margin fades   20
Forever and forever when I move.
How dull it is to pause, to make an end,
To rust unburnished, not to shine in use!
As though to breathe were life! Life piled on life
Were all too little, and of one to me   25
Little remains; but every hour is saved
From that eternal silence, something more,
A bringer of new things; and vile it were
For some three suns to store and hoard myself,
And this grey spirit yearning in desire   30
To follow knowledge like a sinking star,
Beyond the utmost bound of human thought.
    This is my son, mine own Telemachus,
To whom I leave the scepter and the isle—
Well-loved of me, discerning to fulfill   35
This labor, by slow prudence to make mild
A rugged people, and through soft degrees
Subdue them to the useful and the good.
Most blameless is he, centered in the sphere
Of common duties, decent not to fail   40
In offices of tenderness, and pay
Meet adoration to my household gods,
When I am gone. He works his work, I mine.
    There lies the port; the vessel puffs her sail;

---

[2]*Hyades:* A group of stars whose rising was supposedly followed by rain and thus stormy seas.

[3]*Troy:* An ancient city in Asia Minor. According to legend, Paris, king of Troy, abducted Helen, the beautiful wife of Menelaus, king of Sparta, initiating the Trojan War, in which numerous Greek heroes, including Ulysses, fought.

There gloom the dark, broad seas. My mariners,   45
Souls that have toiled, and wrought, and thought with me—
That ever with a frolic welcome took
The thunder and the sunshine, and opposed
Free hearts, free foreheads—you and I are old;
Old age hath yet his honor and his toil.   50
Death closes all; but something ere the end,
Some work of noble note, may yet be done,
Not unbecoming men that strove with Gods.
The lights begin to twinkle from the rocks;
The long day wanes; the low moon climbs; the deep   55
Moans round with many voices. Come, my friends,
'Tis not too late to seek a newer world.
Push off, and sitting well in order smite
The sounding furrows; for my purpose holds
To sail beyond the sunset, and the baths   60
Of all the western stars, until I die.
It may be that the gulfs will wash us down;
It may be we shall touch the Happy Isles,[4]
And see the great Achilles,[5] whom we knew.
Though much is taken, much abides; and though   65
We are not now that strength which in old days
Moved earth and heaven, that which we are, we are—
One equal temper of heroic hearts,
Made weak by time and fate, but strong in will
To strive, to seek, to find, and not to yield.   70

DYLAN THOMAS (1914–1953)

Fern Hill (1946)

Now as I was young and easy under the apple boughs
About the lilting house and happy as the grass was green,
    The night above the dingle[1] starry,
      Time let me hail and climb
      Golden in the heydays of his eyes,   5

---

[4] *Happy Isles:* Elysium, or Paradise, believed to be in the far western ocean.
[5] *Achilles:* Greek hero of the Trojan War.
[1] *dingle:* A small valley or dell, typically wooded.

And honoured among wagons I was prince of the apple towns
And once below a time I lordly had the trees and leaves
    Trail with daisies and barley
    Down the rivers of the windfall light.

And as I was green and carefree, famous among the barns   10
About the happy yard and singing as the farm was home,
    In the sun that is young once only,
      Time let me play and be
    Golden in the mercy of his means,
And green and golden I was huntsman and herdsman, the calves   15
Sang to my horn, the foxes on the hills barked clear and cold,
    And the sabbath rang slowly
    In the pebbles of the holy streams.

All the sun long it was running, it was lovely, the hay
Fields high as the house, the tunes from the chimneys, it was air   20
    And playing, lovely and watery
      And fire green as grass.
    And nightly under the simple stars
As I rode to sleep the owls were bearing the farm away,
All the moon long I heard, blessed among stables, the nightjars[2]   25
    Flying with the ricks,[3] and the horses
      Flashing into the dark.

And then to awake, and the farm, like a wanderer white
With the dew, come back, the cock on his shoulder: it was all
    Shining, it was Adam and maiden,   30
      The sky gathered again
    And the sun grew round that very day.
So it must have been after the birth of the simple light
In the first, spinning place, the spellbound horses walking warm
    Out of the whinnying green stable   35
      On to the fields of praise.

And honoured among foxes and pheasants by the gay house
Under the new made clouds and happy as the heart was long,
    In the sun born over and over,
      I ran my heedless ways,   40
      My wishes raced through the house high hay

---

[2]*nightjars:* A type of nocturnal bird.
[3]*ricks:* A pile of hay or straw.

And nothing I cared, at my sky blue trades, that time allows
In all his tuneful turning so few and such morning songs
  Before the children green and golden
    Follow him out of grace,   45

Nothing I cared, in the lamb white days, that time would take me
Up to the swallow thronged loft by the shadow of my hand,
  In the moon that is always rising,
    Nor that riding to sleep
I should hear him fly with the high fields   50
And wake to the farm forever fled from the childless land.
Oh as I was young and easy in the mercy of his means,
  Time held me green and dying
    Though I sang in my chains like the sea.

KO UN (1933–   )

In the old days a poet once said*

Translated by Brother Anthony, Young-moo Kim, and Gary Gach

In the old days a poet once said
our nation is destroyed
yet the mountains and rivers survive

Today's poet says
the mountains and rivers are destroyed   5
yet our nation survives

Tomorrow's poet will say
the mountains and rivers are destroyed
our nation is destroyed and Alas!
you and I are completely destroyed   10

PHILLIS WHEATLEY (1753–1784)

On Being Brought from Africa
to America (1773)

'Twas mercy brought me from my *Pagan* land,
Taught my benighted soul to understand
That there's a God, that there's a *Saviour* too:

---

*Publication date not available.

Once I redemption neither sought nor knew.
Some view our sable race with scornful eye,   5
"Their colour is a diabolic die."
Remember, *Christians, Negroes*, black as *Cain*,
May be refin'd, and join th' angelic train.

WALT WHITMAN (1819–1892)

I Hear America Singing (1867)

I hear America singing, the varied carols I hear,
Those of mechanics, each one singing his as it should be blithe
    and strong,
The carpenter singing his as he measures his plank or beam,
The mason singing his as he makes ready for work, or leaves
    off work,
The boatman singing what belongs to him in his boat, the   5
    deckhand singing on the steamboat deck,
The shoemaker singing as he sits on his bench, the hatter
    singing as he stands,
The wood-cutter's song, the ploughboy's on his way in the
    morning, or at noon intermission or at sundown,
The delicious singing of the mother, or of the young wife at
    work, or of the girl sewing or washing,
Each singing what belongs to him or her and to none else,
The day what belongs to the day—at night the party of young   10
    fellows, robust, friendly,
Singing with open mouths their strong melodious songs.

WALT WHITMAN (1819–1892)

A Noiseless Patient Spider (1881)

A noiseless patient spider,
I mark'd where on a little promontory it stood isolated,
Mark'd how to explore the vacant vast surrounding,
It launch'd forth filament, filament, filament, out of itself,
Ever unreeling them, ever tirelessly speeding them.   5

And you O my soul where you stand,
Surrounded, detached, in measureless oceans of space,
Ceaselessly musing, venturing, throwing, seeking the spheres to
    connect them,

Till the bridge you will need be form'd, till the ductile anchor hold,
Till the gossamer thread you fling catch somewhere, O my soul.   10

WALT WHITMAN (1819–1892)

from "Song of Myself" (1855)

1

I celebrate myself, and sing myself,
And what I assume you shall assume,
For every atom belonging to me as good belongs to you.

I loafe and invite my soul,
I lean and loafe at my ease observing a spear of summer grass.   5

My tongue, every atom of my blood, form'd from this soil, this air,
Born here of parents born here from parents the same, and their
     parents the same,
I, now thirty-seven years old in perfect health begin,
Hoping to cease not till death.

Creeds and schools in abeyance,   10
Retiring back a while sufficed at what they are, but never forgotten,
I harbor for good or bad, I permit to speak at every hazard,
Nature without check with original energy.

2

Houses and rooms are full of perfumes, the shelves are crowded
     with perfumes,
I breathe the fragrance myself and know it and like it,   15
The distillation would intoxicate me also, but I shall not let it.

The atmosphere is not a perfume, it has no taste of the distillation,
     it is odorless,
It is for my mouth forever, I am in love with it,
I will go to the bank by the wood and become undisguised
     and naked,
I am mad for it to be in contact with me.   20

The smoke of my own breath,
Echoes, ripples, buzz'd whispers, love-root, silk-thread, crotch
     and vine,
My respiration and inspiration, the beating of my heart, the
     passing of blood and air through my lungs,
The sniff of green leaves and dry leaves, and of the shore and
     dark-color'd sea-rocks, and of hay in the barn,

The sound of the belch'd words of my voice loos'd to the eddies   25
    of the wind,
A few light kisses, a few embraces, a reaching around of arms,
The play of shine and shade on the trees as the supple boughs wag,
The delight alone or in the rush of the streets, or along the fields
    and hill-sides,
The feeling of health, the full-noon trill, the song of me rising
    from bed and meeting the sun.

Have you reckon'd a thousand acres much? have you
    reckon'd the
        earth much?   30
Have you practis'd so long to learn to read?
Have you felt so proud to get at the meaning of poems?

Stop this day and night with me and you shall possess the origin
    of all poems,
You shall possess the good of the earth and sun,
    (there are millions
        of suns left,)
You shall no longer take things at second or third hand, nor look
    through the eyes of the dead, nor feed on the
        spectres in books,   35
You shall not look through my eyes either, nor take things
    from me,
You shall listen to all sides and filter them from your self.

WILLIAM WORDSWORTH (1770–1850)

London, 1802 (1802)

Milton![1] thou should'st be living at this hour:
England hath need of thee: she is a fen
Of stagnant waters: altar, sword and pen,
Fireside, the heroic wealth of hall and bower,
Have forfeited their ancient English dower   5
Of inward happiness. We are selfish men;
Oh! raise us up, return to us again;
And give us manners, virtue, freedom, power.
Thy soul was like a star, and dwelt apart:
Thou hadst a voice whose sound was like the sea:

---

[1] *Milton:* John Milton (1608–1674), poet, best known for *Paradise Lost.*

Pure as the naked heavens, majestic, free, 10
So didst thou travel on life's common way,
In cheerful godliness; and yet thy heart
The lowliest duties on herself did lay.

WILLIAM WORDSWORTH (1770–1850)

My heart leaps up when I behold (1807)

My heart leaps up when I behold
   A rainbow in the sky:
So was it when my life began;
So is it now I am a man;
So be it when I shall grow old, 5
   Or let me die!
The Child is father of the Man;
And I could wish my days to be
Bound each to each by natural piety.

WILLIAM BUTLER YEATS (1865–1939)

The Lake Isle of Innisfree (1892)

I will arise and go now, and go to Innisfree,[1]
And a small cabin build there, of clay and wattles[2] made:
Nine bean-rows will I have there, a hive for the honey-bee,
And live alone in the bee-loud glade.

And I shall have some peace there, for peace comes dropping slow, 5
Dropping from the veils of the morning to where the cricket sings;
There midnight's all a glimmer, and noon a purple glow,
And evening full of the linnet's wings.

I will arise and go now, for always night and day
I hear lake water lapping with low sounds by the shore; 10
While I stand on the roadway, or on the pavements grey,
I hear it in the deep heart's core.

---

[1] *Innisfree:* An island in Lough (Lake) Gill, County Sligo, in Ireland.
[2] *wattles:* Stakes interwoven with twigs or branches, used for walls and roofing.

WILLIAM BUTLER YEATS (1865–1939)

Sailing to Byzantium[1] (1927)

That is no country for old men. The young
In one another's arms, birds in the trees
—Those dying generations—at their song,
The salmon-falls, the mackerel-crowded seas,
Fish, flesh, or fowl, commend all summer long   5
Whatever is begotten, born, and dies.
Caught in that sensual music all neglect
Monuments of unaging intellect.

An aged man is but a paltry thing,
A tattered coat upon a stick, unless   10
Soul clap its hands and sing, and louder sing
For every tatter in its mortal dress,
Nor is there singing school but studying
Monuments of its own magnificence;
And therefore I have sailed the seas and come   15
To the holy city of Byzantium.

O sages standing in God's holy fire
As in the gold mosaic of a wall,
Come from the holy fire, perne in a gyre,
And be the singing-masters of my soul.   20
Consume my heart away; sick with desire
And fastened to a dying animal
It knows not what it is; and gather me
Into the artifice of eternity.

Once out of nature I shall never take   25
My bodily form from any natural thing,
But such a form as Grecian goldsmiths make
Of hammered gold and gold enameling
To keep a drowsy Emperor awake;
Or set upon a golden bough to sing   30
To lords and ladies of Byzantium
Of what is past, or passing, or to come.

---

[1] *Byzantium:* Ancient Greek city later rebuilt as Constantinople (now Istanbul).

WILLIAM BUTLER YEATS (1865–1939)

The Second Coming[1] (1921)

Turning and turning in the widening gyre[2]
The falcon cannot hear the falconer;
Things fall apart; the center cannot hold;
Mere anarchy is loosed upon the world,
The blood-dimmed tide is loosed, and everywhere   5
The ceremony of innocence is drowned;
The best lack all conviction, while the worst
Are full of passionate intensity.[3]

Surely some revelation is at hand;
Surely the Second Coming is at hand;   10
The Second Coming! Hardly are those words out
When a vast image out of *Spiritus Mundi*[4]
Troubles my sight: somewhere in sands of the desert
A shape with lion body and the head of a man,
A gaze blank and pitiless as the sun,   15
Is moving its slow thighs, while all about it
Reel shadows of the indignant desert birds.
The darkness drops again; but now I know
That twenty centuries[5] of stony sleep
Were vexed to nightmare by a rocking cradle,   20
And what rough beast, its hour come round at last,
Slouches towards Bethlehem to be born?

---

[1] *The Second Coming:* The phrase usually refers to the return of Christ. Yeats theorized cycles of history, much like the turning of a wheel. Here he offers a poetic comment on his view of the dissolution of civilization at the end of one such cycle.

[2] *gyre:* Spiral.

[3] *Mere... intensity:* Lines 4–8 refer to the Russian Revolution of 1917.

[4] Spiritus Mundi: Literally, "Spirit of the World" (Latin). Yeats believed all souls to be connected by a "Great Memory."

[5] *twenty centuries:* The centuries between the birth of Christ and the twentieth century, in which Yeats was writing.

POETRY SAMPLER: POETRY AND ART

Many poets have found visual art to be a source of inspiration for their poems. In fact, the ancient Greeks used the word *ekphrasis* to denote poetry that focused on paintings, artistic objects, and highly visual scenes. In the *Illiad*, for example, Homer vividly describes the shield of Achilles. The Ancient Romans also saw the connection between art and poetry. The Roman poet Horace made this point in *Ars Poetica* when he observed, "as in painting, so in poetry." Other more contemporary examples of *ekphrasis* occur in John Keats's "Ode on a Grecian Urn" (p. 773) and W. H. Auden's "Musée des Beaux Arts" (p. 696).

A poem about a work of art often expresses a poet's deep emotional response to the work. Sometimes the poet not only gives voice to his or her reactions but also gives voice to the work of art itself. This is true of Keats when he writes about a Grecian urn (which he probably saw in the British Museum in London). In this poem, Keats attempts to come to terms not only with the static images he sees on the urn but also with the effect the urn has on him. For Keats, the quiet majesty of the urn reflects a basic principle of art: "Heard melodies are sweet, but those unheard / Are sweeter; therefore, ye soft pipes, play on" (lines 11–12). For Keats, the message of the urn is simple and very direct: "'Beauty is truth, truth beauty,'—that is all / Ye know on earth, and all ye need to know" (lines 49–50).

A poem about a work of art can also try convey the work's essence to readers. Auden attempts to achieve this in his "Musée des Beaux Arts." By pointing out the inherent contradictions in the Brueghel painting his poem describes, Auden seeks to penetrate the painting and to interpret it for readers. As Icarus plunges to his death into the sea, "dogs go on with their doggy life" (line 12) and the ploughman goes on plowing, never having heard "the splash, the forsaken cry" (line 16). For Auden, Brueghel's painting expresses a truth that the old masters knew: that no matter how momentous an occurrence, life goes on. While someone is suffering—whether it be Christ or Icarus—"someone else is eating or opening a window or just walking dully along" (line 4).

Each of the poems in this sampler is accompanied by the art that inspired it. In "Sonnet in Primary Colors," Rita Dove explores her reactions to paintings by the artist Frida Kahlo. In "Van Gogh's Bed," Jane Flanders describes Vincent Van Gogh's painting of his bedroom in the southern French town of Arles. In "Cézanne's Ports," Alan Ginsberg uses a painting by a well-known impressionist as inspiration just as Robert Hayden does in "Monet's *Waterlilies*." In "The Starry Night," Anne Sexton attempts to convey the intensity of Van Gogh's powerful painting *The Starry Night*. Finally, in "Girl Powdering Her Neck," Cathy Song contemplates a portrait by Kitagawa Utamaro of a geisha preparing herself for her next assignation.

RITA DOVE (1952–)

Sonnet in Primary Colors (1995)

This is for the woman with one black wing
perched over her eyes: lovely Frida,[1] erect
among parrots, in the stern petticoats of the peasant,
who painted herself a present—
wildflowers entwining the plaster corset   5
her spine resides in, that flaming pillar—
this priestess in the romance of mirrors.

Each night she lay down in pain and rose
to the celluloid butterflies of her Beloved Dead,
Lenin[2] and Marx[3] and Stalin[4] arrayed at the footstead.   10
And rose to her easel, the hundred dogs panting
like children along the graveled walks of the garden, Diego's[5]
love a skull in the circular window
of the thumbprint searing her immutable brow.

Self Portrait with Monkey and Parrot (1938) by
Frida Kahlo
© 2015 Banco de México Diego Rivera Frida Kahlo Museums Trust,
Mexico, D.F. / Artists Rights Society (ARS), New York

[1] *Frida:* Frida Kahlo (1907–1954), Mexican painter, feminist and Communist.

[2] *Lenin:* Vladimir Ilyich Lenin (1870–1924), Communist revolutionary and first leader of the Soviet Union.

[3] *Marx:* Karl Marx (1818–1883), political theorist and author of *The Communist Manifesto.*

[4] *Stalin:* Joseph Stalin (1878–1953), second leader of the Soviet Union.

[5] *Diego's:* Diego Rivera (1886–1957), Communist Mexican artist, husband of Frida Kahlo.

JANE FLANDERS (1940–2001)

Van Gogh's Bed (1985)

is orange,
like Cinderella's coach, like
the sun when he looked it
straight in the eye.

is narrow, he sleeps alone, tossing   5
between two pillows, while it carried him
bumpily to the ball.

is clumsy,
but friendly. A peasant
built the frame; an old wife beat   10
the mattress till it rose like meringue.

is empty,
morning light pours in
like wine, melody, fragrance,
the memory of happiness.   15

The Bedroom (1888) by Vincent Van Gogh

ALLEN GINSBERG (1926–1997)

Cézanne's[1] Ports (1961)

In the foreground we see time and life
swept in a race
toward the left hand side of the picture
where shore meets shore.

But that meeting place   5
isn't represented;
it doesn't occur on the canvas.

For the other side of the bay
is Heaven and Eternity,
with a bleak white haze over its mountains.   10

And the immense water of L'Estaque[2] is a go-between
for minute rowboats.

L'Estaque (1883–1885) by Paul Cézanne
Source: ©The Metropolitan Museum of Art/Art Resource, NY

---

[1] *Cézanne's:* Paul Cézanne (1839–1906), French Postimpressionist painter.
[2] *L'Estaque:* Fishing village in France where Cézanne painted many views of the sea.

ROBERT HAYDEN (1913–1980)

Monet's Waterlilies[1]   (1966)

Today as the news from Selma[2] and Saigon[3]
poisons the air like fallout,
I come again to see
the serene, great picture that I love.

Here space and time exist in light   5
the eye like the eye of faith believes.
The seen, the known
dissolve in iridescence, become
illusive flesh of light
that was not, was, forever is.   10

O light beheld as through refracting tears.
Here is the aura of that world
each of us has lost.
Here is the shadow of its joy.

Water Lilies (1914–1917) by Claude Monet
Waterlilies, 1914–17 (see detail 158601) (oil on canvas), Monet, Claude (1840–1926) / Musee Marmottan Monet, Paris, France / Bridgeman Images

---

[1] *"Waterlilies"*: A series of paintings by Claude Monet (1840–1926), a French impressionist painter.

[2] *Selma:* Selma, Alabama. The site of civil rights marches in the mid 1960s, one of which was ended by police violence.

[3] *Saigon:* Capital of South Vietnam from 1954 to 1975; now know as Ho Chi Minh City.

ANNE SEXTON (1928–1974)

The Starry Night[1] (1962)

That does not keep me from having a terrible need of—shall I say the word—
religion. Then I go out at night to paint the stars.
> *—Vincent Van Gogh in a letter to his brother*

The town does not exist
except where one black-haired tree slips
up like a drowned woman into the hot sky.
The town is silent. The night boils with eleven stars.
Oh starry starry night! This is how   5
I want to die.

It moves. They are all alive.
Even the moon bulges in its orange irons
to push children, like a god, from its eye.
The old unseen serpent swallows up the stars.   10
Oh starry starry night! This is how
I want to die:

into that rushing beast of the night,
sucked up by that great dragon, to split
from my life with no flag,   15
no belly,
no cry.

The Starry Night (1889) by Vincent Van Gogh

---

[1] *The Starry Night.* Famous painting (1889) by Dutch Postimpressionist painter Vincent Van Gogh (1853–1890).

CATHY SONG (1955–)

Girl Powdering Her Neck (1983)

from a ukiyo-e[1] print by Utamaro[2]

The light is the inside
sheen of an oyster shell,
sponged with talc and vapor,
moisture from a bath.

A pair of slippers   5
are placed outside
the rice-paper doors.
She kneels at a low table
in the room,
her legs folded beneath her   10
as she sits on a buckwheat pillow.

Her hair is black
with hints of red,
the color of seaweed
spread over rocks.   15

Morning begins the ritual
wheel of the body,
the application of translucent skins.
She practices pleasure:
the pressure of three fingertips   20
applying powder.
Fingerprints of pollen
some other hand will trace.

The peach-dyed kimono
patterned with maple leaves   25
drifting across the silk,
falls from right to left
in a diagonal, revealing
the nape of her neck
and the curve of a shoulder   30
like the slope of a hill
set deep in snow in a country
of huge white solemn birds.

Her face appears in the mirror,
a reflection in a winter pond,   35
rising to meet itself.

She dips a corner of her sleeve
like a brush into water
to wipe the mirror;
she is about to paint herself.   40
The eyes narrow
in a moment of self-scrutiny.
The mouth parts
as if desiring to disturb
the placid plum face;   45
break the symmetry of silence.
But the berry-stained lips,
stenciled into the mask of beauty,
do not speak.

Two chrysanthemums   50
touch in the middle of the lake
and drift apart.

Girl Powdering Her Neck (1790) by
Kitagawa Utamaro
Source: Erich Lessing/Art Resource, NY

[1]ukiyo-e: A type of Japanese woodblock print.

[2]Utamaro: Kitagawa Utamaro (1754–1806), Japanese printmaker.

Reading and Reacting

1. On which features of the work of art does the poet focus? Which aspects does the poet ignore?
2. What purpose is the poet trying to achieve? For example, is the poet expressing emotion, offering an analysis, or attempting to shed light on a particular characteristic or detail of the work?
3. What insight into the work of art do you gain from reading the poem? Do you think the poet is missing anything?
4. What questions about the work of art does the poem raise?
5. Do you disagree with the speaker's interpretation of the work of art? If so, with what do you disagree?
6. **CRITICAL PERSPECTIVE** Writing on the subject of ekphrastic poetry—poetry that takes as its subject a work of visual art—poet and critic Alfred Corn notes both the dangers and the potential rewards of this poetic strategy:

    > A disadvantage...of using very great works of visual art as a subject for ekphrasis is that the comparison between the original and the poem about it may prove too unfavorable. Readers may wonder why they should bother reading a moderately effective poem when they could instead look at the great painting it was based on. If the poem doesn't contain something more than was already available to the audience, it will strike the reader as superfluous, the secondary product of someone too dependent on the earlier, greater work....Once the ambition of producing a complete and accurate description is put aside, a poem can provide new aspects for a work of visual art. It can provide a special angle of approach not usually brought to bear on the original.

    Do the ekphrastic poems in this chapter do what Corn says poems of this kind should do—that is, "provide new aspects for a work of visual art"?

WRITING SUGGESTIONS: Poetry and Art

1. Write a **response** expressing your reactions to either "Monet's *Waterlilies*" or "Van Gogh's Bed."
2. Write an **explication** of "The Starry Night" or "Cezanne's Ports."
3. Write a **comparison-contrast essay** examining the ways the two women are presented in the poems "Sonnet in Primary Colors" and "Girl Powdering Her Neck."
4. Write a **character analysis** of Frida Kahlo as she is depicted in "Sonnet in Primary Colors." Be sure to explore Kahlo's background as well as the hardships she faced. (To prepare for this assignment, do some research on the Web about Kahlo's life and art. Make sure you document the material that you borrow from your sources.)
5. Write an essay about the **cultural context** of "Girl Powdering Her Neck."
6. Write a **comparison-contrast essay** comparing any one of the poems in this chapter to the work of art that inspired it. What details about the work of art does the poet emphasize? Which does the poet downplay or ignore?

4| DRAMA

CHAPTER 25

UNDERSTANDING DRAMA

 Dramatic Literature

The distinctive appearance of a script, with its divisions into acts and scenes, identifies **drama** as a unique form of literature. A play is written to be performed in front of an audience by actors who take on the roles of the characters and who present the story through dialogue and action. (An exception is a **closet drama**, which is meant to be read, not performed.) In fact, the term *theater* comes from the Greek word *theasthai*, which means "to view" or "to see." Thus, drama is different from novels and short stories, which are meant to be read.

 Origins of Modern Drama

The Ancient Greek Theater

The dramatic presentations of ancient Greece developed out of religious rites performed to honor gods or to mark the coming of spring. Playwrights such as Aeschylus (525–456 B.C.), Sophocles (496–406 B.C.), and Euripides (480?–406 B.C.) wrote plays to be performed and judged at competitions held during the yearly Dionysian festivals. Works were chosen by a selection board and evaluated by a panel of judges. To compete in the contest, writers had to submit three tragedies, which could be either based on a common theme or unrelated, and one comedy. Unfortunately, very few of these ancient Greek plays survive today.

The open-air, semicircular ancient Greek theater, built into the side of a hill, looked much like a primitive version of a modern sports stadium. Some Greek theaters, such as the Athenian theater, could seat almost seventeen thousand spectators. Sitting in tiered seats, the audience would look down on the **orchestra**, or "dancing place," occupied by the **chorus**—originally a group of men (led by an individual called the **choragos**) who danced and chanted and later a group of onlookers who commented on the drama.

Grand Theater at Ephesus (3rd century B.C.), a Greek settlement in what is now Turkey
Dave G. Houser/Documentary Value/Corbis

Raised a few steps above the orchestra was a platform on which the actors performed. Behind this platform was a **skene**, or building, that originally served as a resting place or dressing room. (The modern word *scene* is derived from the Greek *skene*.) Behind the skene was a line of pillars called a **colonnade**, which was covered by a roof. Actors used the skene for entrances and exits; beginning with the plays of Sophocles, painted backdrops were hung there. These backdrops, however, were most likely more decorative than realistic. Historians believe that realistic props and scenery were probably absent from the ancient Greek theater. Instead, the setting was suggested by the play's dialogue, and the audience had to imagine the physical details of a scene.

Two mechanical devices were used. One, a rolling cart or platform, was sometimes employed to introduce action that had occurred offstage. For example, actors frozen in position could be rolled onto the roof of the skene to illustrate an event such as the killing of Oedipus's father, which occurred before the play began. Another mechanical device, a small crane, was used to show gods ascending to or descending from heaven. Such devices enabled playwrights to dramatize the myths that were celebrated at the Dionysian festivals.

The ancient Greek theater was designed to enhance acoustics. The flat stone wall of the skene reflected the sound from the orchestra and the stage, and the curved shape of the amphitheater captured the sound, enabling the audience to hear the lines spoken by the actors. Each actor wore a stylized mask, or **persona**, to convey to the audience the personality traits of the particular character being portrayed—a king, a soldier, a wise old man, a young girl (female roles were played by men). The mouths of these masks were probably constructed so they amplified the voice and projected it into the audience. In addition, the actors wore *kothorni*, high shoes that elevated them above the stage, perhaps also helping to project their voices. Due to the excellent acoustics, audiences who see plays performed in these ancient theaters today can hear clearly without the aid of microphones or speaker systems.

Because actors wore masks and because males played the parts of women and gods as well as men, acting methods in the ancient Greek theater were probably not realistic. In their masks, high shoes, and full-length tunics (called *chiton*), actors could not hope to appear natural or to mimic the attitudes of everyday life. Instead, they probably recited their lines while standing in stylized poses, with emotions conveyed more by gesture and tone than by action. Typically, three actors had all the speaking roles. One actor—the **protagonist**—would play the central role and have the largest speaking part. Two other actors would divide the remaining lines between them. Although other characters would come on and off the stage, they would usually not have speaking roles.

Ancient Greek tragedies were typically divided into five parts. The first part was the **prologos**, or prologue, in which an actor gave the background or explanations that the audience needed to follow the rest of the drama. Then came the **párodos**, in which the chorus entered and commented on the events presented in the prologue. Following this were several **episodia**, or episodes, in which characters spoke to one another on the stage and developed the central conflict of the play. Alternating with episodes were **stasimon** (choral odes), in which the chorus commented on the exchanges that had taken place during the preceding episode. Frequently, the choral odes were divided into *strophes*, or stanzas, which were recited or sung as the chorus moved across the orchestra in one direction, and *antistrophes*, which were recited as it moved in the opposite direction. (Interestingly, the chorus stood between the audience and the actors, often functioning as an additional audience, expressing the political, social, and moral views of the community.) The fifth part was the **exodos**, the last scene of the play, during which the conflict was resolved and the actors left the stage.

Using music, dance, and verse—as well as a variety of architectural and technical innovations—the ancient Greek theater was able to convey the traditional themes of tragedy. Thus, the Greek theater powerfully expressed ideas that were central to the religious festivals in which they first appeared: the reverence for the cycles of life and death, the unavoidable dictates of the gods, and the inscrutable workings of fate.

The Elizabethan Theater

The Elizabethan theater, influenced by the classical traditions of Roman and Greek dramatists, traces its roots back to local religious pageants performed at medieval festivals during the twelfth and thirteenth centuries. Town **guilds**—organizations of craftsmen who worked in the same profession—reenacted Old and New Testament stories: the fall of man, Noah and the flood, David and Goliath, and the crucifixion of Christ, for example. Church fathers encouraged these plays because they brought the Bible to a largely illiterate audience. Sometimes these spectacles, called **mystery plays**, were presented in the market square or on the church steps, and at other times actors appeared on movable stages or wagons called **pageants**, which could be wheeled to a given location. (Some of these wagons were quite elaborate, with trapdoors and pulleys and an upper tier that simulated heaven.) As mystery plays became more popular, they were performed in series over several days, presenting an entire cycle of a holiday—the crucifixion and resurrection of Christ during Easter, for example.

Performance of a mystery play
Art Resource

Related to mystery plays are **morality plays**, which developed in the fourteenth and fifteenth centuries. Unlike mystery plays, which depict scenes from the Bible, morality plays allegorize the Christian way of life. Typically, characters representing various virtues and vices struggle or debate over the soul of man. *Everyman* (1500), the best known of these plays, dramatizes the good and bad qualities of Everyman and shows his struggle to determine what is of value to him as he journeys toward death.

By the middle of the sixteenth century, mystery and morality plays had lost ground to a new secular drama. One reason for this decline was that mystery and morality plays were associated with Catholicism and consequently discouraged by the Anglican clergy. In addition, newly discovered plays of ancient Greece and Rome introduced a dramatic tradition that supplanted the traditions of religious drama. English plays that followed the classic model were sensational and bombastic, often dealing with murder, revenge, and blood retribution. Appealing to privileged classes and commoners alike, these plays were extremely popular. (One source estimates that in London, between 20,000 and 25,000 people attended performances each week.)

In spite of the popularity of the theater, actors and playwrights encountered a number of difficulties. First, they faced opposition from city officials who were averse to theatrical presentations because they thought that the crowds attending these performances spread disease. Puritans opposed the theater because they thought plays were immoral and sinful. Finally, some people attached to the royal court opposed the theater because they thought that the playwrights undermined the authority of Queen Elizabeth by spreading seditious ideas. As a result, during Elizabeth's reign, performances were placed under the strict control of the **Master of Revels**, a public official who had the power to censor plays (and did so with great regularity) and to grant licenses for performances.

Acting companies that wanted to put on a performance had to obtain a license—possible only with the patronage of a powerful nobleman—and to perform the play in an area designated by the queen. Despite these difficulties, a number of actors and playwrights gained a measure of financial independence by joining together and forming acting companies. These companies of professional actors performed works such as Christopher Marlowe's *Tamburlaine* and Thomas Kyd's *The Spanish Tragedy* in tavern courtyards and then eventually in permanent theaters. According to scholars, the structures of the Elizabethan theater evolved from these tavern courtyards.

William Shakespeare's plays were performed at the Globe Theatre (a corner of which was unearthed in December 1988). Although scholars do not know the exact design of the original Globe, drawings from the period provide a good idea of its physical features. The major difference between the Globe and today's theaters is the multiple stages on which action could be performed. The Globe consisted of a large main **stage** that extended out into the open-air **yard** where the **groundlings**, or common people, stood. Spectators who paid more sat on small stools in two or three levels of galleries that extended in front of and around the stage. (The theater could probably seat almost two thousand people at a performance.) Most of the play's action occurred on the stage, which had no curtain and could be seen from three sides. Beneath the stage was a space called the **hell**, which could be reached when the floorboards were removed. This space enabled actors to "disappear" or descend into a hole or grave when the play called for such action. Above the stage was a roof called the **heavens**, which protected the actors from the weather and contained ropes and pulleys used to lower props or to create special effects.

At the rear of the stage was a narrow **alcove** covered by a curtain that could be open or closed. This curtain, often painted, functioned as a decorative rather than a realistic backdrop. The main function of this alcove was to enable actors to hide or disappear when the script called for them to do so. Some Elizabethan theaters contained a **rear stage** instead of an alcove. Because the rear stage was concealed by a curtain, props could be arranged on it ahead of time. When the action on the rear stage was finished, the curtain would be closed and the action would continue on the front stage.

On either side of the rear stage was a door through which the actors could enter and exit the front stage. Above the rear stage was a curtained stage called the **chamber**, which functioned as a balcony or as any other setting located above the action taking place on the stage below. On either side of the chamber were casement windows, which actors could use when a play called for a conversation with someone leaning out a window or standing on a balcony. Above the chamber was the **music gallery**, a balcony that housed the musicians who provided musical interludes throughout the play (and that doubled as a stage if the play required it). The **huts**, windows located above the music gallery, could be used by characters playing lookouts or sentries. Because of the many acting sites, more than one action could take place simultaneously. For example, lookouts could stand in the towers of Hamlet's castle while Hamlet and Horatio walked the walls below.

During Shakespeare's time, the theater had many limitations that challenged the audience's imagination. First, young boys—usually between the ages of ten and twelve—played all the women's parts. In addition, there was no artificial lighting, so plays had to be performed in daylight. Rain, wind, or clouds could disrupt a performance or ruin an image—such as "the morn in russet mantle clad"—that the audience was asked to imagine. Finally, because few sets and props were used, the audience often had to visualize the high walls of a castle or the trees of a forest. The plays were performed without intermission, except for musical interludes that occurred at various points. Thus, the experience of seeing one of Shakespeare's plays staged in the Elizabethan theater was different from seeing it staged in a modern theater.

Position of Staircase

D

The Globe Playhouse,

1599-1613

A CONJECTURAL

RECONSTRUCTION

KEY

AA Main entrance
B   The Yard
CC Entrances to lowest gallery
D   Entrances to staircase and upper galleries
E   Corridor serving the different sections of the middle gallery
F   Middle gallery ('Twopenny Rooms')
G   'Gentlemen's Rooms' or 'Lords' Rooms'
H   The stage

J   The hanging being put up round the stage
K   The 'Hell' under the stage
L   The stage trap, leading down to the Hell
MM Stage doors
N   Curtained 'place behind the stage'
O   Gallery above the stage, used as required sometimes by musicians, sometimes by spectators, and often as part of the play
P   Back-stage area (the tiring-house)
Q   Tiring-house door
R   Dressing-rooms
S   Wardrobe and storage
T   The hut housing the machine for lowering enthroned gods, etc., to the stage
U   The 'Heavens'
W   Hoisting the playhouse flag

The Globe Playhouse, 1599–1613; a conjectural reconstruction. From C. Walter
Hodges *The Globe Restored: A Study of the Elizabethan Theatre.* New York: Norton, 1973.
Source: C.W. Hodges. Conjectural Reconstruction of the Globe Playhouse, 1965. Pen & ink.

Aerial view of the reconstructed Globe Theatre in London
Source: ©Jason Hawkes/Corbis

Today, a reconstruction of the Globe Theatre (above) stands on the south bank of the Thames River in London. In the 1940s, the American actor Sam Wanamaker visited London and was shocked to find nothing that commemorated the site of the original Globe. He eventually decided to try to raise enough money to reconstruct the Globe in its original location. The Globe Playhouse Trust was founded in the 1970s, but the actual construction of the new theater did not begin until the 1980s. After a number of setbacks—for example, the Trust ran out of funds after the construction of a large underground "diaphragm" wall needed to keep out the river water—the project was finally completed. The first performance at the reconstructed Globe was given on June 14, 1996, which would have been the late Sam Wanamaker's 77th birthday.

The Modern Theater

Unlike the theaters of ancient Greece and Elizabethan England, seventeenth- and eighteenth-century theaters—such as the Palais Royal, where the great French playwright Molière presented many of his plays— were covered by a roof, beautifully decorated, and illuminated by candles so that plays could be performed at night. The theater remained brightly lit even during performances, partly because there was no easy way to extinguish hundreds of candles and partly because people went to the theater as much to see each other as to see the play.

A curtain opened and closed between acts, and the audience of about five hundred spectators sat in a long room and viewed the play on a **picture-frame stage**. This type of stage, which resembles the stages on which plays are performed today, contained the action within a **proscenium arch** that surrounded the opening through which the audience viewed the performance. Thus, the action seemed to take place in an adjoining room with one of its walls cut away. Painted scenery (some of it quite elaborate), intricately detailed costumes, and stage makeup were commonplace, and for the first time women performed female roles. In addition, a complicated series of ropes, pulleys, and cranks enabled stagehands to change scenery quickly, and sound-effects machines could give audiences the impression that they were hearing a galloping horse or a raging thunderstorm. Because the theaters were small, audiences were relatively close to the stage, so actors could use subtle movements and facial expressions to enhance their performances.

Many of the first innovations in the theater were quite basic. For example, the first stage lighting was produced by candles lining the front of the stage. This method of lighting was not only ineffective—actors were lit from below and had to step forward to be fully illuminated—but also dangerous. Costumes and even entire theaters could (and did) catch fire. Later, covered lanterns with reflectors provided better and safer lighting. In the nineteenth century, a device that used an oxyhydrogen flame directed on a cylinder of lime created extremely bright illumination that could, with the aid of a lens, be concentrated into a spotlight. (It is from this method of stage lighting that we get the expression *to be in the limelight*.)

Eventually, in the twentieth century, electric lights provided a dependable and safe way of lighting the stage. Electric spotlights, footlights, and ceiling light bars made the actors clearly visible and enabled playwrights to create special effects. In Arthur Miller's *Death of a Salesman* (p. 960), for example, lighting focuses attention on action in certain areas of the stage while other areas are left in complete darkness.

Along with electric lighting came other innovations, such as electronic amplification. Microphones made it possible for actors to speak conversationally and to avoid using unnaturally loud "stage diction" to project their voices to the rear of the theater. Microphones placed at various points around the stage enabled actors and actresses to interact naturally and to deliver their lines audibly even without facing the audience. More recently, small wireless microphones have eliminated the unwieldy wires and the "dead spaces" left between upright or hanging microphones, allowing characters to move freely around the stage.

The true revolutions in staging came with the advent of **realism** in the middle of the nineteenth century. Until this time, scenery had been painted on canvas backdrops that trembled visibly, especially when they were intersected by doors through which actors and actresses entered. With realism came settings that were accurate down to the smallest detail. (Improved lighting, which revealed the inadequacies of painted backdrops, made such realistic stage settings necessary.) Backdrops were replaced by the **box set**, three flat panels arranged to form connected walls, with the fourth wall removed to give the audience the illusion of looking into a room. The room itself was decorated with real furniture, plants, and pictures on the walls; the door of one room might connect to another completely furnished room, or a window might open to a garden filled with realistic foliage. In addition, new methods of changing scenery were employed. Elevator stages, hydraulic lifts, and moving platforms enabled directors to make complicated changes in scenery out of the audience's view.

During the late nineteenth and early twentieth centuries, however, some playwrights reacted against what they saw as the excesses of realism. They introduced **surrealistic stage settings**, in which color and scenery mirrored the uncontrolled images of dreams, and **expressionistic stage**

Thrust-Stage Theater. Rendering of the thrust stage at the Guthrie Theatre in Minneapolis. With seats on three sides of the stage area, the thrust stage and its background can assume many forms. Entrances can be made from the aisles, from the sides, through the stage floor, and from the back.
Source: Alvis Upitis/Getty Images

settings, in which costumes and scenery were exaggerated and distorted to reflect the workings of a troubled, even unbalanced mind. In addition, playwrights used lighting to create areas of light, shadow, and color that reinforced the themes of the play or reflected the emotions of the protagonist. Eugene O'Neill's 1920 play *The Emperor Jones,* for example, used a series of expressionistic scenes to show the deteriorating mental state of the terrified protagonist.

Sets in contemporary plays run the gamut from realistic to fantastic, from a detailed re-creation of a room in a production of Tennessee Williams's *The Glass Menagerie* (1945) to dreamlike sets for Eugene O'Neill's *The Emperor Jones* (1920) and Edward Albee's *The Sandbox* (1959). Motorized devices, such as revolving turntables, and *wagons*—scenery mounted on wheels—make possible rapid changes of scenery. The Broadway musical *Les Misérables,* for example, required scores of elaborate sets—Parisian slums, barricades, walled gardens—to be shifted as the audience watched. A gigantic barricade constructed on stage at one point in the play was later rotated to show the carnage that had taken place on both sides of a battle. Light, sound, and smoke were used to heighten the impact of the scene.

Today, as dramatists attempt to break down the barriers that separate audiences from the action they are viewing, plays are not limited to the picture-frame stage; in fact, they are performed on many different kinds of stages. Some plays take place on a **thrust stage** (pictured on the previous page), which has an area that projects out into the audience. Other plays are performed on an **arena stage,** with the audience surrounding the actors. (This kind of performance is often called **theater in the round.**) In addition, experiments have been done with **environmental staging,** in which the stage surrounds the audience or several stages are situated at various locations throughout the audience. Plays may also be performed outdoors, in settings ranging from parks to city streets.

Some playwrights even try to blur the line that divides the audience from the stage by having actors move through or sit in the audience— or even by eliminating the stage entirely. For example, *Tony 'n Tina's Wedding,* a **participatory drama** created in 1988 by the theater group Artificial Intelligence, takes place not in a theater but at a church where a wedding is performed and then at a catering hall where the wedding reception is held. Throughout the play, the members of the audience function as guests, joining in the wedding celebration and mingling with the actors, who improvise freely.

A more recent example of participatory drama is *Sleep No More,* which takes place in a block of warehouses (which has been transformed into the McKittrick Hotel) in the Chelsea neighborhood of New York City. The play is a wordless production of Shakespeare's *Macbeth.* Audience members, who must wear white Venetian carnival masks and remain silent at all times, are

Arena-Stage Theater. The arena theater at the Riverside Community Players in Riverside, California. The audience surrounds the stage area, which may or may not be raised. Use of scenery is limited—perhaps to a single piece of scenery standing alone in the middle of the stage.

Source: Courtesy The Arena Theatre, Riverside Community Players, Riverside, CA

taken by elevator to various floors of the "hotel." Once deposited, they are free to follow any of the actors, who appear and disappear at will, or to explore the hotel's many rooms. The action can be intense, with audience members chasing actors down dark, narrow hallways or up and down stairs to other floors of the hotel, and at times, being pulled into the action of the play.

Scene from the participatory drama *Sleep No More*
Credit: Lucas Jackson/Reuters/Corbis

Today, no single architectural form defines the theater. The modern stage is a flexible space suited to the many varieties of contemporary theatrical production.

 ## Defining Drama

Dramatic works differ from other prose works in a number of fairly obvious ways. For one thing, plays look different on the page: generally, they are divided into **acts** and **scenes**; they include **stage directions** that specify characters' entrances and exits and describe what settings look like and how characters look and act; and they consist primarily of **dialogue**, lines spoken by the characters. And, of course, plays are different from other prose works in that they are written not to be read but to be performed in front of an audience.

Unlike novels and short stories, plays do not usually have narrators to tell the audience what a character is thinking or what happened in the past; for the most part, the audience knows only what characters reveal. To compensate for the absence of a narrator, playwrights can use **monologues** (extended speeches by one character), **soliloquies** (monologues in which a character expresses private thoughts while alone on stage), or **asides** (brief comments by a character who reveals thoughts by speaking directly to the audience without being heard by the other characters). In addition to these dramatic techniques, a play can also use costumes, scenery, props, music, lighting, and other techniques to enhance its impact on the audience.

The play that follows, Anton Chekhov's *The Brute* (1888), is typical of modern drama in many respects. A one-act play translated from Russian, it is essentially a struggle of wills between two headstrong characters, a man and a woman, with action escalating through the characters' increasingly heated exchanges of dialogue. Stage directions briefly describe the setting—"the drawing room of a country house"—and announce the appearance of various props. They also describe the major characters' appearances as well as their actions, gestures, and emotions. Because the play is a **farce**, it features broad physical comedy, asides, wild dramatic gestures, and elaborate figures of speech, all designed to enhance its comic effect.

Source: ©Bettmann/Corbis

ANTON CHEKHOV (1860–1904) is an important nineteenth-century Russian playwright and short story writer. He became a doctor and, as a young adult, supported the rest of his family after his father's bankruptcy. After his early adult years in Moscow, Chekhov spent the rest of his life in the country, moving to Yalta, a resort town in Crimea, for his health (he suffered from tuberculosis). He continued to write plays, mostly for the Moscow Art Theatre, although he could not supervise their production as he would have wished. His plays include *The Seagull* (1896), *Uncle Vanya* (1898), *The Three Sisters* (1901), and *The Cherry Orchard* (1904).

The Brute, or The Bear (1888), is one of a number of one-act farces Chekhov wrote just before his major plays. It is based on a French farce (Les Jurons de Cadillac by Pierre Breton) about a man who cannot refrain from swearing. The woman he loves offers to marry him if he can avoid swearing for one hour; he is unable to do it, but he fails so charmingly that she agrees to marry him anyway.

Cultural Context The custom of dueling has been popular throughout history in many countries. Generally speaking, as in The Brute, duels are fought as a matter of honor—in response to an insult, an offense to one's character, or an affront to one's dignity. Once a challenge to a duel has been issued, negotiators (called seconds) agree on the time, place, and weaponry involved, as well as the point of surrender (first blood drawn or death). In a pistol duel, the participants stand back to back, count off a predetermined number of paces, turn, and fire. Today, dueling is illegal in most countries, and killing someone in the course of a duel is considered murder.

The Brute

A JOKE IN ONE ACT (1888)

Translated by Eric Bentley

CHARACTERS

Mrs. Popov, widow and landowner, small, with dimpled cheeks

Mr. Grigory S. Smirnov, gentleman farmer, middle-aged

Luka, Mrs. Popov's footman, an old man

Gardener

Coachman

Hired Men

SCENE

The drawing room of a country house. Mrs. Popov, in deep mourning, is staring hard at a photograph. Luka is with her.

LUKA: It's not right, ma'am, you're killing yourself. The cook has gone off with the maid to pick berries. The cat's having a high old time in the yard catching birds. Every living thing is happy. But you stay moping here in the house like it was a convent, taking no pleasure in nothing. I mean it, ma'am! It must be a full year since you set foot out of doors.

MRS. POPOV: I must never set foot out of doors again, Luka. Never! I have nothing to set foot out of doors for. My life is done. He is in his grave. I have buried myself alive in this house. We are both in our graves.

LUKA: You're off again, ma'am. I just won't listen to you no more. Mr. Popov is dead, but what can we do about that? It's God's doing. God's will be done. You've cried over him, you've done your share of

mourning, haven't you? There's a limit to everything. You can't go
on weeping and wailing forever. My old lady died, for that matter,
and I wept and wailed over her a whole month long. Well, that was
it. I couldn't weep and wail all my life. She just wasn't worth it. (*He
sighs.*) As for the neighbors, you've forgotten all about them, ma'am.
You don't visit them and you don't let them visit you. You and I are
like a pair of spiders—excuse the expression, ma'am—here we are in
this house like a pair of spiders, we never see the light of day. And it
isn't like there was no nice people around either. The whole county's
swarming with 'em. There's a regiment quartered at Riblov, and
the officers are so good-looking! The girls can't take their eyes off
them—There's a ball at the camp every Friday—The military band
plays most every day of the week—What do you say, ma'am? You're
young, you're pretty, you could enjoy yourself! Ten years from now
you may want to strut and show your feathers to the officers, and it'll
be too late.

MRS. POPOV: (*firmly*) You must never bring this subject up again, Luka.
Since Popov died, life has been an empty dream to me, you know that.
You may think I am alive. Poor ignorant Luka! You are wrong. I am
dead. I'm in my grave. Never more shall I see the light of day, never
strip from my body this . . . raiment of death! Are you listening, Luka?
Let his ghost learn how I love him! Yes, *I* know, and *you* know, he was
often unfair to me, he was cruel to me, and he was unfaithful to me.
What of it? *I* shall be faithful to *him*, that's all. I will show him how *I*
can love. Hereafter, in a better world than this, he will welcome me
back, the same loyal girl I always was—

5 LUKA: Instead of carrying on this way, ma'am, you should go out in the
garden and take a bit of a walk, ma'am. Or why not harness Toby and
take a drive? Call on a couple of the neighbours, ma'am?

MRS. POPOV: (*breaking down*) Oh, Luka!

LUKA: Yes, ma'am? What have I said, ma'am? Oh, dear!

MRS. POPOV: Toby! You said Toby! He adored that horse. When he
drove me out to the Korchagins and the Vlasovs, it was always with
Toby! He was a wonderful driver, do you remember, Luka? So graceful! So strong! I can see him now, pulling at those reins with all his
might and main! Toby! Luka, tell them to give Toby an extra portion
of oats today.

LUKA: Yes, ma'am.

A bell rings.

10 MRS. POPOV: Who is that? Tell them I'm not at home.

LUKA: Very good, ma'am. (*Exit.*)

MRS. POPOV: *(gazing again at the photograph)* You shall see, my Popov, how a wife can love and forgive. Till death do us part. Longer than that. Till death re-unite us forever! *(Suddenly a titter breaks through her tears.)* Aren't you ashamed of yourself, Popov? Here's your little wife, being good, being faithful, so faithful she's locked up here waiting for her own funeral, while you—doesn't it make you ashamed, you naughty boy? You were terrible, you know. You were unfaithful, and you made those awful scenes about it, you stormed out and left me alone for weeks—

Enter Luka.

LUKA: *(upset)* There's someone asking for you, ma'am. Says he must—

MRS. POPOV: I suppose you told him that since my husband's death I see no one?

LUKA: Yes, ma'am. I did, ma'am. But he wouldn't listen, ma'am. He says   15
it's urgent.

MRS. POPOV: *(shrilly)* I see no one!!

LUKA: He won't take no for an answer, ma'am. He just curses and swears and comes in anyway. He's a perfect monster, ma'am. He's in the dining room right now.

MRS. POPOV: In the dining room, is he? I'll give him his come-uppance. Bring him in here this minute.

Exit Luka.

(Suddenly sad again.) Why do they do this to me? Why? Insulting my grief, intruding on my solitude? *(She sighs.)* I'm afraid I'll have to enter a convent. I will, I *must* enter a convent!

Enter Mr. Smirnov and Luka.

SMIRNOV: *(to Luka)* Dolt! Idiot! You talk too much! *(Seeing Mrs. Popov. With dignity.)* May I have the honor of introducing myself, madam? Grigory S. Smirnov, landowner and lieutenant of artillery, retired. Forgive me, madam, if I disturb your peace and quiet, but my business is both urgent and weighty.

MRS. POPOV: *(declining to offer him her hand)* What is it you wish, sir?   20

SMIRNOV: At the time of his death, your late husband—with whom I had the honor to be acquainted, ma'am—was in my debt to the tune of twelve hundred rubles. I have two notes to prove it. Tomorrow, ma'am, I must pay the interest on a bank loan. I have therefore no alternative, ma'am, but to ask you to pay me the money today.

MRS. POPOV: Twelve hundred rubles? But what did my husband owe it to you for?

SMIRNOV: He used to buy his oats from me, madam.

Mrs. Popov: *(to Luka, with a sigh)* Remember what I said, Luka: tell them to give Toby an extra portion of oats today!

Exit Luka.

My dear Mr.—what was the name again?

25 **Smirnov:** Smirnov, ma'am.

Mrs. Popov: My dear Mr. Smirnov, if Mr. Popov owed you money, you shall be paid—to the last ruble, to the last kopeck. But today—you must excuse me, Mr.—what was it?

Smirnov: Smirnov, ma'am.

Mrs. Popov: Today, Mr. Smirnov, I have no ready cash in the house. *(Smirnov starts to speak.)* Tomorrow, Mr. Smirnov, no, the day after tomorrow, all will be well. My steward will be back from town. I shall see that he pays what is owing. Today, no. In any case, today is exactly seven months from Mr. Popov's death. On such a day you will understand that I am in no mood to think of money.

Smirnov: Madam, if you don't pay up now, you can carry me out feet foremost. They'll seize my estate.

30 **Mrs. Popov:** You can have your money. *(He starts to thank her.)* Tomorrow. *(He again starts to speak.)* That is: the day after tomorrow.

Smirnov: I don't need the money the day after tomorrow. I need it today.

Mrs. Popov: I'm sorry, Mr.—

Smirnov: *(shouting)* Smirnov!

Mrs. Popov: *(sweetly)* Yes, of course. But you can't have it today.

35 **Smirnov:** But I can't wait for it any longer!

Mrs. Popov: Be sensible, Mr. Smirnov. How can I pay you if I don't have it?

Smirnov: You don't have it?

Mrs. Popov: I don't have it.

Smirnov: Sure?

40 **Mrs. Popov:** Positive.

Smirnov: Very well. I'll make a note to that effect. *(Shrugging.)* And then they want me to keep cool. I meet the tax commissioner on the street, and he says, "Why are you always in such a bad humor, Smirnov?" Bad humor! How can I help it, in God's name? I need money, I need it desperately. Take yesterday: I leave home at the crack of dawn, I call on all my debtors. Not a one of them pays up. Footsore and weary, I creep at midnight into some little dive, and try to snatch a few winks of sleep on the floor by the vodka barrel. Then today, I come here, fifty miles from home, saying to myself, "At last, at last, I can be sure of something," and you're not in the mood! You give me a mood! Christ, how can I help getting all worked up?

MRS. POPOV: I thought I'd made it clear, Mr. Smirnov, that you'll get your money the minute my steward is back from town.

SMIRNOV: What the hell do I care about your steward? Pardon the expression, ma'am. But it was you I came to see.

MRS. POPOV: What language! What a tone to take to a lady! I refuse to hear another word. (*Quickly, exit.*)

SMIRNOV: Not in the mood, huh? "Exactly seven months since Popov's   45
death," huh? How about me? (*Shouting after her.*) Is there this interest to pay, or isn't there? I'm asking you a question: is there this interest to pay, or isn't there? So your husband died, and you're not in the mood, and your steward's gone off some place, and so forth and so on, but what can *I* do about all that, huh? What do *you* think I should do? Take a running jump and shove my head through the wall? Take off in a balloon? You don't know my *other* debtors. I call on Gruzdeff. Not at home. I look for Yaroshevitch. He's hiding out. I find Kooritsin. He kicks up a row, and I have to throw him through the window. I work my way right down the list. Not a kopeck. Then I come to you, and God damn it to hell, if you'll pardon the expression, you're not in the mood! (*Quietly, as he realizes he's talking to air.*) I've spoiled them all, that's what, I've let them play me for a sucker. Well, I'll show them. I'll show this one. I'll stay right here till she pays up. Ugh! (*He shudders with rage.*) I'm in a rage! I'm in a positively towering rage! Every nerve in my body is trembling at forty to the dozen! I can't breathe, I feel ill, I think I'm going to faint, hey, you there!

Enter Luka.

LUKA: Yes, sir? Is there anything you wish, sir?

SMIRNOV: Water! Water! No, make it vodka.

Exit Luka.

Consider the logic of it. A fellow creature is desperately in need of cash, so desperately in need that he has to seriously contemplate hanging himself, and this woman, this mere chit of a girl, won't pay up, and why not? Because, forsooth, she isn't in the mood! Oh, the logic of women! Come to that, I never have liked them, I could do without the whole sex. Talk to a woman? I'd rather sit on a barrel of dynamite, the very thought gives me gooseflesh. Women! Creatures of poetry and romance! Just to see one in the distance gets me mad. My legs start twitching with rage. I feel like yelling for help.

Enter Luka, handing Smirnov a glass of water.

LUKA: Mrs. Popov is indisposed, sir. She is seeing no one.

SMIRNOV: Get out.

Exit Luka.

Indisposed, is she? Seeing no one, huh? Well, she can see me or not, but I'll be here, I'll be right here till she pays up. If you're sick for a week, I'll be here for a week. If you're sick for a year, I'll be here for a year. You won't get around *me* with your widow's weeds and your schoolgirl dimples. I know all about dimples. (*Shouting through the window.*) Semyon, let the horses out of those shafts, we're not leaving, we're staying, and tell them to give the horses some oats, yes, oats, you fool, what do you think? (*Walking away from the window.*) What a mess, what an unholy mess! I didn't sleep last night, the heat is terrific today, not a damn one of 'em has paid up, and here's this—this skirt in mourning that's not in the mood! My head aches, where's that—(*He drinks from the glass.*) Water, ugh! You there!

Enter Luka.

50 LUKA: Yes, sir. You wish for something, sir?
SMIRNOV: Where's that confounded vodka I asked for?

Exit Luka.

(*Smirnov sits and looks himself over.*) Oof! A fine figure of a man *I* am! Unwashed, uncombed, unshaven, straw on my vest, dust all over me. The little woman must've taken me for a highwayman. (*Yawns.*) I suppose it wouldn't be considered polite to barge into a drawing room in this state, but who cares? I'm not a visitor, I'm a creditor—most unwelcome of guests, second only to Death.

Enter Luka.

LUKA: (*handing him the vodka*) If I may say so, sir, you take too many liberties, sir.
SMIRNOV: What?!
LUKA: Oh, nothing, sir, nothing.
55 SMIRNOV: Who in hell do you think you're talking to? Shut your mouth!
LUKA: (*aside*) There's an evil spirit abroad. The Devil must have sent him. Oh! (*Exit Luka.*)
SMIRNOV: What a rage I'm in! I'll grind the whole world to powder. Oh, I feel ill again. You there!

Enter Mrs. Popov.

MRS. POPOV: (*looking at the floor*) In the solitude of my rural retreat, Mr. Smirnov, I've long since grown unaccustomed to the sound of the human voice. Above all, I cannot bear shouting. I must beg you not to break the silence.

SMIRNOV: Very well. Pay me my money and I'll go.

MRS. POPOV: I told you before, and I tell you again, Mr. Smirnov. I have no cash, you'll have to wait till the day after tomorrow. Can I express myself more plainly? 60

SMIRNOV: And *I* told *you* before, and *I* tell *you* again, that I need the money today, that the day after tomorrow is too late, and that if you don't pay, and pay now, I'll have to hang myself in the morning!

MRS. POPOV: But I have no cash. This is quite a puzzle.

SMIRNOV: You won't pay, huh?

MRS. POPOV: I *can't* pay, Mr. Smirnov.

SMIRNOV: In that case, I'm going to sit here and wait. (*Sits down.*) You'll pay up the day after tomorrow? Very good. Till the day after tomorrow, here I sit. (*Pause. He jumps up.*) Now look, do I have to pay that interest tomorrow, or don't I? Or do you think I'm joking? 65

MRS. POPOV: I must ask you not to raise your voice, Mr. Smirnov. This is not a stable.

SMIRNOV: Who said it was? Do I have to pay the interest tomorrow or not?

MRS. POPOV: Mr. Smirnov, do you know how to behave in the presence of a lady?

SMIRNOV: No, madam, I do not know how to behave in the presence of a lady.

MRS. POPOV: Just what I thought. I look at you, and I say: ugh! I hear you talk, and I say to myself: "That man doesn't know how to talk to a lady." 70

SMIRNOV: You'd like me to come simpering to you in French, I suppose. "*Enchanté, madame! Merci beaucoup* for not paying zee money, *madame! Pardonnez-moi* if I 'ave disturbed you, *madame!* How *charmante* you look in mourning, *madame!*"

MRS. POPOV: Now you're being silly, Mr. Smirnov.

SMIRNOV: (*mimicking*) "Now you're being silly, Mr. Smirnov." "You don't know how to talk to a lady, Mr. Smirnov." Look here, Mrs. Popov, I've known more women than you've known pussy cats. I've fought three duels on their account. I've jilted twelve, and been jilted by nine others. Oh, yes, Mrs. Popov, I've played the fool in my time, whispered sweet nothings, bowed and scraped and endeavored to please. Don't tell me I don't know what it is to love, to pine away with longing, to have the blues, to melt like butter, to be weak as water. I was full of tender emotion. I was carried away with passion. I squandered half my fortune on the sex. I chattered about women's emancipation. But there's an end to everything, dear madam. Burning eyes, dark eyelashes, ripe, red lips, dimpled cheeks, heaving bosoms, soft whisperings, the moon above; the lake below—I don't give a rap for that sort of nonsense any more, Mrs. Popov. I've found out about women. Present company excepted, they're liars. Their behavior is mere play acting; their conversation is sheer gossip. Yes, dear lady, women, young or old, are false, petty, vain, cruel, malicious, unreasonable. As for intelligence, any sparrow could give them points. Appearances, I admit, can be deceptive. In appearance, a woman may be all poetry and romance, goddess and angel, muslin and fluff. To look at her exterior is to be transported to heaven. But I have looked at her interior, Mrs. Popov, and what did I find there—in her very soul? A crocodile. *(He has gripped the back of the chair so firmly that it snaps.)* And, what is more revolting, a crocodile with an illusion, a crocodile that imagines tender sentiments are its own special province, a crocodile that thinks itself queen of the realm of love! Whereas, in sober fact, dear madam, if a woman can love anything except a lapdog you can hang me by the feet on that nail. For a man, love is suffering, love is sacrifice. A woman just swishes her train around and tightens her grip on your nose. Now, you're a woman, aren't you, Mrs. Popov? You must be an expert on some of this. Tell me, quite frankly, did you ever know a woman to be—faithful, for instance? Or even sincere? Only old hags, huh? Though some women are old hags from birth. But as for the others? You're right: a faithful woman is a freak of nature—like a cat with horns.

MRS. POPOV: Who *is* faithful, then? Who *have* you cast for the faithful lover? Not man?

75   SMIRNOV: Right first time, Mrs. Popov: man.

MRS. POPOV: *(going off into a peal of bitter laughter)* Man! Man is faithful! That's a new one! *(Fiercely.)* What right do you have to say this, Mr. Smirnov? Men faithful? Let me tell you something. Of all the men I have ever known my late husband Popov was the best. I loved him, and there are women who know how to love, Mr. Smirnov. I gave him my youth, my happiness, my life, my fortune. I worshipped the ground he trod on—and what happened? The best of men was unfaithful to me, Mr. Smirnov. Not once in a while. All the time. After he died, I found his desk drawer full of love letters. While he was alive, he was always going away for the week-end. He squandered my money. He made love to other women before my very eyes. But, in spite of all, Mr. Smirnov, *I* was faithful. Unto death. And beyond. I am *still* faithful, Mr. Smirnov! Buried alive in this house, I shall wear mourning till the day I, too, am called to my eternal rest.

SMIRNOV: *(laughing scornfully)* Expect me to believe that? As if I couldn't see through all this hocus-pocus. Buried alive! Till you're called to your eternal rest! Till when? Till some little poet—or some little subaltern with his first moustache—comes riding by and asks: "Can that be the house of the mysterious Tamara who for love of her late husband has buried herself alive, vowing to see no man?" Ha!

MRS. POPOV: *(flaring up)* How dare you? How dare you insinuate—?

SMIRNOV: You may have buried yourself alive, Mrs. Popov, but you haven't forgotten to powder your nose.

MRS. POPOV: *(incoherent)* How dare you? How—?   80

SMIRNOV: Who's raising his voice now? Just because I call a spade a spade. Because I shoot straight from the shoulder. Well, don't shout at me, I'm not your steward.

MRS. POPOV: I'm not shouting, you're shouting! Oh, leave me alone!

SMIRNOV: Pay me the money, and I will.

MRS. POPOV: You'll get no money out of me!

SMIRNOV: Oh, so that's it!   85

MRS. POPOV: Not a ruble, not a kopeck. Get out! Leave me alone!

SMIRNOV: Not being your husband, I must ask you not to make scenes with me. *(He sits.)* I don't like scenes.

MRS. POPOV: *(choking with rage)* You're sitting down?

SMIRNOV: Correct, I'm sitting down.

MRS. POPOV: I asked you to leave!   90

SMIRNOV: Then give me the money. *(Aside.)* Oh, what a rage I'm in, what a rage!

MRS. POPOV: The impudence of the man! I won't talk to you a moment longer. Get out. *(Pause.)* Are you going?

SMIRNOV: No.

MRS. POPOV: No?!

SMIRNOV: No.   95

MRS. POPOV: On your head be it. Luka!

Enter Luka.

Show the gentleman out, Luka.

LUKA: *(approaching)* I'm afraid, sir, I'll have to ask you, um, to leave, sir, now, um—

SMIRNOV: *(jumping up)* Shut your mouth, you old idiot! Who do you think you're talking to? I'll make mincemeat of you.

LUKA: *(clutching his heart)* Mercy on us! Holy saints above! *(He falls into an armchair.)* I'm taken sick! I can't breathe!!

MRS. POPOV: Then where's Dasha? Dasha! Dasha! Come here at once!   100
(She rings.)

LUKA: They gone picking berries, ma'am, I'm alone here—Water, water, I'm taken sick!

MRS. POPOV: *(to Smirnov)* Get out, you!

SMIRNOV: Can't you even be polite with me, Mrs. Popov?

MRS. POPOV: *(clenching her fists and stamping her feet)* With you? You're a wild animal, you were never house-broken!

SMIRNOV: What? What did you say?   105

MRS. POPOV: I said you were a wild animal, you were never house-broken.

SMIRNOV: *(advancing upon her)* And what right do you have to talk to me like that?

MRS. POPOV: Like what?

SMIRNOV: You have insulted me, madam.

110 MRS. POPOV: What of it? Do you think I'm scared of you?

SMIRNOV: So you think you can get away with it because you're a woman. A creature of poetry and romance, huh? Well, it doesn't go down with me. I hereby challenge you to a duel.

LUKA: Mercy on us! Holy saints alive! Water!

SMIRNOV: I propose we shoot it out.

MRS. POPOV: Trying to scare me again? Just because you have big fists and a voice like a bull? You're a brute.

115 SMIRNOV: No one insults Grigory S. Smirnov with impunity! And I don't care if you *are* a female.

MRS. POPOV: *(trying to outshout him)* Brute, brute, brute!

SMIRNOV: The sexes are equal, are they? Fine: then it's just prejudice to expect men alone to pay for insults. I hereby challenge—

MRS. POPOV: *(screaming)* All right! You want to shoot it out? All right! Let's shoot it out!

SMIRNOV: And let it be here and now!

120 MRS. POPOV: Here and now! All right! I'll have Popov's pistols here in one minute! *(Walks away, then turns.)* Putting one of Popov's bullets through your silly head will be a pleasure! Au revoir. *(Exit.)*

SMIRNOV: I'll bring her down like a duck, a sitting duck. I'm not one of your little poets, I'm no little subaltern with his first moustache. No, sir, there's no weaker sex where I'm concerned!

LUKA: Sir! Master! *(He goes down on his knees.)* Take pity on a poor old man, and do me a favor: go away. It was bad enough before, you nearly scared me to death. But a duel—!

SMIRNOV: *(ignoring him)* A duel! That's equality of the sexes for you! That's women's emancipation! Just as a matter of principle I'll bring her down like a duck. But what a woman! "Putting one of Popov's bullets through your silly head ..." Her cheeks were flushed, her eyes were gleaming! And, by God, she's accepted the challenge! I never knew a woman like this before!

LUKA: Sir! Master! Please go away! I'll always pray for you!

125 SMIRNOV: *(again ignoring him)* What a woman! Phew!! *She's* no sour puss, *she's* no cry baby. She's fire and brimstone. She's a human cannon ball. What a shame I have to kill her!

LUKA: *(weeping)* Please, kind sir, please, go away!

SMIRNOV: *(as before)* I like her, isn't that funny? With those dimples and all? I like her. I'm even prepared to consider letting her off that debt. And where's my rage? It's gone. I never knew a woman like this before.

Enter Mrs. Popov with pistols.

MRS. POPOV: *(boldly)* Pistols, Mr. Smirnov! *(Matter of fact.)* But before we start, you'd better show me how it's done. I'm not too familiar with these things. In fact I never gave a pistol a second look.

LUKA: Lord, have mercy on us, I must go hunt up the gardener and the coachman. Why has this catastrophe fallen upon us, O Lord? *(Exit.)*

SMIRNOV: *(examining the pistols)* Well, it's like this. There are several   130
makes: one is the Mortimer, with capsules, especially constructed for dueling. What you have here are Smith and Wesson triple-action revolvers, with extractor, first-rate job, worth ninety rubles at the very least. You hold it this way. *(Aside.)* My God, what eyes she has! They're setting me on fire.

MRS. POPOV: This way?

SMIRNOV: Yes, that's right. You cock the trigger, take aim like this, head up, arm out like this. Then you just press with this finger here, and it's all over. The main thing is, keep cool, take slow aim, and don't let your arm jump.

MRS. POPOV: I see. And if it's inconvenient to do the job here, we can go out in the garden.

SMIRNOV: Very good. Of course, I should warn you: I'll be firing in the air.

MRS. POPOV: What? This is the end. Why?   135

SMIRNOV: Oh, well—because—for private reasons.

MRS. POPOV: Scared, huh? *(She laughs heartily.)* Now don't you try to get out of it, Mr. Smirnov. My blood is up. I won't be happy till I've drilled a hole through that skull of yours. Follow me. What's the matter? Scared?

SMIRNOV: That's right. I'm scared.

MRS. POPOV: Oh, come on, what's the matter with you?

SMIRNOV: Well, um, Mrs. Popov, I, um, I like you.   140

MRS. POPOV: *(laughing bitterly)* Good God! He likes me, does he? The gall of the man. *(Showing him the door.)* You may leave, Mr. Smirnov.

SMIRNOV: *(Quietly puts the gun down, takes his hat, and walks to the door. Then he stops and the pair look at each other without a word. Then, approaching gingerly.)* Listen, Mrs. Popov. Are you still mad at me? I'm in the devil of a temper myself, of course. But then, you see—what I mean is—it's this way—the fact is—(Roaring.)* Well, is it my fault, damn it, if I like you? *(Clutches the back of a chair. It breaks.)* Christ, what fragile furniture you have here. I like you. Know what I mean? I could fall in love with you.

Mrs. Popov: I hate you. Get out!

Smirnov: What a woman! I never saw anything like it. Oh, I'm lost, I'm done for, I'm a mouse in a trap.

145 **Mrs. Popov:** Leave this house, or I shoot!

Smirnov: Shoot away! What bliss to die of a shot that was fired by that little velvet hand! To die gazing into those enchanting eyes. I'm out of my mind. I know: you must decide at once. Think for one second, then decide. Because if I leave now, I'll never be back. Decide! I'm a pretty decent chap. Landed gentleman, I should say. Ten thousand a year. Good stable. Throw a kopeck up in the air, and I'll put a bullet through it. Will you marry me?

Mrs. Popov: *(indignant, brandishing the gun)* We'll shoot it out! Get going! Take your pistol!

Smirnov: I'm out of my mind. I don't understand anything any more. *(Shouting.)* You there! That vodka!

Mrs. Popov: No excuses! No delays! We'll shoot it out!

150 **Smirnov:** I'm out of my mind. I'm falling in love. I *have* fallen in love. *(He takes her hand vigorously; she squeals.)* I love you. *(He goes down on his knees.)* I love you as I've never loved before. I jilted twelve, and was jilted by nine others. But I didn't love a one of them as I love you. I'm full of tender emotion. I'm melting like butter. I'm weak as water. I'm on my knees like a fool, and I offer you my hand. It's a shame, it's a disgrace. I haven't been in love in five years. I took a vow against it. And now, all of a sudden, to be swept off my feet, it's a scandal. I offer you my hand, dear lady. Will you or won't you? You won't? Then don't! *(He rises and walks toward the door.)*

Mrs. Popov: I didn't say anything.

Smirnov: *(stopping)* What?

Mrs. Popov: Oh, nothing, you can go. Well, no, just a minute. No, you can go. Go! I detest you! But, just a moment. Oh, if you knew how furious I feel! *(Throws the gun on the table.)* My fingers have gone to sleep holding that horrid thing. *(She is tearing her handkerchief to shreds.)* And what are you standing around for? Get out of here!

Smirnov: Goodbye.

155 **Mrs. Popov:** Go, go, go! *(Shouting.)* Where are you going? Wait a minute! No, no, it's all right, just go. I'm fighting mad. Don't come near me, don't come near me!

Smirnov: *(who is coming near her)* I'm pretty disgusted with myself—falling in love like a kid, going down on my knees like some moongazing whippersnapper, the very thought gives me gooseflesh. *(Rudely.)* I love you. But it doesn't make sense. Tomorrow, I have to pay that interest, and we've already started mowing. *(He puts his arm about her waist.)* I shall never forgive myself for this.

MRS. POPOV: Take your hands off me, I hate you! Let's shoot it out!

A long kiss. Enter Luka with an axe, the Gardener with a rake, the coachman with a pitchfork, hired men with sticks.

LUKA: *(seeing the kiss)* Mercy on us! Holy saints above!

MRS. POPOV: *(dropping her eyes)* Luka, tell them in the stable that Toby is *not* to have any oats today.

*   *   *

 ## A Note on Translations

Many dramatic works that we read or see are translations from other languages. For example, Ibsen wrote in Norwegian, Sophocles in Greek, Molière in French, and Chekhov in Russian. Before English-speaking viewers or readers can evaluate the language of a translated play, they must understand that the language they hear or read is the translator's interpretation of what the playwright intended to communicate. For example, certain words do not have corresponding words in English. In addition, some phrases are idiomatic and cannot be understood outside their original cultural contexts. Finally, some words have specific **connotations**—emotional associations—that the equivalent words in English do not have. For this reason, a translation is always an interpretation, not just a search for literal equivalents; this means that a translation is always different from the original. Moreover, because different translators make different choices when they try to convey a sense of the original, two translations of the same work can vary considerably.

Compare these two versions of an exchange of dialogue from two translations of the same Chekhov play, called *The Brute* in the translation that begins on page 814 and *The Bear* in the alternate version.

From *The Brute*

SMIRNOV: You'd like me to come simpering to you in French, I suppose. "*Enchanté, madame! Merci beaucoup* for not paying zee money, *madame! Pardonnez-moi* if I 'ave disturbed you, *madame!* How *charmante* you look in mourning, *madame!*"

MRS. POPOV: Now you're being silly, Mr. Smirnov.

SMIRNOV: *(mimicking)* "Now you're being silly, Mr. Smirnov." "You don't know how to talk to a lady, Mr. Smirnov." Look here, Mrs. Popov. I've known more women than you've known pussy cats. I've fought three duels on their account. I've jilted twelve, and been jilted by nine others. Oh, yes, Mrs. Popov, I've played the fool in my time, whispered sweet nothings, bowed and scraped and endeavored to please. Don't tell me I don't know what it is to love, to pine away with longing, to have the blues, to melt like butter, to be weak as water. I was full of tender emotion. I was carried away with passion. I squandered half my fortune on the sex. I chattered about women's emancipation. But there's an end to everything, dear madam. . . . (1.71–73)

From *The Bear*

SMIRNOV: Ach, it's astonishing! How would you like me to talk to you? In French, perhaps? *(Lisps in anger.) Madame, je vous prie*. . . . How happy I am that you're not paying me the money. . . . Ah, pardon, I've made you uneasy! Such lovely weather we're having today! And you look so becoming in your mourning dress. *(Bows and scrapes.)*

MRS. POPOV: That's rude and not very clever!

SMIRNOV: *(teasing)* Rude and not very clever! I don't know how to behave in the company of ladies. Madam, in my time I've seen far more women than you've seen sparrows. Three times I've fought duels over women; I've jilted twelve women, nine have jilted me! Yes! There was a time when I played the fool; I became sentimental over women, used honeyed words, fawned on them, bowed and scraped. . . . I loved, suffered, sighed at the moon; I became limp, melted, shivered . . . I loved passionately, madly, every which way, devil take me, I chattered away like a magpie about the emancipation of women, ran through half my fortune as a result of my tender feelings; but now, if you will excuse me, I'm on to your ways! I've had enough!

Although both translations convey Smirnov's anger and frustration, they use different words (with different connotations), different phrasing, and even different stage directions. In *The Bear*, for instance, only one French phrase is used, whereas *The Brute* uses several and specifies a French accent as well; other differences between the two translations include *The Bear*'s use of "teasing," "sparrows," and "I've had enough!" where *The Brute* uses "mimicking," "pussy cats," and "But there's an end to everything, dear madam." (Elsewhere in the play, *The Bear* uses profanity while *The Brute* uses more polite language.)

Recognizing Kinds of Drama

The dramatic tradition stretches back to antiquity, with some of the earliest known plays dating back to the sixth century B.C. This long lifespan has produced numerous developments in the form and conventions of drama.

Traditionally, plays are divided into **acts** and **scenes**. Between acts, there is sometimes an **intermission**, a pause in the action that can be used to heighten the dramatic tension created at the end of the previous scene (as well as to represent the passage of time between one act and the next). The number of acts in a play can range from one to five, depending on the length and scope of the play itself. Shakespeare's *Hamlet* and *A Midsummer Night's Dream* both have five acts, but most full-length contemporary plays have just two or three.

Some shorter plays have only one act. In a **one-act play** such as Chekov's *The Brute*, the playwright is faced with the challenge of creating a dramatic work that includes all the elements that are part of longer plays—exposition, conflict, climax, and resolution. Because these plays are shorter, their imagery and dialogue are often more concise. In fact, because there is less time to devote to character development, subtext, or the consequences of events, one-act plays differ from full-length plays in the same way that short stories differ from novels.

An even more recent development in drama is the **ten-minute play**—a play in which all the actors are onstage and all events take place within a ten-minute time period (see Chapter 26). On an even smaller scale, a **monologue**—an extended speech delivered by one character—can stand alone as a complete dramatic work, as in Joyce Carol Oates's *When I Was a Little Girl and My Mother Didn't Want Me* (1997). Some contemporary plays—including Eve Ensler's *The Vagina Monologues* (1996) and Claudia Shear's *Blown Sideways Through Life* (1994) are composed entirely of a series of interrelated dramatic monologues.

Some contemporary drama is **improvisational**, which means that it is either partially or completely unscripted. This dramatic tradition is a descendant of **commedia dell'arte**, an Italian form of improvisational theater that began in the sixteenth century and was popular until the eighteenth century. Today, many theater actors are trained in "improv" work, which challenges them to sharpen their concentration and to trust in their own instincts rather than relying solely on a script. Some improvisational plays rely on audience participation, requiring actors to improvise in response to audience members' spontaneous contributions to the play.

CHAPTER 26

DRAMA SAMPLER:
TEN-MINUTE PLAYS

Kimberly Pau
Kimberly Pau

Harold Pinter
UPPA/ZUMAPRESS.com/Newscom

Throughout the long history of playwriting, many types and forms of drama have emerged. In recent years, theater has become more experimental, as evidenced by the proliferation of one-act and ten-minute plays, which strive to convey complex ideas in a short amount of time. While traditional one-act plays such as Anton Chekhov's *The Brute* (p. 814) and Susan Glaspell's *Trifles* (p. 867) may have the luxury of unfolding in a more extended period, the **ten-minute play**, which must be performed in ten minutes or less, offers a very small window of opportunity in which the playwright can create meaning. In fact, as director Jon Jory has noted, the ten-minute play is in a sense the dramatic equivalent of the **haiku** in that it is intended to be taken in all at once and thus to have a particularly intense effect on the audience. According to Jory, considered to be the father of the ten-minute play genre, these plays "must, by nature, imply rather than explain. They often depend on metaphor to extend their reach. They stick like glue in the mind because the viewer remembers the *whole* play."

Since a page of script roughly translates into a minute of time onstage, a ten-minute play is generally limited to about ten pages. Despite its brevity, however, a ten-minute play is more than just a scene or an excerpt from a longer play: it is written to stand alone as a complete dramatic work. Although its brief length means it has little or no room for **exposition**, it must introduce a **conflict** (usually relatively early in the play), and it must provide a **resolution**, just as any other play does.

Ten-minute plays are generally staged in groups, allowing the audience to watch several plays in sequence. Casts are usually small; often, the same actors appear in a number of different plays. For this reason, elaborate costumes and staging are impractical (and therefore rare). The most popular venue for a ten-minute play is a drama festival, and numerous competitions offer prizes that include the staging of the winning play. The most prominent contest is sponsored by the Actors Theatre of Louisville, which stages the annual Humana Festival of New American Plays.

The ten-minute plays in this sampler, despite their brief length, manage to treat a variety of provocative subjects. In Jane Martin's *Beauty* (p. 831), the two protagonists trade lives, with unexpected consequences; in Kimberly Pau's *Magic 8 Ball* (p. 837), two college students search for answers about their future; and finally, in Harold Pinter's *Applicant* (p. 840), a job interview does not go as planned.

NOTE *The Blizzard* (p. 854), *Nine Ten* (p. 861), and *Post-its* (p. 955) can also be considered ten-minute plays.

JANE MARTIN, a prize-winning playwright, has never made a public appearance or spoken about any of her works. In fact, she has never given an interview, and no picture of her has ever been published. As one critic wryly observed, Martin is "America's best known, unknown playwright." Martin first came to the attention of American theater audiences with her collection of monologues, *Talking With . . .* , a work that premiered at the 1981 Humana Festival of New American Plays at the Actors Theatre of Louisville, Kentucky. Her other works include *Vital Signs; What Mama Don't Know; Cementville,* the Pulitzer Prize–nominated *Keely and Du* (winner of the 1994 American Theatre Critics Association New Play Award); *Criminal Hearts; Middle Aged White Guys; Jack and Jill; Mr. Bundy; Flaming Guns of the Purple Sage; Good Boys; Flags;* and *Sez She.* Martin's name is widely believed to be a pseudonym. Jon Jory, former artistic director of the Actors Theatre of Louisville—and director of the premieres of all of Martin's plays—is spokesperson for the playwright and, according to some people, may actually be the playwright behind the pen name. Jory has repeatedly denied this; in a 1994 interview, he said that Martin "feels she could not write plays if people knew who she was, regardless of her identity or gender." In Jory's opinion, "The point in the end is the plays themselves.... But if Jane's anonymity is a P. T. Barnum publicity stunt, it's one of the longest circus acts going."

Beauty (2000)

CHARACTERS

Carla
Bethany

An apartment. Minimalist set. A young woman, Carla, on the phone.

CARLA: In love with me? You're in love with me? Could you describe yourself again? Uh-huh. Uh-huh. And you spoke to me? *(A knock at the door.)* Listen, I always hate to interrupt a marriage proposal, but... could you possibly hold that thought? *(Puts phone down and goes to door. Bethany, the same age as Carla and a friend, is there. She carries the sort of Mideastern lamp we know of from Aladdin.)*

BETHANY: Thank God you were home. I mean, you're not going to believe this!

CARLA: Somebody on the phone. *(Goes back to it.)*

BETHANY: I mean, I just had a beach urge, so I told them at work my uncle was dying ...

5 **CARLA:** *(motions to Bethany for quiet)* And you were the one in the leather jacket with the tattoo? What was the tattoo? *(Carla again asks Bethany, who is gesturing wildly that she should hang up, to cool it.)* Look, a screaming eagle from shoulder to shoulder, maybe. There were a lot of people in the bar.

BETHANY: *(gesturing and mouthing)* I have to get back to work.

CARLA: *(on phone)* See, the thing is, I'm probably not going to marry someone I can't remember ... particularly when I don't drink. Sorry. Sorry. Sorry. *(She hangs up.)* Madness.

BETHANY: So I ran out to the beach ...

CARLA: This was some guy I never met who apparently offered me a beer ...

10 **BETHANY:** ... low tide and this ... *(The lamp.)* ... was just sitting there, lying there ...

CARLA: ... and he tracks me down ...

BETHANY: ... on the beach, and I lift this lid thing ...

CARLA: ... and seriously proposes marriage.

BETHANY: ... and a genie comes out.

15 **CARLA:** I mean, that's twice in a ... what?

BETHANY: A genie comes out of this thing.

CARLA: A genie?

BETHANY: I'm not kidding, the whole Disney kind of thing, swirling smoke, and then this twenty-foot-high, see-through guy in like an Arabian outfit.

CARLA: Very funny.

20 **BETHANY:** Yes, funny, but twenty feet high! I look up and down the beach, I'm alone. I don't have my pepper spray or my hand alarm.

You know me, when I'm petrified I joke. I say his voice is too high
for Robin Williams, and he says he's a castrati. Naturally. Who else
would I meet?
CARLA: What's a castrati?
BETHANY: You know ...
The appropriate gesture.
CARLA: Bethany, dear one, I have three modeling calls. I am meeting
Ralph Lauren!
BETHANY: Okay, good. Ralph Lauren. Look, I am not kidding!
CARLA: You're not kidding what?!   25
BETHANY: There is a genie in this thingamajig.
CARLA: Uh-huh. I'll be back around eight.
BETHANY: And he offered me *wishes!*
CARLA: Is this some elaborate practical joke because it's my birthday?
BETHANY: No, happy birthday, but I'm like crazed because I'm on this   30
deserted beach with a twenty-foot-high, see-through genie, so
like sarcastically ... you know how I need a new car ... I said fine,
gimme 25,000 dollars ...
CARLA: On the beach with the genie?
BETHANY: Yeah, right, exactly, and it rains down out of the sky.
CARLA: Oh sure.
BETHANY: *(pulling a wad out of her purse)* Count it, those are thousands.
I lost one in the surf.

*Carla sees the top bill. Looks at Bethany, who nods encouragement. Carla
thumbs through them.*

CARLA: These look real.   35
BETHANY: Yeah.
CARLA: And they rained down out of the sky?
BETHANY: Yeah.
CARLA: You've been really strange lately, are you dealing?
BETHANY: Dealing what, I've even given up chocolate.   40
CARLA: Let me see the genie.
BETHANY: Wait, wait.
CARLA: Bethany, I don't have time to screw around. Let me see the
genie or let me go on my appointments.
BETHANY: Wait! So I pick up the money ... see, there's sand on the
money ... and I'm like nuts so I say, you know, "Okay, look,
ummm, big guy, my uncle is in the hospital" ... because as you
know when I said to the people at work my uncle was dying, I was
on one level telling the truth although it had nothing to do with
the beach, but he was in Intensive Care after the accident, and
that's on my mind, so I say, okay, Genie, heal my uncle ... which
is like impossible given he was hit by two trucks, and the genie

says, "Yes, Master" … like they're supposed to say, and he goes into this like kind of whirlwind, kicking up sand and stuff, and I'm like, "Oh my God!" and the air clears, and he bows, you know, and says, "It is done, Master," and I say, "Okay, whatever-you-are, I'm calling on my cell phone," and I get it out and I get this doctor who is like dumbstruck who says my uncle came to, walked out of Intensive Care and left the hospital! I'm not kidding, Carla.

45   CARLA: On your mother's grave?

BETHANY: On my mother's grave.

They look at each other.

CARLA: Let me see the genie.

BETHANY: No, no, look, that's the whole thing … I was just, like, reacting, you know, responding, and that's already two wishes … although I'm really pleased about my uncle, the $25,000 thing, I could have asked for $10 million, and there is only one wish left.

CARLA: So ask for $10 million.

50   BETHANY: I don't think so. I don't think so. I mean, I gotta focus in here. Do you have a sparkling water?

CARLA: No. Bethany, I'm missing Ralph Lauren now. Very possibly my one chance to go from catalogue model to the very, very big time, so, if you are joking, stop joking.

BETHANY: Not joking. See, see, the thing is, I know what I want. In my guts. Yes. Underneath my entire bitch of a life is this unspoken, ferocious, all-consuming urge …

CARLA: (*trying to get her to move this along*) Ferocious, all-consuming urge …

BETHANY: I want to be like you.

55   CARLA: Me?

BETHANY: Yes.

CARLA: Half the time you don't even like me.

BETHANY: Jealous. The ogre of jealousy.

CARLA: You're the one with the $40,000 job straight out of school. You're the one who has published short stories. I'm the one hanging on by her fingernails in modeling. The one who has creeps calling her on the phone. The one who had to have a nose job.

60   BETHANY: I want to be beautiful.

CARLA: You are beautiful.

BETHANY: Carla, I'm not beautiful.

CARLA: You have charm. You have personality. You know perfectly well you're pretty.

BETHANY: "Pretty," see, that's it. Pretty is the minor leagues of beautiful. Pretty is what people discover about you after they know you.

Beautiful is what knocks them out across the room. Pretty, you get
called a couple of times a year; *beautiful* is twenty-four hours a day.

CARLA: Yeah? So?   65

BETHANY: So?! We're talking *beauty* here. Don't say "So?" Beauty is
the real deal. You are the center of any moment of your life. People
stare. Men flock. I've seen you get offered discounts on makeup for
no reason. Parents treat beautiful children better. Studies show your
income goes up. You can have sex anytime you want it. Men have
to know me. That takes up to a year. I'm continually horny.

CARLA: Bethany, I don't even like sex. I can't have a conversation
without men coming on to me. I have no privacy. I get hassled
on the street. They start pressuring me from the beginning. Half
the time, it never occurs to them to start with a conversation.
Smart guys like you. You've had three long-term relationships, and
you're only twenty-three. I haven't had one. The good guys, the
smart guys are scared to death of me. I'm surrounded by male bim-
bos who think a preposition is when you go to school away from
home. I have no woman friends except you. I don't even want to
talk about this!

BETHANY: I knew you'd say something like this. See, you're "in the
club" so you can say this. It's the way beauty functions as an elite.
You're trying to keep it all for yourself.

CARLA: I'm trying to tell you it's no picnic.

BETHANY: But it's what everybody wants. It's the nasty secret at large   70
in the world. It's the unspoken tidal desire in every room and on
every street. It's the unspoken, the soundless whisper ... millions
upon millions of people longing hopelessly and forever to stop being
whatever they are and be beautiful, but the difference between
those ardent multitudes and me is that I have a goddamn genie and
one more wish!

CARLA: Well, it's not what I want. This is me, Carla. I have never read
a whole book. Page six, I can't remember page four. The last thing
I read was *The Complete Idiot's Guide to WordPerfect*. I leave dinner parties right after the dessert because I'm out of conversation.
You know the dumb blond joke about the application where it
says, "Sign here," she put Sagittarius? I've done that. Only beautiful
guys approach me, and that's because they want to borrow my eye
shadow. I barely exist outside a mirror! You don't want to *be me*.

BETHANY: None of you tell the truth. That's why you have no friends.
We can all see you're just trying to make us feel better because we
aren't in your league. This only proves to me it should be my third
wish. Money can only buy things. Beauty makes you the center of
the universe.

Bethany picks up the lamp.

CARLA: Don't do it. Bethany, don't wish it! I am telling you you'll regret it.

Bethany lifts the lid. There is a tremendous crash, and the lights go out. Then they flicker and come back up, revealing Bethany and Carla on the floor where they have been thrown by the explosion. We don't realize it at first, but they have exchanged places.

CARLA/BETHANY: Oh God.

75 BETHANY/CARLA: Oh God.

CARLA/BETHANY: Am I bleeding? Am I dying?

BETHANY/CARLA: I'm so dizzy. You're not bleeding.

CARLA/BETHANY: Neither are you.

BETHANY/CARLA: I feel so weird.

80 CARLA/BETHANY: Me too. I feel ... *(Looking at her hands.)* Oh, my God, I'm wearing your jewelry. I'm wearing your nail polish.

BETHANY/CARLA: I know I'm over here, but I can see myself over there.

CARLA/BETHANY: I'm wearing your dress. I have your legs!!

BETHANY/CARLA: These aren't my shoes. I can't meet Ralph Lauren wearing these shoes!

CARLA/BETHANY: I wanted to be beautiful, but I didn't want to be you.

85 BETHANY/CARLA: Thanks a lot!!

CARLA/BETHANY: I've got to go. I want to pick someone out and get laid.

BETHANY/CARLA: You can't just walk out of here in my body!

CARLA/BETHANY: Wait a minute. Wait a minute. What's eleven eighteenths of 1,726?

BETHANY/CARLA: Why?

90 CARLA/BETHANY: I'm a public accountant. I want to know if you have my brain.

BETHANY/CARLA: One hundred thirty-two and a half.

CARLA/BETHANY: You have my brain.

BETHANY/CARLA: What shade of Rubenstein lipstick does Cindy Crawford wear with teal blue?

CARLA/BETHANY: Raging Storm.

95 BETHANY/CARLA: You have my brain. You poor bastard.

CARLA/BETHANY: I don't care. Don't you see?

BETHANY/CARLA: See what?

CARLA/BETHANY: We both have the one thing, the one and only thing everybody wants.

BETHANY/CARLA: What is that?

CARLA/BETHANY: It's better than beauty for me; it's better than brains   100
for you.

BETHANY/CARLA: What? What?!

CARLA/BETHANY: Different problems.

Blackout.

*   *   *

Kimberly Pau

KIMBERLY PAU (1981–   ) is a writer and producer of a range of plays, including the experimental one-act play *Bomb Shelter*, which was nominated for eight awards, and the "sci-farce" comedy *Deactivated*, which was a finalist for the 2014 Leah Ryan Fund for Emerging Women Writers. Pau's work also includes a libretto, a music video, and two experimental short films. A founding member of the New York City artistic collective Ouroboros Co., Pau was recognized as one of the Top Ten Off-Off Broadway Theatre Professionals of 2011 by reviewfix.com.

Magic 8 Ball (2012)

CHARACTERS

ELIZABETH and MELISSA are both twenty years old. They are nice girls who grew up well and attend college. They are dressed in somewhat sexy nighties that don't quite flatter them but were probably quite expensive from Victoria's Secret or somewhere else at the mall. They have North Dakota accents.

SETTING: This script was created for the Tiny Theater Festival at the Brick Theater where the pieces were performed in a 6' × 6' × 6' box constructed of PVC pipe—performers and scenic elements were instructed to not exist outside the box at any point during each piece.

The Magic 8 Ball is about 500x larger than the regular toy ones, and it will be used as a device to add in movement. When the characters shake the magic 8 ball they are moving together. The movement is non-literal.

Lights up on a 20 year old girl's bedroom.

OFF STAGE VOICE: The Magic 8 Ball is a hollow plastic sphere resembling an oversized, black and white 8-ball. Inside is a cylindrical reservoir containing a white, plastic, icosahedral[1] die floating in alcohol with dissolved dark blue dye. A random selection device comprising a sealed container having relatively flat window means at least a portion of which is adapted to be substantially horizontally disposed.

Melissa and Elizabeth, both 20, in sexy ill-fitting pajamas play with a giant Magic 8 Ball. They take sexy pics of themselves with their smart phones.

MELISSA: I'm at odds. But I don't know if I should believe in this thing. I know. Oh jeez, ok I know to trust you. I could just trust you couldn't I? Right. I know. I don't know what to ask. (*Pause.*) I do. I do know what to ask. Ready? Do you.

ELIZABETH (*interrupting*):   You have to call it Magic 8 Ball, the first time, it doesn't start to work unless you conjure it by name.

MELISSA: Right. Magic 8 Ball, do you predict the future? (*She shakes the ball*)

5   **MAGIC 8 BALL V.O.:**   It is decidedly so.

ELIZABETH: See I told you so. Watch me. You can get creative with it. Like, am I going to have 4 children with Bradley? (*shakes the ball*)

MAGIC 8 BALL V.O.:   Better not tell you now.

ELIZABETH: Darn. See? It's too clever.

MELISSA: Uh, you probably won't even know Bradley's name by the time you're old enough to have a kid. No. 20's not old enough. It's not. Am I going to have kids? No, wait, better, am I the spinster type? (*shakes the ball*)

10   **MAGIC 8 BALL V.O.:**   You may rely on it.

MELISSA: Huh. Is that an answer to the first question or the second? I guess we have to defer to the latter right? Yeah. Aw jeez.

ELIZABETH: I think you can still have kids if you're a spinster these days.

MELISSA: Oh yeah? Thanks. You go.

ELIZABETH: Should we order pizza? (*shakes the ball*)

15   **MAGIC 8 BALL V.O.:**   My reply is no.

MELISSA: Oh yeah, looking out for our best interest. And our thighs.

ELIZABETH: You see?

MELISSA: We should ask it something important.

ELIZABETH: Oh yeah, like something meaningful.

20   **MELISSA:**   Yeah. Will the world end in our lifetime? (*shakes the ball*)

MAGIC 8 BALL V.O.:   Reply hazy, try again.

ELIZABETH: That question is confusing to me and I'm a human. I think if you're a crystal ball you like to keep it simple.

---

[1] *icosahedral:* Having twenty triangular faces.

MELISSA: Oh yeah. Okay. Will we be friends with the robots? (*shakes the ball*)

MAGIC 8 BALL V.O.: My sources say no.

MELISSA: Oh darn.   25

ELIZABETH: We're not going to like the robots and they're not going to like us. Boring. And predictable! Gosh there's so much I need to know. Is Bradley desperately in love with me? (*shakes the ball*)

MAGIC 8 BALL V.O.: As I see it, yes.

ELIZABETH: YES!!!

MELISSA: As I see it? That's very non-committal.

ELIZABETH: Is he going to propose? (*shakes the ball*)   30

MAGIC 8 BALL V.O.: As I see it, yes.

ELIZABETH: Oh yeah, creepy, twice in a row!

MELISSA: Oh yeah? Did you shake it enough?

ELIZABETH: Um, yeah. Will he do it tomorrow? (*shakes the ball*)

MAGIC 8 BALL V.O.: Don't count on it.   35

ELIZABETH: The next day? (*shakes the ball*)

MAGIC 8 BALL V.O.: Outlook not so good.

ELIZABETH: Darnit! The day after that? (*shakes the ball*)

MAGIC 8 BALL V.O.: Signs point to yes.

ELIZABETH: Uh, thank Gosh.   40

MELISSA: Magic 8 Ball is a mister and he's leading you on.

ELIZABETH: I don't care what you say! It's true! I believe that it's true. Do you want to ask about James?

MELISSA: No. No. I don't want that to be tainted by voodoo.

ELIZABETH: Don't you want to know if you are going to die together?

MELISSA: You think Magic 8 Ball can tell me that?   45

ELIZABETH: Yes, obviously. Magic 8 Ball, are me and Bradley going to die together on the same day in our sleep on the same porch swing? (*shakes the ball*)

MAGIC 8 BALL V.O.: Concentrate and ask again.

ELIZABETH: Magic 8 Ball, are me and Bradley going to die together? (*shakes the ball*)

MAGIC 8 BALL V.O.: Cannot predict now.

MELISSA: Oh jeez, well that's smart. Magic 8 Ball, are you wise and   50
all-knowing? I mean, do you give good advice?

MAGIC 8 BALL V.O.: Yes—definitely.

MELISSA: Then why are you lying to Elizabeth about Bradley like this? (*shakes the ball*)

ELIZABETH: What do you mean?!

MAGIC 8 BALL V.O.: Ask again later.

MELISSA: Oh ok, fair enough, but will you at least admit that you know   55
very well that Bradley and James have discovered this past weekend

that they like to have sex with each other better than us and that's
why they haven't even responded to our text pics of us in our new
fabulous nighties? (*shakes the ball*)

Magic 8 Ball V.O.: It is certain.

Elizabeth: What! No! You liar! Magic 8 Ball you lie!

Melissa: Oh yeah? Is Elizabeth going to blame me for this? Specifically
according to what you once referred to as my gangly lack of sex
appeal? (*shakes the ball*)

Magic 8 Ball V.O.: Without a doubt.

60 **Elizabeth:** Of course it's because of your chopsticks for legs!

Melissa: Is Elizabeth going to find a new boyfriend first or am I? Oh,
wait that's not a yes or no question. Oh jeez. Am I going to fall in
real love first, before Elizabeth? (*shakes the ball*)

Magic 8 Ball V.O.: Yes.

Elizabeth: It's totally broken!

Melissa: Oh yeah? Is Elizabeth going to give up on love after her next
boyfriend goes gay too? (*shakes the ball*)

65 **Magic 8 Ball V.O.:** Most likely.

Elizabeth: Is Melissa going to be sad when I fling myself from the roof
and fall splat on the asphalt? (*shakes the ball*)

Melissa: Oh jeez. Oh crap. Of course I would be devastated!

Magic 8 Ball V.O.: Very doubtful.

Elizabeth: That's it. Now I have absolutely no way of predicting anything.

70 **Melissa:** Dear Magic 8 Ball, will we be able to find happiness without
knowing what's predetermined even if our poor boyfriends like each
other more than they like us? (*shakes the ball*)

Magic 8 Ball V.O.: Outlook good.

Off Stage Voice: A single transparent, fluid bubble is formed in the
liquid between the face carrying the displayed insignia and the
horizontal portion of the window, said single bubble having a predetermined volume such that substantially the entire face carrying
the displayed insignia can be viewed through the bubble and the
horizontally disposed portion of the window.

*   *   *

HAROLD PINTER (1930–2008) was an English playwright,
screenwriter, director, actor, and poet. He won numerous
awards, including the 2005 Nobel Prize in Literature, and held
several honorary university degrees. His work has appeared in
numerous collections, including most recently *Various Voices:
Sixty Years of Prose, Poetry, Politics, 1948–2008* (2009). A
vocal political activist, Pinter often explored absurd and dark
subjects in his work.

Applicant (1961)

An office. Lamb, a young man, eager, cheerful, enthusiastic, is striding nervously, alone. The door opens. Miss Piffs comes in. She is the essence of efficiency.

PIFFS: Ah, good morning.
LAMB: Oh, good morning, miss.
PIFFS: Are you Mr. Lamb?
LAMB: That's right.
PIFFS (*studying a sheet of paper*): Yes. You're applying for this vacant   5
   post, aren't you?
LAMB: I am actually, yes.
PIFFS: Are you a physicist?
LAMB: Oh yes, indeed. It's my whole life.
PIFFS (**languidly**): Good, Now our procedure is, that before we
   discuss the applicant's qualifications we like to subject him to a
   little test to determine his psychological suitability. You've no
   objection?
LAMB: Oh, good heavens, no.   10
PIFFS: Jolly good.

Miss Piffs has taken some objects out of a drawer and goes to Lamb. She places a chair for him.

PIFFS: Please sit down. (*He sits*) Can I fit these to your palms?
LAMB (**affably**): What are they?
PIFFS: Electrodes.
LAMB: Oh yes, of course. Funny little things.   15

She attaches them to his palms.

PIFFS: Now the earphones.

She attaches earphones to his head.

LAMB: I say, how amusing.
PIFFS: Now I plug in.

She plugs in to the wall.

LAMB (**a trifle nervously**): Plug in, do you? Oh yes, of course. Yes, you'd
   have to, wouldn't you?

Miss Piffs perches on a high stool and looks down on Lamb.

   This helps to determine my. . . my suitability does it?

20   **PIFFS:** Unquestionably. Now relax. Just relax. Don't think about a
thing.

    LAMB: No.

    PIFFS: Relax completely. Rela-a-a-x. Quite relaxed?

*Lamb nods. Miss Piffs presses a button on the side of her stool. A piercing
high pitched buzz-hum is heard. Lamb jolts rigid. His hands go to his earphones. He is propelled from the chair. He tries to crawl under the chair.
Miss Piffs watches, impassive. The noise stops. Lamb peeps out from under
the chair, crawls out, stands, twitches, emits a short chuckle and collapses
in the chair.*

    PIFFS: Would you say you were an excitable person?

    LAMB: Not—not unduly, no. Of course, I—

25   **PIFFS:** Would you say you were a moody person?

    LAMB: Moody? No, I wouldn't say I was moody—well, sometimes
occasionally—

    PIFFS: Do you ever get fits of depression?

    LAMB: Well, I wouldn't call them depression exactly—

    PIFFS: Do you often do things you regret in the morning?

30   **LAMB:** Regret? Things I regret? Well, it depends what you mean by
often, really—I mean when you say often—

    PIFFS: Are you often puzzled by women?

    LAMB: Women?

    PIFFS: Men.

    LAMB: Men? Well, I was just going to answer the question about
women—

35   **PIFFS:** Do you often feel puzzled?

    LAMB: Puzzled?

    PIFFS: By women.

    LAMB: Women?

    PIFFS: Men.

40   **LAMB:** Oh, now just a minute, I. . . Look, do you want separate answers
or a joint answer?

    PIFFS: After your day's work do you ever feel tired? Edgy? Fretty? Irri-
table? At a loose end? Morose? Frustrated? Morbid? Unable to concentrate? Unable to sleep? Unable to eat? Unable to remain seated?
Unable to remain upright? Lustful? Indolent? On heat? Randy? Full
of desire? Full of energy? Full of dread? Drained? of energy, of dread?
of desire?

Pause.

Lamb (*thinking*): Well, it's difficult to say really...

Piffs: Are you a good mixer?

Lamb: Well, you've touched on quite an interesting point there—

Piffs: Do you suffer from eczema, listlessness, or falling coat? 45

Lamb: Er . . .

Piffs: Are you virgo intacta?[1]

Lamb: I beg your pardon?

Piffs: Are you virgo intacta?

Lamb: Oh, I say, that's rather embarrassing. I mean—in front of a lady— 50

Piffs: Are you virgo intacta?

Lamb: Yes, I am, actually. I'll make no secret of it.

Piffs: Have you always been virgo intacta?

Lamb: Oh yes, always. Always.

Piffs: From the word go? 55

Lamb: Go? Oh yes, from the word go.

Piffs: Do women frighten you?

She presses a button on the other side of her stool. The stage is plunged into redness, which flashes on and off in time with her questions.

Piffs (*building*): Their clothes? Their shoes? Their voices? Their laughter? Their stares? Their way of walking? Their way of sitting? Their way of smiling? Their way of talking? Their mouths? Their hands? Their feet? Their shins? Their thighs? Their knees? Their eyes? Their (*Drumbeat*). Their (*Drumbeat*). Their (*Cymbal bang*). Their (*Trombone chord*). Their (*Bass note*).

Lamb: (*in a high voice*). Well it depends what you mean really—

The light still flashes. She presses the other button and the piercing buzz-hum is heard again. Lamb's hands go to his earphones. He is propelled from the chair, falls, rolls, crawls, totters and collapses.

Silence.

He lies face upwards. Miss Piffs looks at him then walks to Lamb and bends over him.

Piffs: Thank you very much, Mr. Lamb. We'll let you know. 60

*　　　*　　　*

---

[1]*Virgo intacta:* A virgin.

EARL T. ROSKE is a playwright, short story writer, novelist, and poet. In 2012, he independently published his first novel, *Tale of the Music-Thief.* Roske has written numerous ten-minute plays, which have been produced all over the world. The following play appeared in the 2013 Short + Sweet Festival in Sydney, Australia, the 2013 New Works Winter Festival in Massachusetts, the 2012 Autumn One-Acts in New York, and the Pan Theater's 2011 Ten-Minute Play Festival in California.

Zombie Love (2011)

CHARACTERS

Emily: *Female, early twenties*
Kathy: *Female, early twenties*
Walter: *Male, early twenties, undead*

TIME. PLACE, AND TECHNICAL REQUIREMENTS: Current era, time is now. Park bench, rising moon light, a dead rat, some dying flowers that are edible. Zombie make-up.

Lights up on a park. There is—at minimum—a bench. Emily enters with Walter, a zombie, in tow.

EMILY: Right here! This is perfect, Walter. A bench to sit on and a clear view of the rising moon.
WALTER: (*Always speaks in drawn out syllables and without the use of lips or teeth. The intention is to go with the stereo type.*) Oh. Okay.
EMILY: Come and sit with me. This will be so romantic. You. Me. The moon rising over the hills.
WALTER: Kathy.
5 EMILY: Kathy? No, it's okay. She has no idea—
KATHY: (*Entering*) There you are.
WALTER: Ew . . . nar . . .
WALTER: Trouble.
EMILY: Hello, Kathy.

(Beat)

Lovely evening.
10 KATHY: No hardly. Why are you out here with that?
WALTER: Aw . . .
EMILY: With "him." I'm with "him," Kathy.
KATHY: Whatever. It's not like it has feelings.
WALTER: Do, too . . . .

Emily: See. If you'd just take the time to get to know him.   15
Kathy: I don't want to know a zombie.
Walter: It's okay . . . .
Emily: No it's not, Walter, dear. I'm sorry she doesn't understand.
Kathy: Listen. Emily. We need to talk.
Emily: So talk.   20
Kathy: In private.
Emily: This is private.
Kathy: Not in front of—of him. Okay?
Emily: *(Pause)* Fine. Walter, honey. Give us a moment.
Walter: Um . . . Okay . . .   25
Kathy: Yeah, go eat a bug or something.
Walter: I like bugs . . . .
Kathy: Gross!
Emily: Walter. Remember to chew or they'll just crawl back out.
Walter: Okay   30
Kathy: Doubly gross!
Emily: So . . . ?
Kathy: You need to come home.
Emily: I will. Right after Walter and I watch the moon rise.

*Walter sees something moving around on the ground. He follows it, grunting/
moaning/groaning every few lines of dialogue that follows.*

Kathy: Now.   35
Emily: Really, Kathy, since when are you the boss of me.
Kathy: Someone has to look out for you. Since you've started dating a
    dead guy.
Emily: Undead. And you're going to hold that against him?
Kathy: Yes!
Emily: It's not his fault. He didn't choose to be a zombie. It's just a part   40
    of who he is.
Kathy: Part? Huge part!
Emily: Good.
Kathy: I just don't think he's the right guy for you.
Emily: Well I happen to disagree.
Kathy: People are talking, Emily. You're losing friends.   45

*Walter falls onto a small object on the ground and strangles it with his hands.
Pleased grunting/moaning/groaning sounds. He gets to his feet holding a dead
rat during the next few lines of dialogue. Emily and Kathy are unaware of what
has been happening with Walter.*

Emily: Let them talk. Walter and I are happy together.
Kathy: Oh. come on, Emily! You Can't let this thing—

EMILY: Walter. His name is Walter.

KATHY: This undead Walter come between you and your friends.
Between you and your family.

50 EMILY: Well they'd better not force me to choose, because—

WALTER: (*Presents dead rat to Emily.*) Ook!

KATHY: Ohmygod!

EMILY: Aw, thank you, honey.

WALTER: Or . . . ew . . .

60 KATHY: It's a dead rat!

EMILY: Yes it is. Walter, dear, just put it down over there, sweety.

(*Points to base of bench. Walter puts dead rat next to bench leg.*)

We'll play with it later.

WALTER: Oodie . . . !

KATHY: That's . . . Oh, it's disgusting.

EMILY: It isn't.

(*To Walter*)

(Kathy and I are still talking. Just a bit longer, okay?

65 WALTER: Oon . . . ?

EMILY: (*Looking up.*) The moon hasn't started yet. It'll be okay. Soon.
I promise.

WALTER: Kay . . .

Moves off to one side

KATHY: How can you stand it?

EMILY: What? He brought me a present.

70 KATHY: A dead rat!

EMILY: Well at least he put some effort into it. His own brain power.

WALTER: Bwains . . . !

EMILY: Not now. sweety.

(*To Kathy*)

It wasn't some cheesey crushed velvet rose bought at some quicky-
mart as an afterthought.

KATHY: Dead. Rat.

75 EMILY: You just don't get it. He's not like other guys. He really cares
about me.

KATHY: The undead can't care. Except caring about eating brains.

WALTER: Bwains . . . ?

KATHY: Oh, hush!

EMILY: Don't talk to him like that. At least I know Walter will be there
when I need him. He'll listen when I just need to talk. Can you say
that about other guys?

KATHY: Other guys still have a pulse! 80

(Walter finds some half-dead flowers and "bunches" them into a bouquet.)

EMILY: I don't have to worry about Walter going out and getting drunk—
KATHY: 'Cause he's dead.
EMILY: Forgetting to come home. Sleeping with my best friend.
KATHY: That'd never happen. Thank god.
EMILY: Or just sitting on the couch, hand in his pants, watching sports 85 all day. *(Walter hands Emily the "bunched" flowers.)*

Thank you! Walter likes to take walks with me.
KATHY: 'Cause you order him to go.
EMILY: I don't have to order him.
WALTER: Ind . . . oad . . . ill . . . !
KATHY: Find road-kill? That's disgusting.
EMILY: No guy is perfect, but at least I have something real with Walter. 90
KATHY: Whatever. No one's happy about this but you, Emily. You're driving your friends away. You family is hurt because you won't date somebody nice, and living. Pretty soon all you're going to have left is smelly, undead, rat killing Walter! You won't be happy. You'll grow old regretting your decision.
EMILY: You're the one who sounds unhappy.
KATHY: I'm unhappy that I'm losing my best friend.
EMILY: You haven't lost me, Kathy. I'm right here.
KATHY: I don't think I can stay your friend if you continue to date that! 95
EMILY: Geez, Kathy, you can be such a killjoy. I guess I have no choice.
KATHY: I knew you'd see reason.
EMILY: Walter, dear.
WALTER: Uh . . . ?
EMILY: Kill Kathy for me, please? There's a sweetheart. 100
KATHY: What? No! Wait!

(Walter grabs Kathy who screams. Her scream is choked off as Walter strangles her as they fall to the ground.)

WALTER: Bwains . . . !
EMILY: No, no, Walter. No brains.
WALTER: No . . . bwains . . . ?
EMILY: Just kill her, don't eat her. Okay, honey. 105
WALTER: Aw . . . O . . . A . . .
EMILY: We want to keep her as a friend.
WALTER: Ake . . . end . . . !

(Walter gets up.)

EMILY: The eclipse is about to start, Walter. Come join me?

110 WALTER: E . . . ips . . .

(Sits with Emily)

EMILY: Come join us, Kathy?

KATHY: (*Slowly sitting up. Talks like Walter now.*) Uh . . . ha . . . een . . . ?

EMILY: What happened? Just keeping you as my best friend. Come. Sit with us.

KATHY: O . . . ay . . .

(Kathy sits next to Emily.)

115 EMILY: There. Isn't this perfect?

(Links arms with Kathy and Walter)

What could be better than this?

KATHY & WALTER: Bwains!!!

EMILY: Oh, you, two. Look. It's starting.

They all watch the lunar eclipse.
Lights out

Reading and Reacting

1. Do you think any of the characters in the three plays in this chapter are fully developed, or do you see most (or all) of them as stereotypes? Given the limits of its form, do you think a ten-minute play can ever really develop a character?

2. Most of the plays in this chapter have only one or two characters. Should any additional parts have been written for these plays? Explain.

3. Could the roles in this chapter's plays be portrayed by actors of any gender? of any age? of any race? Why or why not?

4. Identify the central conflict in each play. What do you see as the **climax**, or highest point of tension, in each? Where does the climax generally occur in these plays?

5. Each play in this chapter has a single setting, and each of these settings is described only minimally. Do any settings seem to require more detailed descriptions? If you were going to expand each play, what additional settings might you show?

6. Considering the subject matter of each of the plays in this chapter, what kinds of topics seem to be most appropriate for ten-minute plays? Why do you think this is so? What kinds of topics would *not* be suitable for ten-minute plays?

7. CRITICAL PERSPECIVE The Web site *10-Minute-Plays.com*, whose slogan is "High-octane drama for a fast-food nation," summarizes the structure of a ten-minute play as follows:

> Pages 1 to 2: Set up the world of your main character.
>
> Pages 2 to 3: Something happens to throw your character's world out of balance.
>
> Pages 4 to 7: Your character struggles to restore order to his world.
>
> Page 8: Just when your character is about to restore order, something happens to complicate matters.
>
> Pages 9 to 10: Your character either succeeds or fails in his attempt to restore order.

Although not every play in this chapter is exactly ten pages long, do they all nevertheless conform to the general structure outlined above?

WRITING SUGGESTIONS: Ten-Minute Plays

1. Write a response expressing your reactions to *Magic 8 Ball*.

2. Write an explication of *Applicant*.

3. Assume you are a director providing background for an actor who is to play the role of Carla or Bethany in *Beauty*. Write a character analysis of one of these characters, outlining her background and explaining her emotions, actions, conflicts, and motivation.

4. Write an essay about the cultural context of one of the plays in this chapter.

5. Choose a scene from one of the longer plays in this text that has a definite beginning, middle, and end. Rewrite this scene as a self-contained ten-minute play. (If you like, you can update the scene to the present time, change the characters' names or genders, and make other changes you see as necessary.)

6. Write an original ten-minute play for two characters.

CHAPTER 27

PLOT

David Ives
Evan Agostini/Getty Images
Entertainment/Getty Images

Warren Leight
Scott Gries/Getty Images
Entertainment/Getty Images

Henrik Ibsen
Hulton Archive/Stringer/
Getty Images

Susan Glaspell
AP Images

Plot denotes the way events are arranged in a work of literature. Although the conventions of drama require that the plot of a play be presented somewhat differently from the plot of a short story, the same components of plot are present in both. Plot in a dramatic work, like plot in a short story, is shaped by conflicts that are revealed, intensified, and resolved through the characters' actions. (See Chapter 7 for a discussion of conflict.)

850

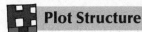

Plot Structure

In 1863, the German novelist and playwright Gustav Freytag devised a pyramid to represent a prototype for the plot of a dramatic work. According to Freytag, a play typically begins with **exposition**, which presents characters and setting and introduces the basic situation in which the characters are involved. Then, during the **rising action**, complications develop, conflicts emerge, suspense builds, and crises occur. The rising action culminates in a **climax**, a point at which the plot's tension peaks. Finally, during the **falling action**, the intensity subsides, eventually winding down to a **resolution**, or **denouement**, in which all loose ends are tied up.

The familiar plot of a detective story follows Freytag's concept of plot: the exposition section includes the introduction of the detective and the explanation of the crime; the rising action develops as the investigation of the crime proceeds, with suspense increasing as the solution approaches; the high point of the action, the climax, comes with the revelation of the crime's solution; and the falling action presents the detective's explanation of the solution. The story concludes with a resolution that typically includes the capture of the criminal and the restoration of order.

The action of Susan Glaspell's one-act play *Trifles* (p. 867), which in many ways resembles a detective story, can be diagrammed like this:

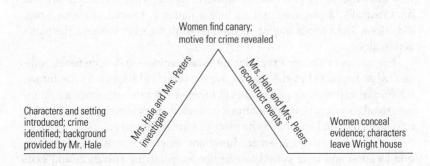

Of course, the plot of a complex dramatic work rarely conforms to the neat pattern represented by Freytag's pyramid. For example, a play can lack exposition entirely. Because long stretches of exposition can be dull, a playwright may decide to arouse audience interest by moving directly into conflict, as Sophocles does in *Oedipus the King* (p. 1182) and as Milcha Sanchez-Scott does in *The Cuban Swimmer* (p. 1166). Similarly, because audiences tend to lose interest after the play's climax is reached, a playwright may choose to dispense with extended falling action. Thus, after Hamlet's death, the play ends quite abruptly, with no real resolution.

Plot and Subplot

While the main plot is developing, a parallel plot, called a **subplot**, may be developing alongside it. This structural device is common in the works of Shakespeare and in many other plays as well. The subplot's function may not immediately be clear, so at first it may seem to draw attention away from the main plot. Ultimately, however, the subplot reinforces elements of the primary plot. In Henrik Ibsen's *A Doll House* (p. 881), for example, the threat of Dr. Rank's impending death parallels the threat of Nora's approaching exposure; for both of them, time is running out.

In Shakespeare's *King Lear*, a more elaborate subplot involves the Earl of Gloucester, who, like Lear, misjudges his children, favoring a deceitful son who does not deserve his support and overlooking a more deserving one. Both families suffer greatly as a result of the fathers' misplaced loyalties. Thus, the parallel plot places additional emphasis on Lear's poor judgment and magnifies the consequences of his misguided acts: both fathers, and all but one of the five children, are dead by the play's end. A subplot can also set up a contrast with the main plot—as it does in *Hamlet* (p. 1043), where Fortinbras acts decisively to avenge his father, an action that underscores Hamlet's hesitation and procrastination when faced with a similar challenge.

 ## Plot Development

In a dramatic work, plot unfolds through **action**: what characters say and do. Generally, a play does not include a narrator. Instead, dialogue, stage directions, and various staging techniques work together to move the play's action along.

Exchanges of **dialogue** reveal what is happening—and, sometimes, indicate what happened in the past or suggest what will happen in the future. Characters can recount past events to other characters, announce an intention to take some action in the future, or summarize events that are occurring offstage. Thus, dialogue takes the place of formal narrative.

On the printed page, **stage directions** efficiently move readers from one location and time period to another by specifying entrances and exits and identifying the play's structural divisions—acts and scenes—and their accompanying changes of setting.

Staging techniques can also advance a play's action. For example, a change in lighting can shift the focus to another part of the stage—and thus to another place and time. An adjustment of scenery or props—for instance, a breakfast table, complete with morning paper, replacing a bedtime setting—can indicate that the action has moved forward in time, as can a change of costumes. Music can also move a play's action along, predicting excitement or doom or a romantic interlude—or a particular character's entrance.

Occasionally, a play does have a formal narrator to move the plot along. For example, in Thornton Wilder's play *Our Town* (1938), a character known as the Stage Manager functions as a narrator, not only describing the play's setting and introducing the characters to the audience but also soliciting questions from characters scattered around the audience, prompting characters, and interrupting dialogue.

Flashbacks

Many plays—such as Arthur Miller's *Death of a Salesman* (p. 960)—include **flashbacks**, which depict events that occurred before the play's main action. Dialogue can also summarize events that occurred earlier, thereby overcoming the limitations set by the time frame in which the play's action unfolds. Thus, Mr. Hale in *Trifles* tells the other characters how he discovered John Wright's murder, and Nora in *A Doll House* confides her secret past to her friend Kristine. As characters on stage are brought up to date, the audience is also given necessary information—facts that are essential to an understanding of the characters' motivation. (In less realistic dramas, characters can interrupt the action to deliver long monologues or soliloquies that fill in background details—or even address the audience directly, as Tom does in Tennessee Williams's *The Glass Menagerie*.)

Foreshadowing

In addition to revealing past events, dialogue can **foreshadow**, or look ahead to, future action. In many cases, seemingly unimportant comments have significance that becomes clear as the play develops. For example, in act 3 of *A Doll House*, Torvald Helmer says to Kristine, "An exit should always be effective, Mrs. Linde, but that's what I can't get Nora to grasp." At the end of the play, Nora's exit is not only effective but also memorable.

Elements of staging—such as props, scenery, lighting, music, and sound effects—can also foreshadow events to come. Finally, various bits of **stage business**—gestures or movements designed to attract the audience's attention—may also foreshadow future events. In *A Doll House*, for example,

Nora's sneaking forbidden macaroons seems at first to suggest her fear of her husband, but her actions actually foreshadow her eventual defiance of his authority.

✔ **CHECKLIST**   **Writing about Plot**

- What happens in the play?

- What is the play's central conflict? How is it resolved? What other conflicts are present?

- What section of the play constitutes its rising action?

- Where does the play's climax occur?

- What crises can you identify?

- How is suspense created?

- What section of the play constitutes its falling action?

- Does the play contain a subplot? What is its purpose? How is it related to the main plot?

- How do characters' actions advance the play's plot?

- How does dialogue advance the play's plot?

- How do stage directions advance the play's plot?

- How do staging techniques advance the play's plot?

- Does the play include a narrator?

- Does the play include flashbacks? foreshadowing? Does the play's dialogue contain summaries of past events or references to events in the future? How does the use of flashbacks or foreshadowing advance the play's plot?

Evan Agostini/Getty Images Entertainment/Getty Images

DAVID IVES (1950–   ), recipient of a Guggenheim Fellowship in playwriting, has published and produced numerous plays, many of which are one-act comedies. His plays are collected in *All in the Timing* (1994), *Mere Mortals* (1998), *Time Flies and Other Short Plays* (2001), *Polish Joke and Other Plays* (2004), and *The Other Woman and Other Short Pieces* (2008). His play *Don Juan in Chicago* (1995) won the Outer Critics Circle Playwriting Award.

Cultural Context The isolated country house is a familiar convention of English and American crime fiction—particularly in classical detective stories in which the number of suspects is limited by the enclosed setting. This genre was defined and popularized by the prolific English mystery writer (and creator of the iconic detective Hercule Poirot) Agatha Christie (1890–1976), who was known as the "queen of crime." By referring to Christie, the characters in this play evoke the well-established tradition of the murder mystery.

The Blizzard (2006)

CHARACTERS

Jenny
Neil
Salim
Natasha

A country house, toward evening. Cold winter light in the windows. In the course of the play, the lights gradually dim around center stage to nighttime. At curtain, Jenny is onstage alone.

JENNY: *(Calls.)* Neil? — Neil! *(Neil enters from outside, stage right.)*
NEIL: It's still coming down. Some of those drifts are three feet deep already. What's the matter?
JENNY: Nothing. I just wondered what happened to you.
NEIL: Got scared, huh?
JENNY: No, I wasn't *scared.* The food's all ready. Do you really think they'll 5
make it up here in this?
NEIL: Joe's got those new chains on the car. The ones that Sandy made him fork out for? Just what you'd expect from Miss Rationality.
JENNY: Right. Mr. *List Maker.* Mr. My-Pencils-Have-To-Be-Laid-Out-In-The-Right-Order-On-My-Desk. No, you're not rational. Sandy is rational.
NEIL: What about the TV?
JENNY: Nothing. Not a thing.
NEIL: The electricity's on. You'd think with a satellite dish we'd pick up 10
*some*thing.
JENNY: The telephone's still out.
NEIL: They've probably been trying us since they left the city.
JENNY: There's no radio either.
NEIL: No *radio?*
JENNY: Isn't it *great?* It's just like an Agatha Christie. 15
NEIL: Thanks for that. I'm still not used to it. Being so remote. Nature's always scared the living crap out of me. Now I'm living in it. Or visiting it on weekends, anyway. You know I saw a bat flapping around out

there? I didn't know there were bats in blizzards. No *radio?* The world
could be ending out there, for Christ's sake. And we'd be the last ones
to hear about it. No *radio* . . .

JENNY: Yes, we have no radio and a beautiful blizzard and a house and
woods and a mountain that are all ours.

NEIL: All ours in twenty-nine years and three months.

JENNY: I kind of wish they weren't coming up tonight. It's so cozy.
I wouldn't mind curling up with a book.

20   NEIL: I wish you hadn't said "Agatha Christie."

JENNY: You inflict *Torturama* One, Two and Three on people and I can't
say "Agatha Christie"?

NEIL: Those are movies, not a real house in the middle of the real country
with the lines down. And *Torturama* paid for our little mansion on a
hill, babe.

JENNY: You know what it is about murder mysteries? No, listen. I think the
reason people like murder mysteries is that, in a murder mystery, everything is *significant.* The people in murder mysteries are living in a *significant world.* A world where everything is there for a reason. Even before
the murder's happened, you know that one is going to happen and you
know that everything is a *clue.* Or rather, you know that some things
are clues and some things are just obfuscation, they're snow. And you
know that everybody has a secret of some kind. A secret that's like a
soul. Murder mysteries are religious, in a way. Don't laugh. They're life
the way you feel it when you're in love. When everything's in a special
light. Incandescent. They're a couple of hours of everything *meaning*
something, for God's sake. And then they're over and you're back to
your old life, to real life. To mortgages and pork loin and potatoes and
making a cherry pie.

NEIL: So real life doesn't feel like it means something to you these days?

25   JENNY: Sure it does. I'm just saying . . . Well, don't we all wish for that in
real life? One of those moments when everything feels charged with
meaning? When the air is electric?

NEIL: Well here's your opportunity. Listen, we're probably going to be totally
snowed in. Why don't we all do something different this weekend.

JENNY: Different, what does different mean?

NEIL: I don't know. Something unusual. Something unexpected. Not you
and Sandy holing yourself up in the kitchen and talking about whatever you talk about, not me and Joe sitting around talking about Mom
and Dad and what happened in the third grade. Not the usual pour-a-
glass-of-Jack-Daniels, bullshit bullshit bullshit, what've you guys been
doing, go in to dinner and break out the Margaux '01, have you seen
any movies, did you catch that episode of blah blah blah. I don't know,
something we've never done before, or let's talk about something we've

never talked about before. Anything, instead of all the things we usually talk about.

JENNY: Okay. Something unusual. I love it.

SALIM: *(Offstage.)* Hello — ? Neil?   30

NEIL: There they are. *(Salim and Natasha enter from the front door at stage
left. Salim carries a black plastic valise.)*

SALIM: Hello! Neil and Jenny, right? Sorry for the cold hand, I'm freezing.
God, you're just like Joe and Sandy described you. I can't believe I'm
finally meeting you, Neil. I am such a fan of *Torturama*. All of them.
Natasha can't watch them, herself. Natasha is squeamish.

NEIL: I'm sorry, I don't understand . . .

SALIM: Salim. And Natasha.

NATASHA: Hello. I'm so happy to encounter you at last. And you, Jenny,   35
you are just as beautiful as Sandy told me. You are exquisite.

SALIM: And God, what a place up here! But so remote! Wow! We brought
this for you. *(Holds up the black valise.)* A little housewarming gift.

NEIL: Whoa, whoa, whoa. I'm sorry, maybe there's been a mistake . . .

SALIM: I mean, this is the place, isn't it? You're Neil and Jenny? Oh, right,
right. *Where are Joe and Sandy.* Middle of a snowstorm. Two strange
people walk in. You're spooked. Totally natural. Natasha?

NATASHA: Joe and Sandy couldn't make it, so they sent us instead.

NEIL: They sent you instead. Wait a minute. They sent *you* instead . . .   40

SALIM: They caught some kind of bug. God, Joe and Sandy have been telling us all about you two for I don't know how long.

NATASHA: A long time.

SALIM: A very long time.

NEIL: I don't think Joe and Sandy ever mentioned knowing a . . . I'm
sorry . . .

SALIM: Salim.   45

NEIL: A Salim and a Natasha.

SALIM: You've been out of touch with your brother for too long, brother.
They were really broken up they couldn't make it tonight. I'd say call
them up and ask them but hey, are your cellphones as down as ours up
here?

JENNY: How do you know Joe and Sandy?

SALIM: *(The black valise.)* You know what's in here? Just for showing us
your hospitality? It's this new tequila, a hundred bucks a bottle. Olé,
right? Let's support those oppressed brothers churning this stuff out for
ten pesos a day. Neil, you want to pour?

JENNY: You didn't answer me.   50

NATASHA: How do we know Joe and Sandy.

SALIM: How do we know Joe and Sandy. How do we know them, Natasha?

NATASHA: Intimately.

SALIM: Intimately. Good word. We know them intimately.

55 JENNY: Neil . . . Neil . . .

NEIL: Look, I'm very sorry, but I'm going to have to ask you to leave.

SALIM: To leave? But . . . okay, I get it, I get it, you want some kind of proof that we're not just what . . .

NATASHA: Imposters.

SALIM: Imposters. Ten points, Natasha. We're not imposters! We're the real thing! I'm sorry if I'm coming on kind of strong, it's my personality, you know what I mean? God, how do you prove that you know somebody? Let's see. Where do I start? Do I start with Joe or Sandy? You know she made him get these hotshot snowchains for the car. That is so Sandy. No imagination, but always thinking ahead. So *rational.* (*Pause.*) Listen. Listen, I'm sorry we barged in on you like this. Maybe we should leave, but . . . hey, are you really going to turn two freezing strangers back out into the storm? Neil, you're the guy who inflicted *Torturama* on the world, more killings per square frame than any movie in history. You're pouring blood in the aisles, man. Don't tell me you're scared. What are you scared of? What am I, the wrong color? And what am I going to do to you, huh? If I was going to do something to you I'd've done it already, wouldn't I? (*Pause.*) So do we leave? Or do we stay? Aw, have a heart, Neil.

60 NEIL: Well, we can't turn you out in this weather . . .

JENNY: Turn them out, Neil.

NEIL: Honey, I . . .

JENNY: Turn them out.

NEIL: It's a blizzard out there, honey.

65 SALIM: Your wife is so sweet. Really. She is a doll.

NATASHA: You know, with so much snow, it's like we're in a murder mystery here.

SALIM: Natasha adores Agatha Christie. You know what I hate about murder mysteries? It's that everybody in them's got a secret. People don't have secrets. People are open books. I don't know you personally, Neil, but just looking at you I'd say you're probably the kind of guy who makes lists, for example. Lines his pencils up on the desk. Likes things neat and tidy. Am I right? A Jack Daniels before dinner kinda guy. You're not the kind of guy who, what, secretly worked for the CIA once upon a time, you're not a guy with a secret history of killing people, I mean *really* killing people, off screen, you don't have any real blood on your hands. You're in the entertainment industry. You have nothing to hide.

JENNY: Send them away, Neil.

SALIM: And Jenny, she probably made her usual dinner for tonight, let's see what would it be, pork loin and some kind of special potato recipe and a cherry-rhubarb pie for dessert. The perfect American housewife. Nothing to conceal. I'm sorry, I'm sorry, there's that personality of mine again. I'm brash. I'm insensitive. I'm loud. Call me American.

NEIL: You know I have a gun in the house.   70

SALIM: Oh, that's rich. What a liar! "I have a gun in the house." Right. That's so cute. This isn't a movie, this is *real life*, Neil. And I'm your brother for the night. I'm a stand-in for Joe. Remember me? Your brother?

JENNY: Where are Joe and Sandy?

SALIM: They're very sick in bed is where they are.

JENNY: What have you done with them?

SALIM: They can't move is what they are. Aren't I your brother? Neil?   75
Come on. *(He puts his arm around Neil's waist.)* Am I your brother?

NEIL: Sure . . .

SALIM: Am I your brother? Am I your brother? Am I your brother?

NEIL: You're my brother.

SALIM: There you see? How hard was that? Now we can talk about all those kids we used to beat up in third grade. Just like old times. Well, brother, what do you say? We're here for the duration. You gonna play the good host here or what? You want to show me around the grounds?

NEIL: Sure.   80

SALIM: Sure what?

NEIL: Sure, brother.

SALIM: Attaboy! *(Salim follows Neil off through the back door. A pause.)*

NATASHA: You know what I love about murder mysteries? Is that everything in them seems to mean something. The people in murder mysteries are living in a significant world. Everything holding it's breath. Waiting. The air is electric. And then, bang, it happens. The irrevocable. Whatever that is. Changing everything. It's a kind of poetry. To me, it's almost a religious feeling.

JENNY: I don't want any more fucking significance. I don't want it. I don't   85
want it.

NATASHA: Poor Jenny. Afraid over nothing. Why? Why?

JENNY: You have the wrong people.

NATASHA: You're the right people. Neil and Jenny. We're just here for dinner with you. And you have nothing to be afraid of. Really. Absolutely nothing.

JENNY: *(Calls out.)* Neil . . . ? Neil . . . ?

NATASHA: Absolutely nothing . . . *(The lights fade.)*   90

*   *   *

Reading and Reacting

1. Using Freytag's pyramid (p. 851) as a model, outline the plot of *The Blizzard*. Does it include all five stages of plot?
2. Neil is a writer whose credits include *Torturama* (presumably a horror movie). Why is this information significant? What else do you know about Neil and Jenny? What more would you like to know?
3. Review the play's stage directions. What kind of information do they provide? Do you think readers need more information? Explain.
4. Which of the following can be considered foreshadowing:

   • The blizzard
   • The fact that, according to the opening stage directions, "*the lights gradually dim*" during the course of the play as night approaches
   • Jenny's statement: "I wish they weren't coming up tonight."
   • Neil's statement: "Why don't we all do something different this weekend."

5. Describe the play's setting. Is the blizzard essential to the play's action and outcome, or could events have unfolded in the same way without it?
6. Jenny says people like murder mysteries because "in a murder mystery, everything is significant"; Natasha later echoes this sentiment. What do they mean? Does this characterization apply to *The Blizzard*?
7. Salim says, "You know what I hate about murder mysteries? It's that everybody in them's got a secret." What secrets might the characters in *The Blizzard* be hiding? Is *The Blizzard* a murder mystery?
8. What do you think might happen to the characters after the play ends? Why? Do you think this outcome is inevitable? Why or why not?

9. **JOURNAL ENTRY** What is the significance of the black valise (the play's only prop)? Do you see it as a symbol?

10. **CRITICAL PERSPECTIVE** In a review of Ives's plays, *New York Times* theater critic Ben Brantley makes the following point:

   > Mr. Ives's theories may owe much to the philosophical arcana of such dense thinkers as Einstein and Derrida, but he is no coolly detached academic. His obsessions with randomness and relativity are translated into revuelike sketches that percolate with comic brio and zesty bits of stagecraft.

   Do you see evidence in *The Blizzard* that Ives is obsessed with "randomness and relativity"?

Related Works: "Accident" (p. 89), "Encounters with Unexpected Animals" (p. 90), "A Good Man Is Hard to Find" (p. 295), "Stopping by Woods on a Snowy Evening" (p. 765)

Scott Gries/Getty Images
Entertainment/Getty Images

WARREN LEIGHT (1957–), a widely acclaimed wr
and director, was a writer/producer for the television seri
Law and Order: Criminal Intent. His play *Side Man* (1998)
was nominated for a Pulitzer Prize and won Broadway's 1999
Tony Award for Best Play. His other plays include *Glimmer,*
Glimmer and *Shine* (2001) and *No Foreigners Beyond This*
Point (2006). His screen credits include *The Night We Never*
Met (1993), *Dear God* (1996), and *Mother's Day* (2010).

Cultural Context The right of the accused to a trial by
jury is stated in the Sixth Amendment to the United States
Constitution as well as in the constitutions of individual states. However, even though it is
a civic duty and an important cultural mainstay, many Americans see jury duty as a burden
because it requires them to take time off from their work and family responsibilities to serve.
Although failing to appear for jury service is a crime, a study conducted by the American
Judicature Society reported that, on any given day, an average of twenty percent of Americans
summoned for jury duty do not appear. (That number drops to fewer than ten percent in some
urban areas.) Some common excuses people use to try to get out of serving include obliga-
tions at school, work, or home; child or elder care; illness or disability; and bias (which may
result from prior knowledge of the case or having a previous or ongoing relationship with
someone involved in the case). In one 2007 criminal case in Miami, Florida, a prospective
juror was dismissed after she told the judge that, if she served, her pet ferret would be left
home alone.

Nine Ten (2001)

CHARACTERS

Leslie
John
Kearrie
Nick
Lyris

Jury Duty Grand Hall. Morning.
John, a slightly awkward bond trader, sits on a bench. Very neat, buttoned down.
He reads a perfectly folded Wall Street Journal. *Lyris Touzet, a dancer, enters,*
almost spills her coffee on him.

LYRIS: Is this Part B?
JOHN: What?
LYRIS: Part B, or not part B?
JOHN: Ah . . . that is the question.
LYRIS: Are you making fun of me? 5
JOHN: No no. Um, let me look at your . . . (*She hands him a slip of paper, he*
reads it.) Where you are is where you're supposed to be.

He needs a little more personal space than she does.

...do they call us at eight-thirty? It's like, nine already, and they ...'t said anything.

They build in a grace period.

...IS: They what?

JOHN: They say eight-thirty so that most people get here by nine. And around nine ten they start calling names.

LYRIS: You knew this, and you came at eight-thirty?

JOHN: Eight actually.

LYRIS: Eight A.M.? You must hate your wife.

JOHN: I don't see her much. We both have to be at work at six.

15 **LYRIS:** You punch in at six?

JOHN: Well, I don't . . . punch in exactly. But, the desk opens at six so. . . .

LYRIS: Your desk opens?

JOHN: Sorry. Trading desk. Bonds. Euros, mostly. From my desk, I'm up so high, on a clear day, you can see Europe.

At a bench opposite, Nick Theron works the Times *crossword puzzle as Leslie Rudin arrives, pissed off and hyper.*

LESLIE: Part B?

20 **NICK:** Must be.

LYRIS: Have they called any—

NICK: Does it look like it? (*She looks to the court officer's desk, downstage left.*) Every once in a while this guy comes out and says we should wait. Which is . . . helpful.

LESLIE: I tried to get out of it on the phone and they said it was my third postponement and I had to come down here in person on the day of and that I wasn't going to get out anyway. And I finally get here—do they just change the names of the subway lines for spite lately?—and there's a line a mile long to get through security and they go through my purse like I'm a serial killer and it turns out if I want to smoke I'm going to have to go down and outside, and then wait on line again for them to check my bag. This just sucks.

NICK: I'm going to tell the judge that I'm a felon. He won't even question it. And he'll tell me felons can't serve. I'll act offended at this. And then he'll just let me go back to my life.

25 **LESLIE:** (*impressed*) That's good.

NICK: Racial profiling. A two-way street.

Over to John and Lyris.

LYRIS: My brother's in the same building. Security guard. You probably don't know him.

Kearrie, a tough businesswoman, enters, rushed.

KEARRIE: Part B?

LYRIS AND JOHN: Or not part B?

KEARRIE: It's too early for cute. (*They look at her, she means it.*) Have they
started to give out postponements yet?

LYRIS: No one gets postponement.

KEARRIE: I'm on a flight tomorrow. (*Pulls something out of her bag.*) I've got
a ticket.

John takes another look at her.

JOHN: Kearrie?

KEARRIE: What?

JOHN: It's me, John. . . .   35

KEARRIE: Right. John. That narrows it down.

JOHN: John McCormack. From Wharton.

Kearrie still doesn't place him.

LYRIS: (*to John*) You sure leave an impression.

JOHN: Story of my life. (*To Kearrie.*) Case study. Euro-economic unity.

KEARRIE: You got an A, I got a B plus. Even though we worked together.   40

JOHN: (*to Lyris*) You know about Irish Alzheimer's . . . you forget everything except your grudges.

KEARRIE: You went to Gold and Strauss when we graduated, right?

JOHN: Still there.

KEARRIE: (*grades him a loser*) You're kidding. You are not still at—

JOHN: Just the last ten years. Kearrie this is—   45

LYRIS: Lyris Touzet. Spiritual dancer. And healer.

JOHN: Lyris this is Kearrie Whitman. We went to Wharton together.
Class of 91.

LYRIS: I must have missed you two by like . . . one year.

*Leslie and Nick. He has no hope of attending to his crossword puzzle. Leslie must
talk or die.*

LESLIE: I'm out in the Hamptons. One week after Labor Day. Paradise found.
The assholes are gone. The beaches are empty. The water is warm.

NICK: Sharks are hungry.   50

LESLIE: No sharks in the Hamptons. Professional courtesy.

NICK: Touché.

LESLIE: I think I'll stay another day. Then I remember . . . fuck me—eight-
thirty summons. Drive in at midnight. Get stuck in traffic. The L.I.E.
has got to be the only road in the world that has traffic jams at two
A.M. By the time I get to my garage it's locked for the night. You ever
try to find a space on the right side of the street at two A.M.?

ris chatting. Kearrie plays with her Palm Pilot.

...y, I always wanted to be a spiritual dancer.

...re making fun of me.

...m not. . . . swear to god. But what is a—

...s: I heal people, through movement. Rhythm. Every person has their
own . . . pulse. Below the surface, that—

KEARRIE: Fuck me!

LYRIS: I help them to get in touch with their inner—

60 **KEARRIE:** (*Turns to them.*) Fuck me fuck me fuck . . .

JOHN: What's hers?

Kearrie now rants in their direction, about her Palm Pilot.

KEARRIE: Money on the table. I've got a watch list. It's programmed to
signal me when there's a discrepancy between euro prices and ADRs.
The spread is sitting there. Sitting there. It's blinking—buy me. Buy
me. I try to buy and my damn signal fades. What's the point of fucking
having a watch list if you can't follow up on it. This whole building
should be wired. This city is . . . in the stone ages.

LYRIS: (*to John*) Some people are harder cases than others.

Over to Nick and Leslie.

NICK: My neighborhood, downtown, they're *always* filming. Some sequel
to a sequel to a disaster flick. *Mortal Danger Times Four.* Whatever.
Which means like—

65 **LESLIE:** They take every parking place. Big lights up—

NICK: —all night long.

LESLIE: Idiots in walkie-talkies saying don't walk there. On your own
street. Call the cops to complain, they don't care. No one in this city
cares. The film crew can be, like, setting off concussion bombs, and
nobody does anything.

Back to John and Lyris.

JOHN: (*to Lyris*) I can't.

LYRIS: Everybody can move. Even you . . . Stand up.

He doesn't.

70 **LYRIS:** (*loud*) STAND UP!

*Nick and Leslie hear this. Look over to John and Lyris. John doesn't want to attract
attention, so he stands. John and Lyris now overlap with Nick and Leslie. Kearrie
is in her own world.*

LYRIS: (*to John*) Just start to, sway a little . . . from your hips.

LESLIE: (*to Nick*) That is sick the way he's flirting with her.

John sits back down.

JOHN: I can't.

LYRIS: Yes you can.

NICK: (*to Leslie*) How do you know it's his fault?   75

LESLIE: (*to Nick*) It's always the guy's fault. I date cops. Believe me. I know.

JOHN: (*to Lyris*) I don't like to. Move. I like things as they are. I've had the same job for ten years.

KEARRIE: (*on her cell phone, to her office*) Here? It's a fucking hellhole. What do you think? Ah-huh. Ah-huh. Ah-huh. Look—keep that on hold.

JOHN: (*to Lyris, oblivious to Kearrie*) Same office, same view. Married my junior high school sweetheart. We take the same train to work. We have the same lunch. Tuna. On rye. No mayo.

LYRIS: No mayo?   80

JOHN: It's not so bad, once you get used to it.

KEARRIE: (*into phone*) Yeah as soon as they call roll, I show my plane ticket . . . and I'm out of here.

Now, from downstage left, a court officer enters.

COURT OFFICER: Hello folks. Welcome to New York County Jury Duty. Before you all come up to me . . .

KEARRIE: Excuse me, I have a flight to—

NICK: I have a record—   85

COURT OFFICER: (*He drowns her out.*)—with your reasons for why you shouldn't be here, let me tell you: I've heard them all. On the bright side, most of you will get to go back to your life in two or three days.

Leslie, Nick, Kearrie, John, and Lyris all groan. Two days is eternity.

COURT OFFICER: And we are as happy to have you, as you are happy to be here. First things first. Check your summons, and be sure you're in the right place. This is Civil Court. Part B. 60 Centre Street. Today is Monday, September 10th . . . Two thousand and one.

Blackout.

*   *   *

Reading and Reacting

1. The exposition provided in the play's stage directions is quite minimal, giving few clues about setting. How do you picture the setting?

2. What basic information does the audience learn about each character? Given the revelation at the end of the play, why is this information important?

3. In the absence of a narrator, how do we learn about each character?

4. This play has a single setting and very little physical action. What moves the plot along?

5. What preconceived ideas do you think most people have about jury duty? How do the characters reinforce these ideas? How does the play use the audience's stereotypical assumptions about jury duty to advance the plot?

6. John complains that he is bored with his life, stuck in a routine. Given the play's ending, these complaints are deeply ironic. What other examples of irony can you identify in this play?

7. Foreshadowing is extremely important in *Nine Ten*. Consider how each of the following details foreshadows the play's ending: John works on a very high floor of his building; Lyris's brother is a security guard in John's building; Kearrie has a ticket for a flight the following day; Nick lives downtown; Leslie dates cops. What is the probable significance of each of these details?

8. At the beginning of the play, John explains the rules for jury duty, saying, "around nine ten they start calling names." Does this statement have any significance beyond its literal meaning?

9. JOURNAL ENTRY Do you think the play's title gives the ending away? Explain. What alternate titles might be appropriate, and why?

10. CRITICAL PERSPECTIVE In her article on literature about the 9/11 terrorist attacks, award-winning novelist Julia Glass tries to find common ground among writers who address her era's "most resounding moments":

> Storytellers who dramatize their own era embrace its most resounding moments, moments when the spiritual compass by which we live (and write) has spun out of alignment. Realigning that compass, searching for a new magnetic north, is some of the best work fiction writers do. We seize something that everyone around us has taken for granted and, whether tenderly or violently, ironically or tragically, we upend it, dissect or shatter it. We write not about *you or them* or *then*. We write about *us*; we write about *now*. Reader, we say, *the view has changed; let me show you how.*

In what sense does *Nine Ten* "upend," "dissect," or "shatter" common perceptions of the world as it was before 9/11?

Related Works: "Going to Work" (p. 601) "The End and the Beginning" (p. 729), *Trifles* (p. 867).

AP Images

SUSAN GLASPELL (1882–1948) was born in Davenport, Iowa, and graduated from Drake University in 1899. First a reporter and then a freelance writer, she lived in Chicago (where she was part of the Chicago renaissance that included poet Carl Sandburg and novelist Theodore Dreiser) and later in Greenwich Village. Her works include two plays in addition to *Trifles*, *The Verge* (1921) and *Alison's House* (1930), and several novels, including *Fidelity* (1915) and *The Morning Is Near Us* (1939). With her husband, George Cram Cook, she founded the Provincetown Players, which became the staging ground for innovative plays by Eugene O'Neill, among others.

Glaspell herself wrote plays for the Provincetown Players, beginning with *Trifles*, which she created for the 1916 season although she had never previously written a drama. The play opened on August 8, 1916, with Glaspell and her husband in the cast. Glaspell said she wrote *Trifles* in one afternoon, sitting in the empty theater and looking at the bare stage: "After a time, the stage became a kitchen—a kitchen there all by itself." She remembered a murder trial she had covered in Iowa in her days as a reporter, and the story began to play itself out on the stage as she gazed. Throughout her revisions, she said, she returned to look at the stage to see whether the events she was recording came to life on it. Although Glaspell later rewrote *Trifles* as a short story called "A Jury of Her Peers," the play remains her most successful and memorable work.

Cultural Context One of the main themes of this play is the contrast between the sexes in terms of their roles, rights, and responsibilities. In 1916, when *Trifles* was first produced, women were not allowed to serve on juries in most states. This circumstance was in accordance with other rights denied to women, including the right to vote, which was not ratified in all states until 1920. Unable to participate in the most basic civic functions, women largely discussed politics only among themselves and were relegated to positions of lesser status in their personal and professional lives.

Trifles (1916)

CHARACTERS

George Henderson, *county attorney*   **Mrs. Peters**
Henry Peters, *sheriff*   **Mrs. Hale**
Lewis Hale, *a neighboring farmer*

SCENE

The kitchen in the now abandoned farmhouse of John Wright, a gloomy kitchen, and left without having been put in order—unwashed pans under the sink, a loaf of bread outside the breadbox, a dish towel on the table—other signs of incompleted work. At the rear the outer door opens and the Sheriff comes in followed

*by the County Attorney and Hale. The Sheriff and Hale are men in middle life,
the County Attorney is a young man; all are much bundled up and go at once
to the stove. They are followed by two women—the Sheriff's wife first; she is a
slight wiry woman, a thin nervous face. Mrs. Hale is larger and would ordinarily
be called more comfortable looking, but she is disturbed now and looks fearfully
about as she enters. The women have come in slowly, and stand close together
near the door.*

COUNTY ATTORNEY: *(rubbing his hands)* This feels good. Come up to the
fire, ladies.

MRS. PETERS: *(after taking a step forward)* I'm not—cold.

SHERIFF: *(unbuttoning his overcoat and stepping away from the stove as if to
mark the beginning of official business)* Now, Mr. Hale, before we move
things about, you explain to Mr. Henderson just what you saw when
you came here yesterday morning.

COUNTY ATTORNEY: By the way, has anything been moved? Are things
just as you left them yesterday?

5   **SHERIFF:** *(looking about)* It's just the same. When it dropped below zero last
night I thought I'd better send Frank out this morning to make a fire
for us—no use getting pneumonia with a big case on, but I told him
not to touch anything except the stove—and you know Frank.

COUNTY ATTORNEY: Somebody should have been left here yesterday.

In this scene from the Provincetown Players' 1917 production of Susan Glaspell's *Trifles,* the
three men discuss the crime while Mrs. Peters and Mrs. Hale look on.

SHERIFF: Oh—yesterday. When I had to send Frank to Morris Center for that man who went crazy—I want you to know I had my hands full yesterday. I knew you could get back from Omaha by today and as long as I went over everything here myself—

COUNTY ATTORNEY: Well, Mr. Hale, tell just what happened when you came here yesterday morning.

HALE: Harry and I had started to town with a load of potatoes. We came along the road from my place and as I got here I said, "I'm going to see if I can't get John Wright to go in with me on a party telephone." I spoke to Wright about it once before and he put me off, saying folks talked too much anyway, and all he asked was peace and quiet—I guess you know about how much he talked himself; but I thought maybe if I went to the house and talked about it before his wife, though I said to Harry that I didn't know as what his wife wanted made much difference to John—

COUNTY ATTORNEY: Let's talk about that later, Mr. Hale. I do want to talk   10
about that, but tell now just what happened when you got to the house.

HALE: I didn't hear or see anything; I knocked at the door, and still it was all quiet inside. I knew they must be up, it was past eight o'clock. So I knocked again, and I thought I heard somebody say, "Come in." I wasn't sure, I'm not sure yet, but I opened the door—this door (*indicating the door by which the two women are still standing*) and there in that rocker—(*pointing to it*) sat Mrs. Wright.

They all look at the rocker.

COUNTY ATTORNEY: What—was she doing?

HALE: She was rockin' back and forth. She had her apron in her hand and was kind of—pleating it.

COUNTY ATTORNEY: And how did she—look?

HALE: Well, she looked queer.   15

COUNTY ATTORNEY: How do you mean—queer?

HALE: Well, as if she didn't know what she was going to do next. And kind of done up.

COUNTY ATTORNEY: How did she seem to feel about your coming?

HALE: Why, I don't think she minded—one way or other. She didn't pay much attention. I said, "How do, Mrs. Wright, it's cold, ain't it?" And she said, "Is it?"—and went on kind of pleating at her apron. Well, I was surprised; she didn't ask me to come up to the stove, or to set down, but just sat there, not even looking at me, so I said, "I want to see John." And then she—laughed. I guess you would call it a laugh. I thought of Harry and the team outside, so I said a little sharp: "Can't I see John?" "No," she says, kind o' dull like. "Ain't he home?" says I. "Yes," says she, "he's home." "Then why can't I see him?" I asked her, out of patience. "'Cause he's dead," says she. *"Dead?"* says I. She just nodded her head, not getting a bit excited, but rockin' back and forth. "Why—where is he?" says I, not knowing what to say. She just pointed upstairs—like that. (*Himself pointing to the room above.*) I got up, with the idea of going up there. I walked from there to here—then I says, "Why, what did he die of?" "He died of a rope round his neck," says she, and just went on pleatin' at her apron. Well, I went out and called Harry. I thought I might—need help. We went upstairs and there he was lyin'—

20 COUNTY ATTORNEY: I think I'd rather have you go into that upstairs, where you can point it all out. Just go on now with the rest of the story.

HALE: Well, my first thought was to get that rope off. It looked . . . (*stops, his face twitches*) . . . but Harry, he went up to him, and he said, "No, he's dead all right, and we'd better not touch anything." So we went back down stairs. She was still sitting that same way. "Has anybody been notified?" I asked. "No," says she, unconcerned. "Who did this, Mrs. Wright?" said Harry. He said it businesslike—and she stopped pleatin' of her apron. "I don't know," she says. "You don't *know?*" says Harry. "No," says she. "Weren't you sleepin' in the bed with him?" says Harry. "Yes," says she, "but I was on the inside." "Somebody slipped a rope round his neck and strangled him and you didn't wake up?" says Harry. "I didn't wake up," she said after him. We must 'a looked as if we didn't see how that could be, for after a minute she said, "I sleep sound." Harry was going to ask her more questions but I said maybe we ought to let her tell her story first to the coroner, or the sheriff, so Harry went fast as he could to Rivers' place, where there's a telephone.

COUNTY ATTORNEY: And what did Mrs. Wright do when she knew that you had gone for the coroner?

HALE: She moved from that chair to this one over here (*pointing to a small chair in the corner*) and just sat there with her hands held together and looking down. I got a feeling that I ought to make some conversation, so I said I had come in to see if John wanted to put in a telephone, and at that she started to laugh, and then she stopped and looked at me—scared. (*The County Attorney, who has had his notebook out, makes a note.*) I dunno, maybe it wasn't scared. I wouldn't like to say it was. Soon Harry got back, and then Dr. Lloyd came, and you, Mr. Peters, and so I guess that's all I know that you don't.

COUNTY ATTORNEY: (*looking around*) I guess we'll go upstairs first—and then out to the barn and around there. (*To the Sheriff.*) You're convinced that there was nothing important here—nothing that would point to any motive.

SHERIFF: Nothing here but kitchen things.   25

The County Attorney, after again looking around the kitchen, opens the door of a cupboard closet. He gets up on a chair and looks on a shelf. Pulls his hand away, sticky.

COUNTY ATTORNEY: Here's a nice mess.

The women draw nearer.

MRS. PETERS: *(to the other woman)* Oh, her fruit; it did freeze. *(To the County Attorney.)* She worried about that when it turned so cold. She said the fire'd go out and her jars would break.

SHERIFF: Well, can you beat the women! Held for murder and worryin' about her preserves.

COUNTY ATTORNEY: I guess before we're through she may have something more serious than preserves to worry about.

HALE: Well, women are used to worrying over trifles.   30

The two women move a little closer together.

COUNTY ATTORNEY: *(with the gallantry of a young politician)* And yet, for all their worries, what would we do without the ladies? *(The women do not unbend. He goes to the sink, takes a dipperful of water from the pail and pouring it into a basin, washes his hands. Starts to wipe them on the roller towel, turns it for a cleaner place.)* Dirty towels! *(Kicks his foot against the pans under the sink.)* Not much of a housekeeper, would you say, ladies?

MRS. HALE: *(stiffly)* There's a great deal of work to be done on a farm.

COUNTY ATTORNEY: To be sure. And yet *(with a little bow to her)* I know there are some Dickson county farmhouses which do not have such roller towels.

He gives it a pull to expose its full length again.

MRS. HALE: Those towels get dirty awful quick. Men's hands aren't always as clean as they might be.

COUNTY ATTORNEY: Ah, loyal to your sex, I see. But you and Mrs. Wright   35 were neighbors. I suppose you were friends, too.

MRS. HALE: *(shaking her head)* I've not seen much of her of late years. I've not been in this house—it's more than a year.

COUNTY ATTORNEY: And why was that? You didn't like her?

MRS. HALE: I liked her all well enough. Farmers' wives have their hands full, Mr. Henderson. And then—

COUNTY ATTORNEY: Yes—?

MRS. HALE: *(looking about)* It never seemed a very cheerful place.   40

COUNTY ATTORNEY: No—it's not cheerful. I shouldn't say she had the homemaking instinct.

Mrs. Hale: Well, I don't know as Wright had, either.

County Attorney: You mean that they didn't get on very well?

Mrs. Hale: No, I don't mean anything. But I don't think a place'd be any cheerfuller for John Wright's being in it.

45 County Attorney: I'd like to talk more of that a little later. I want to get the lay of things upstairs now.

He goes to the left, where three steps lead to a stair door.

Sheriff: I suppose anything Mrs. Peters does'll be all right. She was to take in some clothes for her, you know, and a few little things. We left in such a hurry yesterday.

County Attorney: Yes, but I would like to see what you take, Mrs. Peters, and keep an eye out for anything that might be of use to us.

Mrs. Peters: Yes, Mr. Henderson.

The women listen to the men's steps on the stairs, then look about the kitchen.

Mrs. Hale: I'd hate to have men coming into my kitchen, snooping around and criticizing.

She arranges the pans under sink which the County Attorney had shoved out of place.

50 Mrs. Peters: Of course it's no more than their duty.

Mrs. Hale: Duty's all right, but I guess that deputy sheriff that came out to make the fire might have got a little of this on. (*Gives the roller towel a pull.*) Wish I'd thought of that sooner. Seems mean to talk about her for not having things slicked up when she had to come away in such a hurry.

Mrs. Peters: (*who has gone to a small table in the left rear corner of the room, and lifted one end of a towel that covers a pan*) She had bread set.

Stands still.

Mrs. Hale: (*eyes fixed on a loaf of bread beside the breadbox, which is on a low shelf at the other side of the room. Moves slowly toward it.*) She was going to put this in there. (*Picks up loaf, then abruptly drops it. In a manner of returning to familiar things.*) It's a shame about her fruit. I wonder if it's all gone. (*Gets up on the chair and looks.*) I think there's some here that's all right, Mrs. Peters. Yes—here; (*holding it toward the window*) this is cherries, too. (*Looking again.*) I declare I believe that's the only one. (*Gets down, bottle in her hand. Goes to the sink and wipes it off on the outside.*) She'll feel awful bad after all her hard work in the hot weather. I remember the afternoon I put up my cherries last summer.

*She puts the bottle on the big kitchen table, center of the room. With a sigh, is about
to sit down in the rocking-chair. Before she is seated realizes what chair it is; with a
slow look at it, steps back. The chair which she has touched rocks back and forth.*

MRS. PETERS: Well, I must get those things from the front room closet.
(*She goes to the door at the right, but after looking into the other room, steps
back.*) You coming with me, Mrs. Hale? You could help me carry them.

*They go in the other room; reappear, Mrs. Peters carrying a dress and skirt, Mrs.
Hale following with a pair of shoes.*

MRS. PETERS: My, it's cold in there.   55

She puts the clothes on the big table, and hurries to the stove.

MRS. HALE: (*examining her skirt*) Wright was close. I think maybe that's
why she kept so much to herself. She didn't even belong to the Ladies
Aid. I suppose she felt she couldn't do her part, and then you don't
enjoy things when you feel shabby. She used to wear pretty clothes and
be lively, when she was Minnie Foster, one of the town girls singing in
the choir. But that—oh, that was thirty years ago. This all you was to
take in?

MRS. PETERS: She said she wanted an apron. Funny thing to want, for
there isn't much to get you dirty in jail, goodness knows. But I suppose
just to make her feel more natural. She said they was in the top drawer
in this cupboard. Yes, here. And then her little shawl that always hung
behind the door. (*Opens stair door and looks.*) Yes, here it is.

Quickly shuts door leading upstairs.

MRS. HALE: (*abruptly moving toward her*) Mrs. Peters?

MRS. PETERS: Yes, Mrs. Hale?

MRS. HALE: Do you think she did it?   60

MRS. PETERS: (*in a frightened voice*) Oh, I don't know.

MRS. HALE: Well, I don't think she did. Asking for an apron and her little
shawl. Worrying about her fruit.

MRS. PETERS: (*starts to speak, glances up, where footsteps are heard in the
room above. In a low voice.*) Mr. Peters says it looks bad for her.
Mr. Henderson is awful sarcastic in a speech and he'll make fun of her
sayin' she didn't wake up.

MRS. HALE: Well, I guess John Wright didn't wake when they was slipping
that rope under his neck.

MRS. PETERS: No, it's strange. It must have been done awful crafty and   65
still. They say it was such a—funny way to kill a man, rigging it all up
like that.

MRS. HALE: That's just what Mr. Hale said. There was a gun in the house.
He says that's what he can't understand.

Mrs. Peters: Mr. Henderson said coming out that what was needed for the case was a motive; something to show anger, or—sudden feeling.

Mrs. Hale: *(who is standing by the table)* Well, I don't see any signs of anger around here. *(She puts her hand on the dish towel which lies on the table, stands looking down at table, one half of which is clean, the other half messy.)* It's wiped to here. *(Makes a move as if to finish work, then turns and looks at loaf of bread outside the breadbox. Drops towel. In that voice of coming back to familiar things.)* Wonder how they are finding things upstairs. I hope she had it a little more red-up[1] up there. You know, it seems kind of *sneaking.* Locking her up in town and then coming out here and trying to get her own house to turn against her!

Mrs. Peters: But Mrs. Hale, the law is the law.

70   **Mrs. Hale:** I s'pose 'tis. *(Unbuttoning her coat.)* Better loosen up your things, Mrs. Peters. You won't feel them when you go out.

Mrs. Peters takes off her fur tippet, goes to hang it on hook at back of room, stands looking at the under part of the small corner table.

Mrs. Peters: She was piecing a quilt.

She brings the large sewing basket and they look at the bright pieces.

Mrs. Hale: It's log cabin pattern. Pretty, isn't it? I wonder if she was goin' to quilt it or just knot it?

Footsteps have been heard coming down the stairs. The Sheriff enters followed by Hale and the County Attorney.

Sheriff: They wonder if she was going to quilt it or just knot it!

The men laugh; the women look abashed.

County Attorney: *(rubbing his hands over the stove)* Frank's fire didn't do much up there, did it? Well, let's go out to the barn and get that cleared up.

The men go outside.

75   **Mrs. Hale:** *(resentfully)* I don't know as there's anything so strange, our takin' up our time with little things while we're waiting for them to get the evidence. *(She sits down at the big table smoothing out a block with decision.)* I don't see as it's anything to laugh about.

Mrs. Peters: *(apologetically)* Of course they've got awful important things on their minds.

---

[1]*red-up:* Spruced-up (slang).

Pulls up a chair and joins Mrs. Hale at the table.

MRS. HALE: (*examining another block*) Mrs. Peters, look at this one. Here, this is the one she was working on, and look at the sewing! All the rest of it has been so nice and even. And look at this! It's all over the place! Why, it looks as if she didn't know what she was about!

After she has said this they look at each other, then start to glance back at the door. After an instant Mrs. Hale has pulled at a knot and ripped the sewing.

MRS. PETERS: Oh, what are you doing, Mrs. Hale?

MRS. HALE: (*mildly*) Just pulling out a stitch or two that's not sewed very good. (*Threading a needle.*) Bad sewing always made me fidgety.

MRS. PETERS: (*nervously*) I don't think we ought to touch things.   80

MRS. HALE: I'll just finish up this end. (*Suddenly stopping and leaning forward.*) Mrs. Peters?

MRS. PETERS: Yes, Mrs. Hale?

MRS. HALE: What do you suppose she was so nervous about?

MRS. PETERS: Oh—I don't know. I don't know as she was nervous. I sometimes sew awful queer when I'm just tired. (*Mrs. Hale starts to say something, looks at Mrs. Peters, then goes on sewing.*) Well, I must get these things wrapped up. They may be through sooner than we think. (*Putting apron and other things together.*) I wonder where I can find a piece of paper, and string.

MRS. HALE: In that cupboard, maybe.   85

MRS. PETERS: (*looking in cupboard*) Why, here's a birdcage. (*Holds it up.*) Did she have a bird, Mrs. Hale?

MRS. HALE: Why, I don't know whether she did or not—I've not been here for so long. There was a man around last year selling canaries cheap, but I don't know as she took one; maybe she did. She used to sing real pretty herself.

MRS. PETERS: (*glancing around*) Seems funny to think of a bird here. But she must have had one, or why would she have a cage? I wonder what happened to it.

MRS. HALE: I s'pose maybe the cat got it.

MRS. PETERS: No, she didn't have a cat. She's got that feeling some people   90
have about cats—being afraid of them. My cat got in her room and she was real upset and asked me to take it out.

MRS. HALE: My sister Bessie was like that. Queer, ain't it?

MRS. PETERS: (*examining the cage*) Why, look at this door. It's broke. One hinge is pulled apart.

MRS. HALE: (*looking too*) Looks as if someone must have been rough with it.

MRS. PETERS: Why, yes.

In this scene from a 2010 production of Susan Glaspell's *Trifles,* Mrs. Peters and Mrs. Hale
discuss the discovery of a birdcage.
Prudence Katze

She brings the cage forward and puts it on the table.

95   **MRS. HALE:** I wish if they're going to find any evidence they'd be about it.
     I don't like this place.

  MRS. PETERS: But I'm awful glad you came with me, Mrs. Hale. It would be
     lonesome for me sitting here alone.

  MRS. HALE: It would, wouldn't it? *(Dropping her sewing.)* But I tell you
     what I do wish, Mrs. Peters. I wish I had come over sometimes when
     she was here. I—*(looking around the room)*—wish I had.

  MRS. PETERS: But of course you were awful busy, Mrs. Hale—your house
     and your children.

  MRS. HALE: I could've come. I stayed away because it weren't cheerful—
     and that's why I ought to have come. I—I've never liked this place.
     Maybe because it's down in a hollow and you don't see the road.
     I dunno what it is but it's a lonesome place and always was. I wish
     I had come over to see Minnie Foster sometimes. I can see now—

Shakes her head.

100   **MRS. PETERS:** Well, you mustn't reproach yourself, Mrs. Hale. Somehow
     we just don't see how it is with other folks until—something comes up.

  MRS. HALE: Not having children makes less work—but it makes a quiet
     house, and Wright out to work all day, and no company when he did
     come in. Did you know John Wright, Mrs. Peters?

Mrs. Peters: Not to know him; I've seen him in town. They say he was a good man.

Mrs. Hale: Yes—good; he didn't drink, and kept his word as well as most, I guess, and paid his debts. But he was a hard man, Mrs. Peters. Just to pass the time of day with him—(*Shivers.*) Like a raw wind that gets to the bone. (*Pauses, her eye falling on the cage.*) I should think she would 'a wanted a bird. But what do you suppose went with it?

Mrs. Peters: I don't know, unless it got sick and died.

She reaches over and swings the broken door, swings it again. Both women watch it.

Mrs. Hale: You weren't raised round here, were you? (*Mrs. Peters shakes*   105
her head.*) You didn't know—her?

Mrs. Peters: Not till they brought her yesterday.

Mrs. Hale: She—come to think of it, she was kind of like a bird herself—real sweet and pretty, but kind of timid and—fluttery. How—she—did—change. (*Silence; then as if struck by a happy thought and relieved to get back to everyday things.*) Tell you what, Mrs. Peters, why don't you take the quilt in with you? It might take up her mind.

Mrs. Peters: Why, I think that's a real nice idea, Mrs. Hale. There couldn't possibly be any objection to it, could there? Now, just what would I take? I wonder if her patches are in here—and her things.

They look in the sewing basket.

Mrs. Hale: Here's some red. I expect this has got sewing things in it. (*Brings out a fancy box.*) What a pretty box. Looks like something somebody would give you. Maybe her scissors are in here. (*Opens box. Suddenly puts her hand to her nose.*) Why—(*Mrs. Peters bends nearer, then turns her face away.*) There's something wrapped up in this piece of silk.

Mrs. Peters: Why, this isn't her scissors.   110

Mrs. Hale: (*lifting the silk*) Oh, Mrs. Peters—it's—

Mrs. Peters bends closer.

Mrs. Peters: It's the bird.

Mrs. Hale: (*jumping up*) But, Mrs. Peters—look at it! Its neck! Look at its neck! It's all—other side *to.*

Mrs. Peters: Somebody—wrung—its—neck.

Their eyes meet. A look of growing comprehension, of horror. Steps are heard outside. Mrs. Hale slips the box under quilt pieces, and sinks into her chair. Enter Sheriff and County Attorney. Mrs. Peters rises.

County Attorney: (*as one turning from serious things to little pleasantries*)   115
Well, ladies, have you decided whether she was going to quilt it or knot it?

Mrs. Peters: We think she was going to—knot it.

County Attorney: Well, that's interesting, I'm sure. *(Seeing the birdcage.)* Has the bird flown?

Mrs. Hale: *(putting more quilt pieces over the box)* We think the—cat got it.

County Attorney: *(preoccupied)* Is there a cat?

Mrs. Hale glances in a quick covert way at Mrs. Peters.

120   **Mrs. Peters:** Well, not *now*. They're superstitious, you know. They leave.

County Attorney: *(to Sheriff Peters, continuing an interrupted conversation)* No sign at all of anyone having come from the outside. Their own rope. Now let's go up again and go over it piece by piece. *(They start upstairs.)* It would have to have been someone who knew just the—

Mrs. Peters sits down. The two women sit there not looking at one another, but as if peering into something and at the same time holding back. When they talk now it is in the manner of feeling their way over strange ground, as if afraid of what they are saying, but as if they can not help saying it.

Mrs. Hale: She liked the bird. She was going to bury it in that pretty box.

Mrs. Peters: *(in a whisper)* When I was a girl—my kitten—there was a boy took a hatchet, and before my eyes—and before I could get there—(*Covers her face an instant.*) If they hadn't held me back I would have—(*catches herself, looks upstairs where steps are heard, falters weakly)*—hurt him.

Mrs. Hale: *(with a slow look around her)* I wonder how it would seem never to have had any children around. *(Pause.)* No, Wright wouldn't like the bird—a thing that sang. She used to sing. He killed that, too.

125   **Mrs. Peters:** *(moving uneasily)* We don't know who killed the bird.

Mrs. Hale: I knew John Wright.

Mrs. Peters: It was an awful thing was done in this house that night, Mrs. Hale. Killing a man while he slept, slipping a rope around his neck that choked the life out of him.

Mrs. Hale: His neck. Choked the life out of him.

Her hand goes out and rests on the birdcage.

Mrs. Peters: *(with rising voice)* We don't know who killed him. We don't know.

130   **Mrs. Hale:** *(her own feeling not interrupted)* If there'd been years and years of nothing, then a bird to sing to you, it would be awful—still, after the bird was still.

Mrs. Peters: *(something within her speaking)* I know what stillness is. When we homesteaded in Dakota, and my first baby died—after he was two years old, and me with no other then—

MRS. HALE: *(moving)* How soon do you suppose they'll be through, looking for the evidence?

MRS. PETERS: I know what stillness is. *(Pulling herself back.)* The law has got to punish crime, Mrs. Hale.

MRS. HALE: *(not as if answering that)* I wish you'd seen Minnie Foster when she wore a white dress with blue ribbons and stood up there in the choir and sang. *(A look around the room.)* Oh, I wish I'd come over here once in a while! That was a crime! That was a crime! Who's going to punish that?

MRS. PETERS: *(looking upstairs)* We mustn't—take on.   135

MRS. HALE: I might have known she needed help! I know how things can be—for women. I tell you, it's queer, Mrs. Peters. We live close together and we live far apart. We all go through the same things—it's all just a different kind of the same thing. *(Brushes her eyes; noticing the bottle of fruit, reaches out for it.)* If I was you I wouldn't tell her her fruit was gone. Tell her it *ain't*. Tell her it's all right. Take this in to prove it to her. She—she may never know whether it was broke or not.

MRS. PETERS: *(takes the bottle, looks about for something to wrap it in; takes petticoat from the clothes brought from the other room, very nervously begins winding this around the bottle. In a false voice)* My, it's a good thing the men couldn't hear us. Wouldn't they just laugh! Getting all stirred up over a little thing like a—dead canary. As if that could have anything to do with—with—wouldn't they *laugh!*

The men are heard coming down stairs.

MRS. HALE: *(under her breath)* Maybe they would—maybe they wouldn't.

COUNTY ATTORNEY: No, Peters, it's all perfectly clear except a reason for doing it. But you know juries when it comes to women. If there was some definite thing. Something to show—something to make a story about—a thing that would connect up with this strange way of doing it—

The women's eyes meet for an instant. Enter Hale from outer door.

HALE: Well, I've got the team around. Pretty cold out there.   140

COUNTY ATTORNEY: I'm going to stay here a while by myself. *(To the Sheriff.)* You can send Frank out for me, can't you? I want to go over everything. I'm not satisfied that we can't do better.

SHERIFF: Do you want to see what Mrs. Peters is going to take in?

The County Attorney goes to the table, picks up the apron, laughs.

COUNTY ATTORNEY: Oh, I guess they're not very dangerous things the ladies have picked out. *(Moves a few things about, disturbing the quilt pieces which cover the box. Steps back.)* No, Mrs. Peters doesn't need supervising. For that matter, a sheriff's wife is married to the law. Ever think of it that way, Mrs. Peters?

MRS. PETERS: Not—just that way.

145 SHERIFF: *(chuckling)* Married to the law. *(Moves toward the other room.)* I just want you to come in here a minute, George. We ought to take a look at these windows.

COUNTY ATTORNEY: *(scoffingly)* Oh, windows!

SHERIFF: We'll be right out, Mr. Hale.

Hale goes outside. The Sheriff follows the County Attorney into the other room. Then Mrs. Hale rises, hands tight together, looking intensely at Mrs. Peters, whose eyes make a slow turn, finally meeting Mrs. Hale's. A moment Mrs. Hale holds her, then her own eyes point the way to where the box is concealed. Suddenly Mrs. Peters throws back quilt pieces and tries to put the box in the bag she is wearing. It is too big. She opens box, starts to take bird out, cannot touch it, goes to pieces, stands there helpless. Sound of a knob turning in the other room. Mrs. Hale snatches the box and puts it in the pocket of her big coat. Enter County Attorney and Sheriff.

COUNTY ATTORNEY: *(facetiously)* Well, Henry, at least we found out that she was not going to quilt it. She was going to—what is it you call it, ladies?

MRS. HALE: *(her hand against her pocket)* We call it—knot it, Mr. Henderson.

*   *   *

Reading and Reacting

1. What key events have occurred before the start of the play? Why do you suppose these events are not presented in the play itself?

2. What are the "trifles" to which the title refers? How do these "trifles" advance the play's plot?

3. Glaspell's short story version of *Trifles* is called "A Jury of Her Peers." Who are Mrs. Wright's peers? What do you suppose the verdict would be if she were tried for her crime in 1916, when only men were permitted to serve on juries? If the trial were held today, do you think a jury might reach a different verdict? What would your own verdict be? Do you think Mrs. Hale and Mrs. Peters do the right thing by concealing the evidence?

4. *Trifles* is a one-act play, and all its action occurs in the Wrights' kitchen. What do you see as the advantages and disadvantages of this confined setting?

5. All background information about Mrs. Wright is provided by Mrs. Hale. Do you consider her to be a reliable source of information? Explain.

6. Mr. Hale's summary of his conversation with Mrs. Wright is the reader's only chance to hear her version of events. How might the play be different if Mrs. Wright appeared as a character?

7. How does each of the following events advance the play's action: the men's departure from the kitchen, the discovery of the quilt pieces, the discovery of the dead bird?

8. What assumptions about women do the male characters make? In what ways do the female characters support or challenge these assumptions?

9. JOURNAL ENTRY In what sense is the process of making a quilt an appropriate metaphor for the plot of *Trifles*?

10. CRITICAL PERSPECTIVE In *American Drama from the Colonial Period through World War I*, Gary A. Richardson says that in *Trifles*, Glaspell developed a new structure for her action:

> While action in the traditional sense is minimal, Glaspell is nevertheless able to rivet attention on the two women, wed the audience to their perspective, and make a compelling case for the fairness of their actions. Existing on the margins of their society, Mrs. Peters and Mrs. Hale become emotional surrogates for the jailed Minnie Wright, effectively exonerating her action as "justifiable homicide."
>
> *Trifles* is carefully crafted to match Glaspell's subject matter—the action meanders, without a clearly delineated beginning, middle, or end. . . .

Exactly how does Glaspell "rivet attention on" Mrs. Hale and Mrs. Peters? In what sense is the play's "meandering" structure "carefully crafted to match Glaspell's subject matter"?

Related Works: "I Stand Here Ironing" (p. 217), "Everyday Use" (p. 344), "The Yellow Wallpaper" (p. 434), "Harlem" (p. 577), "Daddy" (p. 589), *A Doll House* (p. 881)

HENRIK IBSEN (1828–1906), Norway's foremost dramatist, was born into a prosperous family; however, his father lost his fortune when Ibsen was six. When Ibsen was fifteen, he was apprenticed to an apothecary away from home and was permanently estranged from his family. During his apprenticeship, he studied to enter the university and wrote plays. Although he did not pass the university entrance exam, his second play, *The Warrior's Barrow* (1850), was produced by the Christiania Theatre in 1850. He began a life in the theater, writing plays and serving as artistic director of a theatrical company. Disillusioned by the public's lack of interest in theater, he left Norway, living with his wife and son in Italy and Germany between 1864 and 1891. By the time he returned to Norway, he was famous and revered. Ibsen's most notable plays include *Brand* (1865), *Peer Gynt* (1867), *A Doll House* (1879), *Ghosts* (1881), *An Enemy of the People* (1882), *The Wild Duck* (1884), *Hedda Gabler* (1890), and *When We Dead Awaken* (1899).

A Doll House marks the beginning of Ibsen's successful realist period, during which he explored the ordinary lives of small-town people—in this case, writing what he called "a

Hulton Archive/Stringer/Getty Images

modern tragedy." Ibsen based the play on a true story, which closely paralleled the main events of the play: a wife borrows money to finance a trip for an ailing husband, repayment is demanded, she forges a check and is discovered. (In the real-life story, however, the husband demanded a divorce, and the wife had a nervous breakdown and was committed to a mental institution.) The issue in *A Doll House*, he said, is that there are "two kinds of moral law, . . . one in man and a completely different one in woman. They do not understand each other. . . ." Nora and Helmer's marriage is destroyed because they cannot comprehend or accept their differences. The play begins conventionally but does not fulfill the audience's expectations for a tidy resolution; as a result, it was not a success when it was first performed. Nevertheless, the publication of *A Doll House* made Ibsen internationally famous.

Cultural Context   During the nineteenth century, the law treated women only a little better than it treated children. Women could not vote, and they were not considered able to handle their own financial affairs. A woman could not borrow money in her own name, and when she married, her finances were placed under the control of her husband. Moreover, working outside the home was out of the question for a middle-class woman. So, if a woman were to leave her husband, she was not likely to have any way of supporting herself, and she would lose the custody of her children. At the time when *A Doll House* was first performed, most viewers were offended by the way Nora spoke to her husband, and Ibsen was considered an anarchist for suggesting that a woman could leave her family in search of herself. However, Ibsen argued that he was merely asking people to look at, and think about, the social structure they supported.

A Doll House   (1879)
Translated by Rolf Fjelde

CHARACTERS

Torvald Helmer, *a lawyer*
Nora, *his wife*
Dr. Rank
Mrs. Linde
A Delivery Boy

Nils Krogstad, *a bank clerk*
The Helmers' three small children
Anne-Marie, *their nurse*
Helene, *a maid*

The action takes place in Helmer's residence.

ACT 1

A comfortable room, tastefully but not expensively furnished. A door to the right in the back wall leads to the entryway; another to the left leads to Helmer's study. Between these doors, a piano. Midway in the left-hand wall a door, and further back a window. Near the window a round table with an armchair and a small sofa. In the right-hand wall, toward the rear, a door, and nearer the foreground a porcelain stove with two armchairs and a rocking chair beside it. Between the stove and the side door, a small table. Engravings on the walls. An étagère with china figures and other small art objects; a small bookcase with richly bound books; the floor carpeted; a fire burning in the stove. It is a winter day.

A bell rings in the entryway; shortly after we hear the door being unlocked. Nora comes into the room, humming happily to herself; she is wearing street clothes and carries an armload of packages, which she puts down on the table to the right. She has left the hall door open; and through it a Delivery Boy is seen, holding a Christmas tree and a basket, which he gives to the Maid who let them in.

NORA: Hide the tree well, Helene. The children mustn't get a glimpse of it till this evening, after it's trimmed. *(To the Delivery Boy, taking out her purse.)* How much?

DELIVERY BOY: Fifty, ma'am.

NORA: There's a crown. No, keep the change. *(The Boy thanks her and leaves. Nora shuts the door. She laughs softly to herself while taking off her street things. Drawing a bag of macaroons from her pocket, she eats a couple, then steals over and listens at her husband's study door.)* Yes, he's home. *(Hums again as she moves to the table right.)*

HELMER: *(from the study)* Is that my little lark twittering out there?

NORA: *(busy opening some packages)* Yes, it is.   5

HELMER: Is that my squirrel rummaging around?

NORA: Yes!

HELMER: When did my squirrel get in?

NORA: Just now. *(Putting the macaroon bag in her pocket and wiping her mouth.)* Do come in, Torvald, and see what I've bought.

HELMER: Can't be disturbed. *(After a moment he opens the door and peers in,*   10
pen in hand.) Bought, you say? All that there? Has the little spendthrift been out throwing money around again?

NORA: Oh, but Torvald, this year we really should let ourselves go a bit. It's the first Christmas we haven't had to economize.

HELMER: But you know we can't go squandering.

NORA: Oh yes, Torvald, we can squander a little now. Can't we? Just a tiny, wee bit. Now that you've got a big salary and are going to make piles and piles of money.

HELMER: Yes—starting New Year's. But then it's a full three months till the raise comes through.

NORA: Pooh! We can borrow that long.   15

HELMER: Nora! *(Goes over and playfully takes her by the ear.)* Are your scatterbrains off again? What if today I borrowed a thousand crowns, and you squandered them over Christmas week, and then on New Year's Eve a roof tile fell on my head, and I lay there—

NORA: *(putting her hand on his mouth)* Oh! Don't say such things!

HELMER: Yes, but what if it happened—then what?

NORA: If anything so awful happened, then it just wouldn't matter if I had debts or not.

HELMER: Well, but the people I'd borrowed from?   20

NORA: Them? Who cares about them! They're strangers.

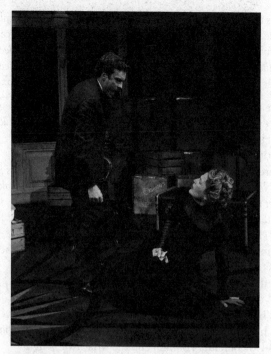

Scene from *A Doll House* with Toby Stephens (as Torvald
Helmer) and Gillian Anderson (as Nora) at The Donmar
Warehouse, London, UK in May 2009
Source: Nigel Norrington/ArenaPal/TopFoto/The Image Works

HELMER: Nora, Nora, how like a woman! No, but seriously, Nora, you know
what I think about that. No debts! Never borrow! Something of freedom's lost—and something of beauty, too—from a home that's founded
on borrowing and debt. We've made a brave stand up to now, the two
of us; and we'll go right on like that the little while we have to.

NORA: *(going toward the stove)* Yes, whatever you say, Torvald.

HELMER: *(following her)* Now, now, the little lark's wings mustn't droop.
Come on, don't be a sulky squirrel. *(Taking out his wallet.)* Nora, guess
what I have here.

25 NORA: *(turning quickly)* Money!

HELMER: There, see. *(Hands her some notes.)* Good grief, I know how costs
go up in a house at Christmastime.

NORA: Ten—twenty—thirty—forty. Oh, thank you, Torvald; I can manage no end on this.

HELMER: You really will have to.

NORA: Oh yes, I promise I will! But come here so I can show you everything I bought. And so cheap! Look, new clothes for Ivar here—and a

sword. Here a horse and a trumpet for Bob. And a doll and a doll's bed here for Emmy; they're nothing much, but she'll tear them to bits in no time anyway. And here I have dress material and handkerchiefs for the maids. Old Anne-Marie really deserves something more.

HELMER: And what's in that package there? 30

NORA: (*with a cry*) Torvald, no! You can't see that till tonight!

HELMER: I see. But tell me now, you little prodigal, what have you thought of for yourself?

NORA: For myself? Oh, I don't want anything at all.

HELMER: Of course you do. Tell me just what—within reason—you'd most like to have.

NORA: I honestly don't know. Oh, listen, Torvald— 35

HELMER: Well?

NORA: (*fumbling at his coat buttons, without looking at him*) If you want to give me something, then maybe you could—you could—

HELMER: Come on, out with it.

NORA: (*hurriedly*) You could give me money, Torvald. No more than you think you can spare; then one of these days I'll buy something with it.

HELMER: But Nora— 40

NORA: Oh, please, Torvald darling, do that! I beg you, please. Then I could hang the bills in pretty gilt paper on the Christmas tree. Wouldn't that be fun?

HELMER: What are those little birds called that always fly through their fortunes?

NORA: Oh yes, spendthrifts; I know all that. But let's do as I say, Torvald; then I'll have time to decide what I really need most. That's very sensible, isn't it?

HELMER: (*smiling*) Yes, very—that is, if you actually hung onto the money I give you, and you actually used it to buy yourself something. But it goes for the house and for all sorts of foolish things, and then I only have to lay out some more.

NORA: Oh, but Torvald— 45

HELMER: Don't deny it, my dear little Nora. (*Putting his arm around her waist.*) Spendthrifts are sweet, but they use up a frightful amount of money. It's incredible what it costs a man to feed such birds.

NORA: Oh, how can you say that! Really, I save everything I can.

HELMER: (*laughing*) Yes, that's the truth. Everything you can. But that's nothing at all.

NORA: (*humming, with a smile of quiet satisfaction*) Hm, if you only knew what expenses we larks and squirrels have, Torvald.

HELMER: You're an odd little one. Exactly the way your father was. You're 50 never at a loss for scaring up money; but the moment you have it, it runs right out through your fingers; you never know what you've done with it. Well, one takes you as you are. It's deep in your blood. Yes, these things are hereditary, Nora.

Nora: Ah, I could wish I'd inherited many of Papa's qualities.

Helmer: And I couldn't wish you anything but just what you are, my sweet little lark. But wait; it seems to me you have a very—what should I call it?—a very suspicious look today—

Nora: I do?

Helmer: You certainly do. Look me straight in the eye.

55 **Nora:** *(looking at him)* Well?

Helmer: *(shaking an admonitory finger)* Surely my sweet tooth hasn't been running riot in town today, has she?

Nora: No. Why do you imagine that?

Helmer: My sweet tooth really didn't make a little detour through the confectioner's?

Nora: No, I assure you, Torvald—

60 **Helmer:** Hasn't nibbled some pastry?

Nora: No, not at all.

Helmer: Nor even munched a macaroon or two?

Nora: No, Torvald, I assure you, really—

Helmer: There, there now. Of course I'm only joking.

65 **Nora:** *(going to the table, right)* You know I could never think of going against you.

Helmer: No, I understand that; and you *have* given me your word. *(Going over to her.)* Well, you keep your little Christmas secrets to yourself, Nora darling. I expect they'll come to light this evening, when the tree is lit.

Nora: Did you remember to ask Dr. Rank?

Helmer: No. But there's no need for that; it's assumed he'll be dining with us. All the same, I'll ask him when he stops by here this morning. I've ordered some fine wine. Nora, you can't imagine how I'm looking forward to this evening.

Nora: So am I. And what fun for the children, Torvald!

70 **Helmer:** Ah, it's so gratifying to know that one's gotten a safe, secure job, and with a comfortable salary. It's a great satisfaction, isn't it?

Nora: Oh, it's wonderful!

Helmer: Remember last Christmas? Three whole weeks before, you shut yourself in every evening till long after midnight, making flowers for the Christmas tree, and all the other decorations to surprise us. Ugh, that was the dullest time I've ever lived through.

Nora: It wasn't at all dull for me.

Helmer: *(smiling)* But the outcome *was* pretty sorry, Nora.

75 **Nora:** Oh, don't tease me with that again. How could I help it that the cat came in and tore everything to shreds.

HELMER: No, poor thing, you certainly couldn't. You wanted so much to please us all, and that's what counts. But it's just as well that the hard times are past.

NORA: Yes, it's really wonderful.

HELMER: Now I don't have to sit here alone, boring myself, and you don't have to tire your precious eyes and your fair little delicate hands—

NORA: (*clapping her hands*) No, is it really true, Torvald, I don't have to? Oh, how wonderfully lovely to hear! (*Taking his arm.*) Now I'll tell you just how I've thought we should plan things. Right after Christmas— (*The doorbell rings.*) Oh, the bell. (*Straightening the room up a bit.*) Somebody would have to come. What a bore!

HELMER: I'm not at home to visitors, don't forget.   80

MAID: (*from the hall doorway*) Ma'am, a lady to see you—

NORA: All right, let her come in.

MAID: (*to Helmer*) And the doctor's just come too.

HELMER: Did he go right to my study?

MAID: Yes, he did.   85

Helmer goes into his room. The Maid shows in Mrs. Linde, dressed in traveling clothes, and shuts the door after her.

MRS. LINDE: (*in a dispirited and somewhat hesitant voice*) Hello, Nora.

NORA: (*uncertain*) Hello—

MRS. LINDE: You don't recognize me.

NORA: No, I don't know—but wait, I think—(*Exclaiming.*) What! Kristine! Is it really you?

MRS. LINDE: Yes, it's me.   90

NORA: Kristine! To think I didn't recognize you. But then, how could I? (*More quietly.*) How you've changed, Kristine!

MRS. LINDE: Yes, no doubt I have. In nine—ten long years.

NORA: Is it so long since we met! Yes, it's all of that. Oh, these last eight years have been a happy time, believe me. And so now you've come in to town, too. Made the long trip in the winter. That took courage.

MRS. LINDE: I just got here by ship this morning.

NORA: To enjoy yourself over Christmas, of course. Oh, how lovely! Yes,   95
enjoy ourselves, we'll do that. But take your coat off. You're not still cold? (*Helping her.*) There now, let's get cozy here by the stove. No, the easy chair there! I'll take the rocker here. (*Seizing her hands.*) Yes, now you have your old look again; it was only in that first moment. You're a bit more pale, Kristine—and maybe a bit thinner.

MRS. LINDE: And much, much older, Nora.

NORA: Yes, perhaps a bit older; a tiny, tiny bit; not much at all. (*Stopping short; suddenly serious.*) Oh, but thoughtless me, to sit here, chattering away. Sweet, good Kristine, can you forgive me?

MRS. LINDE: What do you mean, Nora?

NORA: (*softly*) Poor Kristine, you've become a widow.

100 MRS. LINDE: Yes, three years ago.

NORA: Oh, I knew it, of course: I read it in the papers. Oh, Kristine, you must believe me; I often thought of writing you then, but I kept postponing it, and something always interfered.

MRS. LINDE: Nora dear, I understand completely.

NORA: No, it was awful of me, Kristine. You poor thing, how much you must have gone through. And he left you nothing?

MRS. LINDE: No.

105 NORA: And no children?

MRS. LINDE: No.

NORA: Nothing at all, then?

MRS. LINDE: Not even a sense of loss to feed on.

NORA: (*looking incredulously at her*) But Kristine, how could that be?

110 MRS. LINDE: (*smiling wearily and smoothing her hair*) Oh, sometimes it happens, Nora.

NORA: So completely alone. How terribly hard that must be for you. I have three lovely children. You can't see them now; they're out with the maid. But now you must tell me everything—

MRS. LINDE: No, no, no, tell me about yourself.

NORA: No, you begin. Today I don't want to be selfish. I want to think only of you today. But there *is* something I must tell you. Did you hear of the wonderful luck we had recently?

MRS. LINDE: No, what's that?

115 NORA: My husband's been made manager in the bank, just think!

MRS. LINDE: Your husband? How marvelous!

NORA: Isn't it? Being a lawyer is such an uncertain living, you know, especially if one won't touch any cases that aren't clean and decent. And of course Torvald would never do that, and I'm with him completely there. Oh, we're simply delighted, believe me! He'll join the bank right after New Year's and start getting a huge salary and lots of commissions. From now on we can live quite differently—just as we want. Oh, Kristine, I feel so light and happy! Won't it be lovely to have stacks of money and not a care in the world?

MRS. LINDE: Well, anyway, it would be lovely to have enough for necessities.

NORA: No, not just for necessities, but stacks and stacks of money!

120 MRS. LINDE: (*smiling*) Nora, Nora, aren't you sensible yet? Back in school you were such a free spender.

NORA: (*with a quiet laugh*) Yes, that's what Torvald still says. (*Shaking her finger.*) But "Nora, Nora" isn't as silly as you all think. Really, we've been in no position for me to go squandering. We've had to work, both of us.

MRS. LINDE: You too?

NORA: Yes, at odd jobs—needlework, crocheting, embroidery, and such—(*casually*) and other things too. You remember that Torvald left the department when we were married? There was no chance of promotion in his office, and of course he needed to earn more money. But that first year he drove himself terribly. He took on all kinds of extra work that kept him going morning and night. It wore him down, and then he fell deathly ill. The doctors said it was essential for him to travel south.

MRS. LINDE: Yes, didn't you spend a whole year in Italy?

NORA: That's right. It wasn't easy to get away, you know. Ivar had just   125
been born. But of course we had to go. Oh, that was a beautiful trip, and it saved Torvald's life. But it cost a frightful sum, Kristine.

MRS. LINDE: I can well imagine.

NORA: Four thousand, eight hundred crowns it cost. That's really a lot of money.

MRS. LINDE: But it's lucky you had it when you needed it.

NORA: Well, as it was, we got it from Papa.

MRS. LINDE: I see. It was just about the time your father died.   130

NORA: Yes, just about then. And, you know, I couldn't make that trip out to nurse him. I had to stay here, expecting Ivar any moment, and with my poor sick Torvald to care for. Dearest Papa, I never saw him again, Kristine. Oh, that was the worst time I've known in all my marriage.

MRS. LINDE: I know how you loved him. And then you went off to Italy?

NORA: Yes. We had the means now, and the doctors urged us. So we left a month after.

MRS. LINDE: And your husband came back completely cured?

NORA: Sound as a drum!   135

MRS. LINDE: But—the doctor?

NORA: Who?

MRS. LINDE: I thought the maid said he was a doctor, the man who came in with me.

NORA: Yes, that was Dr. Rank—but he's not making a sick call. He's our closest friend, and he stops by at least once a day. No, Torvald hasn't had a sick moment since, and the children are fit and strong, and I am, too. (*Jumping up and clapping her hands.*) Oh, dear God, Kristine, what a lovely thing to live and be happy! But how disgusting of me—I'm talking of nothing but my own affairs. (*Sits on a stool close by Kristine, arms resting across her knees.*) Oh, don't be angry with me! Tell me, is it really true that you weren't in love with your husband? Why did you marry him, then?

MRS. LINDE: My mother was still alive, but bedridden and helpless—and   140
I had my two younger brothers to look after. In all conscience, I didn't think I could turn him down.

NORA: No, you were right there. But was he rich at the time?

MRS. LINDE: He was very well off, I'd say. But the business was shaky, Nora. When he died, it all fell apart, and nothing was left.

NORA: And then—?

MRS. LINDE: Yes, so I had to scrape up a living with a little shop and a little teaching and whatever else I could find. The last three years have been like one endless workday without a rest for me. Now it's over, Nora. My poor mother doesn't need me, for she's passed on. Nor the boys, either; they're working now and can take care of themselves.

145 NORA: How free you must feel—

MRS. LINDE: No—only unspeakably empty. Nothing to live for now. (*Standing up anxiously.*) That's why I couldn't take it any longer out in that desolate hole. Maybe here it'll be easier to find something to do and keep my mind occupied. If I could only be lucky enough to get a steady job, some office work—

NORA: Oh, but Kristine, that's so dreadfully tiring, and you already look so tired. It would be much better for you if you could go off to a bathing resort.

MRS. LINDE: (*going toward the window*) I have no father to give me travel money, Nora.

NORA: (*rising*) Oh, don't be angry with me.

150 MRS. LINDE: (*going to her*) Nora dear, don't you be angry with me. The worst of my kind of situation is all the bitterness that's stored away. No one to work for, and yet you're always having to snap up your opportunities. You have to live; and so you grow selfish. When you told me the happy change in your lot, do you know I was delighted less for your sakes than for mine?

NORA: How so? Oh, I see. You think Torvald could do something for you.

MRS. LINDE: Yes, that's what I thought.

NORA: And he will, Kristine! Just leave it to me; I'll bring it up so delicately—find something attractive to humor him with. Oh, I'm so eager to help you.

MRS. LINDE: How very kind of you, Nora, to be so concerned over me— doubly kind, considering you really know so little of life's burdens yourself.

155 NORA: I—? I know so little—?

MRS. LINDE: (*smiling*) Well my heavens—a little needlework and such— Nora, you're just a child.

NORA: (*tossing her head and pacing the floor*) You don't have to act so superior.

MRS. LINDE: Oh?

NORA: You're just like the others. You all think I'm incapable of anything serious—

MRS. LINDE: Come now—   160
NORA: That I've never had to face the raw world.
MRS. LINDE: Nora dear, you've just been telling me all your troubles.
NORA: Hm! Trivial! *(Quietly.)* I haven't told you the big thing.
MRS. LINDE: Big thing? What do you mean?
NORA: You look down on me so, Kristine, but you shouldn't. You're proud   165
that you worked so long and hard for your mother.
MRS. LINDE: I don't look down on a soul. But it *is* true: I'm proud—and
happy, too—to think it was given to me to make my mother's last days
almost free of care.
NORA: And you're also proud thinking of what you've done for your
brothers.
MRS. LINDE: I feel I've a right to be.
NORA: I agree. But listen to this, Kristine—I've also got something to be
proud and happy for.
MRS. LINDE: I don't doubt it. But whatever do you mean?   170
NORA: Not so loud. What if Torvald heard! He mustn't, not for anything
in the world. Nobody must know, Kristine. No one but you.
MRS. LINDE: But what is it, then?
NORA: Come here. *(Drawing her down beside her on the sofa.)* It's true—I've
also got something to be proud and happy for. I'm the one who saved
Torvald's life.
MRS. LINDE: Saved—? Saved how?
NORA: I told you about the trip to Italy. Torvald never would have lived if   175
he hadn't gone south—
MRS. LINDE: Of course; your father gave you the means—
NORA: *(smiling)* That's what Torvald and all the rest think, but—
MRS. LINDE: But—?
NORA: Papa didn't give us a pin. I was the one who raised the money.
MRS. LINDE: You? That whole amount?   180
NORA: Four thousand, eight hundred crowns. What do you say to that?
MRS. LINDE: But Nora, how was it possible? Did you win the lottery?
NORA: *(disdainfully)* The lottery? Pooh! No art to that.
MRS. LINDE: But where did you get it from then?
NORA: *(humming, with a mysterious smile)* Hmm, tra-la-la-la.   185
MRS. LINDE: Because you couldn't have borrowed it.
NORA: No? Why not?
MRS. LINDE: A wife can't borrow without her husband's consent.
NORA: *(tossing her head)* Oh, but a wife with a little business sense, a wife
who knows how to manage—
MRS. LINDE: Nora, I simply don't understand—   190
NORA: You don't have to. Whoever said I *borrowed* the money? I could
have gotten it other ways. *(Throwing herself back on the sofa.)* I could

have gotten it from some admirer or other. After all, a girl with my ravishing appeal—

MRS. LINDE: You lunatic.

NORA: I'll bet you're eaten up with curiosity, Kristine.

MRS. LINDE: Now listen here, Nora—you haven't done something indiscreet?

195 NORA: (*sitting up again*) Is it indiscreet to save your husband's life?

MRS. LINDE: I think it's indiscreet that without his knowledge you—

NORA: But that's the point: he mustn't know! My Lord, can't you understand? He mustn't ever know the close call he had. It was to *me* the doctors came to say his life was in danger—that nothing could save him but a stay in the south. Didn't I try strategy then! I began talking about how lovely it would be for me to travel abroad like other young wives; I begged and I cried; I told him please to remember my condition, to be kind and indulge me; and then I dropped a hint that he could easily take out a loan. But at that, Kristine, he nearly exploded. He said I was frivolous, and it was his duty as man of the house not to indulge me in whims and fancies—as I think he called them. Aha, I thought, now you'll just have to be saved—and that's when I saw my chance.

MRS. LINDE: And your father never told Torvald the money wasn't from him?

NORA: No, never. Papa died right about then. I'd considered bringing him into my secret and begging him never to tell. But he was too sick at the time—and then, sadly, it didn't matter.

200 MRS. LINDE: And you've never confided in your husband since?

NORA: For heaven's sake, no! Are you serious? He's so strict on that subject. Besides—Torvald, with all his masculine pride—how painfully humiliating for him if he ever found out he was in debt to me. That would just ruin our relationship. Our beautiful, happy home would never be the same.

MRS. LINDE: Won't you ever tell him?

NORA: (*thoughtfully, half smiling*) Yes—maybe sometime, years from now, when I'm no longer so attractive. Don't laugh! I only mean when Torvald loves me less than now, when he stops enjoying my dancing and dressing up and reciting for him. Then it might be wise to have something in reserve—(*Breaking off.*) How ridiculous! That'll never happen—Well, Kristine, what do you think of my big secret? I'm capable of something too, hm? You can imagine, of course, how this thing hangs over me. It really hasn't been easy meeting the payments on time. In the business world there's what they call quarterly interest and what they call amortization, and these are always so terribly hard to manage. I've had to skimp a little here and there, wherever I could, you know. I could hardly spare anything from my house allowance, because Torvald has to live well. I couldn't let the children go poorly dressed; whatever I got for them, I felt I had to use up completely— the darlings!

MRS. LINDE: Poor Nora, so it had to come out of your own budget, then?

NORA: Yes, of course. But I was the one most responsible, too. Every time   205 Torvald gave me money for new clothes and such, I never used more than half; always bought the simplest, cheapest outfits. It was a godsend that everything looks so well on me that Torvald never noticed. But it did weigh me down at times, Kristine. It *is* such a joy to wear fine things. You understand.

MRS. LINDE: Oh, of course.

NORA: And then I found other ways of making money. Last winter I was lucky enough to get a lot of copying to do. I locked myself in and sat writing every evening till late in the night. Ah, I was tired so often, dead tired. But still it was wonderful fun, sitting and working like that, earning money. It was almost like being a man.

MRS. LINDE: But how much have you paid off this way so far?

NORA: That's hard to say, exactly. These accounts, you know, aren't easy to figure. I only know that I've paid out all I could scrape together. Time and again I haven't known where to turn. (*Smiling.*) Then I'd sit here dreaming of a rich old gentleman who had fallen in love with me—

MRS. LINDE: What! Who is he?   210

NORA: Oh, really! And that he'd died, and when his will was opened, there in big letters it said, "All my fortune shall be paid over in cash, immediately, to that enchanting Mrs. Nora Helmer."

MRS. LINDE: But Nora dear—who *was* this gentleman?

NORA: Good grief, can't you understand? The old man never existed; that was only something I'd dream up time and again whenever I was at my wits' end for money. But it makes no difference now; the old fossil can go where he pleases for all I care; I don't need him or his will— because now I'm free. (*Jumping up.*) Oh, how lovely to think of that, Kristine! Carefree! To know you're carefree, utterly carefree; to be able to romp and play with the children, and to keep up a beautiful, charming home—everything just the way Torvald likes it! And think, spring is coming, with big blue skies. Maybe we can travel a little then. Maybe I'll see the ocean again. Oh yes, it *is* so marvelous to live and be happy!

The front doorbell rings.

MRS. LINDE: (*rising*) There's the bell. It's probably best that I go.

NORA: No, stay. No one's expected. It must be for Torvald.   215

MAID: (*from the hall doorway*) Excuse me, ma'am—there's a gentleman here to see Mr. Helmer, but I didn't know—since the doctor's with him—

NORA: Who is the gentleman?

KROGSTAD: (*from the doorway*) It's me, Mrs. Helmer.

Mrs. Linde starts and turns away toward the window.

NORA: (*stepping toward him, tense, her voice a whisper*) You? What is it? Why do you want to speak to my husband?

220 KROGSTAD: Bank business—after a fashion. I have a small job in the investment bank, and I hear now your husband is going to be our chief—

NORA: In other words, it's—

KROGSTAD: Just dry business, Mrs. Helmer. Nothing but that.

NORA: Yes, then please be good enough to step into the study. (*She nods indifferently as she sees him out by the hall door, then returns and begins stirring up the stove.*)

MRS. LINDE: Nora—who was that man?

225 NORA: That was a Mr. Krogstad—a lawyer.

MRS. LINDE: Then it really was him.

NORA: Do you know that person?

MRS. LINDE: I did once—many years ago. For a time he was a law clerk in our town.

NORA: Yes, he's been that.

230 MRS. LINDE: How he's changed.

NORA: I understand he had a very unhappy marriage.

MRS. LINDE: He's a widower now.

NORA: With a number of children. There now, it's burning. (*She closes the stove door and moves the rocker a bit to one side.*)

MRS. LINDE: They say he has a hand in all kinds of business.

235 NORA: Oh? That may be true: I wouldn't know. But let's not think about business. It's so dull.

Dr. Rank enters from Helmer's study.

RANK: (*still in the doorway*) No, no, really—I don't want to intrude, I'd just as soon talk a little while with your wife. (*Shuts the door, then notices Mrs. Linde.*) Oh, beg pardon. I'm intruding here too.

NORA: No, not at all. (*Introducing him.*) Dr. Rank, Mrs. Linde.

RANK: Well now, that's a name much heard in this house. I believe I passed the lady on the stairs as I came.

MRS. LINDE: Yes, I take the stairs very slowly. They're rather hard on me.

240 RANK: Uh-hm, some touch of internal weakness?

MRS. LINDE: More overexertion, I'd say.

RANK: Nothing else? Then you're probably here in town to rest up in a round of parties?

MRS. LINDE: I'm here to look for work.

RANK: Is that the best cure for overexertion?

MRS. LINDE: One has to live, Doctor.   245

RANK: Yes, there's a common prejudice to that effect.

NORA: Oh, come on, Dr. Rank—you really do want to live yourself.

RANK: Yes, I really do. Wretched as I am, I'll gladly prolong my torment indefinitely. All my patients feel like that. And it's quite the same, too, with the morally sick. Right at this moment there's one of those moral invalids in there with Helmer—

MRS. LINDE: (softly) Ah!

NORA: Who do you mean?   250

RANK: Oh, it's a lawyer, Krogstad, a type you wouldn't know. His character is rotten to the root—but even he began chattering all-importantly about how he had to live.

NORA: Oh? What did he want to talk to Torvald about?

RANK: I really don't know. I only heard something about the bank.

NORA: I didn't know that Krog—that this man Krogstad had anything to do with the bank.

RANK: Yes, he's gotten some kind of berth down there. (To Mrs. Linde.)   255
I don't know if you also have, in your neck of the woods, a type of person who scuttles about breathlessly, sniffing out hints of moral corruption, and then maneuvers his victim into some sort of key position where he can keep an eye on him. It's the healthy these days that are out in the cold.

MRS. LINDE: All the same, it's the sick who most need to be taken in.

RANK: (with a shrug) Yes, there we have it. That's the concept that's turning society into a sanatorium.

Nora, lost in her thoughts, breaks out into quiet laughter and claps her hands.

RANK: Why do you laugh at that? Do you have any real idea of what society is?

NORA: What do I care about dreary old society? I was laughing at something quite different—something terribly funny. Tell me, Doctor—is everyone who works in the bank dependent now on Torvald?

RANK: Is that what you find so terribly funny?   260

NORA: (smiling and humming) Never mind, never mind! (Pacing the floor.)
Yes, that's really immensely amusing: that we—that Torvald has so much power now over all those people. (Taking the bag out of her pocket.) Dr. Rank, a little macaroon on that?

RANK: See here, macaroons! I thought they were contraband here.

NORA: Yes, but these are some that Kristine gave me.

MRS. LINDE: What? I—?

NORA: Now, now, don't be afraid. You couldn't possibly know that   265
Torvald had forbidden them. You see, he's worried they'll ruin my

teeth. But hmp! Just this once! Isn't that so, Dr. Rank? Help yourself!
(*Puts a macaroon in his mouth.*) And you too, Kristine. And I'll also
have one, only a little one—or two, at the most. (*Walking about again.*)
Now I'm really tremendously happy. Now there's just one last thing in
the world that I have an enormous desire to do.

RANK: Well! And what's that?

NORA: It's something I have such a consuming desire to say so Torvald
could hear.

RANK: And why can't you say it?

NORA: I don't dare. It's quite shocking.

270 MRS. LINDE: Shocking?

RANK: Well, then it isn't advisable. But in front of us you certainly can.
What do you have such a desire to say so Torvald could hear?

NORA: I have such a huge desire to say—to hell and be damned!

RANK: Are you crazy?

MRS. LINDE: My goodness, Nora!

275 RANK: Go on, say it. Here he is.

NORA: (*hiding the macaroon bag*) Shh, shh, shh!

Helmer comes in from his study, hat in hand, overcoat over his arm.

NORA: (*going toward him*) Well, Torvald dear, are you through with him?

HELMER: Yes, he just left.

NORA: Let me introduce you—this is Kristine, who's arrived here in town.

280 HELMER: Kristine—? I'm sorry, but I don't know—

NORA: Mrs. Linde, Torvald dear. Mrs. Kristine Linde.

HELMER: Of course. A childhood friend of my wife's, no doubt?

MRS. LINDE: Yes, we knew each other in those days.

NORA: And just think, she made the long trip down here in order to talk
with you.

285 HELMER: What's this?

MRS. LINDE: Well, not exactly—

NORA: You see, Kristine is remarkably clever in office work, and so she's
terribly eager to come under a capable man's supervision and add more
to what she already knows—

HELMER: Very wise, Mrs. Linde.

NORA: And then when she heard that you'd become a bank manager—
the story was wired out to the papers—then she came in as fast as she
could and—Really, Torvald, for my sake you can do a little something
for Kristine, can't you?

290 HELMER: Yes, it's not at all impossible. Mrs. Linde, I suppose you're a
widow?

MRS. LINDE: Yes.

HELMER: Any experience in office work?

Mrs. Linde: Yes, a good deal.

Helmer: Well, it's quite likely that I can make an opening for you—

Nora: (*clapping her hands*) You see, you see!   295

Helmer: You've come at a lucky moment, Mrs. Linde.

Mrs. Linde: Oh, how can I thank you?

Helmer: Not necessary. (*Putting his overcoat on.*) But today you'll have to excuse me—

Rank: Wait, I'll go with you. (*He fetches his coat from the hall and warms it at the stove.*)

Nora: Don't stay out long, dear.   300

Helmer: An hour; no more.

Nora: Are you going too, Kristine?

Mrs. Linde: (*putting on her winter garments*) Yes, I have to see about a room now.

Helmer: Then perhaps we can all walk together.

Nora: (*helping her*) What a shame we're so cramped here, but it's quite   305
impossible for us to—

Mrs. Linde: Oh, don't even think of it! Good-bye, Nora dear, and thanks for everything.

Nora: Good-bye for now. Of course you'll be back this evening. And you too, Dr. Rank. What? If you're well enough? Oh, you've got to be! Wrap up tight now.

In a ripple of small talk the company moves out into the hall; children's voices are heard outside on the steps.

Nora: There they are! There they are! (*She runs to open the door. The children come in with their nurse, Anne-Marie.*) Come in, come in! (*Bends down and kisses them.*) Oh, you darlings—! Look at them, Kristine. Aren't they lovely!

Rank: No loitering in the draft here.

Helmer: Come, Mrs. Linde—this place is unbearable now for anyone but   310
mothers.

Dr. Rank, Helmer, and Mrs. Linde go down the stairs. Anne-Marie goes into the living room with the children. Nora follows, after closing the hall door.

Nora: How fresh and strong you look. Oh, such red cheeks you have! Like apples and roses. (*The children interrupt her throughout the following.*) And it was so much fun? That's wonderful. Really? You pulled both Emmy and Bob on the sled? Imagine, all together! Yes, you're a clever boy, Ivar. Oh, let me hold her a bit, Anne-Marie. My sweet little doll baby! (*Takes the smallest from the nurse and dances with her.*) Yes, yes, Mama will dance with Bob as well. What? Did you throw snowballs? Oh, if I'd only been there! No, don't bother, Anne-Marie—I'll undress them myself. Oh yes, let me. It's such fun. Go in and rest; you look half frozen. There's hot coffee waiting for you on the stove. (*The nurse goes into the room to the left. Nora takes the children's winter things off, throwing them about, while the children talk to her all at once.*) Is that so? A big dog chased you? But it didn't bite? No, dogs never bite little, lovely doll babies. Don't peek in the packages, Ivar! What is it? Yes, wouldn't you like to know. No, no, it's an ugly something. Well? Shall we play? What shall we play? Hide-and-seek? Yes, let's play hide-and-seek. Bob must hide first. I must? Yes, let me hide first. (*Laughing and shouting, she and the children play in and out of the living room and the adjoining room to the right. At last Nora hides under the table. The children come storming in, search, but cannot find her, then hear her muffled laughter, dash over to the table, lift the cloth up and find her. Wild shouting. She creeps forward as if to scare them. More shouts. Meanwhile, a knock at the hall door; no one has noticed it. Now the door half opens, and Krogstad appears. He waits a moment; the game goes on.*)

KROGSTAD: Beg pardon, Mrs. Helmer—

NORA: (*with a strangled cry, turning and scrambling to her knees*) Oh! What do you want?

KROGSTAD: Excuse me. The outer door was ajar; it must be someone forgot to shut it—

315 NORA: (*rising*) My husband isn't home, Mr. Krogstad.

KROGSTAD: I know that.

NORA: Yes—then what do you want here?

KROGSTAD: A word with you.

NORA: With—? (*To the children, quietly.*) Go in to Anne-Marie. What? No, the strange man won't hurt Mama. When he's gone, we'll play some more. (*She leads the children into the room to the left and shuts the door after them. Then, tense and nervous.*) You want to speak to me?

320 KROGSTAD: Yes, I want to.

NORA: Today? But it's not yet the first of the month—

KROGSTAD: No, it's Christmas Eve. It's going to be up to you how merry a Christmas you have.

NORA: What is it you want? Today I absolutely can't—

KROGSTAD: We won't talk about that till later. This is something else. You do have a moment to spare, I suppose?

325 NORA: Oh yes, of course—I do, except—

KROGSTAD: Good. I was sitting over at Olsen's Restaurant when I saw your husband go down the street—

NORA: Yes?

KROGSTAD: With a lady.

NORA: Yes. So?

330 KROGSTAD: If you'll pardon my asking: wasn't that lady a Mrs. Linde?

NORA: Yes.

KROGSTAD: Just now come into town?

NORA: Yes, today.

KROGSTAD: She's a good friend of yours?

NORA: Yes, she is. But I don't see—   335

KROGSTAD: I also knew her once.

NORA: I'm aware of that.

KROGSTAD: Oh? You know all about it. I thought so. Well, then let me ask
you short and sweet: is Mrs. Linde getting a job in the bank?

NORA: What makes you think you can cross-examine me, Mr. Krogstad—
you, one of my husband's employees? But since you ask, you might as
well know—yes, Mrs. Linde's going to be taken on at the bank. And
I'm the one who spoke for her, Mr. Krogstad. Now you know.

KROGSTAD: So I guessed right.   340

NORA: (pacing up and down) Oh, one does have a tiny bit of influence,
I should hope. Just because I am a woman, don't think it means that—
When one has a subordinate position, Mr. Krogstad, one really ought
to be careful about pushing somebody who—hm—

KROGSTAD: Who has influence?

NORA: That's right.

KROGSTAD: (in a different tone) Mrs. Helmer, would you be good enough to
use your influence on my behalf?

NORA: What? What do you mean?   345

KROGSTAD: Would you please make sure that I keep my subordinate position in the bank?

NORA: What does that mean? Who's thinking of taking away your position?

KROGSTAD: Oh, don't play the innocent with me. I'm quite aware that
your friend would hardly relish the chance of running into me again;
and I'm also aware now whom I can thank for being turned out.

NORA: But I promise you—

KROGSTAD: Yes, yes, yes, to the point: there's still time, and I'm advising   350
you to use your influence to prevent it.

NORA: But Mr. Krogstad, I have absolutely no influence.

KROGSTAD: You haven't? I thought you were just saying—

NORA: You shouldn't take me so literally. I! How can you believe that
I have any such influence over my husband?

KROGSTAD: Oh, I've known your husband from our student days. I don't
think the great bank manager's more steadfast than any other married
man.

NORA: You speak insolently about my husband, and I'll show you the door.   355

KROGSTAD: The lady has spirit.

NORA: I'm not afraid of you any longer. After New Year's, I'll soon be done
with the whole business.

KROGSTAD: *(restraining himself)* Now listen to me, Mrs. Helmer. If necessary, I'll fight for my little job in the bank as if it were life itself.

NORA: Yes, so it seems.

360 KROGSTAD: It's not just a matter of income; that's the least of it. It's something else—All right, out with it! Look, this is the thing. You know, just like all the others, of course, that once, a good many years ago, I did something rather rash.

NORA: I've heard rumors to that effect.

KROGSTAD: The case never got into court; but all the same, every door was closed in my face from then on. So I took up those various activities you know about. I had to grab hold somewhere; and I dare say I haven't been among the worst. But now I want to drop all that. My boys are growing up. For their sakes, I'll have to win back as much respect as possible here in town. That job in the bank was like the first rung in my ladder. And now your husband wants to kick me right back down in the mud again.

NORA: But for heaven's sake, Mr. Krogstad, it's simply not in my power to help you.

KROGSTAD: That's because you haven't the will to—but I have the means to make you.

365 NORA: You certainly won't tell my husband that I owe you money?

KROGSTAD: Hm—what if I told him that?

NORA: That would be shameful of you. *(Nearly in tears.)* This secret—my joy and my pride—that he should learn it in such a crude and disgusting way—learn it from you. You'd expose me to the most horrible unpleasantness—

KROGSTAD: Only unpleasantness?

NORA: *(vehemently)* But go on and try. It'll turn out the worse for you, because then my husband will really see what a crook you are, and then you'll *never* be able to hold your job.

370 KROGSTAD: I asked if it was just domestic unpleasantness you were afraid of.

NORA: If my husband finds out, then of course he'll pay what I owe at once, and then we'd be through with you for good.

KROGSTAD: *(a step closer)* Listen, Mrs. Helmer—you've either got a very bad memory, or else no head at all for business. I'd better put you a little more in touch with the facts.

NORA: What do you mean?

KROGSTAD: When your husband was sick, you came to me for a loan of four thousand, eight hundred crowns.

375 NORA: Where else could I go?

KROGSTAD: I promised to get you that sum—

NORA: And you got it.

KROGSTAD: I promised to get you that sum, on certain conditions. You were so involved in your husband's illness, and so eager to finance your trip, that I guess you didn't think out all the details. It might just be a good idea to remind you. I promised you the money on the strength of a note I drew up.

NORA: Yes, and that I signed.

KROGSTAD: Right. But at the bottom I added some lines for your father to   380
guarantee the loan. He was supposed to sign down there.

NORA: Supposed to? He did sign.

KROGSTAD: I left the date blank. In other words, your father would have dated his signature himself. Do you remember that?

NORA: Yes, I think—

KROGSTAD: Then I gave you the note for you to mail to your father. Isn't that so?

NORA: Yes.   385

KROGSTAD: And naturally you sent it at once—because only some five, six days later you brought me the note, properly signed. And with that, the money was yours.

NORA: Well, then; I've made my payments regularly, haven't I?

KROGSTAD: More or less. But—getting back to the point—those were hard times for you then, Mrs. Helmer.

NORA: Yes, they were.

KROGSTAD: Your father was very ill, I believe.   390

NORA: He was near the end.

KROGSTAD: He died soon after?

NORA: Yes.

KROGSTAD: Tell me, Mrs. Helmer, do you happen to recall the date of your father's death? The day of the month, I mean.

NORA: Papa died the twenty-ninth of September.   395

KROGSTAD: That's quite correct; I've already looked into that. And now we come to a curious thing—(*taking out a paper*) which I simply cannot comprehend.

NORA: Curious thing? I don't know—

KROGSTAD: This is the curious thing: that your father co-signed the note for your loan three days after his death.

NORA: How—? I don't understand.

KROGSTAD: Your father died the twenty-ninth of September. But look.   400
Here your father dated his signature October second. Isn't that curious, Mrs. Helmer? (*Nora is silent.*) Can you explain it to me? (*Nora remains silent.*) It's also remarkable that the words "October second" and the year aren't written in your father's hand, but rather in one that I think I know. Well, it's easy to understand. Your father forgot perhaps to date his signature, and then someone or other added it, a bit sloppily, before anyone knew of his death. There's nothing wrong in that. It all comes down to the signature. And there's no question about *that*,

Mrs. Helmer. It really *was* your father who signed his own name here, wasn't it?

NORA: *(after a short silence, throwing her head back and looking squarely at him)* No, it wasn't. I signed Papa's name.

KROGSTAD: Wait, now—are you fully aware that this is a dangerous confession?

NORA: Why? You'll soon get your money.

KROGSTAD: Let me ask you a question—why didn't you send the paper to your father?

405 NORA: That was impossible. Papa was so sick. If I'd asked him for his signature, I also would have had to tell him what the money was for. But I couldn't tell him, sick as he was, that my husband's life was in danger. That was just impossible.

KROGSTAD: Then it would have been better if you'd given up the trip abroad.

NORA: I couldn't possibly. The trip was to save my husband's life. I couldn't give that up.

KROGSTAD: But didn't you ever consider that this was a fraud against me?

NORA: I couldn't let myself be bothered by that. You weren't any concern of mine. I couldn't stand you, with all those cold complications you made, even though you knew how badly off my husband was.

410 KROGSTAD: Mrs. Helmer, obviously you haven't the vaguest idea of what you've involved yourself in. But I can tell you this: it was nothing more and nothing worse than I once did—and it wrecked my whole reputation.

NORA: You? Do you expect me to believe that you ever acted bravely to save your wife's life?

KROGSTAD: Laws don't inquire into motives.

NORA: Then they must be very poor laws.

KROGSTAD: Poor or not—if I introduce this paper in court, you'll be judged according to law.

415 NORA: This I refuse to believe. A daughter hasn't a right to protect her dying father from anxiety and care? A wife hasn't a right to save her husband's life? I don't know much about laws, but I'm sure that somewhere in the books these things are allowed. And you don't know anything about it—you who practice the law? You must be an awful lawyer, Mr. Krogstad.

KROGSTAD: Could be. But business—the kind of business we two mixed up in—don't you think I know about that? All right. Do what you want now. But I'm telling you *this:* if I get shoved down a second time, you're going to keep me company. *(He bows and goes out through the hall.)*

NORA: *(pensive for a moment, then tossing her head)* Oh, really! Trying to frighten me! I'm not so silly as all that. *(Begins gathering up the children's clothes, but soon stops.)* But—? No, but that's impossible! I did it out of love.

THE CHILDREN: *(in the doorway, left)* Mama, that strange man's gone out the door.

NORA: Yes, yes, I know it. But don't tell anyone about the strange man. Do you hear? Not even Papa!

THE CHILDREN: No, Mama. But now will you play again?   420

NORA: No, not now.

THE CHILDREN: Oh, but Mama, you promised.

NORA: Yes, but I can't now. Go inside; I have too much to do. Go in, go in, my sweet darlings. *(She herds them gently back in the room and shuts the door after them. Settling on the sofa, she takes up a piece of embroidery and makes some stitches, but soon stops abruptly.)* No! *(Throws the work aside, rises, goes to the hall door and calls out.)* Helene! Let me have the tree in here. *(Goes to the table, left, opens the table drawer, and stops again.)* No, but that's utterly impossible!

MAID: *(with the Christmas tree)* Where should I put it, ma'am?

NORA: There. The middle of the floor.   425

MAID: Should I bring anything else?

NORA: No, thanks. I have what I need.

The Maid, who has set the tree down, goes out.

NORA: *(absorbed in trimming the tree)* Candles here—and flowers here. That terrible creature! Talk, talk, talk! There's nothing to it at all. The tree's going to be lovely. I'll do anything to please you, Torvald. I'll sing for you, dance for you—

Helmer comes in from the hall, with a sheaf of papers under his arm.

NORA: Oh! You're back so soon?

HELMER: Yes. Has anyone been here?   430

NORA: Here? No.

HELMER: That's odd. I saw Krogstad leaving the front door.

NORA: So? Oh yes, that's true. Krogstad was here a moment.

HELMER: Nora, I can see by your face that he's been here, begging you to put in a good word for him.

NORA: Yes.   435

HELMER: And it was supposed to seem like your own idea? You were to hide it from me that he'd been here. He asked you that, too, didn't he?

NORA: Yes, Torvald, but—

HELMER: Nora, Nora, and you could fall for that? Talk with that sort of person and promise him anything? And then in the bargain, tell me an untruth.

NORA: An untruth—?

440 **HELMER:** Didn't you say that no one had been here? (*Wagging his finger.*) My little songbird must never do that again. A songbird needs a clean beak to warble with. No false notes. (*Putting his arm about her waist.*) That's the way it should be, isn't it? Yes, I'm sure of it. (*Releasing her.*) And so, enough of that. (*Sitting by the stove.*) Ah, how snug and cozy it is here. (*Leafing among his papers.*)

NORA: (*busy with the tree, after a short pause*) Torvald!

HELMER: Yes.

NORA: I'm so much looking forward to the Stenborgs' costume party, day after tomorrow.

HELMER: And I can't wait to see what you'll surprise me with.

445 **NORA:** Oh, that stupid business!

HELMER: What?

NORA: I can't find anything that's right. Everything seems so ridiculous, so inane.

HELMER: So my little Nora's come to *that* recognition?

NORA: (*going behind his chair, her arms resting on its back*) Are you very busy, Torvald?

450 **HELMER:** Oh—

NORA: What papers are those?

HELMER: Bank matters.

NORA: Already?

HELMER: I've gotten full authority from the retiring management to make all necessary changes in personnel and procedure. I'll need Christmas week for that. I want to have everything in order by New Year's.

455 **NORA:** So that was the reason this poor Krogstad—

HELMER: Hm.

NORA: (*still leaning on the chair and slowly stroking the nape of his neck*) If you weren't so very busy, I would have asked you an enormous favor, Torvald.

HELMER: Let's hear. What is it?

NORA: You know, there isn't anyone who has your good taste—and I want so much to look well at the costume party. Torvald, couldn't you take over and decide what I should be and plan my costume?

460 **HELMER:** Ah, is my stubborn little creature calling for a lifeguard?

NORA: Yes, Torvald, I can't get anywhere without your help.

HELMER: All right—I'll think it over. We'll hit on something.

NORA: Oh, how sweet of you. (*Goes to the tree again. Pause.*) Aren't the red flowers pretty—? But tell me, was it really such a crime that this Krogstad committed?

HELMER: Forgery. Do you have any idea what that means?

465 **NORA:** Couldn't he have done it out of need?

HELMER: Yes, or thoughtlessness, like so many others. I'm not so heartless that I'd condemn a man categorically for just one mistake.

NORA: No, of course not, Torvald!

HELMER: Plenty of men have redeemed themselves by openly confessing their crimes and taking their punishment.

NORA: Punishment—?

HELMER: But now Krogstad didn't go that way. He got himself out by sharp   470
practices, and that's the real cause of his moral breakdown.

NORA: Do you really think that would—?

HELMER: Just imagine how a man with that sort of guilt in him has to lie and cheat and deceive on all sides, has to wear a mask even with the nearest and dearest he has, even with his own wife and children. And with the children, Nora—that's where it's most horrible.

NORA: Why?

HELMER: Because that kind of atmosphere of lies infects the whole life of a home. Every breath the children take in is filled with the germs of something degenerate.

NORA: *(coming closer behind him)* Are you sure of that?   475

HELMER: Oh, I've seen it often enough as a lawyer. Almost everyone who goes bad early in life has a mother who's a chronic liar.

NORA: Why just—the mother?

HELMER: It's usually the mother's influence that's dominant, but the father's works in the same way, of course. Every lawyer is quite famil-iar with it. And still this Krogstad's been going home year in, year out, poisoning his own children with lies and pretense; that's why I call him morally lost. *(Reaching his hands out toward her.)* So my sweet little Nora must promise me never to plead his cause. Your hand on it. Come, come, what's this? Give me your hand. There, now. All settled. I can tell you it'd be impossible for me to work alongside of him. I liter-ally feel physically revolted when I'm anywhere near such a person.

NORA: *(withdraws her hand and goes to the other side of the Christmas tree)* How hot it is here! And I've got so much to do.

HELMER: *(getting up and gathering his papers)* Yes, and I have to think   480
about getting some of these read through before dinner. I'll think about your costume, too. And something to hang on the tree in gilt paper, I may even see about that. *(Putting his hand on her head.)* Oh you, my darling little songbird. *(He goes into his study and closes the door after him.)*

NORA: *(softly, after a silence)* Oh, really! It isn't so. It's impossible. It must be impossible.

ANNE-MARIE: *(in the doorway, left)* The children are begging so hard to come in to Mama.

NORA: No, no, no, don't let them in to me! You stay with them, Anne-Marie.

ANNE-MARIE: Of course, ma'am. *(Closes the door.)*

485 **NORA:** *(pale with terror)* Hurt my children—! Poison my home? *(A moment's pause; then she tosses her head.)* That's not true. Never. Never in all the world.

ACT 2

Same room. Beside the piano the Christmas tree now stands stripped of ornaments, burned-down candle stubs on its ragged branches. Nora's street clothes lie on the sofa. Nora, alone in the room, moves restlessly about; at last she stops at the sofa and picks up her coat.

NORA: *(dropping the coat again)* Someone's coming! *(Goes toward the door, listens.)* No—there's no one. Of course—nobody's coming today, Christmas Day—or tomorrow, either. But maybe—*(Opens the door and looks out.)* No, nothing in the mailbox. Quite empty. *(Coming forward.)* What nonsense! He won't do anything serious. Nothing terrible could happen. It's impossible. Why, I have three small children.

Anne-Marie, with a large carton, comes in from the room to the left.

ANNE-MARIE: Well, at last I found the box with the masquerade clothes.
NORA: Thanks. Put it on the table.
ANNE-MARIE: *(does so)* But they're all pretty much of a mess.
5 **NORA:** Ahh! I'd love to rip them in a million pieces!
ANNE-MARIE: Oh, mercy, they can be fixed right up. Just a little patience.
NORA: Yes, I'll go get Mrs. Linde to help me.
ANNE-MARIE: Out again now? In this nasty weather? Miss Nora will catch cold—get sick.
NORA: Oh, worse things could happen—How are the children?
10 **ANNE-MARIE:** The poor mites are playing with their Christmas presents, but—
NORA: Do they ask for me much?
ANNE-MARIE: They're so used to having Mama around, you know.
NORA: Yes. But Anne-Marie, I *can't* be together with them as much as I was.
ANNE-MARIE: Well, small children get used to anything.
15 **NORA:** You think so? Do you think they'd forget their mother if she was gone for good?
ANNE-MARIE: Oh, mercy—gone for good!
NORA: Wait, tell me, Anne-Marie—I've wondered so often—how could you ever have the heart to give your child over to strangers?
ANNE-MARIE: But I had to, you know, to become little Nora's nurse.
NORA: Yes, but how could you *do* it?
20 **ANNE-MARIE:** When I could get such a good place? A girl who's poor and who's gotten in trouble is glad enough for that. Because that slippery fish, he didn't do a thing for me, you know.

Nora: But your daughter's surely forgotten you.

Anne-Marie: Oh, she certainly has not. She's written to me, both when she was confirmed and when she was married.

Nora: *(clasping her about the neck)* You old Anne-Marie, you were a good mother for me when I was little.

Anne-Marie: Poor little Nora, with no other mother but me.

Nora: And if the babies didn't have one, then I know that you'd—What   25
silly talk! *(Opening the carton.)* Go in to them. Now I'll have to—
Tomorrow you can see how lovely I'll look.

Anne-Marie: Oh, there won't be anyone at the party as lovely as Miss Nora. *(She goes off into the room, left.)*

Nora: *(begins unpacking the box, but soon throws it aside)* Oh, if I dared to go out. If only nobody would come. If only nothing would happen here while I'm out. What craziness—nobody's coming. Just don't think. This muff—needs a brushing. Beautiful gloves, beautiful gloves. Let it go. Let it go! One, two, three, four, five, six—*(With a cry.)* Oh, there they are! *(Poises to move toward the door, but remains irresolutely standing. Mrs. Linde enters from the hall, where she has removed her street clothes.)*

Nora: Oh, it's you, Kristine. There's no one else out there? How good that you've come.

Mrs. Linde: I hear you were up asking for me.

Nora: Yes, I just stopped by. There's something you really can help me   30
with. Let's get settled on the sofa. Look, there's going to be a costume party tomorrow evening at the Stenborgs' right above us, and now Torvald wants me to go as a Neapolitan peasant girl and dance the tarantella that I learned in Capri.

Mrs. Linde: Really, are you giving a whole performance?

Nora: Torvald says yes, I should. See, here's the dress. Torvald had it made for me down there; but now it's all so tattered that I just don't know—

Mrs. Linde: Oh, we'll fix that up in no time. It's nothing more than the trimmings—they're a bit loose here and there. Needle and thread? Good, now we have what we need.

Nora: Oh, how sweet of you!

Mrs. Linde: *(sewing)* So you'll be in disguise tomorrow, Nora. You know   35
what? I'll stop by then for a moment and have a look at you all dressed up. But listen, I've absolutely forgotten to thank you for that pleasant evening yesterday.

Nora: *(getting up and walking about)* I don't think it was as pleasant as usual yesterday. You should have come to town a bit sooner, Kristine—Yes, Torvald really knows how to give a home elegance and charm.

MRS. LINDE: And you do, too, if you ask me. You're not your father's daughter for nothing. But tell me, is Dr. Rank always so down in the mouth as yesterday?

NORA: No, that was quite an exception. But he goes around critically ill all the time—tuberculosis of the spine, poor man. You know, his father was a disgusting thing who kept mistresses and so on—and that's why the son's been sickly from birth.

MRS. LINDE: *(lets her sewing fall to her lap)* But my dearest Nora, how do you know about such things?

40 NORA: *(walking more jauntily)* Hmp! When you've had three children, then you've had a few visits from—from women who know something of medicine, and they tell you this and that.

MRS. LINDE: *(resumes sewing; a short pause)* Does Dr. Rank come here every day?

NORA: Every blessed day. He's Torvald's best friend from childhood, and *my* good friend, too. Dr. Rank almost belongs to this house.

MRS. LINDE: But tell me—is he quite sincere? I mean, doesn't he rather enjoy flattering people?

NORA: Just the opposite. Why do you think that?

45 MRS. LINDE: When you introduced us yesterday, he was proclaiming that he'd often heard my name in this house; but later I noticed that your husband hadn't the slightest idea who I really was. So how could Dr. Rank—?

NORA: But it's all true, Kristine. You see, Torvald loves me beyond words, and, as he puts it, he'd like to keep me all to himself. For a long time he'd almost be jealous if I even mentioned any of my old friends back home. So of course I dropped that. But with Dr. Rank I talk a lot about such things, because he likes hearing about them.

MRS. LINDE: Now listen, Nora; in many ways you're still like a child. I'm a good deal older than you, with a little more experience. I'll tell you something: you ought to put an end to all this with Dr. Rank.

NORA: What should I put an end to?

MRS. LINDE: Both parts of it, I think. Yesterday you said something about a rich admirer who'd provide you with money—

50 NORA: Yes, one who doesn't exist—worse luck. So?

MRS. LINDE: Is Dr. Rank well off?

NORA: Yes, he is.

MRS. LINDE: With no dependents?

NORA: No, no one. But—

55 MRS. LINDE: And he's over here every day?

NORA: Yes, I told you that.

MRS. LINDE: How can a man of such refinement be so grasping?

NORA: I don't follow you at all.

MRS. LINDE: Now don't try to hide it, Nora. You think I can't guess who loaned you the forty-eight hundred crowns?

NORA: Are you out of your mind? How could you think such a thing! A 60
friend of ours, who comes here every single day. What an intolerable situation that would have been!

MRS. LINDE: Then it really wasn't him.

NORA: No, absolutely not. It never even crossed my mind for a moment—And he had nothing to lend in those days; his inheritance came later.

MRS. LINDE: Well, I think that was a stroke of luck for you, Nora dear.

NORA: No, it never would have occurred to me to ask Dr. Rank—Still, I'm quite sure that if I had asked him—

MRS. LINDE: Which you won't, of course. 65

NORA: No, of course not. I can't see that I'd ever need to. But I'm quite positive that if I talked to Dr. Rank—

MRS. LINDE: Behind your husband's back?

NORA: I've got to clear up this other thing; *that's* also behind his back. I've *got* to clear it all up.

MRS. LINDE: Yes, I was saying that yesterday, but—

NORA: (*pacing up and down*) A man handles these problems so much better 70
than a woman—

MRS. LINDE: One's husband does, yes.

NORA: Nonsense. (*Stopping.*) When you pay everything you owe, then you get your note back, right?

MRS. LINDE: Yes, naturally.

NORA: And can rip it into a million pieces and burn it up—that filthy scrap of paper!

MRS. LINDE: (*looking hard at her, laying her sewing aside, and rising slowly*) 75
Nora, you're hiding something from me.

NORA: You can see it in my face?

MRS. LINDE: Something's happened to you since yesterday morning. Nora, what is it?

NORA: (*hurrying toward her*) Kristine! (*Listening.*) Shh! Torvald's home. Look, go in with the children a while. Torvald can't bear all this snipping and stitching. Let Anne-Marie help you.

MRS. LINDE: (*gathering up some of the things*) All right, but I'm not leaving here until we've talked this out. (*She disappears into the room, left, as Torvald enters from the hall.*)

NORA: Oh, how I've been waiting for you, Torvald dear. 80

HELMER: Was that the dressmaker?

NORA: No, that was Kristine. She's helping me fix up my costume. You know, it's going to be quite attractive.

HELMER: Yes, wasn't that a bright idea I had?

NORA: Brilliant! But then wasn't I good as well to give in to you?

85 HELMER: Good—because you give in to your husband's judgment? All right, you little goose, I know you didn't mean it like that. But I won't disturb you. You'll want to have a fitting, I suppose.

NORA: And you'll be working?

HELMER: Yes. *(Indicating a bundle of papers.)* See. I've been down to the bank. *(Starts toward his study.)*

NORA: Torvald.

HELMER: *(stops)* Yes.

90 NORA: If your little squirrel begged you, with all her heart and soul, for something—?

HELMER: What's that?

NORA: Then would you do it?

HELMER: First, naturally, I'd have to know what it was.

NORA: Your squirrel would scamper about and do tricks, if you'd only be sweet and give in.

95 HELMER: Out with it.

NORA: Your lark would be singing high and low in every room—

HELMER: Come on, she does that anyway.

NORA: I'd be a wood nymph and dance for you in the moonlight.

HELMER: Nora—don't tell me it's that same business from this morning?

100 NORA: *(coming closer)* Yes, Torvald, I beg you, please!

HELMER: And you actually have the nerve to drag that up again?

NORA: Yes, yes, you've got to give in to me; you *have* to let Krogstad keep his job in the bank.

HELMER: My dear Nora, I've slated his job for Mrs. Linde.

NORA: That's awfully kind of you. But you could just fire another clerk instead of Krogstad.

105 HELMER: This is the most incredible stubbornness! Because you go and give an impulsive promise to speak up for him, I'm expected to—

NORA: That's not the reason, Torvald. It's for your own sake. That man does writing for the worst papers; you said it yourself. He could do you any amount of harm. I'm scared to death of him—

HELMER: Ah, I understand. It's the old memories haunting you.

NORA: What do you mean by that?

HELMER: Of course, you're thinking about your father.

110 NORA: Yes, all right. Just remember how those nasty gossips wrote in the papers about Papa and slandered him so cruelly. I think they'd have had him dismissed if the department hadn't sent you up to investigate, and if you hadn't been so kind and open-minded toward him.

HELMER: My dear Nora, there's a notable difference between your father and me. Your father's official career was hardly above reproach. But mine is; and I hope it'll stay that way as long as I hold my position.

NORA: Oh, who can ever tell what vicious minds can invent? We could be so snug and happy now in our quiet, carefree home—you and I and the children, Torvald! That's why I'm pleading with you so—

HELMER: And just by pleading for him you make it impossible for me to keep him on. It's already known at the bank that I'm firing Krogstad. What if it's rumored around now that the new bank manager was vetoed by his wife—

NORA: Yes, what then—?

HELMER: Oh yes—as long as our little bundle of stubbornness gets her   115
way—! I should go and make myself ridiculous in front of the whole office—give people the idea I can be swayed by all kinds of outside pressure. Oh, you can bet I'd feel the effects of that soon enough! Besides—there's something that rules Krogstad right out at the bank as long as I'm the manager.

NORA: What's that?

HELMER: His moral failings I could maybe overlook if I had to—

NORA: Yes, Torvald, why not?

HELMER: And I hear he's quite efficient on the job. But he was a crony of mine back in my teens—one of those rash friendships that crop up again and again to embarrass you later in life. Well, I might as well say it straight out: we're on a first-name basis. And that tactless fool makes no effort at all to hide it in front of others. Quite the contrary—he thinks that entitles him to take a familiar air around me, and so every other second he comes booming out with his "Yes, Torvald!" and "Sure thing, Torvald!" I tell you, it's been excruciating for me. He's out to make my place in the bank unbearable.

NORA: Torvald, you can't be serious about all this.   120

HELMER: Oh no? Why not?

NORA: Because these are such petty considerations.

HELMER: What are you saying? Petty? You think I'm petty!

NORA: No, just the opposite, Torvald dear. That's exactly why—

HELMER: Never mind. You call my motives petty; then I might as well be   125
just that. Petty! All right! We'll put a stop to this for good. (*Goes to the hall door and calls.*) Helene!

NORA: What do you want?

HELMER: (*searching among his papers*) A decision. (*The Maid comes in.*) Look here; take this letter; go out with it at once. Get hold of a messenger and have him deliver it. Quick now. It's already addressed. Wait, here's some money.

MAID: Yes, sir. (*She leaves with the letter.*)

HELMER: (*straightening his papers*) There, now, little Miss Willful.

NORA: (*breathlessly*) Torvald, what was that letter?   130

HELMER: Krogstad's notice.

NORA: Call it back, Torvald! There's still time. Oh, Torvald, call it back! Do it for my sake—for your sake, for the children's sake! Do you hear, Torvald; do it! You don't know how this can harm us.

HELMER: Too late.

NORA: Yes, too late.

135 **HELMER:** Nora dear, I can forgive you this panic, even though basically you're insulting me. Yes, you are! Or isn't it an insult to think that *I* should be afraid of a courtroom hack's revenge? But I forgive you anyway, because this shows so beautifully how much you love me. (*Takes her in his arms.*) This is the way it should be, my darling Nora. Whatever comes, you'll see: when it really counts, I have strength and courage enough as a man to take on the whole weight myself.

NORA: (*terrified*) What do you mean by that?

HELMER: The whole weight, I said.

NORA: (*resolutely*) No, never in all the world.

HELMER: Good. So we'll share it, Nora, as man and wife. That's as it should be. (*Fondling her.*) Are you happy now? There, there, there—not these frightened dove's eyes. It's nothing at all but empty fantasies—Now you should run through your tarantella and practice your tambourine. I'll go to the inner office and shut both doors, so I won't hear a thing; you can make all the noise you like. (*Turning in the doorway.*) And when Rank comes, just tell him where he can find me. (*He nods to her and goes with his papers into the study, closing the door.*)

140 **NORA:** (*standing as though rooted, dazed with fright, in a whisper*) He really could do it. He will do it. He'll do it in spite of everything. No, not that, never, never! Anything but that! Escape! A way out—(*The doorbell rings.*) Dr. Rank! Anything but that! *Anything*, whatever it is! (*Her hands pass over her face, smoothing it; she pulls herself together, goes over and opens the hall door. Dr. Rank stands outside, hanging his fur coat up. During the following scene, it begins getting dark.*)

NORA: Hello, Dr. Rank. I recognized your ring. But you mustn't go in to Torvald yet; I believe he's working.

RANK: And you?

NORA: For you, I always have an hour to spare—you know that. (*He has entered, and she shuts the door after him.*)

RANK: Many thanks. I'll make use of these hours while I can.

145 **NORA:** What do you mean by that? While you can?

RANK: Does that disturb you?

NORA: Well, it's such an odd phrase. Is anything going to happen?

RANK: What's going to happen is what I've been expecting so long—but I honestly didn't think it would come so soon.

NORA: (*gripping his arm*) What is it you've found out? Dr. Rank, you have to tell me!

RANK: (*sitting by the stove*) It's all over with me. There's nothing to be   150
done about it.

NORA: (*breathing easier*) Is it you—then—?

RANK: Who else? There's no point in lying to one's self. I'm the most miserable of all my patients, Mrs. Helmer. These past few days I've been auditing my internal accounts. Bankrupt! Within a month I'll probably be laid out and rotting in the churchyard.

NORA: Oh, what a horrible thing to say.

RANK: The thing itself is horrible. But the worst of it is all the other horror before it's over. There's only one final examination left; when I'm finished with that, I'll know about when my disintegration will begin. There's something I want to say. Helmer with his sensitivity has such a sharp distaste for anything ugly. I don't want him near my sickroom.

NORA: Oh, but Dr. Rank—   155

RANK: I won't have him in there. Under no condition. I'll lock my door to him—As soon as I'm completely sure of the worst, I'll send you my calling card marked with a black cross, and you'll know then the wreck has started to come apart.

NORA: No, today you're completely unreasonable. And I wanted you so much to be in a really good humor.

RANK: With death up my sleeve? And then to suffer this way for somebody else's sins. Is there any justice in that? And in every single family, in some way or another, this inevitable retribution of nature goes on—

NORA: (*her hands pressed over her ears*) Oh, stuff! Cheer up! Please—be gay!

RANK: Yes, I'd just as soon laugh at it all. My poor, innocent spine, serving   160
time for my father's gay army days.

NORA: (*by the table, left*) He was so infatuated with asparagus tips and *pâté de foie gras*, wasn't that it?

RANK: Yes—and with truffles.

NORA: Truffles, yes. And then with oysters, I suppose?

RANK: Yes, tons of oysters, naturally.

NORA: And then the port and champagne to go with it. It's so sad that all   165
these delectable things have to strike at our bones.

RANK: Especially when they strike at the unhappy bones that never shared in the fun.

NORA: Ah, that's the saddest of all.

RANK: (*looks searchingly at her*) Hm.

NORA: (*after a moment*) Why did you smile?

RANK: No, it was you who laughed.   170

NORA: No, it was you who smiled, Dr. Rank!

RANK: (*getting up*) You're even a bigger tease than I'd thought.

NORA: I'm full of wild ideas today.

RANK: That's obvious.

175 NORA: (*putting both hands on his shoulders*) Dear, dear Dr. Rank, you'll never die for Torvald and me.

RANK: Oh, that loss you'll easily get over. Those who go away are soon forgotten.

NORA: (*looks fearfully at him*) You believe that?

RANK: One makes new connections, and then—

NORA: Who makes new connections?

180 RANK: Both you and Torvald will when I'm gone. I'd say you're well under way already. What was that Mrs. Linde doing here last evening?

NORA: Oh, come—you can't be jealous of poor Kristine?

RANK: Oh yes, I am. She'll be my successor here in the house. When I'm down under, that woman will probably—

NORA: Shh! Not so loud. She's right in there.

RANK: Today as well. So you see.

185 NORA: Only to sew on my dress. Good gracious, how unreasonable you are. (*Sitting on the sofa.*) Be nice now, Dr. Rank. Tomorrow you'll see how beautifully I'll dance; and you can imagine then that I'm dancing only for you—yes, and of course for Torvald, too—that's understood. (*Takes various items out of the carton.*) Dr. Rank, sit over here and I'll show you something.

RANK: (*sitting*) What's that?

NORA: Look here. Look.

RANK: Silk stockings.

NORA: Flesh-colored. Aren't they lovely? Now it's so dark here, but tomorrow—No, no, no, just look at the feet. Oh well, you might as well look at the rest.

190 RANK: Hm—

NORA: Why do you look so critical? Don't you believe they'll fit?

RANK: I've never had any chance to form an opinion on that.

NORA: (*glancing at him a moment*) Shame on you. (*Hits him lightly on the ear with the stockings.*) That's for you. (*Puts them away again.*)

RANK: And what other splendors am I going to see now?

195 NORA: Not the least bit more, because you've been naughty. (*She hums a little and rummages among her things.*)

RANK: (*after a short silence*) When I sit here together with you like this, completely easy and open, then I don't know—I simply can't imagine—whatever would have become of me if I'd never come into this house.

NORA: (*smiling*) Yes, I really think you feel completely at ease with us.

RANK: (*more quietly, staring straight ahead*) And then to have to go away from it all—

NORA: Nonsense, you're not going away.

RANK: *(his voice unchanged)*—and not even be able to leave some poor   200
show of gratitude behind, scarcely a fleeting regret—no more than a
vacant place that anyone can fill.

NORA: And if I asked you now for—? No—

RANK: For what?

NORA: For a great proof of your friendship—

RANK: Yes, yes?

NORA: No, I mean—for an exceptionally big favor—   205

RANK: Would you really, for once, make me so happy?

NORA: Oh, you haven't the vaguest idea what it is.

RANK: All right, then tell me.

NORA: No, but I can't, Dr. Rank—it's all out of reason. It's advice and
help, too—and a favor—

RANK: So much the better. I can't fathom what you're hinting at. Just   210
speak out. Don't you trust me?

NORA: Of course. More than anyone else. You're my best and truest friend,
I'm sure. That's why I want to talk to you. All right, then, Dr. Rank:
there's something you can help me prevent. You know how deeply,
how inexpressibly dearly Torvald loves me; he'd never hesitate a second to give up his life for me.

RANK: *(leaning close to her)* Nora—do you think he's the only one—

NORA: *(with a slight start)* Who—?

RANK: Who'd gladly give up his life for you.

NORA: *(heavily)* I see.   215

RANK: I swore to myself you should know this before I'm gone. I'll never
find a better chance. Yes, Nora, now you know. And also you know
now that you can trust me beyond anyone else.

NORA: *(rising, natural and calm)* Let me by.

RANK: *(making room for her, but still sitting)* Nora—

NORA: *(in the hall doorway)* Helene, bring the lamp in. *(Goes over to the
stove.)* Ah, dear Dr. Rank, that was really mean of you.

RANK: *(getting up)* That I've loved you just as deeply as somebody else?   220
Was *that* mean?

NORA: No, but that you came out and told me. That was quite
unnecessary—

RANK: What do you mean? Have you known—?

The Maid comes in with the lamp, sets it on the table, and goes out again.

RANK: Nora—Mrs. Helmer—I'm asking you: have you known about it?

NORA: Oh, how can I tell what I know or don't know? Really, I don't
know what to say—Why did you have to be so clumsy, Dr. Rank!
Everything was so good.

225 RANK: Well, in any case, you now have the knowledge that my body and soul are at your command. So won't you speak out?

NORA: *(looking at him)* After that?

RANK: Please, just let me know what it is.

NORA: You can't know anything now.

RANK: I have to. You mustn't punish me like this. Give me the chance to do whatever is humanly possible for you.

230 NORA: Now there's nothing you can do for me. Besides, actually, I don't need any help. You'll see—it's only my fantasies. That's what it is. Of course! *(Sits in the rocker, looks at him, and smiles.)* What a nice one you are, Dr. Rank. Aren't you a little bit ashamed, now that the lamp is here?

RANK: No, not exactly. But perhaps I'd better go—for good?

NORA: No, you certainly can't do that. You must come here just as you always have. You know Torvald can't do without you.

RANK: Yes, but *you?*

NORA: You know how much I enjoy it when you're here.

235 RANK: That's precisely what threw me off. You're a mystery to me. So many times I've felt you'd almost rather be with me than with Helmer.

NORA: Yes—you see, there are some people that one loves most and other people that one would almost prefer being with.

RANK: Yes, there's something to that.

NORA: When I was back home, of course I loved Papa most. But I always thought it was so much fun when I could sneak down to the maids' quarters, because they never tried to improve me, and it was always so amusing, the way they talked to each other.

RANK: Aha, so it's *their* place that I've filled.

240 NORA: *(jumping up and going to him)* Oh, dear, sweet Dr. Rank, that's not what I mean at all. But you can understand that with Torvald it's just the same as with Papa—

The Maid enters from the hall.

MAID: Ma'am—please! *(She whispers to Nora and hands her a calling card.)*

NORA: *(glancing at the card)* Ah! *(Slips it into her pocket.)*

RANK: Anything wrong?

NORA: No, no, not at all. It's only some—it's my new dress—

245 RANK: Really? But—there's your dress.

NORA: Oh, that. But this is another one—I ordered it—Torvald mustn't know—

RANK: Ah, now we have the big secret.

NORA: That's right. Just go in with him—he's back in the inner study. Keep him there as long as—

RANK: Don't worry. He won't get away. *(Goes into the study.)*

NORA: *(to the Maid)* And he's standing waiting in the kitchen?   250
MAID: Yes, he came up by the back stairs.
NORA: But didn't you tell him somebody was here?
MAID: Yes, but that didn't do any good.
NORA: He won't leave?
MAID: No, he won't go till he's talked with you, ma'am.   255
NORA: Let him come in, then—but quietly. Helene, don't breathe a word
about this. It's a surprise for my husband.
MAID: Yes, yes, I understand—*(Goes out.)*
NORA: This horror—it's going to happen. No, no, no, it can't happen, it
mustn't. *(She goes and bolts Helmer's door. The Maid opens the hall door
for Krogstad and shuts it behind him. He is dressed for travel in a fur coat,
boots, and a fur cap.)*
NORA: *(going toward him)* Talk softly. My husband's home.
KROGSTAD: Well, good for him.   260
NORA: What do you want?
KROGSTAD: Some information.
NORA: Hurry up, then. What is it?
KROGSTAD: You know, of course, that I got my notice.
NORA: I couldn't prevent it, Mr. Krogstad. I fought for you to the bitter   265
end, but nothing worked.
KROGSTAD: Does your husband's love for you run so thin? He knows every-
thing I can expose you to, and all the same he dares to—
NORA: How can you imagine he knows anything about this?
KROGSTAD: Ah, no—I can't imagine it either, now. It's not at all like my
fine Torvald Helmer to have so much guts—
NORA: Mr. Krogstad, I demand respect for my husband!
KROGSTAD: Why, of course—all due respect. But since the lady's keeping   270
it so carefully hidden, may I presume to ask if you're also a bit better
informed than yesterday about what you've actually done?
NORA: More than you ever could teach me.
KROGSTAD: Yes, I *am* such an awful lawyer.
NORA: What is it you want from me?
KROGSTAD: Just a glimpse of how you are, Mrs. Helmer. I've been thinking
about you all day long. A cashier, a night-court scribbler, a—well, a
type like me also has a little of what they call a heart, you know.
NORA: Then show it. Think of my children.   275
KROGSTAD: Did you or your husband ever think of mine? But never mind.
I simply wanted to tell you that you don't need to take this thing too
seriously. For the present, I'm not proceeding with any action.
NORA: Oh no, really! Well—I knew that.
KROGSTAD: Everything can be settled in a friendly spirit. It doesn't have to
get around town at all; it can stay just among us three.

NORA: My husband must never know anything of this.

280 KROGSTAD: How can you manage that? Perhaps you can pay me the balance?

NORA: No, not right now.

KROGSTAD: Or you know some way of raising the money in a day or two?

NORA: No way that I'm willing to use.

KROGSTAD: Well, it wouldn't have done you any good, anyway. If you stood in front of me with a fistful of bills, you still couldn't buy your signature back.

285 NORA: Then tell me what you're going to do with it.

KROGSTAD: I'll just hold onto it—keep it on file. There's no outsider who'll even get wind of it. So if you've been thinking of taking some desperate step—

NORA: I have.

KROGSTAD: Been thinking of running away from home—

NORA: I have!

290 KROGSTAD: Or even of something worse—

NORA: How could you guess that?

KROGSTAD: You can drop those thoughts.

NORA: How could you guess I was thinking of *that*?

KROGSTAD: Most of us think about *that* at first. I thought about it too, but I discovered I hadn't the courage—

295 NORA: (*lifelessly*) I don't either.

KROGSTAD: (*relieved*) That's true, you haven't the courage? You too?

NORA: I don't have it—I don't have it.

KROGSTAD: It would be terribly stupid, anyway. After that first storm at home blows out, why, then—I have here in my pocket a letter for your husband—

NORA: Telling everything?

300 KROGSTAD: As charitably as possible.

NORA: (*quickly*) He mustn't ever get that letter. Tear it up. I'll find some way to get money.

KROGSTAD: Beg pardon, Mrs. Helmer, but I think I just told you—

NORA: Oh, I don't mean the money I owe you. Let me know how much you want from my husband, and I'll manage it.

KROGSTAD: I don't want any money from your husband.

305 NORA: What do you want, then?

KROGSTAD: I'll tell you what. I want to recoup, Mrs. Helmer; I want to get on in the world—and there's where your husband can help me. For a year and a half I've kept myself clean of anything disreputable—all that time struggling with the worst conditions; but I was satisfied, working my way up step by step. Now I've been written right off, and I'm just not in the mood to come crawling back. I tell you, I want to

move on. I want to get back in the bank—in a better position. Your
husband can set up a job for me—
NORA: He'll never do that!
KROGSTAD: He'll do it. I know him. He won't dare breathe a word of
protest. And once I'm in there together with him, you just wait and
see! Inside of a year, I'll be the manager's right-hand man. It'll be Nils
Krogstad, not Torvald Helmer, who runs the bank.
NORA: You'll never see the day!
KROGSTAD: Maybe you think you can—   310
NORA: I have the courage now—for *that*.
KROGSTAD: Oh, you don't scare me. A smart, spoiled lady like you—
NORA: You'll see; you'll see!
KROGSTAD: Under the ice, maybe? Down in the freezing, coal-black water?
There, till you float up in the spring, ugly, unrecognizable, with your
hair falling out—
NORA: You don't frighten me.   315
KROGSTAD: Nor do you frighten me. One doesn't do these things, Mrs.
Helmer. Besides, what good would it be? I'd still have him safe in my
pocket.
NORA: Afterwards? When I'm no longer—?
KROGSTAD: Are you forgetting that *I'll* be in control then over your final
reputation? (*Nora stands speechless, staring at him.*) Good; now I've
warned you. Don't do anything stupid. When Helmer's read my letter,
I'll be waiting for his reply. And bear in mind that it's your husband
himself who's forced me back to my old ways. I'll never forgive him for
that. Good-bye, Mrs. Helmer. (*He goes out through the hall.*)
NORA: (*goes to the hall door, opens it a crack, and listens*) He's gone. Didn't
leave the letter. Oh no, no, that's impossible too! (*Opening the door
more and more.*) What's that? He's standing outside—not going downstairs. He's thinking it over? Maybe he'll—? (*A letter falls in the mailbox;
then Krogstad's footsteps are heard, dying away down a flight of stairs. Nora
gives a muffled cry and runs over toward the sofa table. A short pause.*) In
the mailbox. (*Slips warily over to the hall door.*) It's lying there. Torvald,
Torvald—now we're lost!
MRS. LINDE: (*entering with the costume from the room, left*) There now,   320
I can't see anything else to mend. Perhaps you'd like to try—
NORA: (*in a hoarse whisper*) Kristine, come here.
MRS. LINDE: (*tossing the dress on the sofa*) What's wrong? You look upset.
NORA: Come here. See that letter? *There!* Look—through the glass in the
mailbox.
MRS. LINDE: Yes, yes, I see it.
NORA: That letter's from Krogstad—   325
MRS. LINDE: Nora—it's Krogstad who loaned you the money!

Nora: Yes, and now Torvald will find out everything.

Mrs. Linde: Believe me, Nora, it's best for both of you.

Nora: There's more you don't know. I forged a name.

330 Mrs. Linde: But for heaven's sake—?

Nora: I only want to tell you that, Kristine, so that you can be my witness.

Mrs. Linde: Witness? Why should I—?

Nora: If I should go out of my mind—it could easily happen—

Mrs. Linde: Nora!

335 Nora: Or anything else occurred—so I couldn't be present here—

Mrs. Linde: Nora, Nora, you aren't yourself at all!

Nora: And someone should try to take on the whole weight, all of the guilt, you follow me—

Mrs. Linde: Yes, of course, but why do you think—?

Nora: Then you're the witness that it isn't true, Kristine. I'm very much myself; my mind right now is perfectly clear; and I'm telling you: nobody else has known about this; I alone did everything. Remember that.

340 Mrs. Linde: I will. But I don't understand all this.

Nora: Oh, how could you ever understand it? It's the miracle now that's going to take place.

Mrs. Linde: The miracle?

Nora: Yes, the miracle. But it's so awful, Kristine. It mustn't take place, not for anything in the world.

Mrs. Linde: I'm going right over and talk with Krogstad.

345 Nora: Don't go near him; he'll do you some terrible harm!

Mrs. Linde: There was a time once when he'd gladly have done anything for me.

Nora: He?

Mrs. Linde: Where does he live?

Nora: Oh, how do I know? Yes. (*Searches in her pocket.*) Here's his card. But the letter, the letter—!

350 Helmer: (*from the study, knocking on the door*) Nora!

Nora: (*with a cry of fear*) Oh! What is it? What do you want?

Helmer: Now, now, don't be so frightened. We're not coming in. You locked the door—are you trying on the dress?

Nora: Yes, I'm trying it. I'll look just beautiful, Torvald.

Mrs. Linde: (*who has read the card*) He's living right around the corner.

355 Nora: Yes, but what's the use? We're lost. The letter's in the box.

Mrs. Linde: And your husband has the key?

Nora: Yes, always.

Mrs. Linde: Krogstad can ask for his letter back unread; he can find some excuse—

Nora: But it's just this time that Torvald usually—

MRS. LINDE: Stall him. Keep him in there. I'll be back as quick as I can.   360
(*She hurries out through the hall entrance.*)

NORA: (*goes to Helmer's door, opens it, and peers in*) Torvald!

HELMER: (*from the inner study*) Well—does one dare set foot in one's own living room at last? Come on, Rank, now we'll get a look—(*In the doorway.*) But what's this?

NORA: What, Torvald dear?

HELMER: Rank had me expecting some grand masquerade.

RANK: (*in the doorway*) That was my impression, but I must have been   365
wrong.

NORA: No one can admire me in my splendor—not till tomorrow.

HELMER: But Nora dear, you look so exhausted. Have you practiced too hard?

NORA: No, I haven't practiced at all yet.

HELMER: You know, it's necessary—

NORA: Oh, it's absolutely necessary, Torvald. But I can't get anywhere   370
without your help. I've forgotten the whole thing completely.

HELMER: Ah, we'll soon take care of that.

NORA: Yes, take care of me, Torvald, please! Promise me that? Oh, I'm so nervous. That big party—You must give up everything this evening for me. No business—don't even touch your pen. Yes? Dear Torvald, promise?

HELMER: It's a promise. Tonight I'm totally at your service—you little helpless thing. Hm—but first there's one thing I want to—(*Goes toward the hall door.*)

NORA: What are you looking for?

HELMER: Just to see if there's any mail.   375

NORA: No, no, don't do that, Torvald!

HELMER: Now what?

NORA: Torvald, please. There isn't any.

HELMER: Let me look, though. (*Starts out. Nora, at the piano, strikes the first notes of the tarantella. Helmer, at the door, stops.*) Aha!

NORA: I can't dance tomorrow if I don't practice with you.   380

HELMER: (*going over to her*) Nora dear, are you really so frightened?

NORA: Yes, so terribly frightened. Let me practice right now; there's still time before dinner. Oh, sit down and play for me, Torvald. Direct me. Teach me, the way you always have.

HELMER: Gladly, if it's what you want. (*Sits at the piano.*)

NORA: (*snatches the tambourine up from the box, then a long, varicolored shawl, which she throws around herself, whereupon she springs forward and cries out*) Play for me now! Now I'll dance!

Helmer plays and Nora dances. Rank stands behind Helmer at the piano and looks on.

385 **Helmer:** *(as he plays)* Slower. Slow down.

Nora: Can't change it.

Helmer: Not so violent, Nora!

Nora: Has to be just like this.

Helmer: *(stopping)* No, no, that won't do at all.

390 **Nora:** *(laughing and swinging her tambourine)* Isn't that what I told you?

Rank: Let me play for her.

Helmer: *(getting up)* Yes, go on. I can teach her more easily then.

Rank sits at the piano and plays; Nora dances more and more wildly. Helmer has stationed himself by the stove and repeatedly gives her directions; she seems not to hear them; her hair loosens and falls over her shoulders; she does not notice, but goes on dancing. Mrs. Linde enters.

Mrs. Linde: *(standing dumbfounded at the door)* Ah—!

Nora: *(still dancing)* See what fun, Kristine!

395 **Helmer:** But Nora darling, you dance as if your life were at stake.

Nora: And it is.

Helmer: Rank, stop! This is pure madness. Stop it, I say!

Rank breaks off playing, and Nora halts abruptly.

Helmer: *(going over to her)* I never would have believed it. You've forgotten everything I taught you.

Nora: *(throwing away the tambourine)* You see for yourself.

400 **Helmer:** Well, there's certainly room for instruction here.

Nora: Yes, you see how important it is. You've got to teach me to the very last minute. Promise me that, Torvald?

Helmer: You can bet on it.

Nora: You mustn't, either today or tomorrow, think about anything else but me; you mustn't open any letters—or the mailbox—

Helmer: Ah, it's still the fear of that man—

405 **Nora:** Oh yes, yes, that too.

Helmer: Nora, it's written all over you—there's already a letter from him out there.

Nora: I don't know. I guess so. But you mustn't read such things now; there mustn't be anything ugly between us before it's all over.

Rank: *(quietly to Helmer)* You shouldn't deny her.

Helmer: *(putting his arm around her)* The child can have her way. But tomorrow night, after you've danced—

410 **Nora:** Then you'll be free.

Maid: *(in the doorway, right)* Ma'am, dinner is served.

Nora: We'll be wanting champagne, Helene.

Maid: Very good, ma'am. *(Goes out.)*

Helmer: So—a regular banquet, hm?

NORA: Yes, a banquet—champagne till daybreak! (*Calling out.*) And some   415
macaroons, Helene. Heaps of them—just this once.

HELMER: (*taking her hands*) Now, now, now—no hysterics. Be my own little
lark again.

NORA: Oh, I will soon enough. But go on in—and you, Dr. Rank. Kristine,
help me put up my hair.

RANK: (*whispering, as they go*) There's nothing wrong—really wrong, is
there?

HELMER: Oh, of course not. It's nothing more than this childish anxiety
I was telling you about. (*They go out, right.*)

NORA: Well?   420

MRS. LINDE: Left town.

NORA: I could see by your face.

MRS. LINDE: He'll be home tomorrow evening. I wrote him a note.

NORA: You shouldn't have. Don't try to stop anything now. After all, it's a
wonderful joy, this waiting here for the miracle.

MRS. LINDE: What is it you're waiting for?   425

NORA: Oh, you can't understand that. Go in to them: I'll be along in a
moment.

*Mrs. Linde goes into the dining room. Nora stands a short while as if composing
herself; then she looks at her watch.*

NORA: Five. Seven hours to midnight. Twenty-four hours to the midnight
after, and then the tarantella's done. Seven and twenty-four? Thirty-
one hours to live.

HELMER: (*in the doorway, right*) What's become of the little lark?

NORA: (*going toward him with open arms*) Here's your lark!

ACT 3

*Same scene. The table, with chairs around it, has been moved to the center of the
room. A lamp on the table is lit. The hall door stands open. Dance music drifts
down from the floor above. Mrs. Linde sits at the table, absently paging through a
book, trying to read, but apparently unable to focus her thoughts. Once or twice
she pauses, tensely listening for a sound at the outer entrance.*

MRS. LINDE: (*glancing at her watch*) Not yet—and there's hardly any time
left. If only he's not—(*Listening again.*) Ah, there he is. (*She goes out in
the hall and cautiously opens the outer door. Quiet footsteps are heard on the
stairs. She whispers:*) Come in. Nobody's here.

KROGSTAD: (*in the doorway*) I found a note from you at home. What's back
of all this?

MRS. LINDE: I just *had* to talk to you.

KROGSTAD: Oh? And it just *had* to be here in this house?

5 MRS. LINDE: At my place it was impossible; my room hasn't a private
entrance. Come in; we're all alone. The maid's asleep, and the Helmers
are at the dance upstairs.

KROGSTAD: *(entering the room)* Well, well, the Helmers are dancing tonight? Really?

MRS. LINDE: Yes, why not?

KROGSTAD: How true—why not?

MRS. LINDE: All right, Krogstad, let's talk.

10 KROGSTAD: Do we two have anything more to talk about?

MRS. LINDE: We have a great deal to talk about.

KROGSTAD: I wouldn't have thought so.

MRS. LINDE: No, because you've never understood me, really.

KROGSTAD: Was there anything more to understand—except what's all too
common in life? A calculating woman throws over a man the moment
a better catch comes by.

15 MRS. LINDE: You think I'm so thoroughly calculating? You think I broke it
off lightly?

KROGSTAD: Didn't you?

MRS. LINDE: Nils—is that what you really thought?

KROGSTAD: If you cared, then why did you write me the way you did?

MRS. LINDE: What else could I do? If I had to break off with you, then it
was my job as well to root out everything you felt for me.

20 KROGSTAD: *(wringing his hands)* So that was it. And this—all this, simply
for money!

MRS. LINDE: Don't forget I had a helpless mother and two small brothers. We
couldn't wait for you, Nils; you had such a long road ahead of you then.

KROGSTAD: That may be; but you still hadn't the right to abandon me for
somebody else's sake.

MRS. LINDE: Yes—I don't know. So many, many times I've asked myself if
I did have that right.

KROGSTAD: *(more softly)* When I lost you, it was as if all the solid ground
dissolved from under my feet. Look at me; I'm a half-drowned man
now, hanging onto a wreck.

25 MRS. LINDE: Help may be near.

KROGSTAD: It was near—but then you came and blocked it off.

MRS. LINDE: Without my knowing it, Nils. Today for the first time
I learned that it's you I'm replacing at the bank.

KROGSTAD: All right—I believe you. But now that you know, will you step
aside?

MRS. LINDE: No, because that wouldn't benefit you in the slightest.

30 KROGSTAD: Not "benefit" me, hm! I'd step aside anyway.

MRS. LINDE: I've learned to be realistic. Life and hard, bitter necessity
have taught me that.

KROGSTAD: And life's taught me never to trust fine phrases.

MRS. LINDE: Then life's taught you a very sound thing. But you do have to trust in actions, don't you?

KROGSTAD: What does that mean?

MRS. LINDE: You said you were hanging on like a half-drowned man to a wreck.   35

KROGSTAD: I've good reason to say that.

MRS. LINDE: I'm also like a half-drowned woman on a wreck. No one to suffer with; no one to care for.

KROGSTAD: You made your choice.

MRS. LINDE: There wasn't any choice then.

KROGSTAD: So—what of it?   40

MRS. LINDE: Nils, if only we two shipwrecked people could reach across to each other.

KROGSTAD: What are you saying?

MRS. LINDE: Two on one wreck are at least better off than each on his own.

KROGSTAD: Kristine!

MRS. LINDE: Why do you think I came into town?   45

KROGSTAD: Did you really have some thought of me?

MRS. LINDE: I have to work to go on living. All my born days, as long as I can remember, I've worked, and it's been my best and my only joy. But now I'm completely alone in the world; it frightens me to be so empty and lost. To work for yourself—there's no joy in that. Nils, give me something—someone to work for.

KROGSTAD: I don't believe all this. It's just some hysterical feminine urge to go out and make a noble sacrifice.

MRS. LINDE: Have you ever found me to be hysterical?

KROGSTAD: Can you honestly mean this? Tell me—do you know every-   50
thing about my past?

MRS. LINDE: Yes.

KROGSTAD: And you know what they think I'm worth around here.

MRS. LINDE: From what you were saying before, it would seem that with me you could have been another person.

KROGSTAD: I'm positive of that.

MRS. LINDE: Couldn't it happen still?   55

KROGSTAD: Kristine—you're saying this in all seriousness? Yes, you are! I can see it in you. And do you really have the courage, then—?

MRS. LINDE: I need to have someone to care for; and your children need a mother. We both need each other. Nils, I have faith that you're good at heart—I'll risk everything together with you.

KROGSTAD: (*gripping her hands*) Kristine, thank you, thank you—Now I know I can win back a place in their eyes. Yes—but I forgot—

MRS. LINDE: *(listening)* Shh! The tarantella. Go now! Go on!

60 KROGSTAD: Why? What is it?

MRS. LINDE: Hear the dance up there? When that's over, they'll be coming down.

KROGSTAD: Oh, then I'll go. But—it's all pointless. Of course, you don't know the move I made against the Helmers.

MRS. LINDE: Yes, Nils, I know.

KROGSTAD: And all the same, you have the courage to—?

65 MRS. LINDE: I know how far despair can drive a man like you.

KROGSTAD: Oh, if I only could take it all back.

MRS. LINDE: You easily could—your letter's still lying in the mailbox.

KROGSTAD: Are you sure of that?

MRS. LINDE: Positive. But—

70 KROGSTAD: *(looks at her searchingly)* Is that the meaning of it, then? You'll save your friend at any price. Tell me straight out. Is that it?

MRS. LINDE: Nils—anyone who's sold herself for somebody else once isn't going to do it again.

KROGSTAD: I'll demand my letter back.

MRS. LINDE: No, no.

KROGSTAD: Yes, of course. I'll stay here till Helmer comes down; I'll tell him to give me my letter again—that it only involves my dismissal— that he shouldn't read it—

75 MRS. LINDE: No, Nils, don't call the letter back.

KROGSTAD: But wasn't that exactly why you wrote me to come here?

MRS. LINDE: Yes, in that first panic. But it's been a whole day and night since then, and in that time I've seen such incredible things in this house. Helmer's got to learn everything; this dreadful secret has to be aired; those two have to come to a full understanding; all these lies and evasions can't go on.

KROGSTAD: Well, then, if you want to chance it. But at least there's one thing I can do, and do right away—

MRS. LINDE: *(listening)* Go now, go, quick! The dance is over. We're not safe another second.

80 KROGSTAD: I'll wait for you downstairs.

MRS. LINDE: Yes, please do; take me home.

KROGSTAD: I can't believe it; I've never been so happy. *(He leaves by way of the outer door; the door between the room and the hall stays open.)*

MRS. LINDE: *(straightening up a bit and getting together her street clothes)* How different now! How different! Someone to work for, to live for—a home to build. Well, it is worth the try! Oh, if they'd only come! (Listening.) Ah, there they are. Bundle up. *(She picks up her hat and coat. Nora's and Helmer's voices can be heard outside; a key turns in the lock, and Helmer brings Nora into the hall almost by force. She is wearing the*

*Italian costume with a large black shawl about her; he has on evening dress,
with a black domino open over it.)*
NORA: *(struggling in the doorway)* No, no, no, not inside! I'm going up
again. I don't want to leave so soon.
HELMER: But Nora dear—   85
NORA: Oh, I beg you, please, Torvald. From the bottom of my heart,
please—only an hour more!
HELMER: Not a single minute, Nora darling. You know our agreement.
Come on, in we go; you'll catch cold out here. *(In spite of her resistance,
he gently draws her into the room.)*
MRS. LINDE: Good evening.
NORA: Kristine!
HELMER: Why, Mrs. Linde—are you here so late?   90
MRS. LINDE: Yes, I'm sorry, but I did want to see Nora in costume.
NORA: Have you been sitting here, waiting for me?
MRS. LINDE: Yes. I didn't come early enough; you were all upstairs; and
then I thought I really couldn't leave without seeing you.
HELMER: *(removing Nora's shawl)* Yes, take a good look. She's worth look-
ing at, I can tell you that, Mrs. Linde. Isn't she lovely?
MRS. LINDE: Yes, I should say—   95
HELMER: A dream of loveliness, isn't she? That's what everyone thought
at the party, too. But she's horribly stubborn—this sweet little thing.
What's to be done with her? Can you imagine, I almost had to use
force to pry her away.
NORA: Oh, Torvald, you're going to regret you didn't indulge me, even for
just a half hour more.
HELMER: There, you see. She danced her tarantella and got a tumultuous
hand—which was well earned, although the performance may have
been a bit too naturalistic—I mean it rather overstepped the propri-
eties of art. But never mind—what's important is, she made a success,
an overwhelming success. You think I could let her stay on after that
and spoil the effect? Oh no; I took my lovely little Capri girl—my
capricious little Capri girl, I should say—took her under my arm; one
quick tour of the ballroom, a curtsy to every side, and then—as they
say in novels—the beautiful vision disappeared. An exit should always
be effective, Mrs. Linde, but that's what I can't get Nora to grasp.
Phew, it's hot in here. *(Flings the domino on a chair and opens the door to
his room.)* Why's it dark in here? Oh yes, of course. Excuse me. *(He goes
in and lights a couple of candles.)*
NORA: *(in a sharp, breathless whisper)* So?
MRS. LINDE: *(quietly)* I talked with him.   100
NORA: And—?
MRS. LINDE: Nora—you must tell your husband everything.

NORA: *(dully)* I knew it.

MRS. LINDE: You've got nothing to fear from Krogstad, but you have to speak out.

105 NORA: I won't tell.

MRS. LINDE: Then the letter will.

NORA: Thanks, Kristine. I know now what's to be done. Shh!

HELMER: *(reentering)* Well, then, Mrs. Linde—have you admired her?

MRS. LINDE: Yes, and now I'll say good night.

110 HELMER: Oh, come, so soon? Is this yours, this knitting?

MRS. LINDE: Yes, thanks. I nearly forgot it.

HELMER: Do you knit, then?

MRS. LINDE: Oh yes.

HELMER: You know what? You should embroider instead.

115 MRS. LINDE: Really? Why?

HELMER: Yes, because it's a lot prettier. See here, one holds the embroidery so, in the left hand, and then one guides the needle with the right— so—in an easy, sweeping curve—right?

MRS. LINDE: Yes, I guess that's—

HELMER: But, on the other hand, knitting—it can never be anything but ugly. Look, see here, the arms tucked in, the knitting needles going up and down—there's something Chinese about it. Ah, that was really a glorious champagne they served.

MRS. LINDE: Yes, good night, Nora, and don't be stubborn any more.

120 HELMER: Well put, Mrs. Linde!

MRS. LINDE: Good night, Mr. Helmer.

HELMER: *(accompanying her to the door)* Good night, good night. I hope you get home all right. I'd be very happy to—but you don't have far to go. Good night, good night. *(She leaves. He shuts the door after her and returns.)* There, now, at last we got her out the door. She's a deadly bore, that creature.

NORA: Aren't you pretty tired, Torvald?

HELMER: No, not a bit.

125 NORA: You're not sleepy?

HELMER: Not at all. On the contrary, I'm feeling quite exhilarated. But you? Yes, you really look tired and sleepy.

NORA: Yes, I'm very tired. Soon now I'll sleep.

HELMER: See! You see! I was right all along that we shouldn't stay longer.

NORA: Whatever you do is always right.

130 HELMER: *(kissing her brow)* Now my little lark talks sense. Say, did you notice what a time Rank was having tonight?

NORA: Oh, was he? I didn't get to speak with him.

HELMER: I scarcely did either, but it's a long time since I've seen him in such high spirits. *(Gazes at her a moment, then comes nearer her.)* Hm—

it's marvelous, though, to be back home again—to be completely alone with you. Oh, you bewitchingly lovely young woman!

NORA: Torvald, don't look at me like that!

HELMER: Can't I look at my richest treasure? At all that beauty that's mine, mine alone—completely and utterly.

NORA: (*moving around to the other side of the table*) You mustn't talk to me   135
that way tonight.

HELMER: (*following her*) The tarantella is still in your blood, I can see—and it makes you even more enticing. Listen. The guests are beginning to go. (*Dropping his voice.*) Nora—it'll soon be quiet through this whole house.

NORA: Yes, I hope so.

HELMER: You do, don't you, my love? Do you realize—when I'm out at a party like this with you—do you know why I talk to you so little, and keep such a distance away; just send you a stolen look now and then— you know why I do it? It's because I'm imagining then that you're my secret darling, my secret young bride-to-be, and that no one suspects there's anything between us.

NORA: Yes, yes; oh, yes, I know you're always thinking of me.

HELMER: And then when we leave and I place the shawl over those fine   140
young rounded shoulders—over that wonderful curving neck—then I pretend that you're my young bride, that we're just coming from the wedding, that for the first time I'm bringing you into my house—that for the first time I'm alone with you—completely alone with you, your trembling young beauty! All this evening I've longed for nothing but you. When I saw you turn and sway in the tarantella—my blood was pounding till I couldn't stand it—that's why I brought you down here so early—

NORA: Go away, Torvald! Leave me alone. I don't want all this.

HELMER: What do you mean? Nora, you're teasing me. You will, won't you? Aren't I your husband—?

A knock at the outside door.

NORA: (*startled*) What's that?

HELMER: (*going toward the hall*) Who is it?

RANK: (*outside*) It's me. May I come in a moment?   145

HELMER: (*with quiet irritation*) Oh, what does he want now? (*Aloud.*) Hold on. (*Goes and opens the door.*) Oh, how nice that you didn't just pass us by!

RANK: I thought I heard your voice, and then I wanted so badly to have a look in. (*Lightly glancing about.*) Ah, me, these old familiar haunts. You have it snug and cozy in here, you two.

HELMER: You seemed to be having it pretty cozy upstairs, too.

RANK: Absolutely. Why shouldn't I? Why not take in everything in life? As much as you can, anyway, and as long as you can. The wine was superb—

150 HELMER: The champagne especially.

RANK: You noticed that too? It's amazing how much I could guzzle down.

NORA: Torvald also drank a lot of champagne this evening.

RANK: Oh?

NORA: Yes, and that always makes him so entertaining.

155 RANK: Well, why shouldn't one have a pleasant evening after a well spent day?

HELMER: Well spent? I'm afraid I can't claim that.

RANK: (*slapping him on the back*) But I can, you see!

NORA: Dr. Rank, you must have done some scientific research today.

RANK: Quite so.

160 HELMER: Come now—little Nora talking about scientific research!

NORA: And can I congratulate you on the results?

RANK: Indeed you may.

NORA: Then they were good?

RANK: The best possible for both doctor and patient—certainty.

165 NORA: (*quickly and searchingly*) Certainty?

RANK: Complete certainty. So don't I owe myself a gay evening afterwards?

NORA: Yes, you're right, Dr. Rank.

HELMER: I'm with you—just so long as you don't have to suffer for it in the morning.

RANK: Well, one never gets something for nothing in life.

170 NORA: Dr. Rank—are you very fond of masquerade parties?

RANK: Yes, if there's a good array of odd disguises—

NORA: Tell me, what should we two go as at the next masquerade?

HELMER: You little featherhead—already thinking of the next!

RANK: We two? I'll tell you what: you must go as Charmed Life—

175 HELMER: Yes, but find a costume for *that*!

RANK: Your wife can appear just as she looks every day.

HELMER: That was nicely put. But don't you know what you're going to be?

RANK: Yes, Helmer, I've made up my mind.

HELMER: Well?

180 RANK: At the next masquerade I'm going to be invisible.

HELMER: That's a funny idea.

RANK: They say there's a hat—black, huge—have you never heard of the hat that makes you invisible? You put it on, and then no one on earth can see you.

HELMER: (*suppressing a smile*) Ah, of course.

RANK: But I'm quite forgetting what I came for. Helmer, give me a cigar, one of the dark Havanas.

HELMER: With the greatest of pleasure. *(Holds out his case.)*   185
RANK: Thanks. *(Takes one and cuts off the tip.)*
NORA: *(striking a match)* Let me give you a light.
RANK: Thank you. *(She holds the match for him; he lights the cigar.)* And now
   good-bye.
HELMER: Good-bye, good-bye, old friend.
NORA: Sleep well, Doctor.   190
RANK: Thanks for that wish.
NORA: Wish me the same.
RANK: You? All right, if you like—Sleep well. And thanks for the light.
   (He nods to them both and leaves.)
HELMER: *(his voice subdued)* He's been drinking heavily.
NORA: *(absently)* Could be. *(Helmer takes his keys from his pocket and goes*   195
   out in the hall.) Torvald—what are you after?
HELMER: Got to empty the mailbox; it's nearly full. There won't be room
   for the morning papers.
NORA: Are you working tonight?
HELMER: You know I'm not. Why—what's this? Someone's been at the
   lock.
NORA: At the lock—?
HELMER: Yes, I'm positive. What do you suppose—? I can't imagine one of   200
   the maids—? Here's a broken hairpin. Nora, it's yours—
NORA: *(quickly)* Then it must be the children—
HELMER: You'd better break them of that. Hm, hm—well, opened it after
   all. *(Takes the contents out and calls into the kitchen.)* Helene! Helene,
   would you put out the lamp in the hall. *(He returns to the room, shutting*
   the hall door, then displays the handful of mail.) Look how it's piled up.
   (Sorting through them.) Now what's this?
NORA: *(at the window)* The letter! Oh, Torvald, no!
HELMER: Two calling cards—from Rank.
NORA: From Dr. Rank?   205
HELMER: *(examining them)* "Dr. Rank, Consulting Physician." They were
   on top. He must have dropped them in as he left.
NORA: Is there anything on them?
HELMER: There's a black cross over the name. See? That's a gruesome
   notion. He could almost be announcing his own death.
NORA: That's just what he's doing.
HELMER: What! You've heard something? Something he's told you?   210
NORA: Yes. That when those cards came, he'd be taking his leave of us.
   He'll shut himself in now and die.
HELMER: Ah, my poor friend! Of course I knew he wouldn't be here much
   longer. But so soon—And then to hide himself away like a wounded
   animal.

NORA: If it has to happen, then it's best it happens in silence—don't you think so, Torvald?

HELMER: *(pacing up and down)* He'd grown right into our lives. I simply can't imagine him gone. He with his suffering and loneliness—like a dark cloud setting off our sunlit happiness. Well, maybe it's best this way. For him, at least. *(Standing still.)* And maybe for us too, Nora. Now we're thrown back on each other, completely. *(Embracing her.)* Oh you, my darling wife, how can I hold you close enough? You know what, Nora—time and again I've wished you were in some terrible danger, just so I could stake my life and soul and everything, for your sake.

215 NORA: *(tearing herself away, her voice firm and decisive)* Now you must read your mail, Torvald.

HELMER: No, no, not tonight. I want to stay with you, dearest.

NORA: With a dying friend on your mind?

HELMER: You're right. We've both had a shock. There's ugliness between us—these thoughts of death and corruption. We'll have to get free of them first. Until then—we'll stay apart.

NORA: *(clinging about his neck)* Torvald—good night! Good night!

220 HELMER: *(kissing her on the cheek)* Good night, little songbird. Sleep well, Nora. I'll be reading my mail now. *(He takes the letters into his room and shuts the door after him.)*

NORA: *(with bewildered glances, groping about, seizing Helmer's domino, throwing it around her, and speaking in short, hoarse, broken whispers)* Never see him again. Never, never. *(Putting her shawl over her head.)* Never see the children either—them, too. Never, never. Oh, the freezing black water! The depths—down—Oh, I wish it were over—He has it now; he's reading it—now. Oh no, no, not yet. Torvald, good-bye, you and the children—*(She starts for the hall; as she does, Helmer throws open his door and stands with an open letter in his hand.)*

HELMER: Nora!

NORA: *(screams)* Oh—!

HELMER: What is this? You know what's in this letter?

225 NORA: Yes, I know. Let me go! Let me out!

HELMER: *(holding her back)* Where are you going?

NORA: *(struggling to break loose)* You can't save me, Torvald!

HELMER: *(slumping back)* True! Then it's true what he writes? How horrible! No, no, it's impossible—it can't be true.

NORA: It *is* true. I've loved you more than all this world.

230 HELMER: Ah, none of your slippery tricks.

NORA: *(taking one step toward him)* Torvald—!

HELMER: What *is* this you've blundered into!

NORA: Just let me loose. You're not going to suffer for my sake. You're not going to take on my guilt.

HELMER: No more playacting. (*Locks the hall door.*) You stay right here and give me a reckoning. You understand what you've done? Answer! You understand?

NORA: (*looking squarely at him, her face hardening*) Yes. I'm beginning to understand everything now.   235

HELMER: (*striding about*) Oh, what an awful awakening! In all these eight years—she who was my pride and joy—a hypocrite, a liar—worse, worse—a criminal! How infinitely disgusting it all is! The shame! (*Nora says nothing and goes on looking straight at him. He stops in front of her.*) I should have suspected something of the kind. I should have known. All your father's flimsy values—Be still! All your father's flimsy values have come out in you. No religion, no morals, no sense of duty—Oh, how I'm punished for letting him off! I did it for your sake, and you repay me like this.

NORA: Yes, like this.

HELMER: Now you've wrecked all my happiness—ruined my whole future. Oh, it's awful to think of. I'm in a cheap little grafter's hands; he can do anything he wants with me, ask for anything, play with me like a puppet—and I can't breathe a word. I'll be swept down miserably into the depths on account of a featherbrained woman.

NORA: When I'm gone from this world, you'll be free.

HELMER: Oh, quit posing. Your father had a mess of those speeches too.   240
What good would that ever do me if you were gone from this world, as you say? Not the slightest. He can still make the whole thing known; and if he does, I could be falsely suspected as your accomplice. They might even think that I was behind it—that I put you up to it. And all that I can thank you for—you that I've coddled the whole of our marriage. Can you see now what you've done to me?

NORA: (*icily calm*) Yes.

HELMER: It's so incredible, I just can't grasp it. But we'll have to patch up whatever we can. Take off the shawl. I said, take if off! I've got to appease him somehow or other. The thing has to be hushed up at any cost. And as for you and me, it's got to seem like everything between us is just as it was—to the outside world, that is. You'll go right on living in this house, of course. But you can't be allowed to bring up the children; I don't dare trust you with them—Oh, to have to say this to someone I've loved so much! Well, that's done with. From now on happiness doesn't matter; all that matters is saving the bits and pieces, the appearance—(*The doorbell rings. Helmer starts.*) What's that? And so late. Maybe the worst—? You think he'd—? Hide, Nora! Say you're sick. (*Nora remains standing motionless. Helmer goes and opens the door.*)

MAID: (*half dressed, in the hall*) A letter for Mrs. Helmer.

Helmer: I'll take it. (*Snatches the letter and shuts the door.*) Yes, it's from him. You don't get it; I'm reading it myself.

245 **Nora:** Then read it.

Helmer: (*by the lamp*) I hardly dare. We may be ruined, you and I. But— I've got to know. (*Rips open the letter, skims through a few lines, glances at an enclosure, then cries out joyfully.*) Nora! (*Nora looks inquiringly at him.*) Nora! Wait—better check it again—Yes, yes, it's true. I'm saved. Nora, I'm saved!

Nora: And I?

Helmer: You too, of course. We're both saved, both of us. Look. He's sent back your note. He says he's sorry and ashamed—that a happy development in his life—oh, who cares what he says! Nora, we're saved! No one can hurt you. Oh, Nora, Nora—but first, this ugliness all has to go. Let me see—(*Takes a look at the note.*) No, I don't want to see it; I want the whole thing to fade like a dream. (*Tears the note and both letters to pieces, throws them into the stove and watches them burn.*) There—now there's nothing left—He wrote that since Christmas Eve you—Oh, they must have been three terrible days for you, Nora.

Nora: I fought a hard fight.

250 **Helmer:** And suffered pain and saw no escape but—No, we're not going to dwell on anything unpleasant. We'll just be grateful and keep on repeating: it's over now, it's over! You hear me, Nora? You don't seem to realize—it's over. What's it mean—that frozen look? Oh, poor little Nora, I understand. You can't believe I've forgiven you. But I have, Nora; I swear I have. I know that what you did, you did out of love for me.

Nora: That's true.

Helmer: You loved me the way a wife ought to love her husband. It's simply the means that you couldn't judge. But you think I love you any the less for not knowing how to handle your affairs? No, no—just lean on me; I'll guide you and teach you. I wouldn't be a man if this feminine helplessness didn't make you twice as attractive to me. You mustn't mind those sharp words I said—that was all in the first confusion of thinking my world had collapsed. I've forgiven you, Nora; I swear I've forgiven you.

Nora: My thanks for your forgiveness. (*She goes out through the door, right.*)

Helmer: No, wait—(*Peers in.*) What are you doing in there?

255 **Nora:** (*inside*) Getting out of my costume.

Helmer: (*by the open door*) Yes, do that. Try to calm yourself and collect your thoughts again, my frightened little songbird. You can rest easy now; I've got wide wings to shelter you with. (*Walking about close by the door.*) How snug and nice our home is, Nora. You're safe here; I'll keep you like a hunted dove I've rescued out of a hawk's claws. I'll bring peace to your poor, shuddering heart. Gradually it'll happen, Nora;

you'll see. Tomorrow all this will look different to you; then everything will be as it was. I won't have to go on repeating I forgive you; you'll feel it for yourself. How can you imagine I'd ever conceivably want to disown you—or even blame you in any way? Ah, you don't know a man's heart, Nora. For a man there's something indescribably sweet and satisfying in knowing he's forgiven his wife—and forgiven her out of a full and open heart. It's as if she belongs to him in two ways now: in a sense he's given her fresh into the world again, and she's become his wife and his child as well. From now on that's what you'll be to me—you little, bewildered, helpless thing. Don't be afraid of anything, Nora; just open your heart to me, and I'll be conscience and will to you both—(*Nora enters in her regular clothes.*) What's this? Not in bed? You've changed your dress?

NORA: Yes, Torvald, I've changed my dress.

HELMER: But why now, so late?

NORA: Tonight I'm not sleeping.

HELMER: But Nora dear—   260

NORA: (*looking at her watch*) It's still not so very late. Sit down, Torvald; we have a lot to talk over. (*She sits at one side of the table.*)

HELMER: Nora—what is this? That hard expression—

NORA: Sit down. This'll take some time. I have a lot to say.

HELMER: (*sitting at the table directly opposite her*) You worry me, Nora. And I don't understand you.

NORA: No, that's exactly it. You don't understand me. And I've never   265
understood you either—until tonight. No, don't interrupt. You can just listen to what I say. We're closing out accounts, Torvald.

HELMER: How do you mean that?

NORA: (*after a short pause*) Doesn't anything strike you about our sitting here like this?

HELMER: What's that?

NORA: We've been married now eight years. Doesn't it occur to you that this is the first time we two, you and I, man and wife, have ever talked seriously together?

HELMER: What do you mean—seriously?   270

NORA: In eight whole years—longer even—right from our first acquaintance, we've never exchanged a serious word on any serious thing.

HELMER: You mean I should constantly go and involve you in problems you couldn't possibly help me with?

NORA: I'm not talking of problems. I'm saying that we've never sat down seriously together and tried to get to the bottom of anything.

HELMER: But dearest, what good would that ever do you?

NORA: That's the point right there: you've never understood me. I've been   275
wronged greatly, Torvald—first by Papa, and then by you.

HELMER: What! By us—the two people who've loved you more than anyone else?

NORA: (*shaking her head*) You never loved me. You've thought it fun to be in love with me, that's all.

HELMER: Nora, what a thing to say!

NORA: Yes, it's true now, Torvald. When I lived at home with Papa, he told me all his opinions, so I had the same ones too; or if they were different I hid them, since he wouldn't have cared for that. He used to call me his doll-child, and he played with me the way I played with my dolls. Then I came into your house—

280 HELMER: How can you speak of our marriage like that?

NORA: (*unperturbed*) I mean, then I went from Papa's hands into yours. You arranged everything to your own taste, and so I got the same taste as you—or I pretended to; I can't remember. I guess a little of both, first one, then the other. Now when I look back, it seems as if I'd lived here like a beggar—just from hand to mouth. I've lived by doing tricks for you, Torvald. But that's the way you wanted it. It's a great sin what you and Papa did to me. You're to blame that nothing's become of me.

HELMER: Nora, how unfair and ungrateful you are! Haven't you been happy here?

NORA: No, never. I thought so—but I never have.

HELMER: Not—not happy!

285 NORA: No, only lighthearted. And you've always been so kind to me. But our home's been nothing but a playpen. I've been your doll-wife here, just as at home I was Papa's doll-child. And in turn the children have been my dolls. I thought it was fun when you played with me, just as they thought it fun when I played with them. That's been our marriage, Torvald.

HELMER: There's some truth in what you're saying—under all the raving exaggeration. But it'll all be different after this. Playtime's over; now for the schooling.

NORA: Whose schooling—mine or the children's?

HELMER: Both yours and the children's, dearest.

NORA: Oh, Torvald, you're not the man to teach me to be a good wife to you.

290 HELMER: And you can say that?

NORA: And I—how am I equipped to bring up children?

HELMER: Nora!

NORA: Didn't you say a moment ago that that was no job to trust me with?

HELMER: In a flare of temper! Why fasten on that?

295 NORA: Yes, but you were so very right. I'm not up to the job. There's another job I have to do first. I have to try to educate myself. You can't help me with that. I've got to do it alone. And that's why I'm leaving you now.

HELMER: (*jumping up*) What's that?

NORA: I have to stand completely alone, if I'm ever going to discover myself and the world out there. So I can't go on living with you.

HELMER: Nora, Nora!

NORA: I want to leave right away. Kristine should put me up for the night—

HELMER: You're insane! You've no right! I forbid you!   300

NORA: From here on, there's no use forbidding me anything. I'll take with me whatever is mine. I don't want a thing from you, either now or later.

HELMER: What kind of madness is this!

NORA: Tomorrow I'm going home—I mean, home where I came from. It'll be easier up there to find something to do.

HELMER: Oh, you blind, incompetent child!

NORA: I must learn to be competent, Torvald.   305

HELMER: Abandon your home, your husband, your children! And you're not even thinking what people will say.

NORA: I can't be concerned about that. I only know how essential this is.

HELMER: Oh, it's outrageous. So you'll run out like this on your most sacred vows.

NORA: What do you think are my most sacred vows?

HELMER: And I have to tell you that! Aren't they your duties to your   310
husband and children?

NORA: I have other duties equally sacred.

HELMER: That isn't true. What duties are they?

NORA: Duties to myself.

HELMER: Before all else, you're a wife and a mother.

NORA: I don't believe in that any more. I believe that, before all else, I'm   315
a human being, no less than you—or anyway, I ought to try to become one. I know the majority thinks you're right, Torvald, and plenty of books agree with you, too. But I can't go on believing what the majority says, or what's written in books. I have to think over these things myself and try to understand them.

HELMER: Why can't you understand your place in your own home? On a point like that, isn't there one everlasting guide you can turn to? Where's your religion?

NORA: Oh, Torvald, I'm really not sure what religion is.

HELMER: What—?

NORA: I only know what the minister said when I was confirmed. He told me religion was this thing and that. When I get clear and away by myself, I'll go into that problem too. I'll see if what the minister said was right, or, in any case, if it's right for me.

HELMER: A young woman your age shouldn't talk like that. If religion can't   320
move you, I can try to rouse your conscience. You do have some moral feeling? Or, tell me—has that gone too?

NORA: It's not easy to answer that, Torvald. I simply don't know. I'm all confused about these things. I just know I see them so differently from you. I find out, for one thing, that the law's not at all what I'd thought—but I can't get it through my head that the law is fair. A woman hasn't a right to protect her dying father or save her husband's life! I can't believe that.

HELMER: You talk like a child. You don't know anything of the world you live in.

NORA: No, I don't. But now I'll begin to learn for myself. I'll try to discover who's right, the world or I.

HELMER: Nora, you're sick; you've got a fever. I almost think you're out of your head.

325 NORA: I've never felt more clearheaded and sure in my life.

HELMER: And—clearheaded and sure—you're leaving your husband and children?

NORA: Yes.

HELMER: Then there's only one possible reason.

NORA: What?

330 HELMER: You no longer love me.

NORA: No. That's exactly it.

HELMER: Nora! You can't be serious!

NORA: Oh, this is so hard, Torvald—you've been so kind to me always. But I can't help it. I don't love you any more.

HELMER: (*struggling for composure*) Are you also clearheaded and sure about that?

335 NORA: Yes, completely. That's why I can't go on staying here.

HELMER: Can you tell me what I did to lose your love?

NORA: Yes, I can tell you. It was this evening when the miraculous thing didn't come—then I knew you weren't the man I'd imagined.

HELMER: Be more explicit; I don't follow you.

NORA: I've waited now so patiently eight long years—for, my Lord, I know miracles don't come every day. Then this crisis broke over me, and such a certainty filled me: *now* the miraculous event would occur. While Krogstad's letter was lying out there, I never for an instant dreamed that you could give in to his terms. I was so utterly sure you'd say to him: go on, tell your tale to the whole wide world. And when he'd done that—

340 HELMER: Yes, what then? When I'd delivered my own wife into shame and disgrace—!

NORA: When he'd done that, I was so utterly sure that you'd step forward, take the blame on yourself and say: I am the guilty one.

HELMER: Nora—!

NORA: You're thinking I'd never accept such a sacrifice from you? No, of course not. But what good would my protests be against you? That was the miracle I was waiting for, in terror and hope. And to stave that off, I would have taken my life.

HELMER: I'd gladly work for you day and night, Nora—and take on pain and deprivation. But there's no one who gives up honor for love.

NORA: Millions of women have done just that.   345

HELMER: Oh, you think and talk like a silly child.

NORA: Perhaps. But you neither think nor talk like the man I could join myself to. When your big fright was over—and it wasn't from any threat against me, only for what might damage you—when all the danger was past, for you it was just as if nothing had happened. I was exactly the same, your little lark, your doll, that you'd have to handle with double care now that I'd turned out so brittle and frail. (*Gets up.*) Torvald—in that instant it dawned on me that for eight years I've been living here with a stranger, and that I'd even conceived three children—oh, I can't stand the thought of it! I could tear myself to bits.

HELMER: (*heavily*) I see. There's a gulf that's opened between us—that's clear. Oh, but Nora, can't we bridge it somehow?

NORA: The way I am now, I'm no wife for you.

HELMER: I have the strength to make myself over.   350

NORA: Maybe—if your doll gets taken away.

HELMER: But to part! To part from you! No, Nora, no—I can't imagine it.

NORA: (*going out, right*) All the more reason why it has to be. (*She reenters with her coat and a small overnight bag, which she puts on a chair by the table.*)

HELMER: Nora, Nora, not now! Wait till tomorrow.

NORA: I can't spend the night in a strange man's room.   355

HELMER: But couldn't we live here like brother and sister—

NORA: You know very well how long that would last. (*Throws her shawl about her.*) Good-bye, Torvald. I won't look in on the children. I know they're in better hands than mine. The way I am now, I'm no use to them.

HELMER: But someday, Nora—someday—?

NORA: How can I tell? I haven't the least idea what'll become of me.

HELMER: But you're my wife, now and wherever you go.   360

NORA: Listen, Torvald—I've heard that when a wife deserts her husband's house just as I'm doing, then the law frees him from all responsibility. In any case, I'm freeing you from being responsible. Don't feel yourself bound, any more than I will. There has to be absolute freedom for us both. Here, take your ring back. Give me mine.

HELMER: That too?

NORA: That too.

HELMER: There it is.

NORA: Good. Well, now it's all over. I'm putting the keys here. The maids   365
know all about keeping up the house—better than I do. Tomorrow,

after I've left town, Kristine will stop by to pack up everything that's mine from home. I'd like those things shipped up to me.

HELMER: Over! All over! Nora, won't you ever think about me?

NORA: I'm sure I'll think of you often, and about the children and the house here.

HELMER: May I write you?

NORA: No—never. You're not to do that.

370 HELMER: Oh, but let me send you—

NORA: Nothing. Nothing.

HELMER: Or help you if you need it.

NORA: No. I accept nothing from strangers.

HELMER: Nora—can I never be more than a stranger to you?

375 NORA: *(picking up the overnight bag)* Ah, Torvald—it would take the greatest miracle of all—

HELMER: Tell me the greatest miracle!

NORA: You and I both would have to transform ourselves to the point that—Oh, Torvald, I've stopped believing in miracles.

HELMER: But I'll believe. Tell me! Transform ourselves to the point that—?

NORA: That our living together could be a true marriage. *(She goes out down the hall.)*

380 HELMER: *(sinks down on a chair by the door, face buried in his hands)* Nora! Nora! *(Looking about and rising.)* Empty. She's gone. *(A sudden hope leaps in him.)* The greatest miracle—?

From below, the sound of a door slamming shut.

*   *   *

Reading and Reacting

1. What is your attitude toward Nora at the beginning of the play? How does your attitude toward her change as the play progresses? What actions and lines of dialogue change your assessment of her?

2. List the key events that occurred before the start of the play. How do we learn of each event?

3. Explain the role of each of the following in advancing the play's action: the Christmas tree, the locked mailbox, the telegram Dr. Rank receives, Dr. Rank's calling cards.

4. In act 2, Torvald says, "Whatever comes, you'll see: when it really counts, I have strength and courage enough as a man to take on the whole weight myself." How does this statement influence Nora's subsequent actions?

5. Explain how each of the following foreshadows events that will occur later in the play: Torvald's comments about Krogstad's children (act 1);

Torvald's attitude toward Nora's father (act 2); Krogstad's suggestions about suicide (act 2).

6. In addition to the play's main plot—which concerns the blackmail of Nora by Krogstad and her attempts to keep her crime secret from Torvald—the play contains several subplots. Some of them began to develop before the start of the play, and some unfold alongside the main plot. Identify these subplots. How do they advance the themes of survival, debt, sacrifice, and duty that run through the play?

7. Is Kristine Linde as much of a "modern woman" as Nora? Is she actually *more* of a modern woman? Is she essential to the play? How might the play be different without her?

8. **JOURNAL ENTRY** Do you see *A Doll House* as primarily about the struggle between the needs of the individual and the needs of society or about the conflict between women's roles in the family and in the larger society? Explain.

9. **CRITICAL PERSPECTIVE** Since its earliest performances, there has been much comment on the conclusion of *A Doll House*. Many viewers have found the play's ending unrealistically harsh. In fact, a famous German actress refused to play the scene as written because she insisted she would never leave her children. (Ibsen reluctantly rewrote the ending for her; in this version, Helmer forces Nora to the doorway of the children's bedroom, and she sinks to the floor as the curtain falls.) Moreover, many critics have found it hard to accept Nora's sudden transformation from, in the words of Elizabeth Hardwick in her essay "Ibsen's Women," "the girlish, charming wife to the radical, courageous heroine setting out alone."

What is your response to the play's ending? Do you think it makes sense in light of what we have learned about Nora and her marriage? Or, do you agree with Hardwick that Nora's abandonment of her children is not only implausible but also a "rather casual" gesture that "drops a stain on our admiration of Nora"?

Related Works: "The Story of an Hour" (p. 127), "The Rocking-Horse Winner" (p. 409), "The Yellow Wallpaper" (p. 434)

WRITING SUGGESTIONS: Plot

1. Central to the plots of both *Trifles* and *A Doll House* is a woman who commits a crime. Compare and contrast the desperate situations that motivate the two women. Then, consider the reactions of other characters in the two plays to each woman's crime.

2. Write an essay in which you discuss the influence of Nora's father on the plot of *A Doll House*.

3. In *The Blizzard*, the action unfolds in a confined, isolated space. Consider this play alongside some other works in which one or more characters are similarly confined—for example, the two people in the car in "Encounters with Unexpected Animals" (p. 90) or the people waiting for jury duty in *Nine Ten* (p. 861). How does the confined setting influence the characters' actions and reactions?

4. Write a monologue for Nora in *A Doll House*, including everything you think she would like to tell her children.

5. Write a play called *Nine Twelve*. Keep all the major characters of *Nine Ten*, but put them together on September 12 in another setting, where they discuss what has happened to them since they last met and how their attitudes toward jury duty, work, and life in general have changed as a result.

CHAPTER 28

CHARACTER

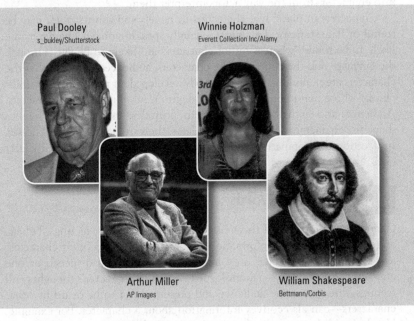

Paul Dooley
s_bukley/Shutterstock

Winnie Holzman
Everett Collection Inc/Alamy

Arthur Miller
AP Images

William Shakespeare
Bettmann/Corbis

In Tennessee Williams's 1945 play *The Glass Menagerie*, the protagonist, Tom Wingfield, functions as the play's narrator. Stepping out of his role as a character and speaking directly to the audience, he directs the play's action, music, lighting, and other elements. In addition, he summarizes characters' actions, explains what motivates them, and discusses the significance of their behavior in the context of the play—commenting on his own character's actions as well. As narrator, Tom also presents useful background information about the characters. For instance, when he introduces his coworker, Jim, he prepares the audience for Jim's entrance and helps them to understand his subsequent actions:

> In high school Jim was a hero. He had tremendous Irish good nature
> and vitality with the scrubbed and polished look of white chinaware. He
> seemed to move in a continual spotlight. . . . But Jim apparently ran into
> more interference after his graduation. . . . His speed had definitely slowed.

943

Six years after he left high school he was holding a job that wasn't much better than mine. (scene 6)

Most plays, however, do not include narrators who present background. Instead, the audience learns about characters from their own words and from comments by others about them, as well as from the characters' actions. When reading a play, we learn about the characters from the playwright's stage directions; when watching a performance, we gain insight into characters from the way actors interpret them.

Characters in plays, like characters in novels and short stories, may be **round** or **flat, static** or **dynamic**. Generally speaking, major characters are likely to be round, whereas minor characters are likely to be flat. Through the language and the actions of the characters, audiences learn whether the characters are multidimensional, skimpily developed, or perhaps merely **foils**: players whose main purpose is to shed light on more important characters. Audiences also learn about the emotions, attitudes, and values that help to shape the characters—their hopes and fears: their strengths and weaknesses. In addition, by comparing characters' early words and actions with later ones, audiences learn whether characters grow and change emotionally.

 ## Characters' Words

Characters' words reveal the most about their attitudes, feelings, beliefs, and values. Sometimes information is communicated (to other characters as well as to the audience) in a **monologue**—an extended speech by one character. A **soliloquy**—a monologue revealing a character's thoughts and feelings, directed at the audience and presumed not to be heard by other characters—can also convey information about a character. For example, Hamlet's well-known soliloquy that begins "To be or not to be" eloquently communicates his distraught mental state—his resentment of his mother and uncle, his confusion about what course of action to take, and his suicidal thoughts. Finally, **dialogue**—an exchange of words between two characters—can reveal misunderstanding or conflict between them, or it can show their agreement, mutual support, or similar beliefs.

In Henrik Ibsen's *A Doll House* (p. 881), dialogue reveals a good deal about the characters. Nora Helmer, the spoiled young wife, has broken the law and kept her crime secret from her husband. Through her words, we learn about her motivation, her values, her emotions, and her reactions to other characters and to her potentially dangerous situation. We learn, for instance, that she is flirtatious: "If your little squirrel begged you, with all her heart and soul . . ." We also see that she is childishly unrealistic about the consequences of her actions. When her husband, Torvald, asks what she would do if he was seriously injured, leaving her in debt, she says, "If anything so awful happened, then it just wouldn't matter if I had debts or not." When Torvald presses, "Well, but the people I'd borrowed from?" she dismisses them: "Them? Who cares about them! They're strangers." As the play progresses, Nora's lack of understanding of the power of the law becomes more and more significant as she struggles with her moral and ethical dilemma.

The inability of both Nora and Torvald to confront ugly truths is also revealed through their words. When, in act 1, Nora tells Krogstad, her black-mailer, that his revealing her secret could expose her to "the most horrible unpleasantness," he responds, "Only unpleasantness?" Yet later on, in act 3, Torvald echoes her language, fastidiously dismissing the horror with, "No, we're not going to dwell on anything unpleasant."

The ease with which Torvald is able to dismiss his dying friend Dr. Rank in act 3 ("He with his suffering and loneliness—like a dark cloud setting off our sunlit happiness. Well, maybe it's best this way.") foreshadows the lack of support he will give Nora immediately thereafter. Especially revealing is his use of *I* and *my* and *me*, which convey his self-centeredness:

> Now you've wrecked all my happiness—ruined my whole future. Oh, it's awful to think of. I'm in a cheap little grafter's hands; he can do anything he wants with me, ask for anything, play with me like a puppet—and I can't breathe a word. I'll be swept down miserably into the depths on account of a featherbrained woman.

Just as Torvald's words reveal that he has not been changed by the play's events, Nora's words show that she has changed significantly. Her dialogue near the end of act 3 shows that she has become a responsible, determined woman—one who understands her situation and her options and is no longer blithely oblivious to her duties. When she says, "I've never felt more clearheaded and sure in my life," she is calm and decisive. When she says, "Our home's been nothing but a playpen. I've been your doll-wife here, just as at home I was Papa's doll-child," she reveals a new self-awareness. And, when she confronts her husband, she displays—perhaps for the first time in their relationship—complete honesty.

Sometimes what other characters say to (or about) a character can reveal more to an audience than the character's own words. For instance, in *A Doll House*, when the dying Dr. Rank says, apparently without malice, "[Torvald] Helmer with his sensitivity has such a sharp distaste for anything ugly," the audience not only thinks ill of the man who is too "sensitive" to visit his sick friend but also questions his ability to withstand situations that may be emotionally or morally "ugly" as well.

When a character is offstage for much (or even all) of the action, the audience must rely on other characters' assessments of the absent character. In Susan Glaspell's *Trifles* (p. 867), the play's focus is on an absent charac-ter, Minnie Wright, who is described solely through other characters' com-ments. The evidence suggests that Mrs. Wright killed her husband, and only

Mrs. Hale's and Mrs. Peters's comments about Mrs. Wright's dreary life can delineate her character and suggest a likely motive for the murder. Although Mrs. Wright never appears on stage, we learn essential information from the other women about her: that as a young girl she liked to sing and that more recently she was so distraught about the lack of beauty in her life that even her sewing revealed her distress.

Whether a character's words are in the form of a monologue, a soliloquy, or dialogue—and whether they reveal information about the character who is speaking or about someone else—words are always revealing. Explicitly or implicitly, they convey a character's nature, attitudes, and relationships with other characters.

Keep in mind that the kind of language characters use can vary widely. A character may, for instance, use learned words, foreign words, elaborate figures of speech, irony or sarcasm, regionalisms, slang, jargon, clichés, or profanity. Words can also be used to indicate tone—for example, to express irony. Any of these uses of language may communicate vital information to the audience about a character's background, attitudes, and motivation. And, of course, a character's language may change as a play progresses, and this change too may be revealing.

Formal and Informal Language

The level of diction a character uses can give audiences a good deal of information. One character in a dramatic work may speak very formally, using absolutely correct grammar, a learned vocabulary, and long, complex sentences; another may speak in an informal style, using conversational speech, colloquialisms, and slang. At times, two characters with different levels of language may be set in opposition for dramatic effect, as they are in Irish playwright George Bernard Shaw's classic play *Pygmalion* (1912), which updates the ancient Greek myth of a sculptor who creates (and falls in love with) a statue of a woman. In Shaw's version, a linguistics professor sets out to teach "proper" speech and manners to a woman who sells flowers on the street. Throughout the play, the contrasting language of Henry Higgins, the professor, and Eliza Doolittle, the flower seller, reveals their differing social standing. The following exchange illustrates this contrast:

LIZA: I ain't got no mother. Her that turned me out was my sixth step-
      mother. But I done without them. And I'm a good girl, I am.
HIGGINS: Very well, then, what on earth is all this fuss about?

A character's accent or dialect may also be significant. In **comedies of manners**, for instance, rustic or provincial characters, identified by their speech, are often objects of humor. In *Pygmalion*, Eliza Doolittle uses cockney dialect, the dialect spoken in the East End of London. At first, her colorful, distinctive language (complete with expressions like *Nah-ow, garn,* and *ah-ah-ah-ow-ow-ow-oo*) and her nonstandard grammatical constructions make her an object of ridicule; later, the transformation of her speech reveals the dramatic changes in her character.

Plain and Elaborate Language

A character's speech may be simple and straightforward or complex and convoluted; it may be plain and unadorned or embellished with elaborate **figures of speech.** The relative complexity or lack of complexity of a character's speech may have different effects on the audience. For example, a character whose language is simple and unsophisticated may seem to be unintelligent, unenlightened, gullible, or naive—especially if he or she also uses slang, dialect, or colloquial expressions. Conversely, a character's plain, down-to-earth language may convey common sense or intelligence. Plain language may also be quite emotionally powerful. For example, Willy Loman's speech in act 2 of *Death of a Salesman* (p. 960), about an eighty-four-year-old salesman named Dave Singleman, moves the audience with its sincerity and directness:

> Do you know? When he died—and by the way he died the death of a salesman, in his green velvet slippers in the smoker of the New York, New Haven and Hartford, going into Boston—when he died, hundreds of salesmen and buyers were at his funeral. Things were sad on a lotta trains for months after that.

Like plain speech, elaborate language may have different effects in different contexts. Sometimes, use of figures of speech can make a character seem to have depth and insight and analytical skills absent in other characters. In the following excerpt from a soliloquy in act 1 scene 2 of *Hamlet,* for example, complex language reveals the depth of Hamlet's anguished self-analysis:

> HAMLET: O, that this too too solid flesh would melt,
> Thaw, and resolve itself into a dew!
> Or that the Everlasting had not fix'd
> His canon 'gainst self-slaughter! O God! O God!
> How weary, stale, flat, and unprofitable
> Seem to me all the uses of this world!
> Fie on't, O fie, 'tis an unweeded garden,
> That grows to seed. . . .

In these lines, Hamlet compares the world to a garden gone to seed. His use of imagery and figures of speech vividly communicates his feelings about the world and his internal struggle against the temptation to commit suicide.

Sometimes, however, elaborate language may make a character seem aloof, pompous, or even untrustworthy. In the following passages from

Shakespeare's *King Lear*, Goneril and Regan, the deceitful daughters, use complicated verbal constructions to conceal their true feelings from their father, King Lear. In contrast, Cordelia—the loyal, loving daughter—uses simple, straightforward language that suggests her sincerity and lack of artifice. Compare the three speeches:

GONERIL: Sir, I love you more than words can wield the matter;
  Dearer than eyesight, space, and liberty;
  Beyond what can be valued, rich or rare;
  No less than life, with grace, health, beauty, honour;
  As much as child e'er lov'd, or father found;
  A love that makes breath poor, and speech unable.
  Beyond all manner of so much I love you. . . .

REGAN: Sir, I am made
  Of the selfsame metal that my sister is,
  And prize me at her worth. In my true heart
  I find she names my very deed of love;
  Only she comes too short, that I profess
  Myself an enemy to all other joys
  Which the most precious square of sense possesses,
  And find I am alone felicitate
  In your dear Highness' love. . . .

CORDELIA: Unhappy that I am, I cannot heave
  My heart into my mouth. I love your Majesty
  According to my bond; no more no less. . . .

Cordelia's unwillingness, even when she is prodded by Lear, to exaggerate her feelings or misrepresent her love through inflated language shows the audience her honesty and nobility. The contrast between her language and that of her sisters makes their very different motives clear.

Tone

Tone reveals a character's mood or attitude. Tone can be flat or emotional, bitter or accepting, affectionate or aloof, anxious or calm. Contrasts in tone can indicate differences in outlook or emotional state between two characters; changes in tone from one point in a play to another can suggest corresponding changes within a character. At the end of *A Doll House*, for instance, Nora is resigned to what she must do, and her language is appropriately controlled. Her husband, however, is desperate to change her mind, and his language reflects this desperation. The following exchanges of dialogue from the end of act 3 illustrate the two characters' contrasting emotional states:

HELMER: But to part! To part from you! No, Nora, no—I can't imagine it.
NORA: *(going out, right)* All the more reason why it has to be.

HELMER: Over! All over! Nora, won't you ever think about me?
NORA: I'm sure I'll think of you often, and about the children and the house here.

In earlier scenes between the two characters, Nora is emotional—at times, hysterical—and her husband is considerably more controlled. As the exchanges above indicate, both Nora and Torvald Helmer change drastically during the course of the play.

Irony

Irony, a contradiction or discrepancy between two levels of meaning, can reveal a great deal about character. **Verbal irony**—a contradiction between what a character says and what he or she means—is very important in drama, where the verbal interplay between characters may carry the weight of the play. For example, when Nora and Dr. Rank discuss the latest news about his health in *A Doll House*, there is deep irony in his use of the phrase "complete certainty." Although the phrase usually suggests reassuring news, here it is meant to suggest death, and both Nora and Dr. Rank understand this.

Dramatic irony depends on the audience's knowing something that a character has not yet realized, or on one character's knowing something that other characters do not know. In some cases, dramatic irony is created by an audience's awareness of historical background or events of which characters are unaware. Familiar with the story of Oedipus, for instance, the audience knows that the man who has caused all the problems in Thebes— the man Oedipus vows to find and take revenge on—is Oedipus himself. In other cases, dramatic irony emerges when the audience learns something— something the characters do not yet know or comprehend—from a play's unfolding action. The central irony in *A Doll House*, for example, is that the family's "happy home" rests on a foundation of secrets, lies, and deception. Torvald does not know about the secrets, and Nora does not understand how they have poisoned her marriage. The audience, however, quickly becomes aware of the atmosphere of deceit—and aware of how it threatens the family's happiness.

Dramatic irony may also be conveyed through dialogue. Typically, dramatic irony is revealed when a character says something that gives the audience information that other characters, offstage at the time, do not know. In *A Doll House*, the audience knows—because Nora has explained her situation to Kristine—that Nora spent the previous Christmas season hard at work, earning money to pay her secret debt. Torvald, however, remains unaware of her activities and believes her story that she was using the time to make holiday decorations, which the cat destroyed. This belief is consistent with his impression of Nora as an irresponsible child, yet the audience has quite a different impression of her. This discrepancy, one of many contradictions between the audience's view of Nora and Torvald's view of her, helps to create dramatic tension in the play.

Finally, **asides** (comments to the audience that other characters do not hear) can create dramatic irony by undercutting dialogue, providing ironic contrast between what the characters on stage know and what the audience knows. In Anton Chekhov's *The Brute* (p. 814), for example, the audience knows that Mr. Smirnov is succumbing to Mrs. Popov's charms because he says, in an aside, "My God, what eyes she has! They're setting me on fire." Mrs. Popov, however, is not yet aware of his infatuation. The discrepancy between the audience's awareness and the character's adds to the play's humor.

 ## Characters' Actions

Through their actions, characters convey their values and attitudes to the audience. Actions also reveal aspects of a character's personality. For example, when Nora in *A Doll House* plays hide-and-seek with her children, eats forbidden macaroons, and takes childish joy in Christmas, her immaturity is apparent.

Audiences also learn about characters from what they do *not* do. Thus, Nora's failure to remain in touch with her friend Kristine, who has had a hard life, reveals her selfishness, and the decision by Mrs. Peters and Mrs. Hale in *Trifles* not to give their evidence to the sheriff indicates their defiant support for Mrs. Wright and their understanding of what motivated her to take such drastic action.

Finally, audiences learn a good deal about characters by observing how they interact with other characters. In William Shakespeare's *Othello*, Iago is the embodiment of evil, and as the play's action unfolds, we discover his true nature. He reveals the secret marriage of Othello and Desdemona to her father; he schemes to arouse Othello's jealousy, making him believe Desdemona has been unfaithful with his lieutenant, Cassio; he persuades Cassio to ask Desdemona to plead his case with Othello, knowing this act will further arouse Othello's suspicions; he encourages Othello to be suspicious of Desdemona's defense of Cassio; he plants Desdemona's handkerchief in Cassio's room; and, finally, he persuades Othello to kill Desdemona and then kills his own wife, Emilia, to prevent her from exposing his role in the intrigue. As the play progresses, then, Iago's dealings with others consistently reveal him to be evil and corrupt.

Stage Directions

When we read a play (rather than see it performed), we also read the playwright's italicized **stage directions**, the notes that concern **staging**—the scenery, props, lighting, music, sound effects, costumes, and other elements that contribute to the way the play looks and sounds to an audience (see Chapter 29). In addition to commenting on staging, stage directions may supply physical details about the characters, suggesting their age, appearance, movements, gestures, and facial expressions. These details may in turn convey additional information about characters: appearance may reveal social position or economic status, expressions may reveal attitudes, and so on. Stage directions may also indicate the manner in which a line of dialogue is to be delivered—*confidently* or *hesitantly*, for instance. The way a line is spoken may reveal a character to be excited, upset, angry, shy, or disappointed. Finally, stage directions may indicate changes in characters—for instance, a character whose speech is described as timid in early scenes may deliver lines emphatically and forcefully later on in the play.

Some stage directions provide a good deal of detail about character; others do little more than list characters' names. Arthur Miller is one playwright who often provides detailed information about character through stage directions. In *Death of a Salesman*, for instance, Miller's stage directions at the beginning of act 1 characterize Willy Loman immediately and specifically:

> He is past sixty years of age, dressed quietly. Even as he crosses the stage to the doorway of the house, his exhaustion is apparent. He unlocks the door, comes into the kitchen, and thankfully lets his burden down, feeling the soreness of his palms. A word-sigh escapes his lips . . .

Subsequent stage directions indicate how lines are to be spoken. For example, in the play's opening lines, Willy's wife Linda calls out to him "*with some trepidation*"; Linda speaks "*very carefully, delicately,*" and Willy speaks "*with casual irritation.*" These instructions to readers (and actors) are meant to suggest the strained relationship between the two characters.

George Bernard Shaw is well known for the full character description in his stage directions. In these directions—seen by readers of the play but of course not heard by audiences—he communicates complex information about characters' attitudes and values, motivation and reactions, and relationships with other characters. In doing so, Shaw himself functions as a kind of narrator, explicitly communicating his own attitudes toward various characters. (The voice in Shaw's stage directions is not the voice of a character in the play; it is the voice of the playwright.) Shaw's stage directions for *Pygmalion* initially describe Eliza Doolittle as follows:

> She is not at all an attractive person. She is perhaps eighteen, perhaps twenty, hardly older. She wears a little sailor hat of black straw that has long been

exposed to the dust and soot of London and has seldom if ever been brushed. Her hair needs washing rather badly; its mousy color can hardly be natural. She wears a shoddy black coat that reaches nearly to her knees and is shaped to her waist. She has a brown skirt with a coarse apron. Her boots are much the worse for wear. She is no doubt as clean as she can afford to be; but compared to the ladies she is very dirty. Her features are no worse than theirs; but their condition leaves something to be desired; and she needs the services of a dentist.

Rather than providing an objective summary of the character's most notable physical attributes, Shaw injects subjective comments (*"seldom if ever brushed"*; *"color can hardly be natural"*; *"no doubt as clean as she can afford to be"*) that reveal his attitude toward Eliza. This initially supercilious attitude, which he has in common with Professor Higgins, is tempered considerably by the end of the play, helping to make Eliza's transformation more obvious to readers than it would be if measured by her words and actions alone. By act 5, the tone of the stage directions characterizing Eliza has changed to admiration: *"Eliza enters, sunny, self-possessed, and giving a staggeringly convincing exhibition of ease of manner."*

Stage directions in most other plays are not nearly as comprehensive. In *Hamlet*, for example, characters are introduced with only the barest identifying tags: *"Claudius, King of Denmark"*; *"Hamlet, Son to the former, and nephew to the present King"*; *"Gertrude, Queen of Denmark, mother to Hamlet."* Most of the play's stage directions do little more than chronicle the various characters' entrances and exits or specify particular physical actions: *"Enter Ghost"*; *"Spreads his arms"*; *"Ghost beckons Hamlet"*; *"He kneels"*; *"Sheathes his sword"*; *"Leaps in the grave."* Occasionally, stage directions specify a prop (*"Puts down the skull"*); a sound effect (*"A noise within"*); or a costume (*"Enter the ghost in his night-gown"*). Such brevity is typical of Shakespeare's plays, in which characters are delineated almost solely by their words—and, not incidentally, by the way actors have interpreted the characters over the years. In fact, because Shakespeare's stage directions only suggest characters' gestures, physical reactions, movements, and facial expressions, actors have been left quite free to experiment, reading various interpretations into Shakespeare's characters.

Actors' Interpretations

When we see a play performed, we gain insight into a character not merely through what the character says and does or how other characters react but also through the way an actor interprets the role. If a playwright does not specify a character's mannerisms, gestures, or movements, or does not indicate how a line is to be delivered, an actor is free to interpret the role as he or she believes it should be played. Even when a playwright *does* specify such actions, the actor has a good deal of freedom to decide which gestures or expressions will convey a particular emotion.

In "Some Thoughts on Playwriting" (1941), American dramatist Thornton Wilder argues that "the theatre is an art which reposes upon the work of many collaborators" rather than on "one governing selecting will." Citing examples from Shakespeare and Ibsen, Wilder illustrates the great degree of "intervention" that may occur in dramatic productions. For instance, Wilder observes, Shakespeare's Shylock (a character in *The Merchant of Venice*) has been portrayed by two different actors as "noble, wronged and indignant" and as "a vengeful and hysterical buffoon"—and both performances were considered plausible interpretations. As noted earlier, the absence of detailed stage directions in Shakespeare's plays makes possible (and perhaps even encourages) such widely divergent interpretations. However, as Wilder points out, even when playing roles created by a dramatist such as Ibsen, whose stage directions are typically quite specific, actors and directors have a good deal of leeway. Thus, actress Janet McTeer, who played the part of Ibsen's Nora in the 1997 London production of *A Doll House*, saw Nora and Torvald, despite their many problems, as "the perfect couple," deeply in love and involved in a passionate marriage. "You have to make that marriage sexually credible," McTeer told the *New York Times*, "to imagine they have a wonderful time in bed, so there becomes something to lose. If you play them as already past it or no longer attracted to each other, then there is no play." This interpretation is not inconsistent with the play, but it does go beyond what Ibsen actually wrote.

Similarly, the role of Catherine in David Auburn's 2001 play *Proof* has been played by several actresses—among them Mary-Louise Parker, Jennifer Jason Leigh, Anne Heche, Gwyneth Paltrow, and Lea Salonga—and each actress has interpreted this complex character in a different way. As *New York Times* theater critic John Rockwell observes, "Catherine can be loopy-ethereal-sexy (Ms. Parker), earthy and even a little bitter (Ms. Leigh), or adorable-needy-fragile (Ms. Heche), and Mr. Auburn's structure and characters and ideas still work."

Irish playwright Samuel Beckett devotes a good deal of attention to indicating actors' movements and gestures and their physical reactions to one another. In his 1952 play *Waiting for Godot*, for example, Beckett's stage directions seem to choreograph every gesture, every emotion, every intention:

- *(he looks at them ostentatiously in turn to make it clear they are both meant)*
- *Vladimir seizes Lucky's hat. Silence of Lucky. He falls. Silence. Panting of the victors.*
- *Estragon hands him the boot. Vladimir inspects it, throws it down angrily.*
- *Estragon pulls, stumbles, falls. Long silence.*
- *He goes feverishly to and fro, halts finally at extreme left, broods.*

Beckett provides full and obviously carefully thought-out stage directions and, in so doing, attempts to retain a good deal of control over his characters. Still, in a 1988 production of *Godot*, director Mike Nichols and comic actors

Robin Williams and Steve Martin felt free to improvise, adding gestures and movements not specified or even hinted at—and most critics believed that this production remained true to the tragicomic spirit of Beckett's existentialist play. In a sense, then, the playwright's words on the page are just the beginning of the characters' lives on the stage.

✔ **CHECKLIST   Writing about Character**

- Does any character serve as a narrator? If so, what information does this narrator supply about the other characters? How reliable is the narrator?

- Who are the major characters? What do we know about them?

- Do the major characters change and grow during the course of the play, or do they remain essentially unchanged?

- What do the minor characters contribute to the play?

- Does the play include monologues or soliloquies? What do these extended speeches reveal about the characters?

- What is revealed about the characters through dialogue?

- Do characters use foreign words, regionalisms, slang, jargon, clichés, or profanity? What does such use of language reveal about the characters? about the play's theme?

- Is the characters' language formal or informal?

- Do characters speak in dialect? Do they have accents?

- Is the characters' language plain or elaborate?

- Do different characters use different kinds of language? What is the significance of these differences?

- How does language reveal characters' emotional states?

- Does the tone of any character's language change significantly as the play progresses? What does this change reveal?

- Does the play include verbal irony? dramatic irony? How is irony conveyed? What purpose does irony achieve?

- What is revealed about the characters through what others say about them?

- What is revealed about characters through their actions?

- What is revealed about characters through the play's stage directions?
- How might different actors' interpretations change an audience's understanding of the characters?

s_bukley/Shutterstock

PAUL DOOLEY (1928–   ) **AND WINNIE HOLZMAN** (1954–   ) are a husband-and-wife playwriting team. Dooley was the co-creator and head writer of the 1970s children's television series *The Electric Company*. He has acted in numerous television shows and films, including *Scrubs* (2009), *Grey's Anatomy* (2008), *Grace under Fire* (1993), *Star Trek: Deep Space Nine* (1993), and *Sixteen Candles* (1984). Holzman wrote the book for the Broadway hit *Wicked* (2003), which was nominated for a 2004 Tony Award. An actor and a screenwriter for numerous television shows, Holzman received a 1995 Emmy Award nomination for writing the television series *My So-Called Life* (1994).

© Everett Collection Inc / Alamy

Cultural Context: The Post-it® brand changed the way Americans wrote notes and reminders. In 1980, Post-it launched the sticky note as a new consumer product. Initially intended for business use, Post-its quickly became a national household staple. Post-it's Web site touts the product's literal and figurative staying power, pointing out, for example, that a Post-it stuck to an evacuated home stayed put for three days during Hurricane Hugo in 1989. Since popularizing sticky notes more than thirty years ago, Post-it has created a wide range of related products, including digital notes.

Post-its (Notes on a Marriage) (1998)

Post-its (Notes on a Marriage) premiered at a benefit performance for the Gilda Radner Cancer Fund, 1998. The cast was as follows:

ACTOR	Paul Dooley
ACTRESS	Winnie Holzman

There is a chair with a small table and a glass of water on either side of the stage, a la A. R. Gurney's Love Letters. *The Actor and Actress enter simultaneously from either wing, dressed simply. Each grasps a handful of Post-its as if it were a script. They sit, modestly acknowledging each other and the audience. Each takes out a pair of reading glasses, puts them on. The Actor lifts his first Post-it to begin . . . and reads. Every line is read from a Post-it.*

ACTOR: Had an early meeting, couldn't bear to wake you. Close front door hard or it won't lock. PS: Last night was incredible.

ACTRESS: Helped myself to breakfast. You need milk. PS: Next time, wake me.

ACTOR: Hey, sleepyhead. Tried to wake you. Not easy. Left you some coffee, hope you like it black.

ACTRESS: Thought 1 should spend at least one night this week at my place. Picked up some milk; you don't have to pay me back.

5   ACTOR: Off to work, extra set of keys on hall table.

ACTRESS: Darling: Went jogging with Lila. If you go out, we need milk. Wow. I can't believe we're a "we"!

ACTOR: Hon: If you have time, could you pick up my shirts? Ticket on hall table. Thanks. PS: Milk.

ACTRESS: Shirts are in your closet. Your mother called. She seemed surprised to hear my voice. You obviously never mentioned me. (*Icy*) Your shirts came to fourteen-fifty.

ACTOR: Gone to florist. Back soon. Hope you liked the chocolates.

10   ACTRESS: Darling, don't go in the den.

ACTOR: Sweetheart, I understand how much it means to you, but at this stage of our relationship I'm just not ready . . . to have a dog.

ACTRESS: (*After a beat.*) We need Milk-Bones. (*Next Post-it.*) Your mother called; call her. (*Next Post-it.*) Did you call your mother? (*Next Post-it.*) Went to lunch with your mother. Back soon.

ACTOR: Your new best friend my mother called. Call her.

ACTRESS: We need milk. Also, your mom mentioned how much you hate Eugene. I don't think Eugene's so bad. You should hear *my* middle name. Thank God *my* mother's dead!

15   ACTOR: Please do not mention the name Eugene to me ever again. Thank you.

ACTRESS: Shopping list: Pistachio ice cream. Sardines. Those tiny little cheeses that come in that cute little net bag . . . They're so adorable, they make me cry.

ACTRESS: We need Pampers. And baby wipes. And we need to get married.

ACTOR: Meet me City Hall, six sharp. You bring old and borrowed; I'll do new and blue. Mom will stay with Eugenia.

ACTRESS: Note to self: Find breast pump.

20   ACTOR: Take cold shower.

ACTRESS: Lose forty pounds.

ACTOR: Redirect sex drive into career. (*Next Post-it.*) Home late. Don't wait up.

ACTRESS: Hey, stranger, if you're not too busy, could you call Eugenia tonight, around bedtime? Just to see if she recognizes your voice?

ACTOR: Hon: Sorry about your birthday. PS: I got the raise!

25   ACTRESS: To the new vice president in charge of marketing. We need milk. Please advise.

ACTOR: Hon: I think we're out of milk. (*Next Post-it.*) Still no milk!

ACTRESS: If you want it so bad, get it yourself. The milk train doesn't stop here anymore.

ACTOR: If you can't even manage to get to the store—get some household help!

ACTRESS: (*Icy.*) Have gone to bed. Dinner is in fridge. If there is something in particular you wish for dinner tomorrow night, please leave note to that effect, and I will have Ursula or Carla or *Jose*, if it's *heavy*, pick it up. (*Beat.*) I can't take this anymore! We barely— (*Turns Post-it over.*)—communicate! There's got to be more to this marriage than a few hastily scribbled words on a small square of pastel paper! (*Beat.*) By the way, we're out of Post-its.

ACTOR: You think I *want* to spend every night at the office? You have   30
absolutely no concept of how a business is run.

ACTRESS: To Whom It May Concern: Regarding your Post-it of June the tenth, allow me to clarify my position—up yours. Eugenia and I will be at your mother's. PS: *You* need milk.

The Actor glances over at the Actress, she sips her water, coolly avoids his gaze. Finally . . .

ACTOR: Call her at my mother's. (*Next Post-it.*) Must call her. (*Next Post-it.*) Reminder: Take out garbage. Call her. (*Next Post-it.*) People to call: Her.

The Actor looks over again at the Actress. She continues to ignore him.

ACTOR: Shopping list: Small loaf bread. Half pint milk. Soup for one. (*Next Post-it.*) Scotch for one. (*Next Post-it.*) Inflatable doll. (*Next Post-it.*) Scotch for two.

The Actress looks at him. He catches her eye. Caught, she hastily looks away.

ACTOR: Things to tell her. That I'm sorry. That I miss her. That all I want—all I ever wanted—for her to be happy.

The Actress turns to him, touched by this. Then . . . takes the next Post-it. Reads.

ACTRESS: We need milk.   35

ACTOR: Dearest—have gone down to the end of the driveway to get the paper—back soon.

ACTRESS: Honey, that therapist called back. He can see you Monday.

ACTOR: Sweetie, your therapist says your Tuesday is now Friday.

ACTRESS: What a session! Dr. K. believes that part of me is locked in unconscious competition with you, and envious of your of masculine role. By the way, we need cucumbers, sausages, and a really big zucchini.

40 ACTOR: At last—a breakthrough today with Dr. G. It all became crystal clear. My mother. My father. *His* mother. You. *Your* mother. (*Turns Post-it over, continues,*) I see our entire marriage in a new light! I must free myself from the past so we can truly have a future. This changes everything.

ACTRESS: Hon: A Diet Coke exploded all over that note you left. Hope it wasn't important.

He stares at her. Oblivious to his reaction, she reads the next Post-it.

Took Eugenia to Brownies. Back soon.

ACTOR: Took Eugenia to kickboxing. Back soon.

ACTRESS: Took Eugenia to therapy. Could be a while.

ACTOR: Someone named Olaf called. Needs your résumé. What résumé?

45 ACTRESS: I landed the job! I start Monday! (*Next Post-it.*) Last-minute meeting. I'll try to call. (*Next Post-it.*) I'll be working late, don't wait up. (*Next Post-it.*) I'm glad you waited. Last night was incredible.

ACTOR: Drove Eugenia to DMV. Hope she doesn't drive me home.

ACTRESS: Eugenia called. Loves college. Mentioned someone named Tyrone. Doesn't miss us at all.

ACTOR: Pick up travel brochures.

ACTRESS: Eugenia called. When can we meet Tyrone?

50 ACTOR: Schedule trip to campus when we get back.

ACTRESS: Sweetheart: Travel agent called. Cruise is confirmed! The honeymoon we never had! A time for us to leave all this behind and enjoy ten glorious days of total togetherness.

A long, silent beat. Very long. Very silent. They both look straight ahead. Finally he lifts the next Post-it.

ACTOR: (*With great relief.*) God, it's good to be home! (*Next Post-it.*) Dinner Wednesday with Eugenia and what's-his-name.

ACTRESS: Tyrone called—it's a boy. Kareem Eugene.

ACTOR: Eugenia called. Loves being a mom.

55 ACTRESS: Off to throw pots! Back soon! (*Next Post-it.*) Don't forget— we're bird-watching Thursday! (*Next Post-it.*) What night is good for square dancing?

ACTOR: Any night you want—we're free! Nothing to tie us down.

ACTOR: Eugenia called. Could we take Kareem for the weekend?

ACTRESS: Tyrone called. Could we take Kareem for spring break?

ACTOR: Kareem called. Could he spend the summer with us? Again. (*Next Post-it.*) Took Kareem to DMV.

60 ACTRESS: Honey—last night was incredible. I couldn't believe how long it went on. You've got to do something about your snoring.

ACTOR: Shopping list: Bengay, Dentucreme. Viagra.
ACTRESS: Wrinkles Away. I-Can't-Believe-It's-Support-Hose. Estrogen
    in a Drum.
ACTOR: We need milk of magnesia.
ACTRESS: Call Medicare.
ACTOR: You left your keys in the door again.   65
ACTRESS: Do you have my keys?
ACTOR: I can't find my glasses.
ACTRESS: Have you seen my cane?
ACTOR: How can I see your cane if I can't find my glasses?
ACTRESS: Gone for walk.   70
ACTOR: Where are you? Next time you go out, leave me a note!
ACTRESS: Sweetheart—dinner in oven. Taking nap. Love ya.

There's a pause as lights slowly fade on the Actress. Then . . .

ACTOR: Call Emily. Also cousin Ruthie. Send note to Father McKay
    and everyone who sent flowers. (*Beat.*) The service was lovely.
    Everybody said so. (*Beat.*) I was looking through your things for that
    locket you said Eugenia should have. I could hardly believe what I
    found. You'd saved every Post-it I ever wrote you. I wish I'd saved
    yours. I could be reading them now. (*Beat.*) Back soon. Going to the
    store. We need milk.

*   *   *

Reading and Reacting

1. Summarize the plot of *Post-its*. What actually happens in this play?
2. What events occur offstage? Identify the references to these events in the characters' dialogue.
3. Read the stage direction at the beginning of the play. What information about the two characters do you get from these stage directions?
4. What facts are revealed in the course of the play about the two characters? What more can you infer about them?
5. In this play, the actors read every line from Post-it notes. What are the advantages and disadvantages of this format?
6. What props are used in this play? What purpose does each prop serve? If you were staging this play, would you use any additional props?
7. Do you think the fact that this play has only two speaking parts is a handicap? Can you suggest a way to add other characters while retaining the "Post-it" format? What other characters do you think could have speaking parts?
8. How much time passes in the course of this play? How can you tell?

9. Do the two characters grow and change over the years? Does their relationship grow and change? Explain.

10. Why is the reference to needing milk repeated over and over again? Is this an effective use of repetition, or does it become annoying? Explain.

11. **JOURNAL ENTRY** Write a series of text messages between this play's two characters, using shorthand and abbreviations as needed. (If you like, you can "translate" some of the play's Post-it messages into text messages.) Does the change of format change the nature of the conversation? If so, how?

12. **CRITICAL PERSPECTIVE** Savanna Dooley, a screenwriter who is also Dooley and Holzman's daughter, describes Holzman's book for the musical *Wicked* as follows: "It is rich with her trademarks: a story about an outsider, fully realized characters, and some subversive political commentary." Does *Post-its* also demonstrate Holzman's "trademarks" as described by Dooley?

Related Works: "Hills Like White Elephants" (p. 74), "Love and Other Catastrophes: A Mix Tape" (p. 84), "The Story of an Hour" (p. 127), "Meeting at Night" (p. 719), "Parting at Morning" (p. 719), "How Do I Love Thee?" (p. 719), *The Brute* (p. 814)

ARTHUR MILLER (1915–2005) was born in New York City and graduated in 1938 from the University of Michigan, where he began to write plays. His first big success, which won the New York Drama Critics Circle Award, was *All My Sons* (1947), about a man who has knowingly manufactured faulty airplane parts during World War II. Other significant plays are *The Crucible* (1953), based on the Salem witch trials of 1692, which Miller saw as parallel to contemporary investigations of suspected Communists by the House Un-American Activities Committee; *A View from the Bridge* (1955); and *After the Fall* (1955). He was married for a time to actress Marilyn Monroe and wrote the screenplay for her movie *The Misfits* (1961). His play *The Last Yankee* opened off-Broadway in 1993, *Broken Glass* was both published and performed in 1994, and *Mr. Peter's Connection* was published in 1998. In 2001, Miller was awarded an NEH fellowship and the John H. Finney Award for Exemplary Service to New York City.

Death of a Salesman is Miller's most significant work, a play that quickly became an American classic. Miller said he was very much influenced by the structure of Greek tragedy, and in his play he shows that a tragedy can also be the story of an ordinary person told in realistic terms. The play is frequently produced, and each production interprets it a bit differently. When Miller directed *Death of a Salesman* in China in 1983, audiences perceived it as primarily the story of the mother. In the 1983 Broadway production, Miller himself realized "at a certain point that it was far more the story of Biff, the son, than it was of Willy Loman, the salesman of the title."

Cultural Context   At the time *Death of a Salesman* was written in 1949, the United States was experiencing the largest economic expansion in its history. After World War II, soldiers returned home, women left the factory jobs they had held while men were at war, and more and more consumer goods were developed and manufactured. As companies expanded and were consolidated, large, impersonal corporations began to replace the mom-and-pop businesses that had dominated the American scene before the war. The foot soldiers of these corporations were the traveling salesmen (today often called "manufacturers' representatives") who moved from town to town and covered large territories in a relentless effort to sign up clients and generate sales. During the same period, the American suburbs began to appear, with a mass movement of population from older urban neighborhoods to massive housing developments such as those constructed in Levittown, Long Island, in 1946. It is against this background that the events of *Death of a Salesman* unfold.

Death of a Salesman   (1949)

CHARACTERS

Willy Loman	**The Woman**
Linda, *his wife*	**Howard Wagner**
Biff ⎫ *his sons*	**Jenny**
Happy ⎭	**Stanley**
Uncle Ben	**Miss Forsythe**
Charley	**Letta**
Bernard	

The action takes place in Willy Loman's house and yard and in various places he visits in the New York and Boston of today.

Throughout the play, in the stage directions, left and right mean stage left and stage right.

ACT 1

A melody is heard, played upon a flute. It is small and fine, telling of grass and trees and the horizon. The curtain rises.

Before us is the Salesman's house. We are aware of towering, angular shapes behind it, surrounding it on all sides. Only the blue light of the sky falls upon the house and forestage; the surrounding area shows an angry glow of orange. As more light appears, we see a solid vault of apartment houses around the small, fragile-seeming home. An air of the dream clings to the place, a dream rising out of reality. The kitchen at center seems actual enough, for there is a kitchen table with three chairs, and a refrigerator. But no other fixtures are seen. At the back of the kitchen there is a draped entrance, which leads to the living room. To the right of the kitchen, on a level raised two feet, is a bedroom furnished only with a brass bedstead and a straight chair. On a shelf over the bed a silver athletic trophy stands. A window opens onto the apartment house at the side.

Behind the kitchen, on a level raised six and a half feet, is the boys' bedroom, at present barely visible. Two beds are dimly seen, and at the back of the room a dormer window. (This bedroom is above the unseen living room.) At the left a stairway curves up to it from the kitchen.

Lee J. Cobb, Mildred Dunnock, Arthur Kennedy, and Cameron Michael in original Broadway production directed by Elia Kazan (1949–50)
© Photofest

The entire setting is wholly or, in some places, partially transparent. The roofline of the house is one-dimensional; under and over it we see the apartment buildings. Before the house lies an apron, curving beyond the forestage into the orchestra. This forward area serves as the back yard as well as the locale of all Willy's imaginings and of his city scenes. Whenever the action is in the present the actors observe the imaginary wall-lines, entering the house only through the door at the left. But in the scenes of the past these boundaries are broken, and characters enter or leave a room by stepping "through" a wall onto the forestage.

From the right, Willy Loman, the Salesman, enters, carrying two large sample cases. The flute plays on. He hears but is not aware of it. He is past sixty years of *age, dressed quietly. Even as he crosses the stage to the doorway of the house, his exhaustion is apparent. He unlocks the door, comes into the kitchen, and thankfully lets his burden down, feeling the soreness of his palms. A word-sigh escapes his lips—it might be "Oh, boy, oh, boy." He closes the door, then carries his cases out into the living room, through the draped kitchen doorway.*

Linda, his wife, has stirred in her bed at the right. She gets out and puts on a robe, listening. Most often jovial, she has developed an iron repression of her exceptions to Willy's behavior—she more than loves him, she admires him, as though his mercurial nature, his temper, his massive dreams and little cruelties, served her only as sharp reminders of the turbulent longings within him, longings which she shares but lacks the temperament to utter and follow to their end.

LINDA: *(hearing Willy outside the bedroom, calls with some trepidation)* Willy!

WILLY: It's all right. I came back.

LINDA: Why? What happened? *(Slight pause.)* Did something happen, Willy?

WILLY: No, nothing happened.

LINDA: You didn't smash the car, did you?   5

WILLY: *(with casual irritation)* I said nothing happened. Didn't you hear me?

LINDA: Don't you feel well?

WILLY: I am tired to the death. *(The flute has faded away. He sits on the bed beside her, a little numb.)* I couldn't make it. I just couldn't make it, Linda.

LINDA: *(very carefully, delicately)* Where were you all day? You look terrible.

WILLY: I got as far as a little above Yonkers. I stopped for a cup of coffee. 10
Maybe it was the coffee.

LINDA: What?

WILLY: *(after a pause)* I suddenly couldn't drive any more. The car kept going onto the shoulder, y'know?

LINDA: *(helpfully)* Oh. Maybe it was the steering again. I don't think Angelo knows the Studebaker.

WILLY: No, it's me, it's me. Suddenly I realize I'm goin' sixty miles an hour and I don't remember the last five minutes. I'm—I can't seem to—keep my mind to it.

LINDA: Maybe it's your glasses. You never went for your new glasses.   15

WILLY: No, I see everything. I came back ten miles an hour. It took me nearly four hours from Yonkers.

LINDA: *(resigned)* Well, you'll just have to take a rest, Willy, you can't continue this way.

WILLY: I just got back from Florida.

LINDA: But you didn't rest your mind. Your mind is overactive, and the mind is what counts, dear.

20 **WILLY:** I'll start out in the morning. Maybe I'll feel better in the morning. (*She is taking off his shoes.*) These goddam arch supports are killing me.

LINDA: Take an aspirin. Should I get you an aspirin? It'll soothe you.

WILLY: (*with wonder*) I was driving along, you understand? And I was fine. I was even observing the scenery. You can imagine, me looking at scenery, on the road every week of my life. But it's so beautiful up there, Linda, the trees are so thick, and the sun is warm. I opened the windshield and just let the warm air bathe over me. And then all of a sudden I'm goin' off the road! I'm tellin' ya, I absolutely forgot I was driving. If I'd've gone the other way over the white line I might've killed somebody. So I went on again—and five minutes later I'm dreamin' again, and I nearly—(*He presses two fingers against his eyes.*) I have such thoughts, I have such strange thoughts.

LINDA: Willy, dear. Talk to them again. There's no reason why you can't work in New York.

WILLY: They don't need me in New York. I'm the New England man. I'm vital in New England.

25 **LINDA:** But you're sixty years old. They can't expect you to keep traveling every week.

WILLY: I'll have to send a wire to Portland. I'm supposed to see Brown and Morrison tomorrow morning at ten o'clock to show the line. Goddammit, I could sell them! (*He starts putting on his jacket.*)

LINDA: (*taking the jacket from him*) Why don't you go down to the place tomorrow and tell Howard you've simply got to work in New York? You're too accommodating, dear.

WILLY: If old man Wagner was alive I'd a been in charge of New York now! That man was a prince, he was a masterful man. But that boy of his, that Howard, he don't appreciate. When I went north the first time, the Wagner Company didn't know where New England was!

LINDA: Why don't you tell those things to Howard, dear?

30 **WILLY:** (*encouraged*) I will, I definitely will. Is there any cheese?

LINDA: I'll make you a sandwich.

WILLY: No, go to sleep. I'll take some milk. I'll be up right away. The boys in?

LINDA: They're sleeping. Happy took Biff on a date tonight.

WILLY: (*interested*) That so?

35 **LINDA:** It was so nice to see them shaving together, one behind the other, in the bathroom. And going out together. You notice? The whole house smells of shaving lotion.

WILLY: Figure it out. Work a lifetime to pay off a house. You finally own it, and there's nobody to live in it.

LINDA: Well, dear, life is a casting off. It's always that way.

WILLY: No, no, some people—some people accomplish something. Did Biff say anything after I went this morning?

LINDA: You shouldn't have criticized him, Willy, especially after he just got off the train. You mustn't lose your temper with him.

WILLY: When the hell did I lose my temper? I simply asked him if he was making any money. Is that a criticism?   40

LINDA: But, dear, how could he make any money?

WILLY: (*worried and angered*) There's such an undercurrent in him. He became a moody man. Did he apologize when I left this morning?

LINDA: He was crestfallen, Willy. You know how he admires you. I think if he finds himself, then you'll both be happier and not fight any more.

WILLY: How can he find himself on a farm? Is that a life? A farmhand? In the beginning, when he was young, I thought, well, a young man, it's good for him to tramp around, take a lot of different jobs. But it's more than ten years now and he has yet to make thirty-five dollars a week!

LINDA: He's finding himself, Willy.   45

WILLY: Not finding yourself at the age of thirty-four is a disgrace!

LINDA: Shh!

WILLY: The trouble is he's lazy, goddammit!

LINDA: Willy, please!

WILLY: Biff is a lazy bum!   50

LINDA: They're sleeping. Get something to eat. Go on down.

WILLY: Why did he come home? I would like to know what brought him home.

LINDA: I don't know. I think he's still lost, Willy. I think he's very lost.

WILLY: Biff Loman is lost. In the greatest country in the world a young man with such—personal attractiveness, gets lost. And such a hard worker. There's one thing about Biff—he's not lazy.

LINDA: Never.   55

WILLY: (*with pity and resolve*) I'll see him in the morning; I'll have a nice talk with him. I'll get him a job selling. He could be big in no time. My God! Remember how they used to follow him around in high school? When he smiled at one of them their faces lit up. When he walked down the street . . . (*He loses himself in reminiscences.*)

LINDA: (*trying to bring him out of it*) Willy, dear, I got a new kind of American-type cheese today. It's whipped.

WILLY: Why do you get American when I like Swiss?

LINDA: I just thought you'd like a change—

WILLY: I don't want a change! I want Swiss cheese. Why am I always being contradicted?   60

LINDA: (*with a covering laugh*) I thought it would be a surprise.

WILLY: Why don't you open a window in here, for God's sake?

LINDA: (*with infinite patience*) They're all open, dear.

WILLY: The way they boxed us in here. Bricks and windows, windows and bricks.

65 LINDA: We should've bought the land next door.

WILLY: The street is lined with cars. There's not a breath of fresh air in the neighborhood. The grass don't grow any more, you can't raise a carrot in the back yard. They should've had a law against apartment houses. Remember those two beautiful elm trees out there? When I and Biff hung the swing between them?

LINDA: Yeah, like being a million miles from the city.

WILLY: They should've arrested the builder for cutting those down. They massacred the neighborhood. (*Lost.*) More and more I think of those days, Linda. This time of year it was lilac and wisteria. And then the peonies would come out, and the daffodils. What fragrance in this room!

LINDA: Well, after all, people had to move somewhere.

70 WILLY: No, there's more people now.

LINDA: I don't think there's more people. I think—

WILLY: There's more people! That's what's ruining this country! Population is getting out of control. The competition is maddening! Smell the stink from that apartment house! And another on the other side . . . How can they whip cheese?

On Willy's last line, Biff and Happy raise themselves up in their beds, listening.

LINDA: Go down, try it. And be quiet.

WILLY: (*turning to Linda, guiltily*) You're not worried about me, are you, sweetheart?

75 BIFF: What's the matter?

HAPPY: Listen!

LINDA: You've got too much on the ball to worry about.

WILLY: You're my foundation and my support, Linda.

LINDA: Just try to relax, dear. You make mountains out of molehills.

80 WILLY: I won't fight with him any more. If he wants to go back to Texas, let him go.

LINDA: He'll find his way.

WILLY: Sure. Certain men just don't get started till later in life. Like Thomas Edison, I think. Or B. F. Goodrich. One of them was deaf. (*He starts for the bedroom doorway.*) I'll put my money on Biff.

LINDA: And Willy—if it's warm Sunday we'll drive in the country. And we'll open the windshield, and take lunch.

WILLY: No, the windshields don't open on the new cars.

85 LINDA: But you opened it today.

WILLY: Me? I didn't. (*He stops.*) Now isn't that peculiar! Isn't that remarkable— (*He breaks off in amazement and fright as the flute is heard distantly.*)

LINDA: What, darling?

WILLY: That is the most remarkable thing.

LINDA: What, dear?

WILLY: I was thinking of the Chevvy. (*Slight pause.*) Nineteen twenty-   90
eight . . . when I had that red Chevvy—(*Breaks off.*) That funny?
I coulda sworn I was driving that Chevvy today.

LINDA: Well, that's nothing. Something must've reminded you.

WILLY: Remarkable. Ts. Remember those days? The way Biff used to simonize that car? The dealer refused to believe there was eighty thousand miles on it. (*He shakes his head.*) Heh! (*To Linda.*) Close your eyes, I'll be right up. (*He walks out of the bedroom.*)

HAPPY: (*to Biff*) Jesus, maybe he smashed up the car again!

LINDA: (*calling after Willy*) Be careful on the stairs, dear! The cheese is on the middle shelf! (*She turns, goes over to the bed, takes his jacket, and goes out of the bedroom.*)

Light has risen on the boys' room. Unseen, Willy is heard talking to himself, "Eighty thousand miles," and a little laugh. Biff gets out of bed, comes downstage a bit, and stands attentively. Biff is two years older than his brother Happy, well built, but in these days bears a worn air and seems less self-assured. He has succeeded less, and his dreams are stronger and less acceptable than Happy's. Happy is tall, powerfully made. Sexuality is like a visible color on him, or a scent that many women have discovered. He, like his brother, is lost, but in a different way, for he has never allowed himself to turn his face toward defeat and is thus more confused and hard-skinned, although seemingly more content.

HAPPY: (*getting out of bed*) He's going to get his license taken away if he   95
keeps that up. I'm getting nervous about him, y'know, Biff?

BIFF: His eyes are going.

HAPPY: No, I've driven with him. He sees all right. He just doesn't keep his mind on it. I drove into the city with him last week. He stops at a green light and then it turns red and he goes. (*He laughs.*)

BIFF: Maybe he's color-blind.

HAPPY: Pop? Why he's got the finest eye for color in the business. You know that.

BIFF: (*sitting down on his bed*) I'm going to sleep.   100

HAPPY: You're not still sour on Dad, are you, Biff?

BIFF: He's all right, I guess.

WILLY: (*underneath them, in the living room*) Yes, sir, eighty thousand miles—eighty-two thousand!

BIFF: You smoking?

105 **HAPPY:** *(holding out a pack of cigarettes)* Want one?

BIFF: *(taking a cigarette)* I can never sleep when I smell it.

WILLY: What a simonizing job, heh!

HAPPY: *(with deep sentiment)* Funny, Biff, y'know? Us sleeping in here again? The old beds. *(He pats his bed affectionately.)* All the talk that went across those two beds, huh? Our whole lives.

BIFF: Yeah. Lotta dreams and plans.

110 **HAPPY:** *(with a deep and masculine laugh)* About five hundred women would like to know what was said in this room.

They share a soft laugh.

BIFF: Remember that big Betsy something—what the hell was her name—over on Bushwick Avenue?

HAPPY: *(combing his hair)* With the collie dog!

BIFF: That's the one. I got you in there, remember?

HAPPY: Yeah, that was my first time—I think. Boy, there was a pig! *(They laugh, almost crudely.)* You taught me everything I know about women. Don't forget that.

115 **BIFF:** I bet you forgot how bashful you used to be. Especially with girls.

HAPPY: Oh, I still am, Biff.

BIFF: Oh, go on.

HAPPY: I just control it, that's all. I think I got less bashful and you got more so. What happened, Biff? Where's the old humor, the old confidence? *(He shakes Biff's knee. Biff gets up and moves restlessly about the room.)* What's the matter?

BIFF: Why does Dad mock me all the time?

120 **HAPPY:** He's not mocking you, he—

BIFF: Everything I say there's a twist of mockery on his face. I can't get near him.

HAPPY: He just wants you to make good, that's all. I wanted to talk to you about Dad for a long time, Biff. Something's—happening to him. He—talks to himself.

BIFF: I noticed that this morning. But he always mumbled.

HAPPY: But not so noticeable. It got so embarrassing I sent him to Florida. And you know something? Most of the time he's talking to you.

125 **BIFF:** What's he say about me?

HAPPY: I can't make it out.

BIFF: What's he say about me?

HAPPY: I think the fact that you're not settled, that you're still kind of up in the air . . .

BIFF: There's one or two other things depressing him, Happy.

130 **HAPPY:** What do you mean?

BIFF: Never mind. Just don't lay it all to me.

HAPPY: But I think if you just got started—I mean—is there any future for you out there?

BIFF: I tell ya, Hap, I don't know what the future is. I don't know— what I'm supposed to want.

HAPPY: What do you mean?

BIFF: Well, I spent six or seven years after high school trying to work   135
myself up. Shipping clerk, salesman, business of one kind or
another. And it's a measly manner of existence. To get on that subway on the hot mornings in summer. To devote your whole life to
keeping stock, or making phone calls, or selling or buying. To suffer
fifty weeks of the year for the sake of a two-week vacation, when all
you really desire is to be outdoors, with your shirt off. And always to
have to get ahead of the next fella. And still—that's how you build
a future.

HAPPY: Well, you really enjoy it on a farm? Are you content out there?

BIFF: (*with rising agitation*) Hap, I've had twenty or thirty different kinds
of jobs since I left home before the war, and it always turns out the
same. I just realized it lately. In Nebraska when I herded cattle, and
the Dakotas, and Arizona, and now in Texas. It's why I came home
now, I guess, because I realized it. This farm I work on, it's spring
there now, see? And they've got about fifteen new colts. There's
nothing more inspiring or—beautiful than the sight of a mare and
a new colt. And it's cool there now, see? Texas is cool now, and it's
spring. And whenever spring comes to where I am, I suddenly get
the feeling, my God, I'm not gettin' anywhere! What the hell am I
doing, playing around with horses, twenty-eight dollars a week! I'm
thirty-four years old, I oughta be makin' my future. That's when I
come running home. And now, I get here, and I don't know what
to do with myself. (*After a pause.*) I've always made a point of not
wasting my life, and every time I come back here I know that all
I've done is to waste my life.

HAPPY: You're a poet, you know that, Biff? You're a—you're an idealist!

BIFF: No, I'm mixed up very bad. Maybe I oughta get married. Maybe I
oughta get stuck into something. Maybe that's my trouble. I'm like a
boy. I'm not married, I'm not in business, I just—I'm like a boy. Are
you content, Hap? You're a success, aren't you? Are you content?

HAPPY: Hell, no!   140

BIFF: Why? You're making money, aren't you?

HAPPY: (*moving about with energy, expressiveness*) All I can do now is
wait for the merchandise manager to die. And suppose I get to
be merchandise manager? He's a good friend of mine, and he just
built a terrific estate on Long Island. And he lived there about two
months and sold it, and now he's building another one. He can't

enjoy it once it's finished. And I know that's just what I would do. I don't know what the hell I'm workin' for. Sometimes I sit in my apartment—all alone. And I think of the rent I'm paying. And it's crazy. But then, it's what I always wanted. My own apartment, a car, and plenty of women. And still, goddammit, I'm lonely.

BIFF: *(with enthusiasm)* Listen, why don't you come out West with me?

HAPPY: You and I, heh?

145 BIFF: Sure, maybe we could buy a ranch. Raise cattle, use our muscles. Men built like we are should be working out in the open.

HAPPY: *(avidly)* The Loman Brothers, heh?

BIFF: *(with vast affection)* Sure, we'd be known all over the counties!

HAPPY: *(enthralled)* That's what I dream about, Biff. Sometimes I want to just rip my clothes off in the middle of the store and outbox that goddam merchandise manager. I mean I can outbox, outrun, and outlift anybody in that store, and I have to take orders from those common, petty sons-of-bitches till I can't stand it any more.

BIFF: I'm tellin' you, kid, if you were with me I'd be happy out there.

150 HAPPY: *(enthused)* See, Biff, everybody around me is so false that I'm constantly lowering my ideals . . .

BIFF: Baby, together we'd stand up for one another, we'd have someone to trust.

HAPPY: If I were around you—

BIFF: Hap, the trouble is we weren't brought up to grub for money. I don't know how to do it.

HAPPY: Neither can I!

155 BIFF: Then let's go!

HAPPY: The only thing is—what can you make out there?

BIFF: But look at your friend. Builds an estate and then hasn't the peace of mind to live in it.

HAPPY: Yeah, but when he walks into the store the waves part in front of him. That's fifty-two thousand dollars a year coming through the revolving door, and I got more in my pinky finger than he's got in his head.

BIFF: Yeah, but you just said—

160 HAPPY: I gotta show some of those pompous, self-important executives over there that Hap Loman can make the grade. I want to walk into the store the way he walks in. Then I'll go with you, Biff. We'll be together yet, I swear. But take those two we had tonight. Now weren't they gorgeous creatures?

BIFF: Yeah, yeah, most gorgeous I've had in years.

HAPPY: I get that any time I want, Biff. Whenever I feel disgusted. The only trouble is, it gets like bowling or something. I just keep knockin' them over and it doesn't mean anything. You still run around a lot?

BIFF: Naa. I'd like to find a girl—steady, somebody with substance.

HAPPY: That's what I long for.

BIFF: Go on! You'd never come home.   165

HAPPY: I would! Somebody with character, with resistance! Like Mom, y'know? You're gonna call me a bastard when I tell you this. That girl Charlotte I was with tonight is engaged to be married in five weeks. (*He tries on his new hat.*)

BIFF: No kiddin'!

HAPPY: Sure, the guy's in line for the vice-presidency of the store. I don't know what gets into me, maybe I just have an overdeveloped sense of competition or something, but I went and ruined her, and furthermore I can't get rid of her. And he's the third executive I've done that to. Isn't that a crummy characteristic? And to top it all, I go to their weddings! (*Indignantly, but laughing.*) Like I'm not supposed to take bribes. Manufacturers offer me a hundred-dollar bill now and then to throw an order their way. You know how honest I am, but it's like this girl, see. I hate myself for it. Because I don't want the girl, and, still, I take it and—I love it!

BIFF: Let's go to sleep.

HAPPY: I guess we didn't settle anything, heh?   170

BIFF: I just got one idea that I think I'm going to try.

HAPPY: What's that?

BIFF: Remember Bill Oliver?

HAPPY: Sure, Oliver is very big now. You want to work for him again?

BIFF: No, but when I quit he said something to me. He put his arm on   175 my shoulder, and he said, "Biff, if you ever need anything, come to me."

HAPPY: I remember that. That sounds good.

BIFF: I think I'll go to see him. If I could get ten thousand or even seven or eight thousand dollars I could buy a beautiful ranch.

HAPPY: I bet he'd back you. 'Cause he thought highly of you, Biff, I mean, they all do. You're well liked, Biff. That's why I say to come back here, and we both have the apartment. And I'm tellin' you, Biff, any babe you want . . .

BIFF: No, with a ranch I could do the work I like and still be something. I just wonder though. I wonder if Oliver still thinks I stole that carton of basketballs.

HAPPY: Oh, he probably forgot that long ago. It's almost ten years.   180 You're too sensitive. Anyway, he didn't really fire you.

BIFF: Well, I think he was going to. I think that's why I quit. I was never sure whether he knew or not. I know he thought the world of me, though. I was the only one he'd let lock up the place.

WILLY: (*below*) You gonna wash the engine, Biff?

HAPPY: Shh!

Biff looks at Happy, who is gazing down, listening. Willy is mumbling in the parlor.

HAPPY: You hear that?

They listen. Willy laughs warmly.

185 BIFF: (*growing angry*) Doesn't he know Mom can hear that?

WILLY: Don't get your sweater dirty, Biff!

A look of pain crosses Biff's face.

HAPPY: Isn't that terrible? Don't leave again, will you? You'll find a job here. You gotta stick around. I don't know what to do about him, it's getting embarrassing.

WILLY: What a simonizing job!

BIFF: Mom's hearing that!

190 WILLY: No kiddin', Biff, you got a date? Wonderful!

HAPPY: Go on to sleep. But talk to him in the morning, will you?

BIFF: (*reluctantly getting into bed*) With her in the house. Brother!

HAPPY: (*getting into bed*) I wish you'd have a good talk with him.

The light on their room begins to fade.

BIFF: (*to himself in bed*) That selfish, stupid . . .

195 HAPPY: Sh . . . Sleep, Biff.

Their light is out. Well before they have finished speaking, Willy's form is dimly seen below in the darkened kitchen. He opens the refrigerator, searches in there, and takes out a bottle of milk. The apartment houses are fading out, and the entire house and surroundings become covered with leaves. Music insinuates itself as the leaves appear.

WILLY: Just wanna be careful with those girls, Biff, that's all. Don't make any promises. No promises of any kind. Because a girl, y'know, they always believe what you tell'em, and you're very young, Biff, you're too young to be talking seriously to girls.

Light rises on the kitchen. Willy, talking, shuts the refrigerator door and comes downstage to the kitchen table. He pours milk into a glass. He is totally immersed in himself, smiling faintly.

WILLY: Too young entirely, Biff. You want to watch your schooling first. Then when you're all set, there'll be plenty of girls for a boy like you. (*He smiles broadly at a kitchen chair.*) That so? The girls pay for you? (*He laughs.*) Boy, you must really be makin' a hit.

Willy is gradually addressing—physically—a point offstage, speaking through the wall of the kitchen, and his voice has been rising in volume to that of a normal conversation.

WILLY: I been wondering why you polish the car so careful. Ha! Don't leave the hubcaps, boys. Get the chamois to the hubcaps. Happy, use newspaper on the windows, it's the easiest thing. Show him how to do it, Biff! You see, Happy? Pad it up, use it like a pad. That's it, that's it, good work. You're doin' all right, Hap. *(He pauses, then nods in approbation for a few seconds, then looks upward.)* Biff, first thing we gotta do when we get time is clip that big branch over the house. Afraid it's gonna fall in a storm and hit the roof. Tell you what. We get a rope and sling her around, and then we climb up there with a couple of saws and take her down. Soon as you finish the car, boys, I wanna see ya. I got a surprise for you, boys.

BIFF: *(offstage)* Whatta ya got, Dad?

WILLY: No, you finish first. Never leave a job till you're finished— remember that. *(Looking toward the "big trees.")* Biff, up in Albany I saw a beautiful hammock. I think I'll buy it next trip, and we'll hang it right between those two elms. Wouldn't that be something? Just swingin' there under those branches. Boy, that would be . . .   200

Young Biff and Young Happy appear from the direction Willy was addressing. Happy carries rags and a pail of water. Biff, wearing a sweater with a block "S," carries a football.

BIFF: *(pointing in the direction of the car offstage)* How's that, Pop, professional?

WILLY: Terrific. Terrific job, boys. Good work, Biff.

HAPPY: Where's the surprise, Pop?

WILLY: In the back seat of the car.

HAPPY: Boy! *(He runs off.)*   205

BIFF: What is it, Dad? Tell me, what'd you buy?

WILLY: *(laughing, cuffs him)* Never mind, something I want you to have.

BIFF: *(turns and starts off)* What is it, Hap?

HAPPY: *(offstage)* It's a punching bag!

BIFF: Oh, Pop!   210

WILLY: It's got Gene Tunney's[1] signature on it!

Happy runs onstage with a punching bag.

BIFF: Gee, how'd you know we wanted a punching bag?

WILLY: Well, it's the finest thing for the timing.

HAPPY: *(lies down on his back and pedals with his feet)* I'm losing weight, you notice, Pop?

---

[1]*Gene Tunney's:* James Joseph ("Gene") Tunney (1897–1978)—American boxer, world heavyweight champion from his defeat of Jack Dempsey in 1926 until his retirement in 1928.

215 WILLY: *(to Happy)* Jumping rope is good too.

BIFF: Did you see the new football I got?

WILLY: *(examining the ball)* Where'd you get a new ball?

BIFF: The coach told me to practice my passing.

WILLY: That so? And he gave you the ball, heh?

220 BIFF: Well, I borrowed it from the locker room. *(He laughs confidentially.)*

WILLY: *(laughing with him at the theft)* I want you to return that.

HAPPY: I told you he wouldn't like it!

BIFF: *(angrily)* Well, I'm bringing it back!

WILLY: *(stopping the incipient argument, to Happy)* Sure, he's gotta practice with a regulation ball, doesn't he? *(To Biff.)* Coach'll probably congratulate you on your initiative!

225 BIFF: Oh, he keeps congratulating my initiative all the time, Pop.

WILLY: That's because he likes you. If somebody else took that ball there'd be an uproar. So what's the report, boys, what's the report?

BIFF: Where'd you go this time, Dad? Gee we were lonesome for you.

WILLY: *(pleased, puts an arm around each boy and they come down to the apron)* Lonesome, heh?

BIFF: Missed you every minute.

230 WILLY: Don't say? Tell you a secret, boys. Don't breathe it to a soul. Someday I'll have my own business, and I'll never have to leave home any more.

HAPPY: Like Uncle Charley, heh?

WILLY: Bigger than Uncle Charley! Because Charley is not—liked. He's liked, but he's not—well liked.

BIFF: Where'd you go this time, Dad?

WILLY: Well, I got on the road, and I went north to Providence. Met the Mayor.

235 BIFF: The Mayor of Providence!

WILLY: He was sitting in the hotel lobby.

BIFF: What'd he say?

WILLY: He said, "Morning!" And I said, "You've got a fine city here, Mayor." And then he had coffee with me. And then I went to Waterbury. Waterbury is a fine city. Big clock city, the famous Waterbury clock. Sold a nice bill there. And then Boston—Boston is the cradle of the Revolution. A fine city. And a couple of other towns in Mass., and on to Portland and Bangor and straight home!

BIFF: Gee, I'd love to go with you sometime, Dad.

240 WILLY: Soon as summer comes.

HAPPY: Promise?

WILLY: You and Hap and I, and I'll show you all the towns. America is full of beautiful towns and fine, upstanding people. And they know me, boys, they know me up and down New England. The finest people. And when I bring you fellas up, there'll be open sesame for all of us, 'cause one thing, boys: I have friends. I can park my car in any street in New England, and the cops protect it like their own. This summer, heh?

BIFF AND HAPPY: *(together)* Yeah! You bet!

WILLY: We'll take our bathing suits.

HAPPY: We'll carry your bags, Pop!   245

WILLY: Oh, won't that be something! Me comin' into the Boston store with you boys carryin' my bags. What a sensation!

Biff is prancing around, practicing passing the ball.

WILLY: You nervous, Biff, about the game?

BIFF: Not if you're gonna be there.

WILLY: What do they say about you in school, now that they made you captain?

HAPPY: There's a crowd of girls behind him everytime the classes   250
change.

BIFF: *(taking Willy's hand)* This Saturday, Pop, this Saturday—just for you, I'm going to break through for a touchdown.

HAPPY: You're supposed to pass.

BIFF: I'm takin' one play for Pop. You watch me, Pop, and when I take off my helmet, that means I'm breakin' out. Then you watch me crash through that line!

WILLY: *(kisses Biff)* Oh, wait'll I tell this in Boston!

Bernard enters in knickers. He is younger than Biff, earnest and loyal, a wor-ried boy.

BERNARD: Biff, where are you? You're supposed to study with me today. 255

WILLY: Hey, looka Bernard. What're you lookin' so anemic about, Bernard?

BERNARD: He's gotta study, Uncle Willy. He's got Regents next week.

HAPPY: *(tauntingly, spinning Bernard around)* Let's box, Bernard!

BERNARD: Biff! *(He gets away from Happy.)* Listen, Biff, I heard Mr. Birnbaum say that if you don't start studyin' math he's gonna flunk you, and you won't graduate. I heard him!

WILLY: You better study with him, Biff. Go ahead now.   260

BERNARD: I heard him!

BIFF: Oh, Pop, you didn't see my sneakers! *(He holds up a foot for Willy to look at.)*

WILLY: Hey, that's a beautiful job of printing!

BERNARD: *(wiping his glasses)* Just because he printed University of Virginia on his sneakers doesn't mean they've got to graduate him, Uncle Willy!

265 WILLY: (*angrily*) What're you talking about? With scholarships to three
    universities they're gonna flunk him?

BERNARD: But I heard Mr. Birnbaum say—

WILLY: Don't be a pest, Bernard! (*To his boys.*) What an anemic!

BERNARD: Okay, I'm waiting for you in my house, Biff.

Bernard goes off. The Lomans laugh.

WILLY: Bernard is not well liked, is he?

270 BIFF: He's liked, but he's not well liked.

HAPPY: That's right, Pop.

WILLY: That's just what I mean. Bernard can get the best marks in
    school, y'understand, but when he gets out in the business world,
    y'understand, you are going to be five times ahead of him. That's
    why I thank Almighty God you're both built like Adonises. Because
    the man who makes an appearance in the business world, the man
    who creates personal interest, is the man who gets ahead. Be liked
    and you will never want. You take me, for instance. I never have to
    wait in line to see a buyer. "Willy Loman is here!" That's all they
    have to know, and I go right through.

BIFF: Did you knock them dead, Pop?

WILLY: Knocked 'em cold in Providence, slaughtered 'em in Boston.

275 HAPPY: (*on his back, pedaling again*) I'm losing weight, you notice, Pop?

Linda enters, as of old, a ribbon in her hair, carrying a basket of washing.

LINDA: (*with youthful energy*) Hello, dear!

WILLY: Sweetheart!

LINDA: How'd the Chevvy run?

WILLY: Chevrolet, Linda, is the greatest car ever built. (*To the boys.*)
    Since when do you let your mother carry wash up the stairs?

280 BIFF: Grab hold there, boy!

HAPPY: Where to, Mom?

LINDA: Hang them up on the line. And you better go down to your
    friends, Biff. The cellar is full of boys. They don't know what to do
    with themselves.

BIFF: Ah, when Pop comes home they can wait!

WILLY: (*laughs appreciatively*) You better go down and tell them what
    to do, Biff.

285 BIFF: I think I'll have them sweep out the furnace room.

WILLY: Good work, Biff.

BIFF: (*goes through wall-line of kitchen to doorway at back and calls
    down*) Fellas! Everybody sweep out the furnace room! I'll be right
    down!

VOICES: All right! Okay, Biff.

BIFF: George and Sam and Frank, come out back! We're hangin' up the wash! Come on, Hap, on the double! (*He and Happy carry out the basket.*)

LINDA: The way they obey him!   290

WILLY: Well, that's training, the training. I'm tellin' you, I was sellin' thousands and thousands, but I had to come home.

LINDA: Oh, the whole block'll be at that game. Did you sell anything?

WILLY: I did five hundred gross in Providence and seven hundred gross in Boston.

LINDA: No! Wait a minute, I've got a pencil. (*She pulls pencil and paper out of her apron pocket.*) That makes your commission . . . Two hundred—my God! Two hundred and twelve dollars!

WILLY: Well, I didn't figure it yet, but . . .   295

LINDA: How much did you do?

WILLY: Well, I—I did—about a hundred and eighty gross in Providence. Well, no—it came to—roughly two hundred gross on the whole trip.

LINDA: (*without hesitation*) Two hundred gross. That's . . . (*She figures.*)

WILLY: The trouble was that three of the stores were half closed for inventory in Boston. Otherwise I woulda broke records.

LINDA: Well, it makes seventy dollars and some pennies. That's very good. 300

WILLY: What do we owe?

LINDA: Well, on the first there's sixteen dollars on the refrigerator—

WILLY: Why sixteen?

LINDA: Well, the fan belt broke, so it was a dollar eighty.

WILLY: But it's brand new.   305

LINDA: Well, the man said that's the way it is. Till they work themselves in, y'know.

They move through the wall-line into the kitchen.

WILLY: I hope we didn't get stuck on that machine.

LINDA: They got the biggest ads of any of them!

WILLY: I know, it's a fine machine. What else?

LINDA: Well, there's nine-sixty for the washing machine. And for the   310
vacuum cleaner there's three and a half due on the fifteenth. Then the roof, you got twenty-one dollars remaining.

WILLY: It don't leak, does it?

LINDA: No, they did a wonderful job. Then you owe Frank for the carburetor.

WILLY: I'm not going to pay that man! That goddam Chevrolet, they ought to prohibit the manufacture of that car!

LINDA: Well, you owe him three and a half. And odds and ends, comes to around a hundred and twenty dollars by the fifteenth.

315 WILLY: A hundred and twenty dollars! My God, if business don't pick up I don't know what I'm gonna do!

LINDA: Well, next week you'll do better.

WILLY: Oh, I'll knock them dead next week. I'll go to Hartford. I'm very well liked in Hartford. You know, the trouble is, Linda, people don't seem to take to me.

They move onto the forestage.

LINDA: Oh, don't be foolish.

WILLY: I know it when I walk in. They seem to laugh at me.

320 LINDA: Why? Why would they laugh at you? Don't talk that way, Willy.

Willy moves to the edge of the stage. Linda goes into the kitchen and starts to darn stockings.

WILLY: I don't know the reason for it, but they just pass me by. I'm not noticed.

LINDA: But you're doing wonderful, dear. You're making seventy to a hundred dollars a week.

WILLY: But I gotta be at it ten, twelve hours a day. Other men—I don't know—they do it easier. I don't know why—I can't stop myself—I talk too much. A man oughta come in with a few words. One thing about Charley. He's a man of few words, and they respect him.

LINDA: You don't talk too much, you're just lively.

325 WILLY: *(smiling)* Well, I figure, what the hell, life is short, a couple of jokes. *(To himself.)* I joke too much! *(The smile goes.)*

LINDA: Why? You're—

WILLY: I'm fat. I'm very—foolish to look at, Linda. I didn't tell you, but Christmas time I happened to be calling on F. H. Stewarts, and a salesman I know, as I was going in to see the buyer, I heard him say something about—walrus. And I—I cracked him right across the face. I won't take that. I simply will not take that. But they do laugh at me. I know that.

LINDA: Darling . . .

WILLY: I gotta overcome it. I know I gotta overcome it. I'm not dressing to advantage, maybe.

330 LINDA: Willy, darling, you're the handsomest man in the world—

WILLY: Oh, no, Linda.

LINDA: To me you are. *(Slight pause.)* The handsomest.

From the darkness is heard the laughter of a woman. Willy doesn't turn to it, but it continues through Linda's lines.

LINDA: And the boys, Willy. Few men are idolized by their children the way you are.

Music is heard as behind a scrim, to the left of the house. The Woman, dimly seen, is dressing.

WILLY: *(with great feeling)* You're the best there is, Linda, you're a pal, you know that? On the road—on the road I want to grab you sometimes and just kiss the life outa you.

The laughter is loud now, and he moves into a brightening area at the left, where The Woman has come from behind the scrim and is standing, putting on her hat, looking into a "mirror" and laughing.

WILLY: 'Cause I get so lonely—especially when business is bad and   335
there's nobody to talk to. I get the feeling that I'll never sell anything again, that I won't make a living for you, or a business, a business for the boys. *(He talks through The Woman's subsiding laughter; The Woman primps at the "mirror.")* There's so much I want to make for—

THE WOMAN: Me? You didn't make me, Willy. I picked you.

WILLY: *(pleased)* You picked me?

THE WOMAN: *(who is quite proper-looking, Willy's age)* I did. I've been sitting at that desk watching all the salesmen go by, day in, day out. But you've got such a sense of humor, and we do have such a good time together, don't we?

WILLY: Sure, sure. *(He takes her in his arms.)* Why do you have to go now?

THE WOMAN: It's two o'clock . . .   340

WILLY: No, come on in! *(He pulls her.)*

THE WOMAN: . . . my sisters'll be scandalized. When'll you be back?

WILLY: Oh, two weeks about. Will you come up again?

THE WOMAN: Sure thing. You do make me laugh. It's good for me. *(She squeezes his arm, kisses him.)* And I think you're a wonderful man.

WILLY: You picked me, heh?   345

THE WOMAN: Sure. Because you're so sweet. And such a kidder.

WILLY: Well, I'll see you next time I'm in Boston.

THE WOMAN: I'll put you right through to the buyers.

WILLY: *(slapping her bottom)* Right. Well, bottoms up!

THE WOMAN: *(slaps him gently and laughs)* You just kill me, Willy. *(He*   350
suddenly grabs her and kisses her roughly.) You kill me. And thanks for the stockings. I love a lot of stockings. Well, good night.

WILLY: Good night. And keep your pores open!

THE WOMAN: Oh, Willy!

The Woman bursts out laughing, and Linda's laughter blends in. The Woman disappears into the dark. Now the area at the kitchen table brightens. Linda is sitting where she was at the kitchen table, but now is mending a pair of silk stockings.

LINDA: You are, Willy. The handsomest man. You've got no reason to feel that—

WILLY: *(coming out of The Woman's dimming area and going over to Linda)* I'll make it all up to you, Linda, I'll—

355 LINDA: There's nothing to make up, dear. You're doing fine, better
than—

WILLY: *(noticing her mending)* What's that?

LINDA: Just mending my stockings. They're so expensive—

WILLY: *(angrily, taking them from her)* I won't have you mending stockings in this house! Now throw them out!

Linda puts the stockings in her pocket.

BERNARD: *(entering on the run)* Where is he? If he doesn't study!

360 WILLY: *(moving to the forestage, with great agitation)* You'll give him
the answers!

BERNARD: I do, but I can't on a Regents! That's a state exam! They're
liable to arrest me!

WILLY: Where is he? I'll whip him, I'll whip him!

LINDA: And he'd better give back that football, Willy, it's not nice.

WILLY: Biff! Where is he? Why is he taking everything?

365 LINDA: He's too tough with the girls, Willy. All the mothers are afraid
of him!

WILLY: I'll whip him!

BERNARD: He's driving the car without a license!

The Woman's laugh is heard.

WILLY: Shut up!

LINDA: All the mothers—

370 WILLY: Shut up!

BERNARD: *(backing quietly away and out)* Mr. Birnbaum says he's
stuck up.

WILLY: Get outa here!

BERNARD: If he doesn't buckle down he'll flunk math! *(He goes off.)*

LINDA: He's right, Willy, you've gotta—

375 WILLY: *(exploding at her)* There's nothing the matter with him! You
want him to be a worm like Bernard? He's got spirit, personality . . .

*As he speaks, Linda, almost in tears, exits into the living room. Willy is alone in
the kitchen, wilting and staring. The leaves are gone. It is night again, and the
apartment houses look down from behind.*

WILLY: Loaded with it. Loaded! What is he stealing? He's giving it
back, isn't he? Why is he stealing? What did I tell him? I never in
my life told him anything but decent things.

*Happy in pajamas has come down the stairs; Willy suddenly becomes aware of
Happy's presence.*

HAPPY: Let's go now, come on.

WILLY: (*sitting down at the kitchen table*) Huh! Why did she have to wax the floors herself? Everytime she waxes the floors she keels over. She knows that!

HAPPY: Shh! Take it easy. What brought you back tonight?

WILLY: I got an awful scare. Nearly hit a kid in Yonkers. God! Why   380 didn't I go to Alaska with my brother Ben that time! Ben! That man was a genius, that man was success incarnate! What a mistake! He begged me to go.

HAPPY: Well, there's no use in—

WILLY: You guys! There was a man started with the clothes on his back and ended up with diamond mines!

HAPPY: Boy, someday I'd like to know how he did it.

WILLY: What's the mystery? The man knew what he wanted and went out and got it! Walked into a jungle, and comes out, the age of twenty-one, and he's rich! The world is an oyster, but you don't crack it open on a mattress!

HAPPY: Pop, I told you I'm gonna retire you for life.   385

WILLY: You'll retire me for life on seventy goddam dollars a week? And your women and your car and your apartment, and you'll retire me for life! Christ's sake, I couldn't get past Yonkers today! Where are you guys, where are you? The woods are burning! I can't drive a car!

Charley has appeared in the doorway. He is a large man, slow of speech, laconic, immovable. In all he says, despite what he says, there is pity, and now, trepidation. He has a robe over his pajamas, slippers on his feet. He enters the kitchen.

CHARLEY: Everything all right?

HAPPY: Yeah, Charley, everything's . . .

WILLY: What's the matter?

CHARLEY: I heard some noise. I thought something happened. Can't we   390 do something about the walls? You sneeze in here, and in my house hats blow off.

HAPPY: Let's go to bed, Dad. Come on.

Charley signals to Happy to go.

WILLY: You go ahead, I'm not tired at the moment.

HAPPY: (*to Willy*) Take it easy, huh? (*He exits.*)

WILLY: What're you doin' up?

CHARLEY: (*sitting down at the kitchen table opposite Willy*) Couldn't sleep   395 good. I had a heartburn.

WILLY: Well, you don't know how to eat.

CHARLEY: I eat with my mouth.

WILLY: No, you're ignorant. You gotta know about vitamins and things like that.

CHARLEY: Come on, let's shoot. Tire you out a little.

400 WILLY: *(hesitantly)* All right. You got cards?

CHARLEY: *(taking a deck from his pocket)* Yeah, I got them. Someplace. What is it with those vitamins?

WILLY: *(dealing)* They build up your bones. Chemistry.

CHARLEY: Yeah, but there's no bones in a heartburn.

WILLY: What are you talkin' about? Do you know the first thing about it?

405 CHARLEY: Don't get insulted.

WILLY: Don't talk about something you don't know anything about.

They are playing. Pause.

CHARLEY: What're you doin' home?

WILLY: A little trouble with the car.

CHARLEY: Oh. *(Pause.)* I'd like to take a trip to California.

410 WILLY: Don't say.

CHARLEY: You want a job?

WILLY: I got a job, I told you that. *(After a slight pause.)* What the hell are you offering me a job for?

CHARLEY: Don't get insulted.

WILLY: Don't insult me.

415 CHARLEY: I don't see no sense in it. You don't have to go on this way.

WILLY: I got a good job. *(Slight pause.)* What do you keep comin' in here for?

CHARLEY: You want me to go?

WILLY: *(after a pause, withering)* I can't understand it. He's going back to Texas again. What the hell is that?

CHARLEY: Let him go.

420 WILLY: I got nothin' to give him, Charley, I'm clean, I'm clean.

CHARLEY: He won't starve. None a them starve. Forget about him.

WILLY: Then what have I got to remember?

CHARLEY: You take it too hard. To hell with it. When a deposit bottle is broken you don't get your nickel back.

WILLY: That's easy enough for you to say.

425 CHARLEY: That ain't easy for me to say.

WILLY: Did you see the ceiling I put up in the living room?

CHARLEY: Yeah, that's a piece of work. To put up a ceiling is a mystery to me. How do you do it?

WILLY: What's the difference?

CHARLEY: Well, talk about it.

430 WILLY: You gonna put up a ceiling?

CHARLEY: How could I put up a ceiling?

WILLY: Then what the hell are you bothering me for?

CHARLEY: You're insulted again.

WILLY: A man who can't handle tools is not a man. You're disgusting.

CHARLEY: Don't call me disgusting, Willy.   435

Uncle Ben, carrying a valise and an umbrella, enters the forestage from around the right corner of the house. He is a stolid man, in his sixties, with a mustache and an authoritative air. He is utterly certain of his destiny, and there is an aura of far places about him. He enters exactly as Willy speaks.

WILLY: I'm getting awfully tired, Ben.

Ben's music is heard. Ben looks around at everything.

CHARLEY: Good, keep playing; you'll sleep better. Did you call me Ben?

Ben looks at his watch.

WILLY: That's funny. For a second there you reminded me of my
brother Ben.

BEN: I have only a few minutes. *(He strolls, inspecting the place. Willy and
Charley continue playing.)*

CHARLEY: You never heard from him again, heh? Since that time?   440

WILLY: Didn't Linda tell you? Couple of weeks ago we got a letter from
his wife in Africa. He died.

CHARLEY: That so.

BEN: *(chuckling)* So this is Brooklyn, eh?

CHARLEY: Maybe you're in for some of his money.

WILLY: Naa, he had seven sons. There's just one opportunity I had with   445
that man . . .

BEN: I must make a train, William. There are several properties I'm
looking at in Alaska.

WILLY: Sure, sure! If I'd gone with him to Alaska that time, everything
would've been totally different.

CHARLEY: Go on, you'd froze to death up there.

WILLY: What're you talking about?

BEN: Opportunity is tremendous in Alaska, William. Surprised you're   450
not up there.

WILLY: Sure, tremendous.

CHARLEY: Heh?

WILLY: There was the only man I ever met who knew the answers.

CHARLEY: Who?

BEN: How are you all?   455

WILLY: *(taking a pot, smiling)* Fine, fine.

CHARLEY: Pretty sharp tonight.

BEN: Is Mother living with you?

WILLY: No, she died a long time ago.

CHARLEY: Who?   460

BEN: That's too bad. Fine specimen of a lady, Mother.

WILLY: (to Charley) Heh?

BEN: I'd hoped to see the old girl.

CHARLEY: Who died?

465 BEN: Heard anything from Father, have you?

WILLY: (unnerved) What do you mean, who died?

CHARLEY: (taking a pot) What're you talkin' about?

BEN: (looking at his watch) William, it's half-past eight!

WILLY: (as though to dispel his confusion he angrily stops Charley's hand) That's my build!

470 CHARLEY: I put the ace—

WILLY: If you don't know how to play the game I'm not gonna throw my money away on you!

CHARLEY: (rising) It was my ace, for God's sake!

WILLY: I'm through, I'm through!

BEN: When did Mother die?

475 WILLY: Long ago. Since the beginning you never knew how to play cards.

CHARLEY: (picks up the cards and goes to the door) All right! Next time I'll bring a deck with five aces.

WILLY: I don't play that kind of game!

CHARLEY: (turning to him) You should be ashamed of yourself!

WILLY: Yeah?

480 CHARLEY: Yeah! (He goes out.)

WILLY: (slamming the door after him) Ignoramus!

BEN: (as Willy comes toward him through the wall-line of the kitchen) So you're William.

WILLY: (shaking Ben's hand) Ben! I've been waiting for you so long! What's the answer? How did you do it?

BEN: Oh, there's a story in that.

Linda enters the forestage, as of old, carrying the wash basket.

485 LINDA: Is this Ben?

BEN: (gallantly) How do you do, my dear.

LINDA: Where've you been all these years? Willy's always wondered why you—

WILLY: (pulling Ben away from her impatiently) Where is Dad? Didn't you follow him? How did you get started?

BEN: Well, I don't know how much you remember.

490 WILLY: Well, I was just a baby, of course, only three or four years old—

BEN: Three years and eleven months.

WILLY: What a memory, Ben!

BEN: I have many enterprises, William, and I have never kept books.

WILLY: I remember I was sitting under the wagon in—was it Nebraska?

BEN: It was South Dakota, and I gave you a bunch of wild flowers.   495

WILLY: I remember you walking away down some open road.

BEN: *(laughing)* I was going to find Father in Alaska.

WILLY: Where is he?

BEN: At that age I had a very faulty view of geography, William. I discovered after a few days that I was heading due south, so instead of Alaska, I ended up in Africa.

LINDA: Africa!   500

WILLY: The Gold Coast!

BEN: Principally, diamond mines.

LINDA: Diamond mines!

BEN: Yes, my dear. But I've only a few minutes—

WILLY: No! Boys! Boys! *(Young Biff and Happy appear.)* Listen to this.   505
This is your Uncle Ben, a great man! Tell my boys, Ben!

BEN: Why, boys, when I was seventeen I walked into the jungle, and when I was twenty-one I walked out. *(He laughs.)* And by God I was rich.

WILLY: *(to the boys)* You see what I been talking about? The greatest things can happen!

BEN: *(glancing at his watch)* I have an appointment in Ketchikan Tuesday week.

WILLY: No, Ben! Please tell about Dad. I want my boys to hear. I want them to know the kind of stock they spring from. All I remember is a man with a big beard, and I was in Mamma's lap, sitting around a fire, and some kind of high music.

BEN: His flute. He played the flute.   510

WILLY: Sure, the flute, that's right!

New music is heard, a high, rollicking tune.

BEN: Father was a very great and a very wild-hearted man. We would start in Boston, and he'd toss the whole family into the wagon, and then he'd drive the team right across the country; through Ohio, and Indiana, Michigan, Illinois, and all the Western states. And we'd stop in the towns and sell the flutes that he'd made on the way. Great inventor, Father. With one gadget he made more in a week than a man like you could make in a lifetime.

WILLY: That's just the way I'm bringing them up, Ben—rugged, well liked, all-around.

BEN: Yeah? *(To Biff.)* Hit that, boy—hard as you can. *(He pounds his stomach.)*

BIFF: Oh, no, sir!   515

BEN: *(taking boxing stance)* Come on, get to me! *(He laughs.)*

WILLY: Go to it, Biff! Go ahead, show him!

BIFF: Okay! (*He cocks his fist and starts in.*)

LINDA: (*to Willy*) Why must he fight, dear?

520 **BEN:** (*sparring with Biff*) Good boy! Good boy!

WILLY: How's that, Ben, heh?

HAPPY: Give him the left, Biff!

LINDA: Why are you fighting?

BEN: Good boy! (*Suddenly comes in, trips Biff, and stands over him, the point of his umbrella poised over Biff's eye.*)

525 **LINDA:** Look out, Biff!

BIFF: Gee!

BEN: (*patting Biff's knee*) Never fight fair with a stranger, boy. You'll never get out of the jungle that way. (*Taking Linda's hand and bowing.*) It was an honor and a pleasure to meet you, Linda.

LINDA: (*withdrawing her hand coldly, frightened*) Have a nice—trip.

BEN: (*to Willy*) And good luck with your—what do you do?

530 **WILLY:** Selling.

BEN: Yes. Well . . . (*He raises his hand in farewell to all.*)

WILLY: No, Ben, I don't want you to think . . . (*He takes Ben's arm to show him.*) It's Brooklyn, I know, but we hunt too.

BEN: Really, now.

WILLY: Oh, sure, there's snakes and rabbits and—that's why I moved out here. Why, Biff can fell any one of these trees in no time! Boys! Go right over to where they're building the apartment house and get some sand. We're gonna rebuild the entire front stoop right now! Watch this, Ben!

535 **BIFF:** Yes, sir! On the double, Hap!

HAPPY: (*as he and Biff run off*) I lost weight, Pop, you notice?

Charley enters in knickers, even before the boys are gone.

CHARLEY: Listen, if they steal any more from that building the watchman'll put the cops on them!

LINDA: (*to Willy*) Don't let Biff . . .

Ben laughs lustily.

WILLY: You shoulda seen the lumber they brought home last week. At least a dozen six-by-tens worth all kinds of money.

540 **CHARLEY:** Listen, if that watchman—

WILLY: I gave them hell, understand. But I got a couple of fearless characters there.

CHARLEY: Willy, the jails are full of fearless characters.

BEN: (*clapping Willy on the back, with a laugh at Charley*) And the stock exchange, friend!

WILLY: (*joining in Ben's laughter*) Where are the rest of your pants?

CHARLEY: My wife bought them.   545

WILLY: Now all you need is a golf club and you can go upstairs and go to sleep. *(To Ben.)* Great athlete! Between him and his son Bernard they can't hammer a nail!

BERNARD: *(rushing in)* The watchman's chasing Biff!

WILLY: *(angrily)* Shut up! He's not stealing anything!

LINDA: *(alarmed, hurrying off left)* Where is he? Biff, dear! *(She exits.)*

WILLY: *(moving toward the left, away from Ben)* There's nothing wrong.   550
What's the matter with you?

BEN: Nervy boy. Good!

WILLY: *(laughing)* Oh, nerves of iron, that Biff!

CHARLEY: Don't know what it is. My New England man comes back and he's bleedin', they murdered him up there.

WILLY: It's contacts, Charley, I got important contacts!

CHARLEY: *(sarcastically)* Glad to hear it, Willy. Come in later, we'll   555
shoot a little casino. I'll take some of your Portland money. *(He laughs at Willy and exits.)*

WILLY: *(turning to Ben)* Business is bad, it's murderous. But not for me, of course.

BEN: I'll stop by on my way back to Africa.

WILLY: *(longingly)* Can't you stay a few days? You're just what I need, Ben, because I—I have a fine position here, but I—well, Dad left when I was such a baby and I never had a chance to talk to him and I still feel—kind of temporary about myself.

BEN: I'll be late for my train.

They are at opposite ends of the stage.

WILLY: Ben, my boys—can't we talk? They'd go into the jaws of hell for   560
me, see, but I—

BEN: William, you're being first-rate with your boys. Outstanding, manly chaps!

WILLY: *(hanging on to his words)* Oh, Ben, that's good to hear! Because sometimes I'm afraid that I'm not teaching them the right kind of— Ben, how should I teach them?

BEN: *(giving great weight to each word, and with a certain vicious audacity)* William, when I walked into the jungle, I was seventeen. When I walked out I was twenty-one. And, by God, I was rich! *(He goes off into darkness around the right corner of the house.)*

WILLY: . . . was rich! That's just the spirit I want to imbue them with! To walk into a jungle! I was right! I was right! I was right!

Ben is gone, but Willy is still speaking to him as Linda, in nightgown and robe, enters the kitchen, glances around for Willy, then goes to the door of the house, looks out and sees him. Comes down to his left. He looks at her.

565 LINDA: Willy, dear? Willy?

WILLY: I was right!

LINDA: Did you have some cheese? (*He can't answer.*) It's very late, darling. Come to bed, heh?

WILLY: (*looking straight up*) Gotta break your neck to see a star in this yard.

LINDA: You coming in?

570 WILLY: What ever happened to that diamond watch fob? Remember? When Ben came from Africa that time? Didn't he give me a watch fob with a diamond in it?

LINDA: You pawned it, dear. Twelve, thirteen years ago. For Biff's radio correspondence course.

WILLY: Gee, that was a beautiful thing. I'll take a walk.

LINDA: But you're in your slippers.

WILLY: (*starting to go around the house at the left*) I was right! I was! (*Half to Linda, as he goes, shaking his head.*) What a man! There was a man worth talking to. I was right!

575 LINDA: (*calling after Willy*) But in your slippers, Willy!

Willy is almost gone when Biff, in his pajamas, comes down the stairs and enters the kitchen.

BIFF: What is he doing out there?

LINDA: Sh!

BIFF: God Almighty, Mom, how long has he been doing this?

LINDA: Don't, he'll hear you.

580 BIFF: What the hell is the matter with him?

LINDA: It'll pass by morning.

BIFF: Shouldn't we do anything?

LINDA: Oh, my dear, you should do a lot of things, but there's nothing to do, so go to sleep.

Happy comes down the stairs and sits on the steps.

HAPPY: I never heard him so loud, Mom.

585 LINDA: Well, come around more often; you'll hear him. (*She sits down at the table and mends the lining of Willy's jacket.*)

BIFF: Why didn't you ever write me about this, Mom?

LINDA: How would I write to you? For over three months you had no address.

BIFF: I was on the move. But you know I thought of you all the time. You know that, don't you, pal?

LINDA: I know, dear, I know. But he likes to have a letter. Just to know that there's still a possibility for better things.

590 BIFF: He's not like this all the time, is he?

LINDA: It's when you come home he's always the worst.

BIFF: When I come home?

LINDA: When you write you're coming, he's all smiles, and talks about the future, and—he's just wonderful. And then the closer you seem to come, the more shaky he gets, and then, by the time you get here, he's arguing, and he seems angry at you. I think it's just that maybe he can't bring himself to—to open up to you. Why are you so hateful to each other? Why is that?

BIFF: (evasively) I'm not hateful, Mom.

LINDA: But you no sooner come in the door than you're fighting!   595

BIFF: I don't know why. I mean to change. I'm tryin', Mom, you understand?

LINDA: Are you home to stay now?

BIFF: I don't know. I want to look around, see what's doin'.

LINDA: Biff, you can't look around all your life, can you?

BIFF: I just can't take hold, Mom. I can't take hold of some kind of a   600
life.

LINDA: Biff, a man is not a bird, to come and go with the springtime.

BIFF: Your hair . . . (He touches her hair.) Your hair got so gray.

LINDA: Oh, it's been gray since you were in high school. I just stopped dyeing it, that's all.

BIFF: Dye it again, will ya? I don't want my pal looking old. (He smiles.)

LINDA: You're such a boy! You think you can go away for a year   605
and . . . You've got to get it into your head now that one day you'll knock on this door and there'll be strange people here—

BIFF: What are you talking about? You're not even sixty, Mom.

LINDA: But what about your father?

BIFF: (lamely) Well, I meant him too.

HAPPY: He admires Pop.

LINDA: Biff, dear, if you don't have any feeling for him, then you can't   610
have any feeling for me.

BIFF: Sure I can, Mom.

LINDA: No. You can't just come to see me, because I love him. (With a threat, but only a threat, of tears.) He's the dearest man in the world to me, and I won't have anyone making him feel unwanted and low and blue. You've got to make up your mind now, darling, there's no leeway any more. Either he's your father and you pay him that respect, or else you're not to come here. I know he's not easy to get along with—nobody knows that better than me—but . . .

WILLY: (from the left, with a laugh) Hey, hey, Biffo!

BIFF: (starting to go out after Willy) What the hell is the matter with him? (Happy stops him.)

LINDA: Don't—don't go near him!   615

BIFF: Stop making excuses for him! He always, always wiped the floor with you. Never had an ounce of respect for you.

HAPPY: He's always had respect for—

BIFF: What the hell do you know about it?

HAPPY: *(surlily)* Just don't call him crazy!

620 **BIFF:** He's got no character—Charley wouldn't do this. Not in his own house—spewing out that vomit from his mind.

HAPPY: Charley never had to cope with what he's got to.

BIFF: People are worse off than Willy Loman. Believe me, I've seen them!

LINDA: Then make Charley your father, Biff. You can't do that, can you? I don't say he's a great man. Willy Loman never made a lot of money. His name was never in the paper. He's not the finest character that ever lived. But he's a human being, and a terrible thing is happening to him. So attention must be paid. He's not to be allowed to fall into his grave like an old dog. Attention, attention must be finally paid to such a person. You called him crazy—

BIFF: I didn't mean—

625 **LINDA:** No, a lot of people think he's lost his—balance. But you don't have to be very smart to know what his trouble is. The man is exhausted.

HAPPY: Sure!

LINDA: A small man can be just as exhausted as a great man. He works for a company thirty-six years this March, opens up unheard-of territories to their trademark, and now in his old age they take his salary away.

HAPPY: *(indignantly)* I didn't know that, Mom.

LINDA: You never asked, my dear! Now that you get your spending money someplace else you don't trouble your mind with him.

630 **HAPPY:** But I gave you money last—

LINDA: Christmas time, fifty dollars! To fix the hot water it cost ninety-seven fifty! For five weeks he's been on straight commission, like a beginner, an unknown!

BIFF: Those ungrateful bastards!

LINDA: Are they any worse than his sons? When he brought them business, when he was young, they were glad to see him. But now his old friends, the old buyers that loved him so and always found some order to hand him in a pinch—they're all dead, retired. He used to be able to make six, seven calls a day in Boston. Now he takes his valises out of the car and puts them back and takes them out again and he's exhausted. Instead of walking he talks now. He drives seven hundred miles, and when he gets there no one knows him any more, no one welcomes him. And what goes through a man's mind, driving seven hundred miles home without having earned a cent? Why shouldn't he talk to himself? Why? When he has to go to Charley and borrow fifty dollars a week and pretend to me that it's his pay? How long can that go on? How long? You see what I'm sitting here and waiting for? And you tell me he has no character? The man who never worked a day but for your benefit? When does he get the medal for that? Is this his reward—to turn around at the age of sixty-three and find his sons, who he loved better than his life, one a philandering bum—

HAPPY: Mom!

LINDA: That's all you are, my baby! *(To Biff.)* And you! What happened to the love you had for him? You were such pals! How you used to talk to him on the phone every night! How lonely he was till he could come home to you!   635

BIFF: All right, Mom. I'll live here in my room, and I'll get a job. I'll keep away from him, that's all.

LINDA: No, Biff. You can't stay here and fight all the time.

BIFF: He threw me out of this house, remember that.

LINDA: Why did he do that? I never knew why.

BIFF: Because I know he's a fake and he doesn't like anybody around who knows!   640

LINDA: Why a fake? In what way? What do you mean?

BIFF: Just don't lay it all at my feet. It's between me and him—that's all I have to say. I'll chip in from now on. He'll settle for half my pay check. He'll be all right. I'm going to bed. *(He starts for the stairs.)*

LINDA: He won't be all right.

BIFF: *(turning on the stairs, furiously)* I hate this city and I'll stay here. Now what do you want?

LINDA: He's dying, Biff.   645

Happy turns quickly to her, shocked.

BIFF: *(after a pause)* Why is he dying?

LINDA: He's been trying to kill himself.

BIFF: *(with great horror)* How?

LINDA: I live from day to day.

BIFF: What're you talking about?   650

LINDA: Remember I wrote you that he smashed up the car again? In February?

BIFF: Well?

LINDA: The insurance inspector came. He said that they have evidence. That all these accidents in the last year—weren't—weren't—accidents.

HAPPY: How can they tell that? That's a lie.

655 **LINDA:** It seems there's a woman . . . (*She takes a breath as—*)

BIFF: (*sharply but contained*) What woman?

LINDA: (*simultaneously*) . . . and this woman . . .

LINDA: What?

BIFF: Nothing. Go ahead.

660 **LINDA:** What did you say?

BIFF: Nothing. I just said what woman?

HAPPY: What about her?

LINDA: Well, it seems she was walking down the road and saw his car. She says that he wasn't driving fast at all, and that he didn't skid. She says he came to that little bridge, and then deliberately smashed into the railing, and it was only the shallowness of the water that saved him.

BIFF: Oh, no, he probably just fell asleep again.

665 **LINDA:** I don't think he fell asleep.

BIFF: Why not?

LINDA: Last month . . . (*With great difficulty.*) Oh, boys, it's so hard to say a thing like this! He's just a big stupid man to you, but I tell you there's more good in him than in many other people. (*She chokes, wipes her eyes.*) I was looking for a fuse. The lights blew out, and I went down the cellar. And behind the fuse box—it happened to fall out—was a length of rubber pipe—just short.

HAPPY: No kidding?

LINDA: There's a little attachment on the end of it. I knew right away. And sure enough, on the bottom of the water heater there's a new little nipple on the gas pipe.

670 **HAPPY:** (*angrily*) That—jerk.

BIFF: Did you have it taken off?

LINDA: I'm—I'm ashamed to. How can I mention it to him? Every day I go down and take away that little rubber pipe. But, when he comes home, I put it back where it was. How can I insult him that way? I don't know what to do. I live from day to day, boys. I tell you, I know every thought in his mind. It sounds so old-fashioned and silly, but I tell you he put his whole life into you and you've turned your backs on him. (*She is bent over in the chair, weeping, her face in her hands.*) Biff, I swear to God! Biff, his life is in your hands!

HAPPY: (*to Biff*) How do you like that damned fool!

BIFF: (*kissing her*) All right, pal, all right. It's all settled now. I've been remiss. I know that, Mom, but now I'll stay, and I swear to you, I'll apply myself. (*Kneeling in front of her, in a fever of self-reproach.*) It's just—you see, Mom, I don't fit in business. Not that I won't try. I'll try, and I'll make good.

675 **HAPPY:** Sure you will. The trouble with you in business was you never tried to please people.

BIFF: I know, I—

HAPPY: Like when you worked for Harrison's. Bob Harrison said you were tops, and then you go and do some damn fool thing like whistling whole songs in the elevator like a comedian.

BIFF: *(against Happy)* So what? I like to whistle sometimes.

HAPPY: You don't raise a guy to a responsible job who whistles in the elevator!

LINDA: Well, don't argue about it now.   680

HAPPY: Like when you'd go off and swim in the middle of the day instead of taking the line around.

BIFF: *(his resentment rising)* Well, don't you run off? You take off sometimes, don't you? On a nice summer day?

HAPPY: Yeah, but I cover myself!

LINDA: Boys!

HAPPY: If I'm going to take a fade the boss can call any number where   685
I'm supposed to be and they'll swear to him that I just left. I'll tell you something that I hate to say, Biff, but in the business world some of them think you're crazy.

BIFF: *(angered)* Screw the business world!

HAPPY: All right, screw it! Great, but cover yourself!

LINDA: Hap, Hap!

BIFF: I don't care what they think! They've laughed at Dad for years, and you know why? Because we don't belong in this nut-house of a city! We should be mixing cement on some open plain, or—or carpenters. A carpenter is allowed to whistle!

Willy walks in from the entrance of the house, at left.

WILLY: Even your grandfather was better than a carpenter. *(Pause. They*   690
watch him.) You never grew up. Bernard does not whistle in the elevator, I assure you.

BIFF: *(as though to laugh Willy out of it)* Yeah, but you do, Pop.

WILLY: I never in my life whistled in an elevator! And who in the business world thinks I'm crazy?

BIFF: I didn't mean it like that, Pop. Now don't make a whole thing out of it, will ya?

WILLY: Go back to the West! Be a carpenter, a cowboy, enjoy yourself!

LINDA: Willy, he was just saying —   695

WILLY: I heard what he said!

HAPPY: *(trying to quiet Willy)* Hey, Pop, come on now . . .

WILLY: *(continuing over Happy's line)* They laugh at me, heh? Go to Filene's, go to the Hub, go to Slattery's, Boston. Call out the name Willy Loman and see what happens! Big shot!

BIFF: All right, Pop.

WILLY: Big!   700

BIFF: All right!

WILLY: Why do you always insult me?

BIFF: I didn't say a word. *(To Linda.)* Did I say a word?

LINDA: He didn't say anything, Willy.

705 **WILLY:** *(going to the doorway of the living room)* All right, good night, good night.

LINDA: Willy, dear, he just decided . . .

WILLY: *(to Biff)* If you get tired hanging around tomorrow, paint the ceiling I put up in the living room.

BIFF: I'm leaving early tomorrow.

HAPPY: He's going to see Bill Oliver, Pop.

710 **WILLY:** *(interestedly)* Oliver? For what?

BIFF: *(with reserve, but trying, trying)* He always said he'd stake me. I'd like to go into business, so maybe I can take him up on it.

LINDA: Isn't that wonderful?

WILLY: Don't interrupt. What's wonderful about it? There's fifty men in the City of New York who'd stake him. *(To Biff.)* Sporting goods?

BIFF: I guess so. I know something about it and—

715 **WILLY:** He knows something about it! You know sporting goods better than Spalding, for God's sake! How much is he giving you?

BIFF: I don't know, I didn't even see him yet, but—

WILLY: Then what're you talkin' about?

BIFF: *(getting angry)* Well, all I said was I'm gonna see him, that's all!

WILLY: *(turning away)* Ah, you're counting your chickens again.

720 **BIFF:** *(starting left for the stairs)* Oh, Jesus, I'm going to sleep!

WILLY: *(calling after him)* Don't curse in this house!

BIFF: *(turning)* Since when did you get so clean!

HAPPY: *(trying to stop them)* Wait a . . .

WILLY: Don't use that language to me! I won't have it!

725 **HAPPY:** *(grabbing Biff, shouts)* Wait a minute! I got an idea. I got a feasible idea. Come here, Biff, let's talk this over now, let's talk some sense here. When I was down in Florida last time, I thought of a great idea to sell sporting goods. It just came back to me. You and I, Biff—we have a line, the Loman Line. We train a couple of weeks, and put on a couple of exhibitions, see?

WILLY: That's an idea!

HAPPY: Wait! We form two basketball teams, see? Two water-polo teams. We play each other. It's a million dollars' worth of publicity. Two brothers, see? The Loman Brothers. Displays in the Royal Palms—all the hotels. And banners over the ring and the basketball court: "Loman Brothers." Baby, we could sell sporting goods!

WILLY: That is a one-million-dollar idea.

LINDA: Marvelous!

BIFF: I'm in great shape as far as that's concerned.   730

HAPPY: And the beauty of it is, Biff, it wouldn't be like a business. We'd be out playin' ball again . . .

BIFF: *(enthused)* Yeah, that's . . .

WILLY: Million-dollar . . .

HAPPY: And you wouldn't get fed up with it, Biff. It'd be the family again. There'd be the old honor, and comradeship, and if you wanted to go off for a swim or somethin'—well, you'd do it! Without some smart cooky gettin' up ahead of you!

WILLY: Lick the world! You guys together could absolutely lick the civilized world.   735

BIFF: I'll see Oliver tomorrow. Hap, if we could work that out . . .

LINDA: Maybe things are beginning to—

WILLY: *(wildly enthused, to Linda)* Stop interrupting! *(To Biff.)* But don't wear sport jacket and slacks when you see Oliver.

BIFF: No, I'll—

WILLY: A business suit, and talk as little as possible, and don't crack any jokes.   740

BIFF: He did like me. Always liked me.

LINDA: He loved you!

WILLY: *(to Linda)* Will you stop! *(To Biff.)* Walk in very serious. You are not applying for a boy's job. Money is to pass. Be quiet, fine, and serious. Everybody likes a kidder, but nobody lends him money.

HAPPY: I'll try to get some myself, Biff. I'm sure I can.

WILLY: I can see great things for you, kids, I think your troubles are over. But remember, start big and you'll end big. Ask for fifteen. How much you gonna ask for?   745

BIFF: Gee, I don't know—

WILLY: And don't say "Gee." "Gee" is a boy's word. A man walking in for fifteen thousand dollars does not say "Gee!"

BIFF: Ten, I think, would be top though.

WILLY: Don't be so modest. You always started too low. Walk in with a big laugh. Don't look worried. Start off with a couple of your good stories to lighten things up. It's not what you say, it's how you say it—because personality always wins the day.

LINDA: Oliver always thought the highest of him—   750

WILLY: Will you let me talk?

BIFF: Don't yell at her, Pop, will ya?

WILLY: *(angrily)* I was talking, wasn't I!

BIFF: I don't like you yelling at her all the time, and I'm tellin' you, that's all.

WILLY: What're you, takin' over this house?   755

LINDA: Willy—

WILLY: *(turning on her)* Don't take his side all the time, goddammit!

BIFF: *(furiously)* Stop yelling at her!

WILLY: *(suddenly pulling on his cheek, beaten down, guilt ridden)* Give my best to Bill Oliver—he may remember me. *(He exits through the living room doorway.)*

760 LINDA: *(her voice subdued)* What'd you have to start that for? *(Biff turns away.)* You see how sweet he was as soon as you talked hopefully? *(She goes over to Biff.)* Come up and say good night to him. Don't let him go to bed that way.

HAPPY: Come on, Biff, let's buck him up.

LINDA: Please, dear. Just say good night. It takes so little to make him happy. Come. *(She goes through the living room doorway, calling upstairs from within the living room.)* Your pajamas are hanging in the bathroom. Willy!

HAPPY: *(looking toward where Linda went out)* What a woman! They broke the mold when they made her. You know that, Biff?

BIFF: He's off salary. My God, working on commission!

765 HAPPY: Well, let's face it: he's no hot-shot selling man. Except that sometimes, you have to admit, he's a sweet personality.

BIFF: *(deciding)* Lend me ten bucks, will ya? I want to buy some new ties.

HAPPY: I'll take you to a place I know. Beautiful stuff. Wear one of my striped shirts tomorrow.

BIFF: She got gray. Mom got awful old. Gee, I'm gonna go in to Oliver tomorrow and knock him for a—

HAPPY: Come on up. Tell that to Dad. Let's give him a whirl. Come on.

770 BIFF: *(steamed up)* You know, with ten thousand bucks, boy!

HAPPY: *(as they go into the living room)* That's the talk, Biff, that's the first time I've heard the old confidence out of you! *(From within the living room, fading off.)* You're gonna live with me, kid, and any babe you want you just say the word . . . *(The last lines are hardly heard. They are mounting the stairs to their parents' bedroom.)*

LINDA: *(entering her bedroom and addressing Willy, who is in the bathroom. She is straightening the bed for him)* Can you do anything about the shower? It drips.

WILLY: *(from the bathroom)* All of a sudden everything falls to pieces! Goddam plumbing, oughta be sued, those people. I hardly finished putting it in and the thing . . . *(His words rumble off.)*

LINDA: I'm just wondering if Oliver will remember him. You think he might?

775 WILLY: *(coming out of the bathroom in his pajamas)* Remember him? What's the matter with you, you crazy? If he'd've stayed with Oliver he'd be on top by now! Wait'll Oliver gets a look at him. You don't know the average caliber any more. The average young man

today—(*he is getting into bed*)—is got a caliber of zero. Greatest thing in the world for him was to bum around.

Biff and Happy enter the bedroom. Slight pause.

WILLY: (*stops short, looking at Biff*) Glad to hear it, boy.
HAPPY: He wanted to say good night to you, sport.
WILLY: (*to Biff*) Yeah. Knock him dead, boy. What'd you want to tell me?
BIFF: Just take it easy, Pop. Good night. (*He turns to go.*)
WILLY: (*unable to resist*) And if anything falls off the desk while you're   780 talking to him—like a package or something—don't you pick it up. They have office boys for that.
LINDA: I'll make a big breakfast—
WILLY: Will you let me finish? (*To Biff.*) Tell him you were in the business in the West. Not farm work.
BIFF: All right, Dad.
LINDA: I think everything—
WILLY: (*going right through her speech*) And don't undersell yourself. No   785 less than fifteen thousand dollars.
BIFF: (*unable to bear him*) Okay. Good night, Mom. (*He starts moving.*)
WILLY: Because you got a greatness in you, Biff, remember that. You got all kinds a greatness . . . (*He lies back, exhausted. Biff walks out.*)
LINDA: (*calling after Biff*) Sleep well, darling!
HAPPY: I'm gonna get married, Mom. I wanted to tell you.
LINDA: Go to sleep, dear.   790
HAPPY: (*going*) I just wanted to tell you.
WILLY: Keep up the good work. (*Happy exits.*) God . . . remember that Ebbets Field game? The championship of the city?
LINDA: Just rest. Should I sing to you?
WILLY: Yeah. Sing to me. (*Linda hums a soft lullaby.*) When that team came out—he was the tallest, remember?
LINDA: Oh, yes. And in gold.   795

Biff enters the darkened kitchen, takes a cigarette, and leaves the house. He comes downstage into a golden pool of light. He smokes, staring at the night.

WILLY: Like a young god. Hercules—something like that. And the sun, the sun all around him. Remember how he waved to me? Right up from the field, with the representatives of three colleges standing by? And the buyers I brought, and the cheers when he came out— Loman, Loman, Loman! God Almighty, he'll be great yet. A star like that, magnificent, can never really fade away!

The light on Willy is fading. The gas heater begins to glow through the kitchen wall, near the stairs, a blue flame beneath red coils.

LINDA: *(timidly)* Willy, dear, what has he got against you?

WILLY: I'm so tired. Don't talk any more.

Biff slowly returns to the kitchen. He stops, stares toward the heater.

LINDA: Will you ask Howard to let you work in New York?

800 WILLY: First thing in the morning. Everything'll be all right.

Biff reaches behind the heater and draws out a length of rubber tubing. He is horrified and turns his head toward Willy's room, still dimly lit, from which the strains of Linda's desperate but monotonous humming rise.

WILLY: *(staring through the window into the moonlight)* Gee, look at the moon moving between the buildings!

Biff wraps the tubing around his hand and quickly goes up the stairs. Curtain.

ACT 2

Music is heard, gay and bright. The curtain rises as the music fades away. Willy, in shirt sleeves, is sitting at the kitchen table, sipping coffee, his hat in his lap. Linda is filling his cup when she can.

WILLY: Wonderful coffee. Meal in itself.

LINDA: Can I make you some eggs?

WILLY: No. Take a breath.

LINDA: You look so rested, dear.

5 WILLY: I slept like a dead one. First time in months. Imagine, sleeping till ten on a Tuesday morning. Boys left nice and early, heh?

LINDA: They were out of here by eight o'clock.

WILLY: Good work!

LINDA: It was so thrilling to see them leaving together. I can't get over the shaving lotion in this house.

WILLY: *(smiling)* Mmm—

10 LINDA: Biff was very changed this morning. His whole attitude seemed to be hopeful. He couldn't wait to get downtown to see Oliver.

WILLY: He's heading for a change. There's no question, there simply are certain men that take longer to get—solidified. How did he dress?

LINDA: His blue suit. He's so handsome in that suit. He could be a— anything in that suit!

Willy gets up from the table. Linda holds his jacket for him.

WILLY: There's no question, no question at all. Gee, on the way home tonight I'd like to buy some seeds.

LINDA: *(laughing)* That'd be wonderful. But not enough sun gets back there. Nothing'll grow any more.

WILLY: You wait, kid, before it's all over we're gonna get a little place   15
out in the country, and I'll raise some vegetables, a couple of
chickens . . .

LINDA: You'll do it yet, dear.

Willy walks out of his jacket. Linda follows him.

WILLY: And they'll get married, and come for a weekend. I'd build a
little guest house. 'Cause I got so many fine tools, all I'd need would
be a little lumber and some peace of mind.

LINDA: *(joyfully)* I sewed the lining . . .

WILLY: I could build two guest houses, so they'd both come. Did he
decide how much he's going to ask Oliver for?

LINDA: *(getting him into the jacket)* He didn't mention it, but I imagine   20
ten or fifteen thousand. You going to talk to Howard today?

WILLY: Yeah. I'll put it to him straight and simple. He'll just have to
take me off the road.

LINDA: And Willy, don't forget to ask for a little advance, because
we've got the insurance premium. It's the grace period now.

WILLY: That's a hundred . . .?

LINDA: A hundred and eight, sixty-eight. Because we're a little short
again.

WILLY: Why are we short?   25

LINDA: Well, you had the motor job on the car . . .

WILLY: That goddam Studebaker!

LINDA: And you got one more payment on the refrigerator . . .

WILLY: But it just broke again!

LINDA: Well, it's old, dear.   30

WILLY: I told you we should've bought a well-advertised machine.
Charley bought a General Electric and it's twenty years old and it's
still good, that son-of-a-bitch.

LINDA: But, Willy—

WILLY: Whoever heard of a Hastings refrigerator? Once in my life I
would like to own something outright before it's broken! I'm always
in a race with the junkyard! I just finished paying for the car and
it's on its last legs. The refrigerator consumes belts like a goddam
maniac. They time those things. They time them so when you
finally paid for them, they're used up.

LINDA: *(buttoning up his jacket as he unbuttons it)* All told, about two
hundred dollars would carry us, dear. But that includes the last
payment on the mortgage. After this payment, Willy, the house
belongs to us.

WILLY: It's twenty-five years!   35

LINDA: Biff was nine years old when we bought it.

WILLY: Well, that's a great thing. To weather a twenty-five year mortgage is—

LINDA: It's an accomplishment.

WILLY: All the cement, the lumber, the reconstruction I put in this house! There ain't a crack to be found in it any more.

40 LINDA: Well, it served its purpose.

WILLY: What purpose? Some stranger'll come along, move in, and that's that. If only Biff would take this house, and raise a family . . . (*He starts to go.*) Good-by, I'm late.

LINDA: (*suddenly remembering*) Oh, I forgot! You're supposed to meet them for dinner.

WILLY: Me?

LINDA: At Frank's Chop House on Forty-eighth near Sixth Avenue.

45 WILLY: Is that so! How about you?

LINDA: No, just the three of you. They're gonna blow you to a big meal!

WILLY: Don't say! Who thought of that?

LINDA: Biff came to me this morning, Willy, and he said, "Tell Dad, we want to blow him to a big meal." Be there six o'clock. You and your two boys are going to have dinner.

WILLY: Gee whiz! That's really somethin'. I'm gonna knock Howard for a loop, kid. I'll get an advance, and I'll come home with a New York job. Goddammit, now I'm gonna do it!

50 LINDA: Oh, that's the spirit, Willy!

WILLY: I will never get behind a wheel the rest of my life!

LINDA: It's changing, Willy, I can feel it changing!

WILLY: Beyond a question. G'by, I'm late. (*He starts to go again.*)

LINDA: (*calling after him as she runs to the kitchen table for a handkerchief*) You got your glasses?

55 WILLY: (*feels for them, then comes back in*) Yeah, yeah, got my glasses.

LINDA: (*giving him the handkerchief*) And a handkerchief.

WILLY: Yeah, handkerchief.

LINDA: And your saccharine?

WILLY: Yeah, my saccharine.

60 LINDA: Be careful on the subway stairs.

She kisses him, and a silk stocking is seen hanging from her hand. Willy notices it.

WILLY: Will you stop mending stockings? At least while I'm in the house. It gets me nervous. I can't tell you. Please.

Linda hides the stocking in her hand as she follows Willy across the forestage in front of the house.

LINDA: Remember, Frank's Chop House.

WILLY: (*passing the apron*) Maybe beets would grow out there.

LINDA: (*laughing*) But you tried so many times.

WILLY: Yeah. Well, don't work hard today. (*He disappears around the right corner of the house.*)   65

LINDA: Be careful!

As Willy vanishes, Linda waves to him. Suddenly the phone rings. She runs across the stage and into the kitchen and lifts it.

LINDA: Hello? Oh, Biff! I'm so glad you called, I just . . . Yes, sure, I just told him. Yes, he'll be there for dinner at six o'clock, I didn't forget. Listen, I was just dying to tell you. You know that little rubber pipe I told you about? That he connected to the gas heater? I finally decided to go down the cellar this morning and take it away and destroy it. But it's gone! Imagine? He took it away himself, it isn't there! (*She listens.*) When? Oh, then you took it. Oh—nothing, it's just that I'd hoped he'd taken it away himself. Oh, I'm not worried, darling, because this morning he left in such high spirits, it was like the old days! I'm not afraid any more. Did Mr. Oliver see you? . . . Well, you wait there then. And make a nice impression on him, darling. Just don't perspire too much before you see him. And have a nice time with Dad. He may have big news too! . . . That's right, a New York job. And be sweet to him tonight, dear. Be loving to him. Because he's only a little boat looking for a harbor. (*She is trembling with sorrow and joy.*) Oh, that's wonderful, Biff, you'll save his life. Thanks, darling. Just put your arm around him when he comes into the restaurant. Give him a smile. That's the boy . . . Good-by, dear. . . . You got your comb? . . . That's fine. Good-by, Biff dear.

In the middle of her speech, Howard Wagner, thirty-six, wheels in a small typewriter table on which is a wire-recording machine and proceeds to plug it in. This is on the left forestage. Light slowly fades on Linda as it rises on Howard. Howard is intent on threading the machine and only glances over his shoulder as Willy appears.

WILLY: Pst! Pst!

HOWARD: Hello, Willy, come in.

WILLY: Like to have a little talk with you, Howard.   70

HOWARD: Sorry to keep you waiting. I'll be with you in a minute.

WILLY: What's that, Howard?

HOWARD: Didn't you ever see one of these? Wire recorder.

WILLY: Oh. Can we talk a minute?

HOWARD: Records things. Just got delivery yesterday. Been driving me   75
crazy, the most terrific machine I ever saw in my life. I was up all
night with it.

WILLY: What do you do with it?

HOWARD: I bought it for dictation, but you can do anything with it. Listen to this. I had it home last night. Listen to what I picked up. The first one is my daughter. Get this. (*He flicks the switch and "Roll out the Barrel" is heard being whistled.*) Listen to that kid whistle.

WILLY: That is lifelike, isn't it?

HOWARD: Seven years old. Get that tone.

80 WILLY: Ts, ts. Like to ask a little favor if you . . .

The whistling breaks off, and the voice of Howard's Daughter is heard.

HIS DAUGHTER: "Now you, Daddy."

HOWARD: She's crazy for me! (*Again the same song is whistled.*) That's me! Ha! (*He winks.*)

WILLY: You're very good!

The whistling breaks off again. The machine runs silent for a moment.

HOWARD: Sh! Get this now, this is my son.

85 HIS SON: "The capital of Alabama is Montgomery; the capital of Arizona is Phoenix; the capital of Arkansas is Little Rock; the capital of California is Sacramento . . ." (*And on, and on.*)

HOWARD: (*holding up five fingers*) Five years old, Willy!

WILLY: He'll make an announcer some day!

HIS SON: (*continuing*) "The capital . . ."

HOWARD: Get that—alphabetical order! (*The machine breaks off suddenly.*) Wait a minute. The maid kicked the plug out.

90 WILLY: It certainly is a—

HOWARD: Sh, for God's sake!

HIS SON: "It's nine o'clock, Bulova watch time. So I have to go to sleep."

WILLY: That really is—

HOWARD: Wait a minute! The next is my wife.

They wait.

95 HOWARD'S VOICE: "Go on, say something." (*Pause.*) "Well, you gonna talk?"

HIS WIFE: "I can't think of anything."

HOWARD'S VOICE: "Well, talk—it's turning."

HIS WIFE: (*shyly, beaten*) "Hello." (*Silence.*) "Oh, Howard, I can't talk into this . . ."

HOWARD: (*snapping the machine off*) That was my wife.

100 WILLY: That is a wonderful machine. Can we—

HOWARD: I tell you, Willy, I'm gonna take my camera, and my bandsaw, and all my hobbies, and out they go. This is the most fascinating relaxation I ever found.

WILLY: I think I'll get one myself.

HOWARD: Sure, they're only a hundred and a half. You can't do without it. Supposing you wanna hear Jack Benny, see? But you can't be at home at that hour. So you tell the maid to turn the radio on when Jack Benny comes on, and this automatically goes on with the radio . . .

WILLY: And when you come home you . . .

HOWARD: You can come home twelve o'clock, one o'clock, any time you   105
like, and you get yourself a Coke and sit yourself down, throw the switch, and there's Jack Benny's program in the middle of the night!

WILLY: I'm definitely going to get one. Because lots of time I'm on the road, and I think to myself, what I must be missing on the radio!

HOWARD: Don't you have a radio in the car?

WILLY: Well, yeah, but who ever thinks of turning it on?

HOWARD: Say, aren't you supposed to be in Boston?

WILLY: That's what I want to talk to you about, Howard. You got a   110
minute?

He draws a chair in from the wing.

HOWARD: What happened? What're you doing here?

WILLY: Well . . .

HOWARD: You didn't crack up again, did you?

WILLY: Oh, no. No . . .

HOWARD: Geez, you had me worried there for a minute. What's the   115
trouble?

WILLY: Well, to tell you the truth, Howard, I've come to the decision that I'd rather not travel any more.

HOWARD: Not travel! Well, what'll you do?

WILLY: Remember, Christmas time, when you had the party here? You said you'd try to think of some spot for me here in town.

HOWARD: With us?

WILLY: Well, sure.   120

HOWARD: Oh, yeah, yeah. I remember. Well, I couldn't think of anything for you, Willy.

WILLY: I tell ya, Howard. The kids are all grown up, y'know. I don't need much any more. If I could take home—well, sixty-five dollars a week, I could swing it.

HOWARD: Yeah, but Willy, see I—

WILLY: I tell ya why, Howard. Speaking frankly and between the two of us, y'know—I'm just a little tired.

HOWARD: Oh, I could understand that, Willy. But you're a road man,   125
Willy, and we do a road business. We've only got a half-dozen salesmen on the floor here.

WILLY: God knows, Howard, I never asked a favor of any man. But I was with the firm when your father used to carry you in here in his arms.

HOWARD: I know that, Willy, but—

WILLY: Your father came to me the day you were born and asked me what I thought of the name of Howard, may he rest in peace.

HOWARD: I appreciate that, Willy, but there just is no spot here for you. If I had a spot I'd slam you right in, but I just don't have a single, solitary spot.

He looks for his lighter. Willy has picked it up and gives it to him. Pause.

130 WILLY: (*with increasing anger*) Howard, all I need to set my table is fifty dollars a week.

HOWARD: But where am I going to put you, kid?

WILLY: Look, it isn't a question of whether I can sell merchandise, is it?

HOWARD: No, but it's a business, kid, and everybody's gotta pull his own weight.

WILLY: (*desperately*) Just let me tell you a story, Howard—

135 HOWARD: 'Cause you gotta admit, business is business.

WILLY: (*angrily*) Business is definitely business, but just listen for a minute. You don't understand this. When I was a boy—eighteen, nineteen—I was already on the road. And there was a question in my mind as to whether selling had a future for me. Because in those days I had a yearning to go to Alaska. See, there were three gold strikes in one month in Alaska, and I felt like going out. Just for the ride, you might say.

HOWARD: (*barely interested*) Don't say.

WILLY: Oh, yeah, my father lived many years in Alaska. He was an adventurous man. We've got quite a little streak of self-reliance in our family. I thought I'd go out with my older brother and try to locate him, and maybe settle in the North with the old man. And I was almost decided to go, when I met a salesman in the Parker House. His name was Dave Singleman. And he was eighty-four years old, and he'd drummed merchandise in thirty-one states. And old Dave, he'd go up to his room, y'understand, put on his green velvet slippers— I'll never forget—and pick up his phone and call the buyers, and without ever leaving his room, at the age of eighty-four, he made his living. And when I saw that, I realized that selling was the greatest career a man could want. 'Cause what could be more satisfying than to be able to go, at the age of eighty-four, into twenty or thirty different cities, and pick up a phone, and be remembered and loved and helped by so many different people? Do you know? when he died—and by the way he died the death of a salesman, in his green velvet slippers in the smoker of the New York, New Haven and Hartford, going into Boston—when he died, hundreds of salesmen and buyers were at his funeral. Things were sad on a lotta trains for months after that. (*He stands up. Howard has not looked at him.*) In those days there was personality in it, Howard. There was respect, and comradeship, and gratitude in it. Today, it's all cut and dried, and there's no chance for bringing friendship to bear—or personality. You see what I mean? They don't know me any more.

HOWARD: (*moving away, to the right*) That's just the thing, Willy.

WILLY: If I had forty dollars a week—that's all I'd need. Forty dollars,   140
Howard.

HOWARD: Kid, I can't take blood from a stone, I—

WILLY: (*desperation is on him now*) Howard, the year Al Smith was nominated, your father came to me and—

HOWARD: (*starting to go off*) I've got to see some people, kid.

WILLY: (*stopping him*) I'm talking about your father! There were promises made across this desk! You mustn't tell me you've got people to see—I put thirty-four years into this firm, Howard, and now I can't pay my insurance! You can't eat the orange and throw the peel away—a man is not a piece of fruit! (*After a pause.*) Now pay attention. Your father—in 1928 I had a big year. I averaged a hundred and seventy dollars a week in commissions.

HOWARD: (*impatiently*) Now, Willy, you never averaged—   145

WILLY: (*banging his hand on the desk*) I averaged a hundred and seventy dollars a week in the year of 1928! And your father came to me—or rather, I was in the office here—it was right over this desk—and he put his hand on my shoulder—

HOWARD: (*getting up*) You'll have to excuse me, Willy, I gotta see some people. Pull yourself together. (*Going out.*) I'll be back in a little while.

On Howard's exit, the light on his chair grows very bright and strange.

WILLY: Pull myself together! What the hell did I say to him? My God, I was yelling at him! How could I! (*Willy breaks off, staring at the light, which occupies the chair, animating it. He approaches this chair, standing across the desk from it.*) Frank, Frank, don't you remember what you told me that time? How you put your hand on my shoulder, and Frank . . . (*He leans on the desk and as he speaks the dead man's name he accidentally switches on the recorder, and instantly—*)

HOWARD'S SON: ". . . of New York is Albany. The capital of Ohio is Cincinnati, the capital of Rhode Island is . . ." (*The recitation continues.*)

150 WILLY: *(leaping away with fright, shouting)* Ha! Howard! Howard! Howard!

HOWARD: *(rushing in)* What happened?

WILLY: *(pointing at the machine, which continues nasally, childishly, with the capital cities)* Shut it off! Shut it off!

HOWARD: *(pulling the plug out)* Look, Willy . . .

WILLY: *(pressing his hands to his eyes)* I gotta get myself some coffee. I'll get some coffee . . .

Willy starts to walk out. Howard stops him.

155 HOWARD: *(rolling up the cord)* Willy, look . . .

WILLY: I'll go to Boston.

HOWARD: Willy, you can't go to Boston for us.

WILLY: Why can't I go?

HOWARD: I don't want you to represent us. I've been meaning to tell you for a long time now.

160 WILLY: Howard, are you firing me?

HOWARD: I think you need a good long rest, Willy.

WILLY: Howard—

HOWARD: And when you feel better, come back, and we'll see if we can work something out.

WILLY: But I gotta earn money, Howard. I'm in no position—

165 HOWARD: Where are your sons? Why don't your sons give you a hand?

WILLY: They're working on a very big deal.

HOWARD: This is no time for false pride, Willy. You go to your sons and tell them that you're tired. You've got two great boys, haven't you?

WILLY: Oh, no question, no question, but in the meantime . . .

HOWARD: Then that's that, heh?

170 WILLY: All right, I'll go to Boston tomorrow.

HOWARD: No, no.

WILLY: I can't throw myself on my sons. I'm not a cripple!

HOWARD: Look, kid, I'm busy this morning.

WILLY: *(grasping Howard's arm)* Howard, you've got to let me go to Boston!

175 HOWARD: *(hard, keeping himself under control)* I've got a line of people to see this morning. Sit down, take five minutes, and pull yourself together, and then go home, will ya? I need the office, Willy. *(He starts to go, turns, remembering the recorder, starts to push off the table holding the recorder.)* Oh, yeah. Whenever you can this week, stop by and drop off the samples. You'll feel better, Willy, and then come back and we'll talk. Pull yourself together, kid, there's people outside.

Howard exits, pushing the table off left. Willy stares into space, exhausted. Now the music is heard—Ben's music— first distantly, then closer, closer. As Willy speaks, Ben enters from the right. He carries valise and umbrella.

WILLY: Oh, Ben, how did you do it? What is the answer? Did you wind up the Alaska deal already?

BEN: Doesn't take much time if you know what you're doing. Just a short business trip. Boarding ship in an hour. Wanted to say good-by.

WILLY: Ben, I've got to talk to you.

BEN: (glancing at his watch) Haven't the time, William.

WILLY: (crossing the apron to Ben) Ben, nothing's working out. I don't   180
know what to do.

BEN: Now, look here, William. I've bought timberland in Alaska and I need a man to look after things for me.

WILLY: God, timberland! Me and my boys in those grand outdoors!

BEN: You've a new continent at your doorstep, William. Get out of these cities, they're full of talk and time payments and courts of law. Screw on your fists and you can fight for a fortune up there.

WILLY: Yes, yes! Linda! Linda!

Linda enters as of old, with the wash.

LINDA: Oh, you're back?   185

BEN: I haven't much time.

WILLY: No, wait! Linda, he's got a proposition for me in Alaska.

LINDA: But you've got— (To Ben.) He's got a beautiful job here.

WILLY: But in Alaska, kid, I could—

LINDA: You're doing well enough, Willy!   190

BEN: (to Linda) Enough for what, my dear?

LINDA: (frightened of Ben and angry at him) Don't say those things to him! Enough to be happy right here, right now. (To Willy, while Ben laughs.) Why must everybody conquer the world? You're well liked, and the boys love you, and someday—(to Ben)—why, old man Wagner told him just the other day that if he keeps it up he'll be a member of the firm, didn't he, Willy?

WILLY: Sure, sure. I am building something with this firm, Ben, and if a man is building something he must be on the right track, mustn't he?

BEN: What are you building? Lay your hand on it. Where is it?

WILLY: (hesitantly) That's true, Linda, there's nothing.   195

LINDA: Why? (To Ben.) There's a man eighty-four years old—

WILLY: That's right, Ben, that's right. When I look at that man I say, what is there to worry about?

BEN: Bah!

WILLY: It's true, Ben. All he has to do is go into any city, pick up the phone, and he's making his living and you know why?

BEN: (picking up his valise) I've got to go.   200

WILLY: (holding Ben back) Look at this boy!

Biff, in his high school sweater, enters carrying suitcase. Happy carries Biff's shoulder guards, gold helmet, and football pants.

WILLY: Without a penny to his name, three great universities are begging for him, and from there the sky's the limit, because it's not what you do, Ben. It's who you know and the smile on your face! It's contacts, Ben, contacts! The whole wealth of Alaska passes over the lunch table at the Commodore Hotel, and that's the wonder, the wonder of this country, that a man can end with diamonds here on the basis of being liked! *(He turns to Biff.)* And that's why when you get out on that field today it's important. Because thousands of people will be rooting for you and loving you. *(To Ben, who has again begun to leave.)* And Ben! when he walks into a business office his name will sound out like a bell and all the doors will open to him! I've seen it, Ben, I've seen it a thousand times! You can't feel it with your hand like timber, but it's there!

BEN: Good-by, William.

WILLY: Ben, am I right? Don't you think I'm right? I value your advice.

205 BEN: There's a new continent at your doorstep, William. You could walk out rich. Rich. *(He is gone.)*

WILLY: We'll do it here, Ben! You hear me? We're gonna do it here!

Young Bernard rushes in. The gay music of the boys is heard.

BERNARD: Oh, gee, I was afraid you left already!

WILLY: Why? What time is it?

BERNARD: It's half-past one!

210 WILLY: Well, come on, everybody! Ebbets Field[1] next stop! Where's the pennants? *(He rushes through the wall-line of the kitchen and out into the living room.)*

LINDA: *(to Biff)* Did you pack fresh underwear?

BIFF: *(who has been limbering up)* I want to go!

BERNARD: Biff, I'm carrying your helmet, ain't I?

HAPPY: No, I'm carrying the helmet.

215 BERNARD: Oh, Biff, you promised me.

HAPPY: I'm carrying the helmet.

BERNARD: How am I going to get in the locker room?

LINDA: Let him carry the shoulder guards. *(She puts her coat and hat on in the kitchen.)*

BERNARD: Can I, Biff? 'Cause I told everybody I'm going to be in the locker room.

---

[1] *Ebbets Field:* The home park of the Brooklyn Dodgers.

HAPPY: In Ebbets Field it's the clubhouse.   220
BERNARD: I meant the clubhouse. Biff!
HAPPY: Biff!
BIFF: (*grandly, after a slight pause*) Let him carry the shoulder guards.
HAPPY: (*as he gives Bernard the shoulder guards*) Stay close to us now.

Willy rushes in with the pennants.

WILLY: (*handing them out*) Everybody wave when Biff comes out on the   225
field. (*Happy and Bernard run off.*) You set now, boy?

The music has died away.

BIFF: Ready to go, Pop. Every muscle is ready.
WILLY: (*at the edge of the apron*) You realize what this means?
BIFF: That's right, Pop.
WILLY: (*feeling Biff's muscles*) You're comin' home this afternoon
captain of the All-Scholastic Championship Team of the City of
New York.
BIFF: I got it, Pop. And remember, pal, when I take off my helmet, that   230
touchdown is for you.
WILLY: Let's go! (*He is starting out, with his arm around Biff, when Charley
enters, as of old, in knickers.*) I got no room for you, Charley.
CHARLEY: Room? For what?
WILLY: In the car.
CHARLEY: You goin' for a ride? I wanted to shoot some casino.
WILLY: (*furiously*) Casino! (*Incredulously.*) Don't you realize what   235
today is?
LINDA: Oh, he knows, Willy. He's just kidding you.
WILLY: That's nothing to kid about!
CHARLEY: No, Linda, what's goin' on?
LINDA: He's playing in Ebbets Field.
CHARLEY: Baseball in this weather?   240
WILLY: Don't talk to him. Come on, come on! (*He is pushing them
out.*)
CHARLEY: Wait a minute, didn't you hear the news?
WILLY: What?
CHARLEY: Don't you listen to the radio? Ebbets Field just blew up.
WILLY: You go to hell! (*Charley laughs. Pushing them out.*) Come on,   245
come on! We're late.
CHARLEY: (*as they go*) Knock a homer, Biff, knock a homer!
WILLY: (*the last to leave, turning to Charley*) I don't think that was funny,
Charley. This is the greatest day of his life.
CHARLEY: Willy, when are you going to grow up?

WILLY: Yeah, heh? When this game is over, Charley, you'll be laughing out of the other side of your face. They'll be calling him another Red Grange.[2] Twenty-five thousand a year.

250 CHARLEY: (kidding) Is that so?

WILLY: Yeah, that's so.

CHARLEY: Well, then, I'm sorry, Willy. But tell me something.

WILLY: What?

CHARLEY: Who is Red Grange?

255 WILLY: Put up your hands. Goddam you, put up your hands!

Charley, chuckling, shakes his head and walks away, around the left corner of the stage. Willy follows him. The music rises to a mocking frenzy.

WILLY: Who the hell do you think you are, better than everybody else? You don't know everything, you big, ignorant, stupid . . . Put up your hands!

Light rises, on the right side of the forestage, on a small table in the reception room of Charley's office. Traffic sounds are heard. Bernard, now mature, sits whistling to himself. A pair of tennis rackets and an overnight bag are on the floor beside him.

WILLY: (offstage) What are you walking away for? Don't walk away! If you're going to say something say it to my face! I know you laugh at me behind my back. You'll laugh out of the other side of your goddam face after this game. Touchdown! Touchdown! Eighty thousand people! Touchdown! Right between the goal posts.

Bernard is a quiet, earnest, but self-assured young man. Willy's voice is coming from right upstage now. Bernard lowers his feet off the table and listens. Jenny, his father's secretary, enters.

JENNY: (distressed) Say, Bernard, will you go out in the hall?

BERNARD: What is that noise? Who is it?

260 JENNY: Mr. Loman. He just got off the elevator.

BERNARD: (getting up) Who's he arguing with?

JENNY: Nobody. There's nobody with him. I can't deal with him any more, and your father gets all upset everytime he comes. I've got a lot of typing to do, and your father's waiting to sign it. Will you see him?

WILLY: (entering) Touchdown! Touch—(He sees Jenny.) Jenny, Jenny, good to see you. How're ya? Workin'? Or still honest?

---

[2]*Red Grange:* Harold Edward ("Red") Grange (1903–1991)—American football player. A running back for the New York Giants football team and the Chicago Bears, Grange was elected to the Football Hall of Fame in 1963.

JENNY: Fine. How've you been feeling?

WILLY: Not much any more, Jenny. Ha, ha! *(He is surprised to see the* 265
rackets.)

BERNARD: Hello, Uncle Willy.

WILLY: *(almost shocked)* Bernard! Well, look who's here! *(He comes*
quickly, guiltily, to Bernard and warmly shakes his hand.)

BERNARD: How are you? Good to see you.

WILLY: What are you doing here?

BERNARD: Oh, just stopped by to see Pop. Get off my feet till my train 270
leaves. I'm going to Washington in a few minutes.

WILLY: Is he in?

BERNARD: Yes, he's in his office with the accountant. Sit down.

WILLY: *(sitting down)* What're you going to do in Washington?

BERNARD: Oh, just a case I've got there, Willy.

WILLY: That so? *(indicating the rackets)* You going to play tennis there? 275

BERNARD: I'm staying with a friend who's got a court.

WILLY: Don't say. His own tennis court. Must be fine people, I bet.

BERNARD: They are, very nice. Dad tells me Biff's in town.

WILLY: *(with a big smile)* Yeah, Biff's in. Working on a very big deal,
Bernard.

BERNARD: What's Biff doing? 280

WILLY: Well, he's been doing very big things in the West. But he
decided to establish himself here. Very big. We're having dinner.
Did I hear your wife had a boy?

BERNARD: That's right. Our second.

WILLY: Two boys! What do you know!

BERNARD: What kind of a deal has Biff got?

WILLY: Well, Bill Oliver—very big sporting-goods man—he wants 285
Biff very badly. Called him in from the West. Long distance, carte
blanche, special deliveries. Your friends have their own private
tennis court?

BERNARD: You still with the old firm, Willy?

WILLY: *(after a pause)* I'm—I'm overjoyed to see how you made the
grade, Bernard, overjoyed. It's an encouraging thing to see a young
man really—really—Looks very good for Biff—very—*(He breaks off,*
then.) Bernard—*(He is so full of emotion, he breaks off again.)*

BERNARD: What is it, Willy?

WILLY: *(small and alone)* What—what's the secret?

BERNARD: What secret? 290

WILLY: How—how did you? Why didn't he ever catch on?

BERNARD: I wouldn't know that, Willy.

WILLY: *(confidentially, desperately)* You were his friend, his boyhood
friend. There's something I don't understand about it. His life ended

after that Ebbets Field game. From the age of seventeen nothing good ever happened to him.

BERNARD: He never trained himself for anything.

295 WILLY: But he did, he did. After high school he took so many correspondence courses. Radio mechanics; television; God knows what, and never made the slightest mark.

BERNARD: (*taking off his glasses*) Willy, do you want to talk candidly?

WILLY: (*rising, faces Bernard*) I regard you as a very brilliant man, Bernard. I value your advice.

BERNARD: Oh, the hell with the advice, Willy. I couldn't advise you. There's just one thing I've always wanted to ask you. When he was supposed to graduate, and the math teacher flunked him—

WILLY: Oh, that son-of-a-bitch ruined his life.

300 BERNARD: Yeah, but, Willy, all he had to do was go to summer school and make up that subject.

WILLY: That's right, that's right.

BERNARD: Did you tell him not to go to summer school?

WILLY: Me? I begged him to go. I ordered him to go!

BERNARD: Then why wouldn't he go?

305 WILLY: Why? Why! Bernard, that question has been trailing me like a ghost for the last fifteen years. He flunked the subject, and laid down and died like a hammer hit him!

BERNARD: Take it easy, kid.

WILLY: Let me talk to you—I got nobody to talk to. Bernard, Bernard, was it my fault? Y'see? It keeps going around in my mind, maybe I did something to him. I got nothing to give him.

BERNARD: Don't take it so hard.

WILLY: Why did he lay down? What is the story there? You were his friend!

310 BERNARD: Willy, I remember, it was June, and our grades came out. And he'd flunked math.

WILLY: That son-of-a-bitch!

BERNARD: No, it wasn't right then. Biff just got very angry, I remember, and he was ready to enroll in summer school.

WILLY: (*surprised*) He was?

BERNARD: He wasn't beaten by it at all. But then, Willy, he disappeared from the block for almost a month. And I got the idea that he'd gone up to New England to see you. Did he have a talk with you then?

Willy stares in silence.

315 BERNARD: Willy?

WILLY: (*with a strong edge of resentment in his voice*) Yeah, he came to Boston. What about it?

BERNARD: Well, just that when he came back—I'll never forget this, it always mystifies me. Because I'd thought so well of Biff, even though he'd always taken advantage of me. I loved him, Willy, y'know? And he came back after that month and took his sneakers—remember those sneakers with "University of Virginia" printed on them? He was so proud of those, wore them every day. And he took them down in the cellar, and burned them up in the furnace. We had a fist fight. It lasted at least half an hour. Just the two of us, punching each other down the cellar, and crying right through it. I've often thought of how strange it was that I knew he'd given up his life. What happened in Boston, Willy?

Willy looks at him as at an intruder.

BERNARD: I just bring it up because you asked me.

WILLY: *(angrily)* Nothing. What do you mean, "What happened?" What's that got to do with anything?

BERNARD: Well, don't get sore.   320

WILLY: What are you trying to do, blame it on me? If a boy lays down is that my fault?

BERNARD: Now, Willy, don't get—

WILLY: Well, don't—don't talk to me that way! What does that mean, "What happened?"

Charley enters. He is in his vest, and he carries a bottle of bourbon.

CHARLEY: Hey, you're going to miss that train. *(He waves the bottle.)*

BERNARD: Yeah, I'm going. *(He takes the bottle.)* Thanks, Pop. *(He picks*   325
up his rackets and bag.) Good-by, Willy, and don't worry about it.
You know, "If at first you don't succeed . . ."

WILLY: Yes, I believe in that.

BERNARD: But sometimes, Willy, it's better for a man just to walk away.

WILLY: Walk away?

BERNARD: That's right.

WILLY: But if you can't walk away?   330

BERNARD: *(after a slight pause)* I guess that's when it's tough. *(Extending his hand.)* Good-by, Willy.

WILLY: *(shaking Bernard's hand)* Good-by, boy.

CHARLEY: *(an arm on Bernard's shoulder)* How do you like this kid?
Gonna argue a case in front of the Supreme Court.

BERNARD: *(protesting)* Pop!

WILLY: *(genuinely shocked, pained, and happy)* No! The Supreme Court!   335

BERNARD: I gotta run, 'By, Dad!

CHARLEY: Knock 'em dead, Bernard!

Bernard goes off.

WILLY: (*as Charley takes out his wallet*) The Supreme Court! And he didn't even mention it!

CHARLEY: (*counting out money on the desk*) He don't have to—he's gonna do it.

340 WILLY: And you never told him what to do, did you? You never took any interest in him.

CHARLEY: My salvation is that I never took any interest in anything. There's some money— fifty dollars. I got an accountant inside.

WILLY: Charley, look . . . (*With difficulty.*) I got my insurance to pay. If you can manage it—I need a hundred and ten dollars.

Charley doesn't reply for a moment; merely stops moving.

WILLY: I'd draw it from my bank but Linda would know, and I . . .

CHARLEY: Sit down, Willy.

345 WILLY: (*moving toward the chair*) I'm keeping an account of everything, remember. I'll pay every penny back. (*He sits.*)

CHARLEY: Now listen to me, Willy.

WILLY: I want you to know I appreciate . . .

CHARLEY: (*sitting down on the table*) Willy, what're you doin'? What the hell is goin' on in your head?

WILLY: Why? I'm simply . . .

350 CHARLEY: I offered you a job. You can make fifty dollars a week. And I won't send you on the road.

WILLY: I've got a job.

CHARLEY: Without pay? What kind of a job is a job without pay? (*He rises.*) Now, look, kid, enough is enough. I'm no genius but I know when I'm being insulted.

WILLY: Insulted!

CHARLEY: Why don't you want to work for me?

355 WILLY: What's the matter with you? I've got a job.

CHARLEY: Then what're you walkin' in here every week for?

WILLY: (*getting up*) Well, if you don't want me to walk in here—

CHARLEY: I am offering you a job.

WILLY: I don't want your goddam job!

360 CHARLEY: When the hell are you going to grow up?

WILLY: (*furiously*) You big ignoramus, if you say that to me again I'll rap you one! I don't care how big you are! (*He's ready to fight.*)

Pause.

CHARLEY: (*kindly, going to him*) How much do you need, Willy?

WILLY: Charley, I'm strapped. I'm strapped. I don't know what to do. I was just fired.

CHARLEY: Howard fired you?

WILLY: That snotnose. Imagine that? I named him. I named him   365
Howard.

CHARLEY: Willy, when're you gonna realize that them things don't
mean anything? You named him Howard, but you can't sell that.
The only thing you got in this world is what you can sell. And the
funny thing is that you're a salesman, and you don't know that.

WILLY: I've always tried to think otherwise, I guess. I always felt that if
a man was impressive, and well liked, that nothing—

CHARLEY: Why must everybody like you? Who liked J. P. Morgan?[3] Was
he impressive? In a Turkish bath he'd look like a butcher. But with
his pockets on he was very well liked. Now listen, Willy, I know you
don't like me, and nobody can say I'm in love with you, but I'll give
you a job because—just for the hell of it, put it that way. Now what
do you say?

WILLY: I—I just can't work for you, Charley.

CHARLEY: What're you, jealous of me?   370

WILLY: I can't work for you, that's all, don't ask me why.

CHARLEY: (angered, takes out more bills) You been jealous of me all your
life, you damned fool! Here, pay your insurance. (He puts the money
in Willy's hand.)

WILLY: I'm keeping strict accounts.

CHARLEY: I've got some work to do. Take care of yourself. And pay your
insurance.

WILLY: (moving to the right) Funny, y'know? After all the highways, and   375
the trains, and the appointments, and the years, you end up worth
more dead than alive.

CHARLEY: Willy, nobody's worth nothin' dead. (After a slight pause.)
Did you hear what I said?

Willy stands still, dreaming.

CHARLEY: Willy!

WILLY: Apologize to Bernard for me when you see him. I didn't mean
to argue with him. He's a fine boy. They're all fine boys, and they'll
end up big—all of them. Someday they'll all play tennis together.
Wish me luck, Charley. He saw Bill Oliver today.

CHARLEY: Good luck.

WILLY: (on the verge of tears) Charley, you're the only friend I got. Isn't   380
that a remarkable thing? (He goes out.)

CHARLEY: Jesus!

---

[3]*J. P. Morgan:* John Pierpont Morgan (1837–1913)—American financier.

Charley stares after him a moment and follows. All light blacks out. Suddenly raucous music is heard, and a red glow rises behind the screen at right. Stanley, a young waiter, appears, carrying a table, followed by Happy, who is carrying two chairs.

STANLEY: *(putting the table down)* That's all right, Mr. Loman, I can handle it myself. *(He turns and takes the chairs from Happy and places them at the table.)*

HAPPY: *(glancing around)* Oh, this is better.

STANLEY: Sure, in the front there you're in the middle of all kinds a noise. Whenever you got a party, Mr. Loman, you just tell me and I'll put you back here. Y'know, there's a lotta people they don't like it private, because when they go out they like to see a lotta action around them because they're sick and tired to stay in the house by theirself. But I know you, you ain't from Hackensack. You know what I mean?

385 HAPPY: *(sitting down)* So, how's it coming, Stanley?

STANLEY: Ah, it's a dog's life. I only wish during the war they'd a took me in the Army. I coulda been dead by now.

HAPPY: My brother's back, Stanley.

STANLEY: Oh, he come back, heh? From the Far West.

HAPPY: Yeah, big cattle man, my brother, so treat him right. And my father's coming too.

390 STANLEY: Oh, your father too!

HAPPY: You got a couple of nice lobsters?

STANLEY: Hundred per cent, big.

HAPPY: I want them with the claws.

STANLEY: Don't worry, I don't give you no mice. *(Happy laughs.)* How about some wine? It'll put a head on the meal.

395 HAPPY: No. You remember, Stanley, that recipe I brought you from overseas? With the champagne in it?

STANLEY: Oh, yeah, sure. I still got it tacked up yet in the kitchen. But that'll have to cost a buck apiece anyways.

HAPPY: That's all right.

STANLEY: What'd you, hit a number or somethin'?

HAPPY: No, it's a little celebration. My brother is—I think he pulled off a big deal today. I think we're going into business together.

400 STANLEY: Great! That's the best for you. Because a family business, you know what I mean?—that's the best.

HAPPY: That's what I think.

STANLEY: 'Cause what's the difference? Somebody steals? It's in the family. Know what I mean? *(Sotto voce.)* Like this bartender here. The boss is goin' crazy what kinda leak he's got in the cash register. You put it in but it don't come out.

HAPPY: (*raising his head*) Sh!

STANLEY: What?

HAPPY: You notice I wasn't lookin' right or left, was I?   405

STANLEY: No.

HAPPY: And my eyes are closed.

STANLEY: So what's the—

HAPPY: Strudel's comin'.

STANLEY: (*catching on, looks around*) Ah, no, there's no—   410

He breaks off as a furred, lavishly dressed Girl enters and sits at the next table. Both follow her with their eyes.

STANLEY: Geez, how'd ya know?

HAPPY: I got radar or something. (*Staring directly at her profile.*) Oooooooo . . . Stanley.

STANLEY: I think that's for you, Mr. Loman.

HAPPY: Look at that mouth. Oh, God. And the binoculars.

STANLEY: Geez, you got a life, Mr. Loman.   415

HAPPY: Wait on her.

STANLEY: (*going to The Girl's table*) Would you like a menu, ma'am?

GIRL: I'm expecting someone, but I'd like a—

HAPPY: Why don't you bring her—excuse me, miss, do you mind? I sell champagne, and I'd like you to try my brand. Bring her a champagne, Stanley.

GIRL: That's awfully nice of you.   420

HAPPY: Don't mention it. It's all company money. (*He laughs.*)

GIRL: That's a charming product to be selling, isn't it?

HAPPY: Oh, gets to be like everything else. Selling is selling, y'know.

GIRL: I suppose.

HAPPY: You don't happen to sell, do you?   425

GIRL: No, I don't sell.

HAPPY: Would you object to a compliment from a stranger? You ought to be on a magazine cover.

GIRL: (*looking at him a little archly*) I have been.

Stanley comes in with a glass of champagne.

HAPPY: What'd I say before, Stanley? You see? She's a cover girl.

STANLEY: Oh, I could see, I could see.   430

HAPPY: (*to The Girl*) What magazine?

GIRL: Oh, a lot of them. (*She takes the drink.*) Thank you.

HAPPY: You know what they say in France, don't you? "Champagne is the drink of the complexion" —Hya, Biff!

Biff has entered and sits with Happy.

BIFF: Hello, kid. Sorry I'm late.

435 HAPPY: I just got here. Uh, Miss—?

GIRL: Forsythe.

HAPPY: Miss Forsythe, this is my brother.

BIFF: Is Dad here?

HAPPY: His name is Biff. You might've heard of him. Great football player.

440 GIRL: Really? What team?

HAPPY: Are you familiar with football?

GIRL: No, I'm afraid I'm not.

HAPPY: Biff is quarterback with the New York Giants.

GIRL: Well, that is nice, isn't it? (*She drinks.*)

445 HAPPY: Good health.

GIRL: I'm happy to meet you.

HAPPY: That's my name. Hap. It's really Harold, but at West Point they called me Happy.

GIRL: (*now really impressed*) Oh, I see. How do you do? (*She turns her profile.*)

BIFF: Isn't Dad coming?

450 HAPPY: You want her?

BIFF: Oh, I could never make that.

HAPPY: I remember the time that idea would never come into your head. Where's the old confidence, Biff?

BIFF: I just saw Oliver—

HAPPY: Wait a minute. I've got to see that old confidence again. Do you want her? She's on call.

455 BIFF: Oh, no. (*He turns to look at The Girl.*)

HAPPY: I'm telling you. Watch this. (*Turning to The Girl.*) Honey? (*She turns to him.*) Are you busy?

GIRL: Well, I am . . . but I could make a phone call.

HAPPY: Do that, will you, honey? And see if you can get a friend. We'll be here for a while. Biff is one of the greatest football players in the country.

GIRL: (*standing up*) Well, I'm certainly happy to meet you.

460 HAPPY: Come back soon.

GIRL: I'll try.

HAPPY: Don't try, honey, try hard.

The Girl exits. Stanley follows, shaking his head in bewildered admiration.

HAPPY: Isn't that a shame now? A beautiful girl like that? That's why I can't get married. There's not a good woman in a thousand. New York is loaded with them, kid!

BIFF: Hap, look —

465 HAPPY: I told you she was on call!

BIFF: *(strangely unnerved)* Cut it out, will ya? I want to say something to you.

HAPPY: Did you see Oliver?

BIFF: I saw him all right. Now look, I want to tell Dad a couple of things and I want you to help me.

HAPPY: What? Is he going to back you?

BIFF: Are you crazy? You're out of your goddam head, you know that?   470

HAPPY: Why? What happened?

BIFF: *(breathlessly)* I did a terrible thing today, Hap. It's been the strangest day I ever went through. I'm all numb, I swear.

HAPPY: You mean he wouldn't see you?

BIFF: Well, I waited six hours for him, see? All day. Kept sending my name in. Even tried to date his secretary so she'd get me to him, but no soap.

HAPPY: Because you're not showin' the old confidence, Biff. He remem-   475
bered you, didn't he?

BIFF: *(stopping Happy with a gesture)* Finally, about five o'clock, he comes out. Didn't remember who I was or anything. I felt like such an idiot, Hap.

HAPPY: Did you tell him my Florida idea?

BIFF: He walked away. I saw him for one minute. I got so mad I could've torn the walls down! How the hell did I ever get the idea I was a salesman there? I even believed myself that I'd been a salesman for him! And then he gave me one look and—I realized what a ridiculous lie my whole life has been! We've been talking in a dream for fifteen years. I was a shipping clerk.

HAPPY: What'd you do?

BIFF: *(with great tension and wonder)* Well, he left, see. And the secretary   480
went out. I was all alone in the waiting-room. I don't know what came over me, Hap. The next thing I know I'm in his office—paneled walls, everything. I can't explain it. I—Hap, I took his fountain pen.

HAPPY: Geez, did he catch you?

BIFF: I ran out. I ran down all eleven flights. I ran and ran and ran.

HAPPY: That was an awful dumb—what'd you do that for?

BIFF: *(agonized)* I don't know, I just—wanted to take something, I don't know. You gotta help me, Hap. I'm gonna tell Pop.

HAPPY: You crazy? What for?   485

BIFF: Hap, he's got to understand that I'm not the man somebody lends that kind of money to. He thinks I've been spiting him all these years and it's eating him up.

HAPPY: That's just it. You tell him something nice.

BIFF: I can't.

HAPPY: Say you got a lunch date with Oliver tomorrow.

490 **BIFF:** So what do I do tomorrow?

HAPPY: You leave the house tomorrow and come back at night and say Oliver is thinking it over. And he thinks it over for a couple of weeks, and gradually it fades away and nobody's the worse.

BIFF: But it'll go on forever!

HAPPY: Dad is never so happy as when he's looking forward to something!

Willy enters.

HAPPY: Hello, scout!

495 **WILLY:** Gee, I haven't been here in years!

Stanley has followed Willy in and sets a chair for him. Stanley starts off but Happy stops him.

HAPPY: Stanley!

Stanley stands by, waiting for an order.

BIFF: (*going to Willy with guilt, as to an invalid*) Sit down, Pop. You want a drink?

WILLY: Sure, I don't mind.

BIFF: Let's get a load on.

500 **WILLY:** You look worried.

BIFF: N-no. (*To Stanley.*) Scotch all around. Make it doubles.

STANLEY: Doubles, right. (*He goes.*)

WILLY: You had a couple already, didn't you?

BIFF: Just a couple, yeah.

505 **WILLY:** Well, what happened, boy? (*Nodding affirmatively, with a smile.*) Everything go all right?

BIFF: (*takes a breath, then reaches out and grasps Willy's hand*) Pal . . . (*He is smiling bravely, and Willy is smiling too.*) I had an experience today.

HAPPY: Terrific, Pop.

WILLY: That so? What happened?

BIFF: (*high, slightly alcoholic, above the earth*) I'm going to tell you everything from first to last. It's been a strange day. (*Silence. He looks around, composes himself as best he can, but his breath keeps breaking the rhythm of his voice.*) I had to wait quite a while for him, and—

510 **WILLY:** Oliver?

BIFF: Yeah, Oliver. All day, as a matter of cold fact. And a lot of— instances—facts, Pop, facts about my life came back to me. Who was it, Pop? Who ever said I was a salesman with Oliver?

WILLY: Well, you were.

BIFF: No, Dad, I was a shipping clerk.

WILLY: But you were practically—

BIFF: (*with determination*) Dad, I don't know who said it first, but I was   515
never a salesman for Bill Oliver.

WILLY: What're you talking about?

BIFF: Let's hold on to the facts tonight, Pop. We're not going to get
anywhere bullin' around. I was a shipping clerk.

WILLY: (*angrily*) All right, now listen to me—

BIFF: Why don't you let me finish?

WILLY: I'm not interested in stories about the past or any crap of that   520
kind because the woods are burning, boys, you understand? There's
a big blaze going on all around. I was fired today.

BIFF: (*shocked*) How could you be?

WILLY: I was fired, and I'm looking for a little good news to tell your
mother, because the woman has waited and the woman has suffered.
The gist of it is that I haven't got a story left in my head, Biff. So
don't give me a lecture about facts and aspects. I am not interested.
Now what've you got to say to me?

Stanley enters with three drinks. They wait until he leaves.

WILLY: Did you see Oliver?

BIFF: Jesus, Dad!

WILLY: You mean you didn't go up there?   525

HAPPY: Sure he went up there.

BIFF: I did. I—saw him. How could they fire you?

WILLY: (*on the edge of his chair*) What kind of a welcome did he give
you?

BIFF: He won't even let you work on commission?

WILLY: I'm out! (*Driving.*) So tell me, he gave you a warm welcome?   530

HAPPY: Sure, Pop, sure!

BIFF: (*driven*) Well, it was kind of—

WILLY: I was wondering if he'd remember you. (*To Happy.*) Imagine,
man doesn't see him for ten, twelve years and gives you that kind of
a welcome!

HAPPY: Damn right!

BIFF: (*trying to return to the offensive*) Pop, look—   535

WILLY: You know why he remembered you, don't you? Because you
impressed him in those days.

BIFF: Let's talk quietly and get this down to the facts, huh?

WILLY: (*as though Biff had been interrupting*) Well, what happened? It's
great news, Biff. Did he take you into his office or'd you talk in the
waiting-room?

BIFF: Well, he came in, see, and—

540 **WILLY:** (*with a big smile*) What'd he say? Betcha he threw his arm around you.

BIFF: Well, he kinda—

WILLY: He's a fine man. (*To Happy.*) Very hard man to see, y'know.

HAPPY: (*agreeing*) Oh, I know.

WILLY: (*to Biff*) Is that where you had the drinks?

545 **BIFF:** Yeah, he gave me a couple of—no, no!

HAPPY: (*cutting in*) He told him my Florida idea.

WILLY: Don't interrupt. (*To Biff.*) How'd he react to the Florida idea?

BIFF: Dad, will you give me a minute to explain?

WILLY: I've been waiting for you to explain since I sat down here! What happened? He took you into his office and what?

550 **BIFF:** Well—I talked. And—and he listened, see.

WILLY: Famous for the way he listens, y'know. What was his answer?

BIFF: His answer was— (*He breaks off, suddenly angry.*) Dad, you're not letting me tell you what I want to tell you!

WILLY: (*accusing, angered*) You didn't see him, did you?

BIFF: I did see him!

555 **WILLY:** What'd you insult him or something? You insulted him, didn't you?

BIFF: Listen, will you let me out of it, will you just let me out of it!

HAPPY: What the hell!

WILLY: Tell me what happened!

BIFF: (*to Happy*) I can't talk to him!

A single trumpet note jars the ear. The light of green leaves stains the house, which holds the air of night and a dream. Young Bernard enters and knocks on the door of the house.

560 **YOUNG BERNARD:** (*frantically*) Mrs. Loman, Mrs. Loman!

HAPPY: Tell him what happened!

BIFF: (*to Happy*) Shut up and leave me alone!

WILLY: No, no! You had to go and flunk math!

BIFF: What math? What're you talking about?

565 **YOUNG BERNARD:** Mrs. Loman, Mrs. Loman!

Linda appears in the house, as of old.

WILLY: (*wildly*) Math, math, math!

BIFF: Take it easy, Pop!

YOUNG BERNARD: Mrs. Loman!

WILLY: (*furiously*) If you hadn't flunked you'd've been set by now!

570 **BIFF:** Now, look, I'm gonna tell you what happened, and you're going to listen to me.

YOUNG BERNARD: Mrs. Loman!

BIFF: I waited six hours—

HAPPY: What the hell are you saying?

BIFF: I kept sending in my name but he wouldn't see me. So finally
he . . . (*He continues unheard as light fades low on the restaurant.*)

YOUNG BERNARD: Biff flunked math!   575

LINDA: No!

YOUNG BERNARD: Birnbaum flunked him! They won't graduate him!

LINDA: But they have to. He's gotta go to the university. Where is he?
Biff! Biff!

YOUNG BERNARD: No, he left. He went to Grand Central.

LINDA: Grand—You mean he went to Boston!   580

YOUNG BERNARD: Is Uncle Willy in Boston?

LINDA: Oh, maybe Willy can talk to the teacher. Oh, the poor, poor
boy!

Light on house area snaps out.

BIFF: (*at the table, now audible, holding up a gold fountain pen*) . . . so I'm
washed up with Oliver, you understand? Are you listening to me?

WILLY: (*at a loss*) Yeah, sure. If you hadn't flunked—

BIFF: Flunked what? What're you talking about?   585

WILLY: Don't blame everything on me! I didn't flunk math—you did!
What pen?

HAPPY: That was awful dumb, Biff, a pen like that is worth—

WILLY: (*seeing the pen for the first time*) You took Oliver's pen?

BIFF: (*weakening*) Dad, I just explained it to you.

WILLY: You stole Bill Oliver's fountain pen!   590

BIFF: I didn't exactly steal it! That's just what I've been explaining
to you!

HAPPY: He had it in his hand and just then Oliver walked in, so he got
nervous and stuck it in his pocket!

WILLY: My God, Biff!

BIFF: I never intended to do it, Dad!

OPERATOR'S VOICE: Standish Arms, good evening!   595

WILLY: (*shouting*) I'm not in my room!

BIFF: (*frightened*) Dad, what's the matter? (*He and Happy stand up.*)

OPERATOR: Ringing Mr. Loman for you!

WILLY: I'm not there, stop it!

BIFF: (*horrified, gets down on one knee before Willy*) Dad, I'll make good,   600
I'll make good. (*Willy tries to get to his feet. Biff holds him down.*) Sit
down now.

WILLY: No, you're no good, you're no good for anything.

BIFF: I am, Dad, I'll find something else, you understand? Now don't
worry about anything. (*He holds up Willy's face.*) Talk to me, Dad.

OPERATOR: Mr. Loman does not answer. Shall I page him?

WILLY: (attempting to stand, as though to rush and silence the Operator) No, no, no!

605 **HAPPY:** He'll strike something, Pop.

WILLY: No, no . . .

BIFF: (desperately, standing over Willy) Pop, listen! Listen to me! I'm telling you something good. Oliver talked to his partner about the Florida idea. You listening? He—he talked to his partner, and he came to me . . . I'm going to be all right, you hear? Dad, listen to me, he said it was just a question of the amount!

WILLY: Then you . . . got it?

HAPPY: He's gonna be terrific, Pop!

610 **WILLY:** (trying to stand) Then you got it, haven't you? You got it! You got it!

BIFF: (agonized, holds Willy down) No, no. Look, Pop. I'm supposed to have lunch with them tomorrow. I'm just telling you this so you'll know that I can still make an impression, Pop. And I'll make good somewhere, but I can't go tomorrow, see?

WILLY: Why not? You simply—

BIFF: But the pen, Pop!

WILLY: You give it to him and tell him it was an oversight!

615 **HAPPY:** Sure, have lunch tomorrow!

BIFF: I can't say that—

WILLY: You were doing a crossword puzzle and accidentally used his pen!

BIFF: Listen, kid, I took those balls years ago, now I walk in with his fountain pen? That clinches it, don't you see? I can't face him like that! I'll try elsewhere.

PAGE'S VOICE: Paging Mr. Loman!

620 **WILLY:** Don't you want to be anything?

BIFF: Pop, how can I go back?

WILLY: You don't want to be anything, is that what's behind it?

BIFF: (now angry at Willy for not crediting his sympathy) Don't take it that way! You think it was easy walking into that office after what I'd done to him? A team of horses couldn't have dragged me back to Bill Oliver!

WILLY: Then why'd you go?

625 **BIFF:** Why did I go? Why did I go? Look at you! Look at what's become of you!

Off left, The Woman laughs.

WILLY: Biff, you're going to go to that lunch tomorrow, or—

BIFF: I can't go. I've got no appointment!

HAPPY: Biff, for . . .!

WILLY: Are you spiting me?

BIFF: Don't take it that way! Goddammit!   630

WILLY: (*strikes Biff and falters away from the table*) You rotten little louse! Are you spiting me?

THE WOMAN: Someone's at the door, Willy!

BIFF: I'm no good, can't you see what I am?

HAPPY: (*separating them*) Hey, you're in a restaurant! Now cut it out, both of you! (*The Girls enter.*) Hello, girls, sit down.

The Woman laughs, off left.

MISS FORSYTHE: I guess we might as well. This is Letta.   635

THE WOMAN: Willy, are you going to wake up?

BIFF: (*ignoring Willy*) How're ya, miss, sit down. What do you drink?

MISS FORSYTHE: Letta might not be able to stay long.

LETTA: I gotta get up very early tomorrow. I got jury duty. I'm so excited! Were you fellows ever on a jury?

BIFF: No, but I been in front of them! (*The Girls laugh.*) This is my father.   640

LETTA: Isn't he cute? Sit down with us, Pop.

HAPPY: Sit him down, Biff!

BIFF: (*going to him*) Come on, slugger, drink us under the table. To hell with it! Come on, sit down, pal.

On Biff's last insistence, Willy is about to sit.

THE WOMAN: (*now urgently*) Willy, are you going to answer the door!

The Woman's call pulls Willy back. He starts right, befuddled.

BIFF: Hey, where are you going?   645

WILLY: Open the door.

BIFF: The door?

WILLY: The washroom . . . the door . . . where's the door?

BIFF: (*leading Willy to the left*) Just go straight down.

Willy moves left.

THE WOMAN: Willy, Willy, are you going to get up, get up, get up, get up?   650

Willy exits left.

LETTA: I think it's sweet you bring your daddy along.

MISS FORSYTHE: Oh, he isn't really your father!

BIFF: (*at left, turning to her resentfully*) Miss Forsythe, you've just seen a prince walk by. A fine, troubled prince. A hard-working, unappreciated prince. A pal, you understand? A good companion. Always for his boys.

LETTA: That's so sweet.

655 HAPPY: Well, girls, what's the program? We're wasting time. Come on, Biff. Gather round. Where would you like to go?

BIFF: Why don't you do something for him?

HAPPY: Me!

BIFF: Don't you give a damn for him, Hap?

HAPPY: What're you talking about? I'm the one who—

660 BIFF: I sense it, you don't give a good goddam about him. (*He takes the rolled-up hose from his pocket and puts it on the table in front of Happy.*) Look what I found in the cellar, for Christ's sake. How can you bear to let it go on?

HAPPY: Me? Who goes away? Who runs off and—

BIFF: Yeah, but he doesn't mean anything to you. You could help him—I can't! Don't you understand what I'm talking about? He's going to kill himself, don't you know that?

HAPPY: Don't I know it! Me!

BIFF: Hap, help him! Jesus . . . help him . . . Help me, help me, I can't bear to look at his face! (*Ready to weep, he hurries out, up right.*)

665 HAPPY: (*starting after him*) Where are you going?

MISS FORSYTHE: What's he so mad about?

HAPPY: Come on, girls, we'll catch up with him.

MISS FORSYTHE: (*as Happy pushes her out*) Say, I don't like that temper of his!

HAPPY: He's just a little overstrung, he'll be all right!

670 WILLY: (*off left, as The Woman laughs*) Don't answer! Don't answer!

LETTA: Don't you want to tell your father—

HAPPY: No, that's not my father. He's just a guy. Come on, we'll catch Biff, and, honey, we're going to paint this town! Stanley, where's the check! Hey, Stanley!

They exit. Stanley looks toward left.

STANLEY: (*calling to Happy indignantly*) Mr. Loman! Mr. Loman!

Stanley picks up a chair and follows them off. Knocking is heard off left. The Woman enters, laughing. Willy follows her. She is in a black slip; he is buttoning his shirt. Raw, sensuous music accompanies their speech.

WILLY: Will you stop laughing? Will you stop?

675 THE WOMAN: Aren't you going to answer the door? He'll wake the whole hotel.

WILLY: I'm not expecting anybody.

THE WOMAN: Whyn't you have another drink, honey, and stop being so damn self-centered?

WILLY: I'm so lonely.

THE WOMAN: You know you ruined me, Willy? From now on, whenever you come to the office, I'll see that you go right through to the
buyers. No waiting at my desk any more, Willy. You ruined me.

WILLY: That's nice of you to say that.   680

THE WOMAN: Gee, you are self-centered! Why so sad? You are the saddest self-centeredest soul I ever did see-saw. (*She laughs. He kisses
her.*) Come on inside, drummer boy. It's silly to be dressing in the
middle of the night. (*As knocking is heard.*) Aren't you going to
answer the door?

WILLY: They're knocking on the wrong door.

THE WOMAN: But I felt the knocking. And he heard us talking in here.
Maybe the hotel's on fire!

WILLY: (*his terror rising*) It's a mistake.

THE WOMAN: Then tell him to go away!   685

WILLY: There's nobody there.

THE WOMAN: It's getting on my nerves, Willy. There's somebody standing out there and it's getting on my nerves!

WILLY: (*pushing her away from him*) All right, stay in the bathroom here,
and don't come out. I think there's a law in Massachusetts about it,
so don't come out. It may be that new room clerk. He looked very
mean. So don't come out. It's a mistake, there's no fire.

*The knocking is heard again. He takes a few steps away from her, and she van-
ishes into the wing. The light follows him, and now he is facing Young Biff, who
carries a suitcase. Biff steps toward him. The music is gone.*

BIFF: Why didn't you answer?

WILLY: Biff! What are you doing in Boston?   690

BIFF: Why didn't you answer? I've been knocking for five minutes,
I called you on the phone—

WILLY: I just heard you. I was in the bathroom and had the door shut.
Did anything happen home?

BIFF: Dad—I let you down.

WILLY: What do you mean?

BIFF: Dad . . .   695

WILLY: Biffo, what's this about? (*Putting his arm around Biff.*) Come on,
let's go downstairs and get you a malted.

BIFF: Dad, I flunked math.

WILLY: Not for the term?

BIFF: The term. I haven't got enough credits to graduate.

WILLY: You mean to say Bernard wouldn't give you the answers?   700

BIFF: He did, he tried, but I only got a sixty-one.

WILLY: And they wouldn't give you four points?

BIFF: Birnbaum refused absolutely. I begged him, Pop, but he won't give me those points. You gotta talk to him before they close the school. Because if he saw the kind of man you are, and you just talked to him in your way, I'm sure he'd come through for me. The class came right before practice, see, and I didn't go enough. Would you talk to him? He'd like you, Pop. You know the way you could talk.

WILLY: You're on. We'll drive right back.

705 BIFF: Oh, Dad, good work! I'm sure he'll change it for you!

WILLY: Go downstairs and tell the clerk I'm checkin' out. Go right down.

BIFF: Yes, Sir! See, the reason he hates me, Pop—one day he was late for class so I got up at the blackboard and imitated him. I crossed my eyes and talked with a lithp.

WILLY: *(laughing)* You did? The kids like it?

BIFF: They nearly died laughing!

710 WILLY: Yeah? What'd you do?

BIFF: The thquare root of thixthy twee is . . . *(Willy bursts out laughing; Biff joins him.)* And in the middle of it he walked in!

Willy laughs and The Woman joins in offstage.

WILLY: *(without hesitating)* Hurry downstairs and—

BIFF: Somebody in there?

WILLY: No, that was next door.

The Woman laughs offstage.

715 BIFF: Somebody got in your bathroom!

WILLY: No, it's the next room, there's a party—

THE WOMAN: *(enters, laughing. She lisps this)* Can I come in? There's something in the bathtub, Willy, and it's moving!

Willy looks at Biff, who is staring open-mouthed and horrified at The Woman.

WILLY: Ah—you better go back to your room. They must be finished painting by now. They're painting her room so I let her take a shower here. Go back, go back . . . *(He pushes her.)*

THE WOMAN: *(resisting)* But I've got to get dressed, Willy, I can't—

720 WILLY: Get out of here! Go back, go back . . . *(Suddenly striving for the ordinary.)* This is Miss Francis, Biff, she's a buyer. They're painting her room. Go back, Miss Francis, go back . . .

THE WOMAN: But my clothes, I can't go out naked in the hall!

WILLY: *(pushing her offstage)* Get outa here! Go back, go back!

Biff slowly sits down on his suitcase as the argument continues offstage.

THE WOMAN: Where's my stockings? You promised me stockings, Willy!

WILLY: I have no stockings here!

THE WOMAN: You had two boxes of size nine sheers for me, and I want   725
them!

WILLY: Here, for God's sake, will you get outa here!

THE WOMAN: (*enters holding a box of stockings*) I just hope there's nobody
in the hall. That's all I hope. (*To Biff.*) Are you football or baseball?

BIFF: Football.

THE WOMAN: (*angry, humiliated*) That's me too. G'night. (*She snatches
her clothes from Willy, and walks out.*)

WILLY: (*after a pause*) Well, better get going. I want to get to the school   730
first thing in the morning. Get my suits out of the closet. I'll get my
valise. (*Biff doesn't move.*) What's the matter? (*Biff remains motionless,
tears falling.*) She's a buyer. Buys for J. H. Simmons. She lives down
the hall—they're painting. You don't imagine— (*He breaks off. After
a pause.*) Now listen, pal, she's just a buyer. She sees merchandise in
her room and they have to keep it looking just so . . . (*Pause. Assuming command.*) All right, get my suits. (*Biff doesn't move.*) Now stop
crying and do as I say. I gave you an order. Biff, I gave you an order!
Is that what you do when I give you an order? How dare you cry!
(*Putting his arm around Biff.*) Now look, Biff, when you grow up you'll
understand about these things. You mustn't—you mustn't overem-
phasize a thing like this. I'll see Birnbaum first thing in the morning.

BIFF: Never mind.

WILLY: (*getting down beside Biff*) Never mind! He's going to give you
those points. I'll see to it.

BIFF: He wouldn't listen to you.

WILLY: He certainly will listen to me. You need those points for the U.
of Virginia.

BIFF: I'm not going there.   735

WILLY: Heh? If I can't get him to change that mark you'll make it up in
summer school. You've got all summer to—

BIFF: (*his weeping breaking from him*) Dad . . .

WILLY: (*infected by it*) Oh, my boy . . .

BIFF: Dad . . .

WILLY: She's nothing to me, Biff. I was lonely, I was terribly lonely.   740

BIFF: You—you gave her Mama's stockings! (*His tears break through and
he rises to go.*)

WILLY: (*grabbing for Biff*) I gave you an order!

BIFF: Don't touch me, you—liar!

WILLY: Apologize for that!

BIFF: You fake! You phony little fake! You fake! (*Overcome, he turns   745
quickly and weeping fully goes out with his suitcase. Willy is left on the
floor on his knees.*)

WILLY: I gave you an order! Biff, come back here or I'll beat you! Come back here! I'll whip you!

Stanley comes quickly in from the right and stands in front of Willy.

WILLY: *(shouts at Stanley)* I gave you an order . . .

STANLEY: Hey, let's pick it up, pick it up, Mr. Loman. *(He helps Willy to his feet.)* Your boys left with the chippies. They said they'll see you home.

A second waiter watches some distance away.

WILLY: But we were supposed to have dinner together.

Music is heard, Willy's theme.

750 STANLEY: Can you make it?

WILLY: I'll—sure, I can make it. *(Suddenly concerned about his clothes.)* Do I—I look all right?

STANLEY: Sure, you look all right. *(He flicks a speck off Willy's lapel.)*

WILLY: Here—here's a dollar.

STANLEY: Oh, your son paid me. It's all right.

755 WILLY: *(putting it in Stanley's hand)* No, take it. You're a good boy.

STANLEY: Oh, no, you don't have to . . .

WILLY: Here—here's some more, I don't need it any more. *(After a slight pause.)* Tell me—is there a seed store in the neighborhood?

STANLEY: Seeds? You mean like to plant?

As Willy turns, Stanley slips the money back into his jacket pocket.

WILLY: Yes. Carrots, peas . . .

760 STANLEY: Well, there's hardware stores on Sixth Avenue, but it may be too late now.

WILLY: *(anxiously)* Oh, I'd better hurry. I've got to get some seeds. *(He starts off to the right.)* I've got to get some seeds, right away. Nothing's planted. I don't have a thing in the ground.

Willy hurries out as the light goes down. Stanley moves over to the right after him, watches him off. The other waiter has been staring at Willy.

STANLEY: *(to the waiter)* Well, whatta you looking at?

The waiter picks up the chairs and moves off right. Stanley takes the table and follows him. The light fades on this area. There is a long pause, the sound of the flute coming over. The light gradually rises on the kitchen, which is empty. Happy appears at the door of the house, followed by Biff. Happy is carrying a large bunch of long-stemmed roses. He enters the kitchen, looks around for Linda. Not seeing her, he turns to Biff, who is just outside the house door, and makes a gesture with his hands, indicating "Not here, I guess." He looks into the living room and freezes. Inside, Linda, unseen, is seated, Willy's coat on her lap. She rises ominously and quietly and moves toward Happy, who backs up into the kitchen, afraid.

HAPPY: Hey, what're you doing up? *(Linda says nothing but moves toward him implacably.)* Where's Pop? *(He keeps backing to the right, and now Linda is in full view in the doorway to the living room.)* Is he sleeping?

LINDA: Where were you?

HAPPY: *(trying to laugh it off)* We met two girls, Mom, very fine types.   765
    Here, we brought you some flowers. *(Offering them to her.)* Put them
    in your room, Ma.

She knocks them to the floor at Biff's feet. He has now come inside and closed the door behind him. She stares at Biff, silent.

HAPPY: Now what'd you do that for? Mom, I want you to have some
    flowers—

LINDA: *(cutting Happy off, violently to Biff)* Don't you care whether he
    lives or dies?

HAPPY: *(going to the stairs)* Come upstairs, Biff.

BIFF: *(with a flare of disgust, to Happy)* Go away from me! *(To Linda.)*
    What do you mean, lives or dies? Nobody's dying around here, pal.

LINDA: Get out of my sight! Get out of here!   770

BIFF: I wanna see the boss.

LINDA: You're not going near him!

BIFF: Where is he? *(He moves into the living room and Linda follows.)*

LINDA: *(shouting after Biff)* You invite him for dinner. He looks forward
    to it all day—*(Biff appears in his parents' bedroom, looks around, and
    exits)*—and then you desert him there. There's no stranger you'd do
    that to!

HAPPY: Why? He had a swell time with us. Listen, when I—*(Linda comes*   775
    back into the kitchen)—desert him I hope I don't outlive the day!

LINDA: Get out of here!

HAPPY: Now look, Mom . . .

LINDA: Did you have to go to women tonight? You and your lousy rot-
    ten whores!

Biff re-enters the kitchen.

HAPPY: Mom, all we did was follow Biff around trying to cheer him up!
    (To Biff.) Boy, what a night you gave me!

LINDA: Get out of here, both of you, and don't come back! I don't   780
    want you tormenting him any more. Go on now, get your things
    together! *(To Biff.)* You can sleep in his apartment. *(She starts to
    pick up the flowers and stops herself.)* Pick up this stuff, I'm not your
    maid any more. Pick it up, you bum, you!

Happy turns his back to her in refusal. Biff slowly moves over and gets down on his knees, picking up the flowers.

LINDA: You're a pair of animals! Not one, not another living soul would have had the cruelty to walk out on that man in a restaurant!

BIFF: *(not looking at her)* Is that what he said?

LINDA: He didn't have to say anything. He was so humiliated he nearly limped when he came in.

HAPPY: But, Mom he had a great time with us—

785 BIFF: *(cutting him off violently)* Shut up!

Without another word, Happy goes upstairs.

LINDA: You! You didn't even go in to see if he was all right!

BIFF: *(still on the floor in front of Linda, the flowers in his hand; with self-loathing)* No. Didn't. Didn't do a damned thing. How do you like that, heh? Left him babbling in a toilet.

LINDA: You louse. You . . .

BIFF: Now you hit it on the nose! *(He gets up, throws the flowers in the wastebasket.)* The scum of the earth, and you're looking at him!

790 LINDA: Get out of here!

BIFF: I gotta talk to the boss, Mom. Where is he?

LINDA: You're not going near him. Get out of this house!

BIFF: *(with absolute assurance, determination)* No. We're gonna have an abrupt conversation, him and me.

LINDA: You're not talking to him!

Hammering is heard from outside the house, off right. Biff turns toward the noise.

795 LINDA: *(suddenly pleading)* Will you please leave him alone?

BIFF: What's he doing out there?

LINDA: He's planting the garden!

BIFF: *(quietly)* Now? Oh, my God!

Biff moves outside, Linda following. The light dies down on them and comes up on the center of the apron as Willy walks into it. He is carrying a flashlight, a hoe and a handful of seed packets. He raps the top of the hoe sharply to fix it firmly, and then moves to the left, measuring off the distance with his foot. He holds the flashlight to look at the seed packets, reading off the instructions. He is in the blue of night.

WILLY: Carrots . . . quarter-inch apart. Rows . . . one-foot rows. *(He measures it off.)* One foot. *(He puts down a package and measures off.)* Beets. *(He puts down another package and measures again.)* Lettuce. *(He reads the package, puts it down.)* One foot—*(He breaks off as Ben appears at the right and moves slowly down to him.)* What a proposition, ts, ts. Terrific, terrific. 'Cause she's suffered, Ben, the woman has suffered. You understand me? A man can't go out the way he came in, Ben, a man has got to add up to something. You can't, you can't—(*Ben moves toward him as though to interrupt.*) You gotta consider, now. Don't answer so quick. Remember, it's a guaranteed twenty-thousand-dollar proposition. Now look, Ben, I want you to go through the ins and outs of this thing with me. I've got nobody to talk to, Ben, and the woman has suffered, you hear me?

BEN: (*standing still, considering*) What's the proposition?   800

WILLY: It's twenty thousand dollars on the barrelhead. Guaranteed, gilt-edged, you understand?

BEN: You don't want to make a fool of yourself. They might not honor the policy.

WILLY: How can they dare refuse? Didn't I work like a coolie to meet every premium on the nose? And now they don't pay off? Impossible!

BEN: It's called a cowardly thing, William.

WILLY: Why? Does it take more guts to stand here the rest of my life   805
ringing up a zero?

BEN: (*yielding*) That's a point, William. (*He moves, thinking, turns.*) And twenty thousand—that *is* something one can feel with the hand, it is there.

WILLY: (*now assured, with rising power*) Oh, Ben, that's the whole beauty of it! I see it like a diamond, shining in the dark, hard and rough, that I can pick up and touch in my hand. Not like—like an appointment! This would not be another damned-fool appointment, Ben, and it changes all the aspects. Because he thinks I'm nothing, see, and so he spites me. But the funeral—(*Straightening up.*) Ben, that funeral will be massive! They'll come from Maine, Massachusetts, Vermont, New Hampshire! All the old-timers with the strange license plates—that boy will be thunder-struck, Ben, because he never realized—I am known! Rhode Island, New York, New Jersey—I am known, Ben, and he'll see it with his eyes once and for all. He'll see what I am, Ben! He's in for a shock, that boy!

BEN: (*coming down to the edge of the garden*) He'll call you a coward.

WILLY: (*suddenly fearful*) No, that would be terrible.

BEN: Yes. And a damned fool.   810

WILLY: No, no, he mustn't, I won't have that! (*He is broken and desperate.*)

BEN: He'll hate you, William.

The gay music of the boys is heard.

WILLY: Oh, Ben, how do we get back to all the great times? Used to be so full of light, and comradeship, the sleigh-riding in winter, and the ruddiness on his cheeks. And always some kind of good news coming up, always something nice coming up ahead. And never even let me carry the valises in the house, and simonizing, simonizing that little red car! Why, why can't I give him something and not have him hate me?

BEN: Let me think about it. (*He glances at his watch.*) I still have a little time. Remarkable proposition, but you've got to be sure you're not making a fool of yourself.

Ben drifts off upstage and goes out of sight. Biff comes down from the left.

815 WILLY: (*suddenly conscious of Biff, turns and looks up at him, then begins picking up the packages of seeds in confusion*) Where the hell is that seed? (*Indignantly.*) You can't see nothing out here! They boxed in the whole goddam neighborhood!

BIFF: There are people all around here. Don't you realize that?

WILLY: I'm busy. Don't bother me.

BIFF: (*taking the hoe from Willy*) I'm saying good-by to you, Pop. (*Willy looks at him, silent, unable to move.*) I'm not coming back any more.

WILLY: You're not going to see Oliver tomorrow?

820 BIFF: I've got no appointment, Dad.

WILLY: He put his arm around you, and you've got no appointment?

BIFF: Pop, get this now, will you? Everytime I've left it's been a fight that sent me out of here. Today I realized something about myself and I tried to explain it to you and I—I think I'm just not smart enough to make any sense out of it for you. To hell with whose fault it is or anything like that. (*He takes Willy's arm.*) Let's just wrap it up, heh? Come on in, we'll tell Mom. (*He gently tries to pull Willy to the left.*)

WILLY: (*frozen, immobile, with guilt in his voice*) No, I don't want to see her.

BIFF: Come on! (*He pulls again, and Willy tries to pull away.*)

825 WILLY: (*highly nervous*) No, no, I don't want to see her.

BIFF: (*tries to look into Willy's face, as if to find the answer there*) Why don't you want to see her?

WILLY: (*more harshly now*) Don't bother me, will you?

BIFF: What do you mean, you don't want to see her? You don't want them calling you yellow, do you? This isn't your fault; it's me, I'm a bum. Now come inside! (*Willy strains to get away.*) Did you hear what I said to you?

Willy pulls away and quickly goes by himself into the house. Biff follows.

LINDA: (*to Willy*) Did you plant, dear?

830 BIFF: (*at the door, to Linda*) All right, we had it out. I'm going and I'm not writing any more.

LINDA: (*going to Willy in the kitchen*) I think that's the best way, dear. 'Cause there's no use drawing it out, you'll just never get along.

Willy doesn't respond.

BIFF: People ask where I am and what I'm doing, you don't know, and you don't care. That way it'll be off your mind and you can start brightening up again. All right? That clears it, doesn't it? (*Willy is silent, and Biff goes to him.*) You gonna wish me luck, scout? (*He extends his hand.*) What do you say?

LINDA: Shake his hand, Willy.

WILLY: (*turning to her, seething with hurt*) There's no necessity to mention the pen at all, y'know.

BIFF: (*gently*) I've got no appointment, Dad.   835

WILLY: (*erupting fiercely*) He put his arm around . . .?

BIFF: Dad, you're never going to see what I am, so what's the use of arguing? If I strike oil I'll send you a check. Meantime forget I'm alive.

WILLY: (*to Linda*) Spite, see?

BIFF: Shake hands, Dad.

WILLY: Not my hand.   840

BIFF: I was hoping not to go this way.

WILLY: Well, this is the way you're going. Good-by.

Biff looks at him a moment, then turns sharply and goes to the stairs.

WILLY: (*stops him with*) May you rot in hell if you leave this house!

BIFF: (*turning*) Exactly what is it that you want from me?

WILLY: I want you to know, on the train, in the mountains, in the val-   845
leys, wherever you go, that you cut down your life for spite!

BIFF: No, no.

WILLY: Spite, spite, is the word of your undoing! And when you're down and out, remember what did it. When you're rotting somewhere beside the railroad tracks, remember, and don't you dare blame it on me!

BIFF: I'm not blaming it on you!

WILLY: I won't take the rap for this, you hear?

Happy comes down the stairs and stands on the bottom step, watching.

BIFF: That's just what I'm telling you!   850

WILLY: (*sinking into a chair at the table, with full accusation*) You're trying to put a knife in me—don't think I don't know what you're doing!

BIFF: All right, phony! Then let's lay it on the line. (*He whips the rubber tube out of his pocket and puts it on the table.*)

HAPPY: You crazy—

LINDA: Biff! (*She moves to grab the hose, but Biff holds it down with his hand.*)

BIFF: Leave it there! Don't move it!   855

WILLY: (*not looking at it*) What is that?

BIFF: You know goddam well what that is.

WILLY: (*caged, wanting to escape*) I never saw that.

BIFF: You saw it. The mice didn't bring it into the cellar! What is this supposed to do, make a hero out of you? This supposed to make me sorry for you?

860 WILLY: Never heard of it.

BIFF: There'll be no pity for you, you hear it? No pity!

WILLY: (*to Linda*) You hear the spite!

BIFF: No, you're going to hear the truth—what you are and what I am!

LINDA: Stop it!

865 WILLY: Spite!

HAPPY: (*coming down toward Biff*) You cut it now!

BIFF: (*to Happy*) The man don't know who we are! The man is gonna know! (*To Willy.*) We never told the truth for ten minutes in this house!

HAPPY: We always told the truth!

BIFF: (*turning on him*) You big blow, are you the assistant buyer? You're one of the two assistants to the assistant, aren't you?

870 HAPPY: Well, I'm practically—

BIFF: You're practically full of it! We all are! And I'm through with it. (*To Willy.*) Now hear this, Willy, this is me.

WILLY: I know you!

BIFF: You know why I had no address for three months? I stole a suit in Kansas City and I was in jail. (*To Linda, who is sobbing.*) Stop crying. I'm through with it.

Linda turns away from them, her hands covering her face.

WILLY: I suppose that's my fault!

875 BIFF: I stole myself out of every good job since high school!

WILLY: And whose fault is that?

BIFF: And I never got anywhere because you blew me so full of hot air I could never stand taking orders from anybody! That's whose fault it is!

WILLY: I hear that!

LINDA: Don't, Biff!

880 BIFF: It's goddam time you heard that! I had to be boss big shot in two weeks, and I'm through with it!

WILLY: Then hang yourself! For spite, hang yourself!

BIFF: No! Nobody's hanging himself, Willy! I ran down eleven flights with a pen in my hand today. And suddenly I stopped, you hear me? And in the middle of that office building, do you hear this? I stopped in the middle of that building and I saw—the sky. I saw the things that I love in this world. The work and the food and time to sit and smoke. And I looked at the pen and said to myself, what the hell am I grabbing this for? Why am I trying to become what I don't want to be? What am I doing in an office, making a contemptuous, begging fool of myself, when all I want is out there, waiting for me the minute I say I know who I am! Why can't I say that, Willy? (*He tries to make Willy face him, but Willy pulls away and moves to the left.*)

WILLY: (*with hatred, threateningly*) The door of your life is wide open!

BIFF: Pop! I'm a dime a dozen, and so are you!

WILLY: (*turning on him now in an uncontrolled outburst*) I am not a dime a 885 dozen! I am Willy Loman, and you are Biff Loman!

Biff starts for Willy, but is blocked by Happy. In his fury, Biff seems on the verge of attacking his father.

BIFF: I am not a leader of men, Willy, and neither are you. You were never anything but a hard-working drummer who landed in the ash can like all the rest of them! I'm one dollar an hour, Willy! I tried seven states and couldn't raise it. A buck an hour! Do you gather my meaning? I'm not bringing home any prizes any more, and you're going to stop waiting for me to bring them home!

WILLY: (*directly to Biff*) You vengeful, spiteful mutt!

Biff breaks from Happy. Willy, in fright, starts up the stairs. Biff grabs him.

BIFF: (*at the peak of his fury*) Pop, I'm nothing! I'm nothing, Pop. Can't you understand that? There's no spite in it any more. I'm just what I am, that's all.

Biff's fury has spent itself, and he breaks down, sobbing, holding on to Willy, who dumbly fumbles for Biff's face.

WILLY: (*astonished*) What're you doing? What're you doing? (*To Linda.*) Why is he crying?

BIFF: (*crying, broken*) Will you let me go, for Christ's sake? Will you 890 take that phony dream and burn it before something happens? (*Struggling to contain himself, he pulls away and moves to the stairs.*) I'll go in the morning. Put him—put him to bed. (*Exhausted, Biff moves up the stairs to his room.*)

WILLY: (*after a long pause, astonished, elevated*) Isn't that remarkable? Biff—he likes me!

LINDA: He loves you, Willy!

HAPPY: (*deeply moved*) Always did, Pop.

WILLY: Oh, Biff! (*Staring wildly.*) He cried! Cried to me! (*He is choking with his love, and now cries out his promise.*) That boy—that boy is going to be magnificent!

Ben appears in the light just outside the kitchen.

895 BEN: Yes, outstanding, with twenty thousand behind him.

LINDA: (*sensing the racing of his mind, fearfully, carefully*) Now come to bed, Willy. It's all settled now.

WILLY: (*finding it difficult not to rush out of the house*) Yes, we'll sleep. Come on. Go to sleep, Hap.

BEN: And it does take a great kind of man to crack the jungle.

In accents of dread, Ben's idyllic music starts up.

HAPPY: (*his arm around Linda*) I'm getting married, Pop, don't forget it. I'm changing everything. I'm gonna run that department before the year is up. You'll see, Mom. (*He kisses her.*)

900 BEN: The jungle is dark but full of diamonds, Willy.

Willy turns, moves, listening to Ben.

LINDA: Be good. You're both good boys, just act that way, that's all.

HAPPY: 'Night, Pop. (*He goes upstairs.*)

LINDA: (*to Willy*) Come, dear.

BEN: (*with greater force*) One must go in to fetch a diamond out.

905 WILLY: (*to Linda, as he moves slowly along the edge of the kitchen, toward the door*) I just want to get settled down, Linda. Let me sit alone for a little.

LINDA: (*almost uttering her fear*) I want you upstairs.

WILLY: (*taking her in his arms*) In a few minutes, Linda. I couldn't sleep right now. Go on, you look awful tired. (*He kisses her.*)

BEN: Not like an appointment at all. A diamond is rough and hard to the touch.

WILLY: Go on now. I'll be right up.

910 LINDA: I think this is the only way, Willy.

WILLY: Sure, it's the best thing.

BEN: Best thing!

WILLY: The only way. Everything is gonna be—go on, kid, get to bed. You look so tired.

LINDA: Come right up.

915 WILLY: Two minutes.

Linda goes into the living room, then reappears in her bedroom. Willy moves just outside the kitchen door.

WILLY: Loves me. (*Wonderingly.*) Always loved me. Isn't that a remarkable thing? Ben, he'll worship me for it!

BEN: (*with promise*) It's dark there, but full of diamonds.

WILLY: Can you imagine that magnificence with twenty thousand dollars in his pocket?

LINDA: (*calling from her room*) Willy! Come up!

WILLY: (*calling from the kitchen*) Yes! Yes! Coming! It's very smart, you   920
  realize that, don't you, sweetheart? Even Ben sees it. I gotta go,
  baby. 'By! By! (*Going over to Ben, almost dancing.*) Imagine? When
  the mail comes he'll be ahead of Bernard again!

BEN: A perfect proposition all around.

WILLY: Did you see how he cried to me? Oh, if I could kiss him, Ben!

BEN: Time, William, time!

WILLY: Oh, Ben, I always knew one way or another we were gonna
  make it, Biff and I!

BEN: (*looking at his watch*) The boat. We'll be late. (*He moves slowly off*   925
  into the darkness.)

WILLY: (*elegiacally, turning to the house*) Now when you kick off, boy,
  I want a seventy-yard boot, and get right down the field under the
  ball, and when you hit, hit low and hit hard, because it's important,
  boy. (*He swings around and faces the audience.*) There's all kinds of
  important people in the stands, and the first thing you know . . .
  (*Suddenly realizing he is alone.*) Ben! Ben, where do I . . . ? (*He makes*
  a sudden movement of search.) Ben, how do I . . . ?

LINDA: (*calling*) Willy, you coming up?

WILLY: (*uttering a gasp of fear, whirling about as if to quiet her*) Sh! (*He*
  turns around as if to find his way; sounds, faces, voices, seem to be
  swarming in upon him and he flicks at them, crying.) Sh! Sh! (*Sud-*
  denly music, faint and high, stops him. It rises in intensity, almost to an
  unbearable scream. He goes up and down on his toes, and rushes off
  around the house.) Shhh!

LINDA: Willy?

There is no answer. Linda waits. Biff gets up off his bed. He is still in his clothes.
Happy sits up. Biff stands listening.

LINDA: (*with real fear*) Willy, answer me! Willy!   930

There is the sound of a car starting and moving away at full speed.

LINDA: No!

BIFF: (*rushing down the stairs*) Pop!

*As the car speeds off, the music crashes down in a frenzy of sound, which
becomes the soft pulsation of a single cello string. Biff slowly returns to his
bedroom. He and Happy gravely don their jackets. Linda slowly walks out
of her room. The music has developed into a dead march. The leaves of day
are appearing over everything. Charley and Bernard, somberly dressed, appear
and knock on the kitchen door. Biff and Happy slowly descend the stairs to
the kitchen as Charley and Bernard enter. All stop a moment when Linda, in
clothes of mourning, bearing a little bunch of roses, comes through the draped*

doorway into the kitchen. She goes to Charley and takes his arm. Now all move toward the audience, through the wall-line of the kitchen. At the limit of the apron, Linda lays down the flowers, kneels, and sits back on her heels. All stare down at the grave.

REQUIEM

CHARLEY: It's getting dark, Linda.

Linda doesn't react. She stares at the grave.

BIFF: How about it, Mom? Better get some rest, heh? They'll be closing the gate soon.

Linda makes no move. Pause.

HAPPY: *(deeply angered)* He had no right to do that! There was no necessity for it. We would've helped him.

CHARLEY: *(grunting)* Hmmm.

5 **BIFF:** Come along, Mom.

LINDA: Why didn't anybody come?

CHARLEY: It was a very nice funeral.

LINDA: But where are all the people he knew? Maybe they blame him.

CHARLEY: Naa. It's a rough world, Linda. They wouldn't blame him.

10 **LINDA:** I can't understand it. At this time especially. First time in thirty-five years we were just about free and clear. He only needed a little salary. He was even finished with the dentist.

CHARLEY: No man only needs a little salary.

LINDA: I can't understand it.

BIFF: There were a lot of nice days. When he'd come home from a trip; or on Sundays, making the stoop; finishing the cellar; putting on the new porch; when he built the extra bathroom; and put up the garage. You know something, Charley, there's more of him in that front stoop than in all the sales he ever made.

CHARLEY: Yeah. He was a happy man with a batch of cement.

15 **LINDA:** He was so wonderful with his hands.

BIFF: He had the wrong dreams. All, all, wrong.

HAPPY: *(almost ready to fight Biff)* Don't say that!

BIFF: He never knew who he was.

CHARLEY: *(stopping Happy's movement and reply. To Biff.)* Nobody dast blame this man. You don't understand: Willy was a salesman. And for a salesman, there is no rock bottom to the life. He don't put a bolt to a nut, he don't tell you the law or give you medicine. He's a man out there in the blue, riding on a smile and a shoe-shine. And when they start not smiling back—that's an earthquake. And then you get yourself a couple of spots on your hat, and you're finished.

Nobody dast blame this man. A salesman is got to dream, boy. It
comes with the territory.

BIFF: Charley, the man didn't know who he was.   20

HAPPY: (*infuriated*) Don't say that!

BIFF: Why don't you come with me, Happy?

HAPPY: I'm not licked that easily. I'm staying right in this city, and I'm
gonna beat this racket! (*He looks at Biff, his chin set.*) The Loman
Brothers!

BIFF: I know who I am, kid.

HAPPY: All right, boy. I'm gonna show you and everybody else that   25
Willy Loman did not die in vain. He had a good dream. It's the only
dream you can have—to come out number-one man. He fought it
out here, and this is where I'm gonna win it for him.

BIFF: (*with a hopeless glance at Happy, bends toward his mother*) Let's
go, Mom.

LINDA: I'll be with you in a minute. Go on, Charley. (*He hesitates.*) I
want to, just for a minute. I never had a chance to say good-by.

*Charley moves away, followed by Happy. Biff remains a slight distance up and
left of Linda. She sits there, summoning herself. The flute begins, not far away,
playing behind her speech.*

LINDA: Forgive me, dear. I can't cry. I don't know what it is, but I can't
cry. I don't understand it. Why did you ever do that? Help me,
Willy, I can't cry. It seems to me that you're just on another trip.
I keep expecting you. Willy, dear, I can't cry. Why did you do it?
I search and search and I search, and I can't understand it, Willy.
I made the last payment on the house today. Today, dear. And
there'll be nobody home. (*A sob rises in her throat.*) We're free and
clear. (*Sobbing more fully, released.*) We're free. (*Biff comes slowly
toward her.*) We're free . . . We're free . . .

*Biff lifts her to her feet and moves out up right with her in his arms. Linda
sobs quietly. Bernard and Charley come together and follow them, followed
by Happy. Only the music of the flute is left on the darkening stage as over the
house the hard towers of the apartment buildings rise into sharp focus, and—*

The Curtain Falls

*   *   *

Reading and Reacting

1. Is Willy a likeable character? What words and actions—both Willy's and
   those of other characters—help you to reach your conclusion?
2. How does the existence of The Woman affect your overall impression of
   Willy? What does she reveal about his character?

3. What does Willy's attitude toward his sons indicate about his character? How is this attitude revealed?

4. In the absence of a narrator, what devices does Miller use to provide exposition—basic information about character and setting?

5. The conversation between Biff and Happy in act 1 reveals many of their differences. List some of the differences between these two characters.

6. In numerous remarks, Willy expresses his philosophy of business. Summarize some of his key ideas about the business world. How realistic do you think these ideas are? How do these ideas help to delineate his character?

7. In act 1, Linda tells Willy, "Few men are idolized by their children the way you are." Is she sincere, is she being ironic, or is she just trying to make Willy feel better?

8. How do the frequent flashbacks help to explain what motivates Willy? How else could this background information have been presented in the play? Are there advantages to using flashbacks instead of the alternative you suggest?

9. Is Linda simply a stereotype of the long-suffering wife, or is she a multidimensional character? Explain.

10. Willy Loman lives in Brooklyn, New York; his "territory" is New England. What is the significance to him of the "faraway places"—Africa, Alaska, California, Texas, and the like—mentioned in the play?

11. What purpose does Bernard serve in the play?

12. The play concludes with a requiem. What is a requiem? What information about each of the major characters is supplied in this brief section? Is this information essential to your understanding or appreciation of the play, or would the play have been equally effective without the requiem? Explain.

13. JOURNAL ENTRY Do you believe Willy Loman is an innocent victim of the society in which he lives, or do you believe there are flaws in his character that make him at least partially responsible for his own misfortune? Explain.

14. CRITICAL PERSPECTIVE Writing just after Miller's death in 2005, playwright David Mamet notes that at the end of *Death of a Salesman*, Miller has offered no solution to Willy's problems but instead "has reconciled us to the notion that there is no solution—that it is the human lot to try and fail, and that no one is immune from self-deception." Mamet goes on to explain the value of Miller's plays by comparing "bad drama" and "good drama":

> Bad drama reinforces our prejudices. It informs us of what we knew when we came into the theater. . . .
>
> The good drama survives because it appeals not to the fashion of the moment, but to the problems both universal and eternal, as they are insoluble.

To find beauty in the sad, hope in the midst of loss, and dignity in failure is great poetic art.

According to Mamet's criteria, does *Death of a Salesman* qualify as "good drama"? Do you think it is great drama?

Related Works: "Those Winter Sundays" (p. 705), "Do not go gentle into that good night" (p. 710), *Oedipus the King* (p. 1182), *Fences* (p. 1270)

Source: ©Bettmann/Corbis

WILLIAM SHAKESPEARE (1564–1616) is recognized as the greatest of English writers, but many details about his life are based on conjecture or tradition. The earliest dependable information concerning Shakespeare is found in the parish registers of Stratford-upon-Avon's Holy Trinity Church, where his baptism was recorded on April 26, 1564. Although his date of birth cannot be determined with certainty, tradition has assigned it to April 23, 1564. Little is known about his early life, but reliable information about significant events is available in church documents. For example, he married Ann Hathaway in 1582 and had three children—Susanna in 1583 and the twins Judith and Hamnet in 1585.

Soon after the birth of his children, Shakespeare left Stratford for London. Upon his arrival in the capital, he set out to establish himself in London's literary world. His first step toward achieving this goal occurred in 1592, when he published his narrative poem *Venus and Adonis*; the following year, he published a second poem, *The Rape of Lucrece*.

By 1594, Shakespeare had become quite involved with the London stage. For approximately twenty years, he enjoyed a successful professional career in London—as actor, playwright, shareholder in the Lord Chamberlain's Men (an acting company), part owner of the Globe Theatre (from 1599), and author of at least thirty-six plays. The income derived from these activities brought him significant wealth and enabled him, sometime between 1610 and 1613, to retire from the theater and to return to Stratford-upon-Avon, where he owned considerable property. On April 23, 1616, Shakespeare died at age fifty-two in Stratford and was buried two days later in Holy Trinity Church.

It is difficult to date many of Shakespeare's plays exactly because they must be dated by records of their first performance (often hard to come by) and by topical references in the text. Shakespeare's company probably first staged *Hamlet* at the Globe Theatre in 1600 or 1601, but some scholars believe the play was composed as early as 1598.

Hamlet has been called Shakespeare's most complex and most confusing play, yet it is also the play most frequently performed, read, and written about. Shakespeare's audience would have recognized *Hamlet* as a **revenge tragedy**—a play in which the hero discovers that a close relative has been murdered, experiences considerable trouble in identifying the murderer, and, after overcoming numerous obstacles, avenges the death by killing the murderer. Frequently, revenge tragedies featured murders, physical mutilations, and ghosts, all enacted with grand style and bold rhetoric. These plays were extremely popular productions that were the action movies of their day.

Hamlet, however, is different from the typical revenge tragedy. Because the ghost gives him the necessary information, Hamlet has no need to search for the cause of his father's death or find the murderer. In fact, the only impediments to Hamlet's revenge are those he himself

An audience at the reconstructed Globe Theatre in London
Source: © Andreas Hub/laif/Redux Pictures

creates. And, by the time the delay ends and Hamlet avenges his father's death, the loss is immense: his mother, the woman he loves, her father and brother, and Hamlet himself are all dead. Although the argument that there would be no play if Hamlet had immediately avenged his father may be valid, it fails to satisfy those who ponder the tragic cost of Hamlet's inaction.

Cultural Context The appearance of a ghost was a longstanding tradition in Renaissance drama. The ghost appeared in Elizabethan revenge tragedies as a plot device to help further the action and prompt a reaction from the hero. For a Renaissance audience, the dramatic representation of a ghost from purgatory would evoke a rich context of legends and lore derived from paintings, illuminated manuscripts, prints, and narratives. Moreover, stories involving ghosts were a frequent element of medieval sermons. However, the ghost in *Hamlet* transcends the traditions of the revenge tragedy. Here, Shakespeare's use of the ghost not only as a plot device but also as a character who may or may not be telling the truth adds depth and complexity to the play.

Hamlet

Prince of Denmark[1] (c. 1600)

CHARACTERS

Claudius, *King of Denmark*	**Reynaldo,** *servant to Polonius*
Hamlet, *son to the former and nephew to the present King*	**Players**
	Two Clowns, *grave-diggers*

---

[1]Note that individual lines are numbered in the following play. When a line is shared by one or more characters, it is counted as one line.

Polonius, *Lord Chamberlain*	**Fortinbras,** *Prince of Norway*
Horatio, *friend to Hamlet*	**A Captain**
Laertes, *son to Polonius*	**English Ambassadors**
Voltimand	**Ghost of Hamlet's Father**
Cornelius	**Gertrude,** *Queen of Denmark and mother*
Courtiers **Rosencrantz**	*of Hamlet*
Guildenstern	**Ophelia,** *daughter to Polonius*
Osric	**Lords, Ladies, Officers,**
A Gentleman	**Soldiers, Sailors,**
A Priest	**Messengers, and other**
Francisco, a soldier	**Attendants**
Officers **Marcellus**	
Bernardo	

Richard Burton as Hamlet
©Bettmann/Corbis

Laurence Olivier as Hamlet
©Bettmann/Corbis

Mel Gibson as Hamlet
Paramount/The Kobal Collection/Picture Desk

ACT 1
SCENE 1

Elsinore. A platform before the castle.

Francisco at his post. Enter to him Bernardo.

BERNARDO: Who's there?
FRANCISCO: Nay, answer me: stand, and unfold yourself.
BERNARDO: Long live the king!
FRANCISCO: Bernardo?
BERNARDO: He.   5
FRANCISCO: You come most carefully upon your hour.
BERNARDO: 'Tis now struck twelve; get thee to bed, Francisco.

FRANCISCO: For this relief much thanks: 'tis bitter cold,
And I am sick at heart.

10 BERNARDO: Have you had quiet guard?

FRANCISCO: Not a mouse stirring.

BERNARDO: Well, good-night.
If you do meet Horatio and Marcellus,
The rivals of my watch, bid them make haste.

15 FRANCISCO: I think I hear them.—Stand, ho! Who is there?

Enter Horatio and Marcellus.

HORATIO: Friends to this ground.

MARCELLUS: And liegemen to the Dane.

FRANCISCO: Give you good-night.

MARCELLUS: O, farewell, honest soldier:

20 Who hath reliev'd you?

FRANCISCO: Bernardo has my place.
Give you good-night.

Exit.

MARCELLUS: Holla! Bernardo!

BERNARDO: Say.

25 What, is Horatio there?

HORATIO: A piece of him.

BERNARDO: Welcome, Horatio:—welcome, good Marcellus.

MARCELLUS: What, has this thing appear'd again to-night?

BERNARDO: I have seen nothing.

30 MARCELLUS: Horatio says 'tis but our fantasy,
And will not let belief take hold of him
Touching this dreaded sight, twice seen of us:
Therefore I have entreated him along
With us to watch the minutes of this night;

35 That, if again this apparition come
He may approve our eyes and speak to it.

HORATIO: Tush, tush, 'twill not appear.

BERNARDO: Sit down awhile,
And let us once again assail your ears,

40 That are so fortified against our story,
What we two nights have seen.

HORATIO: Well, sit we down,
And let us hear Bernardo speak of this.

BERNARDO: Last night of all,

45 When yon same star that's westward from the pole
Had made his course to illume that part of heaven

Where now it burns, Marcellus and myself,
The bell then beating one,—

MARCELLUS: Peace, break thee off; look where it comes again!

Enter Ghost, armed.

BERNARDO: In the same figure, like the king that's dead.   50
MARCELLUS: Thou art a scholar; speak to it, Horatio.
BERNARDO: Looks it not like the king? mark it, Horatio.
HORATIO: Most like:—it harrows me with fear and wonder.
BERNARDO: It would be spoke to.
MARCELLUS: Question it, Horatio.   55
HORATIO: What art thou, that usurp'st this time of night,
Together with that fair and warlike form
In which the majesty of buried Denmark
Did sometimes march? by heaven I charge thee, speak!
MARCELLUS: It is offended.   60
BERNARDO: See, it stalks away!
HORATIO: Stay! speak, speak! I charge thee, speak!

Exit Ghost.

MARCELLUS: 'Tis gone, and will not answer.
BERNARDO: How now, Horatio! you tremble and look pale:
Is not this something more than fantasy?   65
What think you on't?
HORATIO: Before my God, I might not this believe
Without the sensible and true avouch
Of mine own eyes.
MARCELLUS: Is it not like the king?   70
HORATIO: As thou art to thyself:
Such was the very armor he had on
When he the ambitious Norway combated;
So frown'd he once when, in an angry parle,[1]
He smote the sledded Polacks on the ice.   75
'Tis strange.
MARCELLUS: Thus twice before, and just at this dead hour,
With martial stalk hath he gone by our watch.
HORATIO: In what particular thought to work I know not;
But, in the gross and scope of my opinion,   80
This bodes some strange eruption to our state.
MARCELLUS: Good now, sit down, and tell me, he that knows,
Why this same strict and most observant watch
So nightly toils the subject of the land;

[1]*parle:* Parley, or conference.

85   And why such daily cast of brazen cannon,
        And foreign mart for implements of war;
        Why such impress of shipwrights, whose sore task
        Does not divide the Sunday from the week;
        What might be toward, that this sweaty haste
90   Doth make the night joint-laborer with the day:
        Who is't that can inform me?

HORATIO: That can I;
        At least, the whisper goes so. Our last king,
        Whose image even but now appear'd to us,
95   Was, as you know, by Fortinbras of Norway,
        Thereto prick'd on by a most emulate pride,
        Dar'd to the combat; in which our valiant Hamlet,—
        For so this side of our known world esteem'd him,—
        Did slay this Fortinbras; who, by a seal'd compact,
100   Well ratified by law and heraldry,
        Did forfeit, with his life, all those his lands.
        Which he stood seiz'd of,[2] to the conqueror:
        Against the which, a moiety competent[3]
        Was gagéd[4] by our king; which had return'd
105   To the inheritance of Fortinbras,
        Had he been vanquisher; as by the same cov'nant,
        And carriage of the article design'd,
        His fell to Hamlet. Now, sir, young Fortinbras,
        Of unimproved mettle hot and full,
110   Hath in the skirts of Norway, here and there,
        Shark'd up a list of landless resolutes,
        For food and diet, to some enterprise
        That hath a stomach in't: which is no other,—
        As it doth well appear unto our state,—
115   But to recover of us by strong hand,
        And terms compulsatory, those foresaid lands
        So by his father lost: and this, I take it,
        Is the main motive of our preparations,
        The source of this our watch, and the chief head
120   Of this post-haste and romage[5] in the land.

BERNARDO: I think it be no other, but e'en so:
        Well may it sort that this portentous figure
        Comes armed through our watch; so like the king
        That was and is the question of these wars.

---

[2]*seiz'd of:* Possessed.   [3]*moiety competent:* A sufficient portion of his lands.   [4]*gagéd:* Engaged or pledged.   [5]*post-haste and romage:* General activity.

HORATIO: A mote it is to trouble the mind's eye.   125
    In the most high and palmy state of Rome,
    A little ere the mightiest Julius fell,
    The graves stood tenantless, and the sheeted dead
    Did squeak and gibber in the Roman streets:
    As, stars with trains of fire and dews of blood,   130
    Disasters in the sun; and the moist star,
    Upon whose influence Neptune's empire stands,
    Was sick almost to doomsday with eclipse:
    And even the like precurse of fierce events,—
    As harbingers preceding still the fates,   135
    And prologue to the omen coming on,—
    Have heaven and earth together demonstrated
    Unto our climature and countrymen.—
    But, soft, behold! lo, where it comes again!

Re-enter Ghost.

    I'll cross it, though it blast me.—Stay, illusion!   140
    If thou hast any sound or use of voice,
    Speak to me:
    If there be any good thing to be done,
    That may to thee do ease, and grace to me,
    Speak to me: 145
    If thou art privy to thy country's fate,
    Which, happily,[6] foreknowing may avoid,
    O, speak!
    Or if thou has uphoarded in thy life
    Extorted treasure in the womb of earth,   150
    For which, they say, you spirits oft walk in death,

Cock crows.

    Speak of it:—stay, and speak!—Stop it, Marcellus.
MARCELLUS: Shall I strike at it with my partisan?[7]
HORATIO: Do, if it will not stand.
BERNARDO: 'Tis here!   155
HORATIO: 'Tis here!
MARCELLUS: 'Tis gone!

Exit Ghost.

    We do it wrong, being so majestical,
    To offer it the show of violence;

---

[6]*happily:* Haply, or perhaps.   [7]*partisan:* Pike.

160   For it is, as the air, invulnerable,
      And our vain blows malicious mockery.
BERNARDO: It was about to speak when the cock crew.
HORATIO: And then it started like a guilty thing
      Upon a fearful summons. I have heard,
165   The cock, that is the trumpet to the morn,
      Doth with his lofty and shrill-sounding throat
      Awake the god of day; and at his warning,
      Whether in sea or fire, in earth or air,
      The extravagant and erring spirit hies
170   To his confine: and of the truth herein
      This present object made probation.[8]
MARCELLUS: It faded on the crowing of the cock.
      Some say that ever 'gainst that season comes
      Wherein our Saviour's birth is celebrated,
175   The bird of dawning singeth all night long:
      And then, they say, no spirit can walk abroad;
      The nights are wholesome; then no planets strike,
      No fairy takes, nor witch hath power to charm;
      So hallow'd and so gracious is the time.
180 **HORATIO:** So have I heard, and do in part believe.
      But, look, the morn, in russet mantle clad,
      Walks o'er the dew of yon high eastern hill:
      Break we our watch up: and, by my advice,
      Let us impart what we have seen to-night
185   Unto young Hamlet; for, upon my life,
      This spirit, dumb to us, will speak to him:
      Do you consent we shall acquaint him with it,
      As needful in our loves, fitting our duty?
MARCELLUS: Let's do't, I pray; and I this morning know
190   Where we shall find him most conveniently.

Exeunt.

SCENE 2

Elsinore. A room of state in the castle.

Enter the King, Queen, Hamlet, Polonius, Laertes, Voltimand, Cornelius, Lords, and Attendants.

KING: Though yet of Hamlet our dear brother's death
      The memory be green; and that it us befitted
      To bear our hearts in grief, and our whole kingdom

---

[8]*probation:* Proof.

To be contracted in one brow of woe;
Yet so far hath discretion fought with nature   5
That we with wisest sorrow think on him,
Together with remembrance of ourselves.
Therefore our sometime sister, now our queen,
The imperial jointress of this warlike state,
Have we, as 'twere with defeated joy,—   10
With one auspicious and one dropping eye,
With mirth and funeral, and with dirge in marriage,
In equal scale weighing delight and dole,—
Taken to wife: nor have we herein barr'd
Your better wisdoms, which have freely gone   15
With this affair along:—for all, our thanks.
Now follows that you know, young Fortinbras,
Holding a weak supposal of our worth,
Or thinking by our late dear brother's death
Our state to be disjoint and out of frame,   20
Colleagued with the dream of his advantage,
He hath not fail'd to pester us with message,
Importing the surrender of those lands
Lost by his father, with all bonds of law,
To our most valiant brother. So much for him.—   25
Now for ourself, and for this time of meeting:
Thus much the business is:—we have here writ
To Norway, uncle of young Fortinbras,—
Who, impotent and bed-rid, scarcely hears
Of this his nephew's purpose,—to suppress   30
His further gait herein; in that the levies,
The lists, and full proportions, are all made
Out of his subject:—and we here despatch
You, good Cornelius, and you, Voltimand,
For bearers of this greeting to old Norway;   35
Giving to you no further personal power
To business with the king more than the scope
Of these dilated articles allow.
Farewell; and let your haste commend your duty.
CORNELIUS AND VOLTIMAND: In that and all things will we show our duty.   40
KING: We doubt it nothing: heartily farewell.

Exeunt Voltimand and Cornelius.

And now, Laertes, what's the news with you?
You told us of some suit; what is't, Laertes?
You cannot speak of reason to the Dane,

45   And lose your voice: what wouldst thou beg, Laertes,
     That shall not be my offer, nor thy asking?
     The head is not more native to the heart,
     The hand more instrumental to the mouth,
     Than is the throne of Denmark to thy father.
50   What wouldst thou have, Laertes?

LAERTES: Dread my lord,
     Your leave and favor to return to France;
     From whence though willingly I came to Denmark,
     To show my duty in your coronation;
55   Yet now, I must confess, that duty done,
     My thoughts and wishes bend again toward France.
     And bow them to your gracious leave and pardon.

KING: Have you your father's leave? What says Polonius?

POLONIUS: He hath, my lord, wrung from me my slow leave
60   By laborsome petition; and at last
     Upon his will I seal'd my hard consent:
     I do beseech you, give him leave to go.

KING: Take thy fair hour, Laertes; time be thine,
     And thy best graces spend it at thy will!—
65   But now, my cousin Hamlet, and my son,—

HAMLET: [*Aside*] A little more than kin, and less than kind.

KING: How is it that the clouds still hang on you?

HAMLET: Not so, my lord; I am too much i' the sun.

QUEEN: Good Hamlet, cast thy nighted color off,
70   And let thine eye look like a friend on Denmark.
     Do not for ever with thy vailed¹ lids
     Seek for thy noble father in the dust:
     Thou know'st 'tis common,—all that live must die,
     Passing through nature to eternity.

75 HAMLET: Ay, madam, it is common.

QUEEN: If it be,
     Why seems it so particular with thee?

HAMLET: Seems, madam! nay, it is; I know not seems.
     'Tis not alone my inky cloak, good mother,
80   Nor customary suits of solemn black,
     Nor windy suspiration of forc'd breath,
     No, nor the fruitful river in the eye,
     Nor the dejected 'havior of the visage,
     Together with all forms, moods, shows of grief,
85   That can denote me truly: these, indeed, seem;

---

¹*vailed:* Downcast.

    For they are actions that a man might play:
    But I have that within which passeth show;
    These but the trappings and the suits of woe.
KING: 'Tis sweet and cómmendable in your nature, Hamlet,
    To give these mourning duties to your father: 90
    But, you must know, your father lost a father;
    That father lost, lost his; and the survivor bound,
    In filial obligation, for some term
    To do obsequious sorrow: but to persever
    In obstinate condolement is a course   95
    Of impious stubbornness; 'tis unmanly grief:
    It shows a will most incorrect to heaven;
    A heart unfortified, a mind impatient;
    An understanding simple and unschool'd:
    For what we know must be, and is as common   100
    As any the most vulgar thing to sense,[2]
    Why should we, in our peevish opposition,
    Take it to heart? Fie! 'tis a fault to heaven,
    A fault against the dead, a fault to nature,
    To reason most absurd; whose common theme   105
    Is death of fathers, and who still[3] hath cried,
    From the first corse till he that died to-day,
    This must be so. We pray you, throw to earth
    This unprevailing woe; and think of us
    As of a father: for let the world take note   110
    You are the most immediate to our throne;
    And with no less nobility of love
    Than that which dearest father bears his son
    Do I impart toward you. For your intent
    In going back to school in Wittenberg,   115
    It is most retrograde to our desire:
    And we beseech you bend you to remain
    Here, in the cheer and comfort of our eye,
    Our chiefest courtier, cousin, and our son.
QUEEN: Let not thy mother lose her prayers, Hamlet: 120
    I pray thee, stay with us; go not to Wittenberg.
HAMLET: I shall in all my best obey you, madam.
KING: Why, 'tis a loving and a fair reply:
    Be as ourself in Denmark.—Madam, come;
    This gentle and unforc'd accord of Hamlet   125
    Sits smiling to my heart: in grace whereof,

---

[2] *any . . . sense:* Anything that is very commonly seen or heard.   [3] *still:* Ever, or always.

No jocund health that Denmark drinks to-day
But the great cannon to the clouds shall tell;
And the king's rouse[4] the heavens shall bruit[5] again,
130   Re-speaking earthly thunder. Come away.

Exeunt all but Hamlet.

HAMLET: O, that this too too solid flesh would melt,
Thaw, and resolve itself into a dew!
Or that the Everlasting had not fix'd
His canon 'gainst self-slaughter! O God! O God!
135   How weary, stale, flat, and unprofitable
Seem to me all the uses of this world!
Fie on't! O fie! 'tis an unweeded garden,
That grows to seed; things rank and gross in nature
Possess it merely. That it should come to this!
140   But two months dead!—nay, not so much, not two:
So excellent a king; that was, to this,
Hyperion[6] to a satyr: so loving to my mother,
That he might not beteem the winds of heaven
Visit her face too roughly. Heaven and earth!
145   Must I remember? why, she would hang on him
As if increase of appetite had grown
By what it fed on: and yet, within a month,—
Let me not think on't,—Frailty, thy name is woman!—
A little month; or ere those shoes were old
150   With which she follow'd my poor father's body
Like Niobe, all tears;—why she, even she,—
O God! a beast, that wants discourse of reason,
Would have mourn'd longer,—married with mine uncle,
My father's brother; but no more like my father
155   Than I to Hercules: within a month;
Ere yet the salt of most unrighteous tears
Had left the flushing in her galled eyes,
She married:—O, most wicked speed, to post
With such dexterity to incestuous sheets!
160   It is not, nor it cannot come to good;
But break, my heart,—for I must hold my tongue!

Enter Horatio, Marcellus, and Bernardo.

---

[4]*rouse:* Drink.   [5]*bruit:* Echo.   [6]*Hyperion:* The Greek sun-god, the brightest and most beautiful
of the gods.

HORATIO: Hail to your lordship!
HAMLET: I am glad to see you well:
    Horatio,—or I do forget myself.
HORATIO: The same, my lord, and your poor servant ever.   165
HAMLET: Sir, my good friend; I'll change that name with you:
    And what make you from Wittenberg, Horatio?—Marcellus?
MARCELLUS: My good lord,—
HAMLET: I am very glad to see you.—Good even, sir.—
    But what, in faith, make you from Wittenberg?   170
HORATIO: A truant disposition, good my lord.
HAMLET: I would not hear your enemy say so;
    Nor shall you do mine ear that violence,
    To make it truster of your own report
    Against yourself: I know you are no truant.   175
    But what is your affair in Elsinore?
    We'll teach you to drink deep ere you depart.
HORATIO: My lord, I came to see your father's funeral.
HAMLET: I pray thee, do not mock me, fellow-student;
    I think it was to see my mother's wedding.   180
HORATIO: Indeed, my lord, it follow'd hard upon.
HAMLET: Thrift, thrift, Horatio! the funeral-bak'd meats
    Did coldly furnish forth the marriage tables.
    Would I had met my dearest foe[7] in heaven
    Ere I had ever seen that day, Horatio!—   185
    My father,—methinks I see my father.
HORATIO: Where, my lord?
HAMLET: In my mind's eye, Horatio.
HORATIO: I saw him once; he was a goodly[8] king.
HAMLET: He was a man, take him for all in all,   190
    I shall not look upon his like again.
HORATIO: My lord, I think I saw him yester-night.
HAMLET: Saw who?
HORATIO: My lord, the king your father.
HAMLET: The king my father!   195
HORATIO: Season your admiration[9] for awhile
    With an attent ear, till I may deliver,
    Upon the witness of these gentlemen,
    This marvel to you.
HAMLET: For God's love, let me hear.   200
HORATIO: Two nights together had these gentlemen,
    Marcellus and Bernardo, in their watch,

---

[7]*Ddearest foe:* Worst enemy.   [8]*goodly:* Handsome.   [9]*admiration:* Astonishment.

In the dead vast and middle of the night,
Been thus encounter'd. A figure like your father,
205   Arm'd at all points exactly, cap-a-pe,[10]
Appears before them, and with solemn march
Goes slow and stately by them: thrice he walk'd
By their oppress'd[11] and fear-surprised eyes,
Within his truncheon's length; whilst they, distill'd
210   Almost to jelly with the act of fear,
Stand dumb, and speak not to him. This to me
In dreadful secrecy impart they did;
And I with them the third night kept the watch:
Where, as they had deliver'd, both in time,
215   Form of the thing, each word made true and good,
The apparition comes: I knew your father;
These hands are not more like.

HAMLET: But where was this?

MARCELLUS: My lord, upon the platform where we watch'd.

220 HAMLET: Did you not speak to it?

HORATIO: My lord, I did;
But answer made it none: yet once methought
It lifted up its head, and did address
Itself to motion, like as it would speak:
225   But even then the morning cock crew loud,
And at the sound it shrunk in haste away,
And vanish'd from our sight.

HAMLET: 'Tis very strange.

HORATIO: As I do live, my honor'd lord, 'tis true;
230   And we did think it writ down in our duty
To let you know of it.

HAMLET: Indeed, indeed, sirs, but this troubles me.
Hold you the watch to-night?

MARCELLUS and BERNARDO: We do, my lord.

235 HAMLET: Arm'd, say you?

MARCELLUS and BERNARDO: Arm'd, my lord.

HAMLET: From top to toe?

MARCELLUS AND BERNARDO: My lord, from head to foot.

HAMLET: Then saw you not his face?

240 HORATIO: O yes, my lord; he wore his beaver up.

HAMLET: What, look'd he frowningly?

HORATIO: A countenance more in sorrow than in anger.

HAMLET: Pale or red?

---

[10]*cap-a-pe:* From head to toe.   [11]*oppress'd:* Overwhelmed.

HORATIO: Nay, very pale.
HAMLET: And fix'd his eyes upon you?   245
HORATIO: Most constantly.
HAMLET: I would I had been there.
HORATIO: It would have much amaz'd you.
HAMLET: Very like, very like. Stay'd it long?
HORATIO: While one with moderate haste might tell[12] a hundred.   250
MARCELLUS AND BERNARDO: Longer, longer.
HORATIO: Not when I saw't.
HAMLET: His beard was grizzled,—no?
HORATIO: It was, as I have seen it in his life,
      A sable silver'd.   255
HAMLET: I will watch to-night;
      Perchance 'twill walk again.
HORATIO: I warrant it will.
HAMLET: If it assume my noble father's person
      I'll speak to it, though hell itself should gape   260
      And bid me hold my peace. I pray you all,
      If you have hitherto conceal'd this sight,
      Let it be tenable in your silence still;
      And whatsoever else shall hap to-night,
      Give it an understanding, but no tongue: 265
      I will requite your loves. So, fare ye well:
      Upon the platform, 'twixt eleven and twelve,
      I'll visit you.
ALL: Our duty to your honor.
HAMLET: Your loves, as mine to you: farewell.   270

Exeunt Horatio, Marcellus, and Bernardo.

      My father's spirit in arms; all is not well;
      I doubt some foul play: would the night were come!
      Till then sit still, my soul: foul deeds will rise,
      Though all the earth o'erwhelm them, to men's eyes.

Exit.

                              SCENE 3

A room in Polonius' house.
Enter Laertes and Ophelia.

LAERTES: My necessaries are embark'd: farewell:
      And, sister, as the winds give benefit,

---

[12]*tell:* Count

And convoy[1] is assistant, do not sleep,
But let me hear from you.

5 OPHELIA: Do you doubt that?

LAERTES: For Hamlet, and the trifling of his favor,
Hold it a fashion and a toy in blood:
A violet in the youth of primy nature,
Forward, not permanent, sweet, not lasting,

10 The perfume and suppliance of a minute;
No more.

OPHELIA: No more but so?

LAERTES: Think it no more:
For nature, crescent,[2] does not grow alone

15 In thews and bulk; but as this temple[3] waxes,
The inward service of the mind and soul
Grows wide withal. Perhaps he loves you now;
And now no soil nor cautel[4] doth besmirch
The virtue of his will: but you must fear,

20 His greatness weigh'd, his will is not his own;
For he himself is subject to his birth:
He may not, as unvalu'd persons do,
Carve for himself; for on his choice depends
The safety and the health of the whole state;

25 And therefore must his choice be circumscrib'd
Unto the voice and yielding of that body
Whereof he is the head. Then if he says he loves you,
It fits your wisdom so far to believe it
As he in his particular act and place

30 May give his saying deed; which is no further
Than the main[5] voice of Denmark goes withal.
Then weigh what loss your honor may sustain
If with too credent ear you list his songs,
Or lose your heart, or your chaste treasure open

35 To his unmaster'd importunity.
Fear it, Ophelia, fear it, my dear sister;
And keep within the rear of your affection,
Out of the shot and danger of desire.
The chariest maid is prodigal enough

40 If she unmask her beauty to the moon:
Virtue itself scrapes not calumnious strokes:
The canker galls the infants of the spring

---

[1]*convoy:* Means of conveyance.   [2]*crescent:* Growing.   [3]*temple:* Body.   [4]*cautel:* Deceit.
[5]*main:* Strong, or mighty.

Too oft before their buttons be disclos'd;
And in the morn and liquid dew of youth
Contagious blastments are most imminent.   45
Be wary, then; best safety lies in fear:
Youth to itself rebels, though none else near.

OPHELIA: I shall the effect of this good lesson keep
As watchman to my heart. But, good my brother,
Do not, as some ungracious pastors do,   50
Show me the steep and thorny way to heaven;
Whilst like a puff'd and reckless libertine,
Himself the primrose path of dalliance treads,
And recks not his own rede.[6]

LAERTES: O, fear me not.   55
I stay too long:—but here my father comes.

Enter Polonius.

A double blessing is a double grace;
Occasion smiles upon a second leave.

POLONIUS: Yet here, Laertes! aboard, aboard, for shame!
The wind sits in the shoulder of your sail,   60
And you are stay'd for. There,—my blessing with you!

Laying his hand on Laertes' head.

And these few precepts in thy memory
See thou character.[7] Give thy thoughts no tongue,
Nor any unproportion'd thought his act.
Be thou familiar, but by no means vulgar.   65
The friends thou hast, and their adoption tried,
Grapple them to thy soul with hoops of steel;
But do not dull thy palm with entertainment
Of each new-hatch'd, unfledg'd comrade. Beware
Of entrance to a quarrel; but, being in,   70
Bear't that the opposéd may beware of thee.
Give every man thine ear, but few thy voice:
Take each man's censure,[8] but reserve thy judgment.
Costly thy habit as thy purse can buy,
But not express'd in fancy; rich, not gaudy: 75
For the apparel oft proclaims the man;
And they in France of the best rank and station
Are most select and generous chief in that.

---

[6]*rede:* Counsel.   [7]*in . . . character:* Engrave in your mind.   [8]*censure:* Opinion.

Neither a borrower nor a lender be:
80   For a loan oft loses both itself and friend;
And borrowing dulls the edge of husbandry.
This above all,—to thine own self be true;
And it must follow, as the night the day,
Thou canst not then be false to any man.
85   Farewell: my blessing season this in thee!

LAERTES: Most humbly do I take my leave, my lord.

POLONIUS: The time invites you; go, your servants tend.[9]

LAERTES: Farewell, Ophelia; and remember well
What I have said to you.

90 OPHELIA: 'Tis in my memory lock'd,
And you yourself shall keep the key of it.

LAERTES: Farewell. [*Exit.*]

POLONIUS: What is't, Ophelia, he hath said to you?

OPHELIA: So please you, something touching the Lord Hamlet.

95 POLONIUS: Marry, well bethought:
'Tis told me he hath very oft of late
Given private time to you; and you yourself
Have of your audience been most free and bounteous:
If it be so,—as so 'tis put on me,
100   And that in way of caution,—I must tell you,
You do not understand yourself so clearly
As it behoves my daughter and your honor.
What is between you? give me up the truth.

OPHELIA: He hath, my lord, of late made many tenders
105   Of his affection to me.

POLONIUS: Affection! pooh! you speak like a green girl,
Unsifted in such perilous circumstance.
Do you believe his tenders,[10] as you call them?

OPHELIA: I do not know, my lord, what I should think.

110 POLONIUS: Marry, I'll teach you: think yourself a baby;
That you have ta'en these tenders for true pay,
Which are not sterling. Tender yourself more dearly;
Or,—not to crack the wind of the poor phrase,
Wronging it thus,—you'll tender me a fool.

115 OPHELIA: My lord, he hath impórtun'd me with love
In honorable fashion.

POLONIUS: Ay, fashion you may call it; go to, go to.

OPHELIA: And hath given countenance to his speech, my lord,
With almost all the holy vows of heaven.

---

[9] *tend:* Wait.   [10] *tenders:* Offers.

POLONIUS: Ay, springes to catch woodcocks. I do know,   120
 When the blood burns, how prodigal the soul
 Lends the tongue vows: these blazes, daughter,
 Giving more light than heat,—extinct in both,
 Even in their promise, as it is a-making,—
 You must not take for fire. From this time   125
 Be somewhat scanter of your maiden presence;
 Set your entreatments at a higher rate
 Than a command to parley. For Lord Hamlet,
 Believe so much in him, that he is young;
 And with a larger tether may he walk   130
 Than may be given you: in few, Ophelia,
 Do not believe his vows; for they are brokers,[11]—
 Not of that die which their investments show,
 But mere implorators of unholy suits,
 Breathing like sanctified and pious bawds,   135
 The better to beguile. This is for all,—
 I would not, in plain terms, from this time forth,
 Have you so slander any moment leisure
 As to give words or talk with the Lord Hamlet.
 Look to't, I charge you; come your ways.   140
OPHELIA: I shall obey, my lord.

Exeunt.

SCENE 4

The platform.
Enter Hamlet, Horatio, and Marcellus.

HAMLET: The air bites shrewdly; it is very cold.
HORATIO: It is a nipping and an eager air.
HAMLET: What hour now?
HORATIO: I think it lacks of twelve.
MARCELLUS: No, it is struck.   5
HORATIO: Indeed? I heard it not: then it draws near the season
 Wherein the spirit held his wont to walk.

A flourish of trumpets, and ordnance shot off within.

 What does this mean, my lord?
HAMLET: The king doth wake to-night, and takes his rouse,
 Keeps wassail, and the swaggering upspring[1] reels;   10
 And, as he drains his draughts of Rhenish down,

---

[11]*brokers:* Procurers.   [1]*upspring:* A dance.

The kettle-drum and trumpet thus bray out
The triumph of his pledge.[2]

HORATIO: Is it a custom?

15 HAMLET: Ay, marry, is't:
But to my mind,—though I am native here,
And to the manner born,—it is a custom
More honor'd in the breach than the observance.
This heavy-headed revel east and west
20 Makes us traduc'd and tax'd of other nations:
They clepe us drunkards, and with swinish phrase
Soil our addition;[3] and, indeed, it takes
From our achievements, though perform'd at height,
The pith and marrow of our attribute.
25 So oft it chances in particular men
That, for some vicious mole of nature in them,
As in their birth,—wherein they are not guilty,
Since nature cannot choose his origin,—
By the o'ergrowth of some complexion,
30 Oft breaking down the pales and forts of reason;
Or by some habit, that too much o'erleavens
The form of plausive[4] manners;—that these men,—
Carrying, I say, the stamp of one defect,
Being nature's livery or fortune's star,—
35 Their virtues else,—be they as pure as grace,
As infinite as man may undergo,—
Shall in the general censure take corruption
From that particular fault: the dram of evil
Doth all the noble substance of a doubt
40 To his own scandal.

HORATIO: Look, my lord, it comes!

Enter Ghost.

HAMLET: Angels and ministers of grace defend us!—
Be thou a spirit of health or goblin damn'd,
Bring with thee airs from heaven or blasts from hell,
45 Be thy intents wicked or charitable,
Thou com'st in such a questionable shape
That I will speak to thee: I'll call thee Hamlet,
King, father, royal Dane: O, answer me!
Let me not burst in ignorance; but tell
50 Why thy canóniz'd bones, hearsèd in death,

---

[2]*triumph . . . pledge:* The glory of his toasts.   [3]*addition:* Reputation.   [4]*plausive:* Pleasing.

Have burst their cerements;[5] why the sepulchre,
Wherein we saw thee quietly in-urn'd,
Hath op'd his ponderous and marble jaws
To cast thee up again! What may this mean,
That thou, dead corpse, again in còmplete steel,   55
Revisit'st thus the glimpses of the moon,
Making night hideous and we[6] fools of nature
So horridly to shake our disposition
With thoughts beyond the reaches of our souls?
Say, why is this? wherefore? what should we do?   60

Ghost beckons Hamlet.

HORATIO: It beckons you to go away with it,
As if it some impartment did desire
To you alone.
MARCELLUS: Look, with what courteous action
It waves you to a more removed ground: 65
But do not go with it.
HORATIO: No, by no means.
HAMLET: It will not speak; then will I follow it.
HORATIO: Do not, my lord.
HAMLET: Why, what should be the fear?   70
I do not set my life at a pin's fee;
And for my soul, what can it do to that,
Being a thing immortal as itself?
It waves me forth again;—I'll follow it.
HORATIO: What if it tempt you toward the flood, my lord.   75
Or to the dreadful summit of the cliff
That beetles o'er his base into the sea,
And there assume some other horrible form,
Which might deprive your sovereignty of reason,
And draw you into madness? think of it: 80
The very place puts toys of desperation,
Without more motive, into every brain
That looks so many fathoms to the sea
And hears it roar beneath.
HAMLET: It waves me still.—   85
Go on; I'll follow thee.
MARCELLUS: You shall not go, my lord.
HAMLET: Hold off your hands.
HORATIO: Be rul'd; you shall not go.

---

[5]*cerements:* Burial garments.   [6]*we:* Us.

90 HAMLET: My fate cries out,
   And makes each petty artery in this body
   As hardy as the Némean lion's[7] nerve.—

Ghost beckons.

   Still am I call'd;—unhand me, gentlemen;—[*Breaking from them*]
   By heaven, I'll make a ghost of him that lets[8] me.
95 I say, away!—Go on; I'll follow thee.

Exeunt Ghost and Hamlet.

HORATIO: He waxes desperate with imagination.
MARCELLUS: Let's follow; 'tis not fit thus to obey him.
HORATIO: Have after.—To what issue will this come?
MARCELLUS: Something is rotten in the state of Denmark.
100 HORATIO: Heaven will direct it.
MARCELLUS: Nay, let's follow him.

Exeunt.

SCENE 5

A more remote part of the platform.

Enter Ghost and Hamlet.

HAMLET: Where wilt thou lead me? speak, I'll go no further.
GHOST: Mark me.
HAMLET: I will.
GHOST: My hour is almost come,
5   When I to sulphurous and tormenting flames
     Must render up myself.
HAMLET: Alas, poor ghost!
GHOST: Pity me not, but lend thy serious hearing
     To what I shall unfold.
10 HAMLET: Speak; I am bound to hear.
GHOST: So art thou to revenge, when thou shalt hear.
HAMLET: What?
GHOST: I am thy father's spirit;
     Doom'd for a certain term to walk the night,
15   And, for the day, confin'd to waste in fires
     Till the foul crimes[1] done in my days of nature
     Are burnt and purg'd away. But that I am forbid

---

[7]*Némean lion's:* The fierce lion that Hercules was called upon to slay as one of his "twelve labors."
[8]*lets:* Hinders.   [1]*foul crimes:* Sins or faults.

To tell the secrets of my prison-house,
I could a tale unfold whose lightest word
Would harrow up thy soul; freeze thy young blood;   20
Make thy two eyes, like stars, start from their spheres;
Thy knotted and combined locks to part,
And each particular hair to stand on end,
Like quills upon the fretful porcupine:
But this eternal blazon[2] must not be   25
To ears of flesh and blood.—List, list, O, list!—
If thou didst ever thy dear father love,—

HAMLET: O God!

GHOST: Revenge his foul and most unnatural murder.

HAMLET: Murder!   30

GHOST: Murder—most foul, as in the best it is;
But this most foul, strange, and unnatural.

HAMLET: Haste me to know't, that I, with wings as swift
As meditation or the thoughts of love,
May sweep to my revenge.   35

GHOST: I find thee apt;
And duller shouldst thou be than the fat weed
That rots itself in ease on Lethe[3] wharf,
Wouldst thou not stir in this. Now, Hamlet,
'Tis given out that, sleeping in mine orchard,   40
A serpent stung me; so the whole ear of Denmark
Is by a forged process of my death
Rankly abus'd: but know, thou noble youth,
The serpent that did sting thy father's life
Now wears his crown.   45

HAMLET: O my prophetic soul! mine uncle!

GHOST: Ay, that incestuous, that adulterate beast,
With witchcraft of his wit, with traitorous gifts,—
O wicked wit and gifts that have the power
So to seduce!—won to his shameful lust   50
The will of my most seeming virtuous queen:
O Hamlet, what a falling-off was there!
From me, whose love was of that dignity
That it went hand in hand even with the vow
I made to her in marriage: and to decline   55
Upon a wretch whose natural gifts were poor
To those of mine!

---

[2]*eternal blazon:* Disclosure of information concerning the other world.   [3]*Lethe:* The river of forgetfulness of the past, out of which the dead drink.

But virtue, as it never will be mov'd,
Though lewdness court it in a shape of heaven;
60 So lust, though to a radiant angel link'd,
Will sate itself in a celestial bed
And prey on garbage.
But, soft! methinks I scent the morning air;
Brief let me be.—Sleeping within mine orchard,
65 My custom always in the afternoon,
Upon my sécure hour thy uncle stole,
With juice of cursed hebenon[4] in a vial,
And in the porches of mine ears did pour
The leperous distilment; whose effect
70 Holds such an enmity with blood of man
That, swift as quicksilver, it courses through
The natural gates and alleys of the body;
And with a sudden vigor it doth posset[5]
And curd, like eager[6] droppings into milk,
75 The thin and wholesome blood: so did it mine;
And a most instant tetter bark'd about,
Most lazar-like,[7] with vile and loathsome crust,
All my smooth body.
Thus was I, sleeping, by a brother's hand,
80 Of life, of crown, of queen, at once despatch'd:
Cut off even in the blossoms of my sin,
Unhousel'd, unanointed, unanel'd;
No reckoning made, but sent to my account
With all my imperfections on my head:
85 O, horrible! O, horrible! most horrible!
If thou hast nature in thee, bear it not;
Let not the royal bed of Denmark be
A couch for luxury[8] and damned incest.
But, howsoever thou pursu'st this act,
90 Taint not thy mind, nor let thy soul contrive
Against thy mother aught: leave her to heaven,
And to those thorns that in her bosom lodge,
To prick and sting her. Fare thee well at once!
The glowworm shows the matin to be near,
95 And 'gins to pale his uneffectual fire:
Adieu, adieu! Hamlet, remember me. [*Exit.*]
HAMLET: O all you host of heaven! O earth! what else?

---

[4]*hebenon:* Ebony.   [5]*posset:* Coagulate.   [6]*eager:* Acid.   [7]*lazar-like:* Like a leper, whose skin is rough.   [8]*luxury:* Lechery.

And shall I couple hell?—O, fie!—Hold, my heart;
And you, my sinews, grow not instant old,
But bear me stiffly up.—Remember thee! 100
Ay, thou poor ghost, while memory holds a seat
In this distracted globe. Remember thee!
Yea, from the table of my memory
I'll wipe away all trivial fond[9] recórds,
All saws of books, all forms, all pressures past, 105
That youth and observation copied there;
And thy commandment all alone shall live
Within the book and volume of my brain,
Unmix'd with baser matter: yes, by heaven.—
O most pernicious woman! 110
O villain, villain, smiling, damned villain!
My tables,—meet it is I set it down,
That one may smile, and smile, and be a villain;
At least, I am sure, it may be so in Denmark:

Writing.

So, uncle, there you are. Now to my word; 115
It is, *Adieu, adieu! remember me:*
I have sworn't.
HORATIO: [*Within*] My lord, my lord,—
MARCELLUS: [*Within*]   Lord Hamlet,—
HORATIO: [*Within*]   Heaven secure him! 120
MARCELLUS: [*Within*] So be it!
HORATIO: [*Within*] Illo, ho, ho, my lord!
HAMLET: Hillo, ho, ho, boy! come, bird, come.[10]

Enter Horatio and Marcellus.

MARCELLUS: How is't, my noble lord?
HORATIO: What news, my lord? 125
HAMLET: O, wonderful!
HORATIO: Good my lord, tell it.
HAMLET: No; you'll reveal it.
HORATIO: Not I, my lord, by heaven.
MARCELLUS: Nor I, my lord. 130
HAMLET: How say you, then; would heart of man once think it?—
But you'll be secret?
HORATIO AND MARCELLUS: Ay, by heaven, my lord.

---

[9] *fond:* Foolish.   [10] *Hillo . . . come:* Hamlet uses the word "bird" because this is a falconer's call.

HAMLET: There's ne'er a villain dwelling in all Denmark

135 But he's an arrant knave.

HORATIO: There needs no ghost, my lord, come from the grave
To tell us this.

HAMLET: Why, right; you are i' the right;
And so, without more circumstance at all,

140 I hold it fit that we shake hands and part:
You, as your business and desire shall point you,—
For every man has business and desire,
Such as it is;—and for mine own poor part,
Look you, I'll go pray.

145 HORATIO: These are but wild and whirling words, my lord.

HAMLET: I'm sorry they offend you, heartily;
Yes, faith, heartily.

HORATIO: There's no offence, my lord.

HAMLET: Yes, by Saint Patrick, but there is, Horatio,

150 And much offence too. Touching this vision here,—
It is an honest ghost, that let me tell you:
For you desire to know what is between us,
O'ermaster't as you may. And now, good friends,
As you are friends, scholars, and soldiers,

155 Give me one poor request.

HORATIO: What is't, my lord? we will.

HAMLET: Never make known what you have seen to-night.

HORATIO AND MARCELLUS: My lord, we will not.

HAMLET: Nay, but swear't.

160 HORATIO: In faith,
My lord, not I.

MARCELLUS: Nor I, my lord, in faith.

HAMLET: Upon my sword.

MARCELLUS: We have sworn, my lord, already.

165 HAMLET: Indeed, upon my sword, indeed.

GHOST: [Beneath] Swear.

HAMLET: Ha, ha, boy! say'st thou so? art thou there, truepenny?—
Come on,—you hear this fellow in the cellarage,—
Consent to swear.

170 HORATIO: Propose the oath, my lord.

HAMLET: Never to speak of this that you have seen,
Swear by my sword.

GHOST: [Beneath] Swear.

HAMLET: Hic et ubique?[11] then we'll shift our ground.—

175 Come hither, gentlemen,

---

[11]Hic et ubique?: "Here and everywhere" (Latin).

And lay your hands again upon my sword:
Never to speak of this that you have heard,
Swear by my sword.
GHOST: [*Beneath*] Swear.
HAMLET: Well said! old mole! canst work i' the earth so fast?   180
A worthy pioneer![12]—Once more remove, good friends.
HORATIO: O day and night, but this is wondrous strange!
HAMLET: And therefore as a stranger give it welcome.
There are more things in heaven and earth, Horatio,
Than are dreamt of in your philosophy.   185
But come;—
Here, as before, never, so help you mercy,
How strange or odd soe'er I bear myself,—
As I, perchance, hereafter shall think meet
To put an antic disposition on,—   190
That you, at such times seeing me, never shall,
With arms encumber'd[13] thus, or this headshake,
Or by pronouncing of some doubtful phrase,
As, *Well, well, we know;*—or, *We could, an if we would;*—
Or, *If we list to speak;*—or, *There be, an if they might;*—   195
Or such ambiguous giving out, to note
That you know aught of me:—this not to do,
So grace and mercy at your most need help you,
Swear.
GHOST: [*Beneath*] Swear.   200
HAMLET: Rest, rest, perturbed spirit!—So, gentlemen,
With all my love I do commend to you:
And what so poor a man as Hamlet is
May do, to express his love and friending to you,
God willing, shall not lack. Let us go in together;   205
And still your fingers on your lips, I pray.
The time is out of joint:—O cursed spite,
That ever I was born to set it right!—
Nay, come, let's go together.

Exeunt.

ACT 2
SCENE 1

A room in Polonius' house.

Enter Polonius and Reynaldo.

POLONIUS: Give him this money and these notes, Reynaldo.

---

[12] *pioneer:* A soldier who digs trenches and undermines fortresses.   [13] *encumber'd:* Folded.

REYNALDO: I will, my lord.

POLONIUS: You shall do marvelous wisely, good Reynaldo,
Before you visit him, to make inquiry
5   On his behavior.

REYNALDO: My lord, I did intend it.

POLONIUS: Marry, well said; very well said. Look you, sir,
Inquire me first what Danskers[1] are in Paris;
And how, and who, what means, and where they keep,
10   What company, at what expense; and finding,
By this encompassment and drift of question,
That they do know my son, come you more nearer
Than your particular demands will touch it:
Take you, as 'twere, some distant knowledge of him;
15   As thus, *I know his father and his friends,*
And in part him;—do you mark this, Reynaldo?

REYNALDO: Ay, very well, my lord.

POLONIUS: *And in part him;—but, you may say, not well:*
But if t be he I mean, he's very wild;
20   *Addicted so* and so; and there put on him
What forgeries you please; marry, none so rank
As may dishonor him; take heed of that;
But, sir, such wanton, wild, and usual slips
As are companions noted and most known
25   To youth and liberty.

REYNALDO: As gaming, my lord.

POLONIUS: Ay, or drinking, fencing, swearing, quarreling,
Drabbing:[2]—you may go so far.

REYNALDO: My lord, that would dishonor him.

30   POLONIUS: Faith, no; as you may season it in the charge.
You must not put another scandal on him,
That he is open to incontinency;
That's not my meaning: but breathe his faults so quaintly
That they may seem the taints of liberty;
35   The flash and outbreak of a fiery mind;
A savageness in unreclaimed blood,
Of general assault.

REYNALDO: But, my good lord,—

POLONIUS: Wherefore should you do this?

40   REYNALDO: Ay, my lord,
I would know that.

POLONIUS: Marry, sir, here's my drift;

---

[1]*Danskers:* Danes.   [2]*Drabbing:* Going about with loose women.

And I believe it is a fetch of warrant:[3]
You laying these slight sullies on my son.
As 'twere a thing a little soil'd i' the working,   45
Mark you,
Your party in converse, him you would sound,
Having ever seen in the prenominate crimes
The youth you breathe of guilty, be assur'd
He closes with you in this consequence;   50
Good sir, or so; or *friend,* or *gentleman,*—
According to the phrase or the addition[4]
Of man and country.
REYNALDO: Very good, my lord.
POLONIUS: And then, sir, does he this,—he does,—   55
What was I about to say?—By the mass, I was
About to say something:—where did I leave?
REYNALDO: At *closes in the consequence,*
At *friend or so,* and *gentleman.*
POLONIUS: At—closes in the consequence,—ay, marry;   60
He closes with you thus:—I know the gentleman;
I saw him yesterday, or t'other day,
Or then, or then; with such, or such; and, as you say,
There was he gaming; there o'ertook in's rouse;
There falling out at tennis: or perchance,   65
I saw him enter such a house of sale,—
Videlicet,[5] a brothel,—or so forth.—
See you now;
Your bait of falsehood takes this carp of truth:
And thus do we of wisdom and of reach,   70
With windlasses, and with assays of bias,
By indirections find directions out:
So, by my former lecture and advice,
Shall you my son. You have me, have you not?
REYNALDO: My lord, I have.   75
POLONIUS: God b' wi' you; fare you well.
REYNALDO: Good my lord!
POLONIUS: Observe his inclination in yourself.
REYNALDO: I shall, my lord.
POLONIUS: And let him ply his music.   80
REYNALDO: Well, my lord.
POLONIUS: Farewell!

---

[3] *fetch of warrant:* A good device.   [4] *addition:* Form of address.   [5] *Videlicet:* That is; namely (Latin).

Exit Reynaldo.

Enter Ophelia.

How now, Ophelia! what's the matter?

OPHELIA: Alas, my lord, I have been so affrighted.

85 POLONIUS: With what, i' the name of God?

OPHELIA: My lord, as I was sewing in my chamber,
Lord Hamlet,—with his doublet all unbrac'd;
No hat upon his head; his stockings foul'd,
Ungarter'd, and down-gyved[6] to his ankle;
90 Pale as his shirt; his knees knocking each other;
And with a look so piteous in purport
As if he had been loosed out of hell
To speak of horrors,—he comes before me.

POLONIUS: Mad for thy love?

95 OPHELIA: My lord, I do not know;
But truly I do fear it.

POLONIUS: What said he?

OPHELIA: He took me by the wrist, and held me hard;
Then goes he to the length of all his arm;
100 And with his other hand thus o'er his brow,
He falls to such perusal of my face
As he would draw it. Long stay'd he so;
At last,—a little shaking of mine arm,
And thrice his head thus waving up and down,—
105 He rais'd a sigh so piteous and profound
That it did seem to shatter all his bulk
And end his being; that done, he lets me go:
And, with his head over his shoulder turn'd,
He seem'd to find his way without his eyes;
110 For out o' doors he went without their help,
And to the last bended their light on me.

POLONIUS: Come, go with me: I will go seek the king.
This is the very ecstasy[7] of love;
Whose violent property fordoes itself,[8]
115 And leads the will to desperate undertakings,
As oft as any passion under heaven
That does afflict our nature. I am sorry,—
What, have you given him any hard words of late?

OPHELIA: No, my good lord; but, as you did command,
120 I did repel his letters, and denied
His access to me.

---

[6]*down-gyved:* Dangling like chains.   [7]*ecstasy:* Madness.   [8]*fordoes itself:* Destroys itself.

POLONIUS: That hath made him mad.
I am sorry that with better heed and judgment
I had not quoted him: I fear'd he did but trifle,
And meant to wreck thee; but, beshrew my jealousy!   125
It seems it is as proper to our age
To cast beyond ourselves in our opinions
As it is common for the younger sort
To lack discretion. Come, go we to the king:
This must be known; which, being kept close, might move   130
More grief to hide than hate to utter love.

Exeunt.

SCENE 2

A room in the castle.

Enter King, Queen, Rosencrantz, Guildenstern, and Attendants.

KING: Welcome, dear Rosencrantz and Guildenstern!
Moreover that we much did long to see you,
The need we have to use you did provoke
Our hasty sending. Something have you heard
Of Hamlet's transformation; so I call it,   5
Since nor the exterior nor the inward man
Resembles that it was. What it should be,
More than his father's death, that thus hath put him
So much from the understanding of himself,
I cannot dream of: I entreat you both,   10
That being of so young days brought up with him,
And since so neighbor'd to his youth and humor,
That you vouchsafe your rest here in our court
Some little time: so by your companies
To draw him on to pleasures, and to gather,   15
So much as from occasion you may glean,
Whether aught, to us unknown, afflicts him thus,
That, open'd, lies within our remedy.

QUEEN: Good gentlemen, he hath much talk'd of you;
And sure I am two men there are not living   20
To whom he more adheres. If it will please you
To show us so much gentry and good-will
As to expend your time with us awhile,
For the supply and profit of our hope,
Your visitation shall receive such thanks   25
As fits a king's remembrance.

ROSENCRANTZ: Both your majesties
Might, by the sovereign power you have of us,

	Put your dread pleasures more into command
30	Than to entreaty.
	GUILDENSTERN: We both obey,
	And here give up ourselves, in the full bent,
	To lay our service freely at your feet,
	To be commanded.
35	KING: Thanks, Rosencrantz and gentle Guildenstern.
	QUEEN: Thanks, Guildenstern and gentle Rosencrantz:
	And I beseech you instantly to visit
	My too-much-changed son.—Go, some of you,
	And bring these gentlemen where Hamlet is.
40	GUILDENSTERN: Heavens make our presence and our practices
	Pleasant and helpful to him!
	QUEEN: Ay, amen!

Exeunt Rosencrantz, Guildenstern, and some Attendants.

Enter Polonius.

	POLONIUS: The ambassadors from Norway, my good lord,
	Are joyfully return'd.
45	KING: Thou still has been the father of good news.
	POLONIUS: Have I, my lord? Assure you, my good liege,
	I hold my duty, as I hold my soul,
	Both to my God and to my gracious king:
	And I do think,—or else this brain of mine
50	Hunts not the trail of policy[1] so sure
	As it hath us'd to do,—that I have found
	The very cause of Hamlet's lunacy.
	KING: O, speak of that; that do I long to hear.
	POLONIUS: Give first admittance to the ambassadors;
55	My news shall be the fruit to that great feast.
	KING: Thyself do grace to them, and bring them in.

Exit Polonius.

	He tells me, my sweet queen, that he hath found
	The head and source of all your son's distemper.
	QUEEN: I doubt it is no other but the main,—
60	His father's death and our o'erhasty marriage.
	KING: Well, we shall sift him.

Re-enter Polonius, with Voltimand and Cornelius.

---

[1] *trail of policy:* Statecraft.

Welcome, my good friends!
Say, Voltimand, what from our brother Norway?
VOLTIMAND: Most fair return of greetings and desires.
Upon our first, he sent out to suppress   65
His nephew's levies; which to him appear'd
To be a preparation 'gainst the Polack;
But, better look'd into, he truly found
It was against your highness: whereat griev'd,—
That so his sickness, age, and impotence   70
Was falsely borne in hand,—sends out arrests
On Fortinbras; which he, in brief, obeys;
Receives rebuke from Norway; and, in fine,
Makes vows before his uncle never more
To give the assay of arms against your majesty.   75
Whereon old Norway, overcome with joy,
Gives him three thousand crowns in annual fee;
And his commission to employ those soldiers,
So levied as before, against the Polack:
With an entreaty, herein further shown, [*gives a paper*]   80
That it might please you to give quiet pass
Through your dominions for this enterprise,
On such regards of safety and allowance
As therein are set down.
KING: It likes us well;   85
And at our more consider'd time we'll read,
Answer, and think upon this business.
Meantime we thank you for your well-took labor:
Go to your rest; at night we'll feast together:
Most welcome home!   90

Exeunt Voltimand and Cornelius.

POLONIUS: This business is well ended.—
My liege, and madam,—to expostulate
What majesty should be, what duty is,
Why day is day, night night, and time is time,
Were nothing but to waste night, day, and time.   95
Therefore, since brevity is the soul of wit,
And tediousness the limbs and outward flourishes,
I will be brief:—your noble son is mad:
Mad call I it; for to define true madness,
What is't but to be nothing else but mad?   100
But let that go.
QUEEN: More matter with less art.

POLONIUS: Madam, I swear I use no art at all.
That he is mad, 'tis true 'tis pity;
105 And pity 'tis 'tis true: a foolish figure;
But farewell it, for I will use no art.
Mad let us grant him, then: and now remains
That we find out the cause of this effect;
Or rather say, the cause of this defect,
110 For this effect defective comes by cause:
Thus it remains, and the remainder thus.
Perpend.
I have a daughter,—have whilst she is mine,—
Who, in her duty and obedience, mark,
115 Hath given me this: now gather, and surmise

[*Reads*]

> *To the celestial, and my soul's idol, the most beautified Ophelia,—*

That's an ill phrase, a vile phrase,—beautified is a vile phrase: but
you shall hear. Thus:

[*Reads*]

> *In her excellent white bosom, these, &c.*

120 QUEEN: Came this from Hamlet to her?
POLONIUS: Good madam, stay a while; I will be faithful.

[*Reads*]

> *Doubt thou the stars are fire;*
> *Doubt that the sun doth move;*
> *Doubt truth to be a liar;*
125 > *But never doubt I love.*

> *O dear Ophelia, I am ill at these numbers, I have not art to reckon*
> *my groans: but*
> *that I love thee best, O most best, believe it. Adieu.*
> *Thine evermore, most dear lady, whilst this machine is to him,*
> *Hamlet*

This, in obedience, hath my daughter show'd me:
130 And more above, hath his solicitings,
As they fell out by time, by means, and place,
All given to mine ear.
KING: But how hath she
Receiv'd his love?
135 POLONIUS: What do you think of me?

KING: As of a man faithful and honorable.

POLONIUS: I would fain prove so. But what might you think,
    When I had seen this hot love on the wing,—
    As I perceiv'd it, I must tell you that,
    Before my daughter told me,—what might you,   140
    Or my dear majesty your queen here, think,
    If I had play'd the desk or table-book;[2]
    Or given my heart a winking, mute and dumb;
    Or look'd upon this love with idle sight;—
    What might you think? No, I went round to work,   145
    And my young mistress thus I did bespeak:
    Lord Hamlet is a prince out of thy sphere;
    This must not be: and then I precepts gave her,
    That she should lock herself from his resort,
    Admit no messengers, receive no tokens.   150
    Which done, she took the fruits of my advice;
    And he, repulsed,—a short tale to make,—
    Fell into a sadness; then into a fast;
    Thence to a watch; thence into a weakness;
    Thence to a lightness; and, by this declension,   155
    Into the madness wherein now he raves
    And all we wail for.

KING: Do you think 'tis this?

QUEEN: It may be, very likely.

POLONIUS: Hath there been such a time,—I'd fain know that,—   160
    That I have positively said, *'Tis so,*
    When it prov'd otherwise?

KING: Not that I know.

POLONIUS: Take this from this, if this be otherwise: [*Pointing to his head
    and shoulder*]
    If circumstances lead me, I will find   165
    Where truth is hid, though it were hid indeed
    Within the center.

KING: How may we try it further?

POLONIUS: You know, sometimes he walks four hours together
    Here in the lobby.   170

QUEEN: So he does, indeed.

POLONIUS: At such a time I'll loose my daughter to him:
    Be you and I behind an arras[3] then;
    Mark the encounter: if he love her not,
    And be not from his reason fall'n thereon,   175

---

[2]*table-book:* Memorandum pad.   [3]*arras:* Tapestry, hung some distance away from a wall.

Let me be no assistant for a state,
But keep a farm and carters.

KING: We will try it.

QUEEN: But look, where sadly the poor wretch comes reading.

180 POLONIUS: Away, I do beseech you, both away:
I'll board[4] him presently:—O, give me leave.

Exeunt King, Queen, and Attendants.

Enter Hamlet, reading.

How does my good Lord Hamlet?

HAMLET: Well, God-a-mercy.

POLONIUS: Do you know me, my lord?

185 HAMLET: Excellent, excellent well; you're a fishmonger.

POLONIUS: Not I, my lord.

HAMLET: Then I would you were so honest a man.

POLONIUS: Honest, my lord!

HAMLET: Ay, sir; to be honest, as this world goes, is to be one man
190   picked out of ten thousand.

POLONIUS: That's very true, my lord.

HAMLET: For if the sun breed maggots in a dead dog, being a god kissing
carrion,—Have you a daughter?

POLONIUS: I have, my lord.

195 HAMLET: Let her not walk i' the sun: conception is a blessing; but not as
your daughter may conceive:—friend, look to't.

POLONIUS: How say you by that?—[*Aside*] Still harping on my daughter:—
yet he knew me not at first; he said I was a fishmonger: he is far gone,
far gone: and truly in my youth I suffered much extremity for love;
200   very near this. I'll speak to him again.—What do you read, my lord?

HAMLET: Words, words, words.

POLONIUS: What is the matter, my lord?

HAMLET: Between who?

POLONIUS: I mean, the matter that you read, my lord.

205 HAMLET: Slanders, sir: for the satirical slave says here that old men
have gray beards; that their faces are wrinkled; their eyes purging
thick amber and plum-tree gum; and that they have a plentiful lack
of wit, together with most weak hams: all which, sir, though I most
powerfully and potently believe, yet I hold it not honesty to have it
210   thus set down; for you yourself, sir, should be old as I am, if, like a
crab, you could go backward.

---

[4]*board:* Address.

POLONIUS: [*Aside*] Though this be madness, yet there is method in't.—
ill you walk out of the air, my lord?

HAMLET: Into my grave?

POLONIUS: Indeed, that is out o' the air.—[*Aside*] How pregnant[5] some- 215
times his replies are! a happiness that often madness hits on, which
reason and sanity could not so prosperously be delivered of. I will
leave him, and suddenly contrive the means of meeting between
him and my daughter.—More honorable lord, I will most humbly
take my leave of you. 220

HAMLET: You cannot, sir, take from me anything that I will more willingly part withal,—except my life, except my life, except my life.

POLONIUS: Fare you well, my lord.

HAMLET: These tedious old fools!

Enter Rosencrantz and Guildenstern.

POLONIUS: You go to seek the Lord Hamlet; there he is. 225

ROSENCRANTZ: [*To Polonius*] God save you, sir!

Exit Polonius.

GUILDENSTERN: Mine honored lord!

ROSENCRANTZ: My most dear lord!

HAMLET: My excellent good friends! How dost thou, Guildenstern? Ah,
Rosencrantz? Good lads, how do ye both? 230

ROSENCRANTZ: As the indifferent children of the earth.

GUILDENSTERN: Happy in that we are not overhappy; on fortune's cap
we are not the very button.

HAMLET: Nor the soles of her shoe?

ROSENCRANTZ: Neither, my lord. 235

HAMLET: Then you live about her waist, or in the middle of her favors?

GUILDENSTERN: Faith, her privates we.

HAMLET: In the secret parts of fortune? O, most true; she is a strumpet.
What's the news?

ROSENCRANTZ: None, my lord, but that the world's grown honest. 240

HAMLET: Then is doomsday near: but your news is not true. Let me
question more in particular: what have you, my good friends, deserved
at the hands of fortune, that she sends you to prison hither?

GUILDENSTERN: Prison, my lord!

HAMLET: Denmark's a prison. 245

ROSENCRANTZ: Then is the world one.

HAMLET: A goodly one; in which there are many confines, wards, and
dungeons, Denmark being one o' the worst.

---

[5]*pregnant:* Ready, and clever.

ROSENCRANTZ: We think not so, my lord.

250 HAMLET: Why, then, 'tis none to you; for there is nothing either good or bad, but thinking makes it so: to me it is a prison.

ROSENCRANTZ: Why, then, your ambition makes it one; 'tis too narrow for your mind.

HAMLET: O God, I could be bounded in a nutshell, and count myself a 255 king of infinite space, were it not that I have bad dreams.

GUILDENSTERN: Which dreams, indeed, are ambition; for the very substance of the ambitious is merely the shadow of a dream.

HAMLET: A dream itself is but a shadow.

ROSENCRANTZ: Truly, and I hold ambition of so airy and light a quality 260 that it is but a shadow's shadow.

HAMLET: Then are our beggars bodies, and our monarchs and outstretched heroes the beggars' shadows. Shall we to the court? for, by my fay, I cannot reason.

ROSENCRANTZ AND GUILDENSTERN: We'll wait upon you.

265 HAMLET: No such matter: I will not sort you with the rest of my servants, for, to speak to you like an honest man, I am most dreadfully attended. But, in the beaten way of friendship, what make you at Elsinore?

ROSENCRANTZ: To visit you, my lord; no other occasion.

HAMLET: Beggar that I am, I am even poor in thanks; but I thank you: 270 and sure, dear friends, my thanks are too dear a halfpenny. Were you not sent for? Is it your own inclining? Is it a free visitation? Come, deal justly with me: come, come; nay, speak.

GUILDENSTERN: What should we say, my lord?

HAMLET: Why, anything—but to the purpose. You were sent for; and 275 there is a kind of confession in your looks, which your modesties have not craft enough to color: I know the good king and queen have sent for you.

ROSENCRANTZ: To what end, my lord?

HAMLET: That you must teach me. But let me conjure you, by the rights 280 of our fellowship, by the consonancy of our youth, by the obligation of our ever-preserved love, and by what more dear a better proposer could charge you withal, be even and direct with me, whether you were sent for or no?

ROSENCRANTZ: What say you? [*To Guildenstern*]

285 HAMLET: [*Aside*] Nay, then, I have an eye of you.—If you love me, hold not off.

GUILDENSTERN: My lord, we were sent for.

HAMLET: I will tell you why; so shall my anticipation prevent your discovery, and your secrecy to the king and queen moult no feather. 290 I have of late,—but wherefore I know not,—lost all my mirth, forgone all custom of exercises; and, indeed, it goes so heavily with

my disposition that this goodly frame, the earth, seems to me a
sterile promontory; this most excellent canopy, the air, look you,
this brave o'erhanging firmament, this majestical roof fretted[6] with
golden fire,—why, it appears no other thing to me than a foul and   295
pestilent congregation of vapors. What a piece of work is man!
How noble in reason! how infinite in faculties! in form and moving, how express and admirable! in action, how like an angel! in
apprehension, how like a god! the beauty of the world! the paragon
of animals! And yet, to me, what is this quintessence of dust? man   300
delights not me; no, nor woman neither, though by your smiling you
seem to say so.

ROSENCRANTZ: My lord, there was no such stuff in my thoughts.

HAMLET: Why did you laugh, then, when I said, *Man delights not me?*

ROSENCRANTZ: To think, my lord, if you delight not in man, what   305
lenten entertainment[7] the players shall receive from you: we coted[8]
them on the way; and hither are they coming, to offer you service.

HAMLET: He that plays the king shall be welcome,—his majesty shall
have tribute of me; the adventurous knight shall use his foil and
target; the lover shall not sigh gratis; the humorous[9] man shall end   310
his part in peace; the clown shall make those laugh whose lungs are
tickled o' the sere;[10] and the lady shall say her mind freely, or the
blank verse shall halt[11] for't.—What players are they?

ROSENCRANTZ: Even those you were wont to take delight in,—the
tragedians of the city.   315

HAMLET: How chances it they travel? their residence, both in reputation
and profit, was better both ways.

ROSENCRANTZ: I think their inhibition[12] comes by the means of the late
innovation.

HAMLET: Do they hold the same estimation they did when I was in the   320
city? Are they so followed?

ROSENCRANTZ: No, indeed, they are not.

HAMLET: How comes it? do they grow rusty?

ROSENCRANTZ: Nay, their endeavor keeps in the wonted pace; but there
is, sir, an aery[13] of children, little eyases,[14] that cry out on the top of   325
question, and are most tyrannically clapped for't: these are now the

---

[6]*roof fretted:* A roof with fretwork.   [7]*lenten entertainment:* Poor reception.   [8]*coted:* Passed.
[9]*humorous:* Eccentric.   [10]*whose lungs . . . sere:* Whose lungs, for laughter, are easily tickled.
[11]*halt:* Limp.   [12]*inhibition:* Difficulty, preventing them from remaining in the capital.
[13]*aery:* Brood of birds of prey.   [14]*little eyases:* Young hawks; a reference to the boys' companies that
became popular rivals of Shakespeare's company of players.

fashion; and so berattle the common stages,—so they call them,—
that many wearing rapiers are afraid of goose-quills, and dare scarce
come thither.

330 HAMLET: What, are they children? who maintains 'em? how are they
escoted?[15] Will they pursue the quality[16] no longer than they can
sing? will they not say afterwards, if they should grow themselves to
common players,—as it is most like, if their means are no better,—
their writers do them wrong, to make them exclaim against their
335   own succession?

ROSENCRANTZ: Faith, there has been much to do on both sides; and the
nation holds it no sin to tarre[17] them to controversy: there was for
awhile no money bid for argument, unless the poet and the player
went to cuffs in the question.

340 HAMLET: Is't possible?

GUILDENSTERN: O, there has been much throwing about of brains.

HAMLET: Do the boys carry it away?

ROSENCRANTZ: Ay, that they do, my lord; Hercules and his load[18] too.

HAMLET: It is not strange; for mine uncle is king of Denmark, and those
345   that would make mouths at him while my father lived, give twenty,
forty, fifty, an hundred ducats a-piece for his picture in little.
'Sblood, there is something in this more than natural, if philosophy
could find it out.

Flourish of trumpets within.

GUILDENSTERN: There are the players.

350 HAMLET: Gentlemen, you are welcome to Elsinore. Your hands, come:
the appurtenance of welcome is fashion and ceremony: let me
comply with you in this garb; lest my extent[19] to the players, which,
I tell you, must show fairly outward, should more appear like entertainment[20] than yours. You are welcome: but my uncle-father and
355   aunt-mother are deceived.

GUILDENSTERN: In what, my dear lord?

HAMLET: I am but mad north-north-west: when the wind is southerly I
know a hawk from a handsaw.

Enter Polonius.

POLONIUS: Well be with you, gentlemen!

360 HAMLET: Hark you, Guildenstern;—and you too;—at each ear a hearer:
that great baby you see there is not yet out of his swathing-clouts.

---

[15]*escoted:* Financially supported.   [16]*quality:* Profession.   [17]*to tarre:* To egg them on.
[18]*his load:* The globe, or the world.   [19]*extent:* Show of friendliness.   [20]*entertainment:* Welcome.

ROSENCRANTZ: Happily he's the second time come to them; for they say
an old man is twice a child.

HAMLET: I will prophesy he comes to tell me of the players; mark it.
You say right, sir: o' Monday morning; 'twas so indeed.   365

POLONIUS: My lord, I have news to tell you.

HAMLET: My lord, I have news to tell you. When Roscius was an actor in
Rome,—

POLONIUS: The actors are come hither, my lord.

HAMLET: Buzz, buzz!   370

POLONIUS: Upon mine honor,—

HAMLET: Then came each actor on his ass,—

POLONIUS: The best actors in the world, either for tragedy, comedy, history,
pastoral, pastoral-comical, historical-pastoral, tragical-historical,
tragical-comical-historical-pastoral, scene individable,[21] or poem   375
unlimited:[22] Seneca cannot be too heavy nor Plautus too light. For
the law of writ and the liberty,[23] these are the only men.

HAMLET: O Jephthah, judge of Israel, what a treasure hadst thou!

POLONIUS: What a treasure had he, my lord?

HAMLET: Why—   380

> One fair daughter, and no more,
> The which he loved passing well.

POLONIUS: [*Aside*] Still on my daughter.

HAMLET: Am I not i' the right, old Jephthah?

POLONIUS: If you call me Jephthah, my lord, I have a daughter that I   385
love passing well.

HAMLET: Nay, that follows not.

POLONIUS: What follows, then, my lord?

HAMLET: Why—

> As by lot, God wot,   390
> and then, you know,
> It came to pass, as most like it was,

the first row of the pious chanson will show you more; for look
where my abridgement comes.

Enter four or five Players.

---

[21] *scene individable:* A play that observes the unities of time and place.   [22] *poem unlimited:* A typical
multiscene Elizabethan drama, not restricted by the unities; examples are *Hamlet, Macbeth, King
Lear,* and nearly any other play by Shakespeare.   [23] *For the law . . . liberty:* For the laws of the unities
and for playwriting that is not so restricted.

395   You are welcome, masters; welcome, all:—I am glad to see thee
well:—welcome, good friends.—O, my old friend! Thy face is
valanced since I saw thee last; comest thou to beard me in
Denmark?—What, my young lady and mistress! By'r lady, your
ladyship is nearer heaven than when I saw you last, by the altitude
400   of a chopine.[24] Pray God, your voice, like a piece of uncurrent gold,
be not cracked within the ring.—Masters, you are all welcome.
We'll e'en to't like French falconers, fly at anything we see: we'll
have a speech straight: come, give us a taste of your quality; come,
a passionate speech.

405 **1ST PLAYER:** What speech, my lord?

     HAMLET: I heard thee speak me a speech once,—but it was never acted;
or, if it was, not above once; for the play, I remember, pleased not
the million; 'twas caviare to the general: but it was,—as I received
it, and others whose judgments in such matters cried in the top
410   of mine,—an excellent play, well digested in the scenes, set down
with as much modesty as cunning. I remember, one said there were
no sallets in the lines to make the matter savory, nor no matter in
the phrase that might indite the author of affectation; but called it
an honest method, as wholesome as sweet, and by very much more
415   handsome than fine. One speech in it I chiefly loved: 'twas Aeneas'
tale to Dido; and thereabout of it especially where he speaks of
Priam's slaughter: if it live in your memory, begin at this line;—let
me see, let me see:—

     The rugged Pyrrhus, like the Hyrcanian beast,[25]

420 —it is not so:—it begins with Pyrrhus:—

     The rugged Pyrrhus,—he whose sable arms,
     Black as his purpose, did the night resemble
     When he lay couched in the ominous horse,—
     Hath now this dread and black complexion smear'd
425   With heraldry more dismal; head to foot
     Now is he total gules; horridly trick'd
     With blood of fathers, mothers, daughters, sons,
     Bak'd and impasted with the parching streets,
     That lend a tyrannous and damned light
430   To their vile murders: roasted in wrath and fire,

---

[24]*chopine:* A wooden stilt more than a foot high used under a woman's shoe; a Venetian fashion introduced into England.   [25]*The rugged....:* This speech is an example of the declamatory style of drama, which Shakespeare surely must have considered outmoded.

And thus o'er-sized with coagulate gore,
With eyes like carbuncles, the hellish Pyrrhus
Old grandsire Priam seeks.—

So proceed you.

POLONIUS: 'Fore God, my lord, well spoken, with good accent and good   435
discretion.

1ST PLAYER: Anon he finds him
Striking too short at Greeks; his antique sword,
Rebellious to his arm, lies where it falls,
Repugnant to command: unequal match'd,   440
Pyrrhus at Priam drives; in rage strikes wide;
But with the whiff and wind of his fell sword
The unnerved father falls. Then senseless Ilium,
Seeming to feel this blow, with flaming top
Stoops to his base; and with a hideous crash   445
Takes prisoner Pyrrhus' ear: for, lo! his sword,
Which was declining on the milky head
Of reverend Priam, seem'd i' the air to stick:
So, as a painted tyrant, Pyrrhus stood;
And, like a neutral to his will and matter,   450
Did nothing.
But as we often see, against some storm,
A silence in the heavens, the rack stand still,
The blood winds speechless, and the orb below
As hush as death, anon the dreadful thunder   455
Doth rend the region; so, after Pyrrhus' pause,
A roused vengeance sets him new a-work;
And never did the Cyclops' hammers fall
On Mars his armor, forg'd for proof eterne,
With less remorse than Pyrrhus' bleeding sword   460
Now falls on Priam.—
Out, out, thou strumpet, Fortune! All you gods,
In general synod, take away her power;
Break all the spokes and fellies from her wheel,
And bowl the round knave down the hill of heaven,   465
As low as to the fiends!

POLONIUS: This is too long.

HAMLET: It shall to the barber's, with your beard.—Pr'ythee, say on.—He's
for a jig, or a tale of bawdry, or he sleeps:—say on; come to Hecuba.

1ST PLAYER: But who, O, who had seen the mobled queen,—   470

HAMLET: *The mobled queen?*

POLONIUS: That's good; *mobled queen* is good.

1ST PLAYER: Run barefoot up and down, threatening the flames

With bissom rheum; a clout upon that head
475 Where late the diadem stood; and, for a robe,
About her lank and all o'er-teemed loins,
A blanket, in the alarm of fear caught up;—
Who this had seen, with tongue in venom steep'd,
'Gainst Fortune's state would treason have pronounc'd:
480 But if the gods themselves did see her then,
When she saw Pyrrhus make malicious sport
In mincing with his sword her husband's limbs,
The instant burst of clamor that she made,—
Unless things mortal move them not at all,—
485 Would have made milch the burning eyes of heaven,
And passion in the gods.

POLONIUS: Look, whether he has not turn'd his color, and has tears in's
eyes.—Pray you, no more.

HAMLET: 'Tis well; I'll have thee speak out the rest soon.—Good my
490 lord, will you see the players well bestowed? Do you hear, let them
be well used; for they are the abstracts and brief chronicles of the
time; after your death you were better have a bad epitaph than their
ill report while you live.

POLONIUS: My lord, I will use them according to their desert.

495 HAMLET: God's bodikin, man, better: use every man after his desert, and
who should scape whipping? Use them after your own honor and
dignity: the less they deserve the more merit is in your bounty.
Take them in.

POLONIUS: Come, sirs.

500 HAMLET: Follow him, friends: we'll hear a play to-morrow.

Exit Polonius with all the Players but the First.

Dost thou hear me, old friend; can you play the Murder of Gonzago?

1ST PLAYER: Ay, my lord.

HAMLET: We'll ha't to-morrow night. You could, for a need, study a
speech of some dozen or sixteen lines which I would set down and
505 insert in't? could you not?

1ST PLAYER: Ay, my lord.

HAMLET: Very well.—Follow that lord; and look you mock him not.

Exit First Player.

—My good friends, [*to Rosencrantz and Guildenstern*] I'll leave you
till night: you are welcome to Elsinore.

510 ROSENCRANTZ: Good my lord!

Exeunt Rosencrantz and Guildenstern.

HAMLET: Ay, so God b' wi' ye!—Now I am alone.
O, what a rogue²⁶ and peasant slave am I!
Is it not monstrous that this player here,
But in a fiction, in a dream of passion,
Could force his soul so to his own conceit²⁷   515
That from her working all his visage wan'd;
Tears in his eyes, distraction in's aspéct,
A broken voice, and his whole function suiting
With forms to his conceit? And all for nothing!
For Hecuba?   520
What's Hecuba to him or he to Hecuba,
That he should weep for her? What would he do,
Had he the motive and the cue for passion
That I have? He would drown the stage with tears,
And cleave the general ear with horrid speech;   525
Make mad the guilty, and appal the free;
Confound the ignorant, and amaze, indeed,
The very faculties of eyes and ears.
Yet I,
A dull and muddy-mettled rascal, peak,   530
Like John-a-dreams, unpregnant of my cause,
And can say nothing; no, not for a king
Upon whose property and most dear life
A damn'd defeat was made. Am I a coward?
Who calls me villain? breaks my pate across?   535
Plucks off my beard and blows it in my face?
Tweaks me by the nose? gives me the lie i' the throat,
As deep as to the lungs? who does me this, ha?
'Swounds, I should take it: for it cannot be
But I am pigeon-liver'd, and lack gall   540
To make oppression bitter; or ere this
I should have fatted all the region kites
With this slave's offal:—bloody, bawdy villain!
Remorseless, treacherous, lecherous, kindless villain!
O, vengeance!   545
Why, what an ass am I! This is most brave,
That I, the son of a dear father murder'd,
Prompted to my revenge by heaven and hell,
Must, like a whore, unpack my heart with words,
And fall a-cursing like a very drab,   550

---

²⁶*rogue:* Wretched creature.   ²⁷*conceit:* Conception.

A scullion!
Fie upon't! foh!—About, my brain! I have heard
That guilty creatures, sitting at a play,
Have by the very cunning of the scene
555   Been struck so to the soul that presently
They have proclaim'd their malefactions;
For murder, though it have no tongue, will speak
With most miraculous organ. I'll have these players
Play something like the murder of my father
560   Before mine uncle: I'll observe his looks;
I'll tent[28] him to the quick: if he but blench,
I know my course. The spirit that I have seen
May be the devil: and the devil hath power
To assume a pleasing shape; yea, and perhaps
565   Out of my weakness and my melancholy,—
As he is very potent with such spirits,—
Abuses me to damn me: I'll have grounds
More relative than this:—the play's the thing
Wherein I'll catch the conscience of the king. [*Exit.*]

ACT 3
SCENE 1

A room in the castle.

Enter King, Queen, Polonius, Ophelia, Rosencrantz, and Guildenstern.

KING: And can you, by no drift of circumstance,
Get from him why he puts on this confusion,
Grating so harshly all his days of quiet
With turbulent and dangerous lunacy?
5   ROSENCRANTZ: He does confess he feels himself distracted;
But from what cause he will by no means speak.
GUILDENSTERN: Nor do we find him forward to be sounded;
But, with a crafty madness, keeps aloof
When we would bring him on to some confession
10   Of his true state.
QUEEN: Did he receive you well?
ROSENCRANTZ: Most like a gentleman.
GUILDENSTERN: But with much forcing of his disposition.
ROSENCRANTZ: Niggard of question; but, of our demands,
15   Most free in his reply.
QUEEN: Did you assay him

---

[28] *tent:* Probe.

To any pastime?

ROSENCRANTZ: Madam, it so fell out that certain players
We o'er-raught on the way: of these we told him;
And there did seem in him a kind of joy   20
To hear of it: they are about the court;
And, as I think, they have already order
This night to play before him.

POLONIUS: 'Tis most true:
And he beseech'd me to entreat your majesties   25
To hear and see the matter.

KING: With all my heart; and it doth much content me
To hear him so inclin'd.
Good gentlemen, give him a further edge,
And drive his purpose on to these delights.   30

ROSENCRANTZ: We shall, my lord.

Exeunt Rosencrantz and Guildenstern.

KING: Sweet Gertrude, leave us too;
For we have closely sent for Hamlet hither
That he, as 'twere by accident, may here
Affront Ophelia: 35
Her father and myself,—lawful espials,[1]—
Will so bestow ourselves that, seeing, unseen,
We may of their encounter frankly judge;
And gather by him, as he is behav'd,
If't be the affliction of his love or no   40
That thus he suffers for.

QUEEN: I shall obey you:—
And for your part, Ophelia, I do wish
That your good beauties be the happy cause
Of Hamlet's wildness: so shall I hope your virtues   45
Will bring him to his wonted way again,
To both your honors.

OPHELIA: Madam, I wish it may.

Exit Queen.

POLONIUS: Ophelia, walk you here.—Gracious, so please you,
We will bestow ourselves.—[*To Ophelia*] Read on this book;   50
That show of such an exercise may color
Your loneliness.—We are oft to blame in this,—

---

[1] *espials:* Spies.

'Tis too much prov'd,—that with devotion's visage
And pious action we do sugar o'er
55 The devil himself.

KING: [*Aside*]   O, 'tis too true!
How smart a lash that speech doth give my conscience!
The harlot's cheek, beautied with plastering art,
Is not more ugly to the thing that helps it
60 Than is my deed to my most painted word:
O heavy burden!

POLONIUS: I hear him coming: let's withdraw, my lord.

Exeunt King and Polonius.

Enter Hamlet.

HAMLET: To be, or not to be,—that is the question:
Whether 'tis nobler in the mind to suffer
65 The slings and arrows of outrageous fortune,
Or to take arms against a sea of troubles,
And by opposing end them?—To die,—to sleep,—
No more; and by a sleep to say we end
The heart-ache and the thousand natural shocks
70 That flesh is heir to,—'tis a consummation
Devoutly to be wish'd. To die,—to sleep;—
To sleep! perchance to dream:—ay, there's the rub;
For in that sleep of death what dreams may come,
When we have shuffled off this mortal coil,
75 Must give us pause: there's the respect
That makes a calamity of so long life;
For who would bear the whips and scorns of time,
The oppressor's wrong, the proud man's contumely,
The pangs of déspis'd love, the law's delay,
80 The insolence of office, and the spurns
That patient merit of the unworthy takes,
When he himself might his quietus make
With a bare bodkin?[2] who would fardels[3] bear,
To grunt[4] and sweat under a weary life,
85 But that the dread of something after death,—
The undiscover'd country, from whose bourn[5]
No traveler returns,—puzzles the will,
And makes us rather bear those ills we have
Than to fly to others that we know not of?

---

[2]*bodkin:* Stiletto.   [3]*fardels:* Burdens.   [4]*grunt:* Groan.   [5]*bourn:* Boundary.

Thus conscience does make cowards of us all;   90
And thus the native hue of resolution
Is sicklied o'er with the pale cast of thought;
And enterprises of great pith and moment,
With this regard, their currents turn awry,
And lose the name of action.—Soft you now!   95
The fair Ophelia.—Nymph, in thy orisons[6]
Be all my sins remember'd.

OPHELIA: Good my lord,
How does your honor for this many a day?

HAMLET: I humbly thank you; well, well, well.   100

OPHELIA: My lord, I have remembrances of yours,
That I have longed long to re-deliver;
I pray you, now receive them.

HAMLET: No, not I;
I never gave you aught.   105

OPHELIA: My honor'd lord, you know right well you did;
And with them, words of so sweet breath compos'd
As made the things more rich: their perfume lost,
Take these again; for to the noble mind
Rich gifts wax poor when givers prove unkind.   110
There, my lord.

HAMLET: Ha, ha! are you honest?

OPHELIA: My lord?

HAMLET: Are you fair?

OPHELIA: What means your lordship?   115

HAMLET: That if you be honest and fair, your honesty should admit no
discourse to your beauty.

OPHELIA: Could beauty, my lord, have better commerce than with
honesty?

HAMLET: Ay, truly; for the power of beauty will sooner transform   120
honesty from what it is to a bawd than the force of honesty can
translate beauty into his likeness: this was sometime a paradox, but
now the time gives it proof. I did love you once.

OPHELIA: Indeed, my lord, you made me believe so.

HAMLET: You should not have believed me; for virtue cannot so inocu-   125
late our old stock but we shall relish of it: I loved you not.

OPHELIA: I was the more deceived.

HAMLET: Get thee to a nunnery: why wouldst thou be a breeder of sinners? I am myself indifferent[7] honest; but yet I could accuse me of

---

[6] *orisons:* Prayers.   [7] *indifferent:* Tolerably.

130   such things that it were better my mother had not borne me: I am
very proud, revengeful, ambitious; with more offences at my beck
than I have thoughts to put them in, imagination to give them
shape, or time to act them in. What should such fellows as I do
crawling between heaven and earth? We are arrant knaves, all;
135   believe none of us. Go thy ways to a nunnery. Where's your father?

OPHELIA: At home, my lord.

HAMLET: Let the doors be shut upon him, that he may play the fool
nowhere but in's own house. Farewell.

OPHELIA: O, help him, you sweet heavens!

140 HAMLET: If thou dost marry, I'll give thee this plague for thy dowry,—
be thou as chaste as ice, as pure as snow, thou shalt not escape
calumny. Get thee to a nunnery, go: farewell. Or, if thou wilt needs
marry, marry a fool; for wise men know well enough what monsters
you make of them. To a nunnery, go; and quickly too. Farewell.

145 OPHELIA: O heavenly powers, restore him!

HAMLET: I have heard of your paintings too, well enough; God has
given you one face and you make yourselves another: you jig, you
amble, and you lisp, and nickname God's creatures, and make your
wantonness your ignorance. Go to, I'll no more on't; it hath made
150   me mad. I say, we will have no more marriages: those that are married already, all but one, shall live; the rest shall keep as they are.
To a nunnery, go. [*Exit.*]

OPHELIA: O, what a noble mind is here o'erthrown!
The courtier's, soldier's, scholar's eye, tongue, sword:
155   The expectancy and rose of the fair state,
The glass of fashion and the mould of form,
The observ'd of all observers,—quite, quite down!
And I, of ladies most deject and wretched
That suck'd the honey of his music vows,
160   Now see that noble and most sovereign reason,
Like sweet bells jangled, out of tune and harsh;
That unmatch'd form and feature of blown[8] youth
Blasted with ecstasy: O, woe is me,
To have seen what I have seen, see what I see!

Re-enter King and Polonius.

165 KING: Love! his affections do not that way tend;
Nor what he spake, though it lack'd form a little,
Was not like madness. There's something in his soul

---

[8]*blown:* Full-blown.

O'er which his melancholy sits on brood;
And I do doubt[9] the hatch and the disclose
Will be some danger: which for to prevent,   170
I have in quick determination
Thus set it down:—he shall with speed to England
For the demand of our neglected tribute:
Haply, the seas and countries different,
With variable objects, shall expel   175
This something-settled matter in his heart;
Whereon his brains still beating puts him thus
From fashion of himself. What think you on't?
POLONIUS: It shall do well: but yet do I believe
The origin and commencement of his grief   180
Sprung from neglected love.—How now, Ophelia!
You need not tell us what Lord Hamlet said;
We heard it all.—My lord, do as you please;
But if you hold it fit, after the play,
Let his queen mother all alone entreat him   185
To show his grief: let her be round with him;
And I'll be plac'd, so please you, in the ear
Of all their conference. If she finds him not,[10]
To England send him; or confine him where
Your wisdom best shall think.   190
KING: It shall be so:
Madness in great ones must not unwatch'd go.

Exeunt.

SCENE 2

A hall in the castle.

Enter Hamlet and certain Players.

HAMLET: Speak the speech, I pray you, as I pronounced it to you, trip-
pingly on the tongue: but if you mouth it, as many of your players
do, I had as lief the town-crier spoke my lines. Nor do not saw the
air too much with your hand, thus; but use all gently: for in the
very torrent, tempest, and, as I may say, the whirlwind of passion,   5
you must acquire and beget a temperance that may give it smooth-
ness. O, it offends me to the soul, to hear a robustious periwigpated
fellow tear a passion to tatters, to very rags, to split the ears
of the groundlings, who, for the most part, are capable of nothing

---

[9]*doubt:* Fear.   [10]*finds him not:* Does not find him out.

10 but inexplicable dumb shows and noise: I could have such a fellow
whipped for o'erdoing Termagant;[1] it out-herods Herod:[2] pray you,
avoid it.

1ST PLAYER: I warrant your honor.

HAMLET: Be not too tame neither, but let your own discretion be your
15 tutor; suit the action to the word, the word to the action; with this
special observance, that you o'erstep not the modesty of nature: for
anything so overdone is from the purpose of playing, whose end,
both at the first and now, was and is, to hold, as 'twere, the mirror
up to nature; to show virtue her own feature, scorn her own image,
20 and the very age and body of the time his form and pressure. Now,
this overdone or come tardy off, though it make the unskilful laugh,
cannot but make the judicious grieve; the censure of the which one
must, in your allowance, o'erweigh a whole theater of others. O,
there be players that I have seen play,—and heard others praise,
25 and that highly,—not to speak it profanely, that, neither having
the accent of Christians, nor the gait of Christian, pagan, nor man,
have so strutted and bellowed that I have thought some of nature's
journeymen had made men, and not made them well, they imitated
humanity so abominably.

30 1ST PLAYER: I hope we have reformed that indifferently with us, sir.

HAMLET: O, reform it altogether. And let those that play your clowns
speak no more than is set down for them: for there be of them that
will themselves laugh, to set on some quantity of barren spectators
to laugh too; though, in the meantime, some necessary question
35 of the play be then to be considered: that's villainous, and shows a
most pitiful ambition in the fool that uses it. Go, make you ready.

Exeunt Players.

Enter Polonius, Rosencrantz, and Guildenstern.

How now, my lord! will the king hear this piece of work?

POLONIUS: And the queen, too, and that presently.

HAMLET: Bid the players make haste.

Exit Polonius.

40 Will you two help to hasten them?

ROSENCRANTZ AND GUILDENSTERN: We will, my lord. [*Exeunt.*]

HAMLET: What, ho, Horatio!

Enter Horatio.

---

[1]*Termagant:* A violent pagan deity, supposedly Mohammedan. [2]*out-herods Herod:* Outrants the
ranting Herod, who figures in medieval drama.

HORATIO: Here, sweet lord, at your service.

HAMLET: Horatio, thou art e'en as just a man
    As e'er my conversation cop'd withal.   45

HORATIO: O, my dear lord,—

HAMLET: Nay, do not think I flatter;
    For what advancement may I hope from thee,
    That no revénue hast, but thy good spirits,
    To feed and clothe thee? Why should the poor be flatter'd?   50
    No, let the candied tongue lick ábsurd pomp;
    And crook the pregnant hinges of the knee
    Where thrift may follow fawning. Dost thou hear?
    Since my dear soul was mistress of her choice,
    And could of men distinguish, her election   55
    Hath seal'd thee for herself: for thou hast been
    As one, in suffering all, that suffers nothing;
    A man that Fortune's buffets and rewards
    Hast ta'en with equal thanks: and bless'd are those
    Whose blood and judgment are so well commingled   60
    That they are not a pipe for Fortune's finger
    To sound what stop she please. Give me that man
    That is not passion's slave, and I will wear him
    In my heart's core, ay, in my heart of heart,
    As I do thee.—Something too much of this.—   65
    There is a play to-night before the king;
    One scene of it comes near the circumstance
    Which I have told thee of my father's death:
    I pr'ythee, when thou see'st that act a-foot,
    Even with the very comment of thy soul   70
    Observe mine uncle: if this his occulted guilt
    Do not itself unkennel in one speech,
    It is a damned ghost that we have seen;
    And my imaginations are as foul
    As Vulcan's stithy.[3] Give him heedful note: 75
    For I mine eyes will rivet to his face;
    And, after, we will both our judgments join
    In censure of his seeming.

HORATIO: Well, my lord:
    If he steal aught the whilst this play is playing,   80
    And scape detecting, I will pay the theft.

HAMLET: They are coming to the play; I must be idle:[4]
    Get you a place.

---

[3] *stithy:* Smithy.   [4] *idle:* Foolish.

Danish march. A flourish. Enter King, Queen, Polonius, Ophelia, Rosen-crantz, Guildenstern, and others.

KING: How fares our cousin Hamlet?

85 HAMLET: Excellent, i'faith; of the chameleon's dish: I eat the air,[5] promise-crammed: you cannot feed capons so.

KING: I have nothing with this answer, Hamlet; these words are not mine.

HAMLET: No, nor mine now. [*To Polonius*] My lord, you played once i' the university, you say?

90 POLONIUS: That did I, my lord, and was accounted a good actor.

HAMLET: And what did you enact?

POLONIUS: I did enact Julius Caesar: I was killed i' the Capitol; Brutus killed me.

HAMLET: It was a brute part of him to kill so capital a calf there.—Be
95 the players ready.

ROSENCRANTZ: Ay, my lord; they stay upon your patience.

QUEEN: Come hither, my good Hamlet, sit by me.

HAMLET: No, good mother, here's metal more attractive.

POLONIUS: O, ho! do you mark that? [*To the King*]

100 HAMLET: Lady, shall I lie in your lap? [*Lying down at Ophelia's feet*]

OPHELIA: No, my lord.

HAMLET: I mean, my head upon your lap?

OPHELIA: Ay, my lord.

HAMLET: Do you think I meant country matters?

105 OPHELIA: I think nothing, my lord.

HAMLET: That's a fair thought to lie between maids' legs.

OPHELIA: What is, my lord?

HAMLET: Nothing.

OPHELIA: You are merry, my lord.

110 HAMLET: Who, I?

OPHELIA: Ay, my lord.

HAMLET: O, your only jig-maker. What should a man do but be merry? for, look you, how cheerfully my mother looks, and my father died within's two hours.

115 OPHELIA: Nay, 'tis twice two months, my lord.

HAMLET: So long? Nay, then, let the devil wear black, for I'll have a suit of sables. O heavens! die two months ago, and not forgotten yet? Then there's hope a great man's memory may outlive his life half a year: but, by'r lady, he must build churches, then; or else shall he
120 suffer not thinking on, with the hobby-horse, whose epitaph is, *For, O, for, O, the hobby-horse is forgot.*

---

[5]*of the chameleon's . . . the air:* Chameleons were believed to live on air.

Trumpets sound. The dumb show enters.

Enter a King and a Queen, very lovingly; the Queen embracing him and he her. She kneels, and makes show of protestation unto him. He takes her up, and declines his head upon her neck: lays him down upon a bank of flowers: she, seeing him asleep, leaves him. Anon comes in a fellow, takes off his crown, kisses it, and pours poison in the King's ears, and exit. The Queen returns; finds the King dead, and makes passionate action. The Poisoner, with some two or three Mutes, comes in again, seeming to lament with her. The dead body is carried away. The Poisoner woos the Queen with gifts: she seems loth and unwilling awhile, but in the end accepts his love.

Exeunt.

OPHELIA: What means this, my lord?

HAMLET: Marry, this is miching mallecho;[6] it means mischief.

OPHELIA: Belike this show imports the argument of the play.

Enter Prologue.

HAMLET: We shall know by this fellow: the players cannot keep counsel; 125
they'll tell all.

OPHELIA: Will he tell us what this show meant?

HAMLET: Ay, or any show that you'll show him: be not you ashamed to
show, he'll not shame to tell you what it means.

OPHELIA: You are naught, you are naught: I'll mark the play.   130

PROLOGUE:
>   For us, and for our tragedy,
>   Here stooping to your clemency,
>   We beg your hearing patiently.

HAMLET: Is this a prologue, or the posy[7] of a ring?   135

OPHELIA: 'Tis brief, my lord.

HAMLET: As woman's love.

Enter a King and a Queen.

PROLOGUE KING: Full thirty times hath Phoebus' cart gone round
>   Neptune's salt wash and Tellus' orbed ground,[8]
>   And thirty dozen moons with borrow'd sheen   140
>   About the world have times twelve thirties been,
>   Since love our hearts, and Hymen did our hands
>   Unite commutual in most sacred bands.

PROLOGUE QUEEN: So many journeys may the sun and moon
>   Make us again count o'er ere love be done!   145

---

[6]*miching mallecho:* A sneaking misdeed.   [7]*posy:* Motto or inscription.   [8]*orbed ground:* The globe.

But, woe is me, you are so sick of late,
So far from cheer and from your former state
That I distrust you.⁹ Yet, though I distrust,
Discomfort you, my lord, it nothing must:
150   For women's fear and love holds quantity,¹⁰
In neither aught, or in extremity.
Now, what my love is, proof hath made you know;
And as my love is siz'd, my fear is so:
Where love is great, the littlest doubts are fear;
155   Where little fears grow great, great love grows there.
PROLOGUE KING: Faith, I must leave thee, love, and shortly too;
My operant powers their functions leave¹¹ to do:
And thou shalt live in this fair world behind,
Honor'd, belov'd; and haply one as kind
160   For husband shalt thou,—
PROLOGUE QUEEN: O, confound the rest!
Such love must needs be treason in my breast:
In second husband let me be accurst!
None wed the second but who kill'd the first.
165   HAMLET: [*Aside*] Wormwood, wormwood.
PROLOGUE QUEEN: The instances that second marriage move
Are base respects of thrift, but none of love:
A second time I kill my husband, dead,
When second husband kisses me in bed.
170   PROLOGUE KING: I do believe you think what now you speak;
But what we do determine oft we break.
Purpose is but the slave to memory;
Of violent birth, but poor validity:
Which now, like fruit unripe, sticks on the tree;
175   But fall unshaken when they mellow be.
Most necessary 'tis that we forget
To pay ourselves what to ourselves is debt:
What to ourselves in passion we propose,
The passion ending, doth the purpose lose.
180   The violence of either grief or joy
Their own enactures with themselves destroy:
Where joy most revels grief doth most lament;
Grief joys, joy grieves, on slender accident.
This world is not for aye; nor 'tis not strange
185   That even our loves should with our fortunes change;
For 'tis a question left us yet to prove

---

⁹*distrust you:* Worry about you.   ¹⁰*holds quantity:* Correspond in degree.   ¹¹*leave:* Cease.

Whether love lead fortune or else fortune love.
The great man down, you mark his favorite flies;
The poor advanc'd makes friends of enemies.
And hitherto doth love on fortune tend: 190
For who not needs shall never lack a friend;
And who in want a hollow friend doth try,
Directly seasons him his enemy.
But, orderly to end where I begun,—
Our wills and fates do so contrary run   195
That our devices still are overthrown;
Our thoughts are ours, their ends none of our own:
So think thou wilt no second husband wed;
But die thy thoughts when thy first lord is dead.

PROLOGUE QUEEN: Nor earth to me give food, nor heaven light!   200
Sport and repose lock from me day and night!
To desperation turn my trust and hope!
An anchor's[12] cheer in prison be my scope!
Each opposite, that blanks the face of joy,
Meet what I would have well, and it destroy!   205
Both here and hence, pursue me lasting strife,
If, once a widow, ever I be wife!

HAMLET: If she should break it now! [*To Ophelia*]

PROLOGUE KING: 'Tis deeply sworn. Sweet, leave me here awhile;
My spirits grow dull, and fain I would beguile   210
The tedious day with sleep. [*Sleeps*]

PROLOGUE QUEEN: Sleep rock thy brain,
And never come mischance between us twain! [*Exit.*]

HAMLET: Madam, how like you this play?

QUEEN: The lady doth protest too much, methinks.   215

HAMLET: O, but she'll keep her word.

KING: Have you heard the argument? Is there no offence in't?

HAMLET: No, no, they do but jest, poison in jest; no offence i' the world.

KING: What do you call the play?

HAMLET: The Mouse-trap. Marry, how? Tropically.[13] This play is the   220
image of a murder done in Vienna: Gonzago is the duke's name: his
wife, Baptista: you shall see anon; 'tis a knavish piece of work: but
what o' that? your majesty, and we that have free souls, it touches us
not: let the galled jade wince, our withers are unwrung.

Enter Lucianus.

---

[12]*anchor's:* Anchorite's, or hermit's.
[13]*Tropically:* Figuratively, or metaphorically; by means of a "trope."

225   This is one Lucianus, nephew to the king.

OPHELIA: You are a good chorus, my lord.

HAMLET: I could interpret between you and your love, if I could see the puppets dallying.

OPHELIA: You are keen, my lord, you are keen.

230 HAMLET: It would cost you a groaning to take off my edge.

OPHELIA: Still better, and worse.

HAMLET: So you must take your husbands.—Begin, murderer; pox, leave thy damnable faces and begin. Come:—*The croaking raven doth bellow for revenge.*

235 LUCIANUS: Thoughts black, hands apt, drugs fit, and time agreeing;
Confederate season, else no creature seeing;
Thou mixture rank, of midnight weeds collected,
With Hecate's ban[14] thrice blasted, thrice infected,
Thy natural magic and dire property
240   On wholesome life usurp immediately.

Pours the poison into the sleeper's ears.

HAMLET: He poisons him i' the garden for's estate. His name's Gonzago: the story is extant, and writ in choice Italian: you shall see anon how the murderer gets the love of Gonzago's wife.

OPHELIA: The king rises.

245 HAMLET: What, frighted with false fire!

QUEEN: How fares my lord?

POLONIUS: Give o'er the play.

KING: Give me some light:—away!

ALL: Lights, lights, lights!

Exeunt all but Hamlet and Horatio.

250 HAMLET:

Why, let the stricken deer go weep,
The hart ungalled play;
For some must watch, while some must sleep:
So runs the world away.—

255   Would not this, sir, and a forest of feathers, if the rest of my fortunes turn Turk with me, with two Provencial roses on my razed shoes, get me a fellowship in a cry[15] of players, sir?

HORATIO: Half a share.

HAMLET: A whole one, I.

260   For thou dost know, O Damon dear,
This realm dismantled was

---

[14]*Hecate's ban:* The spell of the goddess of witchcraft.   [15]*cry:* Company.

> Of Jove himself; and now reigns here
> A very, very—pajock.[16]

HORATIO: You might have rhymed.

HAMLET: O good Horatio, I'll take the ghost's word for a thousand   265
pound. Didst perceive?

HORATIO: Very well, my lord.

HAMLET: Upon the talk of the poisoning,—

HORATIO: I did very well note him.

HAMLET: Ah, ha!—Come, some music! come, the recorders!—   270

> For if the king like not the comedy,
> Why, then, belike,—he likes it not, perdy.

Come, some music!

Re-enter Rosencrantz and Guildenstern.

GUILDENSTERN: Good my lord, vouchsafe me a word with you.

HAMLET: Sir, a whole history.   275

GUILDENSTERN: The king, sir,—

HAMLET: Ay, sir, what of him?

GUILDENSTERN: Is, in his retirement, marvelous distempered.

HAMLET: With drink, sir?

GUILDENSTERN: No, my lord, rather with choler.   280

HAMLET: Your wisdom should show itself more richer to signify this to
his doctor; for, for me to put him to his purgation would perhaps
plunge him into far more choler.

GUILDENSTERN: Good my lord, put your discourse into some frame, and
start not so wildly from my affair.   285

HAMLET: I am tame, sir:—pronounce.

GUILDENSTERN: The queen, your mother, in most great affliction of
spirit, hath sent me to you.

HAMLET: You are welcome.

GUILDENSTERN: Nay, good my lord, this courtesy is not of the right   290
breed. If it shall please you to make me a wholesome answer, I will
do you mother's commandment: if not, your pardon and my return
shall be the end of my business.

HAMLET: Sir, I cannot.

GUILDENSTERN: What, my lord?   295

HAMLET: Make you a wholesome answer; my wit's diseas'd: but, sir, such
answer as I can make, you shall command; or, rather, as you say, my
mother: therefore no more, but to the matter: my mother, you say,—

---

[16]pajock: Peacock.

ROSENCRANTZ: Then thus she says: your behavior hath struck her into
300   amazement and admiration.

HAMLET: O wonderful son, that can so astonish a mother!—But is there
no sequel at the heels of this mother's admiration?

ROSENCRANTZ: She desires to speak with you in her closet[17] ere you go
to bed.

305 HAMLET: We shall obey, were she ten times our mother. Have you any
further trade with us?

ROSENCRANTZ: My lord, you once did love me.

HAMLET: So I do still, by these pickers and stealers.[18]

ROSENCRANTZ: Good, my lord, what is your cause of distemper? you do,
310   surely, bar the door upon your own liberty if you deny your griefs to
your friend.

HAMLET: Sir, I lack advancement.

ROSENCRANTZ: How can that be, when you have the voice of the king
himself for your succession in Denmark?

315 HAMLET: Ay, but While the grass grows,—the proverb is something musty.

Re-enter the Players, with recorders.

O, the recorders:—let me see one.—To withdraw with you:—why
do you go about to recover the wind of me, as if you would drive me
into a toil?

GUILDENSTERN: O, my lord, if my duty be too bold, my love is too
320   unmannerly.

HAMLET: I do not well understand that. Will you play upon this pipe?

GUILDENSTERN: My lord, I cannot.

HAMLET: I pray you.

GUILDENSTERN: Believe me, I cannot.

325 HAMLET: I do beseech you.

GUILDENSTERN: I know no touch of it, my lord.

HAMLET: 'Tis as easy as lying: govern these ventages[19] with your finger
and thumb, give it breath with your mouth, and it will discourse
most eloquent music. Look you, these are the stops.

330 GUILDENSTERN: But these cannot I command to any utterance of
harmony; I have not the skill.

HAMLET: Why, look you now, how unworthy a thing you make of me!
You would play upon me; you would seem to know my stops; you
would pluck out the heart of my mystery; you would sound me from
335   my lowest note to the top of my compass: and there is much music,
excellent voice, in this little organ; yet cannot you make it speak.
'Sblood, do you think that I am easier to be played on than a pipe?

---

[17]*closet:* Boudoir.   [18]*pickers and stealers:* Fingers.   [19]*ventages:* Holes.

Call me what instrument you will, though you can fret me you cannot play upon me.

Enter Polonius.

God bless you, sir!   340

POLONIUS: My lord, the queen would speak with you, and presently.

HAMLET: Do you see yonder cloud that's almost in shape of a camel?

POLONIUS: By the mass, and 'tis like a camel indeed.

HAMLET: Methinks it is like a weasel.

POLONIUS: It is backed like a weasel.   345

HAMLET: Or like a whale?

POLONIUS: Very like a whale.

HAMLET: Then will I come to my mother by and by.—They fool me to
the top of my bent.—I will come by and by.

POLONIUS: I will say so.   350

HAMLET: By and by is easily said.

Exit Polonius.

Leave me, friends.

Exeunt Rosencrantz, Guildenstern, Horatio, and Players.

'Tis now the very witching time of night,
When churchyards yawn, and hell itself breathes out
Contagion to this world: now could I drink hot blood,   355
And do such bitter business as the day
Would quake to look on. Soft! now to my mother.—
O heart, lose not thy nature; let not ever
The soul of Nero[20] enter this firm bosom:
Let me be cruel, not unnatural: 360
I will speak daggers to her, but use none;
My tongue and soul in this be hypocrites,—
How in my words soever she be shent,
To give them seals never, my soul, consent! [*Exit.*]

SCENE 3

A room in the castle.

Enter King, Rosencrantz, and Guildenstern.

KING: I like him not; nor stands it safe with us
To let his madness range. Therefore prepare you;
I your commission with forthwith despatch,

---

[20] *Nero:* The Roman emperor Nero killed his mother, a crime of which Hamlet does not want to be guilty.

And he to England shall along with you:
5   The terms of our estate may not endure
Hazard so dangerous as doth hourly grow
Out of his lunacies.
   GUILDENSTERN: We will ourselves provide:
Most holy and religious fear it is
10   To keep those many many bodies safe
That live and feed upon your majesty.
   ROSENCRANTZ: The single and peculiar life is bound,
With all the strength and armor of the mind,
To keep itself from 'noyance; but much more
15   That spirit upon whose weal depend and rest
The lives of many. The cease of majesty
Dies not alone; but like a gulf doth draw
What's near it with it: it is a massy wheel,
Fix'd on the summit of the highest mount,
20   To whose huge spokes ten thousand lesser things
Are mortis'd and adjoin'd; which, when it falls,
Each small annexment, petty consequence,
Attends the boisterous ruin. Never alone
Did the king sigh, but with a general groan.
25 KING: Arm you, I pray you, to this speedy voyage;
For we will fetters put upon this fear,
Which now goes too free-footed.
   ROSENCRANTZ AND GUILDENSTERN: We will haste us.

Exeunt Rosencrantz and Guildenstern.

Enter Polonius.

   POLONIUS: My lord, he's going to his mother's closet:
30   Behind the arras I'll convey myself
To hear the process; I'll warrant she'll tax him home:[1]
And, as you said, and wisely was it said,
'Tis meet that some more audience than a mother,
Since nature makes them partial, should o'erhear
35   The speech, of vantage. Fare you well, my liege:
I'll call upon you ere you go to bed,
And tell you what I know.
   KING: Thanks, dear my lord.

Exit Polonius.

---

[1]*tax him home:* Reprove him properly.

O, my offence is rank, it smells to heaven;
It hath the primal eldest curse upon't,—   40
A brother's murder!—Pray can I not,
Though inclination be as sharp as will:
My stronger guilt defeats my strong intent;
And, like a man to double business bound,
I stand in pause where I shall first begin,   45
And both neglect. What if this cursed hand
Were thicker than itself with brother's blood,—
Is there not rain enough in the sweet heavens
To wash it white as snow? Whereto serves mercy
But to confront the visage of offence?   50
And what's in prayer but this twofold force,—
To be forestalled ere we come to fall,
Or pardon'd being down? Then I'll look up;
My fault is past. But, O, what form of prayer
Can serve my turn? Forgive me my foul murder?—   55
That cannot be; since I am still possess'd
Of those effects for which I did the murder,—
My crown, mine own ambition, and my queen.
May one be pardon'd and retain the offence?[2]
In the corrupted currents of this world   60
Offence's gilded hand may shove by justice;
And oft 'tis seen the wicked prize itself
Buys out the law: but 'tis not so above;
There is no shuffling,—there the action lies
In his true nature; and we ourselves compell'd,   65
Even to the teeth and forehead of our faults,
To give in evidence. What then? what rests?[3]
Try what repentance can: what can it not?
Yet what can it when one can not repent?
O wretched state! O bosom black as death!   70
O limed[4] soul, that, struggling to be free,
Art more engag'd! Help, angels! make assay:
Bow, stubborn knees; and, heart, with strings of steel,
Be soft as sinews of the new-born babe!
All may be well. [*Retires and kneels*]   75

Enter Hamlet.

HAMLET: Now might I do it pat, now he is praying;
And now I'll do't—and so he goes to heaven;

---

[2] *retain the offence:* Retain the gains won by the offense.   [3] *rests:* Remains.   [4] *limed:* Snared.

And so am I reveng'd:—that would be scann'd:
A villain kills my father; and for that,
80 I, his sole son, do this same villain send
To heaven.
O, this is hire and salary, not revenge.
He took my father grossly, full of bread;
With all his crimes broad blown, as flush as May;
85 And how his audit stands who knows save heaven?
But in our circumstance and course of thought
'Tis heavy with him: and am I, then, reveng'd,
To take him in the purging of his soul,
When he is fit and season'd for his passage?
90 No.
Up, sword; and know thou a more horrid hent:[5]
When he is drunk, asleep, or in his rage;
Or in the incestuous pleasure of his bed;
At gaming, swearing; or about some act
95 That has no relish of salvation in't;—
Then trip him, that his heels may kick at heaven;
And that his soul may be as damn'd and black
As hell, whereto it goes. My mother stays:
This physic but prolongs thy sickly days. [*Exit.*]

The King rises and advances.

100 KING: My words fly up, my thoughts remain below:
Words without thoughts never to heaven go. [*Exit.*]

SCENE 4

Another room in the castle.

Enter Queen and Polonius.

POLONIUS: He will come straight. Look you lay home to him:
Tell him his pranks have been too broad to bear with,
And that your grace hath screen'd and stood between
Much heat and him. I'll silence me e'en here.
5 Pray you, be round with him.
HAMLET: [*Within*] Mother, mother, mother!
QUEEN: I'll warrant you:
Fear me not:—withdraw, I hear him coming.

Polonius goes behind the arras.

Enter Hamlet.

---

[5]*hent:* Opportunity.

HAMLET: Now, mother, what's the matter?

QUEEN: Hamlet, thou hast thy father much offended.   10

HAMLET: Mother, you have my father much offended.

QUEEN: Come, come, you answer with an idle tongue.

HAMLET: Go, go, you question with a wicked tongue.

QUEEN: Why, how now, Hamlet!

HAMLET: What's the matter now?   15

QUEEN: Have you forgot me?

HAMLET: No, by the rood, not so:
   You are the queen, your husband's brother's wife;
   And,—would it were not so!—you are my mother.

QUEEN: Nay, then, I'll set those to you that can speak.   20

HAMLET: Come, come, and sit you down; you shall not budge;
   You go not till I set you up a glass
   Where you may see the inmost part of you.

QUEEN: What wilt thou do? thou wilt not murder me?—
   Help, help, ho!   25

POLONIUS: [*Behind*] What, ho! help, help, help!

HAMLET: How now! a rat?
   [*Draws.*]
   Dead, for a ducat, dead! [*Makes a pass through the arras*]

POLONIUS: [*Behind*] O, I am slain! [*Falls and dies.*]   30

QUEEN: O me, what hast thou done?

HAMLET: Nay, I know not:
   Is it the king? [*Draws forth Polonius*]

QUEEN: O, what a rash and bloody deed is this!

HAMLET: A bloody deed!—almost as bad, good mother,   35
   As kill a king and marry with his brother.

QUEEN: As kill a king!

HAMLET: Ay, lady, 'twas my word.—
   Thou wretched, rash, intruding fool, farewell! [*To Polonius*]
   I took thee for thy better: take thy fortune;   40
   Thou find'st to be too busy is some danger.—
   Leave wringing of your hands: peace; sit you down,
   And let me wring your heart: for so I shall,
   If it be made of penetrable stuff;
   If damned custom have not braz'd it so   45
   That it is proof and bulwark against sense.

QUEEN: What have I done, that thou dar'st wag thy tongue
   In noise so rude against me?

HAMLET: Such an act
   That blurs the grace and blush of modesty;   50
   Calls virtue hypocrite; takes off the rose

From the fair forehead of an innocent love,
And sets a blister there; makes marriage-vows
As false as dicers' oaths: O, such a deed
55 As from the body of contraction plucks
The very soul, and sweet religion makes
A rhapsody of words: heaven's face doth glow;
Yea, this solidity and compound mass,
With tristful[1] visage, as against the doom,
60 Is thought-sick at the act.
QUEEN: Ah me, what act,
That roars so loud, and thunders in the index?
HAMLET: Look here upon this picture and on this,—
The counterfeit presentment of two brothers.
65 See what grace was seated on this brow;
Hyperion's curls; the front of Jove himself;
An eye like Mars, to threaten and command;
A station like the herald Mercury
New-lighted on a heaven-kissing hill;
70 A combination and a form, indeed,
Where every god did seem to set his seal,
To give the world assurance of a man:
This was your husband.—Look you now, what follows:
Here is your husband, like a mildew'd ear
75 Blasting his wholesome brother. Have you eyes?
Could you on this fair mountain leave to feed,
And batten on this moor? Ha! have you eyes?
You cannot call it love; for at your age
The hey-day in the blood is tame, it's humble,
80 And waits upon the judgment: and what judgment
Would step from this to this? Sense, sure, you have,
Else could you not have motion: but sure that sense
Is apoplex'd: for madness would not err;
Nor sense to ecstasy was ne'er so thrill'd
85 But it reserv'd some quantity of choice
To serve in such a difference. What devil was't
That thus hath cozen'd you at hoodman-blind?[2]
Eyes without feeling, feeling without sight,
Ears without hand or eyes, smelling sans all,
90 Or but a sickly part of one true sense
Could not so mope.
O shame! where is thy blush! Rebellious hell,

---

[1]*tristful:* Gloomy.   [2]*cozen'd . . . hoodman-blind:* Tricked you at blindman's buff.

If thou canst mutine in a matron's bones,
To flaming youth let virtue be as wax,
And melt in her own fire: proclaim no shame   95
When the compulsive ardor gives the charge,
Since frost itself as actively doth burn,
And reason panders[3] will.

QUEEN: O Hamlet, speak no more:
Thou turn'st mine eyes into my very soul;   100
And there I see such black and grained spots
As will not leave their tinct.[4]

HAMLET: Nay, but to live
In the rank sweat of an enseamed bed,
Stew'd in corruption, honeying and making love   105
Over the nasty sty,—

QUEEN: O, speak to me no more;
These words like daggers enter in mine ears;
No more, sweet Hamlet.

HAMLET: A murderer and a villain; 110
A slave that is not twentieth part the tithe
Of your precedent lord; a vice of kings;[5]
A cutpurse of the empire and the rule,
That from a shelf the precious diadem stole,
And put it in his pocket!   115

QUEEN: No more.

HAMLET: A king of shreds and patches,—

Enter Ghost.

Save me, and hover o'er me with your wings,
You heavenly guards!—What would your gracious figure?

QUEEN: Alas, he's mad!   120

HAMLET: Do you not come your tardy son to chide,
That, laps'd in time and passion, lets go by
The important acting of your dread command?
O, say!

GHOST: Do not forget: this visitation   125
Is but to whet thy almost blunted purpose.
But, look, amazement on thy mother sits:
O, step between her and her fighting soul,—
Conceit in weakest bodies strongest works,—
Speak to her, Hamlet.   130

---

[3]*panders:* Becomes subservient to.   [4]*As will not . . . tinct:* As will not yield up their color.
[5]*a vice of kings:* A buffoon among kings; the character "Vice" in morality plays.

HAMLET: How is it with you, lady?
QUEEN: Alas, how is't with you,
          That you do bend your eye on vacancy,
          And with the incorporal air do hold discourse?
135   Forth at your eyes your spirits wildly peep;
          And, as the sleeping soldiers in the alarm,
          Your bedded hair, like life in excrements,[6]
          Starts up and stands on end. O gentle son,
          Upon the heat and flame of thy distemper
140   Sprinkle cool patience. Whereon do you look?
HAMLET: On him, on him! Look you, how pale he glares!
          His form and cause conjoin'd, preaching to stones,
          Would make them capable.—Do not look upon me;
          Lest with this piteous action you convert
145   My stern effects: then what I have to do
          Will want true color; tears perchance for blood.
QUEEN: To whom do you speak this?
HAMLET: Do you see nothing there?
QUEEN: Nothing at all; yet all that is I see.
150 HAMLET: Nor did you nothing hear?
QUEEN: No, nothing but ourselves.
HAMLET: Why, look you there! look, how it steals away!
          My father, in his habit as he liv'd!
          Look, where he goes, even now, out at the portal!

Exit Ghost.

155 QUEEN: This is the very coinage of your brain:
          This bodiless creation ecstasy
          Is very cunning in.
HAMLET: Ecstasy!
          My pulse, as yours, doth temperately keep time.
160   And makes as healthful music: it is not madness
          That I have utter'd: bring me to the test,
          And I the matter will re-word; which madness
          Would gambol from. Mother, for love of grace,
          Lay not that flattering unction to your soul,
165   That not your trespass, but my madness speaks:
          It will but skin and film the ulcerous place,
          Whilst rank corruption, mining all within,
          Infects unseen. Confess yourself to Heaven;
          Repent what's past; avoid what is to come;

---

[6]*in excrements:* In outgrowths or extremities.

And do not spread the compost on the weeds,   170
To make them ranker. Forgive me this my virtue;
For in the fatness[7] of these pursy times
Virtue itself of vice must pardon beg,
Yea, curb and woo for leave to do him good.
QUEEN: O Hamlet, thou hast cleft my heart in twain.   175
HAMLET: O, throw away the worser part of it,
And live the purer with the other half.
Good-night: but go not to mine uncle's bed;
Assume a virtue, if you have it not.
That monster custom, who all sense doth eat,   180
Of habits devil, is angel yet in this,—
That to the use of actions fair and good
He likewise gives a frock or livery
That aptly is put on. Refrain to-night;
And that shall lend a kind of easiness   185
To the next abstinence: the next more easy;
For use almost can change the stamp of nature,
And either curb the devil, or throw him out
With wondrous potency. Once more, good-night:
And when you are desirous to be bless'd,   190
I'll blessing beg of you.—For this same lord [*pointing to Polonius*]
I do repent: but Heaven hath pleas'd it so,
To punish me with this, and this with me,
That I must be their[8] scourge and minister.
I will bestow him, and will answer well   195
The death I gave him. So, again, good-night.—
I must be cruel only to be kind:
Thus bad begins and worse remains behind.—
One word more, good lady.
QUEEN: What shall I do?   200
HAMLET: Not this, by no means, that I bid you do:
Let the bloat king tempt you again to bed;
Pinch wanton on your cheek; call you his mouse;
And let him, for a pair of reechy kisses,
Or paddling in your neck with his damn'd fingers,   205
Make you to ravel all this matter out,
That I essentially am not in madness,
But mad in craft. 'Twere good you let him know;
For who that's but a queen, fair, sober, wise,

---

[7] *fatness:* Corruption.   [8] *their:* Heaven's, or the heavens'.

210   Would from a paddock,[9] from a bat, a gib,[10]
    Such dear concernings hide? who would do so?
    No, in despite of sense and secrecy,
    Unpeg the basket on the house's top,
    Let the birds fly, and, like the famous ape,
215   To try conclusions, in the basket creep,
    And break your own neck down.
  QUEEN: Be thou assur'd, if words be made of breath
    And breath of life, I have not life to breathe
    What thou hast said to me.
220 HAMLET: I must to England; you know that?
  QUEEN: Alack,
    I had forgot: 'tis so concluded on.
  HAMLET: There's letters seal'd: and my two school-fellows,—
    Whom I will trust as I will adders fang'd,
225   They bear the mandate; they must sweep my way,
    And marshal me to knavery. Let it work;
    For 'tis the sport to have the engineer
    Hoist with his own petard: and't shall go hard
    But I will delve one yard below their mines,
230   And blow them at the moon: O, 'tis most sweet,
    When in one line two crafts directly meet.—
    This man shall set me packing:
    I'll lug the guts into the neighbor room.—
    Mother, good-night.—Indeed, this counsellor
235   Is now most still, most secret, and most grave,
    Who was in life a foolish prating knave.
    Come, sir, to draw toward an end with you:—
    Good-night, mother.

Exeunt severally; Hamlet dragging out Polonius.

ACT 4
SCENE 1

A room in the castle.

Enter King, Queen, Rosencrantz, and Guildenstern.

  KING: There's matter in these sighs, these prófound heaves:
    You must translate: 'tis fit we understand them.
    Where is your son?
  QUEEN: Bestow this place on us a little while. [*To Rosencrantz and*
5   *Guildenstern, who go out*]

---

[9]*paddock:* Toad.   [10]*gib:* Tomcat.

Ah, my good lord, what have I seen to-night!
KING: What, Gertrude? How does Hamlet?
QUEEN: Mad as the sea and wind, when both contend
    Which is the mightier: in his lawless fit,
    Behind the arras hearing something stir,   10
    He whips his rapier out, and cries, A *rat, a rat*!
    And, in this brainish apprehension,[1] kills
    The unseen good old man.
KING: O heavy deed!
    It had been so with us had we been there: 15
    His liberty is full of threats to all;
    To you yourself, to us, to every one.
    Alas, how shall this bloody deed be answer'd?
    It will be laid to us, whose providence
    Should have kept short, restrain'd, and out of haunt   20
    This mad young man: but so much was our love,
    We would not understand what was most fit;
    But, like the owner of a foul disease,
    To keep it from divulging, let it feed
    Even on the pith of life. Where is he gone?   25
QUEEN: To draw apart the body he hath kill'd:
    O'er whom his very madness, like some ore
    Among a mineral of metals base,
    Shows itself pure; he weeps for what is done.
KING: O Gertrude, come away!   30
    The sun no sooner shall the mountains touch
    But we will ship him hence: and this vile deed
    We must, with all our majesty and skill,
    Both countenance and excuse.—Ho, Guildenstern!

Enter Rosencrantz and Guildenstern.

    Friends both, go join you with some further aid: 35
    Hamlet in madness hath Polonius slain,
    And from his mother's closet hath he dragg'd him:
    Go seek him out; speak fair, and bring the body
    Into the chapel. I pray you, haste in this.

Exeunt Rosencrantz and Guildenstern.

    Come, Gertrude, we'll call up our wisest friends;   40
    And let them know both what we mean to do
    And what's untimely done: so haply slander,—

---

[1] *brainish apprehension:* Mad notion.

Whose whisper o'er the world's diameter,
As level as the cannon to his blank,
45 Transports his poison'd shot,—may amiss our name,
And hit the woundless air.—O, come away!
My soul is full of discord and dismay.

Exeunt.

SCENE 2

Another room in the castle.

Enter Hamlet.

HAMLET: Safely stowed.
ROSENCRANTZ AND GUILDENSTERN: [*Within*] Hamlet! Lord Hamlet!
HAMLET: What noise? who calls on Hamlet?
O, here they come.

Enter Rosencrantz and Guildenstern.

5 ROSENCRANTZ: What have you done, my lord, with the dead body?
HAMLET: Compounded it with dust, whereto 'tis kin.
ROSENCRANTZ: Tell us where 'tis, that we may take it thence,
And bear it to the chapel.
HAMLET: Do not believe it.
10 ROSENCRANTZ: Believe what?
HAMLET: That I can keep your counsel, and not mine own. Besides, to
be demanded of a sponge!—what replication should be made by the
son of a king?
ROSENCRANTZ: Take you me for a sponge, my lord?
15 HAMLET: Ay, sir; that soaks up the king's countenance, his rewards, his
authorities. But such officers do the king best service in the end: he
keeps them, like an ape, in the corner of his jaw; first mouthed, to
be last swallowed: when he needs what you have gleaned, it is but
squeezing you, and, sponge, you shall be dry again.
20 ROSENCRANTZ: I understand you not, my lord.
HAMLET: I am glad of it: a knavish speech sleeps in a foolish ear.
ROSENCRANTZ: My lord, you must tell us where the body is, and go with
us to the king.
HAMLET: The body is with the king, but the king is not with the body.
25 The king is a thing,—
GUILDENSTERN: A thing, my lord!
HAMLET: Of nothing: bring me to him.
Hide fox, and all after.

Exeunt.

SCENE 3

Another room in the castle.

Enter King, attended.

KING: I have sent to seek him, and to find the body.
How dangerous is it that this man goes loose!
Yet must not we put the strong law on him:
He's lov'd of the distracted multitude,
Who like not in their judgment, but their eyes;   5
And where 'tis so, the offender's scourge is weigh'd,
But never the offence. To bear all smooth and even,
This sudden sending him away must seem
Deliberate pause: diseases desperate grown
By desperate appliance are reliev'd,   10
Or not at all.

Enter Rosencrantz.

                       How now! what hath befallen!
ROSENCRANTZ: Where the dead body is bestow'd, my lord,
   We cannot get from him.
KING: But where is he?   15
ROSENCRANTZ: Without, my lord; guarded, to know your pleasure.
KING: Bring him before us.
ROSENCRANTZ: Ho, Guildenstern! bring in my lord.

Enter Hamlet and Guildenstern.

KING: Now, Hamlet, where's Polonius?
HAMLET: At supper.   20
KING: At supper! where?
HAMLET: Not where he eats, but where he is eaten: a certain convo-
   cation of politic worms are e'en at him. Your worm is your only
   emperor for diet: we fat all creatures else to fat us, and we fat
   ourselves for maggots: your fat king and your lean beggar is but   25
   variable service,—two dishes, but to one table: that's the end.
KING: Alas, alas!
HAMLET: A man may fish with the worm that hath eat of a king, and
   eat of the fish that hath fed of that worm.
KING: What does thou mean by this?   30
HAMLET: Nothing but to show you how a king may go a progress
   through the guts of a beggar.
KING: Where is Polonius?
HAMLET: In heaven; send thither to see: if your messenger find him not
   there, seek him i' the other place yourself. But, indeed, if you find   35

him not within this month, you shall nose him as you go up the
stairs into the lobby.
KING: Go seek him there. [*To some Attendants*]
HAMLET: He will stay till ye come.

Exeunt Attendants.

40 KING: Hamlet, this deed, for thine especial safety,—
    Which we do tender, as we dearly grieve
    For that which thou hast done,—must send thee hence
    With fiery quickness: therefore prepare thyself;
    The bark is ready, and the wind at help,
45 The associates tend, and everything is bent
    For England.
HAMLET: For England!
KING: Ay, Hamlet.
HAMLET: Good.
50 KING: So is it, if thou knew'st our purposes.
HAMLET: I see a cherub that sees them.—But, come; for England!—
    Farewell, dear mother.
KING: Thy loving father, Hamlet.
HAMLET: My mother: father and mother is man and wife; man and wife
55 is one flesh; and so, my mother.—Come, for England! [*Exit.*]
KING: Follow him at foot; tempt him with speed aboard;
    Delay it not; I'll have him hence to-night:
    Away! for everything is seal'd and done
    That else leans on the affair, pray you, make haste.

Exeunt Rosencrantz and Guildenstern.

60 And, England, if my love thou hold'st at aught,—
    As my great power thereof may give the sense,
    Since yet thy cicatrice looks raw and red
    After the Danish sword, and thy free awe
    Pays homage to us,—thou mayst not coldly set
65 Our sovereign process; which imports at full,
    By letters conjuring to that effect,
    The present death of Hamlet. Do it, England;
    For like the hectic in my blood he rages,
    And thou must cure me: till I know 'tis done,
70 Howe'er my haps, my joys will ne'er begin. [*Exit.*]

SCENE 4

A plain in Denmark.

Enter Fortinbras, and Forces marching.

FORTINBRAS: Go, from me greet the Danish king:
Tell him that, by his license, Fortinbras
Craves the conveyance of a promis'd march
Over his kingdom. You know the rendezvous,
If that his majesty would aught with us,   5
We shall express our duty in his eye,
And let him know so.
CAPTAIN: I will do't, my lord.
FORTINBRAS: Go softly on.

Exeunt Fortinbras and Forces.

Enter Hamlet, Rosencrantz, Guildenstern, &c.

HAMLET: Good sir, whose powers are these?   10
CAPTAIN: They are of Norway, sir.
HAMLET: How purpos'd, sir, I pray you?
CAPTAIN: Against some part of Poland.
HAMLET: Who commands them, sir?
CAPTAIN: The nephew to old Norway, Fortinbras.   15
HAMLET: Goes it against the main of Poland, sir,
Or for some frontier?
CAPTAIN: Truly to speak, and with no addition,
We go to gain a little patch of ground
That hath in it no profit but the name.   20
To pay five ducats, five, I would not farm it;
Nor will it yield to Norway or the Pole
A ranker[1] rate should it be sold in fee.
HAMLET: Why, then the Polack never will defend it.
CAPTAIN: Yes, it is already garrison'd.   25
HAMLET: Two thousand souls and twenty thousand ducats
Will not debate the question of this straw:
This is the imposthume[2] of much wealth and peace,
That inward breaks, and shows no cause without
Why the man dies.—I humbly thank you, sir.   30
CAPTAIN: God b' wi' you, sir. [*Exit.*]
ROSENCRANTZ: Will't please you go, my lord?
HAMLET: I'll be with you straight. Go a little before.

Exeunt all but Hamlet.

How all occasions do inform against me,
And spur my dull revenge! What is a man,   35

---

[1] *ranker:* Dearer.   [2] *imposthume:* Ulcer.

If his chief good and market of his time
Be but to sleep and feed? a beast, no more.
Sure he that made us with such large discourse,[3]
Looking before and after, gave us not
40 That capability and godlike reason
To fust[4] in us unus'd. Now, whether it be
Bestial oblivion or some craven scruple
Of thinking too precisely on the event,—
A thought which, quarter'd, hath but one part wisdom
45 And ever three parts coward,—I do not know
Why yet I live to say, *This thing's to do*;
Sith[5] I have cause, and will, and strength, and means
To do't. Examples, gross as earth, exhort me:
Witness this army, of such mass and charge,
50 Led by a delicate and tender prince;
Whose spirit, with divine ambition puff'd,
Makes mouths at the invisible event;
Exposing what is mortal and unsure
To all that fortune, death, and danger dare,
55 Even for an egg-shell. Rightly to be great
Is not to stir without great argument,
But greatly to find quarrel in a straw
When honor's at the stake. How stand I, then,
That have a father kill'd, a mother stain'd,
60 Excitements of my reason and my blood,
And let all sleep? while, to my shame, I see
The imminent death of twenty thousand men,
That, for a fantasy and trick of fame,
Go to their graves like beds; fight for a plot
65 Whereon the numbers cannot try the cause,
Which is not tomb enough and continent[6]
To hide the slain?—O, from this time forth,
My thoughts be bloody, or be nothing worth! [*Exit.*]

SCENE 5

Elsinore. A room in the castle.

Enter Queen and Horatio.

QUEEN: I will not speak with her.
HORATIO: She is importunate; indeed, distract:
Her mood will needs be pitied.

---

[3]*discourse:* Reasoning faculty.   [4]*fust:* Grow musty.   [5]*Sith:* Since.   [6]*continent:* Container.

QUEEN: What would she have?

HORATIO: She speaks much of her father; says she hears   5
  There's tricks i' the world; and hems, and beats her heart;
  Spurns enviously at straws; speaks things in doubt,
  That carry but half sense: her speech is nothing,
  Yet the unshapéd use of it doth move
  The hearers to collection; they aim at it,   10
  And botch the words up fit to their own thoughts;
  Which, as her winks, and nods, and gestures yield them,
  Indeed would make one think there might be thought,
  Though nothing sure, yet much unhappily.
  'Twere good she were spoken with; for she may strew   15
  Dangerous conjectures in ill-breeding minds.
QUEEN: Let her come in.

Exit Horatio.

  To my sick soul, as sin's true nature is,
  Each toy seems prologue to some great amiss:
  So full of artless jealousy is guilt,   20
  It spills itself in fearing to be spilt.

Re-enter Horatio and Ophelia.

OPHELIA: Where is the beauteous majesty of Denmark?
QUEEN: How now, Ophelia!
OPHELIA: [*Sings*]

    How should I your true love know   25
        From another one?
    By his cockle hat and staff,
        And his sandal shoon.

QUEEN: Alas, sweet lady, what imports this song?
OPHELIA: Say you? nay, pray you, mark.   30

[*Sings*]

    He is dead and gone, lady,
        He is dead and gone;
    At his head a grass green turf,
        At his heels a stone.

QUEEN: Nay, but, Ophelia,—   35
OPHELIA: Pray you, mark.

[*Sings*]

    White his shroud as the mountain snow,

Enter King.

Queen: Alas, look here, my lord.
Ophelia: [*Sings*]

40   Larded with sweet flowers;
        Which bewept to the grave did go
        With true-love showers.

King: How do you, pretty lady?
Ophelia: Well, God 'ild you![1] They say the owl was a baker's daughter.
45   Lord, we know what we are, but know not what we may be.
        God be at your table!
King: Conceit upon her father.
Ophelia: Pray you, let's have no words of this; but when they ask you
        what it means, say you this:

[*Sings.*]

50   To-morrow is Saint Valentine's day
            All in the morning betime,
        And I a maid at your window,
            To be your Valentine.
        Then up he rose, and donn'd his clothes,
55   And dupp'd the chamber-door;
        Let in the maid, that out a maid
            Never departed more.

King: Pretty Ophelia!
Ophelia: Indeed, la, without an oath, I'll make an end on't;

[*Sings*]

60   By Gis[2] and by Saint Charity,
            Alack, and fie for shame!
        Young men will do't, if they come to't;
            By cock, they are to blame.
        Quoth she, before you tumbled me,
65   You promis'd me to wed.
        So would I ha' done, by yonder sun,
            An thou hadst not come to my bed.

King: How long hath she been thus?
Ophelia: I hope all will be well. We must be patient: but I cannot
70   choose but weep, to think they should lay him i' the cold ground.
        My brother shall know of it: and so I thank you; for your good

---

[1] *ild you:* Yield you—i.e., reward you.   [2] *Gis:* A contraction for "by Jesus."

counsel.—Come, my coach!—Good-night, ladies; good-night,
sweet ladies; good-night, good-night. [*Exit.*]
KING: Follow her close; give her good watch, I pray you.

Exit Horatio.

O, this is the poison of deep grief; it springs   75
All from her father's death. O Gertrude, Gertrude,
When sorrows come, they come not single spies,
But in battalions! First, her father slain:
Next, your son gone; and he most violent author
Of his own just remove: the people muddied,   80
Thick and unwholesome in their thoughts and whispers
For good Polonius' death; and we have done but greenly
In hugger-mugger[3] to inter him: poor Ophelia
Divided from herself and her fair judgment,
Without the which we are pictures, or mere beasts: 85
Last, and as much containing as all these,
Her brother is in secret come from France;
Feeds on his wonder, keeps himself in clouds,
And wants not buzzers to infect his ear
With pestilent speeches of his father's death;   90
Wherein necessity, of matter beggar'd,
Will nothing stick our person to arraign
In ear and ear. O my dear Gertrude, this,
Like to a murdering piece,[4] in many places
Gives me superfluous death.   95

A noise within.

QUEEN: Alack, what noise is this?
KING: Where are my Switzers?[5] let them guard the door.

Enter a Gentleman.

What is the matter?

GENTLEMAN: Save yourself, my lord:
The ocean, overpeering of his list,   100
Eats not the flats with more impetuous haste
Than young Laertes, in a riotous head,
O'erbears your officers. The rabble call him lord;
And, as the world were now but to begin,
Antiquity forgot, custom not known,   105

---

[3] *in hugger-mugger:* In great secrecy and haste.   [4] *murdering piece:* A cannon.   [5] *Switzers:* Bodyguard
of Swiss mercenaries.

The ratifiers and props of every word,
They cry, *Choose we, Laertes shall be king!*
Caps, hands, and tongues applaud it to the clouds,
Laertes shall be king, Laertes king!

110 QUEEN: How cheerfully on the false trail they cry!
O, this is counter, you false Danish dogs!

KING: The doors are broke.

Noise within.

Enter Laertes armed; Danes following.

LAERTES: Where is this king?—Sirs, stand you all without.

DANES: No, let's come in.

115 LAERTES: I pray you, give me leave.

DANES: We will, we will. [*They retire without the door.*]

LAERTES: I thank you:—keep the door.—O thou vile king,
Give me my father!

QUEEN: Calmly, good Laertes.

120 LAERTES: That drop of blood that's calm proclaims me bastard;
Cries cuckold to my father; brands the harlot
Even here, between the chaste unsmirched brow
Of my true mother.

KING: What is the cause, Laertes,
125   That thy rebellion looks so giant-like?—
Let him go, Gertrude; do not fear our person:
There's such divinity doth hedge a king,
That treason can but peep to what it would,
Acts little of his will.—Tell me, Laertes,
130   Why thou art thus incens'd.—Let him go, Gertrude:—
Speak, man.

LAERTES: Where is my father?

KING: Dead.

QUEEN: But not by him.

135 KING: Let him demand his fill.

LAERTES: How came he dead? I'll not be juggled with:
To hell, allegiance! vows, to the blackest devil!
Conscience and grace, to the profoundest pit!
I dare damnation:—to this point I stand,—
140   That both the worlds I give to negligence,
Let come what comes; only I'll be reveng'd
Most thoroughly for my father.

KING: Who shall stay you?

LAERTES: My will, not all the world:

And for my means, I'll husband them so well,   145
They shall go far with little.
KING: Good Laertes,
If you desire to know the certainty
Of your dear father's death, is't writ in your revenge
That, sweepstake, you will draw both friend and foe,   150
Winner or loser?
LAERTES: None but his enemies.
KING: Will you know them, then?
LAERTES: To his good friends thus wide I'll ope my arms;
And, like the kind life-rendering pelican,[6]   155
Repast them with my blood.
KING: Why, now you speak
Like a good child and a true gentleman.
That I am guiltless of your father's death,
And am most sensible in grief for it,   160
It shall as level to your judgment pierce
As day does to your eye.
DANES: [*Within*]   Let her come in.
LAERTES: How now! what noise is that?

Re-enter Ophelia, fantastically dressed with straws and flowers.

O heat, dry up my brains! tears seven times salt   165
Burn out the sense and virtue of mine eyes!—
By heaven, thy madness shall be paid by weight
Till our scale turn the beam. O rose of May!
Dear maid, kind sister, sweet Ophelia!—
O heavens! is't possible a young maid's wits   170
Should be as mortal as an old man's life!
Nature is fine in love; and where 'tis fine
It sends some precious instance of itself
After the thing it loves.
OPHELIA: [*Sings*]   175

They bore him barefac'd on the bier;
    Hey no nonny, nonny, hey nonny;
And on his grave rain'd many a tear,—
    Fare you well, my dove!

LAERTES: Hadst thou thy wits, and didst persuade revenge,   180
It could not move thus.

---

[6]*life-rendering pelican:* The mother pelican was believed to draw blood from herself to feed her young.

OPHELIA: You must sing, *Down-a-down, and you call him a-down-a.*
O, how the wheel becomes it! It is the false steward, that stole his
master's daughter.

185 LAERTES: This nothing's more than matter.

OPHELIA: There's rosemary, that's for remembrance; pray, love,
remember: and there is pansies that's for thoughts.

LAERTES: A document in madness,—thoughts and remembrance fitted.

OPHELIA: There's fennel for you, and columbines:—there's rue for you;
190 and here's some for me:—we may call it herb-grace o' Sundays:—
O, you must wear your rue with a difference.—There's a daisy:—I
would give you some violets, but they withered all when my father
died:—they say, he made a good end,—

[*Sings*]

> For bonny sweet Robin is all my joy,—

195 LAERTES: Thoughts and affliction, passion, hell itself,
She turns to favor and to prettiness.

OPHELIA: [*Sings*]

> And will he not come again?
> And will he not come again?
200   No, no, he is dead,
>   Go to thy death-bed,
> He never will come again.
>
> His beard was as white as snow
> All flaxen was his poll:
205   He is gone, he is gone,
>   And we cast away moan:
> God ha' mercy on his soul!

And of all Christian souls, I pray God.—God b' wi' ye. [*Exit.*]

LAERTES: Do you see this, O God?

210 KING: Laertes, I must commune with your grief,
Or you deny me right. Go but apart,
Make choice of whom your wisest friends you will,
And they shall hear and judge 'twixt you and me:
If by direct or by collateral hand
215 They find us touch'd, we will our kingdom give,
Our crown, our life, and all that we call ours,
To you in satisfaction; but if not,
Be you content to lend your patience to us,
And we shall jointly labor with your soul
220 To give it due content.

Laertes: Let this be so;
His means of death, his obscure burial,—
No trophy, sword, nor hatchment[7] o'er his bones
No noble rite nor formal ostentation,—
Cry to be heard, as 'twere from heaven to earth,   225
That I must call't in question.
King: So you shall;
And where the offence is, let the great axe fall.
I pray you, go with me.

Exeunt.

SCENE 6

Another room in the castle.

Enter Horatio and a Servant.

Horatio: What are they that would speak with me?
Servant: Sailors, sir: they say they have letters for you.
Horatio: Let them come in.—

Exit Servant.

I do not know from what part of the world
I should be greeted, if not from Lord Hamlet.   5

Enter Sailors.

1st Sailor: God bless you, sir.
Horatio: Let him bless thee too.
1st Sailor: He shall, sir, an't please him. There's a letter for you, sir;
it comes from the ambassador that was bound for England; if your
name be Horatio, as I am let to know it is.   10
Horatio: [*Reads*] *Horatio, when thou shalt have overlooked this, give these
fellows some means to the king: they have letters for him. Ere we were
two days old at sea, a pirate of very warlike appointment gave us chase.
Finding ourselves too slow of sail, we put on a compelled valor; and in
the grapple I boarded them; on the instant they got clear of our ship; so   15
I alone became their prisoner. They have dealt with me like thieves of
mercy: but they knew what they did; I am to do a good turn for them. Let
the king have the letters I have sent; and repair thou to me with as much
haste as thou wouldst fly death. I have words to speak in thine ear will
make thee dumb; yet are they much too light for the bore of the matter.   20
These good fellows will bring thee where I am. Rosencrantz and*

---
[7]*hatchment:* A tablet with coat of arms.

*Guildenstern hold their course for England: of them I have much to tell
thee. Farewell. He that thou knowest thine.*

Hamlet

25 Come, I will give you way for these your letters;
   And do't the speedier, that you may direct me
   To him from whom you brought them.

Exeunt.

SCENE 7

Another room in the castle.

Enter King and Laertes.

KING: Now must your conscience my acquittance seal,
      And you must put me in your heart for friend,
      Sith you have heard, and with a knowing ear,
      That he which hath your noble father slain
5   Pursu'd my life.
LAERTES: It well appears:—but tell me
      Why you proceeded not against these feats,
      So crimeful and so capital in nature.
      As by your safety, wisdom, all things else,
10   You mainly were stirr'd up.
KING: O, for two special reasons;
      Which may to you, perhaps, seem much unsinew'd,
      But yet to me they are strong. The queen his mother
      Lives almost by his looks; and for myself,—
15   My virtue or my plague, be it either which,—
      She's so conjunctive to my life and soul,
      That, as the star moves not but in his sphere,
      I could not but by her. The other motive,
      Why to a public count I might not go,
20   Is the great love the general gender bear him;
      Who, dipping all his faults in their affection,
      Would, like the spring that turneth wood to stone,
      Convert his gyves to graces; so that my arrows,
      Too slightly timber'd for so loud a wind,
25   Would have reverted to my bow again,
      And not where I had aim'd them.
LAERTES: And so have I a noble father lost;
      A sister driven into desperate terms,—
      Whose worth, if praises may go back again,
30   Stood challenger on mount of all the age
      For her perfections:—but my revenge will come.

KING: Break not your sleeps for that: you must not think
That we are made of stuff so flat and dull
That we can let our beard be shook with danger,
And think it pastime. You shortly shall hear more: 35
I lov'd your father, and we love ourself;
And that, I hope, will teach you to imagine,—

Enter a Messenger.

How now! what news?
MESSENGER: Letters, my lord, from Hamlet:
This to your majesty; this to the queen.   40
KING: From Hamlet! Who brought them?
MESSENGER: Sailors, my lord, they say; I saw them not:
They were given me by Claudio,—he receiv'd them
Of him that brought them.
KING: Laertes, you shall hear them.—Leave us.   45

Exit Messenger.

[*Reads*] *High and mighty,—You shall know I am set naked on your kingdom.*
To-morrow shall I beg leave to see your kingly eyes: when I shall, first
asking your pardon thereunto, recount the occasions of my sudden and
more strange return.

Hamlet

What should this mean? Are all the rest come back?
Or is it some abuse,[1] and no such thing?
LAERTES: Know you the hand?
KING: 'Tis Hamlet's character:[2]—*Naked,*—
And in a postscript here, he says, *alone.*   50
Can you advise me?
LAERTES: I am lost in it, my lord. But let him come;
It warms the very sickness in my heart,
That I shall live, and tell him to his teeth,
Thus diddest thou.   55
KING: If it be so, Laertes,—
As how should it be so? how otherwise?—
Will you be rul'd by me?
LAERTES: Ay, my lord:
So you will not o'errule me to a peace.   60
KING: To thine own peace. If he be now return'd,—
As checking at his voyage, and that he means
No more to undertake it,—I will work him

---

[1]*abuse:* Ruse.   [2]*character:* Handwriting.

To an exploit, now ripe in my device,
65   Under the which he shall not choose but fall:
And for his death no wind of blame shall breathe;
But even his mother shall uncharge the practice
And call it accident.
LAERTES: My lord, I will be rul'd;
70   The rather if you could devise it so
That I might be the organ.
KING: It falls right.
You have been talk'd of since your travel much,
And that in Hamlet's hearing, for a quality
75   Wherein they say you shine: your sum of parts
Did not together pluck such envy from him
As did that one; and that, in my regard,
Of the unworthiest siege.
LAERTES: What part is that, my lord?
80 KING: A very riband in the cap of youth,
Yet needful too; for youth no less becomes
The light and careless livery that it wears
Than settled age his sables and his weeds,
Importing health and graveness.—Two months since,
85   Here was a gentleman of Normandy,—
I've seen myself, and serv'd against, the French,
And they can well on horseback: but this gallant
Had witchcraft in't; he grew unto his seat;
And to such wondrous doing brought his horse,
90   As he had been incorps'd and demi-natur'd[3]
With the brave beast: so far he topp'd my thought,
That I, in forgery of shapes and tricks,[4]
Come short of what he did.
LAERTES: A Norman was't?
95 KING: A Norman.
LAERTES: Upon my life, Lamond.
KING: The very same.
LAERTES: I know him well: he is the brooch, indeed,
And gem of all the nation.
100 KING: He made confession of you;
And gave you such a masterly report
For art and exercise in your defence,
And for your rapier most especially,

---

[3] *As . . . demi-natur'd:* Made as one body and formed into half man, half horse—or centaur.
[4] *in forgery . . . tricks:* In imagining tricks of horsemanship.

That he cried out, 'twould be a sight indeed
If one could match you: the scrimers[5] of their nation,   105
He swore, had neither motion, guard, nor eye,
If you oppos'd them. Sir, this report of his
Did Hamlet so envenom with his envy,
That he could nothing do but wish and beg
Your sudden coming o'er, to play with him.   110
Now, out of this,—

LAERTES: What out of this, my lord?

KING: Laertes, was your father dear to you?
Or are you like the painting of a sorrow,
A face without a heart?   115

LAERTES: Why ask you this?

KING: Not that I think you did not love your father;
But that I know love is begun by time;
And that I see, in passages of proof,[6]
Time qualifies the spark and fire of it.   120
There lives within the very flame of love
A kind of wick or snuff that will abate it;
And nothing is at a like goodness still;
For goodness, growing to a pleurisy,[7]
Dies in his own too much: that we would do   125
We should do when we would; for this *would* changes,
And hath abatements and delays as many
As there are tongues, or hands, or accidents;
And then this *should* is like a spendthrift sigh
That hurts by easing. But to the quick o' the ulcer: 130
Hamlet comes back: what would you undertake
To show yourself your father's son in deed
More than in words?

LAERTES: To cut his throat i' the church.

KING: No place, indeed, should murder sanctuarize;   135
Revenge should have no bounds. But, good Laertes,
Will you do this, keep close within your chamber.
Hamlet return'd shall know you are come home:
We'll put on those shall praise your excellence,
And set a double varnish on the fame   140
The Frenchman gave you; bring you, in fine, together,
And wager on yours heads: he, being remiss,[8]
Most generous, and free from all contriving,

---

[5]*scrimers:* Fencers.   [6]*passages of proof:* The evidence of experience.   [7]*pleurisy:* Plethora, an
excess of blood.   [8]*remiss:* Unguarded and free from suspicion.

Will not peruse the foils; so that, with ease,
145 Or with a little shuffling, you may choose
A sword unbated, and, in a pass of practice,
Requite him for your father.
LAERTES: I will do't it:
And, for that purpose, I'll anoint my sword.
150 I bought an unction of a mountebank,
So mortal that but dip a knife in it,
Where it draws blood no cataplasm so rare,[9]
Collected from all simples that have virtue
Under the moon, can save the thing from death
155 That is but scratch'd withal: I'll touch my point
With this contagion, that, if I gall him slightly,
It may be death.
KING: Let's further think of this;
Weigh what convenience both of time and means
160 May fit us to our shape: if this should fail,
And that our drift look through our bad performance,
'Twere better not assay'd: therefore this project
Should have a back or second, that might hold
If this should blast in proof. Soft! let me see:—
165 We'll make a solemn wager on your cunnings,—
I ha't:
When in your motion you are hot and dry,—
As make your bouts more violent to that end,—
And that he calls for drink, I'll have prepar'd him
170 A chalice for the nonce;[10] whereon but sipping,
If he by chance escape your venom'd stuck
Our purpose may hold there.

Enter Queen.

                          How now, sweet queen!
QUEEN: One woe doth tread upon another's heel,
175 So fast they follow:—your sister's drown'd, Laertes.
LAERTES: Drown'd! O, where?
QUEEN: There is a willow grows aslant a brook,
That shows his hoar leaves in the glassy stream;
There with fantastic garlands did she come
180 Of crowflowers, nettles, daisies, and long purples,
That liberal shepherds give a grosser name,

---

[9]*no cataplasm so rare:* No poultice, however remarkably efficacious.   [10]*nonce:* Purpose.

But our cold maids do dead men's fingers call them.
There, on the pendant boughs her coronet weeds
Clambering to hang, an envious[11] sliver broke;
When down her weedy trophies and herself   185
Fell in the weeping brook. Her clothes spread wide;
And, mermaid-like, awhile they bore her up:
Which time she chanted snatches of old tunes;
As one incapable of her own distress,
Or like a creature native and indu'd   190
Unto that element: but long it could not be
Till that her garments, heavy with their drink,
Pull'd the poor wretch from her melodious lay
To muddy death.

LAERTES: Alas, then, she is drown'd?   195
QUEEN: Drown'd, drown'd.
LAERTES: Too much of water hast thou, poor Ophelia,
And therefore I forbid my tears: but yet
It is our trick; nature her custom holds,
Let shame say what it will: when these are gone,   200
The woman will be out.[12]—Adieu, my lord:
I have a speech of fire, that fain would blaze,
But that this folly douts it.[13] [Exit.]
KING: Let's follow, Gertrude;
How much I had to do to calm his rage!
Now fear I this will give it start again;   205
Therefore let's follow.

Exeunt.

ACT 5
SCENE 1

A churchyard.

Enter two Clowns[1] with spades, &c.

1ST CLOWN: Is she to be buried in Christian burial that wilfully seeks
   her own salvation?
2ND CLOWN: I tell thee she is; and therefore make her grave straight:
   the crowner[2] hath sat on her, and finds it Christian burial.
1ST CLOWN: How can that be, unless she drowned herself in her own   5
   defence?

---

[11]*envious:* Malicious.   [12]*The woman . . . out:* I.e., "I shall be ruthless."   [13]*douts it:* Drowns it.
[1]*Clowns:* Rustic fellows.   [2]*crowner:* Coroner.

2ND CLOWN: Why, 'tis found so.

1ST CLOWN: It must be se *offendendo*,³ it cannot be else. For here lies
the point: if I drown myself wittingly, it argues an act: and an act
10 hath three branches; it is to act, to do, and to perform: argal,⁴ she
drowned herself wittingly.

2ND CLOWN: Nay, but hear you, goodman delver,—

1ST CLOWN: Give me leave. Here lies the water; good: here stands the
man; good: if the man go to this water and drown himself, it is, will
15 he, nill he, he goes,—mark you that: but if the water come to him
and drown him, he drowns not himself: argal, he that is not guilty of
his own death shortens not his own life.

2ND CLOWN: But is this law?

1ST CLOWN: Ay, marry, is't; crowner's quest law.

20 2ND CLOWN: Will you ha' the truth on't? If this had not been a gentle-
woman she should have been buried out of Christian burial.

1ST CLOWN: Why, there thou say'st: and the more pity that great folks
should have countenance in this world to drown or hang themselves
more than their even-Christian.⁵—Come, my spade. There is no
25 ancient gentlemen but gardeners, ditchers, and grave-makers; they
hold up Adam's profession.

2ND CLOWN: Was he a gentleman?

1ST CLOWN: He was the first that ever bore arms.

2ND CLOWN: Why, he had none.

30 1ST CLOWN: What, art a heathen? How dost thou understand the Scripture? The Scripture says, Adam digged: could he dig without arms?
I'll put another question to thee: if thou answerest me not to the
purpose, confess thyself,⁶—

2ND CLOWN: Go to.

35 1ST CLOWN: What is he that builds stronger than either the mason, the
shipwright, or the carpenter?

2ND CLOWN: The gallows-maker; for that frame outlives a thousand
tenants.

1ST CLOWN: I like thy wit well, in good faith: the gallows does well; but
40 how does it well? it does well to those that do ill: now thou dost ill
to say the gallows is built stronger than the church: argal, the gallows may do well to thee. To't again, come.

2ND CLOWN: Who builds stronger than a mason, a shipwright, or a
carpenter?

---

³se offendendo: In self-offense; he means *se defendendo*, in self-defense. ⁴*argal*: He means
ergo, therefore. ⁵*even-Christian*: Fellow Christian. ⁶*confess thyself*: "Confess thyself an ass,"
perhaps.

1ST CLOWN: Ay, tell me that, and unyoke.   45

2ND CLOWN: Marry, now I can tell.

1ST CLOWN: To't.

2ND CLOWN: Mass, I cannot tell.

Enter Hamlet and Horatio, at a distance.

1ST CLOWN: Cudgel thy brains no more about it, for your dull ass will
not mend his pace with beating; and when you are asked this ques-   50
tion next, say a grave-maker; the houses that he makes last till
doomsday. Go, get thee to Yaughan: fetch me a stoup of liquor.

Exit Second Clown.

Digs and sings.

> In youth, when I did love, did love,
>   Methought it was very sweet,
> To contract, O, the time, for, ah, my behove,[7]   55
>   O, methought there was nothing meet.

HAMLET: Has this fellow no feeling of his business, that he sings at
grave-making?

HORATIO: Custom hath made it in him a property of easiness.

HAMLET: 'Tis e'en so: the hand of little employment hath the daintier 60
sense.

1ST CLOWN: [*Sings*]

> But age, with his stealing steps,
>   Hath claw'd me in his clutch,
> And hath shipp'd me intil the land,   65
>   As if I had never been such.

Throws up a skull.

HAMLET: That skull had a tongue in it, and could sing once: how the
knave joels[8] it to the ground, as if it were Cain's jawbone, that did
the first murder! This might be the pate of a politician, which this
ass now o'erreaches; one that would circumvent God, might it not?   70

HORATIO: It might, my lord.

HAMLET: Or of a courtier; which could say, *Good-morrow, sweet lord!*
How dost thou, good lord? This might be my lord such-a-one, that
praised my lord such-a-one's horse, when he meant to beg it,—
might it not?   75

HORATIO: Ay, my lord.

---

[7]*behove:* Behoof, or advantage.   [8]*joels:* Throws.

HAMLET: Why, e'en so: and now my Lady Worm's; chapless,[9] and knocked about the mazard[10] with a sexton's spade: here's fine revolution, an we had the trick to see't. Did these bones cost no more the breeding but to play at loggats[11] with 'em? Mine ache to think on't.

80

1ST CLOWN: [Sings]

> A pick-axe and a spade, a spade,
>   For and a shrouding sheet:
> O, a pit of clay for to be made
>   For such a guest is meet.

85

Throws up another.

HAMLET: There's another: why may not that be the skull of a lawyer? Where be his quiddits[12] now, his quillets,[13] his cases, his tenures, and his tricks? why does he suffer this rude knave now to knock him about the sconce with a dirty shovel, and will not tell him of his action of battery? Hum! This fellow might be in's time a great buyer of land, with his statutes, his recognizances, his fines, his double vouchers, his recoveries: is this the fine of his fines, and the recovery of his recoveries, to have his fine pate full of fine dirt? will his vouchers vouch him no more of his purchases, and double ones too, than the length and breadth of a pair of indentures? The very conveyances of his lands will hardly lie in this box; and must the inheritor himself have no more, ha?

90

95

HORATIO: Not a jot more, my lord.

HAMLET: Is not parchment made of sheep-skins?

100 HORATIO: Ay, my lord, and of calf-skins too.

HAMLET: They are sheep and calves which seek out assurance in that. I will speak to this fellow.—Whose grave's this, sir?

1ST CLOWN: Mine, sir.—[Sings]

> O, a pit of clay for to be made
>   For such a guest is meet.

105

HAMLET: I think it be thine indeed; for thou liest in't.

1ST CLOWN: You lie out on't, sir, and therefore it is not yours: for my part, I do not lie in't, and yet it is mine.

HAMLET: Thou dost lie in't, to be in't, and say it is thine: 'tis for the dead, not for the quick; therefore thou liest.

110

1ST CLOWN: 'Tis a quick lie, sir: 'twill away again from me to you.

---

[9]*chapless:* Without a lower jaw. of wood are hurled at a stake. [13]*quillets:* Quibbling distinctions.   [10]*mazard:* Head.   [11]*loggats:* A game in which small pieces [12]*quiddits:* Quiddities, "whatnesses"—that is, hair-splittings.

HAMLET: What man dost thou dig it for?

1ST CLOWN: For no man, sir.

HAMLET: What woman, then?

1ST CLOWN: For none, neither.   115

HAMLET: Who is to be buried in't?

1ST CLOWN: One that was a woman, sir; but, rest her soul, she's dead.

HAMLET: How absolute the knave is! we must speak by the card, or
equivocation will undo us. By the Lord, Horatio, these three years
I have taken note of it; the age is grown so picked[14] that the toe   120
of the peasant comes so near the heel of the courtier, he galls his
kibe.[15]—How long hast thou been a grave-maker?

1ST CLOWN: Of all the days i' the year, I came to't that day that our last
King Hamlet o'ercame Fortinbras.

HAMLET: How long is that since?   125

1ST CLOWN: Cannot you tell that? every fool can tell that: it was the
very day that young Hamlet was born,—he that is mad, and sent
into England.

HAMLET: Ay, marry, why was he sent into England?

1ST CLOWN: Why, because he was mad: he shall recover his wits there;   130
or, if he do not, it's no great matter there.

HAMLET: Why?

1ST CLOWN: 'Twill not be seen in him there; there the men are as mad
as he.

HAMLET: How came he mad?   135

1ST CLOWN: Very strangely, they say.

HAMLET: How strangely?

1ST CLOWN: Faith, e'en with losing his wits.

HAMLET: Upon what ground?

1ST CLOWN: Why, here in Denmark: I have been sexton here, man and   140
boy, thirty years.

HAMLET: How long will a man lie i' the earth ere he rot?

1ST CLOWN: Faith, if he be not rotten before he die,—as we have many
pocky corses now-a-days, that will scarce hold the laying in,—he will
last you some eight year or nine year: a tanner will last you nine year. 145

HAMLET: Why he more than another?

1ST CLOWN: Why, sir, his hide is so tanned with his trade that he will
keep out water a great while; and your water is a sore decayer of
your whoreson dead body. Here's a skull now; this skull has lain in
the earth three-and-twenty years.   150

---

[14]*picked:* Refined or educated.   [15]*galls his kibe:* Rubs and irritates the chilblain sore on the
courtier's heel.

HAMLET: Whose was it?

1ST CLOWN: A whoreson mad fellow's it was: whose do you think it was?

HAMLET: Nay, I know not.

1ST CLOWN: A pestilence on him for a mad rogue! 'a poured a flagon of
155   Rhenish on my head once. This same skull, sir, was Yorick's skull,
the king's jester.

HAMLET: This?

1ST CLOWN: E'en that.

HAMLET: Let me see. [*Takes the skull*]—Alas, poor Yorick!—I knew him,
160   Horatio; a fellow of infinite jest, of most excellent fancy: he hath
borne me on his back a thousand times; and now, how abhorred in
my imagination it is! my gorge rises at it. Here hung those lips that
I have kissed I know not how oft. Where be your gibes now? your
gambols? your songs? your flashes of merriment, that were wont to
165   set the table on a roar? Not one now, to mock your own grinning?
quite chap-fallen? Now get you to my lady's chamber, and tell her,
let her paint an inch thick, to this favor[16] she must come; make her
laugh at that.—Pr'ythee, Horatio, tell me one thing.

HORATIO: What's that, my lord?

170 HAMLET: Dost thou think Alexander looked o' this fashion i' the earth?

HORATIO: E'en so.

HAMLET: And smelt so? pah! [*Throws down the skull*]

HORATIO: E'en so, my lord.

HAMLET: To what base uses we may return, Horatio! Why may not
175   imagination trace the noble dust of Alexander till he find it stopping a bung-hole?

HORATIO: 'Twere to consider too curiously to consider so.

HAMLET: No, faith, not a jot; but to follow him thither with modesty
enough, and likelihood to lead it: as thus; Alexander died, Alex-
180   ander was buried, Alexander returneth into dust; the dust is earth;
of earth we make loam; and why of that loam whereto he was con-
verted might they not stop a beer-barrel?

> Imperious Caesar, dead and turn'd to clay,
>   Might stop a hole to keep the wind away:
185 O, that that earth which kept the world in awe
>   Should patch a wall to expel the winter's flaw!—

But soft! but soft! aside.—Here comes the king.

*Enter Priests, &c., in procession; the corpse of Ophelia, Laertes and Mourners
following; King, Queen, their Trains, &c.*

---

[16]*favor:* Face.

The queen, the courtiers: who is that they follow?
And with such maimed rites? This doth betoken
The corpse they follow did with desperate hand   190
Fordo its own life: 'twas of some estate.
Couch we awhile and mark. [*Retiring with Horatio*]

LAERTES: What ceremony else?

HAMLET: That is Laertes,
A very noble youth: mark.   195

LAERTES: What ceremony else?

1ST PRIEST: Her obsequies have been as far enlarg'd
As we have warrantise: her death was doubtful,
And, but that great command o'ersways the order,
She should in ground unsanctified have lodg'd   200
Till the last trumpet; for charitable prayers,
Shards, flints, and pebbles, should be thrown on her,
Yet here she is allowed her virgin rites,
Her maiden strewments, and the bringing home
Of bell and burial.   205

LAERTES: Must there no more be done?

1ST PRIEST: No more be done:
We should profane the service of the dead
To sing a requiem, and such rest to her
As to peace-parted souls.   210

LAERTES: Lay her i' the earth;—
And from her fair and unpolluted flesh
May violets spring!—I tell thee, churlish priest,
A ministering angel shall my sister be
When thou liest howling.   215

HAMLET: What, the fair Ophelia!

QUEEN: Sweets to the sweet: farewell! [*Scattering flowers*]
I hop'd thou shouldst have been my Hamlet's wife;
I thought thy bride-bed to have deck'd, sweet maid,
And not have strew'd thy grave.   220

LAERTES: O, treble woe
Fall ten times treble on that cursed head
Whose wicked deed thy most ingenious sense
Depriv'd thee of!—Hold off the earth awhile,
Till I have caught her once more in mine arms: 225

Leaps into the grave.

Now pile your dust upon the quick and dead,
Till of this flat a mountain you have made,

To o'er-top old Pelion[17] or the skyish head
Of blue Olympus.

230 HAMLET: [*Advancing*] What is he whose grief
Bears such an emphasis? whose phrase of sorrow
Conjures the wandering stars, and makes them stand
Like wonder-wounded hearers? this is I, Hamlet the
Dane. [*Leaps into the grave*]

235 LAERTES: The devil take thy soul! [*Grappling with him*]
HAMLET: Thou pray'st not well.
I pr'ythee, take thy fingers from my throat;
For, though I am not splenitive and rash,
Yet have I in me something dangerous,
240 Which let thy wiseness fear: away thy hand.
KING: Pluck them asunder.
QUEEN: Hamlet! Hamlet!
ALL: Gentlemen,—
HORATIO: Good my lord, be quiet.

The Attendants part them, and they come out of the grave.

245 HAMLET: Why, I will fight with him upon this theme
Until my eyelids will no longer wag.
QUEEN: O my son, what theme?
HAMLET: I lov'd Ophelia; forty thousand brothers
Could not, with all their quantity of love,
250 Make up my sum.—What wilt thou do for her?
KING: O, he is mad, Laertes.
QUEEN: For love of God, forbear him.
HAMLET: 'Swounds, show me what thou'lt do:
Woul't weep? woul't fight? woul't fast? woul't tear thyself?
255 Woul't drink up eisel?[18] eat a crocodile?
I'll do't.—Dost thou come here to whine?
To outface me with leaping in her grave?
Be buried quick[19] with her, and so will I:
And, if thou prate of mountains, let them throw
260 Millions of acres on us, till our ground,
Singeing his pate against the burning zone,[20]
Make Ossa[21] like a wart! Nay, an thou'lt mouth,
I'll rant as well as thou.
QUEEN: This is mere madness:
265 And thus awhile the fit will work on him;

---

[17]*Pelion:* A mountain in Greece.   [18]*eisel:* Vinegar.   [19]*quick:* Alive.   [20]*burning zone:* The fiery zone of the celestial sphere.   [21]*Ossa:* A high mountain in Greece.

Anon, as patient as the female dove,
When that her golden couplets are disclos'd,[22]
His silence will sit drooping.

HAMLET: Hear you, sir;
What is the reason that you use me thus?   270
I lov'd you ever: but it is no matter;
Let Hercules himself do what he may,
The cat will mew, and dog will have his day. [*Exit.*]

KING: I pray thee, good Horatio, wait upon him.—

Exit Horatio.

[*To Laertes*] Strengthen your patience in our last night's speech;   275
We'll put the matter to the present push.—
Good Gertrude, set some watch over your son.—
This grave shall have a living monument:
An hour of quiet shortly shall we see;
Till then, in patience our proceeding be.   280

Exeunt.

SCENE 2

A hall in the castle.

Enter Hamlet and Horatio.

HAMLET: So much for this, sir: now let me see the other;
You do remember all the circumstance?

HORATIO: Remember it, my lord!

HAMLET: Sir, in my heart there was a kind of fighting
That would not let me sleep: methought I lay   5
Worse than the mutines in the bilboes.[1] Rashly,
And prais'd be rashness for it,—let us know,
Our indiscretion sometimes serves us well,
When our deep plots do fail: and that should teach us
There's a divinity that shapes our ends,   10
Rough-hew them how we will.

HORATIO: This is most certain.

HAMLET: Up from my cabin,
My sea-gown scarf'd about me, in the dark
Grop'd I to find out them: had my desire;   15
Finger'd their packet; and, in fine, withdrew

---

[22]*When . . . are disclos'd:* When the golden twins are hatched.   [1]*mutines . . . bilboes:* Mutineers in
the iron stocks on board ship.

To mine own room again: making so bold,
My fears forgetting manners, to unseal
Their grand commission; where I found, Horatio,
20   O royal knavery! an exact command,—
Larded with many several sorts of reasons,
Importing Denmark's health and England's too,
With, ho! such bugs[2] and goblins in my life,—
That, on the supervise, no leisure bated,
25   No, not to stay the grinding of the axe,
My head should be struck off.

HORATIO: Is't possible?

HAMLET: Here's the commission: read it at more leisure.
But wilt thou hear me how I did proceed?

30 HORATIO: I beseech you.

HAMLET: Being thus benetted round with villainies,—
Ere I could make a prologue to my brains,
They had begun the play,—I sat me down;
Devis'd a new commission; wrote it fair:
35   I once did hold it, as our statists do,
A baseness to write fair, and labor'd much
How to forget that learning; but, sir, now
It did me yeoman's service. Wilt thou know
The effect of what I wrote?

40 HORATIO: Ay, good my lord.

HAMLET: An earnest conjuration from the king,—
As England was his faithful tributary;
As love between them like the palm might flourish;
As peace should still her wheaten garland wear
45   And stand a comma[3] 'tween their amities;
And many such like as's of great charge,—
That, on the view and know of these contents,
Without debatement further, more or less,
He should the bearers put to sudden death,
50   Not shriving-time allow'd.

HORATIO: How was this seal'd?

HAMLET: Why, even in that was heaven ordinant.
I had my father's signet in my purse,
Which was the model of that Danish seal:
55   Folded the writ up in form of the other;
Subscrib'd it; gav't the impression; plac'd it safely,
The changeling never known. Now, the next day

---

[2]*bugs:* Bugbears.   [3]*comma:* Link.

Was our sea-fight; and what to this was sequent
Thou know'st already.

HORATIO: So Guildenstern and Rosencrantz go to't.   60

HAMLET: Why, man, they did make love to this employment;
They are not near my conscience; their defeat
Does by their own insinuation[4] grow:
'Tis dangerous when the baser nature[5] comes
Between the pass and fell[6] incensed points   65
Of mighty opposites.

HORATIO: Why, what a king is this!

HAMLET: Does it not, think'st thee, stand me now upon,[7]
He that hath kill'd my king and whor'd my mother;
Popp'd in between the election and my hopes;   70
Thrown out his angle for my proper life,
And with such cozenage,[8]—is't not perfect conscience
To quit him with this arm? and is't not to be damn'd,
To let this canker of our nature come
In further evil?   75

HORATIO: It must be shortly known to him from England
What is the issue of the business there.

HAMLET: It will be short: the interim is mine;
And a man's life's no more than to say One.
But I am very sorry, good Horatio,   80
That to Laertes I forgot myself;
For by the image of my cause I see
The portraiture of his: I'll court his favors:
But, sure, the bravery[9] of his grief did put me
Into a towering passion.   85

HORATIO: Peace; who comes here?

Enter Osric.

OSRIC: Your lordship is right welcome back to Denmark.

HAMLET: I humbly thank you, sir.—Dost know this water-fly?

HORATIO: No, my good lord.

HAMLET: Thy state is the more gracious; for 'tis a vice to know him. He   90
hath much land, and fertile: let a beast be lord of beasts, and his crib
shall stand at the king's mess: 'tis a chough;[10] but, as I say, spacious
in the possession of dirt.

---

[4]*insinuation:* By their own "sticking their noses" into the business.   [5]*baser nature:* Men of
lower rank.   [6]*fell:* Fierce.   [7]*Does . . . upon:* I.e., "Don't you think it is my duty?"   [8]*cozenage:*
Deceit.   [9]*bravery:* Ostentation.   [10]*his crib . . . chough:* He shall have his trough at the king's table:
he is a chattering fool.

OSRIC: Sweet lord, if your lordship were at leisure, I should impart a
95   thing to you from his majesty.

HAMLET: I will receive it with all diligence of spirit. Put your bonnet to
his right use; 'tis for the head.

OSRIC: I thank your lordship, 'tis very hot.

HAMLET: No, believe me, 'tis very cold; the wind is northerly.

100 OSRIC: It is indifferent cold, my lord, indeed.

HAMLET: Methinks it is very sultry and hot for my complexion.

OSRIC: Exceedingly, my lord; it is very sultry,—as't were,—I cannot tell
how.—But, my lord, his majesty bade me signify to you that he has
laid a great wager on your head. Sir, this is the matter,—

105 HAMLET: I beseech you, remember,—

Hamlet moves him to put on his hat.

OSRIC: Nay, in good faith; for mine ease, in good faith. Sir, here is
newly come to court Laertes; believe me, an absolute gentleman,
full of most excellent differences, of very soft society and great
showing: indeed, to speak feelingly of him, he is the card or
110   calendar of gentry, for you shall find in him the continent of what
part a gentleman would see.

HAMLET: Sir, his definement suffers no perdition in you;—though, I
know, to divide him inventorially would dizzy the arithmetic of
memory, and yet but yaw neither, in respect of his quick sail. But, in
115   the verity of extolment, I take him to be a soul of great article; and
his infusion of such dearth[11] and rareness as, to make true diction of
him, his semblable is his mirror; and who else would trace him, his
umbrage,[12] nothing more.

OSRIC: Your lordship speaks most infallibly of him.

120 HAMLET: The concernancy, sir? why do we wrap the gentleman in our
more rawer breath?

OSRIC: Sir?

HORATIO: Is't not possible to understand in another tongue? You will
do't sir, really.

125 HAMLET: What imports the nomination[13] of this gentleman?

OSRIC: Of Laertes?

HORATIO: His purse is empty already; all's golden words are spent.

HAMLET: Of him, sir.

OSRIC: I know, you are not ignorant,—

130 HAMLET: I would you did, sir; yet, in faith, if you did, it would not much
approve me.[14]—Well, sir.

---

[11]*dearth:* Rareness, or excellence. [12]*umbrage:* Shadow. [13]*nomination:* Naming. [14]*if you . . .
approve me:* If you, who are a fool, thought me not ignorant, that would not be particularly to my credit.

OSRIC: You are not ignorant of what excellence Laertes is,—

HAMLET: I dare not confess that, lest I should compare with him in excellence; but to know a man well were to know himself.

OSRIC: I mean, sir, for his weapon; but in the imputation laid on him by them, in his meed he's unfellowed.[15]   135

HAMLET: What's his weapon?

OSRIC: Rapier and dagger.

HAMLET: That's two of his weapons: but, well.

OSRIC: The king, sir, hath wagered with him six Barbary horses: against the which he has imponed,[16] as I take it, six French rapiers and poniards, with their assigns, as girdle, hangers, and so: three of the carriages, in faith, are very dear to fancy, very responsive to the hilts, most delicate carriages, and of very liberal conceit.   140

HAMLET: What call you the carriages?   145

HORATIO: I knew you must be edified by the margent[17] ere you had done.

OSRIC: The carriages, sir, are the hangers.

HAMLET: The phrase would be more german to the matter if we could carry cannon by our sides: I would it might be hangers till then. But, on: six Barbary horses against six French swords, their assigns, and three liberal conceited carriages; that's the French bet against the Danish: why is this imponed, as you call it?   150

OSRIC: The king, sir, hath laid, that in a dozen passes between you and him he shall not exceed you three hits: he hath laid on twelve for nine; and it would come to immediate trial if your lordship would vouchsafe the answer.   155

HAMLET: How if I answer no?

OSRIC: I mean, my lord, the opposition of your person in trial.[18]

HAMLET: Sir, I will walk here in the hall: if it please his majesty, it is the breathing time of day with me: let the foils be brought, the gentleman willing, and the king hold his purpose, I will win for him if I can; if not, I will gain nothing but my shame and the odd hits.   160

OSRIC: Shall I re-deliver you[19] e'en so?

HAMLET: To this effect, sir; after what flourish your nature will.

OSRIC: I commend my duty to your lordship.   165

HAMLET: Yours, yours.

Exit Osric.

---

[15]*in . . . unfellowed:* In his worth he has no equal.   [16]*imponed:* Staked.   [17]*edified . . . margent:* Informed by a note in the margin of your instructions.   [18]*the opposition . . . trial:* The presence of your person as Laertes' opponent in the fencing contest.   [19]*re-deliver you:* Carry back your answer.

He does well to commend it himself; there are no tongues else for's turn.

HORATIO: This lapwing runs away with the shell on his head.[20]

170 HAMLET: He did comply with his dug before he sucked it.[21] Thus has he,—and many more of the same bevy, that I know the drossy age dotes on,—only got the tune of the time, and outward habit of encounter; a kind of yesty collection,[22] which carries them through and through the most fanned and winnowed opinions; and do but
175 blow them to their trial, the bubbles are out.

Enter a Lord.

LORD: My lord, his majesty commended him to you by young Osric, who brings back to him that you attend him in the hall: he sends to know if your pleasure hold to play with Laertes, or that you will take longer time.

180 HAMLET: I am constant to my purposes; they follow the king's pleasure: if his fitness speaks, mine is ready; now or whensoever, provided I be so able as now.

LORD: The king and queen and all are coming down.

HAMLET: In happy time.

185 LORD: The queen desires you to use some gentle entertainment to Laertes before you fall to play.

HAMLET: She well instructs me.

Exit Lord.

HORATIO: You will lose this wager, my lord.

HAMLET: I do not think so; since he went into France I have been in
190 continual practice: I shall win at the odds. But thou wouldst not think how ill all's here about my heart: but it is no matter.

HORATIO: Nay, good my lord,—

HAMLET: It is but foolery; but it is such a kind of gain-giving[23] as would perhaps trouble a woman.

195 HORATIO: If your mind dislike anything, obey it: I will forestall their repair hither, and say you are not fit.

HAMLET: Not a whit, we defy augury: there's a special providence in the fall of a sparrow. If it be now, 'tis not to come; if it be not to come, it will be now; if it be not now, yet it will come: the readiness

---

[20]*This lapwing . . . head:* This precocious fellow is like a lapwing that starts running when it is barely out of the shell.   [21]*He . . . sucked it:* He paid compliments to his mother's breast before he sucked it.   [22]*yesty collection:* Yeasty or frothy affair.   [23]*gain-giving:* Misgiving.

is all. Since no man has aught of what he leaves, what is't to leave   200
betimes?[24]

Enter King, Queen, Laertes, Lords, Osric, and Attendants with foils, &c.

KING: Come, Hamlet, come, and take this hand from me.

The King puts Laertes' hand into Hamlet's.

HAMLET: Give me your pardon, sir: I have done you wrong:
    But pardon't, as you are a gentleman.
    This presence knows, and you must needs have heard,   205
    How I am punish'd with sore distraction.
    What I have done,
    That might your nature, honor, and exception
    Roughly awake, I here proclaim was madness.
    Was't Hamlet wrong'd Laertes? Never Hamlet: 210
    If Hamlet from himself be ta'en away,
    And when he's not himself does wrong Laertes,
    Then Hamlet does it not, Hamlet denies it.
    Who does it, then? His madness: if't be so,
    Hamlet is of the faction that is wrong'd;   215
    His madness is poor Hamlet's enemy.
    Sir, in this audience,
    Let my disclaiming from a purpos'd evil
    Free me so far in your most generous thoughts
    That I have shot mine arrow o'er the house   220
    And hurt my brother.

LAERTES: I am satisfied in nature,
    Whose motive, in this case, should stir me most
    To my revenge: but in my terms of honor
    I stand aloof; and will no reconcilement   225
    Till by some elder masters of known honor
    I have a voice and precedent of peace
    To keep my name ungor'd. But till that time
    I do receive your offer'd love like love,
    And will not wrong it.   230

HAMLET: I embrace it freely;
    And will this brother's wager frankly play.[25]—
    Give us the foils; come on.

LAERTES: Come, one for me.

---

[24] *what . . . betimes?:* What does an early death matter?   [25] *frankly play:* Fence with a heart free from resentment.

235 HAMLET: I'll be your foil, Laertes; in mine ignorance
Your skill shall, like a star in the darkest night,
Stick fiery off indeed.
LAERTES: You mock me, sir.
HAMLET: No, by this hand.
240 KING: Give them the foils, young Osric.
Cousin Hamlet,
You know the wager?
HAMLET: Very well, my lord;
Your grace hath laid the odds o' the weaker side.
245 KING: I do not fear it; I have seen you both;
But since he's better'd, we have therefore odds.
LAERTES: This is too heavy, let me see another.
HAMLET: This likes me well. These foils have all a length?

They prepare to play.

OSRIC: Ay, my good lord.
250 KING: Set me the stoups of wine upon that table,—
If Hamlet give the first or second hit,
Or quit in answer of the third exchange,
Let all the battlements their ordnance fire;
The king shall drink to Hamlet's better breath;
255 And in the cup an union[26] shall he throw,
Richer than that which four successive kings
In Denmark's crown have worn. Give me the cups;
And let the kettle[27] to the trumpet speak,
The trumpet to the cannoneer without,
260 The cannons to the heavens, the heavens to earth,
Now the king drinks to Hamlet.—Come, begin;—
And you, the judges, bear a wary eye.
HAMLET: Come on, sir.
LAERTES: Come, my lord.

They play.

265 HAMLET: One.
LAERTES: No.
HAMLET: Judgment.
OSRIC: A hit, a very palpable hit.
LAERTES: Well;—again.
270 KING: Stay, give me a drink.—Hamlet, this pearl is thine;

---

[26] *an union:* A pearl.   [27] *kettle:* Kettledrum.

Here's to thy health.—

Trumpets sound, and cannon shot off within.

Give him the cup.

HAMLET: I'll play this bout first; set it by awhile.—
Come.—Another hit; what say you?

They play.

LAERTES: A touch, a touch, I do confess.   275
KING: Our son shall win.
QUEEN: He's fat, and scant of breath.—
Here, Hamlet, take my napkin, rub thy brows:
The queen carouses to thy fortune, Hamlet.
HAMLET: Good madam!   280
KING: Gertrude, do not drink.
QUEEN: I will, my lord; I pray you, pardon me.
KING: [*Aside*] It is the poison'd cup; it is too late.
HAMLET: I dare not drink yet, madam; by and by.
QUEEN: Come, let me wipe thy face.   285
LAERTES: My lord, I'll hit him now.
KING: I do not think't.
LAERTES: [*Aside*] And yet 'tis almost 'gainst my conscience.
HAMLET: Come, for the third, Laertes: you but dally;
I pray you, pass with your best violence: 290
I am afeard you make a wanton of me.
LAERTES: Say you so? come on.

They play.

OSRIC: Nothing, neither way.
LAERTES: Have at you now!

*Laertes wounds Hamlet; then, in scuffling, they change rapiers, and Hamlet
wounds Laertes.*

KING: Part them; they are incens'd.   295
HAMLET: Nay, come, again.

The Queen falls.

OSRIC: Look to the queen there, ho!
HORATIO: They bleed on both sides.—How is it, my lord?
OSRIC: How is't, Laertes?
LAERTES: Why, as a woodcock to my own springe, Osric;   300
I am justly kill'd with mine own treachery.
HAMLET: How does the queen?

KING: She swoons to see them bleed.

QUEEN: No, no, the drink, the drink,—O my dear Hamlet,—
305   The drink, the drink!—I am poison'd. [*Dies.*]

HAMLET: O villainy!—Ho! let the door be lock'd:
    Treachery! seek it out.

Laertes falls.

LAERTES: It is here, Hamlet: Hamlet, thou art slain;
    No medicine in the world can do thee good;
310   In thee there is not half an hour of life;
    The treacherous instrument is in thy hand,
    Unbated and envenom'd: the foul practice
    Hath turn'd itself on me; lo, here I lie,
    Never to rise again: thy mother's poison'd:
315   I can no more:—the king, the king's to blame.

HAMLET: The point envenom'd too!—
    Then venom to thy work. [*Stabs the King.*]

OSRIC AND LORDS: Treason! treason!

KING: O, yet defend me, friends; I am but hurt.

320 HAMLET: Here, thou incestuous, murderous, damned Dane,
    Drink off this potion.—Is thy union here?
    Follow my mother.

King dies.

LAERTES: He is justly serv'd;
    It is a poison temper'd by himself.—
325   Exchange forgiveness with me, noble Hamlet:
    Mine and my father's death come not upon thee,
    Nor thine on me! [*Dies.*]

HAMLET: Heaven make thee free of it! I follow thee.—
    I am dead, Horatio.—Wretched queen, adieu!—
330   You that look pale and tremble at this chance,
    That art but mutes or audience to this act,
    Had I but time,—as this fell sergeant, death,
    Is strict in his arrest,—O, I could tell you,—
    But let it be.—Horatio, I am dead;
335   Thou liv'st; report me and my cause aright
    To the unsatisfied.[28]

HORATIO: Never believe it:
    I am more an antique Roman than a Dane,—
    Here's yet some liquor left.

[28] *the unsatisfied:* The uninformed.

HAMLET: As thou'rt a man,   340
   Give me the cup; let go; by heaven, I'll have't.—
   O good Horatio, what a wounded name,
   Things standing thus unknown, shall live behind me!
   If thou didst ever hold me in thy heart,
   Absent thee from felicity awhile,   345
   And in this harsh world draw thy breath in pain,
   To tell my story.—

March afar off, and shot within.

                          What warlike noise is this?

OSRIC: Young Fortinbras, with conquest come from Poland,
   To the ambassadors of England gives   350
   This warlike volley.

HAMLET: O, I die, Horatio;
   The potent poison quite o'er-crows my spirit:
   I cannot live to hear the news from England;
   But I do prophesy the election lights   355
   On Fortinbras: he has my dying voice;
   So tell him, with the occurrents, more and less,
   Which have solicited.[29]—The rest is silence. [*Dies.*]

HORATIO: Now cracks a noble heart.—Good-night, sweet prince,
   And flights of angels sing thee to thy rest!   360
   Why does the drum come hither?

March within. Enter Fortinbras, the English Ambassadors, and others.

FORTINBRAS: Where is this sight?

HORATIO: What is it you would see?
   If aught of woe or wonder, cease your search.

FORTINBRAS: This quarry cries on havoc.[30]—O proud death,   365
   What feast is toward in thine eternal cell,
   That thou so many princes at a shot
   So bloodily hast struck?

1ST AMBASSADOR: The sight is dismal;
   And our affairs from England come too late: 370
   The ears are senseless that should give us hearing,
   To tell him his commandment is fulfill'd,
   That Rosencrantz and Guildenstern are dead:
   Where should we have our thanks?

---

[29] *So tell him . . . solicited:* So tell him, together with the events, more or less, that have brought on this tragic affair.   [30] *This quarry . . . havoc:* This collection of dead bodies cries out havoc.

375 **HORATIO:** Not from his mouth,
     Had it the ability of life to thank you:
     He never gave commandment for their death.
     But since, so jump[31] upon this bloody question,
     You from the Polack wars, and you from England,
380 Are here arriv'd, give order that these bodies
     High on a stage be placed to the view;
     And let me speak to the yet unknowing world
     How these things came about: so shall you hear
     Of carnal, bloody, and unnatural acts;
385 Of accidental judgments, casual slaughters;
     Of deaths put on by cunning and forc'd cause;
     And, in this upshot, purposes mistook
     Fall'n on the inventors' heads: all this can I
     Truly deliver.
390 **FORTINBRAS:**   Let us haste to hear it,
     And call the noblest to the audience.
     For me, with sorrow I embrace my fortune:
     I have some rights of memory in this kingdom,[32]
     Which now to claim my vantage doth invite me.
395 **HORATIO:** Of that I shall have also cause to speak,
     And from his mouth whose voice will draw on more:
     But let this same be presently perform'd,
     Even while men's minds are wild: lest more mischance
     On plots and errors happen.
400 **FORTINBRAS:**   Let four captains
     Bear Hamlet like a soldier to the stage;
     For he was likely, had he been put on,[33]
     To have prov'd most royally: and, for his passage,
     The soldier's music and the rites of war
405 Speak loudly for him.—
     Take up the bodies.—Such a sight as this
     Becomes the field, but here shows much amiss.
     Go, bid the soldiers shoot.

A dead march.

Exeunt, bearing off the dead bodies: after which a peal of ordnance is shot off.

---

[31] *so jump:* So opportunely.   [32] *I have . . . kingdom:* I have some unforgotten rights to this kingdom.
[33] *put on:* Tested by succession to the throne.

Reading and Reacting

1. What are Hamlet's most notable character traits? Do you see these traits as generally positive or negative?
2. Review each of Hamlet's soliloquies. Do you believe his assessments of his own problems are accurate? Are his assessments of other characters' behavior accurate? Point to examples from the soliloquies that reveal Hamlet's insight or lack of insight.
3. Is Hamlet a sympathetic character? Where (if anywhere) do you find yourself growing impatient with him or disagreeing with him?
4. Why does Hamlet behave so cruelly toward Ophelia after his "To be or not to be" soliloquy (act 3, scene 1)? How does this behavior affect your view of his character?
5. What do other characters' comments reveal about Hamlet's character *before* the key events in the play begin to unfold? For example, in what way has Hamlet changed since he returned to the castle and found out about his father's death?
6. Claudius is presented as the play's villain. Is he all bad, or does he have any redeeming qualities?
7. List those in the play whom you believe to be flat characters. Why do you characterize each individual in this way? What does each of these flat characters contribute to the play?
8. Is Fortinbras simply Hamlet's foil, or does he have another essential role? Explain.
9. Each of the play's major characters has one or more character flaws that influence plot development. What specific weaknesses do you see in Claudius, Gertrude, Polonius, Laertes, Ophelia, and Hamlet himself? Through what words or actions is each weakness revealed? How does each weakness contribute to the play's plot?
10. Why doesn't Hamlet kill Claudius as soon as the ghost tells him what Claudius did? Why doesn't he kill him when he has the chance in act 3? What words and actions reveal Hamlet's motivation for hesitating? What are the implications of his failure to act?
11. Why does Hamlet pretend to be insane? Why does he arrange for the "play within a play" to be performed? Why does he agree to the duel with Laertes? In each case, what words or actions reveal his motivation to the audience?
12. Is the ghost an essential character, or could the information he reveals and the reactions he arouses come from another source? Explain. (Keep in mind that the ghost is a stock character in Elizabethan revenge tragedies.)
13. Describe Hamlet's relationship with his mother. Do you consider this a typical mother/son relationship? Why, or why not?

14. In the graveyard scene (act 5, scene 1), the gravediggers make many ironic comments. How do these comments shed light on the events taking place in the play?

15. JOURNAL ENTRY Both Gertrude and Ophelia are usually seen as weak women, firmly under the influence of the men in their lives. Do you think this characterization of them as passive and dependent is accurate? Explain your views.

16. CRITICAL PERSPECTIVE In *The Meaning of Shakespeare*, (1951), Harold Goddard reads *Hamlet* as, in part, a play about war, with a grimly ironic conclusion in that "all the Elder Hamlet's conquests have been for nothing—for less than nothing. Fortinbras, his former enemy, is to inherit the kingdom! Such is the end to which the ghost's thirst for vengeance has led." Goddard goes on to describe the play's ending:

> The dead Hamlet is borne out "like a soldier" and the last rites over his body are to be the rites of war. The final word of the text is "shoot." The last sounds we hear are a dead march and the reverberations of ordnance being shot off. The end crowns the whole. The sarcasm of fate could go no further. Hamlet, who aspired to nobler things, is treated at death as if he were the mere image of his father: a warrior. Shakespeare knew what he was about in making the conclusion of his play martial. Its theme has been war as well as revenge. It is the story of the Minotaur over again, of that monster who from the beginning of human strife has exacted his annual tribute of youth. No sacrifice ever offered to it was more precious than Hamlet. But he was not the last.
>
> If ever a play seems expressly written for the twentieth century, it is *Hamlet*. It should be unnecessary to underscore its pertinence to an age in which, twice within three decades, the older generation has called on the younger generation to settle a quarrel with the making of which it had nothing to do. So taken, *Hamlet* is an allegory of our time. Imagination or violence, Shakespeare seems to say, there is no other alternative.

Can you find other evidence in the play to support the idea that war (and, more specifically, the futility of war) is one of its major themes? Do you agree that the play is, in this respect, "an allegory of our time"?

Related Works: "The Cask of Amontillado" (p. 249), "Young Goodman Brown" (p. 367), "Referential" (p. 447), *Oedipus the King* (p. 1182)

WRITING SUGGESTIONS: Character

1. In *Death of a Salesman*, each character pursues his or her version of the American Dream. Choose two characters, define their concept of the American Dream, and explain how each tries to make the dream a reality. In each case, consider the obstacles the character encounters, and try to account for the character's success or lack of success. If you like, you may also consider other works in which the American Dream is central—for example, "Two Kinds" (p. 471), *The Cuban Swimmer* (p. 1166), or *Fences* (p. 1270).

2. The key female characters in this chapter's plays—the wife in *Post-its*, Linda in *Death of a Salesman*, and Ophelia in *Hamlet*—are, in one way or another, in conflict with men. Focusing on female characters in two different plays, define each conflict, and consider whether it is resolved in the play. (If you like, you may also discuss a female character who appears in a play in another chapter.)

3. Minor characters are often flat characters; in many cases, their sole function is to advance the plot or to highlight a particular trait in a major character. Sometimes, however, minor characters may be of more than minor importance. Choose one minor character from *Death of a Salesman* or *Hamlet* (or from a play in another chapter), and write an essay in which you discuss what this character contributes and how the play would be different without him or her.

4. Watch a film version of one of the plays in this chapter, and write an essay in which you evaluate the actor's interpretation of the central character.

5. Both *Death of Salesman* and *Hamlet* explore the complex relationships between parents and their children. Write an essay in which you analyze Willy Loman's relationships with his sons or Hamlet's relationship with his mother.

6. In several other plays in this anthology, as in *Hamlet*, the past is an important influence on characters' lives in the present. Write an essay in which you discuss the impact of the past on the present in *Hamlet* and one or two other plays—for example, *A Doll House* (p. 881) or *Oedipus the King* (p. 1182).

CHAPTER 29

STAGING

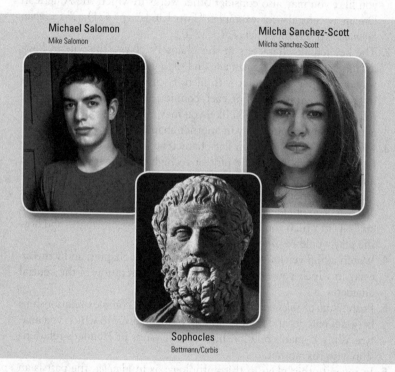

Michael Salomon
Mike Salomon

Milcha Sanchez-Scott
Milcha Sanchez-Scott

Sophocles
Bettmann/Corbis

Staging refers to the physical elements of a play's production that determine how the play looks and sounds to an audience. It encompasses the **stage settings**, or **sets**—furnishings, scenery, props, and lighting—as well as the costumes, sound effects, and music that bring the play to life on the stage. In short, staging is everything that goes into making a written script a performance.

Contemporary staging in the West has traditionally concentrated on recreating the real world. This concept of staging, which has dominated Western theatrical productions for centuries, would seem alien in many non-Western theaters. Japanese **Kabuki dramas** and **No plays**, for example,

1154

depend on staging conventions that make no attempt to mirror reality. Scenery and costumes are largely symbolic, and often actors wear highly stylized makeup or masks. Although some European and American playwrights have been strongly influenced by non-Western staging, the majority of plays being produced in the West still try to create the illusion of reality.

Stage Directions

Usually a playwright presents instructions for the staging of a play in **stage directions**—notes that comment on the scenery, the movements of the performers, the lighting, and the placement of props. (In the absence of detailed stage directions, dialogue can provide information about staging.) Sometimes these stage directions are quite simple, leaving much to the discretion (and imagination) of the director. Consider how little specific information about the setting of the play is provided in these stage directions from act 1 of Samuel Beckett's 1952 absurdist play *Waiting for Godot*:

A country road. A tree. Evening.

Often, however, playwrights furnish more detailed information about staging. Consider these stage directions from act 1 of Anton Chekhov's *The Cherry Orchard*:

A room, which has always been called the nursery. One of the doors leads into Anya's room. Dawn, sun rises during the scene. May, the cherry trees in flower, but it is cold in the garden with the frost of the early morning. Windows closed.
Enter Dunyasha with a candle and Lopahin with a book in his hand.

These comments indicate that the first act takes place in a room with more than one door and that several windows reveal cherry trees in bloom. They also specify that the lighting should simulate the sun rising at dawn and that characters should enter carrying certain props. Still, Chekhov leaves it up to those staging the play to decide on the costumes for the characters and on the furniture to be placed around the room.

Some stage directions are even more specific. Irish playwright George Bernard Shaw's long, complex stage directions are legendary in the theater. Note the degree of detail he provides in these stage directions from his 1906 comedy *The Doctor's Dilemma*:

The consulting-room has two windows looking on Queen Anne Street. Between the two is a marble-topped console, with haunched gilt legs ending in sphinx claws. The huge pier-glass [a long narrow mirror that fits between two windows] which surmounts it is mostly disabled from reflection by elaborate painting on its surface of palms, ferns, lilies, tulips, and sunflowers. The adjoining wall contains the fireplace, with two arm-chairs before it. As we happen to face the corner we see nothing of the other two walls. On the right of the fireplace, or rather on the right of *any person facing the fireplace, is the door. On the left is the writing-table at which Redpenny [a medical student] sits. It is an untidy table with a microscope, several test tubes, and a spirit lamp [an alcohol burner] standing up through its litter of papers. There is a couch in the middle of the room, at right angles to the console, and parallel to the fireplace. A chair stands between the couch and the window. Another in the corner. Another at the other end of the windowed wall. . . . The wallpaper and carpets are mostly green. . . . The house, in fact, was so well furnished in the middle of the XIXth century that it stands unaltered to this day and is still quite presentable.*

Not only does Shaw indicate exactly what furniture is to be placed on stage, but he also includes a good deal of physical description—specifying, for example, "gilt legs ending in sphinx claws" and "test tubes and a spirit lamp" that clutter the writing table. In addition, he defines furniture placement and specifies color.

Regardless of how detailed the stage directions are, they do not eliminate the need for creative interpretations on the part of the producer, director, set designers, and actors (see "Actors' Interpretations," p. 952). Many directors see stage directions as simply suggestions, not requirements, and some consider them more confusing than helpful. Therefore, some directors may choose to interpret a play's stage directions quite loosely—or even to ignore them entirely. For example, in 2007, the Classical Theater of Harlem staged Samuel Beckett's 1952 existentialist drama *Waiting for Godot* in New Orleans. The performances were held outdoors in areas of the city that had been seriously damaged by Hurricane Katrina, and the still-devastated setting gave new power to Beckett's drama of characters' search for meaning against a backdrop of emptiness and despair.

 ## The Uses of Staging

Various elements of staging provide important information about characters and their motivations as well as about the play's theme.

Costumes

Costumes establish the historical period in which a play is set and provide insight into the characters who wear them. For example, when Hamlet first appears on stage, he is profoundly disillusioned and quite melancholy. This fact was immediately apparent to Shakespeare's audience because Hamlet is dressed in sable, which to the Elizabethans signified a melancholy nature. In Tennessee Williams's *The Glass Menagerie* (1945), Laura's dress of soft violet material and her hair ribbon reflect her delicate, childlike innocence. In contrast, her mother's *"imitation velvety-looking cloth [coat] with imitation fur collar"* and her *"enormous black patent-leather pocketbook"* reveal her somewhat pathetic attempt to achieve respectability. Later in the play, awaiting the "gentleman caller," Laura's mother wears a dress that is both outdated and inappropriately youthful, suggesting both her need to relive her own past and her increasingly desperate desire to marry off her daughter.

Props and Furnishings

Props (short for *properties*) can also help audiences interpret a play's characters and themes. For example, the handkerchief in Shakespeare's *Othello* gains significance as the play progresses: it begins as an innocent object and ends as the piece of evidence that convinces Othello his wife is committing adultery. Sometimes props can have symbolic significance. During the Renaissance, for example, flowers had symbolic meaning. In act 4 of *Hamlet*, Ophelia, who is mad, gives flowers to various characters. In a note to the play, the critic Thomas Parrott points out the symbolic significance of her gifts: to Claudius, the murderer of Hamlet's father, she gives fennel and columbines, which signify flattery and ingratitude; to the Queen, she gives rue and daisies, which symbolize sadness and unfaithfulness. Although modern audiences would not understand the significance of these flowers, many people in Shakespeare's Elizabethan audience would have been aware of their meaning.

The **furnishings** in a room can also reveal a lot about a play's characters and themes. Willy Loman's house in Arthur Miller's *Death of a Salesman* (p. 960) is sparsely furnished, revealing the declining financial status of the family. The kitchen contains a table and three chairs and the bedroom only a brass bed and a straight chair. Over the bed on a shelf is Willy's son's silver athletic trophy, a constant reminder of his loss of status. Like Willie Loman's house, the Helmer's living room in *A Doll House*, suggests its inhabitants' social status. The furnishings are typical of "respectable" middle-class families in nineteenth-century Norway. According to the stage directions, the living room is, "A comfortable room, tastefully but not expensively furnished." Everything in it—from the round table with an armchair, to the porcelain stove, to the carpeted floor—is practical and efficient. These furnishings immediately convey to audiences the stability of the family as well as its core values.

Scenery and Lighting

Playwrights often use **scenery** and **lighting** to create imaginative stage settings. In *Death of a Salesman*, the house is surrounded by *"towering angular shapes"* of apartment houses that emphasize the *"small, fragile-seeming home."* Arthur Miller calls for a set that is *"wholly, or in some places, transparent."* Whenever the action is in the present, the actors observe the imaginary boundaries that separate rooms or mark the exterior walls of the house.

When the characters reenact past events, however, they walk over the boundaries and come to the front of the stage. By lighting up and darkening different parts of the stage, Miller shifts from the present to the past and back again.

Contemporary playwrights often use sets that combine realistic and nonrealistic elements. In his Tony Award–winning play M. *Butterfly*, for example, David Henry Hwang uses a **scrim**, a curtain that when illuminated from the front appears solid but when illuminated from the back becomes transparent. He also employs a large red lacquered ramp that runs from the bottom to the top of the stage. The action takes place beneath, on, and above the ramp, creating an effect not unlike that created by Shakespeare's multiple stages. At several points in the play, a character who acts as the narrator sits beneath the ramp, addressing the audience, while at the same time a character on top of the ramp acts out the narrator's words.

Music and Sound Effects

Staging involves more than visual elements such as costumes and scenery; it also involves **music** and **sound effects**. The stage directions for *Death of a Salesman*, for example, begin, "*A melody is heard, played upon a flute.*" Although not specifically identified, the music is described as "*small and fine, telling of grass and trees and the horizon.*" Significantly, this music stands in stark contrast to the claustrophobic urban setting of the play. Music also plays a major role in *The Glass Menagerie*, where a single recurring tune, like circus music, weaves in and out of the play. This musical motif gives emotional impact to certain lines and suggests the fantasy world into which Laura has retreated.

Sound effects play an important part in Henrik Ibsen's *A Doll House* (p. 881). At the very end of the play, after his wife has left him, Torvald Helmer sits alone on the stage. In the following stage directions, the final sound effect cuts short Helmer's attempt at self-deluding optimism:

HELMER: (*sinks down on a chair by the door, face buried in his hands*)
   Nora! Nora! (*Looking about and rising.*) Empty. She's gone. (*A sudden hope leaps in him.*) The greatest miracle—?

From below, the sound of a door slamming shut.

When you read a play, it may be difficult to appreciate the effect that staging can have on a performance. As you read, pay particular attention to the stage directions, and use your imagination to visualize the scenes the playwright describes. In addition, try to imagine the play's sights and sounds, and consider the options for staging that are suggested as characters speak to one another. Although careful reading cannot substitute for seeing a play performed, it can help you imagine the play as it might appear on the stage.

A Final Note

Because of a play's limited performance time, and because of space and financial limitations, not every action or event can be represented on stage. Frequently, incidents that would involve many actors or require elaborate scenery are only suggested. For example, a violent riot may be suggested by a single scuffle, a full-scale wedding by the kiss between bride and groom, a gala evening at the opera by a well-dressed group in box seats, and a trip to an exotic locale by a departure scene. Other events may be suggested by sounds offstage—for example, the roar of a crowd may suggest an athletic event.

✔ **CHECKLIST   Writing about Staging**

- What information about staging is specified in the stage directions of the play?

- What information about staging is suggested by the play's dialogue?

- What information about staging is left to the imagination?

- How might different decisions about staging change the play?

- Do the stage directions provide information about how characters are supposed to look or behave?

- What costumes are specified? In what ways do costumes provide insight into the characters who wear them?

- What props play an important part in the play? Do these props have symbolic meaning?

- Is the scenery special or unusual in any way?

- What kind of lighting is specified by the stage directions? In what way does this lighting affect your reaction to the play?

- How are music and sound effects used in the play? Are musical themes associated with any characters? Do music or sound effects heighten the emotional impact of certain lines?

- What events occur offstage? Why? How are they suggested?

- How does staging help to communicate the play's themes?

Mike Salomon

MICHAEL SALOMON (1988–   ) is a playwright, screenwriter, and short story writer. His plays include *The Tragedy of King James the First* (read by sportscaster Bob Costas on *Slate*'s "*Hang Up and Listen*" podcast) and *RMEO + JULEZ* (winner of the Manhattan Theatre Club's 2009 REALationships Playwright Competition and included in the collection *25 10-Minute Plays for Teens*). The following play appeared in the collection *The Best Ten-Minute Plays 2013*.

CULTURAL CONTEXT   In this play, the characters refer to "alternative casting," a practice in theater and film in which an actor is cast for a role originally intended for someone else. Some examples of alternative casting include the role of Marty McFly in the 1985 movie *Back to the Future* (originally offered to Eric Stoltz, but played by Michael J. Fox) and the role of Clarice Starling in the 1991 movie *The Silence of the Lambs* (played by Jodie Foster, but originally offered to Michelle Pfeiffer). In these examples, the alternative actors are as suited to the roles as the actors they replaced. Some critics, however, have objected to a kind of alternative casting known as "color-blind casting" (and sometimes attacked as "politically correct casting"), a practice in which roles are assigned without regard to race, ethnicity, or even gender. *The Date* tests the boundaries of alternative casting and makes fun of tightly scripted roles—both on and off the stage.

The Date (2012)

CHARACTERS

JACKIE, *female, early twenties, black*
DUQUAN, *male, late fifties, white*
STAGE DIRECTIONS, *male, twenties or thirties (any race except black)*

SETTING

A dimly lit, romantic restaurant.

LIGHTS UP ON JACKIE AND DUQUAN, *sitting at opposite ends of a small, elegantly set dinner table. Both are dressed to the nines. Duquan's sport coat hangs neatly over the back of his chair. On the table are a basket of bread-sticks, a long, burning candle, salt and pepper shakers, and two table settings. Both Jackie and Duquan are reading menus. STAGE DIRECTIONS sits in a folding chair in the front corner of the stage—apart from the others. He faces the audience with a script in hand.*

STAGE DIRECTIONS: *(Reading.)* Setting: a dimly lit, romantic restaurant.
    At one end of the table sits Jackie, a well-dressed, twenty-four year old African American woman. At the other end sits Duquan, a twenty-five year old African American man wearing a shirt and tie.

DUQUAN: See anything that looks good?

Jackie looks up, shocked to see Duquan sitting across from her. She says nothing but stares at him in confusion. Duquan clears his throat.

DUQUAN: *(cont'd)* See anything that looks good?

Jackie glances around the restaurant, unsettled, then back at Duquan. He clears his throat again.

DUQUAN: *(cont'd)* Do you see anything—
JACKIE: I'm—I'm sorry. Is this—? Are you—? Who are you?   5
DUQUAN: I'm Duquan.
JACKIE: Right . . . Seriously, who are you?
DUQUAN: I'm Duquan.

A beat.

DUQUAN: *(cont'd)* So, see anything that looks—
JACKIE: Wait, wait, wait. Hold up. I'm sorry. *You're* Duquan?   10
DUQUAN: Yeah.
JACKIE: Aren't you supposed to be, like, twenty-five? And black?
DUQUAN: Uh-huh.
JACKIE: So . . .
DUQUAN: So what?   15
JACKIE: So why aren't you?
DUQUAN: I am.
JACKIE: You're a black twenty-five year old?
DUQUAN: Mm-hmm.
JACKIE: Really? *You're* a black twenty-five year old?   20
DUQUAN: Yes, ma'am.
JACKIE: *Really?*
DUQUAN: I, um . . .

Duquan begrudgingly stands up and walks over to Stage Directions.

DUQUAN: *(cont'd)* May I?

Duquan takes the script out of Stage Directions hands and flips to the front. He turns to Jackie.

DUQUAN: *(cont'd)* Let's see . . . Yup, that's what it says right here: 25
     "Duquan, a twenty-five year old African American man. Wearing
     a shirt and tie."

He gestures down to his own shirt and tie, then returns the script to Stage Directions and heads back to his seat.

JACKIE: Right, right, right. But *you're* not black.
DUQUAN: I beg your pardon.

JACKIE: You're like some fifty year old white guy.

DUQUAN: Oh. *Oooh!* I see. Yeah, this is a . . . uh . . . oh what do they call it? Alternative casting!

30 JACKIE: What?

DUQUAN: Yeah, I've been alternatively cast.

JACKIE: For our date?

DUQUAN: Mm-hmm.

JACKIE: I'm confused.

35 DUQUAN: Ok, well see, you *are* on a date with a twenty-five-year-old black man, and I am that black man. You get it?

JACKIE: Not particularly.

DUQUAN: Ok. Ok. Uh, let's say this pepper shaker is you, and this salt shaker is me, and so you're on a date with the salt shaker, but it's really a pepper shaker, and—wait, no, that's not right. Hang on. What if *I'm* the pepper shaker and *you're* the—

JACKIE: Hold up. Hold up. I get what you're saying. I just don't understand why.

DUQUAN: Oh. Well it's—I think it's got something to do with the whole date setting and, you know, love, and the way there's, um, deception, and—

40 STAGE DIRECTIONS: It's symbolic of the misrepresentations that we, as humans, purvey in our romantic endeavors.

DUQUAN: Ah. See, there you go. It's symbolism.

JACKIE: It's a date.

DUQUAN: Yes, but it's symbolism too.

JACKIE: Ok. Well what am I symbolic of?

45 DUQUAN: Oh. I don't know. Maybe nothing. Breadstick?

He offers her a breadstick. She doesn't take it.

JACKIE: Nothing?

DUQUAN: Or something. I mean we all have our own layers. I guess you could say mine are just a little more forthright.

JACKIE: I guess so.

DUQUAN: So you're cool, then? Everything settled?

50 JACKIE: What? No. I don't know. I mean, this all still seems kind of messed up to me. Don't get me wrong. I've been on some pretty wacked out dates before, but *this?*

DUQUAN: Hey, you're preaching to the choir here. Talk about your identity crisis, right? I mean, I vote republican.

JACKIE: Yeah, but wait—hang on. This—it is a date, right?

DUQUAN: Uh huh.

JACKIE: And we're supposed to sit here and have a real conversation and, like, really connect like two people, right?

DUQUAN: That's what *I* had in mind. Yeah. 55

JACKIE: Well doesn't it change everything—I mean, doesn't it make any hope of real connection impossible—if you aren't who you're supposed to be?

DUQUAN: But I'm exactly who I'm supposed to be.

JACKIE: You're not a twenty-five year old black man!

DUQUAN: But I *am* a twenty-five year old black man.

JACKIE: Really? Then who's Lil Wayne? 60

DUQUAN: I don't know. A Muppet?

JACKIE: See!

DUQUAN: Look, is it really that big a deal?

JACKIE: Of course it is. I don't want to be on a date with—

DUQUAN: Oh. I see. A white guy? 65

JACKIE: A guy three times my age! And yes, if I'm *supposed* to be on a date with a black guy in the first place, I think it is a little weird to show up and have that black guy be a white guy who apparently *is* a black guy, but he's not really, and he's just been alternatively cast as—

To Stage Directions

I mean, what the hell? Was this *your* idea?

Stage Directions shrugs.

DUQUAN: Look, it's just a simple conceit. You know, like a magic show, or professional wrestling, or fake breasts . . .

JACKIE: I don't want my romantic life to be anything like fake breasts, thank you.

DUQUAN: Ok, well think about it this way: Let's say there really was a twenty-five year old black man sitting here across from you. Does that make the situation any less deceptive? Isn't he just as liable to mislead you about the particular nuances or intricacies of his personality and life? I mean, at least I'm wearing my deceit on my skin.

JACKIE: But how does that make it any better? 70

DUQUAN: Well now you know you can't trust me.

JACKIE: But I want to be able to trust you.

DUQUAN: Ok, then trust me.

JACKIE: How?

DUQUAN: I don't know. Just concede to the illusion. 75

JACKIE: The illusion that you're twenty-five and black?

DUQUAN: That's the one.

JACKIE: But you're not.

DUQUAN: Would it help if I spoke in ebonics?

JACKIE: No. What is wrong with you? 80

DUQUAN: Hey, I will have you know I'm actually a very fun guy. Even for a black man in his twenties. People say I'm quite hip.

JACKIE: No. You aren't. You aren't any of that. Just stop it.

DUQUAN: Fine. I'm sorry, ok? I'm—I'm trying my best here. You know, in a lot of ways I'm probably being more honest than any other guy you'd be out with right now.

JACKIE: Yeah? Well I don't care about that.

85 DUQUAN: Well you probably should care or someone's gonna wind up getting herself into some prickly situations.

JACKIE: But I *don't* care. Look, guy—

DUQUAN: Duquan.

JACKIE: Look. Duquan, I'm sure you're a terrific person and all. Honestly, I do. But I can't deal with all these messed up layers and symbolisms and alternative anythings right now. I just want to be on a normal date with a regular guy, you know? Someone who's roughly my age and has similar interests. Someone I can tell about myself and who can tell me about himself, and then maybe we'll hit it off—or maybe we won't. And yeah, maybe everything he says isn't gonna be the whole honest truth. Maybe he's got a secret drug problem or some creepy fetish or even a wife and kids waiting for him at home, but all of that's up to me to find out for myself. And until I do, I just have to trust him, right? Believe in whatever it is he makes himself out to be and just pray that it's for real.

DUQUAN: Sure, I guess. So then the issue with me is . . . ?

90 JACKIE: I can't believe in you. You're not . . . you're not real.

DUQUAN: So, what you're saying is you'd rather you didn't know if you were being lied to?

JACKIE: In a way.

DUQUAN: I see. Ignorance is bliss, huh?

JACKIE: In this case it is.

95 DUQUAN: I guess so. And so this whole wearing my dishonesty on my sleeve thing: it's a little too much, isn't it?

JACKIE: I'm sorry. I know you were excited to be all symbolic.

DUQUAN: No, no, it's fine. It kind of does all make sense, in a way.

JACKIE: Yeah?

He nods. Beat.

DUQUAN: Hey, what if you just closed your eyes? Tried to pretend—

100 JACKIE: Believe me, I've tried. So many times . . .

DUQUAN: No luck?

JACKIE: No luck.

DUQUAN: I get it. So then all this . . . ?
JACKIE: I can't do it. I'm sorry.

She stands and starts to gather her things.

DUQUAN: Well maybe some other time then.   105
JACKIE: Yeah, maybe.
DUQUAN: And maybe I could just be a fifty-eight year old white guy.
  Named Norm.
JACKIE: And maybe I'll be a twenty-four year-old black girl named
  Jackie.

A beat.

DUQUAN: For what it's worth, I don't have any creepy fetishes. Or a
  wife. Or fake breasts.

Jackie smiles and nods. She exits.

DUQUAN: (*cont'd*) Right.   110

*A long pause. Duquan begins to look around uncomfortably—unsure of what
to do next. Stage Directions appears equally confounded. At last the two make
eye contact. A beat passes. Getting an idea, Stage Directions stands and walks
over to the table, sitting himself in Jackie's former chair.*

STAGE DIRECTIONS: (*Reading from his script.*) Setting: a dimly lit, romantic restaurant. At one end of the table sits Jackie . . .

He gestures to himself. Duquan nods understandingly.

Still reading.
  . . . a well-dressed, twenty-four year old African American woman.
  At the other end sits Duquan, a twenty-five year old African American man wearing a shirt and tie.

Pause.

DUQUAN: See anything that looks good?
STAGE DIRECTIONS: Oh, everything looks amazing. I don't think I'll
  ever be able to choose.

*   *   *

Reading and Reacting

1. Which elements of the play's staging do you consider experimental?
Why? Which do you see as conventional?

2. Why does Salomon make the stage directions a character in the play?

3. What difficulties do you think someone staging this play would encounter? How would you address these difficulties?

4. What is the significance of the play's title? Is it in any way ironic?

5. *The Date* begins with Duquan sitting at a table with Jackie. It ends with Duquan sitting with Stage Directions. What is the significance of this change?

6. What is the central conflict of the play? Can it ever be resolved? Explain.

7. In what ways are the beginning and end of the play similar? How are they different?

8. What is the central theme of *The Date*? Is the play making a point about drama? about race? about dating? about relationships? about something else?

9. JOURNAL ENTRY Assume that there are no stage directions for *The Date*. Write your own set of stage directions, making sure that they reflect your own interpretation of the play.

10. CRITICAL PERSPECTIVE Writing for Northwestern University's online publication *North by Northwestern*, Jennifer Schaefer reviews Michael Solomon's ten-minute play *RMEO + JULEZ*, which won the Manhattan Theater Club's 2009 REALationships Playwright competition. In her review Schaefer observes that the play explores ideas about how technology—especially social media—affects "relationships in the digital age." In what way is the "date" depicted in this play a critique of contemporary romantic relationships? How, if at all, does technology undercut the ability of Jackie and Duquan to relate to each other?

Related Works: "Love and Other Catastrophes: A Mix Tape" (p. 84), "How to Talk to Girls at Parties" (p. 131), "Cathedral" (p. 353), "Castro Moves into the Havana Hilton" (p. 525)

Milcha Sanchez-Scott

MILCHA SANCHEZ-SCOTT (1955–   ) is a Los Angeles–based writer of plays that include *Dog Lady* and *The Cuban Swimmer*, both one-act plays (1984); *Roosters*, published in *On New Ground: Contemporary Hispanic American Plays* (1987) and adapted into the 1993 feature film of the same name; and *Stone Wedding*, produced at the Los Angeles Theater Center (1988). Also produced by the Los Angeles Theater Center was her play *Carmen*, adapted from Georges Bizet's opera of the same title.

Born in Bali, Sanchez-Scott is the daughter of an Indonesian mother and a Colombian-Mexican father. Her early childhood was spent in Mexico, South America, and Britain; her family moved to San Diego when she was fourteen.

Writing in *Time* magazine, William A. Henry observes that the visionary or hallucinatory elements in Sanchez-Scott's plays derive from the Latin American "magic realism" tradition of Jorge Luis Borges and Gabriel García Márquez. For example, Henry notes that in *Roosters*, what seems "a straightforward depiction of the life of farmlands gives way to mysterious visitations, symbolic cockfights enacted by dancers, virginal girls wearing wings, archetypal confrontations between father and son."

In 1984, the New York production of *The Cuban Swimmer* was noteworthy for an ingeniously designed set that realistically re-created on stage Pacific Ocean waves, a helicopter, and a boat. According to the *New York Times*, "The audience [could] almost feel the resisting tides and the California oil slick . . . represented by a watery-blue floor and curtain." Jeannette Mirabel, as the Cuban swimmer, made an "auspicious" debut in the play, according to the *Times:* "In a tour de force of balletic movements, she [kept] her arms fluttering in the imaginary waters throughout the play."

Cultural Context In 1980, in the wake of numerous incidences of dissent and rebellion, Fidel Castro deported a large number of Cubans and encouraged many others to leave. In the resulting exodus, which became known as the Mariel boatlift, more than 120,000 Cuban refugees arrived in Florida, placing tremendous strain on United States resources. In 1984, an agreement was made between the two countries that limited the number of Cuban immigrants to 20,000 per year. Over time, the United States relaxed this quota, but the resulting abundance of refugees prompted the United States government to reinstate the quota in the mid-1990s. In 1996, the Cuban Adjustment Act was passed, stating that Cubans who reached dry land would be allowed to become permanent residents of the United States, but those who were intercepted while still at sea would be returned to Cuba. In 1999, the plight of Cuban refugees was reflected in the story of Elian Gonzalez, a six-year-old boy who was found clinging to an inner tube but was later returned to Cuba in accordance with the 1996 act. Starting in 2009, President Barack Obama, in an effort to open a dialogue with Cuba, eased some travel and economic restrictions.

The Cuban Swimmer (1984)

CHARACTERS

Margarita Suárez, *the swimmer*	**Abuela,** *her grandmother*
Eduardo Suárez, *her father, the coach*	**Voice of Mel Munson**
Simón Suárez, *her brother*	**Voice of Mary Beth White**
Aída Suárez, *her mother*	**Voice of Radio Operator**

SETTING

The Pacific Ocean between San Pedro and Catalina Island.

TIME

Summer.

Live conga drums can be used to punctuate the action of the play.

SCENE 1

Pacific Ocean. Midday. On the horizon, in perspective, a small boat enters upstage left, crosses to upstage right, and exits. Pause. Lower on the horizon, the same boat, in larger perspective, enters upstage right, crosses and exits upstage left. Blackout.

SCENE 2

Pacific Ocean. Midday. The swimmer, Margarita Suárez, is swimming. On the boat following behind her are her father, Eduardo Suárez, holding a megaphone, and Simón, her brother, sitting on top of the cabin with his shirt off, punk sunglasses on, binoculars hanging on his chest.

EDUARDO: (*leaning forward, shouting in time to Margarita's swimming*) Uno, dos, uno, dos. Y uno, dos . . . keep your shoulders parallel to the water.

SIMÓN: I'm gonna take these glasses off and look straight into the sun.

Joanna Liao as Margarita Suárez in a production of *The Cuban Swimmer*
Source: Photo by Mark Garvin.

EDUARDO: (through megaphone) Muy bien, muy bien . . . but punch those arms in, baby.

SIMÓN: (looking directly at the sun through binoculars) Come on, come on, zap me. Show me something. (He looks behind at the shoreline and ahead at the sea.) Stop! Stop, Papi! Stop!

Aída Suárez and Abuela, the swimmer's mother and grandmother, enter running from the back of the boat.

AÍDA AND ABUELA: Qué? Qué es?   5
AÍDA: Es un shark?
EDUARDO: Eh?
ABUELA: Que es un shark dicen?

Eduardo blows whistle. Margarita looks up at the boat.

SIMÓN: No, Papi, no shark, no shark. We've reached the halfway mark.
ABUELA: (looking into the water) A dónde está?   10
AÍDA: It's not in the water.
ABUELA: Oh, no? Oh, no?
AÍDA: No! A poco do you think they're gonna have signs in the water to say you are halfway to Santa Catalina? No. It's done very scientific.
A ver, hijo, explain it to your grandma.
SIMÓN: Well, you see, Abuela—(He points behind.) There's San Pedro. (He points ahead.) And there's Santa Catalina. Looks halfway to me.

Abuela shakes her head and is looking back and forth, trying to make the decision, when suddenly the sound of a helicopter is heard.

ABUELA: (looking up) Virgencita de la Caridad del Cobre. Qué es eso?   15

Sound of helicopter gets closer. Margarita looks up.

MARGARITA: Papi, Papi!

A small commotion on the boat, with everybody pointing at the helicopter above. Shadows of the helicopter fall on the boat. Simón looks up at it through binoculars.

Papi—qué es? What is it?
EDUARDO: (through megaphone) Uh . . . uh . . . uh, un momentico . . . mi hija. . . . Your papi's got everything under control, understand? Uh . . . you just keep stroking. And stay . . . uh . . . close to the boat.
SIMÓN: Wow, Papi! We're on TV, man! Holy Christ, we're all over the fucking U.S.A.! It's Mel Munson and Mary Beth White!
AÍDA: Por Dios! Simón, don't swear. And put on your shirt.

Aída fluffs her hair, puts on her sunglasses and waves to the helicopter. Simón leans over the side of the boat and yells to Margarita.

20 **Simón:** Yo, Margo! You're on TV, man.

Eduardo: Leave your sister alone. Turn on the radio.

Margarita: *Papi! Qué está pasando?*

Abuela: *Que es la televisión dicen? (She shakes her head.) Porque como yo no puedo ver nada sin mis espejuelos.*

Abuela rummages through the boat, looking for her glasses. Voices of Mel Munson and Mary Beth White are heard over the boat's radio.

Mel's Voice: As we take a closer look at the gallant crew of *La Havana* . . . and there . . . yes, there she is . . . the little Cuban swimmer from Long Beach, California, nineteen-year-old Margarita Suárez. The unknown swimmer is our Cinderella entry . . . a bundle of tenacity, battling her way through the choppy, murky waters of the cold Pacific to reach the Island of Romance . . . Santa Catalina . . . where should she be the first to arrive, two thousand dollars and a gold cup will be waiting for her.

25 **Aída:** Doesn't even cover our expenses.

Abuela: *Qué dice?*

Eduardo: Shhhh!

Mary Beth's Voice: This is really a family effort, Mel, and—

Mel's Voice: Indeed it is. Her trainer, her coach, her mentor, is her father, Eduardo Suárez. Not a swimmer himself, it says here, Mr. Suárez is head usher of the Holy Name Society and the owner-operator of Suárez Treasures of the Sea and Salvage Yard. I guess it's one of those places—

30 **Mary Beth's Voice:** If I might interject a fact here, Mel, assisting in this swim is Mrs. Suárez, who is a former Miss Cuba.

Mel's Voice: And a beautiful woman in her own right. Let's try and get a closer look.

Helicopter sound gets louder. Margarita, frightened, looks up again.

Margarita: *Papi!*

Eduardo: *(through megaphone) Mi hija,* don't get nervous . . . it's the press. I'm handling it.

Aída: I see how you're handling it.

35 **Eduardo:** *(through megaphone)* Do you hear? Everything is under control. Get back into your rhythm. Keep your elbows high and kick and kick and kick and kick . . .

Abuela: *(finds her glasses and puts them on) Ay sí, es la televisión . . . (She points to helicopter.) Qué lindo mira . . . (She fluffs her hair,* *gives a big wave.) Aló América! Viva mi Margarita, viva todo los Cubanos en los Estados Unidos!*

AÍDA: Ay *por Dios,* Cecilia, the man didn't come all this way in his helicopter to look at you jumping up and down, making a fool of yourself.

ABUELA: I don't care. I'm proud.

AÍDA: He can't understand you anyway.

ABUELA: *Viva . . . (She stops.) Simón, comó se dice viva?* 40

SIMÓN: Hurray.

ABUELA: Hurray for *mi Margarita y* for all the Cubans living *en* the United States, *y un abrazo . . . Simón, abrazo . . .*

SIMÓN: A big hug.

ABUELA: *Sí,* a big hug to all my friends in Miami, Long Beach, Union City, except for my son Carlos, who lives in New York in sin! He lives . . . *(she crosses herself)* in Brooklyn with a Puerto Rican woman in sin! *No decente . . .*

SIMÓN: Decent. 45

ABUELA: Carlos, *no decente.* This family, *decente.*

AÍDA: Cecilia, *por Dios.*

MEL'S VOICE: Look at that enthusiasm. The whole family has turned out to cheer little Margarita on to victory! I hope they won't be too disappointed.

MARY BETH'S VOICE: She seems to be making good time, Mel.

MEL'S VOICE: Yes, it takes all kinds to make a race. And it's a testimo- 50 nial to the all-encompassing fairness . . . the greatness of this, the Wrigley Invitational Women's Swim to Catalina, where among all the professionals there is still room for the amateurs . . . like these, the simple people we see below us on the ragtag *La Havana,* taking their long-shot chance to victory. *Vaya con Dios!*

Helicopter sound fading as family, including Margarita, watch silently. Static as Simón turns radio off. Eduardo walks to bow of boat, looks out on the horizon.

EDUARDO: *(to himself)* Amateurs.

AÍDA: Eduardo, that person insulted us. Did you hear, Eduardo? That he called us a simple people in a ragtag boat? Did you hear . . .?

ABUELA: *(clenching her fist at departing helicopter)* Mal-Rayo los parta!

SIMÓN: *(same gesture)* Asshole!

Aída follows Eduardo as he goes to side of boat and stares at Margarita.

AÍDA: This person comes in his helicopter to insult your wife, your 55 family, your daughter . . .

MARGARITA: *(pops her head out of the water)* Papi?

AÍDA: Do you hear me, Eduardo? I am not simple.

ABUELA: *Sí.*

AÍDA: I am complicated.

60 ABUELA: *Sí, demasiada complicada.*

AÍDA: Me and my family are not so simple.

SIMÓN: Mom, the guy's an asshole.

ABUELA: (*shaking her fist at helicopter*) Asshole!

AÍDA: If my daughter was simple, she would not be in that water swimming.

65 MARGARITA: Simple? *Papi . . .?*

AÍDA: *Ahora,* Eduardo, this is what I want you to do. When we get to Santa Catalina, I want you to call the TV station and demand an apology.

EDUARDO: *Cállete mujer! Aquí mando yo.* I will decide what is to be done.

MARGARITA: *Papi,* tell me what's going on.

EDUARDO: Do you understand what I am saying to you, Aída?

70 SIMÓN: (*leaning over side of boat, to Margarita*) Yo Margo! You know that Mel Munson guy on TV? He called you a simple amateur and said you didn't have a chance.

ABUELA: (*leaning directly behind Simón.*) Mi hija, insultó a la familia. Desgraciado!

AÍDA: (*leaning in behind Abuela*) He called us peasants! And your father is not doing anything about it. He just knows how to yell at me.

EDUARDO: (*through megaphone*) Shut up! All of you! Do you want to break her concentration? Is that what you are after? Eh?

Abuela, Aída, and Simón shrink back. Eduardo paces before them.

Swimming is rhythm and concentration. You win a race *aquí.* (*Pointing to his head.*) Now . . . (*to Simón*) you, take care of the boat, Aída y Mama . . . do something. Anything. Something practical.

Abuela and Aída get on knees and pray in Spanish.

Hija, give it everything, eh? . . . *por la familia. Uno . . . dos. . . .* You must win.

Simón goes into cabin. The prayers continue as lights change to indicate bright sunlight, later in the afternoon.

SCENE 3

Tableau for a couple of beats. Eduardo on bow with timer in one hand as he counts strokes per minute. Simón is in the cabin steering, wearing his sunglasses, baseball cap on backward. Abuela and Aída are at the side of the boat, heads down, hands folded, still muttering prayers in Spanish.

AÍDA AND ABUELA: (*crossing themselves*) En el nombre del Padre, del Hijo y del Espíritu Santo amén.

EDUARDO: (*through megaphone*) You're stroking seventy-two!

SIMÓN: (*singing*) Mama's stroking, Mama's stroking seventy-two. . . .

EDUARDO: (*through megaphone*) You comfortable with it?

SIMÓN: (*singing*) Seventy-two, seventy-two, seventy-two for you.   5

AÍDA: (*looking at the heavens*) Ay, Eduardo, ven acá, we should be grateful that Nuestro Señor gave us such a beautiful day.

ABUELA: (*crosses herself*) Si, gracias a Dios.

EDUARDO: She's stroking seventy-two, with no problem. (*He throws a kiss to the sky.*) It's a beautiful day to win.

AÍDA: Qué hermoso! So clear and bright. Not a cloud in the sky. Mira! Mira! Even rainbows on the water . . . a sign from God.

SIMÓN: (*singing*) Rainbows on the water . . . you in my arms . . .   10

ABUELA AND EDUARDO: (*Looking the wrong way.*) Dónde?

AÍDA: (*pointing toward Margarita*) There, dancing in front of Margarita, leading her on . . .

EDUARDO: Rainbows on . . . Ay coño! It's an oil slick! You . . . you . . . (*To Simón.*) Stop the boat. (*Runs to bow, yelling.*) Margarita! Margarita!

On the next stroke, Margarita comes up all covered in black oil.

MARGARITA: Papi! Papi . . . !

Everybody goes to the side and stares at Margarita, who stares back. Eduardo freezes.

AÍDA: Apúrate, Eduardo, move . . . what's wrong with you . . . no me   15
oíste, get my daughter out of the water.

EDUARDO: (*softly*) We can't touch her. If we touch her, she's disqualified.

AÍDA: But I'm her mother.

EDUARDO: Not even by her own mother. Especially by her own mother. . . . You always want the rules to be different for you, you always want to be the exception. (*To Simón.*) And you . . . you didn't see it, eh? You were playing again?

SIMÓN: Papi, I was watching . . .

AÍDA: (*interrupting*) Pues, do something Eduardo. You are the big coach,   20
the monitor.

SIMÓN: Mentor! Mentor!

EDUARDO: How can a person think around you? (*He walks off to bow, puts head in hands.*)

ABUELA: (*looking over side*) *Mira como todos los* little birds are dead. (*She crosses herself.*)

AÍDA: Their little wings are glued to their sides.

25 SIMÓN: Christ, this is like the La Brea tar pits.

AÍDA: They can't move their little wings.

ABUELA: *Esa niña tiene que moverse.*

SIMÓN: Yeah, Margo, you gotta move, man.

Abuela and Simón gesture for Margarita to move. Aída gestures for her to swim.

30 ABUELA: *Anda niña, muévete.*

AÍDA: Swim, *hija*, swim or the *aceite* will stick to your wings.

MARGARITA: *Papi?*

ABUELA: (*taking megaphone*) Your *papi* say "move it!"

Margarita with difficulty starts moving.

ABUELA, AÍDA AND SIMÓN: (*laboriously counting*) *Uno, dos . . . uno, dos . . . anda . . . uno, dos.*

EDUARDO: (*running to take megaphone from Abuela*) *Uno, dos . . .*

Simón races into cabin and starts the engine. Abuela, Aída and Eduardo count together.

35 SIMÓN: (*looking ahead*) *Papi*, it's over there!

EDUARDO: Eh?

SIMÓN: (*pointing ahead and to the right*) It's getting clearer over there.

EDUARDO: (*through megaphone*) Now pay attention to me. Go to the right.

Simón, Abuela, Aída and Eduardo all lean over side. They point ahead and to the right, except Abuela, who points to the left.

FAMILY: (*shouting together*) *Para yá! Para yá!*

Lights go down on boat. A special light on Margarita, swimming through the oil, and on Abuela, watching her.

40 ABUELA: *Sangre de mi sangre*, you will be another to save us. En Bolondron, where your great-grandmother Luz Suárez was born, they say one day it rained blood. All the people, they run into their houses. They cry, they pray, *pero* your great-grandmother Luz she had *cojones* like a man. She run outside. She look straight at the sky. She shake her fist. And she say to the evil one, "*Mira . . .* (*beating her chest*) *coño, Diablo, aquí estoy si me quieres.*" And she open her mouth, and she drunk the blood.

Blackout

SCENE 4

Lights up on boat. Aída and Eduardo are on deck watching Margarita swim. We hear the gentle, rhythmic lap, lap, lap of the water, then the sound of inhaling and exhaling as Margarita's breathing becomes louder. Then Margarita's heartbeat is heard, with the lapping of the water and the breathing under it. These sounds continue beneath the dialogue to the end of the scene.

AÍDA: *Dios mío.* Look how she moves through the water. . . .

EDUARDO: You see, it's very simple. It is a matter of concentration.

AÍDA: The first time I put her in water she came to life, she grew before my eyes. She moved, she smiled, she loved it more than me. She didn't want my breast any longer. She wanted the water.

EDUARDO: And of course, the rhythm. The rhythm takes away the pain and helps the concentration.

Pause. Aída and Eduardo watch Margarita.

AÍDA: Is that my child or a seal. . . .   5

EDUARDO: Ah, a seal, the reason for that is that she's keeping her arms very close to her body. She cups her hands, and then she reaches and digs, reaches and digs.

AÍDA: To think that a daughter of mine . . .

EDUARDO: It's the training, the hours in the water. I used to tie weights around her little wrists and ankles.

AÍDA: A spirit, an ocean spirit, must have entered my body when I was carrying her.

EDUARDO: *(to Margarita)* Your stroke is slowing down.   10

Pause. We hear Margarita's heartbeat with the breathing under, faster now.

AÍDA: Eduardo, that night, the night on the boat . . .

EDUARDO: Ah, the night on the boat again . . . the moon was . . .

AÍDA: The moon was full. We were coming to America. . . . *Qué romantico.*

Heartbeat and breathing continue.

EDUARDO: We were cold, afraid, with no money, and on top of everything, you were hysterical, yelling at me, tearing at me with your nails. *(Opens his shirt, points to the base of his neck.)* Look, I still bear the scars . . . telling me that I didn't know what I was doing . . . saying that we were going to die. . . .

AÍDA: You took me, you stole me from my home . . . you didn't give   15
me a chance to prepare. You just said we have to go now, now! Now, you said. You didn't let me take anything. I left everything behind. . . . I left everything behind.

EDUARDO: Saying that I wasn't good enough, that your father didn't raise you so that I could drown you in the sea.

AÍDA: You didn't let me say even a good-bye. You took me, you stole me, you tore me from my home.

EDUARDO: I took you so we could be married.

AÍDA: That was in Miami. But that night on the boat, Eduardo. . . . We were not married, that night on the boat.

20 **EDUARDO:** *No pasó nada!* Once and for all get it out of your head, it was cold, you hated me, and we were afraid. . . .

AÍDA: *Mentiroso!*

EDUARDO: A man can't do it when he is afraid.

AÍDA: Liar! You did it very well.

EDUARDO: I did?

25 **AÍDA:** *Sí.* Gentle. You were so gentle and then strong . . . my passion for you so deep. Standing next to you . . . I would ache . . . looking at your hands I would forget to breathe, you were irresistible.

EDUARDO: I was?

AÍDA: You took me into your arms, you touched my face with your fingertips . . . you kissed my eyes . . . *la esquina de la boca y* . . .

EDUARDO: *Sí, sí,* and then . . .

AÍDA: I look at your face on top of mine, and I see the lights of Havana in your eyes. That's when you seduced me.

30 **EDUARDO:** Shhh, they're gonna hear you.

Lights go down. Special on Aída.

AÍDA: That was the night. A woman doesn't forget those things . . . and later that night was the dream . . . the dream of a big country with fields of fertile land and big, giant things growing. And there by a green, slimy pond I found a giant pea pod and when I opened it, it was full of little, tiny baby frogs.

Aída crosses herself as she watches Margarita. We hear louder breathing and heartbeat.

MARGARITA: Santa Teresa. Little Flower of God, pray for me. San Martín de Porres, pray for me. Santa Rosa de Lima, *Virgencita de la Caridad del Cobre*, pray for me. . . . Mother pray for me.

SCENE 5

Loud howling of wind is heard, as lights change to indicate unstable weather, fog and mist. Family on deck, braced and huddled against the wind. Simón is at the helm.

AÍDA: *Ay Dios mío, qué viento.*

EDUARDO: *(through megaphone)* Don't drift out . . . that wind is pushing you out. *(To Simón.)* You! Slow down. Can't you see your sister is drifting out?

SIMÓN: It's the wind, *Papi.*

AÍDA: Baby, don't go so far. . . .

ABUELA: *(to heaven) Ay Gran Poder de Dios, quita este maldito viento.*   5

SIMÓN: Margo! Margo! Stay close to the boat.

EDUARDO: Dig in. Dig in hard. . . . Reach down from your guts and dig in.

ABUELA: *(to heaven) Ay Virgen de la Caridad del Cobre, por lo más tú quieres a pararla.*

AÍDA: *(putting her hand out, reaching for Margarita)* Baby, don't go far.

Abuela crosses herself. Action freezes. Lights get dimmer, special on Margarita. She keeps swimming, stops, starts again, stops, then, finally exhausted, stops altogether. The boat stops moving.

EDUARDO: What's going on here? Why are we stopping?   10

SIMÓN: *Papi,* she's not moving! Yo Margo!

The family all run to the side.

EDUARDO: *Hija!* . . . *Hijita!* You're tired, eh?

AÍDA: *Por supuesto* she's tired. I like to see you get in the water, waving your arms and legs from San Pedro to Santa Catalina. A person isn't a machine, a person has to rest.

SIMÓN: Yo, Mama! Cool out, it ain't fucking brain surgery.

EDUARDO: *(to Simón)* Shut up, you. *(Louder to Margarita.)* I guess your   15
mother's right for once, huh? . . . I guess you had to stop, eh? . . .
Give your brother, the idiot . . . a chance to catch up with you.

SIMÓN: *(clowning like Mortimer Snerd)* Dum dee dum dee dum ooops, ah shucks . . .

EDUARDO: I don't think he's Cuban.

SIMÓN: *(like Ricky Ricardo) Oye,* Lucy! I'm home! Ba ba lu!

EDUARDO: *(joins in clowning, grabbing Simón in a headlock)* What am I gonna do with this idiot, eh? I don't understand this idiot. He's not like us, Margarita. *(Laughing.)* You think if we put him into your bathing suit with a cap on his head . . . *(He laughs hysterically.)* You think anyone would know . . . huh? Do you think anyone would know? *(Laughs.)*

SIMÓN: *(vamping) Ay, mi amor.* Anybody looking for tits would know.   20

Eduardo slaps Simón across the face, knocking him down. Aída runs to Simón's aid. Abuela holds Eduardo back.

MARGARITA: *Mía culpa! Mía culpa!*

ABUELA: *Qué dices hija?*

MARGARITA: *Papi*, it's my fault, it's all my fault. . . . I'm so cold, I can't move. . . . I put my face in the water . . . and I hear them whispering . . . laughing at me. . . .

AÍDA: Who is laughing at you?

25 MARGARITA: The fish are all biting me . . . they hate me . . . they whisper about me. She can't swim, they say. She can't glide. She has no grace. . . . Yellowtails, bonita, tuna, man-o'-war, snub-nose sharks, *los baracudas* . . . they all hate me . . . only the dolphins care . . . and sometimes I hear the whales crying . . . she is lost, she is dead. I'm so numb, I can't feel. *Papi! Papi!* Am I dead?

EDUARDO: *Vamos*, baby, punch those arms in. Come on . . . do you hear me?

MARGARITA: *Papi* . . . *Papi* . . . forgive me. . . .

All is silent on the boat. Eduardo drops his megaphone, his head bent down in dejection. Abuela, Aída, Simón, all leaning over the side of the boat. Simón slowly walks away.

AÍDA: *Mi hija, qué tienes?*

SIMÓN: Oh, Christ, don't make her say it. Please don't make her say it.

30 ABUELA: Say what? *Qué cosa?*

SIMÓN: She wants to quit, can't you see she's had enough?

ABUELA: *Mira, para eso. Esta niña* is turning blue.

AÍDA: *Oyeme, mi hija.* Do you want to come out of the water?

MARGARITA: *Papi?*

35 SIMÓN: (*to Eduardo*) She won't come out until *you* tell her.

AÍDA: Eduardo . . . answer your daughter.

EDUARDO: *Le dije* to concentrate . . . concentrate on your rhythm. Then the rhythm would carry her . . . ay, it's a beautiful thing, Aída. It's like yoga, like meditation, the mind over matter . . . the mind controlling the body . . . that's how the great things in the world have been done. I wish you . . . I wish my wife could understand.

MARGARITA: *Papi?*

SIMÓN: (*to Margarita*) Forget him.

40 AÍDA: (*imploring*) Eduardo, *por favor.*

EDUARDO: (*walking in circles*) Why didn't you let her concentrate? Don't you understand, the concentration, the rhythm is everything. But no, you wouldn't listen. (*Screaming to the ocean.*) Goddamn Cubans, why, God, why do you make us go everywhere with our families? (*He goes to back of boat.*)

AÍDA: *(opening her arms) Mi hija, ven,* come to Mami. *(Rocking.)* Your *mami* knows.

Abuela has taken the training bottle, puts it in a net. She and Simón lower it to Margarita.

SIMÓN: Take this. Drink it. *(As Margarita drinks, Abuela crosses herself.)*

ABUELA: *Sangre de mi sangre.*

Music comes up softly. Margarita drinks, gives the bottle back, stretches out her arms, as if on a cross. Floats on her back. She begins a graceful backstroke. Lights fade on boat as special lights come up on Margarita. She stops. Slowly turns over and starts to swim, gradually picking up speed. Suddenly as if in pain she stops, tries again, then stops in pain again. She becomes disoriented and falls to the bottom of the sea. Special on Margarita at the bottom of the sea.

MARGARITA: *Ya no puedo* . . . I can't. . . . A person isn't a machine . . .   45
es mi culpa . . . Father forgive me . . . *Papi! Papi!* One, two. *Uno, dos.*
(Pause.) Papi! A dónde estás? (Pause.) One, two, one, two. *Papi!* Ay,
Papi! Where are you . . . ? Don't leave me. . . . Why don't you answer
me? *(Pause. She starts to swim, slowly.) Uno, dos, uno, dos.* Dig in,
dig in. *(Stops swimming.) Por favor, Papi! (Starts to swim again.)* One,
two, one, two. Kick from your hip, kick from your hip. *(Stops swimming. Starts to cry.)* Oh God, please. . . . *(Pause.)* Hail Mary, full
of grace . . . dig in, dig in . . . the Lord is with thee. . . . *(She swims
to the rhythm of her Hail Mary.)* Hail Mary, full of grace . . . dig in,
dig in . . . the Lord is with thee . . . dig in, dig in. . . . Blessed art
thou among women. . . . *Mami,* it hurts. You let go of my hand. I'm
lost. . . . And blessed is the fruit of thy womb, now and at the hour
of our death. Amen. I don't want to die, I don't want to die.

Margarita is still swimming. Blackout. She is gone.

SCENE 6

Lights up on boat, we hear radio static. There is a heavy mist. On deck we see only black outline of Abuela with shawl over her head. We hear the voices of Eduardo, Aída, and Radio Operator.

EDUARDO'S VOICE: *La Havana!* Coming from San Pedro. Over.

RADIO OPERATOR'S VOICE: Right, DT6-6, you say you've lost a swimmer.

AÍDA'S VOICE: Our child, our only daughter . . . listen to me. Her name
is Margarita Inez Suárez, she is wearing a black one-piece bathing
suit cut high in the legs with a white racing stripe down the sides,
a white bathing cap with goggles and her whole body covered with
a . . . with a . . .

EDUARDO'S VOICE: With lanolin and paraffin.
AÍDA'S VOICE: Sí . . . con lanolin and paraffin.

More radio static. Special on Simón, on the edge of the boat.

SIMÓN: Margo! Yo Margo! *(Pause.)* Man don't do this. *(Pause.)* Come
on. . . . Come on. . . . *(Pause.)* God, why does everything have to be
so hard? *(Pause.)* Stupid. You know you're not supposed to die for
this. Stupid. It's his dream and he can't even swim. *(Pause.)* Punch
those arms in. Come home. Come home. I'm your little brother.
Don't forget what Mama said. You're not supposed to leave me behind. *Vamos*, Margarita, take your little brother, hold his hand tight
when you cross the street. He's so little. *(Pause.)* Oh, Christ, give us
a sign. . . . I know! I know! Margo, I'll send you a message . . . like
mental telepathy. I'll hold my breath, close my eyes, and I'll bring you
home. *(He takes a deep breath; a few beats.)* This time I'll beep . . . I'll
send out sonar signals like a dolphin. *(He imitates dolphin sounds.)*

*The sound of real dolphins takes over from Simón, then fades into sound of
Abuela saying the Hail Mary in Spanish, as full lights come up slowly.*

SCENE 7

*Eduardo coming out of cabin, sobbing, Aída holding him. Simón anxiously scan-
ning the horizon. Abuela looking calmly ahead.*

EDUARDO: Es mi culpa, sí, es mi culpa. *(He hits his chest.)*
AÍDA: Ya, ya viejo . . . it was my sin . . . I left my home.
EDUARDO: Forgive me, forgive me. I've lost our daughter, our sister,
our granddaughter, *mi carne, mi sangre, mis ilusiones. (To heaven.)*
Dios mío, take me . . . take me, I say . . . Goddammit, take me!
SIMÓN: I'm going in.
5 AÍDA AND EDUARDO: No!
EDUARDO: *(grabbing and holding Simón, speaking to heaven)* God, take me,
not my children. They are my dreams, my illusions . . . and not this
one, this one is my mystery . . . he has my secret dreams. In him are
the parts of me I cannot see.

Eduardo embraces Simón. Radio static becomes louder.

AÍDA: I . . . I think I see her.
SIMÓN: No, it's just a seal.
ABUELA: *(looking out with binoculars)* Mi nietacita, dónde estás? *(She feels her
heart.)* I don't feel the knife in my heart . . . my little fish is not lost.

*Radio crackles with static. As lights dim on boat, Voices of Mel and Mary Beth
are heard over the radio.*

MEL'S VOICE: Tragedy has marred the face of the Wrigley Invitational   10
Women's Race to Catalina. The Cuban swimmer, little Margarita
Suárez, has reportedly been lost at sea. Coast Guard and divers are
looking for her as we speak. Yet in spite of this tragedy the race
must go on because . . .

MARY BETH'S VOICE: *(interrupting loudly)* Mel!

MEL'S VOICE: *(startled)* What!

MARY BETH'S VOICE: Ah . . . excuse me, Mel . . . we have a winner.   15
We've just received word from Catalina that one of the swimmers is
just fifty yards from the breakers . . . it's, oh, it's . . . Margarita Suárez!

Special on family in cabin listening to radio.

MEL'S VOICE: What? I thought she died!

Special on Margarita, taking off bathing cap, trophy in hand, walking on the water.

MARY BETH'S VOICE: Ahh . . . unless . . . unless this is a tragic . . . No
. . . there she is, Mel. Margarita Suárez! The only one in the race
wearing a black bathing suit cut high in the legs with a racing stripe
down the side.

Family cheering, embracing.

SIMÓN: *(screaming)* Way to go, Margo!

MEL'S VOICE: This is indeed a miracle! It's a resurrection! Margarita
Suárez, with a flotilla of boats to meet her, is now walking on the
waters, through the breakers . . . onto the beach, with crowds of
people cheering her on. What a jubilation! This is a miracle!

Sound of crowds cheering. Lights and cheering sounds fade.

Blackout

*   *   *

Reading and Reacting

1. What lighting and sound effects do the stage directions specify? In
   what way do these effects advance the action of the play? How do they
   help to communicate the play's theme?
2. Although most of the play is in English, the characters frequently
   speak Spanish. What are the advantages and disadvantages of this
   use of Spanish? How does the mixing of English and Spanish reflect
   one of the play's themes?
3. What function do the voices of Mel and Mary Beth serve in the play?
4. What conflicts develop among the family members as the play proceeds? Do you think these conflicts are meant to represent the problems of other immigrant groups?

5. In what sense is Mel's final comment "This is a miracle!" true? In what sense is it ironic?

6. Could this play be seen as an allegory? What is the value of seeing it in this way?

7. During much of the play, Margarita is swimming in full view of the audience. Suggest three ways in which a director could convey this effect on stage. Which way would you choose if you were directing the play? Why?

8. As the headnote to the play explains, the 1984 New York production of *The Cuban Swimmer* had an extremely realistic set. Could the play be staged unrealistically, with the characters on a raised platform instead of a boat? How do you think this kind of set would change the audience's reaction?

9. **JOURNAL ENTRY** Are you able to empathize with Margarita's struggle? What elements of the play make it easy (or difficult) for you to do so?

10. **CRITICAL PERSPECTIVE** In a 1998 article in the *New York Times*, theater critic Brooks Atkinson said, "Nothing is better for good actors than a stage with no scenery."

How do you interpret Atkinson's comment? Do you think this remark could be applied to the staging of *The Cuban Swimmer*?

Related Works: "Snow" (p. 82), "The Secret Lion" (p. 466), "Two Kinds" (p. 471), "Baca Grande" (p. 545), "Harlem" (p. 577), "Mexican Almuerzo in New England" (p. 666), "Isla" (p. 679)

SOPHOCLES (496–406 B.C.), along with Aeschylus and Euripides, is one of the three great ancient Greek tragic dramatists. He lived during the flowering and subsequent decline of fifth-century B.C. Athens—the high point of Greek civilization. Born as Greece struggled against the Persian Empire and moved to adopt democracy, he lived as an adult under Pericles during the golden age of Athens and died as it became clear that Athens would lose the Peloponnesian War. Sophocles was an active participant in the public life of Athens, serving as a collector of tribute from Athenian subjects and later as a general. He wrote at least 120 plays, but only seven have survived, including three plays about Oedipus: *Oedipus the King* (c. 430 B.C.), *Oedipus at Colonus* (411? B.C.), and *Antigone* (441 B.C.).

Oedipus the King, or *Oedipus Rex* (sometimes called *Oedipus the Tyrant*), was performed shortly after a great plague in Athens (probably in 429 or 425 B.C.) and as Athens was falling into decline. The play opens with an account of a plague in Thebes, Oedipus's kingdom. Over the years, *Oedipus the King* has attracted impressive critical attention, from

Bettmann/Corbis

Aristotle's use of it as a model for his definition of tragedy to Freud's use of it when he discusses the Oedipus complex.

Cultural Context During the period in which *Oedipus* was written, the Greeks were especially interested in the relationship between greatness and *hubris*, the excessive pride and ambition that leads to the downfall of a hero in classical tragedy. They were fascinated by the idea that hubris can bring destruction: that the same traits that can elevate a person to greatness can also cause his or her ruin. This theme recurs throughout classical literature and was especially relevant between 431 and 404 B.C., when the second Peloponnesian War (which Athens lost) was being fought between Athens and Sparta. After a Spartan army invaded Attica in 431 B.C., the Athenians retreated behind the walls of their city while the Athenian fleet began raids. Between 430 and 428 B.C., a plague (which the Athenians believed was inflicted upon them by the gods) wiped out at least a quarter of the Athenian population. It was during this tumultuous time that Sophocles wrote of Oedipus and his troubles.

Oedipus the King* (c. 430 B.C.)

Translated by Thomas Gould

CHARACTERS

Oedipus,[1] *the King of Thebes*
Priest of Zeus, *leader of the suppliants*
Creon, *Oedipus's brother-in-law*
Chorus, *a group of Theban elders*
Choragos, *spokesman of the Chorus*

Tiresias, *a blind seer or prophet*
Jocasta, *the queen of Thebes*
Messenger, *from Corinth, once a shepherd*
Herdsman, *once a servant of Laius*
Second Messenger, *a servant of Oedipus*

MUTES

Suppliants, *Thebans seeking Oedipus's help*
Attendants, *for the Royal Family*
Servants, *to lead Tiresias and Oedipus*
Antigone, *daughter of Oedipus and Jocasta*
Ismene, *daughter of Oedipus and Jocasta*

The action takes place during the day in front of the royal palace in Thebes. There are two altars (left and right) on the proscenium and several steps leading down to the orchestra. As the play opens, Thebans of various ages who have come to beg Oedipus for help are sitting on these steps and in part of the orchestra. These suppliants are holding branches of laurel or olive which have strips of wool[2] *wrapped around them. Oedipus enters from the palace (the central door of the skene).*

---

*Note that individual lines are numbered in the following play. When a line is shared by two or more characters, it is counted as one line.

[1] *Oedipus:* The name, meaning "swollen foot," refers to the mutilation of Oedipus's feet by his father, Laius, before the infant was sent to Mount Cithaeron to be put to death by exposure.

[2] *wool:* Branches wrapped with wool are traditional symbols of prayer or supplication.

Laurence Olivier as Oedipus
Merlyn Severn/Picture Post/Getty Images

PROLOGUE[3]

OEDIPUS: My children, ancient Cadmus'[4] newest care,
why have you hurried to those seats, your boughs
wound with the emblems of the suppliant?
The city is weighed down with fragrant smoke,
5   with hymns to the Healer[5] and the cries of mourners.
I thought it wrong, my sons, to hear your words
through emissaries, and have come out myself,
I, Oedipus, a name that all men know.

Oedipus addresses the Priest.

Old man—for it is fitting that you speak
10   for all—what is your mood as you entreat me,
fear or trust? You may be confident
that I'll do anything. How hard of heart
if an appeal like this did not rouse my pity!
PRIEST: You, Oedipus, who hold the power here,
15   you see our several ages, we who sit
before your altars—some not strong enough

---

[3]*Prologue:* The portion of the play containing the exposition, or explanation, of what has gone before and what is now happening.

[4]*Cadmus:* Oedipus's great-great-grandfather (although Oedipus does not know this) and the founder of Thebes.

[5]*Healer:* Apollo, god of prophecy, light, healing, justice, purification, and destruction.

to take long flight, some heavy in old age,
the priests, as I of Zeus,[6] and from our youths
a chosen band. The rest sit with their windings
in the markets, at the twin shrines of Pallas,[7]   20
and the prophetic embers of Ismēnos.[8]
Our city, as you see yourself, is tossed
too much, and can no longer lift its head
above the troughs of billows red with death.
It dies in the fruitful flowers of the soil,   25
it dies in its pastured herds, and in its women's
barren pangs. And the fire-bearing god[9]
has swooped upon the city, hateful plague,
and he has left the house of Cadmus empty.
Black Hades[10] is made rich with moans and weeping.   30
Not judging you an equal of the gods,
do I and the children sit here at your hearth,
but as the first of men, in troubled times
and in encounters with divinities.
You came to Cadmus' city and unbound   35
the tax we had to pay to the harsh singer,[11]
did it without a helpful word from us,
with no instruction; with a god's assistance
you raised up our life, so we believe.
Again now Oedipus, our greatest power,   40
we plead with you, as suppliants, all of us,
to find us strength, whether from a god's response,
or learned in some way from another man.

---

[6] *Zeus:* Father and king of the gods.

[7] *Pallas:* Athena, goddess of wisdom, arts, crafts, and war.

[8] *Ismēnos:* A reference to the temple of Apollo near the river Ismēnos in Thebes. Prophecies were made here by "reading" the ashes of the altar fires.

[9] *fire-bearing god:* Contagious fever viewed as a god.

[10] *Black Hades:* Refers both to the underworld where the spirits of the dead go and to the god of the underworld.

[11] *harsh singer:* The Sphinx, a monster with a woman's head, a lion's body, and wings. The "tax" from which Oedipus freed Thebes was the destruction of all the young men who failed to solve the Sphinx's riddle and were subsequently devoured. The Sphinx always asked the same riddle: "What goes on four legs in the morning, two legs at noon, and three legs in the evening, and yet is weakest when supported by the largest number of feet?" Oedipus discovered the correct answer—man, who crawls in infancy, walks in his prime, and uses a stick in old age—and thus ended the Sphinx's reign of terror. The Sphinx destroyed herself when Oedipus answered the riddle. Oedipus's reward for freeing Thebes of the Sphinx was the throne and the hand of the recently widowed Jocasta.

I know that the experienced among men
45   give counsels that will prosper best of all.
Noblest of men, lift up our land again!
Think also of yourself; since now the land
calls you its Savior for your zeal of old,
oh let us never look back at your rule
50   as men helped up only to fall again!
Do not stumble! Put our land on firm feet!
The bird of omen was auspicious then,
when you brought that luck; be that same man again!
The power is yours; if you will rule our country,
55   rule over men, not in an empty land.
A towered city or a ship is nothing
if desolate and no man lives within.

OEDIPUS: Pitiable children, oh I know, I know
the yearnings that have brought you. Yes, I know
60   that you are sick. And yet, though you are sick,
there is not one of you so sick as I.
For your affliction comes to each alone,
for him and no one else, but my soul mourns
for me and for you, too, and for the city.
65   You do not waken me as from a sleep,
for I have wept, bitterly and long,
tried many paths in the wanderings of thought,
and the single cure I found by careful search
I've acted on: I sent Menoeceus' son,
70   Creon, brother of my wife, to the Pythian
halls of Phoebus,[12] so that I might learn
what I must do or say to save this city.
Already, when I think what day this is,
I wonder anxiously what he is doing.
75   Too long, more than is right, he's been away.
But when he comes, then I shall be a traitor
if I do not do all that the god reveals.

PRIEST: Welcome words! But look, those men have signaled
that it is Creon who is now approaching!
80   OEDIPUS: Lord Apollo! May he bring Savior Luck,
a Luck as brilliant as his eyes are now!

---

[12]*Pythian halls . . . Phoebus:* The temple of Phoebus, Apollo's oracle or prophet at Delphi.

PRIEST: His news is happy, it appears. He comes,
    forehead crowned with thickly berried laurel.[13]
OEDIPUS: We'll know, for he is near enough to hear us.

Enter Creon along one of the parados.

    Lord, brother in marriage, son of Menoeceus!   85
    What is the god's pronouncement that you bring?
CREON: It's good. For even troubles, if they chance
    to turn out well, I always count as lucky.
OEDIPUS: But what was the response? You seem to say
    I'm not to fear—but not to take heart either.   90
CREON: If you will hear me with these men present,
    I'm ready to report—or go inside.

Creon moves up the steps toward the palace.

OEDIPUS: Speak out to all! The grief that burdens me
    concerns these men more than it does my life.
CREON: Then I shall tell you what I heard from the god.   95
    The task Lord Phoebus sets for us is clear:
    drive out pollution sheltered in our land,
    and do not shelter what is incurable.
OEDIPUS: What is our trouble? How shall we cleanse ourselves?   100
CREON: We must banish or murder to free ourselves
    from a murder that blows storms through the city.
OEDIPUS: What man's bad luck does he accuse in this?
CREON: My Lord, a king named Laius ruled our land
    before you came to steer the city straight.
OEDIPUS: I know. So I was told—I never saw him.   105
CREON: Since he was murdered, you must raise your hand
    against the men who killed him with their hands.
OEDIPUS: Where are they now? And how can we ever find
    the track of ancient guilt now hard to read?
CREON: In our own land, he said. What we pursue,   110
    that can be caught; but not what we neglect.
OEDIPUS: Was Laius home, or in the countryside—
    or was he murdered in some foreign land?
CREON: He left to see a sacred rite, he said;
    He left, but never came home from his journey.   115

---

[13] *laurel:* Creon is wearing a garland of laurel leaves, sacred to Apollo.

Oedipus: Did none of his party see it and report—
someone we might profitably question?

Creon: They were all killed but one, who fled in fear,
and he could tell us only one clear fact.

120 **Oedipus:** What fact? One thing could lead us on to more
if we could get a small start on our hope.

Creon: He said that bandits chanced on them and killed him—
with the force of many hands, not one alone.

Oedipus: How could a bandit dare so great an act—
125 unless this was a plot paid off from here!

Creon: We thought of that, but when Laius was killed,
we had no one to help us in our troubles.

Oedipus: It was your very kingship that was killed!
What kind of trouble blocked you from a search?

130 **Creon:** The subtle-singing Sphinx asked us to turn
from the obscure to what lay at our feet.

Oedipus: Then I shall begin again and make it plain.
It was quite worthy of Phoebus, and worthy of you,
to turn our thoughts back to the murdered man,
135 and right that you should see me join the battle
for justice to our land and to the god.
Not on behalf of any distant kinships,
it's for myself I will dispel this stain.
Whoever murdered him may also wish
140 to punish me—and with the selfsame hand.
In helping him I also serve myself.
Now quickly, children: up from the altar steps,
and raise the branches of the suppliant!
Let someone go and summon Cadmus' people:
say I'll do anything.

Exit an Attendant along one of the parados.

145   Our luck will prosper
if the god is with us, or we have already fallen.

Priest: Rise, my children; that for which we came,
he has himself proclaimed he will accomplish.
May Phoebus, who announced this, also come
150 as Savior and reliever from the plague.

*Exit Oedipus and Creon into the palace. The Priest and the Suppliants exit
left and right along the parados. After a brief pause, the Chorus (including the
Choragos) enters the orchestra from the parados.*

PARADOS[1]
STROPHE 1[2]

CHORUS: Voice from Zeus,[3] sweetly spoken, what are you
　　that have arrived from golden
　　Pytho[4] to our shining
　　Thebes? I am on the rack, terror
　　　　shakes my soul.　　　　　　　　　　　　　　　155
　　Delian Healer,[5] summoned by "iē!"
　　I await in holy dread what obligation, something new
　　or something back once more with the revolving years,
　　　　you'll bring about for me.
　　Oh tell me, child of golden Hope,　　　　　　160
　　　　deathless Response!

ANTISTROPHE 1

　　I appeal to you first, daughter of Zeus,
　　　　deathless Athena,
　　　　and to your sister who protects this land,
　　Artemis,[6] whose famous throne is the whole circle　　170
　　　　of the marketplace,
　　and Phoebus, who shoots from afar: iō!
　　Three-fold defenders against death, appear!
　　If ever in the past, to stop blind ruin
　　　　sent against the city,
　　you banished utterly the fires of suffering,
　　　　come now again!

STROPHE 2

　　Ah! Ah! Unnumbered are the miseries
　　I bear. The plague claims all
　　our comrades. Nor has thought found yet a spear　　175
　　by which a man shall be protected. What our glorious
　　earth gives birth to does not grow. Without a birth
　　from cries of labor

---

[1] *Parados:* A song sung by the Chorus on first entering.

[2] *Strophe:* Probably refers to the direction in which the Chorus danced while reciting specific stanzas. *Strophe* may have indicated dance steps to stage left, *antistrophe* to stage right.

[3] *Voice from Zeus:* A reference to Apollo's prophecy. Zeus taught Apollo how to prophesy.

[4] *Pytho:* Delphi.

[5] *Delian Healer:* Apollo.

[6] *Artemis:* Goddess of virginity, childbirth, and hunting.

do the women rise.
180   One person after another
          you may see, like flying birds,
       faster than indomitable fire, sped
       to the shore of the god that is the sunset.[7]

ANTISTROPHE 2

And with their deaths unnumbered dies the city.
185   Her children lie unpitied on the ground,
       spreading death, unmourned.
       Meanwhile young wives, and gray-haired mothers with them,
       on the shores of the altars, from this side and that,
       suppliants from mournful trouble,
190   cry out their grief.
       A hymn to the Healer shines,
          the flute a mourner's voice.
       Against which, golden goddess, daughter of Zeus,
          send lovely Strength.

STROPHE 3

195   Causing raging Ares[8]—who,
          armed now with no shield of bronze,
       burns me, coming on amid loud cries—
       to turn his back and run from my land,
       with a fair wind behind, to the great
200   hall of Amphitritē,[9]
       or to the anchorage that welcomes no one,
       Thrace's troubled sea!
       If night lets something get away at last,
          it comes by day.
205   Fire-bearing god . . .
          you who dispense the might of lightning,
       Zeus! Father! Destroy him with your thunderbolt!

Enter Oedipus from the palace.

ANTISTROPHE 3

Lycēan Lord![10] From your looped
          bowstring, twisted gold,

---

[7] *god . . . sunset:* Hades, god of the underworld.
[8] *Ares:* God of war and destruction.
[9] *Amphitritē:* The Atlantic Ocean.
[10] *Lycēan Lord:* Apollo.

I wish indomitable missiles might be scattered   210
and stand forward, our protectors; also fire-bearing
radiance of Artemis, with which
    she darts across the Lycian mountains.
I call the god whose head is bound in gold,
with whom this country shares its name,   215
Bacchus,[11] wine-flushed, summoned by "euoi!,"
    Maenads' comrade,
to approach ablaze
    with gleaming . . .
pine, opposed to that god-hated god.   220

EPISODE 1[1]

OEDIPUS: I hear your prayer. Submit to what I say
and to the labors that the plague demands
and you'll get help and a relief from evils.
I'll make the proclamation, though a stranger
to the report and to the deed. Alone,   225
had I no key, I would soon lose the track.
Since it was only later that I joined you,
to all the sons of Cadmus I say this:
whoever has clear knowledge of the man   230
who murdered Laius, son of Labdacus,
I command him to reveal it all to me—
nor fear if, to remove the charge, he must
accuse himself: his fate will not be cruel—
he will depart unstumbling into exile.
But if you know another, or a stranger,   235
to be the one whose hand is guilty, speak:
I shall reward you and remember you.
But if you keep your peace because of fear,
and shield yourself or kin from my command,
hear you what I shall do in that event: 240
I charge all in this land where I have throne
and power, shut out that man—no matter who—
both from your shelter and all spoken words,
nor in your prayers or sacrifices make
him partner, nor allot him lustral[2] water.   245
All men shall drive him from their homes: for he
is the pollution that the god-sent Pythian

---

[11] *Bacchus:* Dionysus, god of fertility and wine.
[1] *Episode:* The portion of ancient Greek plays that appears between choric songs.
[2] *lustral:* Purifying.

response has only now revealed to me.
In this way I ally myself in war
250   with the divinity and the deceased.[3]
And this curse, too, against the one who did it,
whether alone in secrecy, or with others:
may he wear out his life unblest and evil!
I pray this, too: if he is at my hearth
255   and in my home, and I have knowledge of him,
may the curse pronounced on others come to me.
All this I lay to you to execute,
for my sake, for the god's, and for this land
now ruined, barren, abandoned by the gods.
260   Even if no god had driven you to it,
you ought not to have left this stain uncleansed,
the murdered man a nobleman, a king!
You should have looked! But now, since, as it happens,
It's I who have the power that he had once,
265   and have his bed, and a wife who shares our seed,
and common bond had we had common children
(had not his hope of offspring had bad luck—
but as it happened, luck lunged at his head);
because of this, as if for my own father,
270   I'll fight for him, I'll leave no means untried,
to catch the one who did it with his hand,
for the son of Labdacus, of Polydōrus,
of Cadmus before him, and of Agēnor.[4]
This prayer against all those who disobey:
275   the gods send out no harvest from their soil,
nor children from their wives. Oh, let them die
victims of this plague, or of something worse.
Yet for the rest of us, people of Cadmus,
we the obedient, may Justice, our ally,
280   and all the gods, be always on our side!
CHORAGOS:[5]   I speak because I feel the grip of your curse:
the killer is not I. Nor can I point
to him. The one who set us to this search,
Phoebus, should also name the guilty man.
285 OEDIPUS: Quite right, but to compel unwilling gods—
no man has ever had that kind of power.

---

[3]*the deceased:* Laius.

[4]*son . . . Agēnor:* Refers to Laius by citing his genealogy.

[5]*Choragos:* Leader of the Chorus and principal commentator on the play's action.

CHORAGOS: May I suggest to you a second way?

OEDIPUS: A second or a third—pass over nothing!

CHORAGOS: I know of no one who sees more of what
Lord Phoebus sees than Lord Tiresias.   290
My Lord, one might learn brilliantly from him.

OEDIPUS: Nor is this something I have been slow to do.
At Creon's word I sent an escort—twice now!
I am astonished that he has not come.

CHORAGOS: The old account is useless. It told us nothing.   295

OEDIPUS: But tell it to me. I'll scrutinize all stories.

CHORAGOS: He is said to have been killed by travelers.

OEDIPUS: I have heard, but the one who did it no one sees.

CHORAGOS: If there is any fear in him at all,
he won't stay here once he has heard that curse.   300

OEDIPUS: He won't fear words: he had no fear when he did it.

Enter Tiresias from the right, led by a Servant and two of Oedipus's Attendants.

CHORAGOS: Look there! There is the man who will convict him!
It's the god's prophet they are leading here,
one gifted with the truth as no one else.

OEDIPUS: Tiresias, master of all omens—   305
public and secret, in the sky and on the earth—
your mind, if not your eyes, sees how the city
lives with a plague, against which Thebes can find
no Saviour or protector, Lord, but you.
For Phoebus, as the attendants surely told you,   310
returned this answer to us: liberation
from the disease would never come unless
we learned without a doubt who murdered Laius—
put them to death, or sent them into exile.
Do not begrudge us what you may learn from birds   315
or any other prophet's path you know!
Care for yourself, the city, care for me,
care for the whole pollution of the dead!
We're in your hands. To do all that he can
to help another is man's noblest labor.   320

TIRESIAS: How terrible to understand and get
no profit from the knowledge! I knew this,
but I forgot, or I had never come.

OEDIPUS: What's this? You've come with very little zeal.

TIRESIAS: Let me go home! If you will listen to me,   325
You will endure your troubles better—and I mine.

OEDIPUS: A strange request, not very kind to the land

that cared for you—to hold back this oracle!

TIRESIAS: I see your understanding comes to you
330   inopportunely. So that won't happen to me . . .
OEDIPUS: Oh, by the gods, if you understand about this,
        don't turn away! We're on our knees to you.
TIRESIAS: None of you understands! I'll never bring
        my grief to light—I will not speak of yours.
335 OEDIPUS: You know and won't declare it! Is your purpose
        to betray us and to destroy this land!
TIRESIAS: I will grieve neither of us. Stop this futile
        cross-examination. I'll tell you nothing!
OEDIPUS: Nothing? You vile traitor! You could provoke
340   a stone to anger! You still refuse to tell?
        Can nothing soften you, nothing convince you?
TIRESIAS: You blamed anger in me—you haven't seen.
        The kind that lives with you, so you blame me.
OEDIPUS: Who wouldn't fill with anger, listening
345   to words like yours which now disgrace this city?
TIRESIAS: It will come, even if my silence hides it.
OEDIPUS: If it will come, then why won't you declare it?
TIRESIAS: I'd rather say no more. Now if you wish,
        respond to that with all your fiercest anger!
350 OEDIPUS: Now I am angry enough to come right out
        with this conjecture: you, I think, helped plot
        the deed; you did it—even if your hand,
        cannot have struck the blow. If you could see,
        I should have said the deed was yours alone.
355 TIRESIAS: Is that right! Then I charge you to abide
        by the decree you have announced: from this day
        say no word to either these or me,
        for you are the vile polluter of this land!
OEDIPUS: Aren't you appalled to let a charge like that
360   come bounding forth? How will you get away?
TIRESIAS: You cannot catch me. I have the strength of truth.
OEDIPUS: Who taught you this? Not your prophetic craft!
TIRESIAS: You did. You made me say it. I didn't want to.
OEDIPUS: Say what? Repeat it so I'll understand.
365 TIRESIAS: I made no sense? Or are you trying me?
OEDIPUS: No sense I understood. Say it again!
TIRESIAS: I say you are the murderer you seek.
OEDIPUS: Again that horror! You'll wish you hadn't said that.
TIRESIAS: Shall I say more, and raise your anger higher?
370 OEDIPUS: Anything you like! Your words are powerless.

TIRESIAS: You live, unknowing, with those nearest to you
            in the greatest shame. You do not see the evil.
OEDIPUS: You won't go on like that and never pay!
TIRESIAS: I can if there is any strength in truth.
OEDIPUS: In truth, but not in you! You have no strength,   375
            blind in your ears, your reason, and your eyes.
TIRESIAS: Unhappy man! Those jeers you hurl at me
            before long all these men will hurl at you.   380
OEDIPUS: You are the child of endless night; it's not
            for me or anyone who sees to hurt you.
TIRESIAS: It's not my fate to be struck down by you.
            Apollo is enough. That's his concern.
OEDIPUS: Are these inventions Creon's or your own?
TIRESIAS: No, your affliction is yourself, not Creon.
OEDIPUS: Oh success!—in wealth, kingship, artistry,   385
            in any life that wins much admiration—
            the envious ill will stored up for you!
            to get at my command, a gift I did not
            seek, which the city put into my hands,
            my loyal Creon, colleague from the start,   390
            longs to sneak up in secret and dethrone me.
            So he's suborned this fortuneteller—schemer!
            deceitful beggar-priest!—who has good eyes
            for gains alone, though in his craft he's blind.
            Where were your prophet's powers ever proved?   395
            Why, when the dog who chanted verse[6] was here,
            did you not speak and liberate this city?
            Her riddle wasn't for a man chancing by
            to interpret; prophetic art was needed,
            but you had none, it seems—learned from birds   400
            or from a god. I came along, yes I,
            Oedipus the ignorant, and stopped her—
            by using thought, not augury from birds.
            And it is I whom you now wish to banish,
            so you'll be close to the Creontian throne.   405
            You—and the plot's concocter—will drive out
            pollution to your grief: you look quite old
            or you would be the victim of that plot!
CHORAGOS: It seems to us that this man's words were said
            in anger, Oedipus, and yours as well.   410
            Insight, not angry words, is what we need,

---

[6]*dog . . . verse:* The Sphinx.

the best solution to the god's response.

TIRESIAS: You are the king, and yet I am your equal
in my right to speak. In that I too am Lord.
415   for I belong to Loxias,[7] not you.
I am not Creon's man. He's nothing to me.
Hear this, since you have thrown my blindness at me:
Your eyes can't see the evil to which you've come,
nor where you live, nor who is in your house.
420   Do you know your parents? Not knowing, you are
their enemy, in the underworld and here.
A mother's and a father's double-lashing
terrible-footed curse will soon drive you out.
Now you can see, then you will stare into darkness.
425   What place will not be harbor to your cry,
or what Cithaeron[8] not reverberate
when you have heard the bride-song in your palace
to which you sailed? Fair wind to evil harbor!
Nor do you see how many other woes
430   will level you to yourself and to your children.
So, at my message, and at Creon, too,
splatter muck! There will never be a man
ground into wretchedness as you will be.

OEDIPUS: Am I to listen to such things from him!
435   May you be damned! Get out of here at once!
Go! Leave my palace! Turn around and go!

Tiresias begins to move away from Oedipus.

TIRESIAS: I wouldn't have come had you not sent for me.
OEDIPUS: I did not know you'd talk stupidity,
or I wouldn't have rushed to bring you to my house.
440 TIRESIAS: Stupid I seem to you, yet to your parents
who gave you natural birth I seemed quite shrewd.
OEDIPUS: Who? Wait! Who is the one who gave me birth?
TIRESIAS: This day will give you birth,[9] and ruin too.
OEDIPUS: What murky, riddling things you always say!
445 TIRESIAS: Don't you surpass us all at finding out?
OEDIPUS: You sneer at what you'll find has brought me greatness.
TIRESIAS: And that's the very luck that ruined you.
OEDIPUS: I wouldn't care, just so I saved the city.
TIRESIAS: In that case I shall go. Boy, lead the way!

---

[7] *Loxias:* Apollo.

[8] *Cithaeron:* The mountain on which Oedipus was to be exposed as an infant.

[9] *This day . . . birth:* On this day, you will learn who your parents are.

OEDIPUS: Yes, let him lead you off. Here, underfoot,   450
    you irk me. Gone, you'll cause no further pain.
TIRESIAS: I'll go when I have said what I was sent for.
    Your face won't scare me. You can't ruin me.
    I say to you, the man whom you have looked for
    as you pronounced your curses, your decrees   455
    on the bloody death of Laius—he is here!
    A seeming stranger, he shall be shown to be
    a Theban born, though he'll take no delight
    in that solution. Blind, who once could see,
    a beggar who was rich, through foreign lands   460
    he'll go and point before him with a stick.
    To his beloved children, he'll be shown
    a father who is also brother; to the one
    who bore him, son and husband; to his father,
    his seed-fellow and killer. Go in   465
    and think this out; and if you find I've lied,
    say then I have no prophet's understanding!

Exit Tiresias, led by a Servant. Oedipus exits into the palace with his Attendants.

STASIMON 1[1]

STROPHE 1

CHORUS: Who is the man of whom the inspired
        rock of Delphi[2] said
    he has committed the unspeakable   470
        with blood-stained hands?
    Time for him to ply a foot
    mightier than those of the horses
        of the storm in his escape;
    upon him mounts and plunges the weaponed   475
    son of Zeus,[3] with fire and thunderbolts,
    and in his train the dreaded goddesses
    of Death, who never miss.

ANTISTROPHE 1

    The message has just blazed,
        gleaming from the snows   480
    of Mount Parnassus: we must track
    everywhere the unseen man.

---

[1] *Stasimon:* Greek choral ode between episodes.
[2] *rock of Delphi:* Apollo's oracle at Delphi.
[3] *son of Zeus:* Apollo.

He wanders, hidden by wild
forests, up through caves
485   and rocks, like a bull,
anxious, with an anxious foot, forlorn.
He puts away from him the mantic[4] words come from earth's
navel,[5] at its center, yet these live
forever and still hover round him.

STROPHE 2

490   Terribly he troubles me,
        the skilled interpreter of birds![6]
I can't assent, nor speak against him.
        Both paths are closed to me.
I hover on the wings of doubt,
495   not seeing what is here nor what's to come.
What quarrel started in the house of Labdacus[7]
or in the house of Polybus,[8]
        either ever in the past
        or now, I never
500   heard, so that . . . with this fact for my touchstone
I could attack the public
        fame of Oedipus, by the side of the Labdaceans
an ally, against the dark assassination.

ANTISTROPHE 2

No, Zeus and Apollo
505   understand and know things
mortal; but that another man
        can do more as a prophet than I can—
for that there is no certain test,
        though, skill to skill,
510   one man might overtake another.
No, never, not until
        I see the charges proved,
when someone blames him shall I nod assent.
For once, as we all saw, the winged maiden[9] came

---

[4] *mantic:* Prophetic.

[5] *earth's navel:* Delphi.

[6] *interpreter of birds:* Tiresias. The Chorus is troubled by his accusations.

[7] *house of Labdacus:* The line of Laius.

[8] *Polybus:* Oedipus's foster father.

[9] *winged maiden:* The Sphinx.

against him: he was seen then to be skilled,   515
   proved, by that touchstone, dear to the people. So,
never will my mind convict him of the evil.

EPISODE 2

Enter Creon from the right door of the skene and speaks to the Chorus.

CREON: Citizens, I hear that a fearful charge
   is made against me by King Oedipus!
   I had to come. If, in this crisis,   520
   he thinks that he has suffered injury
   from anything that I have said or done,
   I have no appetite for a long life—
   bearing a blame like that! It's no slight blow
   the punishment I'd take from what he said: 525
   it's the ultimate hurt to be called traitor
   by the city, by you, by my own people!
CHORAGOS: The thing that forced that accusation out
   could have been anger, not the power of thought.
CREON: But who persuaded him that thoughts of mine   530
   had led the prophet into telling lies?
CHORAGOS: I do not know the thought behind his words.
CREON: But did he look straight at you? Was his mind right
   when he said that I was guilty of this charge?
CHORAGOS: I have no eyes to see what rulers do.   535
   But here he comes himself out of the house.

Enter Oedipus from the palace.

OEDIPUS: What? You here? And can you really have
   the face and daring to approach my house
   when you're exposed as its master's murderer
   and caught, too, as the robber of my kingship?   540
   Did you see cowardice in me, by the gods,
   or foolishness, when you began this plot?
   Did you suppose that I would not detect
   your stealthy moves, or that I'd not fight back?
   It's your attempt that's folly, isn't it—   545
   tracking without followers or connections,
   kingship which is caught with wealth and numbers?
CREON: Now wait! Give me as long to answer back!
   Judge me for yourself when you have heard me!
OEDIPUS: You're eloquent, but I'd be slow to learn   550
   from you, now that I've seen your malice toward me.

CREON: That I deny. Hear what I have to say.

OEDIPUS: Don't you deny it! You are the traitor here!

CREON: If you consider mindless willfulness

555   a prized possession, you are not thinking sense.

OEDIPUS: If you think you can wrong a relative
    and get off free, you are not thinking sense.

CREON: Perfectly just, I won't say no. And yet
    what is this injury you say I did you?

560 OEDIPUS: Did you persuade me, yes or no, to send
    someone to bring that solemn prophet here?

CREON: And I still hold to the advice I gave.

OEDIPUS: How many years ago did your King Laius . . .

CREON: Laius! Do what? Now I don't understand.

565 OEDIPUS: Vanish—victim of a murderous violence?

CREON: That is a long count back into the past.

OEDIPUS: Well, was this seer then practicing his art?

CREON: Yes, skilled and honored just as he is today.

OEDIPUS: Did he, back then, ever refer to me?

570 CREON: He did not do so in my presence ever.

OEDIPUS: You did inquire into the murder then.

CREON: We had to, surely, though we discovered nothing.

OEDIPUS: But the "skilled" one did not say this then? Why not?

CREON: I never talk when I am ignorant.

575 OEDIPUS: But you're not ignorant of your own part.

CREON: What do you mean? I'll tell you if I know.

OEDIPUS: Just this: if he had not conferred with you
    he'd not have told about my murdering Laius.

CREON: If he said that, you are the one who knows.

580   But now it's fair that you should answer me.

OEDIPUS: Ask on! You won't convict me as the killer.

CREON: Well then, answer. My sister is your wife?

OEDIPUS: Now there's a statement that I can't deny.

CREON: You two have equal power in this country?

585 OEDIPUS: She gets from me whatever she desires.

CREON: And I'm a third? The three of us are equals?

OEDIPUS: That's where you're treacherous to your kinsman!

CREON: But think about this rationally, as I do.
    First look at this: do you think anyone

590   prefers the anxieties of being king
    to untroubled sleep—if he has equal power?
    I'm not the kind of man who falls in love
    with kingship. I am content with a king's power.
    And so would any man who's wise and prudent.

I get all things from you, with no distress;   595
as king I would have onerous duties, too.
How could the kingship bring me more delight
than this untroubled power and influence?
I'm not misguided yet to such a point
that profitable honors aren't enough.   600
As it is, all wish me well and all salute;
those begging you for something have me summoned,
for their success depends on that alone.
Why should I lose all this to become king?
A prudent mind is never traitorous.   605
Treason's a thought I'm not enamored of;
nor could I join a man who acted so.
In proof of this, first go yourself to Pytho
and ask if I brought back the true response.
Then, if you find I plotted with that portent   610
reader,[1] don't have me put to death by your vote
only—I'll vote myself for my conviction.
Don't let an unsupported thought convict me!
It's not right mindlessly to take the bad
for good or to suppose the good are traitors.   615
Rejecting a relation who is loyal
is like rejecting life, our greatest love.
In time you'll know securely without stumbling,
for time alone can prove a just man just,
though you can know a bad man in a day.   620

CHORAGOS: Well said, to one who's anxious not to fall.
    Swift thinkers, Lord, are never safe from stumbling.
OEDIPUS: But when a swift and secret plotter moves
    against me, I must make swift counterplot.
    If I lie quiet and await his move,   625
    he'll have achieved his aims and I'll have missed.
CREON: You surely cannot mean you want me exiled!
OEDIPUS: Not exiled, no. Your death is what I want!
CREON: If you would first define what envy is . . .
OEDIPUS: Are you still stubborn? Still disobedient?   630
CREON: I see you cannot think!
OEDIPUS: For me I can.
CREON: You should for me as well!
OEDIPUS: But you're a traitor!

---

[1]*portent reader:* Apollo's oracle or prophet.

CREON: What if you're wrong?
OEDIPUS: Authority must be maintained.
CREON: Not if the ruler's evil.
OEDIPUS: Hear that, Thebes!
635 CREON: It is my city too, not yours alone!
CHORAGOS: Please don't, my Lords! Ah, just in time, I see
          Jocasta there, coming from the palace.
          With her help you must settle your quarrel.

Enter Jocasta from the palace.

    JOCASTA: Wretched men! What has provoked this ill-
340   advised dispute? Have you no sense of shame,
        with Thebes so sick, to stir up private troubles?
        Now go inside! And Creon, you go home!
        Don't make a general anguish out of nothing!
    CREON: My sister, Oedipus your husband here
645   sees fit to do one of two hideous things:
        to have me banished from the land—or killed!
    OEDIPUS: That's right: I caught him, Lady, plotting harm
        against my person—with a malignant science.
    CREON: May my life fail, may I die cursed, if I
650   did any of the things you said I did!
    JOCASTA: Believe his words, for the god's sake, Oedipus,
        in deference above all to his oath
        to the gods. Also for me, and for these men!

<u>KOMMOS[1]</u>
STROPHE 1
    CHORUS: Consent, with will and mind,
655   my king, I beg of you!
    OEDIPUS: What do you wish me to surrender?
    CHORUS: Show deference to him who was not feeble in time past
        and is now great in the power of his oath!
    OEDIPUS: Do you know what you're asking?
    CHORUS: Yes.
    OEDIPUS: Tell me then.
660 CHORUS: Never to cast into dishonored guilt, with an unproved
        assumption, a kinsman who has bound himself by curse.
    OEDIPUS: Now you must understand, when you ask this,
        you ask my death or banishment from the land.

---

[1] *Kommos:* A dirge or lament sung by the Chorus and one or more of the chief characters.

STROPHE 2

CHORUS: No, by the god who is the foremost of all gods,
  the Sun! No! Godless,   665
    friendless, whatever death is worst of all,
  let that be my destruction, if this
    thought ever moved me!
  But my ill-fated soul
    this dying land   670
  wears out—the more if to these older troubles
  she adds new troubles from the two of you!
OEDIPUS: Then let him go, though it must mean my death,
  or else disgrace and exile from the land.
  My pity is moved by your words, not by his—   675
  he'll only have my hate, wherever he goes.
CREON: You're sullen as you yield; you'll be depressed
  when you've passed through this anger. Natures like yours
  are hardest on themselves. That's as it should be.
OEDIPUS: Then won't you go and let me be?   680
CREON: I'll go.
  Though you're unreasonable, they know I'm righteous.

Exit Creon.

ANTISTROPHE 1

CHORUS: Why are you waiting, Lady?
  Conduct him back into the palace!
JOCASTA: I will, when I have heard what chanced.
CHORUS: Conjectures—words alone, and nothing based on thought.   685
  But even an injustice can devour a man.
JOCASTA: Did the words come from both sides?
CHORUS: Yes.
JOCASTA: What was said?
CHORUS: To me it seems enough! enough! the land already troubled,
  that this should rest where it has stopped.
OEDIPUS: See what you've come to in your honest thought,   690
  in seeking to relax and blunt my heart?

ANTISTROPHE 2

CHORUS: I have not said this only once, my Lord.
  That I had lost my sanity,
    without a path in thinking—
  be sure this would be clear   695
    if I put you away

who, when my cherished land
    wandered crazed
with suffering, brought her back on course.
700   Now, too, be a lucky helmsman!
JOCASTA: Please, for the god's sake, Lord, explain to me
    the reason why you have conceived this wrath?
OEDIPUS: I honor you, not them,[2] and I'll explain
    to you how Creon has conspired against me.
705 JOCASTA: All right, if that will explain how the quarrel started.
OEDIPUS: He says I am the murderer of Laius!
JOCASTA: Did he claim knowledge or that someone told him?
OEDIPUS: Here's what he did: he sent that vicious seer
    so he could keep his own mouth innocent.
710 JOCASTA: Ah then, absolve yourself of what he charges!
    Listen to this and you'll agree, no mortal
    is ever given skill in prophecy.
    I'll prove this quickly with one incident.
    It was foretold to Laius—I shall not say
715   by Phoebus himself, but by his ministers—
    that when his fate arrived he would be killed
    by a son who would be born to him and me.
    And yet, so it is told, foreign robbers
    murdered him, at a place where three roads meet.
720   As for the child I bore him, not three days passed
    before he yoked the ball-joints of its feet,[3]
    then cast it, by others' hands, on a trackless mountain.
    That time Apollo did not make our child
    a patricide, or bring about what Laius
725   feared, that he be killed by his own son.
    That's how prophetic words determined things!
    Forget them. The things a god must track
    he will himself painlessly reveal.
OEDIPUS: Just now, as I was listening to you, Lady,
730   what a profound distraction seized my mind!
JOCASTA: What made you turn around so anxiously?
OEDIPUS: I thought you said that Laius was attacked
    and butchered at a place where three roads meet.
JOCASTA: That is the story, and it is told so still.
735 OEDIPUS: Where is the place where this was done to him?

---

[2] *them:* The Chorus.
[3] *ball-joints of its feet:* The ankles.

JOCASTA: The land's called Phocis, where a two-forked road
    comes in from Delphi and from Daulia.

OEDIPUS: And how much time has passed since these events?

JOCASTA: Just prior to your presentation here
    as king this news was published to the city.   740

OEDIPUS: Oh, Zeus, what have you willed to do to me?

JOCASTA: Oedipus, what makes your heart so heavy?

OEDIPUS: No, tell me first of Laius' appearance,
    what peak of youthful vigor he had reached.

JOCASTA: A tall man, showing his first growth of white.   745
    He had a figure not unlike your own.

OEDIPUS: Alas! It seems that in my ignorance
    I laid those fearful curses on myself.

JOCASTA: What is it, Lord? I flinch to see your face.

OEDIPUS: I'm dreadfully afraid the prophet sees.   750
    But I'll know better with one more detail.

JOCASTA: I'm frightened too. But ask: I'll answer you.

OEDIPUS: Was his retinue small, or did he travel
    with a great troop, as would befit a prince?

JOCASTA: There were just five in all, one a herald.   755
    There was a carriage, too, bearing Laius.

OEDIPUS: Alas! Now I see it! But who was it,
    Lady, who told you what you know about this?

JOCASTA: A servant who alone was saved unharmed.

OEDIPUS: By chance, could he be now in the palace?   760

JOCASTA: No, he is not. When he returned and saw
    you had the power of the murdered Laius,
    he touched my hand and begged me formally
    to send him to the fields and to the pastures,
    so he'd be out of sight, far from the city.   765
    I did. Although a slave, he well deserved
    to win this favor, and indeed far more.

OEDIPUS: Let's have him called back in immediately.

JOCASTA: That can be done, but why do you desire it?

OEDIPUS: I fear, Lady, I have already said   770
    too much. That's why I wish to see him now.

JOCASTA: Then he shall come; but it is right somehow
    that I, too, Lord, should know what troubles you.

OEDIPUS: I've gone so deep into the things I feared
    I'll tell you everything. Who has a right   775
    greater than yours, while I cross through this chance?
    Polybus of Corinth was my father,
    my mother was the Dorian Meropē.

I was first citizen, until this chance
780 attacked me—striking enough, to be sure,
but not worth all the gravity I gave it.
This: at a feast a man who'd drunk too much
denied, at the wine, I was my father's son.
I was depressed and all that day I barely
785 held it in. Next day I put the question
to my mother and father. They were enraged
at the man who'd let this fiction fly at me.
I was much cheered by them. And yet it kept
grinding into me. His words kept coming back.
790 Without my mother's or my father's knowledge
I went to Pytho. But Phoebus sent me away
dishonoring my demand. Instead, other
wretched horrors he flashed forth in speech.
He said that I would be my mother's lover,
795 show offspring to mankind they could not look at,
and be his murderer whose seed I am.[4]
When I heard this, and ever since, I gauged
the way to Corinth by the stars alone,
running to a place where I would never see
800 the disgrace in the oracle's words come true.
But I soon came to the exact location
where, as you tell of it, the king was killed.
Lady, here is the truth. As I went on,
when I was just approaching those three roads,
805 a herald and a man like him you spoke of
came on, riding a carriage drawn by colts.
Both the man out front and the old man himself[5]
tried violently to force me off the road.
The driver, when he tried to push me off,
810 I struck in anger. The old man saw this, watched
me approach, then leaned out and lunged down
with twin prongs[6] at the middle of my head!
He got more than he gave. Abruptly—struck
once by the staff in this my hand—he tumbled
815 out, head first, from the middle of the carriage.
And then I killed them all. But if there is

---

[4]*be . . . am:* I would murder my father.
[5]*old man himself:* Laius.
[6]*lunged . . . prongs:* Laius strikes Oedipus with a two-pronged horse goad, or whip.

a kinship between Laius and this stranger,
who is more wretched than the man you see?
Who was there born more hated by the gods?
For neither citizen nor foreigner   820
may take me in his home or speak to me.
No, they must drive me off. And it is I
who have pronounced these curses on myself!
I stain the dead man's bed with these my hands,
by which he died. Is not my nature vile?   825
Unclean?—if I am banished and even
in exile I may not see my own parents,
or set foot in my homeland, or else be yoked
in marriage to my mother, and kill my father,
Polybus, who raised me and gave me birth?   830
If someone judged a cruel divinity
did this to me, would he not speak the truth?
You pure and awful gods, may I not ever
see that day, may I be swept away
from men before I see so great and so   835
calamitous a stain fixed on my person!
CHORAGOS: These things seem fearful to us, Lord, and yet,
  until you hear it from the witness, keep hope!
OEDIPUS: That is the single hope that's left to me,
  to wait for him, that herdsman—until he comes.   840
JOCASTA: When he appears, what are you eager for?
OEDIPUS: Just this: if his account agrees with yours
  then I shall have escaped this misery.
JOCASTA: But what was it that struck you in my story?
OEDIPUS: You said he spoke of robbers as the ones   845
  who killed him. Now: if he continues still
  to speak of many, then I could not have killed him.
  One man and many men just do not jibe.
  But if he says one belted man, the doubt
  is gone. The balance tips toward me. I did it.   850
JOCASTA: No! He told it as I told you. Be certain.
  He can't reject that and reverse himself.
  The city heard these things, not I alone.
  But even if he swerves from what he said,
  he'll never show that Laius' murder, Lord,   855
  occurred just as predicted. For Loxias
  expressly said my son was doomed to kill him.
  The boy—poor boy—he never had a chance
  to cut him down, for he was cut down first.

860   Never again, just for some oracle
      will I shoot frightened glances right and left.
OEDIPUS: That's full of sense. Nonetheless, send a man
      to bring that farm hand here. Will you do it?
JOCASTA: I'll send one right away. But let's go in.
865   Would I do anything against your wishes?

Exit Oedipus and Jocasta through the central door into the palace.

STASIMON 2
STROPHE 1

CHORUS: May there accompany me
      the fate to keep a reverential purity in what I say,
      in all I do, for which the laws have been set forth
      and walk on high, born to traverse the brightest,
870   highest upper air; Olympus[1] only
      is their father, nor was it
      mortal nature
      that fathered them, and never will
      oblivion lull them into sleep;
875   the god in them is great and never ages.

ANTISTROPHE 1

      The will to violate, seed of the tyrant,
      if it has drunk mindlessly of wealth and power,
      without a sense of time or true advantage,
      mounts to a peak, then
880   plunges to an abrupt . . . destiny,
      where the useful foot
      is of no use. But the kind
      of struggling that is good for the city
      I ask the god never to abolish.
885   The god is my protector: never will I give that up.

STROPHE 2

      But if a man proceeds disdainfully
            in deeds of hand or word
      and has no fear of Justice
            or reverence for shrines of the divinities
890   (may a bad fate catch him

---

[1]*Olympus:* Mount Olympus, home of the gods, and treated as a god itself.

for his luckless wantonness!),
if he'll not gain what he gains with justice
and deny himself what is unholy,
or if he clings, in foolishness, to the untouchable
(what man, finally, in such an action, will have strength   895
enough to fend off passion's arrows from his soul?),
if, I say, this kind of
     deed is held in honor—
why should I join the sacred dance?

ANTISTROPHE 2

No longer shall I visit and revere   900
     Earth's navel,[2] the untouchable,
nor visit Abae's [3] temple,
     or Olympia,[4]
if the prophecies are not matched by events
     for all the world to point to.   905
No, you who hold the power, if you are rightly called
Zeus the king of all, let this matter not escape you
and your ever-deathless rule,
for the prophecies to Laius fade . . .
and men already disregard them;   910
nor is Apollo anywhere
     glorified with honors.
Religion slips away.

EPISODE 3

Enter Jocasta from the palace carrying a branch wound with wool and a jar of incense. She is attended by two women.

JOCASTA: Lords of the realm, the thought has come to me
     to visit shrines of the divinities   915
with suppliant's branch in hand and fragrant smoke.
For Oedipus excites his soul too much
with alarms of all kinds. He will not judge
the present by the past, like a man of sense.
He's at the mercy of all terror-mongers.   920

---

[2] *Earth's navel:* Delphi.
[3] *Abae's:* Abae was a town in Phocis where there was another oracle of Apollo.
[4] *Olympia:* Site of the oracle of Zeus.

Jocasta approaches the altar on the right and kneels.

> Since I can do no good by counseling,
> Apollo the Lycēan!—you are the closest—
> I come a suppliant, with these my vows,
> for a cleansing that will not pollute him.
925 For when we see him shaken we are all
> afraid, like people looking at their helmsman.

Enter a Messenger along one of the parados. He sees Jocasta at the altar and then addresses the Chorus.

MESSENGER: I would be pleased if you would help me, stranger.
> Where is the palace of King Oedipus?
> Or tell me where he is himself, if you know.
930 CHORUS: This is his house, stranger. He is within.
> This is his wife and mother of his children.
MESSENGER: May she and her family find prosperity,
> if, as you say, her marriage is fulfilled.
JOCASTA: You also, stranger, for you deserve as much
935 for your gracious words. But tell me why you've come.
> What do you wish? Or what have you to tell us?
MESSENGER: Good news, my Lady, both for your house and husband.
JOCASTA: What is your news? And who has sent you to us?
MESSENGER: I come from Corinth. When you have heard my news
940 you will rejoice, I'm sure—and grieve perhaps.
JOCASTA: What is it? How can it have this double power?
MESSENGER: They will establish him their king, so say
> the people of the land of Isthmia.[1]
JOCASTA: But is old Polybus not still in power?
945 MESSENGER: He's not, for death has clasped him in the tomb.
JOCASTA: What's this? Has Oedipus' father died?
MESSENGER: If I have lied then I deserve to die.
JOCASTA: Attendant! Go quickly to your master,
> and tell him this.

Exit an Attendant into the palace.

> Oracles of the gods!
950 Where are you now? The man whom Oedipus
> fled long ago, for fear that he should kill him—
> he's been destroyed by chance and not by him!

---

[1] *land of Isthmia:* Corinth, Greek city-state situated on an isthmus.

Enter Oedipus from the palace.

OEDIPUS: Darling Jocasta, my beloved wife,
Why have you called me from the palace?

JOCASTA: First hear what this man has to say. Then see   955
what the god's grave oracle has come to now!

OEDIPUS: Where is he from? What is this news he brings me?

JOCASTA: From Corinth. He brings news about your father:
that Polybus is no more! that he is dead!

OEDIPUS: What's this, old man? I want to hear you say it.   960

MESSENGER: If this is what must first be clarified,
please be assured that he is dead and gone.

OEDIPUS: By treachery or by the touch of sickness?

MESSENGER: Light pressures tip agéd frames into their sleep.

OEDIPUS: You mean the poor man died of some disease.   965

MESSENGER: And of the length of years that he had tallied.

OEDIPUS: Aha! Then why should we look to Pytho's vapors,[2]
or to the birds that scream above our heads?[3]
If we could really take those things for guides,
I would have killed my father. But he's dead!   970
He is beneath the earth, and here am I,
who never touched a spear. Unless he died
of longing for me and I "killed" him that way!
No, in this case, Polybus, by dying, took
the worthless oracle to Hades with him.   975

JOCASTA: And wasn't I telling you that just now?

OEDIPUS: You were indeed. I was misled by fear.

JOCASTA: You should not care about this anymore.

OEDIPUS: I must care. I must stay clear of my mother's bed.

JOCASTA: What's there for man to fear? The realm of chance   980
prevails. True foresight isn't possible.
His life is best who lives without a plan.
This marriage with your mother—don't fear it.
How many times have men in dreams, too, slept
with their own mothers! Those who believe such things   985
mean nothing endure their lives most easily.

OEDIPUS: A fine, bold speech, and you are right, perhaps,
except that my mother is still living,
so I must fear her, however well you argue.

JOCASTA: And yet your father's tomb is a great eye.   990

---

[2]*Pytho's vapors:* Prophecies of the oracle at Delphi.

[3]*birds . . . heads:* Prophecies derived from interpreting the flights of birds.

OEDIPUS: Illuminating, yes. But I still fear the living.

MESSENGER: Who is the woman who inspires this fear?

OEDIPUS: Meropē, Polybus' wife, old man.

MESSENGER: And what is there about her that alarms you?

995 OEDIPUS: An oracle, god-sent and fearful, stranger.

MESSENGER: Is it permitted that another know?

OEDIPUS: It is. Loxias once said to me
 I must have intercourse with my own mother
 and take my father's blood with these my hands.

1000 So I have long lived far away from Corinth.
 This has indeed brought much good luck, and yet,
 to see one's parents' eyes is happiest.

MESSENGER: Was it for this that you have lived in exile?

OEDIPUS: So I'd not be my father's killer, sir.

1005 MESSENGER: Had I not better free you from this fear,
 my Lord? That's why I came—to do you service.

OEDIPUS: Indeed, what a reward you'd get for that!

MESSENGER: Indeed, this is the main point of my trip,
 to be rewarded when you get back home.

1010 OEDIPUS: I'll never rejoin the givers of my seed![4]

MESSENGER: My son, clearly you don't know what you're doing.

OEDIPUS: But how is that, old man? For the gods' sake, tell me!

MESSENGER: If it's because of them you won't go home.

OEDIPUS: I fear that Phoebus will have told the truth.

1015 MESSENGER: Pollution from the ones who gave you seed?

OEDIPUS: That is the thing, old man, I always fear.

MESSENGER: Your fear is groundless. Understand that.

OEDIPUS: Groundless? Not if I was born their son.

MESSENGER: But Polybus is not related to you.

1020 OEDIPUS: Do you mean Polybus was not my father?

MESSENGER: No more than I. We're both the same to you.

OEDIPUS: Same? One who begot me and one who didn't?

MESSENGER: He didn't beget you any more than I did.

OEDIPUS: But then, why did he say I was his son?

1025 MESSENGER: He got you as a gift from my own hands.

OEDIPUS: He loved me so, though from another's hands?

MESSENGER: His former childlessness persuaded him.

OEDIPUS: But had you bought me, or begotten me?

MESSENGER: Found you. In the forest hallows of Cithaeron.

1030 OEDIPUS: What were you doing traveling in that region?

---

[4]*givers of my seed:* i.e., "my parents." Oedipus still thinks Meropē and Polybus are his parents.

MESSENGER: I was in charge of flocks which grazed those mountains.
OEDIPUS: A wanderer who worked the flocks for hire?
MESSENGER: Ah, but that day I was your savior, son.
OEDIPUS: From what? What was my trouble when you took me?
MESSENGER: The ball-joints of your feet might testify.   1035
OEDIPUS: What's that? What makes you name that ancient trouble?
MESSENGER: Your feet were pierced and I am your rescuer.
OEDIPUS: A fearful rebuke those tokens left for me!
MESSENGER: That was the chance that names you who you are.
OEDIPUS: By the gods, did my mother or my father do this?   1040
MESSENGER: That I don't know. He might who gave you to me.
OEDIPUS: From someone else? You didn't chance on me?
MESSENGER: Another shepherd handed you to me.
OEDIPUS: Who was he? Do you know? Will you explain!
MESSENGER: They called him one of the men of—was it Laius?   1045
OEDIPUS: The one who once was king here long ago?
MESSENGER: That is the one! The man was shepherd to him.
OEDIPUS: And is he still alive so I can see him?
MESSENGER: But you who live here ought to know that best.
OEDIPUS: Does any one of you now present know   1050
    about the shepherd whom this man has named?
    Have you seen him in town or in the fields? Speak out!
    The time has come for the discovery!
CHORAGOS: The man he speaks of, I believe, is the same
    as the field hand you have already asked to see.   1055
    But it's Jocasta who would know this best.
OEDIPUS: Lady, do you remember the man we just
    now sent for—is that the man he speaks of?
JOCASTA: What? The man he spoke of? Pay no attention!
    His words are not worth thinking about. It's nothing.   1060
OEDIPUS: With clues like this within my grasp, give up?
    Fail to solve the mystery of my birth?
JOCASTA: For the love of the gods, and if you love your life,
    give up this search! My sickness is enough.
OEDIPUS: Come! Though my mothers for three generations   1065
    were in slavery, you'd not be lowborn!
JOCASTA: No, listen to me! Please! Don't do this thing!
OEDIPUS: I will not listen; I will search out the truth.
JOCASTA: My thinking is for you—it would be best.
OEDIPUS: This "best" of yours is starting to annoy me.   1070
JOCASTA: Doomed man! Never find out who you are!
OEDIPUS: Will someone go and bring that shepherd here?
    Leave her to glory in her wealthy birth!

JOCASTA: Man of misery! No other name
1075   shall I address you by, ever again.

Exit Jocasta into the palace after a long pause.

CHORAGOS: Why has your lady left, Oedipus,
            hurled by a savage grief? I am afraid
            disaster will come bursting from this silence.
OEDIPUS: Let it burst forth! However low this seed
1080   of mine may be, yet I desire to see it.
            She, perhaps—she has a woman's pride—
            is mortified by my base origins.
            But I who count myself the child of Chance,
            the giver of good, shall never know dishonor.
1085   She is my mother,[5] and the months my brothers
            who first marked out my lowness, then my greatness.
            I shall not prove untrue to such a nature
            by giving up the search for my own birth.

STASIMON 3
STROPHE

CHORUS: If I have mantic power [1]
1090   and excellence in thought,
            by Olympus,
                you shall not, Cithaeron, at tomorrow's
            full moon,
            fail to hear us celebrate you as the countryman
1095   of Oedipus, his nurse and mother,
            or fail to be the subject of our dance,
                since you have given pleasure
            to our king.
1100   Phoebus, whom we summon by "iē!,"
            may this be pleasing to you!

ANTISTROPHE
Who was your mother, son?
which of the long-lived nymphs
after lying with Pan,[2]

---

[5]*She . . . mother:* Chance is my mother.

[1]*If . . . mantic power:* If I am a prophet.

[2]*Pan:* God of shepherds and woodlands, half man and half goat.

the mountain roaming . . . Or was it a bride
of Loxias?[3]   1105
For dear to him are all the upland pastures.
Or was it Mount Cyllēnē's lord,[4]
or the Bacchic god,[5]
   dweller of the mountain peaks,
who received you as a joyous find   1110
from one of the nymphs of Helicon,
the favorite sharers of his sport?

EPISODE 4

OEDIPUS: If someone like myself, who never met him,
   may calculate—elders, I think I see
   the very herdsman we've been waiting for.   1115
   His many years would fit that man's age,
   and those who bring him on, if I am right,
   are my own men. And yet, in real knowledge,
   you can outstrip me, surely: you've seen him.

*Enter the old Herdsman escorted by two of Oedipus's Attendants. At first, the
Herdsman will not look at Oedipus.*

CHORAGOS: I know him, yes, a man of the house of Laius,   1120
   a trusty herdsman if he ever had one.
OEDIPUS: I ask you first, the stranger come from Corinth:
   is this the man you spoke of?
MESSENGER: That's he you see.
OEDIPUS: Then you, old man. First look at me! Now answer:
   did you belong to Laius' household once?   1125
HERDSMAN: I did. Not a purchased slave but raised in the palace.
OEDIPUS: How have you spent your life? What is your work?
HERDSMAN: Most of my life now I have tended sheep.
OEDIPUS: Where is the usual place you stay with them?
HERDSMAN: On Mount Cithaeron. Or in that district.   1130
OEDIPUS: Do you recall observing this man there?
HERDSMAN: Doing what? Which is the man you mean?
OEDIPUS: This man right here. Have you had dealings with him?
HERDSMAN: I can't say right away. I don't remember.
MESSENGER: No wonder, master. I'll bring clear memory   1135

---

[3]*Loxias:* Apollo.
[4]*Mount Cyllēnē's lord:* Hermes, messenger of the gods.
[5]*Bacchic god:* Dionysus.

to his ignorance. I'm absolutely sure
he can recall it, the district was Cithaeron,
he with a double flock, and I, with one,
lived close to him, for three entire seasons,

1140   six months along, from spring right to Arcturus.[1]
Then for the winter I'd drive mine to my fold,
and he'd drive his to Laius' pen again.
Did any of the things I say take place?

HERDSMAN: You speak the truth, though it's from long ago.

1145 MESSENGER: Do you remember giving me, back then,
a boy I was to care for as my own?

HERDSMAN: What are you saying? Why do you ask me that?

MESSENGER: There, sir, is the man who was that boy!

HERDSMAN: Damn you! Shut your mouth! Keep your silence!

1150 OEDIPUS: Stop! Don't you rebuke his words.
Your words ask for rebuke far more than his.

HERDSMAN: But what have I done wrong, most royal master?

OEDIPUS: Not telling of the boy of whom he asked.

HERDSMAN: He's ignorant and blundering toward ruin.

1155 OEDIPUS: Tell it willingly—or under torture.

HERDSMAN: Oh god! Don't—I am old—don't torture me!

OEDIPUS: Here! Someone put his hands behind his back!

HERDSMAN: But why? What else would you find out, poor man?

OEDIPUS: Did you give him the child he asks about?

1160 HERDSMAN: I did. I wish that I had died that day!

OEDIPUS: You'll come to that if you don't speak the truth.

HERDSMAN: It's if I speak that I shall be destroyed.

OEDIPUS: I think this fellow struggles for delay.

HERDSMAN: No, no! I said already that I gave him.

1165 OEDIPUS: From your own home, or got from someone else?

HERDSMAN: Not from my own. I got him from another.

OEDIPUS: Which of these citizens? What sort of house?

HERDSMAN: Don't—by the gods!—don't, master, ask me more!

OEDIPUS: It means your death if I must ask again.

1170 HERDSMAN: One of the children of the house of Laius.

OEDIPUS: A slave—or born into the family?

HERDSMAN: I have come to the dreaded thing, and I shall say it.

OEDIPUS: And I to hearing it, but hear I must.

HERDSMAN: He was reported to have been—his son.

1175   Your lady in the house could tell you best.

---

[1]*Arcturus:* A star that is first seen in September in the sky over Greece.

OEDIPUS: Because she gave him to you?
HERDSMAN: Yes, my lord.
OEDIPUS: What was her purpose?
HERDSMAN: I was to kill the boy.
OEDIPUS: The child she bore?
HERDSMAN: She dreaded prophecies.
OEDIPUS: What were they?
HERDSMAN: The word was that he'd kill his parents.
OEDIPUS: Then why did you give him up to this old man? 1180
HERDSMAN: In pity, master—so he would take him home,
to another land. But what he did was save him
for this supreme disaster. If you are the one
he speaks of—know your evil birth and fate!
OEDIPUS: Ah! All of it was destined to be true! 1185
Oh light, now may I look my last upon you,
shown monstrous in my birth, in marriage monstrous,
a murderer monstrous in those I killed.

Exit Oedipus, running into the palace.

STASIMON 4
STROPHE 1

CHORUS: Oh generations of mortal men,
while you are living, I will
appraise your lives at zero! 1190
What man
comes closer to seizing lasting blessedness
than merely to seize its semblance,
and after living in this semblance, to plunge? 1195
With your example before us,
with your destiny, yours,
suffering Oedipus, no mortal
can I judge fortunate.

ANTISTROPHE 1

For he,[1] outranging everybody, 1200
shot his arrow[2] and became the lord
of wide prosperity and blessedness,
oh Zeus, after destroying
the virgin with the crooked talons,[3]

---

[1] *he:* Oedipus.
[2] *shot his arrow:* Took his chances; made a guess at the Sphinx's riddle.
[3] *virgin . . . talons:* The Sphinx.

1205   singer of oracles; and against death,
in my land, he arose a tower of defense.
From which time you were called my king
and granted privileges supreme—in mighty
Thebes the ruling lord.

STROPHE 2

1210   But now—whose story is more sorrowful than yours?
Who is more intimate with fierce calamities,
with labors, now that your life is altered?
Alas, my Oedipus, whom all men know:
one great harbor[4]—
1215   one alone sufficed for you,
as son and father,
when you tumbled,[5] plowman[6] of the woman's chamber.
How, how could your paternal
furrows, wretched man,
1220   endure you silently so long.

ANTISTROPHE 2

Time, all-seeing, surprised you living an unwilled life
and sits from of old in judgment on the marriage, not a marriage,
where the begetter is the begot as well.
Ah, son of Laius . . . ,
1225   would that—oh, would that
I had never seen you!
I wail, my scream climbing beyond itself
from my whole power of voice. To say it straight:
from you I got new breath—
1230   but I also lulled my eye to sleep.[7]

EXODOS[1]

Enter the Second Messenger from the palace.

Second Messenger: You who are first among the citizens,
what deeds you are about to hear and see!

---

[4] *one great harbor:* Metaphorical allusion to Jocasta's body.

[5] *tumbled:* Were born and had sex.

[6] *plowman:* Plowing is used here as a sexual metaphor.

[7] *I . . . sleep:* I failed to see the corruption you brought.

[1] *Exodos:* The final scene, containing the play's resolution.

What grief you'll carry, if, true to your birth,
you still respect the house of Labdacus!
Neither the Ister nor the Phasis river   1235
could purify this house, such suffering
does it conceal, or soon must bring to light—
willed this time, not unwilled. Griefs hurt worst
which we perceive to be self-chosen ones.
CHORAGOS: They were sufficient, the things we knew before,   1240
to make us grieve. What can you add to those?
SECOND MESSENGER: The thing that's quickest said and quickest heard:
our own, our royal one, Jocasta's dead.
CHORAGOS: Unhappy queen! What was responsible?
SECOND MESSENGER: Herself. The bitterest of these events   1245
is not for you, you were not there to see,
but yet, exactly as I can recall it,
you'll hear what happened to that wretched lady.
She came in anger through the outer hall,
and then she ran straight to her marriage bed,   1250
tearing her hair with the fingers of both hands.
Then, slamming shut the doors when she was in,
she called to Laius, dead so many years,
remembering the ancient seed which caused
his death, leaving the mother to the son   1255
to breed again an ill-born progeny.
She mourned the bed where she, alas, bred double—
husband by husband, children by her child.
From this point on I don't know how she died,
for Oedipus then burst in with a cry,   1260
and did not let us watch her final evil.
Our eyes were fixed on him. Wildly he ran
to each of us, asking for his spear
and for his wife—no wife: where he might find
the double mother-field, his and his children's.   1265
He raved, and some divinity then showed him—
for none of us did so who stood close by.
With a dreadful shout—as if some guide were leading—
he lunged through the double doors; he bent the hollow
bolts from the sockets, burst into the room,   1270
and there we saw her, hanging from above,
entangled in some twisted hanging strands.
He saw, was stricken, and with a wild roar
ripped down the dangling noose. When she, poor woman,
lay on the ground, there came a fearful sight: 1275

he snatched the pins of worked gold from her dress,
with which her clothes were fastened: these he raised
and struck into the ball-joints of his eyes.[2]
He shouted that they would no longer see
1280   the evils he had suffered or had done,
see in the dark those he should not have seen,
and know no more those he once sought to know.
While chanting this, not once but many times
he raised his hand and struck into his eyes.
1285   Blood from his wounded eyes poured down his chin,
not freed in moistening drops, but all at once
a stormy rain of black blood burst like hail.
These evils, coupling them, making them one,
have broken loose upon both man and wife.
1290   The old prosperity that they had once
was true prosperity, and yet today,
mourning, ruin, death, disgrace, and every
evil you could name—not one is absent.

CHORAGOS: Has he allowed himself some peace from all this grief?

1295 SECOND MESSENGER: He shouts that someone slide the bolts and show
to all the Cadmeians the patricide,
his mother's—I can't say it, it's unholy—
so he can cast himself out of the land,
not stay and curse his house by his own curse.
1300   He lacks the strength, though, and he needs a guide,
for his is a sickness that's too great to bear.
Now you yourself will see: the bolts of the doors
are opening. You are about to see
a vision even one who hates must pity.

Enter the blinded Oedipus from the palace, led in by a household Servant.

1305 CHORAGOS: Terrifying suffering for men to see,
more terrifying than any I've ever
come upon. Oh man of pain
what madness reached you? Which god from far off,
surpassing in range his longest spring,
1310   struck hard against your god-abandoned fate?
Oh man of pain,
I cannot look upon you—though there's so much
I would ask you, so much to hear,

---

[2]*ball-joints of his eyes:* His eyeballs. Oedipus blinds himself in both eyes at the same time.

so much that holds my eyes—
   such is the shudder you produce in me.   1315
OEDIPUS: Ah! Ah! I am a man of misery.
   Where am I carried? Pity me! Where
   is my voice scattered abroad on wings?
     Divinity, where has your lunge transported me?
CHORAGOS: To something horrible, not to be heard or seen.   1320

KOMMOS
STROPHE 1

OEDIPUS: Oh, my cloud
   of darkness, abominable, unspeakable as it attacks me,
   not to be turned away, brought by an evil wind!
   Alas!
   Again alas! Both enter me at once: 1325
   the sting of the prongs,[1] the memory of evils!
CHORUS: I do not marvel that in these afflictions
   you carry double griefs and double evils.

ANTISTROPHE 1

OEDIPUS: Ah, friend,
   so you at least are there, resolute servant!   1330
   Still with a heart to care for me, the blind man.
   Oh! Oh!
   I know that you are there. I recognize
   even inside my darkness, that voice of yours.
CHORUS: Doer of horror, how did you bear to quench   1335
   your vision? What divinity raised your hand?

STROPHE 2

OEDIPUS: It was Apollo there, Apollo, friends,
   who brought my sorrows, vile sorrows to their perfection,
     these evils that were done to me.
   But the one who struck them with his hand,   1340
     that one was none but I, in wretchedness.
   For why was I to see
   when nothing I could see would bring me joy?
CHORUS: Yes, that is how it was.
OEDIPUS: What could I see, indeed,   1345
   or what enjoy—what greeting

---

[1] *prongs:* Refers both to the whip that Laius used and to the two gold pins that Oedipus used to blind himself.

is there I could hear with pleasure, friends?
Conduct me out of the land
    as quickly as you can!
1350 Conduct me out, my friends,
    the man utterly ruined,
    supremely cursed,
        the man who is by gods
    the most detested of all men!
1355 CHORUS: Wretched in disaster and in knowledge:
    oh, I could wish you'd never come to know!

ANTISTROPHE 2

OEDIPUS: May he be destroyed, whoever freed the savage shackles
    from my feet when I'd been sent to the wild pasture,
        whoever rescued me from murder
1360 and became my savior—
    a bitter gift:
    if I had died then,
    I'd not have been such grief to self and kin.
CHORUS: I also would have had it so.
1365 OEDIPUS: I'd not have returned to be my father's
    murderer; I'd not be called by men
    my mother's bridegroom.
    Now I'm without a god,
        child of a polluted parent,
1370 fellow progenitor with him
        who gave me birth in misery.
    If there's an evil that
        surpasses evils, that
    has fallen to the lot of Oedipus.
1375 CHORAGOS: How can I say that you have counseled well?
    Better not to be than live a blind man.
OEDIPUS: That this was not the best thing I could do—
    don't tell me that, or advise me any more!
    Should I descend to Hades and endure
1380 to see my father with these eyes? Or see
    my poor unhappy mother? For I have done,
    to both of these, things too great for hanging.
    Or is the sight of children to be yearned for,
    to see new shoots that sprouted as these did?
1385 Never, never with these eyes of mine!
    Nor city, nor tower, nor holy images
    of the divinities! For I, all-wretched,

most nobly raised—as no one else in Thebes—
deprived myself of these when I ordained
that all expel the impious one—god-shown   1390
to be polluted, and the dead king's son![2]
Once I exposed this great stain upon me,
could I have looked on these with steady eyes?
No! No! And if there were a way to block
the source of hearing in my ears, I'd gladly   1395
have locked up my pitiable body,
so I'd be blind and deaf. Evils shut out—
that way my mind could live in sweetness.
Alas, Cithaeron, why did you receive me?
Or when you had me, not killed me instantly?   1400
I'd not have had to show my birth to mankind.
Polybus, Corinth, halls—ancestral,
they told me—how beautiful was your ward,
a scar that held back festering disease!
Evil my nature, evil my origin.   1405
You, three roads, and you, secret ravine,
you oak grove, narrow place of those three paths
that drank my blood[3] from these hands, from him
who fathered me, do you remember still
the things I did to you? When I'd come here,   1410
what I then did once more? Oh marriages! Marriages!
You gave us life and when you'd planted us
you sent the same seed up, and then revealed
fathers, brothers, sons, and kinsman's blood,
and brides, and wives, and mothers, all the most   1415
atrocious things that happen to mankind!
One should not name what never should have been.
Somewhere out there, then, quickly, by the gods,
cover me up, or murder me, or throw me
to the ocean where you will never see me more!   1420

Oedipus moves toward the Chorus and they back away from him.

Come! Don't shrink to touch this wretched man!
Believe me, do not be frightened! I alone
of all mankind can carry these afflictions.

Enter Creon from the palace with Attendants.

---

[2] *l . . . son:* Oedipus refers to his own curse against the murderer as well as his sins of patricide and incest.
[3] *my blood:* i.e., "the blood of my father, Laius."

CHORAGOS: Tell Creon what you wish for. Just when we need him
1425　　he's here. He can act, he can advise you.
　　　　He's now the land's sole guardian in your place.
OEDIPUS: Ah! Are there words that I can speak to him?
　　　　What ground for trust can I present? It's proved
　　　　that I was false to him in everything.
1430 CREON: I have not come to mock you, Oedipus,
　　　　nor to reproach you for your former falseness.
　　　　You men, if you have no respect for sons
　　　　of mortals, let your awe for the all-feeding
　　　　flames of lordy Hēlius[4] prevent
1435　　your showing unconcealed so great a stain,
　　　　abhorred by earth and sacred rain and light.
　　　　Escort him quickly back into the house!
　　　　If blood kin only see and hear their own
　　　　afflictions, we'll have no impious defilement.
1440 OEDIPUS: By the gods, you've freed me from one terrible fear,
　　　　so nobly meeting my unworthiness:
　　　　grant me something—not for me; for you!
CREON: What do you want that you should beg me so?
OEDIPUS: To drive me from the land at once, to a place
1445　　where there will be no man to speak to me!
CREON: I would have done just that—had I not wished
　　　　to ask first of the god what I should do.
OEDIPUS: His answer was revealed in full—that I,
　　　　the patricide, unholy, be destroyed.
1450 CREON: He said that, but our need is so extreme,
　　　　it's best to have sure knowledge what must be done.
OEDIPUS: You'll ask about a wretched man like me?
CREON: Is it not time you put your trust in the god?
OEDIPUS: But I bid you as well, and shall entreat you.
1455　　Give her who is within what burial
　　　　you will—you'll give your own her proper rites;
　　　　but me—do not condemn my fathers' land
　　　　to have me dwelling here while I'm alive,
　　　　but let me live on mountains—on Cithaeron
1460　　famed as mine, for my mother and my father,
　　　　while they yet lived, made it my destined tomb,
　　　　and I'll be killed by those who wished my ruin!
　　　　And yet I know: no sickness will destroy me,

---

[4]*Hēlius:* The sun.

nothing will: I'd never have been saved
when left to die unless for some dread evil.   1465
Then let my fate continue where it will!
As for my children, Creon, take no pains
for my sons—they're men and they will never lack
the means to live, wherever they may be—
but my two wretched, pitiable girls,   1470
who never ate but at my table, never
were without me—everything that I
would touch, they'd always have a share of it—
please care for them! Above all, let me touch
them with my hands and weep aloud my woes!   1475
Please, my Lord!
Please, noble heart! Touching with my hands,
I'd think I held them as when I could see.

Enter Antigone and Ismene from the palace with Attendants.

What's this?
Oh gods! Do I hear, somewhere, my two dear ones   1480
sobbing? Has Creon really pitied me
and sent to me my dearest ones, my children?
Is that it?
CREON: Yes, I prepared this for you, for I knew
you'd feel this joy, as you have always done.   1485
OEDIPUS: Good fortune, then, and, for your care, be guarded
far better by divinity than I was!
Where are you, children? Come to me! Come here
to these my hands, hands of your brother, hands
of him who gave you seed, hands that made   1490
these once bright eyes to see now in this fashion.

Oedipus embraces his daughters.

He, children, seeing nothing, knowing nothing,
he fathered you where his own seed was plowed.
I weep for you as well, though I can't see you,
imagining your bitter life to come,   1495
the life you will be forced by men to live.
What gatherings of townsmen will you join,
what festivals, without returning home
in tears instead of watching holy rites?
And when you've reached the time for marrying,   1500
where, children, is the man who'll run the risk
of taking on himself the infamy

that will wound you as it did my parents?
What evil is not here? Your father killed
1505   his father, plowed the one who gave him birth,
and from the place where he was sown, from there
he got you, from the place he too was born.
These are the wounds: then who will marry you?
No man, my children. No, it's clear that you
1510   must wither in dry barrenness, unmarried.

Oedipus addresses Creon.

Son of Menoeceus! You are the only father
left to them—we two who gave them seed
are both destroyed: watch that they don't become
poor, wanderers, unmarried—they are your kin.
1515   Let not my ruin be their ruin, too!
No, pity them! You see how young they are,
bereft of everyone, except for you.
Consent, kind heart, and touch me with your hand!

Creon grasps Oedipus's right hand.

You, children, if you had reached an age of sense,
1520   I would have counseled much. Now, pray you may live
always where it's allowed, finding a life
better than his was, who gave you seed.
CREON: Stop this now. Quiet your weeping. Move away, into the house.
OEDIPUS: Bitter words, but I obey them.
CREON: There's an end to all things.
OEDIPUS: I have first this request.
1525 CREON: Tell me. I shall judge when I will hear it.
OEDIPUS: Banish me from my homeland.
CREON: You must ask that of the god.
OEDIPUS: But I am the gods' most hated man!
CREON: Then you will soon get what you want.
OEDIPUS: Do you consent?
CREON: I never promise when, as now, I'm ignorant.
OEDIPUS: Then lead me in.
CREON: Come. But let your hold fall from your children.
OEDIPUS: Do not take them from me, ever!
1530 CREON: Do not wish to keep all of the power.
You had power, but that power did not follow you through life.

Oedipus's daughters are taken from him and led into the palace by Attendants.
Oedipus is led into the palace by a Servant. Creon and the other Attendants
follow. Only the Chorus remains.

CHORUS: People of Thebes, my country, see: here is that Oedipus—
he who "knew" the famous riddle, and attained the highest power,
whom all citizens admired, even envying his luck!
See the billows of wild troubles which he has entered now!   1535
Here is the truth of each man's life: we must wait, and see his end,
scrutinize his dying day, and refuse to call him happy
till he has crossed the border of his life without pain.

Exit the Chorus along each of the parados.

*   *   *

Reading and Reacting

1. The ancient Greeks used no scenery in their theatrical productions. In the absence of scenery, how is the setting established at the beginning of *Oedipus the King*?
2. In some recent productions of *Oedipus the King*, actors wear copies of ancient Greek masks. What are the advantages and disadvantages of using such masks in a contemporary production of the play?
3. In the ancient Greek theater, the *strophe* and *antistrophe* were sung or chanted by the chorus as it danced back and forth across the stage. If you were staging the play today, would you retain the chorus or do away with it entirely? What would be gained or lost with each alternative?
4. Why does Sophocles have Oedipus blind himself offstage? What would be the effect of having Oedipus perform this act in full view of the audience?
5. How does Sophocles observe the unities of time, place, and action? How does Sophocles manage to present information about what happened years before the action of the play while still maintaining the three unities?
6. The ancient Greek audience that viewed *Oedipus the King* was familiar with the plot of the play. Given this situation, how does Sophocles create suspense? What are the advantages and disadvantages of using a story that the audience already knows?
7. By the end of the play, what has Oedipus learned about himself? about the gods? about the quest for truth? Is he a tragic or a pathetic figure?
8. Today, many directors employ **color-blind casting**—that is, they cast an actor in a role without regard to his or her race. Do you think this practice could be used in casting *Oedipus the King*? How, for example, would you react to an African American Oedipus or to an Asian Creon?
9. **JOURNAL ENTRY** Do you think Oedipus deserves his fate? Why, or why not?

10. CRITICAL PERSPECTIVE In "On Misunderstanding the *Oedipus Rex*," F. R. Dodds argues that Sophocles did not intend that Oedipus's tragedy be seen as rising from a "grave moral flaw." Neither, says Dodds, was Oedipus a "mere puppet" of the gods. Rather, "what fascinates us is the spectacle of a man freely choosing, from the highest motives, a series of actions which lead to his own ruin":

> Oedipus is great, not in virtue of a great worldly position—for his worldly position is an illusion which will vanish like a dream—but in virtue of his inner strength: strength to pursue the truth at whatever personal cost, and strength to accept and endure it when found. . . . Oedipus is great because he accepts the responsibility for all his acts, including those which are objectively most horrible, though subjectively innocent.

Do you agree with Dodds's arguments? Do you see Oedipus as someone who has inner strength or as a morally flawed victim of the gods?

Related Works: "Barn Burning" (p. 256), "Young Goodman Brown" (p. 367), "Out, Out—" (p. 596), "Leda and the Swan" (p. 695), "Ulysses" (p. 790), *Hamlet* (p. 1043)

WRITING SUGGESTIONS: Staging

1. Discuss the problems that the original staging of *Oedipus the King* poses for contemporary audiences, and offer some possible solutions.

2. The simplicity of the ancient Greek theater was one of its main strengths. If a scene called for a particular setting—a palace, for example—the setting could be established with dialogue. Find some examples of this technique, and write an essay in which you discuss whether or not such suggestions are as effective in the staging of *Oedipus the King* than special effects or realistic settings would be.

3. Discuss and analyze the staging options for *The Date*—or for a play that is not in this chapter, such as *Beauty* (p. 831) or *Magic 8 Ball* (p. 837).

4. Choose a short story that appears in this anthology, and explain how you would stage it if it were a play. What furnishings, props, costumes, lighting, and sound effects would you choose? What events would occur offstage? Possible subjects for this essay might include "The Story of an Hour" (p. 127), "A&P" (p. 160), or "The Storm" (p. 199).

5. Assume you have a very limited budget for staging *The Cuban Swimmer*. What challenges would you face? Write an essay in which you outline your plans for staging *The Cuban Swimmer*.

CHAPTER 30

THEME

Sophocles
Bettmann/Corbis

August Wilson
AP Images

Like a short story or a poem, a play is open to interpretation. Readers' reactions are influenced by the language of the text, and audiences' reactions are influenced by the performance on stage. As in all works of literature, every element of a play—its title, its conflicts, its dialogue, its characters, and its staging—can shed light on its themes.

 Titles

The **title** of a play can provide insight into its themes. The ironic title of Susan Glaspell's *Trifles* (p. 867), for example, suggests that women's concerns with "trifles" may get to the truth more effectively than the preoccupations of self-important men do. Lorraine Hansberry's *A Raisin in the Sun* (1959), is another title that offers clues to the theme of a play. An allusion to Langston Hughes's poem "Harlem" (p. 577)—which asks, "what happens to a dream deferred? / Does it dry up / like a raisin in the sun?"—the title suggests what happens to an African American family whose dreams are repeatedly crushed. Likewise, the title *Fences* (p. 1270) offers clues to a major theme of August Wilson's play, suggesting that the main character is kept from his goals by barriers that are constructed by himself as well as by society. Finally, the title of Anton Chekhov's *The Brute* (p. 814) calls attention to the play's ideas about male–female relationships. The title may refer to Smirnov, who says that he has never liked women—whom he characterizes as "creatures of poetry and romance." Or, it may refer to Mrs. Popov's late husband, to whose memory she has dedicated her life despite the fact that he was unfaithful. Either alternative reinforces the play's tongue-in-cheek characterization of men as "brutes."

 ## Conflicts

The unfolding plot of a play—especially the **conflicts** that develop—can reveal the play's themes. In Henrik Ibsen's *A Doll House* (p. 881), for example, at least three major conflicts are present: one between Nora and her husband Torvald, one between Nora and Krogstad (an old acquaintance), and one between Nora and society. Each of these conflicts sheds light on the themes of the play.

Through Nora's conflict with Torvald, Ibsen examines the constraints placed on women and men by marriage in the nineteenth century. Both Nora and Torvald are imprisoned within their respective roles: Nora must be passive and childlike, and Torvald must be honorable and always in control. Nora, therefore, expects her husband to be noble and generous and, in a crisis, to sacrifice himself for her. When he fails to live up to her high expectations, she is profoundly disillusioned.

Nora's conflict with Krogstad underscores Ibsen's criticisms of the class system in nineteenth-century Norway. At the beginning of the play, Nora finds it "immensely amusing: that we—that Torvald has so much power over . . . people." Krogstad, a bank clerk who is in the employ of Torvald, visits Nora in act 1 to enlist her aid in saving his job. It is clear that she sees him as her social inferior. For example, when Krogstad questions her about a woman with whom he has seen her, she replies, "What makes you think you can cross-examine me, Mr. Krogstad—you, one of my husband's employees?" Nora does not realize that she and Krogstad are, ironically, very much alike: both occupy subordinate positions and therefore have no power to determine their own destinies.

Finally, through Nora's conflict with society, Ibsen examines the destructive nature of the forces that subjugate women. Nineteenth-century society was male dominated. A married woman had the same legal status as one of her children. She could not borrow money without her husband's signature, own real estate in her own name, or enter into contracts. In addition, all her assets—including inheritances and trust funds—automatically became the property of her husband at the time of marriage. As a result of her sheltered life, Nora at the beginning of the play is completely unaware of the consequences of her actions. Most readers share Dr. Rank's confusion when he asks Nora, "Why do you laugh at that? Do you have any idea of what society is?" It is Nora's disillusionment at finding out that Torvald and the rest of society are not what she has been led to believe they are that ultimately causes her to rebel. By walking out the door at the end of the play, Nora rejects not only her husband and her children (to whom she has no legal right once she leaves), but also society and its laws.

These three conflicts underscore many of the themes that dominate *A Doll House*. First, the conflicts show that marriage in the nineteenth century imprisons both men and women in narrow, constricting roles. They also show that middle-class Norwegian society is narrow, smug, and judgmental. (Krogstad is looked down upon for a crime years after he committed it, and Nora is looked down upon because she borrows money to save her husband's life.) Finally, the conflicts show that society does not offer individuals—especially women—the freedom to lead happy and fulfilling lives. Only when the social and economic conditions that govern society change, Ibsen suggests, can both women and men live together in mutual esteem.

 Dialogue

Dialogue can also give insight into a play's themes. Sometimes a character suggests—or even explicitly states—a theme. In act 3 of *A Doll House*, for example, Nora's friend, Mrs. Linde, comes as close as any character to expressing the central concern of the play when she says, "Helmer's got to learn everything; this dreadful secret has to be aired; those two have to come to a full understanding; all these lies can't go on." As the play goes on to demonstrate, the lies that exist both in marriage and in society are obstacles to love and happiness.

One of the main themes of Arthur Miller's *Death of a Salesman* (p. 960)—the questionable validity of the American Dream, given the nation's social, political, and economic realities—is suggested by the play's dialogue. As his son Biff points out, Willy Loman's stubborn belief in upward mobility and material success is based more on fantasy than on fact:

WILLY: (*with hatred, threatening*) The door of your life is wide open!

BIFF: Pop! I am a dime a dozen, and so are you!

WILLY: (*turning on him now in an uncontrolled outburst*) I am not a dime a
dozen! I am Willy Loman, and you are Biff Loman!

> *Biff starts for Willy, but is blocked by Happy. In his fury, Biff seems on the verge of attacking his father.*

BIFF: I am not a leader of men, Willy, and neither are you. You were never anything but a hard-working drummer who landed in the ash can like all the rest of them! I'm one dollar an hour, Willy! I tried seven states and couldn't raise it. A buck an hour! Do you gather my meaning? I'm not bringing home any prizes any more, and you're going to stop waiting for me to bring them home!

Although it does not explicitly state the theme of the play, this exchange strongly suggests that Biff rejects the desperate optimism to which Willy clings.

 ## Characters

Because a dramatic work focuses on a central character, or **protagonist**, the development of this character can shed light on a play's themes. Willy Loman in *Death of a Salesman* is developed in great detail. At the beginning of the play, he feels trapped, exhausted, and estranged from his surroundings. As Willy gradually sinks from depression into despair, the action of the play shifts from the present to the past, showing the events that shaped his life. His attitudes, beliefs, dreams, and dashed hopes reveal him to be an embodiment of the major theme of the play—that an unquestioning belief in the American Dream of success is both unrealistic and destructive.

Nora in *A Doll House* changes a great deal during the course of the play. At the beginning, she is more her husband's possession than an adult capable of shaping her own destiny. Nora's status becomes apparent in the first act when Torvald gently scolds his "little spendthrift" and refers to her as his "little lark" and his "squirrel." She is reduced to childish deceptions, such as hiding her macaroons when her husband enters the room. After Krogstad accuses her of committing forgery and threatens to expose her, she expects her husband to rise to the occasion and take the blame for her. When Torvald instead accuses her of being a hypocrite, a liar, and a criminal, Nora's neat little world comes crashing down. As a result of this experience, Nora changes; no longer is she the submissive and obedient wife. Instead, she becomes assertive—even rebellious—ultimately telling Torvald that their marriage is a sham and that she can no longer stay with him. This abrupt shift in Nora's personality gives the audience a clear understanding of the major themes of the play.

Unlike Willy and Nora, Antigone in Sophocles's *Antigone* (p. 1234) is a character who changes very little during the course of the play. Fiercely devoted to her brother, Antigone decides to bury her brother's body in violation of Creon's decree that his corpse must be left to rot. Antigone's loyalty to her brother and to the gods makes it impossible for her to compromise. Her stubborn refusal to bend to the will of the king causes her downfall as well as her death. Antigone's inability to change highlights the central conflict of the play: Is a person's main duty to the king, to the gods, or to him- or herself?

 ## Staging

Various staging elements, such as props and furnishings, may also convey the themes of a play. In *Death of a Salesman*, Biff's trophy, which is constantly in the audience's view, is a prop that ironically underscores the futility of Willy's efforts to achieve success. Similarly, the miniature animals in *The Glass Menagerie* suggest the fragility of Laura's character and the futility of her efforts to fit into the modern world. And, in *Trifles*, the depressing farm house, the broken birdcage, and the dead canary hint at Mrs. Wright's misery and the reason she murdered her husband.

Special lighting effects and music can also suggest a play's themes. Throughout *The Glass Menagerie*, for example, words and pictures are projected onto a section of the set between the front room and dining room walls. In scene 1, as Tom's mother, Amanda, tells him about her experiences with her "gentlemen callers," an image of her as a girl greeting callers appears on the screen. As Amanda continues, the words "*Où sont Les Neiges*"—"Where are the snows [of yesteryear]?"—appear on the screen. Later in the play, when Laura and her mother discuss a boy Laura knew, his picture is projected on the screen, showing him as a high school hero carrying a silver cup. In addition to the slides, Williams uses music—a recurring tune, dance music, and "Ave Maria"—to increase the emotional impact of certain scenes. He also uses shafts of light focused on selected areas or characters to create a dreamlike atmosphere for the play. Collectively, the slides, music, and lighting reinforce the theme that those who retreat into the past inevitably become estranged from the present.

 ## A Final Note

As you read, your own values and beliefs influence your interpretation of a play's themes. For instance, your interest in the changing status of women could lead you to focus on the submissive, almost passive, role of Willy's wife, Linda, in *Death of a Salesman*. As a result, you could conclude that the play shows how, in the post–World War II United States, women like Linda often sacrificed their own happiness for that of their husbands. Remember, however, that the play itself, not just your own feelings or assumptions about it, must support your interpretation.

CHAPTER 30 • THEME

✔ CHECKLIST   Writing about Theme

- What is the central theme of the play?

- What other themes can you identify?

- Does the title of the play suggest a theme?

- What conflicts exist in the play? How do they shed light on the themes of the play?

- Do any characters' statements express or imply a theme of the play?

- Do any characters change during the play? How do these changes suggest the play's themes?

- Do certain characters resist change? How does their failure to change suggest a theme of the play?

- Do scenery and props help to communicate the play's themes?

- Does music reinforce certain ideas in the play?

- Does lighting underscore the themes of the play?

SOPHOCLES (496–406 B.C.) (picture and biography on p. 1182) was one of nine generals elected for a military campaign against Samos, a Greek island that was in revolt against Athens. Sophocles' election was due at least in part to the popularity of his play *Antigone*. (Greek plays often centered on problems of the city-state, and the theater was in many ways the center of the state's religious and political life.)

Even though it was written long before *Oedipus the King*, *Antigone* traces the events that befall Oedipus's younger daughter after his banishment from Thebes. Caught between the laws of the gods and the edict of her uncle the king, Antigone follows her conscience despite the fatal consequences to herself. In the 1960s, the story of Antigone was especially meaningful to those Americans who engaged in civil disobedience in struggles for civil rights and in protest against the war in Vietnam.

Cultural Context The central struggle in this play revolves around Antigone's desire to bury her brother in an honorable way. The ancient Greeks believed that at the moment of death, the spirit of the dead person left the body as a little puff of wind. The body was then prepared for burial according to certain rituals, which were primarily performed by female relatives. The burial rituals consisted of three parts: the *prothesis*, or laying out of the body; the *ekphora*, or funeral procession; and the interment of the body or cremated remains of the deceased. Coins were placed over the eyelids of the deceased as payment for the ferryman who would usher the body across the River Styx and into the underworld. The ancient Greeks believed that if the correct methods of burial were not followed, the soul of the deceased would roam between worlds until the proscribed rites were completed.

Antigone* (441 b.c.)

Translation by F. Storr, BA
Formerly Scholar of Trinity College, Cambridge

DRAMATIS PERSONAE

ANTIGONE and ISMENE: *Daughters of Oedipus and sisters of Polyneices and Eteocles*
CREON: *King of Thebes*
HAEMON: *Son of Creon, betrothed to Antigone*
EURYDICE: *Wife of Creon*
TEIRESIAS: *The prophet*
CHORUS: *Theban elders*

A WATCHMAN
A MESSENGER
A SECOND MESSENGER

Scene from a 1999 production of *Antigone* at London's Old Vic Theater
Photo by John Haynes/Lebrecht Music & Arts

PROLOGUE

ANTIGONE and ISMENE before the Palace gates.

ANTIGONE: Ismene, sister of my blood and heart,
See'st thou how Zeus would in our lives fulfill

---

*Note that individual lines are numbered in the following play. When a line is shared by two or more characters, it is counted as one line.

The weird of Oedipus, a world of woes!
For what of pain, affliction, outrage, shame,
5   Is lacking in our fortunes, thine and mine?
And now this proclamation of today
Made by our Captain-General to the State,
What can its purport be? Didst hear and heed,
Or art thou deaf when friends are banned as foes?
10 ISMENE: To me, Antigone, no word of friends
Has come, or glad or grievous, since we twain
Were reft of our two brethren in one day
By double fratricide; and since i' the night
Our Argive leaguers fled, no later news
15   Has reached me, to inspirit or deject.
ANTIGONE: I know 'twas so, and therefore summoned thee
Beyond the gates to breathe it in thine ear.
ISMENE: What is it? Some dark secret stirs thy breast.
ANTIGONE: What but the thought of our two brothers dead,
20   The one by Creon graced with funeral rites,
The other disappointed? Eteocles
He hath consigned to earth (as fame reports)
With obsequies that use and wont ordain,
So gracing him among the dead below.
25   But Polyneices, a dishonored corse,
(So by report the royal edict runs)
No man may bury him or make lament—
Must leave him tombless and unwept, a feast
For kites to scent afar and swoop upon.
30   Such is the edict (if report speak true)
Of Creon, our most noble Creon, aimed
At thee and me, aye me too; and anon
He will be here to promulgate, for such
As have not heard, his mandate; 'tis in sooth
35   No passing humor, for the edict says
Whoe'er transgresses shall be stoned to death.
So stands it with us; now 'tis thine to show
If thou art worthy of thy blood or base.
ISMENE: But how, my rash, fond sister, in such case
40   Can I do anything to make or mar?
ANTIGONE: Say, wilt thou aid me and abet? Decide.
ISMENE: In what bold venture? What is in thy thought?
ANTIGONE: Lend me a hand to bear the corpse away.
ISMENE: What, bury him despite the interdict?

ANTIGONE: My brother, and, though thou deny him, thine   45
    No man shall say that *I* betrayed a brother.
ISMENE: Wilt thou persist, though Creon has forbid?
ANTIGONE: What right has he to keep me from my own?
ISMENE: Bethink thee, sister, of our father's fate,
    Abhorred, dishonored, self-convinced of sin,   50
    Blinded, himself his executioner.
    Think of his mother-wife (ill sorted names)
    Done by a noose herself had twined to death
    And last, our hapless brethren in one day,
    Both in a mutual destiny involved,   55
    Self-slaughtered, both the slayer and the slain.
    Bethink thee, sister, we are left alone;
    Shall we not perish wretchedest of all,
    If in defiance of the law we cross
    A monarch's will? —weak women, think of that,   60
    Not framed by nature to contend with men.
    Remember this too that the stronger rules;
    We must obey his orders, these or worse.
    Therefore I plead compulsion and entreat
    The dead to pardon. I perforce obey   65
    The powers that be. 'Tis foolishness, I ween,
    To overstep in aught the golden mean.
ANTIGONE: I urge no more; nay, wert thou willing still,
    I would not welcome such a fellowship.
    Go thine own way; myself will bury him.   70
    How sweet to die in such employ, to rest,—
    Sister and brother linked in love's embrace—
    A sinless sinner, banned awhile on earth,
    But by the dead commended; and with them
    I shall abide for ever. As for thee,   75
    Scorn, if thou wilt, the eternal laws of Heaven.
ISMENE: I scorn them not, but to defy the State
    Or break her ordinance I have no skill.
ANTIGONE: A specious pretext. I will go alone
    To lap my dearest brother in the grave.   80
ISMENE: My poor, fond sister, how I fear for thee!
ANTIGONE: O waste no fears on me; look to thyself.
ISMENE: At least let no man know of thine intent,
    But keep it close and secret, as will I.
ANTIGONE: O tell it, sister; I shall hate thee more   85
    If thou proclaim it not to all the town.

ISMENE: Thou hast a fiery soul for numbing work.

ANTIGONE: I pleasure those whom I would liefest please.

ISMENE: If thou succeed; but thou art doomed to fail.

90 ANTIGONE: When strength shall fail me, yes, but not before.

ISMENE: But, if the venture's hopeless, why essay?

ANTIGONE: Sister, forbear, or I shall hate thee soon,
And the dead man will hate thee too, with cause.
Say I am mad and give my madness rein
95 To wreck itself; the worst that can befall
Is but to die an honorable death.

ISMENE: Have thine own way then; 'tis a mad endeavor,
Yet to thy lovers thou art dear as ever.

[Exeunt]

PÁRODOS[1]
STROPHE[2] 1

CHORUS: Sunbeam, of all that ever dawn upon
                    Our seven-gated Thebes the brightest ray,
                            O eye of golden day,
            How fair thy light o'er Dirce's fountain shone,
5   Speeding upon their headlong homeward course,
            Far quicker than they came, the Argive force;
                            Putting to flight
            The argent shields, the host with scutcheons white.
            Against our land the proud invader came
10   To vindicate fell Polyneices' claim.
                    Like to an eagle swooping low,
                    On pinions white as new fall'n snow.
            With clanging scream, a horsetail plume his crest,
            The aspiring lord of Argos onward pressed.

ANTISTROPHE[3] 1

15 Hovering around our city walls he waits,
            His spearmen raven at our seven gates.
            But ere a torch our crown of towers could burn,
            Ere they had tasted of our blood, they turn
            Forced by the Dragon; in their rear
20   The din of Ares panic-struck they hear.
            For Zeus who hates the braggart's boast

---

[1] *Párodos:* The song that signifies the entrance of the chorus.

[2] *Strophe:* The first half of an ode, sung by the chorus.

[3] *Antistrophe:* The second half of an ode. Typically a response to the strophe, and also sung by the chorus.

Beheld that gold-bespangled host;
As at the goal the paean they upraise,
He struck them with his forked lightning blaze.

STROPHE 2

To earthy from earth rebounding, down he crashed;   25
    The fire-brand from his impious hand was dashed,
As like a Bacchic reveler on he came,
Outbreathing hate and flame,
And tottered. Elsewhere in the field,
Here, there, great Area like a war-horse wheeled;   30
    Beneath his car down thrust
    Our foemen bit the dust.
Seven captains at our seven gates
Thundered; for each a champion waits,
Each left behind his armor bright,   35
Trophy for Zeus who turns the fight;
Save two alone, that ill-starred pair
One mother to one father bare,
Who lance in rest, one 'gainst the other
Drave, and both perished, brother slain by brother.   40

ANTISTROPHE 2

Now Victory to Thebes returns again
And smiles upon her chariot-circled plain.
    Now let feast and festal should
    Memories of war blot out.
    Let us to the temples throng,   45
    Dance and sing the live night long.

SCENE 1

God of Thebes, lead thou the round.
Bacchus, shaker of the ground!
Let us end our revels here;
Lo! Creon our new lord draws near,
Crowned by this strange chance, our king.   5
What, I marvel, pondering?
Why this summons? Wherefore call
Us, his elders, one and all,
Bidding us with him debate,
On some grave concern of State?   10

[Enter CREON]

CREON: Elders, the gods have righted one again
   Our storm-tossed ship of state, now safe in port.
   But you by special summons I convened
   As my most trusted councilors; first, because
15 I knew you loyal to Laius[1] of old;
   Again, when Oedipus restored our State,
   Both while he ruled and when his rule was o'er,
   Ye still were constant to the royal line.
   Now that his two sons perished in one day,
20 Brother by brother murderously slain,
   By right of kinship to the Princes dead,
   I claim and hold the throne and sovereignty.
   Yet 'tis no easy matter to discern
   The temper of a man, his mind and will,
25 Till he be proved by exercise of power;
   And in my case, if one who reigns supreme
   Swerve from the highest policy, tongue-tied
   By fear of consequence, that man I hold,
   And ever held, the basest of the base.
30 And I contemn the man who sets his friend
   Before his country. For myself, I call
   To witness Zeus, whose eyes are everywhere,
   If I perceive some mischievous design
   To sap the State, I will not hold my tongue;
35 Nor would I reckon as my private friend
   A public foe, well knowing that the State
   Is the good ship that holds our fortunes all:
   Farewell to friendship, if she suffers wreck.
   Such is the policy by which I seek
40 To serve the Commons and conformably
   I have proclaimed an edict as concerns
   The sons of Oedipus; Eteocles
   Who in his country's battle fought and fell,
   The foremost champion—duly bury him
45 With all observances and ceremonies
   That are the guerdon of the heroic dead.
   But for the miscreant exile who returned
   Minded in flames and ashes to blot out
   His father's city and his father's gods,
50 And glut his vengeance with his kinsmen's blood,
   Or drag them captive at his chariot wheels—
   For Polyneices 'tis ordained that none
   Shall give him burial or make mourn for him,

---

[1] *Laius:* A previous King of Thebes, and Oepdius' father.

But leave his corpse unburied, to be meat
For dogs and carrion crows, a ghastly sight. 55
So am I purposed; never by my will
Shall miscreants take precedence of true men,
But all good patriots, alive or dead,
Shall be by me preferred and honored.
CHORUS: Son of Menoeceus,[2] thus thou will'st to deal 60
With him who loathed and him who loved our State.
Thy word is law; thou canst dispose of us
The living, as thou will'st, as of the dead.
CREON: See then ye execute what I ordain. 65
CHORUS: On younger shoulders lay this grievous charge.
CREON: Fear not, I've posted guards to watch the corpse.
CHORUS: What further duty would'st thou lay on us?
CREON: Not to connive at disobedience.
CHORUS: No man is mad enough to court his death.
CREON: The penalty *is* death: yet hope of gain 70
Hath lured men to their ruin oftentimes.

[Enter GUARD]

GUARD: My lord, I will not make pretense to pant
And puff as some light-footed messenger.
In sooth my soul beneath its pack of thought
Made many a halt and turned and turned again; 75
For conscience plied her spur and curb by turns.
"Why hurry headlong to thy fate, poor fool?"
She whispered. Then again, "If Creon learn
This from another, thou wilt rue it worse."
Thus leisurely I hastened on my road; 80
Much thought extends a furlong to a league.
But in the end the forward voice prevailed,
To face thee. I will speak though I say nothing.
For plucking courage from despair methought,
"Let the worst hap, thou canst but meet thy fate." 85
CREON: What is thy news? Why this despondency?
GUARD: Let me premise a word about myself?
I neither did the deed nor saw it done,
Nor were it just that I should come to harm.
CREON: Thou art good at parry, and canst fence about 90
Some matter of grave import, as is plain.
GUARD: The bearer of dread tidings needs must quake.
CREON: Then, sirrah, shoot thy bolt and get thee gone.

---

[2]*Menoeceus:* Father of Creon and father-in-law of Oedipus.

GUARD: Well, it must out; the corpse is buried; someone
95   E'en now besprinkled it with thirsty dust,
             Performed the proper ritual³—and was gone.
CREON: What say'st thou? Who hath dared to do this thing?
GUARD: I cannot tell, for there was ne'er a trace
             Of pick or mattock—hard unbroken ground,
100   Without a scratch or rut of chariot wheels,
             No sign that human hands had been at work.
             When the first sentry of the morning watch
             Gave the alarm, we all were terror-stricken.
             The corpse had vanished, not interred in earth,
105   But strewn with dust, as if by one who sought
             To avert the curse that haunts the unburied dead:
             Of hound or ravening jackal, not a sign.
             Thereat arose an angry war of words;
             Guard railed at guard and blows were like to end it,
110   For none was there to part us, each in turn
             Suspected, but the guilt brought home to none,
             From lack of evidence. We challenged each
             The ordeal, or to handle red-hot iron,
             Or pass through fire, affirming on our oath
115   Our innocence—we neither did the deed
             Ourselves, nor know who did or compassed it.
             Our quest was at a standstill, when one spake
             And bowed us all to earth like quivering reeds,
             For there was no gainsaying him nor way
120   To escape perdition: Ye are bound to tell
             The King ye cannot hide it; so he spake.
             And he convinced us all; so lots were cast,
             And I, unlucky scapegoat, drew the prize.
             So here I am unwilling and withal
125   Unwelcome; no man cares to hear ill news.
CHORUS: I had misgivings from the first, my liege,
             Of something more than natural at work.
CREON: O cease, you vex me with your babblement;
             I am like to think you dote in your old age.
130   Is it not arrant folly to pretend
             That gods would have a thought for this dead man?
             Did they forsooth award him special grace,
             And as some benefactor bury him,
             Who came to fire their hallowed sanctuaries,

---

³*proper ritual:* Rituals and the way they are performed are important in Greek tragedies, especially rituals for death.

To sack their shrines, to desolate their land, 135
And scout their ordinances? Or perchance
The gods bestow their favors on the bad.
No! no! I have long noted malcontents
Who wagged their heads, and kicked against the yoke,
Misliking these my orders, and my rule. 140
'Tis they, I warrant, who suborned my guards
By bribes. Of evils current upon earth
The worst is money. Money 'tis that sacks
Cities, and drives men forth from hearth and home;
Warps and seduces native innocence, 145
And breeds a habit of dishonesty.
But they who sold themselves shall find their greed
Out-shot the mark, and rue it soon or late.
Yea, as I still revere the dread of Zeus,
By Zeus I swear, except ye find and bring 150
Before my presence here the very man
Who carried out this lawless burial,
Death for your punishment shall not suffice.
Hanged on a cross, alive ye first shall make
Confession of this outrage. This will teach you 155
What practices are like to serve your turn.
There are some villainies that bring no gain.
For by dishonesty the few may thrive,
The many come to ruin and disgrace.

GUARD: May I not speak, or must I turn and go 160
  Without a word?—
CREON   Begone! canst thou not see
  That e'en this question irks me?
GUARD   Where, my lord?
  Is it thy ears that suffer, or thy heart? 165
CREON: Why seek to probe and find the seat of pain?
GUARD: I gall thine ears—this miscreant thy mind.
CREON: What an inveterate babbler! Get thee gone!
GUARD: Babbler perchance, but innocent of the crime.
CREON: Twice guilty, having sold thy soul for gain. 170
GUARD: Alas! How sad when reasoners reason wrong.
CREON: Go, quibble with thy reason. If thou fail'st
  To find these malefactors, thou shalt own
  The wages of ill-gotten gains is death.

[Exit CREON]

GUARD: I pray he may be found. But caught or not 175
  (And fortune must determine that) thou never

CHAPTER 30 • THEME

Shalt see me here returning; that is sure.
For past all hope or thought I have escaped,
And for my safety owe the gods much thanks.

ODE[1] 1
STROPHE 1

CHORUS: Many wonders there be, but naught more wondrous than man;
  Over the surging sea, with a whitening south wind wan,
  Through the foam of the firth, man makes his perilous way;
  And the eldest of deities Earth that knows not toil nor decay
5 Ever he furrows and scores, as his team, year in year out,
  With breed of the yoked horse, the ploughshare turneth about.

ANTISTROPHE 1

The light-witted birds of the air, the beasts of the weald and the wood
He traps with his woven snare, and the brood of the briny flood.
Master of cunning he: the savage bull, and the hart
10 Who roams the mountain free, are tamed by his infinite art;
And the shaggy rough-maned steed is broken to bear the bit.

STROPHE 2

Speech and the wind-swift speed of counsel and civic wit,
He hath learnt for himself all these; and the arrowy rain to fly
And the nipping airs that freeze, 'neath the open winter sky.
15 He hath provision for all: fell plague he hath learnt to endure;
Safe whate'er may befall: yet for death he hath found no cure.

ANTISTROPHE 2

Passing the wildest flight thought are the cunning and skill,
That guide man now to the light, but now to counsels of ill.
If he honors the laws of the land, and reveres the Gods of the State
20 Proudly his city shall stand; but a cityless outcast I rate
Whoso bold in his pride from the path of right doth depart;
Ne'er may I sit by his side, or share the thoughts of his heart.

What strange vision meets my eyes,
Fills me with a wild surprise?
25 Sure I know her, sure 'tis she,
The maid Antigone.
Hapless child of hapless sire,
Didst thou recklessly conspire,

---

[1] *Ode:* A type of lyrical stanza that is comprised of three parts: the strophe, the antistrophe, and the epode.

Madly brave the King's decree?
Therefore are they haling thee?   30

SCENE II

[Enter GUARD bringing ANTIGONE]

GUARD: Here is the culprit taken in the act
    Of giving burial. But where's the King?
CHORUS: There from the palace he returns in time.

[Enter CREON]

CREON: Why is my presence timely? What has chanced?
GUARD: No man, my lord, should make a vow, for if   5
    He ever swears he will not do a thing,
    His afterthoughts belie his first resolve.
    When from the hail-storm of thy threats I fled
    I sware thou wouldst not see me here again;
    But the wild rapture of a glad surprise   10
    Intoxicates, and so I'm here forsworn.
    And here's my prisoner, caught in the very act,
    Decking the grave. No lottery this time;
    This prize is mine by right of treasure-trove.
    So take her, judge her, rack her, if thou wilt.   15
    She's thine, my liege; but I may rightly claim
    Hence to depart well quit of all these ills.
CREON: Say, how didst thou arrest the maid, and where?
GUARD: Burying the man. There's nothing more to tell.
CREON: Hast thou thy wits? Or know'st thou what thou say'st?   20
GUARD: I saw this woman burying the corpse
    Against thy orders. Is that clear and plain?
CREON: But how was she surprised and caught in the act?
GUARD: It happened thus. No sooner had we come,
    Driven from thy presence by those awful threats,   25
    Than straight we swept away all trace of dust,
    And bared the clammy body. Then we sat
    High on the ridge to windward of the stench,
    While each man kept he fellow alert and rated
    Roundly the sluggard if he chanced to nap.   30
    So all night long we watched, until the sun
    Stood high in heaven, and his blazing beams
    Smote us. A sudden whirlwind then upraised
    A cloud of dust that blotted out the sky,
    And swept the plain, and stripped the woodlands bare,   35

And shook the firmament. We closed our eyes
And waited till the heaven-sent plague should pass.
At last it ceased, and lo! There stood this maid.
A piercing cry she uttered, sad and shrill,
40 As when the mother bird beholds her nest
Robbed of its nestlings; even so the maid
Wailed as she saw the body stripped and bare,
And cursed the ruffians who had done this deed.
Anon she gathered handfuls of dry dust,
45 Then, holding high a well-wrought brazen urn,
Thrice on the dead she poured a lustral stream.
We at the sight swooped down on her and seized
Our quarry. Undismayed she stood, and when
We taxed her with the former crime and this,
50 She disowned nothing. I was glad—and grieved;
For 'tis most sweet to 'scape oneself scot-free,
And yet to bring disaster to a friend
Is grievous. Take it all in all, I deem
A man's first duty is to serve himself.
55 CREON: Speak, girl, with head bent low and downcast eyes,
Does thou plead guilty or deny the deed?
ANTIGONE: Guilty. I did it, I deny it not.
CREON: (to GUARD) Sirrah, begone whither thou wilt, and thank
Thy luck that thou hast 'scaped a heavy charge.

(To ANTIGONE)

60 Now answer this plain question, yes or no,
Wast thou acquainted with the interdict?

ANTIGONE: I knew, all knew; how should I fail to know?
CREON: And yet wert bold enough to break the law?
ANTIGONE: Yea, for these laws were not ordained of Zeus,
65 And she who sits enthroned with gods below,
Justice, enacted not these human laws.
Nor did I deem that thou, a mortal man,
Could'st by a breath annul and override
The immutable unwritten laws of Heaven.
70 They were not born today nor yesterday;
They die not; and none knoweth whence they sprang.
I was not like, who feared no mortal's frown,
To disobey these laws and so provoke
The wrath of Heaven. I knew that I must die,
75 E'en hadst thou not proclaimed it; and if death
Is thereby hastened, I shall count it gain.

For death is gain to him whose life, like mine,
Is full of misery. Thus my lot appears
Not sad, but blissful; for had I endured
To leave my mother's son unburied there, 80
I should have grieved with reason, but not now.
And if in this thou judgest me a fool,
Methinks the judge of folly's not acquit.
CHORUS: A stubborn daughter of a stubborn sire,
This ill-starred maiden kicks against the pricks. 85
CREON: Well, let her know the stubbornest of wills
Are soonest bended, as the hardest iron,
O'er-heated in the fire to brittleness,
Flies soonest into fragments, shivered through.
A snaffle curbs the fieriest steed, and he 90
Who in subjection lives must needs be meek.
But this proud girl, in insolence well-schooled,
First overstepped the established law, and then—
A second and worse act of insolence—
She boasts and glories in her wickedness. 95
Now if she thus can flout authority
Unpunished, I am woman, she the man.
But though she be my sister's child or nearer
Of kin than all who worship at my hearth,
Nor she nor yet her sister shall escape 100
The utmost penalty, for both I hold,
As arch-conspirators, of equal guilt.
Bring forth the older; even now I saw her
Within the palace, frenzied and distraught.
The workings of the mind discover oft 105
Dark deeds in darkness schemed, before the act.
More hateful still the miscreant who seeks
When caught, to make a virtue of a crime.
ANTIGONE: Would'st thou do more than slay thy prisoner?
CREON: Not I, thy life is mine, and that's enough. 110
ANTIGONE: Why dally then? To me no word of thine
Is pleasant: God forbid it e'er should please;
Nor am I more acceptable to thee.
And yet how otherwise had I achieved
A name so glorious as by burying 115
A brother? so my townsmen all would say,
Where they not gagged by terror, Manifold
A king's prerogatives, and not the least
That all his acts and all his words are law.

120   CREON: Of all these Thebans none so deems but thou.
      ANTIGONE: These think as I, but bate their breath to thee.
      CREON: Hast thou no shame to differ from all these?
      ANTIGONE: To reverence kith and kin[1] can bring no shame.
      CREON: Was his dead foeman not thy kinsman too?
125   ANTIGONE: One mother bare them and the self-same sire.
      CREON: Why cast a slur on one by honoring one?
      ANTIGONE: The dead man will not bear thee out in this.
      CREON: Surely, if good and evil fare alive.
      ANTIGONE: The slain man was no villain but a brother.
130   CREON: The patriot perished by the outlaw's brand.
      ANTIGONE: Nathless the realms below these rites require.
      CREON: Not that the base should fare as do the brave.
      ANTIGONE: Who knows if this world's crimes are virtues there?
      CREON: Not even death can make a foe a friend.
135   ANTIGONE: My nature is for mutual love, not hate.
      CREON: Die then, and love the dead if thou must;
           No woman shall be the master while I live.

[Enter ISMENE]

      CHORUS: Lo from out the palace gate,
             Weeping o'er her sister's fate,
140   Comes Ismene; see her brow,
             Once serene, beclouded now,
             See her beauteous face o'erspread
             With a flush of angry red.
      CREON: Woman, who like a viper unperceived
145   Didst harbor in my house and drain my blood,
            Two plagues I nurtured blindly, so it proved,
            To sap my throne. Say, didst thou too abet
            This crime, or dost abjure all privity?
      ISMENE: I did the deed, if she will have it so,
150   And with my sister claim to share the guilt.
      ANTIGONE: That were unjust. Thou would'st not act with me
            At first, and I refused thy partnership.
      ISMENE: But now thy bark is stranded, I am bold
            To claim my share as partner in the loss.
155   ANTIGONE: Who did the deed the under-world knows well:
            A friend in word is never friend of mine.
      ISMENE: O sister, scorn me not, let me but share
            Thy work of piety, and with thee die.

---

[1] *Kith and kin:* friends and family

ANTIGONE: Claim not a work in which thou hadst no hand;
    One death sufficeth. Wherefore should'st thou die?   160
ISMENE: What would life profit me bereft of thee?
ANTIGONE: Ask Creon, he's thy kinsman and best friend.
ISMENE: Why taunt me? Find'st thou pleasure in these gibes?
ANTIGONE: 'Tis a sad mockery, if indeed I mock.
ISMENE: O say if I can help thee even now.   165
ANTIGONE: No, save thyself; I grudge not thy escape.
ISMENE: Is e'en this boon denied, to share thy lot?
ANTIGONE: Yea, for thou chosed'st life, and I to die.
ISMENE: Thou canst not say that I did not protest.
ANTIGONE: Well, some approved thy wisdom, others mine.   170
ISMENE: But now we stand convicted, both alike.
ANTIGONE: Fear not; thou livest, I died long ago
    Then when I gave my life to save the dead.
CREON: Both maids, methinks, are crazed. One suddenly
    Has lost her wits, the other was born mad.   175
ISMENE: Yea, so it falls, sire, when misfortune comes,
    The wisest even lose their mother wit.
CREON: I' faith thy wit forsook thee when thou mad'st
    Thy choice with evil-doers to do ill.
ISMENE: What life for me without my sister here?   180
CREON: Say not thy sister *here*: thy sister's dead.
ISMENE: What, wilt thou slay thy own son's plighted bride?
CREON: Aye, let him raise him seed from other fields.
ISMENE: No new espousal can be like the old.
CREON: A plague on trulls who court and woo our sons.   185
ANTIGONE: O Haemon, how thy sire dishonors thee!
CREON: A plague on thee and thy accursed bride!
CHORUS: What, wilt thou rob thine own son of his bride?
CREON: 'Tis death that bars this marriage, not his sire.
CHORUS: So her death-warrant, it would seem, is sealed.   190
CREON: By you, as first by me; off with them, guards,
    And keep them close. Henceforward let them learn
    To live as women use, not roam at large.
    For e'en the bravest spirits run away
    When they perceive death pressing on life's heels.   195

ODE II
STROPHE 1

CHORUS: Thrice blest are they who never tasted pain!
    If once the curse of Heaven attaint a race,
    The infection lingers on and speeds apace,

Age after age, and each the cup must drain.
5 So when Etesian blasts from Thrace downpour
Sweep o'er the blackening main and whirl to land
From Ocean's cavernous depths his ooze and sand,
Billow on billow thunders on the shore.

ANTISTROPHE 1

On the Labdacidae I see descending
10   Woe upon woe; from days of old some god
Laid on the race a malison, and his rod
Scourges each age with sorrows never ending.

The light that dawned upon its last born son
Is vanished, and the bloody axe of Fate
15   Has felled the goodly tree that blossomed late.
O Oedipus, by reckless pride undone!

STROPHE 2

Thy might, O Zeus, what mortal power can quell?
Not sleep that lays all else beneath its spell,
Nor moons that never tire: untouched by Time,
20   Throned in the dazzling light
That crowns Olympus' height,
Thou reignest King, omnipotent, sublime.

Past, present, and to be,
All bow to thy decree,
25   All that exceeds the mean by Fate
Is punished, Love or Hate.

ANTISTROPHE 2

Hope flits about never-wearying wings;
Profit to some, to some light loves she brings,
But no man knoweth how her gifts may turn,
30 Till 'neath his feet the treacherous ashes burn.
Sure 'twas a sage inspired that spake this word;
        If evil good appear
        To any, Fate is near;
And brief the respite from her flaming sword.

SCENE III

Hither comes in angry mood
Haemon, latest of thy brood;
Is it for his bride he's grieved,

Or her marriage-bed deceived,
Doth he make his mourn for thee,   5
Maid forlorn, Antigone?

[Enter HAEMON]

CREON: Soon shall we know, better than seer can tell.
    Learning may fixed decree anent thy bride,
    Thou mean'st not, son, to rave against thy sire?
    Know'st not whate'er we do is done in love?   10
HAEMON: O father, I am thine, and I will take
    Thy wisdom as the helm to steer withal.
    Therefore no wedlock shall by me be held
    More precious than thy loving goverance.
CREON: Well spoken: so right-minded sons should feel,   15
    In all deferring to a father's will.
    For 'tis the hope of parents they may rear
    A brood of sons submissive, keen to avenge
    Their father's wrongs, and count his friends their own.
    But who begets unprofitable sons,   20
    He verily breeds trouble for himself,
    And for his foes much laughter. Son, be warned
    And let no woman fool away thy wits.
    Ill fares the husband mated with a shrew,
    And her embraces very soon wax cold.   25
    For what can wound so surely to the quick
    As a false friend? So spue and cast her off,
    Bid her go find a husband with the dead.
    For since I caught her openly rebelling,
    Of all my subjects the one malcontent,   30
    I will not prove a traitor to the State.
    She surely dies. Go, let her, if she will,
    Appeal to Zeus the God of Kindred, for
    If thus I nurse rebellion in my house,
    Shall not I foster mutiny without?   35
    For whoso rules his household worthily,
    Will prove in civic matters no less wise.
    But he who overbears the laws, or thinks
    To overrule his rulers, such as one
    I never will allow. Whome'er the State   40
    Appoints must be obeyed in everything,
    But small and great, just and unjust alike.
    I warrant such a one in either case

Would shine, as King or subject; such a man
45   Would in the storm of battle stand his ground,
A comrade leal and true; but Anarchy—
What evils are not wrought by Anarchy!
She ruins States, and overthrows the home,
She dissipates and routs the embattled host;
50   While discipline preserves the ordered ranks.
Therefore we must maintain authority
And yield to title to a woman's will.
Better, if needs be, men should cast us out
Than hear it said, a woman proved his match.
55 Chorus: To me, unless old age have dulled wits,
Thy words appear both reasonable and wise.
    Haemon: Father, the gods implant in mortal men
Reason, the choicest gift bestowed by heaven.
'Tis not for me to say thou errest, nor
60   Would I arraign thy wisdom, if I could;
And yet wise thoughts may come to other men
And, as thy son, it falls to me to mark
The acts, the words, the comments of the crowd.
The commons stand in terror of thy frown,
65   And dare not utter aught that might offend,
But I can overhear their muttered plaints,
Know how the people mourn this maiden doomed
For noblest deeds to die the worst of deaths.
When her own brother slain in battle lay
70   Unsepulchered, she suffered not his corse
To lie for carrion birds and dogs to maul:
Should not her name (they cry) be writ in gold?
Such the low murmurings that reach my ear.
O father, nothing is by me more prized
75   Than thy well-being, for what higher good
Can children covet than their sire's fair fame,
As fathers too take pride in glorious sons?
Therefore, my father, cling not to one mood,
And deemed not thou art right, all others wrong.
80   For whoso thinks that wisdom dwells with him,
That he alone can speak or think aright,
Such oracles are empty breath when tried.
The wisest man will let himself be swayed
By others' wisdom and relax in time.
85   See how the trees beside a stream in flood
Save, if they yield to force, each spray unharmed,

But by resisting perish root and branch.
The mariner who keeps his mainsheet taut,
And will not slacken in the gale, is like
To sail with thwarts reversed, keel uppermost.   90
Relent then and repent thee of thy wrath;
For, if one young in years may claim some sense,
I'll say 'tis best of all to be endowed
With absolute wisdom; but, if that's denied,
(And nature takes not readily that ply)   95
Next wise is he who lists to sage advice.
CHORUS: If he says aught in season, heed him, King.

(*To* HAEMON)

Heed thou thy sire too; both have spoken well.

CREON: What, would you have us at our age be schooled,
    Lessoned in prudence by a beardless boy?   100
HAEMON: I plead for justice, father, nothing more.
    Weigh me upon my merit, not my years.
CREON: Strange merit this to sanction lawlessness!
HAEMON: For evil-doers I would urge no plea.
CREON: Is not this maid an arrant law-breaker?   105
HAEMON: The Theban commons with one voice say, No.
CREON: What, shall the mob dictate my policy?
HAEMON: 'Tis thou, methinks, who speakest like a boy.
CREON: Am I to rule for others, or myself?
HAEMON: A State for one man is no State at all.   110
CREON: The State is his who rules it, so 'tis held.
HAEMON: As monarch of a desert thou wouldst shine.
CREON: This boy, methinks, maintains the woman's cause.
HAEMON: If thou be'st woman, yes. My thought's for thee.
CREON: O reprobate, would'st wrangle with thy sire?   115
HAEMON: Because I see thee wrongfully perverse.
CREON: And am I wrong, if I maintain my rights?
HAEMON: Talk not of rights; thou spurn'st the due of Heaven
CREON: O heart corrupt, a woman's minion thou!
HAEMON: Slave to dishonor thou wilt never find me.   120
CREON: Thy speech at least was all a plea for her.
HAEMON: And thee and me, and for the gods below.
CREON: Living the maid shall never be thy bride.
HAEMON: So she shall die, but one will die with her.
CREON: Hast come to such a pass as threaten me?   125
HAEMON: What threat is this, vain counsels to reprove?

CREON: Vain fool to instruct thy betters; thou shall rue it.

HAEMON: Wert not my father, I had said thou err'st.

CREON: Play not the spaniel, thou a woman's slave.

130 HAEMON: When thou dost speak, must no man make reply?

CREON: This passes bounds. By heaven, thou shalt not rate
      And jeer and flout me with impunity.
      Off with the hateful thing that she may die
      At once, beside her bridegroom, in his sight.

135 HAEMON: Think not that in my sight the maid shall die,
      Or by my side; never shalt thou again
      Behold my face hereafter. Go, consort
      With friends who like a madman for their mate.

[Exit HAEMON]

CHORUS: Thy son has gone, my liege, in angry haste.

140   Fell is the wrath of youth beneath a smart.

CREON: Let him go vent his fury like a fiend:
      These sisters twain he shall not save from death.

CHORUS: Surely, thou meanest not to slay them both?

CREON: I stand corrected; only her who touched

145   The body.

CHORUS: And what death is she to die?

CREON: She shall be taken to some desert place
      By man untrod, and in a rock-hewn cave,
      With food no more than to avoid the taint

150   That homicide might bring on all the State,
      Buried alive. There let her call in aid
      The King of Death, the one god she reveres,
      Or learn too late a lesson learnt at last:
      'Tis labor lost, to reverence the dead.

ODE III

STROPHE

CHORUS: Love resistless in fight, all yield at a glance of thine eye,
      Love who pillowed all night on a maiden's cheek dost lie,
      Over the upland holds. Shall mortals not yield to thee?

ANTISTROPHE

      Mad are thy subjects all, and even the wisest heart

5   Straight to folly will fall, at a touch of thy poisoned dart.
      Thou didst kindle the strife, this feud of kinsman with kin,
      By the eyes of a winsome wife, and the yearning her heart to win.

For as her consort still, enthroned with Justice above,
Thou bendest man to thy will, O all invincible Love.

SCENE IV

Lo I myself am borne aside,
From Justice, as I view this bride.
(O sight an eye in tears to drown)
Antigone, so young, so fair,
    Thus hurried down   5
Death's bower with the dead to share.

STROPHE 1

ANTIGONE: Friends, countrymen, my last farewell I make;
    My journey's done.
One last fond, lingering, longing look I take
    At the bright sun.   10
For Death who puts to sleep both young and old
    Hales my young life,
And beckons me to Acheron's dark fold,
    An unwed wife.
No youths have sung the marriage song for me,   15
    My bridal bed
No maids have strewn with flowers from the lea,
    'Tis Death I wed.

CHORUS: But bethink thee, thou art sped,
    Great and glorious, to the dead.   20
    Thou the sword's edge hast not tasted,
    No disease thy frame hath wasted.
    Freely thou alone shalt go
    Living to the dead below.

ANTISTROPHE 1

ANTIGONE: Nay, but the piteous tale I've heard men tell   25
    Of Tantalus' doomed child,
Chained upon Siphylus' high rocky fell,
    That clung like ivy wild,
Drenched by the pelting rain and whirling snow,
    Left there to pine,   30
While on her frozen breast the tears aye flow—
    Her fate is mine.

CHORUS: She was sprung of gods, divine,
    Mortals we of mortal line.

35   Like renown with gods to gain
            Recompenses all thy pain.
            Take this solace to thy tomb
            Hers in life and death thy doom.

STROPHE 2

ANTIGONE: Alack, alack! Ye mock me. Is it meet
40   Thus to insult me living, to my face?
            Cease, by our country's altars I entreat,
                Ye lordly rulers of a lordly race.
            O fount of Dirce, wood-embowered plain
                Where Theban chariots to victory speed,
45   Mark ye the cruel laws that now have wrought my bane,
                The friends who show no pity in my need!
            Was ever fate like mine? O monstrous doom,
                Within a rock-built prison sepulchered,
            To fade and wither in a living tomb,
50   And alien midst the living and the dead.

STROPHE 3

CHORUS: In thy boldness over-rash
            Madly thou thy foot didst dash
            'Gainst high Justice' altar stair.
            Thou a father's guild dost bear.

ANTISTROPHE 2

55 ANTIGONE: At this thou touchest my most poignant pain,
                My ill-starred father's piteous disgrace,
            The taint of blood, the hereditary stain,
                That clings to all of Labdacus' famed race.
            Woe worth the monstrous marriage-bed where lay
60   A mother with the son her womb had borne,
            Therein I was conceived, woe worth the day,
                Fruit of incestuous sheets, a maid forlorn,
            And now I pass, accursed and unwed,
                To meet them as an alien there below;
65   And thee, O brother, in marriage ill-bestead,
                'Twas thy dead hand that dealt me this death-blow.

CHORUS: Religion has her chains, 'tis true,
            Let rite be paid when rites are due.
            Yet is it ill to disobey
70   The powers who hold by might the sway.

Thou hast withstood authority,
A self-willed rebel, thou must die.

EPODE[1]

ANTIGONE: Unwept, unwed, unfriended, hence I go,
No longer may I see the day's bright eye;
    Not one friend left to share my bitter woe,   75
And o'er my ashes heave one passing sigh.

CREON: If wail and lamentation aught availed
To stave off death, I trow they'd never end.
Away with her, and having walled her up
In a rock-vaulted tomb, as I ordained,   80
Leave her alone at liberty to die,
Or, if she choose, to live in solitude,
The tomb her dwelling. We in either case
Are guiltless as concerns this maiden's blood,
Only on earth no lodging shall she find.   85

ANTIGONE: O grave, O bridal bower, O prison house
Hewn from the rock, my everlasting home,
Whither I go to join the mighty host
Of kinsfolk, Persephassa's[2] guests long dead,
The last of all, of all more miserable,   90
I pass, my destined span of years cut short.
And yet good hope is mine that I shall find
A welcome from my sire, a welcome too,
From thee, my mother, and my brother dear;
From with these hands, I laved and decked your limbs   95
In death, and poured libations on your grave.
And last, my Polyneices, unto thee
I paid due rites, and this my recompense!
Yet am I justified in wisdom's eyes.
For even had it been some child of mine,   100
Or husband mouldering in death's decay,
I had not wrought this deed despite the State.
What is the law I call in aid? 'Tis thus
I argue. Had it been a husband dead
I might have wed another, and have borne   105
Another child, to take the dead child's place.
But, now my sire and mother both are dead,

---

[1] *Epode:* The third part of an ode.
[2] *Persephassa:* Daughter of Zeus, also know as Persephone.

No second brother can be born for me.
Thus by the law of conscience I was led
110   To honor thee, dear brother, and was judged
By Creon guilty of a heinous crime.
And now he drags me like a criminal,
A bride unwed, amerced of marriage-song
And marriage-bed and joys of motherhood,
115   By friends deserted to a living grave.
What ordinance of heaven have I transgressed?
Hereafter can I look to any god
For succor, call on any man for help?
Alas, my piety is impious deemed.
120   Well, if such justice is approved of heaven,
I shall be taught by suffering my sin;
But if the sin is theirs, O may they suffer
No worse ills than the wrongs they do to me.
CHORUS: The same ungovernable will
125   Drives like a gale the maiden still.
CREON: Therefore, my guards who let her stay
Shall smart full sore for their delay.
ANTIGONE: Ah, woe is me! This word I hear
Brings death most near.
130   CHORUS: I have no comfort. What he saith,
Portends no other thing than death.
ANTIGONE: My fatherland, city of Thebes divine,
Ye gods of Thebes whence sprang my line,
Look, puissant lords of Thebes, on me;
135   The last of all your royal house ye see.
Martyred by men of sin, undone.
Such meed my piety hath won.

[Exit ANTIGONE]

ODE IV
STROPHE 1

CHORUS: Like to thee that maiden bright,
Danae, in her brass-bound tower,
Once exchanged the glad sunlight
For a cell, her bridal bower.
5   And yet she sprang of royal line,
My child, like thine,
And nursed the seed
By her conceived

Of Zeus descending in a golden shower.
Strange are the ways of Fate, her power   10
Nor wealth, nor arms withstand, nor tower;
Nor brass-prowed ships, that breast the sea
    From Fate can flee.

ANTISTROPHE 1

Thus Dryas' child, the rash Edonian King,
For words of high disdain   15
Did Bacchus[1] to a rocky dungeon bring,
To cool the madness of a fevered brain.
    His frenzy passed,
    He learnt at last
'Twas madness gibes against a god to fling.   20
For once he fain had quenched the Maenad's fire;
And of the tuneful Nine[2] provoked the ire.

STROPHE 2

By the Iron Rocks that guard the double main,
    On Bosporus' lone strand,
Where stretcheth Salmydessus' plain   25
    In the wild Thracian land,
    There on his borders Ares[3] witnessed
    The vengeance by a jealous step-dame ta'en
    The gore that trickled from a spindle red,
    The sightless orbits of her step-sons twain.   30

ANTISTROPHE 2

Wasting away they mourned their piteous doom,
The blasted issue of their mother's womb.
But she her lineage could trace
    To great Erecththeus' race;
Daughter of Boreas in her sire's vast caves   35
    Reared, where the tempest raves,
Swift as his horses o'er the hills she sped;
A child of gods; yet she, my child, like thee,
    By Destiny
That knows not death nor age—she too was vanquished.   40

SCENE V

[Enter TEIRESIAS and BOY]

---

[1] *Bacchus:* Another name for Dionysis, God of wine.

[2] *Nine:* The nine muses, who represent knowledge and art.

[3] *Ares:* The Greek god of war.

TEIRESIAS:[1] Princes of Thebes, two wayfarers as one,
　　Having betwixt us eyes for one, we are here.
　　The blind man cannot move without a guide.
CREON: Why tidings, old Teiresias?
5　TEIRESIAS:　　　　　　　　I will tell thee;
　　And when thou hearest thou must heed the seer.
CREON: Thus far I ne'er have disobeyed thy rede.
TEIRESIAS: So hast thou steered the ship of State aright.
CREON: I know it, and I gladly own my debt.
10　TEIRESIAS: Bethink thee that thou treadest once again
　　The razor edge of peril.
CREON:　　　　　　　What is this?
　　Thy words inspire a dread presentiment.
TEIRESIAS: The divination of my arts shall tell.
15　Sitting upon my throne of augury,
　　As is my wont, where every fowl of heaven
　　Find harborage, upon mine ears was borne
　　A jargon strange of twitterings, hoots, and screams;
　　So knew I that each bird at the other tare
20　With bloody talons, for the whirr of wings
　　Could signify naught else. Perturbed in soul,
　　I straight essayed the sacrifice by fire
　　On blazing altars, but the God of Fire
　　Came not in flame, and from the thigh bones dripped
25　And sputtered in the ashes a foul ooze;
　　Gall-bladders cracked and spurted up: the fat
　　Melted and fell and left the thigh bones bare.
　　Such are the signs, taught by this lad, I read—
　　As I guide others, so the boy guides me—
30　The frustrate signs of oracles grown dumb.
　　O King, thy willful temper ails the State,
　　For all our shrines and altars are profaned
　　By what has filled the maw of dogs and crows,
　　The flesh of Oedipus' unburied son.
35　Therefore the angry gods abominate
　　Our litanies and our burnt offerings;
　　Therefore no birds trill out a happy note,
　　Gorged with the carnival of human gore.
　　O ponder this, my son. To err is common
40　To all men, but the man who having erred
　　Hugs not his errors, but repents and seeks

---

[1] *Teiresias:* A blind seer whose visions of the future are often ignored or misinterpreted.

The cure, is not a wastrel nor unwise.
No fool, the saw goes, like the obstinate fool.
Let death disarm thy vengeance. O forbear
To vex the dead. What glory wilt thou win   45
By slaying twice the slain? I mean thee well;
Counsel's most welcome if I promise gain.
CREON: Old man, ye all let fly at me your shafts
Like anchors at a target; yea, ye set
Your soothsayer on me. Peddlers are ye all   50
And I the merchandise ye buy and sell.
Go to, and make your profit where ye will,
Silver of Sardis change for gold of Ind;
Ye will not purchase this man's burial,
Not though the winged ministers of Zeus   55
Should bear him in their talons to his throne;
Not e'en in awe of prodigy so dire
Would I permit his burial, for I know
No human soilure can assail the gods;
This too I know, Teiresias, dire's the fall   60
Of craft and cunning when it tries to gloss
Foul treachery with fair words for filthy gain.
TEIRESIAS: Alas! doth any know and lay to heart—
CREON: Is this the prelude to some hackneyed saw?
TEIRESIAS: How far good counsel is the best of goods?   65
CREON: True, as unwisdom is the worst of ills.
TEIRESIAS: Thou art infected with that ill thyself.
CREON: I will not bandy insults with thee, seer.
TEIRESIAS: And yet thou say'st my prophesies are frauds.
CREON: Prophets are all a money-getting tribe.   70
TEIRESIAS: And kings are all a lucre-loving race.
CREON: Dost know at whom thou glancest, me thy lord?
TEIRESIAS: Lord of the State and savior, thanks to me.
CREON: Skilled prophet art thou, but to wrong inclined.
TEIRESIAS: Take heed, thou wilt provoke me to reveal   75
    The mystery deep hidden in my breast.
CREON: Say on, but see it be not said for gain.
TEIRESIAS: Such thou, methinks, till now hast judged my words.
CREON: Be sure thou wilt not traffic on my wits.
TEIRESIAS: Know then for sure, the coursers of the sun   80
    Not many times shall run their race, before
    Thou shalt have given the fruit of thine own loins
    In quittance of thy murder, life for life;
    For that thou hast entombed a living soul,

85 And sent below a denizen of earth,
And wronged the nether gods by leaving here
A corpse unlaved, unwept, unsepulchered.
Herein thou hast no part, nor e'en the gods
In heaven; and thou usurp'st a power not thine.
90 For this the avenging spirits of Heaven and Hell
Who dog the steps of sin are on thy trail:
What these have suffered thou shalt suffer too.
And now, consider whether bought by gold
I prophesy. For, yet a little while,
95 And sound of lamentation shall be heard,
Of men and women through thy desolate halls;
And all thy neighbor States are leagues to avenge
Their mangled warriors who have found a grave
I' the maw of wolf or hound, or winged bird
100 That flying homewards taints their city's air.
These are the shafts, that like a bowman I
Provoked to anger, loosen at thy breast,
Unerring, and their smart thou shalt not shun.
Boy, lead me home, that he may vent his spleen
105 On younger men, and learn to curb his tongue
With gentler manners than his present mood.

[Exit TEIRESIAS]

CHORUS: My liege, that man hath gone, foretelling woe.
And, O believe me, since these grizzled locks
Were like the raven, never have I known
110 The prophet's warning to the State to fail.
CREON: I know it too, and it perplexes me.
To yield is grievous, but the obstinate soul
That fights with Fate, is smitten grievously.
CHORUS: Son of Menoeceus, list to good advice.
115 Chorus:What should I do. Advise me. I will heed.
CHORUS: Go, free the maiden from her rocky cell;
And for the unburied outlaw build a tomb.
CREON: Is that your counsel? You would have me yield?
CHORUS: Yea, king, this instant. Vengeance of the gods
120 Is swift to overtake the impenitent.
CREON: Ah! what a wrench it is to sacrifice
My heart's resolve; but Fate is ill to fight.
CHORUS: Go, trust not others. Do it quick thyself.
CREON: I go hot-foot. Bestir ye one and all,
125 My henchmen! Get ye axes! Speed away

To yonder eminence! I too will go,
For all my resolution this way sways.
'Twas I that bound, I too will set her free.
Almost I am persuaded it is best
To keep through life the law ordained of old.   130

[Exit CREON]

PAEAN
STROPHE 1

CHORUS: Thou by many names adored,
                    Child of Zeus the God of thunder,
                    Of a Theban bride the wonder,
          Fair Italia's guardian lord;

          In the deep-embosomed glades   5
                    Of the Eleusinian Queen
          Haunt of revelers, men and maids,
                    Dionysus[1], thou art seen.

          Where Ismenus rolls his waters,
                    Where the Dragon's teeth were sown,   10
          Where the Bacchanals thy daughters
                    Round thee roam,
                    There thy home;
          Thebes, O Bacchus, is thine own.

ANTISTROPHE 1

          Thee on the two-crested rock   15
                    Lurid-flaming torches see;
          Where Corisian maidens flock,
                    Thee the springs of Castaly.

          By Nysa's bastion ivy-clad,
          By shores with clustered vineyards glad,   20
          There to thee the hymn rings out,
          And through our streets we Thebans shout,
                    All hall to thee
                    Evoe, Evoe![2]

STROPHE 2

          Oh, as thou lov'st this city best of all,   25
          To thee, and to thy Mother levin-stricken,

---

[1] *Dionysus:* God of wine.
[2] *Evoe, Evoe!:* An exclamation indicating joy.

In our dire need we call;
Thou see'st with what a plague our townsfolk sicken.
        Thy ready help we crave,
30   Whether adown Parnassian heights descending,
Or o'er the roaring straits thy swift was wending,
            Save us, O save!

ANTISTROPHE 2

Brightest of all the orbs that breathe forth light,
        Authentic son of Zeus, immortal king,
35   Leader of all the voices of the night,
        Come, and thy train of Thyiads with thee bring,
        Thy maddened rout
Who dance before thee all night long, and shout,
        Thy handmaids we,
40   Evoe, Evoe!

EXODOS[1]

[Enter MESSENGER]

MESSENGER: Attend all ye who dwell beside the halls
        Of Cadmus and Amphion. No man's life
        As of one tenor would I praise or blame,
        For Fortune with a constant ebb and rise
5   Casts down and raises high and low alike,
        And none can read a mortal's horoscope.
        Take Creon; he, methought, if any man,
        Was enviable. He had saved this land
        Of Cadmus from our enemies and attained
10   A monarch's powers and ruled the state supreme,
        While a right noble issue crowned his bliss.
        Now all is gone and wasted, for a life
        Without life's joys I count a living death.
        You'll tell me he has ample store of wealth,
15   The pomp and circumstance of kings; but if
        These give no pleasure, all the rest I count
        The shadow of a shade, nor would I weigh
        His wealth and power 'gainst a dram of joy.
CHORUS: What fresh woes bring'st thou to the royal house?
20   MESSENGER: Both dead, and they who live deserve to die.
CHORUS: Who is the slayer, who the victim? speak.
MESSENGER: Haemon; his blood shed by no stranger hand.

---

[1] *Exodus:* The closing of the play.

CHORUS: What mean ye? by his father's or his own?

MESSENGER: His own; in anger for his father's crime.

CHORUS: O prophet, what thou spakest comes to pass.   25

MESSENGER: So stands the case; now 'tis for you to act.

CHORUS: Lo! from the palace gates I see approaching
    Creon's unhappy wife, Eurydice.
    Comes she by chance or learning her son's fate?

[Enter EURYDICE]

EURYDICE: Ye men of Thebes, I overheard your talk.   30
    As I passed out to offer up my prayer
    To Pallas[2], and was drawing back the bar
    To open wide the door, upon my ears
    There broke a wail that told of household woe
    Stricken with terror in my handmaids' arms   35
    I fell and fainted. But repeat your tale
    To one not unacquaint with misery.

MESSENGER: Dear mistress, I was there and will relate
    The perfect truth, omitting not one word.
    Why should we gloze and flatter, to be proved   40
    Liars hereafter? Truth is ever best.
    Well, in attendance on my liege, your lord,
    I crossed the plain to its utmost margin, where
    The corse of Polyneices, gnawn and mauled,
    Was lying yet. We offered first a prayer   45
    To Pluto[3] and the goddess of cross-ways,
    With contrite hearts, to deprecate their ire.
    Then laved with lustral waves the mangled corse,
    Laid it on fresh-lopped branches, lit a pyre,
    And to his memory piled a mighty mound   50
    Of mother earth. Then to the caverned rock,
    The bridal chamber of the maid and Death,
    We sped, about to enter. But a guard
    Heard from that godless shrine a far shrill wail,
    And ran back to our lord to tell the news.   55
    But as he nearer drew a hollow sound
    Of lamentation to the King was borne.
    He groaned and uttered then this bitter plaint:
    "Am I a prophet? miserable me!
    Is this the saddest path I ever trod?   60

---

[2]*Pallas:* The Greek goddess Athena.

[3]*Pluto:* The Greek god of the underworld, more commonly known as Hades.

'Tis my son's voice that calls me. On press on,
My henchmen, haste with double speed to the tomb
Where rocks down-torn have made a gap, look in
And tell me if in truth I recognize
65   The voice of Haemon or am heaven-deceived."
So at the bidding of our distraught lord
We looked, and in the craven's vaulted gloom
I saw the maiden lying strangled there,
A noose of linen twined about her neck;
70   And hard beside her, clasping her cold form,
Her lover lay bewailing his dead bride
Death-wedded, and his father's cruelty.
When the King saw him, with a terrible groan
He moved towards him, crying, "O my son
75   What hast thou done? What ailed thee? What mischance
Has reft thee of thy reason? O come forth,
Come forth, my son; thy father supplicates."
But the son glared at him with tiger eyes,
Spat in his face, and then, without a word,
80   Drew his two-hilted sword and smote, but missed
His father flying backwards. Then the boy,
Wroth with himself, poor wretch, incontinent
Fell on his sword and drove it through his side
Home, but yet breathing clasped in his lax arms
85   The maid, her pallid cheek incarnadined
With his expiring gasps. So there they lay
Two corpses, one in death. His marriage rites
Are consummated in the halls of Death:
A witness that of ills whate'er befall
90   Mortals' unwisdom is the worst of all.

[*Exit EURYDICE*]

CHORUS: What makest thou of this? The Queen has gone
         Without a word importing good or ill.
MESSENGER: I marvel too, but entertain good hope.
         'Tis that she shrinks in public to lament
95   Her son's sad ending, and in privacy
         Would with her maidens mourn a private loss.
         Trust me, she is discreet and will not err.
CHORUS: I know not, but strained silence, so I deem,
         Is no less ominous than excessive grief.
100 MESSENGER: Well, let us to the house and solve our doubts,
         Whether the tumult of her heart conceals

Some fell design. It may be thou art right:
Unnatural silence signifies no good.
CHORUS: Lo! the King himself appears.
    Evidence he with him bears   105
    'Gainst himself (ah me! I quake
    'Gainst a king such charge to make)
    But all must own,
    The guilt is his and his alone.
CREON: Woe for sin of minds perverse,   110
    Deadly fraught with mortal curse.
    Behold us slain and slayers, all akin.
    Woe for my counsel dire, conceived in sin.
        Alas, my son,
        Life scarce begun,   115
        Thou wast undone.
    The fault was mine, mine only, O my son!
CHORUS: Too late thou seemest to perceive the truth.
CREON: By sorrow schooled. Heavy the hand of God,
    Thorny and rough the paths my feet have trod,   120
    Humbled my pride, my pleasure turned to pain;
    Poor mortals, how we labor all in vain!

[Enter SECOND MESSENGER]

SECOND MESSENGER: Sorrows are thine, my lord, and more to come,
    One lying at thy feet, another yet
    More grievous waits thee, when thou comest home.   125
CREON: What woe is lacking to my tale of woes?
SECOND MESSENGER: Thy wife, the mother of thy dead son here,
    Lies stricken by a fresh inflicted blow.
CREON: How bottomless the pit!
        Does claim me too, O Death?   130
        What is this word he saith,
    This woeful messenger? Say, is it fit
    To slay anew a man already slain?
        Is Death at work again,
        Stroke upon stroke, first son, then mother slain?   135
CHORUS: Look for thyself. She lies for all to view.
CREON: Alas! another added woe I see.
    What more remains to crown my agony?
    A minute past I clasped a lifeless son,
    And now another victim Death hath won.   140
    Unhappy mother, most unhappy son!
SECOND MESSENGER: Beside the altar on a keen-edged sword
    She fell and closed her eyes in night, but erst

She mourned for Megareus who nobly died
145   Long since, then for her son; with her last breath
She cursed thee, the slayer of her child.
CREON: I shudder with affright
O for a two-edged sword to slay outright
A wretch like me,
150   Made one with misery.
SECOND MESSENGER: 'Tis true that thou wert charged by the dead Queen
As author of both deaths, hers and her son's.
CREON: In what wise was her self-destruction wrought?
SECOND MESSENGER: Hearing the loud lament above her son
155   With her own hand she stabbed herself to the heart.
CREON: I am the guilty cause. I did the deed,
Thy murderer. Yea, I guilty plead.
My henchmen, lead me hence, away, away,
A cipher, less than nothing; no delay!
160 CHORUS: Well said, if in disaster aught is well
His past endure demand the speediest cure.
CREON: Come, Fate, a friend at need,
Come with all speed!
Come, my best friend,
165   And speed my end!
Away, away!
Let me not look upon another day!
CHORUS: This for the morrow; to us are present needs
That they whom it concerns must take in hand.
170 CREON: I join your prayer that echoes my desire.
CHORUS: O pray not, prayers are idle; from the doom
Of fate for mortals refuge is there none.
CREON: Away with me, a worthless wretch who slew
Unwitting thee, my son, thy mother too.
175   Whither to turn I know now; every way
Leads but astray,
And on my head I feel the heavy weight
Of crushing Fate.
CHORUS: Of happiness the chiefest part
180   Is a wise heart:
And to defraud the gods in aught
With peril's fraught.
Swelling words of high-flown might

Mightily the gods do smite.
Chastisement for errors past   185
Wisdom brings to age at last.

*   *   *

Reading and Reacting

1. What ideas does *Antigone* express about duty? about obedience? How do these ideas conform (or fail to conform) to your own concepts of duty and obedience?
2. According to Aristotle, the main character in a tragedy possess a flaw that leads to his or her downfall. Write an essay in which you discuss Antigone's tragic flaw. How does this flaw set up (or make inevitable) the series events that lead to the tragic resolution of the play?
3. Both Creon and Antigone defend rights that they believe are sacred. What rights are in conflict? Is there any room for compromise? Do you sympathize with Antigone or with Creon?
4. Aristotle believed that to be effective, tragic heroes must have elements of both good and evil. Does Antigone conform to Aristotle's requirement? Explain.
5. What is Antigone's fatal flaw? How does this flaw lead to the tragic resolution of the play?
6. As the play progresses, do Creon and Antigone change, or do they remain essentially un changed by events?
7. At the very end of *Antigone*, the Chorus says, "Chastisement for errors past / Wisdom brings to age at last." Do you think Creon has gained wisdom from his experiences? Why, or why not?
8. How does Antigone's gender affect her actions? How does it determine how she is treated? Are the play's attitudes toward women consistent with those of contemporary American society? Explain.
9. JOURNAL ENTRY If you were Antigone, would you have stuck to your principles, or would you have given in? Explain your reasoning.
10. CRITICAL PERSPECTIVE In *Sophocles the Playwright*, S. M. Adams argues that, to the ancient Greek audience, Antigone and Creon were both tragic heroes. Do you agree? If so, do you see the fact that the play has two tragic heroes as a problem?

Related Works: From *Persepolis* (p. 111), "A Worn Path" (p. 386), "Do not go gentle into that good night" (p. 710), "Medgar Evers" (p. 744), *Hamlet* (p. 1043), *Oedipus the King* (p. 1182)

© Ap Images

AUGUST WILSON (1945–2005) was born in Pittsburgh, Pennsylvania, to a German immigrant father and a black mother and lived in the African American neighborhood known as the Hill District. After leaving school at fifteen when he was accused of plagiarizing a paper, he participated in the Black Arts movement in Pittsburgh, submitting poems to local African American publications. In 1969, Wilson and his friend Rob Penny founded the Black Horizons Theatre Company, for which Wilson produced and directed plays. Although Wilson wrote plays while living in Pittsburgh, his work began to gain recognition only after 1978, when he moved to St. Paul, Minnesota. There, in 1982, Lloyd Richards, dean of the Yale School of Drama and artistic director of the Yale Repertory Company, staged a performance of Wilson's *Ma Rainey's Black Bottom*.

Wilson's achievement was epic. Beginning with *Ma Rainey's Black Bottom* in 1984, he wrote a ten-play cycle that chronicled the African American experience in the United States decade by decade. In addition to *Ma Rainey's Black Bottom*, a Tony Award winner, the plays in this cycle include *Fences* (1985), which won a Pulitzer Prize in 1987; *Joe Turner's Come and Gone* (1986); *Two Trains Running* (1989), which won Wilson his fifth New York Drama Critics Circle Award; *The Piano Lesson* (1987), which won a second Pulitzer Prize for Wilson in 1990; *Seven Guitars* (1996); and *Radio Golf*, the last play in the cycle, which opened in 2005, the year of Wilson's death. To honor his achievements, Broadway's Virginia Theater was renamed the August Wilson Theater.

Fences explores how the long-upheld color barrier in professional baseball affected the main character, Troy, who struggles with the pain of never realizing his dream of becoming a big-league player. Throughout the play, Troy retreats behind literal and figurative barriers that impair his relationships with his family.

Cultural Context The history of African Americans in baseball began in the period between emancipation and the civil rights movement. Banned from professional baseball, African American players formed the Negro Leagues, with stars such as Satchel Paige and Josh Gibson emerging in the 1930s. Then, in 1946, Branch Rickey, the club president and general manager of the Brooklyn Dodgers, changed everything when he set out to sign the Negro Leagues' top players to his team. The first player he chose was Jackie Robinson, who broke the racial barrier and debuted at first base for the Dodgers on April 15, 1947, at the age of 28. Robinson's performance earned him the Rookie of the Year award. In 1957, the year in which *Fences* is set, Robinson announced his retirement from baseball after he was traded to the New York Giants. In 1962, he was inducted into the Baseball Hall of Fame.

Fences (1985)

CHARACTERS

Troy Maxson   **Gabriel,** *Troy's brother*
Jim Bono, *Troy's friend*   **Cory,** *Troy and Rose's son*
Rose, *Troy's wife*   **Raynell,** *Troy's daughter*
Lyons, *Troy's oldest son by*
previous marriage

SETTING

The setting is the yard which fronts the only entrance to the Maxson household, an ancient two-story brick house set back off a small alley in a big-city neighborhood. The entrance to the house is gained by two or three steps leading to a wooden porch badly in need of paint.

A relatively recent addition to the house and running its full width, the porch lacks congruence. It is a sturdy porch with a flat roof. One or two chairs of dubious value sit at one end where the kitchen window opens onto the porch. An old-fashioned icebox stands silent guard at the opposite end.

The yard is a small dirt yard, partially fenced, except for the last scene, with a wooden sawhorse, a pile of lumber, and other fence-building equipment set off to the side. Opposite is a tree from which hangs a ball made of rags. A baseball bat leans against the tree. Two oil drums serve as garbage receptacles and sit near the house at right to complete the setting.

THE PLAY

Near the turn of the century, the destitute of Europe sprang on the city with tenacious claws and an honest and solid dream. The city devoured them. They swelled its belly until it burst into a thousand furnaces and sewing machines, a thousand butcher shops and bakers' ovens, a thousand churches and hospitals and funeral parlors and money-lenders. The city grew. It nourished itself and offered each man a partnership limited only by his talent, his guile, and his willingness and capacity for hard work. For the immigrants of Europe, a dream dared and won true.

The descendants of African slaves were offered no such welcome or participation. They came from places called the Carolinas and the Virginias, Georgia, Alabama, Mississippi, and Tennessee. They came strong, eager, searching. The city rejected them and they fled and settled along the riverbanks and under bridges in shallow, ramshackle houses made of sticks and tarpaper. They collected rags and wood. They sold the use of their muscles and their bodies. They cleaned houses and washed clothes, they shined shoes, and in quiet desperation and vengeful pride, they stole, and lived in pursuit of their own dream. That they could breathe free, finally, and stand to meet life with the force of dignity and whatever eloquence the heart could call upon.

By 1957, the hard-won victories of the European immigrants had solidified the industrial might of America. War had been confronted and won with new energies that used loyalty and patriotism as its fuel. Life was rich, full, and flourishing. The Milwaukee Braves won the World Series, and the hot winds of change that would make the sixties a turbulent, racing, dangerous, and provocative decade had not yet begun to blow full.

ACT 1
SCENE 1

It is 1957. Troy and Bono enter the yard, engaged in conversation. Troy is fifty-three years old, a large man with thick, heavy hands; it is this largeness that he strives to fill out and make an accommodation with. Together with his blackness, his largeness informs his sensibilities and the choices he has made in his life.

Of the two men, Bono is obviously the follower. His commitment to their friendship of thirty-odd years is rooted in his admiration of Troy's honesty, capacity for hard work, and his strength, which Bono seeks to emulate.

Scene from the 1987 Broadway production of *Fences* starring James Earl Jones as Troy
Ron Scherl/StageImage/The Image Works

It is Friday night, payday, and the one night of the week the two men engage in a ritual of talk and drink. Troy is usually the most talkative and at times he can be crude and almost vulgar, though he is capable of rising to profound heights of expression. The men carry lunch buckets and wear or carry burlap aprons and are dressed in clothes suitable to their jobs as garbage collectors.

BONO: Troy, you ought to stop that lying!

TROY: I ain't lying! The nigger had a watermelon this big. (*He indicates with his hands.*) Talking about . . . "What watermelon, Mr. Rand?" I liked to fell out! "What watermelon, Mr. Rand?" . . . And it sitting there big as life.

BONO: What did Mr. Rand say?

TROY: Ain't said nothing. Figure if the nigger too dumb to know he carrying a watermelon, he wasn't gonna get much sense out of him. Trying to hide that great big old watermelon under his coat. Afraid to let the white man see him carry it home.

BONO: I'm like you . . . I ain't got no time for them kind of people.   5

TROY: Now what he look like getting mad 'cause he see the man from the union talking to Mr. Rand?

BONO: He come to me talking about . . . "Maxson gonna get us fired." I told him to get away from me with that. He walked away from me calling you a troublemaker. What Mr. Rand say?

TROY: Ain't said nothing. He told me to go down the Commissioner's office next Friday. They called me down there to see them.

BONO: Well, as long as you got your complaint filed, they can't fire you. That's what one of them white fellows tell me.

TROY: I ain't worried about them firing me. They gonna fire me 'cause   10 I asked a question? That's all I did. I went to Mr. Rand and asked him, "Why? Why you got the white mens driving and the colored lifting?" Told him, "what's the matter, don't I count? You think only white fellows got sense enough to drive a truck. That ain't no paper job! Hell, anybody can drive a truck. How come you got all whites driving and the colored lifting?" He told me "take it to the union." Well, hell, that's what I done! Now they wanna come up with this pack of lies.

BONO: I told Brownie if the man come and ask him any questions . . . just tell the truth! It ain't nothing but something they done trumped up on you 'cause you filed a complaint on them.

TROY: Brownie don't understand nothing. All I want them to do is change the job description. Give everybody a chance to drive the truck. Brownie can't see that. He ain't got that much sense.

BONO: How you figure he be making out with that gal be up at Taylors' all the time . . . that Alberta gal?

TROY: Same as you and me. Getting just as much as we is. Which is to say nothing.

BONO: It is, huh? I figure you doing a little better than me . . . and I   15 ain't saying what I'm doing.

TROY: Aw, nigger, look here . . . I know you. If you had got anywhere near that gal, twenty minutes later you be looking to tell somebody. And the first one you gonna tell . . . that you gonna want to brag to . . . is me.

BONO: I ain't saying that. I see where you be eyeing her.

TROY: I eye all the women. I don't miss nothing. Don't never let nobody tell you Troy Maxson don't eye the women.

BONO: You been doing more than eyeing her. You done bought her a drink or two.

TROY: Hell yeah, I bought her a drink! What that mean? I bought you   20 one, too. What that mean 'cause I buy her a drink? I'm just being polite.

BONO: It's all right to buy her one drink. That's what you call being polite. But when you wanna be buying two or three . . . that's what you call eyeing her.

TROY: Look here, as long as you known me . . . you ever known me to chase after women?

BONO: Hell yeah! Long as I done known you. You forgetting I knew you when.

TROY: Naw, I'm talking about since I been married to Rose?

25 BONO: Oh, not since you been married to Rose. Now, that's the truth, there. I can say that.

TROY: All right then! Case closed.

BONO: I see you be walking up around Alberta's house. You supposed to be at Taylors' and you be walking up around there.

TROY: What you watching where I'm walking for? I ain't watching after you.

BONO: I seen you walking around there more than once.

30 TROY: Hell, you liable to see me walking anywhere! That don't mean nothing cause you see me walking around there.

BONO: Where she come from anyway? She just kinda showed up one day.

TROY: Tallahassee. You can look at her and tell she one of them Florida gals. They got some big healthy women down there. Grow them right up out the ground. Got a little bit of Indian in her. Most of them niggers down in Florida got some Indian in them.

BONO: I don't know about that Indian part. But she damn sure big and healthy. Woman wear some big stockings. Got them great big old legs and hips as wide as the Mississippi River.

TROY: Legs don't mean nothing. You don't do nothing but push them out of the way. But them hips cushion the ride!

35 BONO: Troy, you ain't got no sense.

TROY: It's the truth! Like you riding on Goodyears!

Rose enters from the house. She is ten years younger than Troy, her devotion to him stems from her recognition of the possibilities of her life without him: a succession of abusive men and their babies, a life of partying and running the streets, the Church, or aloneness with its attendant pain and frustration. She recognizes Troy's spirit as a fine and illuminating one and she either ignores or forgives his faults, only some of which she recognizes. Though she doesn't drink, her presence is an integral part of the Friday night rituals. She alternates between the porch and the kitchen, where supper preparations are under way.

ROSE: What you all out here getting into?

TROY: What you worried about what we getting into for? This is men talk, woman.

ROSE: What I care what you all talking about? Bono, you gonna stay for supper?

BONO: No, I thank you, Rose. But Lucille say she cooking up a pot of   40
pigfeet.

TROY: Pigfeet! Hell, I'm going home with you! Might even stay the
night if you got some pigfeet. You got something in there to top
them pigfeet, Rose?

ROSE: I'm cooking up some chicken. I got some chicken and collard
greens.[1]

TROY: Well, go on back in the house and let me and Bono finish what
we was talking about. This is men talk. I got some talk for you later.
You know what kind of talk I mean. You go on and powder it up.

ROSE: Troy Maxson, don't you start that now!

TROY: (puts his arm around her) Aw, woman . . . come here. Look here,   45
Bono . . . when I met this woman . . . I got out that place, say,
"Hitch up my pony, saddle up my mare . . . there's a woman out
there for me somewhere. I looked here. Looked there. Saw Rose and
latched on to her." I latched on to her and told her—I'm gonna tell
you the truth—I told her, "Baby, I don't wanna marry, I just wanna
be your man." Rose told me . . . tell him what you told me, Rose.

ROSE: I told him if he wasn't the marrying kind, then move out the way
so the marrying kind could find me.

TROY: That's what she told me. "Nigger, you in my way. You blocking
the view! Move out the way so I can find me a husband." I thought
it over two or three days. Come back—

ROSE: Ain't no two or three days nothing. You was back the same
night.

TROY: Come back, told her . . . "Okay, baby . . . but I'm gonna buy me
a banty rooster and put him out there in the backyard . . . and when
he see a stranger come, he'll flap his wings and crow . . . " Look
here, Bono, I could watch the front door by myself . . . it was that
back door I was worried about.

ROSE: Troy, you ought not talk like that. Troy ain't doing nothing but   50
telling a lie.

TROY: Only thing is . . . when we first got married . . . forget the
rooster . . . we ain't had no yard!

BONO: I hear you tell it. Me and Lucille was staying down there on
Logan Street. Had two rooms with the outhouse in the back. I
ain't mind the outhouse none. But when that goddamn wind blow
through there in the winter . . . that's what I'm talking about! To
this day I wonder why in the hell I ever stayed down there for six
long years. But see, I didn't know I could do no better. I thought
only white folks had inside toilets and things.

---

[1]*collard greens:* A leafy green vegetable.

ROSE: There's a lot of people don't know they can do no better than they doing now. That's just something you got to learn. A lot of folks still shop at Bella's.

TROY: Ain't nothing wrong with shopping at Bella's. She got fresh food.

55 ROSE: I ain't said nothing about if she got fresh food. I'm talking about what she charge. She charge ten cents more than the A&P.

TROY: The A&P ain't never done nothing for me. I spends my money where I'm treated right. I go down to Bella, say, "I need a loaf of bread, I'll pay you Friday." She give it to me. What sense that make when I got money to go and spend it somewhere else and ignore the person who done right by me? That ain't in the Bible.

ROSE: We ain't talking about what's in the Bible. What sense it make to shop there when she overcharge?

TROY: You shop where you want to. I'll do my shopping where the people been good to me.

ROSE: Well, I don't think it's right for her to overcharge. That's all I was saying.

60 BONO: Look here . . . I got to get on. Lucille going be raising all kind of hell.

TROY: Where you going, nigger? We ain't finished this pint. Come here, finish this pint.

BONO: Well, hell, I am . . . if you ever turn the bottle loose.

TROY: (*hands him the bottle*) The only thing I say about the A&P is I'm glad Cory got that job down there. Help him take care of his school clothes and things. Gabe done moved out and things getting tight around here. He got that job . . . He can start to look out for himself.

ROSE: Cory done went and got recruited by a college football team.

65 TROY: I told that boy about that football stuff. The white man ain't gonna let him get nowhere with that football. I told him when he first come to me with it. Now you come telling me he done went and got more tied up in it. He ought to go and get recruited in how to fix cars or something where he can make a living.

ROSE: He ain't talking about making no living playing football. It's just something the boys in school do. They gonna send a recruiter by to talk to you. He'll tell you he ain't talking about making no living playing football. It's a honor to be recruited.

TROY: It ain't gonna get him nowhere. Bono'll tell you that.

BONO: If he be like you in the sports . . . he's gonna be all right. Ain't but two men ever played baseball as good as you. That's Babe Ruth[2]

---

[2]*Babe Ruth:* George Herman Ruth (1895–1948), American baseball player. He played for the New York Yankees during the 1910s and 1920s and is remembered for his home-run hitting and flamboyant lifestyle.

and Josh Gibson.[3] Them's the only two men ever hit more home runs than you.

TROY: What it ever get me? Ain't got a pot to piss in or a window to throw it out of.

ROSE: Times have changed since you was playing baseball, Troy. That   70
was before the war. Times have changed a lot since then.

TROY: How in hell they done changed?

ROSE: They got lots of colored boys playing ball now. Baseball and football.

BONO: You right about that, Rose. Times have changed, Troy. You just come along too early.

TROY: There ought not never have been no time called too early! Now you take that fellow . . . what's that fellow they had playing right field for the Yankees back then? You know who I'm talking about, Bono. Used to play right field for the Yankees.

ROSE: Selkirk?   75

TROY: Selkirk! That's it! Man batting .269, understand? .269. What kind of sense that make? I was hitting .432 with thirty-seven home runs! Man batting .269 and playing right field for the Yankees! I saw Josh Gibson's daughter yesterday. She walking around with raggedy shoes on her feet. Now I bet you Selkirk's daughter ain't walking around with raggedy shoes on her feet! I bet you that!

ROSE: They got a lot of colored baseball players now. Jackie Robinson[4] was the first. Folks had to wait for Jackie Robinson.

TROY: I done seen a hundred niggers play baseball better than Jackie Robinson. Hell, I know some teams Jackie Robinson couldn't even make! What you talking about Jackie Robinson. Jackie Robinson wasn't nobody. I'm talking about if you could play ball then they ought to have let you play. Don't care what color you were. Come telling me I come along too early. If you could play . . . then they ought to have let you play.

Troy takes a long drink from the bottle.

ROSE: You gonna drink yourself to death. You don't need to be drinking like that.

TROY: Death ain't nothing. I done seen him. Done wrassled with him.   80
You can't tell me nothing about death. Death ain't nothing but a

---

[3]*Josh Gibson:* (1911–1947), American baseball player. He played in the Negro Leagues between the 1920s and 1940s and was known as "the Negro Babe Ruth." An unwritten rule against hiring black players kept him out of the major leagues.

[4]*Jackie Robinson:* John Roosevelt Robinson (1919–1972). He became the first African American to play major-league baseball when he was hired by the Brooklyn Dodgers in 1947.

fastball on the outside corner. And you know what I'll do to that! Lookee here, Bono . . . am I lying? You get one of them fastballs, about waist high, over the outside corner of the plate where you can get the meat of the bat on it . . . and good god! You can kiss it good-bye. Now, am I lying?

BONO: Naw, you telling the truth there. I seen you do it.

TROY: If I'm lying . . . that 450 feet worth of lying! (*Pause*.) That's all death is to me. A fastball on the outside corner.

ROSE: I don't know why you want to get on talking about death.

TROY: Ain't nothing wrong with talking about death. That's part of life. Everybody gonna die. You gonna die, I'm gonna die. Bono's gonna die. Hell, we all gonna die.

85 ROSE: But you ain't got to talk about it. I don't like to talk about it.

TROY: You the one brought it up. Me and Bono was talking about baseball . . . you tell me I'm gonna drink myself to death. Ain't that right, Bono? You know I don't drink this but one night out of the week. That's Friday night. I'm gonna drink just enough to where I can handle it. Then I cuts it loose. I leave it alone. So don't you worry about me drinking myself to death. 'Cause I ain't worried about Death. I done seen him. I done wrestled with him.

Look here, Bono . . . I looked up one day and Death was marching straight at me. Like Soldiers on Parade! The Army of Death was marching straight at me. The middle of July, 1941. It got real cold just like it be winter. It seem like Death himself reached out and touched me on the shoulder. He touch me just like I touch you. I got cold as ice and Death standing there grinning at me.

ROSE: Troy, why don't you hush that talk.

TROY: I say . . . what you want, Mr. Death? You be wanting me? You done brought your army to be getting me? I looked him dead in the eye. I wasn't fearing nothing. I was ready to tangle. Just like I'm ready to tangle now. The Bible say be ever vigilant. That's why I don't get but so drunk. I got to keep watch.

ROSE: Troy was right down there in Mercy Hospital. You remember he had pneumonia? Laying there with a fever talking plumb out of his head.

90 TROY: Death standing there staring at me . . . carrying that sickle in his hand. Finally he say, "You want bound over for another year?" See, just like that . . . "You want bound over for another year?" I told him, "Bound over hell! Let's settle this now!"

It seem like he kinda fell back when I said that, and all the cold went out of me. I reached down and grabbed that sickle and threw it just as far as I could throw it . . . and me and him commenced to wrestling.

We wrestled for three days and three nights. I can't say where I
found the strength from. Every time it seemed like he was gonna get
the best of me, I'd reach way down deep inside myself and find the
strength to do him one better.

ROSE: Every time Troy tell that story he find different ways to tell it.
Different things to make up about it.

TROY: I ain't making up nothing. I'm telling you the facts of what happened. I wrestled with Death for three days and three nights and
I'm standing here to tell you about it. (*Pause.*) All right. At the
end of the third night we done weakened each other to where we
can't hardly move. Death stood up, throwed on his robe... had him
a white robe with a hood on it. He threw on that robe and went
off to look for his sickle. Say, "I'll be back." Just like that. "I'll be
back." I told him, say, "Yeah, but . . . you gonna have to find me!"
I wasn't no fool. I wan't going looking for him. Death ain't nothing
to play with. And I know he's gonna get me. I know I got to join his
army . . . his camp followers. But as long as I keep my strength and
see him coming . . . as long as I keep up my vigilance . . . he's gonna
have to fight to get me. I ain't going easy.

BONO: Well, look here, since you got to keep up your vigilance... let
me have the bottle.

TROY: Aw hell, I shouldn't have told you that part. I should have left
out that part.

ROSE: Troy be talking that stuff and half the time don't even know   95
what he be talking about.

TROY: Bono know me better than that.

BONO: That's right. I know you. I know you got some Uncle Remus[5] in
your blood. You got more stories than the devil got sinners.

TROY: Aw hell, I done seen him too! Done talked with the devil.

ROSE: Troy, don't nobody wanna be hearing all that stuff.

*Lyons enters the yard from the street. Thirty-four years old, Troy's son by a
previous marriage, he sports a neatly trimmed goatee, sport coat, white shirt,
tieless and buttoned at the collar. Though he fancies himself a musician, he is
more caught up in the rituals and "idea" of being a musician than in the actual
practice of the music. He has come to borrow money from Troy, and while he
knows he will be successful, he is uncertain as to what extent his lifestyle will
be held up to scrutiny and ridicule.*

---

[5]*Uncle Remus:* The fictional narrator of *Uncle Remus: His Songs and His Sayings* (1880) and a number
of sequels by Joel Chandler Harris. Uncle Remus tells tales about characters such as Brer Rabbit and
the Tarbaby in exaggerated dialect, now widely considered to be a derogatory representation of African
Americans.

100 **LYONS:** Hey, Pop.

TROY: What you come "Hey, Popping" me for?

LYONS: How you doing, Rose? *(He kisses her.)* Mr. Bono. How you doing?

BONO: Hey, Lyons . . . how you been?

TROY: He must have been doing all right. I ain't seen him around here last week.

105 **ROSE:** Troy, leave your boy alone. He come by to see you and you wanna start all that nonsense.

TROY: I ain't bothering Lyons. *(Offers him the bottle.)* Here . . . get you a drink. We got an understanding. I know why he come by to see me and he know I know.

LYONS: Come on, Pop . . . I just stopped by to say hi . . . see how you was doing.

TROY: You ain't stopped by yesterday.

ROSE: You gonna stay for supper, Lyons? I got some chicken cooking in the oven.

110 **LYONS:** No, Rose . . . thanks. I was just in the neighborhood and thought I'd stop by for a minute.

TROY: You was in the neighborhood all right, nigger. You telling the truth there. You was in the neighborhood cause it's my payday.

LYONS: Well, hell, since you mentioned it . . . let me have ten dollars.

TROY: I'll be damned! I'll die and go to hell and play blackjack with the devil before I give you ten dollars.

BONO: That's what I wanna know about . . . that devil you done seen.

115 **LYONS:** What . . . Pop done seen the devil? You too much, Pops.

TROY: Yeah, I done seen him. Talked to him too!

ROSE: You ain't seen no devil. I done told you that man ain't had nothing to do with the devil. Anything you can't understand, you want to call it the devil.

TROY: Look here, Bono . . . I went down to see Hertzberger about some furniture. Got three rooms for two-ninety-eight. That what it say on the radio. "Three rooms . . . two-ninety-eight." Even made up a little song about it. Go down there . . . man tell me I can't get no credit. I'm working every day and can't get no credit. What to do? I got an empty house with some raggedy furniture in it. Cory ain't got no bed. He's sleeping on a pile of rags on the floor. Working every day and can't get no credit. Come back here—Rose'll tell you—madder than hell. Sit down . . . try to figure what I'm gonna do. Come a knock on the door. Ain't been living here but three days. Who know I'm here? Open the door . . . devil standing there bigger than life. White fellow . . . white fellow . . . got on good clothes and everything. Standing there with a clipboard in his hand. I ain't had to say nothing. First words come out of his mouth was . . . "I understand you need some furniture and can't get no credit." I liked to fell over. He say, "I'll give you all the credit you want, but you got to pay the interest on it." I told him, "Give me three rooms worth and charge whatever you want." Next day a truck pulled up here and two men unloaded them three rooms. Man what drove the truck give me a book. Say send ten dollars, first of every month to the address in the book and everything will be all right. Say if I miss a payment the devil was coming back and it'll be hell to pay. That was fifteen years ago. To this day . . . the first of the month I send my ten dollars, Rose'll tell you.

ROSE: Troy lying.

TROY: I ain't never seen that man since. Now you tell me who else that   120
could have been but the devil? I ain't sold my soul or nothing like that, you understand. Naw, I wouldn't have truck with the devil about nothing like that. I got my furniture and pays my ten dollars the first of the month just like clockwork.

BONO: How long you say you been paying this ten dollars a month?

TROY: Fifteen years!

BONO: Hell, ain't you finished paying for it yet? How much the man done charged you?

TROY: Ah hell, I done paid for it. I done paid for it ten times over! The fact is I'm scared to stop paying it.

ROSE: Troy lying. We got that furniture from Mr. Glickman. He ain't   125
paying no ten dollars a month to nobody.

TROY: Aw hell, woman. Bono know I ain't that big a fool.

LYONS: I was just getting ready to say . . . I know where there's a bridge for sale.

TROY: Look here, I'll tell you this . . . it don't matter to me if he was the devil. It don't matter if the devil give credit. Somebody has got to give it.

ROSE: It ought to matter. You going around talking about having truck with the devil . . . God's the one you gonna have to answer to. He's the one gonna be at the Judgment.

LYONS: Yeah, well, look here, Pop . . . let me have that ten dollars. I'll   130
give it back to you. Bonnie got a job working at the hospital.

TROY: What I tell you, Bono? The only time I see this nigger is when he wants something. That's the only time I see him.

LYONS: Come on, Pop, Mr. Bono don't want to hear all that. Let me have the ten dollars. I told you Bonnie working.

TROY: What that mean to me? "Bonnie working." I don't care if she working. Go ask her for the ten dollars if she working. Talking about "Bonnie working." Why ain't you working?

LYONS: Aw, Pop, you know I can't find no decent job. Where am I gonna get a job at? You know I can't get no job.

135 TROY: I told you I know some people down there. I can get you on the rubbish if you want to work. I told you that the last time you came by here asking me for something.

LYONS: Naw, Pop . . . thanks. That ain't for me. I don't wanna be carrying nobody's rubbish. I don't wanna be punching nobody's time clock.

TROY: What's the matter, you too good to carry people's rubbish? Where you think that ten dollars you talking about come from? I'm just supposed to haul people's rubbish and give my money to you 'cause you too lazy to work. You too lazy to work and wanna know why you ain't got what I got.

ROSE: What hospital Bonnie working at? Mercy?

LYONS: She's down at Passavant working in the laundry.

140 TROY: I ain't got nothing as it is. I give you that ten dollars and I got to eat beans the rest of the week. Naw . . . you ain't getting no ten dollars here.

LYONS: You ain't got to be eating no beans. I don't know why you wanna say that.

TROY: I ain't got no extra money. Gabe done moved over to Miss Pearl's paying her the rent and things done got tight around here. I can't afford to be giving you every payday.

LYONS: I ain't asked you to give me nothing. I asked you to loan me ten dollars. I know you got ten dollars.

TROY: Yeah, I got it. You know why I got it? 'Cause I don't throw my money away out there in the streets. You living the fast life . . . wanna be a musician . . . running around in them clubs and things . . . then, you learn to take care of yourself. You ain't gonna find me going and asking nobody for nothing. I done spent too many years without.

145 LYONS: You and me is two different people, Pop.

TROY: I done learned my mistake and learned to do what's right by it. You still trying to get something for nothing. Life don't owe you nothing. You owe it to yourself. Ask Bono. He'll tell you I'm right.

LYONS: You got your way of dealing with the world . . . I got mine. The only thing that matters to me is the music.

TROY: Yeah, I can see that! It don't matter how you gonna eat . . . where your next dollar is coming from. You telling the truth there.

LYONS: I know I got to eat. But I got to live too. I need something that gonna help me to get out of the bed in the morning. Make me feel like I belong in the world. I don't bother nobody. I just stay with the music 'cause that's the only way I can find to live in the world.

Otherwise there ain't no telling what I might do. Now I don't come criticizing you and how you live. I just come by to ask you for ten dollars. I don't wanna hear all that about how I live.

TROY: Boy, your mama did a hell of a job raising you. 150

LYONS: You can't change me, Pop. I'm thirty-four years old. If you wanted to change me, you should have been there when I was growing up. I come by to see you . . . ask for ten dollars and you want to talk about how I was raised. You don't know nothing about how I was raised.

ROSE: Let the boy have ten dollars, Troy.

TROY: *(to Lyons)* What the hell you looking at me for? I ain't got no ten dollars. You know what I do with my money. *(To Rose.)* Give him ten dollars if you want him to have it.

ROSE: I will. Just as soon as you turn it loose.

TROY: *(handing Rose the money)* There it is. Seventy-six dollars and 155 forty-two cents. You see this, Bono? Now, I ain't gonna get but six of that back.

ROSE: You ought to stop telling that lie. Here, Lyons. *(She hands him the money.)*

LYONS: Thanks, Rose. Look . . . I got to run . . . I'll see you later.

TROY: Wait a minute. You gonna say "thanks, Rose" and ain't gonna look to see where she got that ten dollars from? See how they do me, Bono?

LYONS: I know she got it from you, Pop. Thanks. I'll give it back to you.

TROY: There he go telling another lie. Time I see that ten dollars . . . 160 he'll be owing me thirty more.

LYONS: See you, Mr. Bono.

BONO: Take care, Lyons!

LYONS: Thanks, Pop. I'll see you again.

Lyons exits the yard.

TROY: I don't know why he don't go and get him a decent job and take care of that woman he got.

BONO: He'll be all right, Troy. The boy is still young. 165

TROY: The *boy* is thirty-four years old.

ROSE: Let's not get off into all that.

BONO: Look here . . . I got to be going. I got to be getting on. Lucille gonna be waiting.

TROY: *(puts his arm around Rose)* See this woman, Bono? I love this woman. I love this woman so much it hurts. I love her so much . . . I done run out of ways of loving her. So I got to go back to basics. Don't you come by my house Monday morning talking about time to go to work . . . 'cause I'm still gonna be stroking!

170 Rose: Troy! Stop it now!

Bono: I ain't paying him no mind, Rose. That ain't nothing but gin-talk. Go on, Troy. I'll see you Monday.

Troy: Don't you come by my house, nigger! I done told you what I'm gonna be doing.

The lights go down to black.

SCENE 2

The lights come up on Rose hanging up clothes. She hums and sings softly to herself. It is the following morning.

Rose: *(sings)*

> Jesus, be a fence all around me every day
> Jesus, I want you to protect me as I travel on my way.
> Jesus, be a fence all around me every day.

Troy enters from the house.

> Jesus, I want you to protect me
> As I travel on my way.

(To Troy.) 'Morning, You ready for breakfast? I can fix it soon as I finish hanging up these clothes?

Troy: I got the coffee on. That'll be all right. I'll just drink some of that this morning.

Rose: That 651 hit yesterday. That's the second time this month. Miss Pearl hit for a dollar . . . seem like those that need the least always get lucky. Poor folks can't get nothing.

Troy: Them numbers don't know nobody. I don't know why you fool with them. You and Lyons both.

5 Rose: It's something to do.

Troy: You ain't doing nothing but throwing your money away.

Rose: Troy, you know I don't play foolishly. I just play a nickel here and a nickel there.

Troy: That's two nickels you done thrown away.

Rose: Now I hit sometimes . . . that makes up for it. It always comes in handy when I do hit. I don't hear you complaining then.

10 Troy: I ain't complaining now. I just say it's foolish. Trying to guess out of six hundred ways which way the number gonna come. If I had all the money niggers, these Negroes, throw away on numbers for one week—just one week—I'd be a rich man.

Rose: Well, you wishing and calling it foolish ain't gonna stop folks from playing numbers. That's one thing for sure. Besides . . . some good things come from playing numbers. Look where Pope done bought him that restaurant off of numbers.

TROY: I can't stand niggers like that. Man ain't had two dimes to rub together. He walking around with his shoes all run over bumming money for cigarettes. All right. Got lucky there and hit the numbers . . .

ROSE: Troy, I know all about it.

TROY: Had good sense, I'll say that for him. He ain't throwing his money away. I seen niggers hit the numbers and go through two thousand dollars in four days. Man bought him that restaurant down there . . . fixed it up real nice . . . and then didn't want nobody to come in it! A Negro go in there and can't get no kind of service. I seen a white fellow come in there and order a bowl of stew. Pope picked all the meat out the pot for him. Man ain't had nothing but a bowl of meat! Negro come behind him and ain't got nothing but the potatoes and carrots. Talking about what numbers do for people, you picked a wrong example. Ain't done nothing but make a worser fool out of him than he was before.

ROSE: Troy, you ought to stop worrying about what happened at work   15
yesterday.

TROY: I ain't worried. Just told me to be down there at the Commissioner's office on Friday. Everybody think they gonna fire me. I ain't worried about them firing me. You ain't got to worry about that. *(Pause.)* Where's Cory? Cory in the house? *(Calls.)* Cory?

ROSE: He gone out.

TROY: Out, huh? He gone out 'cause he know I want him to help me with this fence. I know how he is. That boy scared of work.

Gabriel enters. He comes halfway down the alley and, hearing Troy's voice, stops.

TROY: *(continues)* He ain't done a lick of work in his life.

ROSE: He had to go to football practice. Coach wanted them to get in a   20
little extra practice before the season start.

TROY: I got his practice . . . running out of here before he get his chores done.

ROSE: Troy, what is wrong with you this morning? Don't nothing set right with you. Go on back in there and go to bed . . . get up on the other side.

TROY: Why something got to be wrong with me? I ain't said nothing wrong with me.

ROSE: You got something to say about everything. First it's the numbers . . . then it's the way the man runs his restaurant . . . then you done got on Cory. What's it gonna be next? Take a look up there and see if the weather suits you . . . or is it gonna be how you gonna put up the fence with the clothes hanging in the yard.

TROY: You hit the nail on the head then.   25

ROSE: I know you like I know the back of my hand. Go on in there and get you some coffee . . . see if that straighten you up. 'Cause you ain't right this morning.

Troy starts into the house and sees Gabriel. Gabriel starts singing. Troy's brother, he is seven years younger than Troy. Injured in World War II, he has a metal plate in his head. He carries an old trumpet tied around his waist and believes with every fiber of his being that he is the Archangel Gabriel.[1] He carries a chipped basket with an assortment of discarded fruits and vegetables he has picked up in the strip district and which he attempts to sell.

GABRIEL: (*singing*)

> Yes, ma'am, I got plums
> You ask me how I sell them
> Oh ten cents apiece
> Three for a quarter
> Come and buy now
> 'Cause I'm here today
> And tomorrow I'll be gone

Gabriel enters.

Hey, Rose!

ROSE: How you doing, Gabe?
GABRIEL: There's Troy . . . Hey, Troy!
30 TROY: Hey, Gabe.

Exit into kitchen.

ROSE: (*To Gabriel.*) What you got there?
GABRIEL: You know what I got, Rose. I got fruits and vegetables.
ROSE: (*looking in basket*) Where's all these plums you talking about?
GABRIEL: I ain't got no plums today, Rose. I was just singing that. Have some tomorrow. Put me in a big order for plums. Have enough plums tomorrow for St. Peter and everybody.

Troy reenters from kitchen, crosses to steps.

(*To Rose.*) Troy's mad at me.
35 TROY: I ain't mad at you. What I got to be mad at you about? You ain't done nothing to me.
GABRIEL: I just moved over to Miss Pearl's to keep out from in your way. I ain't mean no harm by it.
TROY: Who said anything about that? I ain't said anything about that.

---

[1]*Archangel Gabriel:* A messenger of God.

GABRIEL: You ain't mad at me, is you?

TROY: Naw . . . I ain't mad at you, Gabe. If I was mad at you I'd tell you about it.

GABRIEL: Got me two rooms. In the basement. Got my own door too.   40
Wanna see my key? (*He holds up a key.*) That's my own key! Ain't nobody else got a key like that. That's my key! My two rooms!

TROY: Well, that's good, Gabe. You got your own key . . . that's good.

ROSE: You hungry, Gabe? I was just fixing to cook Troy his breakfast.

GABRIEL: I'll take some biscuits. You got some biscuits? Did you know when I was in heaven . . . every morning me and St. Peter[2] would sit down by the gate and eat some big fat biscuits? Oh, yeah! We had us a good time. We'd sit there and eat us them biscuits and then St. Peter would go off to sleep and tell me to wake him up when it's time to open the gates for the judgment.

ROSE: Well, come on . . . I'll make up a batch of biscuits.

Rose exits into the house.

GABRIEL: Troy . . . St. Peter got your name in the book. I seen it. It   45
say . . . Troy Maxson. I say . . . I know him! He got the same name like what I got. That's my brother!

TROY: How many times you gonna tell me that, Gabe?

GABRIEL: Ain't got my name in the book. Don't have to have my name. I done died and went to heaven. He got your name though. One morning St. Peter was looking at his book . . . marking it up for the judgment . . . and he let me see your name. Got it in there under M. Got Rose's name . . . I ain't seen it like I seen yours . . . but I know it's in there. He got a great big book. Got everybody's name what was ever been born. That's what he told me. But I seen your name. Seen it with my own eyes.

TROY: Go on in the house there. Rose going to fix you something to eat.

GABRIEL: Oh, I ain't hungry. I done had breakfast with Aunt Jemima. She come by and cooked me up a whole mess of flapjacks. Remember how we used to eat them flapjacks?

TROY: Go on in the house and get you something to eat now.   50

GABRIEL: I got to sell my plums. I done sold some tomatoes. Got me two quarters. Wanna see? (*He shows Troy his quarters.*) I'm gonna save them and buy me a new horn so St. Peter can hear me when it's time to open the gates. (*Gabriel stops suddenly. Listens.*) Hear that? That's the hellhounds. I got to chase them out of here. Go on get out of here! Get out!

---

[2]*St. Peter:* Disciple of Christ, believed to be the guard at the gates of heaven.

Gabriel exits singing.

> Better get ready for the Judgment
> Better get ready for the Judgment
> My Lord is coming down

Rose enters from the house.

TROY: He's gone off somewhere.

GABRIEL: *(offstage)*

> Better get ready for the Judgment
> Better get ready for the Judgment morning
> Better get ready for the Judgment
> My God is coming down

ROSE: He ain't eating right. Miss Pearl say she can't get him to eat nothing.

55 TROY: What you want me to do about it, Rose? I done did everything I can for the man. I can't make him get well. Man got half his head blown away . . . what you expect?

ROSE: Seem like something ought to be done to help him.

TROY: Man don't bother nobody. He just mixed up from that metal plate he got in his head. Ain't no sense for him to go back into the hospital.

ROSE: Least he be eating right. They can help him take care of himself.

TROY: Don't nobody wanna be locked up, Rose. What you wanna lock him up for? Man go over there and fight the war . . . messin' around with them Japs, get half his head blown off . . . and they give him a lousy three thousand dollars. And I had to swoop down on that.

60 ROSE: Is you fixing to go into that again?

TROY: That's the only way I got a roof over my head . . . 'cause of that metal plate.

ROSE: Ain't no sense you blaming yourself for nothing. Gabe wasn't in no condition to manage that money. You done what was right by him. Can't nobody say you ain't done what was right by him. Look how long you took care of him . . . till he wanted to have his own place and moved over there with Miss Pearl.

TROY: That ain't what I'm saying, woman! I'm just stating the facts. If my brother didn't have that metal plate in his head . . . I wouldn't have a pot to piss in or a window to throw it out of. And I'm fifty-three years old. Now see if you can understand that!

Troy gets up from the porch and starts to exit the yard.

ROSE: Where you going off to? You been running out of here every Saturday for weeks. I thought you was gonna work on this fence?

TROY: I'm gonna walk down to Taylors'. Listen to the ball game. I'll be   65
back in a bit. I'll work on it when I get back.

He exits the yard. The lights go to black.

SCENE 3

The lights come up on the yard. It is four hours later. Rose is taking down the clothes from the line. Cory enters carrying his football equipment.

ROSE: Your daddy like to had a fit with you running out of here this morning without doing your chores.
CORY: I told you I had to go to practice.
ROSE: He say you were supposed to help him with this fence.
CORY: He been saying that the last four or five Saturdays, and then he don't never do nothing, but go down to Taylors'. Did you tell him about the recruiter?
ROSE: Yeah, I told him.   5
CORY: What he say?
ROSE: He ain't said nothing too much. You get in there and get started on your chores before he gets back. Go on and scrub down them steps before he gets back here hollering and carrying on.
CORY: I'm hungry. What you got to eat, Mama?
ROSE: Go on and get started on your chores. I got some meat loaf in there. Go on and make you a sandwich . . . and don't leave no mess in there.

Cory exits into the house. Rose continues to take down the clothes. Troy enters the yard and sneaks up and grabs her from behind.

Troy! Go on, now. You liked to scared me to death. What was the score of the game? Lucille had me on the phone and I couldn't keep up with it.
TROY: What I care about the game? Come here, woman. (*He tries to*   10
kiss her.)
ROSE: I thought you went down Taylors' to listen to the game. Go on, Troy! You supposed to be putting up this fence.
TROY: (*attempting to kiss her again*) I'll put it up when I finish with what is at hand.
ROSE: Go on, Troy. I ain't studying you.
TROY: (*chasing after her*) I'm studying you . . . fixing to do my homework!
ROSE: Troy, you better leave me alone.   15
TROY: Where's Cory? That boy brought his butt home yet?
ROSE: He's in the house doing his chores.
TROY: (*calling*) Cory! Get your butt out here, boy!

Rose exits into the house with the laundry. Troy goes over to the pile of wood, picks up a board, and starts sawing. Cory enters from the house.

TROY: You just now coming in here from leaving this morning?
20 CORY: Yeah, I had to go to football practice.
TROY: Yeah, what?
CORY: Yessir.
TROY: I ain't but two seconds off you noway. The garbage sitting in there overflowing . . . you ain't done none of your chores . . . and you come in here talking about "Yeah."
CORY: I was just getting ready to do my chores now, Pop . . .
25 TROY: Your first chore is to help me with this fence on Saturday. Everything else come after that. Now get that saw and cut them boards.

Cory takes the saw and begins cutting the boards. Troy continues working. There is a long pause.

CORY: Hey, Pop . . . why don't you buy a TV?
TROY: What I want with a TV? What I want one of them for?
CORY: Everybody got one. Earl, Ba Bra . . . Jesse!
TROY: I ain't asked you who had one. I say what I want with one?
30 CORY: So you can watch it. They got lots of things on TV. Baseball games and everything. We could watch the World Series.
TROY: Yeah . . . and how much this TV cost?
CORY: I don't know. They got them on sale for around two hundred dollars.
TROY: Two hundred dollars, huh?
CORY: That ain't that much, Pop.
35 TROY: Naw, it's just two hundred dollars. See that roof you got over your head at night? Let me tell you something about that roof. It's been over ten years since that roof was last tarred. See now . . . the snow comes this winter and sit up there on that roof like it is . . . and it's gonna seep inside. It's just gonna be a little bit . . . ain't gonna hardly notice it. Then the next thing you know, it's gonna be leaking all over the house. Then the wood rot from all that water and you gonna need a whole new roof. Now, how much you think it cost to get that roof tarred?
CORY: I don't know.
TROY: Two hundred and sixty-four dollars . . . cash money. While you thinking about a TV, I got to be thinking about the roof . . . and whatever else go wrong here. Now if you had two hundred dollars, what would you do . . . fix the roof or buy a TV?
CORY: I'd buy a TV. Then when the roof started to leak . . . when it needed fixing . . . I'd fix it.

TROY: Where you gonna get the money from? You done spent it for a
TV. You gonna sit up and watch the water run all over your brand
new TV.

CORY: Aw, Pop. You got money. I know you do.   40

TROY: Where I got it at, huh?

CORY: You got it in the bank.

TROY: You wanna see my bankbook? You wanna see that seventy-three
dollars and twenty-two cents I got sitting up in there.

CORY: You ain't got to pay for it all at one time. You can put a down
payment on it and carry it on home with you.

TROY: Not me. I ain't gonna owe nobody nothing if I can help it. Miss   45
a payment and they come and snatch it right out your house. Then
what you got? Now, soon as I get two hundred dollars clear, then I'll
buy a TV. Right now, as soon as I get two hundred and sixty-four
dollars, I'm gonna have this roof tarred.

CORY: Aw . . . Pop!

TROY: You go on and get you two hundred and buy one if ya want it. I
got better things to do with my money.

CORY: I can't get no two hundred dollars. I ain't never seen two hundred dollars.

TROY: I'll tell you what . . . you get you a hundred dollars and I'll put the
other hundred with it.

CORY: All right, I'm gonna show you.   50

TROY: You gonna show me how you can cut them boards right now.

Cory begins to cut the boards. There is a long pause.

CORY: The Pirates won today. That makes five in a row.

TROY: I ain't thinking about the Pirates. Got an all-white team. Got
that boy . . . that Puerto Rican boy . . . Clemente.[1] Don't even half-
play him. That boy could be something if they give him a chance.
Play him one day and sit him on the bench the next.

CORY: He gets a lot of chances to play.

TROY: I'm talking about playing regular. Playing every day so you can   55
get your timing. That's what I'm talking about.

CORY: They got some white guys on the team that don't play every day.
You can't play everybody at the same time.

TROY: If they got a white fellow sitting on the bench . . . you can bet
your last dollar he can't play! The colored guy got to be twice as

---

[1]*Clemente:* Roberto Clemente (1934–1972), Major League baseball player for the Pittsburg Pirates,
known as much for his humanitarianism as his unique batting style and ability. Clemente received
the Most Valuable Player Award in 1966 and died in a plane crash in 1972 while shuttling supplies to
Nicaraguan earthquake victims.

good before he get on the team. That's why I don't want you to get all tied up in them sports. Man on the team and what it get him? They got colored on the team and don't use them. Same as not having them. All them teams the same.

CORY: The Braves got Hank Aaron[2] and Wes Covington.[3] Hank Aaron hit two home runs today. That makes forty-three.

TROY: Hank Aaron ain't nobody. That what you supposed to do. That's how you supposed to play the game. Ain't nothing to it. It's just a matter of timing . . . getting the right follow-through. Hell, I can hit forty-three home runs right now!

60 CORY: Not off no major-league pitching, you couldn't.

TROY: We had better pitching in the Negro leagues. I hit seven home runs off of Satchel Paige.[4] You can't get no better than that!

CORY: Sandy Koufax.[5] He's leading the league in strikeouts.

TROY: I ain't thinking of no Sandy Koufax.

CORY: You got Warren Spahn[6] and Lew Burdette.[7] I bet you couldn't hit no home runs off of Warren Spahn.

65 TROY: I'm through with it now. You go on and cut them boards. (*Pause.*) Your mama tell me you done got recruited by a college football team? Is that right?

CORY: Yeah. Coach Zellman say the recruiter gonna be coming by to talk to you. Get you to sign the permission papers.

TROY: I thought you supposed to be working down there at the A&P. Ain't you suppose to be working down there after school?

---

[2] *Hank Aaron:* Henry Aaron (1934–   ), American baseball player who broke Babe Ruth's career home run record with a lifetime total of 755 home runs. The holder of 12 other Major League records, Aaron spent his Major League career with the Braves, first in Milwaukee and later in their hometown of Atlanta.

[3] *Wes Covington:* John Wesley Covington (1932–   ), American baseball player known for his ability to frustrate pitchers by wasting time at the plate. In an eleven-year career, Covington played for six Major League teams, beginning with the Milwaukee Braves and retiring with the Los Angeles Dodgers in 1966.

[4] *Satchel Page:* Leroy Robert Paige (1906–1982), American baseball player. He played in the Negro Leagues from the 1920s until 1948, when he joined the Cleveland Indians; he reportedly pitched 55 no-hit games during his career. Joe DiMaggio called him "the best pitcher I have ever faced."

[5] *Sandy Koufax:* Sanford Koufax (1935–   ), left-handed pitcher who won 129 games and lost only 47 for the Los Angeles Dodgers in the six seasons between 1961 and 1966; he won three Cy Young Awards and pitched four no-hit games, the last of which (1965) was a perfect game.

[6] *Warren Spahn:* (1921–2003), left-handed pitcher who at the time of his retirement in 1966 held the National League record of 363 wins; he won 20 or more games in four consecutive seasons (1947–1950) and in several other seasons during the 1950s.

[7] *Lew Burdette:* Selva Lewis Burdette (1926–2007), American baseball player who pitched and won three games for the Milwaukee Braves against the New York Yankees in the 1957 World Series; for that Series, his ERA was an amazingly low .067.

CORY: Mr. Stawicki say he gonna hold my job for me until after the football season. Say starting next week I can work weekends.

TROY: I thought we had an understanding about this football stuff? You suppose to keep up with your chores and hold that job down at the A&P. Ain't been around here all day on a Saturday. Ain't none of your chores done . . . and now you telling me you done quit your job.

CORY: I'm going to be working weekends.   70

TROY: You damn right you are! And ain't no need for nobody coming around here to talk to me about signing nothing.

CORY: Hey, Pop . . . you can't do that. He's coming all the way from North Carolina.

TROY: I don't care where he coming from. The white man ain't gonna let you get nowhere with that football noway. You go on and get your book-learning so you can work yourself up in that A&P or learn how to fix cars or build houses or something, get you a trade. That way you have something can't nobody take away from you. You go on and learn how to put your hands to some good use. Besides hauling people's garbage.

CORY: I get good grades, Pop. That's why the recruiter wants to talk with you. You got to keep up your grades to get recruited. This way I'll be going to college. I'll get a chance . . .

TROY: First you gonna get your butt down there to the A&P and get   75
your job back.

CORY: Mr. Stawicki done already hired somebody else 'cause I told him I was playing football.

TROY: You a bigger fool than I thought . . . to let somebody take away your job so you can play some football. Where you gonna get your money to take out your girlfriend and whatnot? What kind of foolishness is that to let somebody take away your job?

CORY: I'm still gonna be working weekends.

TROY: Naw . . . naw. You getting your butt out of here and finding you another job.

CORY: Come on, Pop! I got to practice. I can't work after school and   80
play football too. The team needs me. That's what Coach Zellman say . . .

TROY: I don't care what nobody else say. I'm the boss . . . you understand? I'm the boss around here. I do the only saying what counts.

CORY: Come on, Pop!

TROY: I asked you . . . did you understand?

CORY: Yeah . . .

TROY: What?!   85

CORY: Yessir.

TROY: You go on down there to that A&P and see if you can get your job back. If you can't do both . . . then you quit the football team. You've got to take the crookeds with the straights.

CORY: Yessir. (*Pause.*) Can I ask you a question?

TROY: What the hell you wanna ask me? Mr. Stawicki the one you got the questions for.

90 CORY: How come you ain't never liked me?

TROY: Liked you? Who the hell say I got to like you? What law is there say I got to like you? Wanna stand up in my face and ask a damn fool-ass question like that. Talking about liking somebody. Come here, boy, when I talk to you.

Cory comes over to where Troy is working. He stands slouched over and Troy shoves him on his shoulder.

Straighten up, goddammit! I asked you a question . . . what law is there say I got to like you?

CORY: None.

TROY: Well, all right then! Don't you eat every day? (*Pause.*) Answer me when I talk to you! Don't you eat every day?

CORY: Yeah.

95 TROY: Nigger, as long as you in my house, you put that sir on the end of it when you talk to me!

CORY: Yes . . . sir.

TROY: You eat every day.

CORY: Yessir!

TROY: Got a roof over your head.

100 CORY: Yessir!

TROY: Got clothes on your back.

CORY: Yessir.

TROY: Why you think that is?

CORY: 'Cause of you.

105 TROY: Ah, hell I know it's 'cause of me . . . but why do you think that is?

CORY: (*hesitant*) 'Cause you like me.

TROY: Like you? I go out of here every morning . . . bust my butt . . . putting up with them crackers[8] every day . . . 'cause I like you? You are the biggest fool I ever saw. (*Pause.*) It's my job. It's my responsibility! You understand that? A man got to take care of his family. You live in my house . . . sleep you behind on my bedclothes . . . fill you belly up with my food . . . 'cause you my son. You my flesh and blood. Not 'cause I like you! 'Cause it's my duty to take care of you.

---

[8]*crackers:* Derogatory term for white people, generally poor southern whites.

I owe a responsibility to you! Let's get this straight right here . . . before it go along any further . . . I ain't got to like you. Mr. Rand don't give me my money come payday cause he likes me. He give me 'cause he owe me. I done give you everything I had to give you. I gave you your life! Me and your mama worked that out between us. And liking your black ass wasn't part of the bargain. Don't you try and go through life worrying about if somebody like you or not. You best be making sure they doing right by you. You understand what I'm saying, boy?

CORY: Yessir.

TROY: Then get the hell out of my face, and get on down to that A&P.

Rose has been standing behind the screen door for much of the scene. She enters as Cory exits.

ROSE: Why don't you let the boy go ahead and play football, Troy? Ain't   110 no harm in that. He's just trying to be like you with the sports.

TROY: I don't want him to be like me! I want him to move as far away from my life as he can get. You the only decent thing that ever happened to me. I wish him that. But I don't wish him a thing else from my life. I decided seventeen years ago that boy wasn't getting involved in no sports. Not after what they did to me in the sports.

ROSE: Troy, why don't you admit you was too old to play in the major leagues? For once . . . why don't you admit that?

TROY: What do you mean too old? Don't come telling me I was too old. I just wasn't the right color. Hell, I'm fifty-three years old and can do better than Selkirk's .269 right now!

ROSE: How's was you gonna play ball when you were over forty? Sometimes I can't go no sense out of you.

TROY: I got good sense, woman. I got sense enough not to let my boy   115 get hurt over playing no sports. You been mothering that boy too much. Worried about if people like him.

ROSE: Everything that boy do . . . he do for you. He wants you to say "Good job, son." That's all.

TROY: Rose, I ain't got time for that. He's alive. He's healthy. He's got to make his own way. I made mine. Ain't nobody gonna hold his hand when he get out there in that world.

ROSE: Times have changed from when you was young, Troy. People change. The world's changing around you and you can't even see it.

TROY: *(slow, methodical)* Woman . . . I do the best I can do. I come in here every Friday. I carry a sack of potatoes and a bucket of lard. You all line up at the door with your hands out. I give you the lint from my pockets. I give you my sweat and my blood. I ain't got no tears. I done spent them. We go upstairs in that room at night . . .

and I fall down on you and try to blast a hole into forever. I get up Monday morning . . . find my lunch on the table. I go out. Make my way. Find my strength to carry me through to the next Friday. (*Pause.*) That's all I got, Rose. That's all I got to give. I can't give nothing else.

Troy exits into the house. The lights go down to black.

SCENE 4

It is Friday. Two weeks later. Cory starts out of the house with his football equipment. The phone rings.

CORY: (*calling*) I got it! (*He answers the phone and stands in the screen door talking.*) Hello? Hey, Jesse. Naw . . . I was just getting ready to leave now.

ROSE: (*calling*) Cory!

CORY: I told you, man, them spikes[1] is all tore up. You can use them if you want, but they ain't no good. Earl got some spikes.

ROSE: (*calling*) Cory!

5 CORY: (*calling to Rose*) Mam? I'm talking to Jesse. (*Into phone.*) When she say that? (*Pause.*) Aw, you lying, man. I'm gonna tell her you said that.

ROSE: (*calling*) Cory, don't you go nowhere!

CORY: I got to go to the game, Ma! (*Into the phone.*) Yeah, hey, look, I'll talk to you later. Yeah, I'll meet you over Earl's house. Later. Bye, Ma.

Cory exits the house and starts out the yard.

ROSE: Cory, where you going off to? You got that stuff all pulled out and thrown all over your room.

CORY: (*in the yard*) I was looking for my spikes. Jesse wanted to borrow my spikes.

10 ROSE: Get up there and get that cleaned up before your daddy get back in here.

CORY: I got to go to the game! I'll clean it up *when I get back.*

Cory exits.

ROSE: That's all he need to do is see that room all messed up.

Rose exits into the house. Troy and Bono enter the yard. Troy is dressed in clothes other than his work clothes.

BONO: He told him the same thing he told you. Take it to the union.

---

[1]*spikes:* Athletic shoes with sharp metal grips set into the soles.

TROY: Brownie ain't got that much sense. Man wasn't thinking about nothing. He wait until I confront them on it . . . then he wanna come crying seniority. (*Calls.*) Hey, Rose!

BONO: I wish I could have seen Mr. Rand's face when he told you.   15

TROY: He couldn't get it out of his mouth! Liked to bit his tongue! When they called me down there to the Commissioner's office . . . he thought they was gonna fire me. Like everybody else.

BONO: I didn't think they was gonna fire you. I thought they was gonna put you on the warning paper.

TROY: Hey, Rose! (*To Bono.*) Yeah, Mr. Rand like to bit his tongue.

Troy breaks the seal on the bottle, takes a drink, and hands it to Bono.

BONO: I see you run right down to Taylors' and told that Alberta gal.

TROY: (*calling*) Hey, Rose! (*To Bono.*) I told everybody. Hey, Rose! I   20
went down there to cash my check.

ROSE: (*entering from the house*) Hush all that hollering, man! I know you out here. What they say down there at the Commissioner's office?

TROY: You supposed to come when I call you, woman. Bono'll tell you that. (*To Bono.*) Don't Lucille come when you call her?

ROSE: Man, hush your mouth, I ain't no dog . . . talk about "come when you call me."

TROY: (*puts his arm around Rose*) You hear this, Bono? I had me an old dog used to get uppity like that. You say, "C'mere, Blue!" . . . and he just lay there and look at you. End up getting a stick and chasing him away trying to make him come.

ROSE: I ain't studying you and your dog. I remember you used to sing   25
that old song.

TROY: (*he sings*)

> Hear it ring! Hear it ring!
> I had a dog his name was Blue.

ROSE: Don't nobody wanna hear you sing that old song.

TROY: (*sings*)

> You know Blue was mighty true.

ROSE: Used to have Cory running around here singing that song.

BONO: Hell, I remember that song myself.   30

TROY: (*sings*)

> You know Blue was a good old dog.
> Blue treed a possum in a hollow log.

That was my daddy's song. My daddy made up that song.

ROSE: I don't care who made it up. Don't nobody wanna hear you sing it.

TROY: (*makes a song like calling a dog*) Come here, woman.

ROSE: You come in here carrying on, I reckon they ain't fired you. What they say down there at the Commissioner's office?

35 TROY: Look here, Rose . . . Mr. Rand called me into his office today when I got back from talking to them people down there . . . it come from up top . . . he called me in and told me they was making me a driver.

ROSE: Troy, you kidding!

TROY: No I ain't. Ask Bono.

ROSE: Well, that's great, Troy. Now you don't have to hassle them people no more.

Lyons enters from the street.

TROY: Aw hell, I wasn't looking to see you today. I thought you was in jail. Got it all over the front page of the *Courier* about them raiding Sefus's place . . . where you be hanging out with all them thugs.

40 LYONS: Hey, Pop . . . that ain't got nothing to do with me. I don't go down there gambling. I go down there to sit in with the band. I ain't got nothing to do with the gambling part. They got some good music down there.

TROY: They got some rogues . . . is what they got.

LYONS: How you been, Mr. Bono? Hi, Rose.

BONO: I see where you playing down at the Crawford Grill tonight.

ROSE: How come you ain't brought Bonnie like I told you? You should have brought Bonnie with you, she ain't been over in a month of Sundays.

45 LYONS: I was just in the neighborhood . . . thought I'd stop by.

TROY: Here he come...

BONO: Your daddy got a promotion on the rubbish. He's gonna be the first colored driver. Ain't got to do nothing but sit up there and read the paper like them white fellows.

LYONS: Hey, Pop . . . if you knew how to read you'd be all right.

BONO: Naw . . . naw . . . you mean if the nigger knew how to *drive* he'd be all right. Been fighting with them people about driving and ain't even got a license. Mr. Rand know you ain't got no driver's license?

50 TROY: Driving ain't nothing. All you do is point the truck where you want it to go. Driving ain't nothing.

BONO: Do Mr. Rand know you ain't got no driver's license? That's what I'm talking about. I ain't asked if driving was easy. I asked if Mr. Rand know you ain't got no driver's license.

TROY: He ain't got to know. The man ain't got to know my business. Time he find out, I have two or three driver's licenses.

LYONS: (*going into his pocket*) Say, look here, Pop . . .

TROY: I knew it was coming. Didn't I tell you, Bono? I know what kind of "Look here, Pop" that was. The nigger fixing to ask me for some money. It's Friday night. It's my payday. All them rogues down there on the avenue . . . the ones that ain't in jail . . . and Lyons is hopping in his shoes to get down there with them.

LYONS: See, Pop . . . if you give somebody else a chance to talk some-   55
times, you'd see that I was fixing to pay you back your ten dollars like I told you. Here . . . I told you I'd pay you when Bonnie got paid.

TROY: Naw . . . you go ahead and keep that ten dollars. Put it in the bank. The next time you feel like you wanna come by here and ask me for something . . . you go on down there and get that.

LYONS: Here's your ten dollars, Pop. I told you I don't want you to give me nothing. I just wanted to borrow ten dollars.

TROY: Naw . . . you go on and keep that for the next time you want to ask me.

LYONS: Come on, Pop . . . here go your ten dollars.

ROSE: Why don't you go on and let the boy pay you back, Troy?   60

LYONS: Here you go, Rose. If you don't take it I'm gonna have to hear about it for the next six months. (*He hands her the money.*)

ROSE: You can hand yours over here too, Troy.

TROY: You see this, Bono. You see how they do me.

BONO: Yeah, Lucille do me the same way.

Gabriel is heard singing offstage. He enters.

GABRIEL: Better get ready for the Judgment! Better get ready for . . .   65
Hey! . . . Hey! . . . There's Troy's boy!

LYONS: How are you doing, Uncle Gabe?

GABRIEL: Lyons . . . The King of the Jungle! Rose . . . hey, Rose. Got a flower for you. (*He takes a rose from his pocket.*) Picked it myself. That's the same rose like you is!

ROSE: That's right nice of you, Gabe.

LYONS: What you been doing, Uncle Gabe?

GABRIEL: Oh, I been chasing hellhounds and waiting on the time to tell   70
St. Peter to open the gates.

LYONS: You been chasing hellhounds, huh? Well . . . you doing the right thing, Uncle Gabe. Somebody got to chase them.

GABRIEL: Oh, yeah . . . I know it. The devil's strong. The devil ain't no pushover. Hellhounds snipping at everybody's heels. But I got my trumpet waiting on the judgment time.

LYONS: Waiting on the Battle of Armageddon, huh?

GABRIEL: Ain't gonna be too much of a battle when God get to waving that Judgment sword. But the people's gonna have a hell of a time trying to get into heaven if them gates ain't open.

75 **LYONS:** *(putting his arm around Gabriel)* You hear this, Pop. Uncle Gabe, you all right!

GABRIEL: *(laughing with Lyons)* Lyons! King of the Jungle.

ROSE: You gonna stay for supper, Gabe? Want me to fix you a plate?

GABRIEL: I'll take a sandwich, Rose. Don't want no plate. Just wanna eat with my hands. I'll take a sandwich.

ROSE: How about you, Lyons? You staying? Got some short ribs cooking.

80 **LYONS:** Naw, I won't eat nothing till after we finished playing. *(Pause.)* You ought to come down and listen to me play, Pop.

TROY: I don't like that Chinese music. All that noise.

ROSE: Go on in the house and wash up, Gabe . . . I'll fix you a sandwich.

GABRIEL: *(to Lyons, as he exits)* Troy's mad at me.

LYONS: What you mad at Uncle Gabe for, Pop?

85 **ROSE:** He thinks Troy's mad at him cause he moved over to Miss Pearl's.

TROY: I ain't mad at the man. He can live where he want to live at.

LYONS: What he move over there for? Miss Pearl don't like nobody.

ROSE: She don't mind him none. She treats him real nice. She just don't allow all that singing.

TROY: She don't mind that rent he be paying . . . that's what she don't mind.

90 **ROSE:** Troy, I ain't going through that with you no more. He's over there cause he want to have his own place. He can come and go as he please.

TROY: Hell, he could come and go as he please here. I wasn't stopping him. I ain't put no rules on him.

ROSE: It ain't the same thing, Troy. And you know it.

Gabriel comes to the door.

Now, that's the last I wanna hear about that. I don't wanna hear nothing else about Gabe and Miss Pearl. And next week . . .

GABRIEL: I'm ready for my sandwich, Rose.

ROSE: And next week . . . when that recruiter come from that school . . . I want you to sign that paper and go on and let Cory play football. Then that'll be the last I have to hear about that.

95 **TROY:** *(to Rose as she exits into the house)* I ain't thinking about Cory nothing.

LYONS: What . . . Cory got recruited? What school he going to?

TROY: That boy walking around here smelling his piss . . . thinking he's grown. Thinking he's gonna do what he want, irrespective of what I say. Look here, Bono . . . I left the Commissioner's office and went down to the A&P . . . that boy ain't working down there. He lying to me. Telling me he got his job back . . . telling me he working weekends . . . telling me he working after school . . . Mr. Stawicki tell me he ain't working down there at all!

LYONS: Cory just growing up. He's just busting at the seams trying to fill out your shoes.

TROY: I don't care what he's doing. When he get to the point where he wanna disobey me . . . then it's time for him to move on. Bono'll tell you that. I bet he ain't never disobeyed his daddy without paying the consequences.

BONO: I ain't never had a chance. My daddy came on through . . . but   100
I ain't never knew him to see him . . . or what he had on his mind or where he went. Just moving on through. Searching out the New Land. That's what the old folks used to call it. See a fellow moving around from place to place . . . woman to woman . . . called it searching out the New Land. Can't say if he ever found it. I come along, didn't want no kids. Didn't know if I was gonna be in one place long enough to fix on them right as their daddy. I figured I was going searching too. As it turned out I been hooked up with Lucille near about as long as your daddy been with Rose. Going on sixteen years.

TROY: Sometimes I wish I hadn't known my daddy. He ain't cared nothing about no kids. A kid to him wasn't nothing. All he wanted was for you to learn how to walk so he could start you to working. When it come time for eating . . . he ate first. If there was anything left over, that's what you got. Man would sit down and eat two chickens and give you the wing.

LYONS: You ought to stop that, Pop. Everybody feed their kids. No matter how hard times is . . . everybody care about their kids. Make sure they have something to eat.

TROY: The only thing my daddy cared about was getting them bales of cotton in to Mr. Lubin. That's the only thing that mattered to him. Sometimes I used to wonder why he was living. Wonder why the devil hadn't come and got him. "Get them bales of cotton in to Mr. Lubin" and find out he owe him money . . .

LYONS: He should have just went on and left when he saw he couldn't get nowhere. That's what I would have done.

TROY: How he gonna leave with eleven kids? And where he gonna go?   105
He ain't knew how to do nothing but farm. No, he was trapped and I think he knew it. But I'll say this for him . . . he felt a responsibility toward us. Maybe he ain't treated us the way I felt he should have . . . but without that responsibility he could have walked off and left us . . . made his own way.

BONO: A lot of them did. Back in those days what you talking about . . . they walk out their front door and just take on down one road or another and keep on walking.

LYONS: There you go? That's what I'm talking about.

BONO: Just keep on walking till you come to something else. Ain't you never heard of nobody having the walking blues? Well, that's what you call it when you just take off like that.

TROY: My daddy ain't had them walking blues! What you talking about? He stayed right there with his family. But he was just as evil as he could be. My mama couldn't stand him. Couldn't stand that evilness. She run off when I was about eight. She sneaked off one night after he had gone to sleep. Told me she was coming back for me. I ain't never seen her no more. All his women run off and left him. He wasn't good for nobody.

When my turn come to head out, I was fourteen and got to sniffing around Joe Canewell's daughter. Had us an old mule we called Greyboy. My daddy sent me out to do some plowing and tied up Greyboy and went to fooling around with Joe Canewell's daughter. We done found us a nice little spot, got real cozy with each other. She about thirteen and we done figured we was grown anyway . . . so we down there enjoying ourselves . . . ain't thinking about nothing. We didn't know Greyboy had got loose and wandered back to the house and my daddy was looking for me. We down there by the creek enjoying ourselves when my daddy come up on us. Surprised us. He had them leather straps off the mule and commenced to whupping me like there was no tomorrow. I jumped up, mad and embarrassed. I was scared of my daddy. When he commenced to whupping on me . . . quite naturally I run to get out of the way. (*Pause.*) Now I thought he was mad 'cause I ain't done my work. But I see where he was chasing me off so he could have that gal for himself. When I see what the matter of it was, I lost all fear of my daddy. Right there is where I become a man . . . at fourteen years of age. (*Pause.*) Now it was my turn to run him off. I picked up them same reins that he had used on me. I picked up them reins and commenced to whupping on him. The gal jumped up and run off . . . and when my daddy turned to face me, I could see why the devil had never come to get him . . . cause he was the devil himself. I don't know what happened. When I woke up, I was laying right there by the creek, and Blue . . . this old dog we had . . . was licking my face. I thought I was blind. I couldn't see nothing. Both my eyes were swollen shut. I laid there and cried. I didn't know what I was gonna do. The only thing I knew was the time had come for me to leave my daddy's house. And right there the world suddenly got big. And it was a long time before I could cut it down to where I could handle it.

Part of that cutting down was when I got to the place where I could feel him kicking in my blood and knew that the only thing that separated us was the matter of a few years.

Gabriel enters from the house with a sandwich.

LYONS: What you got there, Uncle Gabe? 110

GABRIEL: Got me a ham sandwich. Rose gave me a ham sandwich.

TROY: I don't know what happened to him. I done lost touch with everybody except Gabriel. But I hope he's dead. I hope he found some peace.

LYONS: That's a heavy story, Pop. I didn't know you left home when you was fourteen.

TROY: And didn't know nothing. The only part of the world I knew was the forty-two acres of Mr. Lubin's land. That's all I knew about life.

LYONS: Fourteen's kinda young to be out on your own. *(Phone rings.)* 115
I don't even think I was ready to be out on my own at fourteen.
I don't know what I would have done.

TROY: I got up from the creek and walked on down to Mobile.[2] I was through with farming. Figured I could do better in the city. So I walked the two hundred miles to Mobile.

LYONS: Wait a minute . . . you ain't walked no two hundred miles, Pop. Ain't nobody gonna walk no two hundred miles. You talking about some walking there.

BONO: That's the only way you got anywhere back in them days.

LYONS: Shhh. Damn if I wouldn't have hitched a ride with somebody!

TROY: Who you gonna hitch it with? They ain't got no cars and things 120
like they got now. We talking about 1918.

ROSE: *(entering)* What you all out here getting into?

TROY: *(to Rose)* I'm telling Lyons how good he got it. He don't know nothing about this I'm talking.

ROSE: Lyons, that was Bonnie on the phone. She say you supposed to pick her up.

LYONS: Yeah, okay, Rose.

TROY: I walked on down to Mobile and hitched up with some of them 125
fellows that was heading this way. Got up here and found out . . . not only couldn't you get a job . . . you couldn't find no place to live. I thought I was in freedom. Shhh. Colored folks living down there on the riverbanks in whatever kind of shelter they could find for themselves. Right down there under the Brady Street Bridge. Living in shacks made of sticks and tarpaper. Messed around there and went from bad to worse. Started stealing. First it was food. Then I figured, hell, if I steal money I can buy me some food. Buy me some shoes too! One thing led to another. Met your mama. I was young and anxious to be a man. Met your mama and had you. What I do that for? Now I got to worry about feeding you and her. Got to steal

---

[2]*Mobile:* City and seaport in southwestern Alabama.

three times as much. Went out one day looking for somebody to rob . . . that's what I was, a robber. I'll tell you the truth. I'm ashamed of it today. But it's the truth. Went to rob this fellow . . . pulled out my knife . . . and he pulled out a gun. Shot me in the chest. I felt just like somebody had taken a hot branding iron and laid it on me. When he shot me I jumped at him with my knife. They told me I killed him and they put me in the penitentiary and locked me up for fifteen years. That's where I met Bono. That's where I learned how to play baseball. Got out that place and your mama had taken you and went on to make life without me. Fifteen years was a long time for her to wait. But that fifteen years cured me of that robbing stuff. Rose'll tell you. She asked me when I met her if I had gotten all that foolishness out of my system. And I told her, "Baby, it's you and baseball all what count with me." You hear me, Bono? I meant it too. She say, "Which one comes first?" I told her, "Baby, ain't no doubt it's baseball . . . but you stick and get old with me and we'll both outlive this baseball." Am I right, Rose? And it's true.

ROSE: Man, hush your mouth. You ain't said no such thing. Talking about "Baby, you know you'll always be number one with me." That's what you was talking.

TROY: You hear that, Bono. That's why I love her.

BONO: Rose'll keep you straight. You get off the track, she'll straighten you up.

ROSE: Lyons, you better get on up and get Bonnie. She waiting on you.

130 LYONS: (gets up to go) Hey, Pop, why don't you come on down to the Grill and hear me play.

TROY: I ain't going down there. I'm too old to be sitting around in them clubs.

BONO: You got to be good to play down at the Grill.

LYONS: Come on, Pop . . .

TROY: I got to get up in the morning.

135 LYONS: You ain't got to stay long.

TROY: Naw, I'm gonna get my supper and go on to bed.

LYONS: Well, I got to go. I'll see you again.

TROY: Don't you come around my house on my payday.

ROSE: Pick up the phone and let somebody know you coming. And bring Bonnie with you. You know I'm always glad to see her.

140 LYONS: Yeah, I'll do that, Rose. You take care now. See you, Pop. See you, Mr. Bono. See you, Uncle Gabe.

GABRIEL: Lyons! King of the Jungle!

Lyons exits.

TROY: Is supper ready, woman? Me and you got some business to take care of. I'm gonna tear it up too.

ROSE: Troy, I done told you now!

TROY: *(puts his arm around Bono)* Aw hell, woman . . . this is Bono. Bono like family. I done known this nigger since . . . how long I done know you?

BONO: It's been a long time.   145

TROY: I done know this nigger since Skippy was a pup. Me and him done been through some times.

BONO: You sure right about that.

TROY: Hell, I done know him longer than I known you. And we still standing shoulder to shoulder. Hey, look here, Bono . . . a man can't ask for no more than that. *(Drinks to him.)* I love you, nigger.

BONO: Hell, I love you too . . . I got to get home see my woman. You got yours in hand. I got to go get mine.

Bono starts to exit as Cory enters the yard, dressed in his football uniform. He gives Troy a hard, uncompromising look.

CORY: What you do that for, Pop?   150

He throws his helmet down in the direction of Troy.

ROSE: What's the matter? Cory . . . what's the matter?

CORY: Papa done went up to the school and told Coach Zellman I can't play football no more. Wouldn't even let me play the game. Told him to tell the recruiter not to come.

ROSE: Troy . . .

TROY: What you Troying me for. Yeah, I did it. And the boy know why I did it.

CORY: Why you wanna do that to me? That was the one chance I had.   155

ROSE: Ain't nothing wrong with Cory playing football, Troy.

TROY: The boy lied to me. I told the nigger if he wanna play football . . . to keep up his chores and hold down that job at the A&P. That was the conditions. Stopped down there to see Mr. Stawicki . . .

CORY: I can't work after school during the football season, Pop! I tried to tell you that Mr. Stawicki's holding my job for me. You don't never want to listen to nobody. And then you wanna go and do this to me!

TROY: I ain't done nothing to you. You done it to yourself.

CORY: Just cause you didn't have a chance! You just scared I'm gonna   160 be better than you, that's all.

TROY: Come here.

ROSE: Troy . . .

Cory reluctantly crosses over to Troy.

TROY: All right! See. You done made a mistake.

CORY: I didn't even do nothing!

165 TROY: I'm gonna tell you what your mistake was. See . . . you swung at the ball and didn't hit it. That's strike one. See, you in the batter's box now. You swung and you missed. That's strike one. Don't you strike out!

Lights fade to black.

ACT 2
SCENE 1

The following morning. Cory is at the tree hitting the ball with the bat. He tries to mimic Troy, but his swing is awkward, less sure. Rose enters from the house.

ROSE: Cory, I want you to help me with this cupboard.

CORY: I ain't quitting the team. I don't care what Poppa say.

ROSE: I'll talk to him when he gets back. He had to go see about your Uncle Gabe. The police done arrested him. Say he was disturbing the peace. He'll be back directly. Come on in here and help me clean out the top of this cupboard.

Cory exits into the house. Rose sees Troy and Bono coming down the alley.

Troy . . . what they say down there?

TROY: Ain't said nothing. I give them fifty dollars and they let him go. I'll talk to you about it. Where's Cory?

5 ROSE: He's in there helping me clean out these cupboards.

TROY: Tell him to get his butt out here.

Troy and Bono go over to the pile of wood. Bono picks up the saw and begins sawing.

TROY: (*to Bono*) All they want is the money. That makes six or seven times I done went down there and got him. See me coming they stick out their *hands.*

BONO: Yeah. I know what you mean. That's all they care about . . . that money. They don't care about what's right. (*Pause.*) Nigger, why you got to go and get some hard wood? You ain't doing nothing but building a little old fence. Get you some soft pine wood. That's all you need.

TROY: I know what I'm doing. This is outside wood. You put pine wood inside the house. Pine wood is inside wood. This here is outside wood. Now you tell me where the fence is gonna be?

10 BONO: You don't need this wood. You can put it up with pine wood and it'll stand as long as you gonna be here looking at it.

TROY: How you know how long I'm gonna be here, nigger? Hell, I might just live forever. Live longer than old man Horsely.

BONO: That's what Magee used to say.

TROY: Magee's a damn fool. Now you tell me who you ever heard of gonna pull their own teeth with a pair of rusty pliers.

BONO: The old folks . . . my granddaddy used to pull his teeth with pliers. They ain't had no dentists for the colored folks back then.

TROY: Get clean pliers! You understand? Clean pliers! Sterilize them!   15
Besides we ain't living back then. All Magee had to do was walk over to Doc Goldblum's.

BONO: I see where you and that Tallahassee gal . . . that Alberta . . . I see where you all done got tight.

TROY: What you mean "got tight"?

BONO: I see where you be laughing and joking with her all the time.

TROY: I laughs and jokes with all of them, Bono. You know me.

BONO: That ain't the kind of laughing and joking I'm talking about.   20

Cory enters from the house.

CORY: How you doing, Mr. Bono?

TROY: Cory? Get that saw from Bono and cut some wood. He talking about the wood's too hard to cut. Stand back there, Jim, and let that young boy show you how it's done.

BONO: He's sure welcome to it.

Cory takes the saw and begins to cut the wood.

Whew-e-e! Look at that. Big old strong boy. Look like Joe Louis.[1]
Hell, must be getting old the way I'm watching that boy whip through that wood.

CORY: I don't see why Mama want a fence around the yard noways.

TROY: Damn if I know either. What the hell she keeping out with it?   25
She ain't got nothing nobody want.

BONO: Some people build fences to keep people out . . . and other people build fences to keep people in. Rose wants to hold on to you all. She loves you.

TROY: Hell, nigger, I don't need nobody to tell me my wife loves me.
Cory . . . go on in the house and see if you can find that other saw.

CORY: Where's it at?

TROY: I said find it! Look for it till you find it!

Cory exits into the house.

What's that supposed to mean? Wanna keep us in?

---

[1] *Joe Louis:* Joseph Louis Barrow (1914–1981), American boxer known as the "Brown Bomber." In 1937, he became the youngest boxer ever to win the Heavyweight Championship, which he defended twenty-five times; he retired undefeated in 1949.

30   BONO: Troy . . . I done known you seem like damn near my whole life.
You and Rose both. I done know both of you all for a long time. I
remember when you met Rose. When you was hitting them base-
balls out the park. A lot of them gals was after you then. You had
the pick of the litter. When you picked Rose, I was happy for you.
That was the first time I knew you had any sense. I said . . . My man
Troy knows what he's doing . . . I'm gonna follow this nigger . . . he
might take me somewhere. I been following you too. I done learned
a whole heap of things about life watching you. I done learned how
to tell where the shit lies. How to tell it from the alfalfa. You done
learned me a lot of things. You showed me how to not make the
same mistakes . . . to take life as it comes along and keep putting one
foot in front of the other. (Pause.) Rose a good woman, Troy.

TROY: Hell, nigger, I know she a good woman. I been married to her for
eighteen years. What you got on your mind, Bono?

BONO: I just say she a good woman. Just like I say anything. I ain't got
to have nothing on my mind.

TROY: You just gonna say she a good woman and leave it hanging out
there like that? Why you telling me she a good woman?

BONO: She loves you, Troy. Rose loves you.

35   TROY: You saying I don't measure up. That's what you trying to say.
I don't measure up 'cause I'm seeing this other gal. I know what you
trying to say.

BONO: I know what Rose means to you, Troy. I'm just trying to say
I don't want to see you mess up.

TROY: Yeah, I appreciate that, Bono. If you was messing around on
Lucille I'd be telling you the same thing.

BONO: Well, that's all I got to say. I just say that because I love you
both.

TROY: Hell, you know me . . . I wasn't out there looking for nothing.
You can't find a better woman than Rose. I know that. But seems
like this woman just stuck onto me where I can't shake her loose.
I done wrestled with it, tried to throw her off me . . . but she just
stuck on tighter. Now she's stuck on for good.

40   BONO: You's in control . . . that's what you tell me all the time. You
responsible for what you do.

TROY: I ain't ducking the responsibility of it. As long as it sets right in
my heart . . . then I'm okay. 'Cause that's all I listen to. It'll tell me
right from wrong every time. And I ain't talking about doing Rose
no bad turn. I love Rose. She done carried me a long ways and I
love and respect her for that.

BONO: I know you do. That's why I don't want to see you hurt her. But
what you gonna do when she find out? What you got then? If you

try and juggle both of them . . . sooner or later you gonna drop one of them. That's common sense.

TROY: Yeah, I hear what you saying, Bono. I been trying to figure a way to work it out.

BONO: Work it out right, Troy. I don't want to be getting all up between you and Rose's business . . . but work it so it come out right.

TROY: Ah hell, I get all up between you and Lucille's business. When   45 you gonna get that woman that refrigerator she been wanting? Don't tell me you ain't got no money now. I know who your banker is. Mellon don't need that money bad as Lucille want that refrigerator. I'll tell you that.

BONO: Tell you what I'll do . . . when you finish building this fence for Rose . . . I'll buy Lucille that refrigerator.

TROY: You done stuck your foot in your mouth now!

Troy grabs up a board and begins to saw. Bono starts to walk out the yard.

Hey, nigger . . . where you going?

BONO: I'm going home. I know you don't expect me to help you now. I'm protecting my money. I wanna see you put that fence up by yourself. That's what I want to see. You'll be here another six months without me.

TROY: Nigger, you ain't right.

BONO: When it comes to my money . . . I'm right as fireworks on the   50 Fourth of July.

TROY: All right, we gonna see now. You better get out your bankbook.

Bono exits, and Troy continues to work. Rose enters from the house.

ROSE: What they say down there? What's happening with Gabe?

TROY: I went down there and got him out. Cost me fifty dollars. Say he was disturbing the peace. Judge set up a hearing for him in three weeks. Say to show cause why he shouldn't be recommitted.

ROSE: What was he doing that cause them to arrest him?

TROY: Some kids were teasing him and he run them off home. Say he   55 was howling and carrying on. Some folks seen him and called the police. That's all it was.

ROSE: Well, what's you say? What'd you tell the judge?

TROY: Told him I'd look after him. It didn't make no sense to recommit the man. He stuck out his big greasy palm and told me to give him fifty dollars and take him on home.

ROSE: Where's he at now? Where'd he go off to?

TROY: He's gone about his business. He don't need nobody to hold his hand.

60 ROSE: Well, I don't know. Seem like that would be the best place for him if they did put him into the hospital. I know what you're gonna say. But that's what I think would be best.

TROY: The man done had his life ruined fighting for what? And they wanna take and lock him up. Let him be free. He don't bother nobody.

ROSE: Well, everybody got their own way of looking at it I guess. Come on and get your lunch. I got a bowl of lima beans and some corn-bread in the oven. Come and get something to eat. Ain't no sense you fretting over Gabe.

Rose turns to go into the house.

TROY: Rose . . . got something to tell you.

ROSE: Well, come on . . . wait till I get this food on the table.

65 TROY: Rose!

She stops and turns around.

I don't know how to say this. (*Pause.*) I can't explain it none. It just sort of grows on you till it gets out of hand. It starts out like a little bush . . . and the next thing you know it's a whole forest.

ROSE: Troy . . . what is you talking about?

TROY: I'm talking, woman, let me talk. I'm trying to find a way to tell you . . . I'm gonna be a daddy. I'm gonna be somebody's daddy.

ROSE: Troy . . . you're not telling me this? You're gonna be . . . what?

TROY: Rose . . . now . . . see . . .

70 ROSE: You telling me you gonna be somebody's daddy? You telling your *wife* this?

Gabriel enters from the street. He carries a rose in his hand.

GABRIEL: Hey, Troy! Hey, Rose!

ROSE: I have to wait eighteen years to hear something like this.

GABRIEL: Hey, Rose . . . I got a flower for you. (*He hands it to her.*) That's a rose. Same rose like you is.

ROSE: Thanks, Gabe.

75 GABRIEL: Troy, you ain't mad at me is you? Them bad mens come and put me away. You ain't mad at me is you?

TROY: Naw, Gabe, I ain't mad at you.

ROSE: Eighteen years and you wanna come with this.

GABRIEL: (*takes a quarter out of his pocket*) See what I got? Got a brand new quarter.

TROY: Rose . . . it's just . . .

80 ROSE: Ain't nothing you can say, Troy. Ain't no way of explaining that.

GABRIEL: Fellow that give me this quarter had a whole mess of them. I'm gonna keep this quarter till it stop shining.

ROSE: Gabe, go on in the house there. I got some watermelon in the Frigidaire. Go on and get you a piece.

GABRIEL: Say, Rose . . . you know I was chasing hellhounds and them bad mens come and get me and take me away. Troy helped me. He come down there and told them they better let me go before he beat them up. Yeah, he did!

ROSE: You go on and get you a piece of watermelon, Gabe. Them bad mens is gone now.

GABRIEL: Okay, Rose . . . gonna get me some watermelon. The kind with   85 the stripes on it.

Gabriel exits into the house.

ROSE: Why, Troy? Why? After all these years to come dragging this in to me now. It don't make no sense at your age. I could have expected this ten or fifteen years ago, but not now.

TROY: Age ain't got nothing to do with it, Rose.

ROSE: I done tried to be everything a wife should be. Everything a wife could be. Been married eighteen years and I got to live to see the day you tell me you been seeing another woman and done fathered a child by her. And you know I ain't never wanted no half nothing in my family. My whole family is half. Everybody got different fathers and mothers . . . my two sisters and my brother. Can't hardly tell who's who. Can't never sit down and talk about Papa and Mama. It's your papa and your mama and my papa and my mama . . .

TROY: Rose . . . stop it now.

ROSE: I ain't never wanted that for none of my children. And now you   90 wanna drag your behind in here and tell me something like this.

TROY: You ought to know. It's time for you to know.

ROSE: Well, I don't want to know, goddamn it!

TROY: I can't just make it go away. It's done now. I can't wish the circumstance of the thing away.

ROSE: And you don't want to either. Maybe you want to wish me and my boy away. Maybe that's what you want? Well, you can't wish us away. I've got eighteen years of my life invested in you. You ought to have stayed upstairs in my bed where you belong.

TROY: Rose . . . now listen to me . . . we can get a handle on this thing.   95 We can talk this out . . . come to an understanding.

ROSE: All of a sudden it's "we." Where was "we" at when you was down there rolling around with some godforsaken woman? "We" should have come to an understanding before you started making a damn fool of yourself. You're a day late and a dollar short when it comes to an understanding with me.

TROY: It's just . . . She gives me a different idea . . . a different understanding about myself. I can step out of this house and get away from the pressures and problems . . . be a different man. I ain't got to wonder how I'm gonna pay the bills or get the roof fixed. I can just be a part of myself that I ain't never been.

ROSE: What I want to know . . . is do you plan to continue seeing her. That's all you can say to me.

TROY: I can sit up in her house and laugh. Do you understand what I'm saying. I can laugh out loud . . . and it feels good. It reaches all the way down to the bottom of my shoes. *(Pause.)* Rose, I can't give that up.

100 ROSE: Maybe you ought to go on and stay down there with her . . . if she's a better woman than me.

TROY: It ain't about nobody being a better woman or nothing. Rose, you ain't the blame. A man couldn't ask for no woman to be a better wife than you've been. I'm responsible for it. I done locked myself into a pattern trying to take care of you all that I forgot about myself.

ROSE: What the hell was I there for? That was my job, not somebody else's.

TROY: Rose, I done tried all my life to live decent . . . to live a clean . . . hard . . . useful life. I tried to be a good husband to you. In every way I knew how. Maybe I come into the world backwards, I don't know. But . . . you born with two strikes on you before you come to the plate. You got to guard it closely . . . always looking for the curve ball on the inside corner. You can't afford to let none get past you. You can't afford a call strike. If you going down . . . you going down swinging. Everything lined up against you. What you gonna do. I fooled them, Rose. I bunted. When I found you and Cory and a halfway decent job . . . I was safe. Couldn't nothing touch me. I wasn't gonna strike out no more. I wasn't going back to the penitentiary. I wasn't gonna lay in the streets with a bottle of wine. I was safe. I had me a family. A job. I wasn't gonna get that last strike. I was on first looking for one of them boys to knock me in. To get me home.

ROSE: You should have stayed in my bed, Troy.

105 TROY: Then when I saw that gal . . . she firmed up my backbone. And I got to thinking that if I tried . . . I just might be able to steal second. Do you understand after eighteen years I wanted to steal second.

ROSE: You should have held me tight. You should have grabbed me and held on.

TROY: I stood on first base for eighteen years and I thought . . . well, goddamn it . . . go on for it!

ROSE: We're not talking about baseball! We're talking about you going off to lay in bed with another woman . . . and then bring it home to me. That's what we're talking about. We ain't talking about no baseball.

TROY: Rose, you're not listening to me. I'm trying the best I can to explain it to you. It's not easy for me to admit that I been standing in the same place for eighteen years.

ROSE: I been standing with you! I been right here with you, Troy. I got   110
a life too. I gave eighteen years of my life to stand in the same spot with you. Don't you think I ever wanted other things? Don't you think I had dreams and hopes? What about my life? What about me. Don't you think it ever crossed my mind to want to know other men? That I wanted to lay up somewhere and forget about my responsibilities? That I wanted someone to make me laugh so I could feel good? You not the only one who's got wants and needs. But I held on to you, Troy. I took all my feelings, my wants and needs, my dreams . . . and I buried them inside you. I planted a seed and watched and prayed over it. I planted myself inside you and waited to bloom. And it didn't take me no eighteen years to find out the soil was hard and rocky and it wasn't never gonna bloom.

But I held on to you, Troy. I held you tighter. You was my husband. I owed you everything I had. Every part of me I could find to give you. And upstairs in that room . . . with the darkness falling in on me . . . I gave everything I had to try and erase the doubt that you wasn't the finest man in the world. And wherever you was going . . . I wanted to be there with you. 'Cause you was my husband. 'Cause that's the only way I was gonna survive as your wife. You always talking about what you give . . . and what you don't have to give. But you take too. You take . . . and don't even know nobody's giving!

Rose turns to exit into the house; Troy grabs her arm.

TROY: You say I take and don't give!

ROSE: Troy! You're hurting me!

TROY: You say I take and don't give!

ROSE: Troy . . . you're hurting my arm! Let go!

TROY: I done give you everything I got. Don't you tell that lie on me.   115

ROSE: Troy!

TROY: Don't you tell that lie on me!

Cory enters from the house.

CORY: Mama!

ROSE: Troy. You're hurting me.

120 TROY: Don't you tell me about no taking and giving.

Cory comes up behind Troy and grabs him. Troy, surprised, is thrown off balance just as Cory throws a glancing blow that catches him on the chest and knocks him down. Troy is stunned, as is Cory.

ROSE: Troy. Troy. No!

Troy gets to his feet and starts at Cory.

Troy . . . no. Please! Troy!

Rose pulls on Troy to hold him back. Troy stops himself.

TROY: *(to Cory)* All right. That's strike two. You stay away from around me, boy. Don't you strike out. You living with a full count. Don't you strike out.

Troy exits out the yard as the lights go down.

SCENE 2

It is six months later, early afternoon. Troy enters from the house and starts to exit the yard. Rose enters from the house.

ROSE: Troy, I want to talk to you.

TROY: All of a sudden, after all this time, you want to talk to me, huh? You ain't wanted to talk to me for months. You ain't wanted to talk to me last night. You ain't wanted no part of me then. What you wanna talk to me about now?

ROSE: Tomorrow's Friday.

TROY: I know what day tomorrow is. You think I don't know tomorrow's Friday? My whole life I ain't done nothing but look to see Friday coming and you got to tell me it's Friday.

5 ROSE: I want to know if you're coming home.

TROY: I always come home, Rose. You know that. There ain't never been a night I ain't come home.

ROSE: That ain't what I mean . . . and you know it. I want to know if you're coming straight home after work.

TROY: I figure I'd cash my check . . . hang out at Taylors' with the boys . . . maybe play a game of checkers . . .

ROSE: Troy, I can't live like this. I won't live like this. You livin' on borrowed time with me. It's been going on six months now you ain't been coming home.

10 TROY: I be here every Friday. Every night of the year. That's 365 days.

ROSE: I want you to come home tomorrow after work.

TROY: Rose . . . I don't mess up my pay. You know that now. I take my
   pay and I give it to you. I don't have no money but what you give
   me back. I just want to have a little time to myself . . . a little time to
   enjoy life.

ROSE: What about me? When's my time to enjoy life?

TROY: I don't know what to tell you, Rose. I'm doing the best I can.

ROSE: You ain't been home from work but time enough to change   15
   your clothes and run out . . . and you wanna call that the best you
   can do?

TROY: I'm going over to the hospital to see Alberta. She went into the
   hospital this afternoon. Look like she might have the baby early.
   I won't be gone long.

ROSE: Well, you ought to know. They went over to Miss Pearl's and
   got Gabe today. She said you told them to go ahead and lock
   him up.

TROY: I ain't said no such thing. Whoever told you that is telling a lie.
   Pearl ain't doing nothing but telling a big fat lie.

ROSE: She ain't had to tell me. I read it on the papers.

TROY: I ain't told them nothing of the kind.   20

ROSE: I saw it right there on the papers.

TROY: What it say, huh?

ROSE: It said you told them to take him.

TROY: Then they screwed that up, just the way they screw up everything. I ain't worried about what they got on the paper.

ROSE: Say the government send part of his check to the hospital and   25
   the other part to you.

TROY: I ain't got nothing to do with that if that's the way it works.
   I ain't made up the rules about how it work.

ROSE: You did Gabe just like you did Cory. You wouldn't sign the paper
   for Cory . . . but you signed for Gabe. You signed that paper.

The telephone is heard ringing inside the house.

TROY: I told you I ain't signed nothing, woman! The only thing I signed
   was the release form. Hell, I can't read. I don't know what they had
   on that paper! I ain't signed nothing about sending Gabe away.

ROSE: I said send him to the hospital . . . you said let him be free . . . now
   you done went down there and signed him to the hospital for half
   his money. You went back on yourself, Troy. You gonna have to
   answer for that.

TROY: See now . . . you been over there talking to Miss Pearl. She done   30
   got mad cause she ain't getting Gabe's rent money. That's all it is.
   She's liable to say anything.

ROSE: Troy, I seen where you signed the paper.

TROY: You ain't seen nothing I signed. What she doing got papers on
my brother anyway? Miss Pearl telling a big fat lie. And I'm gonna
tell her about it too! You ain't seen nothing I signed. Say . . . you
ain't seen nothing I signed.

Rose exits into the house to answer the telephone. Presently she returns.

ROSE: Troy . . . that was the hospital. Alberta had the baby.

TROY: What she have? What is it?

35 ROSE: It's a girl.

TROY: I better get on down to the hospital to see her.

ROSE: Troy . . .

TROY: Rose . . . I got to go see her now. That's only right . . . what's the
matter . . . the baby's all right, ain't it?

ROSE: Alberta died having the baby.

40 TROY: Died . . . you say she's dead? Alberta's dead?

ROSE: They said they done all they could. They couldn't do nothing
for her.

TROY: The baby? How's the baby?

ROSE: They say it's healthy. I wonder who's gonna bury her.

TROY: She had family, Rose. She wasn't living in the world by herself.

45 ROSE: I know she wasn't living in the world by herself.

TROY: Next thing you gonna want to know if she had any insurance.

ROSE: Troy, you ain't got to talk like that.

TROY: That's the first thing that jumped out your mouth. "Who's gonna
bury her?" Like I'm fixing to take on that task for myself.

ROSE: I am your wife. Don't push me away.

50 TROY: I ain't pushing nobody away. Just give me some space. That's all.
Just give me some room to breathe.

Rose exits into the house. Troy walks about the yard.

TROY: (*with a quiet rage that threatens to consume him*) All right . . .
Mr. Death. See now . . . I'm gonna tell you what I'm gonna do. I'm
gonna take and build me a fence around this yard. See? I'm gonna
build me a fence around what belongs to me. And then I want you
to stay on the other side. See? You stay over there until you're ready
for me. Then you come on. Bring your army. Bring your sickle. Bring
your wrestling clothes. I ain't gonna fall down on my vigilance this
time. You ain't gonna sneak up on me no more. When you ready
for me . . . when the top of your list say Troy Maxson . . . that's when
you come around here. You come up and knock on the front door.
Ain't nobody else got nothing to do with this. This is between you
and me. Man to man. You stay on the other side of the fence until
you ready for me. Then you come up and knock on the front door.
Anytime you want. I'll be ready for you.

The lights go down to black.

SCENE 3

The lights come up on the porch. It is late evening three days later. Rose sits listening to the ball game waiting for Troy. The final out of the game is made and Rose switches off the radio. Troy enters the yard carrying an infant wrapped in blankets. He stands back from the house and calls.

Rose enters and stands on the porch. There is a long, awkward silence, the weight of which grows heavier with each passing second.

TROY: Rose . . . I'm standing here with my daughter in my arms. She ain't but a wee bittie little old thing. She don't know nothing about grownups' business. She innocent . . . and she ain't got no mama.

ROSE: What you telling me for, Troy?

She turns and exits into the house.

TROY: Well . . . I guess we'll just sit out here on the porch.

He sits down on the porch. There is an awkward indelicateness about the way he handles the baby. His largeness engulfs and seems to swallow it. He speaks loud enough for Rose to hear.

A man's got to do what's right for him. I ain't sorry for nothing I done. It felt right in my heart. (*To the baby.*) What you smiling at? Your daddy's a big man. Got these great big old hands. But sometimes he's scared. And right now your daddy's scared 'cause we sitting out here and ain't got no home. Oh, I been homeless before. I ain't had no little baby with me. But I been homeless. You just be out on the road by your lonesome and you see one of them trains coming and you just kinda go like this . . .

He sings a lullaby.

> Please, Mr. Engineer let a man ride the line
> Please, Mr. Engineer let a man ride the line
> I ain't got no ticket please let me ride the blinds

Rose enters from the house. Troy, hearing her steps behind him, stands and faces her.

She's my daughter, Rose. My own flesh and blood. I can't deny her no more than I can deny them boys. (*Pause.*) You and them boys is my family. You and them and this child is all I got in the world. So I guess what I'm saying is . . . I'd appreciate it if you'd help me take care of her.

ROSE: Okay, Troy . . . you're right. I'll take care of your baby for you . . . 'cause . . . like you say . . . she's innocent . . . and you can't visit the sins of the father upon the child. A motherless child has got a hard time. *(She takes the baby from him.)* From right now . . . this child got a mother. But you a womanless man.

Rose turns and exits into the house with the baby. Lights go down to black.

SCENE 4

It is two months later. Lyons enters from the street. He knocks on the door and calls.

LYONS: Hey, Rose! *(Pause.)* Rose!
ROSE: *(from inside the house)* Stop that yelling. You gonna wake up Raynell. I just got her to sleep.
LYONS: I just stopped by to pay Papa this twenty dollars I owe him. Where's Papa at?
ROSE: He should be here in a minute. I'm getting ready to go down to the church. Sit down and wait on him.
5 LYONS: I got to go pick up Bonnie over her mother's house.
ROSE: Well, sit it down there on the table. He'll get it.
LYONS: *(enters the house and sets the money on the table)* Tell Papa I said thanks. I'll see you again.
ROSE: All right, Lyons. We'll see you.

Lyons starts to exit as Cory enters.

CORY: Hey, Lyons.
10 LYONS: What's happening, Cory? Say man, I'm sorry I missed your graduation. You know I had a gig and couldn't get away. Otherwise, I would have been there, man. So what you doing?
CORY: I'm trying to find a job.
LYONS: Yeah I know how that go, man. It's rough out there. Jobs are scarce.
CORY: Yeah, I know.
LYONS: Look here, I got to run. Talk to Papa . . . he know some people. He'll be able to help get you a job. Talk to him . . . see what he say.
15 CORY: Yeah . . . all right, Lyons.
LYONS: You take care. I'll talk to you soon. We'll find some time to talk.

Lyons exits the yard. Cory wanders over to the tree, picks up the bat, and assumes a batting stance. He studies an imaginary pitcher and swings. Dissatisfied with the result, he tries again. Troy enters. They eye each other for a beat. Cory puts the bat down and exits the yard. Troy starts into the house as Rose exits with Raynell. She is carrying a cake.

TROY: I'm coming in and everybody's going out.

ROSE: I'm taking this cake down to the church for the bake sale. Lyons was by to see you. He stopped by to pay you your twenty dollars. It's laying in there on the table.

TROY: *(going into his pocket)* Well . . . here go this money.

ROSE: Put it in there on the table, Troy. I'll get it.   20

TROY: What time you coming back?

ROSE: Ain't no use in you studying me. It don't matter what time I come back.

TROY: I just asked you a question, woman. What's the matter . . . can't I ask you a question?

ROSE: Troy, I don't want to go into it. Your dinner's in there on the stove. All you got to do is heat it up. And don't you be eating the rest of them cakes in there. I'm coming back for them. We having a bake sale at the church tomorrow.

Rose exits the yard. Troy sits down on the steps, takes a pint bottle from his pocket, opens it, and drinks. He begins to sing.

TROY: 25

      Hear it ring! Hear it ring!
      Had an old dog his name was Blue
      You know Blue was mighty true
      You know Blue was a good old dog
      Blue treed a possum in a hollow log
      You know from that he was a good old dog

Bono enters the yard.

BONO: Hey, Troy.

TROY: Hey, what's happening, Bono?

BONO: I just thought I'd stop by to see you.

TROY: What you stop by and see me for? You ain't stopped by in a month of Sundays. Hell, I must owe you money or something.

BONO: Since you got your promotion I can't keep up with you. Used to   30 see you every day. Now I don't even know what route you working.

TROY: They keep switching me around. Got me out in Greentree now . . . hauling white folks' garbage.

BONO: Greentree, huh? You lucky, at least you ain't got to be lifting them barrels. Damn if they ain't getting heavier. I'm gonna put in my two years and call it quits.

TROY: I'm thinking about retiring myself.

BONO: You got it easy. You can *drive* for another five years.

TROY: It ain't the same, Bono. It ain't like working the back of the   35 truck. Ain't got nobody to talk to . . . feel like you working by yourself. Naw, I'm thinking about retiring. How's Lucille?

BONO: She all right. Her arthritis get to acting up on her sometime. Saw Rose on my way in. She going down to the church, huh?

TROY: Yeah, she took up going down there. All them preachers looking for somebody to fatten their pockets. *(Pause.)* Got some gin here.

BONO: Naw, thanks. I just stopped by to say hello.

TROY: Hell, nigger . . . you can take a drink. I ain't never known you to say no to a drink. You ain't got to work tomorrow.

40 BONO: I just stopped by. I'm fixing to go over to Skinner's. We got us a domino game going over his house every Friday.

TROY: Nigger, you can't play no dominoes. I used to whup you four games out of five.

BONO: Well, that learned me. I'm getting better.

TROY: Yeah? Well, that's all right.

BONO: Look here . . . I got to be getting on. Stop by sometime, huh?

45 TROY: Yeah, I'll do that, Bono. Lucille told Rose you bought her a new refrigerator.

BONO: Yeah, Rose told Lucille you had finally built your fence . . . so I figured we'd call it even.

TROY: I knew you would.

BONO: Yeah . . . okay. I'll be talking to you.

TROY: Yeah, take care, Bono. Good to see you. I'm gonna stop over.

50 BONO: Yeah. Okay, Troy.

Bono exits. Troy drinks from the bottle.

TROY:

> Old Blue died and I dig his grave
> Let him down with a golden chain
> Every night when I hear old Blue bark
> I know Blue treed a possum in Noah's Ark.
> Hear it ring! Hear it ring!

Cory enters the yard. They eye each other for a beat. Troy is sitting in the middle of the steps. Cory walks over.

CORY: I got to get by.

TROY: Say what? What's you say?

CORY: You in my way. I got to get by.

55 TROY: You got to get by where? This is my house. Bought and paid for. In full. Took me fifteen years. And if you wanna go in my house and I'm sitting on the steps . . . you say excuse me. Like your mama taught you.

CORY: Come on, Pop . . . I got to get by.

Cory starts to maneuver his way past Troy. Troy grabs his leg and shoves him back.

TROY: You just gonna walk over top of me?

CORY: I live here too!

TROY: (*advancing toward him*) You just gonna walk over top of me in my own house?

CORY: I ain't scared of you.   60

TROY: I ain't asked if you was scared of me. I asked you if you was fixing to walk over top of me in my own house? That's the question. You ain't gonna say excuse me? You just gonna walk over top of me?

CORY: If you wanna put it like that.

TROY: How else am I gonna put it?

CORY: I was walking by you to go into the house 'cause you sitting on the steps drunk, singing to yourself. You can put it like that.

TROY: Without saying excuse me???   65

Cory doesn't respond.

I asked you a question. Without saying excuse me???

CORY: I ain't got to say excuse me to you. You don't count around here no more.

TROY: Oh, I see . . . I don't count around here no more. You ain't got to say excuse me to your daddy. All of a sudden you done got so grown that your daddy don't count around here no more . . . Around here in his own house and yard that he done paid for with the sweat of his brow. You done got so grown to where you gonna take over. You gonna take over my house. Is that right? You gonna wear my pants. You gonna go in there and stretch out on my bed. You ain't got to say excuse me 'cause I don't count around here no more. Is that right?

CORY: That's right. You always talking this dumb stuff. Now, why don't you just get out my way?

TROY: I guess you got someplace to sleep and something to put in your belly. You got that, huh? You got that? That's what you need. You got that, huh?

CORY: You don't know what I got. You ain't got to worry about what   70
I got.

TROY: You right! You one hundred percent right! I done spent the last seventeen years worrying about what you got. Now it's your turn, see? I'll tell you what to do. You grown . . . we done established that. You a man. Now, let's see you act like one. Turn your behind around and walk out this yard. And when you get out there in the alley . . . you can forget about this house. See? 'Cause this is my house. You go on and be a man and get your own house. You can forget about this. 'Cause this is mine. You go on and get yours 'cause I'm through with doing for you.

CORY: You talking about what you did for me . . . what'd you ever give me?

TROY: Them feet and bones! That pumping heart, nigger! I give you more than anybody else is ever gonna give you.

CORY: You ain't never gave me nothing! You ain't never done nothing but hold me back. Afraid I was gonna be better than you. All you ever did was try and make me scared of you. I used to tremble every time you called my name. Every time I heard your footsteps in the house. Wondering all the time . . . what's Papa gonna say if I do this? . . . What's he gonna say if I do that? . . . What's Papa gonna say if I turn on the radio? And Mama, too . . . she tries . . . but she's scared of you.

75 TROY: You leave your mama out of this. She ain't got nothing to do with this.

CORY: I don't know how she stand you . . . after what you did to her.

TROY: I told you to leave your mama out of this!

He advances toward Cory.

CORY: What you gonna do . . . give me a whupping? You can't whup me no more. You're too old. You just an old man.

TROY: (*shoves him on his shoulder*) Nigger! That's what you are. You just another nigger on the street to me!

80 CORY: You crazy! You know that?

TROY: Go on now! You got the devil in you. Get on away from me!

CORY: You just a crazy old man . . . talking about I got the devil in me.

TROY: Yeah, I'm crazy! If you don't get on the other side of that yard . . . I'm gonna show you how crazy I am! Go on . . . get the hell out of my yard.

CORY: It ain't your yard. You took Uncle Gabe's money he got from the army to buy this house and then you put him out.

85 TROY: (*advances on Cory*) Get your black ass out of my yard!

Troy's advance backs Cory up against the tree. Cory grabs up the bat.

CORY: I ain't going nowhere! Come on . . . put me out! I ain't scared of you.

TROY: That's my bat!

CORY: Come on!

TROY: Put my bat down!

90 CORY: Come on, put me out.

Cory swings at Troy, who backs across the yard.

What's the matter? You so bad . . . put me out!

Troy advances toward Cory.

CORY: (*backing up*) Come on! Come on!

TROY: You're gonna have to use it! You wanna draw that bat back on me . . . you're gonna have to use it.

CORY: Come on! . . . Come on!

Cory swings the bat at Troy a second time. He misses. Troy continues to advance toward him.

TROY: You're gonna have to kill me! You wanna draw that bat back on me. You're gonna have to kill me.

Cory, backed up against the tree, can go no farther. Troy taunts him. He sticks out his head and offers him a target.

Come on! Come on!

Cory is unable to swing the bat. Troy grabs it.

TROY: Then I'll show you.   95

Cory and Troy struggle over the bat. The struggle is fierce and fully engaged. Troy ultimately is the stronger and takes the bat away from Cory and stands over him ready to swing. He stops himself.

Go on and get away from around my house.

Cory, stung by his defeat, picks himself up, walks slowly out of the yard and up the alley.

CORY: Tell Mama I'll be back for my things.

TROY: They'll be on the other side of that fence.

Cory exits.

TROY: I can't taste nothing. Helluljah! I can't taste nothing no more. *(Troy assumes a batting posture and begins to taunt Death, the fastball on the outside corner.)* Come on! It's between you and me now! Come on! Anytime you want! Come on! I be ready for you . . . but I ain't gonna be easy.

The lights go down on the scene.

SCENE 5

The time is 1965. The lights come up in the yard. It is the morning of Troy's funeral. A funeral plaque with a light hangs beside the door. There is a small garden plot off to the side. There is noise and activity in the house as Rose, Gabriel, and Bono have gathered. The door opens and Raynell, seven years old, enters dressed in a flannel nightgown. She crosses to the garden and pokes around with a stick. Rose calls from the house.

ROSE: Raynell!

RAYNELL: Mam?

ROSE: What you doing out there?

RAYNELL: Nothing.

Rose comes to the door.

5   ROSE: Girl, get in here and get dressed. What you doing?

RAYNELL: Seeing if my garden growed.

ROSE: I told you it ain't gonna grow overnight. You got to wait.

RAYNELL: It don't look like it never gonna grow. Dag!

ROSE: I told you a watched pot never boils. Get in here and get dressed.

10   RAYNELL: This ain't even no pot, Mama.

ROSE: You just have to give it a chance. It'll grow. Now you come on
   and do what I told you. We got to be getting ready. This ain't no
   morning to be playing around. You hear me?

RAYNELL: Yes, mam.

*Rose exits into the house. Raynell continues to poke at her garden with a stick.
Cory enters. He is dressed in a Marine corporal's uniform, and carries a duffel
bag. His posture is that of a military man, and his speech has a clipped sternness.*

CORY: (*to Raynell*) Hi. (*Pause.*) I bet your name is Raynell.

RAYNELL: Uh huh.

15   CORY: Is your mama home?

Raynell runs up on the porch and calls through the screen door.

RAYNELL: Mama . . . there's some man out here. Mama?

Rose comes to the door.

ROSE: Cory? Lord have mercy! Look here, you all!

*Rose and Cory embrace in a tearful reunion as Bono and Lyons enter from the
house dressed in funeral clothes.*

BONO: Aw, looka here . . .

ROSE: Done got all grown up!

20   CORY: Don't cry, Mama. What you crying about?

ROSE: I'm just so glad you made it.

CORY: Hey Lyons. How you doing, Mr. Bono.

Lyons goes to embrace Cory.

LYONS: Look at you, man. Look at you. Don't he look good, Rose. Got
   them Corporal stripes.

ROSE: What took you so long?

25   CORY: You know how the Marines are, Mama. They got to get all their
   paperwork straight before they let you do anything.

ROSE: Well, I'm sure glad you made it. They let Lyons come. Your Uncle Gabe's still in the hospital. They don't know if they gonna let him out or not. I just talked to them a little while ago.

LYONS: A Corporal in the United States Marines.

BONO: Your daddy knew you had it in you. He used to tell me all the time.

LYONS: Don't he look good, Mr. Bono?

BONO: Yeah, he remind me of Troy when I first met him. (*Pause.*)   30
Say, Rose, Lucille's down at the church with the choir. I'm gonna go down and get the pallbearers lined up. I'll be back to get you all.

ROSE: Thanks, Jim.

CORY: See you, Mr. Bono.

LYONS: (*with his arm around Raynell*) Cory . . . look at Raynell. Ain't she precious? She gonna break a whole lot of hearts.

ROSE: Raynell, come and say hello to your brother. This is your brother, Cory. You remember Cory.

RAYNELL: No, Mam.   35

CORY: She don't remember me, Mama.

ROSE: Well, we talk about you. She heard us talk about you. (*To Raynell.*) This is your brother, Cory. Come on and say hello.

RAYNELL: Hi.

CORY: Hi. So you're Raynell. Mama told me a lot about you.

ROSE: You all come on into the house and let me fix you some break-   40
fast. Keep up your strength.

CORY: I ain't hungry, Mama.

LYONS: You can fix me something, Rose. I'll be in there in a minute.

ROSE: Cory, you sure you don't want nothing? I know they ain't feeding you right.

CORY: No, Mama . . . thanks. I don't feel like eating. I'll get something later.

ROSE: Raynell . . . get on upstairs and get that dress on like I told you.   45

Rose and Raynell exit into the house.

LYONS: So . . . I hear you thinking about getting married.

CORY: Yeah, I done found the right one, Lyons. It's about time.

LYONS: Me and Bonnie been split up about four years now. About the time Papa retired. I guess she just got tired of all them changes I was putting her through. (*Pause.*) I always knew you was gonna make something out yourself. Your head was always in the right direction. So . . . you gonna stay in . . . make it a career . . . put in your twenty years?

CORY: I don't know. I got six already, I think that's enough.

50 LYONS: Stick with Uncle Sam and retire early. Ain't nothing out here. I guess Rose told you what happened with me. They got me down the workhouse. I thought I was being slick cashing other people's checks.

CORY: How much time you doing?

LYONS: They give me three years. I got that beat now. I ain't got but nine more months. It ain't so bad. You learn to deal with it like anything else. You got to take the crookeds with the straights. That's what Papa used to say. He used to say that when he struck out. I seen him strike out three times in a row . . . and the next time up he hit the ball over the grandstand. Right out there in Homestead Field. He wasn't satisfied hitting in the seats . . . he want to hit it over everything! After the game he had two hundred people standing around waiting to shake his hand. You got to take the crookeds with the straights. Yeah, Papa was something else.

CORY: You still playing?

LYONS: Cory . . . you know I'm gonna do that. There's some fellows down there we got us a band . . . we gonna try and stay together when we get out . . . but yeah, I'm still playing. It still helps me to get out of bed in the morning. As long as it do that I'm gonna be right there playing and trying to make some sense out of it.

55 ROSE: (calling) Lyons, I got these eggs in the pan.

LYONS: Let me go on and get these eggs, man. Get ready to go bury Papa. (Pause.) How you doing? You doing all right?

Cory nods. Lyons touches him on the shoulder and they share a moment of silent grief. Lyons exits into the house. Cory wanders about the yard. Raynell enters.

RAYNELL: Hi.

CORY: Hi.

RAYNELL: Did you used to sleep in my room?

60 CORY: Yeah . . . that used to be my room.

RAYNELL: That's what Papa call it. "Cory's room." It got your football in the closet.

Rose comes to the door.

ROSE: Raynell, get in there and get them good shoes on.

RAYNELL: Mama, can't I wear these? Them other ones hurt my feet.

ROSE: Well, they just gonna have to hurt your feet for a while. You ain't said they hurt your feet when you went down to the store and got them.

65 RAYNELL: They didn't hurt then. My feet done got bigger.

ROSE: Don't you give me no backtalk now. You get in there and get them shoes on.

Raynell exits into the house.

Ain't too much changed. He still got that piece of rag tied to that tree. He was out here swinging that bat. I was just ready to go back in the house. He swung that bat and then he just fell over. Seem like he swung it and stood there with this grin on his face . . . and then he just fell over. They carried him on down to the hospital, but I knew there wasn't no need . . . why don't you come on in the house?

CORY: Mama . . . I got something to tell you. I don't know how to tell you this . . . but I've got to tell you . . . I'm not going to Papa's funeral.

ROSE: Boy, hush your mouth. That's your daddy you talking about. I don't want hear that kind of talk this morning. I done raised you to come to this? You standing there all healthy and grown talking about you ain't going to your daddy's funeral?

CORY: Mama . . . listen . . .

ROSE: I don't want to hear it, Cory. You just get that thought out of your head.   70

CORY: I can't drag Papa with me everywhere I go. I've got to say no to him. One time in my life I've got to say no.

ROSE: Don't nobody have to listen to nothing like that. I know you and your daddy ain't seen eye to eye, but I ain't got to listen to that kind of talk this morning. Whatever was between you and your daddy . . . the time has come to put it aside. Just take it and set it over there on the shelf and forget about it. Disrespecting your daddy ain't gonna make you a man, Cory. You got to find a way to come to that on your own. Not going to your daddy's funeral ain't gonna make you a man.

CORY: The whole time I was growing up . . . living in his house . . . Papa was like a shadow that followed you everywhere. It weighed on you and sunk into your flesh. It would wrap around you and lay there until you couldn't tell which one was you anymore. That shadow digging in your flesh. Trying to crawl in. Trying to live through you. Everywhere I looked, Troy Maxson was staring back at me . . . hiding under the bed . . . in the closet. I'm just saying I've got to find a way to get rid of that shadow, Mama.

ROSE: You just like him. You got him in you good.

CORY: Don't tell me that, Mama.   75

ROSE: You Troy Maxson all over again.

CORY: I don't want to be Troy Maxson. I want to be me.

ROSE: You can't be nobody but who you are, Cory. That shadow wasn't nothing but you growing into yourself. You either got to grow into it or cut it down to fit you. But that's all you got to make life with. That's all you got to measure yourself against that world out there. Your daddy wanted you to be everything he wasn't . . . and at the same time he tried to make you into everything he was. I don't know if he was right or wrong . . . but I do know he meant to do more good than he meant to do harm. He wasn't always right. Sometimes when he touched he bruised. And sometimes when he took me in his arms he cut.

When I first met your daddy I thought . . . Here is a man I can lay down with and make a baby. That's the first thing I thought when I seen him. I was thirty years old and had done seen my share of men. But when he walked up to me and said, "I can dance a waltz that'll make you dizzy." I thought, Rose Lee, here is a man that you can open yourself up to and be filled to bursting. Here is a man that can fill all them empty spaces you been tipping around the edges of. One of them empty spaces was being somebody's mother.

I married your daddy and settled down to cooking his supper and keeping clean sheets on the bed. When your daddy walked through the house he was so big he filled it up. That was my first mistake. Not to make him leave some room for me. For my part in the matter. But at that time I wanted that. I wanted a house that I could sing in. And that's what your daddy gave me. I didn't know to keep up his strength I had to give up little pieces of mine. I did that. I took on his life as mine and mixed up the pieces so that you couldn't hardly tell which was which anymore. It was my choice. It was my life and I didn't have to live it like that. But that's what life offered me in the way of being a woman and I took it. I grabbed hold of it with both hands.

By the time Raynell came into the house, me and your daddy had done lost touch with one another. I didn't want to make my blessing off of nobody's misfortune . . . but I took on to Raynell like she was all them babies I had wanted and never had.

The phone rings.

Like I'd been blessed to relive a part of my life. And if the Lord see fit to keep up my strength . . . I'm gonna do her just like your daddy did you . . . I'm gonna give her the best of what's in me.

RAYNELL: *(entering, still with her old shoes)* Mama . . . Reverend Tollivier on the phone.

Rose exits into the house.

80 RAYNELL: Hi.
    CORY: Hi.
    RAYNELL: You in the Army or the Marines?
    CORY: Marines.

RAYNELL: Papa said it was the Army. Did you know Blue?

CORY: Blue? Who's Blue?   85

RAYNELL: Papa's dog what he sing about all the time.

CORY: (*singing*)

> Hear it ring! Hear it ring!
> I had a dog his name was Blue
> You know Blue was mighty true
> You know Blue was a good old dog
> Blue treed a possum in a hollow log
> You know from that he was a good old dog.
> Hear it ring! Hear it ring!

Raynell joins in singing.

CORY AND RAYNELL:

> Blue treed a possum out on a limb
> Blue looked at me and I looked at him
> Grabbed that possum and put him in a sack
> Blue stayed there till I came back
> Old Blue's feets was big and round
> Never allowed a possum to touch the ground.
> Old Blue died and I dug his grave
> I dug his grave with a silver spade
> Let him down with a golden chain
> And every night I call his name
> Go on Blue, you good dog you
> Go on Blue, you good dog you

RAYNELL:

> Blue laid down and died like a man
> Blue laid down and died . . .

BOTH: 90

> Blue laid down and died like a man
> Now he's treeing possums in the Promised Land
> I'm gonna tell you this to let you know
> Blue's gone where the good dogs go
> When I hear old Blue bark
> When I hear old Blue bark
> Blue treed a possum in Noah's Ark[1]
> Blue treed a possum in Noah's Ark.

Rose comes to the screen door.

---

[1]*Noah's Ark:* See Genesis 6.14–20.

Rose: Cory, we gonna be ready to go in a minute.

Cory: (to Raynell) You go on in the house and change them shoes like Mama told you so we can go to Papa's funeral.

Raynell: Okay, I'll be back.

Raynell exits into the house. Cory gets up and crosses over to the tree. Rose stands in the screen door watching him. Gabriel enters from the alley.

Gabriel: (calling) Hey, Rose!

95   Rose: Gabe?

Gabriel: I'm here, Rose. Hey Rose, I'm here!

Rose enters from the house.

Rose: Lord . . . Look here, Lyons!

Lyons: See, I told you, Rose . . . I told you they'd let him come.

Cory: How you doing, Uncle Gabe?

100 Lyons: How you doing, Uncle Gabe?

Gabriel: Hey, Rose. It's time. It's time to tell St. Peter to open the gates. Troy, you ready? You ready, Troy. I'm gonna tell St. Peter to open the gates. You get ready now.

Gabriel, with great fanfare, braces himself to blow. The trumpet is without a mouthpiece. He puts the end of it into his mouth and blows with great force, like a man who has been waiting some twenty-odd years for this single moment. No sound comes out of the trumpet. He braces himself and blows again with the same result. A third time he blows. There is a weight of impossible description that falls away and leaves him bare and exposed to a frightful realization. It is a trauma that a sane and normal mind would be unable to withstand. He begins to dance. A slow, strange dance, eerie and life-giving. A dance of atavistic signature and ritual. Lyons attempts to embrace him. Gabriel pushes Lyons away. He begins to howl in what is an attempt at song, or perhaps a song turning back into itself in an attempt at speech. He finishes his dance and the gates of heaven stand open as wide as God's closet.

That's the way that go!

*   *   *

Reading and Reacting

1. Obviously, fences are a central metaphor in this play. To what different kinds of fences does the play's title refer?

2. How are the fathers and sons in this play alike? How are they different? Does the play imply that sons must inevitably follow in their fathers' footsteps?

3. This play is set in 1957. Given the racial climate of the country at that time, how realistic are Cory's ambitions? Compare the development of

this theme in *Fences* and in another play in this book—for example, *Antigone*, *The Cuban Swimmer*, (p. 1166) or *Hamlet* (p. 1043)?

4. In what ways has Troy's character been shaped by his contact with the white world?

5. Is Troy a tragic hero? If so, what is his flaw?

6. Which of the play's characters, if any, do you consider to be stereotypes? What comment do you think the play makes about stereotypes?

7. How does the conflict between Troy and Cory reflect conflicts within the African American community? Does the play suggest any possibilities for compromise?

8. Do you consider the message of this play to be optimistic or pessimistic? Explain.

9. **JOURNAL ENTRY** Which characters do you like? Which do you dislike? Why?

10. **CRITICAL PERSPECTIVE** Robert Brustein, theater critic and artistic director of Harvard's American Repertory Theater, has criticized Wilson on the ground that "his recurrent theme is the familiar American charge of victimization"; in *Fences*, he argues, "Wilson's larger purpose depends on his conviction that Troy's potential was stunted not [by] 'his own behavior' but by centuries of racist oppression."

   Do you see the central theme of *Fences* as "the familiar American charge of victimization," or do you think another theme is more important?

Related Works: "Discovering America" (p. 93), "Big Black Good Man" (p. 236), "Yet Do I Marvel" (p. 690), *Death of a Salesman* (p. 960)

WRITING SUGGESTIONS: Theme

1. In an interview, writer Lorrie Moore calls *Fences* "an African American *Death of a Salesman*." What do you think she means? Do you agree? Write an essay in which you examine the two plays in light of Moore's comment.

2. Write an essay in which you analyze the baseball images in *Fences*. How do the references to baseball help to develop the play's themes?

3. One of the themes of *Fences* is the dream parents have for their children. Compare the development of this theme in *Fences* and in another play in this book—for example, *The Cuban Swimmer* (p. 1166) or *Hamlet* (p. 1043).

USING LITERARY CRITICISM IN YOUR WRITING

As you become aware of various schools of literary criticism, you see new ways to think—and to write—about fiction, poetry, and drama. Just as you value the opinions of your peers and your instructors, you also will find that the ideas of literary critics can enrich your own reactions to and evaluations of literature. Keep in mind that no single school of literary criticism offers the "right" way of approaching what you read; moreover, no single critic provides the definitive analysis of any short story, poem, or play. As you become aware of the richly varied possibilities of literary criticism, you will begin to ask new questions and discover new insights about the works you read.

 Formalism and New Criticism

Formalism stresses the importance of literary form to the meaning of a work. Formalist scholars consider each work of literature in isolation. They consider biographical, historical, and social matters to be irrelevant to the real meaning of a play, short story, novel, or poem. For example, a formalist would see the relationship between Adam and Eve in *Paradise Lost* as entirely unrelated to John Milton's own marital concerns, and they would view theological themes in the same work as entirely separate from Milton's deep involvement with the Puritan religious and political cause in seventeenth-century England. Formalists would also regard Milton's intentions and readers' responses to the epic poem as irrelevant. Instead, formalists would read the text closely, paying attention to organization and structure, to verbal nuances (suggested by word choice and use of figurative language), and to multiple meanings (often created through the writer's use of paradox and irony). Formalist critics try to reconcile the tensions and oppositions inherent in the text in order to develop a unified reading.

The formalist movement in English-language criticism began in England with I. A. Richards's *Practical Criticism* (1929). To explain and introduce his theory, Richards asked students to interpret famous poems without telling them the poets' names. This strategy encouraged close reading of the text rather than reliance on information about a poet's reputation, the details of a poet's life, or the poem's historical context. The American formalist movement, called **New Criticism**, was made popular by college instructors who realized that formalist criticism provided a useful way for students to work along with an instructor in interpreting a literary work rather than passively listening to a lecture on biographical, literary, and historical influences. The New Critical theorists Cleanth Brooks and Robert Penn Warren put together a series of textbooks (*Understanding Poetry*, *Understanding Fiction*, and *Understanding Drama*, first published in the late 1930s) that were used in colleges for years. After the 1950s, many New Critics began to reevaluate their theories and to broaden their approaches. Although few scholars currently maintain a strictly formalist approach, nearly every critical movement, including feminist, Marxist, psychoanalytic, structuralist, and deconstructionist criticism, owes a debt to the close reading techniques introduced by the formalists.

A New Critical Reading: Kate Chopin's "The Storm" (p. 199)

If you were to apply formalist criticism to Chopin's "The Storm," you might begin by noting the story's three distinctive sections. What relationship do the sections bear to one another? What do we learn from the word choice, the figures of speech, and the symbols in these sections? And, most important, how do these considerations lead readers to a unified view of the story?

In the first section of "The Storm," readers meet Bobinôt and his son Bibi. The description of the approaching clouds as "sombre," "sinister," and "sullen" (200) suggests an atmosphere of foreboding, yet the alliteration of these words also introduces a poetic tone. The conversation between father and son in the final part of this section contrasts, yet does not conflict, with the rather formal language of the introduction. Both Bobinôt and Bibi speak in Cajun dialect, suggesting their humble origins, yet their words have a rhythm that echoes the poetic notes struck in the description of the storm. As the section closes, Bobinôt, thinking of his wife, Calixta, at home, buys a can of the shrimp he knows she likes and holds the treasure "stolidly" (200), ironically suggesting the protection he cannot offer his wife in his separation from her during the coming storm.

The long second section brings readers to the story's central events. Calixta, as she watches the rain, sees her former lover, Alcée, riding up to seek shelter. As in the first section, the language of the narrator is somewhat formal and always poetic, filled with sensuous diction and images. For instance, we see Calixta "unfasten[ing] her white sacque at the throat" (200) and, later, Alcée envisions her lips "as red and moist as pomegranate seed" (202). Again, as in the first section, the conversation of the characters is carried on in dialect, suggesting their lack of sophistication and their connection to the powerful natural forces that surround them.

The lovemaking that follows, then, seems both natural and poetic. There is nothing sordid about this interlude and, as the final sections of the story suggest through their rather ordinary, matter-of-fact language, nothing has been harmed by Calixta and Alcée's yielding to passion.

In the third section, Bobinôt brings home the shrimp, a symbol of his love for Calixta, and, although we recognize the tension between Bobinôt's shy, gentle approach and Alcée's passion, readers can accept the final sentence as literal rather than ironic. The "storms" (both the rain and the storm of passion) have passed, and no one has been hurt. The threat suggested in the opening sentences has been diffused; both the power and the danger evoked by the poetic diction of the first two sections have disappeared, to be replaced entirely by the rhythms of daily life and speech.

For Further Reading: Formalism and New Criticism

Brooks, Cleanth. *The Well Wrought Urn.* 1947.

Empson, William. *Seven Types of Ambiguity.* 1930.

Hartman, Geoffrey H. *Beyond Formalism.* 1970.

Stallman, Robert W. *Critiques and Essays in Criticism. 1920–1948.* 1949.

Wellek, René. *A History of Modern Criticism.* Vol. 6. 1986.

Wimsatt, W. K. *The Verbal Icon.* 1954.

 Reader-Response Criticism

Reader-response criticism opposes formalism, seeing the reader's interaction with the text as central to interpretation. Unlike formalists, reader-response critics do not believe that a work of literature exists as a separate, closed entity. Instead, they consider the reader's contribution to the text as essential. A poem, short story, novel, or play is not a solid piece of fabric but rather a series of threads separated by gaps that readers must fill in, drawing on their own experiences and knowledge.

As readers approach a literary text, they contribute their own interpretations. As they read one sentence and then the next, they develop expectations; and, in realistic stories, these expectations are generally met. Nevertheless, nearly every reader supplies personal meanings and observations, making each reader's experience of a work unique and distinctive from every other reader's experience of the same work. For example, imagine Shakespeare's *Romeo and Juliet* as it might be read by a fourteen-year-old high school student and by her father. The young woman, whose age is the same as Juliet's, is almost certain to identify closely with the female protagonist and to "read" Lord Capulet, Juliet's father, as overbearing and rigid. The young reader's father, however, may be drawn to the poignant passage where Capulet talks with a prospective suitor, urging that he wait while Juliet has time to enjoy her youth. Capulet describes the loss of his other children and calls Juliet "the hopeful lady of my earth." Although the young woman reading this line may interpret it as yet another indication of Capulet's possessiveness, her father may see it as a sign of love and even generosity. The twenty-first-century father may "read" Capulet as a man willing to risk offending a friend in order to keep his daughter safe from the rigors of early marriage (and early childbearing). Whose interpretation is correct? Reader-response theorists would say that both readings are entirely plausible and therefore equally "right."

The differing interpretations produced by different readers can be seen as simply the effect of the different personalities (and personal histories) involved in constructing meaning from the same series of clues. Not only does the reader "create" the work of literature, in large part, but the literature itself may work on the reader as he or she reads, altering the reader's experience and thus the reader's interpretation. For example, the father reading *Romeo and Juliet* may alter his sympathetic view of Capulet as he continues through the play and observes Capulet's later, angry exchanges with Juliet.

Reader-response theorists believe in the importance of **recursive reading**— that is, reading and rereading with the idea that no interpretation is carved in stone. A second or third interaction with the text may well produce a new interpretation. This changing view is particularly likely when the rereading takes place significantly later than the initial reading. For example, if the young woman just described reread *Romeo and Juliet* when she was middle-aged and herself the mother of teenage children, her reaction to Capulet would quite likely be different from her reaction when she read the work at age fourteen.

In one particular application of reader-response theory, called **reception theory**, the idea of developing readings is applied to the general reading public rather than to individual readers. Reception theory, as proposed by Hans Robert Jauss ("Literary History as a Challenge to Literary Theory," *New Literary History*, Vol. 2 [1970–1971]), suggests that each new generation reads the same works of literature differently. Because each generation of readers has experienced different historical events, read different books, and been aware of different critical theories, each generation will view the same works very differently from its predecessors. (Consider, for example, the changing views toward Shakespeare from the seventeenth century to the present.)

Reader-response criticism has received serious attention since the 1960s, when Norman Holland formulated the theory in *The Dynamics of Literary Response* (1968). The German critic Wolfgang Iser (*The Implied Reader*, 1974) argued that in order to be an effective reader, one must be familiar with the conventions and "codes" of writing. This, then, is one reason for studying literature in a classroom: not to produce approved interpretations but to develop strategies and information that will help readers to make sense of a text. Stanley Fish, an American critic, goes even further, arguing that there may not be any "objective" text at all (*Is There a Text in This Class?*, 1980). Fish says that no two readers read the same book, though readers can be trained to have relatively similar responses to a text if they have had relatively similar life experiences. For instance, readers who went to college and took an Introduction to Literature course in which they learned to respond to the various elements of literature, such as character, theme, irony, and figurative language, are likely to have similar responses to a text.

Reader-Response Readings: Kate Chopin's "The Storm" (p. 200)

To demonstrate possible reader-response readings, we can look at the same story previously considered from a formalist perspective. (Of course, if several formalist critics read the story, they too would each write a somewhat different interpretation.)

Written by a twenty-five-year-old man who has studied American literature

In Kate Chopin's "The Storm," attention must be paid to the two adult male characters, Bobinôt and Alcée. Usually, in a love triangle situation, one man is portrayed more sympathetically than the other. But Chopin provides us with a dilemma. Alcée is not a cavalier seducer; he genuinely cares for Calixta. Neither is he a brooding hero. There is nothing gruff or angry about Alcée, and he returns to his family home with no apparent harm done following the passionate interlude. On the other hand, Bobinôt is not a cruel or abusive husband. We can see no clear reason for Calixta's affair except for her desire to fulfill a sexual longing for Alcée.

Written by an eighteen-year-old male student in a first-year literature course

Bibi doesn't seem to be a very important character in the story, but we should pay attention to him as a reflection of his father. At the beginning of the story, Bibi worries about his mother and he expresses his concern to his father. Bobinôt tries to reassure his son, but he gets up and buys a treat for Calixta as much to comfort himself as to get something for her. Then Bibi sits with his father, and it seems as if he has transferred all his worries to Bobinôt. In the third section of the story, after Calixta and Alcée have had their love affair, Bibi and Bobinôt come home. They both seem like children, worried about how Calixta will react. She, of course, is nice to them because she feels so guilty. At the end of the third section, both father and son are happy and enjoying themselves. You can't help but feel great sympathy for them both because they are so loving and simple and because they have been betrayed by Calixta, who has not behaved the way a loving mother and wife should.

Written by a forty-five-year-old woman who has studied Kate Chopin's life and work

A decade after the controversial novel *The Awakening* was published in 1899, one critic protested, "To think of Kate Chopin, who once contented herself with mild yarns about genteel Creole life . . . blowing us a hot blast like that!" (qtd. in Gilbert and Gubar 981). This literary observer was shocked, as one might expect from an early-twentieth-century reader, by Chopin's frank picture of sexual relations, and particularly of the sexual feelings of the novel's heroine. One cannot help but wonder, however, whether the scandalized reader was really widely acquainted with Chopin.

Certainly he could not have read "The Storm." This short story is surprising for many reasons, but primarily because it defies the sexual mores of the late nineteenth century by showing a woman who is neither evil nor doomed enjoying, even glorying in, her sexuality. Calixta is presented as a good wife and loving mother, concerned about her husband and son who are away from home during the storm. Yet her connection to Bobinôt and Bibi does not keep her from passionately enjoying her interlude with Alcée. She goes to his arms unhesitatingly, with no false modesty or guilt (feigned or real) to hold her back. Somehow, this scenario does not seem to fit the definition of "a mild yarn about genteel Creole life."

For Further Reading: Reader-Response Criticism

Bleich, David. *Subjective Criticism.* 1978.

Fish, Stanley. *Is There a Text in This Class?* 1980.

Holland, Norman. *The Dynamics of Literary Response.* 1968.

Iser, Wolfgang. *The Implied Reader.* 1974.

———. *The Act of Reading: A Theory of Aesthetic Response.* 1978.

Rosenblatt, Louise. *The Reader, the Text, the Poem.* 1978.

Sulleiman, Susan, and Inge Crosman, eds. *The Reader in the Text.* 1980.

Tomkins, Jane P., ed. *Reader-Response Criticism.* 1980.

 Feminist Criticism

Throughout the nineteenth century, women such as the Brontë sisters, George Eliot (Mary Ann Evans), Elizabeth Barrett Browning, and Christina Rossetti struggled for the right to be taken as seriously as their male counterparts. Then, in 1929, Virginia Woolf, an experimental novelist and literary critic, published *A Room of One's Own*, which described the difficulties that women writers faced and defined a tradition of literature written by women.

Feminist criticism emerged as a distinct approach to literature only in the late 1960s. Modern feminist criticism began with works such as Mary Ellman's *Thinking about Women* (1968), which focuses on the negative female stereotypes in books authored by men and points out alternative female characteristics suggested by women authors. Another pioneering feminist work was Kate Millet's *Sexual Politics* (1969), which analyzes the societal mechanisms that perpetuate male domination of women. Since that time, feminist writings, though not unified in one theory or methodology, have appeared

in ever-growing numbers. Some feminist critics have adapted psychoanalytic, Marxist, or other poststructuralist theories, and others have broken
new ground. In general, feminist critics take the view that our culture—and
by extension our literature—is primarily patriarchal (controlled by males).

According to feminist critics, what is at issue is not anatomical sex but
gender. As Simone de Beauvoir explained, a person is not born feminine, as
our society defines it, but rather becomes so because of cultural conditioning.
According to feminist critics, paternalist Western culture has defined the
feminine as "other" to the male, as passive and emotional in opposition to
the dominating and rational masculine.

Feminist critics claim that paternalist cultural stereotypes pervade works
of literature in the **canon**—those works generally acknowledged to be the
best and most significant. Feminists point out that the traditional canon
typically consisted of works written by males and about male experiences.
Female characters, when they did appear, were often subordinated to male
characters. A female reader of these works must either identify with the male
protagonist or accept a marginalized role.

One response of feminist critics is to reinterpret works in the traditional
canon. As Judith Fetterley explains in *The Resisting Reader* (1978), the reader
"revisions" the text, focusing on the covert sexual bias in a literary work.
For example, a feminist scholar studying Shakespeare's *Macbeth* might look
closely at the role played by Lady Macbeth and argue that she was not simply
a cold-hearted villain but a victim of the circumstances of her time: women
in her day were not permitted to follow their own ambitions but were relegated to supporting roles, living their lives vicariously through the achievements of their husbands and sons.

A second focus of feminist scholars has been the redefinition of the canon.
By seeking out, analyzing, and evaluating little-known works by women, feminist scholars have rediscovered women writers who were ignored or shunned
by the reading public and by critics of their own times. Thus, writers such as
Kate Chopin and Charlotte Perkins Gilman (see "The Yellow Wallpaper,"
p. 434), who wrote during the late nineteenth and early twentieth centuries,
are now recognized as worthy of serious consideration and study.

A Feminist Reading: Tillie Olsen's "I Stand Here Ironing" (p. 217)

To approach Tillie Olsen's "I Stand Here Ironing" from a feminist perspective, you might focus on the passages in which the narrator describes her
relationships and encounters with men.

> Some readings of Tillie Olsen's "I Stand Here Ironing" suggest that the
> narrator made choices that doomed her oldest daughter to a life of confu-
> sion. If we look at the narrator's relationships with the men in her life,
> however, we can see that she herself is the story's primary victim.
> At nineteen, the narrator was a mother abandoned by her husband,
> who left her a note saying that he "could no longer endure . . . sharing

want" (218) with his wife and infant daughter. This is the first desertion we hear about in the narrator's life, and although she agonizingly describes her painful decisions and the mistakes she made with her daughter Emily, we cannot help but recognize that she was the one who stayed and tried to make things right. Her actions contrast sharply with those of her husband, who ran away, saying that his wife and daughter were burdens too great for him to bear.

The second abandonment is more subtle than the first but no less devastating. After the narrator remarried, she was again left alone to cope with a growing family when her second husband went off to war. True, this desertion was for a "noble" purpose and probably was not voluntary, but the narrator, nevertheless, had to seek one of the low-paying jobs available to women to supplement her allotment checks. She was again forced to leave her children because her husband had to serve the needs of the male-dominated military establishment.

The narrator was alone at crucial points in Emily's life and had to turn away from her daughter in order to survive. She has been brought up in a world that teaches women to depend on men, but she learns that she is ultimately alone. Although the desertions she endured were not always intentional, she had to bear the brunt of circumstances that were not her choice but were foisted on her by the patriarchal society in which she lived.

For Further Reading: Feminist Criticism

Benstock, Shari, ed. *Feminist Issues in Literary Scholarship*. 1987.
Engleton, Mary, ed. *Feminist Issues in Literary Theory: A Reader*. 1986.
Gilbert, Sandra, and Susan Gubar. *The Madwoman in the Attic*. 1979.
————. *No Man's Land*. 3 vols. 1988, 1989, 1994.
————, eds. *The Norton Anthology of Literature by Women*. 1985.
Heilbrun, Carolyn G. *Hamlet's Mother and Other Women*. 1990.
Jacobus, Mary. *Reading Woman: Essays in Feminist Criticism*. 1986.
Miller, Nancy, K., ed. *The Poetics of Gender*. 1986.
————. *Subject to Change*. 1988.
Showalter, Elaine. *A Literature of Their Own*. 1977.
————. *Sister's Choice: Tradition and Change in American Women's Writing*. 1991.

 ## Marxist Criticism

Marxist criticism bases interpretations of literature on the social and economic theories of Karl Marx (*Das Kapital*, 1867–1894) and his colleague and coauthor Friedrich Engels (*The Communist Manifesto*, 1884). Marx and Engels believed that the dominant capitalist middle class would eventually be challenged and overthrown by the working class. In the meantime, however, middle-class capitalists would continue to exploit the working class, who produce excess products and profits yet do not share in the benefits of their labor. Marx and Engels further regarded all parts of the society in which they lived—religious, legal, educational, governmental—as tainted by what they saw as the corrupt values of middle-class capitalists.

Marxist critics apply these views about class struggle to their readings of poetry, fiction, and drama. They tend to analyze the literary works of any historical era as products of the ideology, or network of concepts, that supports the interests of the cultural elite and suppresses those of the working class. Some Marxist critics see all Western literature as distorted by the privileged views of the elite class, but most believe that a few creative writers reject the distorted views of their society and see clearly the wrongs to which working-class people have been subjected. For example, George Lukacs, a Hungarian Marxist critic, proposed that great works of literature create their own worlds and reflect life with clarity. These great works, though not written by Marxists, can be studied for their revealing examples of class conflict and other Marxist concerns. A Marxist critic would look with favor on Charles Dickens, who in nearly every novel pointed out inequities in the political, legal, and educational establishments of his time. Readers who remember Oliver Twist's pitiful plea for "more" workhouse porridge (refused by evil Mr. Bumble, who skims money from funds intended to feed the impoverished inmates) cannot help but see fertile ground for the Marxist critic, who would certainly applaud Dickens's scathing criticism of Victorian social and economic inequality.

Marxist criticism developed in the 1920s and 1930s in Germany and the Soviet Union. Since 1960, British and American Marxism has received greatest attention, with works such as Raymond Williams's *Culture and Society, 1780–1950* (1960) and Terry Eagleton's *Criticism and Ideology* (1976).

A Marxist Reading: Tillie Olsen's "I Stand Here Ironing" (p. 217)

In a Marxist reading of Tillie Olsen's "I Stand Here Ironing," you might concentrate on events that demonstrate how the narrator's and Emily's fates have been directly affected by the capitalist society of the United States.

> Tillie Olsen's "I Stand Here Ironing" stands as a powerful indictment of the capitalist system. The narrator and her daughter Emily are repeatedly exploited and defeated by the pressures of the economic system in which they live.
>
> The narrator's first child, Emily, is born into the world of the 1930s depression—an economic disaster brought on by the excesses and greed of Wall Street. When the young mother is deserted by her first husband, there are no government programs in place to help her. She says it was

the "pre-relief, pre-WPA world of the depression" that forced her away from her child and into "a job hashing at night" (218). Although she is willing to work, she is paid so poorly that she must finally send Emily to live with her husband's family. Raising the money to bring Emily back takes a long time; and after this separation, Emily's health, both physical and emotional, is precarious.

When Emily gets the measles, we get a hard look at what the few social programs that existed during the Depression were like. The child is sent—at the urging of a government social worker—to a convalescent home. The narrator notes bitterly, "They still send children to that place. I see pictures on the society page of sleek young women planning affairs to raise money for it, or dancing at the affairs, or decorating Easter eggs or filling Christmas stockings for the children" (220). The privileged class basks in the artificial glow of their charity work for the poor, yet the newspapers never show pictures of the hospitalized children who are kept isolated from everyone they loved and forced to eat "runny eggs . . . or mush with lumps" (221). Once again the mother is separated from her daughter by a system that discriminates against the poor. Because the family cannot afford private treatment, Emily is forced to undergo treatment in a public institution that not only denies her any contact with her family but also cruelly forbids her to save the letters she receives from home. Normal family relationships are severely disrupted by an uncaring economic structure that only grudgingly offers aid to the poor.

It is clear that the division between mother and daughter is created by, and worsened by, the social conditions in which they live. Because they are poor, they are separated at crucial times and, therefore, never get to know each other fully. Thus, neither can truly understand the ordeals the other has been forced to endure.

For Further Reading: Marxist Criticism

Agger, Ben. *The Discourse of Domination.* 1992.

Bullock, Chris, and David Peck, eds. *Guide to Marxist Literary Criticism.* 1980.

Eagleton, Terry. *Marxism and Literary Criticism.* 1976.

Frow, John. *Marxism and Literary History.* 1986.

Holub, Renate, and Antonio Gramsci. *Beyond Marxism and Postmodernism.* 1992.

Jameson, Fredric. *Marxism and Form.* 1971.

Lentricchia, Frank. *Criticism and Social Change.* 1983.

Ohmann, Richard M. *Politics of Letters.* 1987.

Strelka, Joseph P., ed. *Literary Criticism and Sociology.* 1973.

Williams, Raymond. *Culture and Society, 1780–1950.* 1960.

———. *Marxism and Literature.* 1977.

Psychoanalytic Criticism

Psychoanalytic criticism focuses on a work of literature as an expression in fictional form of the inner workings of the human mind. The premises and procedures used in psychoanalytic criticism were developed by Sigmund Freud (1846–1939), though some critics disagree strongly with his conclusions and their therapeutic and literary applications. Feminists, for example, take issue with Freud's notion that women are inherently masochistic.

Some of the major points of Freud's theories depend on the idea that much of what is most significant to us does not take place in our conscious life. Freud believed that we are forced (mostly by the rigors of having to live in harmony with other people) to repress much of our experience and many of our desires in order to coexist peacefully with others. Some of this repressed experience Freud saw as available to us through dreams and other unconscious structures. He believed that literature could often be interpreted as the reflection of our unconscious life.

Freud was among the first psychoanalytic critics, often using techniques developed for interpreting dreams to interpret literature. Among other analyses, he wrote an insightful study of Dostoevsky's *The Brothers Karamazov* as well as brief commentaries on several of Shakespeare's plays, including *A Midsummer Night's Dream*, *Macbeth*, *King Lear*, and *Hamlet*. The study of *Hamlet* may have inspired a classic of psychoanalytic criticism: Ernest Jones's *Hamlet and Oedipus* (1949), in which Jones explains Hamlet's strange reluctance to act against his uncle Claudius as resulting from Hamlet's unresolved longings for his mother and subsequent drive to eliminate his father. Because Hamlet's own father is dead, Jones argues, Claudius becomes, in the young man's subconscious mind, a father substitute. Hamlet, then, cannot make up his mind to kill his uncle because he sees not a simple case of revenge (for Claudius's murder of his father) but rather a complex web that includes incestuous desire for his own mother (now wed to Claudius). Jones extends his analysis to include the suggestion that Shakespeare himself experienced such a conflict and reflected his own Oedipal feelings in *Hamlet*.

A French psychoanalyst, Jacques Lacan (1901–1981), combined Freudian theories with structuralist literary theories to argue that the essential alienating experience of the human psyche is the acquisition of language. Lacan believed that once you can name yourself and distinguish yourself from others, you enter the difficult social world that requires you to repress your instincts. Like Lacan, who modified and adapted psychoanalytic criticism to connect it to structuralism, many twentieth-century literary scholars, including Marxists and feminists, have found useful approaches in psychoanalytic literary theory (for example, see Mary Jacobus's *Reading Woman: Essays in Feminist Criticism*, 1986).

Psychoanalytic Terms

To fully appreciate psychoanalytic criticism, readers need to understand the following terms:

- *id*—The part of the mind that determines sexual drives and other unconscious compulsions that urge individuals to unthinking gratification.
- *ego*—The conscious mind that strives to deal with the demands of the id and to balance its needs with messages from the superego.
- *superego*—The part of the unconscious that seeks to repress the demands of the id and to prevent gratification of basic physical appetites. The superego is a sort of censor that represents the prohibitions of society, religion, family beliefs, and so on.
- *condensation*—A process that takes place in dreams (and in literature) when several elements from the repressed unconscious are linked together to form a new yet disguised whole.
- *symbolism*—The use of representative objects to stand for forbidden (often sexual) objects. This process takes place in dreams and in literature. For instance, a pole, knife, or gun may stand for the penis.
- *displacement*—The substitution of a socially acceptable desire for a desire that is not acceptable. This process takes place in dreams or in literature. For example, a woman who experiences sexual desires for her son may instead dream of being intimate with a neighbor who has the same first name as (or who looks like) her son.
- *Oedipus complex*—The repressed desire of a son to unite sexually with his mother and kill his father. According to Freud, all young boys go through this stage, but most resolve these conflicts before puberty.
- *projection*—A defense mechanism in which people mistakenly see in others antisocial impulses they fail to recognize in themselves.
- *subject*—The term used in Lacanian theory to designate a speaking person, or a person who has assumed a position within language. The Lacanian subject of language is split, or characterized by unresolvable tension between the conscious perception of the self (Freud's ego) and the unconscious desires that motivate behavior.

A Psychoanalytic Reading: Edgar Allan Poe's "The Cask of Amontillado" (p. 249)

Edgar Allan Poe died in 1849, six years before Freud was born, so Poe could not possibly have known Freud's work. Nevertheless, psychoanalytic critics argue that the principles discovered by Freud and those who followed him are inherent in human nature. Therefore, they believe it is perfectly plausible to use modern psychiatric terms when analyzing a work written before their invention. If you approached Poe's "The Cask of Amontillado" from a psychoanalytic perspective, you might write the following interpretation.

Montresor, the protagonist of Poe's "The Cask of Amontillado," has long fascinated readers who have puzzled over his motives for the story's climactic action when he imprisons his rival, Fortunato, and leaves him to die. Montresor claims that Fortunato insulted him and dealt him a "thousand injuries" (250). Yet when we meet Fortunato, although he appears something of a pompous fool, none of his actions—or even his comments—seems powerful enough to motivate Montresor's thirst for revenge.

If, however, we consider a defense mechanism, first named "projection" and described by Sigmund Freud, we gain a clearer picture of Montresor. Those who employ projection are often people who experience antisocial impulses yet are not conscious of these impulses. It seems highly likely that Fortunato did not persecute Montresor; rather, Montresor himself experienced the impulse to act in a hostile manner toward Fortunato. We know, for instance, that Fortunato belongs to the exclusive Order of Masons because he gives Montresor the secret Masonic sign. Montresor's failure to recognize the sign shows that he is a mason only in the grimmest literal sense. Montresor clearly resents Fortunato's high standing and projects onto Fortunato all of his own hostility toward those who (he thinks) have more or know more than he does. Thus, he imagines that Fortunato's main business in life is to persecute and insult him.

Montresor's obsessive behavior further indicates his pathology. He plans Fortunato's punishment with the cunning one might ordinarily reserve for a major battle, cleverly figuring out a way to keep his servants from the house and to lure the ironically named Fortunato to his death. Each step of the revenge is carefully plotted. This is no sudden crime of passion but rather the diabolically planned act of a deeply disturbed mind.

If we understand Montresor's need to take all of the hatred and anger that is inside himself and to rid himself of those socially unacceptable emotions by projecting them onto someone else, then we can see how he rationalizes a crime that seems otherwise nearly unmotivated. By killing Fortunato, Montresor symbolically kills the evil in himself. It is interesting to note that the final lines of the story support this reading. Montresor observes that "For the half of a century no mortal has disturbed" the bones (255). In other words, the unacceptable emotions have not again been aroused. His last words, a Latin phrase from the Mass for the Dead meaning "rest in peace," suggest that only through his heinous crime has he found release from the torment of his own hatred.

For Further Reading: Psychoanalytic Criticism

Freud, Sigmund. *The Interpretation of Dreams.* 1900.

Gardner, Shirley N., ed. *The (M)other Tongue: Essays in Feminist Psychoanalytic Interpretation.* 1985.

Hartman, Geoffrey H., ed. *Psychoanalysis and the Question of the Text.* 1979.

Kris, Ernst. *Psychoanalytic Explorations in Art.* 1952.

Kristeva, Julia. *Desire in Language.* 1980.

Nelson, Benjamin, ed. *Sigmund Freud on Creativity and the Unconscious.* 1958.

Wright, Elizabeth. *Psychoanalytic Criticism: Theory in Practice.* 1984.

 ## Structuralism

Structuralism, a literary movement with roots in linguistics and anthropology, concentrates on literature as a system of signs that have no inherent meaning except in their agreed-upon or conventional relation to one another. Structuralism is usually described by its proponents not as a new way to interpret literary works but rather as a way to understand how works of literature come to have meaning. Because structuralism developed from linguistic theory, some structuralists use linguistic approaches to literature. When they talk about literary texts, they use the terms (such as *morpheme* and *phoneme*) that linguists use as they study the nature of language. Many structuralists, however, use the linguistic model as an analogy. To understand the analogy, you need to know a bit of linguistic theory.

The French linguist Ferdinand de Saussure (*Course in General Linguistics,* 1915) suggested that the relationship between an object and the name we use to designate it is purely arbitrary. What, for example, makes "C-A-T" signify a small, furry animal with pointed ears and whiskers? Only our learned expectation makes us associate *cat* with the family feline pet. Had we grown up in France, we would make the same association with *chat*, or in Mexico with *gato*. The words we use to designate objects (linguists call these words *signs*) make sense only within the large context of our entire language system and will not be understood as meaningful by someone who does not know that language system. Further, Saussure pointed out, signs become truly useful only when we use them to designate difference. For instance, the word *cat* becomes useful when we want to differentiate a small furry animal that meows from a small furry animal that barks. Saussure was interested in how language, as a structure of conventions, worked. He asked intriguing questions about the underlying rules that allow this made-up structure of signs to work, and, as a result, his pioneering study caught the interest of scholars in many fields.

Many literary scholars saw linguistic structuralism as analogous to the study of literary works. Literary structuralism leads readers to think of poems, short stories, novels, and plays not as self-contained and individual entities that have some kind of inherent meaning but rather as part of a larger literary system. To fully appreciate and analyze the work, the reader must understand the system within which it operates. Like linguistic structuralism, literary structuralism focuses on the importance of difference. We must, for example, understand the difference between the structure of poetry and the structure of prose before we can make sense of William Carlos Williams's "Red Wheelbarrow" (p. 563):

> so much depends
> upon
> a red wheel
> barrow

Readers unacquainted with the conventions of poetry would find those lines meaningless and confusing, although if they knew the conventions of prose, they would readily understand this sentence:

> So much depends upon a red wheelbarrow.

The way we interpret any group of "signs," then, depends on how they are structured and on the way we understand the system that governs their structure.

Structuralists believe that literature is basically artificial because although it uses the same "signs" as everyday language, whose purpose is to give information, the purpose of literature is *not* primarily to relay data. For example, a poem like Dylan Thomas's "Do not go gentle into that good night" (p. 710) is written in the linguistic form of a series of commands, yet the poem goes much further than that. Its meaning is created not only by our understanding the lines as a series of commands but also by our recognition of the poetic form, the rhyming conventions, and the figures of speech that Thomas uses. We can only fully discuss the poem within the larger context of our literary knowledge.

Structuralism also provides the foundation for poststructuralism, a theoretical movement that informs the fields of deconstructionist and New Historicist criticism and has influenced the work of many psychoanalytic and sociological critics. Although structuralists claim that language functions by arbitrarily connecting words (signifiers) to ideas (signifieds), poststructuralists develop the implications of this claim, arguing that because the connection of a word to an idea is purely arbitrary, any operation of language is inherently unstable. Poststructuralists believe that to study a literary text is to study a continuously shifting set of meanings.

A Structuralist Reading: William Faulkner's "Barn Burning" (p. 256)

A structuralist reading tries to bring to light some of the assumptions about language and form that we are likely to take for granted. Looking at the opening paragraph of Faulkner's "Barn Burning," from the point of view of structuralist criticism, you might first look at an interpretation that reads the passage as a stream of Sarty's thoughts. The structuralist critic might then consider the assumptions a reader would have to make to see what Faulkner has written as the thoughts of an illiterate child. Next, the structuralist might look at evidence to suggest the language in this section operates outside the system of language that would be available to Sarty and that, therefore, "Barn Burning" opens not with a simple recounting of the main character's thoughts but rather with something far more complex.

The opening paragraph of William Faulkner's "Barn Burning" is often read as an excursion into the mind of Sarty, the story's young protagonist. When we read the passage closely, however, we note that a supposedly simple consciousness is represented in a highly complex way. For Sarty— uneducated and illiterate—the "scarlet devils" and "silver curve of fish" on the labels of food tins serve as direct signs appealing to his hunger. It is unlikely, however, that Sarty could consciously understand what he sees and express it as metaphor. We cannot, then, read this opening passage as a recounting of the thoughts that pass through Sarty's mind. Instead, these complex sentences and images offer possibilities that reach beyond the limits of Sarty's linguistic system.

Because our own knowledge is wider than Sarty's, the visual images the narrator describes take on meanings for us that are unavailable to the young boy. For example, like Sarty, we know that the "scarlet devils" stand for deviled ham. Yet the devils also carry another possible con-notation. They may indicate evil and thus serve to emphasize the despair and grief Sarty feels are ever present. So we are given images that flash through the mind of an illiterate young boy, apparently intended to sug-gest his poverty and ignorance (he cannot read the words on the labels), yet we are led to see a highly complicated set of meanings. When we encounter later in the passage Sarty's articulated thought, "*our enemy . . . ourn! mine and hisn both! . . .* ," his down-to-earth dialect shows clearly the sharp distinction between the system of language the narrator uses to describe Sarty's view of the store shelves and the system of language Sarty uses to describe what he sees and feels.

For Further Reading: Structuralism

Barthes, Roland. *Critical Essays.* 1964.

Culler, Jonathan. *Structuralist Poetics.* 1975.

Greimas, A. J. *Structured Semantics: An Attempt at a Method.* Trans. McDowell, Schleifer, and Velie. 1983.

Hawkes, Terence. *Structuralism and Semiotics.* 1977.

Lentricchia, Frank. *After the New Criticism.* 1980.

Pettit, Philip. *The Concept of Structuralism: A Critical Analysis.* 1975.

Scholes, Robert. *Structuralism in Literature: An Introduction.* 1974.

Deconstruction

Deconstruction is a literary movement that developed from structuralism. Deconstructionists argue that every text contains within it some ingredient undermining its purported system of meaning. In other words, the structure that seems to hold the text together is unstable because it depends on the conclusions of a particular ideology (for instance, the idea that women are inferior to men or that peasants are content with their lowly position in life), conclusions that are not as natural as the text may pretend. The practice of finding the point at which the text falls apart because of these internal inconsistencies is called deconstruction.

Deconstructive theorists share with formalists and structuralists a concern for the work itself rather than for biographical, historical, or ideological influences. Like formalists, deconstructionists focus on possibilities for multiple meanings within texts. However, while formalists seek to explain paradox by discovering tensions and ironies that can lead to a unified reading, deconstructionists insist on the primacy of multiple possibilities. They maintain that any given text is capable of yielding many divergent readings, all of which are equally valid yet may in some way undermine and oppose one another.

Like structuralists, deconstructionists see literary texts as part of larger systems of discourse. A key structuralist technique is identifying opposites in an attempt to show the structure of language used in a work. Having identified the opposites, the structuralist rests the case. Deconstructionists, however, go further. Jacques Derrida, a French philosopher, noticed that these oppositions do not simply reflect linguistic structures but are the linguistic response to the way people deal with their beliefs (their ideologies). For instance, if you believe strongly that democracy is the best possible form of government, you tend to lump other forms of government into the category "nondemocracies." If a government is nondemocratic, that—not its other distinguishing characteristics—would be significant to you. This typical ideological response operates in all kinds of areas of belief, even ones we are not aware of. Deconstructionists contend that texts tend to give away their ideological biases by means of this opposition.

Derrida called this distinction between "A" and "Not-A" (rather than between "A" and "B") *différance*, a word he coined to suggest a concept represented by the French verb *différer*, which has two meanings: "to be different" and "to defer." (Note that in Derrida's new term an *a* is substituted for an *e*—a distinction that can be seen in writing but not heard in speaking.) When a deconstructionist uncovers *différance* through careful examination of a text, he or she also finds an (often unwitting) ideological bias. Deconstructionists argue that the reader must transcend such ideological biases and must instead acknowledge contradictory possibilities as equally worthy of consideration. No one meaning can or should be designated as correct.

Deconstruction, then, is not really a system of criticism (and, in fact, deconstructionists resist being labeled as a school of criticism). Rather, deconstruction offers a way to take apart a literary text and thereby reveal its separate layers. Deconstructionists often focus on the metaphorical nature of language, claiming that all language is basically metaphoric because the sign we use to designate any given object or action stands apart from the object itself. In fact, deconstructionists believe that all writing is essentially literary and metaphorical because language, by its very nature, can only *stand for* what we call reality or truth; it cannot *be* reality or truth.

A major contribution of deconstructive critics lies in their playful approach to language and to literary criticism. They refuse to accept as absolute any one way of reading poetry, fiction, or drama, and they guard against what they see as the fixed conclusions and arbitrary operating assumptions of many schools of criticism.

A Deconstructionist Reading: Flannery O'Connor's "A Good Man Is Hard to Find" (p. 295)

A deconstructionist reading of Flannery O'Connor's "A Good Man Is Hard to Find" might challenge the essentially religious interpretations the author offered of her own stories in essays and letters. If you were applying deconstructionist criticism to the story, you might argue that the author's reading of the story is no more valid than anyone else's, and that the story can just as legitimately be read as an investigation of the functions of irony in language.

> Flannery O'Connor explained that the grotesque and violent aspects of her stories are intended to shock the reader into recognizing the inhospitable nature of the world and thereby recognizing the universal human need for divine grace. The last sentence of "A Good Man Is Hard to Find" is spoken by The Misfit, who has just murdered a family of travelers: "It's no real pleasure in life" (309). However, the language of O'Connor's stories is extremely ironic—that is, her narrators and characters often say one thing but mean another. So, it is possible that their statements are not empirically true but are representations of a persona or elements of a story they have created using language.
>
> The Grandmother, for example, lives almost entirely in fictions—newspaper clippings, stories for the grandchildren, her belief that The Misfit is a good man. In contrast, The Misfit is more literal than the Grandmother in his perception of reality. He knows, for example, whether the car turned over once or twice. But he too is posing, at first as the tough guy who rejects religious and societal norms by saying, ". . . it's nothing for you to do but enjoy the few minutes you got left the best way you can—by killing somebody or burning down his house or doing some other meanness to him. No pleasure but meanness . . ." (308). Finally, he poses as the pessimist—or, according to O'Connor's reading, the Christian—who claims, "It's no real pleasure in life." The contradictions in The Misfit's language make it impossible to tell which of these facades is "real."

For Further Reading: Deconstruction

Abrams, M. H. "Rationality and the Imagination in Cultural History." *Critical Inquiry* 2 (1976): 447–64. (Abrams claims deconstructionists are parasites who depend on other critics to come up with interpretations that can be deconstructed.)

Arac, Jonathan, Wlad Godzich, and Wallace Martin, eds. *The Yale Critics: Deconstruction in America.* 1983.

Berman, Art. *From the New Criticism to Deconstruction.* 1988.

Culler, Jonathan. *On Deconstruction: Theory and Criticism after Structuralism.* 1982.

Jefferson, Ann. "Structuralism and Post-Structuralism." *Modern Literary Theory: A Comparative Introduction.* 1982.

Johnson, Barbara. *The Critical Difference: Essays in the Contemporary Rhetoric of Reading.* 1980.

Leitsch, Vincent B. *Deconstructive Theory and Practice.* 1982.

Lynn, Steven. "A Passage into Critical Theory." *College English* 52 (1990): 258–71.

Miller, J. Hillis. "The Critic as Host." *Deconstruction and Criticism.* Ed. Harold Bloom et al. 1979. (a response to Abrams's article, listed above)

Norris, Christopher. *Deconstruction: Theory and Practice.* 1982.

 Cultural Studies

Cultural studies is a particularly difficult field of criticism to define for a number of reasons. Chief among these is the scope of the field. Literary theory has typically focused on literature—however defined—while bringing in knowledge about a work's historical context or the life and views of the author as a means of better understanding the work. Cultural studies, on the other hand, treats any and all objects produced by a society as worthy of the same kind of analysis that literary texts receive. Thus, the advertisements for Arthur Miller's *Death of a Salesman*, or the diary of an actual traveling salesman might, to a cultural critic, be as interesting and complex as Miller's play itself.

Given that the work of art no longer occupies a privileged position relative to other artifacts, it is not surprising that cultural critics have tended to call into question the relative merit of what we have traditionally thought of as masterpieces. To say that one work is "better" than another, such critics would argue, is an almost meaningless statement, and one that reveals more about the values of the person making it than about the work itself. Many cultural critics would therefore reject altogether the idea of a literary canon, or a list of great works that an educated person should know. At the very least, cultural critics would argue, any canon must be subject to constant examination and revision.

Cultural studies has roots in both the French structuralism of critics such as Roland Barthes and the Cultural Materialism of British critics such as Raymond Williams. In his classic text *Mythologies* (1957), Barthes began to apply structural analysis not simply to texts but to phenomena in popular culture—professional wrestling, for example. Williams came at similar subject matter from a different angle. Mass culture has traditionally been viewed by Marxists as something imposed on the working classes and the disadvantaged by upper and bourgeoisie classes seeking to maintain their own position. Williams, while acknowledging the truth in such an assertion, distinguished between mass culture and popular culture, noting that the latter can be used by those outside of power as a means of self-expression and even rebellion. It is not surprising that there is a distinctly political edge to cultural studies, and that many of its practitioners see themselves as activists and their research as a means to effect social change.

There are a number of distinct schools—New Historicism, postcolonialism, American multiculturalism, and queer theory—that are often, though not always, placed under the heading of cultural studies. Of these four, the broadest is New Historicism. Its assumptions—that a work cannot be discussed in isolation from the culture that gave rise to it—are shared by most critics in the other schools, and it might be described as much as a method as a school. Postcolonialism, American multiculturalism, and queer theory can all be seen as applications of the principles of cultural studies—particularly its awareness of power relationships and its questioning of traditional canons—to specific geographical areas and cultures.

New Historicism

New Historicism relates a text to the historical and cultural contexts of the period in which it was created and the periods in which it was critically evaluated. These contexts are not considered simply as "background" but as integral parts of a text. According to the New Historicists, history is not objective facts; rather, like literature, history is subject to interpretation and reinterpretation depending on the power structure of a society. Louis Althusser, for example, suggests that ideology intrudes in the discourse of an era, subjecting readers to the interests of the ruling establishment. Michel Foucault argues that the discourse of an era defines the nature of "truth" and what behaviors are acceptable, sane, or criminal. "Truth," according to Foucault, is produced by the interaction of power and the systems in which the power flows, and it changes as society changes. Mikhail Bakhtin suggests that all discourse is dialogic, containing within it many independent and sometimes conflicting voices.

Literature, in the opinion of the New Historicist critics, cannot be interpreted without reference to the time and place in which it was written. Criticism likewise cannot be evaluated without reference to the time and place in which it was written. A flaw of much criticism, according to the New

Historicists, is the consideration of a literary text as if it were an organic whole. Such an approach ignores the diversity of conflicting voices in a text and in the cultural context in which a text is embedded. Indeed, Stephen Greenblatt prefers the term "cultural poetics" to New Historicism because it acknowledges the integral role that literature and art play in the culture of any era. Works of art and literature, according to Greenblatt, actively foster subversive elements or voices but somehow constrain those forces in ways that defuse challenges to the dominant culture.

New Historicists also point out that readers, like texts, are influenced and shaped by the cultural context of their eras and that a thoroughly objective "reading" of a text is therefore impossible. Acknowledging that all readers to some degree "appropriate" a text, some New Historicists present their criticism of texts as "negotiations" between past and present contexts. Thus, criticism of a particular work of literature would draw from both the cultural context of the era in which the text was written and the critic's present cultural context, and the critic would acknowledge how the latter context influences interpretation of the former.

Since the early 1970s, feminist critics have adopted some New Historicist positions, focusing on male–female power conflicts. And critics interested in multicultural texts have stressed the role of the dominant white culture in suppressing or marginalizing the texts of nonwhites. Marxist critics, including Raymond Williams, have adopted the term "cultural materialism" in discussing their mode of New Historicism, which focuses on the political significance of a literary text.

A New Historicist Reading: Charlotte Perkins Gilman's "The Yellow Wallpaper" (p. 434)

A New Historicist scholar might write an essay about "The Yellow Wallpaper" as an illustration of the destructive effects of the patriarchal culture of the late nineteenth century on women. This reading would be vastly different from that of most nineteenth-century critics, who interpreted the story as a harrowing case study of female mental illness. Even some early-twentieth-century readings posited that the narrator's mental illness is the result of her individual psychological problems. In a New Historicist reading, however, you might focus on the social conventions of the time, which produced conflicting discourses that drove the narrator to madness.

> The female narrator of "The Yellow Wallpaper," who is writing in her private journal (which is the text of the short story), explains that her husband, a physician, has diagnosed her as having a "temporary nervous depression—a slight hysterical tendency" (434). She says she should believe such a physician "of high standing" (434) and cooperate with his treatment, which is to confine her to a room in an isolated country estate and compel her to rest and have no visitors and not to write. The "cure" is intended to reduce her nervousness, she further explains. But as the story unfolds, the narrator reveals that she suspects the treatment will not

cure her because it leaves her alone with her thoughts without even her writing to occupy her mind. Her husband's "cure" forces her into a passive role and eliminates any possibility of asserting her own personality. However, she guiltily suggests that her own lack of confidence in her husband's diagnosis may be what is preventing her cure.

The text of "The Yellow Wallpaper" can be divided into at least two conflicting discourses: (1) the masculine discourse of the husband, who has the authority both of a highly respected physician and of a husband, two positions reinforced by the patriarchal culture of the time; and (2) the feminine discourse of the narrator, whose hesitant personal voice contradicts the masculine voice but undermines itself because it keeps reminding her that women should obey their husbands and their physicians. A third discourse underlies the two dominant ones—that of the gothic horror tale, a popular genre of the late nineteenth century. The narrator in "The Yellow Wallpaper" is isolated against her will in a room with barred windows in an almost deserted palatial country mansion she describes as "The most beautiful place!" (435). She is at the mercy of her captor, in this case her husband. She is not sure whether she is hallucinating, and she thinks the mansion may be haunted. She does not know whom to trust, not being sure whether her husband really wants to "cure" her or to punish her for expressing her rebellion.

The narrator learns to hide her awareness of the conflicting discourses. She avoids mentioning her thoughts and fears about her illness or her fancies about the house being haunted, and she hides her writing. She speaks reasonably and in "a very quiet voice" (442). But this inability to speak freely to anyone is a kind of torture, and alone in her room with the barred windows, she takes up discourse with the wallpaper. At first she describes it as "One of those sprawling flamboyant patterns committing every artistic sin" (436). But she is fascinated by the pattern, which has been distorted by mildew and by the tearing away of some sections. The narrator begins to strip off the wallpaper to free a woman she thinks is trapped inside; and, eventually, she visualizes herself as that woman, trapped yet freed by the destruction of the wallpaper. The narrator retreats, or escapes into madness, driven there by the multiple discourses she cannot resolve.

For Further Reading: New Historicist Criticism

Brook, Thomas. *The New Historicism and Other Old Fashioned Topics.* 1991.

Coates, Christopher. "What Was the New Historicism?" *Centennial Review* 32.2 (Spring 1993): 267–80.

Geertz, Clifford. "Thick Description: Toward an Interpretive Theory of Culture." *The Interpretation of Cultures.* By Clifford Geertz. 1973.

Greenblatt, Stephen, ed. *Representing the English Renaissance.* 1988.

Levin, David. "American Historicism: Old and New." *American Literary History* 6.3 (Fall 1994): 527–38.

Rabinov, Paul, ed. *The Foucault Reader.* 1986.

Veeser, H. Aram, ed. *The New Historicism.* 1989.

Queer Theory

The roots of queer theory go back to the 1960s and 1970s, when movements for gay liberation and changing attitudes toward sexuality in general made it easier for artists and critics to identify themselves as gay and lesbian and to deal directly with gay and lesbian themes in their work. Critical examination of these subjects intensified during the 1980s, partly in response to the AIDS crisis. By the early 1990s, the term "queer theory," coined by Teresa de Lauretis, came to be used as an umbrella term for the work being done by critics such as Eve Kosofsky Sedgwick and Judith Butler.

The actual scope of queer theory is significantly broader than the name might imply: queer theorists tend to doubt prevailing notions of sexual identity as something fixed by biology or even by personal inclination since a person might find different means of sexual expression appealing at different points. Queer theory therefore calls into question terms such as *homosexual, heterosexual, bisexual, transsexual,* and *transgender*. It also examines sympathetically those aspects of sexuality that, while not necessarily "queer" in the sense of "gay," have nonetheless been marginalized—cross-dressing, for example, or sadomasochism.

When applying queer theory to texts, critics tend to be particularly interested in those ways in which the text blurs or subverts traditional notions of sexual identity, notions that tend to rely on "heteronormativity"—the idea that heterosexuality is the statistical, and even moral, standard and that all departures from it are perverse or problematic. These blurrings in the text occur not only in contemporary literature but also in works from the past, where they were perhaps missed because of the ideological prejudices of earlier critics.

Given queer theory's emphasis on gender, there are inevitably points of contact with feminist criticism. Critics such as Judith Butler, however, have argued that feminists have been too quick to regard gender, however defined, as something fixed. Queer theory has connections to gay and lesbian activism, but those connections are sometimes strained because activists are often trying to gain recognition or respect for those with a given sexual identity, while queer theorists are more likely to call into question *all* identities. Like other schools within the field of cultural studies, critics employing queer theory often examine cultural artifacts such as film, music, and television programs, in this case for messages that may subtly subvert heteronormativity. For example, there has been considerable interest within queer studies in the ways that Madonna has portrayed sexuality.

In theoretical terms, queer theory's biggest debt has been to the deconstructionists, particularly to Michel Foucault, and to his groundbreaking work, *The History of Sexuality*. Among the foundational works in the field are Butler's *Gender Trouble* and Sedgwick's *Epistemology of the Closet*.

A Queer Theory Reading: Zadie Smith's "The Girl with Bangs" (p. 187)

A queer theory reading of Zadie Smith's "The Girl with Bangs" might focus on the ways in which sexual desire in the story seems related less to gender as it is commonly conceived than to the attraction between individuals. A critic might argue, in fact, that the story as a whole calls into question the validity of gender roles.

In Zadie Smith's "The Girl with Bangs," the narrator enters into her first relationship with another woman, one that leaves her with a new perspective on sexual relationships and on herself. However, the narrator does not think in terms of gay and straight. Rather, she describes herself as being "a boy" in her relationship with Charlotte Greaves.

Male and female, in the eyes of the narrator, are designations that have less to do with physical gender than with gender roles. Because she is the one who pursues Charlotte, and because she is the one who figuratively waits beneath Charlotte's window, she sees herself in the male role, that of the pursuer. Because she finds herself helpless to resist Charlotte— a situation she has never encountered with a man—she thinks, "So this is what it's like being a boy" (190). When Maurice comes to ask her to give up Charlotte, she describes their talk—with only partial irony—as "man-to-man."

The narrator agrees to end her relationship with Charlotte, but when she and Maurice go to speak with Charlotte, they find her in bed with another man. Charlotte's sexual openness—she apparently has sex with anyone, of either gender, whenever she wants—represents another challenge to the heteronormativity of society and to its conventions of monogamy. Her eventual marriage to Maurice might seem at first a surrender to that norm, but the story certainly hints that Maurice will regret the marriage because nothing indicates that Charlotte will suddenly stop sleeping with other people.

Interestingly, the story concludes with the narrator identifying not—as she has during the affair with Charlotte—with men, but with a woman, the woman Maurice has been sleeping with in Thailand. For the duration of the affair, she viewed men as helpless, a view at odds with much of the stereotypical rhetoric of manliness—though not with the conventions of traditional courting. She pictured men, and herself with them, as standing beneath the beloved's window, waiting to catch whatever she might throw down. Now she says that "in the real world, or so it seems to me, it is almost always women and not men who are waiting under windows, and they are almost always disappointed. In this matter Charlotte was unusual" (193).

To say that Charlotte was "unusual" is to say that she was odd, or, in the broadest sense of the word, "queer." What is "queerest" about Charlotte, then, may not be her bisexuality or promiscuity, but her ability to remain free of the negative emotional consequences her existence as a woman in a male-dominated society would typically bring with it.

For Further Reading: Queer Theory

Butler, Judith. *Bodies That Matter: On the Discursive Limits of "Sex."* 1993.

Halperin, David. *Homosexuality: A Cultural Construct.* 1990.

————. *One Hundred Years of Homosexuality.* 1990.

Jagose, Annamarie. *Queer Theory: An Introduction.* 1997.

Parker, Andrew. *After Sex?: On Writing Since Queer Theory.* 2007.

Sedgwick, Eve Kosofsky. *Between Men: English Literature and Male Homosocial Desire.* 1985.

Spargo, Tamsin. *Foucault and Queer Theory.* 1999.

Thomas, Calvin (ed.). *Straight with a Twist: Queer Theory and the Subject of Heterosexuality.* 1999.

Postcolonial Studies

In the years following World War II, the period of European colonization came to a close as first one country and then another gained its independence from the countries—England, France, Belgium—that had controlled them. In most cases, these newly independent countries were substantially different from how they had been prior to colonization; some, in fact, had actually been created by colonization, their borders having been determined by foreign powers. The colonial powers typically introduced their own languages as the languages of government in these countries, and the educational systems they introduced for both the European and native populations of the colonies were likewise modeled on those in Europe.

Writers in former colonies who began to write after the end of colonial rule, then, inherited an often uncomfortable mix of cultural tools and assumptions. On the one hand, many of them had been educated to appreciate European works of literature, and many of them wrote most naturally in European languages. On the other hand, they saw everywhere around them a culture that was very different from that of its former European masters, and which those masters tended to regard as inferior and less civilized. The tension that results from this cultural mix is one of the chief subjects of postcolonial theory and research. In addition, although colonialism has more or less formally ended, many critics would argue that European and other western countries continue to dominate their former colonial possessions in a cultural and economic sense, a domination called **neo-colonialism**.

Postcolonial critics do not necessarily restrict themselves to the literatures of those countries that the European powers have left. Australia, New Zealand, and Canada, for example, were all colonies, and some critics would regard any literature produced in such countries, including that by authors of European descent, to be an appropriate subject of study for postcolonialism. Others would argue that such writers belong to a European tradition and would use the adjective *postcolonial* to describe only the works written by authors from the indigenous populations of those countries.

Nor do postcolonial critics restrict themselves to looking at works produced since the end of the colonial period. Canonical European texts are of special interest to these critics, especially for the light they shed on the ways in which the colonizers viewed the colonized. The character of Caliban in Shakespeare's *The Tempest*, for instance, has been the focus of much debate about what his brutish nature reveals about the views of Shakespeare and the England in which he lived toward the native peoples being encountered by European explorers.

One of the foundational texts of postcolonialism is Edward Said's *Orientalism* (1978), which examined the ways in which Europeans and Americans view, and have viewed, peoples in developing nations (often known as the Third World). Other important works include *The Location of Culture* (1994) by Homi Bhaba and the essay "Under Western Eyes" (1986) by Chandra Talpade Mohanty.

A Postcolonial Reading: Jhumpa Lahiri's 2000 short story "The Third and Final Continent"

A postcolonial reading of "The Third and Final Continent" by Jhumpa Lahiri might look at the differences the narrator notices between his native culture and those of England and the United States. It might also examine the process of his gradual assimilation to American culture, and his own sense of the cultural distance he has traveled.

Jhumpa Lahiri's short story "The Third and Final Continent" relates the thoughts of an Indian emigrant as he adjusts to western society. As a citizen of a country that gained its independence from Great Britain less than twenty years earlier—and after his own birth—the narrator is very much in the position of a provincial visiting the imperial homeland. He lives with other Indians—specifically with other Bengalis—and they eat Indian food and listen to Indian music, but many of their habits are English. For example, they drink tea, smoke English cigarettes, and watch cricket matches.

The narrator arrives in the United States on the day of the first moon landing. The symbolism of this is particularly appropriate since the American astronauts have literally gone to another world, something the narrator does metaphorically. The moment also marks, again literally, the height of American power. At that moment, America is the most powerful country in the world, much as Great Britain was when it first subjugated India. To plant a flag on a piece of land has traditionally been a way of claiming that land for the country represented by the flag.

In the time the narrator spends with Mrs. Croft each evening while staying in her house, the acknowledgment of American supremacy becomes a kind of religious ritual. Each time Mrs. Croft observes that there is an American flag on the moon, the narrator is expected to reply, loudly enough so that the old women can hear him, "Splendid!" The narrator himself had not thought very much about the moon landing despite the reports of it in the paper—and despite the fact that he is a librarian at the

Massachusetts Institute of Technology. His values and the values of the American culture in which he finds himself are very different.

His stay with Mrs. Croft also reveals to him the enormous difference between Indian and American attitudes toward family. It shocks the narrator to learn that a woman one hundred and three years old would be living alone, and the story of her fortitude after the death of her husband is in marked contrast to his own mother's descent into madness after the death of her husband. At the same time, the narrator and Mrs. Croft seem to have a special understanding. The culture he comes from, with its strict rules of propriety, is in some ways reminiscent of the America in which Mrs. Croft lived as a young woman, a point made clear when the old woman, on seeing the narrator's new wife dressed in her traditional Indian clothes, acknowledges that she is truly a lady.

For Further Reading: Postcolonial Studies

Ashcroft, Bill, Gareth Griffiths, and Helen Tiffin. *The Empire Writes Back: Theory and Practice in Post-Colonial Literatures.* 1989.

Chaterjee, Para. *Nationalist Thought in the Colonial World: A Derivative Discourse.* 1993.

Gandhi, Leela. *Postcolonial Theory: A Critical Introduction.* 1998.

Loomba, Ania. *Colonialism/Postcolonialism.* 1998.

Nandy, Ashis. *The Intimate Enemy: Loss and Recovery of Self under Colonialism.* 1983.

Poddar, Prem, and David Johnson. *A Historical Companion of Postcolonial Thought.* 2005.

Said, Edward. *Culture and Imperialism.* 1994.

Williams, Patrick, and Laura Chrisman, eds. *Colonial Discourse and Post-colonial Theory: A Reader.* 1994.

Young, Robert. *Colonial Desire: Hybridity in Theory, Culture, and Race.* 1995.

———. *Postcolonialism: An Historical Introduction.* 2001.

American Multiculturalism

Since its beginnings, America has been home to people from an increasing number of different cultures, many of which have retained distinct identities and traditions over time. Many of these groups came willingly, as immigrants from Europe and other places, while others—African slaves in particular—did not. And, of course, the Native Americans were here before any of the waves of European immigration. That America is multiethnic has long been recognized—it is an unarguable fact. That America is, and ought to be, multicultural—that is, that it is not one culture but many, and that all its cultures are equally valuable—is a position that has gained increasing support in recent decades, particularly since the civil rights movements of the 1950s and 1960s.

One of the chief goals of multicultural critics has been to increase the visibility of literature produced by members of minority groups in the United States. Another has been to create a critical environment in which these works can be properly appreciated. (Since many works by minority authors were written out of a set of assumptions different from those of the dominant culture, such a critical environment could not be assumed.) Multicultural critics have drawn attention to those features of writing by different groups that are distinctive.

Much multicultural criticism so far has focused on the writing of African Americans. The emphasis on this group has been due in part to the sheer number of its members, and in part to the sense that they had been excluded from American public life in a more profound and violent way than any other group. No doubt a further reason is that the African American struggle for equality and freedom has been so central to America's attempts at self-definition. At the same time, Native American, Asian American, and Latino writers, as well as writers of other backgrounds, have attracted an increasing amount of both critical attention and popular success. More recently, the field of ethnic studies has brought attention to the unique accomplishments of groups such as Irish, Italian, and Arab Americans. At the same time, religious studies scholars have looked at the cultures and cultural products of different religious groups, groups that often cut across ethnic and racial boundaries.

Multiculturalism shares many points of contact with cultural studies in general—for example, a willingness to investigate literature traditionally excluded from the canon and a suspicion of the categories of "high" and "low" art. Along with Marxist and New Historicist criticism, it shares an awareness of the ways in which writers and the texts they produce are shaped by societal conditions, and the ways in which those conditions are enforced and defended by those in power.

Important texts in the study of multicultural literature include Henry Louis Gates's *The Signifying Monkey: A Theory of African-American Literary Criticism* (1988), *Beyond Ethnicity: Consent and Descent in American Culture* (1987) by Werner Sollar, and Robert Allen Warrior's *Tribal Secrets: Recovering American Indian Intellectual Traditions* (1995).

An American Multicultural Reading: Alice Walker's "Everyday Use" (p. 344)

A multicultural reading of "Everyday Use" might focus on the quilt that the narrator decides to give to Maggie, rather than to Dee, and on its connection to African American history. Such a reading might also look at the ways in which the narrator's relationship to that history differs from Dee's.

> African American art has often been functional—that is, it is meant to be used. The quilts that become the subject of contention in Alice Walker's "Everyday Use" are an example of this type of art. In fact, the title of the story is a specific reference to the functionality of the handmade things that Dee wants to take with her from her family home. Given Dee's newfound interest in African and African American culture, it is striking that she is unable to appreciate this fact, which seems so obvious to her mother and sister.

Dee seems interested in the history of her people, and of her family, chiefly when she is able to view them as exotic. At times, it seems that she has come to visit her family largely because she sees their home as a kind of museum of black culture. She wants nearly everything in and around the house that she lays eyes on, but she wants them as curios or decorations, not as the functioning butter churns, dashers, and quilts that they are. She was named after her mother's sister, and after her grandmother, but she has taken a new, supposedly more African name: Wangero. She wants the artifacts these women have left behind but not their name.

It would be going too far to say that Walker is simply condemning Dee as shallow. Dee does genuinely admire the artifacts she wants to take with her, and she does want them in part because of the connection they have to members of her own family. Her failing—and this is where the story is at its most subtle—is that, in contrast with Maggie, she *needs* these artifacts to maintain a connection with her family's past. What convinces the narrator of the story to save the quilts for Maggie is the way in which Maggie relinquishes her claim to them: "She can have them, Mama . . . I can 'member Grandma Dee without the quilts" (351).

Dee's last words to her mother and sister neatly sum up her contradictory relationship to them and to the tradition they represent. After saying that her mother doesn't understand her own heritage, she turns to Maggie and says, "You ought to try to make something of yourself, too, Maggie. It's really a new day for us. But from the way you and mama still live you'd never know it" (352). Dee wants to be free of all the negative aspects that have defined the African American experience, yet at the same time she wants to position herself as the heir to that culture. It isn't—it can't be— that simple.

For Further Reading: American Multiculturalism

Allen, Paula Gunn. *The Sacred Hoop: Recovering the Feminine in American Indian Traditions.* 1986.

Anzaldúa, Gloria. *Borderlands/La Frontera: The New Mestiza.* 1987.

Awkward, Michael. *Inspiriting Influences: Tradition, Revision, and Afro-American Literature.* 1989.

Berkovitch, Sacvan. *The Rites of Ascent: Transformations in the Symbolic Construction of America.* 1981.

Ferraro, Thomas J. *Ethnic Passages: Literary Immigrants in Twentieth-Century America.* 1993.

Gates, Henry Louis, Jr. (ed.). *Race, Writing and Difference.* 1985.

Goldberg, David Theo, ed. *Multiculturalism: A Critical Reader.* 1994.

Morrison, Toni. *Playing in the Dark: Whiteness and the Literary Imagination.* 1993.

Pulitano, Elvira. *Toward a Native American Critical Theory.* 2003.

West, Thomas R. *Signs of Struggle: The Rhetorical Politics of Cultural Difference.* 2002.

TEXT CREDITS

Francisco X. Alarcón "'Mexican' Is Not A Noun" from *The Other Side of Night/Del otro lado de la noche*. Copyright © 2002 by Francisco X. Alarcón. Reprinted by permission of University of Arizona Press.

Sherman Alexie reprinted from "The Summer of Black Widows" © 1996 by Sherman Alexie, by permission of Hanging Loose Press.

Sherman Alexie "This Is What It Means to Say Phoenix, Arizona" from THE LONE RANGER AND TONTO FISTFIGHT IN HEAVEN. Copyright © 1993 by Sherman Alexie. Used by permission of Grove/Atlantic, Inc.

Agha Shahid Ali from *A Walk Through the Yellow Pages* by Agha Shahid Ali, published by SUN-Gemini Press. © 1987 by Agha Shahid Ali. Used with permission. All rights reserved.

Julia Alvarez from HOMECOMING. Copyright © 1984, 1996 by Julia Alvarez. Published by Plume, an imprint of The Penguin Group (USA), and originally published by Grove Press. By permission of Susan Bergholz Literary Services, New York, NY and Lamy, NM. All rights reserved.

Julia Alvarez from HOW THE GARCIA GIRLS LOST THEIR ACCENTS. Copyright © 1991 by Julia Alvarez. Published by Algonquin Books of Chapel

Hill. By permission of Susan Bergholz Literary Services, New York, NY and Lamy, NM. All rights reserved.

A. R. Ammons "Coming Right Up," from THE REALLY SHORT POEMS OF A. R. AMMONS by A. R. Ammons. Copyright © 1990 by A. R. Ammons. Used by permission of W. W. Norton & Company.

Margaret Atwood "The City Planners" from THE CIRCLE GAME. Copyright © 1966, 1998 by Margaret Atwood. Reprinted with the permission of House of Anansi Press, Toronto.

Margaret Atwood "you fit into me" from SELECTED POEMS 1965–1975. Copyright © 1976 by Margaret Atwood. Reprinted with the permission of House of Anansi Press, Toronto.

W. H. Auden "*Musée* des Beaux Arts," copyright © 1940 and renewed 1968 by W. H. Auden, from COLLECTED POEMS OF W. H. AUDEN by W. H. Auden. Used by permission of Random House, Inc.

Matsuo Bashō "Four Haiku" from THE PENGUIN BOOK OF JAPANESE VERSE, translated by Geoffrey Bownas and Anthony Thwaite. Translation copyright © 1964, 1998 by Geoffrey Bownas and Anthony Thwaite. Reprinted with the permission of the translators.

QUARTERLY. Reprinted with the permission of the author.

A. E. Housman "Loveliest of Trees," from *Modern British Poetry*, ed. Louis Untermeyer, 1920.

Robert Huff THE VENTRILOQUIST, p. 39. © 1977 by the Rector and Visitors of the University of Virginia. Reprinted by permission of The University of Virginia Press.

Langston Hughes "Harlem (2) ['What happens to a dream deferred...']" from THE COLLECTED POEMS OF LANGSTON HUGHES by Langston Hughes, edited by Arnold Rampersad with David Roessel, Associate Editor, copyright © 1994 by The Estate of Langston Hughes. Used by permission of Alfred A. Knopf, a division of Random House, Inc.

Langston Hughes "Negro" from THE COLLECTED POEMS OF LANGSTON HUGHES by Langston Hughes, edited by Arnold Rampersad with David Roessle, Associate Editor, copyright © 1994 by The Estate of Langston Hughes. Used by permission of Alfred A. Knopf, a division of Random House, Inc.

Langston Hughes "The Negro Speaks of Rivers" from THE COLLECTED POEMS OF LANGSTON HUGHES by Langston Hughes, edited by Arnold Rampersad with David Roessel, Associate Editor, copyright © 1994 by The Estate of Langston Hughes. Used by permission of Alfred A. Knopf, a division of Random House, Inc.

Langston Hughes "Theme for English B" from THE COLLECTED POEMS OF LANGSTON HUGHES by Langston Hughes, edited by Arnold Rampersad with David Roessel, Associate Editor, copyright © 1994 by The Estate of Langston Hughes. Used by permission of Alfred A. Knopf, a division of Random House, Inc.

Leigh Hunt "Jenny Kissed Me," from *The Oxford Book of English Verse: 1250–1900*, ed. Arthur Quiller-Couch, 1919.

David Ives "The Blizzard." Reprinted by permission of the Abrams Artists Agency.

Shirley Jackson "The Lottery" from THE LOTTERY AND OTHER STORIES. Copyright 1948, 1949 by Shirley Jackson. Copyright renewed © 1976, 1977 by Laurence Hyman, Barry Hyman, Mrs. Sarah Webster and Mrs. Joanne Schnurer. Reprinted by permission of Farrar, Straus & Giroux, LLC.

Randall Jarrell "The Death of the Ball Turret Gunner" from THE COMPLETE POEMS. Copyright © 1969, renewed 1997 by Mary von S. Jarrell. Reprinted by permission of Farrar, Straus & Giroux, LLC.

Bret Anthony Johnston "Encounters with Unexpected Animals." Reprinted with permission.

Stephen Graham Jones "Discovering America," *Bleed Into Me: A Book of Stories* (Lincoln: University of Nebraska Press, 2005, 139–42). Reprinted with permission.

David Michael Kaplan "Doe Season" by David Michael Kaplan; first appeared in *The Atlantic Monthly*; also appeared in COMFORT by David Michael Kaplan, and BEST AMERICAN SHORT STORIES, 1986. Copyright © 1985 by David Michael Kaplan. Reprinted with the permission of Brandt & Hochman Literary Agents, Inc.

Jamaica Kincaid "Girl" from AT THE BOTTOM OF THE RIVER. Copyright © 1983 by Jamaica Kincaid. Reprinted by permission of Farrar, Straus & Giroux, LLC.

For performance rights, contact Kimberly Pau (kimberlypau@gmail.com).

Marge Piercy "The secretary chant" from CIRCLES ON THE WATER by Marge Piercy, copyright © 1982 by Middlemarsh, Inc. Used by permission of Alfred A. Knopf, a division of Random House, Inc.

Harold Pinter "Applicant" from REVUE SKETCHES, copyright © 1961 by Harold Pinter. Used by permission of Grove/Atlantic, Inc.

Sylvia Plath "Daddy" from ARIEL. Copyright © 1963 by Ted Hughes. Reprinted by permission of HarperCollins Publishers and Faber and Faber, Ltd.

Sylvia Plath "Morning Song" from ARIEL. Copyright © 1961, 1963 by Ted Hughes. Reprinted by permission of HarperCollins Publishers and Faber and Faber, Ltd.

Dick Pothier and Thomas Gibbons "A Woman's Wintry Death Leads to a Long-Dead Friend" from THE PHILADELPHIA INQUIRER (1987). Reprinted with the permission of The Philadelphia Inquirer.

Ezra Pound from THE CANTOS OF EZRA POUND, copyright © 1948 by Ezra Pound. Reprinted by permission of New Directions Publishing Corp.

Ezra Pound from PERSONAE, copyright © 1926 by Ezra Pound. Reprinted by permission of New Directions Publishing Corp.

Radiohead "Harry Patch (in Memory of)" written by Colin Greenwood, Jonathan Greenwood, Edward O'Brien, Philip Selway, and Thomas Yorke. Reprinted with permission of Kobalt Music Publishing America, Inc.

Henry Reed "Naming of Parts" from HENRY REED: COLLECTED POEMS, edited by Jon Stallworthy. Copyright © 1991. Reprinted with the permission of Oxford University Press, Ltd.

Adrienne Rich "Aunt Jennifer's Tigers." Copyright © 2002, 1951 by Adrienne Rich from THE FACT OF A DOORFRAME: SELECTED POEMS 1950–2001. Used by permission of the author and W. W. Norton & Company, Inc.

Adrienne Rich "Living in Sin." Copyright © 2002, 1955 by Adrienne Rich from THE FACT OF A DOORFRAME: SELECTED POEMS 1950–2001. Used by permission of the author and W. W. Norton & Company, Inc.

Alberto Alvaro Ríos "Nani" from WHISPERING TO FOOL THE WIND. Copyright © 1982 by Alberto Alvaro Ríos. Reprinted with the permission of the author.

Alberto Alvaro Ríos "The Secret Lion" from THE IGUANA KILLER: TWELVE STORIES OF THE HEART. Copyright © 1984 by Alberto Alvaro Ríos. Reprinted with the permission of Confluence Press, www.confluencepress.com.

Theodore Roethke "My Papa's Waltz," copyright 1942 by Hearst Magazines, Inc., from THE COLLECTED POEMS OF THEODORE ROETHKE by Theodore Roethke. Used by permission of Doubleday, a division of Random House, Inc.

Earl T. Roske © 2011 by Earl T. Roske. Reprinted by permission of the author. For performance rights, contact Earl T. Roske (earltroske@yahoo.com).

Cynthia Rylant from "God Went to Beauty School" by Cynthia Rylant. Copyright © 2003 by Cynthia Rylant. Reprinted by permission of HarperCollins Children's Books. All rights reserved.

Jacob Saenz "Evolution of My Block." Reprinted with permission.

THE POEMS, REVISED, by W. B. Yates, edited by Richard J. Finneran. Copyright © 1928 by The Macmillan Company, renewed 1956 by Georgie Yeats. All rights reserved.

William Butler Yeats "The Second Coming." Reprinted with the permission of Scribner, a Division of Simon & Schuster, Inc., from THE COLLECTED WORKDS OF W. B. YEATS, VOLUME I: THE POEMS, REVISED by W. B. Yeats, edited by Richard J. Finneran. Copyright © 1924 by The Macmillan Company, renewed 1962 by Bertha Georgie Yeats. All rights reserved.

GLOSSARY OF
LITERARY TERMS

Action What happens in a drama.

Alexandrine Verse with six iambic feet (iambic hexameter), a common form in French poetry but relatively rare in English poetry.

Allegorical figure or **framework** See **Allegory**.

Allegory Story with two parallel and consistent levels of meaning, one literal and one figurative, in which the figurative level offers a moral or political lesson; John Bunyan's *The Pilgrim's Progress* and Nathaniel Hawthorne's "Young Goodman Brown" are examples of moral allegory. An **allegorical figure** has only one meaning (for instance, it may represent good or evil), as opposed to a **symbol**, which may suggest a complex network of meanings. An **allegorical framework** is the system of ideas that conveys the allegory's message.

Alliteration Repetition of consonant sounds (usually the initial sounds) in a series of words, as in Blake's "The Chimney Sweeper": "So your chimneys I sweep, and in soot I sleep." Alliteration may be reinforced by repeated sounds within and at the ends of words.

Allusion Reference, often to literature, history, mythology, or the Bible, that is unacknowledged in the text but that the author expects a reader to recognize.

Ambiguity Device in which authors intentionally evoke a number of possible meanings of a word or grammatical structure by leaving unclear which meaning they intend.

Anapest See **Meter**.

Antagonist Character who is in conflict with or opposition to the protagonist; the villain. Sometimes the antagonist may be a force or situation (war or poverty) rather than a person.

Antihero Modern character who possesses the opposite attributes of a hero. Rather than being dignified and powerful, the antihero tends to be passive and ineffectual. Willy Loman, the main character in Arthur Miller's *Death of a Salesman*, is an antihero.

Apostrophe Figure of speech in which an absent character or a personified force or object is addressed directly, as if it were present or could comprehend: "O Rose, thou art sick!"

Archetype Image or symbol that is so common or important that it seems to have universal significance. Many archetypes appear in classical myths (for example, a journey to the underworld).

Arena stage Stage on which the actors are surrounded by the audience; also called **theater in the round.**

Aside Brief comment spoken by an actor to the audience (such as, "Here she comes. I'll play a fine trick on her now!") and assumed not to be heard by the other characters.

Assonance Repetition of the same or similar vowel sounds in a series of words: "cr<u>ee</u>p thr<u>ee</u> f<u>ee</u>t."

Atmosphere Tone or mood of a literary work, often established by the setting and language. Atmosphere is the emotional aura that determines readers' expectations about a work—for example, the sense of doom established at the beginning of Shakespeare's *Macbeth*.

Aubade Poem about morning, usually celebrating the dawn.

Ballad Narrative poem, rooted in an oral tradition, usually arranged in quatrains rhyming *abcb* and containing a refrain.

Ballad stanza See **Stanza.**

Beast fable Short tale, usually including a moral, in which animals assume human characteristics—for example, Aesop's "The Tortoise and the Hare."

Beginning rhyme See **Rhyme.**

Black comedy Comedy that relies on the morbid and absurd. Often black comedies (also called *dark comedies*) are so satiric that they become ironic and tragic; examples are Joseph Heller's novel *Catch 22* and Edward Albee's play *The Sandbox.*

Blank verse Lines of unrhymed iambic pentameter in no particular stanzaic form. Because iambic pentameter resembles the rhythms of ordinary English speech, blank verse is often unobtrusive; for instance, Shakespeare's noble characters usually use it, though they may seem to us at

first reading to be speaking in prose. See **Meter.**

Blocking Decisions about how characters move and where they stand on stage in a dramatic production.

Box set Stage setting that gives the audience the illusion of looking into a room.

Cacophony Harsh or unpleasant spoken sound created by clashing consonants such as "The vorpal blade went snicker-snack!" in Lewis Carroll's "Jabberwocky."

Caesura Strong or long pause in the middle of a poetic line, created by punctuation or by the sense of the poem, as in Yeats's "Leda and the Swan": "And Agamemnon dead. Being so caught up. . . ."

Carpe diem Latin for "seize the day"; the philosophy arguing that one should enjoy life today before it passes by, as seen in Herrick's "To the Virgins, to Make Much of Time."

Catastrophe The moment in a tragedy after the climax, when the rising action has ended and the falling action has begun, when the protagonist begins to understand the implications of events that will lead to his or her downfall.

Catharsis Aristotle's term for the emotional reaction or "purgation" that takes place in an audience watching a tragedy.

Character Fictional representation of a person, usually but not necessarily in a psychologically realistic way. E. M. Forster classified characters as **round** (well developed, closely involved in the action and responsive to it) or **flat** (static, stereotypical, or operating as **foils** for the protagonist). Characters can also be classified as **dynamic** (growing and changing in the course of the action) or **static** (remaining unchanged).

Characterization Way in which writers develop their characters and reveal those characters' traits to readers.

Choragos See **Chorus**.

Chorus Group of actors in classical Greek drama who comment in unison on the action and the hero; they are led by the **Choragos**.

Classicism Attitude toward art that values symmetry, clarity, discipline, and objectivity. **Neoclassicism**, practiced in eighteenth-century Europe, appreciated those qualities as found in Greek and Roman art and culture.

Cliché Overused phrase or expression.

Climax Point of greatest tension or importance, where the decisive action of a play or story takes place.

Closed form Type of poetic structure that has a recognizable rhyme scheme, meter, or stanzaic pattern; also called *fixed form*.

Closet drama Play meant to be read instead of performed—for example, Shelley's *Prometheus Unbound*.

Comedy Any literary work, but especially a play, in which events end happily, a character's fortunes are reversed for the better, and a community is drawn more closely together, often by the marriage of one or more protagonists at the end.

Comedy of humours Comedy that focuses on characters whose behavior is controlled by a single characteristic trait, or humour, such as *Volpone* (1606) by Ben Jonson.

Comedy of manners Satiric comedy that achieved great popularity in the nineteenth century. This form focuses on the manners and customs of society and directs its satire against the characters who violate its social conventions and norms. *The Importance of Being Earnest* (1895) by Oscar Wilde is a comedy of manners.

Common measure See **Stanza**.

Conceit See **Metaphor**.

Concrete poem Poem whose typographical appearance on the page reinforces its theme, as with George Herbert's "Easter Wings."

Conflict Struggle between opposing forces (protagonist and antagonist) in a work of literature.

Connotation Meaning that a word suggests beyond its literal, dictionary meaning; its emotional associations, judgments, or opinions. Connotations can be positive, neutral, or negative.

Consonance See **Rhyme**.

Convention See **Literary convention**.

Conventional symbol See **Symbol**.

Cosmic irony See **Irony**.

Couplet See **Stanza**.

Crisis Point at which the decisive action of the plot occurs.

Dactyl See **Meter**.

Denotation Dictionary meaning of a word; its explicit, literal meaning.

Denouement See **Resolution**.

Deus ex machina Latin for "God from a machine": any improbable resolution of plot involving the intervention of some force or agent from outside the story.

Dialect Particular regional variety of language, which may differ from the more widely used standard or written language in its pronunciation, grammar, or vocabulary. Eliza Doolittle's cockney dialect in the George Bernard Shaw play *Pygmalion* is an example.

Dialogue Conversation between two or more characters.

Diction Word choice that determines the level of language used in a piece of literature. **Formal diction** is lofty and elaborate (typical of Shakespearean nobility); **informal diction** is idiomatic and relaxed (like the narrative in John Updike's "A&P").

Jargon is the specialized diction of a professional or occupational group (such as computer scientists). **Idioms** are the colloquial expressions, including slang, of a particular group or society.

Didactic poetry   Poetry whose purpose is to make a point or teach a lesson, particularly common in the eighteenth century.

Double entendre   Phrase or word with a deliberate double meaning, one of which is usually sexual.

Double plot   See **Plot**.

Drama   Literature written to be performed.

Dramatic irony   See **Irony**.

Dramatic monologue   Type of poem perfected by Robert Browning that consists of a single speaker talking to one or more listeners and often revealing much more about the speaker than he or she seems to intend; Browning's "My Last Duchess" is an example of this form.

Dramatis personae   Characters in a play.

Dynamic character   See **Character**.

Elegy   Poem commemorating someone's death, usually in a reflective or mournful tone, such as A. E. Housman's "To an Athlete Dying Young."

Elision   Leaving out an unstressed syllable or vowel, usually in order to keep a regular meter in a line of poetry ("o'er" instead of "over," for example).

End rhyme   See **Rhyme**.

End-stopped line   Line of poetry that has a full pause at the end, typically indicated by a period or semicolon.

Enjambment   See **Run-on line**.

Envoi   Three-line conclusion to a sestina that includes all six of the poem's key words, three placed at the ends of lines and three within the lines. See **Sestina**.

Epic   Long narrative poem, such as the *Iliad* or the *Aeneid*, recounting the adventures of heroes on whose actions the fate of a nation or race depends. Frequently the gods or other supernatural beings take active interest in the events.

Epigram   Short pithy poem or statement— for example, Dorothy Parker's comment on an actress's performance, "She runs the gamut of emotions from A to B."

Epiphany   Term first applied to literature by James Joyce to describe a sudden moment of revelation about the deep meaning of something, such as the boy's realization at the end of "Araby."

Euphemism   Word consciously chosen for its pleasant **connotations**; often used for subjects such as sex and death, whose frank discussion is somewhat taboo in our society. For example, a euphemism for *die* is *pass away*.

Euphony   Pleasant spoken sound created by smooth consonants such as "ripple" or "pleasure."

Exposition   First stage of a plot, where the author presents the information about characters or setting that a reader or viewer will need to understand the subsequent action.

Expressionism   Artistic and literary movement that attempts to portray inner experience. It moves away from realistic portrayals of life and is characterized by violent exaggeration of objective reality and extremes of mood and feeling. In drama, expressionistic stage sets mirror the inner states of the character.

Extended metaphor   See **Metaphor**.

Extended simile   See **Metaphor**. Also see **Conceit**.

Eye rhyme   See **Rhyme**.

Fable   Short tale, often involving animals or supernatural beings and stressing plot above character development, whose object is to teach a pragmatic or moral lesson. See **Beast fable**.

Fairy tale See **Folktale**.

Falling action Stage in a play's plot during which the intensity of the climax subsides.

Falling meter Trochaic and dactylic meters, so called because they move from stressed to unstressed syllables. See **Rising meter**.

Fantasy Work of literature that takes place in an unreal world or contains unreal or incredible characters. J. R. R. Tolkien's *The Lord of the Rings* is one example.

Farce Comedy in which stereotypical characters engage in boisterous horseplay and slapstick humor, as in Chekhov's *The Brute*.

Feminine rhyme See **Rhyme**.

Fiction Form of narrative that is primarily imaginative although its form may resemble types of factual writing such as history and biography.

Figures of speech Expressions—such as **hyperbole, metaphor, metonymy, personification, simile, synechdoche,** and **understatement**—that use words to achieve effects beyond ordinary language.

Flashback Departure from chronological order that presents an event or situation that occurred before the time in which the story's action takes place.

Flat character See **Character**.

Foil Minor character whose role is to highlight the main character by presenting a contrast with him or her.

Folktale Contemporary version of an old, even ancient, oral tale that can be traced back centuries through many different cultures. Folktales include fairy tales, myths, and fables.

Foot See **Meter**.

Foreshadowing Introduction early in a story of situations, characters, or objects that seem to have no special importance but in fact are later revealed to have great significance.

Form Structure or shape of a literary work; the way a work's parts fit together to form a whole. In poetry, form is described in terms of the presence (or absence) of elements like rhyme, meter, and stanzaic pattern. See **Open form** and **Closed form**.

Formal diction See **Diction**.

Free verse See **Open form**.

Freytag's pyramid In his *Technique of the Drama* (1863) Gustav Freytag suggested that the stages of a classic dramatic plot resemble a pyramid, with rising action leading to the climax and giving way to falling action.

Genre Category of literature. Fiction, drama, and poetry are the three major genres; subgenres include the novel, the farce, and the lyric poem.

Haiku Seventeen-syllable, three-line form of Japanese verse that almost always uses concrete imagery and deals with the natural world.

Hamartia Aristotle's term for the "tragic flaw" in characters that eventually causes their downfall in Greek tragedy.

Hermeneutics Traditionally, the use of the Bible to interpret other historical or current events; in current critical theory, the principles and procedures followed to determine the meaning of a text.

Heroic couplet See **Stanza**.

High comedy Term introduced in 1877 by George Meredith to denote comedy that appeals to the intellect, such as Shakespeare's *As You Like It*. See **Low comedy**.

Hubris Tragic flaw of overwhelming pride that exists in the protagonist of a tragedy.

Hyperbole Figurative language that depends on intentional overstatement; Mark Twain often used it to create humor; Jonathan Swift used it for **satire**.

Iamb See **Meter**.

Imagery Words and phrases that
describe the concrete experience
of the five senses, most often sight.
A **pattern of imagery** is a group of
related images developed throughout a work. **Synesthesia** is a form of
imagery that mixes the experience
of the senses (hearing something
visual, smelling something audible,
and so on): "He smelled the blue
fumes of her scent." **Static imagery**
freezes the moment to give it the
timeless quality of painting or sculpture. **Kinetic imagery** attempts to
show motion or change.

Imagism Movement in modern poetry
stressing terseness and concrete
imagery. **Imagists** were a group of
early twentieth-century American
poets, including Ezra Pound, William
Carlos Williams, and Amy Lowell,
who focused on visual images and
created new rhythms and meters.

Imperfect rhyme See **Rhyme.**

In medias res Latin phrase describing
works like Virgil's *Aeneid* that begin
in the middle of the action in order
to catch a reader's interest.

Informal diction See **Diction.**

Internal rhyme See **Rhyme.**

Irony Literary device or situation that
depends on the existence of at least
two separate and contrasting levels
of meaning or experience. **Dramatic**
or **tragic irony**, such as that found
in *Oedipus the King*, depends on the
audience's knowing something the
protagonist has not yet realized.
Situational irony exists when what
happens is at odds with what the
story's situation leads readers to
expect will happen, as in Browning's "Porphyria's Lover." **Cosmic
irony** (or irony of fate) exists when
fate frustrates any effort a character
might make to control or reverse his
or her destiny. **Verbal irony** occurs
when what is said is in contrast
with what is meant. Verbal irony

can be expressed as **understatement,
hyperbole,** or **sarcasm.**

Jargon Specialized language associated
with a particular trade or profession.

Kinetic imagery Imagery that attempts
to show motion or change. See, for
example, William Carlos Williams's
"The Great Figure."

Literary canon Group of literary works
generally acknowledged by critics
and teachers to be the best and most
significant to have emerged from our
history. In the twentieth century,
the canon began to be expanded
to include works by women and by
writers of color.

Literary convention Something whose
meaning is so widely understood
within a society that authors can
expect their audiences to accept and
comprehend it unquestioningly—for
example, the division of plays into
acts or the fact that stepmothers in
fairy tales are likely to be wicked.

Literary criticism Descriptions, analyses, interpretations, or evaluations
of works of literature by experts in
the field.

Literary symbol See **Symbol.**

Low comedy Introduced by George
Meredith, it refers to comedy with
little or no intellectual appeal. Low
comedy is used as comic relief in
Macbeth. See **High comedy.**

Lyric Form of poetry, usually brief
and intense, that expresses a poet's
subjective response to the world.
In classical times, lyrics were set to
music. The romantic poets, particularly Keats, often wrote lyrics about
love, death, and nature.

Masculine rhyme See **Rhyme.**

Meditation Lyric poem that focuses on
a physical object—for example,
Keats's "Ode on a Grecian Urn"—
using this object as a vehicle for
considering larger issues.

Melodrama Sensational play that
appeals shamelessly to the emotions,

contains elements of tragedy but ends happily, and often relies on set plots and stock characters.

Metaphor Concise form of comparison equating two things that may at first seem completely dissimilar, often an abstraction and a concrete image—for example, "My love's a fortress." An **extended metaphor** (or **conceit**) is a comparison used throughout a work; in Tillie Olsen's "I Stand Here Ironing," the mother compares her daughter to a dress waiting to be ironed, thus conveying her daughter's passivity and vulnerability. See **Simile**.

Meter Regular pattern of stressed and unstressed syllables, each repeated unit of which is called a **foot**: an **anapest** has three syllables, two unstressed and the third stressed; a **dactyl** has three syllables, the first stressed and the subsequent ones unstressed. An **iamb** has two syllables, unstressed followed by stressed; a **trochee** has a stressed syllable followed by an unstressed one; a **spondee** has two stressed syllables; and a **pyrrhic** has two unstressed syllables. A poem's meter is described in terms of the kind of foot (anapest, for example) and the number of feet found in each line. The number of feet is designated by the Greek prefix for the number, so one foot per line is called *monometer*, two feet is *dimeter*, followed by *trimeter, tetrameter, pentameter, hexameter*, and so on. The most common meter in English is *iambic pentameter*. See also **Rising meter** and **Falling meter**.

Metonymy Figure of speech in which the term for one thing can be applied to another with which it is closely associated—for example, using "defend the flag" to mean "defend the nation."

Mimesis Aristotle's term for the purpose of literature, which he felt was "imitation" of life.

Monologue Extended speech by one character.

Mood Atmosphere created by the elements of a literary work (setting, characterization, imagery, tone, and so on).

Morality play Medieval Christian allegory, in which personified abstractions, such as Selfishness and Pride, struggle for a person's soul.

Motivation Reasons behind a character's behavior that make us accept or believe that character.

Mystery play Medieval play depicting biblical stories.

Myth Anonymous story reflecting the religious and social values of a culture or explaining natural phenomena, often involving gods and heroes.

Narrative The "storytelling" of a piece of fiction; the forward-moving recounting of episode and description. When an event that occurred earlier is told during a later sequence of events, it is called a **flashback**; suggesting earlier in a narration something that will occur later on is called **foreshadowing**.

Narrator Person who tells the story. See **Point of view**.

Naturalism Nineteenth-century movement whose followers believed that life should not be idealized when depicted in literature. Rather, literature should show that human experience is a continual (and for the most part losing) struggle against the natural world. Émile Zola, Jack London, and Stephen Crane are important practitioners of naturalism.

New Comedy Greek comedies of the fourth and third centuries B.C. that followed **Old Comedy**. They were comedies of romance with stock characters and conventional settings. They lacked the satire, abusive language, and bawdiness of Old Comedy.

Novel Fictional narrative, traditionally realistic, relating a series of events or following the history of a character or group of characters through a period of time.

Novella Extended short story, usually concentrated in episode and action (like a short story) but involving greater character development (like a novel); Franz Kafka's "The Metamorphosis" is a novella.

Octave See **Sonnet**.

Ode Relatively long lyric poem, common in antiquity and adapted by the romantic poets, for whom it was a serious poem of formal diction, often addressed to some significant object (such as a nightingale or the west wind) that has stimulated the poet's imagination.

Old Comedy The first comedies, written in Greece in the fifth century B.C., which heavily satirized the religious and social issues of the day. The chief practitioner of Old Comedy was Aristophanes. See **New Comedy**.

Onomatopoeia Word whose sound resembles what it describes: "snap, crackle, pop." Lewis Carroll's "Jabberwocky" uses onomatopoeia.

Open form Form of poetry that makes use of varying line lengths, abandoning stanzaic divisions, breaking lines in unexpected places, and even dispensing with any pretense of formal structure. Sometimes called *free verse* or *vers libre*. See **Form**.

Ottava rima See **Stanza**.

Oxymoron Phrase combining two seemingly incompatible elements: "crashing silence."

Parable Story that teaches a lesson, such as the parable of the prodigal son in the New Testament.

Paradox Seemingly contradictory situation. Adrienne Rich's "A Woman Mourned by Daughters" uses paradox.

Parody Exaggerated imitation of a serious piece of literature for humorous effect.

Shakespeare's "My mistress' eyes are nothing like the sun" is a parody of traditional Renaissance love poetry.

Pastoral Literary work, such as Christopher Marlowe's lyric poem "The Passionate Shepherd to His Love," that deals nostalgically and usually unrealistically with a simple, preindustrial rural life; the name comes from the fact that traditionally pastorals feature shepherds.

Pastoral romance Prose tale set in an idealized rural world; popular in Renaissance England.

Pathos Suffering that exists simply to satisfy the sentimental or morbid sensibilities of the audience.

Pattern of imagery See **Imagery**.

Perfect rhyme See **Rhyme**.

Persona Narrator or speaker of a poem or story; in Greek tragedy, a persona was a mask worn by an actor.

Personification A figure of speech that endows inanimate objects or abstract ideas with life or human characteristics: "the river wept."

Petrarchan sonnet See **Sonnet**.

Picaresque Episodic, often satirical work, presenting the life story of a rogue or rascal—for example, Cervantes' *Don Quixote*. The form emerged in sixteenth-century Spain.

Picture-frame stage Stage that looks like a room with a missing fourth wall through which the audience views the play. The **proscenium arch** separates the audience from the play.

Plot Way in which the events of the story are arranged. When there are two stories of more or less equal importance, the work has a **double plot**; when there is more than one story but one string of events is clearly the most significant, the other stories are called **subplots**. Plot in fiction often follows the pattern of action in drama, rising to a **climax** and then falling to a **resolution**.

Poetic rhythm See **Rhythm**.

Point of view Perspective from which a story is told. The storyteller may be a major character in the story or a character who witnesses the story's events (*first-person narrator*) or someone who does not figure in the action at all (*third-person narrator*), in which case he or she may know the actions and internal doings of everyone in the story (*omniscient narrator*) or just know some part of these (*limited omniscient narrator*).

The narrator may be an *observer* or a *participant*. If he or she is untrustworthy (stupid or bad, for instance), the story has an *unreliable narrator*; narrators who are unreliable because they do not understand what they are reporting (children, for instance) are called *naive narrators*. If the perspective on the events is the same as one would get by simply watching the action unfold on stage, the point of view is *dramatic* or *objective*.

Popular fiction Works aimed at a mass audience.

Prologue First part of a play (originally of a Greek tragedy) in which the actor gives the background or explanations that the audience needs to follow the rest of the drama.

Props (short for **properties**) Pictures, furnishings, and so on that decorate the stage for a play.

Proscenium arch Arch that surrounds the opening in a **picture-frame stage**; through this arch the audience views the performances.

Prose poem Open form poem whose long lines appear to be prose set in paragraphs—for example, Yusef Komunyakaa's "Nude Interrogation."

Protagonist Principal character of a drama or a work of fiction; the hero. The *tragic hero* is the noble protagonist in classical Greek drama who falls because of a tragic flaw.

Pyrrhic See **Meter**.

Quatrain See **Stanza**.

Realism Writing that stresses life as it really is. Realism relies on careful description of setting and the trappings of daily life, psychological probability, and the lives of ordinary people. Ibsen's *A Doll House* is an example.

Resolution Also called the **denouement**, this is the final stage in the plot of a drama or work of fiction. Here the action comes to an end, and remaining loose ends are tied up.

Rhyme Repetition of concluding sounds in different words, often intentionally used at the ends of poetic lines. In **masculine rhyme** (also called *rising rhyme*) single syllables correspond. In **feminine rhyme** (also called *double rhyme* or *falling rhyme*) two syllables correspond, the second of which is stressed. In **triple rhyme**, three syllables correspond. **Eye rhyme** occurs when words look as though they should rhyme but are pronounced differently ("cough/ tough"). In **perfect rhyme**, the corresponding vowel and consonant sounds of accented syllables must be preceded by different consonants—for example, the *b* and *h* in "born" and "horn." **Imperfect rhyme**, also called *near rhyme*, *slant rhyme*, or *consonance* occurs when consonants in two words are the same but intervening vowels are different—for example, "pick/ pack," "lads/lids." The most common type of rhyme within a poem is **end rhyme**, where the rhyming syllables are placed at the end of a line.
Internal rhyme consists of rhyming words found within a line of poetry.
Beginning rhyme occurs in the first syllable or syllables of a line.

Rhyme royal See **Stanza**.

Rhythm Regular recurrence of sounds in a poem. Ordinarily, rhythm is determined by the arrangement of metrical feet in a line, but sometimes *sprung rhythm*, introduced by Gerard Manley Hopkins, is used. In this type of rhythm, the number of strong stresses in a line determines the rhythm, regardless of how many weak stresses there might be.

Rising action Stage in a play's plot during which the action builds in intensity. See **Freytag's pyramid**.

Rising meter Iambic and anapestic meters, so called because they move from unstressed to stressed syllables. See **Falling meter**.

Romance Type of narrative that deals with love and adventure in a nonrealistic way, most popular in the Middle Ages but sometimes used by more modern authors, such as Hawthorne.

Romantic comedy Comedy such as Shakespeare's *Much Ado about Nothing* in which love is the main subject and idealized lovers endure great difficulties to get to the inevitable happy ending.

Romanticism Eighteenth- and nineteenth-century literary movement that valued subjectivity, individuality, the imagination, nature, excess, the exotic, and the mysterious.

Round character See **Character**.

Run-on line Line of poetry that ends with no punctuation or natural pause and consequently runs over into the next line; also called *enjambment*.

Sarcasm Form of irony in which apparent praise is used to convey strong, bitter criticism.

Satire Literary attack on folly or vanity by means of humor; usually intended to improve society.

Scansion Process of determining the meter of a poem by analyzing the strong and weak stresses in a line to find the unit of **meter** (each recurring pattern of stresses) and the number of these units (or **feet**) in each line.

Scrim Curtain that when illuminated from the front appears solid but when lit from the back becomes transparent.

Sentimental comedy Reaction against the **comedy of manners**. This type of comedy relies on sentimental emotion rather than on wit or humor and focuses on the virtues of life.

Sestet See **Sonnet**.

Sestina Poem composed of six six-line stanzas and a three-line conclusion called an **envoi**. Each line ends with one of six key words. The alternation of these six words in different positions—but always at the ends of lines—in the poem's six stanzas creates a rhythmic verbal pattern that unifies the poem.

Setting Background against which the action of a work takes place: the historical time, locale, season, time of day, weather, and so on.

Shakespearean sonnet See **Sonnet**.

Short-short story Short fictional narrative that is generally under five pages (or fifteen hundred words) in length.

Short story Fictional narrative centered on one climatic event and usually developing only one character in depth; its scope is narrower than that of the **novel**, and it often uses setting and characterization more directly to make its theme clear.

Simile Comparison of two seemingly unlike things using the words *like* or *as*: "My love is like an arrow through my heart." See **Metaphor**.

Situational irony See **Irony**.

Soliloquy Convention of drama in which a character speaks directly to the audience, revealing thoughts and feelings that other characters present on stage are assumed not to hear.

Sonnet Fourteen-line poem, usually a **lyric** in *iambic pentameter* (see **Meter**). It has a strict rhyme scheme in one of two forms: the *Italian*, or

Petrarchan sonnet (an eight-line octave rhymed *abba/abba* with a six-line **sestet** rhymed *cdc/cdc* or a variation) and the *English*, or **Shakespearean sonnet** (three quatrains rhymed *abab/cdcd/efef* with a concluding couplet rhymed *gg*).

Speaker See **Persona**.

Spenserian stanza See **Stanza**.

Spondee See **Meter**.

Stage directions Words in a play that describe an actor's role apart from the dialogue, dealing with movements, attitudes, and so on.

Stage setting (set) Scenery and props in the production of a play. In *expressionist* stage settings, scenery and props are exaggerated and distorted to reflect the workings of a troubled, even abnormal mind. *Surrealistic* stage settings are designed to mirror the uncontrolled images of dreams or nightmares. See **Staging**.

Staging Overall production of a play in performance: the sets, costumes, lighting, sound, music, and so on.

Stanza Group of lines in a poem that forms a metrical or thematic unit. Each stanza is usually separated from others by a blank space on the page. Some common stanzaic forms are the **couplet** (two lines), **tercet** (three lines), **quatrain** (four lines), **sestet** (six lines), and **octave** (eight lines). The **heroic couplet**, first used by Chaucer and especially popular throughout the eighteenth century, notably in Alexander Pope's poetry, consists of two rhymed lines of iambic pentameter, with a weak pause after the first line and a strong pause after the second. **Terza rima**, a form used by Dante, has a rhyme scheme (*aba, bcb, ded*) that creates an interlocking series of stanzas. The **ballad stanza** alternates lines of eight and six syllables. Typically, only the second and fourth lines rhyme.

Common measure is a four-line stanzaic pattern closely related to the ballad stanza. It differs in that its rhyme scheme is *abab* rather than *abcb*.

Rhyme royal is a seven-line stanza (*ababbcc*) set in iambic pentameter.

Ottava rima is an eight-line stanza (*abababcc*) set in iambic pentameter.

The **Spenserian stanza** is a nine-line form (*ababbcbcc*) with the first eight lines in iambic pentameter and the last line in iambic hexameter.

Static character See **Character**.

Static imagery Imagery that freezes a moment to give it the timeless quality of painting or sculpture. Much visual imagery is static.

Stock character Stereotypical character who behaves consistently and whom the audience of a play can recognize and classify instantly: the town drunk, the nerd, and so on.

Stream of consciousness Form of narration controlled not by external events but by the thoughts and subjective impressions of the narrator, commonly found in modern literature, such as the work of Virginia Woolf and James Joyce.

Stress Accent or emphasis, either strong or weak, given to each syllable in a piece of writing, as determined by conventional pronunciation (cárpĕt, not cărpét) and intended emphasis ("going dówn, dówn, dówn tŏ thĕ bóttŏm ŏf thĕ ócĕan"). Strong stresses are marked with a ´ and weak ones with a ˘.

Structure Formal pattern or arrangement of elements to form a whole in a piece of literature.

Style How an author selects and arranges words to express ideas and, ultimately, theme.

Subplot See **Plot**.

Surrealism Literary movement that allows unconventional use of syntax; chronology; juxtaposition;

and bizarre, dreamlike images in prose and poetry.

Symbol Person, object, action, or idea whose meaning transcends its literal or denotative sense in a complex way. A symbol is invested with significance beyond what it could carry on its own. **Universal symbols,** such as the grim reaper, may be called **archetypes; conventional symbols,** such as national flags, evoke a general and agreed-upon response from most people. There are also *private symbols,* such as the "gyre" created by Yeats, which the poet himself invested with extraordinary significance.

Synecdoche Figure of speech in which a part of something is used to represent the whole—for example, "hired hand" represents a laborer.

Synesthesia See **Imagery.**

Tale Short story often involving mysterious atmosphere and supernatural or inexplicable events, such as "The Tell-Tale Heart" by Edgar Allan Poe.

Ten-minute play Short play that can be performed in ten minutes or less.

Tercet See **Stanza.**

Terza rima See **Stanza.**

Theater in the round See **Arena stage.**

Theater of the Absurd Type of drama that discards conventions of plot, character, and motivation in order to depict a world in which nothing makes sense. Edward Albee's *The Sandbox* is an example.

Theme Central or dominant idea of a piece of literature, made concrete by the details and emphasis in the work itself.

Thrust stage Stage that juts out into the audience so the action may be viewed from three sides.

Tone Attitude of the speaker or author of a work toward the subject itself or the audience, as determined by the word choice and arrangement of the piece.

Tragedy Literary work, especially a play, that recounts the downfall of an individual. *Greek tragedy* demanded a noble protagonist whose fall could be traced to a *tragic personal flaw.* *Shakespearean tragedy* also treats noble figures, but the reasons for their tragedies may be less clear-cut than in Greek drama. *Domestic* or *modern tragedy* tends to deal with the fates of ordinary people.

Tragic irony See **Irony.**

Tragicomedy Type of Elizabethan and Jacobean drama that uses elements of both tragedy and comedy.

Triple rhyme See **Rhyme.**

Trochee See **Meter.**

Understatement Intentional downplaying of a situation's significance, often for ironic or humorous effect, as in Mark Twain's famous comment on reading his own obituary, "The reports of my death are greatly exaggerated."

Unities Rules that require a dramatic work to be unified in terms of its time, place, and action. *Oedipus the King* illustrates the three unities.

Universal symbol See **Symbol.**

Verbal irony See **Irony.**

Villanelle A nineteen-line poem composed of five tercets and a concluding quatrain; its rhyme scheme is *aba aba aba aba aba abaa.* Two different lines are systematically repeated in the poem: line 1 appears again in lines 6, 12, and 18, and line 3 reappears as lines 9, 15, and 19. Thus, each tercet concludes with an exact (or close) duplication of either line 1 or line 3, and the final quatrain concludes by repeating both line 1 and line 3.

Visual poetry Poetry that focuses as much on the words' appearance on the page as on what the words say, using a combination of media that may include video, photography, and even sound as well as text.

Wagons Sets mounted on wheels, which make rapid changes of scenery possible.

INDEX OF FIRST LINES OF POETRY

INDEX OF AUTHORS AND TITLES

INDEX OF
LITERARY TERMS